56th Annual Edition

Gun Digest®

2002

Edited by
Ken Ramage

—GUN DIGEST STAFF—

EDITOR
Ken Ramage

ASSOCIATE EDITOR
Ross Bielema

CONTRIBUTING EDITORS

Bob Bell
Holt Bodinson
Raymond Caranta
Doc Carlson
John Haviland

John Malloy
Layne Simpson
Larry S. Sterett
Hal Swiggett

Editorial Comments and Suggestions

We're always looking for feedback on our books. Please let us know what you like about this edition. If you have suggestions for articles you'd like to see in future editions, please contact.

Ken Ramage/Gun Digest
700 East State St.
Iola, WI 54990
email: ramagek@krause.com

Manuscripts, contributions and inquiries, including first class return postage, should be sent to the GUN DIGEST Editorial Offices, Krause Publications, 700 E. State Street, Iola, WI 54990-0001. All materials received will receive reasonable care, but we will not be responsible for their safe return. Material accepted is subject to our requirements for editing and revisions. Author payment covers all rights and title to the accepted material, including photos, drawings and other illustrations. Payment is at our current rates.

CAUTION: Technical data presented here, particularly technical data on the handloading and on firearms adjustment and alteration, inevitably reflects individual experience with particular equipment and components under specific circumstances the reader cannot duplicate exactly. Such data presentations therefore should be used for guidance only and with caution. Krause Publications, Inc., accepts no responsibility for results obtained using this data.

Published by

krause publications

700 E. State Street • Iola, WI 54990-0001
Telephone: 715/445-2214
Web: www.krause.com

Please call or write for our free catalog.

Our toll-free number to place an order or obtain a free catalog is 800-258-0929 or please use our regular business telephone 715-445-2214 for editorial comment and further information.

Library of Congress Catalog Number: 44-32588
ISBN: 0-87349-295-1

TWENTIETH ANNUAL

JOHN T. AMBER LITERARY AWARD

Ken Aiken

Ken Aiken has won the prestigious John T. Amber Award for his article *"Birth of the Modern Firearm,"* a carefully-researched work on the early development of firearms manufacturing in this country, published in *Gun Digest 2001, 55th Edition.* As the 20th winner of this annual award, Aiken joins a very select group of firearms writers.

"Basically I'm a historian," he states, "but for me history is not something abstract. My work has always seemed to center around objects that I can hold."

As a master goldsmith he has worked extensively on restoring ancient treasures from numerous cultural eras and is best known for his work restoring those recovered from sunken shipwrecks; he was in charge of restoration of artifacts recovered from the famous 1641 wreck of the Spanish galleon *Concepcion.* As a horologist he spent years restoring antique and vintage watches for collectors throughout North America.

"Fortunately I'm a quick study and my enthusiasm for a subject encourages people to help me with my projects. Three years ago I knew very little about antique firearms, but while writing a short article about under-hammer firearms I discovered the accepted history of gun manufacturing in Windsor, Vermont was inaccurate and have been unable to leave it alone since."

He is presently the consulting curator to the Norwich University Museum.

The only juried literary award in the firearms field, the John T. Amber Award replaced the Townsend Whelen Award, originated by the late John T. Amber and re-named in his honor. Now, a $1,000 prize goes to the winner of this annual award.

Nominations for the competition are made by the *GUN DIGEST* editor and are judged by a distinguished panel of editors experienced in the firearms field. Entries are evaluated for felicity of expression and illustration, originality and scholarship, and subject importance to the firearms field.

This year's Amber Award nominees, in addition to Aiken, were:

Toby Bridges, *"Modern Maturity...Muzzleloading Enters a New Generation"*

Gordon Bruce, *"Cutaway Collection of the Century"*

Jim Foral, *" John Barlow, the Ideal Man"*

H. Lea Lawrence, *"The Saga of Bo Whoop"*

Rob Lucas, *"Brush-Bucking Bullets...That Didn't"*

Norm Nelson, *"Life with Lil' Lightning"*

Carlos Schmidt, *"Tropical Carabinas"*

W. E. Sprague, *"The AR-7 Explorer: A Survival Tale"*

Dave Ward, *"The 6mm Benchrest – A Dogger's Dream"*

Serving as judges for this year's competition were John D. Acquilino, editor of *Inside Gun News*; James W. Bequette, executive editor of *Shooting Times*; David Brennan, editor of *Precision Shooting*, Sharon Cunningham, director of Pioneer Press; Pete Dickey, former technical editor of *American Rifleman*; the late Robert Elman, former editor-in-chief of Winchester Press, and free-lance editor for Abenake Press and other publications; Jack Lewis, former editor and publisher of *Gun World*; Bill Parkerson, former editor of *American Rifleman*, now director of research and information for the National Rifle Association and Dave Petzal, executive editor of *Field & Stream*.

About Our Covers...

It is the custom of GUN DIGEST to comment on the firearms that illustrate the covers of each edition. This year, a new cartridge shares the front cover with a familiar double-action revolver from Sturm, Ruger and Company.

Front Cover:

Here you see the proven Ruger Super Redhawk double-action revolver, similar to earlier specimens except for the chambering. *New for 2001* – the Super Redhawk is chambered for the 480 Ruger, a brand-new cartridge and the very first to carry the Ruger name. This new cartridge/revolver combination sounds like just the ticket for handgun hunters and silhouette shooters.

Ruger's Super Redhawk was introduced in 1987, chambered for the 44 Magnum cartridge and designed to digest a steady diet of high-intensity magnum loadings without a hitch. Handgun hunters and silhouette shooters were particularly pleased. The Super Redhawk is a heavy, well-built pistol with a strong, extended frame that includes integral scope mounts. Other features include interchangeable insert sight blades, adjustable rear sight and the comfortable Ruger "Cushioned Grip" of Santoprene panels with inset panels of Goncalvo Alves wood.

Until very recently, the Super was chambered only for the 44 Magnum round. That all changed in 1999, when the powerful 454 Casull cartridge was added as a chambering option. The Casull round delivers a tremendous amount of energy, attracting a growing number of shooters interested in high-performance handgunning. The only problem with the cartridge is its 'stout' recoil, which to many handgunners becomes punishing. This led to the development of the new 480 Ruger, which according to developer Hornady Manufacturing and partner Sturm, Ruger & Company, generates approximately half the felt recoil of the 454 Casull while delivering 50 percent more energy than the venerable 44 Magnum.

The newest handgun cartridge on the block – the 480 Ruger.

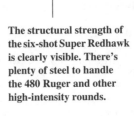

The structural strength of the six-shot Super Redhawk is clearly visible. There's plenty of steel to handle the 480 Ruger and other high-intensity rounds.

Ruger partnered with Hornady Mfg. to bring the 480 Ruger to market.

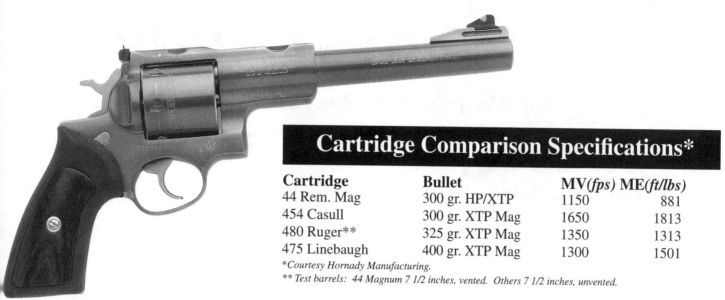

Cartridge Comparison Specifications*

Cartridge	Bullet	MV(fps)	ME(ft/lbs)
44 Rem. Mag	300 gr. HP/XTP	1150	881
454 Casull	300 gr. XTP Mag	1650	1813
480 Ruger**	325 gr. XTP Mag	1350	1313
475 Linebaugh	400 gr. XTP Mag	1300	1501

*Courtesy Hornady Manufacturing.
** Test barrels: 44 Magnum 7 1/2 inches, vented. Others 7 1/2 inches, unvented.

Back Cover:

The Ruger Red Label shotgun is arguably the finest American-made over-and-under shotgun produced today.

Since the basic model's introduction in 1977 (*20 gauge; 12 gauge following in 1982*), shotgunners have enjoyed the reliable, well-made shotgun with the classic lines.

During Ruger's 50th Anniversary in 1999, a limited quantity of Ruger engraved over-and-under shotgun Anniversary Models was produced. These Anniversary Models proved such a success that Sturm, Ruger & Co. decided to offer an engraved series of Red Label shotguns bearing similar-style engraving to that used on the 50th Anniversary models.

These classic shotguns are now available with special scroll engraving that encompasses a 24-carat gold game bird appropriate to each gauge (a pheasant in 12 gauge, a grouse in 20 gauge, a woodcock in 28 gauge–and a duck on the All-Weather 12-gauge stainless steel with synthetic stock model). Additionally, all models of the engraved shotgun carry a Ruger 24-carat gold eagle, machine-engraved on the bottom of the receiver.

These classic shotguns are now available with special scroll engraving that encompasses a 24-carat gold game bird appropriate to each gauge (a pheasant in 12 gauge, a grouse in 20 gauge, a woodcock in 28 gauge–and a duck on the All-Weather 12-gauge stainless steel with synthetic stock model). Additionally, all models of the engraved shotgun carry a Ruger 24-carat gold eagle, machine-engraved on the bottom of the receiver.

The receiver scrollwork was specially designed and proportioned to the unique receiver dimensions of each specific gauge. The engraved designs are cut into the receiver using state-of-the-art computer-controlled equipment and diamond-tipped cutting tools.

The intricacy of the engraving may lead you to expect an extravagant price; however, Ruger's suggested retail prices range from $1,575 to $1,650, depending on the model.

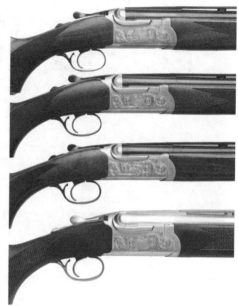

A close look at the well-executed engraving on all four models. Note the proportional size of the frames for (*top to bottom*) the 12 gauge, 20 gauge, 28 gauge and, last, the 12-gauge All Weather.

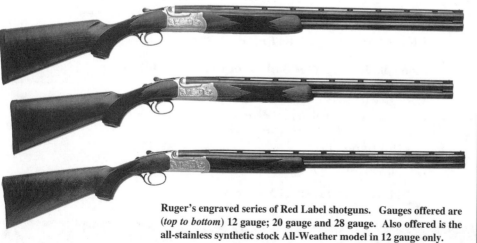

Ruger's engraved series of Red Label shotguns. Gauges offered are (*top to bottom*) 12 gauge; 20 gauge and 28 gauge. Also offered is the all-stainless synthetic stock All-Weather model in 12 gauge only.

> *Correction*
> In the "About Our Covers" report in GUN DIGEST 2001, the back cover rifle and artist were incorrectly reported. The correct description: An 1873 Winchester so good it takes one's breath when seeing it for the first time. Texan Ron Smith executed the unbelievable engraving. His execution and artistry are, in a word, magnificent.
> *Photo by Alan Richmond.*

Gun Digest 2002

~ The World's Greatest Gun Book ~

Page 30

Page 60

Page 85

CONTENTS

REPORTS FROM THE FIELD:

Page 168

Page 174

CATALOG OF ARMS AND ACCESSORIES

The H & R Defender

by John Malloy

The solid-frame H&R American revolver introduced the basic double-action mechanism that would be used in future H&R revolvers. Note the separate sear in the rear of the trigger guard, used in all subsequent H&R revolvers.

THE HARRINGTON & RICHARDSON 38-caliber Defender revolver can be considered that company's first attempt to produce a service-type revolver; some students of firearms think it was the high point of the company's revolver designs.

Beginning in the 1870s, the Massachusetts gunmaker had produced small revolvers for personal protection, and became known for its well-made break-open revolvers. By 1929, H&R had produced a single-shot target pistol placing in the highest ranks of target shooting of the time.

In America, the companies of Colt and Smith & Wesson controlled the service sidearm niche for most of the early 20th century. H&R made no effort to produce a competing service-type arm. However, when the need arose during World War II, H&R did design and produce such a firearm, the 38-caliber Defender revolver. Still of top-break design, and chambered for the 38 S&W cartridge, the Defender showed similarities to the earlier H&R revolvers sold for personal defense. Indeed, the experience of their previous products allowed H&R to produce the Defender, which displayed many improvements.

The Defender entered a category of firearms that falls between true military arms and true commercial arms. A number of such guns were made and used during times of war. They were not military standard or substitute-standard arms, but because they were available, they could free up military arms for military use.

The Harrington & Richardson Defender 38-caliber five-shot revolver revolver fulfilled this function. With its four-inch barrel, it weighed 25 ounces. Its break-open action allowed it to be easily opened and its cylinder easily loaded or unloaded. With a brief training course, almost anyone could become proficient in its operation.

A five-shot revolver chambered for the low-pressure 38 S&W cartridge would be considered rather marginal armament today. However, with a Defender and a handful of cartridges, a person during the Second World War could be an armed Civil Defense leader or a guard at a defense plant. The Defender allowed standard military sidearms to be dedicated to training and to use in the actual battle zones.

This was obviously not the first revolver in 38 S&W the H&R firm had made. In fact, the company had been making revolvers in that caliber since only a few years after the cartridge had been introduced by Smith & Wesson in 1876.

Harrington & Richardson history dates back to 1871. In that year, the firm of Wesson & Harrington was formed. By 1874,

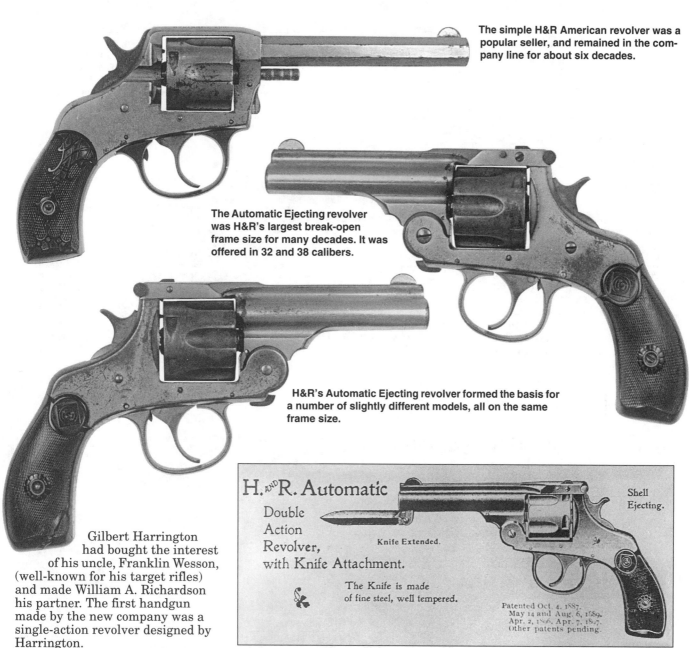

The simple H&R American revolver was a popular seller, and remained in the company line for about six decades.

The Automatic Ejecting revolver was H&R's largest break-open frame size for many decades. It was offered in 32 and 38 calibers.

H&R's Automatic Ejecting revolver formed the basis for a number of slightly different models, all on the same frame size.

H. AND R. Automatic

Double Action Revolver, with Knife Attachment.

The Knife is made of fine steel, well tempered.

Knife Extended.

Shell Ejecting.

Patented Oct. 4, 1887. May 14 and Aug. 6, 1889. Apr. 2, 1896, Apr. 7, 1897. Other patents pending.

One of the most interesting revolvers of H&R's Automatic Ejecting line was a version with a knife blade attached to the lower portion of the barrel.

Gilbert Harrington had bought the interest of his uncle, Franklin Wesson, (well-known for his target rifles) and made William A. Richardson his partner. The first handgun made by the new company was a single-action revolver designed by Harrington.

Dates of introduction of many of Harrington & Richardson's revolvers are in some question. However, reportedly, the H&R single-action revolvers were no longer made after 1880, giving way to new double-action solid-frame designs. The Harrington & Richardson "American" revolver introduced the basic double-action lockwork that was to be used in succeeding H&R revolvers. It featured a separate sear behind the trigger, which pivoted on the rear pin of the trigger guard. This system has been used on all H&R revolvers since. Simple and inexpensive, the American was a popular revolver, staying in production until World War II.

The solid-frame double-actions were made in rimfire chamberings at first, then standardized with chamberings of 32 S&W Long and 38 S&W. A small number were also made for the 44 Webley cartridge.

By at least 1891, the company was marketing a line of hinged-frame break-open revolvers, considered well-made for their time, which incorporated the mechanism for simultaneous ejection of the fired cartridge cases.

Two frame sizes of the break-open revolvers were made, with slight variations in barrel lengths and grips giving rise to a large number of different model names. The "Premier" was the small frame, for 22 and 32 S&W calibers.

The larger frame was designated the "Automatic Ejecting." The name was long, containing seventeen letters, and H&R literature often abbreviated it into other variations, such as "automatic," "auto eject-ing," or "auto eject." This larger

frame size would accomodate a cylinder approximately the diameter of the American cylinder, holding six rounds of 32-caliber cartridges, or five rounds of 38 Smith & Wesson. The Automatic Ejecting was, in a way, the forerunner of the Defender. A number of variations were made during the long production of the Automatic Ejecting, which also stayed in the line until World War II. One of the most interesting variations was a model that incorporated a folding knife under the barrel. The Automatic Ejecting revolver was one of H&R's most popular offerings, staying in the line until World War II.

The company offered "target" grips for the Automatic Ejecting, made of either walnut or hard rubber. These

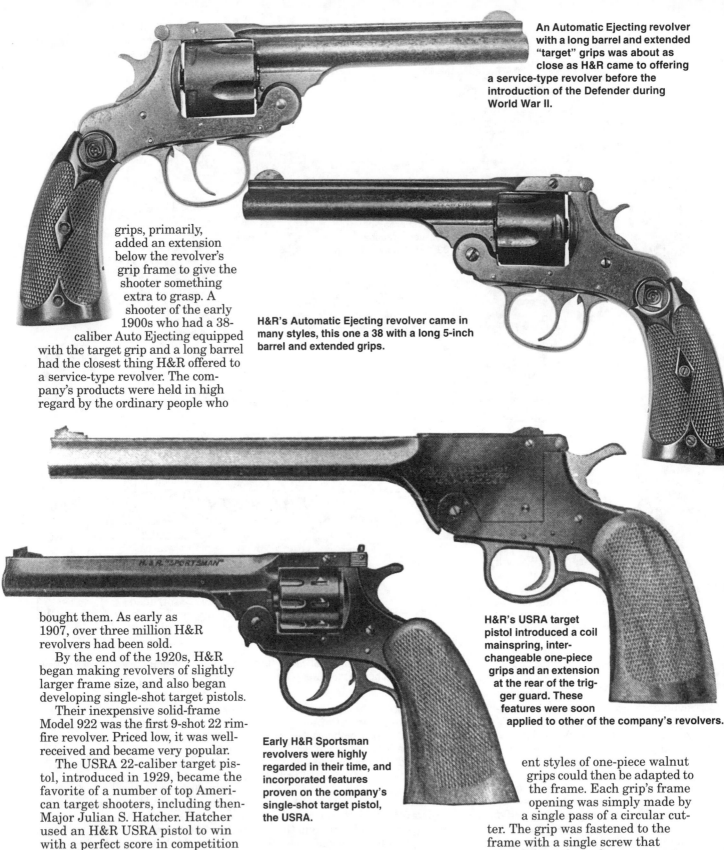

An Automatic Ejecting revolver with a long barrel and extended "target" grips was about as close as H&R came to offering a service-type revolver before the introduction of the Defender during World War II.

H&R's Automatic Ejecting revolver came in many styles, this one a 38 with a long 5-inch barrel and extended grips.

H&R's USRA target pistol introduced a coil mainspring, interchangeable one-piece grips and an extension at the rear of the trigger guard. These features were soon applied to other of the company's revolvers.

Early H&R Sportsman revolvers were highly regarded in their time, and incorporated features proven on the company's single-shot target pistol, the USRA.

grips, primarily, added an extension below the revolver's grip frame to give the shooter something extra to grasp. A shooter of the early 1900s who had a 38-caliber Auto Ejecting equipped with the target grip and a long barrel had the closest thing H&R offered to a service-type revolver. The company's products were held in high regard by the ordinary people who bought them. As early as 1907, over three million H&R revolvers had been sold.

By the end of the 1920s, H&R began making revolvers of slightly larger frame size, and also began developing single-shot target pistols.

Their inexpensive solid-frame Model 922 was the first 9-shot 22 rimfire revolver. Priced low, it was well-received and became very popular.

The USRA 22-caliber target pistol, introduced in 1929, became the favorite of a number of top American target shooters, including then-Major Julian S. Hatcher. Hatcher used an H&R USRA pistol to win with a perfect score in competition at Bisley, England in 1931. Serious shooters began to take notice of what H&R was doing.

The USRA pistol, developed by Walter F. Roper, was named in honor of the United States Revolver Association, which was the coordinating organization for target pistol shooting from 1900 until about the time of World War II, when the National Rifle Association took over that function. Interestingly, the USRA is still a functioning organization, although most competition is done by postal matches now.

H&R's USRA pistol had a novel way of adapting grips to the desires of the individual target shooter. The rear of the steel grip frame was shaped as the arc of a circle. Differ-ent styles of one-piece walnut grips could then be adapted to the frame. Each grip's frame opening was simply made by a single pass of a circular cutter. The grip was fastened to the frame with a single screw that passed through the lower rear portion of the grip. The company cataloged about five or six basic types of grips for the USRA. However, some options combined the features of several different grips. Probably 13 or 14 different grip options were actually available for the USRA.

To improve the grip more, an extension was added to the rear of

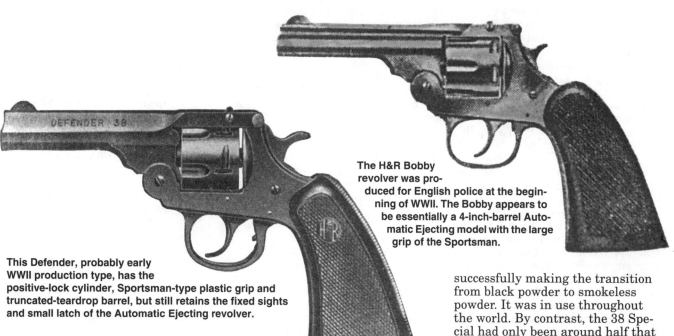

This Defender, probably early WWII production type, has the positive-lock cylinder, Sportsman-type plastic grip and truncated-teardrop barrel, but still retains the fixed sights and small latch of the Automatic Ejecting revolver.

The H&R Bobby revolver was produced for English police at the beginning of WWII. The Bobby appears to be essentially a 4-inch-barrel Automatic Ejecting model with the large grip of the Sportsman.

the trigger guard, providing a rest which allowed part of the weight of the pistol to be supported by the shooter's middle finger.

By the early 1930s, the revolver line had been expanded, based on experience with the USRA. Walter Roper's concept seemed to be to produce a revolver that was much the same size and feel as the single-shot target pistol. Thus, the Sportsman revolver was introduced. The Sportsman was a larger-frame break-open, 9-shot 22 with a 6-inch barrel. The frame, latch and hammer design were similar to those of the successful USRA target pistol. It was logical for H&R to make the grip frame of the Sportsman similar to that of the USRA; the same grip options could then be used on either. The Number 4 grip (generally known as the "Frontier" type) was the one with which the Sportsman ordinarily came, but any other style could be fitted on special order. Both double-action and single-action versions of the Sportsman were made, the single-action bearing model number 199, and the double-action version bearing model number 999. In addition, a variation with a 2-inch barrel and a rounded Number 2 grip was offered. This variant was given model number 299, and was popularly called the New Defender. Although the New Defender had a relatively short life span (about 1936-1941), it provided a catchy name when H&R brought out the wartime revolver that came to be called the Defender.

When World War II began in Europe in 1939, Great Britain was short of all kinds of firearms. Much British military equipment was sub-

sequently lost during the 1940 evacuation of Dunkirk. During the ensuing Battle of Britain, the British developed an understandable concern about possible Nazi activities in England, primarily sabotage. It became desirable for English police, ordinarily not armed at that time, to be armed.

The adoption by Great Britain in 1927 of the 38 S&W cartridge as their standard revolver cartridge allowed Harrington & Richardson to complete a contract for British police revolvers.

The new H&R revolver, named the "Bobby," was a five-shot arm with 4-inch barrel, chambered for the 38 S&W cartridge. Information on the production of the Bobby is difficult to find. It apparently was based on the design of the Automatic Ejecting break-open pocket revolvers, but the new Bobby frame seemed to be similar to the Sportsman frame. The grip portion of the frame apparently was an arc of a circle, so that a number 4 walnut grip could be fitted. Versions in 32 S&W Long have also been reported, but only the 38 could use the British military cartridge.

The British adoption of the low-power 38 S&W round in 1927, albeit in a different loading, seems strange to us now. We must remember, however, that the S&W cartridge with its standard 145-grain bullet had, at that time, been in use for half a century. Smith & Wesson had introduced the cartridge in 1876, using the same ratio of powder to bullet weight as that used by famous 44 Russian cartridge of 1870. The 38 Smith & Wesson became a very popular cartridge,

successfully making the transition from black powder to smokeless powder. It was in use throughout the world. By contrast, the 38 Special had only been around half that time, and its use was primarily limited to the United States.

At any rate, British tests had convinced military planners that bullet weight—not diameter or velocity—was the key factor of stopping power. Accordingly, when they decided on the 38 S&W in 1927, they adopted a 200-grain blunt lead bullet, with a leisurely velocity of just over 600 feet per second. This load was almost a dead ringer for a similar load introduced in America in the same general time period. Introduced by Western, it was called the 38 S&W "Super Police" loading. The 200-grain lead bullet was fully as long as the cartridge case of the 38 S&W, but most of it protruded from the case, leaving just enough room for the powder charge. This actually was an efficient cartridge design.

However, this load was to see only limited use by the British. The 38-caliber cartridge used by the British military was changed in 1937 from the 200-grain lead projectile to a 178-grain jacketed bullet, to meet international standards. The new cartridge was known as the 380 Mark II. The jacketed bullet loading was considered far inferior to the original heavy-bullet lead loading in stopping power. However, the lead-bullet cartridges already produced could be used for home-guard use.

The Bobby 38 revolver could thus chamber either the original 38 S&W loads, the 1927 British lead-bullet loads or the newer jacketed British military rounds. The revolvers probably saw little use, other than being targeted and carried, but apparently they filled the need and were considered satisfactory.

When the United States was drawn into World War II in December

1941, the U.S. military was woefully short of firearms of all types. Standard combat arms could not be spared for guard duty and other non-combat uses. Harrington & Richardson brought out an improved revolver, somewhat similar to the Bobby, for American use. Named the "Defender," the new revolver was made in 38 S&W only, with a 4-inch barrel. The barrel was of heavier design than the sculptured form of previous barrels. In cross-section the barrel is much like a truncated teardrop, with the truncation forming an upper flat of the barrel rib. This design, beside adding weight, was easier and faster to machine than the traditional rounded barrel with distinct rib; its use speeded up production. Both fixed-sight and adjustable-sight variants of the Defenders were made, probably with the fixed-sight version produced first, and then replaced with the adjustable-sight variant. The grip was one-piece molded plastic, shaped like the Number 4 wood grip available with the USRA target pistol and the Sportsman (and interchangeable with it). Shooters of the time praised the feel of the Number 4 grip, and the plastic variant of it was a logical choice.

The Defender was H&R's first 38-caliber revolver with a coil mainspring and a rebounding hammer. It also had a positive cylinder lock and a floating firing pin. A new sear design was incorporated. The front of the trigger guard fit into a machined recess in the frame and eliminated the front trigger guard pin of previous models. All-in-all, the Defender was perhaps the most sophisticated centerfire revolver design the company had produced. It combined the best features of previous models with a substantial number of new innovations.

Probably late WWII or early postwar production, this Defender Special has all the features of the Defender, and has added the finger-rest at the rear of the trigger guard.

The H&R Defender was reportedly purchased by the U.S. government and issued in large numbers to Civil Defense groups and plant security guards. It has been reported that the Post Office and auxiliary police units also used Defenders. It was the only revolver H&R offered for civilian sale for the duration of the war.

The Defender revolver was not H&R's only contribution to the War effort. The company also made Reising submachine guns, 22 training rifles, line-throwing guns, flare pistols and single-shot shotguns and 22 revolvers for training and emergency kits.

The Defender 38 was listed as being suitable for ammunition loaded with either 145- or 200-grain bullets, those being the two standard loads for 38 S&W then made in the United States. It could also use the 38 Colt New Police cartridge. This round used a cartridge case identical to the 38 S&W. However, Colt, reluctant to use the Smith & Wesson name on their revolvers, had, in 1905, developed an almost identical cartridge bearing the Colt name. To distinguish the Colt cartridge, the bullet used was a 150-grain flat-point, which actually gave the New Police round a slight edge in stopping power.

Whatever cartridge used, the Defenders probably saw little actual shooting, but were there when needed and served their purposes adequately. The compact revolvers allowed Civil Defense leaders, plant guards and others to be armed when military weapons could not be spared.

The Defender actually had a lot going for it. The mechanism was simple, the operation easily taught to those who would be issued one. To load, simply open the top latch, insert the cartridges into the five chambers, and close the revolver. Firing could be done either double- or single-action. To eject the empty cartridge cases, the latch was opened again and the barrel and cylinder rocked forward; the star extractor automatically popped out the empties. Then the revolver was ready to be loaded again.

The grip, fairly large for a gun of this size, gave the revolver a good feel. The Defender, for its simplicity, was an accurate revolver. The adjustable sights on some variants were rudimentary, but offered positive adjustment. Windage adjustments were made on the rear sight by loosening a screw on one side, then tightening a corresponding screw on the other side. Elevation was adjusted on the front sight; the

The Defender Special was a good-shooting revolver that feels good in the hand. In May 1971, the writer fired this one in Bullseye competition.

Apparently later during the war, the WWII Defender added adjustable sights and the heavier latch of the Sportsman.

Malloy finds the original Defender to be an easy gun to shoot, with good accuracy. Several decades ago, he used one as his centerfire pistol in a Bullseye target match.

In 1954, the H&R Sportsman came out in a modified version with a different frame shape and two-piece grips. These features were to be used when the Defender was reintroduced a decade later.

Members of the 38 Smith & Wesson family: from left, an original 38 S&W, with 145-grain lead bullet; a British 38/200 load with blunt 200-grain bullet; a WWII British load with 178-grain jacketed bullet; a Western 38 S&W Super Police load with 200-grain bullet, similar to the British 38/200; a 38 Colt New Police cartridge, the same as 38 S&W but with a 150-grain flat-point bullet.

spring-loaded sight was cammed up or down by turning a screw at the front of the barrel, in the rib just above the bore. Somewhat small by modern standards, the square post and notch gave a good sight picture. Your writer can attest to the accuracy of this unlikely revolver. Back in May of 1971 (more-or-less as a stunt, but mostly because I was curious as to how it would do), I fired the centerfire portion of a Bullseye pistol match with a Defender, using my own 38 S&W handloads. It may have been a fluke, but the little revolver turned in an aggregate score within about 15% of my average with my 38-caliber target guns.

The Defender was given the designation Model 25 in H&R literature, although the revolvers were not numbered as such on the guns themselves.

Toward the end of the war, apparently, the Defender was continued in another subtle variation. A finger rest extension was added to the trigger guard, a feature that had appeared also on the Sportsman, and the trigger was grooved. This latest variant of the wartime 38 break-open was available in an adjustable-sight version only. The name of the revolver was changed slightly to Defender Special, and the Model number to 925.

In 1946, the Harrington & Richardson plant was subjected to a lengthly labor strike that lasted for the first seven months of that year. The postwar line was cut down, and just the most popular models were offered for commercial sale. The Model 925, the Defender Special, was dropped from the line.

Only two revolvers were continued in production, both 22-caliber.

The inexpensive solid-frame 922 was probably the best seller of the two. The other offering, the Model 999 Sportsman, continued as the only break-open revolver made by H&R in the postwar years, and was the prestige revolver of the line. In 1954, it was modified. The one-piece grip was dropped, and two-piece grips on a different, more conventional, grip frame were used. (*A revolver of this type, acquired during the latter part of the 1950s, was your writer's first 22 handgun. The revolver shot pretty well, and I have used it on and off for much of my life. In November 1995, on a whim, I used it to fire the 22 portion of an NRA-sanctioned Bullseye pistol match. The old revolver, hopelessly outclassed for competitive target shooting at that time, surprised the assemblage by shooting a score of 99-3x in one timed-fire stage.*)

The Defender looked as if it were to be just a historical footnote. Then, in 1964, almost two decades after it had been dropped, a "second generation" of 38-caliber break-open

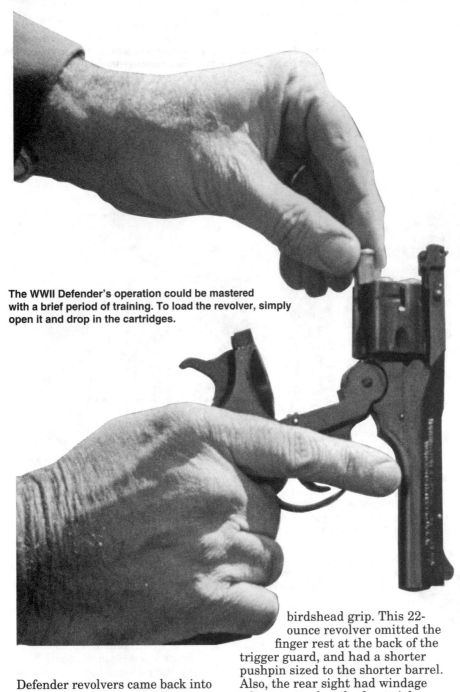

The WWII Defender's operation could be mastered with a brief period of training. To load the revolver, simply open it and drop in the cartridges.

and given the model designation 935. It should be noted that at least a few early birdshead variants were made with 4-inch barrels, but these apparently were not standard production.

The new variations, aside from the pushpin ejection, had other features that differed from the original series of Defender revolvers. Most were minor, but the change to a frame-mounted firing pin was noteworthy. A heavier hammer with a wide spur was used. It should also be noted that the head of the mainspring guide was made of nylon, not metal. This seemed a reasonable change at the time, as it gave smooth operation. The nylon part was used on all the H&R revolvers made during a certain period. Now, with the benefit of hindsight, we know that some of the nylon guide heads cracked with time. When this happened, generally the guns would fire, but the hammer would not rebound. If a shooter is handy with tools, he can easily hand-file a new one from a piece of scrap metal, using the nylon part as a pattern.

The second generation of Defenders filled a need for those who needed a well-made, adjustable-sight centerfire revolver that was relatively inexpensive. Most were probably purchased by individuals for home protection. However, I have heard that at least one small private security firm used the 4-inch version because it cost much less than a Colt or Smith & Wesson, but looked just as good with the butt sticking out of a holster.

The new series of Defender 38 revolvers remained in the H&R line until about 1979, when both 2 1/2- and 4-inch variants were dropped.

There apparently was some confusion of nomenclature caused by some H&R catalogs during the 1970s that listed the 4-inch 38 Defender as Model 926. This designation may have been accurate during some

Defender revolvers came back into the H&R line. Two variants were offered, both cataloged—at least at first—as the Model 925 Defender. One variant had a 4-inch barrel and used the new modernized frame of the Sportsman, with the same two-piece grips. The resultant heavier frame and related parts increased the weight to 31 ounces, a substantial increase of 6 ounces over the original Defender. The automatic-ejection feature had been changed to a simpler ejector pushpin that protruded beneath the barrel. With the revolver open, a separate push on the end of the pin would raise the extractor star and eject the empties. Adjustable sights were of the same type used on the Sportsman and the original Defender.

The second variant came with a 2 1/2-inch barrel and a new type of birdshead grip. This 22-ounce revolver omitted the finger rest at the back of the trigger guard, and had a shorter pushpin sized to the shorter barrel. Also, the rear sight had windage adjustments, but the front sight was fixed. Later, a nickel-finish version of the 2 1/2-inch 925 was produced

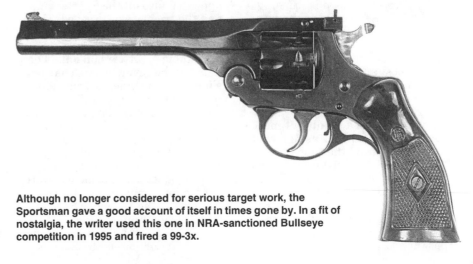

Although no longer considered for serious target work, the Sportsman gave a good account of itself in times gone by. In a fit of nostalgia, the writer used this one in NRA-sanctioned Bullseye competition in 1995 and fired a 99-3x.

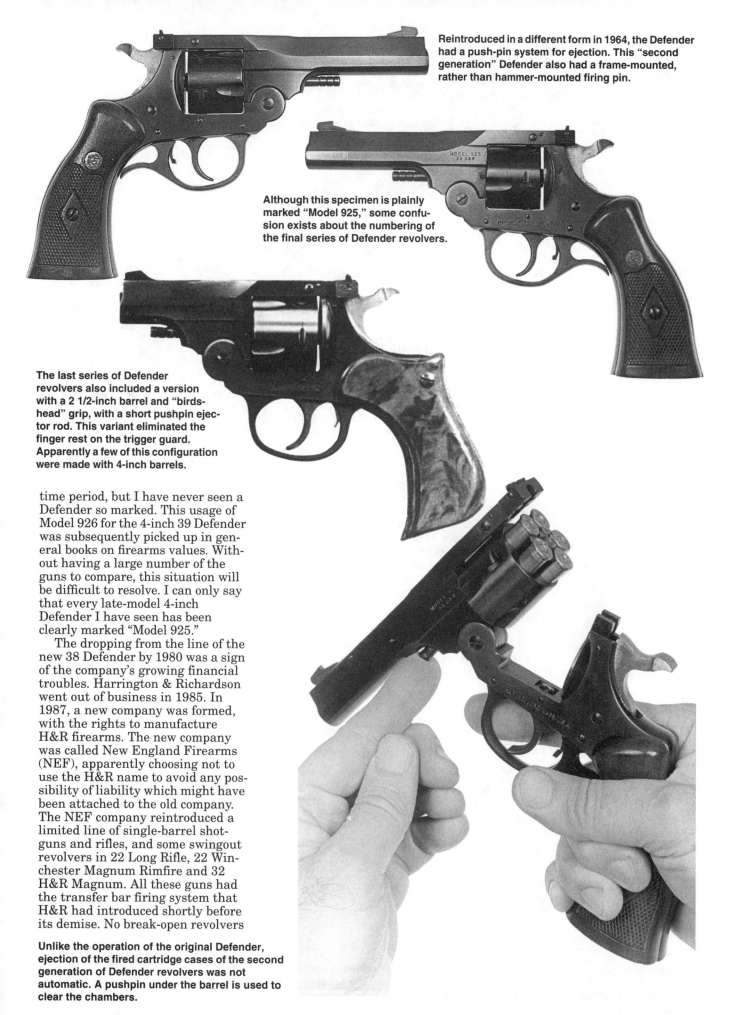

Reintroduced in a different form in 1964, the Defender had a push-pin system for ejection. This "second generation" Defender also had a frame-mounted, rather than hammer-mounted firing pin.

Although this specimen is plainly marked "Model 925," some confusion exists about the numbering of the final series of Defender revolvers.

The last series of Defender revolvers also included a version with a 2 1/2-inch barrel and "birdshead" grip, with a short pushpin ejector rod. This variant eliminated the finger rest on the trigger guard. Apparently a few of this configuration were made with 4-inch barrels.

time period, but I have never seen a Defender so marked. This usage of Model 926 for the 4-inch 39 Defender was subsequently picked up in general books on firearms values. Without having a large number of the guns to compare, this situation will be difficult to resolve. I can only say that every late-model 4-inch Defender I have seen has been clearly marked "Model 925."

The dropping from the line of the new 38 Defender by 1980 was a sign of the company's growing financial troubles. Harrington & Richardson went out of business in 1985. In 1987, a new company was formed, with the rights to manufacture H&R firearms. The new company was called New England Firearms (NEF), apparently choosing not to use the H&R name to avoid any possibility of liability which might have been attached to the old company. The NEF company reintroduced a limited line of single-barrel shotguns and rifles, and some swingout revolvers in 22 Long Rifle, 22 Winchester Magnum Rimfire and 32 H&R Magnum. All these guns had the transfer bar firing system that H&R had introduced shortly before its demise. No break-open revolvers

Unlike the operation of the original Defender, ejection of the fired cartridge cases of the second generation of Defender revolvers was not automatic. A pushpin under the barrel is used to clear the chambers.

The early Defender feels good in the hand, due to the large one-piece grip and in this case, the finger-rest trigger guard. A specimen in good condition is likely to be an accurate shooter.

and no 38-caliber revolvers were included in the new line.

In June of 1991, a new owner took over and brought the H&R name back. Two separate companies were formed. NEF continued a basic line of utilitarian revolvers, rifles and shotguns that could be sold in mass-merchandising outlets. The new company, H&R 1871, Inc., would produce a prestige line of guns for sale by regular firearms dealers. As the leader of the new H&R line, the Model 999 Sportsman 22-caliber revolver was brought back. It would be the last of the long line of H&R top-break revolvers to be produced.

The slightly-redesigned Sportsman continued in production through 1999. By that year, a number of city, county and state governments had initiated lawsuits against members of the firearms industry that made handguns. The Clinton administration saw this as a way to further its anti-gun program. The federal government's Department of Housing and Urban Development threatened to join in suits against manufacturers of handguns.

H&R chose to go out of the handgun business, at least temporaily, until the political climate became clearer. The only handguns in the H&R/NEF line for the year 2000 were non-gun starter revolvers. The proud story of the H&R break-open revolvers that had produced the Defender 38 had reached an end point.

Whether the real high point of the H&R top-break line was actually the Defender or the Sportsman is something that will perhaps be discussed at shooting ranges or collector meetings for times to come. Certainly far more Sportsman revolvers were made and sold, and they were probably used far more often than were the 38s.

Still, the original Defender has the big-bore charm of a centerfire caliber, and a history of actual government purchase and use during World War II. Speculation as to its possible use by different agencies, such as units of the U.S. Post Office and the guards at the Smithsonian Institute, creates an aura of history that sets the Defender apart.

The Harrington & Richardson Defender 38 was an unlikely revolver. When the first Defender was made, the break-open revolver was already obsolescent. The 38 S&W cartridge was losing ground to the more powerful 38 Special. Yet the original Defender filled its niche well. It was not particularly powerful, yet was adequate for its original purpose. It armed guards and others who would probably not have to use a handgun in their duties, but who had the possibility of such a need.

The second generation of Defenders was well behind the times, but had enough appeal to average Americans that the guns continued in production from 1964 to 1979. Perhaps most of them are still sitting in the sock drawers of ordinary people, waiting for an emergency they hope will never happen.

This, then, is the story of the Defender 38. Born in wartime because of a definite need, it combined the best features developed during the company's previous decades of revolver production, and added improvements. The basic design was good enough that similar revolvers were introduced again two decades later, and continued in production another fifteen years.

Then, even after the Defender was dead and gone, and all other top-break revolvers had been discontinued, the basic break-open design was once again resurrected and the 22-caliber Sportsman revolver, with similar features, was made until just recently.

The story of the interesting and unpretentious H&R Defender revolver deserves to be better known.

Like the contemporary USRA and Sportsman, the early Defender revolvers used a coil mainspring and rebounding hammer; the grip frame formed an arc of a circle, so that interchangeable grips could be attached with a single screw.

The operation of both the 22-caliber Sportsman and the original 38-caliber Defender was essentially the same: pull the latch up and pivot the barrel and cylinder forward to clean or load.

The post-1964 "second generation" Model 925 Defender differs from the original in many details, but is a comfortable, good-shooting revolver.

Selected Bibliography:

Amber, John, 1981, History of H&R: *HARRINGTON & RICHARDSON SHOOTING JOURNAL*, 1st ed., p. 26-33.

Askins, Charles, 1950, Handguns Today: *GUN DIGEST*, 5th ed. (1951) p. 112-116.

Baldwin, J.W., 1945, The Manufacturers, Harrington and Richardson: *AMERICAN RIFLEMAN*, v. 93, no. 12 (December 1945) p. 52.

Dickey, Pete, 1979, The Last Top-Break: *AMERICAN RIFLEMAN*, v. 127, no. 3 (March 1979) p. 34-35, 89.

Dickey, Pete, 1981, Sorting Out the .38 Cartridge Confusion: *AMERICAN RIFLEMAN*, v. 129, no. 9 (September 1981) p. 40-41, 70.

Dickey, Pete, 1982, U.S. Cartridge Sidearms: *AMERICAN RIFLEMAN*, v. 130, no. 2 (February 1982) p. 36-39, 80-82.

Fanta, Ladd, 1975, The H&R Free Pistol: *GUN DIGEST*, 30th ed., 1976, p. 80-84.

Hatcher, Maj. Julian S., 1935, *TEXTBOOK OF PISTOLS AND REVOLVERS*: Small Arms Technical Publishing Co., Plantersville, SC.

Hatcher, Maj. Gen. Julian S., 1947, 1947 Production Prospects: *AMERICAN RIFLEMAN*, v. 95, no. 1 (January 1947) p. 7-9, 45.

Hatcher, Maj. Gen. Julian S., 1948, H&R Sportsman 999 Revolver: *AMERICAN RIFLEMAN*, v. 96, no. 9 (September 1948) p. 31.

Hogg, Ian V. and John Weeks, 1982, PISTOLS OF THE WORLD: DBI Books.

Jarrett, William S., editor, 1994, 50 Years Ago in Shooter's Bible: SHOOTER'S BIBLE, No. 86, 1995 edition, p. 8-20.

NRA Staff, 1965, H&R Model 925 Revolver: AMERICAN RIFLEMAN, v. 113, no. 8 (August 1965) p. 62-64.

Rohn, Gerald A., 1984, The H&R Auto Ejecting Revolver: AMERICAN RIFLEMAN, v. 132, no. 4 (April 1984) p. 46-49, 75-76.

Sell, DeWitt E., 1962, Harrington & Richardson Handguns: AMERICAN RIFLEMAN, v. 110, no. 7 (July 1962) p. 40-42.

Stebbins, Henry M., 1961, PISTOLS, A MODERN ENCYCLOPEDIA: Stackpole, Harrisburg, PA.

Suydam, Charles R., 1979, U.S. CARTRIDGES AND THEIR HANDGUNS: Beinfield, N. Hollywood, CA.

Terek, Allen W., 1989, The Single-Shot Target Pistol in the U.S. 1870-1940: GUN COLLECTOR'S DIGEST, 5th ed., p. 186-202.

Waite, M.D., 1974, The H&R Single-Shot Pistol: AMERICAN RIFLEMAN, v. 122, no. 12 (December 1974) p. 36.

Wallack, L.R., 1984, Thirty Million Handguns: GUN DIGEST, 39th ed., 1985, p. 107-112.

Waters, Ken, 1979, 38 Smith & Wesson: HANDLOADER 79, v. 14, no. 3 (May-June 1979) p. 22-25, 45-50.

Most Needed Revolver Wildcat?

Loading the 41 Special!

by Rocky Raab

The lonely 41 Magnum (*center*) is unlike its other magnum stable mates, in that it doesn't have a "Special" version. The 357 (*left*) and the 44 Magnums (*right*) both were developed from their respective Special cartridges. The 41 was created from scratch, and author says it needs a Special version just as much as the other two!

THE SEED THAT grew into my latest wildcat was planted several years ago by an article on the 41 Magnum revolver cartridge. The author bemoaned the fact that the round, as excellent as it is, is virtually moribund. Then came an incisive comment: *"Part of the reason the 41 has never been very popular is that there has never been a 'Special' version for it."* Apparently, more than one experimenter since then has rectified that oversight. Today, articles about the wildcat 41 Special have appeared in several different publications and interest in this well-balanced loading is blooming.

The 41 Magnum is unique among magnum revolver cartridges in that

it was developed from the start as a magnum only. The 357 and 44 Magnums came into existence by lengthening the shorter, less powerful 38 and 44 Specials. Both were created to provide vastly increased power in their respective bore diameters. Cases were lengthened both to hold additional powder and to prevent the more powerful rounds from being chambered in revolvers designed for low-pressure cartridges.

But the 41 is unique. Its case was created from scratch as a magnum. No existing revolvers were chambered for a shorter, lower-powered version. No existing brass was modified. The only reduced-power factory load came in full-length

magnum cases. Even that load churned up some 1050 fps. That's still too powerful for many needs, including routine practice.

So why wasn't a 41 Special developed? Shooters still fire many times more 38 Special cartridges than 357 Magnum, even from their magnum revolvers. Fans abound for the 44 Special as well as its magnum. Both magnum cartridges are truly great rounds. So why are the "Special" versions so darned popular? The simple answer is that the shorter, less powerful versions of magnum cartridges are more pleasant to shoot, easier on firearms, are often more accurate, and are more ballistically efficient at lower velocities. Less recoil, better accuracy and more shootable are three pretty powerful reasons for popularity.

OK, but why not simply load reduced charges in the longer case? Because that approach doesn't often work out as well as we'd hope. Small charges in large cases have been suspected to cause extreme pressures and even burst firearms. No one has definitely explained the phenomenon yet as far as I'm aware, but it has happened. It's also quite easy to get double or even triple charges into a case. At best, such reduced loads often prove inconsistent, giving wide velocity variations and less-than-stellar accuracy. For the "middle magnum" the remedy is obvious: the 41 Special.

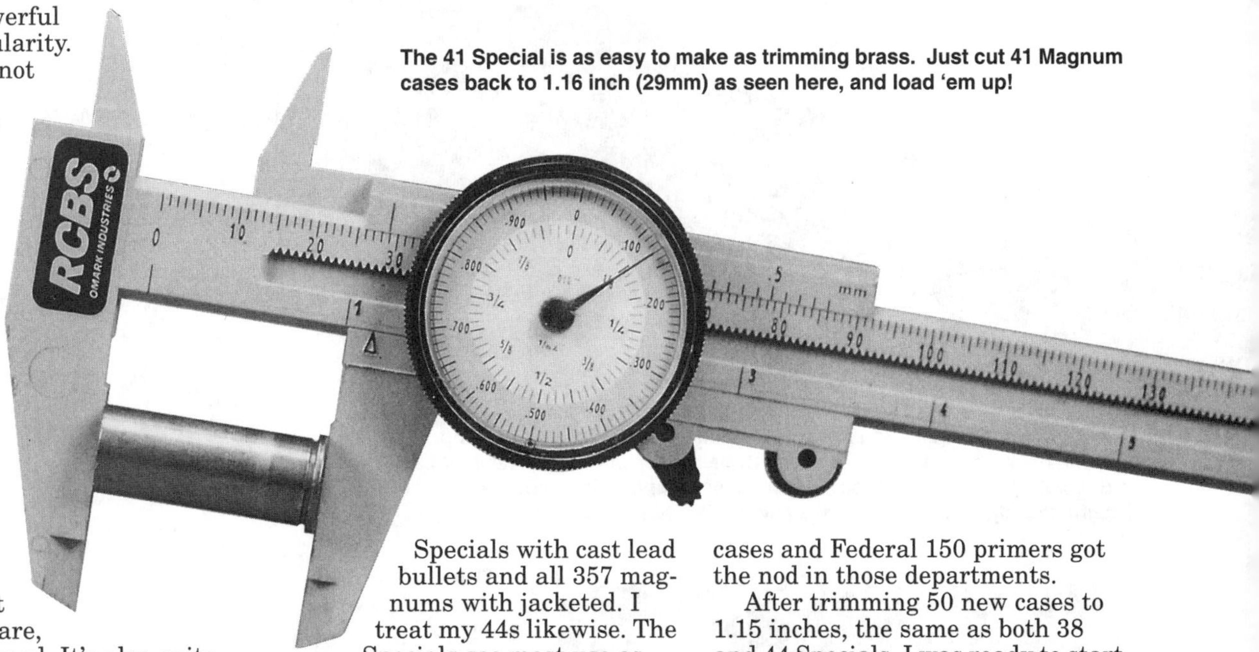

For this project, I reasoned that the whole point of the cartridge is to provide an alternate round for owners of 41 Magnum revolvers. So I simply borrowed a 41 Magnum Ruger Blackhawk from a shooting buddy and started load development.

Mechanically, this is one of the easiest wildcats of all to form. Simply trim 41 Magnum cases back to 'Special' length. But before I trimmed a single case, I researched the prospective round as thoroughly as possible. This was surprisingly difficult despite the fact that my reference shelves fairly sag with reloading books and yearly publications (my loving wife says I'm *annual retentive*). I found not a word on the 41 Special. But I did learn that the long-dead 41 Long Colt was once a popular round. Its ballistics were close to what I had in mind and it was known as a mild, accurate cartridge that hit harder than its paper ballistics would lead one to believe. What doomed the 41 Long Colt wasn't its performance but its outside-lubricated heel-style bullet.

I also found that 41 Magnum cases, components and reloading dies are plentiful. In fact they are sometimes the only items left on the shelf after 357, 44 and 45 shooters have been on buying sprees. Although those supplies include a wide variety of excellent jacketed bullets, I decided to restrict my tests to cast bullets. I load all 38

The 41 Special is as easy to make as trimming brass. Just cut 41 Magnum cases back to 1.16 inch (29mm) as seen here, and load 'em up!

Specials with cast lead bullets and all 357 magnums with jacketed. I treat my 44s likewise. The Specials see most use as practice rounds, casual field loads and general purpose loads where cast bullets are at their best. Only where magnum power and bullet expansion are needed do I select jacketed bullets.

To keep the variables as few as possible, I selected 215-grain SWC plain-based Laser-Cast™ bullets from Oregon Trail as my main bullet. This extremely well-crafted bullet is a Keith-style design with a wide driving band, one lube groove and a sharp shoulder above the crimp groove. Cast of a secret mixture of alloys, including silver, they are harder than your mother-in-law's stare. RCBS carbide dies, Federal

cases and Federal 150 primers got the nod in those departments.

After trimming 50 new cases to 1.15 inches, the same as both 38 and 44 Specials, I was ready to start loading. For powder charges, I used published starting load recipes for the 44 Special with 240-grain cast bullets, but reduced by a half grain. Although case capacity of the 44 is slightly greater than the 41 Special, I reasoned that reducing published starting loads and using lighter bullets would compensate. I selected pistol powders from Accurate, Alliant, Hodgdon, IMR and Winchester. In all, I have developed loads using 14 different powders, and have plans for others as time permits. Why so many? Because I have yet to find a bad load combination for the 41 Special! You read that right. *Everything* I've tried is good — and some are great.

A standard RCBS three-die set was used for all loads. Notice the seating/crimping die (*right*) has been ground shorter by one-eighth inch to allow the crimp shoulder to reach the shortened brass. Some die brands may not need this modification.

After working with a regular Ruger Blackhawk for initial load development, the author had this very early Ruger flattop 357 customized into a 41 Special by Clements Custom Guns of Mississippi. Tolerances are extremely tight, the trigger pull is fabulous and the finish work is superb.

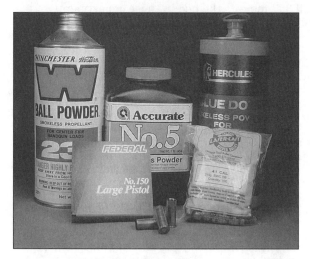

These components are the author's favorites for loads at three different power levels: 700-800 fps, 800-900 fps and 900-1,000 fps.

OK, you don't believe that. I wouldn't have, either. So let me describe my first range session. I took five batches of handloads (10 rounds each) using five different powders, along with boxes of Federal factory 210-grain jacketed hollow points and Remington 210-grain lead semi-wadcutter mid-range ammunition to the range. I fired several groups of both factory loads to establish baseline accuracy, velocity and case expansion parameters. All groups are ten shots at 25 yards from a padded rest. The Federal magnum load shot 2.75-inch groups at 1325 fps with a standard deviation of 19. Pretty good, as I've come to expect from Federal. The Remington mid-range load shot a 3.5-inch average at 1018 fps with an SD of 20. The Remington load was very dirty and left a goodly amount of barrel leading. Not a load I'd be thrilled with as my only alternative to full magnum power.

Then, after cleaning the gun, I started shooting Specials. The very first ten-shot group ran 2.75 inches, the same as the factory magnum load. My Oehler 35 chronograph said the velocity averaged 784 with an SD of 11. Very mild recoil and very clean. Hot dog! The next load clustered into a snug 2.5 inches with a velocity/SD of 918/6. That's a standard deviation of six! For those of you not statistically fluent, that's just short of incredible. Other loads that same day (just educated guesses at loading data, mind you) ran 2.75/821/11, 2.60/882/19 and 2.35/1016/7. Every load was pleasant to shoot, with minimal recoil and muzzle blast. Every group centered just above the point of aim. Was I happy? Is Bill Gates well off?

Back at the loading bench, my micrometer would tell me the Remington midrange and Federal magnum loads expanded cases to 0.4340 and 0.4355 inch respectively, measured just ahead of the case web. My Special loads ranged from 0.4340 to 0.4352 inch, meaning that I'd achieved my goal of a lower velocity cartridge with less-than-factory case expansion. Indeed, the group dimensions and standard deviation numbers said I'd equaled or bettered both factory loads in consistency. In 35 years of reloading, no project has ever met my expectations as well on the first firing. None.

The only hitch so far had been with the loading dies. The excellent RCBS carbide dies were perfectly finished and did their usual superb job. The seating/crimp die was machined for the full-length Magnum, however, so my shorter rounds couldn't be crimped. Instead, I belled cases as little as possible and simply seated the bullets so that the case mouth came to the middle of

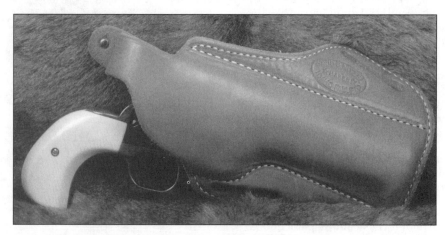

A custom gun deserves a custom holster. This high-ride crossdraw rig is made by Dave Nitzel of Dave's Hide-Out in Idaho Falls, ID. In use, the gun rides above the belt and just inside a half-zipped jacket – out of the way, comfortable yet ready for instant access.

the bullet crimp groove without crimping. I tested every round to make sure that any slight remaining case bell wouldn't hinder chambering. If a round wouldn't chamber, I rolled it on a hard surface while pressing down on the case mouth with the flat edge of a tool shank. I soon had a machinist friend grind an eighth-inch off the bottom of the crimp die. That eliminated the problem, and I can now load and crimp either Special or Magnum cases. I am told that Hornady dies, and perhaps others, will crimp 41 Specials without modification.

Full details are in the accompanying load data chart, but I'll summarize my powder choices here. Let me say again that I have yet to find a truly poor load combination. All of the listed powders produced ten-shot groups of three inches or less with extremely low velocity standard deviations. For the lightest loads, from 750 to 900 fps, the Special thrives on any of the fast-burning powders: Accurate Nitro 100, AA2 or Solo 1000; Alliant Bullseye, Green Dot or Red Dot; Hodgdon Clays; IMR 700X; or Winchester 231 all fit the bill. For loads from 900 to 1050 fps, the medium-speed pistol powders come into their own. Good ones include Accurate Solo 1250 or AA5, Alliant Unique, Blue Dot or their new American Select. Or try

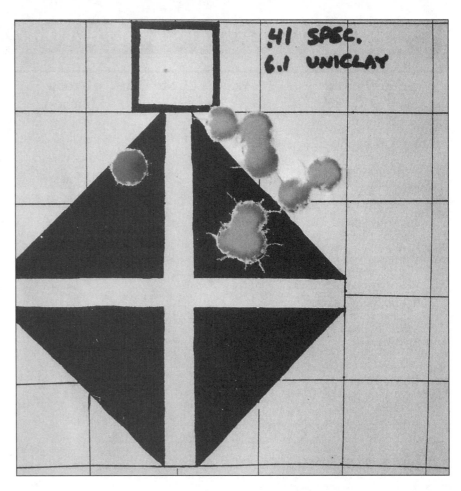

Author says he hasn't found a bad load yet for the 41 Special! This group is typical: Ten shots at 25 yards into 2.5 inches or less. This one develops 950 fps with a standard deviation of just 15.

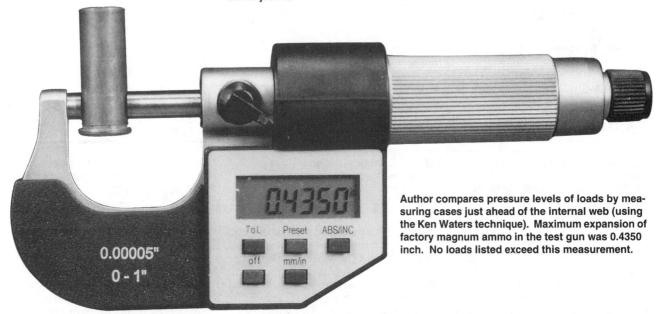

Author compares pressure levels of loads by measuring cases just ahead of the internal web (using the Ken Waters technique). Maximum expansion of factory magnum ammo in the test gun was 0.4350 inch. No loads listed exceed this measurement.

Hodgdon Universal Clays. I have no doubts that old standbys like IMR SR 7625, 4756 or PB would be great. Newer pistol and shotgun propellants like Winchester's Super Target and Super Field or any of the new high performance powders like Alliant Power Pistol or Winchester Action Pistol would likely be good as well. I can't wait to try them all. If

you'd like to experiment with any of these in the 41 Special, I'd suggest you consult published load data for the 44 Special with 240-grain lead bullets. Reduce the lowest listed start load for a selected powder by half a grain. Use standard strength primers only. This procedure has so far proven safe for me when used in the 41 Special with 215-grain lead

bullets. Of course, as in all wildcat cartridges, the results you get from your gun with your components and your loads can be quite different. So use due caution and pay strict attention to all pressure signs.

I didn't try for velocities much above 1000 fps, because that's what the magnum version is for. That being the case, I have no intention

41 Special Load Data

Grains/Powder	Velocity	Std Dev	Group (inches)	Remarks
4.5/Nitro 100	825	14	2.30	Good light load - Very mild recoil
4.5/700X	829	12	2.80	
4.5/Solo 1000	858	8	2.80	Very clean
5.0/W231	812	9	2.75	
5.0/Bullseye	877	10	2.60	
5.0/Clays	920	9	3.30	
5.0/Red Dot	882	19	2.60	
5.0/AA-2	836	11	3.00	
5.5/American Select	918	6	3.20	Very clean
6.0/Unique	934	15	3.50	MAXIMUM
6.5/Universal Clays	1016	7	2.35	MAXIMUM - Accurate
6.5/Solo 1250	1029	8	2.25	
7.5/AA-5	901	19	2.25	Good general load - Accurate an clean
9.5/Blue Dot	1093	11	3.1	Maximum

Note: All loads used Federal cases trimmed to 1.15 inches, Federal 150 primers, and Oregon Trail 215-grain lead semi-wad-cutter bullets. Average of ten-shot groups shot from padded rest at 25 yards over Oehler 35 chronograph. Ruger Blackhawk 41 Magnum revolver with 4 5/8-inch barrel and iron sights. All loads shown were safe in the test firearm. Reduce all loads by one full grain to start and monitor pressure signs.

of working with slow-burning powders like Accurate AA9, Alliant 2400 or Winchester 296. My philosophy has always been to let a cartridge do what it does best and not try to push it into performance levels outside its abilities. When I need more gusto, I reach for a bigger round. But for much of what I do with a revolver, the 41 Special works perfectly.

It works so perfectly that I reconsidered my original limitation of working only with a 41 Magnum Blackhawk. When the time came to return the borrowed Ruger used in this project, I was broken-hearted.

I'd found a wonderful new round but had no gun to shoot it in. I began a search for a 41 of my own. But for weeks and weeks, none appeared at the gun store where I then worked. Murphy's Law applies: When you find a gun you want, you won't have money; when you have money you can't find the gun.

One day, a man came in to sell a wrecked gun. It was a very early Ruger flattop in 357 Magnum. The gun had been in a holster rig and had fallen out of a truck. The belt had somehow caught on something, leaving the gun to drag and bounce down a rocky mountain

road. You can imagine the damage. It was worse.

The grips were gone, the grip frame had been ground almost completely away, the rear sight blade was broken off, and there were major rock dings all over the frame and cylinder. Like I said — a wreck. The storeowner said no thanks. Naturally, I bought it.

My first thoughts were simply to restore it as best I could. After all, dirt-cheap flattops don't fall off trucks every day. Suddenly, a thunderclap hit me. I could have a dedicated 41 Special! With fervor only another *gunophile* would under-

The way it shoulda been! The 357 has its 38 Special (*left group*), The 44 Magnum has its Special (*right group*), and, *center*, the 41 Special and its worthy partner, the 41 Special. What the factories have ignored, the reloader can create!

stand, I pawed through ads of parts suppliers and custom gunsmiths. I called and wrote letters. In the end, I purchased a brass bird's-head grip frame and synthetic ivory grips from Qualité Pistol and Revolver, then shipped the gun to Clements Custom Guns. I included rather broad instructions and followed up with several phone calls to discuss the project with Clement. I opted for his full conversion and accuracy treatment.

When he got it, Clement agreed that the gun was pretty sorry, but that he was confident he could make me happy. I didn't know that Mississippians were inclined to British understatement. Boy, did he make me happy. When the gun came back, I was stunned. This *couldn't* be the same gun I sent off. The only thing the same was the serial number. The photo shows how handsome the gun is, but what doesn't show is the quality of Clement's work.

In his full treatment, Clement re-cuts both frame and barrel threads, fits the new barrel, line-bores the cylinder, installs an oversize base pin with heavy duty catch spring, cuts an 11-degree forcing cone, faces the cylinder and sets the gap at less

than .003-inch, re-times the gun so there is no bolt drag, tunes the trigger to a ice-crisp 2.5 pound pull, smoothes the action, installs a post front sight, removes all original lettering from the frame, polishes and blues. The result is a gun with no endshake, almost no discernible cylinder play when locked, a bolt that drops into the locking cuts precisely on time, a butter-smooth action with a trigger as good as can be had, and a gun that just plain causes jaws to drop when people handle it. Keep in mind — this gun has had the transfer bar conversion! The factory transfer bar conversion makes a gun far safer, but hardly results in a gun with a smooth action and a crisp trigger. After Clement worked his magic, this one is as smooth as can be despite the transfer bar conversion.

As other gun writers often say, a custom gun deserves a custom holster. I chose a very practical and exquisitely constructed rig by the talented Dave Nitzel. It's a high-ride rig he calls the Crossdraw Hunter. I prefer untooled leather, and this one perfectly suits the gun with its oil-tanned elegance. In the field it rides just inside a half-

zipped jacket, out of the way and protected but instantly ready even if I'm scrunched up under sagebrush, calling coyotes. It rides comfortably even when I'm seated in my truck, too. A truly great field rig. It suits my custom Clements. (I can't in all conscience continue to call this gun a Ruger. I dote on Ruger revolvers, but this one goes so far beyond them that it no longer should be called anything but a Clements.)

Finally, does it *shoot*! Any group with more than one ragged hole is caused by the jerk on the trigger. Misses must be attributed to evil spirits or space/time warps. I have been forced to start wearing glasses merely to have a plausible excuse for my mediocre marksmanship. No doubt about it, this is one very Special 41.

Perhaps the time has finally come to commercialize such a round. Both 41 Magnum brass and reloading dies are regular items and can be effortlessly modified to Special length. (I hope RCBS and Starline are reading this!) No additional guns need be made. There is already a good selection of proper bullets. Factory ammo could be produced in no time. I don't know what the potential market is for such ammo, nor do I know that its availability would resuscitate the 41 Magnum. All I know is that the 41 Special is a very accurate, extremely consistent, delightfully pleasant round to shoot. It fills a real need. As a wildcat, it's easy to form, requires only a simple modification to your existing loading dies, and no new components. If you're a 41 Magnum owner, it's a round that you should try. **Finally, the 41 really is Special.** •

Suppliers

Clements Custom Guns
61060 Hatley-Detroit Rd
Greenwood Springs MS 38848
601-256-9626

Qualité Pistol and Revolver
5580 Havana #6A
Denver CO 80239
888-762-3030
qpr@earthlink.net

Dave's Hide-Out
10784 N, 5 E
Idaho Falls ID 83401-5412
208-525-8516

Oregon Trail Bullet Company
PO Box 529
Baker City OR 97814
800-811-0548
www.laser-cast.com

THE MATURE 22 WINCHESTER RIMFIRE MAGNUM

by C. Rodney James

IT WAS WITH prolonged fanfare that Winchester announced, in 1959, the first new rimfire cartridge in 43 years. Prolonged, in that it took them a year to build a gun for it. In light of recent developments, this 42$^{\underline{nd}}$ anniversary of the 22 magnum would seem a good time for a look at the past – and potential future – of this cartridge.

The 22 Winchester Magnum (22 WRM) with its jacketed hollow-point bullet at an advertised 2000 fps velocity, was introduced with great claims of power and flat trajectory — better than the original 22 WCF (predecessor of the Hornet) and shading the nearly obsolete 22 WRF, its nearest rimfire competitor, by well over 500 fps. According to Larry Koller, summarizing rimfire rifles in the 1961 *GUN DIGEST*, early rumors favored a revival of Winchester's Model 43 bolt rifle for the new cartridge. This likely inspired rimfire varmint shooters to think of the WMR as a long-range precision load.

There was plenty of press speculation regarding varmint shooting

potential to 125 yards and beyond, yet the first guns chambered for the WRM were handguns and it was not until 1960 that Winchester offered a rifle. To the disappointment of varmint shooters it was not a varmint gun, but a modified Model 61 — a light pump-action repeater. Stated Koller: *"Winchester's thinking is that the new cartridge is not essentially a long range precision load, that its greatest function will be as a short-to-medium-range rifle for small game, plinking and pests."* Thus began the controversy over what this cartridge was to become.

The idea of long-range (125-plus yards) varmint shooting with the WMR persisted. That first flush of enthusiasm eventually departed as serious shooters discovered that while the early guns and ammunition delivered the velocity and flat trajectories, accuracy was rather lacking and without that, power and velocity weren't much use.

What about the accuracy question? The critics were right, in a way. Top quality 22 LR match rifles, using

match ammunition properly wedded to the rifle produced groups under .5-inch at a hundred yards, with a world's record of .190-inch for five shots set by bench-rest shooter O. M. Dolgem. Since the 22 WMR has never been offered in a match loading, nor have match rifles been produced for this cartridge, this is hardly a justifiable comparison. A lot of bad science (*B.S.*) has been written regarding rimfire accuracy. Anyone seriously interested should read C. E. Harris' fine article "Getting the Best from the 22 Rimfire" in the 1992 *GUN DIGEST*. This blew away such myths as the bullet-weighing and rim-measuring path to accurate shooting, reaffirming such useful strategies as selecting ammunition by maker, type and lot with attention to the role of matching bullet and bore diameter in making the critical difference in accuracy for the premium sporting rifle. Anyone serious about rimfire rifle shooting should try to find a copy of C. S. Landis' *Twenty-two Calibre Rifle Shooting*. This 1932 Samworth book is the best

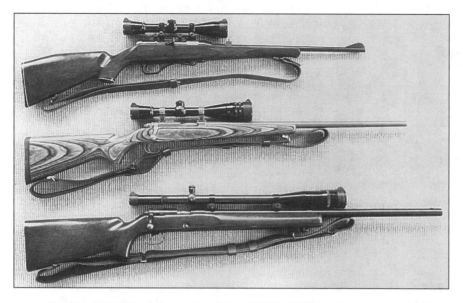

For testing, the H&K 300 autoloader and Ruger K77/22 VBZ bolt action were matched against a bull-barrel Winchester 52C LR target rifle. The 52 is accurate enough to take woodchucks at 100-plus yards. The obvious drawback for the Winchester — 46-inch overall length, weighing 13.5 pounds with the scope.

thing going on hunting and target shooting with the 22 LR.

Many people assume (*wrongly*) that, all other conditions being equal, the expansion of bullet-group size will progress in a simple arithmetical manner, doubling as range doubles. Thus, a nice .5-inch group at fifty yards will be 1-inch at a hundred. With really top-quality, accurate ammunition in a good rifle – in ideal conditions – this will be the case. With every other circumstance somewhere between seventy-five and one hundred yards bad things happen and that .5-inch fifty-yard, .75-inch seventy-five yard group blows out to 2.5, 3 – even 4 inches at a hundred.

Suffice it to say, the only reliable way to determine how your rifle/

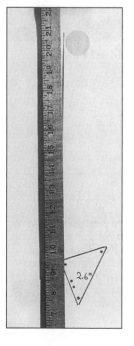

Why taking woodchucks at 150 yards with the LR is nearly impossible — a drop of a foot with the rifle zeroed at 100 yards — though the 2.6-inch group with the WW Power Point is a good one.

ammunition combination will group at longer ranges is to test them at these ranges.

The first generation of WMR rifles were adaptations of existing models of 22 LR sporting rifles. Nobody designed or adapted a rifle of the target/varmint type for this cartridge. As it turned out the WMR was about as accurate as the high-speed LR in the same five-and-a-half to six-pound rifles — producing 1- to 1.5-inch groups at fifty yards and 2-inch or larger groups at one hundred. With a cost of three to four times the LR, it offered greater lethality – but not the hoped-for long-range shots. However, reports began trickling in about a few rifles that actually lived up to some promotional claims of long-range kills on woodchucks and similar game. John Lachuk in his *1978 Gun Digest Book of the 22 Rimfire* offered two one hundred-yard groups for the WMR measuring .5 inch and .75 inch from a JC Higgins 42DLM rifle. The Marlin Model 57 in WMR also gained a reputation for grouping close to an inch – sometimes under – at that range.

The quest for flatter trajectories and long-range accuracy began inspiring various rimfire buffs to experiment with custom-barreled rifles for the magnum and even "reloading" the cartridge by pulling the factory bullets and inserting commercial bullets intended for the 22 Hornet. News of this activity was not greeted with enthusiasm by gun and ammunition manufacturers who discouraged the practice with warnings of excessive pressures and shortened barrel life. That experimenters were "*wildcatting*" the WMR may have provided inspiration for Federal and

Winchester to offer new loadings with precision-made bullets.

In 1988, CCI introduced the +V WMR — a 30-grain bullet with an advertised velocity of 2200 fps. The cartridge was an outgrowth of the 22 Stinger — the hyper-velocity round useable in a Long Rifle chamber. The Stinger had taken some of the edge off the WMR's velocity advantage and sold well. The +V re-established the WMR as a high-velocity competitor at a time the 40-grain round had been scaled back from a (*claimed*) 2000 fps to a (*slightly*) more realistic 1910 fps. The +V's high velocity also gave it a greater rotational speed, which helped keep the short bullet stable at longer ranges. Another innovation was that the jacket was applied by electroplating with pure copper. Early lots were plated, then sized down to the proper diameter. The spring-back factor in the copper resulted in bullets which were not uniform, and accuracy suffered. The problem was solved by making the bullets undersize, then "bumping" them up to the proper .2245-inch diameter.

Federal and Winchester soon followed CCI's lead in producing both light-weight bullets, and those with plated-on jackets, respectively. It also appeared that all three ammunition makers were striving for higher levels of accuracy and flatter trajectories with new bullet designs — Federal with a 30-grain JHP developed by Speer and Winchester with a 34-grain JHP. Remington, after a brief run of WMR in the early 60s, has come back with a 40-grain HP, a 40-grain pointed soft-point and a ballistic tip — a 30-grain bullet with a polymer point.

Imports of the WMR are few. Squires Bingham made 40-grain hollowpoints at one time, but these are no longer available. RWS offers a 40-grain loaded to higher velocities than the average American product.*

At the center of the controversy over WMR accuracy is the question unanswered since it was introduced — that of firearm versus ammunition. Critics claimed the cartridge itself was not particularly accurate, while supporters maintained the fault lay in a lack of really accurate rifles to draw out the round's full potential. In the June '96 issue of *Performance Shooter*, writer Jim Matthews took a major step in providing an answer. Matthews ordered a short, heavy, tight-chambered barrel for his Thompson / Center Contender Carbine from Fred Smith of the Bullberry Barrel Works in Hurricane, Utah. Smith claimed minute-of-angle – or better – groups at a hundred yards for the WMR. This claim was verified by Matthews whose

With far fewer offerings than the Long Rifle, the WMR has expanded from the single 40-grain loading by Winchester to a modest variety with good potential for accuracy. (*L to R*) Original WW 40-grain FMJ and HP; a more recent 40-grain with plated nose; 34 grain-JHP, CCI HP, FMJ, +V 30-grain and shot load. Federal 40 HP and FMJ, 50-grain HP and 30 grain HP. Remington 40-grain PSP and 40-grain HP. Last, RWS 40-grain HP.

hundred-yard groups averaged .6 inch for the Federal 30-grain, .6 inch for the Winchester 40-grain HP, .8 inch for the CCI 40-grain HP and 1 inch for the Federal 50-grain HP.

The next step was for someone to offer an out-of-the-box varmint rifle that would equal – or at least come close to – this level of performance with the new generation of ammunition. First into the field was Ruger with its K77/22 VBZ which came on the market in 1993. Advertised as a "varmint rifle," the Ruger features a 24-inch heavy barrel – hammer-forged for a slick bore – and weighing seven and a quarter pounds, making it the best contender as a precision rifle in this chambering.

The first K77/22VBZ rifle I tested blew 3.5- to 4.0-inch groups outdoors and at no time grouped better than 2 inches at a hundred yards. Some gun writers thought this level of accuracy was fine! A trip to Clark Custom Guns, and a new barrel, made only slight improvements. The rifle was returned to Ruger who tinkered with it a while and, having no success, scrapped it and sent a replacement. Ruger has an excellent, well-deserved reputation in customer relations. The

second rifle proved to be a far better shooter and had a tighter chamber (fired cases *mic* at .242-inch).

For reasons various and sundry the firearms industry has seen fit to bring out a raft of autoloaders in 22WMR. None of these has made news as a tack driver, but one of the more accurate appeared to be the Heckler & Koch Model 300. The H&K features a tight chamber (fired cases mic at .240-inch) and polygonal rifling. I judged it indicative of producing about the best accuracy that could be expected from an autoloader. Just off the line, however, is a new Remington autoloader — the 597 Magnum, which according to *Guns & Ammo* tests is capable of 1.49 inches to 5 inches at 100 yards.

Perhaps the biggest bone of contention in the testing business is the number of shots fired. Most writers condemn three-shot groups in favor of five – and five-shot groups have been demonstrated (*occasionally*) to produce skewed results. Those who think

of themselves as purists favor ten-shot groups. *How many?* Why not twenty-, fifty- or hundred-shot groups? Gary Sitton, in his article "Groups, Statistics, and Practical Facts" in the Sept/Oct 1990 issue of *Handloader magazine* (#147), offered the first statistical analyses of sampling methods in the popular press, based on a monograph by statistician Frank E. Grubs. This document built a case for seven-shot groups as being the smallest number of shots yielding the most reliable results as indicative of the "*true*" dispersion of a large number of groups – assuming the factors of shooter fatigue, heat and fouling were eliminated. Sitton also made a good practical case for three-shot groups with his Model 7 Remington in 243 Winchester, which regularly delivered excellent three-shot groups (close to .5 inch) and poor five-shot groups (close to 1.5 inches) as the thin barrel heated after the third shot. For varmint shooting, where no more than three shots will be taken at a

Fifty-grain Federal delivered this .9-inch group at 100 yards in the Ruger on a calm afternoon. Groups as small as .6 inch have been obtained with the 50-grain Federal in this rifle. The high trajectory of the 50-grain bullet puts it in the LR class in this respect.

			WIN 52-C	RUGER 77/22VBZ	H&K 300
WW	LR Power Pt 40gr		1.6"	—	—
WW	40gr	HP	—	2.2"	1.6"
WW	34gr	HP	—	1.7"	1.9"
Fed	50gr	HP	—	1.3"	2.5"
Fed	30gr	HP	—	1.2"	1.8"
Rem	40gr	SP	—	1.8"	1.3"
RWS	40gr	HP	—	1.9"	1.2"
CCI	40gr	HP	—	1.4"	1.4"
CCI	30gr	HP	—	1.8"	1.5"

TABLE 1.
100 Yard Outdoor Aggregate extreme spread three 5-shot groups

All groups were fired with a sandbag rest. These record groups were fired on a sunny afternoon with the temperature in the 70s; winds 2-7 mph. The H&K rifle likely benefited by being fired later in the day. The discrepancy in the performance of the Federal 50-grain can be explained by the longer-barreled Ruger providing a high enough velocity to stabilize this bullet at longer ranges. These figures can be considered "average" for a "good average" shooting day in the Midwest. Under dead-calm conditions results are much better. On windy days far worse!

target, this is an excellent, accurate rifle and a worthwhile measurement. For sustained, target-shooting activity — terrible!

Gentle reader, the above is included to stimulate your thinking, not to drive you 'round the bend. The tests conducted for this article were designed to give a general indication of optimum accuracy under what might be expected on a reasonably calm day outdoors. To keep fatigue and heat factors to a minimum, I opted for tests of 5-shot groups at 100 yards. For all tests a 22 LR Winchester Model 52C bull-barrel target rifle was fired with Winchester Power-Point hunting ammunition as a benchmark for comparative accuracy since the Power Point is the most accurate hunting cartridge currently available for this particular rifle, grouping .55 inch at 100 yards under ideal conditions and slightly over 1 inch under good conditions — winds under 4 mph. Under fair conditions (winds 5-10 mph,) groups spread to 2 inches.

As can be seen in **Table 1**. the wedding of the proper WMR ammunition to a high-quality bolt-action rifle will produce accuracy levels comparable to a LR match rifle using hollow-point hunting ammunition.

The point where the WMR really shines (in an accurate rifle) is at ranges *in excess* of 100 yards. Less deflection by wind and flatter trajectory are decided advantages.

In three April afternoons of 1998, eight woodchucks were taken with the Ruger using the Federal 30-grain

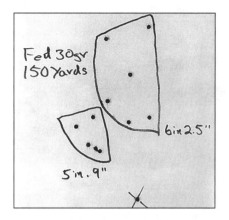

At longer ranges the WMR shines. With a 100-yard zero, the Ruger delivered this 6-shot 2.5-inch group with the Federal 30 grain at 150 yards in mid-afternoon with intermittent tail- and cross-winds of about 4 mph. The 5-shot .9-inch group was fired at 7:15 P.M. when wind had dropped to near zero. Group centers are -3.5 inches and -4.5 inches respectively.

bullet at ranges of 55 to 115 yards. All were one-shot kills, with either head- or heart/spine-shots. I have received reports of chucks killed at 200 yards with the WMR. I don't doubt this since I once drilled a crow dead center with a 40-grain FMJ Winchester WMR in the HK 300 at 225 yards – actual measurement. I did this *ONCE* – under dead-calm conditions and excellent light.

This will probably alienate some readers, but I find limited use for a light sporter/autoloader in this chambering. The only practical value would be for taking large varmints

(coyotes) at ranges of 50 to 60 yards. A few WMR autoloaders (the HK300 and, apparently, the Remington 597) are accurate enough for chuck shooting to 100 yards, but an accurate standard-weight LR target rifle will do that at one-third the ammunition cost. The downside of the target rifle is its length and weight. The autoloader does offer the quick follow-up shot which might have taken the chuck I missed with the Ruger 77.

The notion of the WMR as a "plinking" cartridge at $6.50-plus per box just doesn't compute when Long Rifles can be had for $1.00 at the discount store. Handguns for this cartridge make even less sense since none are particularly accurate and the ballistic performance is only slightly above the Long Rifle - except in very long-barreled (8- to 12-inch) handguns. The construction of the WMR cartridge is such that making a cheap round simply isn't feasible. To expand the usefulness of a rifle of this caliber, a subsonic loading with a lead, hollow-point bullet (ballistically akin to the old Remington Autoloader) would fill a useful niche for short-range pot-hunting where low noise and minimal bullet upset are desired by those who want to buy one multi-purpose rimfire rifle.

Mike Jordan at Winchester proposed a loading of this sort, though more akin to the WRF with a 45-grain bullet, but with the longer WMR case to prevent gas erosion in the magnum chamber that occurs when large numbers of short-length cartridges are fired in a longer chamber. The WRF will function through some actions, but usually not very well. I thought this was a terrific idea, but Jordan described the suggestion as *"falling on deaf ears."*

After four decades, the WMR has evolved from a high-powered rimfire to emerge a good small varmint rifle cartridge to about 100 yards under good shooting conditions (good light, wind 3-5 mph) and to perhaps 150 yards under very good conditions (good light, wind under 3 mph) and 175-200 yards under *ideal* conditions (dead calm, excellent light) in a stiff-barreled bolt-action varmint rifle. On breezy days, accuracy is about like a Long Rifle – with marginally better wind-bucking ability at ranges under a hundred yards for the higher velocity rounds. For the dedicated chuck hunter who does not want to get into reloading and is disciplined enough to pick his shots carefully, a WMR varmint rifle makes good sense. ●

* *The only reliable source for the RWS WMR ammunition is:*

The Old Western Scrounger, Inc.
12924 Highway A-12
Montague, CA 96064
(800) 877-2666

Fired into water at close range, the lightweight bullets exhibit the shattering effect so lethal on varmints. Forty- and fifty-grain bullets expanded well, while offering deeper penetration. *(L to R)* Federal 30-grain JHP, WW 34-grain JHP, WW 40-grain JHP, Rem 40-grain PSP, Rem 40 JHP, Fed 50 JHP.

TABLE 2.
Chronographed Velocities of Ammunition
(5-shot group avg.)

			RUGER 77/22VBZ	H&K 300
WW	40gr	HP	1766	—
WW	34gr	HP	2052	—
Fed	50gr	HP	1443	1329
Fed	30gr	HP	2058	—
Rem	40gr	SP	1777	—
RWS	40gr	HP	1905	—
CCI	40gr	HP	1837	1744
CCI	30gr	HP	2193	2157

All groups were chronographed 12 feet from the muzzle with an Oehler 35P chronograph. Temp 67˚F. As could be expected, the shorter-barreled autoloader produced about 5 percent lower velocity.

The Water-Proof Rifle:

THE BEGINNINGS OF THE WINCHESTER REPEATER

by Ken Aiken

IN A REGION known for the manufacturing of inventive firearms, the development of the first practical rifle using self-contained cartridges wasn't hailed as a historic milestone, but rather as just another variation of the underhammer lock system made famous by another local gunsmith. The importance of the "Water-proof Rifle" becomes evident only when tracing the histories of the Winchester Repeating Rifle Company, Smith & Wesson, and even the Sharps Rifle Manufacturing Company to their common origins. Christopher Spencer once acknowledged that the magazine of his famous repeating rifle was based upon the chambering system of this early firearm, a gun almost entirely unknown to modern collectors.

On February 20, 1839 U.S. patent number 1,084 was jointly awarded to Lebbeus Bailey (Port-

A view of the "Water-Proof" Rifle — brass barrel tapers from breech to muzzle. Some parts appear to have been supplied by N. Kendall & Company. The button to release the hinged magazine door in the buttplate can be seen on the brass plate on the side of the stock.

land, Maine), John B. Ripley (Claremont, New Hampshire), and William B. Smith (Cornish, New Hampshire) for "Bailey, Ripley & Smith's Improvement in Fire Arms." The design was based on the combined experience of three accomplished gunsmiths: Lebbeus Bailey had worked as a gunsmith for Captain John Harris Hall in North Yarmouth, Maine during the years when the Hall breech-loading rifle was invented and first built;[1] William B. Smith was one of the principal partners of N. Kendall & Company in Windsor, Vermont and had patented "Smith's Improved Patented Stud Lock" in 1838;[2] and John B. Ripley was a local gunsmith who produced underhammer rifles.[3] Produced in Ripley's gunshop in

---

1. Captain John H. Hall was granted a patent in 1811 for a breech-loading flint-lock rifle. On March 19, 1819 the U.S. Ordnance Department contracted to manufacture 1,000 of these rifles at Harper's Ferry Armory. Captain Hall was given the position of assistant armorer (with a salary and royalty of one dollar for each gun manufactured). Designated as the United States Rifle Model 1819, it continued to be improved and was manufactured until 1844.

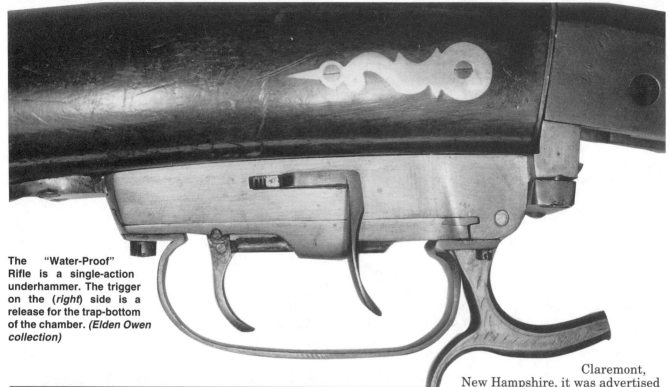

The "Water-Proof" Rifle is a single-action underhammer. The trigger on the (*right*) side is a release for the trap-bottom of the chamber. *(Elden Owen collection)*

The patent drawing for Bailey, Ripley & Smith's gun. *(Elden Owen collection)*

Claremont, New Hampshire, it was advertised as the "Water-proof Rifle."

The concept of a self-contained cartridge wasn't a new idea, in 1812 Jean Samuel Pauly of Paris, France had patented a breech-loading pistol that used a reloadable brass cartridge[4] and a breech-loading German wheel-lock rifle attributed to the late 16th century used reloadable steel cartridges.[5] Nor were multi-shot firearms a new idea: experimentation with multiple-shot firearms dates back at least to 1500 and several American innovations were spurred by the War of 1812. In 1813 Joseph Chambers invented not only a 10-shot flintlock rifle, but also a 224-shot, seven-barrel swivel gun[6] and in 1818 Elisha Collier, Cornelius Coolidge, and Artemus Wheeler, all from Boston, patented a flintlock revolver.[7] But it was the invention of the copper per-

---

2. The dating of underhammer guns, especially those produced by N. Kendall & Company, is difficult since not every firearm was stamped with a serial number. However, any firearm stamped with "Smiths Pat" or "Smiths Pat Improved Lock" can be dated no earlier than 1838. Furthermore, I recently discovered an underhammer rifle in the collection of Terry Tyler that is stamped with the serial number 1 (on the butt plate, barrel, and rear sight) as well "Smiths Pat Improved Lock" — apparently the sequence of serial numbers on N. Kendall & Co. rifles was begun anew sometime in 1838. Coincidentally, rifles produced by Robbins, Kendall & Lawrence are also stamped with a new sequence of serial numbers.

3. An underhammer rifle in the collection of Eldon Owens, which looks very much like a Kendall, is clearly stamped "J.B.Ripley" and "1837" on the barrel.

4. Pauly wasn't the first to develop a cartridge firearm. A German breech-loading wheel-lock rifle that used a reusable steel cartridge and which is dated as late 16th century is pictured on page 30 of *The Great Guns* by Harold L. Peterson and Robert Elman, Grosset & Dunlap, Inc., NY, 1971

5. Two photos of this breech-loading wheel-lock rifle (one with the breech open and a cartridge beside the gun) are shown of page 30 of *The Great Guns* by Harold L. Peterson and Robert Elman, Madison Square Press/Grosset & Dunlap, Inc., NY, 1971

6. Joseph Chambers of Washington, Pennsylvania received a patent in 1813 for "repeating gunnery." The 10-shot sliding-lock rifles were produced by Simeon North in Middletown, Connecticut in the mid-1820s. The producer of the swivel guns is unknown, but they were mounted on the captured frigate *Guerrìere* during a refit by the U.S. Navy in 1814. Both utilized flintlock ignition.

7. The patent model for this revolver incorporated an automatic primer and a cylinder that rotated when the pistol was cocked, but no production models are known to have this feature. E.H. Collier's version of this gun (produced by Samuel Nock in London) used a manually-advanced cylinder (British patent #4315) and was the most successful. Coolidge received a French patent and assigned or licensed it to Perin LePage. Artemus Wheeler continued to produce the gun in Boston, but soon Collier's English version was being exported to the United States where it competed successfully against Wheeler's.

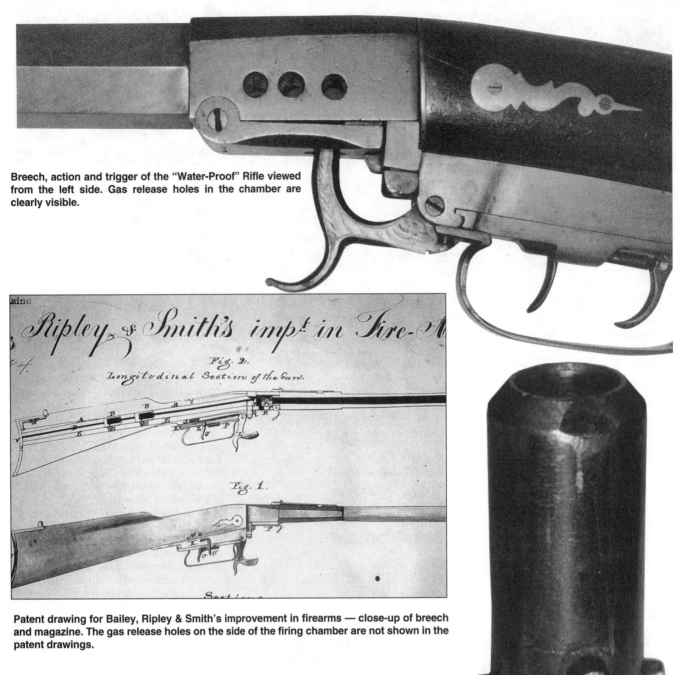

Breech, action and trigger of the "Water-Proof" Rifle viewed from the left side. Gas release holes in the chamber are clearly visible.

Patent drawing for Bailey, Ripley & Smith's improvement in firearms — close-up of breech and magazine. The gas release holes on the side of the firing chamber are not shown in the patent drawings.

An original steel reusable 41-caliber cartridge for the "Water-Proof" Rifle. The protrusion on the side are guide pins; the one in front is the nipple; the beveled front helped to seal the breech.

cussion cap by Joshua Shaw[8] that encouraged the next evolution in gun design in the mid- to late 1830s.

It appears that percussion caps became commercially available in the United States around 1828 — about the time the first percussion underhammer firearms were built.[9] However, it was Nicanor Kendall, working in the shop of Asa Story of West Windsor[10], Vermont, who developed the most popular style of the underhammer lock. Besides being simpler and having fewer parts than sidelock mechanisms, the benefits of having the hammer on the underside of the gun reduced the leakage of moisture down the tube of the nipple into the powder load and provided a clean line of

---

8. Joshua Shaw the artist, not Captain Joshua Shaw of Philadelphia as often erroneously attributed to. Joshua Shaw of London received a U.S. patent for his new application of fulminates on June 19, 1822, but he didn't arrive in this country until 1827. Joshua Shaw first used iron, then pewter, and finally copper for his percussion caps, however, it was the widely published work of E. Goode Wright of Hereford (who, in 1823, substituted fulminate of mercury for the chlorate of potash), that made the copper percussion cap a practical ignition system. An English gunsmith, by the name of Joseph Egg, was the first to commercialize the use of Shaw's percussion cap sometime between 1823 and 1827.

9. A few rare examples of underhammer flintlocks exist, but those with upside-down side-hammer locks are not considered to be underhammers. Although the existence of a true underhammer lock prior to the late 1820s using a pillbox fulminate is probable, and two examples on Kentucky-style pistol stocks are known, I've not found evidence of one ever predating the known New England percussion pistols.

10. In the early 1830s West Windsor was called West Parish; guns stamped "A. STORY W. WINDSOR, VT" date from the 1840s. In some histories Nicanor Kendall is listed as being an apprentice to Asa Story, but my research leads me to believe that because of this prior experience he was hired as an assistant sometime between 1830 and 1832.

The "Water-Proof" Rifle showing the trap. The wedge on the end of the trap door functions to seal the cartridge to the breech and close the magazine from the firing chamber.

sight (without flash) on the upper surface. The underhammer quickly became a regional favorite and in 1835 Nicanor Kendall organized a company that included Asa Story and William Smith as partners in the venture. N. Kendall & Company entered into a contract with the Vermont State Prison at Windsor to establish a shop within its walls for the manufacture of firearms using convict- and paid labor. Using the shop facilities of the prison,[11] the company began to produce underhammer rifles in quantity.[12] By 1838 N. Kendall & Company were producing not only muzzle-loading rifles and "boot" pistols, but also the five-shot Kendall Harmonica Rifle, the twelve-shot Bennett & Haviland "chain" repeater, and the six- to nine-shot Whittier revolver rifle. By 1839 numerous gunsmiths in the region were producing underhammer firearms and, due to the simplicity of the firing mechanism, several styles of multiple-shot underhammer rifles were designed during this era.[13]

However, the rifle designed by Bailey, Ripley and Smith, although an underhammer, didn't resemble any of these other guns; it was, and

remains, a unique firearm. Only two of these guns are known to exist and recently I had the opportunity to examine both of them. One is original while the other has a steel barrel added in 1943 (it was found without one, but the rest of the gun is original). The gun with the new barrel was obviously designed as a fowling piece while the smaller caliber would have been used for game; all measurements and descriptions refer to the smaller caliber gun.

The gun measures 42 inches overall; the 21-inch barrel is made of brass, is octagonal in shape, and tapers in diameter from the breech to the muzzle. It's a 41 caliber and, despite the fact that it's referred to as a rifle, has a smooth bore. It's an underhammer, the stock bears a resemblance to a Kendall, and it appears that certain parts may have been supplied from N. Kendall & Company.

The steel cartridge tube measures 1 1/4 inches long, is flat at the back, has a tapered edge at the front (to form a gas seal with the barrel), and has three protrusions perpendicular to the cylinder position near the rear. Viewed from the back of the cylinder, two of these

protrusions, positioned at 3 and 9 o'clock, are solid pins that are used for alignment; the slightly longer protrusion positioned at 6 o'clock is the nipple for the percussion cap.

The magazine is loaded from a hinged door in the brass butt plate; the door is opened by pressing on a brass button on the left side of the stock near the front of the brass hardware. The tube magazine is drilled through the wood stock and three grooves (the one for the nipple and percussion cap is larger than the other two) keep the cartridges aligned so the percussion cap is in the correct position when each round is chambered.

The trap door is located on the bottom, in front of the brass lock and just behind the barrel. (On the inside lip of the trap door is stamped either "6" or "9.") The hinged trap is fitted on the inside with a flat spring (in a recess, attached by a single screw, on the left side) and a wedge (on the rear inner lip opposite the hinge) of steel with a rectangular base, which tapers from front to back and has a slight curvature to the back surface. A hole, through which the hammer strikes the percussion cap, is in

11. In joint partnership with the prison, Issac Hubbard (not Ashael Hubbard who invented the pump) was producing water pumps (National Hydraulic Company) in a state-of-the-art shop within the prison walls by 1834. The shop included foundries for casting in bronze, pewter, and cast iron; a steam engine for powering machines; a series of blacksmith forges; and a woodworking shop. N. Kendall & Company had access to these facilities in addition to their own specialized machinery. The marketing of the underhammer guns was done through the agents of the National Hydraulic Company.

12. The first contract, made through the Louisiana agent of the pump company in November of 1835, was for several hundred rifles for the Republic of Texas: they were delivered in 1836.

13. Elijah Jacquith of Brattleboro, Vermont designed an underhammer with a revolving cylinder (patent #832 of July 12, 1838); R.B. Moulton of Proctorsville, Vermont was making a harmonica rifle similar to Kendall's; and John Cochran's revolving turret rifle and a version designed by Henry and Charles Daniels were both being manufactured in Springfield, Massachusetts by C.B. Allen.

These rifles were fabricated in Ripley's shop in Claremont, New Hampshire, just a few miles from Windsor, Vermont. How many of the component parts were made in Claremont and how many, if any, were supplied by N. Kendall & Company, is unknown. I was fortunate in being allowed to examine an underhammer rifle made by Ripley in 1837 which is patterned after a Kendall, but the finishing work is crude in comparison. William B. Smith, who was an active partner in N. Kendall & Company in 1838, would have been in a position to supply Ripley's shop with parts cast and fabricated in the shops of the Windsor prison; the sophistication and finishing of the lock case and mechanism suggest this possibility.

This firearm was advertised as the "Water-proof Rifle" and reputed to be popular with local hunters (but probably was quite expensive). How many of these unique "rifles" were produced is unknown, but I was told that Ripley's shop, located in an old woolen mill, was destroyed in a fire a couple of years after the gun began being manufactured, so the numbers were probably very limited.

It is known that after the shop burned, an apprentice who worked on the production of the Water-proof Rifle went to work for N. Kendall & Company and later became a master gunsmith for Robbins, Kendall, & Lawrence. Working on the Jennings Repeating Rifle with Richard S. Lawrence and Daniel Wesson, this master gunsmith continued to apply the knowledge learned in John Ripley's shop to perfect the modern repeating rifle — his name was Benjamin Tyler Henry. ●

front of the wedge and to the side of the spring. Cocking the hammer, then pulling the special "ejection" trigger (located on the right side of the brass lock) releases the catch on the sprung trap and allows the reusable cartridge to fall out. When the hammer is cocked and the trap open, turning the gun over (or bottom up) and tilting it forward, chambers the next round. When the trap is closed, the steel wedge forces the cartridge against the barrel breech, creating a tight gas seal and also isolating the magazine from the firing chamber.

This gun is extremely sophisticated: the first application of a tubular magazine in a percussion gun; the first application of a self-contained cartridge used in a repeating firearm; and the second known application of a reusable steel cartridge are features of note. It also appears easy to use, is not especially heavy, and is better balanced (probably because the barrel is brass) than most guns of the era. It required a lot of hand work to make the parts fit; the trigger system looks especially complicated and appears to be built with horological precision.

SIG SAUER

The Science of Accuracy.

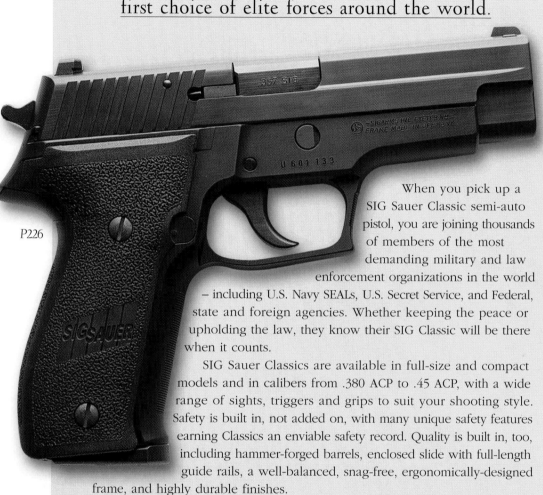

FULLY LOADED

Our most comprehensive line of autoloading shotguns ever.

Gold Camouflage Series
Mossy Oak® Shadow Grass™

Gold Stalker Series, Deer
(Scope not included)

Gold Upland Special

Waterfowl, turkey, upland game, deer, trap, skeet or sporting clays. Whatever your game, there's a Gold autoloading shotgun for you. With 23 different models, the Gold is the most comprehensive line of autoloading shotguns Browning has ever offered.

From specialized target guns to heavy-hitting magnums. Camo,

black synthetic and wood finishes. Each model is fully loaded with standard Gold features, such as a self regulating gas system, back-bored barrel and Invector Plus™ chokes that work together to give you the softest-recoiling shotgun on the market. All Golds also have speed loading and a balance point precisely between the shooter's hands.

Always make sure you store your firearms and ammunition separately and make sure you check out the Gold line — It's fully loaded.

The Gold's self-regulating gas system shoots all loads interchangeably, from 1 oz. light target loads to the heaviest magnums.

BROWNING

www.browning.com

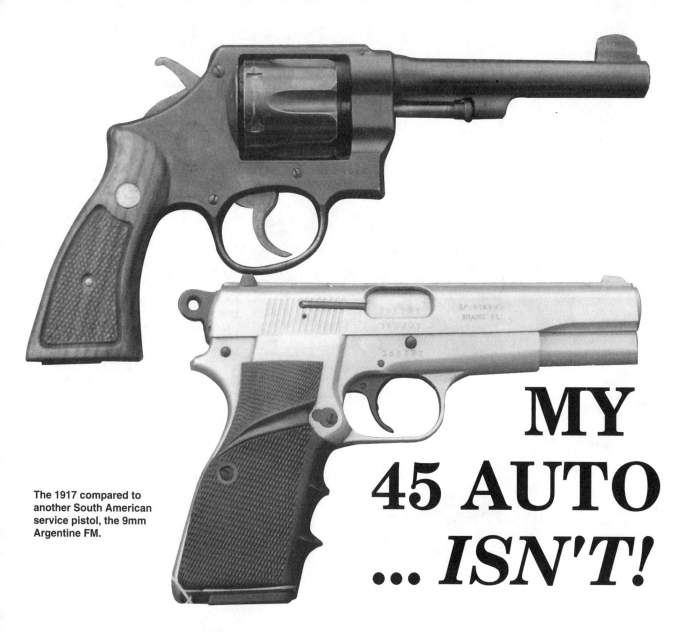

The 1917 compared to another South American service pistol, the 9mm Argentine FM.

MY 45 AUTO ... *ISN'T!*

by Bob Campbell

IN TODAY'S HANDGUNNING world, the revolver is viewed as inherently deficient in accuracy, hit probability and "firepower" – whatever that is. Fact is, the revolver is an excellent choice for many shooters…and a viable fighting tool for anyone in need of life-saving equipment.

Today the revolver is seldom thought of as a military weapon, but Smith & Wesson revolvers are still front-line equipment. Swedish aviators are issued Airweight Model 12 revolvers and Navy *SEALs* carry stainless Combat Magnum revolvers for special use. But the last great revolver war was World War I. Enfields, Colts, Smith & Wessons – and various European military revolvers – barked and drew blood. Some of these revolvers were substitutes for the standard issue sidearm, but revolvers were indeed

front-line equipment with both the British and French armies. America would also find itself with a front-line revolver.

The history of the Smith & Wesson Model 1917 is one of the more interesting tales in handgun lore. If not for the Great War, we would not have the 1917. Under-appreciated today, the 1917 is arguably the finest combat revolver ever produced. Perhaps it came along just a little late in the game, soon to be eclipsed by modern high-capacity auto-loading pistols. But when it was needed, it was needed badly – and most appreciated!

I respectfully submit the best fighting revolver ever produced could not have been manufactured before the advent of autoloading pistols, since the design of this revolver depended upon the avail-

ability of the most effective and widely-used autoloader cartridge – the 45 ACP.

Let's take a look at the history of the Smith & Wesson Model 1917 and, briefly, that of U.S. martial revolvers. There are those who say the Colt Single Action Army was outdated when introduced, but this did not stop the pistol from becoming a legendary sidearm. The gun worked reliably and used a powerful cartridge – the 45 Colt. The potent combination of revolver and cartridge also proved itself in civilian use: The cowboy could drop a problem steer or horse at close range, if need be.

The Army was seduced by the swing-out cylinder of the double-action Colt Model of 1892, and purchased this handgun to replace the Colt SAA. What followed in the field were disastrous *failures to stop*.

Loading a *full-moon* clip into the revolver.

When the ejector rod is pushed, the cases come out – regardless of the orientation of the revolver!

A 38-caliber 152-grain bullet at 750 fps simply did not do the job previously done by the big Colt 45 cartridge. Colt SAAs were reissued; but what the Army really needed was a modern, big-bore repeating pistol. The turn of the century was the heyday of the revolver and, though many

autoloading pistol designs emerged, few were reliable or powerful enough for martial use. While there were a few exceptions, for the most part, revolvers were of sturdy design and reliable function.

Smith & Wesson did an extensive redesign of their revolvers. The break-top simultaneous ejection, so successful in the Webley, did not prove as popular with Americans. If anything, the British were fonder of our revolvers than the opposite.

Smith & Wesson introduced their hand-ejector models just at the turn of the century. The name – *hand-ejector* – comes from the fact that break-top revolvers ejected spent cartridges during opening, whereas the swing-out cylinder revolver required a second, separate action to eject spent cartridges. These new S&W revolvers were offered in several frame sizes. The toughest and most capable were *N*-frame revolvers. These revolvers were chambered for cartridges such as the 44 S&W Special and the 45 Colt. *N*-frame revolvers are robust, accurate handguns capable of tackling real problems. They were fine defense guns but also offered the cowboy and outdoorsman a backup to the rifle, capable of taking large animals at close range.

Colt offered a competitor to the S&W Hand Ejector: the New Service. This is a fine revolver, but my hands fit the Smith & Wesson better.

To understand the advantages of the 1917 we must have a good understanding of the merits of the 45 Colt cartridge. Here was a large-caliber cartridge, throwing a

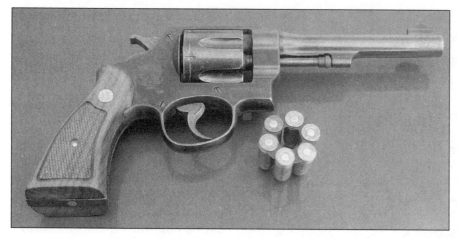

The 45 revolver, with *full-moon* clip.

This revolver, in daily use, has been refinished in tough, durable and attractive *Metalife* finish. Ready for another century of use? Probably.

255-grain .454-inch bullet at 900 fps in popular loadings. The 45 Colt cartridge had one shortcoming. The case rim diameter was a bit undersize for use in a *star-ejecting* DA revolver mechanism. The 45 Colt worked fine in rod-ejecting single-action revolvers, but was prone to slipping past, and jamming beneath, the ejector *star* of a swing-out DA revolver in typical field use. Still, the venerable cartridge was the only game in town – in it's day.

Both Colt and Smith & Wesson large-frame revolvers were in production when pistol-poor Britain found itself fighting the Germans in World War I. Both companies' revolvers, chambered for the British 455 Webley cartridge, were ordered in quantity by British purchasing.

When the United States entered

This holster is well-executed, both structurally and historically.

World War I, peacetime stores of arms were not adequate. Fortunately, our arms industry had been in full production of the Enfield rifle, Smith & Wesson and Colt revolvers. The Army decided to purchase an additional sidearm to supplement production of the Colt 1911 45 Auto. The Colt – and Smith & Wesson – revolvers were certainly suitable, and of proven design.

To avoid the logistics problem of issuing and supplying more than one handgun cartridge, it seemed a simple expedient to chamber revolvers for the 45 ACP cartridge. However, those rimless cartridges had no case rim to be acted upon by a revolver's 'star' ejection mechanism.

An ingenious solution was found in the form of a pair of thin sheet metal 'half-moon' clips which held three cartridges each, allowing the revolver to properly headspace and providing contact with the revolver's ejector 'star.'

The cylinder chambers on early '17s were bored straight through and required the use of *half-moon* clips. Later guns had their chambers revised and bored to properly headspace on the cartridge case mouth. This means the gun could be fired without 'clips and the fired cases picked out singly; no problem for casual shooting.

Since thousands of 1917s were delivered, it is a safe bet many saw use in the trenches. Combat reports from the war show many more mentions of the 1911 auto indicating cavalry and other front-line troops were issued the 1911 when possible.

After the war, many 1917s were sold as surplus. Some went to various federal agencies. including the U.S. Border Patrol. Others went to various banks and post offices, serving to defend against the various robber gangs of the day. Inevitably, the 1917 saw use by Chicago mobsters.

Civilian shooters did not like the 1917's *half-moon* clips, which were seen as a nuisance. Remington answered this problem with a fat, rimmed cartridge known as the 45 Auto Rim. This cartridge headspaces in the normal revolver manner, on the rim.

After World War I, the 1917 continued in production, thanks to a few military contracts, the largest – 30,000 guns – from Brazil. Evidently all the 1917s were not sold as surplus after World War I, since a few saw limited use in World War II.

Because the British had purchased revolvers chambered for the 38 S&W cartridge prior to WWII, the U.S. purchased revolvers chambered for the 38 Special as *substitute standard* issue!

Two of the handiest revolvers of all time: the Smith & Wesson 1917; the Smith & Wesson Model 36.

The 1917 has remained fairly popular in America, with a few die-hard enthusiasts favoring this gun over the 45 Auto. For many reasons, the 1917 is still a viable all-around handgun. I favor handguns that are versatile and, while self-defense is a good reason for owning a handgun, recreation, hunting and pest control are others. The 1917 is up to all of these chores.

Over the years, I have owned most of the handguns manufactured in this century. The 1917 is one of the top two or three, in my opinion. Let's take a look at how the '17 stacks up.

Compared to 45 Colt-chambered revolvers, the Model 1917 chambered for the 45 ACP is more efficient. In factory trim, the 45 ACP round is loaded to a higher intensity than the other cartridge. For the handloader, the 45 ACP beats the 45 Colt with most practical loadings. With a 230-grain bullet at 850 fps, a 200-grain bullet at 950 fps or a 185-grainer at 1050 fps, the 45 ACP will do the job – with less powder and reduced recoil. I don't dispute the 45 Colt is the more powerful round with heavy handloads but, for general use, the 45 ACP is very capable.

Compared to the magnums, the 45 ACP is a superior battle round. It delivers as much terminal effect as any handgun round, but with a minimum of recoil and muzzle flash. But there is more to the equation. There is no revolver faster to load and unload than the Model 1917 using *half-moon* clips. When the ejector rod is stroked, the cylinder contents are ejected whether the gun is held vertical, horizontal – or canted in any direction. The spent cases are leaving the gun – period! There is no chance of a single cartridge slipping past the ejector '*star*,' a considerable advantage over any rimmed revolver cartridge.

The 45 ACP, carried in 3-round *half-moon* clips, is handier and lighter than most charged 6-round speedloaders and more sure in use. Reloads must be done with the barrel of the revolver pointed downward, but we are loading a complete device, not loose cartridges. The 45 ACP revolver can be extremely quick in practiced hands.

Don't confuse these *N*-frame revolvers with modern 'magnum' N-frame revolvers. With fixed sights and a skinny barrel, the 1917 is relatively light and fast-handling. Draws from appropriate holsters are fast and lineup on target sure. For prolonged use with magnum loads, a thick barrel and heavy underlug might make more sense – but the 1917 is easier to carry, day to day.

With practice, good double-action shooting can be accomplished. The old long action differs from more modern actions in its longer hammer throw. I have fired both types and the older long-action is really smoother, just as the old-timers claim. By rocking the double-action trigger just to the breaking point - sighting and squeezing off the last few ounces carefully, long-range hits in the double-action mode are possible.

The 1917 is more than accurate enough for taking small game and medium game at moderate ranges. The accuracy of some examples can be surprising.

My 1917s have been fed a steady diet of handloads over time, which brings us to a fallacy concerning these handguns. More than one writer has mentioned the 45 ACP revolver as a suitable understudy for the 45 Auto, suggesting the revolver will digest handloads not suitable for the autopistol.

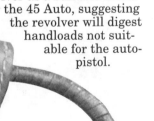

With the 1917/1937 revolver and a good holster, you are ready to go afield – or defend hearth and home – in excellent fashion.

The old revolver, with relics of WWI and WWII.

Actually, the revolver demands care in crimping and proper headspace or it will not perform well.

With care, the revolver will prove more versatile than any autoloader. Few autoloaders will feed and function with a load that sends a 185-grain semi-wadcutter out at 750 fps, then purr along with a 230-grain JHP at 900 fps.

The revolver will. It will also fire shotshells, plastic bullets – even 260-grain full wadcutters – with equal aplomb! The revolver will lie idle for long periods…and come up shooting regardless of lubrication or maintenance.

Speedloaders and 'moon-clips – the latter is much more compact. Two-round clips allow a box of fifty rounds to be clipped up and ready.

Matthew Campbell found the 1917 (vintage 1937) a comfortable-shooting revolver.

I like many modern autos – and own a few. But there is no handgun more capable and useful as an all-around workhorse than my Model 1917. The 1917 was created by one of those fortunate acts of fate, and seems destined to be a handgun important to the genre well into the next century.

Handloading for the 1917

Loading for the 45 ACP revolver is simple. Due to the 45 ACP head-spacing on the case mouth, a heavy roll-crimp cannot be used – unless you always use 'moon clips or you use the 45 Auto Rim case. I have had fine results with the 45 ACP case and moderately heavy loads. But the 1917 is most pleasurable to fire with light target loads. Pen-pal Ted Gillert passed along his favorite target load, which I have appropriated for my own use, while giving credit where credit is due. His load, a pleasant one, is 4.0 grains of Bullseye behind a 185-grain lead bullet.

If you seek a tack-driving load – and who doesn't – try sizing your cast bullets to just under throat diameter. I have done this and – believe me – the 1917 can be an accurate revolver! The 1917 may be an anachronism but its performance is not. Find one while they are still available and give it an honest try. If you appreciate versatility and performance, a 1917 may be the gun for you.

Production of the Model 1917 did not approach the magnitude of the Colt 1911 autoloader – but quite a few were manufactured. Colt's official wartime production totals are 163,476 guns. Our government took over production to speed delivery on September 13 1917, increasing production from 4,000 to as many as 14,000 guns per month.

Commercial sales in the 1921 to 1941 period were weak, although Smith & Wesson cataloged the gun for many years. A bright spot was the sale of some 25,000 guns to Brazil. Known as the 1937 Model, they were delivered in 1938.

After World War II, the Model 1917 was brought back. Smith and Wesson had sold only 991 guns by 1949 and the old war-horse was finally discontinued. Heavy-barrel, target-sighted 45 ACP revolvers continued to enjoy some popularity.

These guns crop up from time to time in the hands of die-hard outdoorsmen – and cops. These folks know what they are about. ●

Reproduction holster source-
International Military Antiques,
PO Box 256
Millington, NJ 07946

The Model 1910 Ross:

"The Best Rifle In The World"

by Jim Foral

"Today we are suffering from the small bore, light bullet, high velocity craze in game shooting," wrote Chauncey Thomas in 1911. E.C. Crossman observed the trend and made a similar statement: "We are on the verge of a high-velocity era." The generation of Thomas and Crossman was witnessing the dawning of the era of high-intensity rifles and the quest for high velocity in rifle cartridges.

THE RIFLEMAN OF the 1920s was experiencing not only the passage of the black powder age, but an almost-overnight transition to the smallbore high velocity approach to rifle ammunition. One rifle/cartridge combination in particular exemplified the abrupt progression to this high velocity outlook, and caused such an electrifying sensation, that it would have a profound influence on how riflemen would continue to regard rifles. The rifle featured a proprietary chambering that would have an equal impact. This new rifle was not the lever gun Americans had learned to shoot with, nor was it made in New England. It was a bolt-action – a straight-pull yet – produced at the unlikely location of the Balnagown, Quebec, plant of the Ross Rifle Company.

The 280 Ross cartridge caused a mild stir with its introduction in 1908 in the little-known Model 1907 Ross rifle. The watchful public's exposure and familiarity was limited until an improved rifle to handle the strenuous chambering was released two years later. The unveiling of the Ross 280, claiming a muzzle velocity of 3,100 fps in the new Model of 1910, was met with the same astonished reception a similar cartridge with a muzzle speed of 4,000 fps might be greeted with these days.

This nearly-new 280 was the former possession of an Iowa doctor who used it to hunt deer and bear in northern Minnesota before World War I.

Just as anyone familiar with the U.S. service rifles – the Krag and Springfield – used the same designation for the rifle and its cartridge, the sporting Ross rifle, cataloged as the Scotch Deer Stalking Model, and the 280 Ross cartridge were commonly referred to as simply *"the Ross."*

The 1910 Ross rifle and its cartridge, in combination, had an enchanting effect on the era's rifle shooters. The sporting literature available was aglow with reports of the Ross' continual conquests in long-range target competition. Canadian 'regulars' shooting the Ross were the winners of the McKinnon Cup Team match in 1909, 1910 and 1911. Every single match rifle event at the 1912 and 1913 Bisley Matches, including the highly coveted King's Prize, was won with a Ross. A Ross match rifle also accounted for the Individual Palma Trophy at Camp Perry in 1913. The list of victories was extensive and impressive. Reports from the game fields of every quarter of the globe were just as flattering. There were claims the Ross had an almost mystical ability to dispatch the largest animal *"no matter where hit."* Ralph Edmunds used his iron-sighted Ross to kill a bighorn sheep at a mile's range. C.C. Luke killed three grizzlies in less than a minute with his Ross. Jim Dyer checked an Alaskan grizzly's charge at thirty feet with his Ross 280. In the hands of the world's sportsmen, the Ross had slain the great beasts of India, Africa and the Arctic. By 1913, every schoolboy and big-game hunter – would-be or otherwise – had fallen under the spell of the Ross. That the sporting Model of 1910 was especially hard to come by outside of Canada, was outrageously expensive, boasted extraordinary ballistics and had been consecrated in the sporting press, contributed to the attraction and allure of the Ross.

Until about 1912, the Ross Rifle Co., concentrating its production efforts on its Canadian and British clients as well as arming the Canadian military, made no effort for the American trade. Accounts were circulated that even simple requests to the factory for catalogs, postmarked from south of the border, were ignored. *"The Ross 280 is not on sale generally in the United States, but your dealer can get full particulars from us"*, a mid-1911 advertisement states. Unable to lay their hands on a Model 1910 Ross, many a salivating American shooter was guilty of coveting his Canadian neighbor's Ross. U.S. demands were met in 1913 when the Ross Rifle Co. appointed the New York City firm of Post and Floto as their exclusive wholesale agents. Ross sporters gradually began to trickle across the border. The 1913 list price, duty paid, was a dear $55. Cartridges sold for $7.50 per hundred. Fifty-five dollars represented several weeks wages for a lot of folks in the high-power rifle market. One 1913 shopper, apparently a few dollars short, complained: *"The price is too high for most of us, and the rifle is not put out in the 280 bore for the poor man."* The Ross firm justified the high price of its products: *"The Ross is not made to compete with the cheapest guns possible to make. It is made to compete with the best ones possible to make."*

Americans yearning for the Ross could attribute their arousal, in large part, to the promotional efforts of American columnist E.C. Crossman. Generally considered the foremost firearms authority of the day, Crossman was capable of influencing a lot of people. Crossman was sent a Ross 280 and a quantity of ammunition early in 1910, and was instantly captivated by the Ross. From the Springfield to the Ross, Crossman's allegiances strayed. He zealously expressed his considerable delight with the newly-introduced rifle with a hearty

barrage of superlatives. *"It would be hard to put out a more perfect arm,"* he wrote in 1910. Crossman repeatedly and unabashedly endorsed the Ross as *"the best rifle in the world,"* and the *"handsomest rifle I have seen."* In a promotional pamphlet circulated by the Ross Rifle Co., Crossman, holding aloft the banner of the Ross, vividly labeled it as the *"rifle of my dreams."* Elsewhere he was moved to say: *"There is no question that the Ross rifle and the Ross 280 cartridge form the finest combination in the world at present,"* and that the Ross was *"head and shoulders above every other arm."* The Ross possessed, according to its Los Angeles champion, *"a perfect trigger pull."* The 280 cartridge was endorsed with equal vigor: *"Without question the 280 cartridge is the most perfect in the world at the present time."* Crossman touted the Ross with such intensity that his enthusiasm was misinterpreted, irritating a segment of his readership. He was openly and repeatedly accused of acting as a paid press agent for the Ross Rifle Co., but no one was surprised when Crossman denied the charges.

At the time, there prevailed a period of dissatisfaction with America's lever-guns and a fascination with some imported rifles that boasted greater power

and vastly better finish. The various Mausers, Mannlichers, and - ultimately - the Ross, made inroads into the American rifle market, alarming and dividing American riflemen. There existed quite a vocal segment of the rifle shooting public that resisted the imported guns and rallied for an avoidance of the intruding foreign rifles affecting sales of the established U.S. arms makers. There were those that felt that *"the goods that come out of New Haven are plenty good enough"* and *"why would anyone want a Ross when we have the Winchester '95"*? In contrast, there were others who couldn't take their eyes off the Ross, drooled over the hand-fitted Mauser or pull their noses from the pages of the importer's catalog with its startling ballistic tables. Americans began to view the mass-produced lever gun in a different light. Some Yankees, whose loyalties to New Haven were not well disguised, complained that since the Ross was invented by a Canadian, it should remain in Canada. A critic to this logic explained that

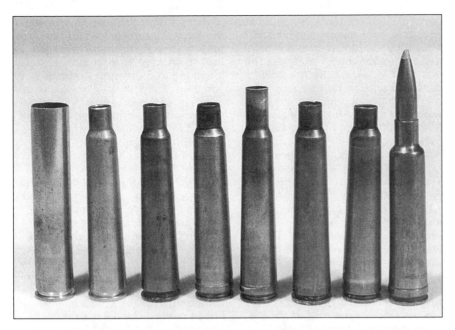

Left to right: B.E.L.L. 280 Ross Basic case – unformed; B.E.L.L. case formed into 280 Ross case; 280 Ross case headstamped R.R. Co. .280 Ross (Ross Rifle Co.); 375 H&H case fireformed to 280 Ross, neck is partially sized; die-formed 375 H&H case, untrimmed; U.S. Cartridge Company case; 30 Newton case die-formed to 280 Ross and 7x61mm Sharpe and Hart cartridge. Case capacities are identical.

the recent invention of wireless telegraphy by an Italian was revolutionizing communications worldwide, and no one demanded that it be restricted to Italy.

Townsend Whelen was a fan. He owned a 1910 Ross equipped with a Lyman #48 sight. As a military man expected to champion the Springfield, Whelen risked being branded a heretic and considered unsupportive of American goods when he publicized his appraisal of the Ross. In 1912 he wrote that *"...it just might be the kingpin of all rifles."* Charles Askins, Sr. wasn't quite as enthusiastic. Askins was basically a shotgunner who reported: *"I am not really interested in the rifle, but in the cartridge and its use in light rifle."* But he also wrote: *"I consider the Ross a good gun, perhaps the finest military rifle made."* Linsey Elliot, a gunwriter from Carbon, Alberta expressed his opinion of the Canadian rifle. He opined that the stocking and checkering was *"of the very best,"* and that the correctly-proportioned shotgun butt with checkered buttplate was a sensible element in managing recoil. *"The balance of the rifle,"* he tells us, *"is perfect."*

The 280 Ross cartridge case had the unusual distinction of being designed from the ground up, and not adapted from an already-existing case. Sir Charles Ross experimented with the .30-1906 case

necked to 28 caliber as early as 1906, but found the 2,700 fps velocities achieved didn't measure up to his goals. By early 1907, Ross was working jointly with the U.S. Cartridge Co. on the design of an enlarged case that would hold enough smokeless powder to propel a bullet of good sectional density to a velocity that would

Rear view of 1910 receiver showing rear bridge, magazine cutoff, safety, and the 'do-nut hole' bolt handle.

exceed the magic 3,000 fps mark. The result of extensive experimentation was a sharply tapered rimmed cartridge that would ultimately be distinguished as the first practical commercial cartridge to break the 3,000 fps barrier.

The Ross has a smokeless powder developed especially for it. Sir Charles' experiments disclosed that no existing powders produced the high velocities he required, and Du Pont was asked to develop a nitrocellulose powder to suit the need of a high-pressure, large-capacity case. Du Pont responded with #10, a Pyro powder, and one of the earliest smokeless varieties not nitroglycerin-based. #10 was slow-burning owing to its rather long (.120-inch) kernels and had a reputation for being cool burning. It was said to be easy on barrel steels. The standardized load for the Ross 280 with a 145-grain bullet was 56 grains, which gave a chronographed velocity of 3,050 fps from the 28-inch Ross barrel. A 180-grain Match bullet was propelled by 52 grains. Before becoming available to the limited handloader's market in 1912, resourceful cartridge developers wanting to determine #10's suitability to their primitive large-capacity experimental cases obtained the powder by purchasing Ross Rifle Co. factory loads and pulling the bullets. Until 1912, it was known as *"Ross powder."*

With the velocity increases of military and sporting cartridges soon after 1900, the drawbacks of existing metal-cased bullets became

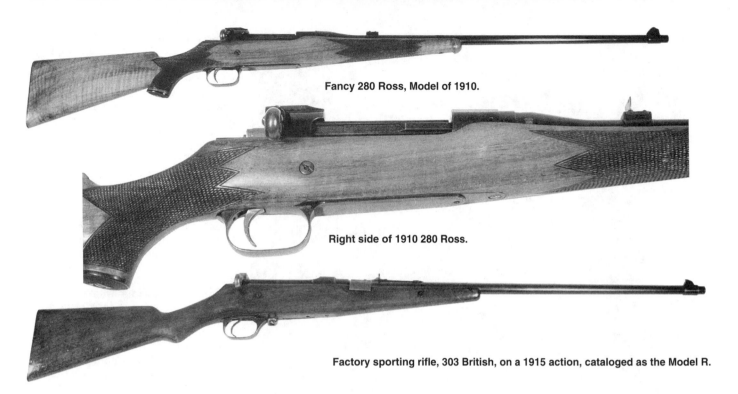

Fancy 280 Ross, Model of 1910.

Right side of 1910 280 Ross.

Factory sporting rifle, 303 British, on a 1915 action, cataloged as the Model R.

very apparent. Bullet jackets simply hadn't progressed to the same degree as other aspects of ordnance. Cupronickel, an alloy comprised of 85 percent copper and 15 percent nickel, was state-of-the-art in 1908, but reached its practical limitation at the 1903 Springfield level of velocity. At the muzzle speed of the Ross, cupronickel fouled terribly. The Ross Rifle Co. experienced considerable difficulty with metallic fouling and accuracy troubles when they first introduced the 280. Until the end of 1909, their cartridges were made for them by an outside concern. When the decision was made to manufacture their own ammunition, a detailed study of the conditions that affected metallic fouling was conducted. Due to the inconsistency of vendor-supplied cupronickel, the degree of fouling varied from lot to lot of ammunition, and the Ross reputation suffered accordingly. The company, in late 1909, experimented with jackets drawn from mild steel, and ultimately adopted this metal for their bullet jackets. These new steel-enveloped bullets were given public trial at the Bisley Matches in 1911. A slightly lower muzzle velocity with the steel jackets was traced to an increase in friction compared to cupro-nickel. Interestingly, a communication from the Ross Rifle Co. in 1914 states the *"firing a shot or two with our steel-jacketed bullets very effectively removed cupro-nickel fouling."*

The Ross 280 had the flattest trajectory of any cartridge available at the time. At 400 yards, the Ross shot as flat as the 30-40 Krag shot

at 200 yards. Sighted an inch high at 200 yards, the Ross bullets struck 3.5 inches low at 300 and eight inches low at 400, which is about on par with the 7mm magnums of today. Ross advertising made marketable use of the flat path followed by the 145-grain Copper-Tube, detailing the gloomy results of what happens to hunters who underestimate the distance to the game.

The Ross Copper-Tube represented the level that jacketed bul-

lets had advanced to by 1910 and was the patented end-product of many attempts by Sir Charles to produce a ballistically efficient bullet that could be depended upon to collapse on impact, not foul unduly and be exceptionally accurate. At its point, a cavity one quarter-inch deep and an eighth-inch wide was lined with a .006-inch thick copper tube, which extended a half-inch into the lead core of the projectile. In theory, the bullet's impact on flesh compressed the air inside the tube and fragmented the forward

part of the bullet. The base and core continued to penetrate. The Ross catalog describes this action as *"literally an explosion."* In practice, the Copper-Tube often behaved like a solid, zipping completely through an animal. Reports from the world's game fields spoke of the extremes of bullet performance. Some hunters reported instantaneous kills, others lost wounded trophies. Taken as a whole, the consensus seems to be one of general satisfaction. W.H.

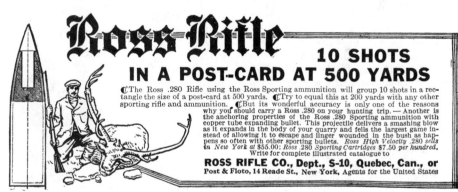

Beasley shot everything the Far North had to offer with the Ross system. Moose, caribou, grizzly and musk-ox fell to his Ross. Complete bullet penetration, in most cases, was his observation. Crossman liked the Copper-Tube, and was impressed with a long string of clean kills made by *"his own fair hand."* He loudly and ardently praised the astonishing accuracy they delivered through his own rifle equipped with a 3 1/2-power Pernox scope sight. By any standards, four to seven inch groups is outstanding

Setting up for steel penetration tests of the Ross and Springfield, summer of 1914. From left: John Colby, E. C. Crossman's range assistant; Crossman is wearing the campaign hat. The lady is Mrs. Crossman. (*from Outers Book, November 1914*)

accuracy, when the range is five hundred yards. After slaying a pair of hard-to-kill goats in 1911, Crossman declared *"the Ross Copper-Tube is a bomb."* Sometime later, he opined the Ross bullet was *"the most murderous missile ever invented, size considered."*

In an age when the 8mm Mauser was considered *"so tremendously powerful,"* hunters who tried the Ross developed almost a reverence for its startling effect on game. Contributors to the outdoor magazines of the period wrote glorifying testimonials to the great shocking effect of the 3,050 fps velocity and the destructive Copper-Tube bullet. A successful moose hunter in 1914 reported the *"powerful Ross knocked the bull down as if it had been struck by lightning."* The well-known Ralph Edmunds wrote: *"I have killed about two dozen elk, but never one in its tracks until I used the Ross."* Chas. Shaffer recommended the Ross 280 *"for anything that wears hair."* A New Zealand hunter used the Ross and Copper-Tube bullets on the local red deer and pigs and recorded: *"I find the game as dead as it can conveniently be on short notice."*

Ross Rifle Co. catalogs and advertising stressed the tremendous accuracy of the 280 Sporter as an enticing sales feature. Some of the claims would represent phenom-

enal accuracy, even by today's standards. The catalogs insist the Model 10 would produce ten-shot groups at 200 yards that generally would not exceed an inch and a half. Other Ross literature states, without humility, that the 280 Ross sporting rifle – with proper ammunition – *"would hit a ten-cent piece every shot at eighty yards,"* and a 1915 ad professed that, with Ross Sporting Ammunition, ten shots would group on a postcard at 500 yards.

With the resounding and thoroughly advertised successes of the Ross Match rifle on the world's target ranges, there appeared to be little reason to refute the company's seemingly extravagant claims. Results of accuracy testing by period analysts present the viewpoint of riflemen not bent on selling rifles. No one in 1913 would have argued that Cap-

tain Townsend Whelen was incapable of testing a rifle. Whelen took six Ross sporters from a dealer's stock, and invested a day shooting ten-shot 200-yard groups. He wrote that the average group he was able to obtain was eight inches. Reports filed by other writers tended to validate what Whelen had determined.

E.C. Crossman was as familiar with the Ross as anyone in North America. Having been once crowned the State High Power Champion of California, he was – if anyone was – capable of wringing out the Ross from a standpoint of accuracy. He repeatedly reported groups of four to seven inches at five hundred yards from his Model 1910 280.

The 280 cartridge was introduced to sporting circles in late 1908. A few rifles were made on the 1905 and the obscure 1907 actions. The Match Mark II rifle, with a heavy 30 1/2-inch barrel, was chambered for the 280 in 1909, and the combination successfully cleaned up every long-range match in Canada, England and Scotland. A remarkable reputation for superior long-range accuracy was quickly and solidly established. A listing of victories won with the Ross included the Waldegrave, the Albert and the

303 British factory load flanked by two partially-fireformed cases fired in oversized 303 Ross chamber.

Edge Cup trophies. A special single-shot variation of the Model 1910 was produced which featured an elaborate optical front sight and a heel-mounted rear sight for use in the back, or supine, position. Using special match cartridges featuring sleek 180-grain hollow-point bullets at 2,800 fps, this model earned the unchallenged reputation as the world's most accurate rifle.

The 1910 action had a multiple-lug bolt head and, like all other Ross rifles, was of straight-pull design. Fundamentally, the mechanism operated on exactly the same principle as the Yankee, or spiral, screwdriver. The bolt sleeve is hollow and five inches long. The bolt handle is integral to the rear of the sleeve and at a right angle to it. The Ross bolt sleeve does not rotate, but slides smoothly in its 'ribways' milled into the receiver, aided in part by a roller to the rear of the sear. The bolt, and bolthead, achieved movement by four opposed helical- or spiral-shaped ribs that followed corresponding grooves in the sleeves. The engagement of the bolt's ribs and the sleeve's grooves transmitted movement to the bolt. Their rate - or twist - was one turn in six inches. When the bolt was pushed forward the last three-quarters of an inch of bolt travel, the lugs rotated into the lug recesses in the receiver, locking the breech. The 1910 bolt glides into the receiver in a horizontal plane, and rotates counter-clockwise to lock in a vertical position. The bolt of the Model of 1905, with its solid lugs, enters the locking lug recesses vertically, and rotates to lock horizontally.

One of the most significant and emphasized characteristics of the Ross was the strength of its action.

Actions of the 1905 (*top*) and 1910 contrasted. The 1905 bolt with solid lugs which slid into the receiver vertically and locked horizontally. The 1910 bolt lugs entered the receiver from the horizontal and locked vertically.

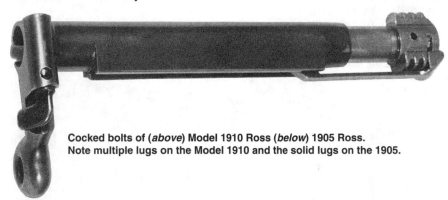

Cocked bolts of (*above*) Model 1910 Ross (*below*) 1905 Ross. Note multiple lugs on the Model 1910 and the solid lugs on the 1905.

Ross advertising dwelled on the breeching system of the M1910 as being similar in construction and principle to the interrupted-thread multiple-lug artillery guns. In-house testing at the Ross factory, generating pressures in the neighborhood of 100,000 psi, failed to damage bolt or receiver. Contemporary experimenters actually attempting to fail a Ross action succeeded in generating pressures that flowed case heads and bent locking lugs, but were defeated in blowing a bolt or destroying a receiver. When Springfield Armory was carburizing Springfield receivers for tensile strength, the Ross receiver and bolt were being heat-treated. Period

Ross advertising claims the then-current rifle strength requirements were exceeded by the 1910 action, and that it was designed to handle whatever the future might bring.

Shooters of the 1910-1915 era had witnessed a headlong succession of ballistic advancements that had occurred very rapidly. Still greater progression was forecast. Unavoidably, there were prophets. An excerpt from the Ross catalog, referring to the Model of 1910 action, effectively capsulizes the expectations of a generation of riflemen: "...*made up particularly to handle the pressure of any cartridge that may be developed within the next decade...to a time when perhaps 4,000 fps velocity, steel cartridge cases and far higher pressures will be the characteristic of military cartridges.*" When the world of ordnance was ready to advance to the higher levels forecast, the Ross 1910 would be found amply strong.

Ross barrels were made of carbon steel. Rifling was four grooves with a twist of 1:8.66 inches. Oddly, the muzzles of Ross barrels were not crowned. Machine rest tests indicated better accuracy was achieved through this method. Purchasers were advised *"a trifle more care must be taken to protect the muzzle from chance blows."* Barrel length for the 303 British sporters was 22 inches. Standard for the 280 Ross Sporting version were 26- and 28-inch barrels. The factory refused to make the 280 barrels shorter than 26 inches on account of *"interference with the ballistics of the arms."*

The Ross magazine was of the staggered type, and capacity was four rounds. A magazine depressor, designed to facilitate dump-loading the magazine, was standard on the 1905 Sporter and also found on some 1910

280 rifles. A flat fingerpiece was positioned on the right side of the rifle just forward of the receiver, so that the fingers of the left hand could press this fingerpiece downward. Depressing this lever drove down the magazine follower, allowing four cartridges to be

dropped into the magazine. Besides being a speedy way to charge the magazine, this mechanism (which Crossman referred to as the "shaker") allowed a person to close the bolt on an empty chamber by depressing the fingerpiece and closing the bolt.

3 GRIZZLIES IN UNDER 1 MINUTE

Feb. 10, 1913—Writing to tell you how pleased I am with the .280 Ross. Last season in Cassiar, B.C. I went after 13 head and bagged the lot, at ranges varying from 60 to 500 yards in 27 shots. My bag consisted of Black Bear, 4 Grizzlies, 2 Goat, 2 Cariboo, 2 Moose. In my estimation there is no rifle to compare with the "Ross .280."

The balance is perfect, the action fast and smooth while the flatness of trajectory quite does away with the judging of distances.

I shot a goat at over 500 Yards with exactly same Sight that I take at 100 yards. The 3 grizzlies were killed in under one minute. Cluny C. Luke, Alberni, B.C. *(Extract letter to Ross Rifle Co.)*

$55.00 The "Ross" .280 High Velocity is now retailed in New York City, duty paid for $55.00 and the Ross .280 Ammunition, with copper tube expanding bullet, patented specially adapted for it, at $7.50 per 100.

Get one NOW for your next trip. If your dealer cannot show one write for illustrated catalogue.

ROSS RIFLE CO., Dept. S-14 QUEBEC, Canada.
Wholesale Agents for U.S.: POST & FLOTO, 14 Reade St., New York City.

Some seldom-seen Ross memorabilia. The catalog is faintly stamped *"Return in five days to Harvey Donaldson, Rome, New; York."* Harvey dated the catalog also – March 5, 1914. At right is a partial box of Ross Rifle Co. factory cartridges. The prudent sportsman didn't leave camp without his Marble's broken-case extractor, this one in 280 Ross.

A nearly noiseless wing-type safety was located at the rear of the bolt sleeve atop the bolt handle. The rear sight is mounted on a barrel band. A single folding leaf has a plain "V" notch in its center. A hair's width platinum wire is inlaid in the leaf, extending vertically from its base to the vertex of the notch. The simple front bead sight is also mounted in a band. Holding the bead in the bottom of the notch zeroed the rifle for close range. A five hundred yard sight setting was obtained by placing the bead at the top of the notch. A slick bridge-mounted peepsight was available as an extra cost option. The peep springs up – absolutely silently – when its lock is pressed. When not in use, it folds down level with the top of the receiver.

The stock is classically elegant in profile. The general lines suggest a degree of pre-WWI British influence. Stock wood was selected Italian walnut. The 1910 Model stocks I have examined all exhibit a moderate amount of figure. Ross literature claims that stocks were given a finish in an *"oil bath."* The forearm terminated in a Schnabel

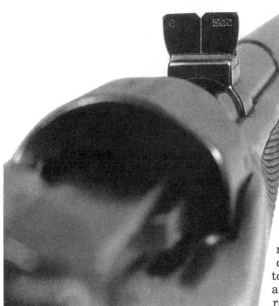

The simple rear folding sight on the Model 10. The vertical line at the bottom of the notch is an inlaid platinum wire.

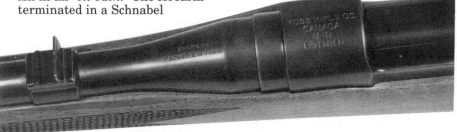

Receiver and barrel stampings on the Model of 1910, 280 Ross.

Magazine depressor of the 1905 Ross, sometimes encountered on the Model 10 sporter.

traditionally found on rifles of this period. A checkered steel buttplate protected the butt. The pistol grip was capped; some in steel, some in hard rubber. Model 1910 rifles destined for the English trade had no buttplates, but featured the butt nicely checkered. A cheekpiece could be added at no extra cost. A wrap-around checkering pattern on the pistol grip was extensive and very nicely executed. The forearm was also checkered. Compared to the generally fair quality of checkering found on most factory sporters of the period, the checkering on the Ross ranks among the very best.

Overall, there is a very apparent sense of quality to the Ross. It is cosmetically and aesthetically appealing to those with classic tastes. Rifle shooters of any generation would be hard-pressed to find a more nicely fitted factory rifle.

By 1912, the Ross company introduced a variation of the 1910 Model to conform with American preferences and intended for the U.S. market. E.C. Crossman introduced the new model to an awaiting American public in the October, 1912 issue of *OUTERS* magazine.

The action was the basic model of 1910, and the changes were

purely cosmetic. The U.S. model had an inch shorter length of pull, a somewhat narrower grip and a significantly higher comb. While still retaining the Schnabel, the forend sported a neater and trimmer appearance.

The stock was patterned after a design the Ross Rifle Co. had solicited from Ludwig Wundhammer, who knew something about American taste in rifle stocks. Aside from the stocking modifications, the bolt handle was turned down closer to the side of the receiver, and the barrel length was reduced to 26 inches.

Crossman expressed his approval for the 1912 Model in his usual fawning manner: *"The rifle is as fine a weapon as one could desire...a splendid and well-fitted weapon."* Crossman added the wood and metal were finished *"without a flaw."* Two targets of ten shots each, shot at the Ross factory's five hundred-yard range, accompanied the test rifle. A postcard would hide one group, and very nearly cover the other.

Sir Charles Ross realized his straight-pull rifle, compared to a turn-bolt design, had a serious shortcoming in its weak extraction capabilities. The Ross lacked the powerful initial camming and shearing effect that raising a bolt handle produces. The action of the locking lugs camming out of their seats, in the first inch of the bolt's rearward movement, provided the model 1910 with the major part of its extractive force. Ross critics pointed out that different and weaker muscles of the hand and arm are used to manipulate a straight-pull rifle as opposed to a turn-bolt. To compensate for inadequacies in the extraction department, Sir Charles contrived adjustments to the 280 cartridge design. The case was rimmed, allowing for greater purchase on the case by the extractor. Secondly, the Ross case benefitted from a distinctly sharp body taper, at the sacrifice of powder space. A somewhat-oversized chamber was employed, seen predominantly in the 303 British combat rifles that saw service in the European trenches, where positive extraction could literally become a life or death proposition. The bullet was undersized. A nominal .288-inch diameter has been widely maintained as the accepted groove dimension.

Depending on which reviewer was doing the reporting – and the source of his information – groove diameters of .289/.292-inch were declared. Bullets, on the other hand, measured .002/.003-inch subcaliber. The Ross 145-grain Copper-Tube measures .2865/.287-inch, as do samples from W.R.A. and the U.S. Cartridge Co. Later Kynoch specimens in my collection are loaded with .288-inch bullets.

The cartridge cases, provided by the U.S. Cartridge Co., loaded at the Ross plant were oiled, according to several well-informed evaluators of rifles in the 1910-era sporting journals. Nowadays, we wouldn't consider this a good practice. Apparently, the consideration of increased thrust on the bolt head generated by greased cartridges fired at 52.000 psi was outweighed in favor of sure extraction. In addition to the attention paid to cartridges, bullets and chambers, the extractor itself was considerably fortified. The width of the 1910 Ross extractor was increased to .450-inch, as opposed to .325-inch for the 1905 Model. The Springfield's extractor width is .390-inch, and a period Mauser Sporter's measures .420-inch.

Information provided by users of the Ross suggest the case design adjustments and other precautions might have forestalled troublesome extraction. Ashley Haines, for one, experienced no trouble in extracting fired cases. In a report in a 1914 issue of *OUTDOOR LIFE*, Haines offered: *"In fact, had one operated the gun with his eyes shut, he could have not have known whether he was manipulating an empty or loaded gun, as the fired cases always came from the chamber so easily."* Crossman's first reports in the April, 1910 *OUTERS* applauded the Ross extraction capabilities. *"With factory ammunition I have used, the bolt came open as though the rifle was empty."* Several cartridges sprinkled with sand, also refused to bind in the chamber of Crossman's Ross. Crossman sang a different tune, however, when he used a lot of overly-soft Dominion cartridges on a hunt in 1911. The fired cases stuck so tenaciously that after finally resorting to hammering the bolt open with a stick, the extractor actually cut through the rim of the shell, and the case had to be driven out with a cleaning rod. *"No Springfield nor Mauser would pull cases that stuck as did these Dominion affairs,"* Crossman announced. Lindsey Elliot reported the Ross extracting system was seriously at fault. Roughly fifteen percent of the cartridges fired in Elliot's Ross stuck so fiercely in the chamber that he was forced to apply *"two or three quite severe jams with my heel to open it."* In each case the extractor held the shell, which was positively withdrawn when the bolt finally opened. Elliot commented that the cartridges, fresh from factory boxes, were oiled and that the grease seemed to contribute to the trouble. Taken as a whole, the Ross impressed Elliot who was moved to say: *"I like the rifle a whole lot and hate it a little bit, the bolt failing to operate is all I have 'agin' it"*. Other period critics spoke of extraction difficulties, but these reports seem to be traceable to a combination of soft cases, second-hand information and what appears to be chronic complainers.

Extraction difficulties in a sporting rifle are, at best, an inconvenience. Deficiencies in a military weapon bear far more serious conse-

My working 280 Ross, set up like a match rifle.

quences. An unrecoverable blow to the reputation of the Ross occurred in the trenches of Europe in World War I. Mark III Ross-equipped Canadian troops experienced a sticking case dilemma so severe that bolts could only be opened by the rather robust application of a mud-encrusted boot, not a pleasant prospect if a clamoring battalion of the godless Hun is storming your trench. A stout cleaning rod must have been the constant companion of these Ross-toting infantrymen. The stuck shells were usually aggravated by the mud and debris that unavoidably accompanied these trench warfare conditions and found their way into the rifle's mechanism. Supplying the Canucks with proper Canadian-made ammunition, rather than the cartridges intended for the British service Lee-Enfield, created a logistical problem as well. Jamming due to a defective bolt stop further affected the soldier's confidence in his rifle. The general unreliability of the Ross under battlefield conditions – coupled with its weight of nearly ten pounds and excessive bayonet-fixed length – led to Canada's rearming with the Lee-Enfield in 1916. The need to standardize the British Empire's combat rifle also weighed heavily in the decision.

The question of safety has regularly arisen when the Ross rifle is brought up. The fact that some Ross bolts have blown back is the only generality well-circulated among riflemen. The Ross has been mentally thrown on the same risky heap and viewed with the same type of apprehension as the low-numbered Springfields and cheap Damascus-barreled shotguns. The fact that the Ross rifle might blow its bolt back into a shooter's face has been disputed since the administration of William Howard Taft, and is largely responsible for the black eye to the Ross that persists to this day. Some authorities claim there has never been an authentic case brought to light, while others claim there have been a couple of dozen shooters killed or disfigured by a wayward Ross bolt. Often, where there is so much smoke, there is usually a fire. Reports in sporting periodicals of the era mention two verifiable incidents, and provide names and locations of the mishaps. Both deaths were traceable to the use of improperly assembled bolts. Linsey Elliot wrote of an episode involving a Canadian soldier who was killed by a blown bolt on a French battlefield.

It is entirely possible to disassemble a Ross bolt, put it back together incorrectly and persuade it

(reportedly with the application of considerable force) to re-enter the rifle and actually fire in an unlocked condition. Purely for the sake of argument, Herbert Cox proved he could do it, and reported he had mastered the technique in a 1945 letter to the 'Dope Bag' section of the *American Rifleman*. At first he got the wrongly-assembled bolt stuck in the receiver, and had a deuce of a time getting it out. He managed to get the job done – after much trouble – by using a screwdriver, both hands and holding the rifle between his knees. Cox's achievement suggests no rifle is foolproof, and folks that insist on trying these stunts should not be entrusted with a high-powered rifle.

If a Ross 1910 is not fully locked when the trigger is pressed, the rifle is designed so that the energy in the compressed mainspring would be expended in closing the bolt, resulting in a misfire. There were, however, a few reports circulated that the Ross

would fire without the bolt being locked. A couple of methods to foolproof the Ross were developed by gunsmiths to prevent the rifle from firing out of battery. One approach involved spot-welding the pawl, which engaged the bolt sleeve, to the sear. A system using setscrews or rivets prevented the firing pin being released from any bolt head position other than positively locked.

Taking the proper precautions, shooting a 1910 Ross is not in the same league as tailgating a '72 Pinto. Anyone considering going cheek-to-cheekpiece with a Ross – and wanting to determine if his bolt is correctly assembled – may do so by watching the bolt lugs rotate into their seats in the last 3/4-inch of bolt travel. You'd better look hard, and you'd better look twice. Also, a bolt that slides queerly – or operates with a 'dead' feeling – should be suspect. The bolt should remain locked forward in the fired position as long as the trigger is held to the

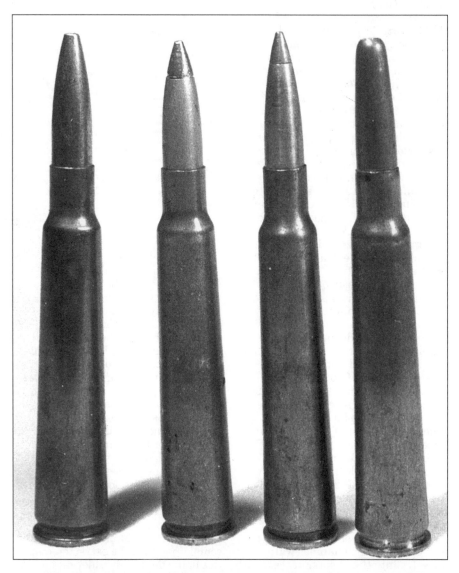

Left to right: **Ross Rifle Co. factory load with Copper-Tube bullet; W.R.A. factory load; U.S. Cartridge Co. factory load and Kynoch I60-grain factory load.**

rear of the guard. Some still-concerned shooters may feel reassured if they would lash the gun to a tire, and pull the trigger for the first shot with a good long string.

That there were misconceptions regarding the Ross rifles collectively is summarized by the statement of one 1940s-era Canadian firearms authority, C.C. Meredith: *"As to the safety of the Ross action, more nonsense has been written than you can shake a stick at."* A fellow Canadian journalist considered the Ross rifles to be *"perfectly safe."* A U.S. contemporary writer, the well-known Phil Sharpe, more than any other individual, was responsible for prolonging and publicizing the bad reputation of the Ross rifles as a group. Sharpe whipped succeeding generations of rifle shooters into a state of paranoia regarding Ross products when he wrote: *"The Ross rifle generally speaking, is not safe."* In *RIFLE IN AMERICA* he states emphatically that he *"would not under any condition shoot the sporting Ross rifle with interrupted screw type lugs and the .280 Ross cartridge."* Repetition for emphasis is found in his *COMPLETE GUIDE TO HANDLOADING* in the section containing loading data. He warns: *"Don't use a Ross rifle in this caliber under any circumstances."*

With the abundance of dire warnings about the 1910 Ross in particular, I have an additional caution for users of Ross rifles chambered for the 303 British. As stated, many of the military rifles had enlarged chambers to aid extraction under battlefield conditions. One would not expect a grossly oversized chamber in a commercial sporting rifle, but the barrel on my factory 303 British sporting rifle has such a chamber, a fact dramatically brought home to me the first time I fired it. The load had a reduced powder charge of 20 grains of Reloader #7 with a Lyman #311291 sized .311-inch. After pulling the trigger, I received a completely unexpected blast of hot gas in my face. The extracted case was too hot to immediately handle, and certainly didn't look like the case I'd chambered. What had happened was that the load used developed insufficient pressure to fully expand the case to the walls of the chamber. Gas flowed between the outside of the case and the chamber wall directly into the shooter's face.

The underside of the 1905 Ross bolthead has a vent, and no doubt a

"It is my opinion

that for Big Game (excluding Pachiderms) the Ross .280 Rifle is the best in the world."

Thus writes Mr. B. K. Miller, of Wild Rose, Wisconsin, to Messrs. Post & Floto, of New York, enclosing at the same time the photo reproduced herewith showing a grizzly who fell dead at the first shot.

Mr. Miller adds: "I have hunted and fished in various parts of the world including British East Africa, but I have never seen a gun the equal of the Ross .280 for big game, as above."

The experience of Mr. Miller has been repeated by many of the keenest hunters throughout the world.

You increase your chances of success on your next trip by taking a Ross .280 with you.

Ross .280 Rifles, in New York · · · · $55.00
Special .280 Sporting Ammunition with copper tube expanding bullet, patented, per 100 · · · · · · · $7.50

At best dealers everywhere.
Catalogue on request.

ROSS RIFLE CO.
Dept. S-12   QUEBEC, CANADA.
or
POST & FLOTO, 14 Reade Street
NEW YORK
Agents for United States

Consult OUTING'S HERBERT WHYTE DEPARTMENT on any of your problems. Its service is absolutely free

portion of the escaping gas was diverted into the empty magazine. In any event, this incident definitely got my attention. A few more shots were fired with the rifle at arm's length, with the same results. Extracted cases had lost their well-defined bottle-necked shape and emerged with a bizarre shoulder-less appearance. The prudent should check the dimensions of a 303 Ross chamber before firing squib loads, and the same warning might be extended for fireforming cases in improved chambers with much-reduced loads. This episode also presents a good case for the habitual use of shooting glasses, no matter what the load. N.R.A. members who purchased surplus Ross military rifles through the D.C.M. in the 1940s often complained that the extracted empties had a double shoulder due to the reamed out chamber, making them difficult to reload.

After a brief but colorful presence, the Ross faded from the sporting scene near war's end. The Ross factory was expropriated by government action in March of 1917. Sir Charles Ross was compensated with a settlement of two million dollars. The intention was to convert the facility to manufacture P-14 Enfields, but the Armistice rolled around before this became necessary. In December of 1919, the plant was demolished and a park built on the site.

After an entire summer of trying, I still haven't seen what those dime-sized groups immodestly claimed by Ross advertising look like. One of my rifles was set up for extended accuracy testing. Originally, this gun came from western Montana where it had seen a lot of use by an owner who cared for his rifles. If rifles could talk, this one would have something to say. It's equipped with a Lyman #48 receiver sight.

The front bead was replaced temporarily with a higher and narrower front sight blade, fashioned from a piece of steel and thinned to .020-inch. Using a six o'clock hold, the blade appears exactly as wide as the 2 1/2-inch bull I like to use at a hun-

makeshift methods. Improvisational methods to caseforming, I suspect, get practiced more than they get publicized. After trimming the shell to 2.600-inches, case taper is approximated by swaging the case in a 270 Winchester sizer. To reshape the shoulder, run the case into a 22-250 FL die until

wholeheartedly recommend this practice. The belted cases make the better shells.

Case capacity of the Ross is exactly the same as the 7x61mm Sharpe & Hart. Loading data for this cartridge can be used in preparing 280 Ross loads.

Shooting and loading for a 280 Ross rifle is an intensely interesting and – if nothing else – different pastime. During a summer of shooting

This is how I spent much of the summer – at the bench with the Ross.

dred yards, allowing for a very precise sight picture.

At one time, Barnes supplied three different weight bullets of full .288-inch diameter. I wasn't able to locate as many of the 140- and 160-grain soft points as I would have liked, but the ones I did send downrange grouped into tight 1- to 1 1/2-inch clusters. The 1.5-inch 195-grain Barnes didn't group nearly as well. Standard, affordable 7mm .284-inch bullets can be safely and efficiently substituted for the proper .287/.288-inch projectiles. I've used the entire range of 120/175-grain weights, with perfectly acceptable results. My own Ross prefers either the 139-grain Hornady Spire Point or the 160-grain Speer. Iron-sighted hundred yard five-shot groups commonly span less than two inches. But correctly-dimensioned .287/.288-inch bullets are available these days from a number of commercial component sources specializing in jacketed bullets for strange diameters – or for obsolete and foreign rifles. I've had good luck with bullets from Schroeder, Hawk and DKT.

Newly-manufactured 280 Ross cases and freshly-loaded ammunition are fairly easy to locate, but are something of an investment. Perfectly usable Ross cases can be formed from any of the belted magnum shells that have the required length. Caseforming, without benefit of the conventional full-length sizing die, can be accomplished by

the bolt will close, then fireform in the usual manner. Other combinations of dies will do the same job, provided a person uses his imagination and has the assortment of dies a handloader generally has available.

One box of reformed 375 H&H cases have been in service for over ten years, and each case has been fired in excess of twenty times. None have ever been full-length resized, just neck-sized about a quarter-inch in a 7mm Magnum neck-sizer die. The cases still chamber effortlessly and primer pockets are still tight. I acquired a box of B.E.L.L. cylindrical, unformed cases and die-formed them in a FL die; these endured five or six firings before heads started to separate. The B.E.L.L. cases stuck so tightly in the chamber, using near maximum loads, that a rubber mallet was required to open the bolt. I have a few old, original U.S. Cartridge Co. cases that have performed magnificently. With the same loads that would bind the B.E.L.L. cases, the U.S. Cartridge Co. shell could be extracted with one finger on the bolt handle. A few cases were formed from 30 Newton brass. Essentially this is a rimless shell with the 280 Ross as its parent case. Despite being rimless, my Ross extracted it without a hitch, even though the Newton shell did tend to bind a bit. Due to the scarcity of this brass, and the fact that the 30 Newton has no rim, I don't

the Ross and single-shot rifles exclusively, I developed the peculiar tendency to try to open all bolt actions with a rearward pull on the bolt handle.

The existence of the Ross represented a challenge to imitators and competitors for increased effectiveness in rifles that was never fully met, an expectation that was never realized. The Ross sparked enthusiasm in a generation of riflemen captivated by the possibilities – never attained – of medium-bore bullets at 4,000 fps. Before World War I, the Ross overcame the obstacles to the 3,000 fps barrier, and stood as the leader of a new era in rifle performance, prepared for whatever advancements the future might bring.

In retrospect, one can't resist wondering how our 1910-era counterparts would have viewed the rifleman's progress in the intervening four score-plus years. We are still shooting metal-cased bullets, and continue to use a century-old ignition system. We never did advance to steel cartridge cases, and just now we are on the threshold of propelling 145-grain 7mm bullets appreciably faster than 3,050 fps.

Was the Ross 1910 the best rifle in the world, as E.C. Crossman supposed back in 1910? Considering what the rest of the world was offering in the way of sporting rifles when the Ross was available, I don't think Crossman was too far off. ●

The Family Colt

An early Colt autoloader serves three generations of the Hurst family in two wars and, in peacetime, as a reliable companion.

by Steve Hurst

WHEN COLT NEEDED a small autoloading pistol for the American market they turned to John Browning; the result was the Model 1903 Pocket Automatic. First produced in 32 ACP and later in 380 ACP, the Pocket Auto was a great success. Colt produced more than 700,000 Pocket Automatics, and kept the gun in production for over 40 years.

In 1913 a Pocket Auto arrived in Garden City, Missouri, where my grandfather James Hurst and his wife Martha were running a restaurant and selling insurance for the Hurst Home Insurance Company. The 32-caliber pistol was the prize in a 25-cents-a-chance punchboard contest. Grandfather saw the cost of the number of places left on the board was less than the $15 price of the gun and, very quickly, the gun was his.

Grandfather sold the restaurant in 1914, moved to Urich, Missouri

James and Martha Hurst in Missouri about 1916, the first owners of the Colt 1903 Pocket Auto 32 ACP.

and started working for the telephone company. World War I created severe manpower shortages, and the phone company found it hard to keep the lines working. Jack, the oldest son, was hired as a lineman at age 14. Grandfather and Jack traveled constantly and the Colt 32 went along to provide security and to take rabbits and other small game.

Hunting was putting food on the table and the Hurst's second son, Edward (my father), was given his first rifle when he was 8 years old. With his Stevens "Little Scout" rifle and Airdale dog 'Pal,' Dad roamed the rural Missouri countryside. Game was plentiful and rabbits sold for 20 cents apiece; 22 rimfire shells were a cent, so hunting was also a profitable business. The Colt 32 went along on some of the rabbit hunts and added more challenge to the close shots.

Father was in college when World War II started, and when he graduated he was immediately drafted – and the Colt 32 went off to war. As Aviation Officer on the seaplane tender *U.S.S. Pine Island*, he served in the Pacific: Okinawa, the Philippines and Japan. The *Pine Island* saw little actual combat. My father related: "*Whenever the Japanese planes got close, the escort ships laid down a smoke screen and we hid under it, so our gunners seldom got a chance to shoot.*"

The Pine Island was too valuable to risk in a shoot-out with Japanese aircraft, but she was right there whenever an island was taken, turning the new anchorage into an instant seaplane base even before the airfield was operating. The *Pine Island* was essentially an aircraft carrier without the landing deck. Huge cranes lifted the seaplanes onto the deck when they needed servicing. Whenever the opportunity arose, the big cranes were used to off-load jeeps stored in the ship's hold, and the crew went out to see how close to the action they could get. Sometimes this was close enough to be fired on by the remaining Japanese defenders. During these adventures – and when exploring Japan after the surrender – the Colt 32 proved comforting to my father on several occasions.

After the war my parents moved from Missouri to Florida, and I grew up in Miami. I first learned to shoot a 22 rifle and a 22 revolver; the Colt 32 was the first center-fire pistol I fired. It was fun to shoot, but did not get much use since a box of shells soaked up all the money I earned in a whole day of lawn work. One of our neighbors, Bill Schoeffler, was a

Edward Hurst and Pal, his Airedale retriever. Ed used the Colt 32 to dispatch rabbits.

The author in the Tourane River valley, October 1965, with M3-AI and the family 32 Auto.

USMC 107562
WE'D RATHER FIGHT— than Switch

handloader and one day I went home from Bill's house with a full reloading kit for the 32. The low-intensity loading of the 32 ACP factory cartridge meant the fired cases did not need to be resized, so reloading was simple: two nails - one knocked out the fired primer and a larger nail seated the new primer. A 22 Short case measured out 2 grains of Bullseye powder and a bag of "O" buckshot provided the bullets that were simply pushed into the case mouth.

My high school friends called these *B.S.* loads (*buckshot*). They were accurate at short range and cycled the action. However, feeding was a sometime-thing and it was unusual to get through a magazine without a jam – which provided lots of practice clearing the gun. A pound of powder loaded more than 3000 rounds of 32 ACP and provided a great introduction to how much inexpensive fun could be had by reloading ammunition. The *B.S.* loads put the Colt 32 back into the *fun-shooting* category and kept us scrambling for the empty cases.

When we were not shooting it for fun, the Colt Pocket Auto was a 'working' gun. Dad worked for the county school system and had to respond when a burglary occurred in a school. The alarm would sound

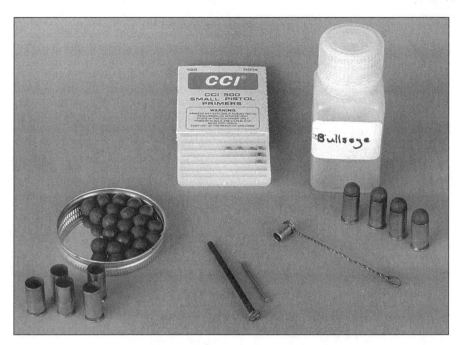

A complete reloading kit for the 32 ACP will fit in your shirt pocket.

Lieutenant (j.g.) Ed Hurst, Air Officer of the *U.S.S. Pine Island*, carried the little Colt 32 on its first trip to Southeast Asia.

at the home of the closest school board representative, who alerted Dad, who in turn called the police and headed for the school – sometimes arriving before the police. The sheriff deputized him so he could make arrests, and the little Colt 32 went along in a shoulder holster.

I joined the Marines after high school and memories of the little pistol faded. The Marines were sending me on a world tour, cut short when Vietnam started to heat up. Our armor battalion was staging to leave from Okinawa and I was surprised when we were not issued pistols. My unit trained with the Model 1911 45 ACP and had been told pistols would be issued for combat operations.

The failure to issue pistols caused me considerable anxiety. I knew how difficult it was to use a rifle aboard an armored personnel carrier. My crew and I kept our M-14s tied down in a rack inside the LVT-P5 Amphibious Tractor – or "Amtrac" – to keep them from bouncing around. Many crew duties required both hands, so it was usually impossible to have a rifle handy. The fact was, I wanted a pistol and Okinawa was not a good place to get one. The old Pocket Auto 32 ACP never entered my thoughts when I wrote my parents, asking them to purchase a pistol and send it to me.

Fortunately, Dad knew what I needed, and when I opened the package, there with the homemade cookies was the Colt 32 Pocket Auto, the shoulder holster and a box of ammunition.

On March 8, 1965, the 9th Marine Expeditionary Brigade of

the 3rd Marine Division made an amphibious landing on the beaches north of Danang and the Colt 32 was in its second war. Tracers, napalm and shells produced a fireworks show as we waited in the pre-dawn hours, increasing our anticipation of the impending landing. As we headed off the ship, the hills were still smoking from the fighting, but the landing was unopposed except for girls selling Coke on the beach. Questions about where the enemy had gone were answered 12 hours later, after the sun set.

I had not anticipated that bringing another gun to Vietnam was like bringing snow to Alaska. The Japanese, Russians, Chinese and French – and now, the Americans – have fought over Vietnam in numerous wars. Because of this, just about any kind of military hardware you can name, past and present, was there. Garands, BARs, Thompsons and M-1 and M-2 carbines were in daily use by the South Vietnamese. The Viet Cong used anything from muzzleloaders and French 8mm Lebel rifles, to Russian Mosin-Nagant bolt actions and the durable and dependable SKS and AK-47. Vietnam looked like a military museum, World War II planes roared through the sky…along with jet planes and helicopters. Soldiers on the ground were using 19th century rifles to fight a 20th century war. Unknown to me, the *U.S.S. Pine Island* was there, too, and in Danang harbor! She had been re-commissioned for, and served in, the Korean conflict and was now active in her third war.

A Martin PBM "Mariner" is hoisted aboard the Pine Island to get new engines. Affectionately called "Dumbo," the PBM was a welcome sight to downed aviators and an unwelcome sight to Japanese submarines.

U.S.S. Pine Island received a battle star in WWII and service medals for Korea and Vietnam.

My Amtrac carried an air-cooled 30-caliber Browning machine gun, and my crew and I had M-14 rifles. The Marine infantry had the M-60 machine gun and the new M-16 rifle, and some troopers made fun of our "museum pieces." However, war is a tough proving ground, and the first M-16s had problems. Soon we were getting offers from troopers who wanted to trade rifles with us, or borrow our M-14s for a patrol. Far from being obsolete, the old designs worked very well, having been perfected over the years and tested in combat. They could be trusted to be both rugged and dependable.

I am sure many of the Garands, BARs and carbines given to the South Vietnamese had been used in both WWII and Korea. The Vietnamese black-market quickly made them available to anyone with money. One of the advantages of being in armor was the opportunity to comfortably carry and try out different weapons over an extended time. For foot patrols, internal camp security and missions, there were always a variety of submachine guns and shotguns available.

I had always wanted a Thompson submachine gun; I guess it was all the Edward G. Robinson gangster movies I had seen. I soon tried one, and found it rugged and reliable, but also big and heavy. It weighs as much as a Garand and, with the 50-round drum magazine, it is even heavier. There was a reason you always see the gangsters shooting out of automobiles – the Thompson was too heavy for the actors to carry

The Colt Pocket Auto holds 8 rounds of 32 ACP in the magazine.

any distance. I quickly decided the Thompson was not what I needed.

The Colt 32 had a lot of company; the decision not to issue pistols caused a huge increase in personal weapons in our unit. Some men decided to stick with the Government Model 1911 for ammunition availability and service by our armorers. Others chose the excellent Browning Hi-Power and Walther P-38 pistols available on the black-market. Revolvers were well represented in a variety of chamberings, but the 38 Special and 357 Magnum were the most popular.

I looked at many other pistols and was sorely tempted by another of John Browning's creations, the Hi-Power. It had a lot going for it: good feeling, accurate and 14 rounds of a more powerful (*than the 32 ACP*) cartridge. Also, 9mm ammo was easy to obtain in Vietnam, whereas 32 ACP ammo was scarce. However, there were drawbacks: the Hi-Power was heavier, wider and had sharp corners. These disadvantages became very apparent in continuous wear, and the Hi-Power never replaced the Colt 32 as my personal weapon.

Browning designed the Model 1903 to be a pocket pistol, and it is an excellent design. First, it is thin; Colt advertised it as *"thin as a book"*, and I guess back then books were pretty thin. Second, it is easy use; on taking it in your hand, you immediately know if it is ready to fire since the extractor protrudes slightly when a round is chambered, and the grip safety extends if the internal hammer is cocked. The good fit in the hand, and low recoil, make fast and accurate shooting easy. Third, and most important, it is slick. There are no sharp corners anywhere on the Colt Pocket Auto 32.

The absence of sharp corners, hammer, levers and protrusions was something I had not appreciated until I started wearing a gun constantly. The only time the Colt 32 came off during the day was when I was bathing – and then it was only a few feet away. At night, I frequently slept wearing the pistol, and this was where the advantages of

The '03 Colt is thin and slick, important qualities some current gun designers have lost sight of.

the little Pocket Auto were very apparent. Because of the slim profile and lack of sharp corners, I could roll on the pistol at night and not wake up, something not possible with a 1911 Government Model or Browning Hi-Power. Tucked away in the shoulder holster, the Colt Pocket Auto was slim and light enough to be easily forgotten.

The holster was a casualty of constant use and the hot, wet climate. It literally rotted to pieces during the monsoon season. I carried the pistol in my pocket and sent a letter off to the Lawrence Leather Company, and shortly a catalog arrived. I chose another shoulder holster, because wearing the Colt '03 under my jacket protected it from the mud and dust that were a constant problem with belt holsters. I sent off a check, and a few weeks later I had my new holster. Mail service in Vietnam was great – cookies usually arrived fresh, along with extra 32 ACP ammo. My supply line was long, but it was efficient!

I would like to be able to tell you about using the Colt '03 in combat but I cannot. A pistol is a weapon of last resort, and I was always able to use my rifle or other, more effective weapons. The one time I did have a use for the Pocket Auto was when a cobra invaded our observation post on the Tourane River. The snake rose up and spread its hood to show us that it meant business. Our radioman responded with a barrage of used radio batteries and the snake beat a hasty retreat. The flying batteries made what had been an already-difficult, stationary skinny target into an impossible fast-moving skinny target – and the snake made good its escape.

It was off the battlefield that the 1903 Pocket Auto was really valuable. The high command decreed that troops on liberty in Danang and Saigon go unarmed. I viewed this with some alarm, since Viet Cong attacks were a frequent occurrence in both cities. In town we were advised to stay in groups of two or three for safety, but to avoid larger groups as these were tempting targets for grenade attacks or motorcycle drive-by shootings. This did not seem like a place that one should go unarmed.

Perhaps the decision to disarm the troops on liberty was a wise one, considering that intoxication was one of their primary objectives. However, I had no intention of drinking in town – I did not want my mind befuddled while in what I considered enemy territory. I could always drink when I was off-duty in our base camp, where I was inside a perimeter guarded by my friends.

It was on liberty that the Pocket Auto 32 really stood out or, more importantly, *did not* stand out. The tight-fitting khaki uniform did not allow room to hide a large revolver, a Browning Hi-Power or a 1911 Government Model. Riding in the shoulder holster, the little 32 passed inspection every time and

Amtracs leave the landing ship, heading for the beach in Vietnam.

went to town. Only once did I need it, when three men approached me with expressions that in any big city spell trouble. A strong-arm robbery was perhaps their intention, until the intended victim put his hand inside his shirt. I did not even have to draw the 32; the trio decided they had important business elsewhere.

A final compliment was paid to the Colt '03 when my tour in Vietnam was over. For $20 you could have a 1911 Government Model or for $50 a Browning Hi-Power. In a land awash with weapons, I was offered $100 for the little Colt that was missing most of its bluing. The other men in my unit who had handled the 1903 Pocket Auto 32 ACP knew its merits. Powerful pistols and high-capacity magazines may be nice, but when you live with a pistol constantly it is best to have one that is easy to live with.

After a tour in Vietnam I was pretty low on sentiment and the slim Colt would have certainly been sold and left in Vietnam. However, my father had made me promise I would bring it home, something I am grateful for now. The Colt '03 Pocket Pistol has served my family for three generations and has been used in two wars. Today it is still doing what John Browning designed it to do almost 100 years ago – be a pocket pistol so it can be in your pocket when you need it.

Rapid fire on a silhouette target at 15 yards. The shooter is over 50 years old, the gun almost 90 – and they still work together just fine.

The Evolution Of Remington Autoloading Shotguns

by R.H.VanDenburg, Jr.

REMINGTON ARMS COMPANY'S entry into the autoloading shotgun market began almost a century ago. In 1900, John Browning was granted a U.S. patent (No. 659,507) for a long-recoil operated, semi-automatic, shotgun mechanism. Because of his long association with the Winchester Repeating Arms Company, Browning offered the design to it. Winchester declined. When the two parties could not reach agreement, Browning terminated his relationship with Winchester and contracted with Fabrique Nationale in Belgium to manufacture the gun. Production began in 1903.

The late General Julian Hatcher, who knew John Browning, and John's son Val, quite well, offered the following in the 8th edition of the GUN DIGEST (1954):

"The Browning automatic shotgun was one of the most difficult inventions Mr. Browning ever worked on, and one of the most successful. When he had it perfected he took it to the Winchester Repeating Arms Company, who had already produced some ten or more different models of rifles and shotguns on Browning's designs, all of them highly successful. But Mr. Browning and Winchester couldn't come to terms on this one. This was most unfortunate for Winchester, for Mr.

Browning, feeling he had been treated unfairly, broke with Winchester completely, and never worked with them again until he was urged by the government to help them out on some machine difficulties during World War I. The story, as told to me by Mr. Browning sometime before his death in 1927, was most interesting."

When he broke with Winchester, Mr. Browning decided to take his gun to Remington and made an appointment with the head of that firm *(Author's note: Marcellus Hartly, Remington's president)*. He was prompt for his appointment but was kept waiting in the office all morning, only to be informed at noontime that the man he was to see had just dropped dead. At a loss what to do he boarded a boat for Belgium, went to the great Fabrique Nationale, of Liege, and offered them his invention.

In 1905 the Remington Arms Company obtained a license to manufacture and market the Browning gun in the United States. Named the Model 11, production began the same year. The initial offering was limited to twelve gauge. Sixteen and twenty gauge variations were also offered, but authorities differ on the exact chronology. Twelve gauge guns weighed about eight pounds; sixteen gauge, seven and one-half pounds;

twenty gauge, seven and one-quarter pounds. Barrel lengths offered were, depending on gauge, 26, 28, 30 and 32 inches. Full, modified, improved cylinder and cylinder chokes were available as well as Skeet choke (26 inch only). Other options included plain or solid rib barrels, Poly Choke and Cutts Compensator. All Model 11s were restricted to a 2 3/4-inch chamber. Several law enforcement models, with shorter barrels, were available as well. A Model 11 No. 0 Riot Gun with 18 1/2-inch barrel was made as early as 1906. The Model 11 Police Special with an 18 1/2-inch barrel bored for buckshot, and with the stock fitted with sling swivels, came along in 1921. All were twelve gauge. Also in 1921, the Model 11 Riot Gun with a 20-inch barrel was available in twelve, sixteen and twenty gauges.

There were some differences in the Remington Model 11 and the Browning parent. Most notably, the Browning had a magazine cutoff assembly, especially popular with waterfowlers; the Remington did not. There were also some slight differences in the shape of the friction parts used to arrest barrel movement.

Interestingly, from 1946 to 1951, when Fabrique Nationale was reorganizing after World War II, Remington produced guns, with the magazine cutoff, under contract for Browning.

These guns were, and are, known as "the American Brownings."

Remington's Model 11, as is the Browning, is known as having a long-action, recoil operation. In use, the breechbolt is locked to the barrel via a locking lug in the bolt engaging a notch in the barrel extension. At firing, the shot charge and wad column are pushed out the muzzle and an equal force attempts to push the case, and everything behind it, in the opposite direction. As the breechbolt and barrel are locked together, both are pushed rearward for a distance that exceeds the length of the shell; about three inches. At the same time, the barrel has a guide ring mounted below it which encircles the magazine tube. As the barrel, and ring, moves rearward, the ring engages a friction piece that grips the magazine tube and serves to retard rearward movement. The friction piece is beveled fore and aft and the forward bevel mates with a corresponding bevel in the rear of the guide ring. The effect is to squeeze the friction piece against the magazine tube. This, plus the compression of the barrel return spring, is all that is necessary for light target or field loads. When heavier loads are used, a friction ring is employed to mate with the friction piece rear bevel to provide an even greater squeezing down of the friction piece. All of these parts are enclosed in the forend.

When the breechbolt and barrel reach the end of their travel, the bolt slams against the inside rear of the receiver. A lever engages the bolt, holding it rearward, while the locking lug is released from its engagement in the barrel extension and the barrel is returned to battery by the force of the compressed barrel return spring. The fired case, which is held to the bolt face by the extractor, is ejected from the gun as the barrel moves forward by the ejector formed in the left side of the barrel extension.

If the magazine contains another round, it is released, striking the carrier latch, which releases the carrier to raise the round in line with the chamber. The breechbolt is simultaneously released and pushed forward by the action spring, chambering the fresh round. The action spring is contained in the stock and was previously compressed as the breechbolt moved rearward.

For most shooters, other characteristics better defined the gun than precisely how it worked. The Browning, the Remington and those made by other companies such as

Remington 11 copy, Remington 11-48 and Remington 11-87.

Savage and Springfield after the initial patents had expired, all showed a common shape. The receiver was squared off at the rear to accommodate the rearward-traveling bolt. This lead to the term "hump-backed" as in "that hump-backed Remington" to describe guns built on the Browning patent. Despite the outward appearance of the gun, which most did not find attractive, many shooters found that the raised receiver forced them to bring the gun to bear in the same manner each time, placing the eye consistently over the barrel, and they simply shot better. The squared receiver also provided a longer sighting plane, quite desirable for long-range shooting. The movement of the parts as the gun

was fired also produced a unique sensation or "feel." Charles Askins, Jr., and perhaps others, referred to it as a *"double shuffle"* and generally detested it. John Amber was known to refer to the gun as the *"Browning clatter box."* At the time, however, the fact that the gun was an autoloader and provided the shooter with three, four or five shots as quickly as he could recover from the recoil and pull the trigger outweighed any other considerations.

All that said, the Remington Model 11 had a pretty good run, remaining in production until 1948, when the Remington 11-48 replaced it. Interestingly, Browning still makes the same gun, little changed over the years, but now in several versions referred to as the Auto-5 or just A-5. (*Author's note: In late 1997 Browning announced the discontinuance of the A-5*).

In 1931, perhaps in response to changing game laws, Remington introduced the Sportsman. It was the same as the Model 11, with some new features and options, except it was offered with only a three-shot shell capacity.

The Remington 11-48 was also a long-action recoil gun. It's most noticeable change was the absence of the "hump-back" receiver shape. By changing the shape of the breechbolt, Remington was able to eliminate the squared-off receiver and in its place introduce a graceful, sloped contour to the receiver rear. The shape has proven to be so universally appealing that it is still used today – a half century later – by Remington and most other manufacturers of autoloading and pump shotguns. A Sportsman-48 version was also offered; as before differing mainly in a three-shot capacity and slightly reduced weight. The 11-48s were initially made in twelve, sixteen and twenty gauges in several grades. In the later years of production, twenty-eight gauge and .410-bore were available in the 11-48 model. The .410 version generated so little recoil it had no friction assembly at all, just the barrel return spring. In fact, the .410-bore Skeet model with ventilated rib came with a special, factory-installed Cutts Compensator with the slots

A copy of the Remington 11/Browning A-5 from Springfield.

pointed forward to increase recoil and ensure positive action functioning. Both the .410 and twenty-eight gauge had a four-shot capacity. Barrel lengths were 25 (twenty-eight and .410 only), 26, 28 and 30 (twelve gauge only) inches.

Chokes included cylinder, improved cylinder, Skeet, modified and full. Extras included custom stocks, beavertail forends, recoil pads, matted receiver top and ventilated ribs. All models were available with factory-installed Poly Choke or Cutts Compensator.

In the 5th edition *GUN DIGEST* (published in 1950) a standard-grade 11-48 cost $99.95 with prices climbing to $564 for a Premier F grade. A Skeet-grade gun was also offered in the Sportsman line that ranged in price from a basic $106.45 to $588.30 for the Premier grade with ventilated rib (1950 prices).

There were several mechanical differences between the Model 11 and the new 11-48 in addition to the receiver/breechbolt shape. The friction, or barrel arresting, mechanism went through three different designs during the life of the 11-48 and Sportsman-48. In the first design the friction piece was a simple split tube with no surrounding friction piece spring. The friction piece remained partly inserted in the barrel guide ring even during disassembly. Behind it was a friction ring. Each end of the friction ring was beveled but at different angles. The degree of friction applied to the magazine tube was determined by which end of the friction ring was forward and mated with the friction piece. The longer bevel was marked to be forward for heavy loads and the shorter bevel to be forward for lighter target or field loads. The barrel recoil spring was of the ribbon type and included a spring cap that fitted between the spring and the friction ring. In a second design the friction ring and cap were replaced with a spring ring and wiper and the recoil spring was changed. In operation the spring was partially inserted into the rear of the recoil spring ring. The bevel in the front of the recoil spring ring and the bevel in the rear of the barrel guide ring were modified to mate with the corresponding bevels in the friction piece in such a manner as to make the assembly self-compensating. The greater the recoil, the more the bevels gripped; no part changing was required.

This second design was introduced in the mid-1950s. A third design, similar to the second, increased the length and weight of the recoil spring ring and shortened the recoil spring. Also the recoil spring threaded into the rear of the recoil spring ring and was staked. The wiper was eliminated.

Other differences between the 11s and the 11-48s included the unloading procedure. In the Model 11, the operator must engage safety, pull back and release the operating handle until magazine and chamber are empty. Then push release button to close the action. In the 11-48, the operator must engage safety and turn the gun bottom-up. Then, pull the operating handle about three-fourths of the way back, depress the carrier and press in the shell stop. This will release a shell from the magazine. Press shell stop again for each shell in the magazine. Pull operating handle completely to rear to remove shell from chamber.

The 11-48s also introduced the pinned trigger assembly which made for easy removal and cleaning. The Sportsman-48 was dropped from the line in 1958 with the introduction of the Sportsman 58. The 11-48 stayed in production until 1969.

The Sportsman 58 was gas-operated, Remington's first attempt at such an approach for autoloading shotguns. As such, it had a relatively short run. It was introduced in 1958 in twelve, sixteen and twenty gauges. It had 2 3/4-inch chambers and a three-shot capacity. A traditional Remington crossbolt safety was placed in the rear of the trigger guard. Barrel lengths were 26 inches (improved cylinder), 28 inches (modified or full choke) and 30 inches (full choke only). Weight was reduced from the previous mechanically operated models with the twelve gauge listed at seven pounds, the sixteen at six and three-quarter and the twenty at six and one-half pounds. A bewildering array of variants was offered, including special trap and Skeet, from the 58 ADL, plain barrel, at $136.45 to the 58F Premier grade at $988.00. The latter offered fancy wood, full engraving and had polished parts.

Actually the Sportsman 58 was quite a visual upgrade from previous models as all 58s had engraved receivers and checkered pistol grips and forends.

In 1959 Remington introduced the Sportsman 58 Magnum in twelve gauge only, with three-inch chamber, 30-inch barrel and a recoil pad. Options included a plain or ventilated rib. Also the same year came the Automaster 878. It was a lower-priced 58 offered in twelve gauge only, with no engraving or checkering. Other Sportsman 58 options introduced in 1958 included a 26-inch barrel with rifle sights, specially bored for rifled slug use. The gun could be purchased with this barrel (Model 58RSS) or the barrel could be purchased separately. Another model had a "Sun Grain," honey-colored stock and forend with checkering and a ventilated rib. It was short-lived, gone by 1961.

The claim to fame of all gas-operated autoloaders is a smoother operation and reduced felt recoil. The Remington Sportsman 58 and its variations met these claims well. First, the barrel did not move during operation, although disassembly, including barrel removal, was quite simple. Second, a small amount of propellant gas was bled from the barrel at a point near the front of the forend. This gas was used to drive a piston, contained inside the magazine tube, to the rear. Actually the piston didn't travel far as it engaged an action bar and slide which, in turn, forced the breechblock to the rear, extracting the fired shell. A recoil, or action, spring housed in the magazine tube forced the piston assembly forward to its original position and another, in the buttstock, pushed the breechbolt back to its loaded position, picking up a fresh shell on the way. Some amount of gas control existed, for the magazine cap was adjustable, with a light and heavy setting. The heavy setting bled off some of the gases headed to the piston to ensure the gun was not subjected to any more force than necessary to operate the action.

The Sportsman 58 was initially well-received with loss of weight, smoother operation and reduced felt recoil pleasing customers and signaling to Remington that gas operation was the wave of the future. On the other hand, placing the gas piston inside the magazine tube limited shell capacity to three shots while recoil-operated guns would often hold four or five shells. Also the gas system produced a powder fouling that caked onto the moving parts, particularly the piston, and had to be removed. A more serious flaw in the 58 was the reported cracking of the receiver behind the bolt handle slot and also at the front of the ejector port. Neither crack rendered the gun unsafe but did nothing to instill customer confidence. This cracking, no doubt, was

partly caused by firing heavy loads with the selector set for light ones.

The Sportsman 58's run ended in 1963 when Remington announced the next generation of autoloading shotgun design, in the form of the famous Remington 1100.

Developed by Remington's design team headed by Wayne Leek, who was also responsible for many of Remington's other successful developments, the Model 1100 set a new standard for autoloading shotgun operation. In his book, "*American Shotgun Design and Performance*," L.R. Wallack had this to say about the 1100:

"The Remington 1100 will eventually go down in history as almost as important an invention as the Browning Auto, because it pioneered a gas system that was sufficiently different and that reduced recoil beyond other known limits. Its system has been copied by so many other guns that its position as the trend-setter is molded in concrete."

Under development almost from the initial release of the Model 58, the 1100 was introduced to firearms writers at a seminar held at Remington headquarters in Bridgeport, CT in November, 1962. Reaction was immediate and positive.

The principal claims Remington made for the new gun were reduced felt recoil, even over other gas-operated models including their own Model 58, and a significantly increased life – up to seven times longer than other autoloaders. While those at the seminar were quick to agree with the former, they had to take Remington's word for the latter, although time seems to suggest Remington was right there, too. The writers were also quick to praise other, cosmetic aspects of the gun. They liked the stock

Remington 11-48, in twenty gauge.

fit and finish - one even praised the impressed checkering. Today such a glossy finish would get mixed reviews and the impressed checkering and white spacers at the buttplate and pistol grip would surely result in negative commentary. At the same time metal finish and a roll-on floral design on the receiver sides were well done and highly praised. The bluing, in particular, was known for its depth and high gloss.

The working mechanism also attracted its share of attention, and rightly so. The barrel underlug that was referred to in earlier models as a guide ring and served to retard the barrel and guide it in its travel (in recoil-operated guns) now became the gas cylinder. On the 58, as gas was taken from twin holes in the barrel during firing it was diverted into the cylinder and pushed against a piston. The difference this time was that the piston was of a ringed design and encircled the magazine tube rather than being contained in it. The piston then pushed back against a piston seal and, in turn, to action bars which served to operate the bolt and ultimately cause ejection of the fired shell and the chambering of a fresh one. The timing of the moving parts was such as to control the amount of gas that reached the piston and prevented undue wear from heavy hunting loads. There were two obvious advantages of the system. First, regaining the full magazine for shell storage (capacity now four, plus one in the chamber). Second, the new piston assembly did not retain powder residue, as did the earlier Model 58.

The claim of reduced recoil was aided by an increase in weight. Nominal weight of a twelve gauge Model 58 was seven pounds; a similar 1100 was seven and one-half. Mostly, though, the elapsed time involved and the movement of some parts not directly associated with the fixed gun, such as the piston, action bars, breechbolt assembly and action sleeve was what did the trick. Total recoil is, of course, always the same for any given load but spreading it over time reduced the sharpness of what was felt. Bob Brister, in his book "*Shotgunning, the Art and the Science*," described all this as *"robbing Peter to pay Paul."*

Remington 11 copy, Remington 11-48 and Remington 11-87 with forends removed to show operating mechanisms.

The shape of the 1100 stock no doubt aided also as stories abound of the stock designers whittling a bit, then having everyone in the shop try the gun, then taking their responses, whittling some more and repeating the process until almost everyone was satisfied. It worked, as the stock fit of the 1100 is about as universally satisfactory as one could hope. Devout lovers of side-by-sides or over-and-unders will often – when pressed – admit that, love aside, they simply shoot better with the 1100.

Some of the things that gave an improved gun life included a stronger receiver, nylon buffers to absorb the shock as rearward bolt travel came to a halt and the improved gas handling system. Better polishing and bluing and a strong wood finish also contributed, at least to the cosmetic side.

In 1963 the 1100 was offered in twelve gauge only. Two receivers (2 3/4 inch or 3 inch) were available and appropriately chambered barrels in cylinder, improved cylinder, modified and full choke. Barrel lengths were 26 inches (cylinder, improved cylinder), 28 inches (modified or full) and 30 inches (full), with or without a ventilated rib. By 1964, sixteen and twenty gauge models were available. The Magnum version (3-inch chambers) was available in twelve and twenty gauges. Also introduced were Skeet and trap models. By 1967 variations included regular, Magnum, Trap, Skeet, Deer, Skeet Mahogany (lighter weight, twenty gauge), Tournament Auto, Premier Auto and Skeet Lightweight (twenty gauge). The Premier Auto was a custom proposition with prices ranging from $1050 to $1750 with gold inlays. Higher grades all had cut checkering. By 1971 a 1100 Small Gauge in twenty-eight gauge and .410 bore were offered with 25-inch barrels. There was also a .410 Skeet version for the 2 1/2-inch shell.

In 1983 a Special Field model was introduced in twelve and twenty gauges with a straight grip stock and a 21-inch barrel. The standard 1100 was now only offered in twelve gauge but a left-hand version was cataloged. The sixteen was gone. If you wanted a twenty gauge, you got the Special Field or the 1100LT-20 (lightweight, 26 or 28 inch barrels, six and one-half pounds). A LT-20 Deer Gun (20 inch barrel, rifle sights) and a LT-20 LTD (23 inch barrel, modified or improved cylinder) were also listed.

Prices had kept up with the times. That basic 1100 in 1963 listed for $174.95 with the top grade rising to $1050. In the 1985 *GUN DIGEST*, the basic price was $463, climbing to $7,247 for the 1100F Premier Auto with all the trimmings. Basic Skeet and trap models started at $555 and $567 respectively.

Prices aside, the 1100 had had a marvelous run. The same *GUN DIGEST* displayed the 3,000,000th 1100, a Premier Skeet gun, fancifully engraved and donated by Remington to support Olympic shooting.

1985 was also the year Remington added the "Special Purpose" Magnum, a three-inch twelve gauge with 26- or 30-inch barrels. Metal was a dull, non-reflective color. The wood had an oil finish, also dull. The gun came with sling swivels and a sling. A final 1985 offering was the Sportsman, a lower-cost 1100 with a hardwood stock. It was limited to twelve gauge, 2 3/4-inch chambers. Price was $390 compared to the then $480 for the basic 1100.

Perhaps the greatest attribute of the 1100 was its handling. Especially with the shorter receiver, shorter-barreled variants with open chokes, balance was firmly "between the hands" and at home in the grouse and woodcock coverts as any side-by-side. The relatively shallow receiver height allowed a grip that many felt kept the hands on a similar plane and aided in gun handling and general responsiveness. The same attributes contributed to its success on the Skeet fields. Other variants made the 1100 popular at trap tournaments, in duck or goose blinds and, generally, anywhere a shotgun was called for. By all accounts, it was not only the most popular autoloading shotgun ever made, it was the best.

But things were about to change, things that would spell the demise of the grand old gun. Remington had decided to make a new twelve gauge autoloading shotgun. It was to be called the Model 11-87.

There were two developments that lead to the decision by Remington to make a new gun. Of principal importance was the advent of steel shot and the requirement that it, not lead, be used when hunting waterfowl. It wasn't that one couldn't shoot steel in an 1100, it was just that steel shot wasn't part of the 1100's design specs. The com-

pany felt it had to build an improved gun that would handle steel shot with aplomb. At the same time, Remington's research team had developed an improved gas-handling system that would allow the same gun to handle the full range of ammo from the lightest 2 3/4-inch target load to the heaviest 3-inch lead or steel load. Previously, all autoloading guns were built on one receiver for 2 3/4-inch shells

Model 11-87 forend. Note fiberglass in inside rear, brass pin in front, cuts for gas release.

and another, if offered at all, for 3-inch shells. The lack of a suitable gas handling system was, at least in part, the reason.

Partly because of steel shot and partly because some felt Remington had resisted the idea long enough, the decision was made to introduce the 11-87 with interchangeable, screw-in choke tubes called REM CHOKES. Steel shot enters into this because it usually takes a more open choke to get optimum performance from steel shot than lead. Guns with a fixed choke designed with lead shot in mind, especially

Remington 11-87 gas cylinder showing two center holes that take gas from barrel and two outside holes that are used to release excess gas.

one bored full, would suffer by comparison. Also, steel shot is hard on barrels, especially where the choke begins its taper. An interchangeable choke tube of special steels and hardness would not only add flexibility and performance, but protection. The same year, the company announced screw-in choke tubes for its other shotguns as well. As far as the 1100

went, this was the last straw. Interchangeable choke tube barrels, by necessity, have thicker barrel walls and the increased weight up front took away the delicate balance that had so identified the 1100. The 3-inch receivered, and chambered, guns with longer barrels were less affected, perhaps even improved, by the slightly heavier barrels with their weight-forward feel aiding follow-through in the duck marshes and goose pits.

The principal differences in the gas system for the 11-87 deal with the release of excess gas. In both the 1100 and the 11-87 systems, gas is taken from the barrel through two holes and directed into the cylinder. In the 11-87 there are two more holes in the cylinder, toward the front, that serve to release gas pressure not needed to operate the action. A spring clip covers these relief holes. A gas cylinder collar fits over the end of the cylinder, covering the spring, and serves to direct the excess gases up and out through a pair of slots cut in the forend.

There was more. The magazine tube on the 11-87 is stainless steel and the magazine tube cap was changed. On the 1100 and, indeed, even back to the Model 11, the cap had serrations on the skirt that engaged a detent ball on the forend that prevented the cap from working loose. On the 11-87, the serrations are inside the cap dome and mate with teeth in a re-designed plastic magazine spring retainer. The spring retainer was designed for easy removal and insertion of a plastic magazine plug, included with each gun, to limit magazine capacity while hunting waterfowl. By contrast, Model 11 and Browning users typically cut a broomstick handle or dowel to length and inserted it in the magazine tube.

The 11-87 extractor was beefed up some 30% over its predecessor and the firing pin retractor spring was made more durable. The feed latch was fastened more securely. The forend, in addition to having a piece of fiberglass cloth on the inside rear, has a brass cross pin up front as further insurance against forend splitting.

Other changes were mostly cosmetic. A solid rubber recoil pad was fitted to a satin-finished stock. Cut checkering, at 20 lines-per-inch, on both pistol grip and forend, was completed in a tasteful design. The wood itself is American walnut with a 14-inch length of pull, a 1 1/2-inch drop at comb and a 2 1/2-inch drop at heel. A black plastic pistol grip cap has a new company logo: in gold color, an "RA" enclosed in a shield. The receiver lacks the roll engraving of the 1100, being plain with the word "Premier" on the right side and "Remington 11-87" and the serial number on the left. The high gloss of the bluing is diminished, suggesting less time spent polishing 11-87 receivers than had been the norm for the 1100s.

All in all the 11-87 gets high marks for attractiveness. It was introduced in 1987 in twelve gauge only with a one-size-fits-all receiver. Barrels were 26, 28 and 30 inches with a ventilated rib and

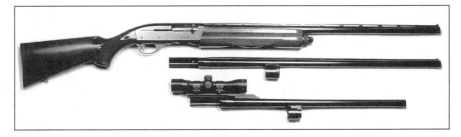

Remington 11-87 with original contour barrel. Below, light contour barrel, rifled barrel with cantilevered scope mount and Simmons 2x32 scope.

interchangeable choke tubes. Included with each gun were improved cylinder, modified and full choke tubes, a spanner wrench for changing tubes, a magazine plug and an Owner's Manual.

Felt recoil was reduced, even over the 1100 but principally due to another weight gain. While, as noted before, a 28-inch barreled Model 58 in twelve gauge weighed seven pounds and a similar 1100 weighed seven and one-half pounds, an 11-87 with the same specs tilted the scales at a whopping eight and one-half pounds. All are nominal weights, of course, and vary slightly depending on wood density, moisture content, etc. The weight gain didn't deter 11-87 customers in the beginning, as most were waterfowl hunters who appreciated the recoil-absorbing heft. Also appreciated were the interchangeable choke tubes, the ability to handle steel shot and the new gas system that allowed shooting light 2 3/4-inch target loads for practice and heavy 3-inch waterfowl or turkey loads from the same gun.

There were other variations introduced that first year as well. In addition to the flagship Premier, there was a Special Purpose Magnum with

Parkerized metal finish and a dull oil-finished stock. The bolt and carrier were dark and the gun came with a 26- or 30-inch barrel, sling swivels and a padded shoulder strap. A Premier Trap had a straight or Monte Carlo stock, different checkering, a 30-inch REM CHOKE barrel and trap chokes (Trap Full, Trap Extra Full, Trap Super Full). The gas system did not include the extra relief holes and was balanced for 2 3/4-inch trap-type ammo only. All trap barrels were back-bored to reduce felt recoil.

A Premier Skeet model had a 26-inch barrel, Skeet stock with a two-piece buttplate and REM CHOKES (Skeet, improved Skeet). Again the gas system was set up for 2 3/4-inch target loads only.

A final early issue was the Special Purpose Deer Gun, with a muted finish, a 21-inch smooth bore barrel with rifle sights and a fixed, improved cylinder slug choke. The barrel and gas system would handle 2 3/4- and 3-inch shells but were not designed for light target or field loads.

The 1100 remained in the line but by 1989 the twelve gauge 1100 was no more except for the Special Field. The rest of the 1100s were there but the twenty, twenty-eight and .410 were all listed as being available in the 1100 Auto with 25-, 26- and 28-inch barrels and in the LT-20 (twenty gauge) and the Small Gauge (twenty-eight and .410) with 25-inch barrels only. Time began to take its toll, however, and by 1995, the twenty-eight and .410 1100s were no longer offered. The 1996 and 1997 catalogs did list a 1100 Skeet in twenty gauge and a 1100 Sporting in twenty-eight. The 1998 catalog added a model 1100 Sporting in twenty gauge with a 28-inch barrel but dropped the 1100 Skeet. If one is interested in a small gauge 1100, the first order of business should be to contact Remington to ascertain what is available.

In 1989, Remington added to its hold on shotgunning by introducing the SP-10 Magnum Auto Shotgun. Actually a re-design of the failed Ithaca ten gauge auto of a few years previous, Remington's offering

Remington REM-CHOKES for 11-87: full, modified, improved cylinder and rifled, with Remington's choke tube wrench.

worked well, but at a cost of eleven and one-quarter pounds and about a thousand dollars. In 1991 the SP-10 line was expanded to include the SP-10 Magnum Turkey Combo. This variant included a 26- or 30-inch ventilated rib barrel and a 22-inch rifle-sighted barrel. Both had REM CHOKE interchangeable tubes. Swivels and sling were part of the package. In 1993, camouflage came to the SP-10 with the SP-10 Magnum-Camo. All surfaces except the bolt and trigger guard were covered with Mossy Oak Bottomland camo finish. The latter two were black. Prices had climbed to over eleven hundred dollars.

By 1992, Remington had begun to take notice of the 11-87's weight and announced the Light Contour barrel (LC) in 26, 28 and 30-inch lengths in the Premier line. The LC barrels were slimmer in profile than the original barrels and therefore required a new forend to keep the gap between the barrel and the forend the same. The actual contour slimmed down the center of the barrel while retaining thickness at the muzzle where the choke tubes threaded into the barrel. One can use the LC barrels with the original forend but looks suffer as well as creating a place for dirt, rain twigs, etc., to hide. Weight loss was touted as one-half pound. With the change to the light contour barrels, the original 11-87 with the heavier barrels was no longer cataloged but the original barrels and forends are still available. A left-handed 11-87 is also available but only with a 28-inch barrel.

Over the first ten years of the 11-87 an astonishing number of variations have been offered. Almost all are contained within a few themes: the basic Premier; the same with a dull finish; with several camo finishes; a shorter barreled deer version with smooth or rifled barrels with rifle sights or a cantilevered

Remington 11-87 SPS (Special Purpose, Synthetic).

scope base; a trap model; a Skeet model; and Sporting Clay models. In addition most barrels are available separately.

Actually, the whole subject of Remington barrels, choke tubes and forends is quite involved, deserving of a separate treatment. Generally speaking, trap barrels are over-bored and for that reason have their own choke tubes. Attempts to use regular REM CHOKES on trap barrels or trap chokes on regular barrels will not prove satisfactory. The company offers an 1100 barrel specifically for use with steel shot. Lead shot may be fired in it but only in the 2 3/4-inch shell length. The shape of the cantilever on deer barrels has also changed over the years. Remington catalogs state that 1100 and 11-87 barrels are not interchangeable. This is good advice but may be overstating the case. Should a gunner have both an 1100 and an 11-87 and wish to interchange barrels, the proper course is to contact Remington. Some interchanging may appear to work but are causing excess wear and possible damage. Additionally, after-market barrels and choke tubes are available from such firms as Hastings, Briley and others.

In spite of Remington's efforts to lighten the 11-87 with contoured barrels, it was never going to be an upland gun. Something had to be done. After some careful consideration, the basic gun was re-designed with a new receiver that was lowered in the rear and with a corresponding change in the bolt. A shorter forend and magazine tube reduced capacity to three rounds in the magazine. This, along with other minor changes, lopped off another half-pound bringing the weight to less than seven and one-half pounds with some 26-inch variants hovering around seven pounds. The receiver remained steel but was thinned slightly. It retained the

length necessary to handle both 2 3/4- and 3-inch shells and was given a floral engraving treatment. The barrels, offered only in 26 and 28 inches, were chrome-lined. The standard gas operating system of the 11-87 was also retained. Further, it was decided to give this gun a separate model number, the Remington 11-96 Euro Lightweight, denoting its year of introduction and the fact that it was first introduced at the IWA trade show in Germany. Most interestingly, the gun would not be manufactured in-house. A contract was let with Bernardelli, the Italian gunmaking firm, to make the gun. Unfortunately things went south in a hurry as Bernardelli went bankrupt. In early 1998 this writer was informed that Bernardelli made fewer than 200 11-96s before their shutdown. However, the gun was well received by those few who had an opportunity to shoot it so production was taken back in-house. Setting up for the new product took some time but, by 1998, 11-96s were in limited production by Remington. Prices for the 11-96 were announced at $852, compared to an 11-87 Premier price of $679.

Because of the new shape, some have opined that Remington should have removed metal from inside rather than outside the receiver. One suspects that would have been easier said than done. The receiver shape does take some getting used to but is, subjectively, quite attractive. Due in part to a reduction in drop at heel from 2 1/2 inches for other 11-87s to 2 1/4 inches for the 11-96, handling is quite good and the stepped receiver does not detract from the ordinary line of sight. (In the November/December, 1997 issue of the *American Rifleman*, a review of the 11-96 gives the weight of the 28-inch specimen being tested as 7 pounds, 5 ounces with a drop at heel as an even 2 inches.) This model does, indeed, show promise as a viable upland gun. Whether it will garner the acclaim the 1100 did from hunters can't be determined until more are actually in the field.

Ninety-three years have passed since Remington first entered the autoloading shotgun market. Ninety-three years, twelve models, millions of guns and hundreds of millions of dollars in sales and, hopefully, many more of each to come.

My own Remington autoloader, an 11-87, was purchased just after the introduction of the Light Con-

Remington 11-87 SPS Camo (Special Purpose, Synthetic, Camo Finish).

TABLE 1

REMINGTON AUTOLOADING SHOTGUN CHRONOLOGY

Model/Variant	Duration	Remarks
11	1905 - 1948	First autoloader
Sportsman	1931-1948	3-shot magazine capacity
S11-48	1948 - 1969	Also long recoil action
Sportsman 48	1948 - 1959	3-shot magazine capacity
Sportsman 58	1958 - 1963	First gas auto
Sportsman 58 Magnum	1959 - 1964	3", 12 gauge only
Automaster 878	1959 - 1963	12 gauge only, cheaper 58
1100	1963 -	Gas operated, outside piston
1100 Special Field	1983 -	Straight grip, 21" barrel
1100 SP Magnum	1985 - 1989	3", dull finish
1100 Sportsman	1985 - 1987	Cheaper 1100
11-87	1987 -	12 gauge only, 3" receiver
SP 10 Magnum	1989 -	10 gauge, 3 1/2"
11-96 Euro Lightweight	1996 -	Lighter weight, similar to 11-87

REMINGTON 11-87 SHOTGUN CHRONOLOGY

Variant	Duration	Remarks
Premier	1987 -	LC in '92, engraving in '96
SP	1987 -	26 and 30", dull, 28" in '90
SP Deer Gun	1987 -	21" RS, dull, cantilever in '89
Premier Trap	1987 -	MC or straight, 30"
Premier Skeet"	1987 -	26"
F Grade	1988 -	Custom shop
175th anniversary	1991 - 1991	Special engraving
Cantilever Deer	1991 -	MC, gloss, rifle barrel option in '93
SPS	1991 -	Synthetic stock, dull finish
SPS-T	1991 -	21" VR, extra full Rem Ck
Sporting Clays	1992 -	28" VR
NWTF	1992 - 1992	Same as SPS-T, Trebark camo
SPS-Camo	1992 -	Mossy Oak Greenleaf, Breakup in '98
SPS-Big Game	1993 - 1993	Mossy Oak Bottomland
SPS-T Camo	1993 -	Mossy Oak Greenleaf, Breakup in '98
SPS-Deer	1993 -	Same as SP-Deer, synthetic
SCNP	1997 -	Sporting Clays with nickel-plated receiver, 28 or 30"
11-96	1996 -	Reshaped receiver, lighter weight, 3-shot magazine

tour variants, although mine has the original contour barrel. Federal regulations had finally succeeded in closing all the loopholes in the laws regarding the use of steel shot on waterfowl, so I was forced to go shopping. I was able to handle guns incorporating several options including varying barrel lengths, light and original contour barrels, gold triggers, silver triggers, blue triggers, etc. Gold triggers, as the late Jack O'Conner used to say, *"give me the vapors."* So I opted for an original contour, 28-inch barrel, blue trigger specimen. The gun was new-in-box but had been sitting on the dealer's shelf for a spell, I suspect, as the asking price was quite attractive. Although the presence of a new gun in the house is not exactly greeted with sorrow, in this case, I can truthfully say *"the gummint made me do it."*

Upon arriving home and familiarizing myself with the Owner's Manual and the 11-87's dis- and re-assembly sequence, I gave the gun a thorough cleaning and lubricating. Even the stock got a bit of wax. The gun looked good; a single flattened diamond on the pistol grip checkering due, no doubt, to less than attentive handling by a clerk or potential customer. No other stock or metal blemishes were found. I've fixed all that, of course. Several waterfowl seasons plus untold trips to the range have added a few "memories."

Several first impressions were quickly formed. First, the gun came to the shoulder well, fit seemingly as if it had been tailor-made for me. Second, it had a trigger pull only a lawyer could love and third, boy, was it heavy.

Out at the range, at many patterning sessions and lots of thrown clays, the gun has demonstrated it shoots at least within an inch or two of where I look, regardless of load, shot weight or choke tube used. The trigger pull smoothed out over the first couple of hundred rounds fired and now drops the hammer with but a pull of 58 ounces on my part. That's three pounds, ten ounces and for an autoloading shotgun used mostly in cold weather, that's O.K. There is some take-up and follow-through that a rifleman would not tolerate, but this is a shotgun.

I did encounter one problem, though. In the process of

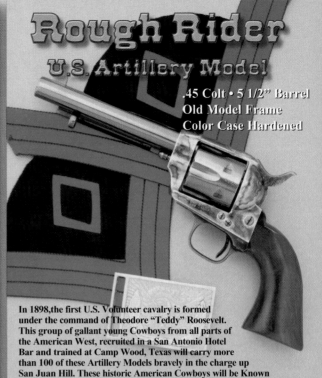

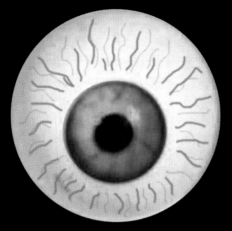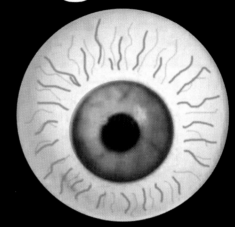

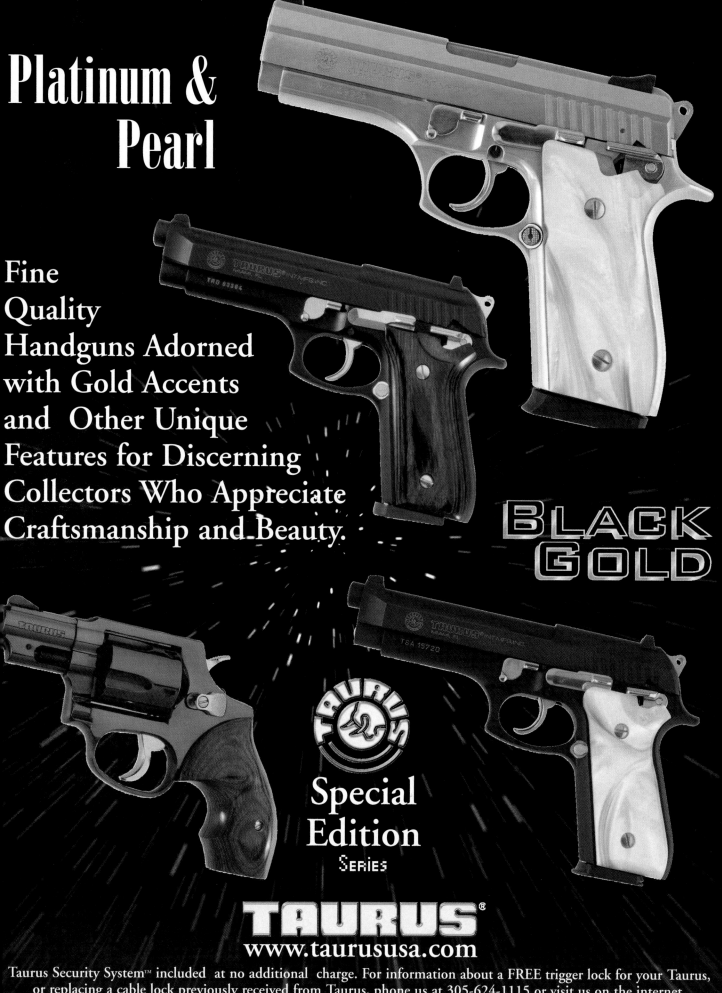

If the gun is special, we make the grips.

Colt .45 Auto
Classic Panel
Diamond
Checkered
with Border
Super Rosewood

Vacquero/Blackhawk,
Fleur-de-lis Checkering
Super Rosewood

Sig 230
Ultima Panel
Super Rosewood

Smith & Wesson
K Frame, with buttcap and checkering, Super Rosewood

Ruger Blackhawk
Classic Panel
Bonded Ivory
Mexican Eagle Carving

Ruger Mark II
Ultima Target
Super Rosewood

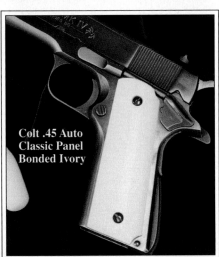

Colt .45 Auto
Classic Panel
Bonded Ivory

For twenty years we have made grips, from sawing the blocks of wood, to the machining, the sanding, the fitting, and the polishing of the finished grips. We have 42,000 square feet of factory space specializing in making grips, handles, and stocks for the handgun, gunstock, archery, and cutlery industries.

We have available a complete catalog of our handgun grips, which showcases our experience, design ideas, and manufacturing skills. We offer handgun shooters, collectors, and enthusiasts a wide range of distinctive grips for their special guns. Our grips are available direct or at your dealer.

901 N. Church St. • *Box 309*
Thomasboro, Illinois 61878
800-626-5774 • *217-643-3125*
Fax: 217-643-7973

Altamont

principally for waterfowling, and because I felt the heavier, original contour barrel produced a smoother swing, I sent the light contour barrel and its forend back.

On the rifled barrel I mounted a Simmons 2x32 scope with their Prodiamond reticle using Weaver medium mounts. The barrel has eight lands and grooves and a twist of one turn in 35 inches. The contour of the barrel requires the use of the original forend. This worked perfectly for me but would have required an additional forend had I only the light contour smooth bore barrel. The barrel handled everything I threw at it - or shot through

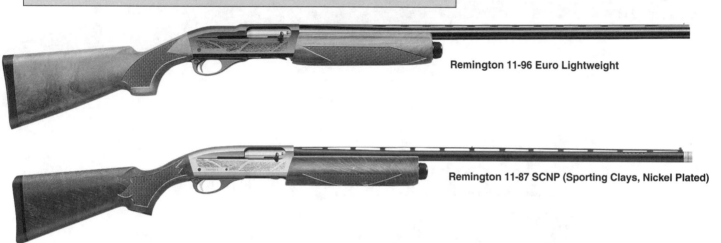

Remington 11-96 Euro Lightweight

Remington 11-87 SCNP (Sporting Clays, Nickel Plated)

examining shells that had been in the magazine, either fired or unfired, I sometimes found shells that had a deep longitudinal cut extending almost the entire length of an unfired shell's body. Examination led me to determine that the shells were rubbing against a sharp point on the forward edge of the intercepter latch, effectively cutting a groove in the shells. I took the gun to a gunsmith who stoned the sharp edge of the part, eliminating the problem.

At a SHOT Show not long afterwards, I discussed the situation with several Remington staffers. Most denied ever having heard of the problem, but one smiled and acknowledged that it was not unheard of. He also said stoning the intercepter latch was the proper remedy. It wasn't until later that I concluded that perhaps I was part of the problem.

Although I shoot shoulder weapons from the right shoulder, I'm nominally left-handed. When I insert shells in the magazine of the 11-87, I push them in with my left thumb, holding the gun in my right hand. By doing this, I push the shells against the intercepter latch as they slide into the magazine.

Any sharp edges that came in contact with the shells would likely result in the cut I found. Were I right-handed, cradling the gun in my left hand and inserting shells with my right thumb, I would have been pushing the shells away from the intercepter latch, and perhaps never experienced the problem. This may help explain why the problem was not so well known. At any rate, the problem is fixed and no shell so cut ever leaked or gave way when fired.

Feeling the desire to learn more about the 11-87, I obtained a 28-inch Light Contour barrel and forend and a 21-inch rifled barrel with a cantilevered scope mount from Remington.

The Light Contour barrel and forend do, indeed, reduce overall weight by one-half pound and shift weight more back between the hands. Felt recoil increases slightly, depending on load type but is not a problem. Point of impact versus point of aim remained the same, as did the performance of the various choke tubes. Still, weight was objectionably heavy for a gun to be carried extensively and called upon to respond quickly upon demand as in hunting upland game. Since I had purchased the gun

it - with ease, as did the scope. This included the traditional Foster-type slugs, the Brenneke style as well as the new saboted types that are inserted inside a standard plastic wad. Groups varied, of course, but the majority ranged from three to five inches, for five shots, at 100 yards. This is reasonably good for slugs generally and well within *"minute of deer"* for the range over which slugs retain sufficient energy for their intended purpose. Buckshot cannot be fired in rifled barrels, of course, nor can any shot. Where shot and slugs are required Remington offers another 21-inch, smooth bore barrel that accepts choke tubes, including a rifled tube. This latter tube also fits regular barrels and works surprisingly well.

By keeping the rifled barrel and scope, along with the regular smooth bore barrel, I've got a pretty versatile outfit. Doves, turkey and waterfowl with the smooth bore, and larger game as well with buckshot; slugs for the rifled barrel cover the big game scene, too. A sling, with quick-detachable swivels, gives added comfort and convenience during long walks to goose pits or the like and is easily removed when desired. ●

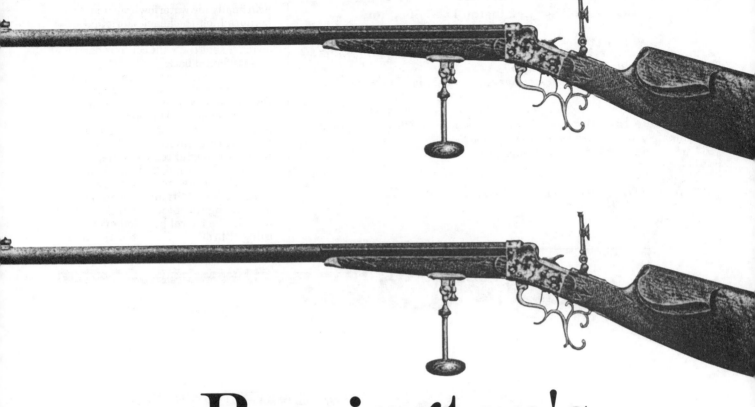

Remington's Number Three Hepburn....

A Single-Shot Rifle of Distinction

by George J. Layman

FOR NEARLY 27 years, until its demise in 1907, the handsome Remington Hepburn breech-loading rifle was a steady favorite with shooters and, like the rolling block, made the transition from black to smokeless powder.

In the 19th century, when firearms inventors were competing vigorously against their contemporaries, gun manufacturers were always happy to entertain the ideas of those mechanically-inclined individuals. Occasionally, relationships were temporary between the inventive geniuses and the firms who purchased the manufacturing rights to their ideas. Lewis Lobdell Hepburn was one such gifted individual who not only displayed a

mechanical background, but was also a highly commended championship long-range marksman. Born in Colton, New York on March 2, 1832, he gained his first job as an apprentice blacksmith, and by 1855 operated a gunsmithing business from his home in upstate New York. Hepburn was later selected to become a member of the U.S. "Elcho Shield" Rifle team in the early 1870s, and later competed in the 1874 Creedmoor matches on Long Island when the U.S. team beat the Irish by a score of 934 to 931.

Hepburn went on to produce some of the finest scores in long-range shooting and he even retired the Remington Diamond Badge after three wins. Lewis Hepburn

became one of the more popular shooters of his day and was soon hired by America's oldest firearms manufacturer, E. Remington and Sons of Ilion, New York. Hepburn became superintendent of their mechanical department and, while under their employ, designed what was to become one of Remington's most popular single-shot sporting rifles, sales of which soon paralleled their already established rolling-block action.

On October 7, 1879, Patent #220,285, a falling-block action from a design submitted by one Lewis L. Hepburn, was assigned to E. Remington and Sons. During that era, it was not uncommon that workers, often through loyalty, would allow their patents to be registered in the name of their employing firm. Thus in 1880, the newly designed single-shot rifle of Lewis Hepburn's namesake was unveiled after a 12 month period of tool-up in readying for full production. It would be introduced as the Remington No. 3 breech-loading rifle – which, ironically, followed the numerical lineup of action size numbers previously assigned to the rolling blocks (i.e. No. 1 large action, and the smaller No. 2 sporting action). The new rifle,

Post-1888 Remington Hepburns had their manufacturer's address –REMINGTON ARMS CO., ILION, N.Y. – stamped ahead of the rear sight dovetail on the barrel. Pre-1888 specimens had the E. REMINGTON address located behind the rear sight.

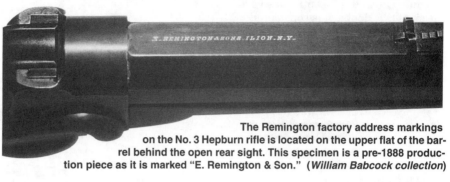

The Remington factory address markings on the No. 3 Hepburn rifle is located on the upper flat of the barrel behind the open rear sight. This specimen is a pre-1888 production piece as it is marked "E. Remington & Son." (*William Babcock collection*)

having been designed by a long-range shooter was, in its first configuration, catalogued as the No. 3 Long Range Creedmoor Model in 44-77 Remington/Sharps caliber. Having a shotgun butt, double-set triggers, long range Vernier tang sight and heel base, it could be ordered in a choice of 32-inch or 34-inch barrels. At the same time, Remington brought out a Mid-Range Creedmoor Rifle which had a shorter 28-inch barrel and the short mid-range Vernier tang sight, but had all other similar features of the long range variant. Lastly, it also differed in caliber, 40-65. The prime ingredient of the new Remington No. 3, however, was the rugged features of its action. The Remington Hepburn, unlike the rolling block, had a side-mounted lever on the right side of the frame which operated the simple, sturdy one-piece falling breech-

block. From its inception, the Remington Hepburn was always noted for its extremely hard steels and, especially, for its rebounding hammer which was an ultra-safe feature that returned the hammer to the safety position after discharge. Throughout its entire production life, the

Remington Hepburn maintained the distinct profile of its checkered pistol-grip stock and the frames were highly finished, with rich case colors and deep-blued barrels. When the sporting Creed-

moor Model Remington Hepburn was offered, the company shortly thereafter introduced a full-size Long Range Military Model, which also had a 34-inch full round barrel, chambered for a special 44-75-520 Remington straight cartridge. Aside from cartridge difference, the major deviation between it and the Creedmoor Sporting Model was that the military version had a straight, plain, full-length two-band stock and was supplied with standard military open sights.

One of the more sought-after variants of the Remington-Hepburn No. 3 is the Match Rifle in either *A* or *B Quality*. Shown is a *B Quality* Hepburn in 40-65 chambering (s/n 5768) that has about 98% finish and an excellent bore. This rifle was sold at auction in August 1998 for $7,000.00 . It is estimated that fewer than 1,000 were manufactured. (*Courtesy J.C. Devine Inc.*)

For years the Remington-Hepburn action has been highly regarded for building up custom single-shot rifles. The example shown is a 45-70, s/n 7050, restocked by E.P. Hinkle in the mid-60s. The elaborate stock is made of laminated Oregon Myrtle; the rifle has been used in the Coors matches by its present owner. (*Photo courtesy of Russell Eckels*)

Made in very small numbers, it also had a fancier counterpart, the high grade Hepburn Long Range Military Model offered concurrently. Primary differences on the fancy grade military model was the checkered pistol grip stock and the elaborate, fully checkered forend. Vernier long range tang sights were included as well. Presently, this variation of the Hepburn is considered quite rare.

By 1882, it was apparent the No. 3 Remington-Hepburn had literally "taken off" from the standpoint of popularity and, as a result, three new models were introduced in 1883. Since everyone was not in the long-range shooting game, Remington now offered the Hepburn in a variety of styles and calibers to suit the different interests and needs of rifle cranks.

The first, most basic variant was the No. 3 Sporting and Target Model. Sold with a choice of full-octagon or full-round barrel, to include the option of part-round, part-octagon barrels as well, the rifle was listed in barrel lengths of 26, 28 or 30 inches. Open sights were standard, but anything could be special-ordered from the Remington custom shop. This particular model usually accounts for the larger numbers of Remington-Hepburn rifles discovered today, and it was chambered for a host of cartridges from 22 through 50-caliber centerfire, with more added as time went on. Also in 1883, the Remington-Hepburn Match Rifle made its debut; a very high grade of target rifle tailor-made for the Schuetzen shooter who concentrated on short to mid-range match events. Chambered for cartridges from 25-20 single-shot through the 40-65, this rifle was offered in two specific grades known as the *"A Quality"* and *"B Quality."*

The features which distinguished the pair were that the *A* grade variant had a plainer variety of wood, uncheckered forend, a standard tang sight and a Beach combination front sight. It also had a cheekrest and nickeled Swiss butt-plate. The *B* grade, on the other hand, was a bit more upscale in its choice of extras. Sold with fancy select-grain walnut stocks, this variant had a larger cheekrest, with Vernier tang sights and a checkered forend as well. Both the *A* and *B Quality* Remington-Hepburn rifles could be ordered with double-set triggers. Though these fine target rifles were produced right up to 1907, informed estimates indicate a total production of less than 1,000 units. As a result, they are among the most sought-after versions of the Remington-

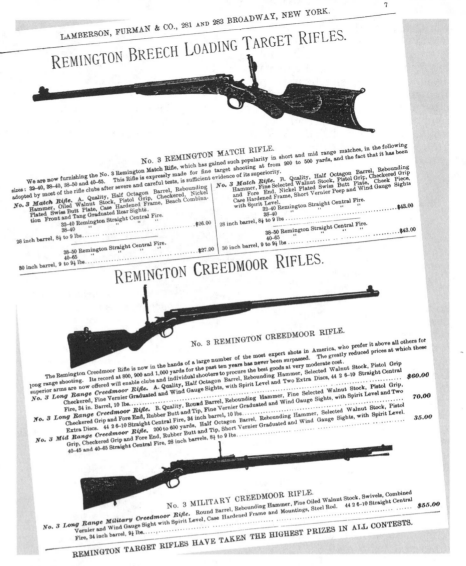

Aside from the Walker-Hepburn, windfall prizes for the collector of the Remington No. 3 are the Creedmoor Long or Mid-Range, the Match Rifle and especially the Military Creedmoor model. Note in this 1887 advertisement that the Creedmoor was also offered in *A* and *B Quality* grades.

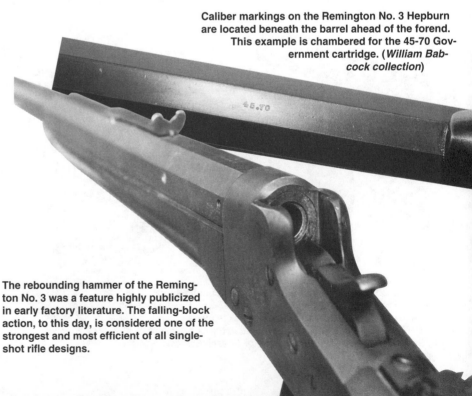

Caliber markings on the Remington No. 3 Hepburn are located beneath the barrel ahead of the forend. This example is chambered for the 45-70 Government cartridge. (*William Babcock collection*)

The rebounding hammer of the Remington No. 3 was a feature highly publicized in early factory literature. The falling-block action, to this day, is considered one of the strongest and most efficient of all single-shot rifle designs.

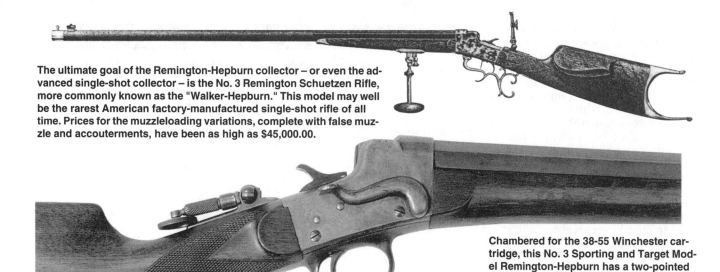

The ultimate goal of the Remington-Hepburn collector – or even the advanced single-shot collector – is the No. 3 Remington Schuetzen Rifle, more commonly known as the "Walker-Hepburn." This model may well be the rarest American factory-manufactured single-shot rifle of all time. Prices for the muzzleloading variations, complete with false muzzle and accouterments, have been as high as $45,000.00.

Chambered for the 38-55 Winchester cartridge, this No. 3 Sporting and Target Model Remington-Hepburn has a two-pointed checkering design on the pistol grip. Often, and for reasons unknown today, early specimens display either a two- or three-point checkering pattern regardless of their grade.

D. H. LAMBERSON & CO., 73 STATE STREET, CHICAGO.

6

REMINGTON
HUNTING, SPORTING AND TARGET RIFLES.

No. 3 REMINGTON RIFLE.

The New Model No. 3 Remington Rifle is especially designed for long range hunting and target purposes, requiring the use of heavy charges. It has a solid breech block, with direct rear support, the convenient side lever action and rebounding hammer, so that the arm always stands with the trigger in the safety notch. rendering premature discharge impossible. It is made with half octagon and full octagon barrel, case hardened frame and mountings, and fine pistol grip walnut stock. Chambered for the new styles of straight shells, as well as other popular sizes, and making a flatter trajectory than other rifles, it is unequalled for target and sporting uses.

Half Octagon or Full Octagon Barrel, Oiled Walnut Stock, Pistol Grip, Checkered, Rebounding Hammer, Case Hardened Frame and Mountings, Open Front and Rear Sights.

No. 3. 32 Caliber Rifles.
32-20 Winchester Central Fire.
32-30 Remington B. N. Central Fire.
32-40 " Straight " $18.00
26 inch barrel, 7¼ to 8¼ lbs. 19.00
28 " " 8 to 8½ lbs. 20.00
30 " " 8½ to 9 lbs.

No. 3. 38 Caliber Rifles.
38-40 Remington Straight Central Fire.
38-50 " $18.00
26 inch barrel, 8 to 8¼ lbs. 19.00
28 " " 8½ to 9 lbs. 20.00
30 " " 8½ to 9¼ lbs.

38-75 Remington Straight Central Fire.
38-90 " $20.00
30 inch barrel, 9 to 10 lbs .

DOUBLE TRIGGERS IN No. 3 RIFLES, EXTRA $2.00.

No. 3. 40 Caliber Rifles.
40-45 Remington Straight Central Fire.
40-65 " " $18.00
26 inch barrel, 8 to 8½ lbs. 19.00
28 " " 8½ to 10 lbs. 20.00
30 " " 9 to 10 lbs.

40-90 Remington Straight Central Fire.
40-90 Sharp's $20.00
30 inch barrel, 9 to 10 lbs.

No. 3. 45 Caliber Rifles.
45-70 Government Central Fire. $18.00
26 inch barrel, 8¼ to 10 lbs. 19.00
28 " " 8½ to 11 lbs. 20.00
30 " " 9 to 11 lbs. 21.00
32 " " 9¼ to 11 lbs.

45-105 Remington Straight Central Fire. $30.00
30 inch barrel, 9 to 10 lbs.

FOR PRICES OF EXTRA SIGHTS, SEE PAGE 9.

No. 3 REMINGTON RIFLES SHOW THE FLATTEST TRAJECTORY.

The wide range of barrel lengths and chamberings of Sporting and Target Models can be seen on this 1887 D.H. Lamberson catalog page. As new cartridges were introduced, the No. 3 was upgraded for them accordingly.

Hepburn. Today's collector is quite aware that few of these rifles follow any sort of strict precedence, and many of each variation offers something different from the next. To cite an example, one of the most unique this writer has owned was a plain No. 3 Sporting and Target Model with an extra-heavy #5 weight full-octagon barrel beveled at the rear where the flats met the frame. The rifle, serial number 1825, was marked 45-2-1/4 which equated to the Sharps 45-100, but the rifle would accept a 45-90 Winchester cartridge. Since the rifle had literally no finish remaining, and was obtained from a five generation-old Wyoming family. It must have been a true Western working gun special-ordered for big game or plains work. It appears old factory literature changed nomenclature for certain variants as time progressed, making inconsistencies commonplace. Though all the foregoing sporting models of the Remington-Hepburn were supposed to have been available right up to their discontinuation, this is questionable due to the limited production numbers of the more specialized types.

It is apparent, however, that as the tastes of shooters evolved into other areas, design of the Remington-Hepburn accommodated these changes as well. When smokeless powder arrived in the 1890s, it took only a brief span of time for the No. 3 Remington to catch up and, between 1893 and 1896, the Remington No. 3 High Power was introduced. Much like their successful rolling-block rifle, Remington felt it was a worthwhile venture to upgrade the No. 3 rifle to meet the requirements of smokeless propellants. Offered in such newly emerged favorites such as the 30-30 Winchester, the 30-40 Krag and the high pressure versions of the 32-40 and 38-55, production numbers on this variation are questionable, with approximate numbers unknown. The No. 3 High Power, though, was still available in the earlier standard configurations that were the hallmark of the Reminton-Hepburn and could still be special-ordered with double set-triggers. The No. 3 High Power was sold in standard barrel lengths of 26, 28 and 30 inches.

With the end of the blackpowder era and the popularity of repeating rifles seeming to overshadow the once-proud reign of the single-shot, one might surmise a smokeless powder version of the Remington-Hepburn would have been the rifle's swan song, but there was still another version in the making. At the turn-of-the-century, Schuetzen shooting in the United States was still a major nationwide activity and, between 1902 to 1904, the Remington No. 3 Schuetzen Match Rifle was unveiled. To meet the standards of the precision off-hand shooter who wanted the very best, Remington offered the ultimate rifle for such a purpose.

The No. 3 Schuetzen Match Rifle, more commonly known today as the "Walker-Hepburn", had a completely redesigned

Chamberings of the Remington No. 3 Hepburn Rifle, by Model

Long Range Creedmoor Rifle	Mid-Range Creedmoor Rifle
44-2-6/10 Remington Straight	40-65 Straight and 40-65 Everlasting

Long Range Military Creedmoor
44-75-520 Remington Straight (2-6/10)

Sporting and Target Model

32-20 WCF	38-40 WCF
32-30 Remington (bottleneck)	38-75 Remington
32-40 Remington Straight	38-90 Winchester (and Remington version)
22 WCF	40-65 Everlasting and Remington Straight
22 Extra Long Maynard Centerfire	40-90 Sharps Straight (and Remington version)
25-20 Stevens Single-Shot	40-60 Marlin/Ballard
25-21 Stevens	40-60 Winchester
25-25 Stevens	40-82 Winchester
38-40 Remington	45-70 Winchester
38-50 Remington Straight 1-3/4	45-90 Winchester
38-55 Ballard	45-105 Remington Straight

Also, the following Sharps calibers could be chambered on special order: 40-50, 40-70, 40-90, and 44-77 Bottleneck. Furthermore, the 45-90, 45-100, 45-105, and 50-90 Sharps Straight cartridges were available as well, to include even the 50-70 Govt.

No. 3 Match Rifle (*A and B Quality*)

32-40 Remington Straight	38-40 Remington Straight
25-20 Stevens	38-55 Ballard
25-25 Stevens	38-50 Remington Straight
25-21 Stevens	40-65 Remington Straight
32-40 Marlin/Ballard	

High Power (smokeless cartridge model)

30-30 Winchester	38-55 High Power Smokeless
30-40 Krag	32 Winchester Special
32-40 High Power Smokeless	38-72 Winchester

Schuetzen Match Rifle (Walker-Hepburn)

32-40 Remington	38-50 Remington Straight
38-40 Remington Straight	40-65 Remington Straight

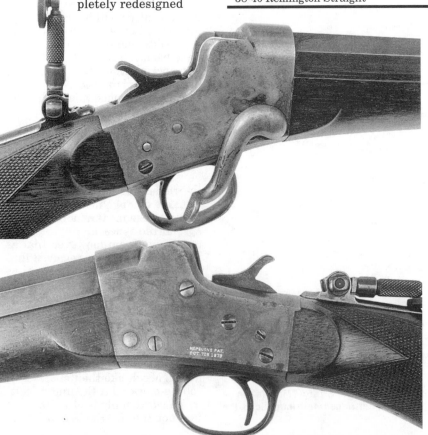

action modified by having its side-lever replaced with an under-lever which operated the sliding breech-block, the design of which would forcefully cam home a cartridge partially inserted into the chamber. The combination finger lever/trigger guard was a fancy scrolled affair and the entire rifle took on a look never before seen on Remington-Hepburn rifles. The beautifully contoured fancy walnut stock with cheek piece and fine-line checkering was standard on this high-grade rifle, and it was equipped with carefully hand adjusted double-set triggers and special windgauge Vernier tang sights. A wide variety of extras were offered on this exquisite firearm, such as optional palm

Left and right views of this Remington-Hepburn indicate that nearly 90 percent of its vivid case colors remain. Another interesting point of Hepburn rifles manufactured after 1888 is that the October 1879 Hepburn patent is marked on the lower left side of the frame whereas earlier pieces have the patent marking on the right side of the frame.

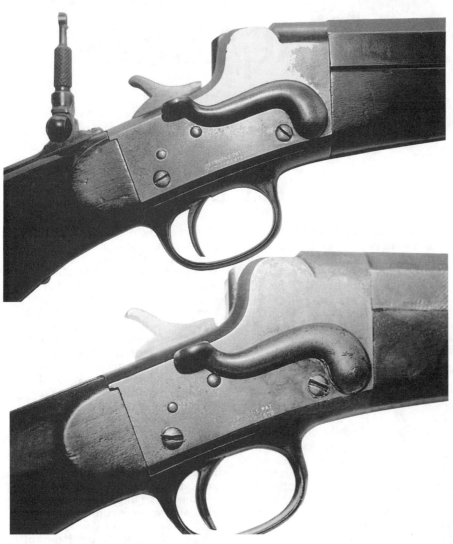

rests and a choice of three different barrel lengths.

The No. 3 Remington Schuetzen Match Rifle (the "Walker-Hepburn") is considered the ultimate 'find' for today's collector searching for the finest of all American single-shot rifles. Though the breechloading versions of the No. 3 Schuetzen rifle have a Walker patent barrel, the muzzleloading variants are the supreme rarity of the association of the Remington-Hepburn and Walker name. Fitted with a patented, removable false muzzle and supplied with a brass bullet starter, barrels were usually marked with the Walker patent beneath the barrel, adjacent to the forend or muzzle. The 11- to 13-pound rifles were chambered in four calibers from 32-40 Remington to 40-65 Remington Straight. Production numbers of this variant are so low they are a distinct rarity all to their own. Norm Flayderman has for years cautioned the collector to be extremely careful in the acquisition of the so-called Walker-Hepburn due to the existence of several spurious or altered specimens. Most collectors and arms historians estimate the total production of all Remington-Hepburn rifles at 10,000 to 13,000 pieces. Today the surviving number of complete, factory-original guns is likely far less since countless specimens must have been destroyed, lost or rebarreled into custom guns.

Universally, all Remington-Hepburn rifles are marked on the right side of the action with HEPBURN'S PAT. OCT. 7TH 1879, with upper barrels having E. REMINGTON & SONS, ILION, NEW YORK and those manufactured after 1888 are stamped, REMINGTON ARMS CO. Caliber markings are located on the underside of the barrel just ahead of the forend. On many earlier No.3 Remington-Hepburn rifles, particularly on the Creedmoor variants, L.L. Hepburn's initials–or even his name–appears stamped under the barrel just under the forend. Though he was a superintendent, he was after all a barrel-maker and no doubt did much work while employed by Remington. It was unfortunate for the Remington company to have lost Lewis L. Hep-

burn after the company went into receivership in 1878.

In 1886, Hepburn relocated to New Haven, Connecticut and accepted a position with John M. Marlin's company. John Marlin was no stranger to Lewis Hepburn as he was quite familiar with a lever-action design patented by Hepburn in 1884 while he still resided in the Ilion, New York area. Hepburn's association with the Marlin Firearms Company proved to be that company's most valuable asset as Hepburn patented numerous lever actions for Marlin, and continued development of several other types of firearms as well.

A very generous individual whose reputation was impeccable, Lewis L. Hepburn remained a dedicated inventor and mechanical expert who designed some of Marlin's best-selling rifles, such as the Models 1888, 1889, 1893 – and many more. All through the 1900s, Hepburn was inexhaustibly loyal to the Marlin company and made his way to work each day no matter how harsh the weather. Unfortunately, this dedication led to his eventual demise. On the icy, cold and sleety morning of January 6, 1910 while walking several blocks from his home to the Marlin factory on Willow Street, he slipped on the sidewalk and fractured his hip. The finest medical treatment of the day could not successfully mend the bones of his broken hip and he was confined to his bed up to his eventual death on August 31, 1914. It is said he remained cheerful and uncomplaining right to the end.

Lewis L. Hepburn should probably be considered one of those rare geniuses, like John Browning, whose designs have yet to be equaled. Though he is probably the father of the modern Marlin lever-action rifle as we know it today, the most famous–and everlasting–tribute to his superb mechanical abilities will always be the Remington-Hepburn single-shot rifle.

*Note** The labels of *A Quality* and *B Quality* were apparently not confined to the Remington-Hepburn Match Rifle alone. Certain advertising literature, as late as 1887, listed the Creedmoor Remington-Hepburn rifles as being sold in grades of *A* and *B Quality* with identical high grade options as those offered for the Match Rifle. ●

Tubular Magazines
...ARE SAFE

by R.W. Ballou

Like many people, I've often wondered about the actual safety of tubular magazines, particularly on rifles chambered for high-power, centerfire cartridges. The idea of one cartridge's bullet resting against the primer of the next cartridge in the magazine, under spring pressure and subjected to the slamming forces created by the gun's recoil is, if you think about it, a little less than comforting. And the oft-repeated warnings about never using pointed – or even round-nose – bullets in one seem to imply that an in-the-magazine discharge is a very real (and very dangerous) possibility.

Actually, the safety record of tubular magazines seems to be exemplary. I've never heard of anyone having an accident involving one, nor have I found any available data on the subject, which is something that can't be said about certain other aspects of firearms design. But the questions still remain—what would happen if some circumstance – such as a defective, incorrectly seated or unusually sensitive primer – caused one of the cartridges in a tubular magazine to fire? It's a known fact that a primer not seated fully into its pocket can cause a slam-fire in a semi-automatic firearm. Could a similar thing happen in the magazine of a heavy-recoiling lever gun? And what about the occasional fool who insists on loading spitzer bullets in his 30-30 in the interest of "improving ballistics?" Is such a person putting himself at risk of some kind of gruesome injury? Is the nose of a bullet capable of acting as a sort-of "firing pin" to indent a primer? And in any case, would a chain-fire in the magazine take place, causing all of the cartridges to fire?

To answer these questions an experiment of some kind seemed in order. This experiment would basically have to determine two things: first, the actual likelihood of a bullet's nose setting off the primer of another cartridge in a tubular magazine due to recoil (or other) forces, and second, the damage – if any – that would result to the magazine, the gun and the shooter.

The first part was easy. A simple procedure was devised that involved placing a primed 30-30 case, neck-down, between the jaws of a vise while hold-

"Under the spreading chestnut tree" photo illustrates the method used to determine the likelihood of a bullet's nose causing a primer to fire in a tubular magazine.

ing a bullet, nose-first, against the primer with a pair of blacksmith's tongs. The base of the bullet was then struck sharply with a two-pound ballpeen hammer. The force generated by this procedure was far greater than anything that might be generated by a gun's recoil; definitely a beyond-worse-case scenario. Three different types of .308-inch bullets were used for this test: a 170-grain cast flat-point (Lyman #311041), a 170-grain jacketed flat-point (Hornady) and a 180-grain jacketed spitzer (Remington). The cast bullet was of a fairly hard alloy; about 16-18 Brinnell. The primers were standard Large Rifle (CCI 200).

With both the cast bullet and the jacketed flat-point, both of which are intended for use in tubular magazines, it was totally impossible to set the primer off. Repeated hard blows with the hammer resulted in nothing more than mutilated bullets, their noses mushroomed to probably twice their original diameter. The spitzer bullet was another story, however. It did actually fire the primer, although it took five hits to do so. Examination of the bullet's nose revealed that the soft lead forming the point absorbed the first few hammer blows. By the fifth blow, the bullet's jacket was in direct contact with the primer, and was rigid enough (as well as small enough in diameter) to act as the "firing pin." Repeating these tests a second time with all three bullet types provided essentially the same results.

A third set of cases was made up with the primers deliberately seated approximately .020-inch above the base of the case. None of the bullet types caused these primers to fire, including the spitzer bullet. The first few blows of the hammer simply seated the primers fully in the cases, by which point the ends of the bullets were flattened to much greater than their original diameter.

The 170-grain cast bullet loads after being subjected to a test firing in the device. Notice how far the bullets have been pushed into the case necks, and the generally sooty condition of the cases. A large amount of the powder in the first (*ruptured*) case was unburned.

I didn't bother trying a full-metal-jacket bullet of any type. The results with the jacketed spitzer bullet indicate that a pointed FMJ bullet would have probably fired the primer on the first whack. And who would be dumb enough to load such bullets in a tubular magazine, anyway?

The second part of this experiment was a little more difficult. What was needed was some kind of device that would enable me to accurately simulate an in-the-magazine discharge, constructed from materials that are typical of tubular magazine guns, and using full-power ammo. Conversion of a Marlin 336C to a half-magazine (in the interest of improved accuracy) provided me with the basis of this device, a leftover piece of magazine tube long enough to hold three 30-30 cartridges, as well as a suitable length of magazine spring. I welded a simple tubular breech to this piece of tube, which I concocted from two different diameters of small pipe, with a T-shaped striker powered by two external coil springs. The magazine spring and end cap hold the cartridges back with sufficient force to enable the point of the striker to indent the primer of the first cartridge in line, positively inducing a discharge in that cartridge. A piece of a discarded SMLE stock serves as a simulated "forearm." To fire the device a length of heavy twine, tied to the striker, is pulled taut and then quickly cut. Very sophisticated! As

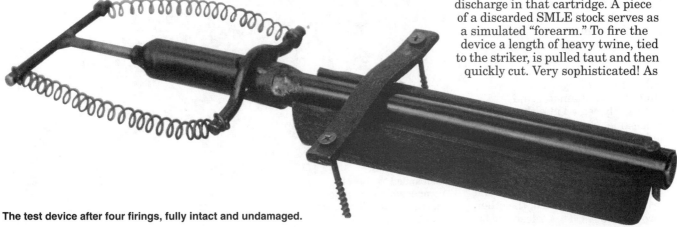

The test device after four firings, fully intact and undamaged.

will be seen, the device's capacity of three cartridges was more than sufficient for this experiment.

Now for the fun part. The device was first fastened to a piece of lumber about four feet long, which was placed on the ground and weighted down with four large stones. A white plastic bucket, sawed in half and with a slot to let the trigger string pass through, was placed over it to contain any possible fragments and also help to indicate how much gas, unburned powder, etc. was escaping. The cord used for the first firing was about 30 feet long: I wanted to be well out of harm's way!

Three different loads (of three cartridges each) were used for this test. These were: the 170-grain cast flat-point bullets (Lyman #311041) over 30 grains of IMR 3031, approximately the working pressure of a factory load; some Remington 170-grain factory loads and the 180-grain Remington spitzer bullets, again over 30 grains of 3031.

Frankly, I was expecting some pretty spectacular results when I first fired the device. What actually happened surprised me, to say the least. First, there was a report about equal in loudness to a child's cap gun, followed by a small amount of smoke drifting out from under the bucket. Waiting a few minutes, I carefully removed the magazine's end plug and slid the contents out. Two cartridges, sooty on the outside and with their bullets telescoped back part way into the cases, were followed by the virtually undamaged bullet of the first cartridge, a lot of unburned powder, and finally the cartridge's case, ruptured for about half of its length. The device, however, was fully intact and undamaged.

Repeating the test with the Remington factory loads produced identical results. Obviously the fired cartridge, loosely contained in a magazine's tube substantially larger than its own diameter and not tightly sealed at either end (the same as on an actual gun), was only able to generate enough pressure to rupture its thin brass case, and propel its bullet forward with the relatively small amount of energy necessary to overcome the crimp and bullet pull of the other two cartridges. This telescoping

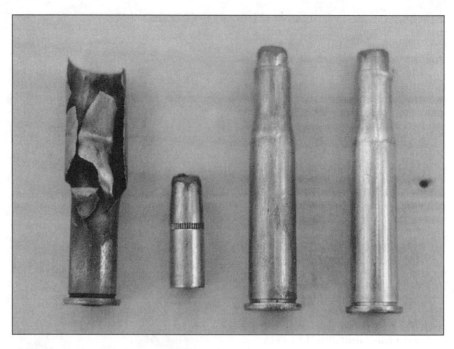

170-grain Remington factory loads after firing in the device.

effect certainly absorbed most of the energy being transmitted. The amount of unburned powder indicated that only partial combustion took place due to the low "chamber" pressure generated. And the white plastic bucket, used as a cover, was still perfectly clean on the inside, indicating that only a relatively small amount of gas had actually escaped.

I was expecting different results with the spitzer bullet loads, but again only the first cartridge fired, with results identical to the other two loads. However, examination of the remains of this firing brought to light an important fact about

tubular magazines: the two unexploded cartridges had noticeable marks on their bases (left by the lead nose of the preceding bullet) that indicated the noses of the bullets were making contact partly on the cartridge bases and only partly on the primers themselves. This makes sense, as virtually all cartridges used in the tubular magazines are tapered to a certain extent or have a pronounced rim, or both, causing them to generally lay at the slight angle when loaded in the magazine. In the case of flat-point bullets that have a *meplat* (nose) that's almost as large in diameter as the primer, probably the bullet's nose will be largely supported by the case itself. This fact alone adds greatly to the safety of the tubular magazine concept.

In a last attempt to create a chain-fire in the magazine I made up three more spitzer loads

The test device dismantled to show its component parts. Notice the "forearm" made from part of an SMLE stock.

and attached small chunks of cardboard to their necks with tape, to act as "shims" to raise the bullet's noses into direct, center-line contact with the primers. These were carefully loaded into the device, verifying their orientation as each was slid down the tube. Still, only one cartridge fired. The second cartridge in line did, however, have a distinct shallow depression in its center produced by the impact of the fired cartridge's bullet – which obviously wasn't enough to set off the primer.

Pointed, FMJ-type bullets could possibly have created a chain-fire, but again, who would ever use such bullets in a tubular magazine? And judging by the results obtained with the loads actually used, I doubt if a chain-fire would have generated sufficient pressure to do any real physical damage to the magazine or anything external to it.

And what did all of this prove? Basically, this experiment demonstrated that a tubular magazine, even on a high-power rifle generating a substantial amount of recoil, is not a potential shrapnel grenade living between the fingers of the shooter's forward hand. With proper bullets, the chances of an in-the-magazine discharge taking place are minute, and in the unlikely event of one happening, the results would not be catastrophic – to the gun, the shooter or any possible bystanders. The real danger to the shooter would be from escaping gas, possibly blowing back into the shooter's face and eyes. And, remember, this experiment in no way quantified how much gas was actually released, although all indications were that it was only a fraction (in terms of volume and pressure) of what might be released by a ruptured cartridge in the chamber of the gun. And the actions of most lever-action rifles are pretty "leaky," especially around the bottom where the lever pivot is. Most of the gas would probably take this route to escape.

None of this is to say that the usual safety precautions regarding tubular magazines (such as never using pointed bullets in one) should be ignored. Far too many people can't be bothered to wear eye protection when they shoot: for them following *all* other safety precautions is doubly important. But tubular magazines *are* safe, possibly even safer than box magazines, which place a number of cartridges seemingly in harm's way directly below the rear of the chambered round. But that's a subject for another experiment! ●

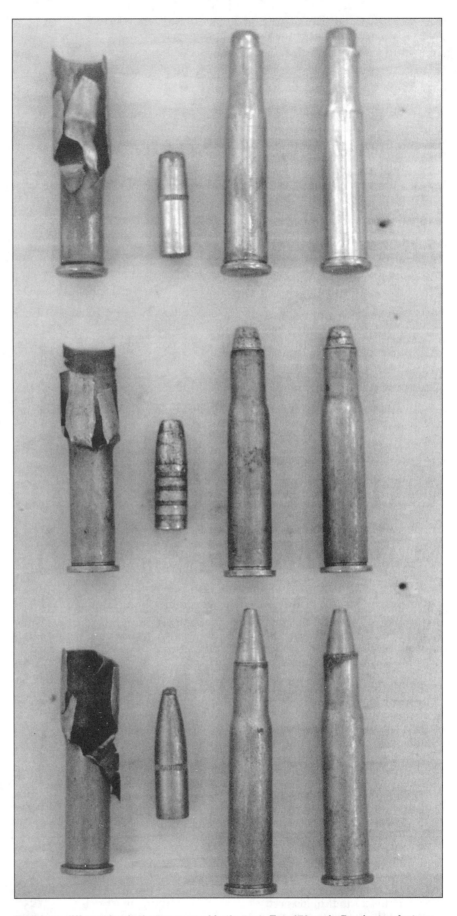

The three different loads that were used in the test. *Top:* 170-grain Remington factory load. *Middle:* 170-grain cast bullets (Lyman #311041) over 30 grains of IMR 3031. *Bottom:* 180-grain spitzer over 30 grains of IMR 3031. Results were virtually identical with all three loads. All bullets were firmly crimped in the case necks.

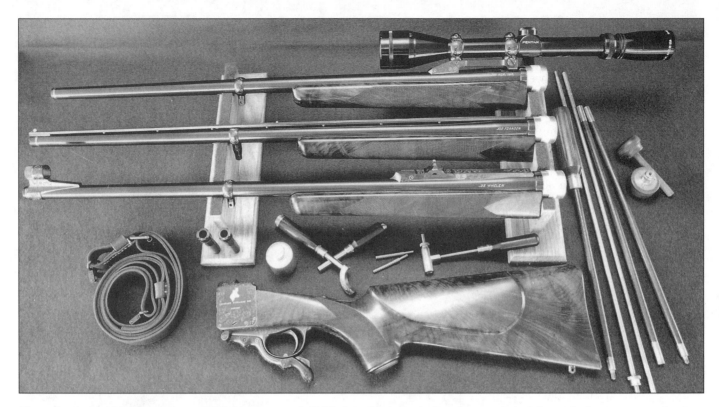

The entire Jenkins/Farquharson set: 280 Ackley Improved, 35 Whelen, .410-bore shotgun, scope, choke tubes, takedown spanner, cleaning rods & sling…

Super-Fine Farquharson

Text and Photos by Scott Key

FOR THIRTY-FIVE YEARS, John Bione had something his friend Red Jenkins wanted. To a gunsmith and rifleman it was a pretty interesting and rare something: an original Westley Richards Farquharson action – a take-down action, no less – no barrel, no stock… just the (arguably) neatest, classiest single-shot action ever designed.

Red offered to buy it. Not for sale. Build a rifle on it for his friend John. Nope. I'll leave it to you, John said. Hell, replied Red, you'll probably outlive me, and it still won't be a rifle!

January 1990, Red gets a phone call. It's John's wife Elaine: "Well, Red, it looks like you got yourself that action…"

So what do you do with it, when you finally get your hands on an original Westley Richards Farquharson? If you're the caliber of craftsman that Red Jenkins is, and can do pretty much anything you want in metal, the question is more what not to do. With an action designed to be a takedown rifle, why not build a multiple-barreled set? Five, three … what?

Red settled on the 280 Ackley Improved, 35 Whelen, and .410 shotgun, a novel but practical combination. There is very little that cannot be successfully hunted with this gun, excepting probably waterfowl and the largest African game. The 280 AI will do for medium game, and the 35 Whelen for any North American big game.

The intention, of course, was not only to produce a practical, eminently shootable longarm, but the finest and handsomest gun possible. And if these photos successfully convey even the slightest indication of it, you can see Mr. "Red" Jenkins most definitely succeeded.

Who was it that wrote "God is in the details."? Everywhere you look on this set, there is something perfectly lovely. There is an obvious sense this gun was built without compromise, by someone who took the time to do it right. Indeed, it looks like whoever built it had all the time in the world, and all the mastery of craft required.

Superfine engraving and gold inlay by Jim White, of Anchorage, Alaska – even on the powder measure.

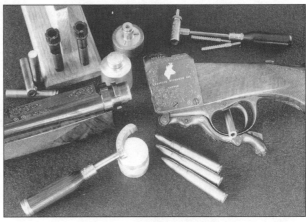

The business end of the three-barreled set, with respective cartridge cases: 280 Ackley Improved, .410 "Forager" and 35 Whelen.

Takedown mechanism, showing tensioning locknut and spanner wrench. Choke tubes, powder measure and custom jag tips in background.

The craftsmanship exercised in the fit and finish of all the pieces and parts is truly amazing. Not obvious in the photos are details like the barrel band/swivel stud assembly on the .410 barrel. It looks like one or two pieces, but is actually six, and can be removed without disturbing the vent rib. The quarter-rib on the 35 Whelen looks like it was milled out of the barrel blank, the fit is so good. Red has a trade secret here that he wishes not divulged; the fine fit is the kind of thing that could drive a good gunsmith a few days worth of crazy.

The story of the .410 barrel alone could fill pages. How do you get an extractor designed for centerfire rimless cartridges to remove a .410 shotshell? You make .410 shotshells out of rifle brass, that's how. Red started by blowing out 240 Weatherby brass, but lost too many cases trying to produce a straight, rimless, belted (it's got to headspace on something, right?) case .430-inch in diameter by 2.5 inches. So he made a set of dies to form a belted case out of 30-06 brass, dies that would swage a belt, and form a near-perfect brass .410 shotgun shell for use in this rifle.

The barrel was obtained before it was rifled for a 416 chambering. The bore was .408-inch, ideal for the .410 smoothbore. The choke tubes are completely custom: cylinder, modified and full. Red made all the reamers and threading tools to produce this choke set just for this one barrel, as well as the special wrench for interchanging them.

The takedown mechanism is also deserving of special note. Westley Richard's takedown design on the Farquharson included no mechanism for adjusting the tension between barrel and action. One of the big problems with any takedown assembly is its tendency to "shoot

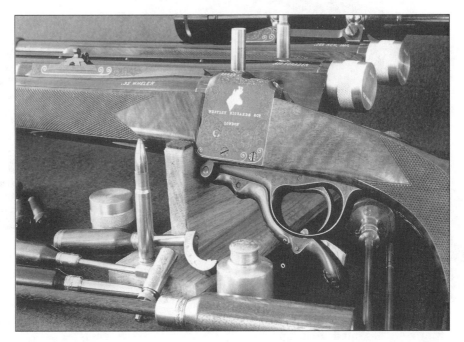

A thing of beauty is a joy…to shoot! Shadows around the quarter-rib conceal the amazing fit. Every item pictured was made from "scratch," except for the action, scope and cartridge brass.

loose" over a period of time. Red added a threaded tensioning collar that tightens and loosens with a spanner wrench (itself a work of art). All three barrels – by Shilen, and each one exactly 27 1/2 inches long – share this feature, a Red Jenkins improvement to the original design.

Even the aluminum dust caps were specially milled for each barrel breech, marked with the chambering/gauge and the serial number "36633," the original action's serial number. Red made special cleaning rods, powder measure (.410), appropriate wrenches, and has only to finish by crafting a case fitted to all these lovely accessories, as well as the gun and barrels.

Stocking of this rifle was by R. M. Johnson of Cheyenne, Wyoming. The walnut is California Claro with a tung oil finish; checkering 18 lpi. Superb.

The engraving and 18k gold inlay is by Jim White, of Anchorage, Alaska and is as perfect as can be imagined – both in coverage and execution. Again, the brilliance of it showing in not only what was done, but also in what was not. Tasteful, elegant, and not excessive.

Rarely, if ever, does one come upon an assemblage of parts and pieces that constitute such a gratifying whole. A rifle like this is rare indeed, but what is really impressive is evidence of the pride the maker had in its creation. Ultimately, it is not the technical expertise alone that impresses, but the great heart it shows. A creation on this order reminds us greatness is not only possible, but intensely important. ●

19th Century Horse Pistols Enter the 21st Century

Nicely tooled & finished holster rig for the circa-1932 Colt SAA with 4 3/4-inch barrel.

by Jim Thompson

The Colt Model P 1873

THE GUN — COLT'S Model P — actually entered production at Colt's Hartford facility in 1872; now, some 130 years later, with hardly a hostile Indian in sight and train robbers virtually gone, the classic revolver design is made in a number of different factories and in more models and chamberings than ever.

In places as far way and foreign to the American West as Russia, East Asia, Europe and Africa, the sleek, classic "cowboy guns" introduced in the 1870s are almost as well known as they were in the U.S. during their 19th century heyday. Some of this has to do with Hollywood movies, some with the very romance of that adventurous era; a little with the unique, sleek designs

– and much with the quantities in which the pistols were produced.

Colt's "*First Generation*" Model P entered full production in 1872, and was taken off assembly lines – the first time – in 1940, by which time some 357,859-plus frames had been produced.

The "*Second Generation*" revolvers, basically updated versions of the original – and a new model with adjustable sights called the New Frontier – consisted of some 90,000-plus of the original design, plus about 4,300 "New Frontiers" in the period 1956-73.

From 1973 until 1989, when the "P" was briefly (and on paper only) ousted from production, 82,000 standard revolvers and 14,500 "New Frontier" variants were produced.

The Model P has always been expensive. At the turn of the century, advertisements showed various models at $18.00-$24.00, roughly wages of a month to a month and a half for a typical middle-income worker of the time. Almost a century later, the same models range from $900-$1500 per copy, still roughly a month's wages for a typical American production worker.

Just the variety of names given the Model P gives some idea how much use it saw and how highly and often it figured in the public mind: *Peacemaker, Single Action Army & Frontier.*

Model P1873 – its catalog designator – was rarely applied to the actual firearm but printed faithfully on every box was the appellation:

First Generation Model P Colt SAA, 7 1/2-inch barrel.

Second Generation Model P Colt SAA 38 Special, circa 1956; 7 1/2-inch barrel.

'*Army Model.*' The informal names popularly bestowed upon guns sold in the United States included *equalizer, thumb-buster, Judge Colt* – to name a few.

Even Colt cannot give a complete list of the cartridges for which the Model 1873 was chambered. 22 Long Rifle and 476 Eley are the extremes among recorded listings, but Colt factory-produced pistols – upon special order – could be chambered for virtually every cartridge which could be engineered into the *First-Generation* guns' cylinders. The original 45 Colt loading was first and probably most popular, but 44/40 (WCF), 38/40, 32/30, 25/20 – even 44 Henry Rimfire – were common in early pistols, when it was often vital to a frontiersman or cowboy that his rifle – most likely a Winchester – and pistol could use the same cartridge. But the Colt Model P was popular in American cities and as a privately-purchased firearm for military and civilian use all over the world, and so the cylinders were chambered for cartridges of all sorts, from virtually everywhere; indeed, since Colt licensed - and even encouraged - licensed exporters to furnish firearms for special applications, chamberings

now considered exotic and obscure show up in authentic Colt specimens...sometimes marked with an overseas importer's identification. Appearing in Colt records, the 44 Russian, 7.5 Nagant – even the Italian Ordnance revolver cartridges and several short-lived British and Australian loadings – as well as an entire list of entries in the vast records which do not denote chambering but, being bound for foreign markets, the revolvers were likely chambered for the locally-popular pistol cartridge.

At the turn of the century, there was not a government in the world whose military had not ordered, in some means or fashion, some quantity of the Model P.

The Bisley Model, with extended grip and improved lock and spring work, was introduced early in the 20th century, and became a very popular target pistol, though never as aesthetically pleasing as the plow-handled original and, even today, not bearing a dollar value to collectors commensurate with its true rarity.

There was a vast market for handguns in the last quarter of the 19th century, and Colt stood atop that market with its first cartridge revolver. Naturally, since there seemed almost no limit to demand, imitators – Colt saw them as usurpers – came along almost immediately.

Remington's Model 1875 and Model 1890 guns were not imita-

tions, however. They followed a continuous line of development from Remington's cap and ball revolvers of the 1850s and 1860s, and were regarded by many shooters as sturdier and more accurate than the Colts. Many said this was due to the "*sail*" under the barrels of the Model 1875s. Others claimed the closer fit between cylinder/forcing cone and better timing accounted for increased accuracy.

Having fired Colts and Remingtons of both original and modern incarnation – my experience indicates the Remingtons, even the Model 1890, with its much-reduced "*sail*" stiffener, are more accurate revolvers.

This is not my opinion alone. Wyatt Earp, who owned many firearms, used Model 1875 Remingtons during most of his tenure in Dodge City, and one of his pistols on display there bears mute testament to his use; its "sail" bears pits and stains from the blood of many a drunken drifter who didn't pay proper attention to Earp's requests to disarm and/or depart. For all the legendary violence involving the Earps and their pistols – and the reports are largely correct – it is a well-documented fact he was far more inclined to bludgeon an opponent than to shoot him down. And for his purposes, the "sail" beneath the barrel of the Model 1875 was ideal.

Spanish and Mexican copies of the Colt – and even the Remington

– appeared in the U.S. as early as 1895. Seldom well-made and never highly thought of, these guns were a budget item, often delivered with no markings at all, not even a serial number. It is perhaps fortunate - given the indifferent metallurgy of many early copies - that they seem to have been shot little, if at all. In other parts of the world, loosely Colt-inspired single-action guns – and even Nagant-styled revolvers – were stamped "*Frontier*" and sold as "American-style."

But when Colt's production line closed in 1940, in order to tool up for less labor-intensive military weapons sold in far more lucrative quantities, a door was opened for the serious copyists. By the 1950s, Western movies and television series were very popular, shooters and collectors began to seek "a piece of the West," and prices on Colt originals began to skyrocket. Early on, the Hy Hunter Corporation, in the U.S., commissioned Germany's Sauer to initiate production of Colt-inspired single actions.

As late as the early 1980s, Hawes in the United States and others in Europe were still selling these guns which, by then, had become cosmetically much more like Colts with their rainbow-hued, case-hardened frames, although internally some coil springs had been substituted.

Ruger's Blackhawk series was never a true Colt clone, but as even Bill Ruger will assure you, the whole series was inspired by the Colt, or perhaps more accurately, by the absence of the big single action from the marketplace.

When Colt marketing people noticed a current product based on an 'ancient' design outselling many of their more 'modern' current catalog items, a very simple marketing decision was made: In 1954, Colt announced the "P" would re-enter production in 1955. First deliveries were made from late '55 to early '56. These products utilized a whole new series of serial numbers, followed by the letters "SA," and were a faithful continuation of the original, in which only small contours of the grip internals and pin and the geometry of the firing pin were altered. In fact, among collectors who shoot and admire the "P" the general feeling is that very late *First Generation* and very early *Second Generation* guns are the best made and finished pistols of the entire run. The later *Third Generation* added safety features to the

hammer/trigger interface, requiring many internal parts changes, and began another serial number set, using "SA" as a prefix. A very few *Second Generation* guns – those numbered above #99,999 – also used the "SA" number prefix.

While sales of the "new" Colt were brisk, the idea of budget-priced, high-quality Colt Single Action copies was too good to resist. Val Forgett of Navy Arms correctly analyzed the then-emerging wave of Western Americana nostalgia, and after early spates of Belgian and Spanish-built black powder replicas, contracted with Italian gunmaker Aldo Uberti to produce Colt and Remington cap and ball replicas. It was a short step from there to production of the later cartridge revolvers, sold worldwide as the "Cattleman" series. Uberti's products have proliferated, and the Colt variants include versions featuring the original ca.1880 solid frame, unusual barrel lengths, special "magnum" frames, etc., etc. — many only loosely based on the originals. Likewise, Armi Jager, originally contracted by Intercontinental Arms of Los Angeles, now imported to the U.S. by EMF of Santa Ana, California, began to produce many Colt copies – even the Bisley

Bisley Model, circa 1912.

Bisley Model, circa 1916, with 4 3/4-inch barrel.

version – in chambering options which do credit to the diversity of the venerable originals. These revolvers, too, are now sold worldwide under a variety of brand names and by many different distributors. If imitation comprises the sincerest form of flattery, then the P Model is one of the most complimented designs of all time. And the ancient horse pistol earned every accolade. It is still earning praise.

Five major and countless minor books comprise the literature of what is really nothing more than two and a half models of a single basic design. Every book devoted to Colt spends a very high percentage of its pages discussing the company's first dedicated cartridge design. While the original frame is produced with only tiny changes by Colt and others, only the Bisley really represents any change in configuration or mechanical arrangements.

A footnote should be made, however, that Interarms' last stainless steel Uberti-parts/Hammerli-proofed and adjusted guns used speeded-up lockwork and coil springs before production was canceled in 1987. For a product deemed moribund more than 50 years ago, the proliferation of new

models, variants, and copies is rather startling.

Still, it is accurate to say that any Colt-like single action is essentially purchased in obedience to some combination of glands and hormones, a purchase decision driven by nostalgia rather than dispassionate technical assessment.

The Model P's shortcomings are as well known as the legend:

Short grips – so short that a man with big hands finds at least one, often two fingers dangling as if oh-so-properly sipping a cup of tea.

Hammer fall (Bisley Model excepted) – not quite slow enough to read the instructions between trigger release and ignition, but sluggish enough that the shooter's job of aiming is not even close to finished when the trigger is squeezed.

Powerful flat springs – drive small notched cams, especially at quarter cock, which means the gun's own internal leverage can cause chips and breakage...complaints even Western cowboys lodged against Colt's most famous product.

At the time the Model P was introduced, of course, the self-contained cartridge was new and seemed handy in any version. Today the rather elaborate reloading oper-

ation seems inconvenient compared to that of modern double-action revolvers with swing-out cylinders, and absolutely archaic when compared to a magazine-fed autoloader with easily swapped magazines.

Sam Colt didn't invent ergonomics. Legend says he was left-handed, and that seems to have been true, for the gun on which he did only very early prototypical work is, essentially, *backwards* for a right-hander. But like the later P.08, the swept grip contour of the early black powder Colts - shortened - accounts for a lot of fast, instinctive accurate shooting.

Again, contrary to logic, many shooters can shoot more accurately pointing the Model 1873 like a finger than they can using the sights and, with practice, the legendary capability of the old pistol to hit a man-sized target with a minimum of training can become awesome. In the 1960s, when electronic timing took the old "*guesstimates*" of fast draw times into the realm of hard data, it became fairly common in competition for shooters to draw, fire, and hit – in a vital area – man-sized targets in under a half second; the very best American competitors such as Steven A. Benson and Thell Reed were able to hit multiple tar-

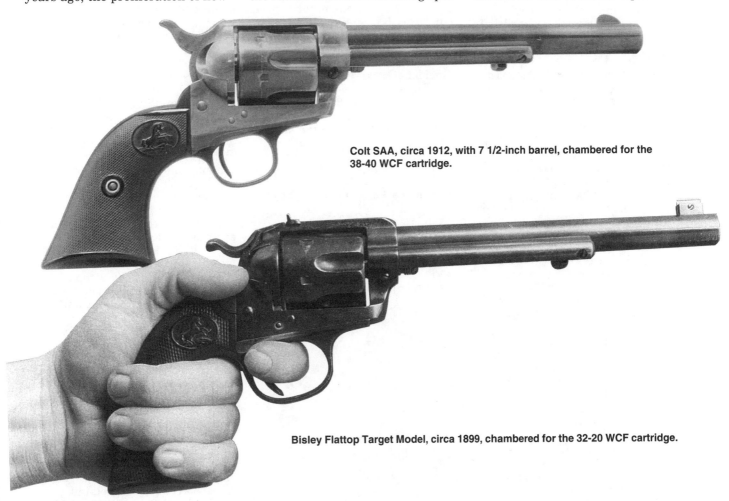

Colt SAA, circa 1912, with 7 1/2-inch barrel, chambered for the 38-40 WCF cartridge.

Bisley Flattop Target Model, circa 1899, chambered for the 32-20 WCF cartridge.

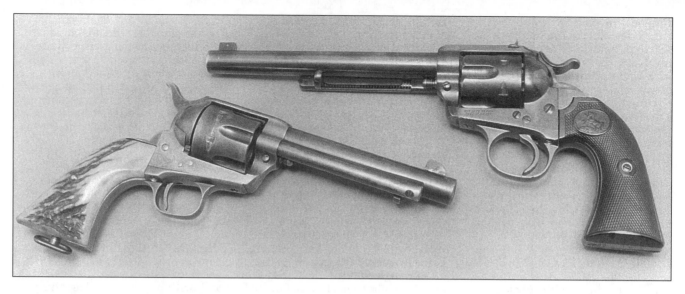

Mexican contract SA (*left*) and (*right*) Bisley Flattop Target Model, circa 1915.

gets in that time, executing the basic draw-fire-hit sequence from an electronic signal in less than one-tenth of a second.

This data gave new credence to the previously disregarded claim that the best shooters of the 1870s and 1880s could "beat the drop" - that is, confronted by an armed opponent whose pistol was already drawn, cocked and carefully aimed, kill him before he was able to discharge his weapon. Of course, students of the era had already learned the phenomenon was real: At least two prosecuting attorneys, questioning defendants in criminal cases, died from attempting to re-enact such scenarios in courtrooms, in front of witnesses.

As far as has been recorded, however, none of the historical "debunkers" of the 1950s-60s ever expired from experiments similar to the courtroom re-enactments held in the Old West. What is important is the failure, in about 40-plus years of experimentation and curiosity, to duplicate the fast draw times with any other firearm. Even the Remington, with faster lock time, does not handle as quickly or point as well as does the Colt and its clones.

The Colt Model P design had to be a maid-of-all-work, and so there were many variations. The U.S. Government was the first customer, adopting the 45 Colt Government version in 1872. The standard version was had a 7 1/2-inch barrel and was fitted with one-piece wood grips. The Government cartridge was similar to current 45 Colt, but almost 4mm shorter, and would also chamber in the S&W Schofield. Only Fiocchi now manufactures the original cartridge, though handloaders can duplicate the original round easily.

The 45 Colt cartridge was introduced about 1888, primarily for the civilian market; although in the 1890s, when the Government-owned guns were rebuilt, virtually all cylinders were adjusted as necessary (many accommodated the later cartridge with no adjustment at all).

Colt operates a historical department and will furnish, for about $100, a letter of documentation if your Model P is on file. Most early guns went out with barrel length "unnoted" and were almost always 7 1/2-inch tubes. However, custom barrel lengths were always available. Standard lengths next introduced were 4 3/4 inch (*sometimes listed as 4 5/8 inch, this is the same barrel, but the thread shank is not measured fully*) and 5 1/2 inch – often called the "*artillery*" length, because rebuilt Government single

---

A close look at Remington ejector tubes.

actions were trimmed to - or rebarreled to - that length primarily for artillery use. The cavalry continued to use the 7 1/2 inch length for the gun's entire service duration.

An exception was when older guns were drawn from stocks years later for isolated service in overseas posts. Then, one simply carried whatever "came through the system" as occurred during the U.S. anti-guerilla campaign against the Moros in the Philippines before World War I.

Colt records show tubes from 2 inches to 16 inches, and 8-inch barrels were very common on Bisleys, especially in the "target" calibers. The standard Sheriff's Model, introduced in the 1890s, was a 3 1/2-inch barreled gun, dispensing entirely with the ejector tube, though a 2 - inch barreled model was also fairly common, and also sometimes called the "Sheriff's Model."

Flat-tops and even the primitive-but-effective adjustable sights of the period could be ordered as early as the 1880s for "*target models*," but did not become common features until the 20th century Bisleys. Only about 976 flattop Bisleys were built; many with long target barrels. The practical but unattractive Bisley disappeared from most catalogs about 1921, though guns may have been delivered afterward. It was more than a little strange to eyes accustomed to the graceful P Model, and by then its place in Colt's catalog and the target shooter's heart had been usurped by the Shooting Master and Officer's Model Target.

The first identifiable physical change on the Model P was the 1892 introduction of the spring-loaded, cross-bolt cylinder pin retaining mechanism, at about SN#144,000.

Colt Bisley Model.

Uberti's version of the Remington 1890 SA, paired with tooled buscadero rig.

Unlike scarce originals, replicas see a lot of range use; (*top*) blued SA replica with 4 3/4-inch barrel and (*below*) an 1875 Remington replica with plated finish.

Conveniently, this marks the introduction of smokeless powder and better metallurgy in cylinders, which is why those guns with the cross-bolt/spring bolt release are called "*smokeless*" guns. That release provided faster access to the cylinder for cleaning, without need for a screwdriver, and dispensed with the frame-fitted cylinder pin retaining screw, which sometimes shot loose. However, the "*smokeless*" setup was not truly standardized until about SN# 163,000, and a very few odd solid-frame models appear even after that. Collectors should realize from the onset of their activities that Colt hated to throw out parts for obvious sensible business reasons, and the "rules" of tidy feature changes at given serial number blocks are about as notable for the exceptions as for the conformance of individual guns to the general rules. While there were many subtle changes in the pistols over the years – the elimination of detailed serial numbering of small parts, for example, about 1920 – few

of these were more than small notations in the *First Generation's* 67-68 year run of production. As late as 1947-48, Colt was preparing, for presentation and upon special V.I.P. order, pre-war frames. This should have told management that demand was not dormant.

Perhaps ironically, perhaps appropriately, this 130-year-old design – and even its clones and copies – are evolving backwards. As this article is finished, the biggest seller among *Third Generation* Colts and Uberti copies is the "Old Model" - a solid-frame blackpowder-style gun bearing the early "incomplete" patent dates just as a gun would've been delivered about 1876, complete with the maroon-magenta finish *aficionados* recognize as the ancient, original - and quite fragile - charcoal blue finish which was "*state-of-the-art*" in 1880.

Colt's Model P was connected with all those things which smell and feel of horses and sand; black powder, big bullets, cheap whiskey – and times very bad and very good.

Remington Single Actions Model 1875 & Model 1890

It's hard to even visualize now, but there was a time when the "third player" in the two-party American firearms business of the 19th century had a fleeting opportunity to dominate the pistol market. The old saw "*pistols come from Colt, rifles come from Winchester*" may have been firmly established in the public's mind, but Remington had as good a reputation as either, produced a greater variety of products than either and, in 1875, introduced a revolver which, had it been on the market about three years earlier, might be the one we today call "*The Gun That Tamed The West*."

But it didn't happen that way. The beefy Remington '75 sold just about 25,000 units from its introduction until 1890, during which time Colt sold over 110,000 Model Ps. The successor Model 1890, mechanically identical but somewhat more streamlined and lighter, proved to be the last conventional Remington heavy-caliber revolver; slightly over 2000 were made. As far as any stateside researchers can tell, the Model 1890 was produced only in 44 W.C.F. (44/40), whereas the Model 1870 was built for 44 Remington Center Fire, 44/40 and 45 Colt. There are reports of both guns being shipped abroad in other calibers and, while the reports are probably true, there is no evidence that Remington built those guns; they were most likely converted by companies in the import/export business and therefore, to the collector, are not "original."

The rarity of original Remingtons is such that they are seldom fired. Back in the mid-60s, I discovered a pair of nickel-plated Model 1875s in wonderful condition, part of the estate of their original owner. They were 45s and would not quite chamber modern 45 Colt ammunition, After trimming about 1/32-inch off the cases and loading with black powder, I found the cannons fired high under 100 yards, and actually made wonderful groups at the range.

Indeed, they shot as well as any modern or vintage 45 I have ever owned, and much better than all my Colts, including an 8-inch barreled flat-top Target Bisley lent to me for comparison by a friend. I didn't shoot them much and, in 1969, sold the pair to finance my daughter Anna's arrival to this earth. Even then, their price was enough to provide the hospital with full payment, do some of the repairs on the pile of amalgamated junk I tried to drive,

pay the rent – and cover a few unplanned contingencies. Today, most any decent, original 1875 reaches into four digits; proven, authentic Model 1890s bring two or three times the older model.

The Model 1875 retains most of the lines – and almost all the lock-work – of Remington's cap 'n ball revolvers. Even in the 19th century, serious shooters tended to favor them over the better known - but older - Colt design. Part of this had to do with the *sail* under the barrel, which was rumored to keep the barrel more rigid, and which was surely handy for bashing opponents. Cylinder and barrel alignment really was tighter than on the Colt of similar vintage.

But the public's confidence and imagination was firmly held by the Hartford firm, and *aficionados* don't buy enough hardware to keep a production model in a prominent market position. Remington's advertising was not well-developed and, even today, Remington collectors bemoan the fact that both in-house and third party literature on the firearms and their use is sadly lacking.

Inspecting and photographing some of the vintage Remingtons from Frank Deimerly's collection reminded me that Remingtons tend to change patterns abruptly on parts, and parts fit and shape; switch back and forth, not necessarily according to any pattern – and the general assumption one has to make is that many of the changes to the hammer and cylinder manufacturing technique and finish were simply made at random.

Most common barrel lengths were 7 1/2 inches and 5 1/2 inches on the Model 1875 though, as with Colts, there were enough exceptions to spark a lot of collector interest. Most common barrel lengths on 1890s seem to be 5 inch and 71/2 inch, though I've seen a 4 inch which might be authentic – and quite a few others which must've been field-modified by gunsmiths of the time.

Lately, Uberti has been manufacturing both the models in versions that look like, shoot like and handle like the originals – but whose parts

interchange with 19th century guns only in very limited instances. Frank and I did some playing, and the cylinder and bushing might interchange, as might the barrels, with some fitting – but little else is close enough to fit without major rework. Frames are of the "*smokeless*" Colt cross-pin type, which Remington never produced. As in the originals, maximum-length 45 Colt ammunition cause blockages in the replica by hanging the bullet out the cylinder front and blocking cylinder rotation. I shot mostly Silvertips and Federal's 225-grain SWC and, with reloads, got brilliant results with Speer's deep-dish 185-grain hollow-point. The bore is .452-inch, so you need have no worries about using bullets you may have considered more appropriate to 45 ACP. My other Uberti Remington is a 357, and it prospers on a similar diet, gobbling up 180-grain Federal hollow-point loads and NyClads.

The Model 1890 Uberti "Outlaw" ("*Army Model" from some importers*) is a 357 and, while not as accurate as the Model 1875, is very handy and still shoots better than my recent Colts or Colt copies.

Some of this superior accuracy can be attributed to the much quicker lock time than Colt's "P". The grip is, if anything, shorter. This doesn't bother me much with my small hands, but a big-handed man might fumble with the gun. Many original guns are found with homemade grips which extend the backstrap contour almost an inch below the metal and use the screw only to align with the backstrap.

Remington's wheel-guns are long out of production, but like so many modern firearms, those who've used them find themselves pondering why other less accurate, seemingly less durable guns were used in such quantities by individuals and governments, when in fact this particular thumb-buster actually sold for a bit less than its better-known competitor. Sam Colt and P.T. Barnum understood, though: NEVER UNDERESTIMATE THE VALUE OF ADVERTISING!

●

OLD ELI AND OLD SAM: MY LIFE'S COMPANIONS

by R. C. House

THE TWO OLD geezers had been around a long time before they came into my life. I wasn't much more than a kid myself when we met, and they're still with me. I'm older, and I show it. So are they, but they're not much different. Then again, they're made of sterner stuff than I. Old Eli's been my pal for forty years; as for Old Sam, it's maybe a few years less than that. But, like I say, with each it's been a while.

To clear the air right off the bat, they're original percussion revolvers; "Eli" is an 1858 Remington Army, and "Sam," an 1860 Colt Army. Both, of course, 44 caliber.

Old Eli showed up like the answer to a maiden's prayer. Long before there was any such thing as reliable reproductions, we shot original muzzleloaders. Sure they were more or less valuable antiques, but with proper care in shooting and cleaning, there was no reason they'd lose anything in value. And I couldn't afford anything fancy or of great value anyway; found a couple of reasonably sound small-bore eastern squirrel rifles in local antique shops, stocked up on proper powder, patches, balls and caps and went out and had some fun.

Then I got the *craves* to have a percussion revolver. Everything I'd read and heard pointed to the Remington Army as having a slight edge over its nearest rival, the legendary Colt Army with its attractive fluid, flowing lines.

The Remington was more angular; with its sturdy top strap over the cylinder and an octagonal barrel that screwed into the frame, it seemed – and the experts agreed – the more substantial of the two. Remingtons I saw at gun shows, though, were 'way out of my price range. So, I decided to start haunting the shows and the gun shops where I might find a frame or a barrel; a loading lever, backstrap and other *innards*. I'd piece one together and maybe whittle a set of grips out of any old wood. I didn't want a museum piece; I wanted a hand-held charcoal burner of Civil War vintage. Make-do would have to do.

My plan hadn't progressed much when all the pieces magically fell into place. A guy where I worked in Cleveland walked into the office one Monday morning with Sunday's classifieds. "See this 'old Colt' for sale in the want ads?" he asks.

Sure enough, an "old Colt pistol" was advertised for $35. I called the number. Yeah, the guy said, he still had it, but somebody was coming at one o'clock ready to pay him the thirty-five smackers sight unseen. I said I'd be there at noon on my lunch hour. I had no earthly idea how I'd juggle things to manage that much money. Probably go without lunches for a few weeks.

He took me into his cellar and pulled this thing out of a big tool box where it had lain for God knows how long among files and planes and chisels and drill bits. I wanted to rebuke this guy for his negligence, then I remembered I was there to talk him into selling me an old gun. Oh, it was a sorry sight, and it wasn't an "old Colt." It was a sure-enough 1858 Remington New Model Army! He didn't know the difference, so I figured I had the upper hand right there. Served him right, after what he'd done to that once fine old veteran!

As for the gun, internal parts were missing or broken and the cylinder spun randomly on the arbor. Probably kids playing with it over the years had snapped the hammer, mashing the cylinder stop metal between the cap wells. It had dings here and there from all those years knocking around in that tool box. It looked badly rusted and grungy and I had no way of knowing the condition of the bore; sick and tired is the best way I can describe it. Still, I had to have it. It'd be a start; and it was mostly "all

Almost forty years later, the two guns are still up to their old tricks — this time far out in southern California's Mojave Desert.

there." Coincidentally, this was in 1958, the centennial year of the 1858 Remington style.

He'd bought it, he said, in a Montana hock shop in the '30s as a souvenir of a trip West. I told him because of its rough condition I couldn't pay more than twenty-five bucks.

"Guy's coming at one with thirty-five up front," he said.

"You're bettin' he'll be here," I said. "I'll give you thirty right now. He may come here with thirty-five, or he may not come at all. What do you say?" He reached for my thirty.

A buddy from work had come with me; he knew a thing or three about old guns too. As we got in the car he grinned slyly at me and spoke softly: "You lucky stiff! And they called Jesse James a thief!" I just possum-grinned back at him.

The next weekend, I took Old Eli down to Wes Kindig's Log Cabin Gun Shop in Lodi, Ohio. I bought all my blackpowder supplies from Wes in those days. And now and then an old frontstuffer. For what Wes didn't have on hand, he referred me to a fellow named Turner Kirkland down in Union City, Tennessee, who was doing pretty well starting up a mail-order muzzle-loader supply business. Called his outfit Dixie Gun Works.

Anyway, Wes had his gunsmith put in new parts where needed and make sure the cylinder rotation timing was proper. I guess maybe we put in a new set of nipples, too. Cost twelve bucks total as I remember — and I had my shooter, however rough it might have looked. With solvents and gentle abrasives I cleaned the metal carefully, and scoured the chambers and the bore...finding some light pitting in the latter, but not enough to discourage me.

The grips have two definite notches, and another that may be intentional, but may also be a chip from neglect. What those mean, I have no way of knowing. Just that it's so. Old Eli may have been there in some of the Old West's dramatic

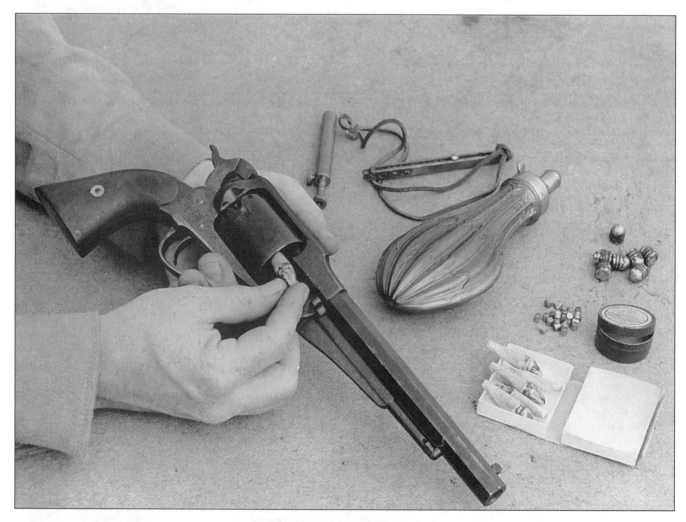

After years of neglect and abuse, a restored "Old Sam" is again ready for business.

moments. I like to think so. Beyond that is anybody's guess.

With time, I discovered a wondrous thing. Old Eli started going along on primitive camping trips or one-day

At one time, the author experimented with cigarette-paper cartridges for "Old Eli."

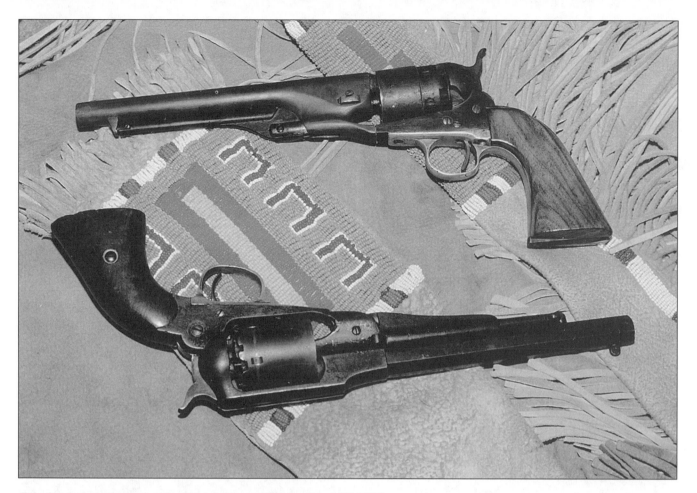

Enjoying a *siesta* on beadwork and buckskin are "Old Sam" and "Old Eli."

shooting outings. Then it was always thoroughly and carefully cleaned and lightly oiled at home. So help me, the metal responded with use. On the frame particularly, quite a bit of the original blue has emerged. Other metal areas have also smoothed and mellowed. As with humans, exercise energized lazy muscles. I figure Old Eli was just showing his gratitude at being rescued from too many years in oblivion.

Old Sam came along a few years later. My brother-in-law did some painting and handyman work for a widow acquaintance. This woman's late husband had fooled around with guns a little. When my brother-in-law was helping her clean out the garage, he found an old dusty and grimy cigar box under the work bench, and told me it was a full of what looked like gun parts. The widow asked if I'd make an offer on them.

Next time I visited, my brother-in-law produced this box. In it was a disassembled, nearly complete 1860 Colt Army. Only one problem. When I said the late husband had "fooled" around with guns, I didn't realize how plumb-center I was! He had subjected the barrel and frame to a wire wheel....probably in some mis-

guided notion that rebluing the thing would add to its value. I've often wondered how many fine old pieces, stored tenderly by the unknowing-but-caring for a century and more, found their way into such destructive hands.

I've been a *'beer budget'* gun collector all my life. Fortune – or lack of same – forced me to concentrate on the marginal guns...and often on the 'rejects.' My restorations don't create museum pieces, and I don't claim they do. My goal has been to return as much dignity as I can manage to some great old American arms.

Careful to avoid casting too many aspersions on a dead husband, I gently pointed out to the widow that the antiquity of the parts had been destroyed; I offered fifty bucks for the "parts" and she was delighted. So was I, but my work was cut out for me. I wasn't trying to cheat her, I just didn't have any more dough; and besides, the "stuff" wasn't worth much more.

On close inspection, most of the serial numbers (and they matched) were intact; the top-of-barrel address had been ground away by the evil wheel. Everything else was there, though: all parts, screws, springs and such.

The cylinder and loading lever were still lightly pitted, proof they'd managed to avoid the wire wheel; the ambitious "restorer" probably ground the light pitting off the frame and barrel. Totally unnecessary.

The grips were gone. The bore was a little like Old Eli's; some pitting. But what the hell. I'm not a big handgun man. I just like to heft the things, to feel in my grip the spirit of the old times and the old-timers, take a sight and enjoy feeling her buck against my hand and arm, and hear that magnificent bark...and that's enough for me. If I print on the paper at twenty-five yards, Whoopee! If a ball punches into the black, I'm ecstatic. I'm a moist-eyed romantic, not a wild-eyed perfectionist.

A regular screwdriver maniac had been at work on the Colt's frame and backstrap screws. All the slots were badly burred. A good friend who'd worked on guns all his life told me they could be salvaged; said most all the metal was intact, that it was just upset. And he offered his savvy to move my restoration along. In a piece of pine two-by-four, he bored holes about the size of the screw shanks. With the damaged screw head and slot left

On one of their first joint camping trips, in about 1960, at a backwoods camp near the Ohio River, Old Sam and Old Eli sounded off together.

exposed but secure, he tapped the head very, very carefully and lightly with a small hammer, patiently coaxing the disturbed metal into place. Often, he might need to deepen or refresh the slot with a very thin hacksaw blade. But the gun went back together looking like it had a set of new screws. *'Twarn't. Them's the originals.*

The brass trigger guard had missed the wire wheel as well, and I was grateful.

None of the working parts were badly worn; the revolver went back together easy as pie and the cylinder cycled precisely. I dismantled it again and tried to minimize the coarse grooves and scratches with fine emery cloth; hated to, but those deep, angry wire-brush scars had to be healed, softened, smoothed over, toned down. A browning solution completed the job, giving it overall an aged-brown look. Patina it ain't, but in looks, it's the next best thing. I found a set of modern-made one-

piece wood grips for a couple of bucks at a gun shop; fit wasn't great, but acceptable. I was in business! I'd brought back at least a little dignity to another old frontstuffer fogie.

Neither of these old soldiers will class as museum-grade or even as collectibles. Old Eli showed up when there were no replicas. Old Sam had been so disfigured that there was little harm I could do with my restoration and occasional shooting.

So, this two-gun man went forth; when roughing it in back-country camps where we could plink, I hauled them along and stoked, stroked and exercised them. They started in Ohio in various primitive camps and back-country hikes; they had memorable outings for a few years on Michigan farmlands. Later, and for a year or more, we roamed and roared away – out in the saguaro cactus and jumping cholla-infested Arizona deserts. Then,

about thirty-five years ago, we three began a long and memorable string of primitive forays way to hell and gone into the wild and wide-open spaces of southern California's Mojave Desert. There we can still find places of solitude that passeth understanding, and shoot with no one to object (we may leave a little lead and a few footprints, but take out only photographs; often we lug out trash left by the less concerned!).

Back to the guns. Their names? The original Remington gunmaker's first name was the jaw-breaker, Eliphalet. And everybody knows that Colonel Colt's first name was Samuel, so the nicknames "Eli" and "Sam" came naturally.

So what if they are not big on accuracy or looks? They sure are feel-good guns. I made survivors of them and in return they have provided me years of primitive, back-country shooting fun.

To me, that's all that matters. ●

WARHORSES

by Carlos Schmidt

SOMETIMES THE ACTS done by a country – as much as acts performed by an individual – have unexpected results. So it is with almost a of century of American presence in Nicaragua. While many aspects of the US presence are well known (most recently the confrontation with a far-leftist government in the 1980s), what is less well known is that every significant involvement the United States undertook in Nicaragua resulted in American arms of that era being imported to this small, Central American country – and then left behind.

Perusing little-known nooks and crannies, usually looking for old and rare books, has provided an interesting source for aging American military weapons. And with a bit of ingenuity, sweat – and a very able machinist – I now have several of those old battle rifles – a Krag, Springfield, Garand and M-14 – up and shooting; in some cases shooting very well.

"Civilize 'em with a Krag"

When I first started hanging around gunshops back in Michigan at the tender age of about 12, I got to know some old machinists and gunsmiths, usually of German background, who spoke English with an accent, chewed tobacco, were cranky, and knew their business. Chronologically, that was about the end of the Eisenhower administration; a world much simpler, when most gunshops were awash with old WWII *gaspipes* – and some older pieces, like the Krag. I remember selling from the gun rack several sporterized Krags for $25. The word, from my tobacco-chewing mentors, was that they were a 'smooth action' but pretty old and

High-power shooters always benefit from position practice. Here Tim Cornish limbers up with his 8mm Persian Mauser.

therefore not worth much. Also, even in those days, there were a lot of Krags with rotted barrels. There was still floating around some of the original GI ammo with corrosive primers that would *frost* a barrel overnight if it wasn't cleaned with soap and water soon after shooting. Still in all, I liked the Krag, especially when loaded with the venerable Lyman cast bullet design *#311284*. I decided one day I would have one of those elderly rifles.

Fast-forward through the decades to a time much later… in the spring of 2000 I was in Masaya, a regional town about 20 miles from Managua, looking for some old books. There had been a series of earthquakes caused by a local volcano that had shaken up many of the old adobe

houses. People began cleaning out their back rooms and selling a few things. Quite by accident I found a house where the owner had an old collection of very rusty rifles. In looking them over, they appeared to be a collection of rifles that had been used in every revolution (*of which there have been many*) – successful and unsuccessful – since the 19th century. The collection began with an Erfurt Mauser Model 71/84, a Remington rolling block 7mm, a Model 1916 Spanish Mauser, a rusty (but still functioning) Model 1892 Winchester in 32-20, and a couple of really rusty Krags – one with bolt and action intact, but missing most of the furniture. The barrel was so rusty, light would barely shine down it. As usual, I paid too much for that piece, went next door to my favorite Mexican restaurant and celebrated with some fine *mole*.

The stock had termites, but I gassed them and found that with some judicious glass bedding I could make that stock work again, especially as a carbine. The major problem was the barrel – it simply had to be replaced. I soon found that Krag barrels in good condition are just about impossible to find. Even William Brophy's fine **The Krag Rifle** proved to be of little help in obtaining the dimensions of the Krag barrel at the shank end, where everything mattered.

In desperation I e-mailed Brownells and asked their advice. I said I wanted to communicate with an old, cranky gunsmith, who

chewed tobacco and who remembered how to rebarrel a Krag. Four days later I got a response from old Reid Coffield, member of the staff of Brownells and gunsmith *extraordinaire*. He said he did not chew tobacco but otherwise met the bill as he was pretty old, remembered perfectly how to rebarrel Krags, and surely was cranky. *Aha!* I thought, *a blast from the past*. As one would figure, the Springfield barrel shank is really quite close to the Krag's, with a slightly different diameter and pitch of thread. Also, the extractor cut in the Krag barrel is on the top and completely unlike that of the Mauser-type Springfield. And, the chamber of the 30-40 Krag is different enough from the 30-06 so that it had to be rechambered if one used a Springfield barrel.

I found, in the old *bodega* of Somoza's army, a couple of Springfield barrels

and so had only to find a machinist who could do the work that 'Doctor' Coffield suggested. As it turns out, the tropics had an allure not just for me, but also for a semi-retired master machinist *Catalunian*, Don José Sanchez. Hailing from Barcelona, long Spain's manufacturing center, Don José simply knew his business. In his front room he has a large lathe, and he can make most anything out of metal that is required. I gave him the rusty Krag, the barrel, a chambering reamer for 30-40 Krag, a translation of 'Doctor' Coffield's missive, Brophy's book – and a week later I had a Krag barreled action with a new barrel.

I specified that I wanted him to duplicate the Model 1898 carbine, complete with a 22-inch barrel and cut-down stock. He was able to cut down the stock, plug the termite holes, form a new handguard and

Escorting the body of a deceased Conservative Party politician, a Nicaraguan honor guard unit marches between onlookers and another unit of the Nicaraguan Army. This photo was taken in 1926, on the dock at the freshwater port of Granada; the 1898 Krag rifles - with fixed bayonets - are clearly visible.

braze on the original front sight – all without breaking into a sweat. The rear sight is still the 2nd model of the Model 1902 rifle sight, but I can live with that. I have not installed the saddle ring as they make noise and I use this carbine for deer hunting down here.

At the range, the virtue of a new barrel tightly bedded into the stock became apparent as, from the first, the carbine grouped 1 inches at 100 meters. The load? An FN 30-caliber 147-grain FMJ in front of a reasonable charge of 4064. Velocity? Probably 2400 fps. The result? A fine deer rifle that shoots well and handles surprisingly well. In fact, the Krag carbine, with its 22-inch barrel and shortened stock, handles very nicely, much like the trapdoor Springfield carbine. It is simply a lovely carbine, and one that is a pleasure to shoot. It would be at home in the forests of my native Michigan or in the black timber of the Yellowstone country, and would make a dandy rifle for the hunter that wants to put the hunt back into hunting and leave his *'digital'* rifle at home.

The M1903 Springfield in Action

As much as anything, Paul Mauser's Model 1898 bolt-action 8mm spelled the end of the Krag's career in the United States Army. By 1903 the Army had adopted a modified Mauser action that retained some of the lines and furniture of the Krag. The quaint side box magazine was changed into a conventional Mauser-type staggered box magazine fed by 5-round stripper clips. The action was straight Mauser, with the distinctive knurled cocking piece retained from the Krag. The barrel was set at 24 inches in length and the sights included a modified late-model Krag rear sight calibrated for a 30-caliber bullet of 150 grains at about 2750 feet per second.

The result was a rifle that was surprisingly light and that made a very fine target rifle. For horse cavalrymen like Col. Frank Tompkins, who led the chase after Pancho Villa after his raid on Columbus, New Mexico in 1916, the M1903 was a bit long for cavalry use. Later, writing of the incident, he evaluated the equipment he had used in north and central Chihuahua. He noted, regarding the rifle, " *The present rifle* [the M1903 Springfield] *is too long and too heavy for the cavalry. I suggest a carbine about the size of the old Krag carbine chambered to shoot same ammunition as the infantry rifle.*" (Tompkins: 235).

Still, the Model 1903 did have an interesting moment at the little-known encounter at Hidalgo de Parral. Known as the place where Pancho Villa was assassinated in 1923, in 1916 it was the scene of one fine shot by a good rifleman and a Springfield. Col. Tompkins and his mounted troopers had just been run out of Parral by irregular Mexican cavalry. The Mexican troops stopped on a hill about a half-mile from the Americans and appeared to ponder what to do next. One Captain Lippincott, a member of Tompkins' squadron, laid down on top of an adobe house and prepared to fire at one of the horsemen, a target he calculated to be 800 yards distant. He adjusted the Springfield's sights, slipped into the prone position, correctly used a tight sling and, with one shot, dropped one of the cavalrymen from his saddle.

In Nicaragua, the era when the Springfield spoke was the Marine intervention to fight against Cesar Augusto Sandino, 1927-1933. Much has been written about this guerrilla action, and much of what has been written is a bit fanciful. Total Marine casualties in the field for that six-year period were 43 dead; more died in brothels, barroom brawls, of disease, and suicide than died on the battlefield.

In the field the Marines used two weapons, the M1903 and the M1921 Thompson sub machine gun. The native troops were given the Krags. Due to the heavy growth on many of the mountains, the arm of choice of the Marines was the Thompson. Probably the last Marine living in Nicaragua was Mr. George Smith. He was the Marine provincial commandant of Esteli while his friend Chesty Puller was the Marine provincial commandant of Matagalpa, the next province to the east. Interviewed by the author in 1991 a month before his death, old George was emphatic that he went into battle and ambushes with a

Thompson with four 50-round drums of ammo and left his Springfield at home. He was never sorry.

Still, the Springfield had its uses; one imaginatively applied by Matthew Ridgway, in the 1930s a young officer on duty at Managua. He developed a passion for hunting the Central American alligator, or caiman, that abounded in the waters of Lake Managua. He evidently spent many a happy afternoon crawling through the mud on the shores of Lake Managua drilling caimans with the Springfield. He even lost his West Point ring in that slime.

A more important use of the Marine Springfields occurred in the July 16, 1927 Sandinista attack on the Marine headquarters in the northern mountain town of Ocotal. The Marine commander, one Capt. G.D. Hatfield, with 34 Marines under his direct command, entered into an exchange of telegrams with Augusto Sandino a few days prior to the attack. The exchange ended with Sandino writing, *"I remain your most obedient servant, who ardently desires to put you in a handsome tomb with beautiful bouquets of flowers."* Hatfield replied, " *Bravo General. If words were bullets and phrases were soldiers you would be a field marshal instead of a mule thief*". The attack came a couple of days later; with hundreds of Sandinistas attacking the Marine bar-

Reading mirage, doping wind... or simply relaxing? Mrs. Nellie Luna, distinguished rifle and pistol shot, considers her distant target.

Inspecting his 300-meter target, along with others on the same relay, is Evelio Gutierrez (*third from left*), a member of Nicaragua's Olympic shooting team at the Sidney games. Author Schmidt notes " *I glass-bedded his rifle… and then he beat me with it!*"

racks in the town hall (and the town hall of Ocotal still today). The Marines fought off the Sandinistas with a couple of BARs, but mostly Springfields. The native troops, the nascent *Guardia Nacional*, were holed up two blocks away and fought

began dive-bombing the troops, dropping small bombs. The air attack lasted only 45 minutes but it broke the back of the Sandinista attack. It also wrote a new page in military history by being the first organized dive-bombing attack in history, years before the German air force was credited with inventing this new use of the warplane.

Having fired all four "warhorse" rifles, Ms. Shany Perez reports the '03 Springfield kicks the most.

off the attackers with their Krags. The fighting was fierce and the Marines were in a difficult position until a couple of Marine bi-planes flew up from Managua, saw the situation and returned to Managua for reinforcements. By middle afternoon five DeHavilands appeared over the Sandinista troops and

By chance I ran across remnants of a Springfield, built by Rock Island Arsenal. As usual, the barrel was rotted out, there was no stock, and the action was not exactly in mint condition. No matter, I checked with all of the gun repair shops in Managua and found the parts I needed: a stock, and a barrel in good shape. Again, old Don José Sanchez came to the rescue and installed the barrel. I did the rest, installed the stock, handguard and furniture, glass-bedded the action into the stock, and put on a Lyman aperture sight, much lamenting they no longer make the great #48 sight. The result is what you would call a *parts gun*, but one that had the potential to shoot.

More interestingly, the action was made at Rock Island Armory, with a serial number of 374XXX. That rifle was made at - or shortly after - the end of WWI and may have taken part in the Marine activities in the U.S. intervention of 1929-1933. At least the serial number is correct for that period. And, judging from the deep pits in the action, that rifle had been in tropical America for a long time. Unfortunately, when I took the rifle to the range to test-fire it, I could not get it to shoot worth beans. I then had to enter into the voodoo world of Springfield bedding.

There are (or were, since few people still shoot the Springfield in its military condition – and especially at 300 meters, as was my intent) two schools of thought on Springfield bedding. One school, represented by the eloquent writings of Col. Townsend Whelan, argues for a free-floating (*more or less*) barrel within the military stock, including the handguard. The other school of thought was impressed on my tender sensibilities by some of the old WWII vets that shot at the local rifle club and who, in the early '60s were in their 50s. One old boy, Salvatore, told me that Springfields always shot better with a lot of upward pressure on the barrel under where the front band and bayonet lug was located. He told me to hang a coffee can of lead shot under

the front of the stock and apply glass-bedding so that when the glass 'set up,' constant pressure upward on the barrel would dampen barrel vibrations and improve accuracy.

On my second foray into glass-bedding with Brownell's original recipe, the kind you had to add in the glass fibers and dye powder – and that set up with a puff of smoke, I got the job done but it did not look good. My father, who thought my brother's and my enthusiasm for guns was a perversion of youth, found the sight of my Springfield, dripping that runny glass-bedding onto the floor – and with a coffee can of lead shot hanging from the front of the stock, complete with glass fingerprints all over the rifle – a funny sight indeed.

That was my first experience with what '*Professor*' Jerry Kuhnhausen calls 'mechanical locking.' After not so gently separating the

stock from the action and getting rid of the hard drips of glass, I took the rifle to the range. I found that Salvatore was right because that Springfield would really shoot and keep all of its shots inside of the old 5-ring at 300 yards, with many in the 5V-ring.

Forty years later I found myself in the same predicament. I forwent the coffee can treatment and decided to use shims and a system of bedding that I found that worked on an old Model 52 Winchester and the 7.62x54Rmm Nagant carbine. The Winchester was one of the first ones, without the speed lock, and was bedded - mostly - with a very tight front barrel band and a tight forward screw. The action was almost loose in the stock. That old rifle would shoot inside of an inch at 50 yards with iron sights, with many groups approaching a half-inch. The Nagant was bedded the same way, with the barrel completely shimmed so that it could not flop, or vibrate very much at all.

I took the Springfield to the range with some file folder shims and tested out a couple of thicknesses until the Springfield began shooting sub-two-inch groups at 100 meters, with a couple groups approaching one inch. The accumulated thickness of the shims was 0.015 inches and the barrel within the front band was tight. I then substituted tuna fish tin-can shims for the paper shims - cut to the same thickness - and went back to the range. The Springfield easily shot into 1 1/2 inches on a regular basis. With a 100 meter 'zero' the Springfield is sighted for the NRA 300-yard slow-fire target with 23 clicks elevation on the Lyman #57 sight. The Springfield, silent for over 70 years, was again honorably punching holes - in paper - in Nicaragua.

In the newly-ordained rifle matches down here held at 300 meters, shot from the sitting position and using the NRA 300-yard slow-fire target the Springfield, using old ball ammo, holds its own against the newer Garand and M-14. And, it is a pleasure to hear the *bark* of a Springfield that has been down here for almost 80 years and see the precision with which it can still punch 30-caliber holes in a target more than three football fields away.

The M1 Garand

During the long, sleepy 40-year interlude of the Somoza family's political control of Nicaragua the prevalent arm of their army, the *Guardia Nacional*, was the M1 Garand. All of them were supplied by the United

With the Masaya volcano in the background, the rebuilt Krag gets the once-over from an admirer.

States. The *Guardia* carried their Garands everywhere. Later, after the *Sandinistas* drove out Somoza in 1979, the arm of choice became the AK 47 and the Garands were relegated to guard duty, and finally oblivion. In fact, in the last 10 years it has become hard to locate an intact Garand. After some considerable efforts I located two junkers and began to rebuild them. As with the Krag and Springfield, the barrels were rotted and some parts inside were broken or missing. For some reason, both had parts of the rear sights missing, and the top of the safety lever broken off.

I must admit that I had, for years, a prejudice against

Clearly putting in a full day at the range, author's *compadre* Tim Cornish holds two classic U. S. battle rifles: the M14 (*left*) and the venerable M1 Garand (*right*).

Garands. While a young lad, I began sighting-in rifles for deer season at the local gun shop and had the opportunity to get to know many different rifles. At the range I never could get a Garand to group better than three inches, and I thought that all Garands were mediocre in the accuracy department. Then one day I had that youthful illusion shattered. While at the 300-yard range test-firing an FN 270 Winchester, I noticed that one Johnny Zajac came to the firing line with a Garand in good shape. Old Johnny was the city plumbing inspector, spoke English with a plainly Polish accent, and always chewed cigars, usually unlit. But old Johnny could shoot. I watched him, from the sitting position, shoot 10 rounds in one minute with his Garand. I then drove him down to the target and saw nine shots in a circle of about three inches, with one shot that had 'leaked' two inches outside of the group. He was furious with that leaked shot and used cusswords in both languages. I became converted to the accuracy possibility of the Garand.

In Nicaragua, parts for the Garand can still be found locally and I rebarreled both rifles. Since, like the Springfield, I intended to use both rifles for high-power target shooting at 200 and 300 meters, I had to do something to improve their 4-inch groups. The answer was simple. I bought one of the first copies of 'Professor' Jerry Kuhnhausen's book on accurizing the M1 and M14. I read the book several

times and went to work. The result was two highly accurate Garands that will shoot 5- to 6-inch groups at 300 meters, with the 'issue' iron sights. And they will probably shoot better than that, but my eyes don't see the front sight as clearly as they once did.

'Professor' Kuhnhausen's theory is that by tightening up everything that hangs from the barrel, including the entire gas system (and ensuring the gas system hangs *directly* under the barrel assembly, what he calls *centerlining*), and by glass-bedding the action into the stock so that it is drawn down tightly into the stock by closing the trigger guard, the Garand will shoot as well as any bolt gun and do so for many rounds without changing point of impact. One of his secrets is 'pressure bedding,' or glass-bedding the action in such a fashion that the barrel is flexed downward by some 25 to 40 pounds of pressure. Obviously, with the gas system, one cannot speak of a free-floating Garand barrel, so the service armorers began to experiment with ways to dampen barrel vibration – exactly as I had done with the Springfield. Their solution - and Kuhnhausen's - was to apply *Rube Goldberg* technology. A small fixture is made and placed under the barrel so that, when the action is glass-bedded, the back of the action must be forced down to the stock – by either a clamp, fixture or surgical elastic tubing. It really looks weird but it works like gangbusters.

The result is a rifle that must be assembled with some force, but which will not change its point of impact even under repeated shot strings. It changes the Garand from being a run-of-the-mill battle rifle, that will group 3-4 inches with a good barrel, into a precision instrument that will group between 1-2 inches – even with the half-century-old ball ammo that I shoot – and not change its point of impact, regardless of barrel temperature. The Garand becomes every bit as accurate as the Springfield.

The M14

The last of the American battle rifles commonly found in Nicaragua is the M14. How it came to Nicaragua has to do with one of the more colorful Contra *commandantes*, Eden Pastora, "*Commandante Zero.*" Never one to suffer from an inferiority complex, during a couple of years in the Contra War he had considerable support of the United States government. He was known for his unorthodox manner of waging war. For example, he would perform amorous interludes with known Sandinista spies in the hopes of converting them by means of his prowess. He also had the Contra headquarters with the most information leaks. When he decided to attack the southern border town of Greytown in the middle 1980s, he scrounged a bunch of M14s from some American warehouse, some in almost-new condition. The Sandinista Army, of course, knew all about it and confiscated the arms cache of about 1500 rifles. A decade later many of them were sold to Century Arms. A few of those rifles made their way into civilian hands and the Nicaraguan army retained a small amount.

I was asked to accurize several M14s and so I turned to 'Professor' Kuhnhausen again. In dissembling the M14 it occurred to me that it is nothing so much as an M1 with a much-improved gas system and with the ability to accept a magazine from the

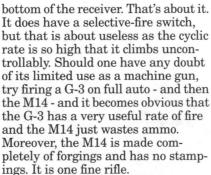

My rebuilt Krag balances nicely in the experienced hands of Ms. Perez. She took up shooting to share an activity with her boyfriend – and she now shoots better than he does.

bottom of the receiver. That's about it. It does have a selective-fire switch, but that is about useless as the cyclic rate is so high that it climbs uncontrollably. Should one have any doubt of its limited use as a machine gun, try firing a G-3 on full auto - and then the M14 - and it becomes obvious that the G-3 has a very useful rate of fire and the M14 just wastes ammo. Moreover, the M14 is made completely of forgings and has no stampings. It is one fine rifle.

To accurize the M14, the exact same theory that was useful with the M1 can be applied. The process involves tightening up the gas system in relation to the barrel, and pressure-bedding the barreled action tightly into the service stock with adequate 'draw' from the trigger guard. In fact, of all three American battle rifles the M14, at least to me, is the easiest to accurize. And they really do shoot. From the bench, with iron sights, several that I have worked on will group 5-7 inches at 300 meters. And I am sure that younger eyes could improve on that grouping. It seems to shoot best with either FN ball ammo or Portuguese ammo that was imported into Nicaragua in the early 1980s. And, like the Garand, when properly glass-bedded the point of impact does not change in slow- or timed-fire. As good as is the Garand, the M14 is a bit better.

Regarding Ammunition, Ergonomics, And Rifle Use

One of the more interesting, but little-known facts about the 30-06 and 7.62mm NATO rounds is that they are ballistically identical. Frank Barnes, some time ago, collected all of the ordnance data on U.S. military cartridges, including powder charges, and found that the standard load was a 150-grain (*or thereabouts*) bullet traveling at 2750 feet per second at the muzzle. That appears to be the case from WWI, except for a

time when the M72 bullet of 172 grains with a boattail was substituted for the 150-grain ball. The common charge was 50 grains of 4895, a hotter load than found in modern loading manuals. That load became the standard load for WWII and afterward; when the 7.62mm NATO was adopted in 1957 it was loaded to the same, exact ballistics – which leads to some unanticipated advantages.

For example, when the M1 is sighted correctly to shoot off the front sight at 100 yards and the rear sight is indexed on the 100-yard setting, the ability to sight for longer distances is made very easy with the aperture rear sights, which have one-minute clicks and are calibrated to distances past 1200 yards. The sights on the M14 are almost the same, being set for 100-meter intervals and the clicks being one minute at 100 meters, rather than yards. But they are set up the same fashion as the Garand sights. And since they shoot equal weight bullets at the same velocity, the trajectory is the same.

At 300 meters, and shooting at the 18-inch bullseye of the 300-yard slow-fire target, my sight setting, using a 6 o'clock hold, for the Garand is the 300-yard setting, plus three clicks. The center of the target is nine inches, or three minutes of angle, above the point of aim. Ditto for the M14, where my sight setting is also the 300-meter setting, plus three clicks. No other battle rifle known to me has this facility for changing sight setting, or returning to an old sight setting, with no change in point of impact.

After going through the exercise of reconditioning old American warhorses, the inevitable question is which rifle shoots the best. In answering the question, some consideration should be given to the type of shooting in which the rifles have been used. The Springfield, Garand and M14 all have been used with iron sights in offhand, sitting, and prone positions; the last two positions with a tight sling. The common range has been 300 meters at the Nicaraguan regular rifle matches, and the target is the NRA 300 yard slow-fire target. The Krag sits in a class by itself. It is a fine offhand rifle - *period*. Of the four American battle rifles, it handles most like an American sporting rifle. It is my choice for hunting the small Nicaraguan whitetail deer in thick forest. Its smooth bolt action is unparalleled and it is the most fun of all the battle rifles to use to kill rocks and tin cans. And it is, to my eyes, the most nostalgic and attractive of all American bolt-action rifles. No gun collection can be complete without a Krag.

For me, the Springfield is the most difficult rifle to shoot, for two reasons. First, it is the lightest, making it very easy to throw a shot into the white, or beyond. Secondly, its stock has a lot of 'drop' and so the recoil, during a shot string, is more noticeable than with the other two rifles. The Springfield has the most nostalgia and the best trigger – but I don't shoot it as well as the others, I am sad to say.

The Garand is muzzle-heavy and some days seems to just go to sleep under the bullseye. My Garand has a better trigger than the M14 and the scores I shoot with it and the M14 are almost identical. But I average a few points more with the M14 than the Garand. Why? I dunno. Finally, when the pressure of a match approaches and my friends all become enthusiastic competitors, I reach for the Winchester M14 that I got, courtesy of some governmental agency and Eden Pastora. It is the first M14 that I ever glass-bedded and I made a bunch of mistakes in that first attempt. But occasionally I will get a one-inch group from a benchrest at 100 meters, and at 300 meters I can call almost every shot – even the bad ones that go wandering toward Masaya volcano. It is a bit lighter towards the muzzle than the Garand and should be a bit more difficult to hold steady from the sitting position. But it is the rifle that somehow shoots the best for me, and in which I have confidence. It goes to every match and always shoots better than I. It is much rifle.

Lastly, a few words are in order about modern rifle use. One of the biggest impediments to getting shooters to participate in the Nicaraguan national rifle matches has been "shooter shock" at shooting at 300 meters and shooting with iron sights. Many of my friends read English-language gun magazines, reload and can quote the latest article about the 300 Dragon Killer Diller that shoots a 150-grain bullet at almost 4000 fps. They also are adept at benchresting such flamethrowers at 100 meters, and discussing the fine points of pillar-bedding, rifle powders, etc. But get them off the bench, suggest they learn to use a sling and shoot at 300 meters – and some folks become plainly nervous. When some folks try shooting at the bullseye with scope sights, they discover that the scope is not necessarily superior sighting equipment, if you have a fixed point of aim for iron sights and

The '03 Springfield, proudly wearing faded military markings and showing some wear and tear on the forearm, now sports a fully adjustable aperture receiver sight.

those iron sights are properly sighted in. With its image vibrations the scope may actually be a hindrance.

Times change and fashion changes. The old riflemen at the Bay City Rifle Club that got me shooting decades ago are long departed. Somehow the idea of teaching the basics of rifle shooting with 3- or 4-position shooting of the 22 long rifle at 50 feet got lost in America, as did the idea of shooting high-power rifles – using the same theory of position, sight alignment and trigger control – as for the 22 rimfire. The use of the tight sling becomes almost a lost art. More velocity, synthetic stocks, and other innovations cannot replace the pure theory and practice of rifle fire, and no medium has reduced rifle fire to its essence, or to its classic simplicity, as does shooting the American battle rifle from position, at extended ranges and with iron sights. 'Digital' guns have their use, and are now most popular, but somehow the magic and skill of directed rifle fire has gotten lost in technological developments. A return to using American battle rifles, those dependable warhorses, so much a part of the American past of target shooting and history,

should once again become a part of the present and future of shooting. There can be no more elegant use for a centerfire rifle. ●

For further Reading:

Brophy, Lt. Col. William S. USAR Ret.
1985 **The Krag Rifle**, The Gun Room Press, Highland Park, NJ

Kuhnhausen, Jerry
1985 **The Gas Operated Service Rifles A Shop Manual, Volumes I&II**, VSP Publishers, McCall, ID

Macaulay, Neill
1985 **The Sandino Affair**, Duke University Press, Chapel Hill, NC

Tompkins, Frank, Col.
1995[1934] **Chasing Villa**, J.M. Carroll & Company, Bryan, TX

Whelen, Townsend, Col.
2000[1946] **Small Arms Design And Ballistics, Volume II: Ballistics**, Palladium Press, Birmingham, AL

Art of the Engraver & Custom Gunmaker

by Tom Turpin

A Beretta 682 O/U shotgun stocked and extensively metalsmithed by gunmaker Jay McCament. The engraving is by Bob Evans and the photography by Turk's Head Productions.

Texan Terry Theis did the Germanically-styled engraving and gold inlay work on this floorplate. Terry studied under German Master Engraver and dear friend of mine, the late Erich Boessler. *Photo courtesy of the engraver.*

A magnificent 500 NE double rifle from Dakota Arms. The wonderful engraving was executed by Creative Arts of Italy, who also supplied the photography.

This lovely custom Mauser chambered for the 280 Remington is the work of young custom maker Shane Thompson. His work is clean and crisp and his styling and execution above reproach. This quality of work, coming from a relative youngster, is proof-positive that custom gunmaking is not a dying art. *Photo by Steven Dodd Hughes.*

A ornately decorated Winchester Model 95 from the shop of Joe Rundell. Joe did all the work on this Winchester, to include the exquisite engraving and rarely seen woodcarving. It is a magnificent piece of work. *Photo by Weyer of Toledo*

A highly upgraded Dakota Model 10 single-shot rifle. The rifle has about all of the available options offered by Dakota and has been wonderfully adorned by the engravers at Creative Arts in Italy. *Photo by Turk's Head Productions.*

A beautiful Winchester Model 94 from the Michigan shop of Joe Rundell. Joe selected the figures engraved on the rifle - Gen. Douglas MacArthur, John Wayne, Audie Murphy as well as Presidents Harry S. Truman, Franklin D. Roosevelt, Theodore Roosevelt, Thomas Jefferson and George Washington, because they were all Masons as is Rundell. He donated the rifle to his Lodge to be used as a raffle prize to purchase life-saving equipment for the Clio, Michigan police and fire departments. Rundell did all the work on this wonderful rifle. *Photo by Weyer of Toledo.*

A beautiful Dakota double shotgun that has been lavishly embellished by Creative Arts Engravers of Italy. This beautiful round-action SxS was photographed by Turk's Head Productions.

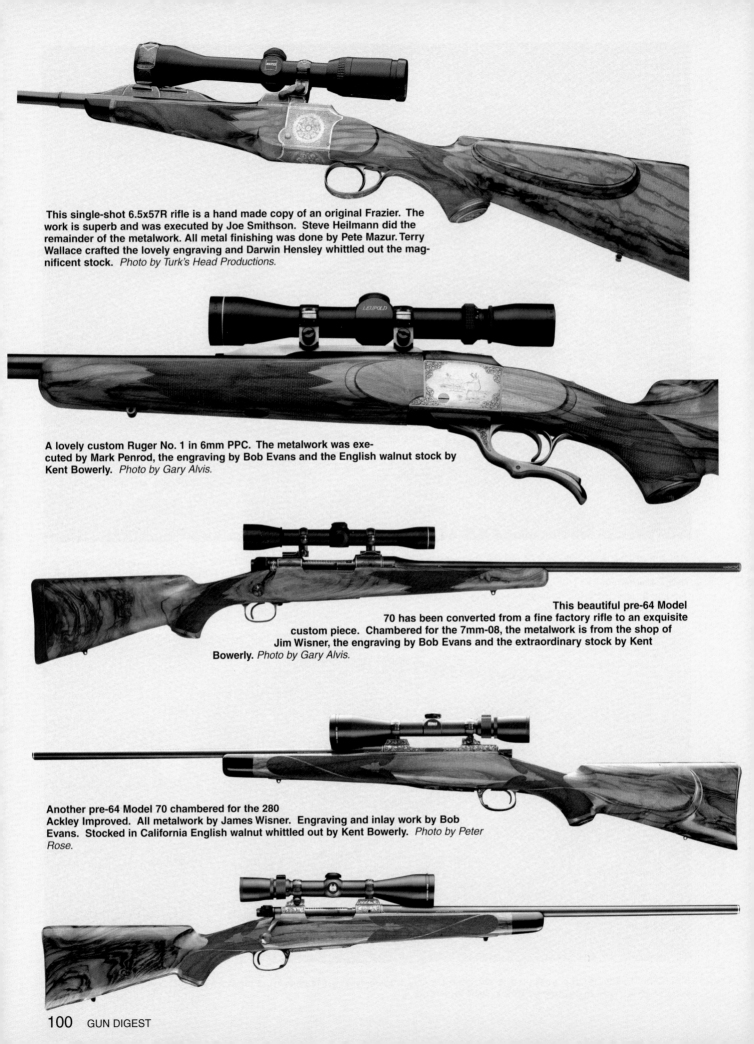

This single-shot 6.5x57R rifle is a hand made copy of an original Frazier. The work is superb and was executed by Joe Smithson. Steve Heilmann did the remainder of the metalwork. All metal finishing was done by Pete Mazur. Terry Wallace crafted the lovely engraving and Darwin Hensley whittled out the magnificent stock. *Photo by Turk's Head Productions.*

A lovely custom Ruger No. 1 in 6mm PPC. The metalwork was executed by Mark Penrod, the engraving by Bob Evans and the English walnut stock by Kent Bowerly. *Photo by Gary Alvis.*

This beautiful pre-64 Model 70 has been converted from a fine factory rifle to an exquisite custom piece. Chambered for the 7mm-08, the metalwork is from the shop of Jim Wisner, the engraving by Bob Evans and the extraordinary stock by Kent Bowerly. *Photo by Gary Alvis.*

Another pre-64 Model 70 chambered for the 280 Ackley Improved. All metalwork by James Wisner. Engraving and inlay work by Bob Evans. Stocked in California English walnut whittled out by Kent Bowerly. *Photo by Peter Rose.*

This 416 Rigby is built on a highly-modified Enfield action. Tom Burgess executed the superb metalwork. It included removing the rear half of the action and welding on a revamped rear bridge. There is a fold-down peep sight just above the bolt notch that is adjustable for windage and elevation. The front sight folds into itself to protect the blade when not in use and is also adjustable for elevation. Burgess also fitted a set of his detachable rings that truly return the scope to 'zero' every time it is removed and replaced. D'Arcy Echols crafted the stock from a very hard piece of Old World French walnut, fitted a grip cap of his design and checkered the stock 26 lpi. *Photo by Hazen Photography.*

A lovely Martini that was barreled, stocked and engraved by Ed DeLorge. Ed also did the photography.

One of the very nicest 1886 Winchesters that one is apt to ever come across. Jerry Fisher did the exquisite stock and also a good bit of the metalwork as well. Pete Mazur also worked on the metal and did the finish work. Robert Swartley created the engraving artistry in metal, an outstanding example of bulino execution. *Photos by David Wesbrook.*

This miniature express rifle is crafted around a Winchester Model 52 action. The metalwork is by Steve Heilmann, the metal finish work by Pete Mazur, the engraving by Terry Wallace and the elegant stock by Darwin Hensley. *Photo by Turk's Head Productions.*

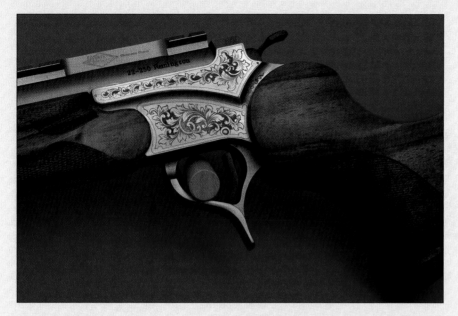

This Virgin Valley custom 22-250 was checkered and engraved by Ed DeLorge. *Photo by DeLorge.*

A right and left side view of a 1st Generation Colt single action that has been restored, engraved and custom-gripped by Ed DeLorge. *Photos by DeLorge.*

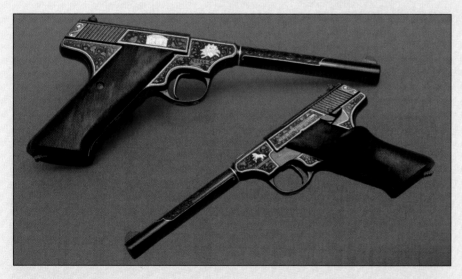

Left and right side views of a Colt Challenger that was restored, custom-stocked and engraved by Ed DeLorge. *Photos by DeLorge.*

This Dakota 76 chambered for the 416 Rigby cartridge is the work of Al Lind. Al did both metalwork and crafted the gorgeous Turkish walnut stock in his Tacoma, WA shop. Al checkered the stock in a lovely point pattern, 24 lpi. *Photo by Turk's Head Productions.*

This lovely 6mm PPC High Wall is the work of four superb artisans. Jim Blair did the wonderful engraving, Steve Heilmann the superb metalwork, Pete Mazur did the finishing and Darwin Hensley crafted the stock. This photo shows how really difficult it is, even for a master like Mustafa Bilal, to fully capture delicate bulino engraving on film. *Photo by Turk's Head Productions.*

Starting on this rifle, Californian Steve Heilmann first cut down a Mauser action to a length suitable for the 22 R Lovell cartridge, scaling the rest of the metalwork in proportion. Darwin Hensley then whittled the stock from a superb piece of English walnut and Sam Welch added the elegant scroll engraving. Finally, Pete Mazur completed the piece with his superb metal finishing. *Photo by Turk's Head Productions.*

This lovely trigger guard and floorplate was engraved and gold-inlaid by Ed DeLorge. Judging from the gold elephant inlaid on the floorplate, the bottom metal is for a heavy caliber express rifle. *Photo by Ed DeLorge.*

Colorado custom gunmaker Gene Simillion started this rifle with a pre-64 Model 70 action barreled and chambered for the 416 Taylor cartridge. The wonderful French walnut stock is checkered in a point pattern at 26 lpi and features a leather-covered pad and trap grip cap. The rifle has a fitted quarter rib with standing rear sight, checkered bolt knob, and custom mounts and rings. All the work, including the photography, was accomplished by Gene Simillion.

This lovely custom 338 Winchester was crafted around a new Model 70 action and Krieger cut-rifled 26-inch barrel. It also features custom bottom metal, scope mounts and Talley rings. The English walnut stock is fitted with a steel grip cap, recoil pad, ebony forend tip, and is checkered in a point pattern. Gene Simillion accomplished all the outstanding work. *Photo by Gene Simillion.*

Both sides of a European combination gun that has been wonderfully engraved by German engraver Andreas Scholz. Herr Scholz is currently employed by the old German manufacturer, F.W. Heym. *Photo courtesy of the engraver.*

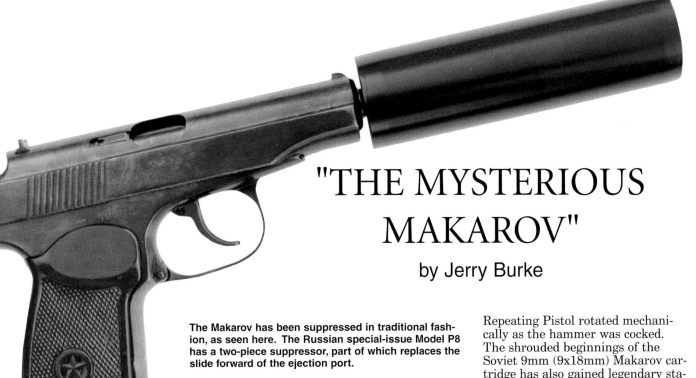

"THE MYSTERIOUS MAKAROV"

by Jerry Burke

The Makarov has been suppressed in traditional fashion, as seen here. The Russian special-issue Model P8 has a two-piece suppressor, part of which replaces the slide forward of the ejection port.

IT WAS A tumultuous time, and the entire world was watching. Freedom was riding the crest of an emotional tidal wave, driven by the indomitable human spirit. The year was 1989, and the decades-long Cold War was ending where it began… in the German city of Berlin. Throughout the DDR (*Deutsche Demokratische Republik,* or East Germany) and elsewhere, Communism was collapsing. Worldwide media rushed to report joyous scenes of reunited families, as reveling throngs hacked away at the hated concrete monstrosity known as the Berlin Wall. In a dark shadowy corner of this chaos lurked a high-ranking counterintelligence officer of the *Ministerium fur Staatssicherheit*… the *Stasi* (The East German Secret Police)… fearing reprisals from those he had long held under his boot heel. Helped into the West in exchange for a wealth of State secrets, this purveyor of fear and torture brought with him a Soviet-designed semi-automatic pistol known in Russia as the *Pistolet Makarova*.

With the reunification of Germany in October of 1990, as many as 270,000 of these service pistols… named for their Soviet designer (Nikolay Fyedorovich Makarov)… were turned over to the *Bundeswehr*. Soon, everything from former East German military mess kit forks to MIG jet fighter clocks found their way to the worldwide surplus market. A significant number of primarily East German-manufactured Makarov semi-automatic military pistols soon started making their way to the United States. In those early days, American handgunners knew virtually nothing about this Cold War instrument of totalitarianism. With little to go on, reports on the Makarov started appearing in print, and with those reports came speculation Soviet weapons specialists had grappled with for decades, sometimes innocently offered-up as fact.

Handgun Myths Turned Legend

Popular myths that have gained legendary status are part of firearms lore. Perhaps the most enduring is the misconception that Samuel Colt invented the revolving firearm. This is simply not true. A certain Mr. Collier of Boston had an English patent for such a device by 1813. As a young seaman with an established firearms interest, Colt roamed the streets of Calcutta, India in 1830, where Collier's invention was in use by British forces. There can be no doubt that on a one-way voyage under sail of seventeen thousand miles, seaman Samuel Colt spent countless hours noting the gear that locked a capstan in place to keep cable from running wild. Sam's real claim-to-mechanical-fame was applying that existing sailing ship pawl and ratchet gear to the existing revolving firearm. The cylinder on a Colt's Repeating Pistol rotated mechanically as the hammer was cocked. The shrouded beginnings of the Soviet 9mm (9x18mm) Makarov cartridge has also gained legendary status, and it all begins with a sexy-sounding, pre-WWII experimental German endeavor dubbed the "Ultra Project".

The Ultra Enigma

This is the most often repeated theory on the birth of the 9x18mm Makarov pistol cartridge, the one receiving the majority of related firearms coverage in the 1990s. It is a fact that, in the late 1930s, the German munitions firm of Gustav Genschow (*Geco*, by trade name) set out to develop a proprietary cartridge for Hermann Goring's *Luftwaffe* (Air Force), christened the "Ultra Project". However, the significance of this effort has been blown out of all proportion, as if on the level of significant secret Nazi projects like the atom bomb, ballistic missiles and jet aircraft. In pre-WWII Nazi Germany, this was a minor-league project, a tip-of-the-hat to the burgeoning ego of Germany's Air Force Commander. If nothing else, an aircrew sidearm does not an air force make. The Ultra Project was an attempt to develop a cartridge… and a pistol to fire it… that would be more potent than the 9mm *Kurz* (380 ACP) but could function in a handgun smaller than service pistols like the 9mm (9x19mm) Luger or the Walther P-38. The origin of this theory is a Soviet Ph.D. candidate's thesis, dated 1967, covering 50 years of Russian small arms. According to the student, when the Russians were gained control of the Zella-Mehlis area containing the Walther factory, design information on the Geco 9mm Ultra cartridge and cor-

Military Makarovs were produced in (*top-to-bottom*) the D.D.R. (East Germany), U.S.S.R. (Russia), the PRC (Communist China) and Bulgaria. They remain the service sidearm of Russia and Communist China.

Some scholars claim the Russian Makarov (*top*) was patterned after the German Walther PPK (*bottom*); others strongly disagree. As noted in the text, both are correct.

responding experimental Walther pistols were unearthed. Supposedly, the post-WWII Soviets used this obscure proprietary cartridge/pistol experiment as the launching pad for developing the 9mm Makarov cartridge.

But this theory has a number of problems associated with it. To begin with, we have neither verification of this thesis by anyone directly associated with development of the 9mm Makarov cartridge, nor access to relevant official documents. Secondly, the Russian academic's work was officially sanctioned by Communist authorities not exactly known for sharing weapons development information or techniques. The Ph.D. paper was even made available to Western booksellers. While it could be true, all this makes facts contained in the doctoral work of questionable value. The third problem with the "*we got it from the Walther factory*" theory is doubt as to what the Russians actually found when they took possession of the famous German weapons plant. When Patton's Third U.S. Army captured the region near the end of WWII, American GIs had full run of the Walther facility for a considerable period of time. Hundreds, perhaps thousands, of Walther pistols and related paraphernalia were appropriated as war trophies… everything from engraved presentation handguns to prototypical pieces and unfinished handguns. If that isn't enough to cast doubt on the value of the Walther factory to the Russians, prior to the takeover in 1945, American technical intelligence personnel worked with a passion to remove everything of potential value to our former ally. In the process, they even spirited Fritz Walther himself to safety. Dark clouds of the coming Cold War were already forming. As a result, the Russians primarily acquired gunmaking machinery and – perhaps – expertise from any local plant employees they could lay their hands upon.

If the 9x18mm Russian Makarov cartridge did have its beginnings in the shelved pre-WWII German attempt to improve on the pocket pistol, the Soviets may have had a better source than the stripped Walther facility. Near war's end, Russian troops captured whatever remained of Geco corporate headquarters at Durlach, designers of the 9mm Ultra cartridge as well as an 8mm version. Everyone originally concerned with the Ultra Project... the German Air Force, Geco and Walther... had long-since shelved the project as a waste of time and effort. If anything remained intact at the Geco offices, the Russians may have had better odds of finding reference material and/or sample cartridges where the chambering was developed. And, since it was a two-company effort, the Geco facility may have been home to one or more of the experimental Walther Ultra pistols as well.

Most cartridge scholars would agree that while the pre-WWII German 9mm Ultra cartridge and the post-War 9mm Makarov cartridges appear dimensionally similar to each other, they are not. They

From a shooter's standpoint, little separates military Makarov pistols produced in four Communist countries except minor variations in grips, magazines and markings. Seen here, genuine Russian-made martial Makarov (*top*) and the version produced in the D.D.R. (East Germany).

Genuine Communist Chinese-produced military Makarovs carry the arsenal code "66" inside a triangle on the left side of the frame, as seen here.

are, however, alike in ballistic performance. Taking this view, there is yet another, less dramatic and certainly more mundane theory to explain how the 9mm Makarov cartridge may have come into being. Professional designers, whether striving to improve the corn flake or create a medical miracle, are well schooled and steeped in all that has already been accomplished in their chosen field. Soviet munitions and weapons designers did not work in a vacuum. In European tradition, the pistol was more a badge of rank than a serious combat weapon. The Soviets wanted a cartridge that would be more effective than the 9mm *Kurz* (380 ACP), but could still be used in a blowback system, as exemplified by the Walther PP/PPK

A Russian military Makarov and Soviet issue holster and cleaning rod. Rare collectibles, like this Russian KGB uniform patch and KGB Duty Service badges, can cost as much as a surplus pistol!

East German-produced Makarov with military-issue rain pattern canvas holster. Produced from 1960-65, these pistols served Communist East Germany until the Germanys were reunited in 1989.

The Bulgarian-produced Makarov pistol and holster are nearly identical to the Russian original, except for markings. The Bulgarian arsenal code is the number "10" inside two concentric circles behind the slide stop on the left side of the frame.

Southeast Asian war relic holsters add interest to any military Makarov collection. Seen here (*bottom-to-top*): locally-produced Viet Cong product of artificial leather, thick leather model with Khmer Rouge provenance and Russian version with Viet Cong badge device. Note cleaning rod loops on two outside holsters.

series developed in the late 1920s. Given the popular pistol calibers of the day, Russian cartridge designers had two obvious perspectives from which to proceed. They could beef-up the 9mm *Kurz* or downsize the 9mm Parabellum. Since the 9mm Parabellum cartridge requires a recoil-operated, rather than the less-expensive-to-produce blow-back operating system, the 9mm *Kurz* was the more practical place to start. Whether the Russians began with the work German designers had done on the pre-WWII 9mm Ultra cartridge, or simply started with the most powerful blow-back pistol cartridge of the day, will probably never be known for sure. But once the 9mm Makarov pistol cartridge came into being, what type of blow-back pistol could be created to accommodate it?

Makarov Pistol Design

It is certainly possible, even likely, that the German firms of Geco and Walther worked on the Ultra assignment somewhat simultaneously; it would make perfect sense. Compared to recoil-operated service pistols like the 45-caliber Colt M1911/A1 Automatic, the 9mm Makarov is considerably less powerful but decidedly handier. The Russian invention is something of a large pocket pistol, as seen in the accompanying Specifications Chart. But now we come to another dilemma regarding the Makarov… not only is the origin of the chambering a murky mire, but whether-or-not it was based on an existing, non-Soviet design continues to be debated. Some contend the Makarov is nothing more than a Soviet knock-off of the Walther PPK pistol. Others denounced such a notion, pointing to such minor differences as the "*fire/safe*" position of the slide-mounted manual safeties of the two handguns. Taking it to the extreme, it could be argued the Russian Makarov is a copy of the Walther PPK, since both are hand-held devices from which to launch a projectile, and the PPK was produced first. Of course, a slingshot would also qualify. At the other end of the argumentative scale, grip color has never been the same on both pistols. Thus, you could conclude the Makarov was not patterned after the PPK. As is often the case, there is merit to both sides of this argument. But as with the

9mm Makarov cartridge, we will probably never know for a certainty. An accompanying photo displays both a field-stripped Walther PPK and a Makarov, with the grips removed. Like the PPK, the Makarov is equipped with a one-piece, three-sided grip. The action on both pistols is what we today call a "traditional double-action." A prominent feature of the PP/PPK-series Walther pistols is the disassembly procedure, employing a trigger guard hinged at the front. The Makarov follows the Walther example in this feature as well. Other design similarities between the Walther PPK and the Makarov include a knurled external hammer, fixed barrel, blow-back operating system and bottom magazine release (on some early Walther PP & PPK specimens). Both pistols have a hammer drop safety activated when the manual safety lever is applied - if the hammer in the cocked position; sights on both pistols are similar. However, the design of these two pistols does vary in other ways. The "safe/fire" positions on the pistols are indeed reversed, and only the Makarov has an external slide stop/release lever. Disconnectors on the two handguns differ, and only the Makarov has the highly desirable chrome-lined barrel. Of course, the calibers are also different. The PPK has been chambered for the 22 LR rimfire, 25 and 32 ACP cartridges - as well as the 9mm *Kurz* (380 ACP); other than a 22LR conversion kit mentioned

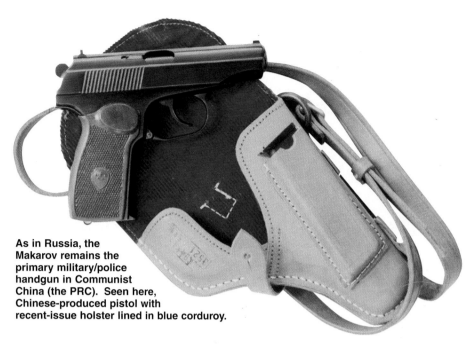

As in Russia, the Makarov remains the primary military/police handgun in Communist China (the PRC). Seen here, Chinese-produced pistol with recent-issue holster lined in blue corduroy.

below, a military Makarov is a one-caliber pistol (9x18mm Makarov). As a result of its more powerful chambering, the Makarov is a larger pistol, stretching the original concept of a pocket pistol. Only one grip screw is needed to secure the Makarov's 3-sided grip to the frame; the Walther PPK grip is held in place by a grip screw on each side. The lanyard ring or loop on a Walther PPK is located at the rear base of the gripframe, behind the magazine well. On the Makarov, the lanyard loop is permanently affixed to the left rear side of

the grip. The Makarov has an 8-round magazine capacity while the maximum load for a Walther PPK varies depending on chambering.

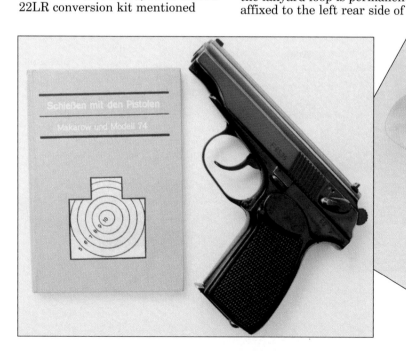

Black plastic grip sans lanyard loop gives Makarovs produced by the former D.D.R. (East Germany) a sleek appearance. Hardcover manual covers everything from parts nomenclature to approved shooting stances for the *"Makarow"* and a secondary issue pistol, both in 9x18mm Makarov caliber.

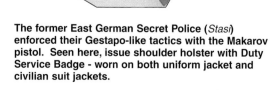

The former East German Secret Police (*Stasi*) enforced their Gestapo-like tactics with the Makarov pistol. Seen here, issue shoulder holster with Duty Service Badge - worn on both uniform jacket and civilian suit jackets.

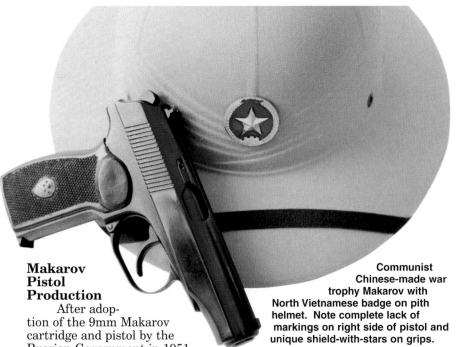

Makarov Pistol Production

After adoption of the 9mm Makarov cartridge and pistol by the Russian Government in 1951, production was eventually spun-off to other satellite countries, including East Germany, Bulgaria and Communist China. Reports circulate from time-to-time regarding Makarov production in other countries, including Communist Cuba, but in the end only a limited number of critical replacement parts seem to have been locally manufactured. Similar markings appear on the left side of frame and slide on military Makarovs from each country-of-origin, and require a bit of interpretation. To the right of the serial number, a Russian Makarov is marked with an arsenal code consisting of a circle surrounding a triangle with a vertical line drawn down the middle. On most Russian Makarovs encountered in the U.S., the last two digits of the production year follow the manufacturing location; on others, a year code appears using Cyrillic letters. A series of "punch" marks at the rear of the frame, representing various inspections, completes the line of markings.

On Makarovs produced in East Germany (the D.D.R.), markings are similar and in the same general locations, but a mark consisting of "K100" inside a rectangle precedes the serial number. A circle inside a 4-sided diamond is the mark of the Ernst Thaelmann Werke. The factory is named in honor and memory of a Communist activist who operated inside Nazi Germany. Known production years for these D.D.R. Makarovs are from 1958 to 1965. Bulgarian specimens reflect a factory code consisting of the number

Communist Chinese-made war trophy Makarov with North Vietnamese badge on pith helmet. Note complete lack of markings on right side of pistol and unique shield-with-stars on grips.

"10" enclosed in two concentric circles. However, as with some Russian Makarovs, the Bulgarian model has a year-of-production alpha code, rather than the easy-to-interpret year codes found on most Russian and East German Makarovs. Military/police Makarovs produced in the Peoples Republic of China exhibit the factory code of the number "66" inside a triangle; and, "59SHI" follows near the back of the frame on the left side. Some Makarovs from each country of origin have as many as the last four digits of the serial number stamped

on the manual safety. Additionally, the color of both hammers and/or manual safeties on some Makarovs is reddish - or even purple-hued, in direct contrast to the bluing that covers the rest of the metal parts. Partial serial and assembly numbers are also often found on the frame under the grips, as well as elsewhere on some internal parts.

There is some variance in Makarov grips. Original on Russian, Chinese and Bulgarian military models is a rusty red composite similar to what older Americans know by the trade name, Bakelite.

On Russian and Bulgarian grips, a single Communist star in a circle adorns both sides of the grip, which is checkered on all three sides. A muted thumb rest also appears on both sides of the grip, with a single grip screw at the rear holding it in place. A unique feature which guards against the grip screw working loose during firing is a notched metal spring collar inside the grip screw hole. There are four sides to the cloverleaf-like grip screw head and, as the grip screw is tightened, the notched protrusion in the metal collar inside the grip screw hole locks the grip screw in place, an arrangement not unlike some modern adjustable rear sights.

The Chinese martial Makarov follows the same grip pattern, except the Red Star is replaced by a shield containing one large star with a cluster of four smaller ones below in a semi-circle. The thumb rest is smaller and not as smoothly integrated into the grip design.

The East Germans went their own way in grip design, using a black checkered plastic composite with thumb rests similar to their Russian and Bulgarian counterparts. Although an ordnance shop post-

A pair of Russian-made Makarovs. *Top*, 9x18mm Soviet military issue. *Bottom*, CO2 BB pistol, available through the website, "makarov.com".

production procedure was implemented to accommodate a lanyard at the rear of the grip, East German grips do not include a "staple"-style lanyard loop.

Left-to-right: **9mm** *Kurz* **(380 ACP), 9mm Ultra, 9mm Makarov, 9mm Makarov training dummy, 9mm Police and 9x19mm Parabellum. Makarov cartridge is dimensionally different from the 9mm Ultra cartridge but ballistically similar.**

A variety of American-made and foreign 9x18mm Makarov cartridges were used for testing. Military Makarovs from all countries of manufacture performed admirably.

Specification Chart *(East German Mfg.)*

Action:	Traditional double-action semi-auto pistol.
Caliber:	9x18mm Makarov
Finish:	Blue
Barrel:	3.75 inches
Capacity:	8-round magazine + 1 in the chamber
Trigger:	13 lbs. double-action; 5 lbs. single-action
Sights:	Front sight integral with slide; rear sight drift-adjustable
Weight:	25 ounces, unloaded
Height:	5 inches
Width:	1 3/8 inches
Length:	6 3/8 inches

Retail Surplus Cost: Approximately $225 as-new, with spare magazine and holster.

Pistol Comparison Chart

Pistol	Cartridge	Ammunition	Group(inches)*
Makarov (E.G.)	9x18mm Makarov	Hornady JHP	**1.75 / 4.25**
SIG P232	9mm Kurz (380 ACP)	Black Hills JHP	**1.54 / 3.73**
S&W 3913	9mm Parabellum	Winchester JHP	**1.24 / 3.51**
RUGER P93	9mm Parabellum	CORBON JHP	**1.52 /3.82**

Results: Best of five 5-shot groups measured from center-to-center of two widest shots.
Distance: 7 yards offhand / 25 yards from solid rest.

Makarov magazines are skeletonized to reduce weight, as well as limit production costs. When originally issued, they were marked to match the pistol with which they were issued, and two were issued per pistol. On East German magazines, there is a vertical "hump" on the bottom left which adds rigidity to the design. While early Russian Makarov magazines had this feature, most encountered today... as well as magazines from Bulgaria and Communist China... simply have a break in the sheet metal where that "hump" once appeared. Either style magazine will function in any military Makarov from any country of manufacture. Except for the Chinese military Makarov, the last three digits of the serial number are typically etched onto the left side of Makarov magazines. The Chinese stamp the digits on the base of the floorplate. However, the matching of magazines to a specific pistol had nothing to do with the functioning of the pistol. It was a way of ensuring that whomever was assigned that Makarov was also responsible for the care and maintenance of those specific magazines. Magazines from all producing nations are found with the numeral "1" or "2" stamped or etched on the magazine spine, indicating issue as either the primary or back-up magazine for a specific pistol.

An exceptionally smart feature on all military Makarovs, but not post-Cold War export or so-called "tourist" pistols, is the chrome-lined barrel. With plenty of harsh-weather combat experience acquired by the Russians, and regular maintenance difficult under prolonged periods of engagement, the extra cost of the chrome job was worth every ruble. Of the many Makarovs I have examined, including battlefield returns from operations in Grenada and the Gulf War, all had excellent bores.

Each nation producing the Makarov provided their forces with a quality product, but I rate the East German Makarov as the best. The primary differences are in the care of parts manufacture, fit and finish. Surprisingly, the Chinese military Makarov rates a close second in my experience. Next in line for quality assurance is an original Russian military Makarov, followed by the quite serviceable Bulgarian issue. However, I suspect some of these variations have to do with the years of manufacture. Again, the D.D.R. manufactured Makarovs

Accuracy tests were conducted among (*left-to-right*) **Ruger P93, S&W 3913, East German Makarov and SIG P232.** Makarov proved its worth as a potential budget home defense/legal concealed carry pistol.

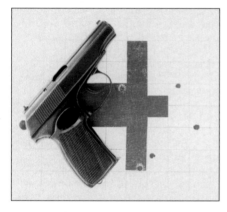

At 25 yards from a solid rest, Makarov performance lagged slightly behind more modern pistols tested, but proved more than adequate.

At 7 yards offhand, this East German Makarov easily produced 1.75-inch groups using Hornady's 95-grain JHP ammunition.

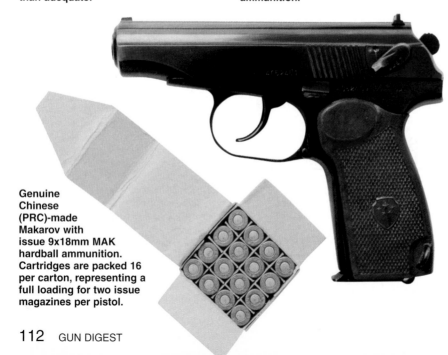

Genuine Chinese (PRC)-made Makarov with issue 9x18mm MAK hardball ammunition. Cartridges are packed 16 per carton, representing a full loading for two issue magazines per pistol.

between 1958 and 1965. Most Soviet Makarov examples available for examination were produced more than two decades later, when money was tight and Communist economies were on the wane. At this writing, the once-scarce Bulgarian Makarov is becoming very common; but while eminently serviceable, fit and finish on the Bulgarian specimens is not quite up to the quality of other producing nations, with slightly inferior slide-to-frame fit.

The Quiet Makarov

Especially interesting variations of the Makarov are the seldom seen suppressed versions. The Makarov has been suppressed in traditional fashion through special threaded barrels and screw-on tube devices. However, of greater interest is the special-purpose Makarov P8, on which a portion of the suppressor tube is an integral part of the pistol itself. The suppressor tube starts just forward of the barrel chamber, running nearly the same length as a standard slide/barrel combination. The Model P8 can be fired with or without the tube extension attached. Sights are of increased, non-standard height to allow for sighting over the integral suppressor tube and extension. The Model P8 comes standard with a leather holster equipped with a separate compartment forward of the pistol pouch to accommodate the detachable suppressor tube. How many of these P8 Makarovs were produced and whether-or-not they are still in service is not known for a certainty, but in-service P8s have been reliably reported as recently as 1996.

Mil Spec Ammunition

The primary producers of military issue 9x18mm Makarov ammunition have predictably been the nations producing the pistol. Each country of manufacture… Russia, East Germany, The Peoples Republic of China (PRC) and Bulgaria… developed standard "ball" or full-metal jacket cartridges. Bullet cores may be of lead or steel, where lead is in short supply. Steel bullet cores are mushroom-shaped, and are placed near the nose of the bullet. Production of 9x18mm Makarov ammunition has also been accomplished in Hungary, Poland and Czechoslovakia, to name a few. Case material has been of both brass and mild steel. Some authorities believe a steel case is better in a blow-back pistol system due to the greater "sticking power" of steel in the barrel chamber, absorbing more of the recoil energy than brass. Typical muzzle velocity of these rounds is 1,050 fps from a bullet weighing 93.7 grains. Variations abound for the cartridge collector, as at least 100 different headstamps are known to exist, with the earliest specimen thus far dated 1949. A variety of dummy – or "drill" – rounds exist, usually identifiable by plastic bullets, drilled or indented shell casings or a combination thereof.

Perhaps the most interesting 9x18mm Makarov cartridge variations are those produced in Czechoslovakia. That nation was the last of the Soviet Bloc countries to issue the Makarov cartridge and pistol. Not satisfied with the power of the Russian-developed cartridge, the Czechs developed their own load, featuring a lighter bullet which boosted muzzle velocity by as much as 300 fps. They then developed and adopted the Vzor 82 pistol to accommodate the hotter "Makarov" cartridge.

Mil Spec Makarov Equipment

The Soviet military Makarov was, and still is, issued in a full-flap brown leather holster with open-top spare magazine pouch sewn to the face. The flap covers the open end of the magazine pouch. A relatively thin leather strap is sewn or riveted to the inside back of the holster and fits through a slot on the face of the holster. This is a device to allow easier access to the pistol when

9x18mm Makarov cartridges tested included Chinese-made Norinco FMJ plus the Russian JSC Barnaul-brand JHP, aluminum-cased CCI/Blazer JHP and JHPs by Hornady and CORBON.

removing it from the holster. The leather strap runs under the triggerguard, and when the tab on the loose end of the strap is pulled, it shortens the amount of strap inside the holster and boosts the pistol up higher into the holster. Two leather straps on the back of the holster accommodate a variety of belt widths. On the front of the Russian and Bulgarian-issue holsters, parallel to the holstered pistol's sight plane, are two leather loops to receive a steel cleaning rod; the East Germans saw fit to eliminate this feature. Typical Russian and Bulgarian military issue holsters are brown, with the East Germans preferring more of a maroon look; the Bulgarians are also known to have employed black leather during some of their history with the Makarov.

A Southeast Asian war trophy. Communist Chinese Makarov pistol (note shield with stars on grip) and Russian holster with Viet Cong badge device.

Makarov Cartridge History Chart

Cartridge:	9mm Kurz (380) (Belgian)	9mm Ultra (German)	9mm Makarov (Russian)	9mm Parabellum (German)
Year Developed	1908	1938	1946	1902
Case Length	.680"	.727"	.710"	.760"
Case Diameter (at neck)	.373"	.374"	.384"	.380"
Case Diameter (at base)	.373"	.374"	.389"	.392"
Case Diameter (at rim)	.374	.374"	.396"	.393"
Bullet Diameter	.356"	.354"	.363"	.355"
Bullet Weight (mil spec jacketed)	95 grs.	108 grs.	93.7 grs.	115 grs.
Bullet Type	round nose	flat nose	round nose	round nose
Muzzle Velocity	.98"	1.023"	.97"	1.16"
Muzzle Velocity	955 fps.	984 fps.	1,050 fps.	1,140 fps.

At the exclusive website, "makarov.com", you'll find everything your heart desires from genuine collectibles and repair parts to top-quality legal concealed-carry products.

The Makarov After "The Fall"

As indicated, it wasn't long after the Berlin Wall ceased to separate the two Germanys that surplus military and police equipment of the former D.D.R. was on the market, along with a smattering of Soviet-produced Makarovs. And, the availability of inexpensive imported surplus ammunition helped move plenty of hardware off dealers' shelves. However, some of the surplus ammunition was known to be corrosive and other batches were described as "mildly corrosive"… a term I don't acknowledge as legitimate for use in any firearm I own.

As European Communism collapsed, the capitalistic instinct kicked in, and post-Cold War Makarov pistols, called "tourist" Makarovs by purists, started to make an appearance. The Russian commercial export version was equipped with a civilian-friendly grip and fully adjustable rear sight. An increased-capacity 9mm Makarov was also created, with a thicker grip frame than the original military issue, and these have already become collectible. While importation of these post-Cold War pistols was still in full swing, the Russian Makarov was also produced in 9mm *Kurz* (380 ACP). The Germans resumed Makarov production briefly in the 1990s, but they were only produced in the hundreds, and have become the most desirable of all commercial Makarovs. The Chinese certainly had no intention of being left out of this commercial opportunity, and NORINCO also began producing commercial Makarov pistols for export. Most of the Chinese imports can be identified by the "ZZ" serial number prefix on the left side of the frame and slide. Most post-Cold War Makarov imports are easily identified by various telltale markings on the right side of the slide and/or frame.

In addition to the standard leather military/police full-flap holster, the D.D.R. also issued a treated canvas Makarov holster in a camouflage rain pattern. The overall color scheme is gray, and every manner of equipment was produced in this pattern from fatigue blouses to mess kit covers. Also full-flap in design, the rain-pattern holster includes a spare magazine pouch but again, not an accommodation for a cleaning rod. The East Germans also issued a shoulder holster in limited quantities, but the holster pouch is rather thin and shapeless. In some specimens, a full leather flap is employed while a thin rubberized material is used on other samples; a strap secures the flap to the holster by way of a metal post, and the rig is obviously not designed for quick-draw. Straps are of cloth, with spare magazine pouch attached. An additional strap is stitched to the bottom rear of the holster toe, with a leather tab for securing the holster to a belt stud or belt loop. The magazine pouch also has a flap with stud retainer.

While a variety of steel Makarov cleaning rods exist, all have a somewhat sharp point at the end of the cleaning cloth slot to aid in pistol disassembly. A short screwdriver blade is at the finger loop end of the cleaning rod, designed to provide easy removal of the grip screw. More than one cleaning kit has been issued for the Makarov,

including a version in a metal container resembling an old tobacco tin. Another kit is packaged in a treated canvas roll-up pouch, and was also issued for the AK-47 assault rifle.

An extremely rare Makarov accessory is the 22 Long Rifle conversion kit. Packaged in a dovetailed wooden box, the kit consists of a 22 LR barrel insert, a reduced-weight slide, special recoil spring and a quantity of hollow metal 9mm Makarov cartridge dummies in which 22 Long Rifle rimfire cartridges are placed for firing. Standard 9mm Makarov magazines are utilized. The device was designed for training purposes, and only a few have surfaced from the former East Germany. Designed to function as a semi-automatic pistol, each cartridge dummy and spent 22 rimfire cartridge case ejects from the converted Makarov as a unit.

Modern 9x18mm Makarov cartridges tested include (*L to R*): JHPs by CORBON, Hornady, CCI/Blazer and Russian-made JSC Barnaul plus Norinco's FMJ produced in the PRC (Peoples Republic of China). Historic cartridges covered in the text include (*center-to-right*): 9x19mm Parabellum, 9mm Police, 9mm Makarov practice dummy, 9x18mm Makarov, 9mm Ultra and 9mm Kurz (380 ACP).

My favorite post-Cold War Makarov is Russian-made on the hi-capacity frame, but fires standard BBs of Red Ryder fame, rather than the 9mm Makarov cartridge. This CO2 air pistol, imported by European American Arms and available through the website makarov.com is great fun, as well as accurate. Reasonably priced for the quality provided, the Russian CO2 Makarov is delivered standard with steel cleaning rod, a starter-quantity of BBs, replacement O-rings and an owner's manual. Powered by CO2 cartridges with BB magazine capacity of 13, the double-action Russian Makarov air pistol actually cycles with each shot fired. However, never forget that an air gun has the potential to be dangerous and harmful if improperly handled. Virtually every safety rule associated with cartridge pistols relates directly to the safe securing and handling of air-guns.

The Makarov In The Field

The first U.S. ammunition manufacturer to recognize the impending demand for American-made 9x18mm Makarov ammunition was CCI, who introduced a jacketed hollow-point round to their Blazer cartridge line-up. Since then, CORBON, Federal, Hornady and Winchester have cataloged this cartridge with jacketed hollow-points. CCI has since added a TMJ version to their Blazer line, and in case you're wondering, CCI uses the term "TMJ" to identify their bullet

Russian KGB uniform patch (*top*). **KGB Duty Service Badge** (*left*). **Stasi/East German Secret Police 40-Year Service Badge** (*right*). **Historic cartridges** (*L to R*): 9mm Kurz (380 ACP), 9mm Ultra, 9x18mm Makarov, Makarov dummy practice round, 9mm Police and 9x19mm Parabellum.

type, which is completely surrounded with gilding metal - including the base of the projectile. Newest of all is Winchester's offering… a brass-cased cartridge with 95-grain round-nose FMJ bullet. Foreign 9mm Makarov commercial offerings include a FMJ produced by NORIN-

CO of the Peoples Republic of China, as well as a jacked hollow-point by JSC Barnaul of Russia.

For accuracy and function testing, I used commercial Makarov ammunition from each company listed above, declining to subject the test pistols to questionable surplus fodder. Included was CCI/Blazer's 95-grain TMJ aluminum-cased cartridge and CORBON's JHP of the same weight. Federal's 9x18mm MAK cartridge uses a lighter 90-grain bullet, and Hornady's 95-grain jacketed hollowpoint and Winchester's round-nose FMJ of the same weight completed the list of American-made test ammunition. Included on the import side, Norinco's green carton is filled with full-metal jacketed bullets topping lacquered steel cases; bullet weight is 94 grains. The Russian-made JSC Barnaul hollowpoint with, again, a bullet weight of 95 grains was also included in the test. In addition to shooting from a solid rest at 25 yards, I also tried each load from 7 yards. A nearly mint-condition Makarov was tested from each country of major manufacture… Russia, East Germany, The Peoples Republic of China and Bulgaria. In total, five groups of five rounds were fired from each pistol, using each variety of test ammunition.

One military Makarov pistol from each country of manufacture (Russia, East Germany, Bulgaria and Communist China) was fired initially. With the test pistols in literally as-new-issue condition and test ammunition second to none, results seen in the accompanying chart put the Makarov in the best possible light. There was not enough variance from pistol-to-pistol to be meaningful, given the performance expected from a military sidearm, but the East German version performed best, and results are displayed in the accompanying chart. I suspect at least two factors contributed to the German product proving to be the most accurate. First, greater care in manufacture and finishing are evident on the former D.D.R. pistol, reflecting the time-honored German reputation for quality craftsmanship. Second, the E.G. test Makarov was produced

Makarov Ballistics Test

FACTORY AMMUNITION

Manufacturer	Case Material	Bullet *(grs./type)*	MV (fps)	Group* *(inches)*
CCI/Blazer	Aluminum	95/TMJ	946	**1.93/4.64**
CORBON	Brass	95/JHP	1,035	**2.25/4.57**
Federal	Brass	90/JHP	975	**2.30/5.03**
Hornady	Brass	95/JHP	981	**1.75/4.25**
JSC *(Russia)*	Steel	95/JHP	951	**2.64/6.05**
Norinco *(PRC)*	Steel	94/FMJ	986	**2.26/5.88**
Winchester	Brass	95/FMJ	973	**1.98/4.51**

LEGEND: JHP = Jacketed Hollowpoint; **FMJ** = Full Metal Jacket; **TMJ** = Total Metal Jacket *(core completely jacketed)*.

*Results: Best of five 5-shot strings. Group size measured center-to-center of two widest shots. SHOOTING CHRONY chronograph used to determine velocity, placed 8 feet from the muzzle. **Distance:** 7 yards offhand / 25 yards from a solid rest.

in 1960, rather than decades later for two of the other test Makarovs. As economic conditions in the Communist countries declined, some production shortcuts were utilized which had little-or-no negative effect on the serviceability of the Makarov as a military pistol.

From the field test, it is clear the Soviet-designed 9mm Makarov cartridge/service pistol combination is accurate and reliable, especially when you remember this duo went into production in 1951. Offhand groups fired at 7 yards produced repetitive groups of under 2 inches, and more than one at 1 3/4 inches, with the E.G. Makarov preferring Hornady's 95-grain JHP cartridges. However, all of the test ammunition preformed admirably, with groups running between that 1 3/4-inch grouping to under 4 inches.

And then it was on to the considerably more challenging 25-yard mark, but from a decidedly solid rest position. Once again, performance was more than acceptable for a service pistol, with most groups fired using American-made ammunition averaging about 4 1/2 inches. However, the Norinco military-style ball ammunition produced groups as wide as 8 inches from the widest two shots in a 5-shot group. The Russian commercial JHPs tended toward 7-inch groups at 25-yards. Again, the E.G. specimen preformed best, with the Chinese military model a close second. The Russian Makarov generally fired 1-inch wider 5-shot groups at 25 yards, while the Bulgarian version produced groups a full 2 inches wider than the D.D.R.-produced pistol. But like anything else, pistols vary from handgun-to-handgun. I even tested the military Makarov against three of my favorite modern pistols... a SIG P232, the S&W 3913 (which is just about the size of a Makarov) and a hi-capacity Ruger P93. Results are in the related chart, but you can see the military Makarov can hold its own against modern products.

Aftermarket Makarov Accessories

Some will be satisfied with the opportunity to add Makarov military Cold War trophies to their collection, whether they ever enjoy shooting them or not. The time is right, as prices remain low for the three European variations. I consider a true Russian military Makarov the best buy, as this original-among-originals is still the Soviet service pistol and not seen

regularly in the U.S. At retail, little more than $200 should land you a military Makarov... most likely an East German or Bulgarian version... in new or nearly new condition. If you locate one, a true Russian-produced military Makarov will be similarly priced. But whether you're going to just display your prize Makarov under glass or enjoy shooting and possibly legally packing it, you will probably want to acquire some accessories. You'll find firing-up the ol' computer and going to "makarov.com" – a simple, convenient and efficient way to acquire everything-Makarov from collectible surplus items like cleaning kits in a tobacco-style can, and modern

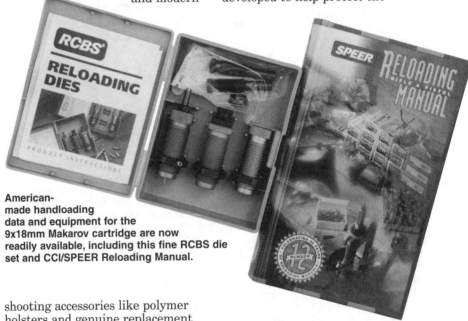

American-made handloading data and equipment for the 9x18mm Makarov cartridge are now readily available, including this fine RCBS die set and CCI/SPEER Reloading Manual.

shooting accessories like polymer holsters and genuine replacement parts. Many makarov.com products are exclusives; prices are great and so is the service. You'll also be lead into a message board where "Makarovniks" (Makarov enthusiasts) exchange information on their varied experiences and requests for information to the tune of an average 75 messages per day!

The Makarov And Legal Concealed Carry

The military Makarov is reliable, accurate and packs enough power to just qualify as a legitimate option for legal civilian concealed carry. The 1950s design is more snag-proof than many a more modern design, and the addition of a ramped rear sight would make the Makarov near-perfect in that category. However, the most readily available version, those produced in East Germany, are now between 35 and 40 years old. I am also leery of the metallurgical quality of these foreign military surplus sidearms,

although parts failures on unaltered military Makarovs seem few and far between. If your budget for a house gun or legal concealed carry handgun is severely limited, it is hard to argue against the military Makarov. However, given the option, I heartily recommend something new out-of-the-box from the product lines of long-standing commercial handgun producers like Beretta, Glock, H&K, Ruger, Smith & Wesson or Walther.

The Makarov In A Nutshell

Designed in the early days of the post-WWII Cold War and officially adopted in 1951, the 9x18mm Makarov cartridge and the *Pistolet Makarova* (Makarov pistol) were developed to help protect the

Communist Government of Mother Russia from the evil, decadent West. In no small measure, it aided in the suppression of the Russian people and through design-sharing and production proliferation, the suppression of a variety of Soviet Bloc nations, Communist China... even Castro-dominated Cuba. An extensive variety of 9x18mm Makarov military ammunition has been produced and scores of minor variations in the military pistols themselves will forever keep collectors busy. The military surplus Makarov pistol is truly a Cold War war trophy. Each time I fire a military Makarov, I can almost hear the Liberty Bell ringing for millions of people I will never know. There is only one more military Makarov I hope to add to my collection; one of former Communist Cuban provenance, when the people of that beautiful island nation are free people once again. ●

The M16-series rifles have served the U.S. military, law enforcement and sportsman with distinction for nearly 40 years. They have become the world's standard for comparison. Here is the latest, the M16A2 assault rifle.

The AR15/M16: The Rifle That Was Never Supposed To Be.

How The "Mattel Toy" Became America's Assault Rifle.

by Christopher R. Bartocci

Photos by Lawrence Ventura. Property of the Wisconsin Department of Justice, State Crime Laboratory-Milwaukee.

IN MARCH OF 1965, the first U.S. troops landed in Vietnam. They were carrying the M14 rifle, chambered for the 7.62x51mm NATO (M80 Ball) cartridge, which had a detachable 20-round magazine and was capable of semi- and full-automatic fire. The military soon learned the M14 on full auto was extremely difficult to control; most burst fire was ineffective. As a result, many M14

rifles were issued with the selector levers removed, making the rifle – effectively – an M1 Garand with a 20-round magazine. The M14 was accurate but heavy, weighing nearly nine pounds, empty. As U.S. involvement in the Vietnam War escalated, our troops encountered North Vietnamese as well as the Vietcong carrying the Soviet-designed AK47 (**A**vtomat **K**alashnikova model **47**), chambered

for the 7.62x39mm Soviet cartridge, and had a 30-round magazine. The AK's light recoil permitted controllable, accurate full-auto bursts and American troops began to feel outgunned. The United States needed it's own assault rifle – and needed it fast.

During the early 1950s, ArmaLite, a division of Fairchild Engine and Airplane Corporation of Hollywood, California, was working on a new assault rifle. The chief engineer was Eugene M. Stoner (1922-1997), described by many as the most gifted firearms designer since John Browning. His first attempt to create a new assault rifle was designated the AR10 (**A**rmaLite **R**ifle model **10**).

The AR10 was the first weapon to incorporate Gene Stoner's patented (*U.S. Patent No. 2,951,424*) gas system. This system uses a port in the barrel to bleed gas from the fired cartridge into a tube that runs under the handguard, from the front sight assembly to the upper receiver and into the carrier key on the bolt carrier. The pressure gives a hammer-like blow to the bolt carrier, pushing it rearward while simultaneously unlocking the eight-lug bolt from the barrel extension. The bolt and bolt carrier, continuing to move rearward, extract and eject the spent cartridge case and the buffer and recoil/buffer spring return the bolt assembly forward, stripping a cartridge off the magazine, chambering it and locking the bolt into the barrel extension. Using expertise gained in the aircraft industry, Stoner designed the upper and lower receivers of the AR10 to be made of lightweight aircraft aluminum.

The first AR10 prototype, chambered for the 7.62x51mm NATO cartridge carried in a 20-round magazine, was completed in 1955. The rifle proved *extremely* accurate for a gas-operated weapon. In December 1955, the first AR10 was presented to the Infantry Board and School at Fort Benning, Georgia, by Gene Stoner and George Sullivan, an ArmaLite executive. Stoner demonstrated his new weapon concept to General William Wyman at Fort Benning on May 6th, just five days after the announcement of the adoption of the M14. Subsequently, the Board recommended further investigation into the AR10. In 1957 General Wyman, impressed by the merits and performance of the AR10, went to the ArmaLite Company and asked Gene Stoner to join a weapons program, offering ArmaLite financial support for future development of ArmaLite rifles in exchange for proprietary rights to the final product. Subsequently, ArmaLite introduced a totally new

concept for the modern battlefield, a 22-caliber battle rifle. As a result, the 30-caliber AR10 was to have a short history with the U.S. military.

The AR10, scaled down to fire the popular 222 Remington cartridge, had little recoil in semi-auto mode and was amazingly controllable on full-auto. There was heavy resistance to the radical new design from the Ordnance Corps, especially from Dr. Frederick Carten. Dr. Carten was adamantly opposed to weapons developed by commercial companies outside the Ordnance Corps and Springfield Armory – as well as guns made of aluminum and plastic. General Wyman ordered 10 of these new rifles, along with 100,000 rounds of ammunition, for Infantry Board trials. ArmaLite's focus was thus changed to the 22-caliber rifle and the AR15 (ArmaLite Rifle model 15) was born. In 1958, General Wyman ordered the Army to conduct the first tests on the new AR15.

Among the changes from the AR10 to the AR15 were revised sights to accommodate the flatter-shooting 22-caliber cartridge; elevation to be adjusted via a threaded front post sight rather than within the rear sight, where a less expensive

The original AR15; the weapon configuration that Colt bought from ArmaLite. Notice the three-prong suppressor, the fibrite stock/pistol/grip/firearm grips, the absent forward assist and the smooth bolt carrier without forward-assist grooves. This was the model used in the Department of Defense testing which launched the weapon's reputation for durability, reliability and accuracy.

The Army/Marine version adopted towards the middle of the Vietnam War to serve the U.S. Marines (*until 1983*) and the Army (*until 1986*). Note the forward assist, magazine release fence "*Boss*" and the "*bird cage*" flash suppressor. Note the 25-meter 'zeroing' target.

L-shaped peep sight was substituted. The resulting rifle was 37 1/2 inches long and weighed an incredible 6 pounds empty; 6.12 pounds with a loaded 25-round magazine.

The AR15 made use of high-impact fibrite stocks, pistol grips and handguards. A selector lever on the left side of the rifle could be manipulated with the shooter's right thumb without removing the hand from the pistol grip. The magazine release, on the right side of the receiver, could be operated with the trigger finger; when pressed, the magazine would drop free. A fresh magazine, requiring no camming – or 'rocking' – could be inserted straight into the magazine well. This attribute contributed significantly to speedy reloading in combat situations compared to its closest rival, the AK47/AKM. These are two of the main reasons why the AR15/M16-series rifles are considered the finest human-engineered assault rifles in the world.

A bolt catch mechanism is located on the left side of the rifle. When the last round was fired, the magazine follower would elevate the bolt catch and lock the bolt to the rear. After inserting a full magazine, the rifleman would push in on the upper portion of the bolt catch to release the bolt and load the rifle. The receivers, produced from 7075 T6 aircraft aluminum, which helps keep the rifle lightweight and dissipates heat better than conventional metals, are hard-anodized with a non-reflective matte gray weather-resistant finish.

Stoner went to Aberdeen Proving Ground for ammunition assistance. He enlisted the expertise of Robert Hutton, known as the father of the 5.56x45mm round. The pressures involved were more than the 222 Remington case could handle, so the 222 Special was developed. Sierra Bullet Co. made the 55-grain full metal jacket boat-tail bullet and the first "222 Special" ammunition was loaded by Remington Arms. This cartridge, with a muzzle velocity of 3,250 fps and a maximum effective range of 460 meters, became the 5.56x45mm Ball M193/223 Remington.

Tests by the Infantry Board and School at Fort Benning went very well for the AR15. Stoner personally delivered the weapons and conducted training and familiarization classes for all involved in the testing. In March of 1958, the Board found some *"bugs"* in the AR15 system. Some of the resultant changes incorporated in the first rifles were reduction of the trigger pull to seven

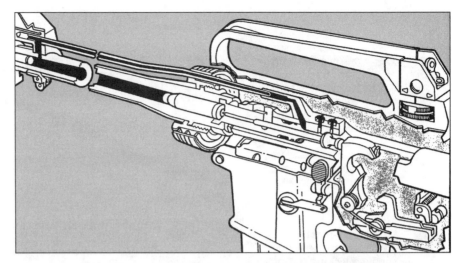

The firing sequence of Gene Stoner's design. After the hammer strikes the primer and fires the round, the bullet travels down the barrel and reaches the gas port where gas is bled into the gas tube and back into the bolt carrier assembly. The diverted gas delivers a hammer-like blow and moves the carrier to the rear, unlocking the bolt, extracting and ejecting the fired cartridge. The buffer spring returns the bolt carrier forward, chambering a fresh round and locking the bolt into the barrel extension – the rifle is now ready to fire again. *Printed with permission of Colt Firearms.*

pounds; replacement of the one-piece handguard with a two-piece triangular handguard; magazine capacity reduced from 25 to 20 rounds and the switching of the selector lever settings. The Board found the AR15 to be nearly three times more reliable than the M14 in the development stages. Despite the positive conclusion of the test, Dr. Carten's report stated the AR15 had not demonstrated sufficient technical merit and should not be developed by the Army. Accordingly, the Ordnance Corps lost interest in the AR15.

When Bill Davis, at the time Chief of the Small Arms Branch at Aberdeen Proving Ground, first encountered the AR15, he was quite impressed and found it had no shortcomings that would not

be worked out in the normal course of development. Davis thought Carten's decision to drop the AR15 rifle was a bad one and that the weapon held great promise.

On February 19, 1959, Colt's Patent Firearms Manufacturing Company of Hartford, Connecticut purchased the rights to the AR15 and AR10 from Fairchild Stratos (ArmaLite) for a lump sum of $75,000 plus a royalty of four and a half percent on all further production of the AR15 and AR10. Colt also paid Cooper & Macdonald (a sales group who did a lot of work in Southeast Asia) $250,000 and a one percent royalty on all production of AR15 and AR10 rifles.

In July of 1960, Air Force General Curtis LeMay attended a Fourth of

The forward assist bolt closure mechanism. The M16A1 (*shown*) had the "*tear drop*" style while the new M16A2 has a round button style.

The evolution of the M16 to the M16A1 is very evident when the rifles are compared side by side. The M16 (*top*) and the M16A1 (*bottom*). Note the addition of the forward bolt assist, magazine fence guard "*BOSS*" and the "*birdcage*" flash suppressor on the M16A1.

July celebration where a Colt salesman placed three watermelons on a firing range at distances of 50, 100 and 150 yards – then gave General LeMay an AR15 and loaded magazines. Following this hands-on range evaluation, General LeMay ordered 80,000 rifles on the spot. However, Congress put the General's order on hold.

Concurrently, Colt had requested a re-trial from the Ordnance Corps to demonstrate improvements to the rifle. Initially the request was denied, the Ordnance Corps saying the military had no use for such a weapon. However, a request arrived at the Pentagon from Lackland Air Force Base requesting the AR15 be qualified as a candidate to replace M2 carbines. This turn of events caused Congress to investigate why the Ordnance Corps had boycotted the AR15. Subsequently, the Ordnance Corps set up the test without delay.

The test was concluded in November 1960. Three rifles were subjected to a light machine-gun test and two to accuracy tests. There were a total of 24,443 rounds fired. One rifle in the accuracy test delivered an amazing 10-round group at 100 yards that measured only 1.5 inches; any group under six inches at 100 yards being acceptable for an assault rifle. The rifle also performed admirably in the unlubricated, dust, extreme cold and rain tests. The final results indicated the AR15 was superior to all competitors, including the M14. The rifle was then approved for Air Force trial.

It took General LeMay three tries before his request was approved. In the summer of 1961, the Deputy Defense Secretary approved 8,500 AR15 rifles for the Air Force, pending congressional approval...which Congress withheld. General LeMay then brought the issue to President Kennedy, without

success. Finally, in May of 1962, the purchase was approved. With things warming up in Southeast Asia, the AR15 was about to meet the Army.

Many of the U.S. advisors in Vietnam were equipped with the new AR15 rifle. Rifles began to surface throughout Vietnam, totally outside the normal small arms procurement process. The first troops using the AR15 under combat conditions were very enthusiastic, preferring it to all other weapons. The South Vietnamese were impressed with the rifle, as well. In December 1961, Secretary of Defense Robert McNamara authorized a purchase of 1000 AR15s. There was further testing (Project AGILE) to explore the compatibility of the AR15 rifle to the smaller Vietnamese. The results indicated the AR15 was more suitable for the South Vietnamese military than the M2 carbine. In actual combat, the new 5.56x45mm cartridge was found to be more lethal than its 30-caliber counterparts.

While Project AGILE testing was being conducted, the Army completed the Hitch Report, which was a comparison of the AR15, AK47, M14 and M1 Garand. The report concluded that the AR15 was superior to the weapons to which it was compared.

Testing of the AR15 weapon system had met with contempt from the Ordnance Corps. In one test in the Arctic, weapons were malfunctioning at alarming rates. As soon as Gene Stoner heard, he was on the next plane to Fort Greeley, Alaska. He found parts misaligned, front sights

The combat 5.56x45mm. The M193 Ball Cartridge (*left*), 55-grain full metal jacket boattail bullet. The M855/SS109 Ball Cartridge (*right*), 62-grain full metal jacket boattail with a hardened steel penetrator core. Identified by the green tip.

removed (front sights held in with taper pins have no reason to ever be removed) and replaced with pieces of welding rod. With missing and damaged parts, there was no way the weapons would function properly and, with welding rod replacing the front sight, accuracy suffered. The arctic test was, in fact, rigged to make the AR15 look inadequate. Gene Stoner repaired all the weapons; the test resumed and the weapons performed admirably.

Fortunately, Defense Secretary McNamara was fond of the AR15, knew the Ordnance Corps was dragging its feet on the weapon and on January 23, 1963, halted all procurements of the M14. Finally, in 1964, Defense Secretary McNamara ordered the Ordnance Corps to work with all branches of the armed forces to get the AR15 ready for issue to all military personnel...one rifle for all branches. The Army purchased 100,000 rifles for issue to the Air Assault, Airborne, Ranger and Special Forces units.

After the AR15 – now, the M16 rifle – went into circulation, more was learned about how to improve the rifle. The rifling twist was changed from 1:14 inches to 1:12 inches. The Army wanted a manual bolt closure device added so, if the bolt failed to lock, it could be manually closed – and the forward assist assembly was born. The firing pin was lightened to prevent slam-fires (caused by the inertia of the firing pin when the bolt closed on a round). The buffer was changed from the original hollow version to one with weights in it to prevent the bolt from bouncing back when it slammed into the barrel extension.

On November 4, 1963, Colt was awarded a contract worth $13.5 million dollars for the procurement of

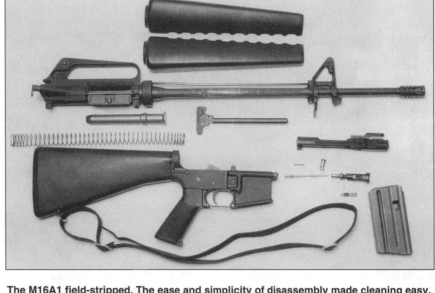

The M16A1 field-stripped. The ease and simplicity of disassembly made cleaning easy. All AR15/M16-series weapons disassemble in the same manner.

104,000 rifles...the legendary "*One Time Buy.*" Of those rifles, 19,000 were M16s for the Air Force and 85,000 were the XM16E1 (with the bolt closure device/forward assist assembly) for the Army and Marines. The XM16E1 was adopted as the M16A1 rifle. Steps were taken to procure ammunition.

Procurement of the ammunition is one of the main factors in the rifle's performance early in the Vietnam War. The initial ammunition used by DOD was made to Armalite/Colt specifications that called for IMR 4475 propellant. The weapon's reputation for durability and reliability was based on this ammo/extruded propellant combination. However, the military wanted to standardize propellants and the propellant used in the established 7.62x51mm NATO cartridge was Ball powder manufactured by Olin Corporation. So, when ammunition was ordered, Olin's Ball powder was used for the new 5.56x45mm M193 Ball

cartridge. Both powders created the desired 50,750 psi.

Ball (*spherical)* powder reaches its peak pressure significantly faster than extruded IMR powder. Ball powder generates larger amounts of carbon residue that clogs the gas tube and barrel port, causing the firearm to malfunction. The most serious malfunctions, during the early use of Ball powder, involved extraction problems and a significant increase in the cyclic rate of fire. Despite having this information, the Department Of Defense still approved use of Ball powder. Gene Stoner was approach by Frank Vee of the OSD Comptrollers office after the package was approved and asked what he (Gene Stoner) thought of the use of Ball powder. Stoner asked, "*Why are you asking me now?*" Vee said, "*I would have felt better if you would have approved the package.*" Stoner replied, "*Well, now we both don't feel so good.*"

The "*One-Time Buy*" was now a thing of the past. The original $13.5 million contract turned into a $17,994,694.23 contract. There were an additional 33,500 rifles that went to the Air Force, 240 to the Navy and 82 to the Coast Guard. Over $517,000 worth of spare parts was ordered.

The first field performance reports, from the 5th Special

The battle cartridges of the 20th Century (*left to right*): 7.62x63mm (30-06 Springfield); 8mm Mauser; 7.62x54mm Russian; 7.92x33mm Kurtz; 30 US Carbine; 7.62x51mm NATO (308 Winchester); 7.62x39mm Soviet; 5.56x45mm NATO (223 Remington) and the 5.45x39mm Soviet.

Which is the better assault rifle? The M16A1 (*top*) or the AKM/AK47 (*bottom*)? Both are the most prolific military rifles of the last half of the 20th century; the most tested and most produced all over the world. Author feels hands-down winner is the M16 series.

Forces in Vietnam, were excellent. The rifle had been well received and was very popular, although instruction manuals were in "short supply." During the investigation by the Ichord Subcommittee of the M-16 Rifle Program, Honorable Richard Ichord said – regarding the rifle's reputation with the North Vietnamese Army and Vietcong – *"I understand that they refer to this rifle as "black rifle,"...I have heard their motto is "Beware of the units with the black rifles"*... they have been possessed with deadly fear." In September 1965, General Westmoreland ordered an additional 100,000 rifles and requested all U.S. ground forces in Vietnam be equipped with the new M16A1 rifles. Colt now signed an additional contract to deliver 25,000 rifles a month by December 1966. In 1968, GM Hydramatic Division and Harrington & Richardson were awarded second-source contracts from the Department of Defense.

Letters from the field began reporting the rifles were malfunctioning at an alarming rate, with U.S. troops found dead next to jammed M16 rifles. Spent cartridge cases were becoming lodged in the chamber and the only way to remove them was to knock them out with a cleaning rod. Requests were made for Colt to send a representative to the field to solve this problem. This turn of events was highly publicized by the media.

A representative from Colt, Mr. Kanemitsu Ito, went to Vietnam and claimed to be shocked, having never seen equipment in such poor shape. He claimed to have looked down the barrel of one rifle and not seen 'daylight' due to severe rusting and pitting. Many of the troops he spoke to said they were never trained to maintain their rifle, that the rifle was "*self-cleaning*" and that they had not handled an M16/M16A1 rifle until they arrived "*In-Country.*" Subsequently, Mr. Ito gave classes on maintenance all over South Vietnam.

Seeking an independent, unbiased report of the true field performance situation, the Ichord Congressional Subcommittee selected a retired officer, Colonel Crossman, as their representative and sent him to Vietnam. In the course of his investigation, he interviewed 250 soldiers and Marines throughout South Vietnam – fully 50 percent of whom reported malfunctions with their M16/M16A1 rifles. Of these malfunctions, 90 percent were failures to extract. Col. Crossman found 22-caliber cleaning kits in short supply and concluded many of the problems were due to lack of maintenance and cleaning. He also felt there was room for improvement in the rifle. He concluded, *"It was not possible to correlate ammunition make or type with malfunctions."* His findings report, dated June 16, 1967, included the state-

ment that the rifle needed a complete overhaul in design and manufacture.

According to Gene Stoner, there were hardly any 22-caliber cleaning kits in Vietnam – and no instruction manuals. The 'cleanup' began: The military developed bore and chamber cleaning brushes and began to distribute 22-caliber cleaning kits, firearm maintenance cards and instruction manuals, for the M16/M16A1 rifles.

From May 15th through August 22nd, 1967, the much-publicized Ichord Congressional Subcommittee (*Honorable Richard Ichord, Chairman*) investigated the history, development, testing, procurement and foreign sales of the M16 rifle. During the investigation, the subcommittee visited U.S. military training installations – of all branches – where the committee members interviewed hundreds of Vietnam returnees on their experiences with the M16/M16A1 rifle. They also visited South Vietnam to interview troops in combat zones. Several people were called to testify before the subcommittee. Two topics, not identified until after the subcommittee returned from Vietnam, were the propellant and high cyclic rate issues; the subcommittee would focus most of their attention on these two aspects.

Reports from Vietnam of failures to extract in the field caused the subcommittee great concern. They investigated; finding the major contributor to malfunctions was ammunition assembled using Ball powder. The change from IMR extruded powder to Ball powder in 1964 for the 5.56mm ammunition was neither justified nor supported by test data, they found. The subcommittee also found the Ball propellant sole-source position enjoyed by Olin Mathieson for many years – and their close relationship with the Army – may have influenced Army Materiel Command. They felt the AR15/M16 rifle, as initially developed, was an excellent and reliable weapon. Further, certain modifications made to the rifle at the insistence of the Army – also unsupported by test data – were unnecessary. For example, both the Air Force and the Marine Corps found no evidence to support the expense and possible problems of the manual bolt closure (*forward assist*) device.

Gene Stoner was called to testify at the congressional hearings to explain the extraction problem; he explained the failure to extract was due to the use of ball powder.

Gene Stoner [To Mr. Bray]: *"Well, the cartridge tends to stick-under high residual pressure in the barrel, and of course with this too-soon action you also have a higher bolt velocity. In other words, your bolt is trying to open at higher speeds, so you have a aggravated condition where the cartridge is tending to stick in there a little longer or a little harder, and you are also giving it a harder jerk by driving the bolt faster."*

Mr. Bray [To Gene Stoner]: *"Then a faster rate of fire could cause that situation (failure to extract)?"*

Gene Stoner [To Mr. Bray]: *"This is probably one of the worst conditions you can get, by increasing the cyclic rate."*

Basically, Ball propellant causes the bolt to open prematurely, before the spent cartridge case has had sufficient time to contract. The result is the extractor shears off the rim of the spent cartridge case – which sticks in the chamber. Ball and IMR powders create the same peak pressure but the Ball powder reaches its peak much faster than IMR powder, causing a significant increase in the cyclic rate of fire. Ball powder leaves significantly more fouling in the chamber and bolt assembly. Gene Stoner also pointed out the rifle had gone through more than 22 changes from his original design and neither Colt nor the Department of Defense consulted him on how some changes would impact his design.

The forward assist was one of the changes on which he was not con-

Specifications Table

	M16/M16A1 Rifles	M16A2 Rifles
Caliber	5.56x45mm NATO	5.56x45mm NATO
	M193 Ball	M855 Ball/M193 Ball
Method of Operation	Gas	Gas
Locking System	Rotating Bolt	Rotating Bolt
Type of Fire	Selective	Semi/ 3-Shot Burst
Weight Empty	7 pounds	7.9 pounds
Magazine Capacity	20 & 30 Rounds	20 & 30 Rounds
Barrel Length	20 inches	20 inches
Overall Length	39 inches	39.624 inches
Technical Data	Rifling: 6 grooves, right hand twist, 1 turn in 12 inches	Rifling: 6 grooves, right hand twist, 1 turn in 7 inches
Sights	**Front;** post with elevation adj.	**Front;** post with elevation adj.
	Rear; L-type aperture windage adj. only.	**Rear;** L-type aperture adj. windage and elevation
Cyclic Rate	750 to 950 RPM	750 to 950 RPM
Practical Rate of Fire	150-200 RPM, Automatic	150-200 RPM, Automatic
Muzzle Velocity	M193 Ball- 3,250 fps.	M193 Ball- 3,250 fps. M855 Ball- 3,100 fps.
Muzzle Energy	M193 Ball- 1,270 ft/lb	M193 Ball- 1,270 ft/lb M855 Ball- 1,302 ft/lb
Cooling	Air	Air
Maximum Effective	460 Meters/ 503 yards	M193 Ball-460 meters/ 503 yards
Range	(Individual / Point Targets)	M855 Ball-550 meters/ 600 yards
	(Area Target)	M855 Ball-800 meters/ 875 yards
Maximum Range	2,653 Meters/ 2,902 yards	M193 Ball-2, 653 meters/ 2,902 yards
		M855 Ball-3, 600 meters/ 3,935 yards

sulted and Mr. Ichord asked Gene Stoner his opinion of the device.

Gene Stoner [To Mr. Ichord]: *"I wasn't in on that, except I was told the Army insisted on it. There were reasons for it. One reason was that they felt that due to the fact that the M-1, and the M-14 rifle, and the carbine had always had something for a soldier to push on; that maybe this would be a comforting feeling to him, or something. I could never quite get it through my mind that it was necessary. I did not really advise it. I thought it was a*

mistake, myself. But I made my thought known to the people-"

He explained the last thing you want to do is force a round into a dirty chamber, which quickly leads to function failures. The chamber fouling tends to embed in the soft brass cartridge case and lock it in, causing a fired cartridge case to be – literally – locked into the chamber at the moment of extraction. Gene Stoner was able to prove the rifle and ammunition combination he furnished to Armalite/Colt was a totally reliable weapon system and the change the military made, without his consent, caused the malfunctions. He told the committee he expressed these concerns to the OSD Comptrollers office and was ignored. The subcommittee accepted this as the reason for the condition.

M16 rifle project manager, Col. Yout, was of particular interest to the subcommittee. Throughout the hearing he was accused of making irresponsible decisions as to the direction of the program.

Mr.Ichord[to Col. Yout]: *We have evidence and are advised by our experts…that Ball propellant, which you apparently speak so highly of, does have an adverse affect upon the operation of the M16 rifle. It speeded up the cyclic rate. It is dirtier burning…When we are also advised that the Army was cautioned against making this change from IMR to Ball propellant…Naturally, we would be quite concerned. Apparently you aren't so concerned. I don't understand your explanation. I just haven't been able to understand you - but perhaps you haven't offered the information in words I can understand. Would you care to say something?* He never replied to the question.

The Army made a statement on July 27, 1967: *"From the vantage point of retrospect, it has sometimes been suggested that the particular behavior of Ball propellant should have been predicted…Had the Army anticipated these develop-*

The CAR15 (*Colt Automatic Rifle 15*) gained major popularity with the development of the new M4 and M4A1 carbine. Note the telescoping stock and the shorter barrel. Most CAR15 rifles were issued with a 14.5-inch barrel.

ments, it is most unlikely that the course chosen in January, 1964, would probably have been the same. A decision to reduce the velocity requirement, and continue loading IMR4475 propellant would probably have been made instead, and development of alternate propellants could have been pursued more deliberately."

This is the closest to an admission of negligence by the Army for the decision to use Ball powder. Gene

Stoner warned them long before it got to this point; who would know more about the rifle's performance and design intent than the man who designed it? In the end, the rifle was not the problem; instead, this was an ammunition-driven problem that altered the design intent of the rifle.

In August 1967, the hearings ended, and in October 1967, the subcommittee concluded *"Grave mismanagement, errors of judgment and lack of responsibility had characterized the Army's handling of the entire M16 program."* They stated the officials in the Department of the Army were aware of the adverse affect of Ball propellant on the cyclic rate of the M16 rifle as early as March 1964, yet continued to accept delivery of additional thousands of rifles that were not subjected to acceptance or endurance tests using Ball propellant. All Colt endurance testing was done using IMR 4475. The subcommittee also concluded

"The failure on the part of officials with authority in the Army to cause action to be taken to correct the deficiencies of the 5.56mm ammunition borders on criminal negligence."

The cyclic rate of the rifle was increased 10 to 15 percent (approximately 200 rounds per minute), resulting in higher stress on certain components caused by the higher velocity of the bolt carrier assembly. As a result, there were parts driven beyond their working parameters – as well as the bolt opening prematurely. Many parts were changed to more stringent specifications to help deal with the higher pressure curve and harder impact. To solve the chamber corrosion and failure-to-extract issues, all future production rifle barrels would be chrome-lined. Even though chrome-lining barrels is a military specification, Ordinance failed to require this basic requirement on the AR15/M16 rifle system.

Chrome-lining the barrels gave three major improvements to the

standard barrel. First, the chrome-lined barrel was corrosion resistant. Second, chrome is slippery in nature and assists in extraction and ejection. When chromed, the walls of the chamber are harder; sand and mud don't 'iron' into them. Thirdly, chrome is 2 to 3 times harder than standard barrel steel so the barrel lasts significantly longer. The new, improved M16 / M16A1 barrel assemblies would have stamped on the barrel, in front of the front sight assembly: "**C**" (*Chrome Chamber Only*), "**C MP B**" (*Chrome Chamber, Barrel & Magnetic Resonance Tested*) or "**C MP Chrome Bore**"(*Chrome Chamber, Barrel & Magnetic Resonance Tested*).

Many experts, including Bill Davis, felt the failure to chrome the chamber was responsible for many of the early malfunctions in Vietnam.

The flash hider was changed from the early three-prong to the new *"bird cage"* style. The three-prong suppressor was superior to the new design, but was snag-prone in the field. With these modifications in place, the M16/M16A1 rifle was *"perfected"* and performing to the Department of Defense acceptance standards.

The AR15/M16 Carbines

Soon there was a demand for a smaller, more compact, version of the rifle. Early in 1966, the Army expressed interest for a carbine for its special operation units, placing an order totaling some 2,050 carbines. Lt. Col. Yout later ordered an additional 765 Colt "Commandos" – and a new name was coined for the carbine project. The first carbines were known as CAR15 (Colt Automatic Rifle). These first designs incorporated a 10-inch barrel and a sliding butt stock. Later the barrel was changed to 11.4 inches to permit the weapon to launch grenades. The Army signed a contract for 2,815 *"Commando model"* submachine guns on June 28, 1966.

As expected, the CAR15 – now the XM177E2 – successfully passed all testing phases at Aberdeen Proving Ground. However, a new problem appeared: the deafening noise and large fireball from the muzzle, thanks to the CAR15's higher cyclic rate of 700 to 1,000 rounds per minute. As a remedy, many of these rifles were equipped with 14.5-inch barrels, a practice that carried over to the M4 project of the early 1980s.

Product Improvement (PIP)

On October 28, 1980, there was a new 5.56x45mm cartridge on the block. NATO (Northern Atlantic Treaty Organization) had adopted the Belgian-made SS109. This new bullet had two major differences from the GI 5.56x45mm M193 Ball cartridge:

First, the bullet weighed 62 grains instead of 55 grains.

Second, this new bullet had a hardened steel penetrator core, giving this new 5.56x45mm round better penetration at all distances than the 7.62x51mm NATO (M80 Ball) round. This new SS109 round penetrated three 3.5mm mild steel plates at 640 meters and a U.S. issue helmet at 1,300 meters.

The new 5.56x45mmNATO round revolutionized military small arms ammunition all over the world. In 1974, the Soviet Union switched from the 7.62x39mm (AK47/AKM) to the 5.45x39mm Soviet round of the new AK74 rifle. This new round was a .221-inch diameter 52-grain full metal jacket boat-tail armor-piercing bullet with a velocity of 3000 fps.

The new SS109 round was more lethal than the original M193 Ball round due to the faster 'spin' and fragmentation upon impact with soft tissue.

The SR25, perhaps the most accurate autoloader on the face of the earth. Gene Stoner revives his original AR10 design, with some added features of the M16A2, to build this semi-automatic 7.62x51mm sniper rifle.

Military surgeons all over the world have asked the United Nations to ban small caliber high-velocity rounds in combat – including the 5.56x45mm and the 5.45x39mm cartridges – which they believe cause unnecessary pain and suffering.

Switzerland re-designed the M855/SS109 round with a thicker jacket to stop fragmentation upon impact. This new cartridge, however, was significantly more accurate at longer ranges than the M193 Ball cartridge, boosting the maximum effective range to 800 meters. To accommodate this new cartridge, a new barrel twist – from 1:12 inches to 1:7 inches – was required to stabilize the heavier 62-grain bullet.

There was a catch: the SS109 ammunition could not be fired accurately in an M16/M16A1 rifle due to its slower rifling twist. The bullet would not stabilize and would *"keyhole"* in flight. This new cartridge was about to be adopted as the M855 Ball cartridge of the U.S. military and the new PIP project would re-design the M16A1 rifle around this cartridge.

The United States Marine Corps began negotiations with Colt in January of 1980, asking for three modified rifles that would make use of the new FN SS109/XM855 cartridge and would incorporate four Marine-designated changes:

- The sights must be adjustable to 800 meters.
- The bullet must be accurate to 800 meters and possess the capability to penetrate all known steel helmets and body armor at 800 meters.
- The strength of the plastic stock, pistol grip and handguards – as well as the strength of the exposed portion of the barrel – must be improved.
- The rifle must have the full-auto capability replaced with a 3-shot burst mode.

The Joint Services Small Arms Program (JSSAP) PIP

The first rifles arrived from Colt in November of 1981. The USMC Firepower Division at Quantico, Virginia, would lead the PIP project. On November 11th, 20 Marines and 10 soldiers from the 197th Infantry Brigade at Fort Benning, Georgia, would take 30 M16A1 rifles and 30 M16A1E1 (PIP rifles) and test them for a month. The test report was issued on December 11th and the conclusions were as follows:

- The sights were easily adjusted in the field by hand rather than with a bullet tip.
- Increased the effectiveness at long range, more so than the M16A1.
- More durable plastic furniture on the M16A1E1, for hand-to-hand combat.
- Sights were better for low-light conditions thanks to a larger-diameter (5mm) close-range aperture in the rear sight.
- Increased ammunition conservation and more effective fire with the 3-round burst than with full-auto fire.
- Utilized the XM855 NATO (SS109) ammunition, which improves the accuracy and penetration at all ranges.

The product-improvement (PIP) "M16A1E1" was classified as the **M16A2** in September of 1982 and was adopted by the United States Marine Corps in November of 1983. The Marines ordered 76,000 M16A2 rifles from Colt. The Army did not adopt the M16A2 until 1986.

The M16A2 Rifle

There were twelve major changes from the M16A1 to the M16A2 and, although the rifles seem similar at first glance, they are two totally different weapons. Many improvements were necessary to accommodate the new M855 Ball and M856 tracer rounds. The twelve major variances – between the A1 and A2 – are as follows:

1. The flash suppresser of the M16A1 is now a muzzle brake/compensator on the M16A2. Instead of having vents all around the flash suppresser, the bottom has been left solid, which reduces muzzle climb and prevents dust from flying when firing from the prone position.
2. The barrel, from the front sight assembly to the flash suppressor/compensator, is heavier. The M16A1 rifles barrels were known to bend when paratroopers landed and the barrels hit the ground. When the A1 barrels would heat up, sling tension could bend them. The new M16A2 barrels had a rifling twist of 1:7 inches to accommodate the SS109/M855 cartridge.
3. The front sight post on the M16A2 is square, contrasted to the round post of the M16A1.

The M16A2 is mechanically identical to the M16 and the M16A1. The only difference is the 3-round burst selector setting in lieu of full-auto. All the changes were improvements to accuracy, more durable stock and grips as well as some structural reinforcements.

4. The M16A2 handguard was redesigned to have an interchangeable, upper and lower, round ribbed handguard.

5. The slip-ring *"delta ring"* was redesigned and is now canted for easier removal of the handguards.

6. A spent shell deflector was added to the upper receiver behind the ejection port of the M16A2 to accommodate left-hand shooters and, as well, the pivot pin area of the upper receiver has been strengthened. The area around the buffer tube extension (takedown pin area) was strengthened to prevent cracking during hand-to-hand combat or from impact on the butt of the weapon while cushioning one's fall.

7. The rear sight was redesigned. The 1.75mm and 5mm apertures made adjustable for windage as well as elevation. The maximum elevation setting is 800 meters. There is still an "L-shaped" sight aperture, and there is a 5mm aperture battle sight effective to 200 meters.

8. The forward assist assembly was changed from the "tear drop" style of the M16A1 to the new round "button" style forward assist assembly of the M16A2.

9. The pistol grip is now made of a stronger plastic (™Zytel), and incorporates a "swell" below the middle finger position.

10. The three-shot Burst selector lever setting of the M16A2 replaced the Auto setting of the M16A1.

11. The 5/8-inch longer M16A2 stock is made from foam-filled nylon, said to be ten to twelve times stronger than the fibrite stocks of the M16 /M16A1.

12. The buttplate has been made stronger (™Zytel), and the entire buttplate is checkered. The trapdoor can be opened by hand rather requiring the tip of a cartridge.

Critics Attack the M16A2

There were critics who still found problems with the M16A2. One of the greatest criticisms was the substitution of the *Burst* mode for the *Automatic* mode selector option. The critics reasoned the M16 rifle was adopted because U.S. troops felt outgunned by the North Vietnamese Army /Viet Cong who were equipped with full-auto AK47s. While, theoretically, the 3-round burst was more effective than full-auto fire, there was no substitute for a well-trained automatic rifleman. More recently, infantry units have noticed it takes more time to clear rooms and buildings in the MOUT environment (Military Operations in Urban Terrain) with the three-round burst versus the full-auto mode and feel the full-auto option is desirable in those circumstances.

Not only was the conceptual validity of the three-round *Burst* under scrutiny, but the mechanical design as well. The burst mechanism does not recycle. If only two rounds were fired – because the trigger was not held long enough or the weapon ran out of ammunition – the next time the trigger was pulled only one round would fire.

Further, some critics found the sighting system too complex. The Canadian military addressed many of the issues brought up by American military critics. When Canada replaced their aging FN FAL 7.62mmNATO rifles, they modeled the new rifle after the M16A2. Their Diemaco-manufactured C7 was, virtually, an M16A2 that retained the rear sight and the full-auto setting of the M16A1. Some critics did not like the fact that the new M855 cartridge could not be fired in the current issue M16 /M16A1 rifles without raising concerns that the fast 1:7-inch rifling twist would more quickly burn out barrels during extended rapid fire.

The "Shorty" Program Revisited: The M4 Carbine.

In 1994, the Army adopted the second carbine of the 20th century and the first general issue carbine since 1941: The M4 - perhaps the finest carbine ever developed. They were, at first, to be used by special operation units – but then were selected for use in many other units. Deliveries began in August of 1994, from Colt's Manufacturing, for 24,000 M4 carbines contracted at $11 million; another contract followed in 1995 for 16,217 M4A1 carbines.

The M4 is basically a M16A2 with a telescoping butt stock and a 14.5-inch barrel. The barrel has the heavy profile of the M16A2 barrel with a modified groove to accommodate the M203 grenade launcher. With its 14.5-inch barrel, the M4 fires the M855 Ball round at 2900 fps. The M4

The latest in the M16 family: the M16A2. The standard by which all assault rifles are judged. Note major changes: fully adjustable rear sight, round handguards, longer stock, finger swell on pistol grip and cartridge case deflector. Note the 25-meter 'zeroing' target.

incorporates the M16A2 fully adjustable rear sight. Colt's Manufacturing claims there is little, if any, difference in accuracy at ranges up to 500/600 meters. M4 carbines can be found with either full-auto or burst settings. The M4 duplicates the reliability and accuracy of the full-size rifle and weighs only 5.65 pounds.

The M4 has two variants: the standard M4 and the M4A1. The M4A1 is identical to the M4 with the exception of its removable carrying handle, which is attached to a Picatinny Weaver Rail system. This arrangement enables easy attachment of optical sighting systems or, by reattaching the carrying handle, use of the iron sights.

Rebirth of the AR10, Further Developments by Gene Stoner

The legacy of the ArmaLite rifles is far from over. The great weapons designer, Eugene Stoner, never stopped working on his AR10 design. He, along with C. Reed Knight of Knight's Manufacturing, perfected the AR10 and added many design features of the M16A2, to build the SR25 (**S**toner **R**ifle model **25**). The model number comes from adding the 10 from the AR10 and the 15 from the AR15. Basically the SR25 looks like an M16 on steroids, beefed up to accommodate the 30-caliber round. The SR25 Match rifle is a 7.62x51mmNATO sniper rifle. Knight's Manufacturing is one of the only manufacturers that guarantee their rifle will shoot one minute of angle at 100 yards using factory 168-grain Match 7.62x51mm NATO/308 Winchester ammunition. This rifles incorporates the 5R rifling sniper barrel manufactured by Remington

Arms for the M24 sniper rifle. Knight's Manufacturing is the only company to which Remington has ever sold these precision barrel blanks. The 5R rifling is designed to optimize the use of 168-grain Match 7.62x51mmNATO/308 Winchester ammunition. Many firearms experts claim the SR25 is the most accurate semi-automatic rifle in the world.

In May of 2000, the U.S. Navy SEALS adopted the SR25 – now classified as the Mk 11 Mod 0 – as a full weapons system: rifle, Leupold scope, back-up pop-up iron sights and a sound suppresser. This is a modified SR25 Match rifle, which has a 20-inch barrel instead of 24-inch barrel. Following this sale, the U.S. Army Rangers also purchased SR25 rifles.

Production Sources of Civilian/Military Versions of the AR15/M16

The AR15 rifle has been copied all over the world, in military and sporting configurations. The Canadian military adopted the C7 as it's main battle rifle. The C7, literally a modified M16A2 rifle, is manufactured by Diemaco of Ontario, Canada, an unknown company to most of the world but a large player in this weapon system. Diemaco has supplied their C7 and C8 weapons systems to Denmark, Norway, New Zealand and the Netherlands. They also equip the legendary British SAS and SBS with their SFW (Special Forces Weapon), designated the British L119A1 Assault Rifle. There have also been other military copies of the M16-series rifle made by Elisco Tool Company of the Philippines and Chartered Industries of Singapore.

Currently manufacturing the M16A2 and M4 carbines for the U.S.

military are Colt's Manufacturing Inc, Hartford, Connecticut and FN Manufacturing of Columbia, South Carolina. Quality Parts/Bushmaster Firearms of Windham, Maine have manufactured approximately 400 complete M4 carbines for the United States Department of Defense as well as an additional (approximately) 400 complete M4 upper receivers assemblies.

The semi-automatic Colt AR15/Sporter-series rifles have become very popular in the world of competitive shooters. Colt's Manufacturing Company, Inc. manufactures more civilian versions of the rifle than any other manufacturer, even though there are many other semi-auto clones produced. One of the finest is the XM15E2S, made by Quality Parts/Bushmaster Firearms. Some other manufacturers are Olympic Arms of Olympia, Washington and ArmaLite, Inc., a division of Eagle Arms of Coal Valley, Illinois.

The AR15/M16 rifle has come a long way, surviving political opposition and its troubles in Vietnam to become one of the finest military rifles ever produced, with more than 9 million M16-series rifles in service throughout the world, equipping the troops of more than 20 nations. The U.S. military has always been a military of marksmen, and the M16A2 complements this philosophy, setting a standard of accuracy very few assault rifles can match while enjoying the reputation of being the finest human-engineered assault rifle in the world. The M16-series rifle continues to be the rifle of choice of SWAT teams and police departments all over the country, and it will be the main battle rifle of the United States well into the new millennium. ●

Charles Newton and His Big Game 22 Rifle

by Hollis M. Flint

"The present and ever growing scarcity of game, with the ever increasing army of hunters, makes the shots farther apart than they used to be. Therefore it becomes more and more important that, when a shot is offered, the weapon at hand will not only hit but kill cleanly and quickly."

Charles Newton, Outdoor Life, August 1912

LAID OUT NEATLY on the bedroom floor were about two dozen rifles and shotguns. *"Bob has gotten too old to shoot anymore."* my friend told me. *"These are from his collection and I am selling them for him."* I surveyed the spread, mostly current models, until I came to a vaguely familiar bolt-action rifle in the middle of one row. *"Is that a Newton?"* I asked, pointing to the rifle. I had seen my first and only Newton rifle two months before, a gift from

author Zane Grey to his hunting guide "Babe" Haught. That Newton, a 30-06, hangs in the Payson, Arizona, Historical Museum. *"Yes, but it*

Charles Newton, President, Newton Arms Company. Newton was born into a farming family in New York state in 1868. His endeavors included school teacher, lawyer, national guardsman and finally firearms inventor, promoter, and manufacturer. The picture is taken from Newton's 1914 catalog.

has been rebarreled." "What caliber is it now?" I inquired. *"The barrel is marked P.O. Ackley .22 Newton."* my friend responded. I bought the rifle, knowing nothing at all about Newton rifles or the 22 Newton cartridge. For sure I planned to shoot it.

The first step toward appreciating my Newton rifle was to figure out how it went together and functioned. I discovered the instructions I needed in the chapter "Newton Original Turnbolt" in Frank De Haas' book *Bolt Action Rifles*. Suffice to say you need these instructions as disassembly is not like the Mauser system and is not self-evident. It is in disassembly that the advanced design of the Newton action is revealed.

The Newton action features a one piece bolt with multiple interrupted screw-type front locking lugs and recessed bolt face. Newton held that multiple lugs greatly reduce the shock load on each lug and thus the possibility of fracturing the bolt head. Also, multiple lugs increase the extractive force of bolt lift. Other features include Mauser-type extractor, one-piece striker, staggered column box magazine, and an extremely strong flat top receiver with square threads to receive the barrel shank. Unlike the 1903 Springfield and Mauser, the receiver is entirely free of projections above the stock. The rear contour of the receiver accepts 1903 Springfield receiver sights. Like the Mauser, the bolt sleeve seals the rear of the action. The bolt sleeve holds a three-position safety that blocks the striker and prevents bolt lift. Feeding is of the controlled-round type of the Mauser action. However, the bolt can be closed on a chambered round. Bolt lift does not interfere with a low mounted scope but the original receiver was not drilled and tapped. Newton's 1915 catalog states that "— *a telescopic sight [may be] mounted above the center of the receiver and just as close to the receiver as may be desired.*" The action is fitted with an excellent double-set

trigger of Newton's design that functions much like those used in European Mauser sporting rifles. Pulling the front trigger allows removal of the bolt. Bolt disassembly, clever but simple, is outlined by De Haas. De Haas concluded that the original Newton action was a superior design.

My Ackley barrel is 26 inches long and fitted with a front sight which appears to be original Newton. The bore is rifled with five square-cut grooves with the correct 1-in-8 inch twist. Original 22 Newton barrels were 24 inches long and cut with Newton-Pope "segmental rifling" having five rounded shallow grooves. Newton noted that his barrels with segmental rifling (the grooves are segments of a circle) have "*greater durability, increased accuracy, less strain on bullet jackets, and clean as easily as a shotgun.*" Newton mounted a rear sight, with one upright and one folding leaf, by means of a barrel band and set screw. Or you could order Newton's "bull strong" bolt peep sight.

The stock of my rifle is original and numbered to the action as are all major parts except the barrel. The Newton stock was developed in cooperation with Fred Adolph and Ludwig Wundhammer, well-known gunsmiths of the time, and follows the classic German style with gentle pistol grip curve and *schnable*

pounds with steel buttplate and grip cap. With a heavier barrel, my rifle weighs seven and one half pounds without scope. Rifles in 30 to 35 Newton weighed close to eight pounds. The price in 1918 was $76.50, more than three times the cost of a Model 94 Winchester.

The take-down system allows disassembly without tools. The hinged magazine floorplate acts as a lever and unscrews from a stud in the square recoil lug of the receiver. The barrel and receiver are then lifted and removed from a dovetailed metal tang fixed to the stock at the rear of the receiver. A long bolt through the metal pistol grip cap, combined with the rear trigger guard screw, holds the tang in place. This arrangement strengthens the vulnerable grip area of the stock.

I found that there are several variations of the Newton rifle. Newton, a lawyer by trade, organized his first company in 1914 in Buffalo, N.Y. Initially German Mauser 98 actions were to be barreled to 256, 30, 33, and 35 Newton proprietary cartridges. Note that none of Newton's magnum-class cartridges were encumbered with a headspacing belt, and all were 30-06 length. The extensive 1915 Newton catalog first described the 22 Newton cartridge, designed in 1913, which was based on the 7mm Mauser cartridge. The war soon brought an end to the supply of Mauser actions, only one shipment of 256 Newton Mausers was delivered. Springfield 1903 actions were considered, but also were not

Barrel inscription on my rebarreled Newton rifle leaves no doubt about who did the work.

The Newton rifle is modern except for excessive drop at comb and small knob on bolt handle. It handles very nicely.

forend tip. My stock has neither cheek piece nor Wundhammer palm swell. The wood is straight-grained walnut and has the dimensions advertised by Newton: 14-inch length of pull and drop at comb and heel of 1 3/4 and 2 7/8 inches, respectively. The complete rifle was listed at seven

readily available. Newton assembled kits containing 256 Newton barrels and sporting stocks produced by Marlin Firearms to fit 1903 Springfield actions. Jim Foral described his 256 Newton Springfield, built from one of these kits, in the 1998 issue of *GUNS ILLUSTRATED*.

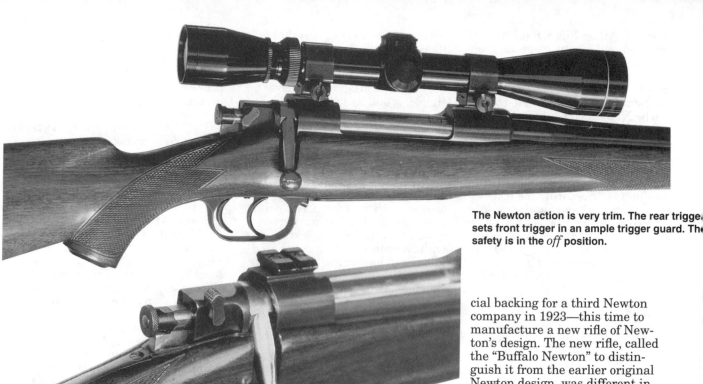

The Newton action is very trim. The rear trigger sets front trigger in an ample trigger guard. The safety is in the *off* position.

The three-position safety is shown in the *safe* position with the bolt locked. The firing position is obtained by flipping the safety to the rear and down.

Newton next turned his inventive genius to designing and manufacturing his own rifle. The "original" Newton rifle was the result and is described above. Production of the original Newton rifle began in 1917 at Newton's factory in Buffalo, New York. As previously noted, the 30-06 was an option to Newton's proprietary cartridges. Cartridges were manufactured by Newton from brass supplied by Remington and U.S. Cartridge Company. Under Newton's direction, the rifle was made of quality materials and high standards were set. All parts were interchangeable by the owner, *"whether he be located in Buffalo or China,"* according to Newton. Machining chrome vanadium steel receivers and bolts, complicated inletting of walnut stocks and extensive gauging of parts required considerable effort in manufacture. Newton's rifle did not lend itself to mass production and his company went bankrupt in 1918. He had turned out about 2400 rifles. The receiver of the company assets completed an additional 1600 rifles of the original design. Only 400 of these receivership rifles passed inspection by the receiver and were sold. The dubious remaining rifles were sold to a group of New York dealers in 1919. These dealers then retailed them for $5.00 each because the workmanship was so poor (thereby soiling Newton's reputation). Thus, a total of about 4000 original Newton rifles went into circulation. My rifle, serial number 1537, was likely one of those produced under Newton's direction in 1917. Its workmanship is of the highest quality. However, serial numbers cannot be used to determine production dates according to Bruce Jennings.

For the record, the world's expert on Charles Newton and his rifles is Bruce Jennings of Sheridan, Wyoming. His 1984 book *Charles Newton, Father of High Velocity* contains a 480-page collection of just about everything published on Newton and his rifles including articles by Newton, catalogs, and related correspondence. Mr. Jennings has an extensive collection of Newton rifles and ammunition for reference. I found him very willing to answer questions about my Newton rifle and handloading 22 Newton cartridges.

Newton started his second company in 1919, again in Buffalo, N.Y. The new rifles were to be made on Mauser 98 actions for 256, 30 and 35 Newton cartridges and ammunition to be manufactured by Western Cartridge Co. Again, a hesitant supply of imported actions lead to undelivered orders and stalemate. The orders, however, brought the finan-cial backing for a third Newton company in 1923—this time to manufacture a new rifle of Newton's design. The new rifle, called the "Buffalo Newton" to distinguish it from the earlier original Newton design, was different in several respects. However, the results of the endeavor ended the same way as Newton's first company: bankruptcy. About 1000 Buffalo Newton rifles were manufactured between 1925 and 1929.

Phil Sharpe, in his book *The Rifle in America*, attributed Newton's failures to lack of uniform quality because *"He did not know precision manufacturing methods."* Bruce Jennings takes exception to Sharpe: *"I do not feel it is fair for Sharpe to label Newton as an incompetent manufacturer because of the defective and inferior rifles manufactured by others and beyond his control."* Jennings further notes *"— rifles that passed [Newton's] inspection were nicely fitted and well made —."*

Undaunted, Newton approached Marlin to produce a third Newton rifle design, the "LeverBolt." In the final chapter, Newton's LeverBolt Rifle Company, with rifles to be produced by Marlin, never got into production. Newton died in 1932, at the age of 63, at his home in New Haven, Connecticut. Bruce Jennings owns the only extant prototype of the LeverBolt (Jennings 1996). A detailed account by M. D. Waite of Newton's rifle business appeared in the *American Rifleman*, May, 1971.

The 22 Newton, like all of Newton's cartridge designs, stressed high velocity. The original catalog description of the 22 Newton cartridge indicates a muzzle velocity of 3100 fps with a 90-grain .228 diameter spitzer bullet. To stabilize the long bullet, Newton used a 1-in-8 inch twist. Although Newton intended his 22 cartridge for big game, very few Newton rifles of any model were

Detail of the stud and floor plate lever that allows takedown of the Newton rifle into two pieces. Zeroing of the rifle is not effected by takedown and reassembly.

chambered for it. Bruce Jennings has seen or heard of about a dozen original 22 Newton rifles. Phil Sharpe, who interviewed Newton in 1926, indicates that the inventor manufactured few of his rifles in 22 Newton because he felt his 256 Newton cartridge was superior for big game. The 256 Newton was obviously a better cartridge for general big game hunting. With a .264 diameter 120-grain bullet at an advertised 3100 fps, it is not far behind the 270 Winchester (Haviland, 1997). The 256, 30 and 35 Newton cartridges became the standard bearers for Newton. The 280 and 33 Newton cartridges, listed in early catalogs, joined the 22 Newton in relative obscurity. In fact, the 280 and 33 Newton cartridges may never have seen fruition in saleable rifles. The 22 Newton was dropped in 1918 according to Phil Sharpe. The 256, 30 and 35 Newton were loaded by Western Cartridge Company as late as 1938.

Why the 22 Newton ended up with a quoted .228-inch bullet (or the 256 Newton with a .264 diameter bullet for that matter) is unclear. Some suggest that the odd diameter bullets precluded re-chambering existing .22 and .25 caliber rifles for Newton's proprietary cartridges. In fact, Newton later confirmed this was to avoid "— *every Tom, Dick, and Harry rechambering .25 caliber barrels for our ammunition.*" Newton's 22 Hi-Power cartridge, developed in 1905 and adopted by Savage Arms Corporation for its Model 99 in 1911, used a bastard .227 diameter 70-grain bullet in a necked down 25-35 Winchester case. Newton wanted a 90-grain bullet for the Hi-Power, his first big game 22 rifle. Savage chose the lighter bullet because it could be driven to 2800 fps, 100 fps faster than the 150-grain bullet from the popular 30-06

Springfield. A lesser known Newton development, the 22 long range pistol cartridge, used the .227 diameter 70-grain Hi-Power bullet in a modified 28-30 Stevens center fire rifle cartridge. The 22 long range pistol cartridge was chambered in a falling block single shot pistol produced by Fred Adolph.

More appropriately named, Newton's 250-3000 was developed in 1912 and adapted to the Savage Model 99 rifle in 1915. Newton figured a 100-grain bullet at 2800 fps was right, but Savage opted for 87 grains at 3000 fps. Another 1912 development, the 25 Newton Special, is found today as the 25-06 Remington. Newton similarly developed the 7mm 06 (280 Remington) about the same time. All these cartridges were anachronisms in an era when many considered killing power proportional to bore diameter and lever actions were popular. Newton noted resistance to bolt action rifles: "*We are aware the fact that this rifle is not a lever action will be a disappointment to some.*" Newton's bolt action rifles and high velocity car-

tridges were not popular with shooters of the period.

There is no doubt that Newton originally envisioned his 22 Newton cartridge as suitable for big game rather than for small game and varmints. His 1915 catalog states: "At all ranges beyond the muzzle it is more powerful than the well known Krag or 30-40 U.S.A. cartridge." Newton further stated, "Think of a 22 caliber rifle of the power equal to the 405 [Winchester] at 300 yards and more powerful beyond that range." Summing up, "It is ample for deer and efficient against all our heavier game." Indeed, the modern 6mm Remington and 243 Winchester are comparable with .015-inch larger diameter bullets of nearly the same weight, sectional density and velocity.

Reloading the 22 Newton is surprisingly easy. Newton necked down the 7mm Mauser case to produce his 22 cartridge. The 257 Roberts and 6mm Remington cases work as well but the need to inside-ream case necks is avoided by using the 6mm case as a starting point. Dies for the 22 Newton were purchased from RCBS (an in-stock item!). One hundred 6mm Remington cases were run through the sizing die and the necks trimmed to 2.225 inches overall cartridge length (Nonte, 1967). These cases would not enter the Ackley cut chamber of my rifle. The case ahead of the extractor groove was too large. I ran the cases through a 30-06 small base sizing die which only reduces the base of the shorter 6mm case. The cases were still too large at the base. A machinist friend took an eighth of an inch off the 30-06 small base sizing die (not easy to do as the die is very hard). Cases well lubed

Pre-World War II .22 caliber hot shots: 22-3000/2 R Lovell, 219 Zipper, 22 Hi-Power, 22-250, 220 Swift and 22 Newton. Only the Hi-Power and Newton were ever intended for big game.

smaller. His bullets were left over from handloading experiments and tests with the 228 Ackley Magnum and 228 Hawk. These two hotshots are made from cut-down 30-06 cases (there were several versions) and 6mm Remington cases, respectively. Both cases are about the same length and are ballistically comparable to the 22 Newton (surprisingly, there are several other comparable 22 cartridges, see Simpson, 1991). The Ackley round dates to the late 40s and gunsmith Wayne Schwartz developed the Hawk in the late 60s. Ken Waters did his testing of the two cartridges using .226/.227-inch bullets swaged by Schwartz (Waters, 1970). Ken obtained top velocities with these heavy bullets using slow burning powders, including 4831 and IMR 4350.

Besides the bullets, Ken also sent me an article by Ralph Avery on loading the 22 Newton (Avery 1990). Mr. Avery obtained his best results with then new IMR 7828 and an 84-grain bullet. Frank C. Barnes in his book *Cartridges of the World*, lists loads for the 22 Newton with 70 and 90-grain bullets and IMR 4350 powder. Considering the data from these sources, I decided to develop my loads with the proven successful slow burning powders.

I fitted my rifle with a 3-9X Leupold scope in low Weaver rings for accuracy tests. The receiver already had Weaver No. 26 bases front and rear. The bolt handle easily cleared the ocular lens of the scope and the low mounting of the scope minimized the effect of the stock's low comb. All shooting was done at 100 yards from the bench. The unset trigger breaks at seven pounds. I gladly used the set trigger feature for a crisp two-pound pull. Three or more five-shot groups were used for accuracy measurements. A Beta Chrony chronograph set 10 feet from the muzzle was used to obtain velocities for experimental loads. The standard deviations of the velocities were calculated for 15 or more shots for each load. The standard deviation indicates that 95% of all velocities sampled for a particular load should fall between the upper and lower limits established by the deviation. Lower standard deviations indicate more uniform velocities.

I fire-formed the full-length resized 6mm Remington cases using the load suggested by Nonte: 32 grains of IMR 4895 and the 70-grain .227 Hornady bullet. CCI BR-2 primers were used in these and all subsequent loads. Fire forming reduces the angle of the shoulder and

The head of the Newton bolt has seven lugs. Not shown are two additional safety lugs at the rear of the bolt and gas vent hole on the opposite side of the bolt head.

and run through the shortened 30-06 die chambered easily. Cases so sized also fit the chamber after firing. Case problem solved.

The only commercial 22-caliber bullet near the .228 diameter is the 70-grain .227-inch bullet for the 22 Hi-Power. This bullet is designed for 2800 fps velocity and it turned out that is about as fast as it can be

driven through the 1-in-8 inch twist without coming apart. More of that later. Bruce Jennings suggested I contact Ken Waters to see if he had any .228 caliber bullets. No, but Ken did have some miscellaneous small lots of .226- and .227-inch diameter bullets weighing 83 to 90 grains. Ken also indicated that 22 Newton barrels he had measured were .227 or

Ballistics of Newton Cartridges Circa 1920

Cartridge-bullet (gr.)	Velocity (fps)		Energy (ft-lbs)	
	Muzzle	200 yards	Muzzle	200 yards
22-90	3103	2689	1921	1445
256-140	2920	2552	2660	2030
30-172	3000	2618	3440	2631
33-200	3000	2530	4000	2852
35-250	2975	2512	4925	3500

Bullet	IMR Powder	Grains	Velocity fps± sd	Avg. group inches
Hornady	4895	32	2892± 18	1.22
70-gr./.227	4064	32	2847±30	1.19
	4831	40	3018±28	1.11
	4350	40	3093±17	3.32[1]
83-gr./.226	7828	44	2920± 26	2
		46	3054± 20	2
		47	3185± 29	2.83
85-gr./.227	7828	44	2845±26	2
		46	3111±13	2
		47	3266±30	3.15
90-gr./.227	7828	45	3065±18	2.65
		46	3105±16	1.40
Hornady	4895	32	2783±25	1.71
68-gr. BTM	4064	35	3049±7	1.51
		38	3290± 24	2.15
		40	3373±11	2
Hornady	4350	40	3079± 26	1.51
75-gr. V MAX	4831	44	3160± 17	2
	7828	41	2731± 28	2.45
		46	3178±20	3.75
Berger	4350	40	2980± 27	1.92
80-gr. VLD	4831	44	3141±21	2
	7828	41	2672± 27	2.79
		46	3197±10	2

Selected loads for the 22 Newton.

Averages are for three or more five-shot groups at 100 yards

[1]Vertical stringing, faint comet tails some bullet holes

[2] Some targets missing one or more bullet holes

Bullets used in tests with the 22 Newton include .224 diameter 68 and 75-grain Hornady and 80-grain Berger match bullets. Bullets .226/.227-inch are 70-grain Hornady and 83, 85 and 90-grain bullets from Ken Waters.

Newton's offerings included the 30-06 Springfield, 22, 256, 30, 33 and 35 Newton. The case diameter of the 30, 33 and 35 Newton are very close to the belt diameter of the 338 Winchester magnum. *Cartridges courtesy of Bruce Jennings.*

shortens the case neck. These loads averaged 2892 ±18 fps. Four measured five shot groups of the fire-forming loads averaged 1.22 inches at 100 yards.

Encouraged, I proceeded to work up maximum loads using the 70-grain Hornady bullet and IMR 4350, 4831 and 7828. Newton stated *"We load to 54000 pounds per square inch"*, a reasonable limit but difficult to define without laboratory equipment. Also, Newton incorporated a relatively long throat in his barrels to accommodate the long bullets he used. My Ackley chamber has the long throat and all bullets were seated to maximum length minus a few thousandths. Loads were prepared in two-grain increments from about 10 grains below the anticipated maximum. Three cartridges with weighed charges were fired for each load. Velocity was measured, primers examined for signs of high pressure indicated by flattening and extrusion back around the firing pin, and bolt lift was noted for each shot. Firing was discontinued when any signs of high pressure were encountered. The maximum load was then taken to be two grains less than the load showing signs of high pressure. In this way I determined that the 70-grain Hornady bullet could be propelled to three-shot average velocities of 3354, 3391 and 3478 fps with 44, 48 or 50 grains of IMR 4350, 4831 and 7828, respectively. None of these bullets hit the target.

An observant friend noted a blue streak from the Hornady bullet was plainly visible at velocities above 3000 fps. A lead *comet tail* appeared around each bullet hole in targets set at 25 yards. The lead cores were obviously melting due to the heat produced by barrel friction. Newton also noted the problem of bullet core melt with his high-velocity cartridges. All Newton ammunition after about 1915 was loaded with bullets containing paper-insulated cores. Phil Sharpe found these "heat insulated" bullets worked as claimed. The 70-grain Hornady bullet was tested with reduced loads.

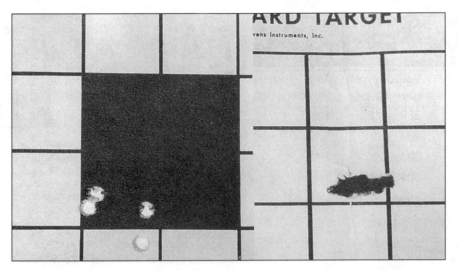

A stability problem occurred when .226/.227-inch bullets were not driven to maximum velocities. In this case an 83-grain bullet departed from a nice grouping of four shots to land sideways elsewhere on the target.

M15 rifles chambered for the 223 Remington currently popular in high-power rifle competition. The accuracy of the .003-inch smaller bullets was not expected to be good. Nevertheless, I selected three bullets for testing: 68-grain Hornady BTM, 75-grain Hornady V MAX and 80-grain Berger VLD.

Overall, the .224-inch bullets provided 1 1/2 to 2-inch groups with selected loads. However, the results for the .224-inch bullets contrast with those for the .226/.227-inch bullets in apparent stability at high velocity. The .226-.227 bullets, excluding the 70-grain Hornady, did not consistently hit the targets if driven at less than about 3200 fps. The .224 bullets did not consistently hit the targets if driven near or above about 3100 fps. A comparison of the profiles of the 83-grain bullet obtained from Ken Waters and the 80-grain Berger bullet shows a substantial difference in bullet length and bearing area. I have to conclude that different rifling twists are appropriate for each: the 1 in 8 inch twist of my rifle and original Newton barrels is appropriate for high velocity with the comparatively blunt 90-grain game bullet.

I cannot see any reason why the 22 Newton or similar sized .22-caliber cartridge could not be used for game the size of antelope and deer *if* a controlled expanding bullet of 80 to

I proceeded to determine maximum loads for 83, 85 and 90-grain .226/.227-inch bullets. Maximum and reduced loads with IMR 7828 were fired for accuracy and velocity measurements. However, it was the 90-grain softpoint that was of most interest, since it fulfills Newtons original vision of his big game 22 cartridge. I was pleased to achieve 3100 fps with this weight bullet, as Newton claimed in 1917. I recently learned both P. O. Ackley and Phil Sharpe duplicated Newton's ballistics before World War II. Some have questioned Newton's published velocities with the powders of his day. Not surprisingly, Newton developed a progressive-burning coated powder, patented, for use in his own cartridges. This powder, made by Du Pont, was not commercially available and may have allowed the velocities Newton claimed.

Out of curiosity, I decided to try some of the heavy .224-inch bullets now available. These match-grade bullets are designed for fast-twist

A lot of powder burning in a small tube creates heat. I allowed fifteen minutes between groups for cooling the barrel.

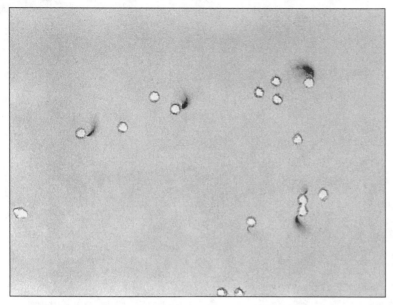

Comet tails around bullet holes at 25 yards occurred when the 70-grain Hornady bullet was driven above about 3100 fps. The greater the velocity, the more lead deposited.

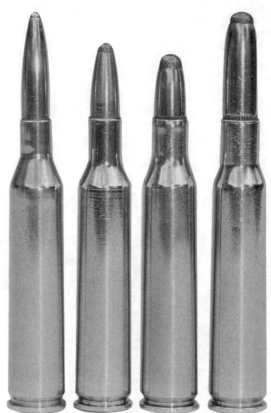

The 7mm Mauser family: 22 Newton, 6mm Remington, 257 Roberts and 7mm Mauser.

90 grains was available. Certainly the 22 Newton would be a superb "windy day" long-range varmint cartridge. However, no factory cartridge with the case capacity of the 22 Newton and appropriate twist for heavy bullets is available, or likely to be in the future. The reason is that the 243 Winchester and 6mm Remington are better choices for deer-size game. Newton wisely touted his 256 Newton cartridge as the *"all around cartridge"* for big game. In today's magnum-crazy world, Newton would likely be pointing to his .30-caliber cartridge for this purpose.

Charles Newton envisioned a complete rifle-shooting package to achieve the *"greatest advancement in ballistic efficiency so far accomplished."* To this end Newton borrowed from existing technology and freely admitted doing so. However, you cannot study Newton's rifle and ammunition without concluding that the man was an inventive genius. There is little in today's bolt-action hunting rifles and ammunition that was not presaged in the fertile mind of Charles Newton.

It is clear that Newton's rifles and cartridges were far ahead of the time in which he tenaciously tried to establish them. However, it was the Newton rifle action which most impressed me. M. D. Waite declared *"Even by today's standards, the design of the original Newton rifle action was notably neat and clean cut with no excess metal in any area."* Phil Sharpe opined: *"The original Newton was a mighty fine rifle and some of his earlier guns were built with extreme precision."* To my mind, Frank DeHaas

summed it perfectly when he asked, *"Why has not somebody revived the Newton rifle? And if this is ever done, the revival should be complete: action with set-triggers, stock design and in calibers originally designed by Newton to include the 250-3000, 256 Newton, 30 Newton and 35 Newton."* Strong praise from a man who was very well acquainted with bolt action rifle design. Whether you think Newton's big-game 22 cartridge should be included in a revival or not, Charles Newton is a man to whom much is owed for the inspiration leading to modern high velocity rifle cartridges. Phil Sharpe perhaps has his epitaph: *"He was an intelligent man. He was a man of great vision—but he couldn't manufacture."* It is too bad he did not take on a partner with that necessary talent. On the other hand, maybe it would have made no difference eighty-plus years ago. ●

Bibliography

Avery, Ralph. .22 Newton and IMR-7828. *Handloader.* May—June, 1990.

Barnes, Frank C. *Cartridges of the World.* Eighth Edition. Krause Publications Inc., Iola, WI, 1997.

De Haas, Frank. *Bolt Action Rifles.* Third Edition. DBI Books Inc., Northbrook, IL, 1995.

Foral, Jim. The 256 Newton Sporting Springfield. *Guns Illustrated.* Krause Publications Inc., Iola, WI, 1998.

Haviland, John. Shooting a Newton. *Gun Digest.* Krause Publications Inc., Iola, WI, 1997.

Jennings, Bruce M. Jr. Charles Newton's Leverbolt. *Gun Digest.* Krause Publications Inc., Iola, WI, 1996.

Jennings, Bruce M. Jr. *Charles Newton, Father of High Velocity.* Fenske Printing, Inc., Rapid City, SD, 1984.

Nonte, George C. Jr. *The Home Guide to Cartridge Conversions.* Stackpole Co., Harrisburg, PA, 1967.

Sharpe, Philip B. *The Rifle in America.* Third Edition. Funk and Wagnalls Co., New York, NY. 1953.

Simpson, Layne. Shooting the Big 22's. *Handloaders Digest.* DBI Books Inc., Northbrook, IL, 1991.

Waite, M. D. Charles Newton, Father of the .25-06. *American Rifleman.* May, 1971.

Waters, Ken. Pitting Two .228's. *Handloader,* Sept.-Oct., 1970.

Author's custom 40/65 Remington Rolling Block Rifle and cartridges loaded with his hollow-point bullets from converted RCBS mould. Accessories shown include C. Sharps Arms tang sight; leather cartridge carrier made by author and pull-through cleaner.

HOMEMADE "EXPRESS" BULLETS FOR THE 40/65 WINCHESTER

by Harvey T. Pennington

I WAS CERTAINLY excited when I received a letter confirming I had been successful in the 1999 Montana drawing for antelope licenses. Having anticipated the hunt for months, there was no doubt about the rifle I would use. At the June, 1999, Quigley Buffalo Rifle Match in Forsyth, Montana, I had acquired a beautiful, custom 40/65 Remington

Rolling Block (Creedmore style) built by my friend, Dick Kutzler, from nearby Glendive, Montana.

The rifle was built around an old, original No. 1 action that had been flawlessly re-color-casehardened; its 34-inch, half-round Green Mountain barrel proved to be a tack-driver with the RCBS 40-400-CSA bullet over 57-58 grains of GOEX car-

tridge-grade black powder. However, I felt the 400-grain bullet was simply too heavy (and a little slow, at 1200 fps) for the small-bodied antelope, so I decided to obtain a mould for a lighter-weight bullet that would better suit my needs.

I ordered an RCBS 40-300-CSA double-cavity mould and, although its bullets shot well, I felt for my proposed use on antelope it needed a broader flat point (*meplat*) to provide greater initial impact and promote faster expansion. As a matter of fact, it seemed a hollow-point design might be even more effective on the lightweight pronghorn. A couple of books in my home firearms library reinforced my theory; illustrations of the original 40/65 W.C.F. cartridge (and the apparently interchangeable 40/60 Marlin) in Frank Barnes' *Cartridges of the World* showed that, indeed, their factory 260-grain bullets had noticeably broader flat points than those of the bullets cast in my RCBS 40-300-CSA mould. Further, in *The Ideal Handbook, No. 15* (reprint by Wolfe Publishing Company, October, 1991), the Ideal Company illustrated at least two different hollow-point ("express") moulds suitable for the 40/65 W.C.F., boasting that "*Every person owning one of these rifles should have an express mould, as they greatly increase the killing power for large game.*"

Granted, several custom mould manufacturers are in existence today, and they can provide moulds for almost any design of cast bullet that a hunter or target-shooter desires. But I didn't have enough time to wait for a custom mould, nor was I aware of anyone who manufactured hollow-point moulds suitable for my rifle. As a matter of fact, there seems to be a very limited selection of hunting bullets available for the 40/65 today, even though target bullets and moulds are readily available. Certainly, the 40/65 is an outstanding target cartridge – both for silhouette and long-range matches – but it must not be forgotten that its original purpose was for hunting; a purpose for which it is as well-suited today as it was over 100 years ago.

As a result, I began looking at ways I could modify my existing mould to better suit my needs. An examination of an old Lyman hollow-point mould gave me ideas for the type of modification I had in mind. That mould had a hole extending through the nose-end (bottom) of the cavity and had a separate pin (to form the cavity for the hollow point of the bullet) inserted through the same hole from the bottom of the closed mould; of course, there was a latch to hold the pin in place while the cavity was being filled with lead, and to allow the pin to be released and pulled from the cavity before the mould was opened to remove the bullet. It seemed that all this could be accomplished with the tools I had available.

Converted RCBS 40-300-CSA mould showing cavity on left after drilling, as described in article.

First, a broader flat point seemed in order. After measuring the widths of the meplats on several of my cast bullets for both handguns and rifles, I decided that a diameter of .250-inch for the flat portion of the nose of the bullet should work fine. Keeping in mind the design of the Lyman hollow-point mould, it seemed the first step should be to drill through the nose portion of my mould cavity. After removing the sprue plate, I firmly set the closed RCBS

Bottom of converted mould showing rod inserted into drilled hole, positioning of E-clip on rod and the screw which – together with the E-clip – provides the latch to hold rod in place during casting; to remove the rod, the rod is turned so the open side of the E-clip will permit it to be pulled past the screw head.

40-300-CSA mould in my drill press vise, being careful to level it. When I was satisfied with its position, and satisfied it was secure for drilling, I tightened a .250-inch bit in the chuck and centered it in one of the cavities at the top of the mould (where the base of the bullet is formed). After lowering the bit into the cavity to ensure it was centered, I applied cutting oil to the bit and drilled through the center of the cavity and out through the bottom of the blocks (where the nose of the bullet is formed).

Next, I measured the distance from the nose-end of the ogive (at the point where the newly-drilled hole began) to the bottom surface of the mould blocks. This distance was then transferred to a 2.50-inch diameter steel rod I had obtained at a local hardware store; measuring from the flat end of the rod, that distance (.550-inch) was marked on the rod using Dykem Blue Layout Fluid and scribed line. I cut that section of the rod to a length of 3.5 inches and set it in my lathe chuck. While turning the rod in the lathe, a hacksaw blade was used to cut a shallow groove around the circumference of the rod at the scribed line. The purpose of this groove was to hold an E-clip, as part of the latch which would hold the rod in place when the cavity was being filled with lead alloy.

Once the E-clip was placed on the rod, I then needed a place on the bottom of the mould blocks to fasten the rod in position. On the bottom of one of the blocks, a measurement was made from the edge of the rod's position to the point where an 8x32 hole would be drilled and tapped. The flat bottom of the head of the 8x32 screw would be the other part of the latch, which would hold the rod in position.

The hole for this screw was drilled in the bottom of the block a distance of .345-inch from the edge of the hole where the rod would be placed. This would allow sufficient clearance for the open side of the E-clip to pass by the head of the screw as it was inserted into the mould; then, by turning the rod, the E-clip's solid side would be positioned between the bottom of the mould block and the bottom of the head of the screw, retaining the rod. To remove the rod from the mould, the process is reversed; the rod is turned so the open side of the E-clip will miss the edge of the head of the screw while the rod is being withdrawn (pulled) from the mould. After threading the screw hole with an 8x32 tap and inserting the screw, the screw was

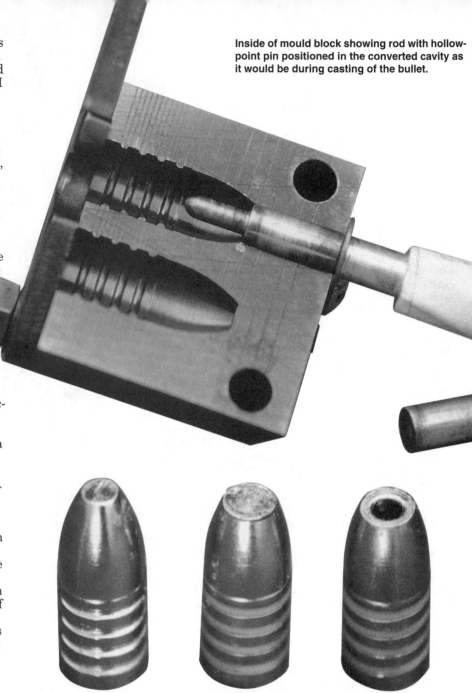

Inside of mould block showing rod with hollow-point pin positioned in the converted cavity as it would be during casting of the bullet.

Left: bullet cast from unaltered RCBS 40-300-CSA mould cavity. *Middle*: author's .250-inch flat-point bullet cast from altered cavity. *Right*: author's hollow-point bullet cast from altered cavity.

adjusted so that it allowed just enough clearance for the E-clip on the rod to be turned without binding between the screw head and the bottom of the mould block.

Of course, the rod itself needed a handle – not just to keep the rod from getting too hot during the casting procedure – but also to allow the rod to be more easily turned, and to allow leverage to withdraw and insert the rod after each bullet had been cast. To accomplish this, I simply drilled a .10-inch diameter hole through the center of the rod at a 90-degree angle about half an inch from the end of the handle-end of

the rod. A .10-inch diameter steel pin, two inches long, was slipped through the hole, forming a T-handle. The handle, and the end of the rod, were then generously wrapped with masking tape to provide some insulation and to prevent the T-handle from slipping in its hole.

With that accomplished, I was ready for casting! It was very satisfying to know the simple alteration I had completed made such a difference. The new bullet had the look of a very fine bullet for the smaller big-game species such as antelope and whitetail deer. It still weighed 300 grains (with my 1-40 alloy) and its new, quarter-inch flat point gave the impression of being a serious hunting bullet. Further, accuracy with the new bullet did not seem to suffer at all in comparison to the bullets cast in the original factory cavity.

So, what about the hollow-point version? That was easy! All

that was required at this point was to use another 3.5-inch section of quarter-inch rod for the hollow-point pin. On the lathe, I turned one end of the rod down to a diameter of .140-inch for a length of .380-inch; this part of the rod would become the "pin" to form the hollow-point cavity itself. The pin portion was then given a slight taper to its end and smoothly rounded, using a file and

grains (with 1-40 alloy), and proved pleasingly accurate with either 23.5 grains of AA 5744 or 65 grains of GOEX Cartridge Grade black powder. Groups with either of those loads were less than 5 inches at 200 yards. With my soft alloy, which I thought would be best for antelope, these bullets mushroomed to an average diameter of over nine-tenths of an inch when they struck

about 15 inches by the time it reaches the target at 200 yards.

Luckily, my chance came at a doe antelope at about 150 yards. Because of the height of the grass between us, I had to take the shot from a standing position. The hit was just behind the diaphragm, but the force of the impact and the sound of the hit were amazing. Even with this less-than-ideal hit, the doe ran only about 40-50 yards and stopped; it was obvious she could go no farther. My second shot went into the chest and she was down for good.

When I returned home after the hunt and reported on the bullet's success to my good friend Dennis Human, he made it known he would like the same kind of conversion to his RCBS 40-350-CSA single-cavity mould. I agreed to do so, and had his mould ready well before for the Kentucky deer season in November. Dennis used his hollow-point version (which weighs about 330 grains) and a black-powder load to harvest a nice whitetail buck, with one shot, at about 30 yards. His rifle was a Model 1875 chambered for the 40-65, built by C. Sharps Arms of Big Timber, Montana.

Author's hollow-point bullet from converted mould, and two expanded bullets recovered from 200-yard dirt backstop.

crocus cloth as the rod was being turned in the lathe, so the pin could be easily removed from the cast bullet. From the point on the rod where the "pin" ended and the diameter returned to .250-inch, I measured back up the rod to the same distance (.550-inch) that I had on the first rod and, again using Dykem Blue, scribed a line around the rod. Again, I used the hacksaw while the rod was being turned in the lathe and cut a shallow groove at that point to accommodate another E-clip. When the E-clip was seated, and the T-handle was installed as before, I was ready to cast hollow-point bullets out of the same cavity of the mould that I had previously altered!

The hollow-point bullets cast in the altered cavity weighed 280

my dirt backstop at 200 yards, with very little fragmentation.

When the time came for the antelope hunt, it was this 280-grain hollow-point version that went along. I opted for the black powder load mentioned above, with a card wad between the powder and the base of the bullet. My bullet lubricant was homemade: a mixture consisting of one-half Vaseline, one-half paraffin and (for each pound of that mixture) one teaspoon of RCBS Case Lube. Overall cartridge length was 2.67 inches. Velocity with this combination was about 1400 fps and, after some experimentation, I decided on a hunting zero of 150 yards. Beyond that distance, the trajectory of the bullet definitely becomes quite pronounced, falling

The nice thing about this type of conversion is that it takes a minimum of equipment and can be accomplished in just a couple of hours. Although I had a small lathe to work with, everything I have mentioned here (with the possible exception of making the hollow-point pin) can be accomplished by anyone who has access to a good drill press with a sturdy table vise. With a little care, the finished product will allow the casting of highly effective hunting bullets for black-powder cartridge rifles, with the option of hollow-point bullets for the lighter species of big game.

Interested? Go ahead - give it a try!

●

ONE GOOD GUN

by Charles W. Overstreet

The Overstreet Winchester

The Overstreet Winchester.

I CAME INTO this world back in 1937 in New Haven, Connecticut. At a very early age, I headed west to Oklahoma, settling in a small gun shop in Fairfax, a small town in Osage County. One day, a fellow named Clyde Overstreet dropped into the store, decided we were meant for each other and took me home to live with him and his family on a cattle ranch south of town.

Those were great times for me. Deer weren't plentiful, although Clyde and I got our share. But the coyote population was out of control, a real threat to all the ranchers. Those pesky varmints killed more baby calves, sheep and goats than one could imagine! We also had more than our share of fox and raccoon; those sneaky devils raided the chicken house, killed laying hens and ate eggs. Clyde kept me pretty busy as we worked hard to keep the varmints in check. I was never one to keep score, but we nailed our share of those troublesome pests.

I was sort of wild back in those early days. I had some crazy habits. Guess you might say, I still have them. You see, I never minded going to the field and taking down a critter when the occasion and need came up. But I always liked to be cleaned and oiled real good when we got back to the house.

Like I said, life was good back in those days. Clyde's son, Charles, grew up and developed a good feel for hunting. I will say this about old Clyde, he did a dandy job with Charles' gun training. I listened while he talked of safety, sight pictures, proper breathing and squeezing — as well as cleaning the rifle after the hunt. When the youngster graduated from the single-shot .22, I introduced him to the thrill of bigger game and guns. We had some fine times together, but more about him later.

In addition to hunting, I had other duties around the ranch. When butchering time rolled around, I was called upon to put down a hog or calf, sometimes both. But one of my saddest duties came one day when Clyde's favorite cow pony stepped in a hole and broke a leg. Clyde and I hated having to send him on; Clyde was almost in tears, but it was a job that had to be done.

A few years later we got back into serious deer hunting. During the late Forties and early Fifties, Clyde and some of his friends made several hunting trips to Texas. One thing you have to know about Texas whitetail — they are just a tad bit larger than the average Irish setter and are quick as greased lightning. In spite of that speed, we did ourselves proud on those trips.

During the next few years, Clyde got pretty busy and didn't have time for much hunting; Charles went away to college and then to the army for a few years, so I spent my time just hanging around the house resting in my favorite gun rack. In the late Fifties, Clyde and his friends traveled back to Texas for another deer hunt and we had a great time. I was my old straight-shooting self and brought down a buck on the first day. That evening Clyde cleaned me real good and placed me next to the door where he wouldn't forget me when they loaded up for the drive back to Oklahoma. But just as you would imagine, he walked out the door and left me standing there.

The way it worked out, that was our last hunt together. A couple of weeks later, the host of the hunt found me, picked me up and — not knowing who I was — put me in his gun closet with the rest of his guns. All were 30/30 Winchesters; nary a telescopic sight in the entire bunch.

Years passed and my services were never called for. Once every month, with the other guns, I was faithfully given a good cleaning. Life was good!

Clyde passed on to his just reward in 1962. In 1967, Charles and his family were living in California. He tracked me down and learned I was alive and well in Texas, so he wrote asking I be returned. I was carefully wrapped, boxed and shipped first class to Santa Monica, California.

Charles was in the advertising business and didn't have much time for hunting. We went to a rifle range from time to time and I taught his sons, Mark and Mike, a thing or two about rifle shooting. But most of the time, Charles displayed me on a nice rack and kept me clean and oiled. He always spoke highly of me; said I brought back wonderful memories of ranch life in Oklahoma.

In 1979, Charles moved back to Oklahoma and I made the trip with the family. We settled on a small acreage east of Stillwater, where I now reside in a new gun rack. A couple of months before hunting season in 1993, a huge hunting bug stung old Charlie and, once again, he got real interested in the Oklahoma whitetail!

Charles took me out to the range and fired a few shots at a target to make sure he and I were looking at the same thing.

We joined a bunch of Charles' friends at Kaw Lake in northern Oklahoma. As we set up our hunting camp, the other fellows started taking their guns out of their cases and I swear, those were the strangest-looking deer rifles I had ever seen; not a 30/30 in the bunch. All had telescopic sights. A few had fancy engravings — and one had a weird-looking stock with a hole near where a shooter's thumb fit. Charles wasn't any more impressed with that sort of stuff than I was.

Before dawn the following morning, we were at our stand, ready for action. It was good to be back in the woods again; I couldn't remember when I had seen my last daybreak. A flock of geese flew over, breaking the quiet dawn with their incessant honking. A wild tom turkey was raising a ruckus on the other side of the hill, attempting to get his hens together — and all around busy squirrels hustled here and there gathering acorns for the coming winter.

The air was fresh and there was a tingle along my barrel as the cold, northern wind blew gently across the lake and brushed past us. I thought, "This is just like the old days with Clyde. Now I have to do my best and help Charles get his deer."

Nothing happened the first day, it's like that sometimes; everything has to be just right before those bucks show themselves. Back in camp that night I laid there smelling the smoke

Clyde lashing a load of Texas whitetails in 1948.

from the campfire and listened to Charlie and his friends laughing and telling their hunting stories and as usual, a few lies. This was why I was made, the reason for my being! I remembered how it was in the old days with Clyde; memories, wonderful memories.

The sun poked up over the blackjacks about 6:00 a.m. and found Charles and me sitting on a rock overlooking a little pasture of buffalo grass. About 10:00 a.m. Charles saw a doe bounding out of a plum thicket followed by a nice five-point buck, prancing along with

nothing but romance on his mind. It was about a 75-yard shot, not much for me but I wasn't too sure about Charlie. I could feel his heart pumping rapidly as he picked up his sight picture, breathed just right and gently began to squeeze my trigger. Charles has a fine touch; he was so smooth it startled me when my hammer fell.

Oops, it was a lung shot; the buck now had other things to consider. He dropped the love idea like a hot potato and broke back to the sumac brush. Quick as a flash Charles racked up the next round and squeezed off

a second shot. I watched the buck fall — a perfect heart shot!

I didn't do any crowing when we got back to camp that night. Seems all those fancy young guns still had their first shot to fire. I just grinned as they stared at my buck hanging in the blackjack oak next to the campsite. The next morning, Charles and I headed back to Stillwater with a little meat for the freezer.

I'm back home now, resting easy in my rack and waiting for next year when Charles and I go out again. But this isn't the last of my story. It seems I'm going to be around the Overstreet's for a good long time. Charlie has two sons, and an Overstreet grandson, so I've sort of become an Overstreet tradition. Like all traditions, there's no telling how long I'll be around, teaching young Overstreets the finer art of rifle shooting.

Charles had a brass plate engraved and nailed on the side of my stock. It reads:

The Overstreet Winchester Model 94

Clyde E. — Charles Wm. — Mark Wm. — Michael L. — Andrew Wm.

So, don't expect to see me in a pawn shop. If you want to look at a 30/30 Winchester who has had a long and happy career, I'll be resting in my rack waiting for another Overstreet to take me out to the woods to make more memories. ●

Charles with his buck, in 1993.

ONE GOOD GUN

I wanted a gun that was invulnerable to bad weather, powerful and accurate enough for any species of North American game, and not too heavy to carry in rough country. My quest led me to...

OLD UGLY

I DIDN'T ACTUALLY need another rifle, but you know how it is. Back in 1960 I'd had a 338 Magnum built on a 400-series FN Mauser action, which had a sliding safety and an underslung bolt handle for scope clearance. An adjustable trigger was installed, as well as a 22-inch barrel, one of the last tubes John Buhmiller made. I got a fair to middlin' walnut blank from Flaig's in Pittsburgh and Earl Hock finished and full-length glass-bedded it.

It became my favorite rifle for big game in rough, thick-cover country. I used it from Pennsylvania to Canada to Idaho to Alaska. It took tons of game for me – elk, bear, whitetails, mulies, whatever – with never a bobble. In fact, in the hunting seasons of well over three decades, I killed every critter I shot at but one. That miss was at a Colorado buck at more than half a mile. It came out of a narrow stand of aspens and started across a high alpine meadow. I couldn't see any antlers with the Redfield set at 2x but when I cranked it up to 7x there was a big high-standing rack. I knew I couldn't hit him that far but thought the report might confuse him and turn him my way. It didn't, he didn't; so I had my only miss with that old 338.

I shot it a lot. Mostly on the bench, of course, testing different loads for accuracy and trajectory, checking the zero, chronographing, etc. Now, after some 2500 rounds with heavy powder charges, it doesn't group as well as it used to, particularly with spitzer bullets, though it still does OK with round noses. They're OK in the woods. Once with the 275-grain Speer I popped a 5-point Colorado bull through the

Though most at home in the Rockies, the 338 can be handloaded down to a level reasonable for deer.

spine between the shoulders, from above on a steep sidehill, and the bullet angled back through the rear of the lungs and most of the paunch. I didn't weigh it afterward and didn't measure the penetration, but the Speer did the job.

Another time in Idaho, after a week of cold hunting in wet snow, my only chance was at an elk one step from vanishing in a dense tangle – and its rear end was toward me. Its head was down, feeding, I guess, so I had no shot at that. If I'd been carrying a 270, say, I wouldn't have fired, but with the 338 I did. The 250-grain Nosler Partition missed the anus by less than an inch and the elk collapsed, never moving a

step. I dunno where the bullet ended up, but it did all that was required.

Anyway, you can understand why I like the 338. The Buhmiller barrel was plenty accurate, too. When new, it made groups as small as 7/8-inch at 100, though 1-1/2 or so for 5 shots was more common. Once I had 7 rounds left after zeroing +3 inches at 100 with the Nosler 250-grain and a maximum load of H4831, so I shot them at 300 yards to check drop and accuracy. The group was just 4-1/2 inches low and measured just over 4 inches, which I don't think is bad for a load that churns up some 4000 foot-pounds of muzzle energy. I mean, does anyone ever need better than 1.3 *moa* groups for elk when they have a vital area big as a bushel basket?

With scope and full magazine, though, my 338 Mauser weighted 9-1/2 pounds, and this, plus the deteriorating barrel, some years ago convinced me that another gun in this chambering was necessary. A new barrel would handle the long spitzers from Hornady, Sierra and Nosler for open country use.

So I did some thinking. First consideration of course was the action. The FN was fine, but I'd always thought about getting an old Model 70 Winchester, the pre-64 style with its controlled feeding system, Mauser-type extractor and great trigger. Gunsmith Al Wardrop had one he was willing to part with, so that matter was settled.

Al came up with a suggestion for a barrel, too. He had a shot-out Hart 30-caliber target tube which could be rebored. I liked the idea for various reasons, including the fact it was stainless steel. October weather in the Rockies can be miserable and nobody can clean a barrel as often as he wants in elk camp, so the stainless eliminated one problem. So it was rebored to 338, rifled with a 1:10 twist, and turned down to sporter weight, finishing up at 22 inches from the front of

and zeroed them in first, then the little Redfield. I've had no trouble with the scope after using it for years now (*knock wood*), but it's comforting to know the irons are there.

I didn't have to do as much shooting with this 338 as with my earlier one, for it had given me a good idea of accurate loads and ballistics. So this barrel should last

forever. After all, even in several decades, how many shots can anyone fire at game?

At eight pounds, woods-ready, my M70 338 is almost

▲ "Old Ugly" — Bell's rebored, Rustoleum-painted, fiberglass-stocked, Lo-Swing-mounted, Redfield-scoped elk killer.

the receiver ring. By the time that was done, a fiberglass stock arrived from Chet Brown. A gun as light as this one was shaping up to be might kick too much, so I had the barrel Mag-Na-Ported.

Then a 1-4x Redfield was latched to the top deck with a Lo-Swing Pachmayr mount. The weakest point of any mounting system is the base-to-receiver attachment, so a small-diameter hardened steel rod was driven into a hole drilled through the rear of the mount base and the bridge of the receiver. With such an arrangement, regardless of recoil, the scope couldn't move.

Still, because this was a backcountry gun and there was a remote but real possibility I might booger up the scope somehow, I had Wardrop take a little flop-down peep sight that Redfield used to offer as an addition to their mount, and install it on the vertical rear face of the Pachmayr base. With a flat ivory-faced front sight, it provided immediate emergency backup in case the scope should ever be damaged – as once happened on a northern Ontario moose hunt when the mud on a steep sidehill gave way under my boots and my scope smashed into a tree when I tried to catch myself. It's only a few lost hours if something goes wrong on a deer hunt close to home, but it's another matter if you're 75 bush-plane miles back of nowhere when it happens.

So I got the metallic sights as backups on the Model 70,

▲ Scope swung aside to show how aperture sight can be used in emergency.

▲ Here's the 250-gr. Nosler Partition semi-point loaded in Bell's 338. This handful of cartridges represents 20,000 foot pounds of energy.

two pounds lighter than the FN, which makes a noticeable difference as the hills get higher and steeper. But, due to the Mag-Na-Porting, recoil seems about the same – so I'm happy.

My second 338 isn't a pretty gun. Stainless steel can be blued, sort of, though it's complicated. I found it easier to spray-paint the barrel with black Rustoleum. And no one would confuse the fiberglass stock with Circassian walnut. In fact, my hunting buddy Bob Wise took one look at the finished gun and nicknamed it "Old Ugly." But it shoots as well as the first one did when it was new, and kills as well, so what do looks matter?

So my "one good gun" is actually two. They're not identical twins – more like siblings – but at least they're both chambered for the same cartridge, and I doubt if there's a better one for North American big game. ●

The Browning A-Bolt, coupled with a Kahles scope, makes an ideal lightweight package for the field.

THE YEAR OF THE SHORT MAGNUMS

by Holt Bodinson

SHORT SPORTING CAR-TRIDGES designed for big-game rifles aren't new. The 250/3000 and the 300 Savage have been around a *LONG* time and even Winchester's 243-308-358 series is beginning to show a little gray around the temples. What is very new is the commercial appearance of wee, little, beltless, 30-caliber magnums. After hunting with short magnums for the last three years, I must report that they are sensational.

The first 30-caliber short magnum appeared a little over four years ago in the form of Lazzeroni's 7.82(308) Patriot. With an overall case length of 2.050 inches, a 30-degree shoulder, and a head size of 0.580 inch, the Patriot looks ever so much like a blown-out PPC case formed on a 416 Rigby body. It's a stout case, too. Drawn by MAST (Bell) Technology, the Lazzeroni brass is capable of being reloaded 10-15 times, even at a working pressure of 65,000 psi. Ballistically, the Patriot really performs. From a 24-inch Savage barrel at 70-degrees, my Oehler check chronograph recorded the following 5-shot, average velocities:

125-grain Sierra ProHunter: 3596 fps

130-grain Barnes-X (Lazzeroni plated): 3549 fps

168-grain Sierra MatchKing (moly lubed): 3207 fps

180-grain Nosler Partition (Lazzeroni plated): 3119 fps

220-grain Sierra RN: 2877 fps

You'll notice the "Lazzeroni plated" designation with sev-

eral bullets. Lazzeroni orders both Nosler and Barnes-X bullets slightly undersized and has them hard-plated with NP3 by Robar. The effect is similar to lubricating the bullets with moly. Shot-to-shot variations are very low in the Patriot, typically under 10 fps. As a result, accuracy runs to sub-minute of angle, and the squat little magnum is already beginning to make waves in 1000-yard benchrest competition.

The latest entry into the short-action magnum category is Winchester's 300 WSM ("Winchester Short Magnum"). In designing their case with an overall length of 2.1 inches, Winchester essentially adopted a 404 Jeffery case diameter, added a rebated rim of 0.532 inch, a 35-degree shoulder, and a 0.300-inch long neck. In style, it's reminiscent of the 284 Winchester with which it shares the 35-degree shoulder and rebated rim. Whereas Lazzeroni gained powder capacity by going to a larger-bodied case, Winchester did it by lengthen-

The 300 WSM is offered in (*L*) the Browning A-Bolt and (*R*) the Winchester Model 70 Featherweight.

ing the case body as much as possible, and using a sharper shoulder. Ballistically, the result is a cartridge that equals the standard factory-loaded 300 Win Mag.

Currently, Winchester offers three factory loads: a 150-grain Ballistic Silvertip at 3300 fps; and either a 180-grain Power-Point or Fail Safe at 2970 fps. I have chronographed all three loads in both a Winchester Model 70 Featherweight with a 24-inch barrel and a Browning A-Bolt with a 23-inch barrel. Factory quoted velocities are right there,

The 300 WSM is factory loaded with 180-grain Fail Safes and Power-Points and 150-grain Ballistic Silvertips.

and the two 180s shoot to the same point-of-impact. Once again, shot-to-shot velocity variations are very low; accuracy is sub-minute of angle and the difference in velocity between a 23- and a 24-inch barrel is insignificant.

One of the endearing qualities of the Lazzeroni and Winchester short 30-caliber magnums is their efficiency. Taking less powder than a 300 Win Mag., they equal or exceed the velocity of the standard magnum and do it in a barrel only 23 inches long. In fact, when I chronographed the Lazzeroni Patriot in a 26-inch barrel, there were no significant velocity gains to be made. In theory, the short, fat, sharp-shouldered cases provide improved powder combustion within the case body itself. The facts seem to support the theory. The efficiency of either case makes them prime candidates for chambering in single-shot pistols.

Because the short-action magnums require less powder, recoil – even in the light 6 1/2 to 6 3/4-pound Lazzeroni, Winchester and Browning rifles – is much reduced. My subjective impression is that the recoil and muzzle blast levels are more along the lines of the 30-06 or 308, than the 300 Winchester Magnum. The short magnums are simply a pleasure to shoot and the light, short-action rifles in which they are chambered a real joy when you're huffing up the mountains after deer, elk or sheep.

Winchester indicates that reloaders will find Winchester 760 Ball powder ideal for the 300 WSM. The Lazzeroni case does well with Reloder 15 with the 125/130-grain bullets; H4350 with the 168s; Reloder 19 with the 180s. The latter loads being

Light rifles and short magnum cartridges, like the Lazzeronis, are ideal for scaling mountains after Coues deer.

The Patriot is currently chambered in the reasonably priced Lazzeroni/Savage Model 16LZ.

assembled with standard Federal 210M primers.

Having successfully taken desert mule deer, Coues deer and elk with the Lazzeroni Patriot and Nilgai with the 300 WSM, I can report these new short magnums and the delightful rifles they're chambered for leave nothing to be desired in terms of field performance. What impresses me most is the inherent accuracy of these short-powder-column cases and the lack of magnum-level recoil with any bullet weight selected.

Lazzeroni has gone one step further than Winchester and created a whole family of short-action magnums in 243, 264, 284, 338, and 416 calibers. You can view their ballistic performance by going to: www.lazzeroni.com.

But don't expect Winchester to sit on their laurels. I imagine they're giving a 270 WSM some very serious thought.

The Patriot is currently chambered in both a stainless steel Lazzeroni /Savage Model 16LZ and a Lazzeroni Mountain Rifle. The 300 WSM is chambered in at least three different Browning A-Bolt designs as well as the Model 70 Featherweight. www.browning.com and www.winchester-guns.com.

Lazzeroni and Winchester have rewritten the chapter on big game ammunition. The short, beltless, magnum revolution is just beginning. ●

The short Lazzeroni Patriot(C) exceeds the performance (L) of the 300 Win. Mag. and is based (R) on a cut-down 30-caliber Warbird.

by **JOHN MALLOY**

HANDGUNS TODAY:

AUTOLOADERS

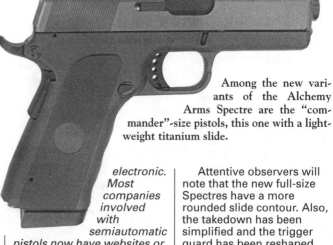

Among the new variants of the Alchemy Arms Spectre are the "commander"-size pistols, this one with a lightweight titanium slide.

*T*HE PAST YEAR was one of great uncertainty for both makers and users of autoloading handguns.

There were many aspects. Lawsuits against firearms manufacturers (primarily those making semi-auto pistols), misuse of authority by public officials, media assaults against firearms ownership, and proposed anti-gun legislation at state and federal levels—all of these things played a part.

As the year 2000 went on, the November 7, 2000 elections were seen as a climax that would give an indication as to what the future might hold.

But even the elections added to the uncertainty, and it was over a month later before George W. Bush was finally acknowledged the President-elect. The election of Bush, who is basically pro-gun, should provide needed relief from the anti-gun policies of the Clinton-Gore administration. In the meantime, however, some state legislators and bureaucrats decided they were firearms experts, even when they had no understanding of handgun or ammunition terminology. States such as California, Maryland and Massachusetts initiated differing standards as to what pistols could be sold within their borders. The arbitrary and sometimes conflicting rules baffled many manufacturers. If other states come up with even different criteria, how can any handgun meet them all?

Some manufacturers have held off spending research time or money on new developments due to this uncertainty. Some have suspended certain models from production.

Yet, there is still much going on in the world of autoloading handguns. There are many new offerings. Most of these are variations on the 1911 theme, and the 45 ACP cartridge remains the most popular chambering for new offerings. Polymer frames have not lost their charm, and some interesting polymer/aluminum combinations have been introduced. Small 45s are very popular, but some new full-size variants have been introduced also. However, everything is not 1911 45s. There are also brand-new designs and brand-new cartridges being introduced. The 22-caliber pistol remains popular—both new pistols and conversion units are being introduced in the 22 Long Rifle (22 LR) chambering. New U. S. companies have been set up to market foreign products.

Due to litigation possibilities and state requirements, many manufacturers are offering or designing locking devices that can incapacitate their pistols.

The aftermarket industry is active and creative. Many new accessories for autoloading handguns are being offered.

The industry has become more involved with things electronic. Most companies involved with semiautomatic pistols now have websites or e-mail addresses to provide information about their products. To show that your writer is up with the times, these electronic contacts will be provided here.

Now, let's take a look at what the companies are doing:

ALCHEMY ARMS

Alchemy Arms' Spectre pistol was introduced only a year ago, but already variations are being introduced. The original 4.5-inch full-size model has been joined by a 4-inch version. The carbon- and stainless-steel slides in both lengths are now joined by those made of titanium. Titanium reduces the weight of a Spectre to 22 ounces.

Express sights (large bead, shallow notch) are standard now. Alchemy also plans to introduce new wide sights of their own design.

Attentive observers will note that the new full-size Spectres have a more rounded slide contour. Also, the takedown has been simplified and the trigger guard has been reshaped slightly. A notch in the front of the trigger guard serves as what the company calls a "digital safety." When not ready to shoot, the user can place his finger on the notch instead of on the trigger.
www.alchemyltd.com

ARMSCOR

This Philippine manufacturer makes a line of 1911-type pistols. The line consists of full-size (5"), "commander" (4") and compact (3.5") in blue, stainless and dual-tone finishes. Calibers are 45, 40 and 9mm. New for 2001 was a full-size 45-caliber "meltdown" variation, with all the edges rounded off.
www.armscor.com.ph

ARMS MORAVIA

The recently introduced CZ-G 2000 pistol now has a new U. S. importer. Anderson and Richardson Arms Co., of Fort Worth, TX, will handle the Czech-made pistol. The

Beretta offers a nifty new holster for their 9000S pistols—it can be used left or right, straight or tilted, narrow belt or wide.

Beretta's Cathy Williams demonstrates the new 9000S pistol, this version a double-action-only (DAO).

distinctively shaped pistol has a polymer frame and is available in 9mm and 40. It is a conventional Double Action (DA) with the decocker recessed into the slide.
arms@arms-moravia.cz

BERETTA

Beretta is celebrating its 475th anniversary in 2001, and rightfully considers itself the oldest firearms company in existence. Records in the company's archives show that in 1526, Bartolomeo Beretta sold 185 arquebus barrels to the Arsenal of Venice. (He received 296 ducats as payment.) From that point, the Beretta line has expanded.

The biggest news is the new Model 92 Millennium pistol. Based on the Model 92 design, it is single action, has a steel frame, frame-mounted safety (it can be carried cocked-and-locked), carbon-fiber grips and adjustable rear sight. The slide is the reinforced "Brigadier" type. It is finished in nickel alloy, with special engraving. Production will be limited to 2000 pistols, 1000 of which will be sold in the United States.

The 92/96 series pistols are now available in a Black Inox (black on stainless) variant. Finish is matte black with gray wraparound rubber grips.

On the smaller end, the 3022 Alley Cat variation of its little Tomcat 32 is offered. It has Big Dot tritium express sights, and comes with a special inside-the-pants holster.

The Model 87 22-caliber target pistol has its adjustable sights mounted in a full-length top bar that will accept optical or electronic sights. A nice feature is that the pistol will stand upright when placed on a flat surface.

The 9000S, Beretta's first polymer-frame pistol, is now in full production. The 9000S, the first Beretta with a tilting-barrel locking system, now makes the company the only one to offer all three common locked-breech systems (the 92/96 series has the dropping block, and the Cougar has the rotating barrel system). To retain the traditional Beretta open-top configuration, Beretta engineers moved the locking lugs from the top to the lower side of the 9000S barrel. A clever holster is available for the 9000S—it can be used either right or left side, straight up or tilted forward, small belt or large belt.

A 22-caliber conversion kit is now offered for the 92/96 series 9mm and 40 S&W pistols.
www.berettausa.com

BROWNING

Browning is celebrating its 25th year of 22-caliber pistol production in Utah. Accordingly, this year the company is producing a 25th Anniversary Buck Mark pistol with a 6.75-inch barrel and bonded ivory grips with a scrimshaw pattern. 1000 will be made.

Other new items in the pistol line include Buck Mark "Color Camper" pistols. These will be made with red, blue or green frames. A limited run of 1200 pistols will be made in colors.

It is not really a pistol, but the Buck Mark line has also been expanded to include a semiautomatic carbine. By

Malloy tries out a 40-caliber conventional DA Beretta 9000S in single-action mode. A separate DAO variant is also offered.

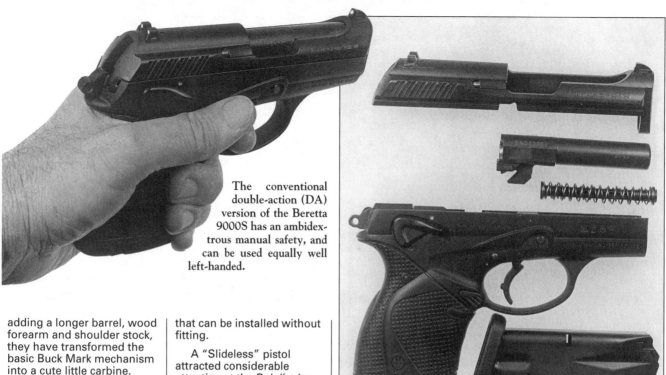

The conventional double-action (DA) version of the Beretta 9000S has an ambidextrous manual safety, and can be used equally well left-handed.

The 9000S is Beretta's first tilting barrel locking system. It is cam-operated, and the lugs are at the bottom to maintain the traditional Beretta open-top appearance.

adding a longer barrel, wood forearm and shoulder stock, they have transformed the basic Buck Mark mechanism into a cute little carbine.
www.browning.com

BUL

Bul Transmark, of Israel, introduced a new 10-shot small 45 at the January 2001 SHOT Show. It uses a polymer frame and was so new Bul had not named it yet. It will not be sold in the U. S. under the Bul name. The company is also marketing parts for 1911-type pistols. Their "Warp Speed" kit of hammer, sear and disconnector is a high-quality, low-price set of parts

that can be installed without fitting.

A "Slideless" pistol attracted considerable attention at the Bul display. The custom 9mm pistol had so much metal removed from the slide it almost seemed a cutaway model. It is claimed to have a very fast action, and the specimen shown was actually used in competition.
www.bultransmark.com

►Century International has a new line of 45 automatics. This variation is the ported Blue Thunder model, with distinctive trigger guard and various enhancements.

◄To celebrate the 25th year of production of 22-caliber pistols in Utah, Browning has introduced a 25th Anniversary commemorative pistol. 1000 will be made.

◄Browning's Buck Mark pistol is the basis for the new Buck Mark carbine. Not really a pistol, but sort of cute.

CASULL

Casull Arms, noted for big revolvers and powerful cartridges, has entered the world of semiautomatic pistols. The new Casull autoloader is a 1911-style pistol for, of course, a powerful new cartridge. The new bottleneck round is called the 38 Casull. It reportedly pushes a 124-grain bullet out at about 1800 feet per second (fps), while a

The new Dan Wesson 1911-type Pointman pistols have given the company a position in the autoloader field as well as in revolvers.

The new Firestorm 22 is a Bersa-style pistol handling the popular 22 Long Rifle (22LR) cartridge. Operation is conventional DA and capacity is 10+1.

147-grain projectile leaves at about 1650 fps.

www.casullarms.com

CENTURY INTERNATIONAL

Century International's big news is their new line of 45-caliber 1911-style pistols. The guns are available in full-size and "commander" lengths in two styles. The standard model has a beavertail grip safety and extended controls. The Blue Thunder variant adds combat sights, full-length guide rod, a notched front strap, distinctively reshaped trigger guard and (in the full-size versions) an optional ported barrel.

Century also offers the Korean Daewoo "Tri-fire" pistols, in the full-size version, in 9mm and 40 S&W. The Arcus 9mm pistol is made in Bulgaria, and is available in full-size and compact versions. It is based on the venerable Browning High-Power mechanism, but includes a *DA* trigger and extended safety lever.

www.centuryarms.com

COLT

Colt continues to make its line of 1911-style pistols in 45 ACP only. One special edition model was displayed at the January 2001 SHOT Show, considered by some a reissue. It is a genuine Colt 1911A1 as it was made at the beginning of World War II. It is Parkerized, has the original mechanical construction (no late-model changes), and has

the old wide hammer, and—glory be—a lanyard ring. The markings are the same as those of the original Colts of the early WWII period. However, if you look closely, you'll see the serial number has a "WK" prefix. They are the initials of Lt. Gen. William Keyes, Colt's new head man, who supported the project.

It is a little off the subject of autoloading handguns, but many were glad to see a Python 357 revolver back in Colt's display. Plans were to reintroduce the Python during the second quarter of 2001, in a 6-inch stainless-steel version.

www.colt.com

CZ-USA

The CZ 75 and its variants continue to dominate the line for CZ. New at the 2001 SHOT Show were the CZ 75 Compact, now in 40 S&W as well as 9mm, and the CZ 75D (decocker) variants. The new decocker model eases the hammer down in two steps; this could be of real interest to those who have never really felt comfortable with the hammer of a loaded pistol slamming forward, no matter what assurances the safety devices provided.

Also available is a CZ 75 Compact "carry" pistol. This is a smooth-edged "meltdown" that many shooters seem to like nowadays. A new CZ 75M

IPSC pistol has been introduced. In 40 S&W caliber, it is designed to meet MII frame of the 45-caliber CZ 97, and has extended magazine release, compensator, blast deflector and other niceties.

The polymer-frame CZ 100, previously scheduled for United States introduction, will not be imported.

CZ offers a FirePoint sight with a red dot that stays permanently on. The expected life is over five years.

If you have looked at CZ pistols and have wondered why some models have the letter B suffix in the designation, be aware that it indicates that a new firing pin safety is installed. If you see a pin-filled hole in the rear

portion of the slide, that also indicates the new safety.

www.cz-usa.com

DAN WESSON

Dan Wesson, a name associated with modern revolvers since 1968, introduced a line of 1911-type pistols in the year 2000. By January 2001, the variety of "Pointman" pistols had

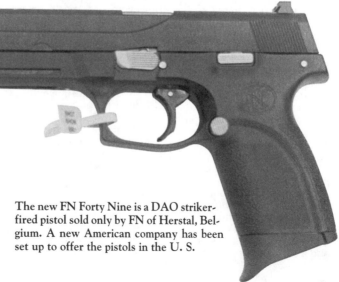

The new FN Forty Nine is a DAO striker-fired pistol sold only by FN of Herstal, Belgium. A new American company has been set up to offer the pistols in the U. S.

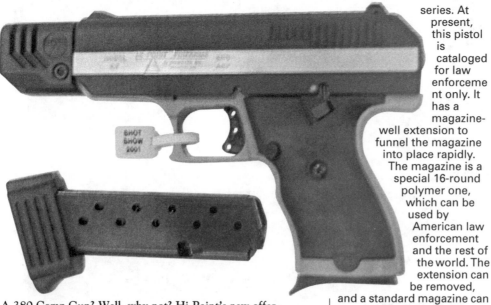

A 380 Comp Gun? Well, why not? Hi-Point's new offering gives a new shooter a low-recoil way to get started. Two magazines are provided—an 8-shot finger-rest version, and a 10-shot extended one.

series. At present, this pistol is cataloged for law enforcement only. It has a magazine-well extension to funnel the magazine into place rapidly. The magazine is a special 16-round polymer one, which can be used by American law enforcement and the rest of the world. The extension can be removed, and a standard magazine can be used. So, it is possible that a 10-round "civilian" version might be forthcoming if the interest warrants it.

www.hecklerkoch-usa.com

HERITAGE

The nice little Heritage Stealth polymer-frame pistol has taken a sabbatical for now. Cowboy Action shooting has become popular enough that Heritage has expanded its single-action "Rough Rider" revolver line, and temporarily suspended production of the semiautos. A number of shooters have expressed the hope that the Stealth pistols—which have received good reviews for exceptional accuracy—will soon become available again.

www.heritagemfg.com

HIGH STANDARD

High Standard is offering a "Safety/Fast" shooting kit for its new line of 1911-type pistols. From the full-cock position, the hammer can be pushed forward, a bit like a Daewoo. However, the similarity ends there. The Safety/Fast system automatically engages the thumb safety when the hammer is pushed forward. Now, everything is locked—the hammer cannot be recocked, the trigger cannot be pulled, the slide cannot be moved. At this time a transfer-bar system prevents the hammer from contacting the firing pin. To get the pistol back into action, simply push the thumb safety down. The hammer is automatically recocked, and the pistol is ready to shoot. Pretty nifty.

www.highstandard.com

HI-POINT

Hi-Point Firearms has introduced a new 380 Comp Gun. The new pistol has a 4-inch barrel, adjustable sights and compensator on the muzzle. It comes with two magazines—an 8-round version with a finger rest, and a 10-round extended model. Why a 380? Hi-Point claims it is extremely accurate with very low recoil; perhaps a good way for a new shooter to get started at low cost. Unlike most previous models, the new pistol has a magazine disconnect safety and last-round hold-open. It is also available with a laser mounted to the compensator.

www.high pointFirearms.com

grown to eleven different models.

www.danwessonfirearms. com

FIRESTORM

FireStorm is a new name in the shooting world, introduced just last year, which offers new twists in established designs. Its first offering was a line of 1911-styled 45-caliber pistols. A new introduction in early 2001 was a new FireStorm pistol chambered for the 22LR cartridge. Based on the Bersa design, the new pistol has 10+1 capacity and measures about 4.7x6.6 inches. Matte and duo-tone finishes are offered. The FireStorm pistols are available through SGS Importers.

www.firestorm-sgs.com

FN

FN Herstal, of Belgium, sells some handguns in the rest of the world that Browning sells in the United States. The new FN Forty-Nine pistol (*note that the first letters of the company name and the pistol model are the same*), however, is sold only by FN. It is a departure from the traditional pistols based on the Browning 1935 "High Power." The FN is *DAO*, striker-fired – and with a polymer frame, yet.

The pistol feels good in the hand, with a *slantier* grip angle than that of the 1935-type pistols. The slide and barrel are of stainless steel, and a semigloss black finish

is available. The polymer frame's forward edge is slotted for whatever accessories the shooter might desire.

The new pistol is offered in 9mm for now. Size is 5.7x7.7 inches, with a 4.25" barrel. Empty weight is about 26 ounces. Magazine capacity is 16 rounds for the rest of the world, 10 for the common folk in America. The Forty-Nine is offered through a new company, FN Manufacturing, Inc. of Columbia, SC.

billf@fnmfg.com

GLOCK

Having filled most of the niches in its autoloading handgun plans, Glock has taken a temporary break from introducing new models this year. However, the company is working on a new internal lock, a prototype of which was present at the 2001 SHOT Show in New Orleans. This prototype device locked with a key through the butt, in the space behind the magazine. When locked, a protrusion at the rear of the grip can be seen or felt.

www.glock.com

HK

Heckler & Koch have introduced a new 40-caliber pistol in their USP Expert

IAI offers new features such as extended controls and large beavertail grip safety on its line of 1911-type pistols. This is a full-size pistol with a 5-inch barrel.

IAI

IAI offers new features on its line of 1911-type pistols such as extended slide stop, safety and magazine release, beavertail grip safety, ambidextrous safety and beveled magazine well. The Houston-based company is now also the sole distributor for the South African RAP 401 (9mm) and RAP 440 (40 S&W) pistols, which are marketed as the IAI M-3000 and IAI M-4000 models, respectively.
www.israelarms.com

Kahr Arms has expanded its polymer-frame offerings with the new P40, a lightweight pistol chambered for the 40 S&W cartridge.

Auto-Ordnance, now operated by Kahr, offers three 1911-style pistols, including this variant with wrap-around grips.

HS AMERICA

The HS 2000 pistol, introduced just last year, is now in production in 9mm. 40-caliber versions were scheduled for mid-2001. Recall that the Croatian-designed pistol has a polymer frame, a "Glock-type" trigger, and locks by a cam-operated tilting-barrel system. New features such as an accessory rail, front slide serrations, a shorter trigger pull and an outlined stippled grip are now standard. They will be phased in on current production.

Also added is a "*read this*" instruction notice of which American shooters have grown so fond. When bored with shooting, we can just stop and read our guns.
www.hsarms.com

KAHR

Kahr introduced its first polymer-frame 9mm pistol last year, and is filling out its polymer lineup. The new 40 S&W-caliber Kahr P40 was introduced at the January 2001 SHOT Show. The P40 weighs in at less than 19 ounces and measures about 4.5x6 inches, with a 3.5-inch barrel. The single-column 6-round magazine keeps the width down to less than an inch. Two magazines come with each pistol.

Recall that Kahr bought Auto-Ordnance two years ago, and with it the right to the 1911-type A-O Thompson pistols. Three versions are now in production: a Parkerized military version, a standard blued version, and a deluxe variant with wrap-around grips and 3-dot sights.
www.kahr.com

KEL-TEC

Kel-Tec has had such good response to the little 6.5-ounce P-32 pistol that they are trying to fill all possible niches of their customers' wants. The P-32 slide may now be had in a hard chrome finish as well as the standard black. The polymer frame is now available in a choice of five

Kel-Tec's Renee Goldman holds two of the many options of the company's popular lightweight P-32 pistol.

◀ To help preserve our firearms rights, Kimber offered a special Heritage Fund pistol. The company donated to the Hunting and Shooting Sports Heritage Foundation for each pistol sold.

▶ Kimber believes their new Ultra Ten II is the smallest, lightest 10-shot 45 around. The new pistol is the first to utilize Kimber's new grip-operated safety system.

Wildlife Artist Jocelyn Lillpop Russell takes a break at the 2001 SHOT Show to examine the new Kimber Ultra Ten II pistol.

10-round magazine for 10+1 capacity. Did you notice the "II" in the name? It is the first Kimber produced with the new safety system.
www.kimberamerica.com

KORTH

At its first SHOT Show display in recent years was the elegant German Korth pistol. A new company, Korth USA, has been formed to market the Korth in the United States. The clever design and beautiful machine work on the Korth variant displayed allows the use of four

colors, in addition to the basic black. Options are silver grey, light blue, dark blue, tan and olive. Mix and match the slides and frames, and it would be possible to have an extensive collection of just P-32s.
www.kel-tec.com

KIMBER

Kimber, reportedly the largest maker of 1911-style pistols, has added a new safety system. The firing pin block is now deactivated by movement of the grip safety, rather than the trigger. This allows the trigger to do the original job of releasing the hammer,

without any additional parts going along for the ride that might change the pull. There is no difference in external appearance. The change was scheduled to be phased in during 2001, and the modified pistols will have a "II" designation after the model number.

Kimber designed a special Heritage Fund Edition 45 to help preserve our firearms rights. For each pistol purchased, the company donated $200 to the Hunting and Shooting Sports Heritage Foundation. Each owner also received an individual Heritage Fund membership.

Who offers the smallest, lightest 10-shot 45? Kimber believes their brand-new Ultra Ten II fits that description. At 24 ounces, with its aluminum-insert polymer frame, the new pistol holds a

A new company, Korth USA, has been formed to market the elegant German Korth pistol in the United States.

Lots of people still like full-size 45s, and Llama has brought its MAX-1 pistol out of temporary retirement and back into the product line.

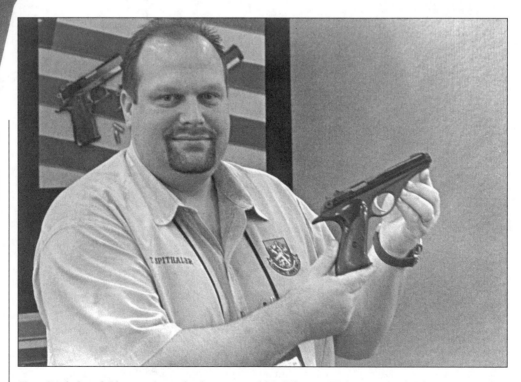

calibers to be used in a single pistol, with only changes of barrels. Even though they are of different dimensions and shapes, 9x19mm, 9x21mm, 357 SIG and 40 S&W cartridges can be handled in the Korth with the same magazine, slide, extractor, ejector and springs. A lot of thought went into this pistol.
www.korthusa.com

LES BAER

Les Baer Custom is offering a new variation of their 45-caliber Monolith pistol, which was introduced in 2000. Recall that the Monolith frame extends all

the way forward to the front of the slide. The new variant is a 4.25-inch barrel pistol called the Comanche. It is available in standard weight and heavyweight styles, and is guaranteed to shoot 3-inch groups at 50 yards. Tritium night sights are included.
www.lesbaer.com

LLAMA

Some years ago, the trend to smaller carry pistols, especially in 45 ACP, became evident. Llama got in on that trend and concentrated on their compact and sub-compact "Minimax" 45s. But there are always those who like the original 1911 size and style. To appeal to them,

Llama has reintroduced the government-size 45-caliber MAX-1 pistol, which has a matte black finish.
www.bersa-llama.com

MAGNUM RESEARCH

Polymer is "in," and Magnum Research has added a polymer-frame pistol to their Baby Eagle lineup.

Their big boomer, the Desert Eagle, now offers components to switch from one caliber to another almost instantly. Owners of Mark XIX Desert Eagles in 44 Magnum, 440 Cor-Bon, or 50

North American Arms figures that if a small 32 is good, why not a small 380? The new NAA Guardian 380 is only fractions of an inch larger than their 32.

Action Express (50 AE) can now have the other calibers with just a barrel and magazine change. The 357 Magnum Desert Eagle can also convert to the other calibers, but that swap requires a bolt assembly change also. All chamberings are available with 6- or 10-inch barrels.

Titanium Gold finishes are now available on most of the pistol line, one of eight different finishes the company can provide.

www.magnumresearch.com

NAA

North American Arms, long a maker of mini-revolvers, was a recent entry into the semi-auto pistol field just a few years ago. Its single offering—the 25-sized 32 Guardian pistol—was well received, so now the company has added another. If a small 32 is good, company officers apparently reasoned, would not a small 380 be better? Their new offering, displayed for the first time at the January 2001 SHOT Show, is the NAA Guardian 380. The new 380 measures 3.5x4.75 inches, with a 2.5-inch barrel.

Tom Spithaler of Olympic Arms displays a 22-caliber Whitney Wolverine pistol. The company plans to bring back the neat little pistol, long out of production.

Introduced during the 1950s, the Whitney Wolverine was considered far ahead of its time. Now, Olympic Arms plans to reintroduce the racy-looking little pistol.

Pacific Armament's Joel Steinberg (*right*) points out features of the company's new line of 1911-type pistols to Gayle Grissett. Long a maker of parts, Pacific Armament now offers a variety of complete pistols.

Kristi McGaha of Professional Ordnance demonstrates the new quick-detachable muzzle brake on the company's big 223-caliber pistol. Using carbon-fiber receivers, the 20-inch pistol weighs only 46 ounces.

Also available is an attachable laser that fastens to the front of the pistol and acts as a "*deprinter*," concealing the shape of the pistol when it is carried in a pocket.
www.naaminis.com

NOWLIN

The 40 Super cartridge, introduced last year, has great potential, and Nowlin has brought out a pistol for that recent cartridge. The new Maximum Hunter model was so new, only one sample was available to observe at the SHOT Show. With its 6-inch barrel, velocities are reported to be in the 1800 fps range.

Nowlin also demonstrated other new variations. The company's Compact Carry guns are 6+1 short-grip 1911 variants with 4.25-inch barrels.

A World Cup PPC pistol is available in 9mm, 38 Super, 9x23, 10mm, 40 S&W and 45 ACP. A nice feature is a set of sights that allows preset adjustments for the different PPC ranges.
www.nowlinguns.com

OLYMPIC ARMS

Remember the Whitney Wolverine, the racy-looking 22 pistol made back in the 1950s? Many said it was 50 years ahead of its time. Now that the half-century has passed, Olympic Arms believes it should be offered again. Olympic had actually made most of the parts to begin manufacture, when disaster struck. The factory burned down, and the Wolverine project was dealt a big setback. As of early 2001, a new building was being constructed, and the Whitney Wolverine is indeed

Weight is less than 19 ounces. For comparison, the 32 is 3.3x4.35 inches, so the difference is about .4-inch longer grip and about .2-inch longer slide. Capacity of both pistols is 6+1.

A new version of the 32, the Guttersnipe, was unveiled at the same time. The catchy name comes from a hollow gutter along the tip of the slide. At the end of the gutter is a white dot. At the

rear of the slide, on the sides of the gutter, are two white dots. Thus, the little pistol offers a 3-dot sight system without using any sights. Nothing protrudes and there is nothing to snag.

Shooters Arms Manufacturing, located in the Philippines, offers 1911-type pistols. S.A.M.'s Richard Yuson holds the new Falcon, with frame extended to the front of the slide.

versions with 38 Super chambering in the works.
gunparts@att.net

PARA-ORDNANCE

Para-Ordnance, which began with—and gained recognition for—its double-column high-capacity 1911 frames, has introduced its first single-stack pistols. Designed to be slimmer for concealed carry, the first of the new series to be presented are compact, short-barrel *DAO* versions. The L6.45S is a 3.5-inch-barrel version, and the LL6.45S is a 3-incher. They have spurless "snag-free" hammers.

New variants of the LDA (Light Double Action) line, which was introduced two years ago, will be offered with manual safeties.
www.paraord.com

PROFESSIONAL ORDNANCE

Professional Ordnance, makers of the large but relatively light 223-caliber pistols, now offer a quick-detachable compensator for their new pistols. The company uses carbon-fiber upper and lower receivers to make a pistol fully 20 inches long that only weighs 46 ounces. The new compensator reduces muzzle rise, and so makes the pistol easier to shoot. A ball-type lock lets it go on or off the muzzle in seconds.
www.professional-ordnance.com

RUGER

Sturm, Ruger & Co.'s P-series polymer-frame guns have become mainstays in the firm's pistol line. One new variant was introduced at the 2001 SHOT Show. It is a P-95 DA with a conventional manual safety. The safety is ambidextrous and can be operated from either side.
www.ruger-firearms.com

S.A.M.

Shooters Arms Manufacturing, located in the Philippines, is offering a new long-frame 1911 variant. The front of the polymer double-stack frame extends to the front of the slide. The Falcon, as the new series is called, is available in full-size (5" barrel) or compact (4.25" barrel) variants. S.A.M. makes several variations of semiautomatic pistols, all based on the Colt 1911, and

scheduled to reappear. Minor modifications to the safety will be made, but essentially the pistol will be an exact continuation of the original.
www.olyarms.com

PACIFIC ARMAMENT

A new line of 45-caliber 1911-type pistols has been introduced by Pacific Armament Corp. The company has been making FAL rifle receivers and 1911 parts, and is now offering it own series of complete pistols. Full-size (5") and commander-size (4.25") variants were available in early 2001, with shorter officer-size pistols and

Sigarm's Laura Burgess displays a Mauser M2 pistol, which is marketed by Sigarms, along with the company's extensive line of SIG pistols.

This closeup of the new Mauser M2 shows a lug that functions in the pistol's rotating-barrel locking system.

In recent years, full-size service pistols seem not to have received much attention. However, the reliable full-size SIG P220, in 45 ACP, has been quietly available since 1975 while other models got the fanfare. Now, a new stainless-steel version has been introduced. The new P220ST is, like its blued predecessor, a 5.6x7.8-inch conventional DA pistol, with a 4.5-inch barrel.

The P226 is now also available as a 9mm Sport pistol for competition in which the lower recoil of the 9mm offers a recovery-time advantage. The new P226 has a heavy 5.6-inch barrel

►The 45-caliber SIG P220 has been quietly available for over a quarter-century without much fanfare. Now the full-size pistol is available in a new stainless-steel version. Here, Malloy fires an early P220, one of the first imported.

◄The nice SIG P210 is back in the catalog, in a new version that includes a push-button magazine release.

◄For competition in which fast recovery time is important, SIG offers the P226 Sport, a 9mm with 51-ounce weight.

all chambered for the 45 ACP cartridge.
www.shootersarms.com.ph

SIGARMS

In 2000, two German investors acquired Sigarms. The purchase included the Exeter, NH operation in the United States. As might be expected, some changes are taking place.

The elegant 9mm single-action P210, scheduled last year to fade into history, is now back in the line, and in a version with a new "American-style" pushbutton magazine release to replace the catch at the base of the grip. This new P210 has wood grips and adjustable sights. Three other variations are also offered with the original butt magazine release and different options of sights and barrel lengths.

◄SIG's standby 45-caliber pistol, the venerable P220, is now available in a stainless-steel version.

Some models of the S&W 22-caliber pistol line are now offered with "Hi-Viz" sights.

There is now a ported S&W Sigma. The new SW40P and SW9P have barrel porting, three-dot sights and an accessory rail.

with a weighted frame extension. The weight is upped to over 51 ounces. Capacity is the legal limit of 10+1.

SIG also offers the new rotating-barrel Mauser M2 pistol, a compact 5x6.8-inch size with a 3.5-inch barrel. At about 32 ounces, the M2 comes as a 45, 40S&W or 357 SIG. Capacity is 8+1 in 45, 10+1 in the other calibers.

www.sigarms.com

SMITH & WESSON

Smith & Wesson created considerable discussion in mid-2000 when the company reached an agreement with the Clinton administration. Ostensibly about safety, it actually concerned what they could make, how those products would be marketed and how the company would spend its money. The

firearms community apparently did not favor such government control of a private industry. In October 2000, S&W's parent company, the Tomkins group, announced that Ed Schultz had stepped down as president and CEO. He was replaced by George Colclough, a 25-year S&W employee.

By early 2001, the company had dropped a

number of items from the line, but had added some new ones, too. Several new semiautomatic pistols were added.

The SW9P (9mm) and SW40P (40S&W) are ported pistols in the Sigma series. The new ported guns feature 3-dot sights and an accessory or equipment rail on the forward frame. The sides of the slides are polished bright.

For those who want something less bright, S&W

has also gone the other way with its unported SW9G and SW40G pistols. Specifications are basically the same, but these are not bright. The polymer frame is NATO green, and a coating of Melonite black hides the stainless slide.

The 22-caliber models 22A and 22S pistols are now offered with "Hi-Viz" sights. They use light-gathering rods at the front sights that appear to the shooter as a bright orange or bright green dot.

www.smith-wesson.com

Sommer & Ockenfuss developed the 224 HV cartridge (*left*) for their new P21 pistol. The new SO pistol will also be chambered for the traditional 9mm and 40 S&W cartridges.

▶Here is the prototype of the new Sommer & Ockenfuss P21 pistol. The grip safety at the front of the grip allows the gun to fire as a conventional DA pistol. When the grip safety is released, the hammer lowers automatically.

At first observation, the pistol reminds one of the HK P7, as it has a long pivoted bar in the front strap of the grip frame. On the HK pistol, this was a cocking lever; on the SO P21, the lever is called a grip safety. When the SO pistol is grasped, it operates as a conventional double-action (*DA*) arm, that is, *DA* for the first shot, SA for succeeding shots. The difference with the P21 is that when the grip safety is released, the hammer is automatically uncocked and drops to the safety position.

As a compact pistol of about 4.7x6.5 inches, the P21 has its 3.1-inch barrel offered in more-or-less standard 9mm and 40 chamberings. However, SO also offers it with a new cartridge, the 224 HV. The new round is essentially an elongated 9mm case necked down to 22 caliber. The overall length is about that of the standard 9mm cartridge. A 40-grain jacketed bullet reportedly goes out at about 2000 feet per second. For comparison, that is faster than the 40-grain 22 Winchester Magnum Rimfire (22 WMR) fired from a rifle. Pretty zippy.

www.sommer-ockenfuss.de

Springfield's Donna Rahn displays the armsmaker's new TRP Operator, a 45 with a special frame for accessory attachment. This specimen has a light installed.

The new Integral Locking System (ILS) from Springfield Armory is a patented locking device that can disable a 1911-type pistol. It is contained entirely within the mainspring housing.

SPRINGFIELD

Springfield has introduced an Internal Locking System (ILS) for their line of 1911-type pistols. The locking device uses a special key to make the pistol inoperable; a reverse turn of the key can put it back into service. The interesting thing about this system is that it is completely contained within the mainspring housing.

Springfield began phasing these in on their products in February 2001 and planned to offer a retrofit kit soon afterwards. The installation requires no modification to the pistol.

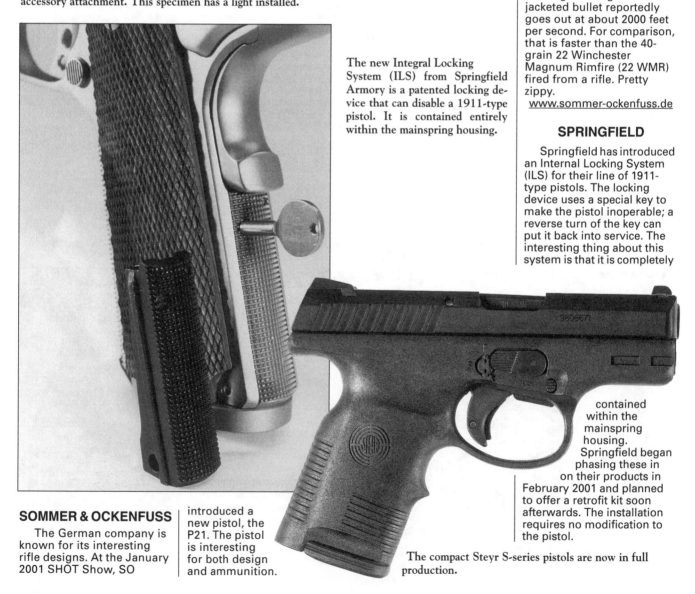

The compact Steyr S-series pistols are now in full production.

SOMMER & OCKENFUSS

The German company is known for its interesting rifle designs. At the January 2001 SHOT Show, SO introduced a new pistol, the P21. The pistol is interesting for both design and ammunition.

A new pistol, the TRP Operator, was introduced by Springfield at the January 2001 SHOT Show. The initials stand for Tactical Response Pistol, and the gun is based around the FBI-contract-pistol specifications. The "Operator" portion of the name refers to a special frame with a forged light/accessory rail at the front. The pistol carries most of Springfield's current enhancements, and it has the adjustable rear sight mounted in a forward position on the slide to prevent damage or snagging.
www.springfieldarmory.com

STEYR

The smaller "S" series Steyr pistol, introduced last year, is now in production. The first shipment of 9mms reached the United States in January 2001, with the 40 S&W variant coming soon after.

Steyr's importer, GSI of Trussville, AL, has offered an upgrade of a more consistent trigger assembly for the first group of "M"- series pistols sold. They have the serial numbers of the ones eligible for the upgrade.

The triangular sight system remains standard, but Steyr is considering more sight options for the future.
www.GSIfirearms.com

STI

The V.I.P., a new 45 ACP pistol, was STI's offering for 2001. Based on the 1911, of course, the V.I.P. has an interesting aluminum frame with a double-stack polymer grip. The slide is stainless steel, sized to fit the 3.9-inch barrel. The combination of materials, says STI, makes a potent, lightweight, corrosion-resistant personal-defense firearm. Available in 45 ACP, the capacity is 10+1 and the weight is 25 ounces.
www.stiguns.com

TALON

A new company from Ennis, MT, Talon Industries has introduced pistols in the recent category of inexpensive subcompact polymer-frame carry pistols. Two models, the T-100 (380) and the T-200 (9mm) are offered. Each has a 10-round magazine, with a weight of 17 ounces. Overall size is 4.4x6 inches, and the barrel length is 3.3 inches. Locking is by a tilting-barrel system. Trigger mechanism is DAO.
talonind@3rivers.net

TAURUS

Handy little pistols and more ammunition options have given the 32 ACP a new lease on life in recent years. Now Taurus will have a 32 Automatic in their line. The new Taurus 32 is included in the polymer-frame Millennium series, and is designated PT 132. The little gun was too new to make it into the company's 2001 catalog, so keep an eye peeled for it.

The compact Millenium 45, the PT 145, was introduced last year, but ran into production delays. Quantity delivery of the compact 23-ounce 45 was rescheduled for summer 2001. For those who like a variety of sight options, it may be worth the wait, as night sights will be available when it arrives
www.taurususa.com

VALTRO

Whatever happened to the Valtro 45, the nice Italian-made 1911 design that was

The subcompact Talon pistol is a new entry in the field of inexpensive polymer-frame carry pistols. It is available in 9mm and 380.

introduced several years ago? It had a slow manufacturing start, but is now in production. As of early 2001, the guns were coming out of Italy at the rate of about 100 a month. The pistols are offered in the United States by Valtro USA, of San Rafael, CA.

WALTHER USA

Some changes have been taking place at Walther USA since last year. The Hungarian-made PPK/E, announced last year to replace the PPK/S, will not be imported after all. Instead, the PPK/S, which was destined to fade into history, was slightly redesigned and was scheduled to be available by late summer 2001. The

Talon's Sharon Edwards points out the features of the Talon 9mm pistol to Sean Gilthorpe at the 2001 SHOT Show.

Pearce Grips offers easily installed 1911 front-strap finger grooves that can be used with the pistol's original grips or with Pearce's big-diamond rubber grips. Here, a combination is used to spruce up the writer's nice old 45 Government Model.

With the trend to legal-limit magazine capacity in smaller-size pistols, it sometimes becomes harder to load the magazines. There are good magazine loaders available, but generally different ones are required for different magazines. Magloader has introduced a clever new loading aid that will work with all magazines in calibers 32 through 45. The simple loader fits on the shooter's thumb, is easy to carry around, and works great. www.magloader.com

How about a magazine for magazines? The Redi-Clip is a nylon dispenser that holds five loaded magazines and allows them to be withdrawn one at a time. It can clip to a belt or can be otherwise mounted. www.Redi-Clip.com

The Safety Fast shooting kit is available from Numrich Gun Parts for Colt 1911 and Browning High Power pistols. The modified pistol can be safely carried with hammer down on a chambered round. By depressing the manual safety, the hammer is automatically cocked and the pistol is ready to shoot. The kit comes with complete instructions and can be installed without modification to the gun. info@gunpartscorp.com

"Pre-ban" high capacity pistol magazines are treasured items for those with high-capacity pistols. Yet, the magazines can lead a hard life, especially when used in certain types of pistol competition. It is a tragic loss if one is damaged beyond use. Now, the LaPrade Company offers legal replacement magazine bodies for damaged high-capacity Glock magazines. A shooter can put the internal parts of the unusable magazine into the new body and be back in action.

These are just a few of the accessories available for those who enjoy shooting autoloading pistols. A shooter can find an array of metallic sights, optical sights, electronic sights, lasers, grips, holsters, safety devices, specialized parts and magazines, not to mention such staples as ammunition and targets. We should never lose sight of the fact that autoloading handguns and their accessories provide both a creative and an economic boost to our nation.

remaining stocks of the original-design PPK/S will be sold until they are gone.

Walther realizes that just about everyone can use a 22 pistol. A new offering, a 22-caliber version of the company's P99 pistol, was introduced in January 2001, with availability planned for April 2001. The new P22 is about 25 % smaller than the P99, but retains the same general appearance, although there are mechanical differences. The takedown, ambidextrous magazine release and interchangeable grip backstraps are similar, but the new 22 is hammer-operated, rather than striker-fired. Two versions were announced, a plinker with a 3.4-inch barrel and a more serious version with a weighted 5-inch barrel. The barrels are interchangeable, and the first 1000 will be offered in a kit with both barrels.
www.walther-usa.com

WILSON

Wilson Combat has introduced their KZ-45, a polymer-frame compact carry pistol. A prototype was shown at the January 2001 SHOT Show, and availability was planned for sometime in 2002. A 9+1 45, the new compact Wilson, based on the 1911 design, sports a 4.1-inch barrel. Although the magazine is of the staggered double-column type, the width is as thin as a standard 1911. The KZ-45 will come with an accuracy guarantee of 1.5 inches at 25 yards.
www.wilsoncombat.com

POSTSCRIPT

Innovative accessories for semiautomatic handguns have been recently introduced. Here are just a few of them:

Pearce Grips offers new items for the ever-popular 1911 pistols. A shooter who likes his present grip panels but would like front-strap finger grooves can get just the rubber front grooves. The Pearce product is a clever way to adapt the finger grooves without modification of the gun. Pearce also offers rubber grip panels, with moulded big-diamond checkering. These can be used by themselves or combined with the finger grooves for a good-feeling grip. www.pearcegrip.com

Among a plethora of new accessories is the Redi-Clip, sort of a magazine for pistol magazines.

by HAL SWIGGETT

HANDGUNS TODAY:

SIXGUNS AND OTHERS

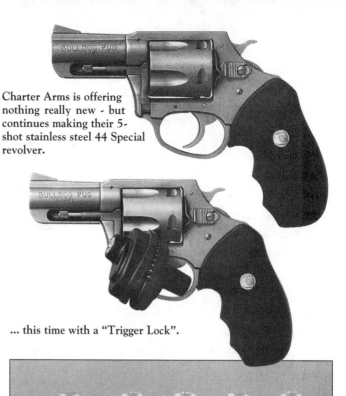

Charter Arms is offering nothing really new - but continues making their 5-shot stainless steel 44 Special revolver.

... this time with a "Trigger Lock".

Anschutz Model 64P Magnum.

... and it is STILL a 5-shot, double action revolver.

Anschutz

Long noted for super-accurate rifles, this German manufacturer does in fact produce bolt-action pistols that equal their rifles: The 64 P is chambered 22 Long Rifle; the 64 P Magnum is chambered for the 22 Winchester Magnum. Magazine capacity for the LR is five; the Magnum, four. Barrel length is 9.8 inches and weight is 3.5 pounds for both. Stocks are black, ergonomic, weatherproof and non-slip synthetic. Both are delivered with sights;

both are grooved for scope mounting.

I have been shooting their wood-stocked pistols chambered 22 LR and 22 WMR for many years; both scoped – and they have served well. I look forward to trying the new Anschutz synthetic model.

Casull Arms

Dick Casull, inventor of the 454 Casull cartridge and builder of the single-action revolver to handle it, has come up with another "winner" – the Casull Arms Model CA 2000. This is a tiny

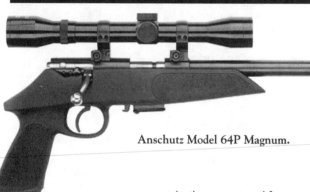

Casull Arms, at least to this gun-writer, little 22 Long Rifle-chambered 5-shot re-volver is, by far, the "cut-est" little revolver I've ever seen. With its fold-up trigger it can, easily, fit in a shirt pocket, behind a note-book.

little 5-shot revolver with a fold-up trigger and enclosed hammer that could, very easily, fit in a shirt pocket behind a notebook. It's chambered for the 22 Long Rifle, weighs 8 to 9 ounces and is truly palm-size.

Colt

This Hartford, Connecticut company started manufacturing single-action revolvers in 1836 in Paterson, New Jersey. After two moves they ended up in Hartford in 1848 – and are still in Connecticut.

Their first revolver was the Pocket Model Paterson No. 1, a 28-caliber, 5-shooter. Should you have one in 98-percent original condition it could be worth upwards of $30,000 according to the current edition of *Flayderman's Guide to Antique American Arms and their Values...*

Their current single-action revolver line includes two models – Cowboy Single Action (CSA) and Single Action Army (SAA).

The Cowboy Single Action is blue color-case finished with a 5 1/2-inch barrel, chambered for the 45 Colt.

The Single Action Army line offers eight different "models."

Blue color-case finish (*P1840*) or Nickel finish (*P1841*) with 4 3/4-inch barrels. Model (*P1850*) and (*P1856*) are chambered .45 Colt and carry 5 1/2-inch barrels. Models (*P1940*) and (*P1956*) are chambered for the 44-40 WCF, with 4 3/4-inch barrels [(*40*) blue (*41*) nickel]. Models (*P1950*) and (*P1956*), in that same order, are blue- or nickel-finished with 5 1/2-inch barrels and also chambered for the 44-40 WCF.

Competitor Corporation, Inc.

Al Straitiff and his wife run this "outfit." They produce a single-shot, cannon-breech pistol and chamber it for any cartridge you might be able to come up with.

Mine is many, many years old and chambered 223 Remington. Al's

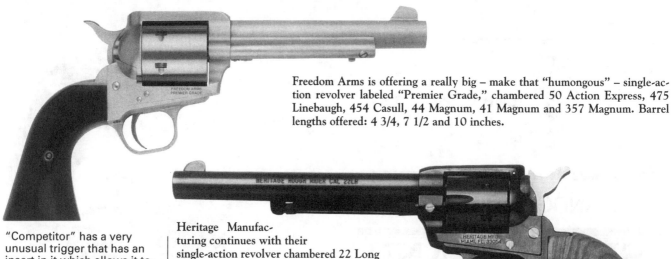

Freedom Arms is offering a really big – make that "humongous" – single-action revolver labeled "Premier Grade," chambered 50 Action Express, 475 Linebaugh, 454 Casull, 44 Magnum, 41 Magnum and 357 Magnum. Barrel lengths offered: 4 3/4, 7 1/2 and 10 inches.

"Competitor" has a very unusual trigger that has an insert in it which allows it to fire with only 1 1/4 lbs of pressure – not for the casual handgunner.

Dan Wesson Arms

This company has gone through some difficult years but is still turning out their fine Model 360/7360 double-action revolvers. Model 360 is carbon steel with black-oxide bluing. Model 7360 is stainless steel with satin-brushed finish. Their 10-inch barreled double-action revolvers have achieved great success in Silhouette shooting.

Freedom Arms

I have been shooting this company's 454 Casull single-action 5-shot revolvers since their very first production. My lengthy barrel measures 9 1/4 inches (including SSK Industries' ported "Recoil

Heritage Manufacturing continues with their single-action revolver chambered 22 Long Rifle or 22 Winchester Magnum.

Reducer"). This one wears a Simmons 1.5-4x scope in a 4-ring mount (yes – you will know when FA's 454 Casull does fire!).

Freedom Arms has grown! Currently they are offering Premier Grade single actions chambered for the 50 Action Express, 475 Linebaugh, 454 Casull, 44 Magnum, 41 Magnum and 357 Magnum with barrel lengths of 4 3/4, 7 1/2 and 10 inches.

Their Field Grade is available in barrel lengths of 4 3/4, 7 1/2 and 10 inches.

They have not neglected rimfire handgunners. Freedom Arms catalogs a 22 Long Rifle revolver with a 7 1/2-inch barrel.

There are now four Silhouette models: 22 Long Rifle/10 inch; 357 Magnum/9 inch; 41 Magnum/10 inch and 44 Magnum/10 inch.

If you are a handgunner you really do need this manufacturer's catalog.

Heritage Manufacturing, Inc.

This Florida-based manufacturer offers their single-action revolver chambered 22 Long Rifle or 22 Winchester Magnum rimfire. Barrel lengths are 3 3/4, 4 1/2, 6 1/2 and 9 inches. Rough Rider's frame is manufactured from 4140 steel; sights are adjustable. Grips are manufactured from exotic hardwood.

Lasergrips

Crimson Trace Corporation offers grips for revolvers that, when "squeezed", send out a red beam that is easily seen and lets the handgunner know exactly where his bullet will hit.

Though I've never had reason to use it, there is one of my handguns, so rigged, under my pillow every night as I sleep.

Magnum Research

Magnum Research offers their Magnum BFR in two models: Maxine and Little Max – both stainless steel with two cylinder lengths.

Maxine, the larger model, chambers the potent 45/70 Government round, 444 Marlin and 45 Colt/.410.

Little Max is available chambered for the 454 Casull, 45 Colt, 50 A.E. and 22 Hornet. Available barrel lengths are 6 1/2, 7 1/2 or 10 inches.

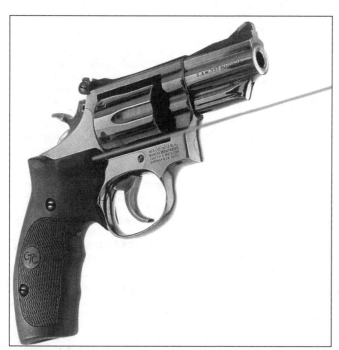

Lasergrips offers a *"beam shooting light"* that lets the shooter know exactly where his bullet will hit.

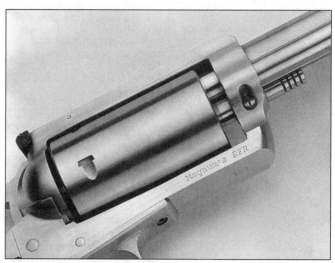

Magnum's BFR boasts a large, rugged frame to accommodate the unusually long cylinder chambered for the 45/70 Government, and others.

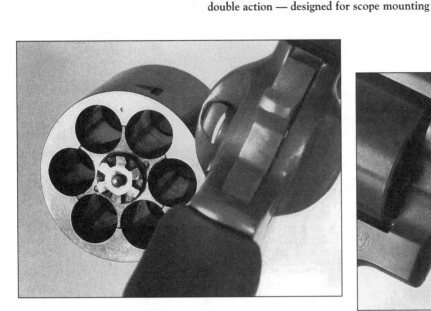

Ruger, this time around, is offering a double action — designed for scope mounting —

... 6-shot revolver —

... chambered 480 Ruger (an entirely new cartridge) —

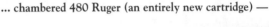

... manufactured by Hornady.

M.O.A. "Maximum"

Richard R. Mertz, president of this company, has manufactured his "Falling Block Single Shot" pistol for more than a few years. It has won many silhouette titles and taken critters from wild hogs to elk; kudu to moose.

The one I've been shooting is chambered for the 250 Savage Improved and topped with Simmons' 4x32 scope. With its 14-inch long, 3/4-inch diameter barrel it weighs 4 lbs., 15 oz. Trigger pull is 2 1/2 lbs. It has taken antelope in Wyoming – plus deer (both whitetail and mulies), javelina – and many coyotes.

North American Arms

I mention this manufacturer every year for a reason. They are the only manufacturer of a handgun that can be with you totally concealed at all times. All 22s or 22 WMRs with barrel lengths 1 1/8, 1 5/8, 2 and 4 inches. Though I have a concealed carry-license here in Texas, I have – lots of times – had one of these tiny revolvers in my left-side shirt pocket, behind my always-present note book.

Ruger

Their newest, near as I can tell, is a double-action GP100 chambered 357 Magnum offered in blue or stainless steel with barrel lengths of 3, 4 or 6 inches. Plus, your choice of fixed or adjustable sights.

Ruger introduced their Redhawk/Super Redhawk a few years back with the buyer's choice of blue or stainless steel. For 2001 Ruger offers the Super Redhawk chambered for a new cartridge of their design – the 480 Ruger.

Here I quote page 31 in their new catalog: "*The new 480 Ruger cartridge is an exciting new development in handgun hunting cartridges. It offers approximately a third more energy than the powerful 44 Magnum, able to stop big game reliably at typical handgun range.*" Ruger's new innovation is offered with the buyer's choice of 7 1/2- or 9 1/2-inch barrels. Finish is SSTG (stainless steel target gray). I will have to have one of these!

Page 36 of the Ruger catalog lists as *NEW*, their Ruger Vaquero with a "Birds Head" grip. Ruger still catalogs their precious little Bearcat.

You need one of their new catalogs.

Savage Arms

I have been shooting one of Savage Arms' Model 516 bolt-action "*short rifles*" (my term because I have found I can do anything with these pistols most riflemen can with their long barrels).

Why am I so fond of it? They made it ever so much easier to shoot because their designer put the bolt on the left side! Plus – its integral muzzle brake allows any shooter to see where the bullets are hitting.

Mine is chambered for the 22-250 Remington. Magazine capacity is 2, making it a 3-shooter. Trigger pull is "*crisp as breaking glass*" at 1 3/4 lbs. A Burris 3-9x scope is mounted on its 14 1/2-inch barrel (including muzzle brake).

Savage describes Striker's stock as "*dual pillar-bedded ambidextrous mid-grip synthetic*".

Now, I understand, they are offering a Sportsman model chambered for the 22 Long Rifle. I know I will have to have one of these, too, because it is the only one I would ever consider in any survival situation.

One 500-round carton of 22 Long Rifle cartridges weighs 5-plus pounds. Yet those 500 rounds would feed a family many, many moons.

Rossi /Braztech

For 2001 this Miami company is offering several new revolvers, chambered for the 38 Special or 357 Magnum, depending on the model.

Model 351 is blue steel; Model 352 is stainless. Both with 2-inch barrels, 5-round cylinders chambered for the 38 Special.

Model 461 is blue steel, chambered to accept six 357 Magnum cartridges. Model 462 is stainless steel-constructed; both with 2-inch barrels. Both will accept 38 Special ammunition, along with 357s.

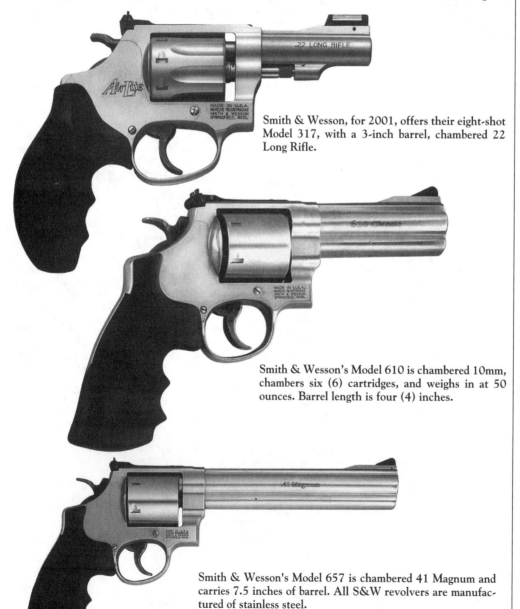

Savage, for 2001, is offering a "Sportsman Model," chambered 22 Long Rifle.

Model 851 is chambered for the 38 Special; blue steel, 6-round capacity with a 4-inch barrel.

Model 971 and Model 972 are chambered for the 357 Magnum. '71 is blue-finished and wears a 4-inch barrel. '72 – of stainless steel – carries a 6-inch barrel.

Models R351 (*blued*) and R352 (*stainless*) are short-barreled, 5-shot, 38 Specials.

Model R461 is also short-barreled, blued – but its cylinder accepts six 357 Magnum cartridges. All are delivered with key locks.

Smith & Wesson

Though this Springfield, Massachusetts, company specializes in *self-shuckers* (autoloaders) they are offering three new revolvers for 2001. Model 317 is chambered 22 Long Rifle, with an 8-shot cylinder. Built on S&W's "J" frame with a 3-inch barrel and target hammer – believe it or not – it weighs only 11.9 ounces. It is manufactured of aluminum alloy and stainless steel to save weight.

S&W's Model 610 is chambered for the 10mm round, chambers six cartridges, and weighs 50 ounces. This revolver has a 4-inch underlug barrel with a ramp front and adjustable rear sight.

Their Model 657 is chambered for the 41 Magnum. This one is fitted with a 7.5-inch barrel, target hammer, smooth trigger – in stainless steel.

Taurus

Up front in their catalog was Titanium Tracker. "*Now available in Total Titanium, the Tracker adds weight and durability benefits of Total Titanium to its list of exclusive features, including rubber grip and extended ejector rod. The Tracker family is available in 41 Magnum and 357 Magnum. All feature adjustable sights.*" Titanium is featured in their Model 85 38 Special, Model 6171 357 Magnum and Model 627 Tracker. They offer a 9-shot 22 rimfire or 8-shot 22 Magnum – their Model 941SS2 – with your choice of 2-, 4- or 5-inch barrel. Taurus' Model 85B2GRC 5-shot is chambered for the 38 Special – another of their short-barreled series.

Taurus' mid-frame service revolver is chambered for the 357 Magnum and is, in their words, "*A Tack Driver*". Their Model 65 is a 6-shot service revolver with fixed sights. Taurus offers another 41 Magnum labeled "Tracker". It, too, is of titanium construction and offered with a 4- or 6-barrel. Cylinder capacity is 5 rounds; weight 24.3 ounces.

Taurus is still cataloging their Raging Bull chambered for the 454 Casull or, if you prefer, 44 Magnum. Barrel lengths offered are: 4, 6 1/2 and 8 3/8 inches. Scope mounts to match barrel lengths and finish (*they offer both blue or stainless*) are also offered for 6 1/2-inch or 8 3/8-inch barrels.

The Raging Hornet wears a 10-inch barrel, carries an 8-shot cylinder and is chambered to accept eight 22 Hornet cartridges.

I've said it before – and I do mean it – you readers really do need catalogs from each of these manufacturers. ●

Smith & Wesson, for 2001, offers their eight-shot Model 317, with a 3-inch barrel, chambered 22 Long Rifle.

Smith & Wesson's Model 610 is chambered 10mm, chambers six (6) cartridges, and weighs in at 50 ounces. Barrel length is four (4) inches.

Smith & Wesson's Model 657 is chambered 41 Magnum and carries 7.5 inches of barrel. All S&W revolvers are manufactured of stainless steel.

THE GUNS OF EUROPE

by **RAYMOND CARANTA**

ALAIN VAUSSENAT AND HIS "V.98" SINGLE SHOT RIFLE

ALAIN VAUSSENAT IS a skilled gunmaker, living near the French village Chantemerle, high in the Alp Mountains near the Swiss border.

From the windows of Alain Vaussenat's small chalet, where he designs and crafts his custom guns, there is a magnificent view of the Alps: to the right, the *Vercors*; front, the *Oisans*, famous "Resistance" strongholds during World War II and, left, the *Belledonne* high

The Vaussenat "V98" sample tested, was chambered for the 7mm-08 Remington and fitted with a Kahles "Helia" 3-9X42 scope.

peak, with *Champrousse* ski station, home of earlier winter Olympics games where Jean-Claude Killy once won three gold medals.

- Alain Vaussenat's facilities.

If the artist is great, his facilities are small; a situation

often encountered in these mountainous regions and this workshop is no exception. Within, the walls are covered with traditional hand-tools and many drawers are filled with them. Vaussenat also uses several machine tools; a small high-precision Swiss Schaublin "*SV12*" milling machine, a French Crouzet "*86-105*" universal lathe and a special LIP grinder, originally intended for watch manufacture.

In front of the workshop, there is an open shooting range equipped with two Oehler and Chrony chronographs, for measuring muzzle velocities at 65 and 130 yards (60 and 120 meters).

Ballistic considerations.

Vaussenat is very interested in bullet design and velocities; perfectly conscious that, for hunting, it is the terminal velocity that counts, rather than the muzzle velocity. His hunting experience, aided by the use

of a laser range finder, teaches him a 2,460 fps (*750 m/s*) impact velocity is required – but rarely attained in long-range shooting – to drop game in its tracks.

However, he is not impressed with those cartridges burning a great amount of powder and producing even more noise, flash and recoil – such as the 7mm Remington Magnum – feeling they are not superior to properly-loaded, less 'ambitious' cartridges.

Preferred chamberings are, for instance, the 243 Winchester, 260 Remington, 6.5x57mm Mauser, 270 Winchester, 7mm-08 Remington and the 30-06 Springfield, for both European and North American game.

For African – or otherwise dangerous game, such as the bear – Vaussenat considers the 300 Winchester Magnum, 300 H&H, 8x68S, 375 H&H and 416 Rigby the most efficient and useful chamberings.

The 375 H&H is, for instance, one of the best selections against the most dangerous beasts, provided the first hit is properly placed. The highly praised "*Mega-Magnums*" can be totally ineffective, if the shooter closes his eyes (anticipating recoil) before pulling the trigger, and hits the quarry in a non-

vital place. Vaussenat's motto is simple: "*Workmanship.*" During the last twelve years he has handcrafted more than fifty bolt-action rifles of the very best quality, based on the classic Mauser action and fitted with a fast thumb-operated safety. These rifles are individually made to the customer's specifications, precisely fitted and hand-finished in the smallest details.

Some of these rifles are takedown designs, which permit easy transportation to the shooting ranges and hunting grounds. These rifles can be quickly re-assembled and fired accurately – without re-zeroing – thanks to a

When the knife is gripped for cutting downwards, the thumb position, firmly pressing the blade back, provides accurate guiding for an easy cutting up of the game.

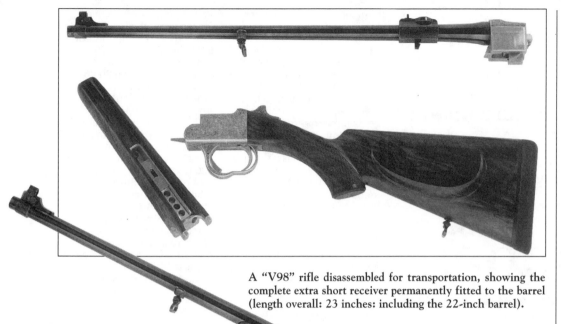

A "V98" rifle disassembled for transportation, showing the complete extra short receiver permanently fitted to the barrel (length overall: 23 inches: including the 22-inch barrel).

and cost a minimum of F.F. 8,500 (US $1,200 approximately) – plus delivery costs.

Why the "V98" single-shot-rifle

A mountain hunter since he was seventeen, Vaussenat's favorite game is the *chamois* – so much that he is now president of the "International Chamois Club," which is comprised of distinguished French, Swiss and Spanish *aficionados*.

For this kind of challenging alpine hunt Vaussenat has, for thirty years, carried an attractive 6.5x57mm Austrian Mannlicher Schoenauer *stuetzen* repeater, requiring re-zeroing quite often since, while they look fine, the full-length forearms are sensitive to dampness and temperature variations – both inconsistent with long-lasting 'zeros.'

Seeking improvement, he shifted to the single-shot rifle for this kind of hunting and purchased, initially, a nice Ferlach *Heeren* rifle chambered for the 7x65R cartridge. Next, a Ferlach 300 Winchester Magnum *Kipplauf*, followed by a fixed-barrel gun, in the same chambering, with a

special barrel-bedding compound.

The stocks are made of the best French walnut, seasoned twenty years and handpicked by the gunmaker. The stocks of African-caliber rifles are hand-checkered 20 lines-per-inch around the wrist and upon the pistol grip; for conventional chamberings, a finer 30 lines-per-inch checkering is available on request. The stock finish is English-style oil – an old turn-of-the-century procedure – that will not change over the years. The forend tip and grip cap are cut from the best available ebony.

Trigger mechanisms are hand-made, with crisp let-off, unless otherwise specified.

Magazines are fixed and internal, with a standard five-round capacity. Vaussenat is strongly opposed to removable magazines since, in emergencies, they can easily turn the best repeater into a single-shot rifle.

Scope mounts are the European claw-type, for dependable accuracy and fast removal, when required. The gun's balance, open sights and stock design are optimized to permit the fastest instinctive shooting. Available chamberings include the 243 Winchester, 7x64mm, 270 Winchester, 300 Winchester Magnum, 8x68S and 375 H&H.

Prices vary, according to specific customer requirements, from F.F. 50,000 to F.F. 100,000 (US $7,000.00 to $14,000.00, at the December 2000 rate) – plus delivery – quite reasonable, in view of the extensive handwork involved and first-class materials used throughout.

Vaussenat also makes custom hunting knives; most with fixed blades, shaped according to the wishes of his hunter friends. The exceptionally sturdy Vaussenat knife has been designed for field dressing and cutting up European game. Exceptionally sturdy, and forged of a French steel in "D2"-class, with a full-width tang and thick blade, these knives are available with engraving matching that of the customer's rifle and with matching serial numbers. They are delivered in a custom leather sheath – also made by Vaussenat –

The first "V98" single-shot prototype, finished in white.

Left side view of an engraved "V98" single-shot rifle showing the elegant stock lines and wood quality.

Farquharson action. This potent chambering was selected since, at that time, only single-shot rifles of at least 30-caliber were allowed for hunting the Swiss *Valais* area.

By the way, the Swiss 7.5x55mm service cartridge was then prohibited – despite being actually a .30-inch/30-caliber – because it was designated "7.5mm" (nominally .295-inch)...typical of the Swiss mentality.

Finally, he finally purchased a 30-06 *Kipplauf*. Highly

accurate at the beginning, the accuracy slowly decayed after firing only a thousand rounds. Subsequently, after a careful evaluation of the available

single-shot rifle systems, in 1981 Vaussenat established his own parameters for "*the ideal gun*" – his "V98" single-shot rifle design.

The "V98" single-shot rifle design fulfills seven basic requirements:

1) Ease of transportation - fast disassembly, via simple barrel removal, reduces overall length.

2) Ease of loading - an action enabling loading, or unloading, without

is both simple and foolproof, without undue variation.

7) Self-cocking, with hand-cocking option - the "V98" rifle features a highly sophisticated cocking device, simple to operate, which consists of an outside two-position selector (which also acts as a cocking indicator felt by the thumb of the right hand as the gun is gripped).

On "**F**" position, the internal hammer cocks automatically when the action is opened. If the selector is pushed to "**S**", the mainspring is relaxed and the rifle is deactivated. Simply push the selector back to "**F**" to restore the firing configuration.

With the selector on "**S**", the gun can be loaded, but the inside hammer uncocked – the selector has to be pushed to

The hooded "V98" front sight in transport configuration.

The "V98" bead front sight ready for shooting.

requiring excessive manipulation as is the case with *Kipplauf*-style guns, when rested or prone. Under such shooting circumstances, operation is much easier with a fixed-barrel – rather than a break-action arm – and does not alert the game.

3) Sturdiness - use of a falling-block action, the stiffer and sturdier choice, for best accuracy and durability.

4) Barrel interchangeability - the breechblock unit, specific to each barrel, remains attached to it during field-stripping, ensuring barrel interchangeability without adverse effect on accuracy.

5) Free barrel expansion - there is no contact between the free-floating barrel and the forearm, for optimum accuracy.

6) Trigger mechanism steadiness: the "V98" rifle is fitted with a single trigger featuring a single-stage mechanism, only adjustable on a bench. This mechanism

On this engraved sample, note the breechblock in closed configuration and the selector located in front of the right-hand thumb.

"**F**" for shooting. Moreover, this selector acts also as an unfailing cocking indicator felt by the right-hand thumb, when gripping the gun.

The final "V98" rifle design.

Vaussenat settled upon a modified single-trigger *Heeren*-style falling-block action featuring interchangeable barrels; each fitted with an individual breechblock, as mentioned earlier.

In this design, barrel removal is controlled by an inside lever, exposed when the forearm is removed. To open the action, push forward on the front lever

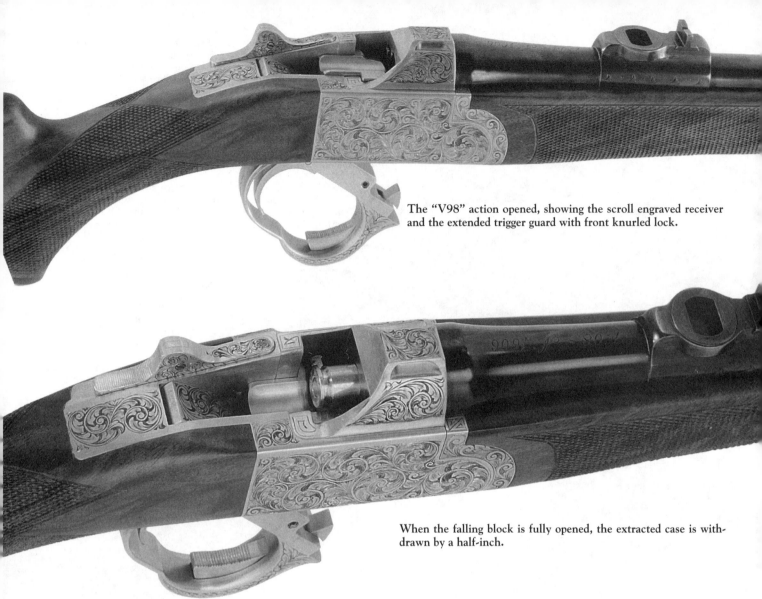

The "V98" action opened, showing the scroll engraved receiver and the extended trigger guard with front knurled lock.

When the falling block is fully opened, the extracted case is withdrawn by a half-inch.

located inside the trigger-guard; then pull down the trigger guard, which controls the breechblock vertical travel. Vaussenat wisely increased the trigger guard length, to eliminate a known drawback of the original *Heeren* gun.

The "V98" single-shot rifle is of the extractor type; ejectors being noisy in the field. The pivoting extractor is located in the left wall of the receiver, in front of the breechblock. When the action is opened, the shell is extracted a half-inch, for easy removal and reloading. Any chambering is available, up to the 416 Rigby.

The standard trigger-pull setting is two pounds, which can be factory-adjusted – as required – down to one pound. Maurice Riocreux, the great French artist and former pupil of the Saint-Etienne Fine Arts School, expertly engraves the "V98" rifles to customer requirements.

Our test sample No 1.

The "V98" *No 1* was delivered to this writer on Sunday, December 16, 2000 – four days past the promised date – quite precise for what is, literally, a prototype specimen...and we were not disappointed!

Chambered in 7mm-08 Remington, it was a wonderful handy carbine 37 inches long, with a 22-inch barrel and weighing 6.2 pounds.

The stock, including a one-inch recoil pad, looked shorter than it actually was; the length was perfect for a five-foot, nine-inch hunter dressed in thick winter garb – and its styling was rich, indeed!

The *squarish* steel receiver was less than three inches long. The open rear sight, with a comfortable U-notch, was dovetailed into a custom-shaped barrel rib and the ramp-style removable-bead front sight was protected by a folding hood.

An Austrian Kahles "Helia" 3-9x42 scope, with a beautiful 5X field of view at 100 meters, added some twenty ounces to the overall weight, bringing the scoped rifle to 7.4 pounds. With the scope, overall steadiness was improved – but the mount would be better, if lower.

The rifle's workmanship was perfect, with velvet-smooth operation, but special mention is deserved by the buttstock and forend burl walnut that reflects its aristocratic French heritage. What a pity for the highly praised Circassian – and other Mohammedan – gunstock woods! Fortunately, in this old European country, we still have treasures other than our cathedrals.

For fast offhand shooting, with the open sights, the gun balanced two inches forward of the trigger, for excellent stability; the 'off' hand drawing the slender,

ebony-capped forearm into the shoulder.

At 130 yards, the standard Vaussenat mountain rifle range – after careful zeroing – our best three-round grouping was .36-inch between centers, using a proprietary handload featuring a Nosler "Ballistic Tip" 120-grain bullet propelled by 46 grains of Hodgdon "Varget" powder, delivering 3,100 fps (Remington case and Federal No. 215 primer).

Now, we are awaiting the bill for a fine custom-engraved sample...but Vaussenat has just advised he is not yet able to state a firm price.

Alain Vaussenat's address:

Mr. Alain Vaussenat
Armes de Qualite
50, Chemin de Chantemerle
F-38700 LA TRONCHE - France
Fax: (33).476.88.04.28_
www.alainvaussenat.com

by LAYNE SIMPSON

RIFLE REVIEW

Beretta

THERE ARE A number of advantages to having the name, Beretta. For one, you appear first in my column – and you always will unless Anschutz has something new or until someone forms the Acme Gun Co., or Albacore Firearms, Inc., or something like that.

Beretta's Mato, a rifle that ranks right up there with the best of 'em in looks, quality and performance is now available in 270 Winchester, 7mm Remington Magnum,

30-06, 300 Winchester Magnum and 375 H&H Magnum. All of those chamberings are available in the synthetic-stocked Mato Synthetic but the 375 H&H Magnum is not available in the wood-stocked Mato Deluxe. The 375-caliber Synthetic rifle comes with a muzzle brake. At the very top of the line is the Mato Deluxe Extra with a steel trapdoor gripcap on its fancy English walnut stock. The bottom edge of the stock has a spare magazine compartment with hinged steel cover.

Renaissance-style engraving covers trigger guard, floorplate of the detachable magazine and other parts of the rifle. Sights consist of an express-style folding leaf at the rear and a ramped blade with interchangeable beads up front. This fine rifle comes with its own leather carrying case and it is veeeery expensive.

Browning

The first thought that came to my mind as I reached for Browning's new Buck Mark Sporter was, "*now why would they want to go and do a thing like that?*" The answer came as I handled it. Regardless of how unorthodox this Buck Mark pistol with its 18-inch barrel and nondetachable walnut buttstock might appear to some, it is rather a neat little rig. The Sporter has fiber-optic sights and an integral Weaver-style scope mounting rail on its receiver; the Target is the same except for its heavier barrel and no open sights. Also new from Browning is the BAR Stalker with synthetic forearm and buttstock. Three barrel lengths are available; 20 inches in 243 and 308; 22 inches in 270 and 30-06, and 24 inches in its three magnum chamberings, 7mm Remington, 300 Winchester and 338 Winchester. The Stalker comes with or without open sights, and with or without the BOSS muzzle brake.

Back in September of 2000 I had the opportunity to hunt caribou in Alaska with an A-Bolt Stainless Stalker chambered for the 300 Winchester Short Magnum, a new beltless magnum introduced by Winchester. Think of the 300 Remington Ultra Mag shortened enough to work in short-action rifles and capable of equaling the velocity of the longer 300 Winchester Magnum and you have the new 300 WSM. It is also available in the wood-stocked A-Bolt Hunter. The caribou didn't cooperate but I shot enough Winchester ammo loaded with the 180-grain Fail-Safe bullet on paper to know that I could have hit one a long way off if given the opportunity. Actually, the trip didn't turn out too badly. While everyone else was off looking for caribou that never showed up, I was busy shooting ptarmigan and gadwall with a 28-gauge Model 12 pump gun I had brought along.

Charter 2000

Charter 2000 has introduced a new bolt-action called the Field King. Available in 243, 308, 25-06, 270 and 30-06 Springfield, it has a 22-inch Shaw barrel, M17-type extractor, adjustable trigger, black synthetic stock and a magazine capacity of four rounds. Other features include a one-piece bolt with

Browning Buck Mark Sporter.

Browning BAR Stalker with synthetic forearm and buttstock.

Browning A-Bolt Stainless Stalker.

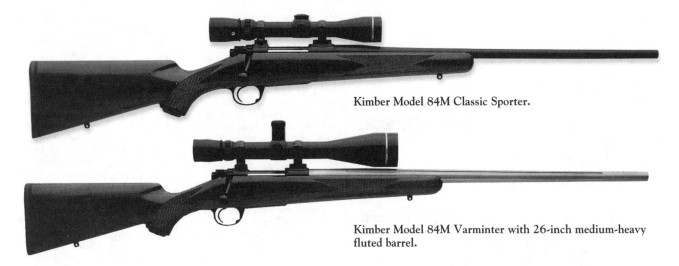

Kimber Model 84M Classic Sporter.

Kimber Model 84M Varminter with 26-inch medium-heavy fluted barrel.

recessed face and anti-bind groove on one locking lug.

Heckler & Koch

New at Heckler and Koch is an interesting gas-operated autoloading big-game rifle called the SLB 2000. It has interchangeable 22-inch barrels in 7x64mm Brenneke, 30-06 Springfield and 9.3x62mm. Modular in design, the new rifle has a lightweight alloy receiver, a tang-mounted sliding safety button that blocks both hammer and trigger and a premium-grade, oil-finished buttstock and forearm replete with cut checkering. The rifle handles and feels great but I'm not sure American sportsmen will become too excited about the exaggerated curve of its buttstock grip. I failed in my efforts to come up with an official weight but the SLB 2000 felt lighter than any other semiauto I have handled lately.

Kimber

In a previous report I cast my vote for the 22-caliber Kimber Model 82C as the most exciting new rifle of the year. I'm voting in the same direction in 2001 except this time it is for the new Model 84M centerfire. Rated at only 5-3/4 pounds, it should not greatly exceed 6-1/2 pounds when equipped with a light scope such as the Burris Mini or Leupold Compact and George Miller's Conetrol mount. Any sheep hunter who does not lust for one of these hasn't seen how nice it is, nor has he climbed any really steep sheep mountains. My wife doesn't hunt sheep but I am sure she will expect to see her very own Model 84M beneath the tree come Christmas. It will also be ideal for a youngster's first grownup rifle.

Among other dandy things, the Model 84M has a Model 70-type, two-position safety lever on its bolt shroud and a steel trigger guard/floorplate assembly, the latter hinged and with its release at the inside front of the trigger guard. Controlled cartridge feeding is there, compliments of Paul Mauser's nonrotating, claw-type extractor. The blued steel receiver is pillar-bedded into the stock. The Model 84M Classic has a 22-inch chrome-moly barrel with a lightweight contour and is chambered to 243 Winchester, 260 Remington, 7mm-08 and 308 Winchester. Barrels are air-gauged to ensure dimensional integrity of bore and groove diameter to within .001 inch and their chambers are hand-polished to a mirror-smooth finish for ease of spent case extraction. The walnut stock has cut checkering at wrist and forearm, steel gripcap, quick-detach sling swivels and a one-inch Pachmayr Decelerator pad. As far as I know, the Model 84M is the lightest all-steel, wood-stocked big-game rifle available. God willing and the creek doesn't rise above the tops of my hip boots, I will have hunted red stag in New Zealand with a Model 84M in 308 several months before you read this.

Two additional versions of the Sporter are planned for the future, Model 84S with shorter action for the 223 Remington and such, and Model 84L with longer action for the 25-06, 270, 280, 30-06 and others of their breed. Also slated for a 2001 introduction is the Model 84M Varminter with 26-inch medium-heavy fluted barrel in 22-250. Actually, the first 100 will have 24-inch barrels, something Kimber collectors will want to know about.

Kimber's Model 82, the rifle that reintroduced quality and superb accuracy back into the world of small-game rifles, is now available in four versions, Classic for hunting, plinking and target shooting; Hunter Silhouette for NRA metallic silhouette competition; Super America for those who choose to own the world's most handsome standard-production rifle in 22 rimfire, and Short Varmint/Target for everything else.

Lazzeroni

John Lazzeroni is offering Sako TRGS and Savage Model 112 rifles in several of his proprietary chamberings. The Savage has a 24-inch barrel in 308 Patriot and 284 Tomahawk while you can buy the Sako with a 26-inch barrel in 308 Warbird and 284 Firebird.

Les Baer Custom

Les Baer claims half-inch accuracy for five-shot groups at 100 yards from the new

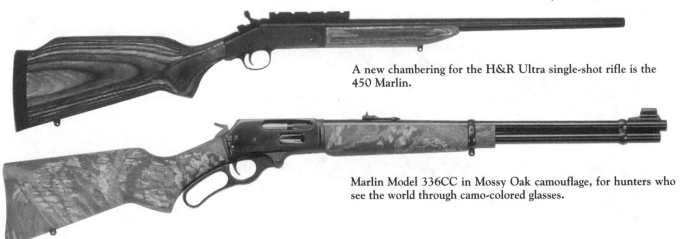

A new chambering for the H&R Ultra single-shot rifle is the 450 Marlin.

Marlin Model 336CC in Mossy Oak camouflage, for hunters who see the world through camo-colored glasses.

Marlin Model 1895 Cowboy, with the old square-shaped finger lever, chambered for the 45/70 Government.

Super Custom Varmint version of his 223-chambered AR15 and I can assure you it's no brag. He sent me one along with a supply of Federal Premium ammo loaded with a 52-grain hollow-point bullet and the stuff averaged only a hair over half an inch at 100 long paces. One of my handloads with the 50-grain Nosler Ballistic Tip averaged .482 inch. To be honest, I had to work mighty hard to maintain that level of accuracy because its tubular handguard makes the rifle difficult to stabilize consistently atop a sandbag. I suggested to Les that he offer the option of a detachable, flat, metal plate secured to the bottom of the handguard, and wide enough to snuggle uniformly into a rabbit-ear style bag. He was a step ahead of me because that option was already in the works. An idea he did go for was to build a few rifles in 6x45mm, an extremely accurate little cartridge easily made by necking up the 223 Remington case for 6mm bullets. I still have some Euber match-grade bullets left over from my benchrest shooting days and am looking forward to trying them in one of Les' ARs.

Magnum Research, Inc.

Most of those who own Mountain Eagle rifles made by Magnum Research, Inc. are probably aware of the fact that its action is made by the Finnish company of Sako. Or I should say it was made by Sako because all MRI bolt guns are now built around blueprinted Remington Model 700 actions. I shot the Tactical Rifle version with a 27-inch composite barrel in 308 Winchester and it averaged

.702 inch at 100 yards for five-shot groups with Federal 168-grain Gold Match ammo. When fed my handload consisting of a benchrest-prepared Federal case, Federal 210M primer and 42.0 grains of H4895 behind the Nosler 168-grain match bullet, the rifle averaged .510 inch for a 10-group average. Who knows how accurately I might have shot it had it been equipped with the optional Jewell trigger. Comb height and length-of-pull of the synthetic stock are adjustable and after jacking up the comb a bit the stock felt like it was tailor-made for me. The Tactical Rifle in 223 or 22-250 is also not a bad varmint rig and in 300 Winchester Magnum it would not be a bad choice for sitting in one spot all day and occasionally taking a poke at deer on the other side of a bean field.

Marlin

Biggest news from Marlin for 2001 is the company's acquisition of H&R 1871, Inc. which claims to be the world's largest manufacturer of break-action, single-shot rifles and shotguns. They are sold under the brand names of Harrington & Richardson, New England Firearms and Wesson & Harrington. Additional chamberings from H&R in its Ultra rifle line is the 450 Marlin and 22 WMR. It has a 22-inch barrel, cut-checkered stock and forearm of cinnamon laminate, ventilated recoil pad, and sling swivel posts. No open sights are there but the rifle comes with a factory-installed scope mounting base and an offset hammer spur. The 22 WMR is also now available in a rifle from New England Arms. Adult and youth versions of the

NEF Sporter are available, both with black synthetic stock and forearm, automatic case ejection, and an exposed hammer replete with a transfer bar-type safety system.

Conservative folks like me winced and groaned loudly when we got our first look at an old classic like the Marlin 336 with its stock and forearm decked out in Mossy Oak camouflage but it will sell like hotcakes to a rapidly growing number of hunters who believe the outcome of a hunt is greatly dependent on how much camo they and their equipment wear. Called the Model 336CC, it has a 20-inch Micro-Groove barrel, six-round magazine and is available only in 30-30 Winchester.

Marlin's new Model 1894CP in 357 Magnum has an American walnut stock with rubber butt pad, semi-buckhorn rear sight, 16 1/4-inch ported barrel and 8-round magazine. It weighs only 5-3/4 pounds. Moving on up to more punch at both ends, the Model 1895GS is the old Model 1895G Guide Gun with a 18 1/2-inch ported, stainless steel barrel with Ballard-style cut rifling and in 45-70 Government. Other features include walnut stock, 4-round magazine and semi-buckhorn, folding rear sight. Then we have the Model 1895 Cowboy, another rifle in 45-70 that should have all those *buckaroos* and *buckarettes* out there making quick draws for their wallets. It has a straight-grip stock with the old square-shaped finger lever, black walnut stock with no checkering, 9-round magazine, semi-buckhorn sight and a 26-inch tapered octagon barrel with Ballard-style rifling.

With its economical price, 22-inch barrel, 12-round tubular magazine, screw-adjustable open rear sight and fiberglass-reinforced polycarbonate stock, the new TS version of Marlin's famous Model 84 bolt-action rifle is sure to be a hit among shooters on the lookout for a knock-about rifle in 22 WMR. Add Mossy Oak's Break-Up camo finish to the hardwood stock of the old Model 25MN and you have a new version called the Model 25MNC in 22 WMR. It also has a 7-round detachable magazine, 22-inch Micro-Groove barrel and adjustable rear sight.

One last thing. If you haven't already obtained a copy of the 2001 Marlin catalog you really should because its cover is one of the more handsome seen in recent years. Inside are photos of previous covers dating back to 1899.

Remington

When it comes to introducing new stuff each year, nobody can out-introduce Remington. This is great news to me because I like Remington products and the vast number of new ones unveiled each year go a long way toward filling up this column with things that increase a rifleman's pulse rate.

At the top of this year's introductions is the all-new Model 710 rifle in 270 Winchester and 30-06 for now. For starters, the three-lug bolt with its 60-degree rotation locks up into the barrel rather than the receiver ring and this allows Remington to make the receiver from steel tubing. Rather than being threaded into the receiver, the 22-inch cold-forged, button-rifled

Remington's all-new Model 710 rifle.

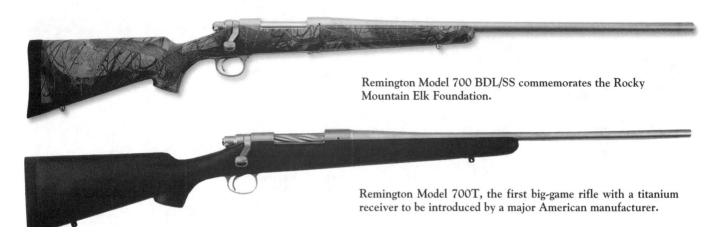

Remington Model 700 BDL/SS commemorates the Rocky Mountain Elk Foundation.

Remington Model 700T, the first big-game rifle with a titanium receiver to be introduced by a major American manufacturer.

barrel is permanently installed by a very large factory worker with a very strong hydraulic press. When engaged, Remington's new key-operated Integrated Security System on the bolt shroud prevents the bolt from closing. Inside the receiver is a fiberglass-reinforced nylon insert within which the bolt travels fro and to. One side of the trigger components housing is injection-molded integrally with the insert. The Model 710 has a gray-colored synthetic stock replete with recoil pad, quick-detach sling swivel posts and an integral triggerguard. I shot one in 30-06 with Remington's 180-grain Core-Lokt ammo and the first five shots on paper measured 1.68 inches between the least friendly two in the group. Four of those shots went into 0.725 inch and three of them snuggled into 0.312 inch. The fellows in green I talked to said their goal was to make the Model 710 just as accurate as the Model 700 – and looks like they did it. So why did Remington go to all of this trouble when they already had the best-selling Model 700? So they could sell an accurate, seven-pound big-game rifle complete with a factory-installed Bushnell 3-9X Sharpshooter scope for less than $375, that's why.

Just as I said they would last year, Remington has now added 7mm- and 375-caliber members to the Ultra Mag family of cartridges. All told, 12 new Model 700 variations in those two calibers as well as the 300 and 338 Ultra Mags have been added to the list. I shot a couple of 375 Ultra Mag factory loads in a Model 700 LSS with a 26-inch barrel. Three-shot groups fired with the 300-grain A-Frame load averaged 1.87

inches with velocity at 2740 fps, only 20 fps slower than Remington claims. The load with the 300-grain Barnes Super Solid clocked 2792 fps and averaged 1.32 inches on paper. That won't win a benchrest match but it will topple over a African Cape buffalo or Alaskan brown bear in no time flat.

The 7mm Ultra Mag I shot was a Model 77 African Plains Rifle with a 26-inch barrel and laminated wood stock. The 140-grain Core-Lokt factory ammo averaged 2.11 inches at 100 yards and 3377 fps on the chronograph. The 140-grain Nosler Partition averaged 1.32 inches and 3374 fps. This, by the way, is quite comparable to Remington's 140-grain 7mm STW factory ammo as it usually averages just over 3400 fps in a 26-inch barrel. How do you choose between the two? One has a belt, the other doesn't; Remington offers both choices. Before leaving the subject of Ultra Mags, the .338 version is now available in the left-hand Model 700BDL.

Latest from Remington's custom shop is the Model 700 African Big Game Rifle with laminated wood stock, fully-adjustable machined rear sight, ramped and hooded front sight with changeable bead, *perch-belly* magazine, a barrel band-type detachable sling swivel up front, and a three-shot detachable magazine, all wrapped around the 375 H&H Magnum, 375 Ultra Mag, 416 Remington Magnum or 458 Winchester Magnum. And speaking of commemorative rifles, Remington hasn't built many through the years so the Model 700 BDL/SS in 300 Ultra Mag cooked up for the Rocky Mountain Elk Foundation might be worth a serious look. It has the RMEF

logo laser-etched into the stock and is covered from butt to forearm tip with Realtree Hardwoods camo. Part of the money from each one sold will go to the foundation.

Twenty-first in a series of classic Model 700 classics started with the 7x57mm Mauser back in 1981 is the 2001 edition in a classic deer cartridge, the 7mm-08 Remington. I believe this is the first standard-weight Model 700 hunting rifle to be offered in this chambering with a 24-inch barrel. I keep asking for the 8x57mm Mauser and 35 Remington but they continue to ignore me. Remington's extremely successful family of Model 97 22 rimfire autoloaders has a heavy-barrel addition. The new baby has a 20-inch carbon steel barrel in 22 Long Rifle or 22 WMR, a brown laminated wood stock and it weighs six pounds.

Last but most certainly not least - nor heaviest - is the first big-game rifle with a titanium receiver to be introduced by a major American manufacturer. Barrel and bolt are stainless steel while the triggerguard/floorplate assembly is made of aluminum. Called the Model 700T, the short-action version weighs 5-1/4 pounds while the long-action version weighs only a quarter-pound more. The titanium receiver is only about 60 percent as heavy as a steel receiver and, in addition to that, a bit more weight disappeared when Remington design engineers decided to go with spiral-cut lightning flutes in the bolt body and to hollow out the bolt handle knob. The rifle got even lighter when they decided to use the lightest Kevlar-reinforced, carbon-fiber, composite stock ever from Remington. Contour of the 22-inch barrel looks to me

to be about the same as that of the Model 700 Mountain rifle. Other chamberings are sure to follow but for now there are enough in the 260 Remington, 270 Winchester, 7mm-08 and 30-06 Springfield.

In the *things-every-Model 700-rifle-owner-should-have department* is an inexpensive new bolt takedown tool made of a synthetic material that won't scratch the bolt. Your friendly neighborhood Remington dealer should have it in stock by now.

Ruger

Not a lot of exciting news from Ruger this year except I noticed quite a bit of wood has been trimmed from the stock of the Model 77 Magnum in 375 H&H and 416 Rigby, a long-awaited modification that greatly improves the handling and feel of the rifle. There is a new version of Ruger's incredibly successful 10/22. It has a stainless steel barreled action in 22 LR only and a thumbhole-style stock of laminated wood and, most unusual for Ruger, Star Wars styling. There is also the rumor of a Model 77 compact with short barrel and stock for shooters with short arms but I have yet to actually see one.

Sako

Now owned by Beretta, the Finnish firm of Sako is introducing a new version of the excellent Model 75 rifle called the Finnlight. Three action sizes are available, No. 3 for the 243, 7mm-08 and 308; No. 4 for the 25-06, 6.5x55mm Swedish, 270, 30-06 and 280 Remington, and No. 5 for the 7mm Remington Magnum and 300 Winchester Magnum. All metal parts of the barreled action are stainless steel with a special coating to prevent wear and oxidation when exposed to the elements. Lengths of the fluted barrels range from 24 to 26 inches, depending on caliber. Weight ranges from six to seven pounds with a few of the missing ounces due to a trigger guard/floorplate assembly made of hard anodized aluminum. The bolt has Sako's latest *Key Concept* deactivation system which can make the rifle inoperable in unauthorized hands. The magazine is detachable, the single-stage trigger is factory-set at about three pounds and the chamber can be loaded or unloaded while the side-mounted safety switch is engaged. Of all the synthetic stocks I have handled on factory rifles, I'll have to say the one made by Sako is my favorite. Injection-molding the stock in two steps allows the insertion of soft rubber-like inserts in the grip and forearm for a comfortable no-slip grip with hands made slippery by a sudden downpour.

Samco Global Arms

I have been writing this report for GUN DIGEST since the 1982 edition and I don't recall ever covering a military-surplus firearm in it. I have been so impressed by a Model 1898 Persian Mauser I received from Samco, I just had to make it the first exception. Several grades are available ranging from a "collector-quality" rifle in unissued condition (which comes with its original factory target fired when it was built) to the "special select" rifle. I have been shooting the latter grade and with the exception of a few minor storage dings on its stock it was absolutely brand-spanking new when I first received it. If you have ever wanted to go beyond worn-out Mausers with pitted bores and mismatched serial numbers, here is your chance to add something really special to your collection. Accuracy with every factory load I could round up plus handloads with about every bullet available ranged from 1.48 inches to 4.66 inches for five-shot averages at 100 yards, and that with the original barleycorn front sight. I'll leave it that way because it is so much fun to shoot as-is, plus I wouldn't dare spoil that untouched Persian lion crest on its receiver by drilling and tapping it for a scope.

Savage

The receiver of the Savage Model 110 rifle has always been long enough to handle full-length magnum cartridges such as the 300 H&H Magnum and 300 Weatherby Magnum but the length of its magazine box restricted it to the use of medium-length magnums such as the 7mm Remington and 300 Winchester. This no longer is true as the latest lineup of Model 116 Weather Warrior rifles have magazine boxes long enough to take the 7mm STW and 300 Remington Ultra Mag, two new chamberings for 2001. Rifles in those two chamberings have 26-inch barrels; those in the shorter magnums have 24-inchers while the barrels of those in standard-performance cartridges such as 270 and 30-06 are two inches shorter than that. The 7mm STW is also available in the wood-stocked Model 114 Ultra with a 24-inch barrel. Other news from Savage is the Model 114CE with European-style wood stock and a left-hand version of the Model 93G in 22 rimfire.

Springfield, Inc.

Springfield recently hosted an event during which a few writers, including yours truly, were told there was no way we could shoot up all the ammo on hand in two days. We came very close to proving them wrong and probably would have had the temperature ever made it above freezing and if the wind had dropped below 50 mph. I shot my share of the ammo in 1911-A1 pistols of various calibers and then switched to shooting reactive steel targets at long range with several versions of the 308-caliber M1A rifle. Most incredible of all was the new M32 Tactical Rifle with comb-height adjustable wood stock, folding tripod, Springfield 4-14X mil-dot scope, premium-grade Hart or Krieger barrel and other features too numerous to mention. If you can see it with your naked eyes you can hit it with this rifle! Who would ever have thought such a homely old battle rifle could average half-minute-of-angle with match ammo? I don't know about the other shooters but I really wasn't surprised by such a level of accuracy because I have owned a M1A Super Match with a Hart barrel for several years.

If you haven't read the life story of Marine legend Carlos Hathcock, you owe it to yourself to do so. A recipient of the Silver Star for saving the lives of seven comrades, he spent most of his tour in Vietnam as a sniper which is why the sniper range at Camp Lejeune, NC was named in his honor. The Vietcong who had a $30,000 bounty on his head referred to Hathcock as "*Long Trang*" (The White Feather) because he often wore one in his bush hat. Hathcock passed on in February 2000 and in a special arrangement with his estate and family, Springfield has introduced a special edition of the M1A/M5 with a likeness of his signature and a white feather logo etched on its receiver. Among many other things, the rifle has a heavy Krieger match-grade barrel, Harris folding bipod, National Match operating rod, adjustable match trigger and a McMillan fiberglass stock.

My friends at Springfield keep promising to bring back the M1 carbine with quality equal to that of the M1A they are now building and I keep looking forward to rolling the clock back to my youth while shooting it.

Steyr

The Steyr family of hunting rifles continues to grow and a number of less-than-ordinary features are available. They include a three-position, roller-type tang safety that blocks the firing pin, ice and residue grooves upon the outside of the bolt body, butt spacers that allow length of pull to be adjusted and a steel bushing that supports the spring-loaded extractor when the bolt is closed. Many of the standard chamberings are there, including the 6.5 Swede and 376 Steyr.

Tristar Sporting Arms Ltd.

Previously known mainly for its line of Italian-made over-under and side-by-side shotguns, Tristar is now importing Uberti-built Colt single-action clones in 45 Colt, as well as four different center-fire rifles. Three of the latter are modern reproductions of lever actions of yesteryear, the 1860 Henry, Winchester Model 1866 and Winchester Model 1873 – all available in 44-40 or 45 Colt. Two variations of the Henry are offered, standard rifle with 24 1/4-inch barrel and Trapper with 18 1/2-inch barrel. The Henry also has a brass frame, forged steel tubular magazine and straight-grip walnut buttstock with brass buttplate. The Winchester '66 is available in Sporting and Yellowboy versions and is dressed quite similar to the Henry. The Winchester '73 is available in Sporting makeup only but with a color-case-hardened steel frame, walnut stock with curved steel buttplate and 24 1/4- or 30-inch barrels. The other new rifle is a very nicely done reproduction of the Winchester Model 1885 Hi-Wall. It has a walnut stock with shotgun-style steel buttplate, case-colored frame and underlever, and a 28-inch octagon barrel in 45-70 Government. Weight is 8-3/4 pounds and, at a suggested

The Winchester Model 9410.

Model 70 Custom Safari Express.

Winchester Model 94 Custom Limited Edition in 38-55 Winchester.

retail price of $765, it is bound to sell quite well.

Ultra Light Arms

Ultra Light Arms is back and Melvin Forbes is at the wheel. Since his catalog looks the same as it did before he became involved with Colt, I am sure everything will be the same as it used to be, including high quality and superb accuracy wrapped up in a trim little 5-1/4 pound rifle chambered for about any center-fire cartridge you can think of. The Model 22RF in

22 rimfire is also back in production.

U.S. Repeating Arms Co.

There was a time, many years ago, when both Savage and Marlin offered lever-action rifles chambered for the .410 shotshell but with the exception of a few custom rifles built by gunsmiths, the Winchester Model 94 has never been available so chambered. Until now, that is. Chambered only for the 2 1/2-inch cartridge, the Model 9410 (*darned neat name*) has

a smooth-bored barrel with no choke constriction. A repeater, its tubular magazine holds eight or nine rounds depending on the brand of ammo used. Why it has an adjustable rear sight and ramped front sight is totally beyond me – but it does.

Several paragraphs back I mentioned hunting caribou in Alaska with a Browning Stainless Stalker in 300 WSM. Since Browning and U.S. Repeating Arms Company (USRAC) are owned by the same parent company, it didn't surprise me to see a Model 70 or two chambered for the 300 WSM on that same trip. That chambering is slated to be available during 2001 in Classic Featherweight, Classic Stainless and Classic Laminated versions of the short-action Model 70. Whereas Browning rifles in this caliber have 23-inch barrels, the Winchesters have 24-inchers. Other additions are the 25-06 and 338 Winchester Magnum in the Classic Super Grade, and 300 Remington Ultra Mag in the Classic Stainless Composite.

I keep seeing more and more interesting projects coming from the Winchester custom shop. One is the Model 70 Custom African Express in 416 Rigby and 470 Capstick. A couple of other nice Model 70s are the Custom Safari Express in 375 Remington Ultra Mag and 416 Rigby and the Custom Ultimate Classic in 7mm Remington Ultra Mag, 338 Remington Ultra Mag and 6.5x55mm Swedish. Then there is the short-action Model 70 Classic Custom, the first factory bolt-action rifle to be offered in 450 Marlin. You can also buy a takedown version of the Model 70 in a variety of calibers.

My favorite Winchester for 2001 is the new Model 94 Custom Limited Edition with

fancy cut-checkered walnut, case-colored hammer, receiver and finger lever and 26-inch half-octagon barrel in 38-55 caliber. The good folks in the custom shop, by the way, were first among major rifle builders to offer my 7mm STW and they continue to chamber the Model 70 it and for my 358 STA.

Tom Volquartsen

One of my recent projects was to see how much, if any, the accuracy of 22 WMR ammunition would improve if I sorted it by weight, rim thickness, overall length and a few other things. The autoloading rifle I used in those tests was built by Tom Volquartsen, has a bolt and receiver precision-machined from stainless steel and uses Ruger 10/22 magazines. It also has a match-grade stainless steel barrel and McMillan fiberglass stock. One of Volquartsen's heavier models, it and its Burris 6-24X scope weigh exactly 10 pounds. Reporting on everything in detail about the ammo experiments would fill up an entire article, and it did, so I'll keep it short by saying I ended up with one load that averaged 0.68 inch for 10 five-shot groups at 100 yards. Some groups measured less than half an inch. Only those of us who have seriously worked with the 22 WMR know how fantastic that really is.

Weatherby

Weatherby rifles are now available in two excellent new chamberings. One, called the 338-06 A-Square, is simply the old 338-06 wildcat that was registered with SAAMI by A-Square a few years back. Except for a small difference in bullet diameter between the two, it is also the same cartridge as the old 333 OKH of the 1930s. As its name implies, the 338-06 is

In addition to averaging less than half an inch at 100 yards, the Weatherby Super VarmintMaster was also deadly on California ground squirrels at long range.

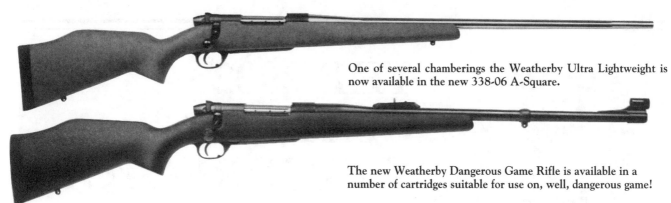

One of several chamberings the Weatherby Ultra Lightweight is now available in the new 338-06 A-Square.

The new Weatherby Dangerous Game Rifle is available in a number of cartridges suitable for use on, well, dangerous game!

the 30-06 case necked down for 338-caliber bullets. It is a great cartridge and not too far behind the 338 Winchester Magnum in everything except recoil. Weatherby is offering ammunition loaded with the 210-grain Nosler Partition at a muzzle velocity of 2750 feet per second. For now, the only rifle to be chambered for it is the Mark V Ultra Lightweight. I just received one of the first rifles built by Weatherby in this caliber but the cartridges are still a few weeks away so I'll wait and report on its performance the next time we meet.

Also headed back to the game fields is another excellent old classic called the 375 Weatherby Magnum. It was one of the first cartridges designed by Roy Weatherby back in the 1940s and was dropped from production soon after he

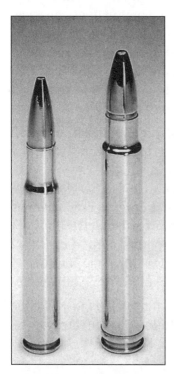

Weatherby 338-06 A-Square (*Left*) and 375 Magnum.

introduced his bigger 378 Weatherby Magnum in 1953. The 375 Weatherby Magnum case is nothing less than an improved version of the grand old 375 H&H Magnum with less body taper and Weatherby's familiar double-radius shoulder. In a pinch, 375 H&H Magnum ammo can be fired in a rifle chambered for the Weatherby cartridge, something nice to know if you run out of ammo while on safari. Initially to be loaded with the 300-grain Nosler Partition at 2800 fps, I won't be surprised to eventually see this grand old cartridge from Weatherby loaded with at least one other bullet of lighter weight.

The first Mark V to be chambered to 375 Weatherby Magnum is the new Dangerous Game Rifle (*Where have I seen that name before?*). Among other things, this one includes a Bell & Carlson synthetic stock replete with CNC-machined aluminum bedding block and Pachmayr Decelerator pad, 24-inch barrel, pre-'64 Winchester Model 70 Super Grade-style express rear sight and ramped and hooded front sight with a large gold-colored bead. Other chambering options include the 375 H&H Magnum, 416 Remington Magnum, 458 Winchester Magnum and the entire line of Weatherby cartridges of .378, .416 and .460 calibers. Average weight is 8-3/4 pounds except it is increased to 9-1/2 pounds for the 460 Weatherby Magnum. I'll probably be hunting Asian buffalo and other things in Australia this year and may use a Mark V DGR in 375 Weatherby Magnum or the Mark V Ultra Lightweight in 338-06 A-Square.

You might recall that, quite a few years ago, Weatherby beat all of its major-power competition to the punch by

being first to offer a big-game rifle with a synthetic stock. It was called the Mark V Fibermark and after being discontinued for several years it is back in 19 different chamberings ranging from the 22-250, 243 Winchester, 270 Winchester and 30-06 on the standard-size Mark V action to the 30-378 Weatherby Magnum, 338 Winchester Magnum, 340 Weatherby Magnum and 375 H&H Magnum on the magnum-size action. Barrel lengths are 26 inches for the Weatherby cartridges and 24 inches for everything else. Barrel contours are No. 4 for the 458 and 460 and No. 3 for the others. Actually, two versions of the Fibermark are available, one with a stainless steel barreled action, the other of blued steel.

Last year, I told you about a Weatherby Super VarmintMaster in 22-250 that had averaged .517-inch for over 50, five-shot groups at 100 yards with a variety of handloads and factory ammo. As it turned out, it was the most accurate off-the-shelf factory rifle I tested during 2000. Well, I just finished testing a Super VarmintMaster in 220 Swift and it averaged .486-inch. A new offspring of that rifle is called Super PredatorMaster and is available in 223, 22-250, 243, 7mm-08 and 308 Winchester. At 6-1/2 pounds it is a couple of pounds lighter than its papa, most of the difference being in their barrels. The Super VarmintMaster has a rather heavy 26-inch barrel while the barrel of PredatorMaster measures 24 inches and is lighter in contour. There you have them, two great varmint rifles from Weatherby, one for shooters who sit a lot and walk very little, the other for those who would rather walk than sit. Other news for 2001 is the 7mm STW and 338-378

Magnum chamberings in the Mark V Synthetic. The 7mm STW is also available in both right- and left-handed versions of the Mark V Accumark.

Wilson Combat

I am not exactly sure if a nifty item Bill Wilson sent to me belongs to me or to our pistol editor because it converts a 45-caliber 1911 pistol into a carbine with a 18-inch barrel – and no modifications are necessary. Simply remove the top assembly from your 1911, slide the frame into the conversion unit, install the slide latch and the job is done. It comes with equipped with a Weaver-style scope mounting rail and works with single-stack pistols made by Kimber, Springfield, Colt and others, as well as double-stackers made by Kimber, Springfield, Para Ordnance and others. I just burned up a variety of factory loads in one attached to a 14-shot Kimber polymer frame and wearing a Tasco red dot sight and everything stayed well inside the palm of your hand, with several groups measuring as small as two inches. Outdoors, it's a fun-gun, maybe even a hog-gun if you like to get close before shooting like I do. Indoors, its compact 33 1/4-inch length and seven-pound heft make it something for someone who cannot shoot a pistol accurately to consider for home defense. ●

Editor's note. *Layne is Field Editor for* Shooting Times *magazine. Autographed copies of his book* "The Custom 1911 Government Model Pistol" *are available for $30 from High Country Press, 104 Holly Tree Lane, Simpsonville, SC.*

THE 2002 GUN DIGEST WEB DIRECTORY

by Holt Bodinson

OUR GUN DIGEST Web Directory is in its third year of publication, and it continues to grow at a remarkable pace. During the past year, firearm manufacturers and purveyors, organizations and forums, even enthusiastic private parties have added new sites, improved existing sites, increased security protection, and converted E-mail addresses into full-blown web pages.

How important is it to have access to firearms information on the Internet? Essential! Take one example. Barnes just released the latest version of its ballistics program. Did they burn disks to mail out to consumers? No. The only way this powerful and easy-to-use program is available is via a download over the Internet.

The firearms industry really should receive some kudos for how well it has adapted to and adopted the Internet. Using the web site addresses contained in this directory, one can create a virtual, international "SHOT Show" that is more comprehensive than any on-the-ground exposition could ever be.

The following index of current Web sites is offered to our readers as a convenient jumping-off point. The Internet is such a dynamic and changing environment that half the fun is just exploring what's out there. Considering that most of the Web sites have hot links to other firearm-related Web sites, the Internet trail just goes on-and-on once you've taken the initial step to go online.

Here are a few pointers:

If the web site you desire is not listed, try using the full name of the company or product, typed without spaces, between **www.-** and **-.com,** for example, **www.krause.com.** Probably 95 percent of current Web sites are based on this simple, self-explanatory format.

Try a variety of search engines like *Microsoft Internet Explorer, Metacrawler, GoTo.com, Yahoo, HotBot, AltaVista, Lycos, Excite, InfoSeek, Looksmart, Google*, and *WebCrawler* while using key words such as gun, firearm, rifle, pistol, blackpowder, shooting, hunting— frankly, any word that relates to the sport. Each search engine seems to comb through the World Wide Web in a different fashion and produces different results. We find *Metacrawler* to be among the best.

While the Internet has been a bastion of freedom without censors, *AOL* has eliminated some firearm sites and often seems to search without luck for firearm-related information. That's why having the option to use alternative search engines is so important. Accessing the various search engines is simple. Just type **www.yahoo.com** for example, and you're on your way.

Finally, the best introduction to firearms-related Web sites is a large, specialized Web site like *Shooter's Online Services* located at **www.shooters.com**. There are enough firearm-related links at **www.shooters.com** to make your initial trips down the Internet highway a rewarding adventure.

A whole world is just a "click" away. Enjoy our Directory!

WEB DIRECTORY

AMMUNITION AND COMPONENTS

3-D Ammunition www.3dammo.com
Accurate Arms Co. Inc www.accuratepowder.com
ADCO/Nobel Sport Powder www.adcosales.com
Aguila Ammunition www.aguilaammo.com
All Purpose Ammunition www.dragonbreath.com
Alliant Powder www.alliantpowder.com
Ammo Depot www.ammodepot.com
Arizona Ammunition, Inc. www.arizonaammunition.com
A-Zoom Ammo www.a-zoom.com
Ballard Rifle & Cartridge LLC www.ballardrifles.com
Ballistic Products,Inc. www.ballisticproducts.com
Barnes Bullets www.barnesbullets.com
Baschieri & Pellagri www.baschieri-pellagri.com
Berger Bullets, Ltd. www.bergerbullets.com
Berry's Mfg., Inc. www.berrysmfg.com
Big Bore Bullets of Alaska www.awloo.com/bbb/index.htm
Bismuth Cartridge Co. www.bismuth-notox.com
Black Hills Ammunition, Inc. www.black-hills.com
Brenneke of America Ltd. www.brennekeusa.com
Buffalo Arms www.buffaloarms.com
Bull-X inc. www.bull-x.com
Calhoon, James, Bullets www.jamescalhoon.com
CCI-Blount www.blount.com
Century Arms www.centuryarms.com
Cheaper Than Dirt www.cheaperthandirt.com
Claybuster Wads www.claybuster.com
Clean Shot Powder www.cleanshot.com
Cole Distributing www.cole-distributing.com
Cor-Bon www.cor-bon.com
Denver Bullet Co. denbullets@aol.com
Dillon Precision www.dillonprecision.com
DKT, Inc. www.dktinc.com
Dynamit Nobel RWS Inc. www.dnrws.com
Elephant Black Powder www.elephantblackpowder.com
Eley Ammunition www.gzanders.com/eley
Eley Hawk Ltd. www.eleyhawk.com
Eley Limited www.eley.co.uk
Federal Cartridge Co. www.federalcartridge.com
Fiocchi of America www.fiocchiusa.com
Fowler Bullets www.benchrest.com/fowler
Glaser Safety Slug, Inc. www.safetyslug.com
GOEX Inc. www.goexpowder.com
Graf & Sons graf@ktis.net
Hi-Tech Ammunition www.iidbs.com/hitech
Hirtenberger kengsfirearms@mindspring.com
Hodgdon Powder www.hodgdon.com
Hornady www.hornady.com
Hull Cartridge www.hullcartridge.com
Huntington Reloading Products www.huntingtons.com
Impact Bullets www.impactbullets.com
IMR Smokeless Powders www.imrpowder.com

ION Industries, Inc. www.trutracer.com
Keng's Firearms Specialty kengsfirearms@mindspring.com
Kent Cartridge America www.kentgamebore.com
Kynoch Ammunition kynamco@aol.com
Lapua www.lapua.com
Lawrence Brand Shot www.metalico.com
Lazzeroni Arms Co. www.lazzeroni.com
Lightfield Ammunition Corp www.lightfieldammo.com
Lomont Precision Bullets www.klomont.com/kent
Lost River Ballistic Technologies,Inc.
    www.lostriverballistic.com
Lyman www.lymanproducts.com
Magnus Bullets www.magnusbullets.com
Magtech www.magtechammunition.com
Mast Technology www.bellammo.com
Masterclass Bullet Co. www.mastercast.com
Meister Bullets www.meisterbullets.com
Midway USA www.midwayusa.com
Miltex,Inc. www.miltexusa.com
MK Ballistic Systems www.mkballistics.com
Mullins Ammunition www.mullinsammunition.com
National Bullet Co. www.nationalbullet.com
Nobel Sport www.adcosales.com
Nosler Bullets Inc www.nosler.com
Old Western Scrounger www.ows-ammunition.com
Oregon Trail/Laser-Cast Bullets www.laser-cast.com
Pattern Control www.patterncontrol.com
PMC-Eldorado Cartridge www.pmcammo.com
Polywad www.polywad.com
Primex Technologies Inc. ksstase11@primextech.com
Pro Load Ammunition www.proload.com
Rainier Ballistics www.rainierballistics.com
Ram Shot Powder www.ramshot.com
Reloading Specialties Inc. www.reloadingspecialties.com
Remington www.remington.com
Sauvestre Slug kengsfirearms@mindspring.com
Sellier & Bellot USA inc. www.sb-usa.com
Shilen www.shilen.com
Sierra www.sierrabullets.com
Speer-Blount www.blount.com
Sporting Supplies Int'l Inc. www.ssiintl.com
Starline www.starlinebrass.com
Triton Cartridge www.triton-ammo.com
Tru-Tracer www.trutracer.com
Vihtavuori Lapua www.lapua.com
Western Powders Inc. www.westernpowders.com
Widener's Reloading & Shooters Supply www.wideners.com
Winchester Ammunition www.winchester.com
Wolf Ammunition www.wolfammo.com
Woodleigh Bullets zedfield@apollo.ruralnet.net.au
Zanders Sporting Goods www.gzanders.com

CASES, SAFES, GUN LOCKS, AND CABINETS

Ace Case Co. www.acecase.com
AG English Sales Co. www.agenglish.com
All Americas' Outdoors www.innernet.net/gunsafe
Alpine Cases www.alpinecases.com
Aluma Sport by Dee Zee www.deezee.com
American Security Products www.amsecusa.com

Americase www.americase.com
Avery Outdoors, Inc. www.averyoutdoors.com
Bear Track Cases www.beartrackcases.com
Boyt Harness Co. www.boytharness.com
Bulldog Gun Safe Co. www.gardall.com
Cannon Safe Co. www.cannonsafe.com

WEB DIRECTORY

CCL Security Products **www.cclsecurity.com**
Concept Development Corp. **www.saf-t-blok.com**
Fort Knox Safes **www.ftknox.com**
Franzen Security Products **www.securecase.com**
Frontier Safe Co. **www.frontiersafe.com**
Granite Security Products **www.granitesafe.com**
Gunlocker Phoenix USA Inc. **www.gunlocker.com**
GunVault **www.gunvault.com**
Hakuba USA Inc. **www.hakubausa.com**
Heritage Safe Co. **www.heritagesafecompany.com**
Hide-A-Gun **www.hide-a-gun.com**
Hunter Company **www.huntercompany.com**
Knouff & Knouff, Inc. **www.kkair.com**
Kolpin Mfg. Co. **www.kolpin.com**
Liberty Safe & Security **www.libertysafe.com**
New Innovative Products **www.starlightcases.com**
Noble Security Systems Inc. **www.noble.co.ll**
Phoenix USA Inc. **www.gunlocker.com**

Rhino Gun Cases **www.rhinoguns.com**
Rocky Mountain Safe Inc. **www.rockymountainsafe.com**
Safe Tech, Inc. **www.safrgun.com**
Saf-T-Hammer **www.saf-t-hammer.com**
Saf-T-Lok Corp. **www.saf-t-lok.com**
San Angelo All-Aluminum Products Inc.
   sasptuld@x.netcom.com
Securecase **www.securecase.com**
Shot Lock Corp. **www.shotlock.com**
Smart Lock Technology Inc. **www.smartlock.com**
Sportsmans Steel Safe Co. **www.sportsmansteelsafes.com**
Stack-On Products Co. **www.stack-on.com**
T.Z. Case Int'l **www.tz-case.com**
Treadlock Security Safes **www.treadlok.com**
Versatile Rack Co. **www.versatilegunrack.com**
V-Line Industries **www.vlineind.com**
Winchester Safes **www.fireking.com**
Ziegel Engineering **www.ziegeleng.com**

CHOKE DEVICES, RECOIL REDUCERS, AND ACCURACY DEVICES

100 Straight Products **www.100straight.com**
Answer Products Co. **www.answerrifles.com**
Briley Mfg **www.briley.com**

Carlson's **www.carlsonschokes.com**
Colonial Arms **www.colonialarms.com**
Mag-Na-Port Int'l Inc. **www.magnaport.com**

CHRONOGRAPHS

Competitive Edge Dynamics **www.cedhk.com**
Oehler Research Inc. **www.oehler-research.com**
PACT **www.pact.com**

ProChrony **www.competitionelectronics.com**
Shooting Chrony Inc **www.shootingchrony.com**

CLEANING PRODUCTS

Accupro **www.accupro.com**
Ballistol USA **www.ballistol.com**
Birchwood Casey **www.birchwoodcasey.com**
Bore Tech **www.boretech.com**
Break-Free, Inc. **break-free@worldnet.att.net**
Bruno Shooters Supply **www.brunoshooters.com**
Butch's Bore Shine **www.bbsindustries.com**
Clenzoil **www.clenzoil.com**
Corrosion Technologies **www.corrosionx.com**
Dewey Mfg. **www.deweyrods.com**
Eezox Inc. **www.xmission.com**
G 96 **www.g96.com**
Hoppes **www.hoppes.com**
Hydrosorbent Products **www.dehumidify.com**
Iosso Products **www.iosso.com**
KG Industries **www.kgproducts.com**
Kleen-Bore Inc. **www.kleen-bore.com**

L&R Mfg. **www.lrultrasonics.com**
Mpro7 Gun Care **www.mp7.com**
Otis Technology, Inc. **www.otisgun.com**
Outers **www.outers-guncare.com**
Ox-Yoke Originals Inc. **www.oxyoke.com**
Prolix Lubricant **www.prolixlubricant.com**
ProShot Products **www.proshotproducts.com**
ProTec Lubricants **www.proteclubricants.com**
Rusteprufe Labs **www.rusteprufe.com**
Sagebrush Products **www.sagebrushproducts.com**
Sentry Solutions Ltd. **www.sentrysolutions.com**
Shooters Choice Gun Care **www.shooters-choice.com**
Silencio **www.silencio.com**
Stony Point Products **www.stoneypoint.com**
Tetra Gun **www.tetraproducts.com**
World's Fastest Gun Bore Cleaner **www.michaels-oregon.com**

FIREARM MANUFACTURERS AND IMPORTERS

AAR, Inc. **www.iar-arms.com**
Accuracy Rifle Systems **www.mini-14.net**
Ace Custom 45's **www.acecustom45.com**
Advanced Weapons Technology **www.AWT-Zastava.com**
Airgun Express **www.airgunexpress.com**
Alchemy Arms **www.alchemyltd.com**
American Derringer Corp. **www.amderringer.com**
AMT **www.amtguns.com**
Answer Products Co. **www.answerrifles.com**
AR-7 Industries,LLC **www.ar-7.com**

Armalite **www.armalite.com**
Armscorp USA Inc. **www.armscorpusa.com**
Arnold Arms **www.arnoldarms.com**
Arthur Brown Co. **www.eabco.com**
Autauga Arms,Inc. **www.autaugaarms.com**
Auto-Ordnance Corp. **www.auto-ordnance.com**
Axtell Rifle Co. **www.riflesmith.com**
Aya **www.webstudio.net/aya**
Ballard Rifle & Cartridge LLC **www.ballardrifles.com**
Barrett Firearms Mfg. **www.barrettrifles.com**

Beeman Precision Airguns **www.beeman.com**
Benelli USA Corp. **www.benelliusa.com**
Benjamin Sheridan **www.crosman.com**
Beretta U.S.A. Corp. **www.berettausa.com**
Bill Hanus Birdguns **www.billhanusbirdguns.com**
Blackstar **www.benchrest.com/blackstar**
Bond Arms **www.bondarms.com**
Borden's Rifles, Inc. **www.bordensrifles.com**
Bowen Classic Arms **www.bowenclassicarms.com**
Briley Mfg **www.briley.com**
BRNO Arms **www.zbrojouka.com**
Brolin Arms **www.shooters.com/brolin/**
Brown, Ed Products **www.edbrown.com**
Browning **www.browning.com**
BUL Transmark, Ltd. **www.aquanet.co.il/bul_m5**
Bushmaster Firearms/Quality Parts **www.bushmaster.com**
Cape Outfitters **www.doublegun.com**
Carbon 15 **www.professional-ordnance.com**
Casull Arms Corp. **www.casullarms.com**
Century Arms **www.centuryarms.com**
Chadick's Ltd. **www.chadicks-ltd.com**
Champlin Firearms **www.champlinarms.com**
Charles Daly **www.charlesdaly.com**
Charter2000, Inc. **www.charterfirearms.com**
Christensen Arms **www.christensenarms.com**
Cimarron Firearms Co. **www.cimarron-firearms.com**
Clark Custom Guns **www.clarkcustomguns.com**
Colt Mfg Co. **www.colt.com**
Connecticut Valley Arms **www.cva.com**
Coonan Arms **www.uslink.net/~cruzer/main/htm**
Cooper Firearms **www.cooperfirearms.com**
Crosman **www.crosman.com**
Crossfire, L.L.C. **www.crossfirellc.com**
C.Sharp Arms Co. **www.csharparms.com**
CZ USA **www.cz-usa.com**
Daisy Mfg Co. **www.daisy.com**
Dakota Arms Inc. **www.dakotaarms.com**
Dan Wesson Firearms **www.danwesson-firearms.com**
Davis Industries **www.davisindguns.com**
Dixie Gun Works **www.dixiegun.com**
Dlask Arms Corp. **www.dlask.com**
D.S. Arms, Inc. **www.dsarms.com**
DZ Arms **www.tool-fix.com/dzarms.html**
Eagle Imports,Inc. **www.bersa-llama.com**
Enterprise Arms **www.enterprise.com**
European American Armory Corp. **www.eaacorp.com**
Fabarm **www.fabarm.com**
Freedom Arms **www.freedomarms.com**
Gamo **www.gamo.com**
Gary Reeder Custom Guns **www.reeder-customguns.com**
Gibbs Rifle Company **www.gibbsrifle.com**
Glock **www.glock.com**
Griffin & Howe **www.griffinhowe.com**
Griffon USA, Inc. **griffonusa@aol.com**
Grizzly Big Boar Rifle **www.largrizzly.com**
GSI Inc. **www.gsifirearms.com**
H&R 1871, Inc., New England Firearms,H&R
  hr1871@hr1871.com
Hammerli **www.hammerli.com**
Harris Gunworks **www.harrisgunworks.com**
Heavy Express, Inc. **www.heavyexpress.com**

Heckler and Koch **www.hecklerkoch-usa.com**
Henry Repeating Arms Co. **www.henryrepeating.com**
High Standard Mfg. **www.highstandard.com**
Hi-Point Firearms **www.hi-pointfirearms.com**
H-S Precision **www.hsprecision.com**
IAR Inc. **www.iar-arms.com**
Imperial Miniature Armory **www.1800miniature.com**
Interarms **www.interarms.com**
Inter Ordnance **www.inter-ordnance.com**
Intrac Arms International LLC **defence@dldnet.com**
Israel Arms **www.israelarms.com**
Ithaca Gun Co. **www.ithacagun.com**
Izhevsky Mekhanichesky Zavod **www.baikalinc.ru**
JP Enterprises, Inc. **www.jpar15.com**
Kahr Arms **www.kahr.com**
Kel-Tec CNC Ind., Inc. **www.kel-tec.com**
Kimber **www.kimberamerica.com**
Knight's Mfg. Co. **kacsr25@aol.com**
Knight Rifles **www.knightrifles.com**
Krieghoff GmbH **www.krieghoff.de**
Krieghoff Int'l **www.shootingsports.com**
L.A.R Mfg **www.largrizzly.com**
Lazzeroni Arms Co. **www.lazzeroni.com**
Les Baer Custom, Inc. **www.lesbaer.com**
Lone Star Rifle Co. **www.lonestarrifle.com**
Magnum Research **www.magnumresearch.com**
Markesbery Muzzleloaders **www.markesbery.com**
Marksman Products **www.marksman.com**
Marlin **www.marlinfirearms.com**
McMillan Bros Rifle Co. **www.mcfamily.com**
Merkel **www.gsifirearms.com**
Miltech **www.miltecharms.com**
Miltex, Inc. **www.miltexusa.com**
Navy Arms **www.navyarms.com**
Nesika Actions **www.nesika.com**
New England Arms Corp. **www.newenglandarms.com**
New England Custom Gun Svc, Ltd.
  www.newenglandcustomgun.com
North American Arms **www.naaminis.com**
Nowlin Mfg. Inc. **www.nowlinguns.com**
O.F. Mossberg & Sons **www.mossberg.com**
Olympic Arms **www.olyarms.com**
Para-Ordnance **www.paraord.com**
Pedersoli Davide & Co. **www.davide-pedersoli.com**
Power Custom **www.powercustom.com**
Remington **www.remington.com**
Republic Arms Inc. **www.republicarmsinc.com**
Rizzini Di Rizzini **www.rizzini.it**
Robar Companies, Inc. **www.robarguns.com**
Robinson Armament Co. **www.robarm.com**
Rock River Arms, Inc. **www.rockriverarms.com**
Rogue Rifle Co. Inc. **www.chipmunkrifle.com**
Rossi Arms **www.rossiusa.com**
RPM **www.rpmxlpistols.com**
RWS **www.dnrws.com**
Sabatti SpA **info@sabatti.it**
Saco Defense **www.sacoinc.com**
Safari Arms **www.olyarms.com**
Samco Global Arms Inc. **www.samcoglobal.com**
Sarco Inc. **www.sarcoinc.com**
Savage Arms Inc. **www.savagearms.com**

WEB DIRECTORY

Scattergun Technologies Inc. **www.scattergun.com**
SIG Arms,Inc. **www.sigarms.com**
Simpson Ltd. **www.simpsonltd.com**
SKB Shotguns **www.skbshotguns.com**
Smith & Wesson **www.smith-wesson.com**
Springfield Armory **www.springfield-armory.com**
SSK Industries **www.sskindustries.com**
Steyr Mannlicher **www.gsifirearms.com**
STI Int'l **sales@sti-guns.com**
Strayer-Voigt Inc. **www.sviguns.com**
Sturm,Ruger & Company **www.ruger-firearms.com**
Tar-Hunt Slug Guns, Inc. **www.tar-hunt.com**
Taurus **www.taurususa.com**
Tennessee Guns **www.tennesseeguns.com**

The 1877 Sharps Co. **www.1877sharps.com**
Thompson Center Arms **www.tcarms.com**
Traditions **www.traditionsmuzzle.com**
Uberti USA,Inc. **www.uberti.com**
U.S. Fire-Arms Mfg. Co. **www.usfirearms.com**
U.S. Repeating Arms Co. **www.winchester-guns.com**
Vektor USA **vektorusa@series2000.com**
Volquartsen Custom Ltd. **www.volquartsen.com**
Weatherby **www.weatherby.com**
Webley Scott Ltd. **www.webley.g.uk**
Wild West Guns **www.wildwestguns.com**
William Larkin Moore & Co. **www.doublegun.com**
Wilson's Gun Shop Inc. **www.wilsoncombat.com**
Winchester Firearms **www.winchester-guns.com**

GUN PARTS, BARRELS, AFTER-MARKET ACCESSORIES

300 Below **www.300below.com**
Accuracy Speaks, Inc. **www.accuracyspeaks.com**
American Spirit Arms Corp. **www.gunkits.com**
Badger Barrels, Inc. **www.badgerbarrels.com**
Bar-Sto Precision Machine **www.barsto.com**
Belt Mountain Enterprises **www.beltmountain.com**
Blackstar **www.benchrest.com/blackstar**
Buffer Technologies **www.buffertech.com**
Bullberry Barrel Works **www.bullberry.com**
Bushmaster Firearms/Quality Parts **www.bushmaster.com**
Butler Creek Corp **www.butler-creek.com**
Caspian Arms Ltd. **caspianarm@aol.com**
Cheaper Than Dirt **www.cheaperthandirt.com**
Chesnut Ridge **www.chestnutridge.com/**
Chip McCormick Corp **www.chipmccormickcorp.com**
Colonial Arms **www.colonialarms.com**
Cylinder & Slide Shop **www.cylinder-slide.com**
Dixie Gun Works **www.dixiegun.com**
DPMS **www.dpmsinc.com**
D.S.Arms,Inc. **www.dsarms.com**
Ed Brown Products **www.edbrown.com**
EFK Marketing/Fire Dragon Pistol Accessories
   www.flmfire.com
Federal Arms **www.fedarms.com**
Forrest Inc. **www.gunmags.com**
Gentry, David **www.gentrycustom.com**
Gun Parts Corp. **www.gunpartscorp.com**
Hart Rifle Barrels **www.hartbarrels.com**
Hastings Barrels **www.hastingsbarrels.com**
Heckman Specialties **www.members.tripod.com/~heckspec**
Heinie Specialty Products **www.heinie.com**
Jarvis, Inc. **www.jarvis-custom.com**
J&T Distributing **www.jtdistributing.com**
Jonathan Arthur Ciener, Inc. **www.22lrconversions.com**
JP Enterprises **www.jpar15.com**
King's Gunworks **www.kingsgunworks.com**

Les Baer Custom, Inc. **www.lesbaer.com**
Lilja Barrels **www.riflebarrels.com**
Lothar Walther Precision Tools Inc. **www.lothar-walther.de**
M&A Parts, Inc. **www.m-aparts.com**
Marvel Products, Inc. **www.marvelprod.com**
MEC-GAR SrL **www.mec-gar.it**
Michaels of Oregon Co. **www.michaels-oregon.com**
Pachmayr **www.pachmayr.com**
Pac-Nor Barreling **www.pac-nor.com**
Para Ordinance Pro Shop **www.ltms.com**
Point Tech Inc. **pointec@ibm.net**
Promag Industries **www.promagindustries.com**
Power Custom, Inc. **www.powercustom.com**
Rocky Mountain Arms **www.rockymountainarms.com**
Royal Arms Int'l **www.royalarms.com**
R.W. Hart **www.rwhart.com**
Sarco Inc. **www.sarcoinc.com**
Scattergun Technologies Inc. **www.scattergun.com**
Shilen **www.shilen.com**
Smith & Alexander Inc. **www.smithandalexander.com**
Speed Shooters Int'l **www.shooternet.com/ssi**
Sprinco USA Inc. **sprinco@primenet.com**
SSK Industries **www.shooters.com/apg/members.htm**
Tapco **www.tapco.com**
Trapdoors Galore **www.trapdoors.com**
Triple K Manufacturing Co. Inc. **www.triplek.com**
U.S.A. Magazines Inc. **www.usa-magazines.com**
Verney-Carron SA **www.verney-carron.com**
Volquartsen Custom Ltd. **www.volquartsen.com**
W.C. Wolff Co. **www.gunsprings.com**
Waller & Son **www.wallerandson.com**
Weigand Combat Handguns **www.weigandcombat.com**
Western Gun Parts **www.westerngunparts.com**
Wilson Combat **www.wilsoncombat.com**
Wisner's Inc. **www.gunpartsspecialist.com**
Z-M Weapons **www.zmweapons.com/home.htm**

GUNSMITHING SUPPLIES AND INSTRUCTION

American Gunsmithing Institute
   www.americangunsmith.com
Brownells, Inc. **www.brownells.com**
B-Square Co. **www.b-square.com**
Clymer Mfg. Co. **www.clymertool.com**
Craftguard Metal Finishing **crftgrd@aol.com**
Dem-Bart **www.dembartco.com**

Du-Lite Corp. **www.dulite.com**
Dvorak Instruments **www.dvorakinstruments.com**
Gradiant Lens Corp. **www.gradientlens.com**
Gunline Tools **www.gunline.com**
JGS Precision Tool Mfg. LLC **www.jgstools.com**
Midway **www.midwayusa.com**
Olympus America Inc. **www.olympus.com**

WEB DIRECTORY

HANDGUN GRIPS

Ajax Custom Grips, Inc. **www.ajaxgrips.com**
Altamont Co. **altamont@net66.com**
Barami Corp. **www.baramihipgrip.com**
Crimson Trace Corp. **www.crimsontrace.com**
Eagle Grips **www.eaglegrips.com**
Fitz Pistol Grip Co. **johnpaul@snowcrest.net**

Hogue Grips **www.getgrip.com**
Lett Custom Grips **www.lettgrips.com**
Pachmayr **www.pachmayr.com**
Pearce Grips **www.pearcegrip.com**
Trausch Grips Int.Co. **www.erausch.com**
Uncle Mike's: **www.uncle-mikes.com**

HOLSTERS AND LEATHER PRODUCTS

Aker Leather Products **www.akerleather.com**
Alessi Distributor R&F Inc. **www.alessiholsters.com**
Alfonso's of Hollywood **www.alfonsogunleather.com**
Armor Holdings **www.holsters.com**
Bagmaster **www.bagmaster.com**
Bianchi **www.bianchiint.com**
Blackhills Leather **www.blackhillsleather.com**
BodyHugger Holsters **www.nikolais.com**
Brigade Gun Leather **www.brigadegunleather.com**
Chimere **www.chimere.com**
Classic Old West Styles **www.cows.com**
Conceal It **www.conceal-it.com**
Conceal 'N Draw **www.themetro.om/03/fempro**
Concealment Shop Inc. **www.theconcealmentshop.com**
Coronado Leather Co. **www.coronadoleather.com**
Creedmoor Sports, Inc. **www.creedmoorsports.com**
Custom Leather Wear **www.customleatherwear.com**
Defense Security Products **www.thunderwear.com**
DeSantis Holster **www.desantisholster.com**
Dillon Precision **www.dillonprecision.com**
Don Hume Leathergoods, Inc. **www.donhume.com**
Ernie Hill International **www.erniehill.com**
Fist **www.fist-inc.com**
Front Line Ltd. **frontlin@internet-zahav.net**
Galco **www.usgalco.com**
Gilmore's Sports Concepts **www.gilmoresports.com**
Gould & Goodrich **www.goulduse.com**
Gunmate Products **www.gun-mate.com**

Hellweg Ltd. **www.hellwegltd.com**
Hide-A-Gun **www.hide-a-gun.com**
Holsters.Com **www.holsters.com**
Horseshoe Leather Products **www.horseshoe.co.uk**
Hunter Co. **www.huntercompany.com**
Kirkpatrick Leather Company **www.kirkpatrickleather.com**
Kramer Leather **www.kramerleather.com**
Law Concealment Systems **www.handgunconcealment.com**
Levy's Leathers Ltd. **www.levysleathers.com**
Michaels of Oregon Co. **www.michaels-oregon.com**
Milt Sparks Leather **www.miltsparks.com**
Mitch Rosen Extraordinary Gunleather **www.mitchrosen.com**
Old World Leather **www.gun-mate.com**
Pager Pal **www.pagerpal.com**
Phalanx Corp. **www.phalanxarms.com**
PWL **www.pwlusa.com**
Rumanya Inc. **www.rumanya.com**
Safariland Ltd. Inc. **www.safariland.com**
Shooting Systems Group Inc. **www.shootingsystems.com**
Strictly Anything Inc. **www.strictlyanything.com**
Strong Holster Co. **www.strong-holster.com**
The Belt Co. **www.conceal-it.com**
The Leather Factory Inc. **lflandry@flash.net**
The Outdoor Connection **www.outdoorconnection.com**
Top-Line USA inc. **www.toplineusa.com**
Triple K Manufacturing Co. **www.triplek.com**
Wilson Combat **www.wilsoncombat.com**

MISCELLANEOUS SHOOTING PRODUCTS

10X Products Group **www.10Xwear.com**
Aero Peltor **www.aearo.com**
Beartooth **www.beartoothproducts.com**
Dalloz Safety **www.cdalloz.com**
Deben Group Industries Inc. **www.deben.com**
Decot Hy-Wyd Sport Glasses **www.sportglasses.com**
E.A.R., Inc. **www.earinc.com**

Johnny Stewart Wildlife Calls **www.stewartoutdoors.com**
North Safety Products **www.northsafety-brea.com**
Second Chance Body Armor Inc. **email@secondchance.com**
Silencio **www.silencio.com**
Smart Lock Technologies **www.smartlock.com**
Walker's Game Ear Inc. **www.walkersgameear.com**

MUZZLELOADING FIREARMS AND PRODUCTS

Austin & Halleck, Inc. **austinhal@aol.com**
CVA **www.cva.com**
Davis, Vernon C. & Co. **www.mygunroom/vcdavis&co/**
Dixie Gun Works, Inc. **www.dixiegun.com**
Elephant Black Powder **www.elephantblackpowder.com**
Goex Black Powder **www.goexpowder.com**
Jedediah Starr Trading Co. **www.jedediah-starr.com**
Jim Chambers Flintlocks **www.flintlocks.com**
Knight Rifles **www.knightrifles.com**

Log Cabin Shop **www.logcabinshop.com**
Lyman **www.lymanproducts.com**
Millennium Designed Muzzleloaders
   www.m2kmuzzleloaders.com
Mountain State Muzzleloading
   www.mtnstatemuzzleloading.com
MSM, Inc. **www.msmfg.com**
Muzzleloading Technologies, Inc.
   www.mtimuzzleloading.com

WEB DIRECTORY

Navy Arms **www.navyarms.com**
October Country Muzzleloading **www.oct-country.com**
Ox-Yoke Originals Inc. **www.oxyoke.com**
Rightnour Mfg. Co. Inc. **www.rmcsports.com**

The Rifle Shop **trshoppe@aol.com**
Thompson Center Arms **www.tcarms.com**
Traditions Performance Muzzleloading
   www.traditionsmuzzle.com

PUBLICATIONS, VIDEOS, AND CD'S

Airgun Letter **www.airgunletter.com**
American Firearms Industry **www.amfire.com**
American Handgunner **www.americanhandgunner.com**
American Hunter **www.americanhunter.org**
American Shooting Magazine **www.americanshooting.com**
Blacksmith **bcbooks@glasscity.net**
Blackpowder Hunting **www.98.net/ibha/**
Black Powder Journal **www.blackpowderjournal.com**
Blue Book Publications **www.bluebookinc.com**
Combat Handguns **www.combathandguns.com**
Countrywide Press **www.countrysport.com**
DBI Books/Krause Publications **www.krause.com**
Delta Force **www.infogo.com/delta**
Discount Gun Books **www.discountgunbooks.com**
Gun List **www.gunlist.com**
Gun Video **www.gunvideo.com**
GUNS Magazine **www.gunsmagazine.com**
Gunweb Magazine WWW Links **www.imags.com**
Harris Publications **www.harrispublications.com**
Heritage Gun Books **www.gunbooks.com**
Krause Publications **www.krause.com**
Moose Lake Publishing **MooselakeP@aol.com**
Munden Enterprises Inc. **www.bob-munden.com**

Outdoor Videos **www.outdoorvideos.com**
Precision Shooting **www.precisionshooting.com**
Rifle and Handloader Magazines **www.riflemagazine.com**
Rifle and Shotgun Magazine/Gun Journal
   www.natcom-publications.com
Safari Press Inc. **www.safaripress.com**
Shooters News **www.shootersnews.com**
Shooting Industry **www.shootingindustry.com**
Shooting Sports Retailer **ssretailer@ad.com**
Shotgun News **www.shotgunnews.com**
Shotgun Report **www.shotgunreport.com**
Shotgun Sports Magazine **www.shotgun-sports.com**
Small Arms Review **www.smallarmsreview.com**
Sporting Clays Web Edition **www.sportingclays.com**
Sports Afield **www.sportsafield.comm**
Sports Trend **www.sportstrend.com**
Sportsmen on Film **www.sportsmenonfilm.com**
The Gun Journal **www.shooters.com**
The Shootin Iron **www.off-road.com/4x4web/si/si.html**
The Single Shot Exchange Magazine
   singleshot@earthlink.net
Voyageur Press **www.voyageurpress.com**
VSP Publications **www.gunbooks.com**

RELOADING TOOLS AND SUPPLIES

Ballisti-Cast Mfg. **www.powderandbow.com/ballist**
Bruno Shooters Supply **www.brunoshooters.com**
CH Tool & Die **www.cdhd.com**
Corbin Mfg & Supply Co. **www.corbins.com**
Dillon Precision **www.dillonprecision.com**
Forster Precision Products **www.forsterproducts.com**
Hanned Line **www.hanned.com**
Harrell's Precision **www.harrellsprec.com**
Hornady **www.hornady.com**
Huntington Reloading Products **www.huntingtons.com**
J & J Products Co. **www.jandjproducts.com**
Lee Precision,Inc. **www.leeprecision.com**
Littleton Shotmaker **www.leadshotmaker.com**
Lyman **www.lymanproducts.com**
Magma Engineering **www.magmaengr.com/magma.htm**
Mayville Engineering Co. (MEC) **www.mecreloaders.com**
Midway **www.midwayusa.com**

Moly-Bore **www.molybore.com**
MTM Case-Guard **www.mtmcase-guard.com**
NECO **www.neconos.com**
NEI Handtools Inc. **www.neihandtools.com**
Neil Jones Custom Products **www.neiljones.com**
Ponsness/Warren **www.reloaders.com**
Ranger Products
   www.pages.prodigy.com/rangerproducts.home.htm
Rapine Bullet Mold Mfg Co. **www.bulletmolds.com**
RCBS **www.rcbs.com**
Redding Reloading Equipment **www.redding-reloading.com**
Russ Haydon's Shooting Supplies **www.shooters-supply.com**
Sinclair Int'l Inc. **www.sinclairintl.com**
Stoney Point Products Inc **www.stoneypoint.com**
Thompson Bullet Lube Co. **www.thompsonbulletlube.com**
Wilson(L.E. Wilson) **www.lewilson.com**

RESTS— BENCH, PORTABLE, ATTACHABLE

B-Square **www.b-square.com**
Desert Mountain Mfg. **www.bench-master.com**
Harris Engineering Inc.
   www.cyberteklabs.com/harris/main/htm
Kramer Designs **www.snipepod.com**
L Thomas Rifle Support **www.ltsupport.com**
Level-Lok **www.levellok.com**
Midway **www.midwayusa.com**
Ransom International **www.ransom-intl.com**

R.W. Hart **www.rwhart.com**
Sinclair Intl, Inc. **www.sinclairintl.com**
Stoney Point Products **www.stoneypoint.com**
Varmint Masters **www.varmintmasters.com**
Versa-Pod **www.versa-pod.com**

WEB DIRECTORY

SCOPES, SIGHTS, MOUNTS AND ACCESSORIES

Accusight www.accusight.com
ADCO www.shooters.com/adco/index/htm
Aimpoint www.aimpointusa.com
Aim Shot, Inc. www.hi-techoptics.com
Aimtech Mount Systems www.aimtech-mounts.com
Alpec Team, Inc. www.alpec.com
American Technologies Network, Corp. www.atncorp.com
AO Sight Systems Inc. www.aosights.com
Ashley Outdoors, Inc. www.ashleyoutdoors.com
ATN www.atncorp.com
BSA Optics www.bsaoptics.com
B-Square Company, Inc. www.b-square.com
Burris www.burrisoptics.com
Bushnell Corp. www.bushnell.com
Carl Zeiss Optical Inc. www.zeiss.com
C-More Systems www.cmore.com
Conetrol Scope Mounts www.conetrol.com
Crimson Trace Corp. www.crimsontrace.com
Crossfire L.L.C. www.amfire.com/hesco/html
DCG Supply Inc. www.dcgsupply.com
EasyHit, Inc. www.easyhit.com
EAW www.eaw.de
Electro-Optics Technologies www.eotechmdc.com/holosight
Europtik Ltd. www.europtik.com
Gilmore Sports www.gilmoresports.com
Hakko Co. Ltd. www.hakko-japan.co.jp
Hesco www.hescosights.com
Hitek Industries www.nightsight.com
HIVIZ www.northpass.com
Innovative Weaponry,Inc. www.ptnightsights.com
Ironsighter Co. www.ironsighter.com
ITT Night Vision www.ittnightvision.com
Kahles www.kahlesoptik.com
Kowa Optimed Inc. www.kowascope.com
Laser Bore Sight www.laserboresight.com
Laser Devices Inc. www.laserdevices.com
Lasergrips www.crimsontrace.com
LaserLyte www.laserlyte.com

LaserMax Inc. www.lasermax-inc.com
Laser Products www.surefire.com
Leapers, Inc. www.leapers.com
Leica Camera Inc. www.leica-camera.com/usa
Leupold www.leupold.com
Lyman www.lymanproducts.com
Marble Arms www.marblearms.com
Micro Sight Co. www.microsight.com
Millett www.millettsights.com
Miniature Machine Corp. www.mmcsight.com
NAIT www.nait.com
Newcon International Ltd. newconsales@newcon-optik.com
Night Owl Optics www.jnltrading.com
Nikon Inc. www.nikonusa.com
North American Integrated Technologies www.nait.com
O.K. Weber, Inc. www.okweber.com
Pentax Corp. www.pentaxlightseeker.com
Premier Reticle www.premierreticles.com
R&R Int'l Trade www.nightoptic.com
Schmidt & Bender www.schmidt-bender.com
Scopecoat www.scopecoat.com
Scopelevel www.scopelevel.com
Segway Industries www.segway-industries.com
Shepherd Scope Ltd. www.shepherdscopes.com
Sightron www.sightron.com
Simmons-Blount www.blount.com
S&K www.scopemounts.com
Springfield Armory www.springfield-armory.com
Sure-Fire www.surefire.com
Swarovski/Kahles www.swarovskioptik.com
Swift Instruments Inc. www.swift-optics.com
Tasco www.tascosales.com
Trijicon Inc. www.trijicon-inc.com
Truglo Inc. www.truglosights.com
U.S. Optics Technologies Inc. www.usoptics.com
Weaver-Blount www.blount.com
Wilcox Industries Corp www.wilcoxind.com
Williams Gun Sight Co. www.williamsgunsight.com

SHOOTING ORGANIZATIONS, SCHOOLS AND RANGES

Amateur Trapshooting Assoc. www.shootata.com
American Custom Gunmakers Guild www.acgg.org
American Gunsmithing Institute
    www.americangunsmith.com
American Pistolsmiths Guild www.americanpistol.com
American Shooting Sports Council www.assc.com
BATF www.atf.ustreas.gov
Blackwater Lodge and Training Center
    www.blackwaterlodge.com
Boone and Crockett Club www.boone-crockett.org
Buckmasters, Ltd. www.buckmasters.com
Citizens Committee for the Right to Keep & Bear Arms
    www.ccrkba.org
Civilian Marksmanship Program www.odcmp.com
Colorado School of Trades cstinfo@uswest.net
Ducks Unlimited www.ducks.org
Firearms Coalition www.nealknox.com
Front Sight Firearms Training Institute www.frontsight.com
Gun Clubs www.associatedgunclubs.org

Gun Owners' Action League www.goal.org
Gun Owners of America www.gunowners.org
Gun Trade Asssoc. Ltd. www.brucepub.com/gta
Gunsite Training Center,Inc. www.gunsite.com
International Defense Pistol Assoc. www.idpa.com
International Handgun Metallic Silhouette Assoc. www.ihmsa.org
International Hunter Education Assoc. www.ihea.com
Murray State College (gunsmithing) darnold@msc.cc.ok.us
National 4-H Shooting Sports kesabo@nmsu.edu
National Benchrest Shooters Assoc. www.benchrest.com
National Muzzle Loading Rifle Assoc. www.nmlra.org
National Reloading Manufacturers Assoc
    www.reload-nrma.com
National Rifle Assoc. www.nra.org
National Rifle Assoc. ILA www.nraila.org
National Shooting Sports Foundation www.nssf.org
National Skeet Shooters Association www.nssa-nsca.com
National Sporting Clays Assoc. www.nssa-nsca.com
National Wild Turkey Federation www.nwtf.com

WEB DIRECTORY

North American Hunting Club **www.huntingclub.com**
Pennsylvania Gunsmith School **www.pagunsmith.com**
Quail Unlimited **www.qu.org**
Right To Keep and Bear Arms **www.rkba.org**
Rocky Mountain Elk Foundation **www.rmef.org**
SAAMI **www.saami.org**
Second Amendment Foundation **www.saf.org**
Shooting Ranges Int'l **www.shootingranges.com**
Single Action Shooting Society **www.sassnet.com**
S&W Academy and Nat'l Firearms Trng. Center
   www.sw-academy.com

Ted Nugent United Sportsmen of America **www.tnugent.com**
Thunder Ranch **www.thunderranchinc.com**
Trapshooters Homepage **www.trapshooters.com**
Trinidad State Junior College **www.tsjc.cccoes.edu**
U.S. Int'l Clay Target Assoc. **www.usicta.com**
United States Fish and Wildlife Service **www.fws.gov**
U.S. Practical Shooting Assoc. **www.uspsa.org**
USA Shooting **www.usashooting.com**
Varmint Hunters Assoc. **www.varminthunter.org**
Wildlife Legislative Fund of America **www.wlfa.org**
Women's Shooting Sports Foundation **www.wssf.org**

STOCKS

Bell & Carlson, Inc. **www.bellandcarlson.com**
Boyd's Gunstock Industries, Inc. **www.boydboys.com**
Butler Creek Corp **www.butler-creek.com**
Calico Hardwoods, Inc. **www.calicohardwoods.com**
Choate Machine **www.riflestock.com**
Elk Ridge Stocks **www.reamerrentals.com/elk_ridge.htm**
Great American Gunstocks **www.gunstocks.com**
Lone Wolf **www.lonewolfriflestocks.com**

McMillan Fiberglass Stocks **www.mcmfamily.com**
MPI Stocks **www.mpistocks.com**
Ram-Line- Blount Inc. **www.blount.com**
Rimrock Rifle Stock **www.rimrockstocks.com**
Royal Arms Gunstocks **www.imt.net/~royalarms**
Tiger-Hunt Curly Maple Gunstocks **www.gunstockwood.com**
Wenig Custom Gunstocks Inc. **www.wenig.com**

TARGETS AND RANGE EQUIPMENT

Action Target Co. **www.actiontarget.com**
Advanced Interactive Systems **www.ais-sim.com**
Birchwood Casey **www.birchwoodcasey.com**
Caswell Detroit Armor Companies **www.bullettrap.com**
MTM Products **www.mtmcase-gard.com**
Natiional Target Co. **www.nationaltarget.com**
Newbold Target Systems **www.newboldtargets.com**

Range Management Services Inc. **www.casewellintl.com**
Reactive Target Systems Inc. **chrts@primenet.com**
Super Trap Bullet Containment Systems **www.supertrap.com**
Thompson Target Technology
   www.cantorweb.com/thompsontargets
Visible Impact Targets **www.crosman.com**
White Flyer **www.whiteflyer.com**

TRAP AND SKEET SHOOTING EQUIPMENT AND ACCESSORIES

Auto-Sporter Industries **www.auto-sporter.com**
10X Products Group **www.10Xwear.com**
Claymaster Traps **www.claymaster.com**
Do-All Traps, Inc. **www.do-alltraps.com**

Laporte USA **www.laporte-shooting.com**

Outers **www.blount.com**

Trius Products Inc. **www.triustraps.com**

TRIGGERS

Shilen **www.shilen.com**
Timney Triggers **www.timneytrigger.com**

Brownells **www.brownells.com**

MAJOR SHOOTING WEB SITES AND LINKS

All Outdoors **www.alloutdoors.com**
Alphabetic Index of Links **www.gunsgunsguns.com**
Auction Arms **www.auctionarms.com**
Firearms Internet Database **www.savannahlane.com**
Gun Broker Auctions **www.gunbroker.com**
Gun Games Online **www.gungames.com**
Gun Index **www.gunindex.com**
Gun Industry **www.gunindustry.com**
Gun Talk **www.shooters.com/guntalkactivitiesframe.html**
GunLinks **www.gunlinks.com**
Guns For Sale **www.gunsamerica.com**
Gunweb **www.gunweb.com**
GunXchange **www.gunxchange.com**
Hunting Digest **www.huntingdigest.com**

Hunting Information(NSSF) **www.huntinfo.org**
Hunting Network **www.huntingnetwork.com**
Real Guns **www.realguns.com/links/glinks.htm**
Rec.Guns **www.recguns.com**
Shooters' Gun Calendar **www.guncalendar.com/index.cfm**
Shooter's Online Services **www.shooters.com**
Shooters Search **www.shooterssearch.com**
Shotgun Sports Resource Guide **www.shotgunsports.com**
Sportsman's Web **www.sportsmansweb.com**
TUCO's Firearms Forums **www.paradise-web.com/plus/**
   plus.mirage?who=tuco10&all=yes
Where To Shoot **www.wheretoshoot.com**
Xoutdoors **www.xoutdoors.com**

by JOHN HAVILAND

SHOTGUN REVIEW

NOT MANY YEARS ago the canvas coat was the mantle of upland bird and waterfowl hunters. The coats faded from the days afield to match the tans of frosted alder leaves and cattails. The hunters who wore these coats had lived through the Great Depression or had been told by their parents how tough times had been. They saved their money, made do with what they had and turned off the lights every time they walked out of the room.

Nearly every one of these bird hunters owned one shotgun for all their hunting, from grouse to geese to keeping the eyes tuned up on clay pigeons. The gun was most likely a pump-action Winchester Model 12 or Remington 870, or maybe an autoloader like the Browning A-5. The guns were 12 gauge, the 16 and 20 reserved for young shooters in training. The 12 gauge 2 3/4-inch shell held

plenty of lead shot to kill any bird that flew. While three-inch guns, like the Winchester Model 12 Heavy Duck gun, were available, most considered the extra shot as superfluous and shells downright expensive.

That was then. Now 'more' is modern.

Scott Granger, of Browning and Winchester, says he sees two types of shotgunners today. *"There's still a lot of hunters who want one gun to do it all,* Granger says. "*Those hunters want a 12 gauge 3 1/2-inch magnum in a gas-operated autoloader that softens recoil somewhat. They want that 3 1/2-inch magnum for shooting steel shot at geese. Now a lot of guys will never shoot those big shells, but they still want that versatility just in case,"* he says.

"The second type of shotgunner is what I call the technical group," Granger says. *"These guys also go with an autoloader in 3 1/2-*

inch magnum for hunting. But they're also interested in target shooting and you just can't dismiss the influence sporting clays has had on shotguns."

The over/under in 12 gauge is the first choice for sporting clays. *"This is the gun these technical guys have always wanted,"* Granger says. The gun has a somewhat higher rib and a fiber optic front sight to help provide a quicker sight picture.

Eddie Stevens, of Remington Arms, says most hunters these days own at least two shotguns. *"One is a work gun they carry in the boat or in the blind,"* he says. *"The other is a target gun for the trap or sporting clays range."*

Stevens says the working gun is probably a pump or an autoloader. Stock choice is split 50/50 between wood or synthetic – and interchangeable chokes are a necessity. The gun must be chambered for the 12 gauge 3 1/2-inch magnum. *"Sales of the 3 1/2 inch have just skyrocketed,"* Stevens says. *"People want the versatility of being able to shoot all the 12 gauge loads in one gun."*

The second shotgun must be a good-looking gun that can be displayed at the target range. For this show gun, most shotgunners go with an over/under or an autoloader with a checkered stock of figured wood and metal polished bright and deep-blued.

Stevens predicts in the future shotgunners will buy a different shotgun for targets, upland birds, turkeys, waterfowl and deer. *"Of course, we love that,"* he says.

Let's see what manufacturers have new that shotgunners must have this year.

B.C. Outdoors/Verona

B.C. Outdoors is hooked up with PMC Ammunition, Docter Sport Optics and now a line of Verona 12 gauge semiautomatic and competition over/under shotguns imported from Italy.

The over/unders come stocked in dimensions for skeet, trap or sporting. Common features on all three guns include single selective triggers adjustable for length of pull; bores with extended forcing cones, back-boring, porting and four Briley Spectrum chokes.

The Verona semiautomatics are gas-operated and based on the design of the SPAS-12 shotguns. The three Verona semi-auto models are available with a black composite stock or a Turkish walnut stock. All feature aluminum receivers and a chromed bolt assembly. The guns accept 2 3/4- or 3-inch magnum shells and have a magazine cutoff. Barrels are 28 or 26 inches and come equipped with a screw-in choke.

Benelli

Benelli sells 72 different versions of its shotguns for law enforcement, home defense, hunting, target and competition – as well as the largest selection of left-hand semiautomatics in the world.

Benelli engineers started with a clean computer screen when they designed the new Nova, a 3 1/2-inch 12-gauge pump-action shotgun. In place of a conventional steel receiver and separate buttstock is a single unit that incorporates a light - but rigid - steel liner molded inside a glass-reinforced polymer shell. Molded-in ribs around the grip provide a secure hold. The recoil pad

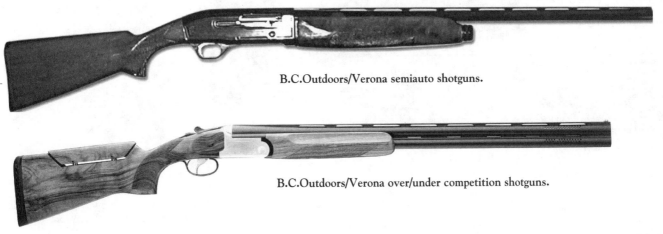

B.C.Outdoors/Verona semiauto shotguns.

B.C.Outdoors/Verona over/under competition shotguns.

twists off for access to a recess in the buttstock for installation of a recoil reducer to absorb some of the recoil from heavy 3 1/2-inch loads.

Beretta

Beretta has redesigned its S682 Gold E-series of competition over/unders. The four guns include features such as Beretta's Optima-Bore and an adjustable comb. The Optima-Bore consists of chrome-lined bores with lengthened forcing cones, over-boring and extended choke tubes. The comb is adjustable for height and cast – and an indicator scale facilitates easy, accurate adjustments. The triggers are adjustable to vary length of pull 3/8 of an inch from the grip to the trigger. Two trigger shoes are supplied, one with a surface canted for right-hand shooters and the other with a wide, symmetrical face. The guns are the S682 Gold E Trap, Trap Combo, Skeet and Sporting and are shipped in a new ABS hard case.

Engraving is now included on Beretta's 686E Sporting and 687EL Gold Pigeon II over/unders. The Sporting has an ellipsis pattern on its receiver while the Pigeon II is engraved with a game scene. The guns rest in Giugiaro Design cases which include five Beretta Mobilchokes, disassembly tools, interchangeable plastic or rubber recoil pads and oil.

The Beretta ES100 Rifle Slug semiautomatic comes with a 24-inch rifled barrel. This year Beretta has added a 28-inch smooth-bored barrel to go along with the Rifle Slug gun to make the ES100 Rifle Slug Combo good for hunters after bucks in the morning and birds in the afternoon.

Ouch! Last week I was patterning several loads from a 12 gauge 3 1/2-inch magnum. The hard rubber recoil pad on the

Beretta S682 Gold Receiver

Above, from left to right: Beretta S682 Gold E Sporting, S682 Gold E Skeet, S682 Gold E Trap, and S682 Gold E Trap Combo.

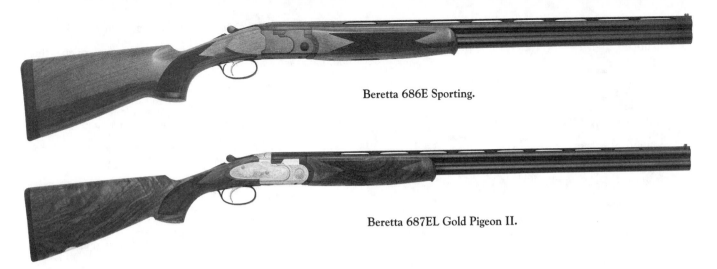

Beretta 686E Sporting.

Beretta 687EL Gold Pigeon II.

pump gun whacked my shoulder with every ounce of recoil. Immediately after the 15th round a sharp pain shot through my shoulder. After three days I can barely hold my arm straight out. Beretta has created the GEL*TEK recoil pad with people like me in mind. The pad is made with a silicone gel core to soak up recoil. The pad fits the stocks of most Beretta guns and has a clasp that allows easy attachment and removal.

Browning

Browning has brought out a bunch of new guns which are mostly existing models that have been slimmed down or had features added.

Browning teamed with the National Wild Turkey Federation to bring out the NWTF Shotgun Series. The guns are dressed-up Gold autoloading or Browning Pump Shotguns chambered in 10 gauge, 12 gauge 3 1/2-inch or 3-inch. The guns come with a 24-inch barrel with an *Extra-Full* extended choke and Hi-Viz fiber-optic sights atop the muzzle. The NWTF logo is on the side of the buttstock of the guns with the lock, stock and barrels done up in Mossy Oak Breakup Camouflage.

The Browning Gold Upland 12 gauge autoloader shaves 12 ounces from the standard Gold Hunter. That weight savings comes from a straight-grip stock and cutting the barrel back to 24 inches. The 20-gauge Gold Upland is the same weight as the standard Gold in that gauge and is fitted with 26-inch barrels.

The Gold Fusion is a new, trimmed, Gold Hunter 12 gauge. The gun weighs seven pounds four ounces, which is eight ounces lighter than the Gold Hunter. The lighter weight is a result of a slimmer stock and a magazine tube made of aluminum with a steel liner.

The gun is shipped in a hard case containing all sorts of goodies. The accessories include a set of shims that fit between the head of the grip and the receiver to adjust cast and drop of the comb, Hi-Viz fiber-optic sights with different light '*pipes*' and five choke tubes – from *Skeet to Full*.

Early this year I had a chance to shoot a Fusion at a variety of flying targets in Mississippi. I worried the recoil would be a bit much, from such a light gun with a plastic buttplate, shooting Winchester Supreme High Velocity loads of 1 1/4 ounces of steel *BBs* or *2s*. But the gas-operated gun was pleasant to shoot while hunting ducks and geese along the Coldwater River in northern Mississippi. also carried the Fusion during a brisk afternoon shooting pen-raised bobwhite quail. The birds kept to the pines and shots were short – at 10 to 15

New Browning Fusion in the Mississippi duck blind.

New Browning Fusion and a green-winged teal.

The new Browning Fusion as a saddle gun on a Mississippi bobwhite quail hunt.

Browning Fusion after bobwhite quail.

yards. The Fusion's light weight helped on those quick point-and-fire shots. I really liked the fiber-optic sights. The illuminated dot helped remind me to keep my cheek planted on the comb and served as a reference point on crossing shots.

No fault of the Fusion's, but sporting clays that same outing at The Willows was a humbling experience for me.

It's a fun course with targets diving from towers in the timber and springing from tall grass. Again, I liked the fiber-optic sight. If there was one negative, it was that the Fusion was a bit light for a smooth swing on hard crossing shots at fast singles and doubles.

This has little to do with new shotguns, but I'll tell you anyway. Duck Flush is a

Shooting a round of Duck Flush at the Willow Sporting Clays range.

game at Willows. It is the most fun I've ever had with a shotgun. Three shooters stand abreast, each with 25 cartridges. When the shooting starts five traps from different positions in front hurl 75 clay targets toward the shooters in two minutes. All three shooters fire and reload as fast as possible because the targets come quickly in ones or twos, or in a cloud of six or seven. A clay is considered 'lost' when it lands unbroken on the pond in front of the shooters.

Back to Browning shotguns....

Another lightweight is the Gold Ten Gauge Light Camo. The gun's receiver is aluminum alloy, which cuts one pound off the standard model for a weight of 9 pounds 7 ounces. The Ten Gauge Light Camo has a 26- or 28-inch barrel and is covered in Mossy Oak Shadow Grass or Break-Up camouflage patterns.

Browning has five new 20-gauge guns. The development of sabot-type slugs has made the 20 gauge much more effective on big game. With that in mind Browning has introduced the Gold Deer Hunter in 20 gauge. The gun features a three-inch chamber in a rifled 22-inch barrel with a cantilever scope base.

The sideplates of the Citori Privilege 20 gauge are engraved with a ringneck pheasant flushing from under a pointer on the left side and alighting woodcocks on the right. The over/under's barrels are 26- or 28-inches and the stock is hand-oiled walnut with a schnabel forearm.

The Citori Ultra XS Skeet 20 gauge is the little brother to the 12 gauge introduced last year. The Ultra has slim lines, vented side ribs and a high post rib on 28- or 30-inch barrels. Stocks are either fixed or come with an adjustable comb.

The Micro designation has been placed on the 20-gauge autoloading Gold and Browning Pump Shotgun. The Gold has a smaller circumference grip, a shortened 13 7/8-inch length of pull and 26-inch barrels, all wrapped up at 6 pounds 10 ounces. The BPS also has a thinner grip and an easier-to-reach forearm – along with a 22-inch barrel, which is back-bored and threaded

for Invector Plus, choke tubes.

A final elegant touch is the Browning Side Lock side-by-side. The 12 or 20 gauge gun is made for Browning by Lebeau-Courally. As its name implies, it features sidelocks, double triggers and automatic ejectors. You can choose from grayed or blued metal finish.

Ithaca Gun

For over 50 years my father's Ithaca Model 37 pump-action 12 gauge has been in continual use shooting waterfowl and upland birds. With the idea of having the gun refinished after all that duty, I took the gun to gunsmith Doug Wells to have it checked. Wells said the 37's working parts showed no appreciable wear, although the chipped and oil-soaked butt stock needed replacing. I bought a new walnut butt stock and forearm for the gun. While I finished the wood, Wells went ahead and started work restoring the gun. He polished the screw heads that had been burred by ill-fitting screwdrivers, re-blued the metal and reamed out its full choke to between modified and improved cylinder. (That has proved a good choice for today's tight patterning upland and nontoxic waterfowl loads.) The refinished gun sparkled. My father said the gun looks even better than the day he bought it in 1947. My son shot ruffed grouse and ducks with the 37 this past fall. It never missed a beat. No doubt in another 50 years his grandson will be shooting the Ithaca 37.

The popularity of last year's Ithaca's Model 37 16 gauge has resulted in a 16-gauge deer gun from Ithaca. The Deerslayer II has a fully rifled barrel that is free-floated. The lack of a barrel attachment at the end of the magazine tube removes any stress that might alter alignment between the barrel and receiver. The buttstock has a Monte Carlo comb that positions the eye higher to easily see through a scope mounted on the drilled and tapped receiver.

A good slug load was the only way a 16-gauge slug gun would fly. Lightfield's new 16-gauge sabot ammunition develops energy comparable to a 12-gauge slug, and at a faster velocity.

Above, top to bottom: FABARM Classic Lion English, FABARM Silver Lion Cub, FABARM Field Pump 12 Gauge, FABARM Tactical and FABARM Field Pump 12 Gauge/Camouflage.

Ithaca has new 37s stocked to fit women and benefit the NRA Foundation's Women's Programs Endowment. The Ithaca Model 37 Women's Endowment Shotguns in 16 and 20 gauge are straight-stocked with American black walnut with dimensions to fit the average-size woman. An Ithaca stockmaker will make stocks of specific dimensions to order on these or any Model 37. A portion of the money from the sales of these guns will be donated to the NRA Foundation's Women's Programs Endowment.

FABARM

Heckler & Koch is adding four new models to its FABARM shotgun line.

The Classic Lion English is the latest addition to the FABARM Classic Lion shotgun side-by-side family. The Classic Lion English features an English straight-grip stock and double

triggers. The gun is a boxlock with automatic ejectors and safeties and weighs right at seven pounds. Barrels are 26, 28 or 30 inches, complete with *Cylinder, Improved Cylinder, Modified, Improved Modified* and *Full* choke tubes. This 12-gauge gun also has three-inch chambers just in case your upland birds tend toward the huge.

Previously available only in 20 gauge with a 24-inch barrel, the short-stocked FABARM Silver Lion Cub is now also available in 12 and 20 gauge with a standard 26-inch ported barrel and a mid-rib bead.

Joining the FABARM pump-action shotguns is the Field Pump 12 Gauge featuring a 12 gauge three-inch chamber in a 28-inch vent-ribbed barrel or a 24-inch rifled barrel with sights. The Field is based on FABARM police shotguns. The aluminum receiver keeps the gun's weight at seven pounds. The guns come with a black sandblasted matte

finish or in Mossy Oak Breakup camouflage – with *Cylinder, Modified* and *Full* choke tubes.

The Tactical semiautomatic is based on their gas-operated sporting shotguns. The Tactical handles all 12-gauge shells, from light 2 3/4-inch to three-inch slugs. The gun weighs 6.6 pounds with a 20-inch barrel. Picatinny rails can be screwed to the barrel, receiver and bottom of the forearm to attach accessories like a scope, ghost-ring rear sight, heat shields, lights and other necessities to help initiate tactical movements against weasels and skunks raiding the hen house.

All FABARM shotguns are made with the Tribore Barrel System, which consists of three internal bore profiles. An over-bore region of .7401-inch in 12 gauge begins at the front of the forcing cone to soften recoil. The bore gradually narrows at the middle of the barrel's length to a standard *cylinder* bore of

.7244-inch. This leads to a gradual increase in velocity to the shot column. The shot column then passes through a standard choke, followed by a short *cylinder* profile at the muzzle. The *cylinder* dimension between the choke and muzzle acts as a port to bleed off excess powder gas.

Mossberg

Thank goodness for abbreviations, or this section would be taken up spelling out 'Single Shot Interchangeable Rifle/ Shotgun.' Last year Mossberg introduced the SSI-One break-action that interchanges rifle cartridge barrels in a matter of minutes.

This year the SSI-One Slug and Turkey guns have been added. The rifled slug barrel is 24 inches long and accepts 12-gauge 2 3/4 or 3-inch slugs. A Weaver-style scope base is provided. Guns average 7.5 pounds in

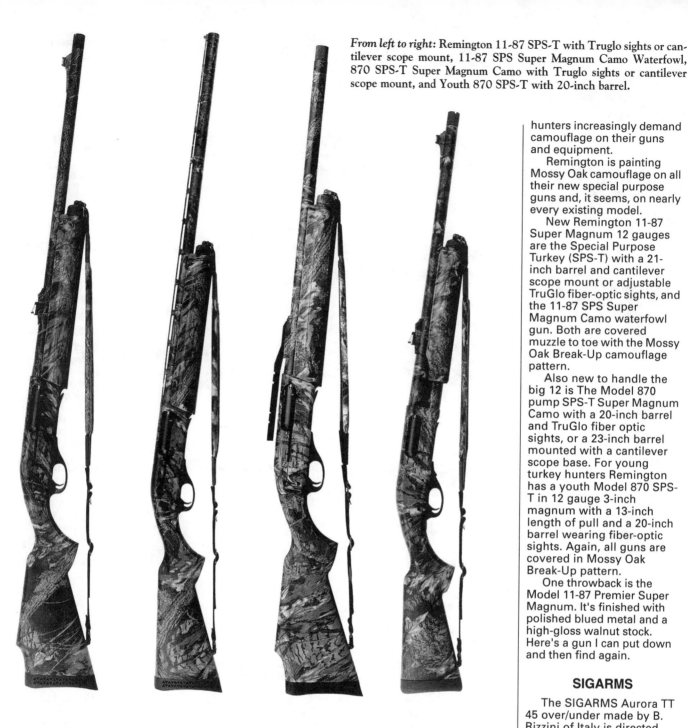

From left to right: Remington 11-87 SPS-T with Truglo sights or cantilever scope mount, 11-87 SPS Super Magnum Camo Waterfowl, 870 SPS-T Super Magnum Camo with Truglo sights or cantilever scope mount, and Youth 870 SPS-T with 20-inch barrel.

hunters increasingly demand camouflage on their guns and equipment.

Remington is painting Mossy Oak camouflage on all their new special purpose guns and, it seems, on nearly every existing model.

New Remington 11-87 Super Magnum 12 gauges are the Special Purpose Turkey (SPS-T) with a 21-inch barrel and cantilever scope mount or adjustable TruGlo fiber-optic sights, and the 11-87 SPS Super Magnum Camo waterfowl gun. Both are covered muzzle to toe with the Mossy Oak Break-Up camouflage pattern.

Also new to handle the big 12 is The Model 870 pump SPS-T Super Magnum Camo with a 20-inch barrel and TruGlo fiber optic sights, or a 23-inch barrel mounted with a cantilever scope base. For young turkey hunters Remington has a youth Model 870 SPS-T in 12 gauge 3-inch magnum with a 13-inch length of pull and a 20-inch barrel wearing fiber-optic sights. Again, all guns are covered in Mossy Oak Break-Up pattern.

One throwback is the Model 11-87 Premier Super Magnum. It's finished with polished blued metal and a high-gloss walnut stock. Here's a gun I can put down and then find again.

SIGARMS

The SIGARMS Aurora TT 45 over/under made by B. Rizzini of Italy is directed toward sporting clays shooters with an eye for style.

The Aurora's steel receiver is case-colored; with gold overlay game scenes flowing forward to a ventilated rib atop blued barrels. Internally, the boxlock action is machined from chrome-nickel molybdenum steel. Five-inch long forcing cones treat the shot column gently to improve patterns. The gun's walnut stock is finished with satin oil and checkered 20 lines per inch on the palm-swell grip and schnable forearm.

According to a SIGARMS press statement, the Aurora

weight. The SSI-One Turkey has a ported 24-inch smoothbore barrel with a 12 gauge 3 1/2-inch chamber. An extended Accu-Mag turkey tube *Extra Full* choke is included with the SSI-One Turkey barrel.

The mandatory use of nontoxic shot (read *steel*) for waterfowl hunting has fairly well removed gauges smaller than the 12 from waterfowl hunting. That can be a problem in selecting a gun for smaller-framed shooters. Mossberg has solved that problem with its Model 500 Field 12 gauge Bantam. The Bantam has a shortened buttstock to fit younger shooters, a grip contoured to

move the hand closer to the trigger and the forearm moved closer to the rear for an easier reach. The Bantam also comes with a half-price certificate for a full-size buttstock and forearm when the shooter has outgrown the Bantam.

A few final words on Mossberg: The 835 Ulti-Mag has a covering of Realtree Advantage Timber camouflage for hunters after sharp-eyed turkey and waterfowl.

Also, Mossberg now has a stock-drop spacer system. One, or all, of four spacers fit between the rear of the receiver and the head of the stock grip to raise the vertical

angle of the stock up to 1/2-inch. This adjustment allows easier eye alignment when shooting with a scope or rifle sights. It also raises the point of pattern impact for shooting rising targets, like pheasants.

Remington

I'm not so sure hunters over 40 (like me) should use guns or gear covered with camouflage unless it is buckled or tied to them. They might put it down somewhere, forget it about for a while – and then never be able to find it again. Still, a marketing director for a large firearm manufacturer said

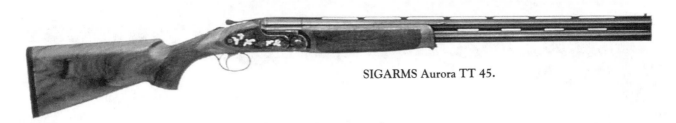

SIGARMS Aurora TT 45.

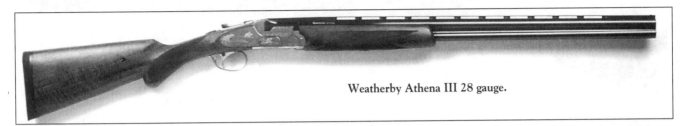

Weatherby Athena III 28 gauge.

"stock dimensions have been specifically designed with the American shooter in mind." The stock has 1 1/2 inches of drop at the head of the comb and only 1/2-inch more drop to the heel and is slightly cast off. The length of pull is 14 3/4-inches. That length of pull seems a bit long, until you try it. A SIG SA5 over/under I had came with that length pull. I'm pretty much average size and, for the first few rounds of clay targets, I had to make an extra effort to push the gun well ahead while bringing the stock comb up to my cheek. But after a while I became used to the long pull – and liked it because it helped me keep my cheek planted on the comb.

In 2000 SIGARMS and L.L. Bean introduced the New Englander B. Rizzini over/under shotgun in 12 and 20 gauge. This year the gun will also be chambered in 28 gauge and .410-bore.

The New Englander is a lightweight field gun with a low profile casehardened receiver enclosing a box lock. The barrel bores are chrome lined with three-inch chambers (2 3/4-inches in 28 gauge.) Five screw-in chokes from *Full* to *Skeet* are included. The forearm is beavertail-shaped and stocks are sized proportionately for each gauge. The guns are shipped in an aluminum hard case. They are available through SIGARMS and L.L. Bean in Freeport, Maine.

Weatherby

Weatherby introduced the Athena III in 1999 and this year has added the 28 gauge to its line of Athena Grade III Classic Field over/under shotguns. The 28-gauge model comes with 26- or 28-inch barrels with overall lengths of 43 or 45 inches. The Athena III's stock is oil-finished Claro walnut with hand-cut checkering, a comb with 3/4-inch drop along its length, a rounded grip and slender forearm. The butt is castoff. The Athena III weighs between 6 1/2 and 7 pounds and has a 14 1/4-inch length of pull.

Winchester

A few refinements and one new shotgun from Winchester this year.

A sporting clays model of the Super X2 is now offered. It features a set of shims to adjust the drop and cast of the comb. Two gas pistons are included to ensure cycling of all loads. One is for light target loads and the other for heavy three-inch field loads. In addition to a synthetic stock, the Super X2 Field now has a walnut stock.

Winchester has dressed up its Super X2 3 1/2-inch magnum and Model 1300 pump three-inch magnum

Above, top to bottom: Winchester Super X2 3 1/2-inch in Mossy Oak Shadow Grass, Super X2 NWTF Turkey 3 1/2-inch with Truglo sights, and Super X2 Sporting Clays.

Winchester Model 1300 NWTF Turkey Superflauge Camo.

Winchester Model 9410.

Winchester Super X2 Field gun with new walnut stock and a bobwhite quail.

12 gauges to promote the National Wild Turkey Federation. The "Team NWTF" logo is printed on the buttstock of these guns and three-dot TruGlo sights are standard on the Super X2 24-inch barrel and the Model 1300's 22-inch barrel. Each gun comes with a NWTF membership form, a video, hat and six issues of *Turkey Call* magazine.

Winchester's new gun is the Model 9410, which stands for a Model 94 lever action chambered for the .410-bore 2 1/2-inch shell. The 6 3/4 pound rifle – I mean, shotgun – has a smooth bore, *Cylinder*-choked 24-inch barrel. The opening of the rear sight has been enlarged and a TruGlo front sight installed for quick pointing on flying targets. The tube magazine holds nine rounds and will more than take care of any carrot-nibbling rabbits in the garden and grouse along the trail.

Winchester Super X2 Field gun with new walnut stock.

by DOC CARLSON

BLACKPOWDER REVIEW

BLACKPOWDER SHOOTERS ARE one of the most diverse groups in the shooting sports. Re-enactors and the historical periods they enjoy run the gamut from the French-Indian War, through the Fur Trade Era to the Civil War. Hunters range from the very traditional flintlock/patched round ball shooters to those using the latest in-line technology. The blackpowder cartridge *aficionados* include those involved in Cowboy Action Shooting, Black Powder Cartridge Silhouette, Long Range - and a fair sprinkling of those who hunt with firearms of the black-powder cartridge era. Firearms and accessories for blackpowder shooters show the same wide diversity.

Savage Arms

Probably the biggest news to hit the blackpowder field recently is the introduction by Savage Arms of an in-line type muzzle-loading rifle that is designed for a diet of smokeless powder. For years the watchword of muzzle loading has been "*black powder only.*" This new offering by Savage will modify that a bit.

Savage has taken their basic Model 110 bolt-action rifle and adapted it into a 50-caliber muzzle-loading rifle. So far, nothing too innovative; Remington and

Ruger have done, basically, the same thing. What makes the Savage different – and has stirred up quite a bit of controversy among muzzleloader shooters and manufacturers – is the use of smokeless powder as a propellant. As stated before, smokeless powder has always been a "*no-no*" in muzzleloaders, so this rifle is certainly a departure from conventional muzzle loading arms and shooting.

The key to the system is a special, heat-treated breech plug that takes a patented "percussion module." The module fits very closely into a chamber in the breech plug and effectively seals against gas leakage when the bolt is closed. The 209 shotgun primer in the module ignites the powder charge through a small orifice when the gun is fired. This system, which restricts the powder gas and pressure to the barrel, sets the Savage Model 10MLSS apart from any other muzzle-loading arm on the market.

The rifle is supplied, at present, in matte blue finish or stainless steel with a synthetic stock. The heavy-contour barrel is 24 inches long with a 1:24-inch twist, intended for conical bullet projectiles, not round ball. Savage recommends the use of 45-caliber bullets and heavy-duty sabots. Many of the sabots on the market will

not hold up to the higher pressures of smokeless powders and tend to leak, with the accompanying loss of accuracy. Savage recommends several different smokeless powder and bullet combinations in the brochure supplied with each gun. The rifle comes with two percussion modules, breech plug wrench, ball starter and a de-capper. Extra percussion modules can be purchased for a nominal price.

Reports of shooting tests show the new Savage offering to be very accurate, with proper loads. It easily holds two-minutes-of-angle groups. The weak link seems to be the sabot. If the barrel gets overly hot – or if the weather is extremely hot – the sabots tend to soften, making it easy for gas to 'blow by,' with resulting loss of accuracy. This should be of little consequence under hunting conditions, but is something to keep in mind during load workups. It is also very important to stay with Savage's recommended loads. Smokeless powder is much less forgiving of overloads than black powder and it's replicas.

For those who aren't comfortable with smokeless powder in muzzleloaders – or in those states that don't allow the use of smokeless – the new Savage works just fine with blackpowder or Pyrodex, including the Pyrodex pellets. There will, of course, be a certain amount of fouling buildup with these propellants, something not seen with smokeless.

With the various recommended smokeless powder loads, muzzle velocities of 2200 to 2300 fps are generated with 240-grain 45-caliber bullets and heavy-duty sabots. These loadings deliver energy in the 3000 foot/pounds range, making the rifle a definite "player" for most big game.

Because of the potential of smokeless powder to generate very significant pressures, the recommended loadings should be followed with as much care as reloaders exercise when

reloading rifle cartridges. Pre-measured loads, carried in quick-load tubes, will be the most practical for hunting, I imagine.

How hunters and game departments will receive this Savage innovation remains to be seen. I suspect that the total lack of fouling, with the accompanying reduction of cleaning chores, will appeal to many. The higher velocities and somewhat flatter trajectories will also be well received by many muzzle-loading hunters. The introduction of this rifle certainly proves that innovation and invention continues among American firearms makers.

White Rifles

White Rifles has taken their in-line guns into the space age by the addition of a carbon fiber-wrapped stainless steel barrel to their standard in-line action. The advantage of this barrel type is reduced heat buildup during shooting and more barrel stability over wide temperature ranges. Hunters, if your rifle is sighted in during warm weather and then taken to a hunting area that is very cold, there will be very little effect on the point of impact due to the temperature variation. The carbon fiber-wrapped barrel is very stable and ballistically "*quiet.*"

This new rifle is bedded in a thumbhole laminated wood stock. The breech plug is equipped with a musket-size nipple for reliable ignition under all conditions. The 50-caliber barrel is set up to use the White System, as are all the While line of firearms. Under this system, undersize bullets are especially designed to load easily down the bore of the rifle and, upon firing, to shorten and upset into the rifling to give a good gas seal and grip the rifling well. This has proven to be a very accurate, hard-hitting and easy-loading system in the hunting field.

Also new this year from White is a series of their bullets sized to load easily in the barrels of Knight, Remington, Ruger,

Savage Model 10 ML 50-caliber muzzleloader.

Knight Super Disc Rifle, new in 45 caliber.

Thompson/Center and other muzzle-loading rifles. Of particular interest to hunters, this product addition allows the use of a full bore-size bullet, of 360 to 430 grains, in most 45, 50 or 54-caliber muzzleloaders.

There seems to be the beginnings of a trend towards the 45-caliber in the in-line rifles. White is making their Whitetail Hunter and Elite Hunter rifles available in this caliber. They join several other manufacturers who are reintroducing this caliber. The 45 fell from favor when most guns on the market were designed to shoot round ball. The smaller ball is short on energy and penetration, beyond 50 yards or so, on deer-size animals. With the increasing use of bullet-type projectiles in hunting muzzleloaders, the 45 caliber is getting a new lease on life. In conical bullet shapes, weighing 350 to 450 grains, this caliber has plenty of long-range energy for the hunting field.

Knight Rifles

Knight Rifles has entered the 45-caliber club also. They are offering the popular D.I.S.C. rifle in 45 caliber, as well as the standard 50 caliber. They are making a sabot-type bullet of 40 caliber to match this new bore diameter. The sabot material is heavy duty to stand up to heavy loads of black powder or Pyrodex. Called the "Red Hot" Barnes bullet, it can be had in 150- or 175-grain weights. A 240-grain "Precision" bullet of lead with a plastic insert in the hollow point to aid expansion is also available, along with a 180-grain pure lead hollow point. The advantage to the 40/45-caliber projectile is, of course, higher velocities and flatter trajectories. The 150-grain Red Hot bullet can be pushed at over 2600 fps (*at the muzzle*) and will deliver in excess of 1700 fps and 1000 ft./lbs. energy at 150 yards, when loaded over 150 grains of Pyrodex pellets and fired by a 209 primer. If zeroed at 100 yards, drop (*below line of sight*) will be 2 1/4 inches at 150 yards and 7 1/4 inches at 200 yards. Pretty darn good ballistics for something that loads from the front with blackpowder – or its substitute.

Called the Knight Super DISC Rifle, this new 45-caliber offering is available in standard composite stock styles, finished in Mossy Oak Break Up, Advantage Timber HD or basic black. If desired, a thumbhole stock can be ordered in black also. The Knight bolt-action DISC system is used, which utilizes a thin plastic disc to hold the 209 shotgun primer. The primed disc is inserted in a slot at the front of the action and, as the bolt is lowered, the bolt body cams ahead to force the disc tightly against an ignition orifice in the rear of the breech plug.

The action is coupled with a fluted Green Mountain barrel in either blued or stainless steel finish. The 1:20-inch twist is matched to the 45-caliber projectiles, producing the exceptional accuracy that Knight rifles are known for. The barrel is topped with fully adjustable TruGlo sights for outstanding sight pictures in all kinds of light conditions. Those fiber-optic sights are a great help to those of us who seem to have lost the ability to see a clear rear sight—some say due to advancing years. *Myself, I think it's due to interference by the guardian angel of deer and other critters.*

Traditions Performance Firearms

Traditions Performance Firearms is another well-known name in the muzzle-loading field that has gotten on the 45-caliber bandwagon. They call their offering the Lightning 45 LD, the 'LD' standing for *long distance*. The bolt-action gun is available with either blue- or C-Nickel-finished fluted barrel, rifled 1:20 inches. The blue version is fitted with a black synthetic stock and the C-Nickel model can be had with either the black - or a High Definition Advantage Timber camouflage pattern - stock. The gun comes with a three-way ignition system using number 11 caps, musket caps or the 209 shotgun primer and is recommended for loads up to 150 grains of black powder or Pyrodex. This rifle also sports the TruGlo fiber-optic sights. This will be a popular addition to Traditions' rather complete line of in-line guns.

True to their name, Traditions also makes a wide range of the traditional side-hammer guns. Their Magnum Plains Percussion Rifle has the look of the half-stock plains rifle of old, but features an ignition system designed to handle the Pyrodex pellets – as well as up to 150 grains of loose black powder or Pyrodex. The gun features double set-triggers, brass butt plate and trigger guard, blued octagon barrel and adjustable fiber-optic sights. The twist of the rifling is 1:32 inches, primarily intended for conical/slug bullets. The barrel is held in the hardwood stock by two barrel keys, typical of Plains-type rifles. The overall style matches the half-stock working gun of the past.

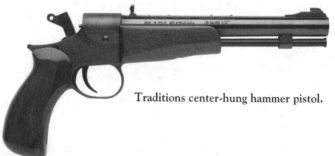

Traditions center-hung hammer pistol.

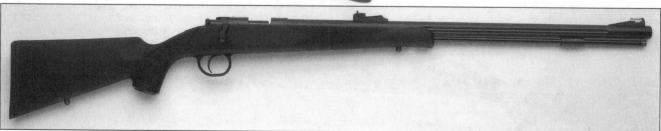

Traditions 45-caliber Lightning LD Rifle.

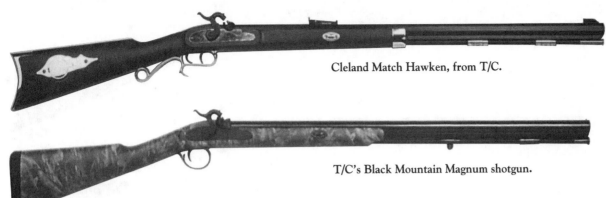

Cleland Match Hawken, from T/C.

T/C's Black Mountain Magnum shotgun.

Traditions also make a hybrid-type gun called the Thunder Magnum. This is a Monte Carlo, pistol-grip stock side-hammer gun that also has an ignition system designed for Pyrodex pellets as well as loose powder. The side-hammer lock features a thumb safety. The half-stock rifle has a "*first in the industry*" (according to Traditions) removable stainless steel breech plug so the barrel can be cleaned from the breech end – *ala* in-line action guns. The rifle is available finished in either C-Nickel or blued, with a hardwood stock. The barrel is held in the stock by a easily removable barrel band. This gun is a side-hammer with many of the features of the popular in-line guns to appeal to those who like both styles.

Unique to Traditions is their Crockett rifle. This very traditional-looking half-stock percussion gun is made in 32 caliber—a rarity among the many guns of 45 caliber and up. The trim rifle has a blued octagon barrel, double set triggers and brass fittings. The twist is 1:48 inches, which will handle patched round ball quite well for hunting small game or targets. The Crockett rifle fits well with Traditions' line of flint and percussion full-stock rifles. These other rifles are, almost without exception, equipped with barrels rifled 1:66—obviously intended for round ball.

In the pistol line, Traditions features a group of modernistic muzzleloaders with center-hung hammers. These guns, in 50-caliber percussion, are available with barrel lengths of 14 3/4 inches to 20 inches, in either C-Nickel or blue finish. The 20-inch model is even available with a muzzle brake to cut down on recoil and muzzle rise. Stocks are either walnut or black-finish hardwood. Equipped with target sights, these pistols are for serious hunters or target shooters. Traditions also have several pistol models in the more traditional designs. Pretty much something for everyone in the Traditions line.

Thompson/Center Arms

For many years, before the proliferation of all the reproductions that we have available today, the standard bore size for most repro muzzleloaders was 40 caliber. It was the caliber most seen on the firing line at the various shoots around the country. A great many of the original guns for target and small game hunting also were of this caliber. The reason was that this is a very accurate caliber for a round-ball gun and recoil is nonexistent. This fine caliber has been pushed into obscurity by the recent trend to 50- and 54-caliber guns.

Thompson/Center has brought back this once-popular caliber in their Cleland Match Hawken rifle. This is a 40-caliber version of the ever-popular Hawken series of T/C rifles. The rifle utilizes an American walnut stock with all brass furniture. The percussion lock and double set triggers are the same as found on the Hawken models. The 1-inch across-the-flats octagon barrel is blued and 31 inches long. The 40-caliber bore is rifled 1:48 inches. This results in a barrel of good weight for steady offhand hold and exceptional accuracy with patched round ball.

Sights are a bead-type front, coupled with an open target rear with knurled windage and elevation screws that are finger-adjustable; no tools are needed to change settings. This target rear sight is also available as an accessory that can be added to any T/C rifle. Advice on design and building this new addition to the T/C line was supplied by Chad Cleland, an NMLRA National Champion, hence the name of the rifle.

Also new this year from the T/C folks is their Black Mountain Magnum in 12 gauge. The blued barrel is 27 inches long, round and comes with a screw-in turkey choke for tight patterns. Loaded with 100 grains of black powder or Pyrodex, behind 1 1/4 oz. of shot, this muzzleloader should be big medicine for the turkey hunter. It should do well on the trap field, also.

The percussion shotgun features a composite stock with Advantage Timber Camo finish and blued hardware with, of course, a single trigger. It is of standard side-hammer lock design with a rubber recoil pad and aluminum ramrod. A no-nonsense shotgun designed with the serious hunter in mind.

Connecticut Valley Arms

CVA has substantially upgraded one of their in-lines

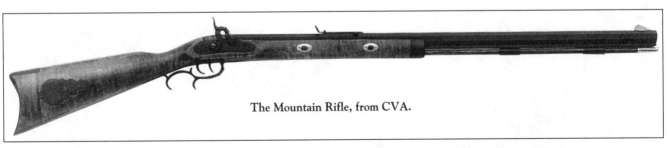

The Mountain Rifle, from CVA.

CVA's Firebolt 209 UltraMag.

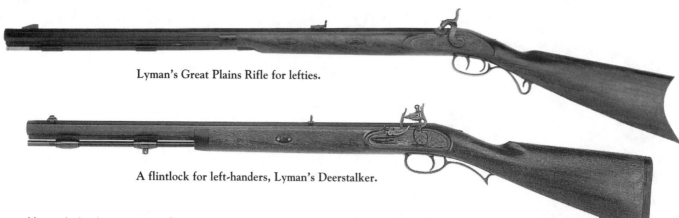

Lyman's Great Plains Rifle for lefties.

A flintlock for left-handers, Lyman's Deerstalker.

and brought back a traditional favorite. The bolt-action Firebolt rifle series now features a 26-inch fluted barrel with 209-primer ignition and loading recommendations up to 150-grain charges. It is made in both 50-, and the newly popular 45-calibers. The action is housed in a heavier, resin-filled stock with rubber recoil pad to cut down on felt recoil. The standard stocks have a soft rubber coating over a FiberGrip cosmetic finish, making them quiet in the woods and easy to grip with cold, wet or gloved hands. The stocks are also available in rubber-coated Break Up camo patterns. The muzzle of the barrel is rebated for ease of loading. The receiver is drilled and tapped for scope mounting, if one wishes, and open sights are of the fiber optic variety.

The updated FireBolt is available in nickel or blued finish with either of the stock finishes previously noted... a good-looking, practical arm for the hunter.

On the traditional side, CVA is reintroducing their Mountain Rifle that was a very popular part of their line some years back. This reasonably priced, traditional half-stock rifle was dropped from the line some years back. It was reinstated a year or so ago as a high-priced, special issue gun and has finally made it back into the line as a middle-priced offering.

The Mountain Rifle starts with a figured hard maple stock showing an oil-type finish. The browned steel barrel is 50 caliber, 32 inches long, with a 1:66-inch twist – definitely a traditional round-ball gun. Browned steel trigger guard, butt plate, forend cap and patchbox add to the traditional look and feel of this rifle. The percussion lock is a Manton style, which was one of the first reproduction locks to come on the market for custom builders back in the 1960s. It was called the Hamm lock after the maker, Russ Hamm. The rifle is

made in the USA and will be available in limited quantities.

The sights are a traditional buckhorn rear coupled with a silver blade front, as was typical of the type. This was one of the better-looking reproduction rifles on the market a decade ago and the new offering certainly loses nothing of the look and feel of its predecessor. I think the shooter looking for a gun with the look of an original will find this one to his (or her) liking.

Lyman Products Corporation

Lyman has added a drop-in barrel with a 1:32-inch twist for their Great Plains series of rifles. This will convert the 1:60 round-ball rifles to shoot the slug-type projectiles. The barrels are available to fit both flint and percussion guns in either right or left hand configurations. This will give an added dimension to these popular rifles.

Lyman is also introducing a left-hand version of the Deerstalker rifle in flintlock. This makes this company one of the leaders in catering to traditionalists that shoot from the "*wrong*" side. There are a high percentage of

shooters out there that handle rifles from the left shoulder and it's good to see a company that works to meet their needs.

Lyman is probably best known for supplying reloading equipment. They can trace their roots in this area well back into the 1800s. Last year they added three-die reloading sets for many of the classic calibers that blackpowder cartridge folks are shooting. These include 40-65, 40-70 Sharps Straight, 45-90, 45-100-2.6, 45-110-2 7/8, 45-120-3 1/4 and 50-90. Now they have added neck-sizer die sets in 40 cal., 45 cal. Short (for up to 45-100), and 45 cal. long (for 45s from 45-110 and longer). These die sets allow the neck of the case to be sized to provide good bullet tension, while maintaining the fire-formed dimensions of the rest of the case. This will extend case life as well as contribute to accuracy. Along with the very complete line of bullet moulds for blackpowder shooters of all stripes, these new dies make Lyman the complete shopping store for the blackpowder cartridge shooter, as well as the muzzleloader.

Lyman's Black Powder Handbook, Second Edition.

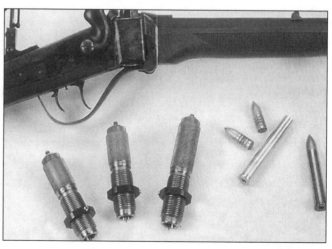

New neck-sizing dies from Lyman.

Tasco's World-Class 1x32mm riflescope for muzzleloaders.

Also new from Lyman is the new 2nd edition of the *Lyman Black Powder Handbook*. In addition to complete coverage of loads for muzzle-loading firearms – which include Pyrodex pellets, sabotted bullets and conical-type projectiles – the latest *Handbook* contains a section on loads for blackpowder cartridges for both rifles and pistols. Anyone who shoots blackpowder or its substitute, Pyrodex, in any kind of firearm needs a copy of this book. A copy of the annual Lyman catalog will delight the heart of such shooters also.

Tasco

Many states are beginning to allow the use of telescopic sights on muzzleloaders. All of the in-line rifles are drilled and tapped for scopes and most scope mount manufacturers are making mounts to fit the various front loaders on the market. Many states, including my home state of Nebraska, allow the use of scopes only if there is no magnification. Tasco has added a line of scopes specifically designed for muzzleloading guns. Part of their World Class model line, the muzzleloader scopes are made in 1 x 32, 1.75 x 20, 2-7x 32, and 3-9 x 32 – all with 1-inch tubes and 30/30-type reticle. All are finished in blue and have good eye relief, as well as a wide field of view.

Dixie Gun Works

Dixie Gun Works has brought back a great shotgun accessory from days of yore. They are now carrying a double, over-the-shoulder *shot snake* of the type that was a "must have" accessory for the well-equipped muzzle-loading shotgun shooter of years past. The unit consists of two long narrow shot containers made of soft leather and tipped with shutter-type shot measures. The whole works is mounted on a wide shoulder strap and includes a small pouch for wads, capper – or whatever. The wide strap distributes the load evenly and makes carrying shot comfortable and practical. The shutter-type shot dispensers are adjustable for the amount of shot dropped and hang pointing downward for ease of dispensing the shot into the muzzle of the shotgun – a very handy thing for the m/l shotgun shooter to carry in the field.

If you are into any type of blackpowder shooting and don't have a copy of the Dixie Gun Works catalog, you are missing a real treat. Started by Turner Kirkland in the 1950s, Dixie carries anything the blackpowder shooter could want. The catalog also contains the world's premiere listing of antique gun parts – both original and newly made. Five bucks sent to Dixie for a copy of this 700-plus-page bible for blackpowder shooters is money very well spent.

The blackpowder cartridge shooters and cowboy action aficionados have quite a bit to celebrate this year. There are some great replicas being imported for these folks.

Tristar Sporting Arms, Ltd.

Tristar Sporting Arms, Ltd. is importing a reproduction of the Winchester 1887 12-gauge lever-action shotgun. Made by the Lithgow Small Arms factory in Australia, the shotgun is actually a scaled-down version of the 1901 Winchester 10 gauge lever gun. The 1901 was a much-improved version of the 1887 and incorporated many safety features that are needed for shooting today's smokeless shotshells. The gun is made to shoot only 2 3/4-inch 12 gauge shotshells and will handle either smokeless or blackpowder loadings of same.

The gun will be offered with a 22-inch barrel with *Improved Cylinder* choking. Walnut stocks, oil finished, with steel butt plate and blued metal parts make this shotgun a dead ringer for the original. The guns will be coming into this country starting in February of 2001. They will be imported on a limited basis the first year, with production of around 4000 guns over the next two or three years. I expect we'll see many of these guns on the firing lines of the Cowboy Action shoots around the country.

Interstate Arms Corporation

Another old-timer that is coming back - again a Winchester shotgun - is the venerable Model 1897. Imported by Interstate Arms Corporation, this one is made in China and is a very good replica of this well-known scattergun. Made with a 20-inch *Cylinder-bore* barrel, hardwood stocks finished with a walnut oil color and blued steel; this is another shotgun that should find favor with the Cowboy Action folks. The gun is made with a solid frame, rather than the takedown frame, of the original. This holds the price down to a reasonable level. The only gauge will be 12, at least for the foreseeable future. After an absence of over half a century, it's good to see another of the classic shotguns back on the market.

Navy Arms

The Navy Arms Company is another of those companies that have become a household word among re-enactors, muzzleloading *aficionados* and lovers of reproduction arms. They have one of the more complete lines of reproduction arms – from the very early matchlock to 1900-period guns. Re-enactors portraying nearly all periods of the history of United States use the firearms available from this pioneering company.

The latest addition to this fine line of reproduction guns is the Smith & Wesson Third Model Russian revolver. Smith & Wesson manufactured this gun between 1874 and 1878 for both the Russian military and the civilian commercial market. It is a top-break revolver similar to the famous 1875 Schofield. It is chambered, of course, for the 44 Russian cartridge. It features a blued frame, cylinder and barrel with the hammer and spur trigger guard being casehardened, as original. Walnut grips complete the picture. A lanyard ring is attached to the butt of this very nicely made revolver. Among the well-known shootists of the Old West who reportedly carried this revolver was Pat Garrett, the nemesis of Billy the Kid. I'm sure the Cowboy Action Shooters will welcome this one.

Taylor's & Company, Inc.

One of the more famous guns of the Civil War was "*That damn Yankee rifle you load on Sunday and shoot all week*" – the Spencer. Made in both rifle and carbine versions, the best known is the carbine version that was issued to Union cavalry troops. This was the first really successful cartridge repeater to arrive on the scene in any numbers and

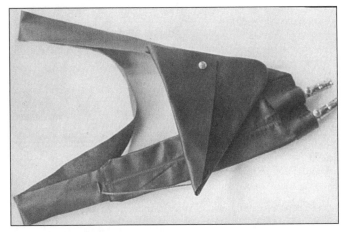

The Shot Snake, from Dixie Gunworks.

TriStar's new reproduction of the 1887 Winchester 12 gauge. A beauty, made in Australia.

was contemporary with the Henry rifle.

Taylor's & Company, Inc., is now importing a reproduction Spencer carbine that is a real beauty. Made by Armi Sport in Italy, the gun is the Model 1865... which corrected some of the faults of the original 1860 rifle. It holds seven cartridges in a tubular buttstock magazine and feeds them into the chamber by way of a lever action. The hammer must be cocked manually for each shot. This reproduction is very nicely done. I have spent some time with the manufacturer on various occasions and he is very committed to capturing the finest detail of any reproduction guns that he makes.

The carbine features a walnut stock, blued barrel and casehardened lock and action. The barrel length is 20 inches and overall length is 37 inches. The gun will be available chambered for the original 56/50 (*in reloadable centerfire rather than the original rimfire, however*), 44 Russian and 45 Schofield.

Also available will be a very nice reproduction of the original Blakeslee six-tube cartridge carrier that was originally issued with the carbine. This cartridge box was carried under the trooper's left arm and gave a fast reload by use of the tubes, each holding seven cartridges. A shoulder sling with hook to carry the carbine will also be available.

Goex Powder Company

Blackpowder shooting would not amount to much without the powder to shoot. We are lucky to have several suppliers of quality blackpowder and it's replicas.

Goex Powder Co., formerly owned by Du Pont, is probably the oldest American powder company still around. They make Goex black powder in 1Fg, 2Fg, 3Fg, 4 Fg and Cannon grades – as well as Cartridge, which is intended for black-powder cartridge shooting. They have recently brought a reproduction blackpowder, called Clear Shot, on the market that will give black powder pressures without the fouling and clean up requirements associated with the original powder. This is a ball-type powder, which meters nicely through any type of measure. They are

also importing a blackpowder from Slovenia called KIK. This will be offered in 2Fg and 3 Fg only, at present.

Luna Tech, Inc.

A company called Luna Tech, Inc. is importing a German powder called Wano. This is available in all the standard grades, with the addition of unglazed 4Fg as an option. This is called '*pan powder*'

to be used to prime the pan of flintlock guns—the idea being that unglazed powder will catch the sparks better, giving faster and more reliable ignition.

Petro Explo Co.

Petro Explo Co. brings in Elephant Black Powder in all four Fg grades, and Cannon. They also import Swiss blackpowder that is especially popular with the blackpowder cartridge silhouette shooters. It is available in 1Fg, 1 1/2Fg, 2Fg, 3Fg and 4Fg, with the 1 1/2Fg being the one used in large-capacity black powder cartridges.

Hodgdon Powder Company

Hodgdon Powder Company continues to expand the offerings of their compressed Pyrodex pellets to cover more calibers and charges. Their Pyrodex was the first replica blackpowder on the market and continues to be the one by which all other replica powders are judged.

Clean Shot Technologies, Inc.

Clean Shot Technologies, Inc. makes a replica powder called, of all things, Clean Shot. It is an ascorbic acid-based powder that also duplicates black powder pressures with little or no fouling. This powder is popular with the Cowboy Action crowd due to the lack of clean-up hassle—something that's important when shooting blackpowder loads in a lever gun.

The blackpowder sport continues to prosper. Technology continues to impact the sport also, much to the consternation of some of the traditional shooters. We are free to utilize the advancements or not, as we wish. So, pick the part of the black-powder sport that appeals to you – and do it. Also recognize that others may like something different. That doesn't make either one wrong – just different. Enjoy your sport—and keep an eye on your back trail. ●

The S&W Third Model, in 44 Russian, from Navy Arms.

Another beauty, the Spencer carbine from Taylor's, Inc.

by BOB BELL

SCOPES AND MOUNTS

WHEN OLD SHOOTERS like me were young – back in the '30s, say – scopes were just gaining some notice, and although metallic sights still were being used by the vast majority of hunters, a few were dabbling with those "*fragile glass sights.*" Everyone wondered why those glass lenses didn't break under the forces of recoil, but some of us were willing to experiment; certain advantages seemed possible and we wanted to benefit from them. To save time, money and effort, we looked to experts like Townsend Whelen, Elmer Keith and others for advice. It was surprisingly similar, regardless of who gave it.

For big-game hunting, get the best 2 1/2x you can afford; something like the Weaver 330, Noske, or Lyman Alaskan.

For open country game like pronghorns, a 4x like the Weaver 440 might be OK, but the hunter should have considerable earlier experience with a 2 1/2x and its bigger field.

A 6x scope was thought to be just the ticket for sit-still varmints, and higher powers were rarely if ever seen, except some target models on competitive rifles used for bullseye punching.

This attitude was still common after World War II ended in 1945. In fact, I remember trading a new Weaver K6, which only recently had been introduced, to a fellow who wanted to mount it on his Model 70 Swift, for 'chucks. He had been using an aperture sight and thought that bright 6x was wonderful, a real improvement. (*In return he gave me a M65 Winchester 218 Bee with a 440 Weaver in Stith Streamline mount. I'd like to make a swap like that now!*)

A good 2 1/2x or 4x would still do for most big game, as almost all such critters are killed within a couple of hundred yards, but hunting conditions and techniques have changed for most of us, and these changes have made higher power scopes practicable. Back in the '30s and early '40s, most hunting for deer – the most popular big game species – was done by gangs of men working cooperatively as drivers and watchers. Almost invariably they carried open-sighted, poorly zeroed rifles. Woods hunting was the norm, and most chances came at short range at moving animals. It wasn't unusual for a lot of shots to be fired at one animal as it ran past a line of hunters, and if someone finally dropped it, it might have three or four scratch hits besides the one that killed it.

As scopes gained limited acceptance and hunters learned about zeroing in, strings of shots became rare, for one or two bullets usually did the job. However, the gangs were still hunting in the woods. Ranges were short and the deer fast, which meant that a large field of view which gave easier target acquisition was more important than high magnification. So a 2 1/2x or 4x scope was more than sufficient.

But when millions of servicemen came home after WWII and Korea, they'd had enough years of enforced togetherness, coordinated movements and massed firepower. They wanted to be alone, even in the woods... especially in the woods, for the solitude they found there was a great healer.

So the style of hunting changed. The number of hunters grew in total, but they were individuals scattered across the vastness, not concentrated in groups. And their effect on game was different. Instead of deliberately frightening animals into movement, hoping to shove them past a line of watchers, the hunters became silent parts of the environment, moving slowly only at intervals or just waiting and looking, with carefully sighted-in scoped rifles in their hands. Their mindset became more that of the sniper than the assault team. They let their targets expose themselves by natural movements.

As a result, a deer often was seen first, unafraid, moving slowly or not at all. And the hunter in his hidden position, with some kind of natural support for his rifle, found it easy to place his crosshairs properly and squeeze. For such shooting, he didn't need an exceptionally big field in his scope, but he could benefit from higher magnification than he had previously chosen. That allowed him to see more detail, pick a tunnel through thick cover for his bullet, fire deliberately when conditions were optimum.

Fortunately, that was the time when modern variable powers began to come along. With one of these, a hunter could adapt his scope to his needs of the moment. Early variables had all sorts of mechanical problems, but their potential was obvious. The 2 1/2-8x Bausch & Lomb was the best of the time, though not the earliest. It was the first to attract a large following, although its unusual externally-adjustable mount occasionally gave problems.

Since then, countless variables have been introduced worldwide; they're now more common than straight powers. Early problems have been eliminated in most; excellent adjustments are now internal, which means the scope can be solidly mounted, and power spreads have been increased, usually from a 3:1 to 4:1 ratio.

For those who still prowl the hardwood ridges and brushy hollows, low power compact variables are available, and even occasional 2 1/2x or 4x straight powers can be found. (I can't imagine parting with the 4x Zeiss Diatal C that tops my old 338 Magnum.) But for years the overall trend in scopes has been upward, not only in magnification but also in size and weight. Simple observation shows that.

I've no idea when or if that movement is going to stop. There's no doubt that a group of smart optical engineers in a well-lighted, computer-equipped design room can keep coming up with new features for scopes. But every time they do, the scopes seem to get larger and heavier, and that means problems for the ultimate user; be he hunter, soldier or SWATman. It's one thing to think only of the design of a scope, but it's another thing when you stop to realize the scope is only part of the complete rig, that it still has to go on a gun. Otherwise, what use is it? So it's important to realize the scope has a real effect on a gun's weight, bulkiness, balance, and handiness... everything.

That brings up another matter. Obviously, putting any scope on any gun requires a mount. And that mount has to hold the scope in a constant, unvarying relationship to the gun. It daren't move the slightest amount if the gun is to remain in zero – the rings have to hold the scope so no slippage can occur, and they must fit the base(s) so tightly there can be no movement there. Then the base must attach just as solidly to the receiver.

That's asking a lot. I'm surprised that mounts work as well as they do.

A tiny reference mark made on the main tube near a mount ring can let you check if the scope has slipped at all after zeroing. But it's nearly impossible to tell if there is a tiny movement in the base-receiver connection. Many mount makers like to point out how firmly their mounts hold the scope and the rings fit the bases (*which, admittedly, is very important*), but I can't recall anyone bragging about how solid their base-receiver joint is. Yet this is the weakest point in the whole scope mounting system.

A few riflemakers must have pondered this, for they've done something about it. For instance, some Sako actions have bases that are part of the action itself; integral tapered dovetails, broad ends forward so that recoil tightens the base-ring joint if there's any movement at all. This alone is enough reason for using a Sako action to build a custom rifle. It's the best system I know for attaching a mount to a rifle.

Might mention that some six decades ago, on a visit to the Smithsonian Institution in Washington, D.C., I saw a hunting rifle built for a man named Ralph G. Packard. Don't know if it was unique or not, but I've never seen another one like it. The scope mount was an integral part of the handmade action. It was machined right in, so obviously couldn't move at all. I doubt if many hunters would want to pay the price this must have cost, but it shows that at least one shooter way back in the 1930s had already recognized a mounting weakness... the tendency of recoil effect to shear the mounting screws. (*And if something like a 30-06, say, could cause such a problem, what's to be thought about today's monster magnums?*)

I've never had a scope come off a rifle like that, but years ago when Smith & Wesson brought out the 44 Magnum, Earl Hock and I tried to mount a K4 on one. (*There were no handgun scopes or mounts back then.*) The third or fourth shot would shear the screws of the Weaver bases and send the scope flying. We admitted defeat after this happened several times.

A big part of the mounting problem always has been the use of small diameter 6-48 screws. These worked fine when installing aperture sights in earlier years, so were automatically used to attach scope mounts, especially the install-it-yourself types. These worked OK when scopes were small and light, though even then some shooters went to the stronger 8-40 size, even though this required a trip to a gunsmith for drilling and tapping.

An integral recoil shoulder on the base to engage the action seemed logical; this would leave the screws only the job of holding the base down, not also having to resist recoil. The Redfield Jr. base has had this design since early in the last century, and its several clones carry it on to this day, though nobody seems to talk about it much. That, plus its opposing windage screws which allowed horizontal adjustment for early scopes which had none, was a most important feature. I've heard reports in recent years that the Redfield's rear ring attachment, being held to the base by only the windage screws, left the mount too weak for some of today's heavy-recoiling cartridges. I've never had this problem, even with heavy loads in a light 338 Magnum, but that's the most powerful load I usually shoot. If necessary, you can get bases which have the dovetail connection for both fore and aft rings, though then there is no windage in the mount... which probably doesn't matter nowadays since most scopes have good internal adjustments.

But with scopes getting heavier and recoil getting greater all the time, I can't help wondering about the ability of the mount, especially those with 2-piece bases, to hold the scope onto the gun. Some makers advise using 8-40 screws, and perhaps that's all it takes to do the job. But I'd feel more comfortable if the rear of the front base extended downward about an eighth of an inch to contact the rear face of the receiver ring and thus absorb the rifle's recoil. I don't know whether this would be practicable or not – the action's dimensions and placement of the factory scope mounting holes might not be consistent enough to allow it – but it ought to be worth looking into.

By coincidence, just as I was writing this section, Jim Leatherwood called about another matter. I happened to mention my feelings about the need for a recoil lug on the mount base. He told me that some Marine Corps riflemen felt the same, and that one bridge-type mount developed by the Corps for a military weapon had not one but two integral lugs: the forward lug contacting the rear of the receiver ring; the rear lug, the front of the bridge. This perfectly illustrates the point I was trying to make... and it left me feeling pretty good about being in sync with a bunch of real riflemen like the Marines.

Well, I've gone on long enough with my personal ideas, so it's time to get on to this year's scopes. They're listed in random order.

Leupold

Leupold's Premiere Scope (LPS) line now includes a 2.5-10x45, which is intended to meet any need a big-game hunter might have. The power spread obviously covers any situation which might arise, from the 2.5x setting for whitetails in the brush to the 10x for bighorns on the next ridge, Even at top magnification this scope delivers a 4.5mm exit pupil, and that means good light in any reasonable shooting situation. Maintube diameter is 30mm, the *DiamondCoat* lens coating brings light transmission to over 99% of the lens surface, and eye relief at all powers is 4 inches. That's more than most scopes have, which is good on hard-kicking magnums if taken advantage of: some mounts, however, don't allow positioning the scope that far ahead. Use a mount that does, and put the scope as far forward as will still give a full field of view from offhand while wearing hunting clothing; any other shooting position will move your eye closer. Remember, eye relief is intended to keep the ocular lens housing from smacking you in the eyebrow during recoil, so benefit from Leupold's longer-than-normal design by mounting it properly.

Some hunters undoubtedly will use the larger 3.5-14x50 Side Focus LPS for big game too, but I don't follow their thinking. I've never needed that much power for large critters and the added bulk and weight were nuisances, affecting a sporter-weight rifle's balance noticeably, especially for quick shots. I'd expect this size scope to be chosen for a heavier rifle that's used for stand hunting on deer, say, and also for chucks in the summer. This scope is named for an adjustment dial on the left side of the turret that allows focusing for range without getting out of shooting position, as an adjustable objective scope requires.

The 3.5-14x50 has the same high light transmission, *Diamond* coating, 4-inch eye relief, etc., as other scopes in the LPS line and weighs 18.5 oz. To the existing Fine and Heavy Duplex reticles in their Vari-X III 4.5-14x Golden Ring scopes, Leupold has added the option of a Standard Duplex. Heavy post subtension is 1.5 *moa* at bottom power, 0.5 *moa* at 14x. Also, a German #4 Dot can be had in the Vari-X III 1.5-5x20, 3.5-l0x50, and 4.5-14x50 AO Illuminated Reticle scopes.

Another new Leupold item of interest to riflemen of all classes is a Magnetic Boresighter, It works on any caliber and, because it uses magnets instead of barrel spuds, there's no need to be concerned about possible bore damage.

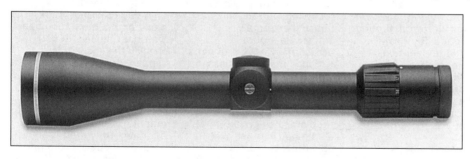

The Leupold 3.5-14x50 has a dial on the left side of the turret to adjust for range. It and the similar 2.5-10x45 have 30mm main tubes, *DiamondCoating.*

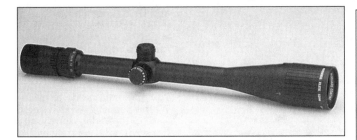

Bushnell's 6-24x40 Elite 4200 is great for varmints at any range, even if you get caught in the rain, for it's treated with *RainGuard*.

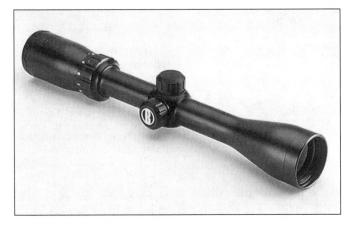

Overall, the 3-9x is still the most popular variable for big game. This is one of several Bushnell supplies.

Laser rangefinders have taken much of the problem out of long-range shooting. This Bushnell Yardage Pro Scout can be used with one hand.

Bushnell

Bushnell now offers six full lines of scopes – the Elite 4200 and 3200, Trophy, Banner, Scopechief and Sportsman, the latter a successor to the popular Sportview series – plus the unusual HOLOsight, which doesn't fit into any of the above lines. Magnifications range from a 1x red dot sight for handgunners to a 36x for benchresters. Almost all are variables and all conventional powers are represented, so if any shooter can't find one to fill his needs, they must be very unusual indeed.

New this year in the Elite 3200 series are a 3-9x40 and 3-9x50 with 3-2-1 Low Light reticle. This is basically a *Plex* design but the extreme inner ends of the four posts reduce significantly in thickness before becoming crosshairs. Other reticles are available, including the Mil-Dot in the 6-24x 4200; this style is especially useful on long range, deliberately aimed and fired rifles. The dots of known size and spacing on both vertical and horizontal crosshairs help greatly with range estimation and hold-off for bullet drop and wind deflection. Both Elite lines have Bushnell's *RainGuard* treatment, a permanent repellant coating applied to the external surfaces of the objective and ocular lenses that prevents moisture from affecting the target image.

I've been using a 2.5-10x40 Elite for well over a year now, in all kinds of weather, and it has performed exactly as specified.

The Yardage Pro Scout is an addition to Bushnell's laser rangefinder line. Measuring 1.5x4x2.75 in. and weighing less than 7 oz., the YPS is held vertically and can be operated with one hand. It has a 6x eyepiece and gives readings of +/- one yard out to 700 yards on highly reflective targets.

Swarovski

Swarovski's latest addition is the 6-18x50 AV (American Variable). It's intended primarily for ultra-long range cartridges such as the 7mm STW, 30-378, or Winchester 30 WSM, according to the manufacturer, although its adaptability to the bigger varmint cartridges also is obvious. Unlike many other European scopes, this Austrian model has its reticle in the second focal plane, so the amount it subtends is inversely proportional to the magnification.

To simplify waterproofing and add strength, this scope's objective bell, middle tube, turret housing and ocular bell connection are machined out of a solid piece of special alloy bar stock. The maintube is 1-inch diameter to fit most American mounts. Other Swarovski models in the AV series are the 3-9x36, 3-10x42, and 4-12x50, all having features that appeal to riflemen on this side of the Atlantic.

A new entry in Swarovski's A-V series is this 6-18x50. It has a hardened aluminum main tube; can be ordered with three posts – and CH or Plex reticle.

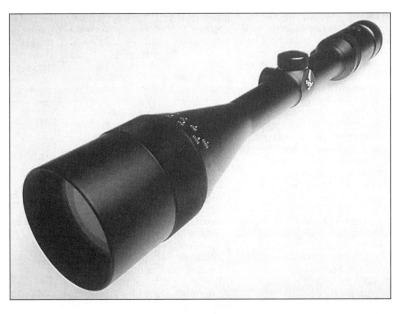

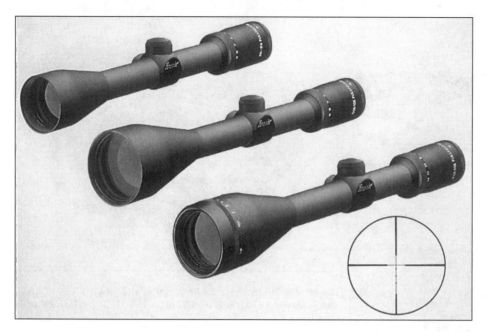

Burris 3-9x40, 3.5-10x50, and 4.5-14x42 are just three of dozens of high-grade scopes from this Colorado company.

All of the AV scopes have 3.5 inch eye relief, the others 3.15 inches, and there's a large choice of reticles, some illuminated. Except for a 6x42 and a pair of 8xs with 50mm and 56mm objectives, all Swarovskis are variables, ranging from 1.25-4x24 to 6-24x50. All have diopter compensation (binocular type) eyepieces, which are quicker and easier to use than tube-threaded eyepieces.

Burris

Burris has added a 4-16x to their Black Diamond line, which already included a 3-12x, 6-24x, 8-32x and a straight 6x. The new scope is available with the Ballistic Mil-Dot reticle; in this design the bottom half of the vertical crosshair has short horizontal lines to indicate approximate points of impacts at 100-yard increments out to 700 yards. The other three crosshair sections have Mil-Dots to help with range estimation and windage correction. All Black Diamonds have 30mm maintubes, 50mm objectives, and can be had with Plex, Mil-Dot or Ballistic Mil-Dot reticle.

The 3-9x Fullfield II now is offered with the Electro-Dot reticle. Aiming under the worst of light conditions is made possible by simply twisting a rotary switch to create a tiny spot of light at the crosshair intersection. Being able to see your exact aiming point can make the difference between a hit and a miss – between success or failure – when it's late on the last day of a hunt. I know. The Electro-Dot has two intensity settings and is powered by a common camera battery, which lasts a minimum of 12 hours – and usually 24 to 36 on full power.

A new Fullfield II 6.5-20x50 is due out right about now. It will be built on an inch maintube, and prototypes weigh only 19 oz. (*The name Fullfield, incidentally, came along in the mid-'70s when Burris first offered scopes that gave larger-than-ordinary fields which were round rather than the TV-shape of other scope manufacturers.*)

Nightforce

Nightforce scopes are bulky and heavy – even the smallest, a 1.7-6x42, weighs 22 oz. and the 5.5-22x56 goes 38.5 oz.– but optically they're unsurpassed. At least I've never looked through anything superior to them. Reticles range from a simple crosshair to the highly sophisticated Varminter Ranging that takes a bit of study, but then makes a deadly unit on an ultra-long-range outfit. The rifleman who specializes in such shooting could well find a Nightforce that fills his needs. Not intended for boars in the swamps or even whitetails in the woods, the Nightforces are at home on precision, heavy-barrel rifles intended for the longest shots at game, or on a serious tactical rifle.

Conetrol

Conetrol mounts are made for countless rifle-scope combinations and are particularly popular with riflemen who like the smooth look of their *projectionless* rings, which are locked with a fitted cap instead of screws, As well as being made for 1-inch and 30mm tubes, these are also available for old European scopes with 26mm or 26 1/2mm tubes, in three heights. For shooters who use scopes with very large objectives, there are Extra High horizontally split 1-inch rings. For rifles such as Sako and Dubiel, which have integral dovetails atop the action, Conetrol bases are made to fit, which gives an unusually strong connection at what is the weakest point of any mounting system. They are also made to fit Warne bases.

George Miller, honcho at Conetrol, advises they will soon have a quick-detachable unit which includes windage adjustment, an unusual feature in QD mounts.

Pentax

Pentax has joined with Whitetails Unlimited, Inc. to offer a new line of scopes called – interestingly enough – the Whitetails Unlimited series. Of the same high quality we've come to expect from Pentax, the new line consists of four variables: 2-5x, 3-9x, 3.7-11x and 4.5-14x. All have one piece 1-inch maintubes, 7-layer coating, and eye relief of 3.1 to 3.8 inches, and all have Twilight Plex reticles for dim light use. With objectives ranging from 20mm to 50mm and large fields of view, one of these will doubtless fill anyone's needs on a whitetail rifle, be it a light lever-action carbine or a heavy beanfield bolt action. A portion of every WU purchase goes to WTU to better whitetail environment.

Pentax also presents their new generation of Lightseeker-30 scopes. Three models, 4-16x, 6-24x and 8.5-32x, all with adjustable objective units, have 30mm tubes and 50mm objectives. The maintubes, larger than the original Lightseekers, allow increased *w&e* adjustment range, and the eyepiece focusing mechanism also has been improved. The LS-30s are available with Mil-Dot

The Kahles 2-7x36 American Hunter has its reticle in the second focal plane, as most hunters here prefer.

reticles or one of the Plex designs.

Kahles

Kahles, the old Austrian optical company now part of Swarovski, has just added a 2-7x36 to their American Hunter line. Its built on a 1-inch one-piece hardened aluminum tube and has its reticle in the second focal plane. Only 11 inches long and weighing less than 12 oz., this size scope is what I believe most big-game rifles should be wearing.

Shepherd

Shepherd's 6-18x40 is their newest, and gives hunters a fairly high magnification scope with the unusual and efficient reticle system I detailed in GUNS ILLUSTRATED many years ago (see "*Shepherd's Super-Sophisticated Scope,*" 18th ed. 1986). Basically, this reticle is a series of open circles that subtend 18 inches at hundred-yard intervals out to 1000 yards. They're spaced to match the drop of high-velocity cartridges, so you just find the circle that fits a deer's depth, aim with it and shoot, For a long time Shepherd scopes were made in 2-7x, 3-9x and 3-10x only. I've used all these sizes with good results, but the 6-18x offers even higher magnification for those who need or want it.

Warne

Warne recently introduced the Maxima series of permanently attached mounts. Rings are made for 1 inch and 30mm tubes, in three heights and finishes. They're made by the sintered steel process, which allows complicated shapes to be produced at much less than the cost of traditional methods. The scope is locked into the rings by four high tensile socket head cap screws: two at top, two at bottom. The lower ones also hold the ring to the base. A solid steel key in the bottom of the ring engages a notch in the base to eliminate the possibility of fore or aft movement. Maxima rings also for Weaver or Picatinny bases. Warne Magnum mounts accommodate heavy scopes with 50mm or 56mm objectives. Either permanently attached or

quick detachable, they come with High or Extra High rings and accept 1 inch or 30mm maintubes. They fit Maxima steel bases or the Weaver style. Ultra High models are made specifically for sporter versions of the Colt M16 and the Heckler & Koch SL7.

Simmons

Simmons' Aetec scope is now available in 2.8-10x and 3.8-12x; both with an Illuminated Reticle and 44mm objective. This is the first scope I ever knew about to have an aspherical lens system. This gives a flatter – and thus improved – target image at the extreme outer edge of the field. The Aetec, of course, has all the good features of today's high-grade scopes - it's waterproof and shockproof and has multi-coated optics and quarter-minute clicks.

Weaver

Weaver Grand Slam scopes have been around for a bit over a year now, and they're probably the best scopes to ever wear the long-popular Weaver name. There are half a dozen Grand Slams, all variables, ranging from 1.5-5x32 to the 6-20x40 with adjustable objective, and a straight 4.7x40. The 3-l0x40 seems a reasonable size for the average big-game rifle; big enough to give good light transmission at top power without seeming to overpower the gun as scopes with 50mm or 56mm objectives can do on a sporter. It's 12 inches long and weighs 13.8 oz., has 1/4-*moa* clicks and binocular-type focusing for the eye.

Redfield

Redfield scopes, which many expected to vanish when that old Colorado company died a few years ago, are back. Along with the Weaver and Simmons lines mentioned above, Redfield scopes are now available from Blount, Inc., which has to make that company one of the biggest scope suppliers anywhere.

Four familiar Redfield lines are being offered – Golden Five Star, Tracker, Widefield and Illuminator. The Widefields have low-profile objectives, which lets them sit low on the receiver, and is their only line to have a straight power, a 4x. The

Nikon pushes their 4-12x40 AO as a top choice for either big game or varmints, and their logic is not debatable.

variables come in all conventional powers from 2-7x to 6-18x, most with a choice of matte, gloss or silver finish.

A lot of hunters will be glad to know the Redfields are back. They were just too good to fade away, I guess.

Tasco

Tasco has added a pair of variables to their extensive hunting scope line – a 1.5-5x and a 3-9x. Called the EXP (Extreme Performance) models, there's nothing unusual about their power spreads, but the noticeable feature is their objective units. These are horizontal ovals, maxing at 32x44 in the former, 42x54mm in the 3-9x. The purpose, of course, is to get the high light transmission of a large objective – *Tasco calls it an Oval* – without having to use high mounts. Tasco points out these scopes were unaffected by 500 rounds on a McMillan 50-caliber rifle, so a 338 or whatever should be no problem. Tasco also offers many varmint and tactical scopes.

Nikon

Nikon is pretty much standing pat on their Monarch UCC, Titanium and Buckmaster lines this year– why not? they cover practically all any hunter might need–but they do have one new Buckmaster due out right about the time this *GD* appears in bookstores. This is the 1x20

Black Powder, and its name should make it obvious which hunter group it's slanted for. Black powder shooters become more numerous every year, but they don't need long-range scopes because they're not using long-range rifles. But in dim woods they do need lots of light, and this little model has 88% transmission, with a 20mm exit pupil and a huge field to make target acquisition fast and easy.

Mitchell

Mitchell Optics is a comparatively new scope company, having been formed in Illinois about 1995, with the goal of producing updated versions of the full-length, return-to-battery target scopes that were popular for so long. For several decades now, there has been a strong movement toward the comparatively short action-mounted scopes demanded by benchresters, but there has always been a percentage of shooters who preferred the externally-adjusted target types made by Fecker, Unertl, Lyman and others. Maybe they grew up using them or seeing their fathers use them. Those old favorites have been gone for years but, in the Mitchell, shooters have another high-quality make to play with if they want.

As background, George Mitchell, president of the company, has a PhD in biochemistry from Harvard, was cofounder and - for over a quarter-century - vice president of research and development for an analytical instrument company specializing in advanced electro-optical instrumentation for fluorescence spectroscopy. What this means is, he knows optics.

With the input of James Miller, a nationally recognized smallbore prone competitor and the guy one of the scopes is named for, Mitchell Optics produces three target scopes: 11/2- and 2-inch objectives, both in 20x or 27x, and a 2 1/2-inch in 24x or 32x. All have 1-inch maintubes, 30mm oculars and 70mm eye relief, and all use Mitchell's own external mounts with thick, CNC-milled aluminum frames, and 1/4-*moa* micrometer-grade *w&e* adjustments. Scope lengths range from 24 to 26 inches; weights from 28 to 52 oz.

Leatherwood

Leatherwood Auto-Ranging Telescopes (ART) were conceived by Jim Leatherwood while still a college student in the early '60s. After testing by the military, they were used by U.S. Army snipers in Vietnam and elsewhere, and commercial models were produced by Realist Inc. Currently a 3-9x40 having ART features and called the Sporter is offered to hunters. It comes with a unique lever-operated QD mount that latches solidly to Weaver-style bases.

After zeroing at 200 yards with the scope's internal 1/4-*moa* clicks, the range/calibration/power ring unit located just ahead of the

Fixed-power 6x42mm from Sightron.

Sightron's new 2.5-7x32mm variable.

eyepiece is synchronized with your load's trajectory (*following simple instructions that come with the scope*). Then it's only a matter of bracketing the target with tick marks on the reticle, holding where you want to hit – and shooting. There's no need to estimate range, no need to hold high. The scope automatically takes care of everything out to 600 yards, which is as far as Leatherwood thinks anyone should be shooting at animals. (*I agree fully with him on that.*) His military scopes work to a greater distance, but they have other purposes. For more detailed info, check Leatherwood's website at http:/www.leatherwoodoptics.com

Jim is currently adapting his Sporter scope for use with muzzleloading rifles, too, which could well make it compatible with rifled slug

The new Sightron 1.5-6x50mm variable works for both woods and field shooting.

shotguns, I expect – though not to 600 yards, of course.

21st Century Technologies

21st Century Technologies of Ft. Worth, TX, in January announced they have acquired all assets of the highly regarded Unertl Optical Co. of Mars, PA. For sixty years various Unertl scopes were favorites of many hunters, competitive marksmen, and snipers. How many of these scopes will be available is not yet known. First offering of the new company will be the internally-adjustable l0x Unertl that was long made for the USMC, FBI and other governmental agencies. It's due to appear in the second quarter of 2001.

Sightron

Sightron has a whole line of new offerings this year. A 6x42 is the only straight power, and comes in answer to the requests of Western

hunters who want the simplicity and durability of such a scope for their average hunting – much like a straight 4x serves so many in the East. There are also Variables in the ever-popular 3-9x50 size, a 3-13x50 for those who often have extra-long shots, 2.5-7x32 and 1.5-6x50 for normal woods and field shooting. Sightron also has many Competition/Tactical scopes, Compact, Shotgun and Pistol models. All have ZACT-7 *Revcoat*, a seven-layer broadband coating, and *ExacTrack* adjustments, a unique system that keeps click values consistent even at the limit of their range.

BSA Optics

BSA Optics has a new series of variables called the Mil-Dot. That's the kind of reticle they have, of course, black in 4-16x40 and 6-24x40, or illuminated red in the same scopes. An 11-position rheostat makes it easy to adjust the reticle as

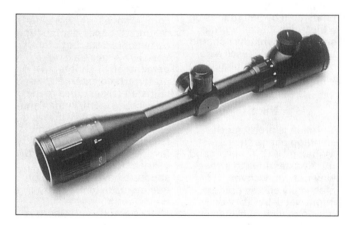

BSA's Mil-Dot scopes are made in 4-16x, 6-24x and 8-32x – all with 40mm objectives.

Thompson/Center's 2.5-7x28 on their 22 Classic rifle.

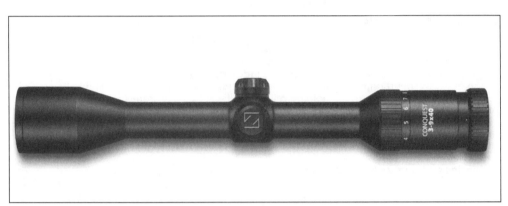

Zeiss' 3-9x40mm variable, one of the new Conquest line.

bright or dim as required for the best contrast. There's also an 8-32x40 with black mil-dot. Other features include adjustable objectives, finger-adjustable "reset to zero" *w&e* knobs, and 1/8-*moa* clicks. Also new in the BSA Deerhunter series is a 3-9x40 with illuminated reticle.

Thompson/Center

Thompson/Center has a couple of new scopes, a 2.5-7x designed particularly - but not exclusively - for the T/C 22 LR Classic rifle, and a 1.25-4x Recoil Proof pistol scope for use on Encore and Contender single-shot pistols.

Springfield Armory

Springfield Armory's high-grade Government model scopes are intended primarily as tactical designs for serious shooting, but they also serve as long-range hunting models. Most are variables – 4-14x40, 4-14x56, and 6-20x56, but there are a couple of

straight-powers: a 6x40 and a 10x56. All have detailed range-finder reticles; some of which are illuminated, calibrated for either the 7.62mm (308 Win.) or 5.56mm (223 Rem.). Some also are made with mil-dot reticle, and all have an internal bubble level and 1/4-*moa* clicks.

Zeiss

Zeiss has a new line of scopes aimed at the American hunter. Called the Conquests, all are built on 1-inch, one-piece hardened alloy tubes with matte or stainless finish. Four scopes make up the line: a 3-9x40 for big game; 3-9x40S for shotguns, high-grade airguns and muzzleloaders; 3.5-10x44 and 4.5-14x44 for those who have to deal with ultra-long range critters much of the time.

Eye relief is long – 4 inches in both 3-9s, 3.5 inches in the higher powers, and is constant at all magnifications. There's a choice of half a dozen reticles, and they're

positioned in the second focal plane, so subtend less of the target as power is increased. All air/glass surfaces are multi-coated of course, and *w&e* adjustments have a range of up to 66 inches. Weights go from 15 to 17+ oz., lengths from 12.7 to 13.9 inches. All Conquests have 1/4-*moa* clicks right now, but the two larger ones will have the option of 1/8 *moa* shortly.

The 4.5-14x44 offers the first turret-mounted parallax adjustment from Zeiss. This means focusing for distant targets can be made from a normal shooting position, rather than lowering the gun to screw the objective in or out.

Another new Zeiss is the VariPoint 1.5-6x42 T*, a power range that will handle all normal big game hunting and which, at bottom power, will be suitable for dangerous game at short range. The VariPoint's reticle arrangement features an illuminated dot (which turns black if the battery runs out), as well as a post that

magnifies with the power for use as a ranging reticle. Like the Conquests, the VariPoint's ocular unit has a diopter adjustment of +2/-3 to quickly focus for individual eyesight.

Zeiss has been a leader in all phases of optics since 1894. They introduced their first riflescope in 1904, and many Zeiss scopes were used extensively for hunting in the last century and by the German military in both World Wars. (*The late John Unertl, Sr., incidentally, was a German sniper in WWI, many years before he started making his own well-known scopes in this country.*)

In the late '30s a 2 1/4x Zeiss Zielklein happened to be the first good scope I ever used, and in 1945 I liberated a 6x Zeiss Zielsechs in northern Germany which I've used on many rifles ever since. And years ago I got the 4x Zeiss Diatal C which has a permanent home on my favorite 338. So I've had well over a half-century's experience with one Zeiss or another. I guess it's fair to say I like 'em. ●

by **LARRY S. STERETT**

HANDLOADING UPDATE

JUST AS IT has for the past few years, interest in handloading continues to increase. As this shooter sees it, much of the increase is concentrated in three major areas: Cowboy action shooting, 50 BMG shooting and long-range precision shooting. Trap, skeet, sporting clays, varmint and big game hunters, and target shooters – plus the various metallic silhouette shooters, practical pistol, and combat shooters – all handload, although likely not increasing at the rate of the others.

For the 50 BMG shooters, Hornady, RCBS and The Old Western Scrounger have both presses and die sets available. Forester Products has a special trimmer for the 50 BMG, while The OW Scrounger has a 50 BMG file trim die. The OW Scrounger also has loading dies, and shell holders for the 12.7mm and 14.5mm Russian cartridges, the .5 Boyes and a number of 20mm cartridges, plus bullet pullers for several of these calibers.

Barnes Bullets not only has several new bullets this year, but a new edition, Number 3, of the *Barnes Bullets Reloading Manual* is available. New also is the next generation of ballistics software, Barnes Ballistics Program Version 2.0, compatible with Windows 95 and 98. The manual contains new how-to articles, new cartridge data including material on Barnes XLC and VLC coated bullets, and lots of photos. The ballistics program can be downloaded at **www.barnesbullets.com**

and the information is displayed in both table and graph form. By inputting a few specifics about the gun and the load, the program will calculate the trajectory, energy, wind drift, time-of-flight, and more. You can also calculate recoil forces, determine optimum *zero*, store loading data, etc.

Beartooth Bullets has a spiral-wound *Technical Guide* for those handloaders doing their own bullet casting. It's thorough and covers barrel lapping, proper bullet fit, bullet selection, loading records, range data, load development and trouble-shooting, with the last discussing such topics as bullet seating, crimping and powder selection. The *Guide* has no index, but in addition to a table of contents, it has at the end a Table of Figures and a Table of Tables. Beartooth suggests a way in which loading data may be kept, and the full-size version of their form may be downloaded from **www.beartoothbullets.com** along with the full-size version of their quartered target form.

Beartooth has a loading manual in the works for their line of bullets. It may be available by the time you read this, but look for a full report in the next edition.

Dillon Precision Products continues to add to their line of 'blue' reloading presses, dies and accessories. New for the AT 500 or Advanced Turret 500 is a '500 Package Deal' that features accessories a handloader needs, but would normally

have to purchase separately. Included are a Reloading Handbook, dial caliper, bench wrench, cartridge bin, strong mount bracket to raise the press, mounting hardware, Eliminator scale, safety glasses, and a primer flip tray. The AT 500 is based on the 550B frame and features an 'indexable' shellplate and interchangeable toolheads, but is not progressive. It is capable of loading over 40 calibers and can be upgraded to an RL 500B later if desired.

Also new in the Dillon line is the Super 1050. Featuring a lengthened frame and a new crank assembly to accommodate long cartridges, the Super 1050 has all the features of the RL 1050, but with greater strength and smoother operation. It comes with factory-adjusted dies and is currently available for six of the most popular cartridges.

Form Plus Industries has a handy new 'PocketPak' for holding reloaded rifle cartridges. Produced from translucent plastic in a choice of orange, green or clear, the PocketPaks are available in

four sizes to fit most cartridges from the 243 Winchester to the 416 Remington Magnum. Paks for cartridges the size of the 270 Winchester or 30-06 will hold five rounds, while Paks for magnum-size cartridges are designed to handle four rounds. No PocketPaks are currently available to fit cartridges based on the 404 or 416 cases, such as the 378 and 460 Weatherby Magnums. (*The PocketPaks can withstand a good bit of wear, but are completely recyclable when no longer usable.*)

Each PocketPak comes with a gummed label for recording the loading data: cartridge, case, bullet type and weight; powder brand and weight (*charge*), primer and date of loading. Additional labels can be obtained.

Designed to slip into a jacket, shirt, hunting vest, or pants pocket, the PocketPak protects the loaded cartridge from damage, particularly the soft point bullet tips. The covers snap closed - friction tight - and when

Beartooth Bullets' *Technical Guide* is a handy reference for handloaders of cast bullets. Spiral-bound to lay flat, it's loaded with information.

The PocketPak from Form Plus Industries holds five reloaded rifle cartridges and is available in three colors and four sizes to fit most cartridges from the 243 Winchester to the 416 Remington Magnum.

opened, the cartridges can easily be removed by pushing on the base, or slipping a finger under the bullet tip and pulling upward.

Forester Products' Co-Ax loading press has featured a spring-loaded universal "S" jaws shell holder which would handle most rifle and handgun cartridge cases from 218 Bee to the 458 Winchester Magnum,

Hodgdon's new *Basic Reloaders Manual* features up-to-date data for the latest cartridges, plus for many of the older calibers. Data for the Titegroup and Longshot powders are included.

the 22 Remington Jet to the 45 Colt. An optional "*LS*" jaws holder was available to handle a few cartridges the "*S*" holder would not accept. Now there's a new shell holder adapter plate which will accept regular shell holders. This will facilitate the reloading of some non-standard cartridges, which the "*S*" and "*LS*" jaws will not accept, but for which a regular-style shell holder is available.

Forester has also added three new chamberings: 6.5/284, 300 Remington Ultra Mag and 30/378 Weatherby to their line of Bench Rest and Ultra-micrometer dies sets. The new offerings are available as a complete set or as individual full-length sizer and seater dies.

Hodgdon Powder Company has a new *Basic Reloaders Manual* that provides loads for 12 and 16 gauge shotshells using Titegroup and Longshot powders, respectively – plus new loads for the 338 Remington Ultra, 338/378 Weatherby, 450 Marlin and 376 Steyr. In addition there are a host of new Longshot powder loads for a "baker's dozen" handgun cartridges from the 32 H & R Magnum to the 458 Casull. No data in this edition for the 480 Ruger, but the next manual will no doubt have it and data is provided for the 475 Linebaugh. (*Loads for the 475 Linebaugh should not be used for the 480 Ruger.*)

Hornady Manufacturing Company not only introduced a new cartridge this year – the 480 Ruger with a 325-grain XTP-MAG jacketed hollow-point bullet – but, as well, additional equipment for handloaders. Foremost is the new 'Cam Lock' Case Trimmer, which comes with seven of the most popular pilots, from 22 to 45 caliber.

This new trimmer features a redesigned handle knob, a taller base to reduce knuckle banging, a one-finger case cam lock, and a micro-adjustable cutting head. The 'Cam Lock' Trimmer finish is, naturally, '*Hornady Red.*' Also new from the Grand Island firm is a Neck-Turning Tool that permits uniform case neck-turning in 0.001-inch increments. Mandrels are sold separately, and five

sizes – .22, 6mm, 6.5mm, 7mm, and .308 – are currently available. To obtain the most accurate loads, uniformity in case neck thickness is required, making 'turning' a must.

Lee Precision, Inc. has several new items for handloaders, with the biggest news being a new four-hole Turret Press. The three-hole Lee Turret Press has been on the market for two decades, and the Lee firm has worn out two casting dies, and is now on the third, turning them out. The new four-hole model turret can be retrofitted to many of the earlier versions for a double sawbuck, using an Update Kit, and in only a couple of minutes. Or, an entire new four-hole Turret Press can be purchased, with the three-hole press as a backup or set up for another cartridge. Extra turrets for either model are also available. All the great features of the original press have been retained in the new model, including rapid changing of dies, shell holders and primer arm – without tools.

The Lee Zip Trim Power Head case trimmer was introduced last year, but now it can be even better. An optional Universal 3-jaw chuck is available that will hold any cartridge case from the 25 ACP to the 460 Weatherby Magnum. There's also a "spinner stud" so the 3-jaw chuck can be used with an electric drill, if desired. The Lee Case Trimmer can now be obtained with a cutter and lock stud for the shell holder, or the cutter only with a handy Ball Grip.

In the Lee LP Pacesetter rifle die line the 338 Remington Ultra Mag has been added, bringing the total to more than eighty cartridges overall in the various lines. Free shell holders are included with three of the pistol die lines: carbide, steel and speed – and four of the rifle die lines: Pacesetter, LP Pacesetter, Collet and Deluxe.

New dust-tight housings for thermostat life unique infinite heat controls have been added to several of the Lee Electric Melters for bullet casting. This will extend the life of the controls, which

Hornady Manufacturing's new Neck-Turning Tool permits neck turning in 0.001-inch increments. Mandrels are available separately in five sizes from .22- to .308-inch.

permit full power until the metal has melted.

Lyman Products Corporation now has 3-die sets for the 450 Marlin and 454 Casull cartridges, plus neck-sizing dies in 40 and 45 caliber to fit many of the black powder cartridges utilized in Cowboy Action Shooting. The 40 caliber will handle the 40-65, 40-77, etc. cartridges, while the 45 dies are available in *short* and *long* versions to handle cases from the 45-70 to the 45-120, along with a host of others. There's also a new double-cavity mold (*#454647*) to cast 285-grain truncated, gas-check bullets for the 454 Casull. (Cowboy action shooters will appreciate the 2nd edition of the *Black Powder Handbook*, with hundreds of tested loads for black powder cartridges, in addition to loads for muzzleloaders.)

Every handloader needs a good caliper, and Lyman has a new electronic 4-inch Pocket Caliper. It will measure length, and depth, outside and inside diameters in mm/inch functions and is accurate to 0.001 inch. An added 'plus' is the on/off push button to save the battery when the caliper is not being used.

Micro Technologies, LLC., manufacturer of the Duster Series of replacement wads for shotshells, has a new handy *Reloading Guide* to go with their line of blue, green, yellow, orange and red wads. The loads feature the most popular powders and CCI, Federal, Fiocchi, Remington and Winchester primers. Various brands of 12, 20 and 28 gauge – plus .410-bore –

hulls are included but no suggested 16 gauge loads are provided. In addition to the regular loads, there are tables on the inside cover of the Guide for powder conversion, chilled shot conversion with the approximate number of pellets per load, downrange velocity of various sizes of lead shot, and an illustration of the space occupied by an ounce of lead shot in various gauges.

Nostalgia Enterprises Co. has a host of items for handloaders, including a portable shooting bench that weighs only 14 pounds, and a device to enable clamping the Wilson Case Trimmer to the loading bench. One useful item is the new Case Gauge Companion, which permits cartridge cases to be permanently marked on the head-stamp surface. After those special cases have been determined, it is placed in the Companion and accurately and precisely embossed with a choice of symbols, letters or digits. Each Companion comes with a complete set of stamps, and an anvil of the customer's choice. One anvil will suffice for a number of cases; currently anvils are available to fit nearly five-dozen different cartridges, including the 416 Rigby and the 50 BMG.

Quinetics Corp. has been known for their kinetic bullet puller for at least three decades. It pulls most bullets with one or two strikes, and without damage to the bullet or case. Now Quinetics has what they call the 'Ultimate Model' with a new "*Twist*" chuck assembly. After the

bullet and powder are free from the case, twist the cap 1/4-turn and lightly tap the head of the puller on the bottom of a receptacle. The case, powder, and bullet will drop out, without having to pull the case out manually and empty out the powder and bullet. It's simple to operate, and quick.

Molds for casting bullets are available from a number of manufacturers, including **Lyman Products, Lee Precision**, and **Magma Engineering**. Another firm which has a large number of molds available, including ones for calibers from the Civil War era and the last half of the 19th century is **Rapine Bullet Mold Mfg.** Shooters who need to cast bullets for use in their original or reproduction Smith, Smith-Maynard, Burnside, Sharps, Spencer, Gallagher, or 11mm Mauser should check Rapine's list. The firm also has molds for the more common calibers, even a 'collar button' design for the 45-70, and a couple of semi-wadcutter designs for 12 gauge slugs – plus .58 and .69 caliber for use with muskets.

RCBS, long known for the C-frame and 0-frame loading presses, now has a new turret press to add to a line which currently includes the Pro 2000 Progressive, Rock Chucker, Reloader Special-5, Partner, AmmoMaster Single Stage and the AmmoMaster 50 BMG Pack. All the presses are available separately, or as part of a complete kit with everything necessary to start reloading, except the components. The turret press features cast-iron

construction, a six-station turret head that provides the option of installing two die sets adjusted for different cartridges. (*Additional turret heads are available and switching heads requires the removal of only one bolt.*)

For RCBS Rock Chucker, Reloader Special-3 or Reloader Special-5 owners who want to up their output without buying another press, there's a new Piggyback III. This unit changes the single stage to a 5-station, manual indexing, progressive reloader in one step and can increase the output from 50 rounds per hour to well over 400 rounds. The Piggyback handles all 7/8"x14 dies, utilizes APS priming and an optional Star Wheel can be obtained to allow quick caliber changeover. Extra Pro 2000 Piggyback III die plates can be obtained to allow permanent die setup, eliminating the need to install and adjust dies for each caliber change; just change the die plate. There's also a new Case-Activated Linkage Kit for the Uniflow Powder Measure. This Kit allows the Uniflow to be used on most of the four or five-station progressive presses. The drop tube portion is fully adjustable for all case length variations, and three pistol, are provided with each kit.

Several new chamberings have been added to the RCBS die line. These include the 376 Steyr, 7mm Remington Ultra Magnum, the 338-378 Weatherby Magnum, 450 Marlin and the 38 Casull.

Redding Reloading Equipment's newest item for handloaders is an "Instant Indicator" Headspace and Bullet Comparator to permit rapid checking of headspace. This allows sizing dies to be properly adjusted to prevent incorrect headspace, and the case length can quickly be checked to determine if trimming (bushings, small rifle/large rifle, come with each kit) is necessary. The Indicator is currently available for 28 cartridges, from the 222 Remington to the 338 Winchester Magnum. Other new Redding items include additional reloading dies, 300 Winchester Short Magnum, 7mm and 375 Remington Ultra Magnums, the 450 Marlin Magnum, and the new 480 Ruger. Depending on the cartridge, standard and deluxe two- and three-die sets are available, plus Type S neck-

and full-length sizing dies. A Deluxe Reloading Kit with all the tools necessary to produce quality reloads is now available, as is an accessory power screwdriver adaptor for the Model 1400 Case Trimmer. New titanium-coated cutters are available for the Redding 1400 Trimmer also.

Handloaders reloading cartridges originally purchased in the factory boxes do not have a problem with what to do with the reloaded cartridges. Put them back in the original box, with a new label indicating the primer, powder/charge and bullet type/weight. Reloading brass or shotgun hulls from a commercial shooting range, or purchased as surplus, presents a slight problem. If you purchase 500 once-fired brass cases packed in bulk in a steel ammo can, it would be handy to have it in 20-round packs when you get it reloaded. Or what about the 500 empty shotshell hulls you purchased at the Grand American?

Scharch Mfg. Inc. has the answer. Not only does this firm have components – pulled bullets and once-fired military and commercial brass – they also have containers for the reloaded ammunition. Plastic and cardboard boxes and trays are available to hold 20 or 50 rounds of the most popular metallic cartridges, or cardboard boxes to hold 25 shotshells. The cardboard boxes are available in plain white or red-printed boxes. The trays for the metallic cartridge are black if plastic, white if cardboard. The trays may be purchased separately, or with red or white cardboard boxes. Plastic slip-top or hinge-top ammo boxes are also available for the most popular handgun and rifle cartridges. The slip-top boxes hold 20 rounds, and the hinge-top boxes are available to hold 50 or 100 rounds.

Scharch handles a few other items for handloaders, including primer sealant, bullet lube and case-sizing lubricant. In addition the firm distributes the RangeMaster line of machinery and reloading equipment for those individuals, gun clubs, law enforcement, shooting ranges or firms wanting to increase their production of reloads.

Kaltron-Pettibone, distributors of VihtaVuori smokeless powders and Lapua ammunition, has a new reloading manual available. Unlike most American manuals, the VihtaVuori manual features some cartridges common in Europe, Russia or the Scandinavian countries – but not often seen in the U. S. It's an excellent reference for the

Kaltron-Pettibone has a 38-minute *"Reloading With the Masters"* video with in-depth coverage of case preparation, resizing, trimming, powder burning rates – and a host of other useful information. Narrated by competitive shooter Matt Burkett, with champions Rob Leatham, Brian Enos and Angus Hobdell assisting, it may provide the reloading hints necessary to win major shooting matches.

Lee Precision's latest is a new four-hole turret press, one up from the previous three-hole turret. An Update Kit is available to ret-rofit the previous model, if desired.

loading data using VihtaVuori powders, but the ballistics it features are useful.

Huntington Die Services, the original RCBS firm, distributes RCBS products, but also has more special-order reloading dies and case-forming dies than you can literally 'shake a stick at.' From the 14 Carbine and 14 Flea to the 700 Nitro in loading dies and case-forming dies from the 14 Walker Hornet to the 585 Nyatti. If someone just has to have cases for a 577 Snider or 577/450 Martini-Henry, Huntington can provide both the forming dies and the loading dies. Just remember, unusual items are not located in the economy section. Custom products are not inexpensive.

Another item useful to handloaders is the new, revised and expanded 9th edition of *Cartridges of the World* by the publishers of the *Gun Digest*. It features more than 1,500 of the world's cartridges: current production, obsolete, smokeless and black powder, proprietary, wildcat, military and domestic, centerfire and rimfire, metric, English and American. Some loading data is provided for most of the centerfire cartridges, and dimensioned drawings are provided for the current production U. S. calibers. Loading data is not provided for rimfires, or the shotshells. In addition to the loading data and information on the cartridges (most of which are illustrated by photographs), there are a number of informative articles and an excellent section on cartridge identification by measurement, from the 2.7mm Kolibri to the 70-150 Winchester. There's also a similar section on shotshells.

Handloading continues to gain in popularity. Every time a new cartridge is introduced the aftermarket takes over to provide loading components and the necessary equipment to reload the cartridge. (*New shotshell gauges do not appear with any regularity. New loads are introduced, and new components, and equipment to increase the ease and rate of reloading, but the last new reloadable shotshell of any degree of popularity was probably the .410-bore, and that was more than three-quarters of a century ago.*) Thankfully, the handloading of metallic rifle and handgun cartridges, and regular shotshells, is enough to keep us occupied. ●

by HOLT BODINSON

AMMUNITION, BALLISTICS & COMPONENTS

NOTHING HAS BEEN more exciting lately than the appearance of Winchester's and Lazzeroni's short magnum cartridges. These squat, fat, big-game cartridges seem to do exactly what the makers say they will do: provide the performance levels of the larger magnums with less powder, less recoil and, typically, improved accuracy. Equally intriguing is the appearance of Aguila's 17-caliber rimfire for the small-game enthusiast. Whether your interest runs to rifles, shotguns or handguns, you'll find some interesting new cartridges and components here from the world's leading makers.

Aguila

While it's been whispered about for years, the 17-caliber rimfire is now being commercially produced by Aguila in Mexico. The diminutive small-game round, based on a necked-down 22 LR case, made its debut at this year's SHOT Show – along with drop-in barrels for the Ruger series of rimfire rifles. Ballistics are rather impressive, with a 20-grain soft point or FMJ being launched at 1850 fps. If you've never fussed with a sub-caliber rifle, this might be the one for you. Aguila's "silent" primer-fueled 22 LR Colibri has proven popular

indeed for indoor target shooting and backyard pest control, so this year Aguila is introducing the "Super Colibri" with a 20-grain bullet at 500 fps. And two more radical 22 rimfires make their debuts – the "223 RF" featuring a 43-grain FMJ at 1000 fps, and the "22 Goliah" loaded with a 75-grain lead bullet at 1000 fps. This year brings the introduction of Aguila's "smart bullet," the "IQ." The IQ is a dual-purpose, non-lead alloy bullet that breaks into 3 or 4 projectiles when fired directly at a gelatin block while, at the same time, offering cohesion and excellent penetration against hard surfaces such as glass and plastic. The IQ bullet is currently loaded in the 9mm, 45 ACP, and 40 S&W and will soon be released as a 170-grain, 2400 fps loading in the 454 Casull. www.aguilaammo.com

Accurate Arms

No new powders this year--instead, AA has issued the 2nd Edition of its thoroughly unique "*Loading Guide*." In it is data for the XMP-5744 reduced load powder and XMR-4064. Both powders were developed after *Guide* Number 1 was published. A whole new section devoted to Cowboy Action Shooting loads has been added – plus loading data for the 300 Whisper, 7.62x25 Tokarev, 357 Sig, 400 CorBon, 44 Russian, 45 S&W Schofield, 460 Rowland, 260 Rem., 300 and 338 Rem. Ultra Mags, 45-90, 45-110, 45-120 and 50-110. Lots of new bullets have been added, including the Remington 30-caliber Sabot! This is a "must have" reloading manual. www.accuratepowder.com

Alliant Powder

Making a major push to improve the clean-burning characteristics of some to its classic powders, Alliant has reduced powder fouling by 50 percent in its Green Dot and Unique canister grades. Significantly, Reloder 15 was selected by the Army as its powder of choice for the 7.62 M118 Special Ball Long-Range Sniper round. In Army trials, canister grade Reloder 15 provided superior performance in the four test categories – accuracy,

chamber pressure, ballistic performance and lot-to-lot consistency with temperature ranges from 125'F to -40' F and distances out to 1000 yards. Try some in your 308 Winchester! www.alliantpowder.com

Ballistic Products

This is *THE* one-stop shop for shotshell reloaders. If it's not in their extensive catalog, it probably does not exist for any gauge. New offerings include a plastic X-treme spreader wad that will fit all shells from 20-thru-10 gauge; a 16 gauge Trap Commander wad, and the availability of a wider selection of Fiocchi hulls that can be shipped without additional HAZMAT fees including the 12 gauge 3 1/2 inch and 24, 28 and 32 gauges. The company's line of highly informative and rigorously tested handloading manuals has been updated with new editions this year of "*The Sixteen Gauge Manual;*" "*Statistics & Pellet Ballistics;*" "*High Performance for Clays;*" "*The Powder Manual;*" and "*Handloading Steel Shotshells.*" If you load any shotgun gauges at all, do send for BPI's catalog and don't overlook their terrific

Alliant's Green Dot is still Green Dot but it burns 50 percent cleaner.

▶Following rigorous testing, Alliant's Reloder-15 was selected as the new propellant for the Army's 7.62mm sniper round.

handloading manuals and monographs. www.ballisticproducts.com.

Barnes Bullets

Most computer-based ballistic programs seem to be developed by technocrats or computer nerds – not the Barnes program. Here is the easiest to use, most logical ballistics program available, and Barnes has just revised it. It's available as a download from Barnes' web site after one pays a reasonable fee for a user ID number. *Highly recommended.* Barnes X-Bullets are now factory loaded by Lazzeroni, Federal, Sako, PMC and Weatherby, and the new coated X-Bullets being released this year are a 120-grain/6.5mm; 130-grain/ 308 and a 210-grain/338. Look for the 3rd edition of Barnes reloading manual to make its appearance mid-year – new data will include the XLC and VLC lines. www.barnesbullets.com

Bell Brass (MAST Technology)

Making some of the toughest brass ever produced, Bell is adding the following new cases this year: 505 Gibbs; 450 NE; 500/ 465; 475 #2; 450 #2; 577 NE; 405 Win; 7mm Dakota; and 338 Lapua. Keep those boomers booming! www.bellammo.com

Berger Bullets

Founders Walt and Eunice Berger, have sold the business to Spiveco Inc., manufacturer of those jewel-quality J4 bullet jackets. The new owner, J.R. Spivey, is the son of one of the founders of Sierra Bullets, so the fine Berger line is in good hands. During the move of the manufacturing equipment from Phoenix, AZ

to Fullerton, CA this past year, Berger bullets have been in short supply. Now, the manufacturing process has been upgraded and automated, so look for Berger benchrest-quality bullets to be back in inventory this year. www.bergerbullets.com

Big Bore Express, Ltd.

Ballistic points for muzzleloading bullets? You bet. Big Bore now has a complete line of saboted, ballistic-pointed bullets for the 45, 50 and 54-caliber muzzle-stuffers. www.bigbore.com

Bismuth

Bismuth has transferred its non-toxic shotgun shell technology to the realm of frangible, non-toxic handgun ammunition. Their new 9mm, 40 S&W and 45 ACP projectiles are created by casting, swaging and then copper-plating a pure Bismuth core, thereby approximating the weight and recoil of lead ammunition. Upon impact, the Bismuth bullets disintegrate into Bismuth dust. Labeled "Bismuth Reduced Hazard Ammunition," the new loads are recommended for high-risk environments – including nuclear, biological, chemical, precious cargo and personal defense situations – where ricochet and over-penetration is to be avoided. www-bismuth-notox.com

Black Hills Ammunition

Loading the 6.5-284 originally for Norma, Black Hills has now released this exceptional target cartridge under its own label. The Black Hill loads feature either a 142-grain Sierra or 140-grain Hornady A-Max

match bullet in Norma brass. As an option, either load can be furnished with molycoated bullets. Also new this year, are a 9mm 124-grain JHP+P load at 1250 fps; a 165-grain Gold Dot or FMJ loading for the 40 S&W at maximum velocities; a 45 ACP +P load featuring the 230-grain Hornady XTP bullet at 950 fps; and for the cowboys and cowgirls, a 32 H&R Magnum(!) load featuring a 90-grain lead bullet at 750 fps. Anyway, Black Hills offers superior ammo at great prices. www.black-hills.com

Brenneke

Called the "SuperSabot", Brenneke's latest 12 gauge slug design features a hollow brass cylinder of 63 caliber with an aluminum piston that slides forward during flight to form a pointed nose, increasing the slug's overall aerodynamic qualities. Upon impact, the piston is driven to rear so the brass body forms a 63-caliber *cookie cutter.* The 425-grain slug is loaded to 1,690 fps in the 3-inch hull and 1,542 fps in the 2 3/4-inch case. www.brennekeusa.com

Black Hills' 40 S&W load of a 165-grain Gold Dot bullet at 1150 fps is the hottest available within industry pressure standards.

With the return of the 32 H&R to the Ruger Vaquero line, Black Hills offers the perfect cowboy action load – a 90-grain lead bullet at 750 fps.

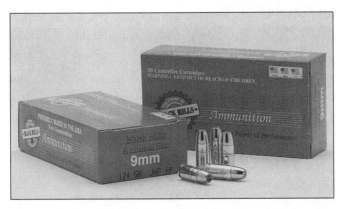

Black Hills' new 9mm+P load features a 124-grain Speer Gold Dot at a sizzling 1250 fps.

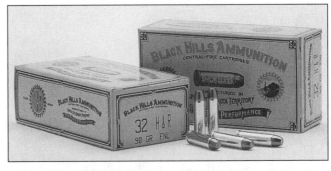

Black Hills, which originally loaded the 6.5-284 for Norma, now offers the ammunition under its own label.

◄ CCI is reviving the 22 WRF load with a 45-grain Gold Dot at 1300 fps.

◄ CCI has added 38 Special, 44 Special and 45 Colt cowboy action loads to its Blaser line.

Bull-X Bullets

Renowned for their non-leading CSJ series of cast bullets, Bull-X is fielding three new conventional cast bullets this year – a 245-grain 38-55 bullet sized properly to 0.379" ; a 300-grain 44-caliber LBT design and a 435-grain 45-70 FP. If you haven't tried the CSJ line of dry film-lubed rifle and pistols bullets, you're missing a technological breakthrough. www.bull-x.com

CCI-Speer

How do you improve the 22 rimfire? Design three new loads for it. CCI is reviving the 22 WRF load with a 45-grain Gold Dot HP at 1300 fps – perfect for those old Winchester 1890 and 1906 models; as well as a reduced load in 22 WMRs. Also added this year are a 50-grain Gold Dot 22 WMR load at 1525 fps and a pre-fragmented 32-grain "QuickShok" 22 RF loading at 1640 fps. The aluminum-cased Blaser line is being expanded with 38 Special, 44 Special and 45 Colt "cowboy" loads. On the Speer side of the shop, the high-performance Gold Dot

handgun line has been extended to include the 44 Special, 454 Casull and 50 Action Express, while the 25 and 32 auto cartridges with FMJs now grace the Lawman line. Speer has developed several new bullets this year – a 170-grain Gold Dot SP .357; a 225-grain Grand Slam for the .338; a 300-grain African Grand Slam SP in .375; and a 130-grain FNSP for the 7-30 Waters cartridge. www.cci-ammunition.com

Cfventures

Here's a small mail order operation with a unique product--a "*soft*" gas check that can reduce leading significantly. Actually it's a thin waxy sheet that is pressed cookie-cutter-style into the mouth of the case just before seating the bullet. Worth trying. Reach them at 509 Harvey Drive, Bloomington, IN 47403-1715.

Clean Shot Technologies

Clean Shot, the black powder substitute, is now offered in easy-to-handle 30- and 50-grain pellets for muzzleloading, or loading those cowboy action cartridges. Here's the smoke without the mess. www.cleanshot.com

Double Impact

This is a curious new 12 gauge loading invented by Muninord of Italy. The shot column in these loads is packaged within two different wads that project

two distinct patterns with each shot – one at close range – the other out to 100 meters! www.newballisticsdoubleimpact.com

Federal

Federal was purchased by Blount recently and will continue to produce fine ammunition under the Federal label. New this year in the rifle ammunition line are a Gold Medal 22 RF load that duplicates the ballistics of their award-winning UltraMatch at a much less price; a 223 match cartridge featuring Sierra's 77-grain Matchking at 2750 fps; the 338 Rem. UltraMag with a 250-grain Trophy Bonded Bear Claw at 2860 fps; and two new loadings of the Barnes XLC bullet--the 7mm Rem Mag. with a 160-grain pill at 2940 fps and the 338 Win. Mag. with 225-grains at 2800 fps. The 9mm and 40 S&W have been given a revolutionary bullet that is actually an expanding FMJ featuring a collapsing internal rubber tip just under the nose. Lots of new 12 gauge shotgun loads including a layered tungsten iron and steel loading; a 1 3/8 oz. copper-coated shot load in #s 4,5 and 6 at 1400 fps; a 1 1/8 oz. Handicap load at 1235 fps; and a 3/4 oz. Barnes sabot slug at 1900 fps. New Federal components offered this year are Tungsten-polymer #4 and #6 bulk shot as well as 45- and 50-grain Barnes Expander muzzleloading sabot slugs. www.federalcartridge.com

FNM

This Portuguese maker is loading two hard-to-get cartridges – the 7.5 MAS and 7.5x55 Swiss. Cole Distributing in Bowling Green, KY is importing both loads at very reasonable

prices. www.cole-distributing.com

Garrett Cartridges

If you own a 45-70 or 44 Magnum revolver, Garrett delivers all the power you'll ever need for big-game hunting. Garrett loads super-hard cast bullets with broad meplats and of a weight-forward Hammerhead design that leaves adequate room in the case for powder. Want to use your 45-70 for elephant, Cape buffalo or coastal brown bear? Garrett's 540-grain load at 1550 fps will shoot through Cape buffalo lengthwise. Don't quite need that level of power? How about a 420-grain loading at 1850 fps that will provide the same level of performance on elk, moose and heavy bear. Garrett's 44 Magnum handgun loads are equally impressive--a 310-grain bullet at 1325 fps and a 330-grain bullet at 1385 fps. www.garrettcartridges.com

Hevishot

The latest, USFWS-approved non-toxic shot is Hevishot-composed of an alloy of tungsten, nickel and iron. It's heavier than lead, about as hard as steel, produces tight patterns and high pellet energies at long ranges. It was used to win this year's National Wild Turkey Federation's Still Target World Championships. www.hevishot.com

Hodgdon

No new powders this year but lots of new loading data in their "*Basic Reloaders Manual*" including the 376 Steyr, 450 Marlin, 460 Rowland, 'Longshot' pistol loads. and 'Titegroup' shotgun data. www.hodgdon.com

Federal's expanding FMJ features a collapsing nose over an internal rubber core and is designed for police departments that prohibit HP ammo.

Hornady is introducing the new Ruger 480 cartridge, featuring a 325-grain XTP bullet at 1,350 fps.

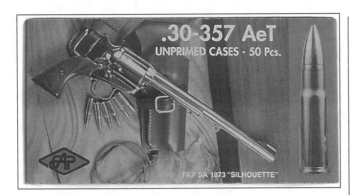

With a 123-grain bullet at 1992 fps, the 30-357 Aet should really perform in Pietta's new silhouette six-shooter.

Hornady

As a joint project with Ruger, Hornady released the 480 Ruger cartridge featuring a 325-grain XTP magnum bullet at 1,350 fps. Another impressive joint venture is the 376 Steyr that almost duplicates 375 H&H performance in a standard-length action and non-belted case. A 165- and a 180-grain 30-caliber SST bullet have been added to the component line this year. www.hornady.com

ITD Enterprises

ITD is working with Murom, Russia's largest primer maker, to market a line of non-hygroscopic, lead- and heavy metal-free primers that have at least a 25 year shelf life and which, according to HP White tests, exhibit uniform sensitivity and reliability. Stay tuned. itdprime@aol.com

Lapua

In addition to its new 6.5-284 brass, Lapua is introducing some very unique handgun cartridges this year. There's a rimmed, bottle-necked, 30-357 AeT cartridge sporting a 123-grain bullet at 1992 fps to be chambered in a single-action silhouette revolver made by Fratelli Pietta of Italy. In conjunction with Tanfoglio, Lapua has designed a heavy-walled 9mm case called the 9mm FAR. The purpose of the reinforced case is to permit the manufacture of a high velocity, in-line barrel, blowback action pistol that will offer improved accuracy and performance. Finally, there's a rimless, heavy duty, 38 Super Comp version of the 38 Super Auto cartridge that should minimize reloading problems in progressive presses. Speaking about reloading, Lapua and Vihtavuori have released a 38-minute video entitled "*Reloading with the Masters*" featuring the champs – Leatham, Enos and Hobdell, who do some show-and-tell about reloading for competition. www.lapua.com

Lazzeroni

In this, the year of the short, non-belted magnums, Lazzeroni's 30-caliber Patriot is being factory-loaded with 168-grain moly-coated Sierra Matchkings at 3200 fps from a 24-inch barrel. The compact little Patriot has proven an outstanding 1000-yard target round and surprisingly Sierra's 168-grain MatchKings perform very well on deer-class big game. Watch for the release, mid-year, of Lazzeroni's short 7mm magnum, the Tomahawk, that produces 3,379 fps with a 140-grain bullet. www.lazzeroni.com

Lightfield

Specializing in high-performance shotgun slug designs, Lightfield has developed a complete family of full weight, high-performance slugs for the 12 and 16 gauges. Called the Commander Impact Discarding Sabot, the design features a sabot that stays with the hollowpoint lead slug until impact, thereby stabilizing the slug in flight – and particularly at the critical moment when it becomes subsonic (under 1200 fps). The 16 gauge Commander features a 15/16 oz. slug at 1610 fps. The 12 gauge 3-inch Commander sports a 1-oz. slug at 1800 fps; coming soon is a 3 1/2-inch loading at 2000 fps. Reports coming from municipal deer control programs rate the Lightfield slugs as superior one-shot stoppers. www.lightfield-ammo.com

Lost River Ballistic Technologies

Lost River makes a family of streamlined, high ballistic coefficient, hunting bullets under their "J36" label and a parallel match grade line known as the "J40." Their hollowpoint, boattail bullets are machined on a CNC lathe from a copper/nickel alloy and then fitted with a sharp copper tip. The maker indicates the bullets expand to 1.5-1.75 times their diameter upon impact and do not shed weight. Available in calibers 224 thru 510. www.lostriverballistic.com

Norma

Lots of plentiful new brass this year including the 6.5-284, 404 Jeffery, and 45 Basic – the latter case being drawn slightly oversize so it can be sized properly to sloppy old chambers. In cooperation with Krieghoff, Norma has designed a long, skinny rimmed 6mm case designated the 6x70R. The low-pressure cartridge is loaded with a 90-grain Nosler Ballistic Tip at 2460 fps and is chambered in Krieghoff's combination guns. www.norma.cc

North Fork Technologies

Using CNC-turned jackets and a bonded lead core, North Fork produces a sophisticated line of big-game hunting bullets in

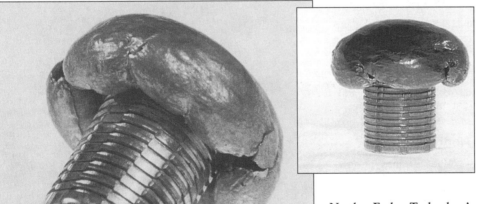

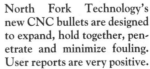

North Fork Technology's new CNC bullets are designed to expand, hold together, penetrate and minimize fouling. User reports are very positive.

Based on precision J4 jackets, Nosler's new 155-grain 308-caliber match bullet is designed for Palma, service and silhouette competition.

Responding to requests for a streamlined 9.3mm hunting bullet, Nosler is introducing a 250-grain 9.3mm Ballistic Tip.

calibers 284-416. These are unusual-looking bullets in that the bearing portion of the solid alloy shank is grooved to reduce copper fouling. Reports from African *PH*s indicate the bullet can be driven through a Cape buffalo from stem-to-stern with excellent expansion and weight retention. Tel: (307)436-2726

Northern Precision

Never at a loss for new custom bullet designs, William Noody has developed a 30-caliber "Versatile Benchrest" bullet in 180-230 grain weights. The bullets feature a low-fouling, tapered jacket; a bonded core and can double as a hunting bullet. A similar bonded-core design – but with a heavier

For handgun hunters, Nosler has designed a 90-grain 6mm Ballistic Tip that expands at more moderate velocities.

jacket for the sizzling velocities of the Lazzeroni Warbird, 300 Ultra Mag and 30-378 Weatherby – is also being offered this year. The company is also offering 50- and 54-caliber muzzleloading sabots featuring spitzer-tipped, bonded-core, 44-caliber bullets in 240 to 350 grain weights. I've been shooting Noody's 150- and 160-grain bonded core, J4-jacketed, "Whitetail" bullets this past year in a 308 Winchester and I've been very pleased with their accuracy, performance and low fouling qualities. Tel: (315)493-1711

Nosler

This is a "Ballistic Tip" year for Nosler with the introduction of some great new calibers and grain weights. In the expanded Ballistic Tip line, there's a 90-grain 243 handgun hunting bullet; a 80-grain 243 varmint bullet; a 180-grain 8mm and a 250-grain 9.3mm. Being added to the competition bullet line is a 30-caliber, 155-grain JHP based on the precision J4 jacket. www.nosler.com

Old Western Scrounger

Dangerous Dave now carries the full Kynoch line, so if you need anything from 700 Nitro to 318 Wesley Richards, the *OWS* has it. Several new calibers have been added to the "obsolete" ammunition line – the 7.92x33 *Kurz*; 11mm French Ordnance Revolver and, for you Chicago Palm Pistol owners, the 32 Extra Short Rimfire. OWS is producing loaded ammunition and brass for the 405 Winchester, featuring a 300-grain Woodleigh bullet at 2200 fps. Dave is considering contracting for 1,000,000 round runs of the 5mm Rem. Rimfire Mag. and the 25 Stevens Long Rimfire, so ring him up later. The new catalog's a scream, and filled with rare goodies. www.ows-ammunition.com

Laser-Cast's latest 170-grain 30-caliber gas-checked cast bullet is economical and suitable for everything from 30-30s to 300 magnums.

Remington continues to expand its UMC Leadless line with the addition of the 40 S&W.

Oregon Trail Laser-Cast Bullets

Three sensational new rifle bullets have been added to the Laser Cast lineup. First, there's a gas-check, 170-grain 30-caliber RNFP sized to .309" that is perfect for any 30-caliber. I've been using this bullet in a 30-30 at velocities up to 1970 fps with little or no leading. Its accuracy has been outstanding. Then there are two plain-base bullets – a 170-grain 32-caliber RNFP

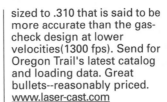

sized either .321" or .323", making it useful for the 32-40, 32 Special, and 8mms; plus a 165-grain 30-caliber RNFP

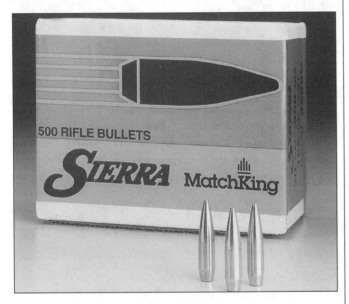

Sierra's latest MatchKing offering is a sleek 250-grain .338-caliber bullet with extremely high ballistic coefficients.

sized to .310 that is said to be more accurate than the gas-check design at lower velocities(1300 fps). Send for Oregon Trail's latest catalog and loading data. Great bullets--reasonably priced. www.laser-cast.com

Remington

Big Green has been highly focussed on rounding out their Ultra Mag line with the addition of new premium bullet loads for the 7mm, 300, 338 and 375 Ultra Mags. At the same time, a new Sirocco Bonded bullet line has been added in 270 Win., 7mm Rem. Mag., 308 Win., and 30-06. In the Premier centerfire line, the 22-250 and the 7mm-08 have been added — loaded with Nosler Partitions. With the interest in lead-free ammunition accelerating, Remington has added a UMC Leadless line that includes the 9mm, 380 Auto, 38 Special, 40 S&W and 45 Auto – and developed leadless frangible loads for the 38 Special and 357 Sig. For large volume varmint hunters, inexpensive 223 and 22-250 loadings have been added to the UMC-brand label. Velocity is up in their Premier copper-plated turkey loads with the 3- and 3 1/2-inch shell in #4, 5, and 6 shot at 1300 fps while 2 3/4-inch 12 and 20 gauge loadings in the Upland Express line are now launched at 1400 and 1300 fps, respectively. Finally, a new 1-oz loading of #7 1/2 and #8 at 1290 fps has been added as a 12 gauge Nitro 27 Handicap load. www.remington.com

Sellier & Bellot

Here's a step back in history, S&B has introduced a complete, across-the-gauges line of paper shotshells and a full line of 7/8 and 1 oz. loadings for the 28 gauge. There's also a 174-grain HPBT target load for the 7.62x54mmR and a 196-grain FMJ loading for the 8mm Mauser. www.sb-usa.com

Sierra

The 'Bulletsmiths' have been playing catch-up ball with their extensive lines. The new product this year is a 250-grain 338 HPBT MatchKing. See their informative catalog and series of technical newsletters at www.sierrabullets.com

Simunition

Simunition makes and distributes highly refined lines of non-lethal practice ammunition that can be fired in a trainee's personal service weapon. Some of the products are designed for face-to-face combat practice with padded clothing while others are for close-quarter combat target ranges. www.simunition.com

SSK

JD Jones continues to expand his "Whisper" series--this year with a 510 Whisper that is based on the 333 Lapua case. Loaded with only 25 grains of powder and the 750-grain Hornady A-MAX bullet, this subsonic round is reportedly capable of 6-inch groups at 600 yards. SSK's radically "*blown-out*" '06-based single-shot pistol

SSK's diminutive 510 Whisper takes 25 grains of powder and generates 1500 fps with a 600-grain bullet.

The 270 JDJ#2 is SSK's radically "improved" case that is also available as a 257 or 6.5mm.

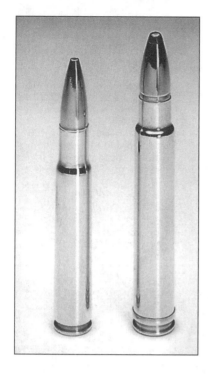

Weatherby is the first major manufacturer to offer the excellent 338-06 A-Square as a standard chambering.

Winchester's radical 300 Short Magnum delivers 300 Win. Mag. performance in a compact, accurate cartridge – perfect for short-action rifles.

rounds now include the 257, 6.5 and 270 calibers. Finally, Jones reports he's working on a 40mm practice round, using a 30-caliber tracer to duplicate the 40mm's trajectory.
www.sskindustries.com

Swift Bullets

Three new Sirocco bullets make their debut this year: 165- and 180-grain 308s and a 130-grain 270 pill.
www.swiftbullets.com

Weatherby

Weatherby will be the first major firm to offer the 338-06 A-Square as a factory round. Loaded with a 210-grain Nolser, the legitimized 338 wildcat produces 2750 fps at the muzzle. Returning to the Weatherby line, after being absent for too many years, is the ever-effective 375 Weatherby Magnum, loaded with a 300-grain Nosler Partition at 2800 fps. See these exciting new loads at www.weatherby.com

Winchester

Big news this year has been the introduction of Winchester's new rifle cartridge, the 300 Winchester Short Magnum, dubbed the 300 WSM. Chambered initially in short-action Browning A-Bolts and Winchester Model 70 Featherweights, this highly efficient round features a 35-degree shoulder, rebated rim

and a short overall length of 2.8 inches. Initial factory loads feature 180-grain Failsafes and Power-Points at 2970 fps and a 150-grain Ballistic Silvertip at 3300 fps. I'm predicting we may see a 270 WSM in the future.

Winchester has launched a new line of shotshells called Western Target and Field Loads in 12 and 20 gauges and with #7 1/2 and #8 shot for the sporting clays market. For slug hunters, there's an interesting new 20 gauge loading featuring a 260-grain Partition Gold slug at 1900 fps. Some of the most reasonable plinking loads around are Winchester's USA brand 223 with either a 55- or 62-grain FMJ and the 147-grain FMJ in the 30-06. The economical USA Brand line also has been upgraded with the addition of jacketed hollow points for the 38 Special, 9mm, 357 SIG, 40 S&W and 45 Auto. And, to satisfy the demand for leadless loads, the WinClean pistol ammunition line has been expanded to include the 9mm Luger with either a 124- or 147-grain bullet and the 357 SIG loaded with a 125-grain WinClean projectile.
www.winchester.com

Wolf

As an importer of ammunition from Russia's Tula Cartridge Works, Wolf continues to expand the line of non-corrosive, steel-cased ammunition. A number of new loads and calibers are

Winchester's new 20 gauge Partition Gold slug, at 1900 fps, offers a flat trajectory – plus excellent penetration of light big game.

Sporting clays shooters should be pleased with Winchester's new Western Target and Field Loads available in #7 1/2 and #8 shot.

being added this year, including the 40 S&W, 223 Rem. HP, 7.62x39mm SP, 7.62x54mmR HP, and match-

grade brass-cased 22 rimfire.
www.wolfammo.com
It's been a busy year. ●

AVERAGE CENTERFIRE RIFLE CARTRIDGE BALLISTICS AND PRICES

Many manufacturers do not supply suggested retail prices. Others did not get their pricing to us before press time. All pricing can vary dependent on the exact brand and style of ammo selected and/or the retail outlet from which you make your purchase. Pricing has been rounded to the nearest dollar and represents our best estimate of average pricing. An * after the cartridge means these loads are available with Nosler Partition or Swift A-Frame bullets. Listed pricing may or may not reflect this bullet type. ** = these are packed 50 to box, all others are 20 to box. Wea. Mag.= Weatherby Magnum. Spfd. = Springfield. A-A-Sq. = A-Square. N.E.=Nitro Express.

Cartridge	Bullet Weight Grains	VELOCITY (fps)					ENERGY (ft. lbs.)					TRAJ. (in.)				Approx. Price per box
		Muzzle	100 yds.	200 yds.	300 yds.	400 yds.	Muzzle	100 yds.	200 yds.	300 yds.	400 yds.	100 yds.	200 yds.	300 yds.	400 yds.	
17 Remington	25	4040	3284	2644	2086	1606	906	599	388	242	143	+2.0	+1.7	-4.0	-17.0	$17
221 Fireball	50	2800	2137	1580	1180	988	870	507	277	155	109	+0.0	-7.0	-28.0	NA	$14
22 Hornet	34	3050	2132	1415	1017	852	700	343	151	78	55	+0.0	-6.6	-15.5	-29.9	NA
22 Hornet	35	3100	2278	1601	1135	929	747	403	199	100	67	+2.75	0.0	-16.9	-60.4	NA
22 Hornet	45	2690	2042	1502	1128	948	723	417	225	127	90	+0.0	-7.7	-31.0	NA	$27**
218 Bee	46	2760	2102	1550	1155	961	788	451	245	136	94	+0.0	-7.2	-29.0	NA	$46**
222 Remington	40	3600	3117	2673	2269	1911	1151	863	634	457	324	++1.07	0.0	-6.13	-18.9	NA
222 Remington	50	3140	2602	2123	1700	1350	1094	752	500	321	202	++2.0	-0.4	-11.0	-33.0	$11
222 Remington	55	3020	2562	2147	1773	1451	1114	801	563	384	257	+2.0	-0.4	-11.0	-33.0	$12
22 PPC	52	3400	2930	2510	2130	NA	1335	990	730	525	NA	+2.0	1.4	-5.0	NA	NA
223 Remington	40	3650	3010	2450	1950	1530	1185	805	535	340	265	+2.0	+1.0	-6.0	-22.0	$14
223 Remington	40	3800	3305	2845	2424	2044	1282	970	719	522	371	0.84	0.0	-5.34	-16.6	NA
223 Remington	50	3300	2874	2484	2130	1809	1209	917	685	504	363	1.37	0.0	-7.05	-21.8	NA
223 Remington	52/53	3330	2882	2477	2106	1770	1305	978	722	522	369	+2.0	+0.6	-6.5	-21.5	$14
223 Remington	55	3240	2748	2305	1906	1556	1282	922	649	444	296	+2.0	-0.2	-9.0	-27.0	$12
223 Remington	60	3100	2712	2355	2026	1726	1280	979	739	547	397	+2.0	+0.2	-8.0	-24.7	$16
223 Remington	64	3020	2621	2256	1920	1619	1296	977	723	524	373	+2.0	-0.2	-9.3	-23.0	$14
223 Remington	69	3000	2720	2460	2210	1980	1380	1135	925	750	600	+2.0	+0.8	-5.8	-17.5	$15
223 Remington	75	2790	2554	2330	2119	1926	1296	1086	904	747	617	2.37	0.0	-8.75	-25.1	NA
223 Remington	77	2750	2584	2354	2169	1992	1293	1110	948	804	679	1.93	0.0	-8.2	-23.8	NA
222 Rem. Mag.	55	3240	2748	2305	1906	1556	1282	922	649	444	296	+2.0	-0.2	-9.0	-27.0	$14
225 Winchester	55	3570	3066	2616	2208	1838	1556	1148	836	595	412	+2.0	+1.0	-5.0	-20.0	$19
224 Wea. Mag.	55	3650	3192	2780	2403	2057	1627	1244	943	705	516	+2.0	+1.2	-4.0	-17.0	$32
22-250 Rem.	40	4000	3320	2720	2200	1740	1420	980	660	430	265	+2.0	+1.8	-3.0	-16.0	$14
22-250 Rem.	50	3725	3264	2641	2455	2103	1540	1183	896	669	491	0.89	0.0	-5.23	-16.3	NA
22-250 Rem.	52/55	3680	3137	2656	2222	1832	1654	1201	861	603	410	+2.0	+1.3	-4.0	-17.0	$13
22-250 Rem.	60	3600	3195	2826	2485	2169	1727	1360	1064	823	627	+2.0	+2.0	-2.4	-12.3	$19
220 Swift	40	4200	3678	3190	2739	2329	1566	1201	904	666	482	+0.51	0.0	-4.0	-12.9	NA
220 Swift	50	3780	3158	2617	2135	1710	1586	1107	760	506	325	+2.0	+1.4	-4.4	-17.9	$20
220 Swift	50	3850	3396	2970	2576	2215	1645	1280	979	736	545	0.74	0.0	-4.84	-15.1	NA
220 Swift	55	3800	3370	2990	2630	2310	1765	1390	1090	850	650	0.8	0.0	-4.7	-14.4	NA
220 Swift	55	3650	3194	2772	2384	2035	1627	1246	939	694	506	+2.0	+2.0	-2.6	-13.4	$19
220 Swift	60	3600	3199	2824	2475	2156	1727	1364	1063	816	619	+2.0	+1.6	-4.1	-13.1	$19
22 Savage H.P.	71	2790	2340	1930	1570	1280	1225	860	585	390	190	+2.0	-1.0	-10.4	-35.7	NA
6mm BR Rem.	100	2550	2310	2083	1870	1671	1444	1185	963	776	620	+2.5	-0.6	-11.8	NA	$22
6mm Norma BR	107	2822	2667	2517	2372	2229	1893	1690	1506	1337	1181	+1.73	0.0	-7.24	-20.6	NA
6mm PPC	70	3140	2750	2400	2070	NA	1535	1175	895	665	NA	+2.0	+1.4	-5.0	NA	NA
243 Winchester	55	4025	3597	3209	2853	2525	1978	1579	1257	994	779	+0.6	0.00	-4.0	-12.2	NA
243 Winchester	60	3600	3110	2660	2260	1890	1725	1285	945	680	475	+2.0	+1.8	-3.3	-15.5	$17
243 Winchester	70	3400	3040	2700	2390	2100	1795	1435	1135	890	685	1.1	0.0	-5.9	-18.0	NA
243 Winchester	75/80	3350	2955	2593	2259	1951	1993	1551	1194	906	676	+2.0	+0.9	-5.0	-19.0	$16
243 Winchester	85	3320	3070	2830	2600	2380	2080	1770	1510	1280	1070	+2.0	+1.2	-4.0	-14.0	$18
243 Winchester	90	3120	2871	2635	2411	2199	1946	1647	1388	1162	966	1.4	0.0	-6.4	-18.8	NA
243 Winchester*	100	2960	2697	2449	2215	1993	1945	1615	1332	1089	882	+2.5	+1.2	-6.0	-20.0	$16
243 Winchester	105	2920	2689	2470	2261	2062	1988	1686	1422	1192	992	+2.5	+1.6	-5.0	-18.4	$21
243 Light Mag.	100	3100	2839	2592	2358	2138	2133	1790	1491	1235	1014	+1.5	0.0	-6.8	-19.8	NA
6mm Remington	80	3470	3064	2694	2352	2036	2139	1667	1289	982	736	+2.0	+1.1	-5.0	-17.0	$16
6mm Remington	100	3100	2829	2573	2332	2104	2133	1777	1470	1207	983	+2.5	+1.6	-5.0	-17.0	$16
6mm Remington	105	3060	2822	2596	2381	2177	2105	1788	1512	1270	1059	+2.5	+1.1	-3.3	-15.0	$21
6mm Rem. Light Mag.	100	3250	2997	2756	2528	2311	2345	1995	1687	1418	1186	1.59	0.0	-6.33	-18.3	NA
6.17(.243) Spitfire	100	3350	3122	2905	2698	2501	2493	2164	1874	1617	1389	2.4	3.20	0	-8	NA
240 Wea. Mag.	87	3500	3202	2924	2663	2416	2366	1980	1651	1370	1127	+2.0	+2.0	-2.0	-12.0	$32
240 Wea. Mag.	100	3395	3106	2835	2581	2339	2559	2142	1785	1478	1215	+2.5	+2.8	-2.0	-11.0	$43
25-20 Win.	86	1460	1194	1030	931	858	407	272	203	165	141	0.0	-23.5	NA	NA	$32**
25-35 Win.	117	2230	1866	1545	1282	1097	1292	904	620	427	313	+2.5	-4.2	-26.0	NA	$24
250 Savage	100	2820	2504	2210	1936	1684	1765	1392	1084	832	630	+2.5	+0.4	-9.0	-28.0	$17

17
22

6mm
(24)

25

Many manufacturers do not supply suggested retail prices. Others did not get their pricing to us before press time. All pricing can vary dependent on the exact brand and style of ammo selected and/or the retail outlet from which you make your purchase. Pricing has been rounded to the nearest dollar and represents our best estimate of average pricing. An * after the cartridge means these loads are available with Nosler Partition or Swift A-Frame bullets. Listed pricing may or may not reflect this bullet type. ** = these are packed 50 to box, all others are 20 to box. Wea. Mag.= Weatherby Magnum. Spfd. = Springfield. A-A-Sq. = A-Square. N.E.=Nitro Express.

Cartridge	Bullet Weight Grains	VELOCITY (fps)					ENERGY (ft. lbs.)					TRAJ. (in.)				Approx. Price per box
		Muzzle	100 yds.	200 yds.	300 yds.	400 yds.	Muzzle	100 yds.	200 yds.	300 yds.	400 yds.	100 yds.	200 yds.	300 yds.	400 yds.	
25 cont.																
257 Roberts	100	2980	2661	2363	2085	1827	1972	1572	1240	965	741	+2.5	-0.8	-5.2	-21.6	$20
257 Roberts+P	117	2780	2411	2071	1761	1488	2009	1511	1115	806	576	+2.5	-0.2	-10.2	-32.6	$18
257 Roberts+P	120	2780	2560	2360	2160	1970	2060	1750	1480	1240	1030	+2.5	+1.2	-6.4	-23.6	$22
257 Roberts	122	2600	2331	2078	1842	1625	1831	1472	1169	919	715	+2.5	0.0	-10.6	-31.4	$21
257 Light Mag.	117	2940	2694	2460	2240	2031	2245	1885	1572	1303	1071	+1.7	0.0	-7.6	-21.8	NA
25-06 Rem.	87	3440	2995	2591	2222	1884	2286	1733	1297	954	686	+2.0	+1.1	-2.5	-14.4	$17
25-06 Rem.	90	3440	3043	2680	2344	2034	2364	1850	1435	1098	827	+2.0	+1.8	-3.3	-15.6	$17
25-06 Rem.	100	3230	2893	2580	2287	2014	2316	1858	1478	1161	901	+2.0	+0.8	-5.7	-18.9	$17
25-06 Rem.	117	2990	2770	2570	2370	2190	2320	2000	1715	1465	1246	+2.5	+1.0	-7.9	-26.6	$19
25-06 Rem.*	120	2990	2730	2484	2252	2032	2382	1985	1644	1351	1100	+2.5	+1.2	-5.3	-19.6	$17
25-06 Rem.	122	2930	2706	2492	2289	2095	2325	1983	1683	1419	1189	+2.5	+1.8	-4.5	-17.5	$23
257 Wea. Mag.	87	3825	3456	3118	2805	2513	2826	2308	1870	1520	1220	+2.0	+2.7	-0.3	-7.6	$32
257 Wea. Mag.	100	3555	3237	2941	2665	2404	2806	2326	1920	1576	1283	+2.5	+3.2	0.0	-8.0	$32
257 Scramjet	100	3745	3450	3173	2912	2666	3114	2643	2235	1883	1578	+2.1	+2.77	0.0	-6.93	NA
6.5																
6.5x50mm Jap.	139	2360	2160	1970	1790	1620	1720	1440	1195	985	810	+2.5	-1.0	-13.5	NA	NA
6.5x50mm Jap.	156	2070	1830	1610	1430	1260	1475	1155	900	695	550	+2.5	-4.0	-23.8	NA	NA
6.5x52mm Car.	139	2580	2360	2160	1970	1790	2045	1725	1440	1195	985	+2.5	0.0	-9.9	-29.0	NA
6.5x52mm Car.	156	2430	2170	1930	1700	1500	2045	1630	1285	1005	780	+2.5	-1.0	-13.9	NA	NA
6.5x55mm Light Mag.	129	2750	2549	2355	2171	1994	2166	1860	1589	1350	1139	+2.0	0.0	-8.2	-23.9	NA
6.5x55mm Swe.	140	2550	NA	NA	NA	NA	2020	NA	NA	NA	NA	NA	NA	NA	NA	$18
6.5x55mm Swe.*	139/140	2850	2640	2440	2250	2070	2525	2170	1855	1575	1330	+2.5	+1.6	-5.4	-18.9	$18
6.5x55mm Swe.	156	2650	2370	2110	1870	1650	2425	1950	1550	1215	945	+2.5	0.0	-10.3	-30.6	NA
260 Remington	125	2875	2669	2473	2285	2105	2294	1977	1697	1449	1230	1.71	0.0	-7.4	-21.4	NA
260 Remington	140	2750	2544	2347	2158	1979	2351	2011	1712	1448	1217	+2.2	0.0	-8.6	-24.6	NA
6.5-284 Norma	142	3025	2890	2758	2631	2507	2886	2634	2400	2183	1982	1.13	0.0	-5.7	-16.4	NA
6.71 (264) Phantom	120	3150	2929	2718	2517	2325	2645	2286	1969	1698	1440	+1.3	0.0	-6.0	-17.5	NA
6.5 Rem. Mag.	120	3210	2905	2621	2353	2102	2745	2248	1830	1475	1177	+2.5	+1.7	-4.1	-16.3	Disc.
264 Win. Mag.	140	3030	2782	2548	2326	2114	2854	2406	2018	1682	1389	+2.5	+1.4	-5.1	-18.0	$24
6.71 (264) Blackbird	140	3480	3261	3053	2855	2665	3766	3307	2899	2534	2208	+2.4	+3.1	0.0	-7.4	NA
27																
270 Winchester	100	3430	3021	2649	2305	1988	2612	2027	1557	1179	877	+2.0	+1.0	-4.9	-17.5	$17
270 Winchester	130	3060	2776	2510	2259	2022	2702	2225	1818	1472	1180	+2.5	+1.4	-5.3	-18.2	$17
270 Win. Supreme	130	3150	2881	2628	2388	2161	2865	2396	1993	1646	1348	1.3	0.0	-6.4	-18.9	NA
270 Winchester	135	3000	2780	2570	2369	2178	2697	2315	1979	1682	1421	+2.5	+1.4	-6.0	-17.6	$23
270 Winchester*	140	2940	2700	2480	2260	2060	2685	2270	1905	1590	1315	+2.5	+1.8	-4.6	-17.9	$20
270 Win. Light Magnum	130	3215	2998	2790	2590	2400	2983	2594	2246	1936	1662	1.21	0.0	-5.83	-17.0	NA
270 Winchester*	150	2850	2585	2336	2100	1879	2705	2226	1817	1468	1175	+2.5	+1.2	-6.5	-22.0	$17
270 Win. Supreme	150	2930	2693	2468	2254	2051	2860	2416	2030	1693	1402	1.7	0.0	-7.4	-21.6	NA
270 Wea. Mag.	100	3760	3380	3033	2712	2412	3139	2537	2042	1633	1292	+2.0	+2.4	-1.2	-10.1	$32
270 Wea. Mag.	130	3375	3119	2878	2649	2432	3287	2808	2390	2026	1707	+2.5	-2.9	-0.9	-9.9	$32
270 Wea. Mag.*	150	3245	3036	2837	2647	2465	3507	3070	2681	2334	2023	+2.5	+2.6	-1.8	-11.4	$47
7mm																
7mm BR	140	2216	2012	1821	1643	1481	1525	1259	1031	839	681	+2.0	-3.7	-20.0	NA	$23
7mm Mauser*	139/140	2660	2435	2221	2018	1827	2199	1843	1533	1266	1037	+2.5	0.0	-9.6	-27.7	$17
7mm Mauser	145	2690	2442	2206	1985	1777	2334	1920	1568	1268	1017	+2.5	+0.1	-9.6	-28.3	$18
7mm Mauser	154	2690	2490	2300	2120	1940	2475	2120	1810	1530	1285	+2.5	+0.8	-7.5	-23.5	$17
7mm Mauser	175	2440	2137	1857	1603	1382	2313	1774	1340	998	742	+2.5	-1.7	-16.1	NA	$17
7x57 Light Mag.	139	2970	2730	2503	2287	2082	2722	2301	1933	1614	1337	+1.6	0.0	-7.2	-21.0	NA
7x30 Waters	120	2700	2300	1930	1600	1330	1940	1405	990	685	470	+2.5	-0.2	-12.3	NA	$18
7mm-08 Rem.	120	3000	2725	2467	2223	1992	2398	1979	1621	1316	1058	+2.0	0.0	-7.6	-22.3	$18
7mm-08 Rem.*	140	2860	2625	2402	2189	1988	2542	2142	1793	1490	1228	+2.5	+0.8	-6.9	-21.9	$18
7mm-08 Rem.	154	2715	2510	2315	2128	1950	2520	2155	1832	1548	1300	+2.5	+1.0	-7.0	-22.7	$23
7mm-08 Light Mag.	139	3000	2790	2590	2399	2216	2777	2403	2071	1776	1515	+1.5	0.0	-6.7	-19.4	NA
7x64mm Bren.	140	Not Yet Announced														$17
7x64mm Bren.	154	2820	2610	2420	2230	2050	2720	2335	1995	1695	1430	+2.5	+1.4	-5.7	-19.9	NA
7x64mm Bren.*	160	2850	2669	2495	2327	2166	2885	2530	2211	1924	1667	+2.5	+1.6	-4.8	-17.8	$24
7x64mm Bren.	175	Not Yet Announced														$17

Many manufacturers do not supply suggested retail prices. Others did not get their pricing to us before press time. All pricing can vary dependent on the exact brand and style of ammo selected and/or the retail outlet from which you make your purchase. Pricing has been rounded to the nearest dollar and represents our best estimate of average pricing. An * after the cartridge means these loads are available with Nosler Partition or Swift A-Frame bullets. Listed pricing may or may not reflect this bullet type. ** = these are packed 50 to box, all others are 20 to box. Wea. Mag.= Weatherby Magnum. Spfd. = Springfield. A-A-Sq. = A-Square. N.E.=Nitro Express.

Cartridge	Bullet Weight Grains	VELOCITY (fps)					ENERGY (ft. lbs.)					TRAJ. (in.)				Approx. Price per box
		Muzzle	100 yds.	200 yds.	300 yds.	400 yds.	Muzzle	100 yds.	200 yds.	300 yds.	400 yds.	100 yds.	200 yds.	300 yds.	400 yds.	
284 Winchester	150	2860	2595	2344	2108	1886	2724	2243	1830	1480	1185	+2.5	+0.8	-7.3	-23.2	$24
280 Remington	120	3150	2866	2599	2348	2110	2643	2188	1800	1468	1186	+2.0	+0.6	-6.0	-17.9	$17
280 Remington	140	3000	2758	2528	2309	2102	2797	2363	1986	1657	1373	+2.5	+1.4	-5.2	-18.3	$17
280 Remington*	150	2890	2624	2373	2135	1912	2781	2293	1875	1518	1217	+2.5	+0.8	-7.1	-22.6	$17
280 Remington	160	2840	2637	2442	2556	2078	2866	2471	2120	1809	1535	+2.5	+0.8	-6.7	-21.0	$20
280 Remington	165	2820	2510	2220	1950	1701	2913	2308	1805	1393	1060	+2.5	+0.4	-8.8	-26.5	$17
7x61mm S&H Sup.	154	3060	2720	2400	2100	1820	3200	2520	1965	1505	1135	+2.5	+1.8	-5.0	-19.8	NA
7mm Dakota	160	3200	3001	2811	2630	2455	3637	3200	2808	2456	2140	+2.1	+1.9	-2.8	-12.5	NA
7mm Rem. Mag.*	139/140	3150	2930	2710	2510	2320	3085	2660	2290	1960	1670	+2.5	+2.4	-2.4	-12.7	$21
7mm Rem. Mag.	150/154	3110	2830	2568	2320	2085	3221	2667	2196	1792	1448	+2.5	+1.6	-4.6	-16.5	$21
7mm Rem. Mag.*	160/162	2950	2730	2520	2320	2120	3090	2650	2250	1910	1600	+2.5	+1.8	-4.4	-17.8	$34
7mm Rem. Mag.	165	2900	2699	2507	2324	2147	3081	2669	2303	1978	1689	+2.5	+1.2	-5.9	-19.0	$28
7mm Rem Mag.	175	2860	2645	2440	2244	2057	3178	2718	2313	1956	1644	+2.5	+1.0	-6.5	-20.7	$21
7mm Wea. Mag.	140	3225	2970	2729	2501	2283	3233	2741	2315	1943	1621	+2.5	+2.0	-3.2	-14.0	$35
7mm Wea. Mag.	154	3260	3023	2799	2586	2382	3539	3044	2609	2227	1890	+2.5	+2.8	-1.5	-10.8	$32
7mm Wea. Mag.*	160	3200	3004	2816	2637	2464	3637	3205	2817	2469	2156	+2.5	+2.7	-1.5	-10.6	$47
7mm Wea. Mag.	165	2950	2747	2553	2367	2189	3188	2765	2388	2053	1756	+2.5	+1.8	-4.2	-16.4	$43
7mm Wea. Mag.	175	2910	2693	2486	2288	2098	3293	2818	2401	2033	1711	+2.5	+1.2	-5.9	-19.4	$35
7.21(.284) Tomahawk	140	3300	3118	2943	2774	2612	3386	3022	2693	2393	2122	2.3	3.20	0.0	-7.7	NA
7mm STW	140	3325	3064	2818	2585	2364	3436	2918	2468	2077	1737	+2.3	+1.8	-3.0	-13.1	NA
7mm STW Supreme	160	3150	2894	2652	2422	2204	3526	2976	2499	2085	1727	1.3	0.0	-6.3	-18.5	NA
7mm Rem. Ultra Mag.	140	3425	3184	2956	2740	2534	3646	3151	2715	2333	1995	1.7	1.60	-2.6	-11.4	NA
7mm Firehawk	140	3625	3373	3135	2909	2695	4084	3536	3054	2631	2258	+2.2	+2.9	0.0	-7.03	NA
7.21 (.284) Firebird	140	3750	3522	3306	3101	2905	4372	3857	3399	2990	2625	1.6	2.4	0.0	-6	NA
30 Carbine	110	1990	1567	1236	1035	923	977	600	373	262	208	0.0	-13.5	NA	NA	$28**
303 Savage	190	1890	1612	1327	1183	1055	1507	1096	794	591	469	+2.5	-7.6	NA	NA	$24
30 Remington	170	2120	1822	1555	1328	1153	1696	1253	913	666	502	+2.5	-4.7	-26.3	NA	$20
7.62x39mm Rus.	123/125	2300	2030	1780	1550	1350	1445	1125	860	655	500	+2.5	-2.0	-17.5	NA	$13
30-30 Win.	55	3400	2693	2085	1570	1187	1412	886	521	301	172	+2.0	0.0	-10.2	-35.0	$18
30-30 Win.	125	2570	2090	1660	1320	1080	1830	1210	770	480	320	-2.0	-2.6	-19.9	NA	$13
30-30 Win.	150	2390	1973	1605	1303	1095	1902	1296	858	565	399	+2.5	-3.2	-22.5	NA	$13
30-30 Win. Supreme	150	2480	2095	1747	1446	1209	2049	1462	1017	697	487	0.0	-6.5	-24.5		NA
30-30 Win.	160	2300	1997	1719	1473	1268	1879	1416	1050	771	571	+2.5	-2.9	-20.2	NA	$18
30-30 PMC Cowboy	170	1300	1198	1121			638	474				0.0	-27.0			NA
30-30 Win.*	170	2200	1895	1619	1381	1191	1827	1355	989	720	535	+2.5	-5.8	-23.6	NA	$13
300 Savage	150	2630	2354	2094	1853	1631	2303	1845	1462	1143	886	+2.5	-0.4	-10.1	-30.7	$17
300 Savage	180	2350	2137	1935	1754	1570	2207	1825	1496	1217	985	+2.5	-1.6	-15.2	NA	$17
30-40 Krag	180	2430	2213	2007	1813	1632	2360	1957	1610	1314	1064	+2.5	-1.4	-13.8	NA	$18
7.65x53mm Arg.	180	2590	2390	2200	2010	1830	2685	2280	1925	1615	1345	+2.5	0.0	-27.6	NA	NA
307 Winchester	150	2760	2321	1924	1575	1289	2530	1795	1233	826	554	+2.5	-1.5	-13.6	NA	Disc.
307 Winchester	180	2510	2179	1874	1599	1362	2519	1898	1404	1022	742	+2.5	-1.6	-15.6	NA	$20
7.5x55 Swiss	180	2650	2450	2250	2060	1880	2805	2390	2020	1700	1415	+2.5	+0.6	-8.1	-24.9	NA
308 Winchester	55	3770	3215	2726	2286	1888	1735	1262	907	638	435	-2.0	+1.4	-3.8	-15.8	$22
308 Winchester	150	2820	2533	2263	2009	1774	2648	2137	1705	1344	1048	+2.5	+0.4	-8.5	-26.1	$17
308 Winchester	165	2700	2440	2194	1963	1748	2670	2180	1763	1411	1199	+2.5	0.0	-9.7	-28.5	$20
308 Winchester	168	2680	2493	2314	2143	1979	2678	2318	1998	1713	1460	+2.5	0.0	-8.9	-25.3	$18
308 Winchester	178	2620	2415	2220	2034	1857	2713	2306	1948	1635	1363	+2.5	0.0	-9.6	-27.6	$23
308 Winchester*	180	2620	2393	2178	1974	1782	2743	2288	1896	1557	1269	+2.5	-0.2	-10.2	-28.5	$17
308 Light Mag.*	150	2980	2703	2442	2195	1964	2959	2433	1986	1606	1285	+1.6	0.0	-7.5	-22.2	NA
308 Light Mag.	165	2870	2658	2456	2263	2078	3019	2589	2211	1877	1583	+1.7	0.0	-7.5	-21.8	NA
308 High Energy	165	2870	2600	2350	2120	1890	3020	2485	2030	1640	1310	+1.8	0.0	-8.2	-24.0	NA
308 Light Mag.	168	2870	2658	2456	2263	2078	3019	2589	2211	1877	1583	+1.7	0.0	-7.5	-21.8	NA
308 High Energy	180	2740	2550	2370	2200	2030	3000	2600	2245	1925	1645	+1.9	0.0	-8.2	-23.5	NA
30-06 Spfd.	55	4080	3485	2965	2502	2083	2033	1483	1074	764	530	+2.0	+1.9	-2.1	-11.7	$22
30-06 Spfd.	125	3140	2780	2447	2138	1853	2736	2145	1662	1279	953	+2.0	+1.0	-6.2	-21.0	$17

Many manufacturers do not supply suggested retail prices. Others did not get their pricing to us before press time. All pricing can vary dependent on the exact brand and style of ammo selected and/or the retail outlet from which you make your purchase. Pricing has been rounded to the nearest dollar and represents our best estimate of average pricing. An * after the cartridge means these loads are available with Nosler Partition or Swift A-Frame bullets. Listed pricing may or may not reflect this bullet type. ** = these are packed 50 to box, all others are 20 to box. Wea. Mag.= Weatherby Magnum. Spfd. = Springfield. A-A-Sq. = A-Square. N.E.=Nitro Express.

Cartridge	Bullet Weight Grains	VELOCITY (fps)					ENERGY (ft. lbs.)					TRAJ. (in.)				Approx. Price per box
		Muzzle	100 yds.	200 yds.	300 yds.	400 yds.	Muzzle	100 yds.	200 yds.	300 yds.	400 yds.	100 yds.	200 yds.	300 yds.	400 yds.	
30-06 Spfd.	150	2910	2617	2342	2083	1853	2820	2281	1827	1445	1135	+2.5	+0.8	-7.2	-23.4	$17
30-06 Spfd.	152	2910	2654	2413	2184	1968	2858	2378	1965	1610	1307	+2.5	+1.0	-6.6	-21.3	$23
30-06 Spfd.*	165	2800	2534	2283	2047	1825	2872	2352	1909	1534	1220	+2.5	+0.4	-8.4	-25.5	$17
30-06 Spfd.	168	2710	2522	2346	2169	2003	2739	2372	2045	1754	1497	+2.5	+0.4	-8.0	-23.5	$18
30-06 Spfd.	178	2720	2511	2311	2121	1939	2924	2491	2111	1777	1486	+2.5	+0.4	-8.2	-24.6	$23
30-06 Spfd.*	180	2700	2469	2250	2042	1846	2913	2436	2023	1666	1362	-2.5	0.0	-9.3	-27.0	$17
30-06 Spfd.	220	2410	2130	1870	1632	1422	2837	2216	1708	1301	988	+2.5	-1.7	-18.0	NA	$17
30-06 Light Mag.	150	3100	2815	2548	2295	2058	3200	2639	2161	1755	1410	+1.4	0.0	-6.8	-20.3	NA
30-06 Light Mag.	180	2880	2676	2480	2293	2114	3316	2862	2459	2102	1786	+1.7	0.0	-7.3	-21.3	NA
30-06 High Energy	180	2880	2690	2500	2320	2150	3315	2880	2495	2150	1845	+1.7	0.0	-7.2	-21.0	NA
7.82 (308) Patriot	150	3250	2999	2762	2537	2323	3519	2997	2542	2145	1798	+1.2	0.0	-5.8	-16.9	NA
300 WSM	150	3300	3061	2834	2619	2414	3628	3121	2676	2285	1941	1.1	0.0	-5.4	-15.9	NA
300 WSM	180	2970	2741	2524	2317	2120	3526	3005	2547	2147	1797	1.6	0.0	-7.0	-20.5	NA
308 Norma Mag.	180	3020	2820	2630	2440	2270	3645	3175	2755	2385	2050	+2.5	+2.0	-3.5	-14.8	NA
300 Dakota	200	3000	2824	2656	2493	2336	3996	3542	3131	2760	2423	+2.2	+1.5	-4.0	-15.2	NA
300 H&H Magnum*	180	2880	2640	2412	2196	1990	3315	2785	2325	1927	1583	+2.5	+0.8	-6.8	-21.7	$24
300 H&H Magnum	220	2550	2267	2002	1757	NA	3167	2510	1958	1508	NA	-2.5	-0.4	-12.0	NA	NA
300 Peterson	180	3500	3319	3145	2978	2817	4896	4401	3953	3544	3172	+2.3	+2.9	0.0	-6.8	NA
300 Win. Mag.	150	3290	2951	2636	2342	2068	3605	2900	2314	1827	1424	+2.5	+1.9	-3.8	-15.8	$22
300 Win. Mag.	165	3100	2877	2665	2462	2269	3522	3033	2603	2221	1897	+2.5	+2.4	-3.0	-16.9	$24
300 Win. Mag.	178	2900	2760	2568	2375	2191	3509	3030	2606	2230	1897	+2.5	+1.4	-5.0	-17.6	$29
300 Win. Mag.*	180	2960	2745	2540	2344	2157	3501	3011	2578	2196	1859	+2.5	+1.2	-5.5	-18.5	$22
300 W.M. High Energy	180	3100	2830	2580	2340	2110	3840	3205	2660	2190	1790	+1.4	0.0	-6.6	-19.7	NA
300 W.M. Light Mag.	180	3100	2879	2668	2467	2275	3840	3313	2845	2431	2068	+1.39	0.0	-6.45	-18.7	NA
300 Win. Mag.	190	2885	1691	2506	2327	2156	3511	3055	2648	2285	1961	+2.5	+1.2	-5.7	-19.0	$26
300 W.M. High Energy	200	2930	2740	2550	2370	2200	3810	3325	2885	2495	2145	+1.6	0.0	-6.9	-20.1	NA
300 Win. Mag.*	200	2825	2595	2376	2167	1970	3545	2991	2508	2086	1742	-2.5	+1.6	-4.7	-17.2	$36
300 Win. Mag.	220	2680	2448	2228	2020	1823	3508	2927	2424	1993	1623	+2.5	0.0	-9.5	-27.5	$23
300 Rem. Ultra Mag.	150	3450	3208	2980	2762	2556	3964	3427	2956	2541	2175	1.7	1.5	-2.6	-11.2	NA
300 Rem. Ultra Mag.	180	3250	3037	2834	2640	2454	4221	3686	3201	2786	2407	2.4		-3.0	-12.7	NA
300 Rem. Ultra Mag.	200	3025	2826	2636	2454	2279	4063	3547	3086	2673	2308	2.4	0.0	-3.4	-14.6	NA
300 Wea. Mag.	100	3900	3441	3038	2652	2305	3714	2891	2239	1717	1297	+2.0	+2.6	-0.6	-8.7	$32
300 Wea. Mag.	150	3600	3307	3033	2776	2533	4316	3642	3064	2566	2137	+2.5	+3.2	0.0	-8.1	$32
300 Wea. Mag.	165	3450	3210	3000	2792	2593	4360	3796	3297	2855	2464	+2.5	+3.2	0.0	-7.8	NA
300 Wea. Mag.	178	3120	2902	2695	2497	2308	3847	3329	2870	2464	2104	+2.5	-1.7	-3.6	-14.7	$43
300 Wea. Mag.	180	3330	3110	2910	2710	2520	4430	3875	3375	2935	2540	+1.0	0.0	-5.2	-15.1	NA
300 Wea. Mag.	190	3030	2830	2638	2455	2279	3873	3378	2936	2542	2190	+2.5	+1.6	-4.3	-16.0	$38
300 Wea. Mag.	220	2850	2541	2283	1964	1736	3967	3155	2480	1922	1471	+2.5	+0.4	-8.5	-26.4	$35
300 Warbird	180	3400	3180	2971	2772	2582	4620	4042	3528	3071	2664	+2.59	+3.25	0.0	-7.95	NA
300 Pegasus	180	3500	3319	3145	2978	2817	4896	4401	3953	3544	3172	+2.28	+2.89	0.0	-6.79	NA
32-20 Win.	100	1210	1021	913	834	769	325	231	185	154	131	0.0	-32.3	NA	NA	$23**
303 British	150	2685	2441	2210	1992	1787	2401	1984	1627	1321	1064	+2.5	+0.6	-8.4	-26.2	$18
303 British	180	2460	2124	1817	1542	1311	2418	1803	1319	950	687	+2.5	-1.8	-16.8	NA	$18
303 Light Mag.	150	2830	2570	2325	2094	1884	2667	2199	1800	1461	1185	+2.0	0.0	-8.4	-24.6	NA
7.62x54mm Rus.	146	2950	2730	2520	2320	NA	2820	2415	2055	1740	NA	+2.5	+2.0	-4.4	-17.7	NA
7.62x54mm Rus.	180	2580	2370	2180	2000	1820	2650	2250	1900	1590	1100	+2.5	0.0	-9.8	-28.5	NA
7.7x58mm Jap.	180	2500	2300	2100	1920	1750	2490	2105	1770	1475	1225	+2.5	0.0	-10.4	-30.2	NA
8x57mm JS Mau.	165	2850	2520	2210	1930	1670	2965	2330	1795	1360	1015	+2.5	+1.0	-7.7	NA	NA
32 Win. Special	170	2250	1921	1626	1372	1175	1911	1393	998	710	521	+2.5	-3.5	-22.9	NA	$14
8mm Mauser	170	2360	1969	1622	1333	1123	2102	1464	993	671	476	+2.5	-3.1	-22.2	NA	$18
8mm Rem. Mag.	185	3080	2761	2464	2186	1927	3896	3131	2494	1963	1525	+2.5	+1.4	-5.5	-19.7	$30
8mm Rem. Mag.	220	2830	2581	2346	2123	1913	3912	3254	2688	2201	1787	+2.5	+0.6	-7.6	-23.5	Disc.
338-06	200	2750	2553	2364	2184	2011	3358	2894	2482	2118	1796	+1.9	0.0	-8.22	-23.6	NA
330 Dakota	250	2900	2719	2545	2378	2217	4668	4103	3595	3138	2727	+2.3	+1.3	-5.0	-17.5	NA
338 Lapua	250	2963	2795	2640	2493	NA	4842	4341	3881	3458	NA	+1.9	0.0	-7.9	NA	NA
338 Win. Mag.	200	2960	2658	2375	2110	1862	3890	3137	2505	1977	1539	+2.5	+1.0	-6.7	-22.3	$27
338 Win. Mag.*	210	2830	2590	2370	2150	1940	3735	3130	2610	2155	1760	+2.5	+1.4	-6.0	-20.9	$33
338 Win. Mag.*	225	2785	2517	2266	2029	1808	3871	3165	2565	2057	1633	+2.5	+0.4	-8.5	-25.9	$27

30

30 Mag.

31

8mm

33

Many manufacturers do not supply suggested retail prices. Others did not get their pricing to us before press time. All pricing can vary dependent on the exact brand and style of ammo selected and/or the retail outlet from which you make your purchase. Pricing has been rounded to the nearest dollar and represents our best estimate of average pricing. An * after the cartridge means these loads are available with Nosler Partition or Swift A-Frame bullets. Listed pricing may or may not reflect this bullet type. ** = these are packed 50 to box, all others are 20 to box. Wea. Mag.= Weatherby Magnum. Spfd. = Springfield. A-A-Sq. = A-Square. N.E.=Nitro Express.

Cartridge	Bullet Weight Grains	VELOCITY (fps)					ENERGY (ft. lbs.)					TRAJ. (in.)				Approx. Price per box
		Muzzle	100 yds.	200 yds.	300 yds.	400 yds.	Muzzle	100 yds.	200 yds.	300 yds.	400 yds.	100 yds.	200 yds.	300 yds.	400 yds.	
338 W.M. Heavy Mag.	225	2920	2678	2449	2232	2027	4259	3583	2996	2489	2053	+1.75	0.0	-7.65	-22.0	NA
338 W.M. High Energy	225	2940	2690	2450	2230	2010	4320	3610	3000	2475	2025	+1.7	0.0	-7.5	-22.0	NA
338 Win. Mag.	230	2780	2573	2375	2186	2005	3948	3382	2881	2441	2054	+2.5	+1.2	-6.3	-21.0	$40
338 Win. Mag.*	250	2660	2456	2261	2075	1898	3927	3348	2837	2389	1999	+2.5	+0.2	-9.0	-26.2	$27
338 W.M. High Energy	250	2800	2610	2420	2250	2080	4350	3775	3260	2805	2395	+1.8	0.0	-7.8	-22.5	NA
338 Ultra Mag.	250	2860	2645	2440	2244	2057	4540	3882	3303	2794	2347	1.7	0.0	-7.6	-22.1	NA
8.59(.338) Galaxy	200	3100	2899	2707	2524	2347	4269	3734	3256	2829	2446	3	3.80	0.0	-9.3	NA
340 Wea. Mag.*	210	3250	2991	2746	2515	2295	4924	4170	3516	2948	2455	+2.5	+1.9	-1.8	-11.8	$56
340 Wea. Mag.*	250	3000	2806	2621	2443	2272	4995	4371	3812	3311	2864	+2.5	+2.0	-3.5	-14.8	$56
338 A-Square	250	3120	2799	2500	2220	1958	5403	4348	3469	2736	2128	+2.5	+2.7	-1.5	-10.5	NA
338-378 Wea. Mag.	225	3180	2974	2778	2591	2410	5052	4420	3856	3353	2902	3.1	3.80	0.0	-8.9	NA
338 Titan	225	3230	3010	2800	2600	2409	5211	4524	3916	3377	2898	+3.07	+3.80	0.0	-8.95	NA
338 Excalibur	200	3600	3361	3134	2920	2715	5755	5015	4363	3785	3274	+2.23	+2.87	0.0	-6.99	NA
338 Excalibur	250	3250	2922	2618	2333	2066	5863	4740	3804	3021	2370	+1.3	0.0	-6.35	-19.2	NA
348 Winchester	200	2520	2215	1931	1672	1443	2820	2178	1656	1241	925	+2.5	-1.4	-14.7	NA	$42
357 Magnum	158	1830	1427	1138	980	883	1175	715	454	337	274	0.0	-16.2	-33.1	NA	$25**
35 Remington	150	2300	1874	1506	1218	1039	1762	1169	755	494	359	+2.5	-4.1	-26.3	NA	$16
35 Remington	200	2080	1698	1376	1140	1001	1921	1280	841	577	445	+2.5	-6.3	-17.1	-33.6	$16
356 Winchester	200	2460	2114	1797	1517	1284	2688	1985	1434	1022	732	+2.5	-1.8	-15.1	NA	$31
356 Winchester	250	2160	1911	1682	1476	1299	2591	2028	1571	1210	937	+2.5	-3.7	-22.2	NA	$31
358 Winchester	200	2490	2171	1876	1619	1379	2753	2093	1563	1151	844	+2.5	-1.6	-15.6	NA	$31
358 STA	275	2850	2562	2292	2039	NA	4958	4009	3208	2539	NA	+1.9	0.0	-8.6	NA	NA
350 Rem. Mag.	200	2710	2410	2130	1870	1631	3261	2579	2014	1553	1181	+2.5	-0.2	-10.0	-30.1	$33
35 Whelen	200	2675	2378	2100	1842	1606	3177	2510	1958	1506	1145	+2.5	-0.2	-10.3	-31.1	$20
35 Whelen	225	2500	2300	2110	1930	1770	3120	2650	2235	1870	1560	+2.6	0.0	-10.2	-29.9	NA
35 Whelen	250	2400	2197	2005	1823	1652	3197	2680	2230	1844	1515	+2.5	-1.2	-13.7	NA	$20
358 Norma Mag.	250	2800	2510	2230	1970	1730	4350	3480	2750	2145	1655	+2.5	+1.0	-7.6	-25.2	NA
358 STA	275	2850	2562	229*2	2039	1764	4959	4009	3208	2539	1899	+1.9	0.0	-8.58	-26.1	NA
9.3x57mm Mau.	286	2070	1810	1590	1390	1110	2710	2090	1600	1220	955	+2.5	-2.6	-22.5	NA	NA
9.3x62mm Mau.	286	2360	2089	1844	1623	NA	3538	2771	2157	1670	1260	+2.5	-1.6	-21.0	NA	NA
9.3x64mm	286	2700	2505	2318	2139	1968	4629	3984	3411	2906	2460	+2.5	+2.7	-4.5	-19.2	NA
9.3x74Rmm	286	2360	2089	1844	1623	NA	3538	2771	2157	1670	NA	+2.5	-2.0	-11.0	NA	NA
38-55 Win.	255	1320	1190	1091	1018	963	987	802	674	587	525	0.0	-23.4	NA	NA	$25
375 Winchester	200	2200	1841	1526	1268	1089	2150	1506	1034	714	527	+2.5	-4.0	-26.2	NA	$27
375 Winchester	250	1900	1647	1424	1239	1103	2005	1506	1126	852	676	+2.5	-6.9	-33.3	NA	$27
376 Steyr	225	2600	2331	2078	1842	1625	3377	2714	2157	1694	1319	2.5	0.0	-10.6	-31.4	NA
376 Steyr	270	2600	2372	2156	1951	1759	4052	3373	2787	2283	1855	2.3	0.0	-9.9	-28.9	NA
375 Dakota	300	2600	2316	2051	1804	1579	4502	3573	2800	2167	1661	+2.4	0.0	-11.0	-32.7	NA
375 N.E. 2-1/2"	270	2000	1740	1507	1310	NA	2398	1815	1362	1026	NA	+2.5	-6.0	-30.0	NA	NA
375 Flanged	300	2450	2150	1886	1640	NA	3998	3102	2369	1790	NA	+2.5	-2.4	-17.0	NA	NA
375 H&H Magnum	250	2670	2450	2240	2040	1850	3955	3335	2790	2315	1905	+2.5	-0.4	-10.2	-28.4	NA
375 H&H Magnum	270	2690	2420	2166	1928	1707	4337	3510	2812	2228	1747	+2.5	0.0	-10.0	-29.4	$28
375 H&H Magnum*	300	2530	2245	1979	1733	1512	4263	3357	2608	2001	1523	+2.5	-1.0	-10.5	-33.6	$28
375 H&H Hvy. Mag.	270	2870	2628	2399	2182	1976	4937	4141	3451	2150	1845	+1.7	0.0	-7.2	-21.0	NA
375 H&H Hvy. Mag.	300	2705	2386	2090	1816	1568	4873	3793	2908	2195	1637	+2.3	0.0	-10.4	-31.4	NA
375 Rem. Ultra Mag.	270	2900	2558	2241	1947	1678	5041	3922	3010	2272	1689	1.9	2.7	-8.9	-27	NA
375 Rem. Ultra Mag.	300	2760	2505	2263	2035	1822	5073	4178	3412	2759	2210	2.0	0.0	-8.8	-26.1	NA
375 Wea. Mag.	300	2700	2420	2157	1911	1685	4856	3901	3100	2432	1891	+2.5	-.04	-10.7	-	NA
378 Wea. Mag.	270	3180	2976	2781	2594	2415	6062	5308	4635	4034	3495	+2.5	+2.6	-1.8	-11.3	$71
378 Wea. Mag.	300	2929	2576	2252	1952	1680	5698	4419	3379	2538	1881	+2.5	+1.2	-7.0	-24.5	$77
375 A-Square	300	2920	2626	2351	2093	1850	5679	4594	3681	2917	2281	+2.5	+1.4	-6.0	-21.0	NA
38-40 Win.	180	1160	999	901	827	764	538	399	324	273	233	0.0	-33.9	NA	NA	$42**
450/400-3"	400	2150	1932	1730	1545	1379	4105	3316	2659	2119	1689	+2.5	-4.0	-9.5	-30.0	NA
416 Dakota	400	2450	2294	2143	1998	1859	5330	4671	4077	3544	3068	+2.5	-0.2	-10.5	-29.4	NA
416 Taylor	400	2350	2117	1896	1693	NA	4905	3980	3194	2547	NA	+2.5	-1.2	15.0	NA	NA
416 Hoffman	400	2380	2145	1923	1718	1529	5031	4087	3285	2620	2077	+2.5	-1.0	-14.1	NA	NA
416 Rigby	350	2600	2449	2303	2162	2026	5253	4661	4122	3632	3189	+2.5	-1.8	-10.2	-26.0	NA

33 cont.

34 35

9.3 mm

375

40 41

AVERAGE CENTERFIRE RIFLE CARTRIDGE BALLISTICS & PRICES, continued

Many manufacturers do not supply suggested retail prices. Others did not get their pricing to us before press time. All pricing can vary dependent on the exact brand and style of ammo selected and/or the retail outlet from which you make your purchase. Pricing has been rounded to the nearest dollar and represents our best estimate of average pricing. An * after the cartridge means these loads are available with Nosler Partition or Swift A-Frame bullets. Listed pricing may or may not reflect this bullet type. ** = these are packed 50 to box, all others are 20 to box. Wea. Mag.= Weatherby Magnum. Spfd. = Springfield. A-A-Sq. = A-Square. N.E.=Nitro Express.

	Cartridge	Bullet Weight Grains	VELOCITY (fps)					ENERGY (ft. lbs.)					TRAJ. (in.)				Approx. Price per box
			Muzzle	100 yds.	200 yds.	300 yds.	400 yds.	Muzzle	100 yds.	200 yds.	300 yds.	400 yds.	100 yds.	200 yds.	300 yds.	400 yds.	
	416 Rigby	400	2370	2210	2050	1900	NA	4990	4315	3720	3185	NA	+2.5	-0.7	-12.1	NA	NA
40	416 Rigby	410	2370	2110	1870	1640	NA	5115	4050	3165	2455	NA	+2.5	-2.4	-17.3	NA	$110
	416 Rem. Mag.*	350	2520	2270	2034	1814	1611	4935	4004	3216	2557	2017	+2.5	-0.8	-12.6	-35.0	$82
	416 Rem. Mag.*	400	2400	2175	1962	1763	1579	5115	4201	3419	2760	2214	+2.5	-1.5	-14.6	NA	$80
	416 Wea. Mag.*	400	2700	2397	2115	1852	1613	6474	5104	3971	3047	2310	+2.5	0.0	-10.1	-30.4	$96
	10.57 (416) Meteor	400	2730	2532	2342	2161	1987	6621	5695	4874	4147	3508	+1.9	0.0	-8.3	-24.0	NA
	404 Jeffrey	400	2150	1924	1716	1525	NA	4105	3289	2614	2064	NA	+2.5	-4.0	-22.1	NA	NA
425	425 Express	400	2400	2160	1934	1725	NA	5115	4145	3322	2641	NA	+2.5	-1.0	-14.0	NA	NA
	44-40 Win.	200	1190	1006	900	822	756	629	449	360	300	254	0.0	-33.3	NA	NA	$36**
44	44 Rem. Mag.	210	1920	1477	1155	982	880	1719	1017	622	450	361	0.0	-17.6	NA	NA	$14
	44 Rem. Mag.	240	1760	1380	1114	970	878	1650	1015	661	501	411	0.0	-17.6	NA	NA	$13
	444 Marlin	240	2350	1815	1377	1087	941	2942	1753	1001	630	472	+2.5	-15.1	-31.0	NA	$22
	444 Marlin	265	2120	1733	1405	1160	1012	2644	1768	1162	791	603	+2.5	-6.0	-32.2	NA	Disc.
	45-70 Govt.	300	1810	1497	1244	1073	969	2182	1492	1031	767	625	0.0	-14.8	NA	NA	$21
45	45-70 Govt. Supreme	300	1880	1558	1292	1103	988	2355	1616	1112	811	651	0.0	-12.9	-46.0	-105	NA
	45-70 Govt. CorBon	350	1800	1526	1296			2519	1810	1307			0.0	-14.6			NA
	45-70 Govt.	405	1330	1168	1055	977	918	1590	1227	1001	858	758	0.0	-24.6	NA	NA	$21
	45-70 Govt. PMC Cowboy	405	1550	1193				1639	1280				0.0	-23.9			NA
	45-70 Govt. Garrett	415	1850					3150					3.0	-7.0			NA
	45-70 Govt. Garrett	530	1550	1343	1178	1062	982	2828	2123	1633	1327	1135	0.0	-17.8			NA
	450 Marlin	350	2100	1774	1488	1254	1089	3427	2446	1720	1222	922	0.0	-9.7	-35.2		NA
	458 Win. Magnum	350	2470	1990	1570	1250	1060	4740	3065	1915	1205	870	+2.5	-2.5	-21.6	NA	$43
	458 Win. Magnum	400	2380	2170	1960	1770	NA	5030	4165	3415	2785	NA	+2.5	-0.4	-13.4	NA	$73
	458 Win. Magnum	465	2220	1999	1791	1601	NA	5088	4127	3312	2646	NA	+2.5	-2.0	-17.7	NA	NA
	458 Win. Magnum	500	2040	1823	1623	1442	1237	4620	3689	2924	2308	1839	+2.5	-3.5	-22.0	NA	$61
	458 Win. Magnum	510	2040	1770	1527	1319	1157	4712	3547	2640	1970	1516	+2.5	-4.1	-25.0	NA	$41
	450 Dakota	500	2450	2235	2030	1838	1658	6663	5544	4576	3748	3051	+2.5	-0.6	-12.0	-33.8	NA
	450 N.E. 3-1/4"	465	2190	1970	1765	1577	NA	4952	4009	3216	2567	NA	+2.5	-3.0	-20.0	NA	NA
	450 N.E. 3-1/4"	500	2150	1920	1708	1514	NA	5132	4093	3238	2544	NA	+2.5	-4.0	-22.9	NA	NA
	450 No. 2	465	2190	1970	1765	1577	NA	4952	4009	3216	2567	NA	+2.5	-3.0	-20.0	NA	NA
	450 No. 2	500	2150	1920	1708	1514	NA	5132	4093	3238	2544	NA	+2.5	-4.0	-22.9	NA	NA
	458 Lott	465	2380	2150	1932	1730	NA	5848	4773	3855	3091	NA	+2.5	-1.0	-14.0	NA	NA
	458 Lott	500	2300	2062	1838	1633	NA	5873	4719	3748	2960	NA	+2.5	-1.6	-16.4	NA	NA
	450 Ackley Mag.	465	2400	2169	1950	1747	NA	5947	4857	3927	3150	NA	+2.5	-1.0	-13.7	NA	NA
	450 Ackley Mag.	500	2320	2081	1855	1649	NA	5975	4085	3820	3018	NA	+2.5	-1.2	-15.0	NA	NA
	460 Short A-Sq.	500	2420	2175	1943	1729	NA	6501	5250	4193	3319	NA	+2.5	-0.8	-12.8	-	NA
	460 Wea. Mag.	500	2700	2404	2128	1869	1635	8092	6416	5026	3878	2969	+2.5	+0.6	-8.9	-28.0	$72
475	500/465 N.E.	480	2150	1917	1703	1507	NA	4926	3917	3089	2419	NA	+2.5	-4.0	-22.2	-	NA
	470 Rigby	500	2150	1940	1740	1560	NA	5130	4170	3360	2695	NA	+2.5	-2.8	-19.4	NA	NA
	470 Nitro Ex.	480	2190	1954	1735	1536	NA	5111	4070	3210	2515	NA	+2.5	-3.5	-20.8	NA	NA
	470 Nitro Ex.	500	2150	1890	1650	1440	1270	5130	3965	3040	2310	1790	+2.5	-4.3	-24.0	NA	$177
	475 No. 2	500	2200	1955	1728	1522	NA	5375	4243	3316	2573	NA	+2.5	-3.2	-20.9	NA	NA
	505 Gibbs	525	2300	2063	1840	1637	NA	6166	4922	3948	3122	NA	+2.5	-3.0	-18.0	NA	NA
50	500 N.E.-3"	570	2150	1928	1722	1533	NA	5850	4703	3752	2975	NA	+2.5	-3.7	-22.0	NA	NA
58	500 N.E.-3"	600	2150	1927	1721	1531	NA	6158	4947	3944	3124	NA	+2.5	-4.0	-22.0	NA	NA
	495 A-Square	570	2350	2117	1896	1693	NA	5850	4703	3752	2975	NA	+2.5	-1.0	-14.5	NA	NA
	495 A-Square	600	2280	2050	1833	1635	NA	6925	5598	4478	3562	NA	+2.5	-2.0	-17.0	NA	NA
	500 A-Square	600	2380	2144	1922	1766	NA	7546	6126	4920	3922	NA	+2.5	-3.0	-17.0	NA	NA
	500 A-Square	707	2250	2040	1841	1567	NA	7947	6530	5318	4311	NA	+2.5	-2.0	-17.0	NA	NA
	500 BMG PMC	660	3080	2854	2639	2444	2248	13688	500 yd. zero				+3.1	+3.90	+4.7	+2.8	NA
	577 Nitro Ex.	750	2050	1793	1562	1360	NA	6990	5356	4065	3079	NA	+2.5	-5.0	-26.0	NA	NA
	577 Tyrannosaur	750	2400	2141	1898	1675	NA	9591	7633	5996	4671	NA	+3.0	0.0	-12.9	NA	NA
600	600 N.E.	900	1950	1680	1452	NA	NA	7596	5634	4212	NA	NA	+5.6	0.0	NA	NA	NA
700	700 N.E.	1200	1900	1676	1472	NA	NA	9618	7480	5774	NA	NA	+5.7	0.0	NA	NA	NA

CENTERFIRE HANDGUN CARTRIDGES — BALLISTICS & PRICES

Notes: Blanks are available in 32 S&W, 38 S&W and 38 Special. "V" after barrel length indicates test barrel was vented to produce ballistics similar to a revolver with a normal barrel-to-cylinder gap. Ammo prices are per 50 rounds except when marked with an ** which signifies a 20 round box; *** signifies a 25-round box. Not all loads are available from all ammo manufacturers. Listed loads are those made by Remington, Winchester, Federal, and others. DISC. is a discontinued load. Prices are rounded to nearest whole dollar and will vary with brand and retail outlet. † = new bullet weight this year; "c" indicates a change in data.

Cartridge	Bullet Wgt. Grs.	VELOCITY (fps)			ENERGY (ft. lbs.)			Mid-Range Traj. (in.)		Bbl. Lgth. (in.)	Est. Price/ box
		Muzzle	50 yds.	100 yds.	Muzzle	50 yds.	100 yds.	50 yds.	100 yds.		
221 Rem. Fireball	50	2650	2380	2130	780	630	505	0.2	0.8	10.5"	$15
25 Automatic	35	900	813	742	63	51	43	NA	NA	2"	$18
25 Automatic	45	815	730	655	65	55	40	1.8	7.7	2"	$21
25 Automatic	50	760	705	660	65	55	50	2.0	8.7	2"	$17
7.5mm Swiss	107	1010	NA	NA	240	NA	NA	NA	NA	NA	NEW
7.62mmTokarev	87	1390	NA	NA	365	NA	NA	0.6	NA	4.5"	NA
7.62 Nagant	97	1080	NA	NA	350	NA	NA	NA	NA	NA	NEW
7.63 Mauser	88	1440	NA	NA	405	NA	NA	NA	NA	NA	NEW
30 Luger	93†	1220	1110	1040	305	255	225	0.9	3.5	4.5"	$34
30 Carbine	110	1790	1600	1430	785	625	500	0.4	1.7	10"	$28
30-357 AeT	123	1992	NA	NA	1084	NA	NA	NA	NA	10"	NA
32 S&W	88	680	645	610	90	80	75	2.5	10.5	3"	$17
32 S&W Long	98	705	670	635	115	100	90	2.3	10.5	4"	$17
32 Short Colt	80	745	665	590	100	80	60	2.2	9.9	4"	$19
32 H&R Magnum	85	1100	1020	930	230	195	165	1.0	4.3	4.5"	$21
32 H&R Magnum	95	1030	940	900	225	190	170	1.1	4.7	4.5"	$19
32 Automatic	60	970	895	835	125	105	95	1.3	5.4	4"	$22
32 Automatic	60	1000	917	849	133	112	96			4"	NA
32 Automatic	65	950	890	830	130	115	100	1.3	5.6	NA	NA
32 Automatic	71	905	855	810	130	115	95	1.4	5.8	4"	$19
8mm Lebel Pistol	111	850	NA	NA	180	NA	NA	NA	NA	NA	NEW
8mm Steyr	112	1080	NA	NA	290	NA	NA	NA	NA	NA	NEW
8mm Gasser	126	850	NA	NA	200	NA	NA	NA	NA	NA	NEW
380 Automatic	60	1130	960	NA	170	120	NA	1.0	NA	NA	NA
380 Automatic	85/88	990	920	870	190	165	145	1.2	5.1	4"	$20
380 Automatic	90	1000	890	800	200	160	130	1.2	5.5	3.75"	$10
380 Automatic	95/100	955	865	785	190	160	130	1.4	5.9	4"	$20
38 Super Auto +P	115	1300	1145	1040	430	335	275	0.7	3.3	5"	$26
38 Super Auto +P	125/130	1215	1100	1015	425	350	300	0.8	3.6	5"	$26
38 Super Auto +P	147	1100	1050	1000	395	355	325	0.9	4.0	5"	NA
9x18mm Makarov	95	1000	NA	NA	NA	NA	NA	NA	NA	NA	NEW
9x18mm Ultra	100	1050	NA	NA	240	NA	NA	NA	NA	NA	NEW
9x23mm Largo	124	1190	1055	966	390	306	257	0.7	3.7	4"	NA
9x23mm Win.	125	1450	1249	1103	583	433	338	0.6	2.8	NA	NA
9mm Steyr	115	1180	NA	NA	350	NA	NA	NA	NA	NA	NEW
9mm Luger	88	1500	1190	1010	440	275	200	0.6	3.1	4"	$24
9mm Luger	90	1360	1112	978	370	247	191	NA	NA	4"	$26
9mm Luger	95	1300	1140	1010	350	275	215	0.8	3.4	4"	NA
9mm Luger	100	1180	1080	NA	305	255	NA	0.9	NA	4"	NA
9mm Luger	115	1155	1045	970	340	280	240	0.9	3.9	4"	$21
9mm Luger	123/125	1110	1030	970	340	290	260	1.0	4.0	4"	$23
9mm Luger	140	935	890	850	270	245	225	1.3	5.5	4"	$23
9mm Luger	147	990	940	900	320	290	265	1.1	4.9	4"	$26
9mm Luger +P	90	1475	NA	NA	437	NA	NA	NA	NA	NA	NA
9mm Luger +P	115	1250	1113	1019	399	316	265	0.8	3.5	4"	$27
9mm Federal	115	1280	1130	1040	420	330	280	0.7	3.3	4"V	$24
9mm Luger Vector	115	1155	1047	971	341	280	241	NA	NA	4"	NA
9mm Luger +P	124	1180	1089	1021	384	327	287	0.8	3.8	4"	NA
38 S&W	146	685	650	620	150	135	125	2.4	10.0	4"	$19
38 Short Colt	125	730	685	645	150	130	115	2.2	9.4	6"	$19
39 Special	100	950	900	NA	200	180	NA	1.3	NA	4"V	NA
38 Special	110	945	895	850	220	195	175	1.3	5.4	4"V	$23

Side tabs: 22, 25, 30, 32, 9mm 38, 38

Notes: Blanks are available in 32 S&W, 38 S&W and 38 Special. "V" after barrel length indicates test barrel was vented to produce ballistics similar to a revolver with a normal barrel-to-cylinder gap. Ammo prices are per 50 rounds except when marked with an ** which signifies a 20 round box; *** signifies a 25-round box. Not all loads are available from all ammo manufacturers. Listed loads are those made by Remington, Winchester, Federal, and others. DISC. is a discontinued load. Prices are rounded to nearest whole dollar and will vary with brand and retail outlet. † = new bullet weight this year; "c" indicates a change in data.

Cartridge	Bullet Wgt. Grs.	VELOCITY (fps)			ENERGY (ft. lbs.)			Mid-Range Traj. (in.)		Bbl. Lgth. (in).	Est. Price/box
		Muzzle	50 yds.	100 yds.	Muzzle	50 yds.	100 yds.	50 yds.	100 yds.		
38 Special	110	945	895	850	220	195	175	1.3	5.4	4"V	$23
38 Special	130	775	745	710	175	160	120	1.9	7.9	4"V	$22
38 Special Cowboy	140	800	767	735	199	183	168			7.5" V	NA
38 (Multi-Ball)	140	830	730	505	215	130	80	2.0	10.6	4"V	$10**
38 Special	148	710	635	565	165	130	105	2.4	10.6	4"V	$17
38 Special	158	755	725	690	200	185	170	2.0	8.3	4"V	$18
38 Special +P	95	1175	1045	960	290	230	195	0.9	3.9	4"V	$23
38 Special +P	110	995	925	870	240	210	185	1.2	5.1	4"V	$23
38 Special +P	125	975	929	885	264	238	218	1	5.2	4"	NA
38 Special +P	125	945	900	860	250	225	205	1.3	5.4	4"V	#23
38 Special +P	129	945	910	870	255	235	215	1.3	5.3	4"V	$11
38 Special +P	130	925	887	852	247	227	210	1.3	5.50	4"V	NA
38 Special +P	147/150(c)	884	NA	NA	264	NA	NA	NA	NA	4"V	$27
38 Special +P	158	890	855	825	280	255	240	1.4	6.0	4"V	$20
357 SIG	115	1520	NA	NA	593	NA	NA	NA	NA	NA	NA
357 SIG	124	1450	NA	NA	578	NA	NA	NA	NA	NA	NA
357 SIG	125	1350	1190	1080	510	395	325	0.7	3.1	4"	NA
357 SIG	150	1130	1030	970	420	355	310	0.9	4.0	NA	NA
356 TSW	115	1520	NA	NA	593	NA	NA	NA	NA	NA	NA
356 TSW	124	1450	NA	NA	578	NA	NA	NA	NA	NA	NA
356 TSW	135	1280	1120	1010	490	375	310	0.8	3.50	NA	NA
356 TSW	147	1220	1120	1040	485	410	355	0.8	3.5	5"	NA
357 Mag., Super Clean	105	1650									NA
357 Magnum	110	1295	1095	975	410	290	230	0.8	3.5	4"V	$25
357 (Med.Vel.)	125	1220	1075	985	415	315	270	0.8	3.7	4"V	$25
357 Magnum	125	1450	1240	1090	585	425	330	0.6	2.8	4"V	$25
357 (Multi-Ball)	140	1155	830	665	420	215	135	1.2	6.4	4"V	$11**
357 Magnum	140	1360	1195	1075	575	445	360	0.7	3.0	4"V	$25
357 Magnum	145	1290	1155	1060	535	430	360	0.8	3.5	4"V	$26
357 Magnum	150/158	1235	1105	1015	535	430	360	0.8	3.5	4"V	$25
357 Mag. Cowboy	158	800	761	725	225	203	185				NA
357 Magnum	165	1290	1189	1108	610	518	450	0.7	3.1	8-3/8"	NA
357 Magnum	180	1145	1055	985	525	445	390	0.9	3.9	4"V	$25
357 Magnum	180	1180	1088	1020	557	473	416	0.8	3.6	8"V	NA
357 Mag. CorBon F.A.	180	1650	1512	1386	1088	913	767	1.66	0.0		NA
357 Mag. CorBon	200	1200	1123	1061	640	560	500	3.19	0.0		NA
357 Rem. Maximum	158	1825	1590	1380	1170	885	670	0.4	1.7	10.5"	$14**
40 S&W	135	1140	1070	NA	390	345	NA	0.9	NA	4"	NA
40 S&W	155	1140	1026	958	447	362	309	0.9	4.1	4"	$14***
40 S&W	165	1150	NA	NA	485	NA	NA	NA	NA	4"	$18***
40 S&W	180	985	936	893	388	350	319	1.4	5.0	4"	$14***
40 S&W	180	1015	960	914	412	368	334	1.3	4.5	4"	NA
400 Cor-Bon	135	1450	NA	NA	630	NA	NA	NA	NA	5"	NA
10mm Automatic	155	1125	1046	986	436	377	335	0.9	3.9	5"	$26
10mm Automatic	170	1340	1165	1145	680	510	415	0.7	3.2	5"	$31
10mm Automatic	175	1290	1140	1035	650	505	420	0.7	3.3	5.5"	$11**
10mm Auto. (FBI)	180	950	905	865	361	327	299	1.5	5.4	4"	$16**
10mm Automatic	180	1030	970	920	425	375	340	1.1	4.7	5"	$16**
10mm Auto H.V.	180†	1240	1124	1037	618	504	430	0.8	3.4	5"	$27
10mm Automatic	200	1160	1070	1010	495	510	430	0.9	3.8	5"	$14**
10.4mm Italian	177	950	NA	NA	360	NA	NA	NA	NA	NA	NEW

Notes: Blanks are available in 32 S&W, 38 S&W and 38 Special. "V" after barrel length indicates test barrel was vented to produce ballistics similar to a revolver with a normal barrel-to-cylinder gap. Ammo prices are per 50 rounds except when marked with an ** which signifies a 20 round box; *** signifies a 25-round box. Not all loads are available from all ammo manufacturers. Listed loads are those made by Remington, Winchester, Federal, and others. DISC. is a discontinued load. Prices are rounded to nearest whole dollar and will vary with brand and retail outlet. † = new bullet weight this year; "c" indicates a change in data.

Cartridge	Bullet Wgt. Grs.	VELOCITY (fps)			ENERGY (ft. lbs.)			Mid-Range Traj. (in.)		Bbl. Lgth. (in).	Est. Price/box
		Muzzle	50 yds.	100 yds.	Muzzle	50 yds.	100 yds.	50 yds.	100 yds.		
41 Action Exp.	180	1000	947	903	400	359	326	0.5	4.2	5"	$13**
41 Rem. Magnum	170	1420	1165	1015	760	515	390	0.7	3.2	4"V	$33
41 Rem. Magnum	175	1250	1120	1030	605	490	410	0.8	3.4	4"V	$14**
41 (Med. Vel.)	210	965	900	840	435	375	330	1.3	5.4	4"V	$30
41 Rem. Magnum	210	1300	1160	1060	790	630	535	0.7	3.2	4"V	$33
44 S&W Russian	247	780	NA	NA	335	NA	NA	NA	NA	NA	NA
44 S&W Special	180	980	NA	NA	383	NA	NA	NA	NA	6.5"	NA
44 S&W Special	180	1000	935	882	400	350	311	NA	NA	7.5"V	NA
44 S&W Special	200†	875	825	780	340	302	270	1.2	6.0	6"	$13**
44 S&W Special	200	1035	940	865	475	390	335	1.1	4.9	6.5"	$13**
44 S&W Special	240/246	755	725	695	310	285	265	2.0	8.3	6.5"	$26
44-40 Win. Cowboy	225	750	723	695	281	261	242				NA
44 Rem. Magnum	180	1610	1365	1175	1035	745	550	0.5	2.3	4"V	$18**
44 Rem. Magnum	200	1400	1192	1053	870	630	492	0.6	NA	6.5"	$20
44 Rem. Magnum	210	1495	1310	1165	1040	805	635	0.6	2.5	6.5"	$18**
44 (Med. Vel.)	240	1000	945	900	535	475	435	1.1	4.8	6.5"	$17
44 R.M. (Jacketed)	240	1180	1080	1010	740	625	545	0.9	3.7	4"V	$18**
44 R.M. (Lead)	240	1350	1185	1070	970	750	610	0.7	3.1	4"V	$29
44 Rem. Magnum	250	1180	1100	1040	775	670	600	0.8	3.6	6.5"V	$21
44 Rem. Magnum	250	1230	1132	1057	840	711	620	0.8	2.9	6.5"V	NA
44 Rem. Magnum	275	1235	1142	1070	931	797	699	0.8	3.3	6.5"	NA
44 Rem. Magnum	300	1200	1100	1026	959	806	702	NA	NA	7.5"	$17
44 Rem. Magnum	330	1385	1297	1220	1406	1234	1090	1.83	0.00	NA	NA
440 CorBon	260	1700	1544	1403	1669	1377	1136	1.58	NA	10"	NA
450 Short Colt/450 Revolver	226	830	NA	NA	350	NA	NA	NA	NA	NA	NEW
45 S&W Schofield	180	730	NA	NA	213	NA	NA	NA	NA	NA	NA
45 S&W Schofield	230	730	NA	NA	272	NA	NA	na			
45 Automatic	165	1030	930	NA	385	315	NA	1.2	NA	5"	NA
45 Automatic	185	1000	940	890	410	360	325	1.1	4.9	5"	$28
45 Auto. (Match)	185	770	705	650	245	204	175	2.0	8.7	5"	$28
45 Auto. (Match)	200	940	890	840	392	352	312	2.0	8.6	5"	$20
45 Automatic	200	975	917	860	421	372	328	1.4	5.0	5"	$18
45 Automatic	230	830	800	675	355	325	300	1.6	6.8	5"	$27
45 Automatic	230	880	846	816	396	366	340	1.5	6.1	5"	NA
45 Automatic +P	165	1250	NA	NA	573	NA	NA	NA	NA	NA	NA
45 Automatic +P	185	1140	1040	970	535	445	385	0.9	4.0	5"	$31
45 Automatic +P	200	1055	982	925	494	428	380	NA	NA	5"	NA
45 Super	185	1300	1190	1108	694	582	504	NA	NA	5"	NA
45 Win. Magnum	230	1400	1230	1105	1000	775	635	0.6	2.8	5"	$14**
45 Win. Magnum	260	1250	1137	1053	902	746	640	0.8	3.3	5"	$16**
45 Win. Mag. CorBon	320	1150	1080	1025	940	830	747	3.47			NA
455 Webley MKII	262	850	NA	NA	420	NA	NA	NA	NA	NA	NA
45 Colt	200	1000	938	889	444	391	351	1.3	4.8	5.5"	$21
45 Colt	225	960	890	830	460	395	345	1.3	5.5	5.5"	$22
45 Colt + P CorBon	265	1350	1225	1126	1073	884	746	2.65	0.0		NA
45 Colt + P CorBon	300	1300	1197	1114	1126	956	827	2.78	0.0		NA
45 Colt	250/255	860	820	780	410	375	340	1.6	6.6	5.5"	$27
454 Casull	250	1300	1151	1047	938	735	608	0.7	3.2	7.5"V	NA
454 Casull	260	1800	1577	1381	1871	1436	1101	0.4	1.8	7.5"V	NA
454 Casull	300	1625	1451	1308	1759	1413	1141	0.5	2.0	7.5"V	NA
454 Casull CorBon	360	1500	1387	1286	1800	1640	1323	2.01	0.0		NA
475 Linebaugh	400	1350	1217	1119	1618	1315	1112	NA	NA	NA	NA
480 Ruger	325	1350	1191	1076	1315	1023	835	2.6	0.0	7.5"	NA
50 Action Exp.	325	1400	1209	1075	1414	1055	835	0.2	2.3	6"	$24**

40, 10mm cont.

44

45, 50

Note: The actual ballistics obtained with your firearm can vary considerably from the advertised ballistics. Also, ballistics can vary from lot to lot with the same brand and type load.

Cartridge	Bullet Wt. Grs.	Velocity (fps) 22-1/2" Bbl.		Energy (ft. lbs.) 22-1/2" Bbl.		Mid-Range Traj. (in.)	Muzzle Velocity 6" Bbl.
		Muzzle	100 yds.	Muzzle	100 yds.	100 yds.	
17 Aguila	20	1850	NA	NA	NA	NA	NA
22 Short Blank	—	—	—	—	—	—	—
22 Short CB	29	727	610	33	24	NA	706
22 Short Target	29	830	695	44	31	6.8	786
22 Short HP	27	1164	920	81	50	4.3	1077
22 Colibri	20	375	183	6	1	NA	NA
22 Super Colibri	20	500	441	11	9	NA	NA
22 Long CB	29	727	610	33	24	NA	706
22 Long HV	29	1180	946	90	57	4.1	1031
22 LR Ballistician	25	1100	760	65	30	NA	NA
22 LR Pistol Match	40	1070	890	100	70	4.6	940
22 LR Sub Sonic HP	38	1050	901	93	69	4.7	NA
22 LR Standard Velocity	40	1070	890	100	70	4.6	940
22 LR HV	40	1255	1016	140	92	3.6	1060
22 LR Silhoutte	42	1220	1003	139	94	3.6	1025
22 SSS	60	950	802	120	86	NA	NA
22 LR HV HP	40	1280	1001	146	89	3.5	1085
22 LR Hyper HP	32/33/34	1500	1075	165	85	2.8	NA
22 LR Stinger HP	32	1640	1132	191	91	2.6	1395
22 LR Hyper Vel	30	1750	1191	204	93	NA	NA
22 LR Shot #12	31	950	NA	NA	NA	NA	NA
22 WRF JHP	45	1300	1015	169	103	3	NA
22 Win. Mag.	30	2200	1373	322	127	1.4	1610
22 Win. Mag. V-Max BT	33	2000	1495	293	164	0.60	NA
22 Win. Mag. JHP	34	2120	1435	338	155	1.4	NA
22 Win. Mag. JHP	40	1910	1326	324	156	1.7	1480
22 Win. Mag. FMJ	40	1910	1326	324	156	1.7	1480
22 Win. Mag. JHP	50	1650	1280	300	180	1.3	NA
22 Win. Mag. Shot #11	52	1000	—	NA	—	—	NA

SHOTSHELL LOADS & PRICES

NOTES: * = 10 rounds per box. ** = 5 rounds per box. Pricing variations and number of rounds per box can occur with type and brand of ammunition. Listed pricing is the average nominal cost for load style and box quantity shown. Not every brand is available in all shot size variations. Some manufacturers do not provide suggested list prices. All prices rounded to nearest whole dollar. The price you pay will vary dependent upon outlet of purchase. # = new load spec this year; "C" indicates a change in data.

Dram Equiv.	Shot Ozs.	Load Style	Shot Sizes	Brands	Avg. Price/box	Velocity (fps)
10 Gauge 3-1/2" Magnum						
4-1/2	2-1/4	premium	BB, 2, 4, 5, 6	Win., Fed., Rem.	$33	1205
Max	2	premium	4, 5, 6	Fed., Win.	NA	1300
4-1/4	2	high velocity	BB, 2, 4	Rem.	$22	1210
4-1/2	2-1/4	duplex	4x6	Rem.	$14*	1205
Max	18 pellets	premium	00 buck	Fed., Win.	$7**	1100
Max	1-7/8	Bismuth	BB, 2, 4	Win., Bis.	NA	1225
Max	1-3/4	Tungsten-Polymer	4, 6	Fed.	NA	1325
4-1/4	1-3/4	steel	TT, T, BBB, BB, 1, 2, 3	Win., Rem.	$27	1260
Mag	1-5/8	steel	T, BBB	Win.	$27	1285
4-5/8	1-5/8	steel	F, T, BBB	Fed.	$26	1350
Max	1-5/8	Tungsten - Iron	BBB, BB, 2, 4	Fed.		1300
Max	1-5/8	Bismuth	BB, 2, 4	Bismuth	NA	1375
Max	1-1/2	Tungsten - Iron & steel	2xBB	Fed.	NA	1375
Max	1-3/8	steel	T, BBB, BB, 2	Fed., Win.	NA	1450
Max	1-3/8	Tungsten - Iron	BBB, BB, 2, 4	Fed.		1450
Max	1-3/4	slug, rifled	slug	Fed.	NA	1280
Max	24 Pellets	Buckshot	1 Buck	Fed.	NA	1100
Max	54 pellets	Super-X	4 Buck	Win.	NA	1150
12 Gauge 3-1/2" Magnum						
Max	2-1/4	premium	4, 5, 6	Fed., Rem., Win.	$13*	1150
Max	2	Lead	4, 5, 6	Fed.	NA	1275
Max	2	Copper plated turkey	4, 5	Rem.	NA	1300
Max	18 pellets	premium	00 buck	Fed., Win., Rem.	$7**	1100
Max	1-7/8	Bismuth	BB, 2, 4	Win., Bis.	NA	1225
Max	1-3/4	Tungsten-Polymer	4, 6	Fed.	NA	1275
4-1/8	1-9/16	steel	TT, F, T, BBB, BB, 1, 2	Rem., Win., Fed.	$22	1335
Max	1-3/8	steel	T, BBB, BB, 2, 4	Fed., Win.	NA	1450
Max	1-3/8	Tungsten - Iron	BBB, BB, 2, 4	Fed.	NA	1450
Max	1-3/8	Tungsten - Iron & steel	2xBB	Fed.	NA	1375
Max	24 pellets	Premium	1 Buck	Fed.	NA	1100
Max	54 pellets	Super-X	4 Buck	Win.	NA	1050
12 Gauge 3" Magnum						
4	2	premium	BB, 2, 4, 5, 6	Win., Fed., Rem.	$9*	1175
4	2	duplex	4x6	Rem.	$10	1175
4	1-7/8	premium	BB, 2, 4, 6	Win., Fed., Rem.	$19	1210
4	1-7/8	duplex	4x6	Rem., Fio.	$9*	1210
Max	1-3/4	turkey	4, 5, 6	Fed., Fio., Win., Rem.	NA	1300
4	1-3/4	duplex	2x4, 4x6	Fio.	NA	1150
4	1-5/8	premium	2, 4, 5, 6	Win., Fed., Rem.	$18	1290
Max	1-5/8	Bismuth	BB, 2, 4, 5, 6	Win., Bis.	NA	1250
4	24 pellets	buffered	1 buck	Win., Fed., Rem.	$5**	1040
4	15 pellets	buffered	00 buck	Win., Fed., Rem.	$6**	1210
4	10 pellets	buffered	000 buck	Win., Fed., Rem.	$6**	1225
4	41 pellets	buffered	4 buck	Win., Fed., Rem.	$6**	1210

Dram Equiv.	Shot Ozs.	Load Style	Shot Sizes	Brands	Avg. Price/box	Velocity (fps)
12 Gauge 3" Magnum (cont.)						
Max	1-3/8	Tungsten - Polymer	4, 6	Fed.	NA	1330
Max	1-3/8	Tungsten-Iron	4	Fed.	NA	1300
Max	1-1/4	Tungsten - Iron & steel	4x2, 4x4	Fed.	NA	1400
Max	1-3/8	slug	slug	Bren.	NA	1476
Max	1-1/4	slug, rifled	slug	Fed.	NA	1600
Max	1-3/16	saboted slug	copper slug	Rem.	NA	1500
Max	1-1/8	Tungsten - Iron	BBB, BB, 2, 4	Fed.	NA	1400
Max	1	steel	4, 6	Fed.		1330
Max	1	slug, rifled	slug, magnum	Win., Rem.	$5**	1760
Max	1	saboted slug	slug	Rem., Win., Fed.	$10**	1550
3-5/8	1-3/8	steel	TT, F, T, BBB, BB, 1, 2, 3, 4	Win., Fed., Rem.	$19	1275
Max	1-1/8	steel	T, BBB, BB, 2, 4, 5, 6	Fed., Win.	NA	1450
Max	1-1/8	steel	BB, 2	Fed.	NA	1400
4	1-1/4	steel	TT, F, T, BBB, BB, 1, 2, 3, 4, 6	Win., Fed., Rem.	$18	1375
Max	1-1/4	Tungsten-Iron and Steel	4x2	Fed.	NA	1400
Max	1-1/8	Tungsten - Polymer	4, 6	Fed.	NA	1375
Max	1-3/8	Tungsten - Polymer	4, 6	Fed.	NA	1330
12 Gauge 2-3/4"						
Max	1-5/8	magnum	4, 5, 6	Win., Fed.	$8*	1250
Max	1-3/8	turkey	4, 5, 6	Fio.	NA	1250
Max	1-3/8	duplex	2x4, 4x6	Fio.	NA	1200
Max	1-3/8	Bismuth	BB, 2, 4, 5, 6	Win., Bis.	NA	1280
3-3/4	1-1/2	magnum	BB, 2, 4, 5, 6	Win., Fed., Rem.	$16	1260
3-3/4	1-1/2	duplex	BBx4, 2x4, 4x6	Rem., Fio.	$9*	1260
Max	1-1/4	Supreme H-V	4, 6, 7-1/2	Win. Rem.	NA	1400
3-3/4	1-1/4	high velocity	BB, 2, 4, 5, 6, 7-1/2, 8, 9	Win., Fed., Rem., Fio.	$13	1330
Max	1-1/4	Tungsten - Polymer	4, 6	Fed.	NA	1330
3-1/2	1-1/4	mid-velocity	7, 8, 9	Win.	Disc.	1275
3-1/4	1-1/4	standard velocity	6, 7-1/2, 8, 9	Win., Fed., Rem., Fio.	$11	1220
Max	1-1/4	Bismuth	4, 6	Win.		1220
3-1/4	1-1/8	standard velocity	4, 6, 7-1/2, 8, 9	Win., Fed., Rem., Fio.	$9	1255
Max	1	steel	BB, 2	Fed.	NA	1450
Max	1	Tungsten - Iron	BB, 2, 4	Fed.	NA	1450
3-1/4	1	standard velocity	6, 7-1/2, 8	Rem., Fed., Fio., Win.	$6	1290
3-1/4	1-1/4	target	7-1/2, 8, 9	Win., Fed., Rem.	$10	1220
3	1-1/8	spreader	7-1/2, 8, 8-1/2, 9	Fio.	NA	1200
3	1-1/8	duplex target	7-1/2x8	Rem.	NA	1200
3	1-1/8	target	7-1/2, 8, 9, 7-1/2x8	Win., Fed., Rem., Fio.	$7	1200
3	1-1/8	duplex clays	7-1/2x8-1/2	Rem.	NA	1200
2-3/4	1-1/8	target	7-1/2, 8, 8-1/2, 9, 7-1/2x8	Win., Fed., Rem., Fio.	$7	1145
2-3/4	1-1/8	duplex target	7-1/2x8	Rem.	NA	1145
2-3/4	1-1/8	low recoil	7-1/2, 8	Rem.	NA	1145

Dram Equiv.	Shot Ozs.	Load Style	Shot Sizes	Brands	Avg. Price/box	Velocity (fps)
12 Gauge 2-3/4" (cont.)						
2-1/2	26 grams	low recoil	8	Win.	NA	980
2-1/4	1-1/8	target	7-1/2, 8, 8-1/2, 9	Rem., Fed.	$7	1080
Max	1	spreader	7-1/2, 8, 8-1/2, 9	Fio.	NA	1300
3-1/4	28 grams (1 oz)	target	7-1/2, 8, 9	Win., Fed., Rem., Fio.	$8	1290
3	1	target	7-1/2, 8, 8-1/2, 9	Win., Fio.	NA	1235
2-3/4	1	target	7-1/2, 8, 8-1/2, 9	Fed., Rem., Fio.	NA	1180
3-1/4	24 grams	target	7-1/2, 8, 9	Fed., Win., Fio.	NA	1325
3	7/8	light	8	Fio.	NA	1200
3-3/4	8 pellets	buffered	000 buck	Win., Fed., Rem.	$4**	1325
4	12 pellets	premium	00 buck	Win., Fed., Rem.	$5**	1290
3-3/4	9 pellets	buffered	00 buck	Win., Fed., Rem., Fio.	$19	1325
3-3/4	12 pellets	buffered	0 buck	Win., Fed., Rem.	$4**	1275
4	20 pellets	buffered	1 buck	Win., Fed., Rem.	$4**	1075
3-3/4	16 pellets	buffered	1 buck	Win., Fed., Rem.	$4**	1250
4	34 pellets	premium	4 buck	Fed., Rem.	$5**	1250
3-3/4	27 pellets	buffered	4 buck	Win., Fed., Rem., Fio.	$4**	1325
Max	1	saboted slug	slug	Win., Fed., Rem.	$10**	1450
Max	1-1/4	slug, rifled	slug	Fed.	NA	1520
Max	1-1/4	slug	slug	Lightfield		1440
Max	1	slug, rifled	slug, magnum	Rem., Fed.	$5**	1680
Max	1	slug, rifled	slug	Win., Fed., Rem.	$4**	1610
Max	1	sabot slug	slug	Sauvestre		1640
Max	385 grains	Partition Gold Slug	slug	Win.	NA	1900
Max	325 grains	Barnes Sabot	slug	Fed.	NA	1900
3	1-1/8	steel target	6-1/2, 7	Rem.	NA	1200
2-3/4	1-1/8	steel target	7	Rem.	NA	1145
3	1#	steel	7	Win.	$11	1235
3-1/2	1-1/4	steel	T, BBB, BB, 1, 2, 3, 4, 5, 6	Win., Fed., Rem.	$18	1275
3-3/4	1-1/8	steel	BB, 1, 2, 3, 4, 5, 6	Win., Fed., Rem., Fio.	$16	1365
3-3/4	1	steel	2, 3, 4, 5, 6, 7	Win., Fed., Rem., Fio.	$13	1390
Max	7/8	steel	7	Fio.	NA	1440
16 Gauge 2-3/4"						
3-1/4	1-1/4	magnum	2, 4, 6	Fed., Rem.	$16	1260
3-1/4	1-1/8	high velocity	4, 6, 7-1/2	Win., Fed., Rem., Fio.	$12	1295
Max	1-1/8	Bismuth	4, 5	Win., Bis.	NA	1200
2-3/4	1-1/8	standard velocity	6, 7-1/2, 8	Fed., Rem., Fio.	$9	1185
2-1/2	1	dove	6, 7-1/2, 8, 9	Fio., Win.	NA	1165
2-3/4	1		6, 7-1/2, 8	Fio.	NA	1200
Max	15/16	steel	2, 4	Fed., Rem.	NA	1300
Max	7/8	steel	2, 4	Win.	$16	1300
3	12 pellets	buffered	1 buck	Win., Fed., Rem.	$4**	1225
Max	4/5	slug, rifled	slug	Win., Fed., Rem.	$4**	1570
Max	.92	sabot slug	slug	Sauvestre		1560
20 Gauge 3" Magnum						
3	1-1/4	premium	2, 4, 5, 6, 7-1/2	Win., Fed., Rem.	$15	1185
Max	1-1/4	Tungsten-Polymer	4, 6	Fed.	NA	1185

Dram Equiv.	Shot Ozs.	Load Style	Shot Sizes	Brands	Avg. Price/box	Velocity (fps)
20 Gauge 3" Magnum (cont.)						
3	1-1/4	turkey	4, 6	Fio.	NA	1200
Max	18 pellets	buck shot	2 buck	Fed.	NA	1200
Max	24 pellets	buffered	3 buck	Win.	$5**	1150
2-3/4	20 pellets	buck	3 buck	Rem.	$4**	1200
3-1/4	1	steel	1, 2, 3, 4, 5, 6	Win., Fed., Rem.	$15	1330
Max	1-1/16	Bismuth	2, 4, 5, 6	Bismuth	NA	1250
Max	7/8	Tungsten - Iron	2, 4	Fed.	NA	1375
Mag	5/8	saboted slug	275 gr.	Fed.	NA	1450
20 Gauge 2-3/4"						
2-3/4	1-1/8	magnum	4, 6, 7-1/2	Win., Fed., Rem.	$14	1175
Max	1-1/8	Tungsten-Polymer	4, 6	Fed.	NA	1175
2-3/4	1	high velocity	4, 5, 6, 7-1/2, 8, 9	Win., Fed., Rem., Fio.	$12	1220
Max	1	Bismuth	4, 6	Win., Bis.	NA	1200
Max	1	Supreme H-V	4, 6, 7-1/2	Win. Rem.	NA	1300
Max	7/8	Steel	2, 3, 4	Fio.	NA	1500
2-1/2	1	standard velocity	6, 7-1/2, 8	Win., Rem., Fed., Fio.	$6	1165
2-1/2	7/8	clays	8	Rem.	NA	1200
2-1/2	7/8	promotional	6, 7-1/2, 8	Win., Rem., Fio.	$6	1210
2-1/2	1	target	8, 9	Win., Rem.	$8	1165
2-1/2	7/8	target	8, 9	Win., Fed., Rem.	$8	1200
2-1/2	7/8	steel - target	7	Rem.		1200
Max	5/8	Saboted Slug	Copper Slug	Rem.	NA	1500
Max	20 pellets	buffered	3 buck	Win., Fed.	$4	1200
Max	5/8	slug, saboted	slug	Win.,	$9**	1400
2-3/4	5/8	slug, rifled	slug	Rem.	$4**	1580
Max	3/4	saboted slug	copper slug	Fed., Rem.	NA	1450
Max	3/4	slug, rifled	slug	Win., Fed., Rem., Fio.	$4**	1570
Max	.9	sabot slug	slug	Sauvestre		1480
Max	260 grains	Partition Gold Slug	slug	Win.	NA	1900
Max	3/4	steel	2, 3, 4, 6	Win., Fed., Rem.	$14	1425
28 Gauge 2-3/4"						
2	1	high velocity	6, 7-1/2, 8	Win.	$12	1125
2-1/4	3/4	high velocity	6, 7-1/2, 8, 9	Win., Fed., Rem., Fio.	$11	1295
2	3/4	target	8, 9	Win., Fed., Rem.	$9	1200
Max	5/8	Bismuth	4, 6	Win., Bis.	NA	1250
410 Bore 3"						
Max	11/16	high velocity	4, 5, 6, 7-1/2, 8, 9	Win., Fed., Rem., Fio.	$10	1135
Max	9/16	Bismuth	4	Win., Bis.	NA	1175
410 Bore 2-1/2"						
Max	1/2	high velocity	4, 6, 7-1/2	Win., Fed., Rem.	$9	1245
Max	1/5	slug, rifled	slug	Win., Fed., Rem.	$4**	1815
1-1/2	1/2	target	8, 8-1/2, 9	Win., Fed., Rem., Fio.	$8	1200

SHOOTER'S MARKETPLACE

INTERESTING PRODUCT NEWS FOR THE ACTIVE SHOOTING SPORTSMAN

The companies represented on the following pages will be happy to provide additional information – feel free to contact them.

SWEETSHOOTER™ PREVENTS METAL CORROSION

Sweetshooter's micro-thin film penetrates the pores of barrels and other metal surfaces of firearms, blackpowder arms and knives to prevent corrosion and fouling. Once Sweetshooter™ fills the pores of these metal surfaces, there is no place for copper, lead, carbon and other deposits to collect, except on the film surface. Simply wipe them away! Users have found that Sweetshooter™ smoothes actions, reduces jamming, extends barrel life and improves accuracy. There is no need for immediate cleanup. Soaking of gun parts in solvent is eliminated, too.

While Sweetshooter™ is great for firearms and muzzleloaders, it will also prevent corrosion on knives, fishing tackle and tools, too.

NO MORE FOULING...GUARANTEED!

For information, call 1-800-932-4445 or visit their website at www.tecrolan.com

TECROLAN INC.

P.O. Box 14916, Fort Worth, TX 76117 • Phone: 940-325-6688 • Fax: 940-325-3636

FRIENDLY CLAY TARGET THROWERS

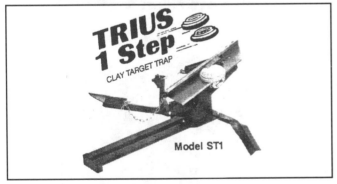

Model ST1

Trius Traps offer shooters superior quality, easy cocking, manual clay target traps. Singles, doubles plus piggy back doubles. Traps are factory-assembled and tested. Attach mount and main spring and you're ready to shoot. All adjustments made without tools. Birdshooter — quality at a budget price. Trius Model 92R — the original "Foot trap." Trapmaster — sit down comfort with pivoting action. The innovative 1-Step (shown) — almost effortless to use. Set arm without tension, place targets on arm and step on pedal to put tension on main spring and release target. High angle target retainer on all traps. Trius, satisfying shooters since 1955.

TRIUS TRAPS, INC.

Attn: Dept. SM'2001, P.O. Box 25, Cleves, OH 45002
Phone: 513-941-5682 • Web: www.triustraps.com

RAZOR SHARP

Finland has a harsh and challenging environment. Long ago, Finns developed a multi-purpose survival knife "the puukko." These basic tools are very sharp, lightweight and durable. Used for many daily tasks, these knives are still being used today. Kellam Knives began to bring these knives into the worldwide marketplace. The "puukko" is an excellent tool that will endure for many decades. This year, one of their makers from the KP Smithy won Best Knifemaker in Finland. His family has been making knives since 1610 and comes from an award-winning tradition.

Kellam Knives offers the largest selection of quality knives made by the most respected knifemakers in Finland.

902 S. Dixie Hwy., Lantana, FL 33462
Phone: 561-588-3185 or 800-390-6918
Fax: 561-588-3186
Web: www.kellamknives.com
Email: info@kellamknives.com

SHOOTER'S MARKETPLACE

RIFLE AND PISTOL MAGAZINES

Still in stock: High Caps for AR-7, AR-10, 10-22, etc.

Forrest, Inc. offers shooters one of the largest selections of standard and extended high-capacity magazines in the United States. Whether you're looking for a few spare magazines for that obsolete 22 rifle or pistol, or wish to replace a reduced-capacity ten-shot magazine with the higher-capacity pre-ban original, all are available from this California firm. They offer competitive pricing especially for dealers wanting to buy in quantity. Gun show dealers are our specialty. G.I., O.E.M., factory or aftermarket.

Forrest Inc. also stocks parts and accessories for the Colt 1911 45 Auto pistol, the SKS and MAK-90 rifles as well as many U.S. military rifles. One of their specialty parts is firing pins for obsolete weapons.

Call or write Forrest, Inc. for more information and a free brochure. Be sure and mention *Shooter's Marketplace*.

FORREST, INC.
P.O. Box 326, Dept: #100, Lakeside, CA 92040
Phone: 619-561-5800 • Fax: 888-GUNCLIP
Web: www.gunmags.com

NEW MANUAL AVAILABLE

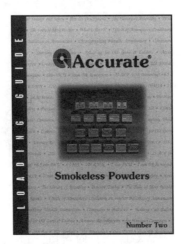

Accurate Powder's newest manual, Number Two, contains new data on powders XMR 4064 and XMP 5744, as well as a special section on Cowboy Action Shooting. In addition, the 400-page manual has loads for new cartridges, such as the .260 Rem., .300 Rem. Ultra Mag., .338 Rem. Ultra Mag., .357 Sig., .300 Whisper, .400 Corbon and more. It also includes many new bullets for the most popular cartridges as well as data for sabots in selected calibers. The price for the book is $16.95, plus $2.00 for shipping and handling in the continental U.S. To order a copy, call or write to:

ACCURATE ARMS
5891 Hwy. 230 W., McEwen, TN 37101
Phone: 1-800-416-3006 • Web: www.accuratepowder.com

6x18x40 VARMINT/TARGET SCOPE

Send for
Free Catalog

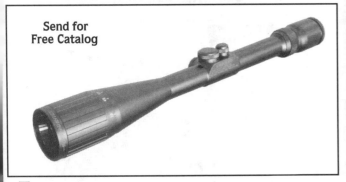

The Shepherd 6x18x40 Varmint/Target Scope makes long-range varmint and target shooting child's play. Just pick the ranging circle that best fits your target (be it prairie dogs, coyotes or paper varmints) and Shepherd's exclusive, patented Dual Reticle Down Range System does the rest. You won't believe how far you can accurately shoot, even with rimfire rifles.

Shepherd's superior lens coating mean superior light transmission and tack-sharp resolution.

This new shockproof, waterproof scope features 1/4 minute-of-angle clicks on the ranging circles and friction adjustments on the crosshairs that allow fine-tuning to 0.001 MOA. A 40mm adjustable objective provides a 5.5-foot field of view at 100 yards (16x setting). 16.5 FOV @ 6X.

SHEPHERD ENTERPRISES, INC.
Box 189, Waterloo, NE 68069
Phone: 402-779-2424 • Fax: 402-779-4010
E-mail: shepherd@shepherdscopes.com • Web: www.shepherdscopes.com

NYLON COATED GUN CLEANING RODS

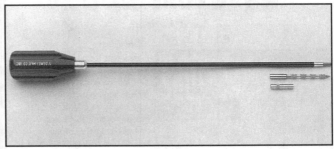

J. Dewey cleaning rods have been used by the U.S. Olympic shooting team and the benchrest community for over 20 years. These one-piece, spring-tempered, steel-base rods will not gall delicate rifling or damage the muzzle area of front-cleaned firearms. The nylon coating elmininates the problem of abrasives adhering to the rod during the cleaning operation. Each rod comes with a hard non-breakable plastic handle supported by ball-bearings, top and bottom, for ease of cleaning.

The brass cleaning jags are designed to pierce the center of the cleaning patch or wrap around the knurled end to keep the patch centered in the bore.

Coated rods are available from 17-caliber to shotgun bore size in several lengths to meet the needs of any shooter. Write for more information.

J. DEWEY MFG. CO., INC.
P.O. Box 2014, Southbury, CT 06488
Phone: 203-264-3064 • Fax: 203-262-6907
Web: www.deweyrods.com

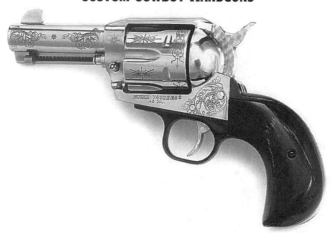

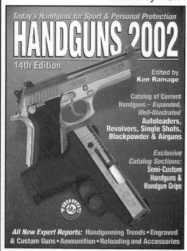

SHOOTER'S MARKETPLACE

ADVANCED MULTI-FUNCTION RIFLE

DSA offers a complete line of new U.S.-manufactured SA58 rifles. The SA58 rifle is a 21st-century version of the battle proven FAL. DSA is the only U.S. manufacturer of FAL-type rifles with upper and lower receivers machined from solid billets.

Firearm durability, reliability and shooter safety are vital components of the DSA design and manufacturing process. H.P. White Laboratory, Inc. excess pressure tested a SA58 rifle to 101,000 CUP with the receiver remaining undamaged! The SA58 is an incredibly strong and accurate multi-function rifle that can be accessorized to fit the personal needs of each shooter. Available in .308, .243, .260 and 7mm-08 calibers.

DSA carries a huge selection of FAL/SA58 parts and accessories, including two new, DSA exclusive items. The FAL Rail Interface Handguard has a 1913 Picatinny rail on all four sides for attaching accessories where the shooter wants them. The X Series FAL Buttstock gives the shooter a better rifle grip for precision shooting.

For more information, call for a catalog or check out the DSA Web site.

DSA, INC.
P.O. Box 370, Barrington, IL 60011
Phone: 847-277-7258 • Fax: 847-277-7259
Web: www.dsarms.com

ALASKAN HUNTER

Gary Reeder Custom Guns, builder of full custom guns, including custom cowboy guns, hunting handguns, African hunting rifles, custom Encores and Encore barrels, has a free brochure available or you can check out the large Web site at www.reedercustomguns.com. One of our most popular series is our Alaskan Hunter. This beefy 5-shot 454 Casull is for the serious handgun hunter and joins our 475 Linebaugh and 500 Linebaugh as our most popular hunting handguns. For more information contact:

GARY REEDER CUSTOM GUNS
2710 N Steve's Blvd., Suite 22, Flagstaff, AZ 86004
Phone: 520-526-3313

HIGH QUALITY OPTICS

One of the best indicators of quality is a scope's resolution number. The smaller the number, the better. Our scope has a resolution number of 2.8 seconds of angle. This number is about 20% smaller (better) than other well-known scopes costing much more. It means that two .22 caliber bullets can be a hair's breadth apart and edges of each still be clearly seen. With a Shepherd at 800 yards, you will be able to tell a four inch antler from a four inch ear and a burrowing owl from a prairie dog. Bird watchers will be able to distinguish a Tufted Titmouse from a Ticked-Off Field Mouse. Send for free catalog.

SHEPHERD ENTERPRISES, INC.
Box 189, Waterloo, NE 68069
Phone: 402-779-2424 • Fax: 402-779-4010
E-mail: shepherd@shepherdscopes.com • Web: www.shepherdscopes.com

COMBINATION RIFLE AND OPTICS REST

The Magna-Pod weighs less than two pounds, yet firmly supports more than most expensive tripods. It will hold 50 pounds at its low 9-inch height and over 10 pounds extended to 17 inches. It sets up in seconds where there is neither time nor space for a tripod and keeps your expensive equipment safe from knock-overs by kids, pets, pedestrians, or even high winds. It makes a great mono-pod for camcorders, etc., and its carrying box is less than 13" x 13" x 3 1/4" high for easy storage and access.

Attached to its triangle base it becomes an extremely stable table pod or rifle bench rest. The rifle yoke pictured in photo is included.

It's 5 pods in 1: Magna-Pod, Mono-Pod, Table-Pod, Shoulder-Pod and Rifle Rest. Send for free catalog.

SHEPHERD ENTERPRISES, INC.
Box 189, Waterloo, NE 68069
Phone: 402-779-2424 • Fax: 402-779-4010
E-mail: shepherd@shepherdscopes.com • Web: www.shepherdscopes.com

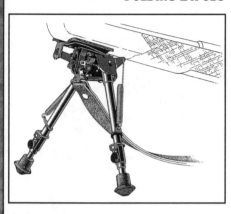

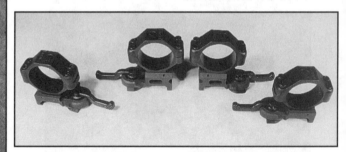

SHOOTER'S MARKETPLACE

AO PRO EXPRESS SIGHTS

Uses proven Express Sight Principle with Big Dot Tritium or Standard Dot Tritium Front Sight with a vertical Tritium Bar within the Express Rear Sight. Ideal "flash sight alignment" stressed in defensive handgun courses. The tritium Express Rear enhances low-light sight alignment and acquisition. This improves a handgun for fastest sight picture in both normal and low light. Professional trainers rate it as the fastest acquisition sight under actual stress situations. Improves front sight acquisition for IDPA and IPSC shooting competition. Fits most handguns with factory dovetails; other models require dovetail front cuts. Also available in Adjustable Express Rear for Bomar, LPA, and Kimber.

Price: Pro Express Big Dot Tritium (or Standard Dot Tritium): $120.00

Price: Adjustable Pro Express Big Dot Tritium (or Standard Dot Tritium): $150.00

AO SIGHT SYSTEMS INC.
(Formerly: Ashley Outdoors)
2401 Ludelle, Fort Worth, TX 76105
Phone: 817-536-0136 • Fax: 800-536-3517

CUSTOM LEATHER

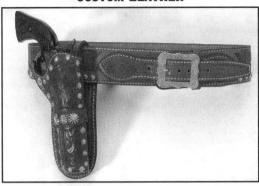

Rod Kibler Saddlery applies 25 years of saddle-making experience to the construction of fine holsters and belts. Kibler has found working on gun leather was a natural extension of saddle work.

Kibler, himself an active cowboy-action shooter, listens to other shooters and incorporates their ideas into his leatherwork for shooters.

Each of his rigs is extensively field-tested to ensure it will perform for the buyer. Several top national competitors have used Rod Kibler rigs for years.

Kibler adheres to old-time methods and quality standards. This commitment assures gun leather that meets the customer's standards, as well as Kibler's.

Only select, oak-tanned skirting leather is used.

The pictured rig is fully hand carved and lined with top-grain leather. The hardware includes solid sterling siver conchos and buckle.

ROD KIBLER SADDLERY
2307 Athens Road, Royston, GA 30662-3231 • Phone: 706-246-0487

e-GunParts.com

Numrich Gun Parts Corporation has expanded its website to include full e-commerce purchasing. Our new virtual storefront allows shopping for all your firearms parts and accessories by manufacturer and model. 180,000 items are available to purchase from our secure site, 24 hours a day, from anywhere in the world. You can now browse and buy within four clicks. The updated e-commerce site will also offer specials, new products, and inventory closeouts.

NUMRICH GUN PARTS CORPORATION
226 Williams Lane, West Hurley, NY 12491
Orders: 845-679-2417 • Customer Svc: 845-679-4867
Toll Free Fax: 877-Gun Parts • E-mail: info@gunpartscorp.com

The Gun Digest® Book of Modern Gun Values
11th Edition
Edited by Ken Ramage

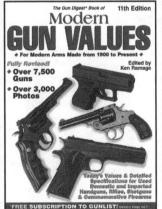

Identify, evaluate and price any of the commonly encountered firearms made from 1900 to present. This specialized, heavily illustrated, expanded edition helps you easily identify and value older firearms found in gun shops, auctions, advertisements-or that old family gun you've just inherited. More than 7,500 post-1900 models are gathered by type then listed alphabetically. All prices are fully updated to mid-year. Includes more photos, and new sections covering mechanical inspection and (full-color) condition evaluation. New reference section lists books and associations for collectors.

Softcover • 8-1/2 x 11 • 640 pages
3,000+ b&w photos
Item# MGV11 • $24.95

To place a credit card order or for a FREE all-product catalog call

 800-258-0929 *Offer DLB1*

M-F 7am - 8pm • Sat 8am - 2pm, CST

DBI BOOKS
a division of Krause Publications, Inc.

Krause Publications, Offer DLB1
P.O. Box 5009, Iola WI 54945-5009 • **www.krausebooks.com**

Shipping & Handling: $4.00 first book, $2.00 each additional. Non-US addresses $20.95 first book, $5.95 each additional.
Sales Tax: CA, IA, IL, PA, TN, VA, WI residents please add appropriate sales tax.

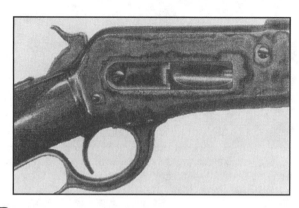

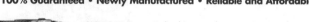

SHOOTER'S MARKETPLACE

NEW YOUTH SHOTGUN

The Ithaca Model 37 Ultra Featherlight Youth model is based on the classic Model 37 pump-action shotgun, with bottom ejection and adaptability to either right- or left-handed shooters via a simple safety change. This new model uses a receiver machined from aircraft-grade aluminum to keep the gun's unloaded weight below five pounds, a definite benefit to younger shooters. The Youth model features a 22-inch barrel with interchangeable choke tubes and a vent rib. The American black walnut stock has a 12 3/4-inch length of pull over the ventilated recoil pad. For information, please contact:

ITHACA GUN® CO., LLC
901 Route 34B, King Ferry, NY 13081
Phone: 315-364-7171 • Fax: 315-364-5134
Web: www.ithacagun.com

NEW DEER GUN IN 16-GAUGE

Ithaca Gun is introducing a new 16-gauge fixed-barrel Deerslayer II pump-action shotgun based on the proven Model 37 design.

Like the 12-gauge Deerslayer II, the new 16-gauge version is designed with scope use in mind, featuring a factory drilled and tapped receiver, a Monte Carlo stock and incorporates a free-floated, rifled barrel mated to the all-steel receiver to deliver rifle-like accuracy. The new Ithaca, and Lightfield's 16-gauge impact-discarding sabot ammunition, makes a hard-hitting, flat-shooting combination delivering energy comparable to that of a 12 gauge - from a lighter, easier-to-carry gun.

ITHACA GUN® CO., LLC
901 Route 34B, King Ferry, NY 13081
Phone: 315-364-7171 • Fax: 315-364-5134
Web: www.ithacagun.com

VERSATILE SCOPE
WATERPROOF; MULTI-COATED; SPEED FOCUS

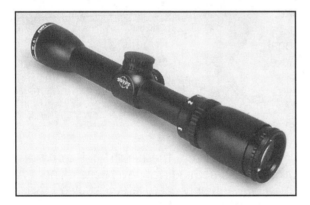

The 1.5-4.5x, 32mm Model 648M Swift *PREMIER.*
Considered by many to be the most versatile scope in our *Premier* line, works well on a shotgun or used as a black powder scope. It is often used in wooded areas for turkeys. It is effective on deer where rifles are permitted. Eye relief from 3.05 to 3.27. Crosshair and circle reticle make this rifle scope easy to focus on target, and ideal for turkey hunting. With black matte finish.

For more information, contact:

SWIFT INSTRUMENTS, INC.
952 Dorchester Avenue, Dept: GD, Boston, MA 02125
Phone: 617-436-2960 • Fax: 617-436-3232
E-mail: info@swiftoptics.com • Web: www.swift-optics.com

MODEL 676S SWIFT PREMIER
4-12X, 40 – WA – WATERPROOF – MULTI-COATED – SPEED FOCUS

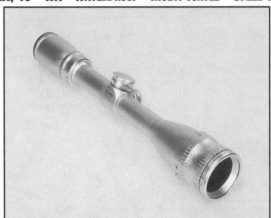

With a parallax adjustment from 10 yards to infinity this scope is highly adaptable and excellent for use as a varminting scope or on gas powered air rifles. Elevation and windage adjustments are full saddle on the hard anodized 1-inch tube. *Speed Focus* adjustment brings you on target easily. The objectives are multi-coated and the self-centering reticle in Quadraplex. Available in regular (676), matte (676M), and silver finish (676S). Gift boxed.

For more information, contact:

SWIFT INSTRUMENTS, INC.
952 Dorchester Avenue, Dept: GD, Boston, MA 02125
Phone: 617-436-2960 • Fax: 617-436-3232
E-mail: info@swiftoptics.com • Web: www.swift-optics.com

SHOOTER'S MARKETPLACE

COWBOY ACTION

The closest you'll get to the Old West short of a time machine.

Join SASS® and preserve the spirit of the Old West. Members receive a numbered shooter's badge, alias registration, an annual subscription to *The Cowboy Chronicle*, and much more.

SINGLE ACTION SHOOTING SOCIETY™

Phone Toll Free: 1-877-411-SASS
Web: www.sassnet.com

JP ENTERPRISES, INC.

Manufacturer of professional grade semi-auto rifles for competitive shooters and law enforcement. In addition, they offer modifications on bolt rifles, Remington shotguns and Glock pistols using proprietary components and techniques to enhance performance. They also offer their complete line of high performance parts for rifles, pistols and shotguns for sale direct or through several major distributors such as Brownell's. In particular, their recoil eliminators for rifles and the JP precision trigger system for AR-type rifles are known for their outstanding performance and have become the choice for many professional level shooters. Last year, they introduced a new coil reduction system for Remington series shotguns that has received excellent feed back from the action shooting community. Their extensive web site can be seen at www.jpar15.com.

JP ENTERPRISES, INC.
P.O. Box 378, Hugo, MN 55378
Phone: 651-426-9196 • Fax: 651-426-2472

DO-ALL TRAPS

Do-All Traps has a variety of traps and targets for the weekend shooter or commercial range.

The heart of the Do-All Trap is a patented, pivoting adjustable throwing arm. Three simple adjusting bolts allow the arm to be positioned to throw any clay target from a 90-degree vertical springing teal to a ground-bouncing rabbit or standard pair of doubles, and everything in-between.

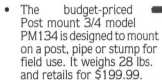

A sliding, adjustable-tension spring clip on the throwing arm adapts to standard, rabbit, 90mm (midi), 60mm (mini) or battue clays, and allows them to be thrown as singles, stacked doubles or nesting pairs. By varying spring tension, target selection and position of the targets on the throwing arms, the Do-All Trap can create any target presentation desired.

The frame of each Do-All Trap is 3-inch, heavy-duty steel tubing with robotic welds and a durable power-coat paint finish. Each model assembles in seconds and includes an adjusting wrench, protective ring-guard and 15-minute instructional video.

- The budget-priced Post mount 3/4 model PM134 is designed to mount on a post, pipe or stump for field use. It weighs 28 lbs. and retails for $199.99.

- The Single Trap model ST200 includes a fold-down chair, includes legs and also fits a trailer hitch. It weighs 47 lbs. and retails for $139.99.

- The Double Trap 3/4 Trap model DT534 has the same features as the Single Trap, but includes an extra throwing arm for report pairs. It can throw four targets at once. It weighs 94 lbs. and retails for $399.99.

Weekend rifle and airgun shooters will enjoy the fun of swinging targets with The Plinker and Plinker Jr.

- The Plinker, designed to withstand .22 rimfire rounds, has four pendulum targets that swing up when shot. To reset, simply shoot the fifth "reset" target at the top. The 10-lb. steel unit retails for $34.99.

- The Plinker Jr. is similar to The Plinker, but made to withstand airgun pellets. It weighs 1 lb. and retails for $13.99.

8113 Moores Ln., Suite 1900-154, Brentood, TN 37027
Phone: 1-800-252-9247 or 615-269-4889
Fax: 800-633-3172 or 615-269-4434
E-mail: sales@do-alltraps.com • Web: www.do-alltraps.com

SHOOTER'S MARKETPLACE

PERFORMANCE AMMUNITION

For serious enthusiasts who demand quality and accuracy, Black Hills Ammunition offers high quality ammo at a reasonable price with good service. Black Hills Ammunition has been producing high quality rounds for over 20 years. They sell dealer-direct and pay all freight to the continental U.S. Minimum order in only one case. Satisfaction is guaranteed. Black Hills Ammunition specializes in match-quality 223 (both new and remanufactured), .308 Match, cowboy ammo and more. Performance is so good that the U.S. Army, Navy, Air Firce and Marines all use Black Hills.

Ask for it at your dealer, or contact them directly for purchase information.

BLACK HILLS AMMUNITION
P.O. Box 3090, Rapid City, SD 57709
Phone: 1-605-348-5150 • Fax: 1-605-348-9827

ADJUSTABLE APERTURE FOR GLASSES

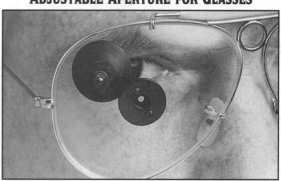

The Merit Optical Attachment is an instantly adjustable iris aperture that allows shooters to see their iron sights and target clearly. The adjustable aperture dramatically increases the eye's depth of focus, eliminating a fuzzy sight picture.

The Optical Attachment works with all types of glasses including bifocals and trifocals. It attaches securely with a small rubber suction cup. The aperture instantly adjusts from .022- to .156-inch in diameter to accommodate different light conditions. It is compact and lightweight.

Merit Corporation makes a full line of adjustable apertures for mounting in peep sights as well. Contact Merit Corporation for information and a free catalog.

MERIT CORPORATION
P.O. Box 9044, Schnectady, NY 12309
Phone: 518-346-1420
Web: www.meritcorporation.com

OBSOLETE AND HARD-TO-FIND AMMO

The Old Western Scrounger has been in the firearms business for 40 years, providing obsolete and hard-to-find ammunition and components, including European and double-rifle calibers. The company now carries the Kynoch line of ammo, ranging from the 318 Westley Richards to the 700 Nitro Express. Old Western Scrounger's own line of ammo covers almost any obsolete rifle or pistol caliber, including a 1 million-round run of the 5mm Remington Mag. (coming soon). The firm also is the exclusive carrier of RWS brass and other reloading components. In addition, Scrounger carries Fiocchi, Norma, Eley and RWS ammunition, as well as some old favorites. Free catalogs and free shipping are provided on orders over $25.00. Call the company if you need help determining which ammo is needed for a particular gun.

OLD WESTERN SCROUNGER, INC.
1540 Lucas Road, Yreka, CA 96097
Phone: 800-UPS-AMMO • Web: www.ows-ammunition.com

QUALITY CUSTOM KNIVES

Mike Schirmer's lifelong interest in knives stems from his passion for hunting and since he lives in the heart of Montana's best big-game country, he has had plenty of opportunity to test his blades. Mike has also worked as an elk guide and a "buffalo skinner." (Call him to book a buffalo hunt.) All of Mike's knives, no matter how beautiful, are made to use. D2 is his favorite type of steel, but he will use other steels (including damascus) on special order. All types of handle material are available, as is engraving.

While the majority of his business is hunting knives, Mike also makes camp, fighting, and Old West Period knives. When you purchase a Mike Schirmer knife, you are getting a one-of-a-kind piece of working art that is destined to be a family heirloom. Mike usually has a few knives on hand for immediate delivery, or if you prefer, he will make a custom knife to your design.

For more information, contact Mike at:

RUBY MOUNTAIN KNIVES
P.O. Box 534,
Twin Bridges, MT 59754
Phone: 406-684-5868 • Email:
schirmer@3rivers.net

SHOOTER'S MARKETPLACE

CNC MACHINED TRIGGER GUARD

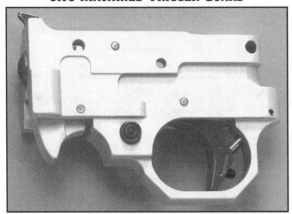

This is a complete CNC machined trigger guard equipped with precision EDM parts. It features an internal pretravel adjustment that is set at the factory in order to greatly reduce pretravel. This new match trigger guard is CNC machined from a solid billet of high strength aircraft aluminum. The hammer is a precision ground 440C stainless steel. The sear and disconnector are EDM manufactured parts. The trigger is black anodized and equipped with an overtravel adjustment screw. The trigger is reset internally. An automatic bolt release and an extended magazine release are also included.

VOLQUARTSEN CUSTOM LTD.
24276 240th Street, P.O. Box 397, Carroll, IA 51401
Phone: 712-792-4238 • Fax: 712-792-2542
E-mail: info@volquartsen.com • Web: www.volquartsen.com

CNC MACHINED STEEL COMPETITION BOLT

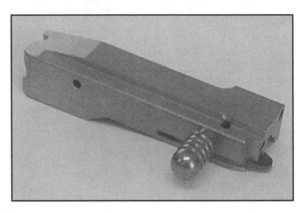

This bolt features hardened (60Rc) and tuned extractor for positive, consistent extraction. It also includes Volquartsen's own unique round titanium firing pin for faster lock time and to assure positive ignition. The new bolt also features interchangeable bolt handles. It is available with their streamline, compact stainless steel handle or a target knob (red or black) for easy cocking control. The bolt comes with Volquartsen's recoil rod and spring for ease of installation in either their stainless steel receiver or for the factory Ruger 10/22® receiver.

VOLQUARTSEN CUSTOM LTD.
24276 240th Street, P.O. Box 397, Carroll, IA 51401
Phone: 712-792-4238 • Fax: 712-792-2542
E-mail: info@volquartsen.com • Web: www.volquartsen.com

BREAK-FREE®
An Armor Holdings Company

Break-Free® is a leading manufacturer of synthetic-based cleaners, lubricants and preservative compounds for military weapon maintenance, law enforcement, civilian firearms, high performance sports equipment and industrial machinery. Break-Free's flagship product Break-Free CLP® was specifically developed to provide reliable weapon lubrication in battlefield conditions and to remove firing residues, carbon deposits and other firing contaminants. Moreover, Break-Free CLP® repels water and dirt and prevents corrosion, and keeps weapons combat ready in any condition – rain, snow, ice, mud, or sand.

Break-Free® has been an approved qualified source and quality supplier to militaries around the globe for over 20 years. To learn more about the Break-Free family of products, visit www.break-free.com or buy online at holsters.com.

BREAK-FREE®, INC.
13386 International Parkway
Jacksonville, FL 32218
Phone: 800-428-0588

M36 PLUSONE™ EXTENSION

Pearce Grip Inc., originators of the popular grip extension line for the Glock® sub-compact auto pistols, introduces the M36 PlusOne™ extension. This unit converts the Glock® model 36 (45 Auto) factory six-round magazine to a seven-round capacity and provides the extra finger groove for shooting comfort and control. The PlusOne™ replaces the factory magazine floor plate and is held securely to the magazine body with an external locking device that doubles as a contour blending feature completing the rear of the grip. This new extension is made from a high-impact polymer and incorporates the same texture and checkering pattern found on the pistol frame for a factory appearance. For more information or for a dealer near you contact:

PEARCE GRIP, INC.
P.O. Box 40367, Fort Worth, TX 76140
Phone: 800-390-9420 • Fax: 817-568-9707

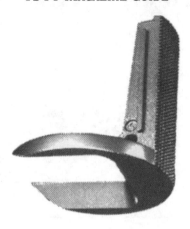

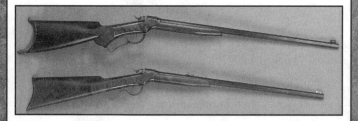
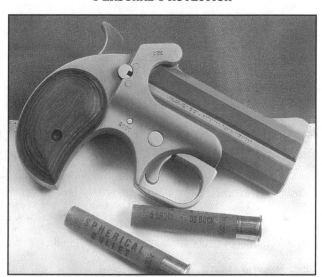

2002
GUN DIGEST
Complete Compact
CATALOG

GUNDEX

HANDGUNS

RIFLES

SHOTGUNS

BLACKPOWDER

AIRGUNS

ACCESSORIES

REFERENCE

DIRECTORY OF THE ARMS TRADE

GUNDEX

GUNDEX

GUNDEX

GUNDEX

GUNDEX

Includes models suitable for several forms of competition and other sporting purposes.

Accu-Tek BL-9

Accu-Tek AT-380

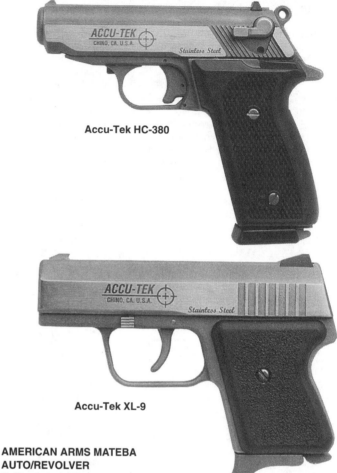

Accu-Tek HC-380

Accu-Tek XL-9

ACCU-TEK BL-9 AUTO PISTOL

Caliber: 9mm Para., 5-shot magazine. **Barrel:** 3". **Weight:** 22 oz. **Length:** 5.6" overall. **Stocks:** Black pebble composition. **Sights:** Fixed. **Features:** Double action only; black finish. Introduced 1997. Price includes cleaning kit and gun lock, two magazines. Made in U.S. by Accu-Tek.
Price: $232.00

Accu-Tek Model AT-32SS Auto Pistol

Same as the AT-380SS except chambered for 32 ACP. Introduced 1991. Price includes cleaning kit and gun lock.
Price: Satin stainless $221.00

ACCU-TEK MODEL AT-380 AUTO PISTOL

Caliber: 380 ACP, 5-shot magazine. **Barrel:** 2.75". **Weight:** 20 oz. **Length:** 5.6" overall. **Stocks:** Grooved black composition. **Sights:** Blade front, rear adjustable for windage. **Features:** Stainless steel frame and slide. External hammer; manual thumb safety; firing pin block, trigger disconnect. Introduced 1991. Price includes cleaning kit and gun lock. Made in U.S. by Accu-Tek.
Price: Satin stainless $221.00

ACCU-TEK MODEL HC-380 AUTO PISTOL

Caliber: 380 ACP, 10-shot magazine. **Barrel:** 2.75". **Weight:** 26 oz. **Length:** 6" overall. **Stocks:** Checkered black composition. **Sights:** Blade front, rear adjustable for windage. **Features:** External hammer; manual thumb safety with firing pin and trigger disconnect; bottom magazine release. Stainless steel construction. Introduced 1993. Price includes cleaning kit and gun lock. Made in U.S. by Accu-Tek.
Price: Satin stainless $231.00

ACCU-TEK XL-9 AUTO PISTOL

Caliber: 9mm Para., 5-shot magazine. **Barrel:** 3". **Weight:** 24 oz. **Length:** 5.6" overall. **Stocks:** Black pebble composition. **Sights:** Three-dot system; rear adjustable for windage. **Features:** Stainless steel construction; double-action-only mechanism. Introduced 1999. Price includes cleaning kit and gun lock, two magazines. Made in U.S. by Accu-Tek.
Price: $248.00

AMERICAN ARMS MATEBA AUTO/REVOLVER

Caliber: 357 Mag., 6-shot. **Barrel:** 4", 6", 8". **Weight:** 2.75 lbs. **Length:** 8.77" overall. **Stocks:** Smooth walnut. **Sights:** Blade on ramp front, adjustable rear. **Features:** Double or single action. Cylinder and slide recoil together upon firing. All-steel construction with polished blue finish. Introduced 1995. Imported from Italy by American Arms, Inc.
Price: $1,295.00
Price: 6" $1,349.00

AMT AUTOMAG II AUTO PISTOL

Caliber: 22 WMR, 9-shot magazine (7-shot with 3-3/8" barrel). **Barrel:** 3-3/8", 4-1/2", 6". **Weight:** About 32 oz. **Length:** 9-3/8" overall. **Stocks:** Grooved carbon fiber. **Sights:** Blade front, adjustable rear. **Features:** Made of stainless steel. Gas-assisted action. Exposed hammer. Slide flats have brushed finish, rest is sandblast. Squared trigger guard. Introduced 1986. From Galena Industries, Inc.
Price: $429.00

AMT AUTOMAG III PISTOL

Caliber: 30 Carbine, 8-shot magazine. **Barrel:** 6-3/8". **Weight:** 43 oz. **Length:** 10-1/2" overall. **Stocks:** Carbon fiber. **Sights:** Blade front, adjustable rear. **Features:** Stainless steel construction. Hammer-drop safety. Slide flats have brushed finish, rest is sandblasted. Introduced 1989. From Galena Industries, Inc.
Price: $529.00

AMT AUTOMAG IV PISTOL

Caliber: 45 Winchester Magnum, 6-shot magazine. **Barrel:** 6.5". **Weight:** 46 oz. **Length:** 10.5" overall. **Stocks:** Carbon fiber. **Sights:** Blade front, adjustable rear. **Features:** Made of stainless st3578eel with brushed finish. Introduced 1990. Made in U.S. by Galena Industries, Inc.
Price: $599.00

AMT Backup

Auto-Ordnance Deluxe

Auto-Ordnance 1911A1 Standard

Auto-Ordnance Pit Bull

AMT 45 ACP HARDBALLER II

Caliber: 45 ACP. **Barrel:** 5". **Weight:** 39 oz. **Length:** 8-1/2" overall. **Stocks:** Wrap-around rubber. **Sights:** Adjustable. **Features:** Extended combat safety, serrated matte slide rib, loaded chamber indicator, long grip safety, beveled magazine well, adjustable target trigger. All stainless steel. From Galena Industries, Inc.

Price: **$425.00**
Price: Government model (as above except no rib, fixed sights) . **$399.00**
Price: 400 Accelerator (400 Cor-Bon, 7" barrel) **$549.00**
Price: Commando (40 S&W, Government Model frame) **$435.00**

AMT 45 ACP HARDBALLER LONG SLIDE

Caliber: 45 ACP. **Barrel:** 7". **Length:** 10-1/2" overall. **Stocks:** Wrap-around rubber. **Sights:** Fully adjustable rear sight. **Features:** Slide and barrel are 2" longer than the standard 45, giving less recoil, added velocity, longer sight radius. Has extended combat safety, serrated matte rib, loaded chamber indicator, wide adjustable trigger. From Galena Industries, Inc.

Price: **$529.00**

AMT BACKUP PISTOL

Caliber: 357 SIG (5-shot); 38 Super, 9mm Para. (6-shot); 40 S&W, 400 Cor-Bon; 45 ACP (5-shot). **Barrel:** 3". **Weight:** 23 oz. **Length:** 5-3/4" overall. **Stocks:** Checkered black synthetic. **Sights:** None. **Features:** Stainless steel construction; double-action-only trigger; dust cover over the trigger transfer bar; extended magazine; titanium nitride finish. Introduced 1992. Made in U.S. by Galena Industries.

Price: 9mm, 40 S&W, 45 ACP **$319.00**
Price: 38 Super, 357 SIG, 400 Cor-Bon **$369.00**

AMT 380 DAO Small Frame Backup

Similar to the DAO Backup except has smaller frame, 2-1/2" barrel, weighs 18 oz., and is 5" overall. Has 5-shot magazine, matte/stainless finish. Made in U.S. by Galena Industries.

Price: **$319.00**

AUTO-ORDNANCE 1911A1 AUTOMATIC PISTOL

Caliber: 45 ACP, 7-shot magazine. **Barrel:** 5". **Weight:** 39 oz. **Length:** 8-1/2" overall. **Stocks:** Checkered plastic with medallion. **Sights:** Blade front, rear adjustable for windage. **Features:** Same specs as 1911A1 military guns—parts interchangeable. Frame and slide blued; each radius has non-glare finish. Made in U.S. by Auto-Ordnance Corp.

Price: 45 ACP, blue **$447.00**
Price: 45 ACP, Parkerized **$462.00**
Price: 45 ACP Deluxe (three-dot sights, textured rubber
wraparound grips) **$455.00**

Auto-Ordnance 1911A1 Custom High Polish Pistol

Similar to the standard 1911A1 except has a Videki speed trigger, extended thumb safety, flat mainspring housing, Acurod recoil spring guide system, rosewood grips, custom combat hammer, beavertail grip safety. High-polish blue finish. Introduced 1998. Made in U.S. by Auto-Ordnance Corp.

Price: **$585.00**

Auto-Ordnance ZG-51 Pit Bull Auto

Same as the 1911A1 except has 3-1/2" barrel, weighs 36 oz. and has an over-all length of 7-1/4". Available in 45 ACP only; 7-shot magazine. Introduced 1989.

Price: **$470.00**

AUTAUGA 32 AUTO PISTOL

Caliber: 32 ACP, 6-shot magazine. **Barrel:** 2". **Weight:** 11.3 oz. **Length:** 4.3" overall. **Stocks:** Black polymer. **Sights:** Fixed. **Features:** Double-action-only mechanism. Stainless steel construction. Uses Winchester Silver Tip ammunition.

Price: . . . . **NA**

Baer Custom Carry

Beretta 96

Baer Premium II

BAER 1911 CUSTOM CARRY AUTO PISTOL

Caliber: 45 ACP, 7- or 10-shot magazine. **Barrel:** 5". **Weight:** 37 oz. **Length:** 8.5" overall. **Stocks:** Checkered walnut. **Sights:** Baer improved ramp-style dovetailed front, Novak low-mount rear. **Features:** Baer forged NM frame, slide and barrel with stainless bushing; fitted slide to frame; double serrated slide (full-size only); Baer speed trigger with 4-lb. pull; Baer deluxe hammer and sear, tactical-style extended ambidextrous safety, beveled magazine well; polished feed ramp and throated barrel; tuned extractor; Baer extended ejector, checkered slide stop; lowered and flared ejection port, full-length recoil guide rod; recoil buff. Partial listing shown. Made in U.S. by Les Baer Custom, Inc.

Price: Standard size, blued **$1,640.00**
Price: Standard size, stainless **$1,690.00**
Price: Comanche size, blued **$1,640.00**
Price: Comanche size, stainless. **$1,690.00**
Price: Comanche size, aluminum frame, blued slide **$1,923.00**
Price: Comanche size, aluminum frame, stainless slide **$1,995.00**

BAER 1911 PREMIER II AUTO PISTOL

Caliber: 9x23, 38 Super, 400 Cor-Bon, 45 ACP, 7- or 10-shot magazine. **Barrel:** 5". **Weight:** 37 oz. **Length:** 8.5" overall. **Stocks:** Checkered rosewood, double diamond pattern. **Sights:** Baer dovetailed front, low-mount Bo-Mar rear with hidden leaf. **Features:** Baer NM forged steel frame and barrel with stainless bushing; slide fitted to frame; double serrated slide; lowered, flared ejection port; tuned, polished extractor; Baer extended ejector, checkered slide stop, aluminum speed trigger with 4-lb. pull, deluxe Commander hammer and sear, beavertail grip safety with pad, beveled magazine well, extended ambidextrous safety; flat mainspring housing; polished feed ramp and throated barrel; 30 lpi checkered front strap. Made in U.S. by Les Baer Custom, Inc.

Price: Blued **$1,428.00**
Price: Stainless. **$1,558.00**
Price: 6" model, blued, from **$1,595.00**

BAER 1911 S.R.P. PISTOL

Caliber: 45 ACP. **Barrel:** 5". **Weight:** 37 oz. **Length:** 8.5" overall. **Stocks:** Checkered walnut. **Sights:** Trijicon night sights. **Features:** Similar to the

F.B.I. contract gun except uses Baer forged steel frame. Has Baer match barrel with supported chamber, Wolff springs, complete tactical action job. All parts Mag-na-fluxed; deburred for tactical carry. Has Baer Ultra Coat finish. Tuned for reliability. Contact Baer for complete details. Introduced 1996. Made in U.S. by Les Baer Custom, Inc.

Price: Government or Comanche length **$2,240.00**

BERETTA MODEL 92FS PISTOL

Caliber: 9mm Para., 10-shot magazine. **Barrel:** 4.9". **Weight:** 34 oz. **Length:** 8.5" overall. **Stocks:** Checkered black plastic. **Sights:** Blade front, rear adjustable for windage. Tritium night sights available. **Features:** Double action. Extractor acts as chamber loaded indicator, squared trigger guard, grooved front- and backstraps, inertia firing pin. Matte or blued finish. Introduced 1977. Made in U.S. and imported from Italy by Beretta U.S.A.

Price: With plastic grips **$669.00**

Beretta Model 92FS/96 Brigadier Pistols

Similar to the Model 92FS/96 except with a heavier slide to reduce felt recoil and allow mounting removable front sight. Wrap-around rubber grips. Three-dot sights dovetailed to the slide, adjustable for windage. Weighs 35.3 oz. Introduced 1999.

Price: 9mm or 40 S&W, 10-shot. **$716.00**
Price: Inox models (stainless steel) **$771.00**

Beretta Model 92FS 470th Anniversary Limited Edition

Similar to the Model 92FS stainless except has mirror polish finish, smooth walnut grips with inlaid gold-plated medallions. Special and unique gold-filled engraving includes the signature of Beretta's president. The anniversary logo is engraved on the top of the slide and the back of the magazine. Each pistol identified by a "1 of 470" gold-filled number. Special chrome-plated magazine included. Deluxe lockable walnut case with teak inlays and engraving. Only 470 pistols will be sold. Introduced 1999.

Price: **$2,082.00**

Beretta Model 92FS Compact and Compact Type M Pistol

Similar to the Model 92FS except more compact and lighter: overall length 7.8"; 4.3" barrel; weighs 30.9 oz. Has Bruniton finish, chrome-lined bore, combat trigger guard, ambidextrous safety/decock lever. Single column 8-shot magazine (Type M), or double column 10-shot (Compact), 9mm only. Introduced 1998. Imported from Italy by Beretta U.S.A.

Price: Compact (10-shot) **$669.00**
Price: Compact Type M (8-shot). **$669.00**
Price: Compact Inox (stainless) **$734.00**
Price: Compact Type M Inox (stainless). **$721.00**

Beretta Model 96 Pistol

Same as the Model 92FS except chambered for 40 S&W. Ambidextrous safety mechanism with passive firing pin catch, slide safety/decocking lever, trigger bar disconnect. Has 10-shot magazine. Available with three-dot sights. Introduced 1992.

Price: Model 96, plastic grips **$669.00**
Price: Stainless, rubber grips **$734.00**

Beretta 950 Jetfire

Beretta M8000/8040 Cougar

Bersa Thunder 380

BERETTA MODEL 80 CHEETAH SERIES DA PISTOLS

Caliber: 380 ACP, 10-shot magazine (M84); 8-shot (M85); 22 LR, 7-shot (M87). **Barrel:** 3.82". **Weight:** About 23 oz. (M84/85); 20.8 oz. (M87). **Length:** 6.8" overall. **Stocks:** Glossy black plastic (wood optional at extra cost). **Sights:** Fixed front, drift-adjustable rear. **Features:** Double action, quick takedown, convenient magazine release. Introduced 1977. Imported from Italy by Beretta U.S.A.

Price: Model 84 Cheetah, plastic grips $576.00
Price: Model 84 Cheetah, wood grips, nickel finish $652.00
Price: Model 85 Cheetah, plastic grips, 8-shot $545.00
Price: Model 85 Cheetah, wood grips, nickel, 8-shot $609.00
Price: Model 87 Cheetah, wood, 22 LR, 7-shot $576.00
Price: Model 87 Target, plastic grips $669.00

Beretta Model 86 Cheetah

Similar to the 380-caliber Model 85 except has tip-up barrel for first-round loading. Barrel length is 4.4", overall length of 7.33". Has 8-shot magazine, walnut grips. Introduced 1989.
Price: $578.00

BERETTA MODEL 950 JETFIRE AUTO PISTOL

Caliber: 25 ACP, 8-shot. **Barrel:** 2.4". **Weight:** 9.9 oz. **Length:** 4.7" overall. **Stocks:** Checkered black plastic or walnut. **Sights:** Fixed. **Features:** Single action, thumb safety; tip-up barrel for direct loading/unloading, cleaning. From Beretta U.S.A.
Price: Jetfire plastic, matte finish $226.00
Price: Jetfire plastic, stainless $267.00

Beretta Model 21 Bobcat Pistol

Similar to the Model 950 BS. Chambered for 22 LR or 25 ACP. Both double action. Has 2.4" barrel, 4.9" overall length; 7-round magazine on 22 cal.; 8 rounds in 25 ACP, 9.9 oz., available in nickel, matte, engraved or blue finish. Plastic grips. Introduced in 1985.
Price: Bobcat, 22 or 25, blue $285.00
Price: Bobcat, 22, stainless $307.00
Price: Bobcat, 22 or 25, matte $252.00

BERETTA MODEL 3032 TOMCAT PISTOL

Caliber: 32 ACP, 7-shot magazine. **Barrel:** 2.45". **Weight:** 14.5 oz. **Length:** 5" overall. **Stocks:** Checkered black plastic. **Sights:** Blade front, drift-adjustable rear. **Features:** Double action with exposed hammer; tip-up barrel for direct loading/unloading; thumb safety; polished or matte blue finish. Imported from Italy by Beretta U.S.A. Introduced 1996.
Price: Blue $370.00
Price: Matte $340.00
Price: Stainless $418.00
Price: Titanium $572.00

BERETTA MODEL 8000/8040/8045 COUGAR PISTOL

Caliber: 9mm Para., 10-shot, 40 S&W, 10-shot magazine; 45 ACP, 8-shot. **Barrel:** 3.6". **Weight:** 33.5 oz. **Length:** 7" overall. **Stocks:** Checkered plastic. **Sights:** Blade front, rear drift adjustable for windage. **Features:** Slide-mounted safety; rotating barrel; exposed hammer. Matte black Bruniton finish. Announced 1994. Imported from Italy by Beretta U.S.A.
Price: $709.00

Price: D model, 9mm, 40 S&W $739.00
Price: D model, 45 ACP $739.00

BERETTA MODEL 9000S COMPACT PISTOL

Caliber: 9mm Para., 40 S&W; 10-shot magazine. **Barrel:** 3.4". **Weight:** 26.8 oz. **Length:** 6.6". **Grips:** Soft polymer. **Sights:** Windage-adjustable white-dot rear, white-dot blade front. **Features:** Glass-reinforced polymer frame; patented tilt-barrel, open-slide locking system; chrome-lined barrel; external serrated hammer; automatic firing pin and manual safeties. Introduced 2000. Imported from Italy by Beretta USA.
Price: 9000S Type F (single and double action, external hammer) $551.00
Price: 9000S Type D (double-action only, no external hammer or safety) $551.00

Beretta Model 8000/8040/8045 Mini Cougar

Similar to the Model 8000/8040 Cougar except has shorter grip frame and weighs 27.6 oz. Introduced 1998. Imported from Italy by Beretta U.S.A.
Price: 9mm or 40 S&W $709.00
Price: 9mm or 40 S&W, DAO $739.00
Price: 45 ACP, 6-shot $739.00
Price: 45 ACP DAO $739.00

BERSA THUNDER 380 AUTO PISTOLS

Caliber: 380 ACP, 7-shot (Thunder 380 Lite), 9-shot magazine (Thunder 380 DLX). **Barrel:** 3.5". **Weight:** 23 oz. **Length:** 6.6" overall. **Stocks:** Black polymer. **Sights:** Blade front, notch rear adjustable for windage; three-dot system. **Features:** Double action; firing pin and magazine safeties. Available in blue or nickel. Introduced 1995. Distributed by Eagle Imports, Inc.
Price: Thunder 380, 7-shot, deep blue finish $248.95
Price: Thunder 380 Deluxe, 9-shot, satin nickel $291.95

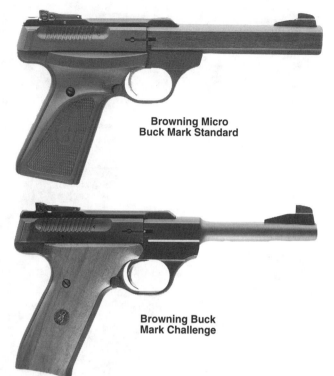

Browning Micro Buck Mark Standard

Calico M-110

Browning Buck Mark Challenge

BLUE THUNDER/COMMODORE 1911-STYLE AUTO PISTOLS

Caliber: 45 ACP, 7-shot magazine. **Barrel:** 4-1/4", 5". **Weight:** NA. **Length:** NA. **Grips:** Checkered hardwood. **Sights:** Blade front, drift-adjustable rear. **Features:** Extended slide release and safety, spring guide rod, skeletonized hammer and trigger, magazine bumper, beavertail grip safety. Imported from the Philippines by Century International Arms Inc.
Price: . . . . **$464.80 to $484.80**

BROWNING HI-POWER 9mm AUTOMATIC PISTOL

Caliber: 9mm Para.,10-shot magazine. **Barrel:** 4-21/32". **Weight:** 32 oz. **Length:** 7-3/4" overall. **Stocks:** Walnut, hand checkered, or black Polyamide. **Sights:** 1/8" blade front; rear screw-adjustable for windage and elevation. Also available with fixed rear (drift-adjustable for windage). **Features:** External hammer with half-cock and thumb safeties. A blow on the hammer cannot discharge a cartridge; cannot be fired with magazine removed. Fixed rear sight model available. Includes gun lock. Imported from Belgium by Browning.
Price: Fixed sight model, walnut grips **$680.00**
Price: Fully adjustable rear sight, walnut grips **$730.00**
Price: Mark III, standard matte black finish, fixed sight, moulded grips,
ambidextrous safety **$662.00**

Browning Hi-Power Practical Pistol

Similar to the standard Hi-Power except has silver-chromed frame with blued slide, wrap-around Pachmayr rubber grips, round-style serrated hammer and removable front sight, fixed rear (drift-adjustable for windage). Available in 9mm Para. Includes gun lock. Introduced 1991.
Price: **$717.00**

BROWNING BUCK MARK STANDARD 22 PISTOL

Caliber: 22 LR, 10-shot magazine. **Barrel:** 5-1/2". **Weight:** 32 oz. **Length:** 9-1/2" overall. **Stocks:** Black moulded composite with checkering. **Sights:** Ramp front, Browning Pro Target rear adjustable for windage and elevation. **Features:** All steel, matte blue finish or nickel, gold-colored trigger. Buck Mark Plus has laminated wood grips. Includes gun lock. Made in U.S. Introduced 1985. From Browning.
Price: Buck Mark Standard, blue **$286.00**
Price: Buck Mark Nickel, nickel finish with contoured rubber grips **$338.00**
Price: Buck Mark Plus, matte blue with laminated wood grips . . . **$350.00**
Price: Buck Mark Plus Nickel, nickel finish, laminated wood grips **$383.00**

Browning Buck Mark Camper

Similar to the Buck Mark except 5-1/2" bull barrel. Weight is 34 oz. Matte blue finish, molded composite grips. Introduced 1999. From Browning.
Price: **$258.00**
Price: Camper Nickel, nickel finish, molded composite grips **$287.00**

Browning Buck Mark Challenge

Similar to the Buck Mark except has a lightweight barrel and smaller grip diameter. Barrel length is 5-1/2", weight is 25 oz. Introduced 1999. From Browning.
Price: **$320.00**

Browning Buck Mark Micro

Same as the Buck Mark Standard and Buck Mark Plus except has 4" barrel. Available in blue or nickel. Has 16-click Pro Target rear sight. Introduced 1992.
Price: Micro Standard, matte blue finish. **$286.00**
Price: Micro Nickel, nickel finish **$338.00**
Price: Buck Mark Micro Plus, matte blue, lam. wood grips . . . **$350.00**
Price: Buck Mark Micro Plus Nickel **$383.00**

Browning Buck Mark Bullseye

Same as the Buck Mark Standard except has 7-1/4" fluted barrel, matte blue finish. Weighs 36 oz.
Price: Bullseye Standard, molded composite grips **$420.00**
Price: Bullseye Target, contoured rosewood grips **$541.00**

Browning Buck Mark 5.5

Same as the Buck Mark Standard except has a 5-1/2" bull barrel with integral scope mount, matte blue finish.
Price: 5.5 Field, Pro-Target adj. rear sight, contoured walnut grips **$459.00**
Price: 5.5 Target, hooded adj. target sights, contoured walnut grips
. . . . **$459.00**

Buck Mark Commemorative

Same as the Buck Mark Standard except has a 6-3/4" Challenger-style barrel, matte blue finish and scrimshaw-style, bonded ivory grips. Includes pistol rug. Limited to 1,000 guns.
Price: Commemorative. **$437.00**

CALICO M-110 AUTO PISTOL

Caliber: 22 LR. **Barrel:** 6". **Weight:** 3.7 lbs. (loaded). **Length:** 17.9" overall. **Stocks:** Moulded composition. **Sights:** Adjustable post front, notch rear. **Features:** Aluminum alloy frame; compensator; pistol grip compartment; ambidextrous safety. Uses same helical-feed magazine as M-100 Carbine. Introduced 1986. Made in U.S. From Calico.
Price: **$570.00**

CARBON-15 (Type 97) PISTOL

Caliber: 223, 10-shot magazine. **Barrel:** 7.25". **Weight:** 46 oz. **Length:** 20" overall. **Stock:** Checkered composite. **Sights:** Ghost ring. **Features:** Semi-automatic, gas-operated, rotating bolt action. Carbon fiber upper and lower receiver; chromemoly bolt carrier; fluted stainless match barrel; mil. spec. optics mounting base; uses AR-15-type magazines. Introduced 1992. From Professional Ordnance, Inc.
Price: **$1,600.00**
Price: Type 20 pistol (light-profile barrel, no compensator,
weighs 40 oz.). **$1,500.00**

Carbon-15

Colt 1991 Model O Compact

Charles Daly M-1911-A1P

Colt XS Model O Commander

Colt XS Lightweight Commander

CHARLES DALY M-1911-A1P AUTOLOADING PISTOL

Caliber: 45 ACP, 7- or 10-shot magazine. **Barrel:** 5". **Weight:** 38 oz. **Length:** 8-3/4" overall. **Stocks:** Checkered. **Sights:** Blade front, rear drift adjustable for windage; three-dot system. **Features:** Skeletonized combat hammer and trigger; beavertail grip safety; extended slide release; oversize thumb safety; Parkerized finish. Introduced 1996. Imported from the Philippines by K.B.I., Inc.
Price: **$469.95**

COLT MODEL 1991 MODEL O AUTO PISTOL

Caliber: 45 ACP, 7-shot magazine. **Barrel:** 5". **Weight:** 38 oz. **Length:** 8.5" overall. **Stocks:** Checkered black composition. **Sights:** Ramped blade front, fixed square notch rear, high profile. **Features:** Matte finish. Continuation of serial number range used on original G.I. 1911 A1 guns. Comes with one magazine and moulded carrying case. Introduced 1991.
Price: **$645.00**
Price: Stainless. **$800.00**

Colt Model 1991 Model O Commander Auto Pistol

Similar to the Model 1991 A1 except has 4-1/4" barrel. Overall length is 7-3/4". Comes with one 7-shot magazine, molded case.
Price: Blue **$645.00**
Price: Stainless steel **$800.00**

COLT XSE SERIES MODEL O AUTO PISTOLS

Caliber: 45 ACP, 8-shot magazine. **Barrel:** 4.25", 5". **Weight:** NA. **Length:** NA. **Grips:** Checkered, double diamond rosewood. **Sights:** Drift-adjustable three-dot combat. **Features:** Brushed stainless finish; adjustable, two-cut aluminum trigger; extended ambidextrous thumb safety; upswept beavertail with palm swell; elongated slot hammer; beveled magazine well. Introduced 1999. From Colt's Manufacturing Co., Inc.
Price: XSE Government (5" barrel) **$950.00**
Price: XSE Commander (4.25" barrel) **$950.00**

COLT XSE LIGHTWEIGHT COMMANDER AUTO PISTOL

Caliber: 45 ACP, 8-shot. **Barrel:** 4-1/4". **Weight:** 26 oz. **Length:** 7-3/4" overall. **Stocks:** Double diamond checkered rosewood. **Sights:** Fixed, glare-proofed blade front, square notch rear; three-dot system. **Features:** Brushed stainless slide, nickeled aluminum frame; McCormick elongated-

slot enhanced hammer, McCormick two-cut adjustable aluminum hammer. Made in U.S. by Colt's Mfg. Co., Inc.
Price: 45, stainless **$950.00**

COLT DEFENDER

Caliber: 40 S&W, 45 ACP, 7-shot magazine. **Barrel:** 3". **Weight:** 22-1/2 oz. **Length:** 6-3/4" overall. **Stocks:** Pebble-finish rubber wraparound with finger grooves. **Sights:** White dot front, snag-free Colt competition rear. **Features:** Stainless finish; aluminum frame; combat-style hammer; Hi Ride grip safety, extended manual safety, disconnect safety. Introduced 1998. Made in U.S. by Colt's Mfg. Co.
Price: **$773.00**

HANDGUNS

Colt Lightweight Commander

Colt Defender

Coonan 357 Magnum

CZ 75B 9mm

CZ 75B Decocker

COONAN 357 MAGNUM, 41 MAGNUM PISTOLS

Caliber: 357 Mag., 41 Magnum, 7-shot magazine. **Barrel:** 5". **Weight:** 42 oz. **Length:** 8.3" overall. **Stocks:** Smooth walnut. **Sights:** Interchangeable ramp front, rear adjustable for windage. **Features:** Stainless steel construction. Unique barrel hood improves accuracy and reliability. Link-less barrel. Many parts interchange with Colt autos. Has grip, hammer, half-cock safeties, extended slide latch. Made in U.S. by Coonan Arms, Inc.

Price: 5" barrel, from **$735.00**
Price: 6" barrel, from **$768.00**
Price: With 6" compensated barrel **$1,014.00**
Price: Classic model (Teflon black two-tone finish, 8-shot magazine,
   fully adjustable rear sight, integral compensated barrel) **$1,400.00**
Price: 41 Magnum Model, from **$825.00**

Coonan Compact Cadet 357 Magnum Pistol

Similar to the 357 Magnum full-size gun except has 3.9" barrel, shorter frame, 6-shot magazine. Weight is 39 oz., overall length 7.8". Linkless bull barrel, full-length recoil spring guide rod, extended slide latch. Introduced 1993. Made in U.S. by Coonan Arms, Inc.

Price: **$855.00**

CZ 75B AUTO PISTOL

Caliber: 9mm Para., 40 S&W, 10-shot magazine. **Barrel:** 4.7". **Weight:** 34.3 oz. **Length:** 8.1" overall. **Stocks:** High impact checkered plastic. **Sights:** Square post front, rear adjustable for windage; three-dot system. **Features:** Single action/double action design; firing pin block safety; choice of black polymer, matte or high-polish blue finishes. All-steel frame. Imported from the Czech Republic by CZ-USA.

Price: Black polymer **$472.00**
Price: Glossy blue **$486.00**
Price: Dual tone or satin nickel **$486.00**
Price: 22 LR conversion unit **$279.00**

CZ 75B Decocker

Similar to the CZ 75B except has a decocking lever in place of the safety lever. All other specifications are the same. Introduced 1999. Imported from the Czech Republic by CZ-USA.

Price: 9mm, black polymer **$467.00**
New! **Price:** 40 S&W **$481.00**

CZ 75D Compact

CZ 85

CZ 83B

CZ 97B

CZ 75B Compact Auto Pistol

Similar to the CZ 75 except has 10-shot magazine, 3.9" barrel and weighs 32 oz. Has removable front sight, non-glare ribbed slide top. Trigger guard is squared and serrated; combat hammer. Introduced 1993. Imported from the Czech Republic by CZ-USA.

Price: 9mm, black polymer **$499.00**
Price: Dual tone or satin nickel **$513.00**
Price: D Compact, black polymer **$526.00**

CZ 75M IPSC Auto Pistol

Similar to the CZ 75B except has a longer frame and slide, slightly larger grip to accommodate new heavy-duty magazine. Ambidextrous thumb safety, safety notch on hammer; two-port in-frame compensator; slide racker; frame-mounted Firepoint red dot sight. Introduced 2001. Imported from the Czech Republic by CZ USA.

Price: 40 S&W, 10-shot mag. **$1,498.00**
Price: CZ 75 Standard IPSC (40 S&W, adj. sights) **$1,038.00**

CZ 85B Auto Pistol

Same gun as the CZ 75 except has ambidextrous slide release and safety-levers; non-glare, ribbed slide top; squared, serrated trigger guard; trigger stop to prevent overtravel. Introduced 1986. Imported from the Czech Republic by CZ-USA.

Price: Black polymer **$483.00**
Price: Combat, black polymer **$540.00**
Price: Combat, dual tone **$487.00**
Price: Combat, glossy blue **$499.00**

CZ 85 Combat

Similar to the CZ 85B (9mm only) except has an adjustable rear sight, adjustable trigger for overtravel, free-fall magazine, extended magazine catch. Does not have the firing pin block safety. Introduced 1999. Imported from the Czech Republic by CZ-USA.

Price: 9mm, black polymer **$540.00**
Price: 9mm, glossy blue **$561.00**
Price: 9mm, dual tone or satin nickel **$561.00**

CZ 83B DOUBLE-ACTION PISTOL

Caliber: 9mm Makarov, 32 ACP, 380 ACP, 10-shot magazine. **Barrel:** 3.8". **Weight:** 26.2 oz. **Length:** 6.8" overall. **Stocks:** High impact checkered plastic. **Sights:** Removable square post front, rear adjustable for windage; three-dot system. **Features:** Single action/double action; ambidextrous magazine release and safety. Blue finish; non-glare ribbed slide top. Imported from the Czech Republic by CZ-USA.

Price: Blue **$378.00**
Price: Nickel **$378.00**

CZ 97B AUTO PISTOL

Caliber: 45 ACP, 10-shot magazine. **Barrel:** 4.85". **Weight:** 40 oz. **Length:** 8.34" overall. **Stocks:** Checkered walnut. **Sights:** Fixed. **Features:** Single action/double action; full-length slide rails; screw-in barrel bushing; linkless barrel; all-steel construction; chamber loaded indicator; dual transfer bars. Introduced 1999. Imported from the Czech Republic by CZ-USA.

Price: Black polymer **$607.00**
Price: Glossy blue **$621.00**

CZ 75/85 Kadet

CZ 100

Davis P-380

Davis P-32

Desert Eagle Mark XIX

CZ 75/85 KADET AUTO PISTOL

Caliber: 22 LR, 10-shot magazine. **Barrel:** 4.88". **Weight:** 36 oz. **Length:** NA. **Stocks:** High impact checkered plastic. **Sights:** Blade front, fully adjustable rear. **Features:** Single action/double action mechanism; all-steel construction. Duplicates weight, balance and function of the CZ 75 pistol. Introduced 1999. Imported from the Czech Republic by CZ-USA.

Price: Black polymer. $486.00

CZ 100 AUTO PISTOL

Caliber: 9mm Para., 40 S&W, 10-shot magazine. **Barrel:** 3.7". **Weight:** 24 oz. **Length:** 6.9" overall. **Stocks:** Grooved polymer. **Sights:** Blade front with dot, white outline rear drift adjustable for windage. **Features:** Double action only with firing pin block; polymer frame, steel slide; has laser sight mount. Introduced 1996. Imported from the Czech Republic by CZ-USA.

Price: 9mm Para. $405.00
Price: 40 S&W $405.00

DAVIS P-380 AUTO PISTOL

Caliber: 380 ACP, 5-shot magazine. **Barrel:** 2.8". **Weight:** 22 oz. **Length:** 5.4" overall. **Stocks:** Black composition. **Sights:** Fixed. **Features:** Choice of chrome or black Teflon finish. Introduced 1991. Made in U.S. by Davis Industries.

Price: $98.00

DAVIS P-32 AUTO PISTOL

Caliber: 32 ACP, 6-shot magazine. **Barrel:** 2.8". **Weight:** 22 oz. **Length:** 5.4" overall. **Stocks:** Laminated wood. **Sights:** Fixed. **Features:** Choice of black Teflon or chrome finish. Announced 1986. Made in U.S. by Davis Industries.

Price: $107.00

DESERT EAGLE MARK XIX PISTOL

Caliber: 357 Mag., 9-shot; 44 Mag., 8-shot; 50 Magnum, 7-shot. **Barrel:** 6", 10", interchangeable. **Weight:** 357 Mag.—62 oz.; 44 Mag.—69 oz.; 50 Mag.— 72 oz. **Length:** 10-1/4" overall (6" bbl.). **Stocks:** Rubber. **Sights:** Blade on ramp front, combat-style rear. Adjustable available. **Features:** Interchangeable barrels; rotating three-lug bolt; ambidextrous safety; adjustable trigger. Military epoxy finish. Satin, bright nickel, hard chrome, polished and blued finishes available. 10" barrel extra. Imported from Israel by Magnum Research, Inc.

Price: 357, 6" bbl., standard pistol $1,199.00
Price: 44 Mag., 6", standard pistol $1,199.00
Price: 50 Magnum, 6" bbl., standard pistol $1,199.00
Price: 440 Cor-Bon, 6" bbl. $1,389.00

HANDGUNS

Desert Eagle Baby Eagle

E.A.A. Witness

Entréprise Elite P500

Entréprise Boxer P500

DESERT EAGLE BABY EAGLE PISTOLS

Caliber: 9mm Para., 40 S&W, 45 ACP, 10-round magazine. **Barrel:** 3.5", 3.7", 4.72". **Weight:** NA. **Length:** 7.25" to 8.25" overall. **Grips:** Polymer. **Sights:** Drift-adjustable rear, blade front. **Features:** Steel frame and slide; polygonal rifling to reduce barrel wear; slide safety; decocker. Reintroduced in 1999. Imported from Israel by Magnum Research Inc.

Price: Standard (9mm or 40 cal.; 4.72" barrel, 8.25" overall) . . . **$499.00**
Price: Semi-Compact (9mm, 40 or 45 cal.; 3.7" barrel,
7.75" overall) **$499.00**
Price: Compact (9mm or 40 cal.; 3.5" barrel, 7.25" overall) **$499.00**
Price: Polymer (9mm or 40 cal; polymer frame; 3.25" barrel,
7.25" overall) **$499.00**

E.A.A. WITNESS DA AUTO PISTOL

Caliber: 9mm Para., 10-shot magazine; 38 Super, 40 S&W, 10-shot magazine; 45 ACP, 10-shot magazine. **Barrel:** 4.50". **Weight:** 35.33 oz. **Length:** 8.10" overall. **Stocks:** Checkered rubber. **Sights:** Undercut blade front, open rear adjustable for windage. **Features:** Double-action trigger system; round trigger guard; frame-mounted safety. Introduced 1991. Imported from Italy by European American Armory.

Price: 9mm, blue. **$351.00**
Price: 9mm, Wonder finish **$366.00**
Price: 9mm Compact, blue, 10-shot **$351.00**
Price: As above, Wonder finish **$366.60**
Price: 40 S&W, blue **$366.60**
Price: As above, Wonder finish **$366.60**
Price: 40 S&W Compact, 9-shot, blue **$366.60**
Price: As above, Wonder finish **$366.60**
Price: 45 ACP, blue. **$351.00**
Price: As above, Wonder finish **$366.60**
Price: 45 ACP Compact, 8-shot, blue. **$351.00**
Price: As above, Wonder finish **$366.60**

E.A.A. EUROPEAN MODEL AUTO PISTOLS

Caliber: 32 ACP or 380 ACP, 7-shot magazine. **Barrel:** 3.88". **Weight:** 26 oz. **Length:** 7-3/8" overall. **Stocks:** European hardwood. **Sights:** Fixed blade front, rear drift-adjustable for windage. **Features:** Chrome or blue finish; magazine, thumb and firing pin safeties; external hammer; safety-lever takedown. Imported from Italy by European American Armory.

Price: Blue **$132.60**
Price: Wonder finish **$163.80**

ENTRÉPRISE ELITE P500 AUTO PISTOL

Caliber: 45 ACP, 10-shot magazine. **Barrel:** 5". **Weight:** 40 oz. **Length:** 8.5" overall. **Stocks:** Black ultra-slim, double diamond, checkered synthetic. **Sights:** Dovetailed blade front, rear adjustable for windage; three-dot system. **Features:** Reinforced dust cover; lowered and flared ejection port; squared trigger guard; adjustable match trigger; bolstered front strap; high grip cut; high ride beavertail grip safety; steel flat mainspring housing; extended thumb lock; skeletonized hammer, match grade sear, disconnector; Wolff springs. Introduced 1998. Made in U.S. by Entréprise Arms.

Price: **$739.90**

Entréprise Boxer P500 Auto Pistol

Similar to the Medalist model except has adjustable Competizione "melded" rear sight with dovetailed Patridge front; high mass chiseled slide with sweep cut; machined slide parallel rails; polished breech face and barrel channel. Introduced 1998. Made in U.S. by Entréprise Arms.

Price: $1,399.00

Entréprise Medalist P500 Auto Pistol

Similar to the Elite model except has adjustable Competizione "melded" rear sight with dovetailed Patridge front; machined slide parallel rails with polished breech face and barrel channel; front and rear slide serrations; lowered and flared ejection port; full-length one-piece guide rod with plug; National Match barrel and bushing; stainless firing pin; tuned match extractor; oversize firing pin stop; throated barrel and polished ramp; slide lapped to frame. Introduced 1998. Made in U.S. by Entréprise Arms.

Price: 45 ACP. **$979.00**
Price: 40 S&W $1,099.00

Entréprise Tactical 500

Felk MTF 450

FEG PJK-9HP

Glock 17C

Entréprise Tactical P500 Auto Pistol

Similar to the Elite model except has Tactical2 Ghost Ring sight or Novak lo-mount sight; ambidextrous thumb safety; front and rear slide serrations; full-length guide rod; throated barrel, polished ramp; tuned match extractor; fitted barrel and bushing; stainless firing pin; slide lapped to frame; dehorned. Introduced 1998. Made in U.S. by Entréprise Arms.

Price: **$979.90**
Price: Tactical Plus (full-size frame, Officer's slide) **$1,049.00**

ERMA KGP68 AUTO PISTOL

Caliber: 32 ACP, 6-shot, 380 ACP, 5-shot. **Barrel:** 4". **Weight:** 22-1/2 oz. **Length:** 7-3/8" overall. **Stocks:** Checkered plastic. **Sights:** Fixed. **Features:** Toggle action similar to original "Luger" pistol. Action stays open after last shot. Has magazine and sear disconnect safety systems.

Price: **$499.95**

FEG PJK-9HP AUTO PISTOL

Caliber: 9mm Para., 10-shot magazine. **Barrel:** 4.75". **Weight:** 32 oz. **Length:** 8" overall. **Stocks:** Hand-checkered walnut. **Sights:** Blade front, rear adjustable for windage; three dot system. **Features:** Single action; polished blue or hard chrome finish; rounded combat-style serrated hammer. Comes with two magazines and cleaning rod. Imported from Hungary by K.B.I., Inc.

Price: Blue **$259.95**
Price: Hard chrome. **$259.95**

FEG SMC-380 AUTO PISTOL

Caliber: 380 ACP, 6-shot magazine. **Barrel:** 3.5". **Weight:** 18.5 oz. **Length:** 6.1" overall. **Stocks:** Checkered composition with thumbrest. **Sights:** Blade front, rear adjustable for windage. **Features:** Patterned af-

ter the PPK pistol. Alloy frame, steel slide; double action. Blue finish. Comes with two magazines, cleaning rod. Imported from Hungary by K.B.I., Inc.

Price: **$224.95**

FELK MTF 450 AUTO PISTOL

Caliber: 9mm Para. (10-shot); 40 S&W (8-shot); 45 ACP (9-shot magazine). **Barrel:** 3.5". **Weight:** 19.9 oz. **Length:** 6.4" overall. **Stocks:** Checkered. **Sights:** Blade front; adjustable rear. **Features:** Double-action-only trigger, striker fired; polymer frame; trigger safety, firing pin safety, trigger bar safety; adjustable trigger weight; fully interchangeable slide/barrel to change calibers. Introduced 1998. Imported by Felk Inc.

Price: **$395.00**
Price: 45 ACP pistol with 9mm and 40 S&W slide/barrel
assemblies **$999.00**

GLOCK 17 AUTO PISTOL

Caliber: 9mm Para., 10-shot magazine. **Barrel:** 4.49". **Weight:** 22.04 oz. (without magazine). **Length:** 7.32" overall. **Stocks:** Black polymer. **Sights:** Dot on front blade, white outline rear adjustable for windage. **Features:** Polymer frame, steel slide; double-action trigger with "Safe Action" system; mechanical firing pin safety, drop safety; simple takedown without tools; locked breech, recoil operated action. Adopted by Austrian armed forces 1983. NATO approved 1984. Imported from Austria by Glock, Inc.

Price: Fixed sight, with extra magazine, magazine loader, cleaning kit
. . . . **$641.00**
Price: Adjustable sight **$671.00**
Price: Model 17L (6" barrel) **$800.00**
Price: Model 17C, ported barrel (compensated) **$646.00**

Glock 22

Glock 30

Glock 26

Glock 31

Glock 19 Auto Pistol

Similar to the Glock 17 except has a 4" barrel, giving an overall length of 6.85" and weight of 20.99 oz. Magazine capacity is 10 rounds. Fixed or adjustable rear sight. Introduced 1988.

Price: Fixed sight **$641.00**
Price: Adjustable sight **$671.00**
Price: Model 19C, ported barrel **$646.00**

Glock 20 10mm Auto Pistol

Similar to the Glock Model 17 except chambered for 10mm Automatic cartridge. Barrel length is 4.60", overall length is 7.59", and weight is 26.3 oz. (without magazine). Magazine capacity is 10 rounds. Fixed or adjustable rear sight. Comes with an extra magazine, magazine loader, cleaning rod and brush. Introduced 1990. Imported from Austria by Glock, Inc.

Price: Fixed sight **$700.00**
Price: Adjustable sight **$730.00**

Glock 21 Auto Pistol

Similar to the Glock 17 except chambered for 45 ACP, 10-shot magazine. Overall length is 7.59", weight is 25.2 oz. (without magazine). Fixed or adjustable rear sight. Introduced 1991.

Price: Fixed sight **$700.00**
Price: Adjustable sight **$730.00**

Glock 22 Auto Pistol

Similar to the Glock 17 except chambered for 40 S&W, 10-shot magazine. Overall length is 7.28", weight is 22.3 oz. (without magazine). Fixed or adjustable rear sight. Introduced 1990.

Price: Fixed sight **$641.00**
Price: Adjustable sight **$671.00**
Price: Model 22C, ported barrel **$646.00**

Glock 23 Auto Pistol

Similar to the Glock 19 except chambered for 40 S&W, 10-shot magazine. Overall length is 6.85", weight is 20.6 oz. (without magazine). Fixed or adjustable rear sight. Introduced 1990.

Price: Fixed sight **$641.00**
Price: Model 23C, ported barrel **$646.00**
Price: Adjustable sight **$671.00**

GLOCK 26, 27 AUTO PISTOLS

Caliber: 9mm Para. (M26), 10-shot magazine; 40 S&W (M27), 9-shot magazine. **Barrel:** 3.46". **Weight:** 21.75 oz. **Length:** 6.29" overall. **Stocks:** Integral. Stippled polymer. **Sights:** Dot on front blade, fixed or fully adjustable white outline rear. **Features:** Subcompact size. Polymer frame, steel slide; double-action trigger with "Safe Action" system, three safeties. Matte black Tenifer finish. Hammer-forged barrel. Imported from Austria by Glock, Inc. Introduced 1996.

Price: Fixed sight **$641.00**
Price: Adjustable sight **$671.00**

GLOCK 29, 30 AUTO PISTOLS

Caliber: 10mm (M29), 45 ACP (M30), 10-shot magazine. **Barrel:** 3.78". **Weight:** 24 oz. **Length:** 6.7" overall. **Stocks:** Integral. Stippled polymer. **Sights:** Dot on front, fixed or fully adjustable white outline rear. **Features:** Compact size. Polymer frame steel slide; double-recoil spring reduces recoil; Safe Action system with three safeties; Tenifer finish. Two magazines supplied. Introduced 1997. Imported from Austria by Glock, Inc.

Price: Fixed sight **$700.00**
Price: Adjustable sight **$730.00**

Glock 31/31C Auto Pistols

Similar to the Glock 17 except chambered for 357 Auto cartridge; 10-shot magazine. Overall length is 7.32", weight is 23.28 oz. (without magazine). Fixed or adjustable sight. Imported from Austria by Glock, Inc.

Price: Fixed sight **$641.00**
Price: Adjustable sight **$671.00**
Price: Model 31C, ported barrel **$646.00**

Glock 35

Hammerli Trailside PL 22

Heckler & Koch USP Compact

Heckler & Koch USP45

Glock 32/32C Auto Pistols

Similar to the Glock 19 except chambered for the 357 Auto cartridge; 10-shot magazine. Overall length is 6.85", weight is 21.52 oz. (without magazine). Fixed or adjustable sight. Imported from Austria by Glock, Inc.

Price: Fixed sight **$616.00**
Price: Adjustable sight **$644.00**
Price: Model 32C, ported barrel **$646.00**

Glock 33 Auto Pistol

Similar to the Glock 26 except chambered for the 357 Auto cartridge; 9-shot magazine. Overall length is 6.29", weight is 19.75 oz. (without magazine). Fixed or adjustable sight. Imported from Austria by Glock, Inc.

Price: Fixed sight **$641.00**
Price: Adjustable sight **$671.00**

GLOCK 34, 35 AUTO PISTOLS

Caliber: 9mm Para. (M34), 40 S&W (M35), 10-shot magazine. **Barrel:** 5.32". **Weight:** 22.9 oz. **Length:** 8.15" overall. **Stocks:** Integral. Stippled polymer. **Sights:** Dot on front, fully adjustable white outline rear. **Features:** Polymer frame, steel slide; double-action trigger with "Safe Action" system; three safeties; Tenifer finish. Imported from Austria by Glock, Inc.

Price: Model 34, 9mm. **$770.00**
Price: Model 35, 40 S&W **$770.00**

GLOCK 36 AUTO PISTOL

Caliber: 45 ACP, 6-shot magazine. **Barrel:** 3.78". **Weight:** 20.11 oz. **Length:** 6.77" overall. **Stocks:** Integral. Stippled polymer. **Sights:** Dot on front, fully adjustable white outline rear. **Features:** Polymer frame, steel slide; double-action trigger with "Safe Action" system; three safeties; Tenifer finish. Imported from Austria by Glock, Inc.

Price: Fixed sight **$700.00**
Price: Adj. sight **$730.00**

HAMMERLI TRAILSIDE PL 22 TARGET PISTOL

Caliber: 22 LR, 10-shot magazine. **Barrel:** 4.5", 6". **Weight:** 28 oz. (4.5" barrel). **Length:** 7.75" overall. **Stocks:** Wood target-style. **Sights:** Blade front, rear adjustable for windage. **Features:** One-piece barrel/frame unit; two-stage competition-style trigger; dovetail scope mount rail. Introduced 1999. Imported from Switzerland by SIGARMS, Inc.

Price: . . . . **NA**

HECKLER & KOCH USP AUTO PISTOL

Caliber: 9mm Para., 10-shot magazine, 40 S&W, 10-shot magazine. **Barrel:** 4.25". **Weight:** 28 oz. (USP40). **Length:** 6.9" overall. **Stocks:** Non-slip stippled black polymer. **Sights:** Blade front, rear adjustable for windage. **Features:** New HK design with polymer frame, modified Browning action with recoil reduction system, single control lever. Special "hostile environment" finish on all metal parts. Available in SA/DA, DAO, left- and right-hand versions. Introduced 1993. Imported from Germany by Heckler & Koch, Inc.

Price: Right-hand **$699.00**
Price: Left-hand **$714.00**
Price: Stainless steel, right-hand **$749.00**
Price: Stainless steel, left-hand **$799.00**

Heckler & Koch USP Compact Auto Pistol

Similar to the USP except has 3.58" barrel, measures 6.81" overall, and weighs 1.60 lbs. (9mm). Available in 9mm Para. 357 SIG or 40 S&W with 10-shot magazine. Introduced 1996. Imported from Germany by Heckler & Koch, Inc.

Price: Blue **$759.00**
Price: Blue with control lever on right. . . . **$784.00**
Price: Stainless steel **$849.00**
Price: Stainless steel with control lever on right **$874.00**

Heckler & Koch USP45 Auto Pistol

Similar to the 9mm and 40 S&W USP except chambered for 45 ACP, 10-shot magazine. Has 4.13" barrel, overall length of 7.87" and weighs 30.4 oz. Has adjustable three-dot sight system. Available in SA/DA, DAO, left- and right-hand versions. Introduced 1995. Imported from Germany by Heckler & Koch, Inc.

Price: Right-hand **$799.00**
Price: Left-hand **$824.00**
Price: Stainless steel right-hand. **$859.00**
Price: Stainless steel left-hand. **$884.00**

Heckler & Koch USP45 Tactical

Heckler & Koch P7M8

Heckler & Koch USP Expert

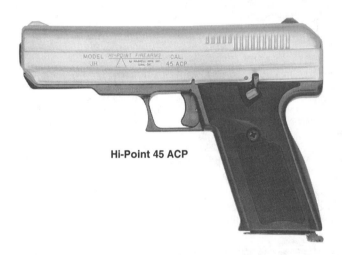

Hi-Point 45 ACP

Heckler & Koch USP45 Compact

Similar to the USP45 except has stainless slide; 8-shot magazine; modified and contoured slide and frame; extended slide release; 3.80" barrel, 7.09" overall length, weighs 1.75 lbs.; adjustable three-dot sights. Introduced 1998. Imported from Germany by Heckler & Koch, Inc.

Price: With control lever on left, stainless **$879.00**
Price: As above, blue **$879.00**
Price: With control lever on right, stainless **$904.00**
Price: As above, blue **$854.00**

HECKLER & KOCH USP45 TACTICAL PISTOL

Caliber: 45 ACP, 10-shot magazine. **Barrel:** 4.92". **Weight:** 2.24 lbs. **Length:** 8.64" overall. **Stocks:** Non-slip stippled polymer. **Sights:** Blade front, fully adjustable target rear. **Features:** Has extended threaded barrel with rubber O-ring; adjustable trigger; extended magazine floorplate; adjustable trigger stop; polymer frame. Introduced 1998. Imported from Germany by Heckler & Koch, Inc.

Price: **$1,069.00**

HECKLER & KOCH MARK 23 SPECIAL OPERATIONS PISTOL

Caliber: 45 ACP, 10-shot magazine. **Barrel:** 5.87". **Weight:** 43 oz. **Length:** 9.65" overall. **Stocks:** Integral with frame; black polymer. **Sights:** Blade front, rear drift adjustable for windage; three-dot. **Features:** Polymer frame; double action; exposed hammer; short recoil, modified Browning action. Civilian version of the SOCOM pistol. Introduced 1996. Imported from Germany by Heckler & Koch, Inc.

Price: **$2,289.00**

Heckler & Koch USP Expert Pistol

Combines features of the USP Tactical and HK Mark 23 pistols with a new slide design. Chambered for 45 ACP; 10-shot magazine. Has adjustable target sights, 5.20" barrel, 8.74" overall length, weighs 1.87 lbs. Match-grade single- and double-action trigger pull with adjustable stop; ambidextrous control levers; elongated target slide; barrel O-ring that seals and centers barrel. Suited to IPSC competition. Introduced 1999. Imported from Germany by Heckler & Koch, Inc.

Price: **$1,449.00**

HECKLER & KOCH P7M8 AUTO PISTOL

Caliber: 9mm Para., 8-shot magazine. **Barrel:** 4.13". **Weight:** 29 oz. **Length:** 6.73" overall. **Stocks:** Stippled black plastic. **Sights:** Blade front, adjustable rear; three dot system. **Features:** Unique "squeeze cocker" in frontstrap cocks the action. Gas-retarded action. Squared combat-type trigger guard. Blue finish. Compact size. Imported from Germany by Heckler & Koch, Inc.

Price: P7M8, blued **$1,369.00**

HI-POINT FIREARMS 40 S&W AUTO

Caliber: 40 S&W, 8-shot magazine. **Barrel:** 4.5". **Weight:** 39 oz. **Length:** 7.72" overall. **Stocks:** Checkered acetal resin. **Sights:** Adjustable; low profile. **Features:** Internal drop-safe mechanism; alloy frame. Introduced 1991. From MKS Supply, Inc.

Price: Matte black **$159.00**

HI-POINT FIREARMS 45 CALIBER PISTOL

Caliber: 45 ACP, 7-shot magazine. **Barrel:** 4.5". **Weight:** 39 oz. **Length:** 7.95" overall. **Stocks:** Checkered acetal resin. **Sights:** Adjustable; low profile. **Features:** Internal drop-safe mechanism; alloy frame. Introduced 1991. From MKS Supply, Inc.

Price: Matte black **$159.00**
Price: Chrome slide, black frame **$169.00**

Hi-Point 9MM Comp

Kahr K9

Kahr MK40

HI-POINT FIREARMS 9MM COMP PISTOL

Caliber: 9mm, Para., 10-shot magazine. **Barrel:** 4". **Weight:** 39 oz. **Length:** 7.72" overall. **Stocks:** Textured acetal plastic. **Sights:** Adjustable; low profile. **Features:** Single-action design. Scratch-resistant, nonglare blue finish, alloy frame. Muzzle brake/compensator. Compensator is slotted for laser or flashlight mounting. Introduced 1998. From MKS Supply, Inc.
Price: Matte black **$159.00**

HI-POINT FIREARMS MODEL 9MM COMPACT PISTOL

Caliber: 9mm Para., 8-shot magazine. **Barrel:** 3.5". **Weight:** 29 oz. **Length:** 6.7" overall. **Stocks:** Textured acetal plastic. **Sights:** Combat-style adjustable three-dot system; low profile. **Features:** Single-action design; frame-mounted magazine release; polymer or alloy frame. Scratch-resistant matte finish. Introduced 1993. Made in U.S. by MKS Supply, Inc.
Price: Black, alloy frame **$137.00**
Price: With polymer frame (29 oz.), non-slip grips **$137.00**
Price: Aluminum with polymer frame **$137.00**

Hi-Point Firearms Model 380 Polymer Pistol

Similar to the 9mm Compact model except chambered for 380 ACP, 8-shot magazine, adjustable three-dot sights. Weighs 29 oz. Polymer frame. Introduced 1998. Made in U.S. by MKS Supply.
Price: **$99.95**

Hi-Point Firearms 380 Comp Pistol

NEW! Similar to the 380 Polymer Pistol except has a 4" barrel with muzzle compensator; action locks open after last shot. Includes a 10-shot and an 8-shot magazine; trigger lock. Introduced 2001. Made in U.S. by MKS Supply Inc.
Price: **$125.00**
Price: With laser sight **$190.00**

HS AMERICA HS 2000 PISTOL

Caliber: 9mm Para., 357 SIG, 40 S&W, 10-shot magazine. **Barrel:** 4.08". **Weight:** 22.88 oz. **Length:** 7.2" overall. **Grips:** Integral black polymer. **Sights:** Drift-adjustable white dot rear, white dot blade front. **Features:** Incorporates trigger, firing pin, grip and out-of-battery safeties; firing-pin status and loaded chamber indicators; ambidextrous magazine release; dual-tension recoil spring with stand-off device; polymer frame; black finish with chrome-plated magazine. Imported from Croatia by HS America.
Price: **$419.00**

IAI M-3000 AUTO PISTOL

Caliber: 9mm Para., 7-shot magazine. **Barrel:** 3-1/2". **Weight:** 32 oz. **Length:** 6-1/2" overall. **Grips:** Plastic. **Sights:** High-contrast fixed. **Features:** Double-action; all-steel construction; automatic firing-pin safety; field strips without tools; slide stays open after last shot. Imported by IAI Inc.
Price: **$373.70**

IAI M-4000 AUTO PISTOL

Similar to IAI M-3000 Pistol above, except chambered in 40 S&W. All-steel construction; 7-shot magazine.
Price: **$373.70**

IAI M-5000 AUTO PISTOL

Caliber: 45 ACP, 8-shot magazine. **Barrel:** 4.25". **Weight:** 36 oz. **Length:** 6" overall. **Grips:** Plastic. **Sights:** Fixed. **Features:** 1911-style; blued steel frame and slide; beavertail grip safety; extended slide stop, safety and magazine release; beveled feed ramp; combat-style hammer; beveled magazine well; ambidexterous safety. Imported from the Philippines by IAI Inc.
Price: **$447.40**

IAI M-6000 AUTO PISTOL

Caliber: 45 ACP, 8-shot magazine. **Barrel:** 5". **Weight:** 36 oz. **Length:** 8-1/2" overall. **Grips:** Plastic. **Sights:** Fixed. **Features:** 1911-style; blued steel frame and slide; beavertail grip safety; extended slide stop, safety and magazine release; beveled feed ramp and magazine well; combat-style hammer; ambidexterous safety. Imported from the Philippines by IAI Inc.
Price: **$447.40**

KAHR K9, K40 DA AUTO PISTOLS

Caliber: 9mm Para., 7-shot, 40 S&W, 6-shot magazine. **Barrel:** 3.5". **Weight:** 25 oz. **Length:** 6" overall. **Stocks:** Wrap-around textured soft polymer. **Sights:** Blade front, rear drift adjustable for windage; bar-dot combat style. **Features:** Trigger-cocking double-action mechanism with passive firing pin block. Made of 4140 ordnance steel with matte black finish. Contact maker for complete price list. Introduced 1994. Made in U.S. by Kahr Arms.
Price: E9, black matte finish **$399.00**
Price: Matte black, night sights 9mm **$640.00**
Price: Matte stainless steel, 9mm **$580.00**
Price: 40 S&W, matte black **$550.00**
Price: 40 S&W, matte black, night sights **$640.00**
Price: 40 S&W, matte stainless **$580.00**
Price: K9 Elite 98 (high-polish stainless slide flats, Kahr combat trigger), from **$631.00**
Price: As above, MK9 Elite 98, from **$631.00**
Price: As above, K40 Elite 98, from **$631.00**

Kel-Tec P-11

Kimber Custom 45

Kel-Tec P-32

Kimber Compact Custom

Kahr K9 9mm Compact Polymer Pistol

Similar to K9 steel frame pistol except has polymer frame, matte stainless steel slide. Barrel length 3.5"; overall length 6"; weighs 17.9 oz. Includes two 7-shot magazines, hard polymer case, trigger lock. Introduced 2000. Made in U.S. by Kahr Arms.

Price: **$527.00**

Kahr MK9/MK40 Micro Pistol

Similar to the K9/K40 except is 5.5" overall, 4" high, has a 3" barrel. Weighs 22 oz. Has snag-free bar-dot sights, polished feed ramp, dual recoil spring system, DA-only trigger. Comes with 6- and 7-shot magazines. Introduced 1998. Made in U.S. by Kahr Arms.

Price: Matte stainless **$580.00**
Price: Elite 98, polished stainless, tritium night sights **$721.00**

KEL-TEC P-11 AUTO PISTOL

Caliber: 9mm Para., 10-shot magazine. **Barrel:** 3.1". **Weight:** 14 oz. **Length:** 5.6" overall. **Stocks:** Checkered black polymer. **Sights:** Blade front, rear adjustable for windage. **Features:** Ordnance steel slide, aluminum frame. Double-action-only trigger mechanism. Introduced 1995. Made in U.S. by Kel-Tec CNC Industries, Inc.

Price: Blue **$309.00**
Price: Hard chrome. **$363.00**
Price: Parkerized **$350.00**

KEL-TEC P-32 AUTO PISTOL

Caliber: 32 ACP, 7-shot magazine. **Barrel:** 2.68". **Weight:** 6.6 oz. **Length:** 5.07" overall. **Stocks:** Checkered composite. **Sights:** Fixed. **Features:** Double-action-only mechanism with 6-lb. pull; internal slide stop. Textured composite grip/frame. Made in U.S. by Kel-Tec CNC Industries, Inc.

Price: **$295.00**

KIMBER CUSTOM AUTO PISTOL

Caliber: 45 ACP, 7-shot magazine. **Barrel:** 5", match grade. **Weight:** 38 oz. **Length:** 8.7" overall. **Stocks:** Checkered black rubber (standard), or rosewood. **Sights:** McCormick dovetailed front, low combat rear. **Features:** Slide, frame and barrel machined from steel forgings; match-grade barrel, chamber, trigger; extended thumb safety; beveled magazine well; beveled front and rear slide serrations; high-ride beavertail safety; checkered flat mainspring housing; kidney cut under trigger guard; high cut grip design; match-grade stainless barrel bushing; Commander-style hammer; lowered and flared ejection port; Wolff springs; bead blasted black oxide finish. Made in U.S. by Kimber Mfg., Inc.

Price: Custom. **$730.00**
Price: Custom Walnut (double-diamond walnut grips) **$752.00**
Price: Custom Stainless **$832.00**
Price: Custom Stainless 40 S&W. **$870.00**
Price: Custom Stainless Target 45 ACP (stainless, adj. sight) **$944.00**
Price: Custom Stainless Target 40 S&W **$974.00**

Kimber Compact Auto Pistol

Similar to the Custom model except has 4" bull barrel fitted directly to the slide without a bushing; full-length guide rod; grip is .400" shorter than full-size gun; no front serrations. Steel frame models weigh 34 oz., aluminum 28 oz. Introduced 1998. Made in U.S. by Kimber Mfg., Inc.

Price: 45 ACP, matte black. **$764.00**
Price: Compact Stainless 45 ACP **$871.00**
Price: Compact Stainless 40 S&W. **$902.00**
Price: Compact Aluminum Stainless 45 ACP (aluminum frame, stainless slide) **$837.00**
Price: Compact Aluminum Stainless 40 S&W **$873.00**

Kimber Ultra Carry

Kimber High Capacity Polymer

Kimber Pro CDP

Kimber Pro Carry Auto Pistol

Similar to the Compact model except has aluminum frame with full-length grip. Has 4" bull barrel fitted directly to the slide without bushing. Introduced 1998. Made in U.S. by Kimber Mfg., Inc.

Price: 45 ACP **$773.00**
Price: 40 S&W **$808.00**
Price: Pro Carry Stainless 45 ACP **$845.00**
Price: Pro Carry Stainless 40 S&W **$881.00**

Kimber Ultra Carry Auto Pistol

Similar to the Compact Aluminum model except has 3" balljoint spherical bushingless cone barrel; aluminum frame; beveling at front and rear of ejection port; relieved breech face; tuned ejector; special slide stop; dual captured low-effort spring system. Weighs 25 oz. Introduced 1999. made in U.S. by Kimber Mfg., Inc.

Price: 45 ACP **$808.00**
Price: 40 S&W **$847.00**
Price: Stainless, 45 ACP **$886.00**
Price: Stainless, 40 S&W **$931.00**

KIMBER HIGH CAPACITY POLYMER PISTOL

Caliber: 45 ACP, 10- and 14-shot magazine. **Barrel:** 5". **Weight:** 34 oz. **Length:** 8.7" overall. **Stocks:** Integral; checkered black polymer. **Sights:** McCormick low profile front and rear. **Features:** Polymer frame with steel insert. Comes with 10-shot magazine. Checkered front strap and mainspring housing; polymer trigger; stainless high ride beavertail grip safety; hooked trigger guard. Introduced 1997. Made in U.S. by Kimber Mfg., Inc.

Price: Polymer Custom, matte black finish **$795.00**
Price: Polymer Stainless (satin-finish stainless slide) **$856.00**
Price: Polymer Pro Carry (compact slide, 4" bull barrel) **$814.00**
Price: Polymer Pro Carry Stainless **$874.00**
New! **Price:** Polymer Ultra Ten II (polymer/stainless) **$896.00**

Kimber Gold Match Auto Pistol

Similar to the Custom model except has Kimber adjustable sight with rounded and blended edges; stainless steel match-grade barrel hand-fitted to spherical barrel bushing; premium aluminum trigger; extended ambidextrous thumb safety; hand-checkered double diamond rosewood grips. Hand-fitted by Kimber Custom Shop. Made in U.S. by Kimber Mfg., Inc.

Price: Gold Match 45 ACP **$1,169.00**
Price: Gold Match Stainless 45 ACP (highly polished flats) **$1,315.00**
Price: Gold Match Stainless 40 S&W **$1,345.00**

Kimber Polymer Gold Match Auto Pistol

Similar to the Polymer model except has Kimber adjustable sight with rounded and blended edges; stainless steel match-grade barrel hand-fitted to spherical barrel bushing; premium aluminum trigger; extended ambidextrous thumb safety. Hand-fitted by Kimber Custom Shop. Introduced 1999. Made in U.S. by Kimber Mfg., Inc.

Price: **$1,041.00**
Price: Polymer Stainless Gold Match (polished stainless slide). **$1,177.00**

Kimber Gold Combat Auto Pistol

Similar to the Gold Match except designed for concealed carry. Has two-piece extended and beveled magazine well, tritium night sights; premium aluminum trigger; 30 lpi front strap checkering; special Custom Shop markings; Kim Pro black finish. Introduced 1999. Made in U.S. by Kimber Mfg., Inc.

Price: 45 ACP **$1,682.00**
Price: Gold Combat Stainless (satin-finished stainless frame
and slide, special Custom Shop markings) **$1,623.00**

KIMBER PRO CDP AUTO PISTOL

Caliber: 45 ACP, 7-shot magazine. **Barrel:** 4". **Weight:** 28 oz. **Length:** 7.7" overall. **Grips:** Hand-checkered. double diamond rosewood. **Sights:** Tritium three-dot. **Features:** Matte black, machined aluminum frame; satin stainless steel slide; match-grade barrel and chamber; beveled magazine well; extended ejector; high-ride beavertail grip safety; match-grade trigger group; ambidextrous safety; checkered frontstrap; meltdown treatment. Introduced 2000. Made in U.S. by Kimber.

Price: **$1,142.00**

KIMBER ULTRA CDP AUTO PISTOL

Caliber: 45 ACP, 6-shot magazine. **Barrel:** 3". **Weight:** 25 oz. **Length:** 6.8" overall. **Grips:** Hand-checkered. double diamond rosewood. **Sights:** Tritium three-dot. **Features:** Matte black, machined aluminum frame; satin stainless steel slide; match-grade barrel and chamber; beveled magazine well and ejection port; dual recoil spring system for reliability and ease of manual slide operation; match-grade barrel, chamber and trigger; ambidextrous safety; checkered frontstrap; meltdown treatment. Introduced 2000. Made in U.S. by Kimber.

Price: **$1,142.00**

Llama Minimax

Llama Max-1

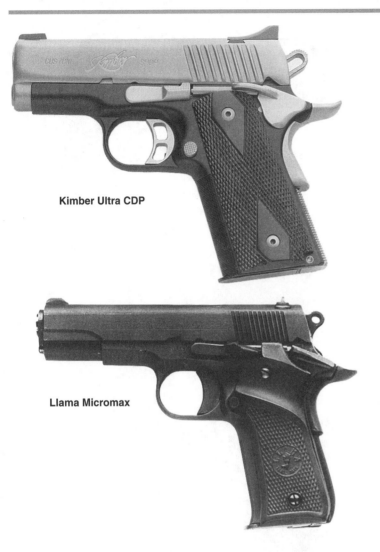

Kimber Ultra CDP

Llama Micromax

LLAMA MICROMAX 380 AUTO PISTOL

Caliber: 32 ACP, 8-shot, 380 ACP, 7-shot magazine. **Barrel:** 3-11/16". **Weight:** 23 oz. **Length:** 6-1/2" overall. **Stocks:** Checkered high impact polymer. **Sights:** 3-dot combat. **Features:** Single-action design. Mini custom extended slide release; mini custom extended beavertail grip safety; combat-style hammer. Introduced 1997. Imported from Spain by Import Sports, Inc.

Price: Matte blue. **$281.95**
Price: Satin chrome (380 only) **$298.95**

LLAMA MINIMAX SERIES

Caliber: 9mm Para., 8-shot; 40 S&W, 7-shot; 45 ACP, 6-shot magazine. **Barrel:** 3-1/2". **Weight:** 35 oz. **Length:** 7-1/3" overall. **Stocks:** Checkered rubber. **Sights:** Three-dot combat. **Features:** Single action, skeletonized combat-style hammer, extended slide release, cone-style barrel, flared ejection port. Introduced 1996. Imported from Spain by Import Sports, Inc.

Price: Blue **$316.95**
Price: Duo-Tone finish (45 only) **$324.95**
Price: Satin chrome **$333.95**

Llama Minimax Sub-Compact Auto Pistol

Similar to the Minimax except has 3.14" barrel, weighs 31 oz.; 6.8" overall length; has 10-shot magazine with finger extension; beavertail grip safety. Introduced 1999. Imported from Spain by Import Sports, Inc.

Price: 45 ACP, matte blue. **$331.95**
Price: As above, satin chrome **$349.95**
Price: Duo-Tone finish (45 only) **$341.95**

LLAMA MAX-I AUTO PISTOLS

Caliber: 45 ACP, 7-shot. **Barrel:** 5-1/8". **Weight:** 36 oz. **Length:** 8-1/2" overall. **Stocks:** Black rubber. **Sights:** Blade front, rear adjustable for windage; three-dot system. **Features:** Single-action trigger; skeletonized combat-style hammer; steel frame; extended manual and grip safeties. Introduced 1995. Imported from Spain by Import Sports, Inc.

Price: 45 ACP, 7-shot, Government model. **$310.95**

NORTH AMERICAN ARMS GUARDIAN PISTOL

Caliber: 32 ACP, 6-shot magazine. **Barrel:** 2.1". **Weight:** 13.5 oz. **Length:** 4.36" overall. **Stocks:** Black polymer. **Sights:** Fixed. **Features:** Double-action-only mechanism. All stainless steel construction; snag-free. Introduced 1998. Made in U.S. by North American Arms.

Price: **$359.00**

OLYMPIC ARMS OA-96 AR PISTOL

Caliber: 223. **Barrel:** 6", 8", 4140 chrome-moly steel. **Weight:** 5 lbs. **Length:** 15-3/4" overall. **Stocks:** A2 stowaway pistol grip; no buttstock or receiver tube. **Sights:** Flat-top upper receiver, cut-down front sight base. **Features:** AR-15-type receivers with special bolt carrier; short aluminum hand guard; Vortex flash hider. Introduced 1996. Made in U.S. by Olympic Arms, Inc.

Price: **$858.00**

Olympic Arms OA-98 AR Pistol

Similar to the OA-93 except has removable 7-shot magazine, weighs 3 lbs. Introduced 1999. Made in U.S. by Olympic Arms, Inc.

Price: **$990.00**

North American Arms Guardian

One Pro .45

ONE PRO .45 AUTO PISTOL

Caliber: 45 ACP or 400 Cor-Bon, 10-shot magazine. **Barrel:** 3.75" **Weight:** 31.1 oz. **Length:** 7.04" overall. **Stocks:** Textured composition. **Sights:** Blade front, drift-adjustable rear; three-dot system. **Features:** All-steel construction; decocking lever and automatic firing pin lock; DA or DAO operation. Introduced 1997. Imported from Switzerland by Magnum Research, Inc.

Price: **$649.00**
Price: Conversion kit, 45 ACP/400, 400/45 ACP **$249.00**

ONE PRO 9 AUTO PISTOL

Caliber: 9mm Para., 10-shot magazine. **Barrel:** 3.01". **Weight:** 25.1 oz. **Length:** 6.06" overall. **Stocks:** Smooth wood. **Sights:** Blade front, rear adjustable for windage. **Features:** Rotating barrel; short slide; double recoil springs; double-action mechanism; decocking lever. Introduced 1998. Imported from Switzerland by Magnum Research.

Price: **$649.00**

Para-Ordnance P12.45

PARA-ORDNANCE P-SERIES AUTO PISTOLS

Caliber: 9mm Para., 40 S&W, 45 ACP, 10-shot magazine. **Barrel:** 3", 3-1/2", 4-1/4", 5". **Weight:** From 24 oz. (alloy frame). **Length:** 8.5" overall. **Stocks:** Textured composition. **Sights:** Blade front, rear adjustable for windage. High visibility three-dot system. **Features:** Available with alloy, steel or stainless steel frame with black finish (silver or stainless gun). Steel and stainless steel frame guns weigh 40 oz. (P14.45), 36 oz. (P13.45), 34 oz. (P12.45). Grooved match trigger, rounded combat-style hammer. Beveled magazine well. Manual thumb, grip and firing pin lock safeties. Solid barrel bushing. Contact maker for full details. Introduced 1990. Made in Canada by Para-Ordnance.

Price: P14.45ER (steel frame) **$750.00**
Price: P14.45RR (alloy frame) **$740.00**
Price: P12.45RR (3-1/2" bbl., 24 oz., alloy) **$740.00**
Price: P13.45RR (4-1/4" barrel, 28 oz., alloy) **$740.00**
Price: P12.45ER (steel frame) **$750.00**
Price: P16.40ER (steel frame) **$750.00**
Price: P10-9RR (9mm, alloy frame) **$740.00**
Price: Stainless receiver (40, 45) **$799.00**
Price: Stainless receiver (9mm) **$850.00**

Para-Ordnance Limited Pistols

Similar to the P-Series pistols except with full-length recoil guide system; fully adjustable rear sight; tuned trigger with overtravel stop; beavertail grip safety; competition hammer; front and rear slide serrations; ambidextrous safety; lowered ejection port; ramped match-grade barrel; dovetailed front sight. Introduced 1998. Made in Canada by Para-Ordnance.
Price: 9mm, 40 S&W, 45 ACP . . . . **$865.00 to $899.00**

Para-Ordnance LDA

HANDGUNS — AUTOLOADERS, SERVICE & SPORT

Peters Stahl High Capacity

Phoenix Arms HP22

Peters Stahl Trophy Master

Peters Stahl Millenium

Para-Ordnance LDA Auto Pistols
Similar to the P-series except has double-action trigger mechanism. Steel frame with matte black finish, checkered composition grips. Available in 9mm Para., 40 S&W, 45 ACP. Introduced 1999. Made in Canada by Para-Ordnance.
Price: **$775.00**

Para-Ordnance LDA Limited Pistols
Similar to the LDA except has ambidextrous safety, adjustable rear sight, front slide serrations and full-length recoil guide system. Made in Canada by Para-Ordnance.
Price: Black finish **$899.00**
Price: Stainless **$929.00**

PETERS STAHL AUTOLOADING PISTOLS
Caliber: 9mm Para., 45 ACP. **Barrel:** 5" or 6". **Weight:** NA. **Length:** NA. **Grips:** Walnut or walnut with rubber wrap. **Sights:** Fully adjustable rear, blade front. **Features:** Stainless steel extended slide stop, safety and extended magazine release button; speed trigger with stop and approx. 3-lb. pull; polished ramp. Introduced 2000. Imported from Germany by Phillips & Rogers.
Price: High Capacity (accepts 15-shot magazines in 45 cal.; includes 10-shot magazine) **$1,695.00**
Price: Trophy Master (blued or stainless, 7-shot in 45, 8-shot in 9mm) **$1,995.00**
Price: Millenium Model (titanium coating on receiver and slide) **$2,195.00**

PHOENIX ARMS HP22, HP25 AUTO PISTOLS
Caliber: 22 LR, 10-shot (HP22), 25 ACP, 10-shot (HP25). **Barrel:** 3". **Weight:** 20 oz. **Length:** 5-1/2" overall. **Stocks:** Checkered composition. **Sights:** Blade front, adjustable rear. **Features:** Single action, exposed hammer; manual hold-open; button magazine release. Available in satin nickel, polished blue finish. Introduced 1993. Made in U.S. by Phoenix Arms.
Price: With gun lock and cable lanyard **$128.00**
Price: HP Rangemaster kit with 5" bbl., locking case and accessories **$169.00**
Price: HP Deluxe Rangemaster kit with 3" and 5" bbls., 2 mags., case **$199.00**

PSA-25 AUTO POCKET PISTOL
Caliber: 25 ACP, 6-shot magazine. **Barrel:** 2-1/8". **Weight:** 9.5 oz. **Length:** 4-1/8" overall. **Stocks:** Checkered black polymer, ivory, checkered transparent carbon fiber-filled polymer. **Sights:** Fixed. **Features:** All steel construction; striker fired; single action only; magazine disconnector; cocking indicator. Introduced 1987. Made in U.S. by Precision Small Arms, Inc.
Price: Traditional (polished black oxide) **$269.00**
Price: Nouveau-Satin (brushed nickel) **$269.00**
Price: Nouveau-Mirror (highly polished nickel) **$309.00**
Price: Featherweight (aluminum frame, nickel slide) **$405.00**
Price: Diplomat (black oxide with gold highlights, ivory grips) **$625.00**
Price: Montreaux (gold plated, ivory grips) **$692.00**
Price: Renaissance (hand engraved nickel, ivory grips) **$1,115.00**
Price: Imperiale (inlaid gold filigree over blue, scrimshawed ivory grips) **$3,600.00**

PSA-25 Auto

Rock River Standard Match

Republic Patriot

Ruger P89

REPUBLIC PATRIOT PISTOL

Caliber: 45 ACP, 6-shot magazine. **Barrel:** 3". **Weight:** 20 oz. **Length:** 6" overall. **Stocks:** Checkered. **Sights:** Blade front, drift-adjustable rear. **Features:** Black polymer frame, stainless steel slide; double-action-only trigger system; squared trigger guard. Introduced 1997. Made in U.S. by Republic Arms, Inc.
Price: About **$325.00**

ROCK RIVER ARMS STANDARD MATCH AUTO PISTOL

Caliber: 45 ACP. **Barrel:** NA. **Weight:** NA. **Length:** NA. **Grips:** Cocobolo, checkered. **Sights:** Heine fixed rear, blade front. **Features:** Chrome-moly steel frame and slide; beavertail grip safety with raised pad; checkered slide stop; ambidextrous safety; polished feed ramp and extractor; aluminum speed trigger with 3.5 lb. pull. Made in U.S. From Rock River Arms.
Price: **$1,025.00**

ROCKY MOUNTAIN ARMS PATRIOT PISTOL

Caliber: 223, 10-shot magazine. **Barrel:** 7", with muzzle brake. **Weight:** 5 lbs. **Length:** 20.5" overall. **Stocks:** Black composition. **Sights:** None furnished. **Features:** Milled upper receiver with enhanced Weaver base; milled lower receiver from billet plate; machined aluminum National Match handguard. Finished in DuPont Teflon-S matte black or NATO green. Comes with black nylon case, one magazine. Introduced 1993. From Rocky Mountain Arms, Inc.
Price: With A-2 handle top . . . . **$2,500.00 to $2,800.00**
Price: Flat top model. . . . . **$3,000.00 to $3,500.00**

RUGER P89 AUTOLOADING PISTOL

Caliber: 9mm Para., 10-shot magazine. **Barrel:** 4.50". **Weight:** 32 oz. **Length:** 7.84" overall. **Stocks:** Grooved black Xenoy composition.

Sights: Square post front, square notch rear adjustable for windage, both with white dot inserts. **Features:** Double action with ambidextrous slide-mounted safety-levers. Slide is 4140 chrome-moly steel or 400-series stainless steel, frame is a lightweight aluminum alloy. Ambidextrous magazine release. Blue or stainless steel. Introduced 1986; stainless introduced 1990.
Price: P89, blue, with extra magazine and magazine loading tool, plastic case with lock **$452.00**
Price: KP89, stainless, with extra magazine and magazine loading tool, plastic case with lock **$499.00**

Ruger P89D Decocker Autoloading Pistol

Similar to the standard P89 except has ambidextrous decocking levers in place of the regular slide-mounted safety. The decocking levers move the firing pin inside the slide where the hammer can not reach it, while simultaneously blocking the firing pin from forward movement—allows shooter to decock a cocked pistol without manipulating the trigger. Conventional thumb decocking procedures are therefore unnecessary. Blue or stainless steel. Introduced 1990.
Price: P89D, blue with extra magazine and loader, plastic case with lock **$452.00**
Price: KP89D, stainless, with extra magazine, plastic case with lock **$499.00**

Ruger P89 Double-Action-Only Autoloading Pistol

Same as the KP89 except operates only in the double-action mode. Has a spurless hammer, gripping grooves on each side of the rear of the slide; no external safety or decocking lever. An internal safety prevents forward movement of the firing pin unless the trigger is pulled. Available in 9mm Para., stainless steel only. Introduced 1991.
Price: With lockable case, extra magazine, magazine loading tool **$499.00**

Ruger P90

Ruger KP95DAO

Ruger P93D

RUGER P90 MANUAL SAFETY MODEL AUTOLOADING PISTOL

Caliber: 45 ACP, 7-shot magazine. **Barrel:** 4.50". **Weight:** 33.5 oz. **Length:** 7.87" overall. **Stocks:** Grooved black Xenoy composition. **Sights:** Square post front, square notch rear adjustable for windage, both with white dot inserts. **Features:** Double action with ambidextrous slide-mounted safety-levers which move the firing pin inside the slide where the hammer can not reach it, while simultaneously blocking the firing pin from forward movement. Stainless steel only. Introduced 1991.

Price: KP90 with extra magazine, loader, plastic case

with lock **$539.00**

Price: P90 (blue). **$499.00**

Ruger KP90 Decocker Autoloading Pistol

Similar to the P90 except has a manual decocking system. The ambidextrous decocking levers move the firing pin inside the slide where the hammer can not reach it, while simultaneously blocking the firing pin from forward movement—allows shooter to decock a cocked pistol without manipulating the trigger. Available only in stainless steel. Overall length 7.87", weighs 34 oz. Introduced 1991.

Price: KP90D with lockable case, extra magazine, and magazine

loading tool **$539.00**

RUGER P93 COMPACT AUTOLOADING PISTOL

Caliber: 9mm Para., 10-shot magazine. **Barrel:** 3.9". **Weight:** 31 oz. **Length:** 7.3" overall. **Stocks:** Grooved black Xenoy composition. **Sights:** Square post front, square notch rear adjustable for windage. **Features:**

Front of slide is crowned with a convex curve; slide has seven finger grooves; trigger guard bow is higher for a better grip; 400-series stainless slide, lightweight alloy frame; also in blue. Decocker-only or DAO-only. Includes hard case with lock. Introduced 1993. Made in U.S. by Sturm, Ruger & Co.

Price: KP93DAO, double-action-only **$546.00**
Price: KP93D ambidextrous decocker, stainless **$546.00**
Price: P93D, ambidextrous decocker, blue **$467.00**

Ruger KP94 Autoloading Pistol

Sized midway between the full-size P-Series and the compact P93. Has 4.25" barrel, 7.5" overall length and weighs about 33 oz. KP94 is manual safety model; KP94DAO is double-action-only (both 9mm Para., 10-shot magazine); KP94D is decocker-only in 40-caliber with 10-shot magazine. Slide gripping grooves roll over top of slide. KP94 has ambidextrous safety-levers; KP94DAO has no external safety, full-cock hammer position or decocking lever; KP94D has ambidextrous decocking levers. Matte finish stainless slide, barrel, alloy frame. Also available in blue. Includes hard case and lock. Introduced 1994. Made in U.S. by Sturm, Ruger & Co.

Price: P94, P944, blue (manual safety) **$467.00**
Price: KP94 (9mm), KP944 (40-caliber) (manual

safety-stainless) **$546.00**
Price: KP94DAO (9mm), KP944DAO (40-caliber) **$546.00**
Price: KP94D (9mm), KP944D (40-caliber)-decock only **$546.00**

RUGER P95 AUTOLOADING PISTOL

Caliber: 9mm Para., 10-shot magazine. **Barrel:** 3.9". **Weight:** 27 oz. **Length:** 7.3" overall. **Stocks:** Grooved; integral with frame. **Sights:** Blade front, rear drift adjustable for windage; three-dot system. **Features:** Moulded polymer grip frame, stainless steel or chrome-moly slide. Suitable for +P+ ammunition. Safety model, decocker or DAO. Introduced 1996. Made in U.S. by Sturm, Ruger & Co. Comes with lockable plastic case, spare magazine, loading tool.

Price: P95 DAO double-action-only **$407.00**
Price: P95D decocker only **$407.00**
Price: KP95 stainless steel. **$453.00**
Price: KP95DAO double-action only, stainless steel **$453.00**
Price: KP95 safety model, stainless steel **$453.00**
Price: P95 safety model, blued finish **$407.00**

RUGER P97 AUTOLOADING PISTOL

Caliber: 45ACP 8-shot magazine. **Barrel:** 4-1/8". **Weight:** 30-1/2 oz. **Length:** 7-1/4" overall. Grooved: Integral with frame. **Sights:** Blade front, rear drift adjustable for windage; three dot system. **Features:** Moulded polymer grip frame, stainless steel slide. Decocker or DAO. Introduced 1997. Made in U.S. by Sturm, Ruger & Co. Comes with lockable plastic case, spare magaline, loading tool. .

Price: (KP97D decock-only) **$483.00**
Price: (KP97DAO double-action only) **$483.00**

Ruger KMK-4

Ruger KP512

Ruger 22/45-P4

RUGER MARK II STANDARD AUTOLOADING PISTOL

Caliber: 22 LR, 10-shot magazine. **Barrel:** 4-3/4" or 6". **Weight:** 25 oz. (4-3/4" bbl.). **Length:** 8-5/16" (4-3/4" bbl.). **Stocks:** Checkered plastic. **Sights:** Fixed, wide blade front, fixed rear. **Features:** Updated design of the original Standard Auto. Has new bolt hold-open latch. 10-shot magazine, magazine catch, safety, trigger and new receiver contours. Introduced 1982.
Price: Blued (MK 4, MK 6) $278.00
Price: In stainless steel (KMK 4, KMK 6) $364.00

Ruger 22/45 Mark II Pistol

Similar to the other 22 Mark II autos except has grip frame of Zytel that matches the angle and magazine latch of the Model 1911 45 ACP pistol. Available in 4" bull, 4-3/4" standard and 5-1/2" bull barrels. Comes with extra magazine, plastic case, lock. Introduced 1992.
Price: P4, 4" bull barrel, adjustable sights $275.00
Price: KP 4 (4-3/4" barrel), stainless steel, fixed sights $305.00
Price: KP512 (5-1/2" bull barrel), stainless steel, adj. sights $359.00
Price: P512 (5-1/2" bull barrel, all blue), adj. sights $275.00

SAFARI ARMS ENFORCER PISTOL

Caliber: 45 ACP, 6-shot magazine. **Barrel:** 3.8", stainless. **Weight:** 36 oz. **Length:** 7.3" overall. **Stocks:** Smooth walnut with etched black widow spider logo. **Sights:** Ramped blade front, LPA adjustable rear. **Features:** Extended safety, extended slide release; Commander-style hammer; beavertail grip safety; throated, polished, tuned. Parkerized matte black or satin stainless steel finishes. Made in U.S. by Safari Arms.
Price: $630.00

SAFARI ARMS GI SAFARI PISTOL

Caliber: 45 ACP, 7-shot magazine. **Barrel:** 5", 416 stainless. **Weight:** 39.9 oz. **Length:** 8.5" overall. **Stocks:** Checkered walnut. **Sights:** G.I.-style blade front, drift-adjustable rear. **Features:** Beavertail grip safety; extended thumb safety and slide release; Commander-style hammer. Parkerized finish. Reintroduced 1996.
Price: $439.00

SAFARI ARMS CARRIER PISTOL

Caliber: 45 ACP, 7-shot magazine. **Barrel:** 6", 416 stainless steel. **Weight:** 30 oz. **Length:** 9.5" overall. **Stocks:** Wood. **Sights:** Ramped blade front, LPA adjustable rear. **Features:** Beavertail grip safety; extended controls; full-length recoil spring guide; Commander-style hammer. Throated, polished and tuned. Satin stainless steel finish. Introduced 1999. Made in U.S. by Safari Arms, Inc.
Price: $714.00

SAFARI ARMS COHORT PISTOL

Caliber: 45 ACP, 7-shot magazine. **Barrel:** 3.8", 416 stainless. **Weight:** 37 oz. **Length:** 8.5" overall. **Stocks:** Smooth walnut with laser-etched black widow logo. **Sights:** Ramped blade front, LPA adjustable rear. **Features:** Combines the Enforcer model, slide and MatchMaster frame. Beavertail grip safety; extended thumb safety and slide release; Commander-style hammer. Throated, polished and tuned. Satin stainless finish. Introduced 1996. Made in U.S. by Safari Arms, Inc.
Price: $654.00

SAFARI ARMS MATCHMASTER PISTOL

Caliber: 45 ACP, 7-shot. **Barrel:** 5" or 6", 416 stainless steel. **Weight:** 38 oz. (5" barrel). **Length:** 8.5" overall. **Stocks:** Smooth walnut. **Sights:** Ramped blade, LPA adjustable rear. **Features:** Beavertail grip safety; extended controls; Commander-style hammer; throated, polished, tuned. Parkerized matte-black or satin stainless steel. Made in U.S. by Olympic Arms, Inc.
Price: 5" barrel $594.00
Price: 6" barrel $654.00

Safari Arms Carry Comp Pistol

Similar to the Matchmaster except has Wil Schueman-designed hybrid compensator system. Made in U.S. by Olympic Arms, Inc.
Price: $1,067.00

SEECAMP LWS 32 STAINLESS DA AUTO

Caliber: 32 ACP Win. Silvertip, 6-shot magazine. **Barrel:** 2", integral with frame. **Weight:** 10.5 oz. **Length:** 4-1/8" overall. **Stocks:** Glass-filled nylon. **Sights:** Smooth, no-snag, contoured slide and barrel top. **Features:** Aircraft quality 17-4 PH stainless steel. Inertia-operated firing pin. Hammer fired double-action-only. Hammer automatically follows slide down to safety rest position after each shot—no manual safety needed. Magazine safety disconnector. Polished stainless. Introduced 1985. From L.W. Seecamp.
Price: $425.00

SIG SAUER P220 SERVICE AUTO PISTOL

Caliber: 45 ACP, (7- or 8-shot magazine). **Barrel:** 4-3/8". **Weight:** 27.8 oz. **Length:** 7.8" overall. **Stocks:** Checkered black plastic. **Sights:** Blade front, drift adjustable rear for windage. Optional Siglite nightsights. **Features:** Double action. Decocking lever permits lowering hammer onto locked firing pin. Squared combat-type trigger guard. Slide stays open after last shot. Imported from Germany by SIGARMS, Inc.
Price: Blue SA/DA or DAO $790.00
Price: Blue, Siglite night sights $880.00
Price: K-Kote or nickel slide $830.00
Price: K-Kote or nickel slide with Siglite night sights $930.00

SIG Sauer P220

SIG Arms Pro 2009

SIG Arms P245 Compact

SIG Sauer P229S

SIG Sauer P220 Sport Auto Pistol

Similar to the P220 except has 4.9" barrel, ported compensator, all-stainless steel frame and slide, factory-tuned trigger, adjustable sights, extended competition controls. Overall length is 9.9", weighs 43.5 oz. Introduced 1999. From SIGARMS, Inc.

Price: **$1,320.00**

SIG Sauer P245 Compact Auto Pistol

Similar to the P220 except has 3.9" barrel, shorter grip, 6-shot magazine, 7.28" overall length, and weighs 27.5 oz. Introduced 1999. From SIGARMS, Inc.

Price: Blue **$780.00**
Price: Blue, with Siglite sights. **$850.00**
Price: Two-tone. **$830.00**
Price: Two-tone with Siglite sights **$930.00**
Price: With K-Kote finish. **$830.00**
Price: K-Kote with Siglite sights **$930.00**

SIG Sauer P229 DA Auto Pistol

Similar to the P228 except chambered for 9mm Para., 40 S&W, 357 SIG. Has 3.86" barrel, 7.08" overall length and 3.35" height. Weight is 30.5 oz. Introduced 1991. Frame made in Germany, stainless steel slide assembly made in U.S.; pistol assembled in U.S. From SIGARMS, Inc.

Price: **$795.00**
Price: With nickel slide **$890.00**
Price: Nickel slide Siglite night sights **$935.00**

SIG PRO AUTO PISTOL

Caliber: 9mm Para., 40 S&W, 10-shot magazine. **Barrel:** 3.86". **Weight:** 27.2 oz. **Length:** 7.36" overall. **Stocks:** Composite and rubberized one-piece. **Sights:** Blade front, rear adjustable for windage. Optional Siglite night sights. **Features:** Polymer frame, stainless steel slide; integral frame accessory rail; replaceable steel frame rails; left- or right-handed magazine release. Introduced 1999. From SIGARMS, Inc.

Price: SP2340 (40 S&W) **$596.00**
Price: SP2009 (9mm Para.) **$596.00**
Price: As above with Siglite night sights. **$655.00**

SIG Sauer P226 Service Pistol

Similar to the P220 pistol except has 4.4" barrel, and weighs 28.3 oz. 357 SIG or 40 S&W. Imported from Germany by SIGARMS, Inc.

Price: Blue SA/DA or DAO **$830.00**
Price: With Siglite night sights **$930.00**
Price: Blue, SA/DA or DAO 357 SIG **$830.00**
Price: With Siglite night sights **$930.00**
Price: K-Kote finish, 40 S&W only or nickel slide **$830.00**
Price: K-Kote or nickel slide Siglite night sights **$930.00**
Price: Nickel slide 357 SIG. **$875.00**
Price: Nickel slide, Siglite night sights **$930.00**

SIG Sauer P229 Sport Auto Pistol

Similar to the P229 except available in 357 SIG only; 4.8" heavy barrel; 8.6" overall length; weighs 40.6 oz.; vented compensator; adjustable target sights; rubber grips; extended slide latch and magazine release. Made of stainless steel. Introduced 1998. From SIGARMS, Inc.

Price: **$1,320.00**

SIG SAUER P232 PERSONAL SIZE PISTOL

Caliber: 380 ACP, 7-shot. **Barrel:** 3-3/4". **Weight:** 16 oz. **Length:** 6-1/2" overall. **Stocks:** Checkered black composite. **Sights:** Blade front, rear adjustable for windage. **Features:** Double action/single action or DAO. Blowback operation, stationary barrel. Introduced 1997. Imported from Germany by SIGARMS, Inc.

Price: Blue SA/DA or DAO **$505.00**
Price: In stainless steel. **$545.00**
Price: With stainless steel slide, blue frame **$525.00**
Price: Stainless steel, Siglite night sights, Hogue grips **$585.00**

SIG Sauer P232

Smith & Wesson 4013 TSW

Smith & Wesson 457

SIG SAUER P239 PISTOL

Caliber: 9mm Para., 8-shot, 357 SIG 40 S&W, 7-shot magazine. **Barrel:** 3.6". **Weight:** 25.2 oz. **Length:** 6.6" overall. **Stocks:** Checkered black composite. **Sights:** Blade front, rear adjustable for windage. Optional Siglite night sights. **Features:** SA/DA or DAO; blackened stainless steel slide, aluminum alloy frame. Introduced 1996. Made in U.S. by SIGARMS, Inc.
Price: SA/DA or DAO **$620.00**
Price: SA/DA or DAO with Siglite night sights **$720.00**
Price: Two-tone finish **$665.00**
Price: Two-tone finish, Siglite sights **$765.00**

SMITH & WESSON MODEL 22A SPORT PISTOL

Caliber: 22 LR, 10-shot magazine. **Barrel:** 4", 5-1/2", 7". **Weight:** 29 oz. **Length:** 8" overall. **Stocks:** Two-piece polymer. **Sights:** Patridge front, fully adjustable rear. **Features:** Comes with a sight bridge with Weaver-style integral optics mount; alloy frame; .312" serrated trigger; stainless steel slide and barrel with matte blue finish. Introduced 1997. Made in U.S. by Smith & Wesson.
Price: 4" **$230.00**
Price: 5-1/2" **$255.00**
Price: 7" **$289.00**

SMITH & WESSON MODEL 457 TDA AUTO PISTOL

Caliber: 45 ACP, 7-shot magazine. **Barrel:** 3-3/4". **Weight:** 29 oz. **Length:** 7-1/4" overall. **Stocks:** One-piece Xenoy, wrap-around with straight backstrap. **Sights:** Post front, fixed rear, three-dot system. **Features:** Aluminum alloy frame, matte blue carbon steel slide; bobbed hammer; smooth trigger. Introduced 1996. Made in U.S. by Smith & Wesson.
Price: **$563.00**

SMITH & WESSON MODEL 908 AUTO PISTOL

Caliber: 9mm Para., 8-shot magazine. **Barrel:** 3-1/2". **Weight:** 26 oz. **Length:** 6-13/16". **Stocks:** One-piece Xenoy, wrap-around with straight backstrap. **Sights:** Post front, fixed rear, three-dot system. **Features:** Alu-

minum alloy frame, matte blue carbon steel slide; bobbed hammer; smooth trigger. Introduced 1996. Made in U.S. by Smith & Wesson.
Price: **$509.00**

SMITH & WESSON 9mm RECON AUTO PISTOL MODEL

Caliber: 9mm Para. **Barrel:** 3-1/2". **Weight:** 27 oz. **Length:** 7" overall. **Stocks:** Hogue wrap-around, finger-groove rubber. **Sights:** Three-dot Novak Low Mount, drift adjustable. **Features:** Traditional double-action mechanism. Tuned action, hand-crowned muzzle, polished feed ramp, hand-lapped slide, spherical barrel bushing. Checkered frontstrap. Introduced 1999. Made by U.S. by Smith & Wesson.
Price: **$1,150.00**

SMITH & WESSON MODEL 2213, 2214 SPORTSMAN AUTOS

Caliber: 22 LR, 8-shot magazine. **Barrel:** 3". **Weight:** 18 oz. **Length:** 6-1/8" overall. **Stocks:** Checkered black polymer. **Sights:** Patridge front, fixed rear; three-dot system. **Features:** Internal hammer; serrated trigger; single action. Model 2213 is stainless with alloy frame, Model 2214 is blued carbon steel with alloy frame. Introduced 1990. Made in U.S. by Smith & Wesson.
Price: Model 2213 .... **$340.00**
Price: Model 2214 .... **$292.00**

SMITH & WESSON MODEL 4013, 4053 TSW AUTOS

Caliber: 40 S&W, 9-shot magazine. **Barrel:** 3-1/2". **Weight:** 26.4 oz. **Length:** 6-7/8" overall. **Stocks:** Xenoy one-piece wrap-around. **Sights:** Novak three-dot system. **Features:** Traditional double-action system; stainless slide, alloy frame; fixed barrel bushing; ambidextrous decocker; reversible magazine catch. Introduced 1997. Made in U.S. by Smith & Wesson.
Price: Model 4013 TSW **$844.00**
Price: Model 4053 TSW, double-action-only **$844.00**

Smith & Wesson Model 22S Sport Pistols

Similar to the Model 22A Sport except with stainless steel frame. Available only with 5-1/2" or 7" barrel. Introduced 1997. Made in U.S. by Smith & Wesson.
Price: 5-1/2" standard barrel **$312.00**
Price: 5-1/2" bull barrel, wood target stocks with thumbrest **$379.00**
Price: 7" standard barrel **$344.00**
Price: 5-1/2" bull barrel, two-piece target stocks with thumbrest .. **$353.00**

SMITH & WESSON MODEL 410 DA AUTO PISTOL

Caliber: 40 S&W, 10-shot magazine. **Barrel:** 4". **Weight:** 28.5 oz. **Length:** 7.5 oz. **Stocks:** One-piece Xenoy, wrap-around with straight backstrap. **Sights:** Post front, fixed rear; three-dot system. **Features:** Aluminum alloy frame; blued carbon steel slide; traditional double action with left-side slide-mounted decocking lever. Introduced 1996. Made in U.S. by Smith & Wesson.
Price: **$563.00**

Smith & Wesson 3913 TSW

Smith & Wesson 4506

Smith & Wesson 3913 LadySmith

SMITH & WESSON MODEL 910 DA AUTO PISTOL

Caliber: 9mm Para., 10-shot magazine. **Barrel:** 4". **Weight:** 28 oz. **Length:** 7-3/8" overall. **Stocks:** One-piece Xenoy, wrap-around with straight backstrap. **Sights:** Post front with white dot, fixed two-dot rear. **Features:** Alloy frame, blue carbon steel slide. Slide-mounted decocking lever. Introduced 1995.
Price: Model 910 . . . . **$509.00**

SMITH & WESSON MODEL 3913 TRADITIONAL DOUBLE ACTION

Caliber: 9mm Para., 8-shot magazine. **Barrel:** 3-1/2". **Weight:** 26 oz. **Length:** 6-13/16" overall. **Stocks:** One-piece Delrin wrap-around, textured surface. **Sights:** Post front with white dot, Novak LoMount Carry with two dots, adjustable for windage. **Features:** Aluminum alloy frame, stainless slide (M3913) or blue steel slide (M3914). Bobbed hammer with no half-cock notch; smooth .304" trigger with rounded edges. Straight backstrap. Extra magazine included. Introduced 1989.
Price: **$662.00**

Smith & Wesson Model 3913-LS LadySmith Auto

Similar to the standard Model 3913 except has frame that is upswept at the front, rounded trigger guard. Comes in frosted stainless steel with matching gray grips. Grips are ergonomically correct for a woman's hand. Novak LoMount Carry rear sight adjustable for windage, smooth edges for snag resistance. Extra magazine included. Introduced 1990.
Price: **$744.00**

Smith & Wesson Model 3953 DAO Pistol

Same as the Model 3913 except double-action-only. Model 3953 has stainless slide with alloy frame. Overall length 7"; weighs 25.5 oz. Extra magazine included. Introduced 1990.
Price: **$724.00**

Smith & Wesson
Model 3913TSW/3953TSW Auto Pistols

Similar to the Model 3913 and 3953 except TSW guns have tighter tolerances, ambidextrous manual safety/decocking lever, flush-fit magazine, delayed-unlock firing system; magazine disconnector. Compact alloy frame, stainless steel slide. Straight backstrap. Introduced 1998. Made in U.S. by Smith & Wesson.
Price: Single action/double action **$724.00**
Price: Double action only **$724.00**

SMITH & WESSON MODEL 4006 TDA AUTO

Caliber: 40 S&W, 10-shot magazine. **Barrel:** 4". **Weight:** 38.5 oz. **Length:** 7-7/8" overall. **Stocks:** Xenoy wrap-around with checkered panels. **Sights:** Replaceable post front with white dot, Novak LoMount Carry fixed rear with two white dots, or micro. click adjustable rear with two white dots. **Features:** Stainless steel construction with non-reflective finish. Straight back-strap. Extra magazine included. Introduced 1990.
Price: With adjustable sights **$899.00**
Price: With fixed sight **$864.00**
Price: With fixed night sights **$991.00**

Smith & Wesson Model 4043, 4046 DA Pistols

Similar to the Model 4006 except is double-action-only. Has a semi-bobbed hammer, smooth trigger, 4" barrel; Novak LoMount Carry rear sight, post front with white dot. Overall length is 7-1/2", weighs 28 oz. Model 4043 has alloy frame. Extra magazine included. Introduced 1991.
Price: Model 4043 (alloy frame) **$844.00**
Price: Model 4046 (stainless frame) **$864.00**
Price: Model 4046 with fixed night sights **$991.00**

SMITH & WESSON MODEL 4500 SERIES AUTOS

Caliber: 45 ACP, 8-shot magazine. **Barrel:** 5" (M4506). **Weight:** 41 oz. (4506). **Length:** 8-1/2" overall. **Stocks:** Xenoy one-piece wrap-around, arched or straight backstrap. **Sights:** Post front with white dot, adjustable or fixed Novak LoMount Carry on M4506. **Features:** M4506 has serrated hammer spur. All have two magazines. Contact Smith & Wesson for complete data. Introduced 1989.
Price: Model 4506, fixed sight **$822.00**
Price: Model 4506, adjustable sight **$855.00**
Price: Model 4566 (stainless, 4-1/4", traditional DA, ambidextrous
safety, fixed sight) **$897.00**
Price: Model 4586 (stainless, 4-1/4", DA only) **$897.00**

SMITH & WESSON MODEL 4513TSW/4553TSW PISTOLS

Caliber: 45 ACP, 6-shot magazine. **Barrel:** 3-3/4". **Weight:** 28 oz. (M4513TSW). **Length:** 6-7/8" overall. **Stocks:** Checkered Xenoy; straight backstrap. **Sights:** White dot front, Novak Lo Mount Carry 2-Dot rear. **Features:** Model 4513TSW is traditional double action, Model 4553TSW is double action only. TSW series has tighter tolerances, ambidextrous manual safety/decocking lever, flush-fit magazine, delayed-unlock firing system; magazine disconnector. Compact alloy frame, stainless steel slide. Introduced 1998. Made in U.S. by Smith & Wesson.
Price: Model 4513TSW **$880.00**
Price: Model 4553TSW **$837.00**

Smith & Wesson 4553 TSW

Springfield 1911A1 Standard

Smith & Wesson Sigma SW40V

Springfield Full-Size 1911A1

SMITH & WESSON MODEL 5900 SERIES AUTO PISTOLS

Caliber: 9mm Para., 10-shot magazine. **Barrel:** 4". **Weight:** 28-1/2 to 37-1/2 oz. (fixed sight); 38 oz. (adjustable sight). **Length:** 7-1/2" overall. **Stocks:** Xenoy wrap-around with curved backstrap. **Sights:** Post front with white dot, fixed or fully adjustable with two white dots. **Features:** All stainless, stainless and alloy or carbon steel and alloy construction. Smooth .304" trigger, .260" serrated hammer. Introduced 1989.
Price: Model 5906 (stainless, traditional DA, adjustable sight,
  ambidextrous safety) **$861.00**
Price: As above, fixed sight **$822.00**
Price: With fixed night sights **$948.00**
Price: Model 5946 DAO (as above, stainless frame and slide) . . **$822.00**

SMITH & WESSON ENHANCED SIGMA SERIES PISTOLS

Caliber: 9mm Para., 40 S&W, 10-shot magazine. **Barrel:** 4". **Weight:** 26 oz. **Length:** 7.4" overall. **Stocks:** Integral. **Sights:** White dot front, fixed rear; three-dot system. Tritium night sights available. **Features:** Ergonomic polymer frame; low barrel centerline; internal striker firing system; corrosion-resistant slide; Teflon-filled, electroless-nickel coated magazine. Introduced 1994. Made in U.S. by Smith & Wesson.
Price: SW9E, 9mm, 4" barrel, black finish, fixed sights **$657.00**
Price: SW9V, 9mm, 4" barrel, satin stainless, fixed night sights . . **$447.00**
Price: SW40E, 40 S&W, 4" barrel, black finish, fixed sights **$657.00**
Price: SW40V, 40 S&W, 4" barrel, black polymer, fixed sights . . . **$447.00**

SMITH & WESSON SIGMA SW380 AUTO

Caliber: 380 ACP, 6-shot magazine. **Barrel:** 3". **Weight:** 14 oz. **Length:** 5.8" overall. **Stocks:** Integral. **Sights:** Fixed groove in the slide. **Features:** Polymer frame; double-action-only trigger mechanism; grooved/serrated front and rear straps; two passive safeties. Introduced 1995. Made in U.S. by Smith & Wesson.
Price: **$328.00**

Smith & Wesson Model 6906 Double-Action Auto

Similar to the Model 5906 except with 3-1/2" barrel, 10-shot magazine, fixed rear sight, .260" bobbed hammer. Extra magazine included. Introduced 1989.
Price: Model 6906, stainless **$720.00**
Price: Model 6906 with fixed night sights **$836.00**
Price: Model 6946 (stainless, DA only, fixed sights) **$720.00**

SMITH & WESSON MODEL CS9 CHIEFS SPECIAL AUTO

Caliber: 9mm Para., 7-shot magazine. **Barrel:** 3". **Weight:** 20.8 oz. **Length:** 6-1/4" overall. **Stocks:** Hogue wrap-around rubber. **Sights:** White dot front, fixed two-dot rear. **Features:** Traditional double-action trigger mechanism. Alloy frame, stainless or blued slide. Introduced 1999. Made in U.S. by Smith & Wesson.
Price: Blue or stainless **$648.00**

Smith & Wesson Model CS40 Chiefs Special Auto

Similar to the CS9 except chambered for 40 S&W (7-shot magazine), has 3-1/4" barrel, weighs 24.2 oz., and measures 6-1/2" overall. Introduced 1999. Made in U.S. by Smith & Wesson.
Price: Blue or stainless **$683.00**

Smith & Wesson Model CS45 Chiefs Special Auto

Similar to the CS40 except chambered for 45 ACP, 6-shot magazine, weighs 23.9 oz. Introduced 1999. Made in U.S. by Smith & Wesson.
Price: Blue or stainless **$683.00**

SPRINGFIELD, INC. FULL-SIZE 1911A1 AUTO PISTOL

Caliber: 9mm Para., 9-shot; 38 Super, 9-shot; 40 S&W, 9-shot; 45 ACP, 8-shot. **Barrel:** 5". **Weight:** 35.6 oz. **Length:** 8-5/8" overall. **Stocks:** Checkered plastic or walnut. **Sights:** Fixed three-dot system. **Features:** Beveled magazine well; lowered and flared ejection port. All forged parts, including frame, barrel, slide. All new production. Introduced 1990. From Springfield, Inc.
Price: Mil-Spec 45 ACP, Parkerized **$559.00**
Price: Standard, 45 ACP, blued **$770.00**
Price: Standard, 45 ACP, stainless. **$828.00**
Price: Lightweight 45 ACP (28.6 oz., matte finish, night sights) . . **$832.00**
Price: 40 S&W, stainless **$812.00**
Price: 9mm, stainless **$837.00**

Springfield TRP

Stoeger American Eagle Luger

Springfield
V10 Ultra Compact

Springfield, Inc. TRP Pistols

Similar to the 1911A1 except 45 ACP only; has checkered front strap and mainspring housing; Novak Night Sight combat rear sight and matching dovetailed front sight; tuned, polished extractor; oversize barrel link; lightweight speed trigger and combat action job; match barrel and bushing; extended ambidextrous thumb safety and fitted beavertail grip safety; Carry bevel on entire pistol; checkered cocobolo wood grips; comes with two Wilson 8-shot magazines. Frame is engraved "Tactical," both sides of frame with "TRP." Introduced 1998. From Springfield, Inc.

Price: Standard with Armory Kote finish. $1,395.00
Price: Standard, stainless steel $1,265.00
Price: Champion, Armory Kote, adj. sights. $1,407.00

Springfield, Inc. 1911A1 High Capacity Pistol

Similar to the Standard 1911A1 except available in 45 ACP with 10-shot magazine. Has Commander-style hammer, walnut grips, beveled magazine well, plastic carrying case. Introduced 1993. From Springfield, Inc.

Price: Mil-Spec 45 ACP $807.00
Price: 45 ACP Ultra Compact (3-1/2" bbl.) $812.00
Price: As above, stainless steel $884.00

Springfield, Inc. 1911A1 V-Series Ported Pistols

Similar to the standard 1911A1 except comes with scalloped slides with 10, 12 or 16 matching barrel ports to redirect powder gasses and reduce recoil and muzzle flip. Adjustable rear sight, extended thumb safety, Videki speed trigger, and beveled magazine well. Checkered walnut grips standard. Available in 45 ACP, stainless or bi-tone. Introduced 1992.

Price: V-16 Long Slide, stainless $1,080.00
Price: Target V-12, stainless. $878.00
Price: V-10 (Ultra-Compact, bi-tone) $853.00
Price: V-10 stainless. . . . . NA

Springfield, Inc. 1911A1 Champion Pistol

Similar to the standard 1911A1 except slide is 4.025". Novak Night Sights. Comes with Delta hammer and cocobolo grips. Available in 45 ACP only; Parkerized or stainless. Introduced 1989.

Price: Parkerized $817.00
Price: Stainless. $870.00
Price: Lightweight, matte finish. $867.00

Springfield Inc. Ultra Compact Pistol

Similar to the 1911A1 Compact except has shorter slide, 3.5" barrel, beavertail grip safety, beveled magazine well, Novak Low Mount or Novak Night Sights, Videki speed trigger, flared ejection port, stainless steel frame, blued slide, match grade barrel, rubber grips. Introduced 1996. From Springfield, Inc.

Price: Parkerized 45 ACP, Night Sights $817.00
Price: Stainless 45 ACP, Night Sights $884.00
Price: Lightweight, matte finish. $867.00
Price: Lightweight, 9mm, stainless. $853.00

Springfield Inc. Long Slide 1911 A1 Pistol

Similar to the Full Size model except has a 6" barrel and slide for increased sight radius and higher velocity, fully adjustable sights, muzzle-forward weight distribution for reduced recoil and quicker shot-to-shot recovery. From Springfield, Inc.

Price: Target, 45 ACP, stainless with Night Sights $1,002.00
Price: Trophy Match, stainless with adj. sights. $1,399.00

STEYR M & S SERIES AUTO PISTOLS

Caliber: 9mm Para., 40 S&W, 357 SIG; 10-shot magazine. **Barrel:** 4" (3.58" for Model S). **Weight:** 28 oz. (22.5 oz. for Model S). **Length:** 7.05" overall (6.53" for Model S). **Grips:** Ultra-rigid polymer. **Sights:** Drift-adjustable, white-triangle rear; white-triangle blade front. **Features:** Polymer frame; trigger-drop firing pin, manual and key-lock safeties; loaded chamber indicator; 5.5-lb. trigger pull; 111-degree grip angle enhances natural pointing. Introduced 2000. Imported from Austria by GSI Inc.

Price: Model M (full-sized frame with 4" barrel) $609.95
Price: Model S (compact frame with 3.58" barrel) $609.95
Price: Extra 10-shot magazines (Model M or S) $39.00

STOEGER AMERICAN EAGLE LUGER

Caliber: 9mm Para., 7-shot magazine. **Barrel:** 4", 6". **Weight:** 32 oz. **Length:** 9.6" overall. **Stocks:** Checkered walnut. **Sights:** Blade front, fixed rear. **Features:** Recreation of the American Eagle Luger pistol in stainless steel. Chamber loaded indicator. Introduced 1994. From Stoeger Industries.

Price: 4", or 6" Navy Model $720.00
Price: With matte black finish $798.00

Taurus PT 22

Taurus PT92B

TAURUS MODEL PT 22/PT 25 AUTO PISTOLS

Caliber: 22 LR, 8-shot (PT 22); 25 ACP, 9-shot (PT 25). **Barrel:** 2.75". **Weight:** 12.3 oz. **Length:** 5.25" overall. **Stocks:** Smooth rosewood or mother-of-pearl. **Sights:** Blade front, fixed rear. **Features:** Double action. Tip-up barrel for loading, cleaning. Blue, nickel, duotone or blue with gold accents. Introduced 1992. Made in U.S. by Taurus International.
Price: 22 LR or 25 ACP, blue, nickel or with duo-tone finish with rosewood grips **$215.00**
Price: 22 LR or 25 ACP, blue with gold trim, rosewood grips **$230.00**
Price: 22 LR or 25 ACP, blue, nickel or duotone finish with checkered wood grips. $190.00
Price: 22 LR or 25 ACP, blue with gold trim, mother of pearl grips
. . . . **$230.00**

TAURUS MODEL PT92B AUTO PISTOL

Caliber: 9mm Para., 15-shot magazine. **Barrel:** 5". **Weight:** 34 oz. **Length:** 8.5" overall. **Stocks:** Black rubber. **Sights:** Fixed notch rear. Three-dot sight system. Also offered with micrometer-click adjustable night sights. **Features:** Double action, exposed hammer, chamber loaded indicator, ambidextrous safety, inertia firing pin. Imported by Taurus International.
Price: Blue **$575.00**
Price: Stainless steel **$595.00**
Price: Blue with gold trim, rosewood grips **$625.00**
Price: Blue with gold trim, mother-of-pearl grips. **$645.00**
Price: Stainless steel with gold trim, rosewood grips **$645.00**
Price: Stainless steel with gold trim, mother-of-pearl grips. **$655.00**
Price: Blue with checkered rubber grips, night sights. **$655.00**
Price: Stainless steel with checkered rubber grips, night sights. . . **$670.00**

Taurus Model PT99 Auto Pistol

Similar to the PT92 except has fully adjustable rear sight, smooth Brazilian walnut stocks and is available in stainless steel or polished blue. Introduced 1983.
Price: Blue **$595.00**
Price: Stainless steel **$610.00**
Price: 22 Conversion kit for PT 92 and PT99 (includes barrel and slide)
. . . . **$266.00**

TAURUS MODEL PT-100B AUTO PISTOL

Caliber: 40 S&W, 10-shot magazine. **Barrel:** 5". **Weight:** 34 oz. **Length:** 8-1/2". **Grips:** Checkered rubber, rosewood or mother-of-pearl. **Sights:** 3-dot fixed or adjustable; night sights available. **Features:** Single/double action with three-position safety/decocker. Re-introduced in 2001. Imported by Taurus International.
Price: Blued finish. **$575.00**
Price: Stainless steel **$595.00**
Price: Blue with gold accents, rosewood grips **$625.00**
Price: Blue with gold accents, mother-of-pearl grips **$645.00**
Price: Stainless w/gold accents, mother-of-pearl grips **$655.00**

TAURUS MODEL PT-111 MILLENNIUM AUTO PISTOL

Caliber: 9mm Para., 10-shot magazine. **Barrel:** 3.25". **Weight:** 18.7 oz. **Length:** 6.0" overall. **Stocks:** Polymer. **Sights:** 3-dot fixed; night sights available. Low profile, three-dot combat. **Features:** Double action only. Firing pin lock; polymer frame; striker fired; push-button magazine release. Introduced 1998. Imported by Taurus International.
Price: Blue **$425.00**
Price: Stainless. **$435.00**
Price: With night sights, blue slide **$500.00**
Price: With night sights, stainless slide **$520.00**

Taurus Model PT-111 Millennium Titanium Pistol

Similar to the PT-111 except with titanium slide, night sights.
Price: **$585.00**

TAURUS PT-132 MILLENIUM AUTO PISTOL

Caliber: 32 ACP, 10-shot magazine. **Barrel:** 3.25". **Weight:** 18.7 oz. **Length:** NA. **Grips:** Polymer. **Sights:** 3-dot fixed; night sights available. **Features:** Double-action only; polymer frame; matte stainless or blue steel slide; manual safety; integral key-lock action. Introduced 2001.
Price: . . . . **$422.00 to $438.00**

Taurus Model PT-138 Auto Pistol

Similar to the PT-111 except chambered for 380 ACP, with 10-shot magazine. Double-action-only mechanism. Has black polymer frame with blue or stainless slide. Introduced 1999. Imported by Taurus International.
Price: Blue . . . . **$425.00 ($500.00** with night sights)
Price: Stainless. . . . . **$435.00 ($520.00** with night sights)

TAURUS PT-140 MILLENIUM AUTO PISTOL

Caliber: 40 S&W, 10-shot magazine. **Barrel:** 3.25". **Weight:** 18.7 oz. **Length:** NA. **Grips:** Checkered polymer. **Sights:** 3-dot fixed; night sights available. **Features:** Double-action only; matte stainless or blue steel slide; black polymer frame; manual safety; integral key-lock action. From Taurus International.
Price: . . . . **$455.00 to $555.00**

TAURUS PT-145 MILLENIUM AUTO PISTOL

Caliber: 45 ACP, 10-shot magazine. **Barrel:** 3.27". **Weight:** 23 oz. **Length:** NA. **Stock:** Checkered polymer. **Sights:** 3-dot fixed; night sights available. **Features:** Double-action only; matte stainless or blue steel slide; black polymer frame; manual safety; integral key-lock action. From Taurus International.
Price: . . . . **$490.00 to $575.00**

TAURUS MODEL PT-911 AUTO PISTOL

Caliber: 9mm Para., 10-shot magazine. **Barrel:** 4". **Weight:** 28.2 oz. **Length:** 7" overall. **Stocks:** Black rubber. **Sights:** Fixed. Low profile, three-dot combat. **Features:** Double action, exposed hammer; ambidextrous hammer drop; chamber loaded indicator. Introduced 1997. Imported by Taurus International.

Taurus PT-911

Taurus PT-940

Taurus PT-938

Taurus PT-945

Taurus PT-957

Price: Blue $505.00
Price: Stainless. $525.00
Price: Blue with gold accents, rosewood grips $555.00
Price: Stainless with gold accents, rosewood grips $570.00
Price: Blue/gold accents, mother-of-pearl grips $570.00
Price: Stainless/gold accents, mother-of-pearl grips $585.00
Price: Blue finish, night sights. $585.00
Price: Stainless finish, night sights $600.00

TAURUS MODEL PT-938 AUTO PISTOL

Caliber: 380 ACP, 10-shot magazine. **Barrel:** 3.72". **Weight:** 27 oz. **Length:** 6.5" overall. **Grips:** Black rubber. **Sights:** Fixed. Low profile, three-dot combat. **Features:** Double-action only. Chamber loaded indicator; firing pin block; ambidextrous hammer drop. Introduced 1997. Imported by Taurus International.
Price: Blue $500.00
Price: Stainless. $530.00

TAURUS MODEL PT-940 AUTO PISTOL

Caliber: 40 S&W, 10-shot magazine. **Barrel:** 3.35". **Weight:** 28.2 oz. **Length:** 7.05" overall. **Grips:** Checkered rubber, rosewood or mother-of-pearl. **Sights:** Drift-adjustable front and rear; three-dot combat. **Features:** Single/double action, exposed hammer; manual ambidextrous hammer-drop; inertia firing pin; chamber loaded indicator. Introduced 1996. Imported by Taurus International.
Price: Blue $525.00
Price: Stainless steel $535.00
Price: Blue with gold accents, rosewood grips $570.00
Price: Stainless with gold accents, rosewood grips $600.00

TAURUS MODEL PT-945 AUTO PISTOL

Caliber: 45 ACP, 8-shot magazine. **Barrel:** 4.25". **Weight:** 29.5 oz. **Length:** 7.48" overall. **Grips:** Checkered black rubber, rosewood or mother-of-pearl. **Sights:** Drift-adjustable front and rear; three-dot system. **Features:** Single/double-action mechanism. Has manual ambidextrous hammer drop safety, intercept notch, firing pin block, chamber loaded indicator, integral key-lock, last-shot hold-open. Introduced 1995. Imported by Taurus International.

Price: Blue $560.00
Price: Stainless. $580.00
Price: Blue, ported $600.00
Price: Stainless, ported $620.00
Price: Blue with gold accents, rosewood grips $610.00
Price: Blue with gold accents, mother-of-pearl grips $625.00
Price: Stainless w/gold accents, mother-of-pearl grips $645.00

TAURUS MODEL PT-957 AUTO PISTOL

Caliber: 357 SIG, 10-shot magazine. **Barrel:** 3-5/8". **Weight:** 28 oz. **Length:** 7" overall. **Stocks:** Checkered rubber. **Sights:** Fixed, low profile, three-dot combat; night sights optional. **Features:** Single/double action mechanism; blue, stainless steel, blue with gold accents or stainless with gold accents; exposed hammer; ported barrel/slide; three-position safety with decocking lever and ambidextrous safety. Introduced 1999. Imported by Taurus International.
Price: Blue $560.00
Price: Stainless. $575.00
Price: Blue with gold accents, rosewood grips $610.00
Price: Stainless with gold accents, rosewood grips $625.00

Vektor SP1

Walther PP

Walther PPK/S

Vektor Ultra with Tasco Scope

VEKTOR SP1 SPORT PISTOL
Caliber: 9mm Para., 10-shot magazine. **Barrel:** 5 ".**Weight:** 38 oz. **Length:** 9-3/8" overall. **Stocks:** Checkered black composition. **Sights:** Combat-type blade front, adjustable rear. **Features:** Single action only with adjustable trigger stop; three-chamber compensator; extended magazine release. Introduced 1999. Imported from South Africa by Vektor USA.
Price: **$829.95**

Vektor SP1 Tuned Sport Pistol
Similar to the Vektor Sport except has fully adjustable straight trigger, LPA three-dot sight system, and hard nickel finish. Introduced 1999. Imported from South Africa by Vektor USA.
Price: **$1,199.95**

Vektor SP1 Target Pistol
Similar to the Vektor Sport except has 5-7/8" barrel without compensator; weighs 40-1/2 oz.; has fully adjustable straight match trigger; black slide, bright frame. Introduced 1999. Imported from South Africa by Vektor USA.
Price: **$1,299.95**

Vektor SP1, SP2 Ultra Sport Pistols
Similar to the Vektor Target except has three-chamber compensator with three jet ports; strengthened frame with integral beavertail; lightweight polymer scope mount (Weaver rail). Overall length is 11", weighs 41-1/2 oz. Model SP2 is in 40 S&W. Introduced 1999. Imported from South Africa by Vektor USA.
Price: SP1 (9mm) **$2,149.95**
Price: SP2 (40 S&W) **$2,149.95**

VEKTOR SP1 AUTO PISTOL
Caliber: 9mm Para., 40 S&W (SP2), 10-shot magazine. **Barrel:** 4-5/8". **Weight:** 35 oz. **Length:** 8-1/4" overall. **Stocks:** Checkered black composition. **Sights:** Combat-type fixed. **Features:** Alloy frame, steel slide; traditional double-action mechanism; matte black finish. Introduced 1999. Imported from South Africa by Vektor USA.
Price: SP1 (9mm) **$599.95**
Price: SP1 with nickel finish **$629.95**
Price: SP2 (40 S&W) **$649.95**

Vektor SP1, SP2 Compact General's Model Pistol
Similar to the 9mm Para. Vektor SP1 except has 4" barrel, weighs 31-1/2 oz., and is 7-1/2" overall. Recoil operated. Traditional double-action mechanism. SP2 model is chambered for 40 S&W. Introduced 1999. Imported from South Africa by Vektor USA.
Price: SP1 (9mm Para.) **$649.95**
Price: SP2 (40 S&W) **$649.95**

VEKTOR CP-1 COMPACT PISTOL
Caliber: 9mm Para., 10-shot magazine. **Barrel:** 4". **Weight:** 25.4 oz. **Length:** 7" overall. **Stocks:** Textured polymer. **Sights:** Blade front adjustable for windage, fixed rear; adjustable sight optional. **Features:** Ergonomic grip frame shape; stainless steel barrel; delayed gas-buffered blowback action. Introduced 1999. Imported from South Africa by Vektor USA.
Price: With black slide **$479.95**
Price: With nickel slide **$499.95**
Price: With black slide, adjustable sight **$509.95**
Price: With nickel slide, adjustable sight **$529.95**

WALTHER PP AUTO PISTOL
Caliber: 380 ACP, 7-shot magazine. **Barrel:** 3.86". **Weight:** 23-1/2 oz. **Length:** 6.7" overall. **Stocks:** Checkered plastic. **Sights:** Fixed, white markings. **Features:** Double action; manual safety blocks firing pin and drops hammer; chamber loaded indicator on 32 and 380; extra finger rest magazine provided. Imported from Germany by Carl Walther USA.
Price: 380 . . . . **$999.00**

Walther PPK/S American Auto Pistol
Similar to Walther PP except made entirely in the United States. Has 3.27" barrel with 6.1" length overall. Introduced 1980.
Price: 380 ACP only, blue **$540.00**
Price: As above, 32 ACP or 380 ACP, stainless **$540.00**

Walther PPK

Walther P99

Walther TPH

Dan Wesson Pointman Major

Walther PPK American Auto Pistol

Similar to Walther PPK/S except weighs 21 oz., has 6-shot capacity. Made in the U.S. Introduced 1986.
Price: Stainless, 32 ACP or 380 ACP **$540.00**
Price: Blue, 380 ACP only **$540.00**

WALTHER MODEL TPH AUTO PISTOL

Caliber: 22 LR, 25 ACP, 6-shot magazine. **Barrel:** 2-1/4". **Weight:** 14 oz. **Length:** 5-3/8" overall. **Stocks:** Checkered black composition. **Sights:** Blade front, rear drift-adjustable for windage. **Features:** Made of stainless steel. Scaled-down version of the Walther PP/PPK series. Made in U.S. Introduced 1987. From Carl Walther USA.
Price: Blue or stainless steel, 22 or 25 . . . . **$440.00**

WALTHER P88 COMPACT PISTOL

Caliber: 9mm Para., 10-shot magazine. **Barrel:** 3.93". **Weight:** 28 oz. **Length:** NA. **Stocks:** Checkered black polymer. **Sights:** Blade front, drift adjustable rear. **Features:** Double action with ambidextrous decocking lever and magazine release; alloy frame; loaded chamber indicator; matte blue finish. Imported from Germany by Carl Walther USA.
Price: **$900.00**

WALTHER P99 AUTO PISTOL

Caliber: 9mm Para., 9x21, 40 S&W,10-shot magazine. **Barrel:** 4". **Weight:** 25 oz. **Length:** 7" overall. **Stocks:** Textured polymer. **Sights:** Blade front (comes with three interchangeable blades for elevation adjustment), micrometer rear adjustable for windage. **Features:** Double-action mechanism with trigger safety, decock safety, internal striker safety; chamber loaded indicator; ambidextrous magazine release levers; polymer frame with interchangeable backstrap inserts. Comes with two magazines. Introduced 1997. Imported from Germany by Carl Walther USA.
Price: **$799.00**

Walther P990 Auto Pistol

Similar to the P99 except is double action only. Available in blue or silver tenifer finish. Introduced 1999. Imported from Germany by Carl Walther USA.
Price: **$749.00**

WALTHER P-5 AUTO PISTOL

Caliber: 9mm Para., 8-shot magazine. **Barrel:** 3.62". **Weight:** 28 oz. **Length:** 7.10" overall. **Stocks:** Checkered plastic. **Sights:** Blade front, adjustable rear. **Features:** Uses the basic Walther P-38 double-action mechanism. Blue finish. Imported from Germany by Carl Walther USA.
Price: **$900.00**

DAN WESSON POINTMAN MAJOR AUTO PISTOL

Caliber: 45 ACP. **Barrel:** 5". **Weight:** NA. **Length:** NA. **Grips:** Rosewood checkered. **Sights: Features:** Blued or stainless steel frame and serrated slide; Chip McCormick match-grade trigger group, sear and disconnect; match-grade barrel; high-ride beavertail safety; checkered slide release; high rib; interchangeable sight system; laser engraved. Introduced 2000. Made in U.S. by Dan Wesson Firearms.
Price: Model PM1-B (blued) **$789.00**
Price: Model PM1-S (stainless) **$799.00**

Dan Wesson Pointman Minor Auto Pistol

Similar to Pointman Major except has blued frame and slide with fixed rear sight. Introduced 2000. Made in U.S. by Dan Wesson Firearms.
Price: Model PM2-P **$579.00**

HANDGUNS

Dan Wesson
Pointman Seven

Dan Wesson Pointman Guardian

Dan Wesson Pointman Seven Auto Pistols

Similar to Pointman Major except has dovetail adjustable target rear sight and dovetail target front sight. Available in blued or stainless finish. Introduced 2000. Made in U.S. by Dan Wesson Firearms.

Price: PM7 (blued frame and slide) **$999.00**
Price: PM7S (stainless finish). **$1,099.00**

Dan Wesson Pointman Guardian Auto Pistols

Similar to Pointman Major except has a more compact frame with 4.25" barrel. Avaiable in blued or stainless finish with fixed or adjustable sights. Introduced 2000. Made in U.S. by Dan Wesson Firearms.

Price: PMG-FS (blued frame and slide, fixed sights) **$769.00**
Price: PMG-AS (blued frame and slide, adjustable sights). **$779.00**
Price: PMGD-FS Guardian Duce (stainless frame and blued slide,
    fixed sights) **$829.00**
Price: PMGD-AS Guardian Duce (stainless frame and blued slide,
    adj. sights). **$839.00**

Dan Wesson Pointman Hi-Cap Auto Pistol

NEW! Similar to Pointman Minor except has full-size high-capacity (10-shot) magazine with 5" chromed barrel, blued finish and dovetail fixed rear sight. Match adjustable trigger, ambidextrous extended thumb safety, beavertail safety. Introduced 2001. From Dan Wesson Firearms.

Price: PMHC (Pointman High-Cap) **$669.00**

Dan Wesson Pointman Dave Pruitt Signature Series

NEW! Similar to other full-sized Pointman models except customized by Master Pistolsmith and IDPA Grand Master Dave Pruitt. Alloy carbon-steel from with black oxide bluing and bead-blast matte finish. Front and rear chevron cocking serrations; dovetail-mount fixed Novak style sights; match trigger group, sear and hammer; exotic hardwood grips. Introduced 2001. From Dan Wesson Firearms.

Price: PMDP (Pointman Dave Pruitt) **$899.00**

Wilkinson Sherry

WILKINSON SHERRY AUTO PISTOL

Caliber: 22 LR, 8-shot magazine. **Barrel:** 2-1/8". **Weight:** 9-1/4 oz. **Length:** 4-3/8" overall. **Stocks:** Checkered black plastic. **Sights:** Fixed, groove. **Features:** Cross-bolt safety locks the sear into the hammer. Available in all blue finish or blue slide and trigger with gold frame. Introduced 1985.

Price: **$195.00**

WILKINSON LINDA AUTO PISTOL

Caliber: 9mm Para. **Barrel:** 8-5/16". **Weight:** 4 lbs., 13 oz. **Length:** 12-1/4" overall. **Stocks:** Checkered black plastic pistol grip, walnut forend. **Sights:** Protected blade front, aperture rear. **Features:** Fires from closed bolt. Semi-auto only. Straight blowback action. Cross-bolt safety. Removable barrel. From Wilkinson Arms.

Price: **$533.33**

Includes models suitable for several forms of competition and other sporting purposes.

Baer 1911 Ultimate Master

Beretta Model 89

Baer 1911 Bullseye Wadcutter

Beretta Model 96 Combat

BAER 1911 ULTIMATE MASTER COMBAT PISTOL
Caliber: 9x23, 38 Super, 400 Cor-Bon 45 ACP (others available), 10-shot magazine. **Barrel:** 5", 6"; Baer NM. **Weight:** 37 oz. **Length:** 8.5" overall. **Stocks:** Checkered rosewood. **Sights:** Baer dovetail front, low-mount Bo-Mar rear with hidden leaf. **Features:** Full-house competition gun. Baer forged NM blued steel frame and double serrated slide; Baer triple port, tapered cone compensator; fitted slide to frame; lowered, flared ejection port; Baer reverse recoil plug; full-length guide rod; recoil buff; beveled magazine well; Baer Commander hammer, sear; Baer extended ambidextrous safety, extended ejector, checkered slide stop, beavertail grip safety with pad, extended magazine release button; Baer speed trigger. Made in U.S. by Les Baer Custom, Inc.
Price: Compensated, open sights. **$2,476.00**
Price: 6" Model 400 Cor-Bon **$2,541.00**

BAER 1911 NATIONAL MATCH HARDBALL PISTOL
Caliber: 45 ACP, 7-shot magazine. **Barrel:** 5". **Weight:** 37 oz. **Length:** 8.5" overall. **Stocks:** Checkered walnut. **Sights:** Baer dovetail front with undercut post, low-mount Bo-Mar rear with hidden leaf. **Features:** Baer NM forged steel frame, double serrated slide and barrel with stainless bushing; slide fitted to frame; Baer match trigger with 4-lb. pull; polished feed ramp, throated barrel; checkered front strap, arched mainspring housing; Baer beveled magazine well; lowered, flared ejection port; tuned extractor; Baer extended ejector, checkered slide stop; recoil buff. Made in U.S. by Les Baer Custom, Inc.
Price: **$1,335.00**

Baer 1911 Bullseye Wadcutter Pistol
Similar to the National Match Hardball except designed for wadcutter loads only. Has polished feed ramp and barrel throat; Bo-Mar rib on slide; full-length recoil rod; Baer speed trigger with 3-1/2-lb. pull; Baer deluxe hammer and sear; Baer beavertail grip safety with pad; flat mainspring housing checkered 20 lpi. Blue finish; checkered walnut grips. Made in U.S. by Les Baer Custom, Inc.
Price: From. **$1,495.00**
Price: With 6" barrel, from **$1,690.00**

BENELLI MP90S WORLD CUP PISTOL
Caliber: 22 Long Rifle, 6- or 9-shot magazine. **Barrel:** 4.4" **Weight:** 2.5 lbs. **Length:** 11.75". **Grip:** Walnut. **Sights:** Blade front, fully adjustable rear. **Features:** Single-action target pistol with fully adjustable trigger and adjustable heel rest; integral scope rail mount; attachment system for optional external weights.
Price: **$1,190.00**

Benelli MP95E Atlanta Pistol
Similar to MP90S World Cup Pistol, but available in blue finish with walnut grip or chrome finish with laminate grip. Overall length 11.25". Trigger overtravel adjustment only.
Price: (blue finish, walnut grip) **$740.00**
Price: (chrome finish, laminate grip) **$810.00**

BERETTA MODEL 89 GOLD STANDARD PISTOL
Caliber: 22 LR, 8-shot magazine. **Barrel:** 6". **Weight:** 41 oz. **Length:** 9.5" overall. **Stocks:** Target-type walnut with thumbrest. **Sights:** Interchangeable blade front, fully adjustable rear. **Features:** Single action target pistol. Matte black, Bruniton finish. Imported from Italy by Beretta U.S.A.
Price: **$802.00**

BERETTA MODEL 96 COMBAT PISTOL
Caliber: 40 S&W, 10-shot magazine. **Barrel:** 4.9" (5.9" with weight). **Weight:** 34.4 oz. **Length:** 8.5" overall. **Stocks:** Checkered black plastic. **Sights:** Blade front, fully adjustable target rear. **Features:** Uses heavier Brigadier slide with front and rear serrations; extended frame-mounted safety; extended, reversible magazine release; single-action-only with competition-tuned trigger with extra-short let-off and over-travel adjustment. Comes with tool kit. Introduced 1997. Imported from Italy by Beretta U.S.A.
Price: **$1,593.00**
Price: 4.9" barrel. **$1,341.00**
Price: 5.9" barrel. **$1,634.00**
Price: Combo **$1,599.00**

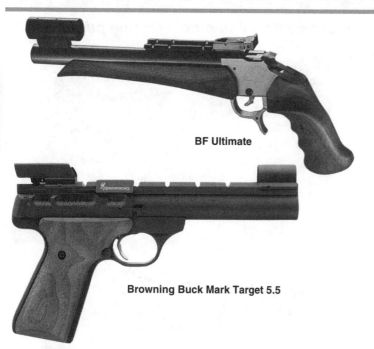

BF Ultimate

Browning Buck Mark Target 5.5

Browning Buck Mark Bullseye

Colt Gold Cup Trophy

Beretta Model 96 Stock Pistol

Similar to the Model 96 Combat except is single/double action, with half-cock notch. Has front and rear slide serrations, rubber magazine bumper, replaceable accurizing barrel bushing, ultra-thin fine-checkered grips (aluminum optional), checkered front and back straps, radiused back strap, fitted case. Weighs 35 oz., 8.5" overall. Introduced 1997. Imported from Italy by Beretta U.S.A.

Price: **$1,700.00**

BF ULTIMATE SILHOUETTE HB SINGLE SHOT PISTOL

Caliber: 7mm U.S., 22 LR Match and 100 other chamberings. **Barrel:** 10.75" Heavy Match Grade with 11-degree target crown. **Weight:** 3 lbs., 15 oz. **Length:** 16" overall. **Stocks:** Thumbrest target style. **Sights:** Bo-Mar/Bond ScopeRib I Combo with hooded post front adjustable for height and width, rear notch available in .032", .062", .080" and .100" widths; 1/2-MOA clicks. **Features:** Designed to meet maximum rules for IHMSA Production Gun. Falling block action gives rigid barrel-receiver mating. Hand fitted and headspaced. Etched receiver; gold-colored trigger. Introduced 1988. Made in U.S. by E. Arthur Brown Co. Inc.

Price: **$669.00**

Classic BF Hunting Pistol

Similar to BF Ultimate Silhouette HB Single Shot Pistol, except no sights; drilled and tapped for scope mount. Barrels from 8 to 15". Variety of options offered. Made in U.S. by E. Arthur Brown Co. Inc.

Price: **$599.00**

BROWNING BUCK MARK SILHOUETTE

Caliber: 22 LR, 10-shot magazine. **Barrel:** 9-7/8". **Weight:** 53 oz. **Length:** 14" overall. **Stocks:** Smooth walnut stocks and forend, or finger-groove walnut. **Sights:** Post-type hooded front adjustable for blade width and height; Pro Target rear fully adjustable for windage and elevation. **Features:** Heavy barrel with .900" diameter; 12-1/2" sight radius. Special sighting plane forms scope base. Introduced 1987. Made in U.S. From Browning.

Price: **$448.00**

Browning Buck Mark Target 5.5

Same as the Buck Mark Silhouette except has a 5-1/2" barrel with .900" diameter. Has hooded sights mounted on a scope base that accepts an optical or reflex sight. Rear sight is a Browning fully adjustable Pro Target, front sight is an adjustable post that customizes to different widths, and can be adjusted for height. Contoured walnut grips with thumbrest, or finger-groove walnut. Matte blue finish. Overall length is 9-5/8", weighs 35-1/2 oz. Has 10-shot magazine. Introduced 1990. From Browning.

Price: **$425.00**
Price: Target 5.5 Gold (as above with gold anodized frame and top rib) **$477.00**
Price: Target 5.5 Nickel (as above with nickel frame and top rib). **$477.00**

Browning Buck Mark Field 5.5

Same as the Target 5.5 except has hoodless ramp-style front sight and low profile rear sight. Matte blue finish, contoured or finger-groove walnut stocks. Introduced 1991.

Price: **$425.00**

Browning Buck Mark Bullseye

Similar to the Buck Mark Silhouette except has 7-1/4" heavy barrel with three flutes per side; trigger is adjustable from 2-1/2 to 5 lbs.; specially designed rosewood target or three-finger-groove stocks with competition-style heel rest, or with contoured rubber grip. Overall length is 11-5/16", weighs 36 oz. Introduced 1996. Made in U.S. From Browning.

Price: With ambidextrous moulded composite stocks **$389.00**
Price: With rosewood stocks, or wrap-around finger groove **$500.00**

COLT GOLD CUP MODEL O PISTOL

Caliber: 45 ACP, 8-shot magazine. **Barrel:** 5", with new design bushing. **Weight:** 39 oz. **Length:** 8-1/2". **Stocks:** Checkered rubber composite with silver-plated medallion. **Sights:** Patridge-style front, Bomar-style rear adjustable for windage and elevation, sight radius 6-3/4". **Features:** Arched or flat housing; wide, grooved trigger with adjustable stop; ribbed-top slide, hand fitted, with improved ejection port.

Price: Blue **$1,050.00**
Price: Stainless. **$1,116.00**

COMPETITOR SINGLE SHOT PISTOL

Caliber: 22 LR through 50 Action Express, including belted magnums. **Barrel:** 14" standard; 10.5" silhouette; 16" optional. **Weight:** About 59 oz. (14" bbl.). **Length:** 15.12" overall. **Stocks:** Ambidextrous; synthetic (standard) or laminated or natural wood. **Sights:** Ramp front, adjustable rear. **Features:** Rotary canon-type action cocks on opening; cammed ejector; interchangeable barrels, ejectors. Adjustable single stage trigger, sliding thumb safety and trigger safety. Matte blue finish. Introduced 1988. From Competitor Corp., Inc.

Price: 14", standard calibers, synthetic grip **$414.95**
Price: Extra barrels, from **$159.95**

Competitor Single Shot

E.A.A. Witness Gold Team

Freedom Arms 252 Silhouette

Hammerli SP 20

CZ 75 CHAMPION COMPETITION PISTOL

Caliber: 9mm Para., 9x21, 40 S&W, 10-shot magazine. **Barrel:** 4.49". **Weight:** 35 oz. **Length:** 9.44" overall. **Stocks:** Black rubber. **Sights:** Blade front, fully adjustable rear. **Features:** Single-action trigger mechanism; three-port compensator (40 S&W, 9mm have two port) full-length guide rod; extended magazine release; ambidextrous safety; flared magazine well; fully adjustable match trigger. Introduced 1999. Imported from the Czech Republic by CZ USA.
Price: 9mm Para., 9x21, 40 S&W, dual-tone finish. **$1,484.00**

CZ 75 ST IPSC AUTO PISTOL

Caliber: 40 S&W, 10-shot magazine. **Barrel:** 5.12". **Weight:** 2.9 lbs. **Length:** 8.86" overall. **Stocks:** Checkered walnut. **Sights:** Fully adjustable rear. **Features:** Single-action mechanism; extended slide release and ambidextrous safety; full-length slide rail; double slide serrations. Introduced 1999. Imported from the Czech Republic by CZ-USA.
Price: Dual-tone finish **$1,038.00**

EAA/BAIKAL IZH35 AUTO PISTOL

Caliber: 22 LR, 5-shot magazine. **Barrel:** 6". **Weight:** NA. **Length:** NA. **Grips:** Walnut; fully adjustable right-hand target-style. **Sights:** Fully adjustable rear, blade front; detachable scope mount. **Features:** Hammer-forged target barrel; machined steel receiver; adjustable trigger; manual slide hold back, grip and manual trigger-bar disconnect safeties; cocking indicator. Introduced 2000. Imported from Russia by European American Armory.
Price: Blued finish. **$519.00**

E.A.A. WITNESS GOLD TEAM AUTO

Caliber: 9mm Para., 9x21, 38 Super, 40 S&W, 45 ACP. **Barrel:** 5.1". **Weight:** 41.6 oz. **Length:** 9.6" overall. **Stocks:** Checkered walnut, competition style. **Sights:** Square post front, fully adjustable rear. **Features:** Triple-chamber cone compensator; competition SA trigger; extended safety and magazine release; competition hammer; beveled magazine well; beavertail grip. Hand-fitted major components. Hard chrome finish. Match-grade barrel. From E.A.A. Custom Shop. Introduced 1992. From European American Armory.
Price: **$2,150.00**

E.A.A. Witness Silver Team Auto

Similar to the Witness Gold Team except has double-chamber compensator, oval magazine release, black rubber grips, double-dip blue finish. Comes with Super Sight and drilled and tapped for scope mount. Built for the intermediate competition shooter. Introduced 1992. From European American Armory Custom Shop.
Price: 9mm Para., 9x21, 38 Super, 40 S&W, 45 ACP **$968.00**

ENTRÉPRISE TOURNAMENT SHOOTER MODEL I

Caliber: 45 ACP, 10-shot magazine. **Barrel:** 6". **Weight:** 40 oz. **Length:** 8.5" overall. **Stocks:** Black ultra-slim double diamond checkered synthetic. **Sights:** Dovetailed Patridge front, adjustable Competizione "melded" rear. **Features:** Oversized magazine release button; flared magazine well; fully machined parallel slide rails; front and rear slide serrations; serrated top of slide; stainless ramped bull barrel with fully supported chamber; full-length guide rod with plug; stainless firing pin; match extractor; polished ramp; tuned match extractor; black oxide. Introduced 1998. Made in U.S. by Entréprise Arms.
Price: **$2,300.00**
Price: TSMIII (Satin chrome finish, two-piece guide rod) **$2,700.00**

Excel Industries CP-45 Auto Pistol

Caliber: 45 ACP, 6-shot magazine. **Barrel:** 3-1/4 inches. **Weight:** 31 oz. **Length:** 6-3/8 inches overall. **Grips:** Checkered black nylon. **Sights:** Fully adjustable rear, three-dot; blade front. **Features:** Stainless steel frame and slide; single action with external hammer and firing pin block, manual thumb safety; last-shot hold open. Includes gun lock and cleaning kit. Introduced 2001. Made in U.S. by Excel Industries Inc.
Price: **$425.00**

FREEDOM ARMS MODEL 83 FIELD GRADE SILHOUETTE CLASS

Caliber: 22 LR, 5-shot cylinder. **Barrel:** 10". **Weight:** 63 oz. **Length:** 15.5" overall. **Stocks:** Black Micarta. **Sights:** Removable patridge front blade; Iron Sight Gun Works silhouette rear, click adjustable for windage and elevation (optional adj. front sight and hood). **Features:** Stainless steel, matte finish, manual sliding-bar safety system; dual firing pins, lightened hammer for fast lock time, pre-set trigger stop. Introduced 1991. Made in U.S. by Freedom Arms.
Price: Silhouette Class **$1,765.00**
Price: Extra fitted 22 WMR cylinder **$264.00**

GAUCHER GP SILHOUETTE PISTOL

Caliber: 22 LR, single shot. **Barrel:** 10". **Weight:** 42.3 oz. **Length:** 15.5" overall. **Stocks:** Stained hardwood. **Sights:** Hooded post on ramp front, open rear adjustable for windage and elevation. **Features:** Matte chrome barrel, blued bolt and sights. Other barrel lengths available on special order. Introduced 1991. Imported by Mandall Shooting Supplies.
Price: **$425.00**

HAMMERLI SP 20 TARGET PISTOL

Caliber: 22 LR, 32 S&W. **Barrel:** 4.6". **Weight:** 34.6-41.8 oz. **Length:** 11.8" overall. **Stocks:** Anatomically shaped synthetic Hi-Grip available in five sizes. **Sights:** Integral front in three widths, adjustable rear with changeable notch widths. **Features:** Extremely low-level sight line; anatomically shaped trigger; adjustable JPS buffer system for different recoil characteristics. Receiver available in red, blue, gold, violet or black. Introduced 1998. Imported from Switzerland by SIGARMS, Inc and Hammerli Pistols USA.
Price: . . . . **NA**

High Standard Trophy

High Standard Victor

HARRIS GUNWORKS SIGNATURE JR. LONG RANGE PISTOL

Caliber: Any suitable caliber. **Barrel:** To customer specs. **Weight:** 5 lbs. **Stock:** Gunworks fiberglass. **Sights:** None furnished; comes with scope rings. **Features:** Right- or left-hand benchrest action of titanium or stainless steel; single shot or repeater. Comes with bipod. Introduced 1992. Made in U.S. by Harris Gunworks, Inc.

Price: $2,700.00

HIGH STANDARD TROPHY TARGET PISTOL

Caliber: 22 LR, 10-shot magazine. **Barrel:** 5-1/2" bull or 7-1/4" fluted. **Weight:** 44 oz. **Length:** 9.5" overall. **Stock:** Checkered hardwood with thumbrest. **Sights:** Undercut ramp front, frame-mounted micro-click rear adjustable for windage and elevation; drilled and tapped for scope mounting. **Features:** Gold-plated trigger, slide lock, safety-lever and magazine release; stippled front grip and backstrap; adjustable trigger and sear. Barrel weights optional. From High Standard Manufacturing Co., Inc.

Price: 5-1/2", scope base $510.00
Price: 7.25" $650.00
Price: 7.25", scope base $591.00

HIGH STANDARD VICTOR TARGET PISTOL

Caliber: 22 LR, 10-shot magazine. **Barrel:** 4-1/2" or 5-1/2"; push-button takedown. **Weight:** 46 oz. **Length:** 9.5" overall. **Stock:** Checkered hardwood with thumbrest. **Sights:** Undercut ramp front, micro-click rear adjustable for windage and elevation. Also available with scope mount, rings, no sights. **Features:** Stainless steel construction. Full-length vent rib. Gold-plated trigger, slide lock, safety-lever and magazine release; stippled front grip and backstrap; polished slide; adjustable trigger and sear. Comes with barrel weight. From High Standard Manufacturing Co., Inc.

Price: $591.00
Price: With Weaver rib $532.00

KIMBER SUPER MATCH AUTO PISTOL

Caliber: 45 ACP, 7-shot magazine. **Barrel:** 5". **Weight:** 38 oz. **Length:** 18.7" overall. **Sights:** Blade front, Kimber fully adjustable rear. **Features:** Guaranteed to have shot 3" group at 50 yards. Stainless steel frame, black KimPro slide; two-piece magazine well; premium aluminum match-grade trigger; 30 lpi front strap checkering; stainless match-grade barrel; ambidextrous safety; special Custom Shop markings. Introduced 1999. Made in U.S. by Kimber Mfg., Inc.

Price: $1,927.00

MORINI MODEL 84E FREE PISTOL

Caliber: 22 LR, single shot. **Barrel:** 11.4". **Weight:** 43.7 oz. **Length:** 19.4" overall. **Stocks:** Adjustable match type with stippled surfaces. **Sights:** Interchangeable blade front, match-type fully adjustable rear. **Features:** Fully adjustable electronic trigger. Introduced 1995. Imported from Switzerland by Nygord Precision Products.

Price: $1,450.00

PARDINI MODEL SP, HP TARGET PISTOLS

Caliber: 22 LR, 32 S&W, 5-shot magazine. **Barrel:** 4.7". **Weight:** 38.9 oz. **Length:** 11.6" overall. **Stocks:** Adjustable; stippled walnut; match type. **Sights:** Interchangeable blade front, interchangeable, fully adjustable rear. **Features:** Fully adjustable match trigger. Introduced 1995. Imported from Italy by Nygord Precision Products.

Price: Model SP (22 LR)............................. $950.00
Price: Model HP (32 S&W)........................... $1,050.00

PARDINI GP RAPID FIRE MATCH PISTOL

Caliber: 22 Short, 5-shot magazine. **Barrel:** 4.6". **Weight:** 43.3 oz. **Length:** 11.6" overall. **Stocks:** Wrap-around stippled walnut. **Sights:** Interchangeable post front, fully adjustable match rear. **Features:** Model GP Schuman has extended rear sight for longer sight radius. Introduced 1995. Imported from Italy by Nygord Precision Products.

Price: Model GP $1,095.00
Price: Model GP Schuman........................... $1,595.00

PARDINI K22 FREE PISTOL

Caliber: 22 LR, single shot. **Barrel:** 9.8". **Weight:** 34.6 oz. **Length:** 18.7" overall. **Stocks:** Wrap-around walnut; adjustable match type. **Sights:** Interchangeable post front, fully adjustable match open rear. **Features:** Removable, adjustable match trigger. Barrel weights mount above the barrel. New model introduced in 1999. Imported from Italy by Nygord Precision Products.

Price: $1,295.00

RUGER MARK II TARGET MODEL AUTOLOADING PISTOL

Caliber: 22 LR, 10-shot magazine. **Barrel:** 6-7/8". **Weight:** 42 oz. **Length:** 11-1/8" overall. **Stocks:** Checkered hard plastic. **Sights:** .125" blade front, micro-click rear, adjustable for windage and elevation. Sight radius 9-3/8". Comes with lockable plastic case with lock. **Features:** Introduced 1982.

Price: Blued (MK-678) $336.00
Price: Stainless (KMK-678) $420.00

Ruger Mark II Government Target Model

Same gun as the Mark II Target Model except has 6-7/8" barrel, higher sights and is roll marked "Government Target Model" on the right side of the receiver below the rear sight. Identical in all aspects to the military model used for training U.S. Armed Forces except for markings. Comes with factory test target. Comes with lockable plastic case and lock. Introduced 1987.

Price: Blued (MK-678G)............................. $405.00
Price: Stainless (KMK-678G) $485.00

Ruger Stainless Competition Model Pistol

Similar to the Mark II Government Target Model stainless pistol except has 6-7/8" slab-sided barrel; the receiver top is fitted with a Ruger scope base of blued, chrome moly steel; comes with Ruger 1" stainless scope rings for mounting a variety of optical sights; has checkered laminated grip panels with right-hand thumbrest. Has blued open sights with 9-1/4" radius. Overall length is 11-1/8", weight 45 oz. Comes with lockable plastic case and lock. Introduced 1991.

Price: KMK-678GC................................. $499.00

Ruger Mark II Bull Barrel

Same gun as the Target Model except has 5-1/2" or 10" heavy barrel (10" meets all IHMSA regulations). Weight with 5-1/2" barrel is 42 oz., with 10" barrel, 51 oz. Comes with lockable plastic case with lock.

Price: Blued (MK-512) $336.00
Price: Blued (MK-10) $340.00
Price: Stainless (KMK-10) $425.00
Price: Stainless (KMK-512) $420.00

Ruger Mark II Bull Barrel - MK10

Safari Arms Big Deuce

Smith & Wesson Model 41

Springfield 1911A1 Trophy Match

SAFARI ARMS BIG DEUCE PISTOL

Caliber: 45 ACP, 7-shot magazine. **Barrel:** 6", 416 stainless steel. **Weight:** 40.3 oz. **Length:** 9.5" overall. **Stocks:** Smooth walnut. **Sights:** Ramped blade front, LPA adjustable rear. **Features:** Beavertail grip safety; extended thumb safety and slide release; Commander-style hammer. Throated, polished and tuned. Parkerized matte black slide with satin stainless steel frame. Introduced 1995. Made in U.S. by Safari Arms, Inc.
Price: **$714.00**

SMITH & WESSON MODEL 41 TARGET

Caliber: 22 LR, 10-shot clip. **Barrel:** 5-1/2", 7". **Weight:** 44 oz. (5-1/2" barrel). **Length:** 9" overall (5-1/2" barrel). **Stocks:** Checkered walnut with modified thumbrest, usable with either hand. **Sights:** 1/8" Patridge on ramp base; micro-click rear adjustable for windage and elevation. **Features:** 3/8" wide, grooved trigger; adjustable trigger stop.
Price: S&W Bright Blue, either barrel **$801.00**

SMITH & WESSON MODEL 22A TARGET PISTOL

Caliber: 22 LR, 10-shot magazine. **Barrel:** 5-1/2" bull. **Weight:** 38.5 oz. **Length:** 9-1/2" overall. **Stocks:** Dymondwood with ambidextrous thumbrests and flared bottom or rubber soft touch with thumbrest. **Sights:** Patridge front, fully adjustable rear. **Features:** Sight bridge with Weaver-style integral optics mount; alloy frame, stainless barrel and slide; matte black finish. Introduced 1997. Made in U.S. by Smith & Wesson.
Price: **$320.00**

Smith & Wesson Model 22S Target Pistol

Similar to the Model 22A except has stainless steel frame. Introduced 1997. Made in U.S. by Smith & Wesson.
Price: **$379.00**

Springfield, Inc. 1911A1 Trophy Match Pistol

Similar to the 1911A1 except factory accurized, Videki speed trigger, skeletonized hammer; has 4- to 5-1/2-lb. trigger pull, click adjustable rear sight, match-grade barrel and bushing. Comes with cocobolo grips. Introduced 1994. From Springfield, Inc.
Price: Blue **$1,089.00**
Price: Stainless steel **$1,149.00**
Price: High Capacity (stainless steel, 10-shot magazine, front slide serrations, checkered slide serrations) **$1,118.00**

Springfield, Inc. Expert Pistol

Similar to the Competition Pistol except has triple-chamber tapered cone compensator on match barrel with dovetailed front sight; lowered and flared ejection port; fully tuned for reliability; fitted slide to frame; extended ambidextrous thumb safety, extended magazine release button; beavertail grip safety; Pachmayr wrap-around grips. Comes with two magazines, plastic carrying case. Introduced 1992. From Springfield, Inc.

Price: 45 ACP, Duotone finish **$1,724.00**
Price: Expert Ltd. (non-compensated) **$1,624.00**

Springfield, Inc. Distinguished Pistol

Has all the features of the 1911A1 Expert except is full-house pistol with deluxe Bo-Mar low-mounted adjustable rear sight; full-length recoil spring guide rod and recoil spring retainer; checkered frontstrap; S&A magazine well; walnut grips. Hard chrome finish. Comes with two magazines with slam pads, plastic carrying case. From Springfield, Inc.
Price: 45 ACP **$2,445.00**
Price: Distinguished Limited (non-compensated) **$2,345.00**

SPRINGFIELD, INC. 1911A1 BULLSEYE WADCUTTER PISTOL

Caliber: 38 Super, 45 ACP. **Barrel:** 5". **Weight:** 45 oz. **Length:** 8.59" overall (5" barrel). **Stocks:** Checkered walnut. **Sights:** Bo-Mar rib with undercut blade front, fully adjustable rear. **Features:** Built for wadcutter loads only. Has full-length recoil spring guide rod, fitted Videki speed trigger with 3.5-lb. pull; match Commander hammer and sear; beavertail grip safety; lowered and flared ejection port; tuned extractor; fitted slide to frame; recoil buffer system; beveled and polished magazine well; checkered front strap and steel mainspring housing (flat housing standard); polished and throated National Match barrel and bushing. Comes with two magazines with slam pads, plastic carrying case, test target. Introduced 1992. From Springfield, Inc.
Price: **$1,499.00**

Springfield, Inc. Basic Competition Pistol

Has low-mounted Bo-Mar adjustable rear sight, undercut blade front; match throated barrel and bushing; polished feed ramp; lowered and flared ejection port; fitted Videki speed trigger with tuned 3.5-lb. pull; fitted slide to frame; recoil buffer system; checkered walnut grips; serrated, arched mainspring housing. Comes with two magazines with slam pads, plastic carrying case. Introduced 1992. From Springfield, Inc.
Price: 45 ACP, blue, 5" only **$1,295.00**

Springfield, Inc. 1911A1 N.M. Hardball Pistol

Has Bo-Mar adjustable rear sight with undercut front blade; fitted match Videki trigger with 4-lb. pull; fitted slide to frame; throated National Match barrel and bushing, polished feed ramp; recoil buffer system; tuned extractor; Herrett walnut grips. Comes with two magazines, plastic carrying case, test target. Introduced 1992. From Springfield, Inc.
Price: 45 ACP, blue **$1,336.00**

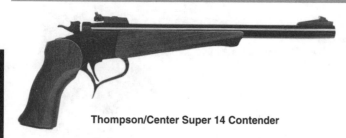

Thompson/Center Super 14 Contender

Wichita Silhouette

Unique D.E.S. 69U

STI EAGLE 5.0 PISTOL
Caliber: 9mm Para., 38 Super, 40 S&W, 45 ACP, 10-ACP, 10-shot magazine. **Barrel:** 5", bull. **Weight:** 34 oz. **Length:** 8.62" overall. **Stocks:** Checkered polymer. **Sights:** Bo-Mar blade front, Bo-Mar fully adjustable rear. **Features:** Modular frame design; adjustable match trigger; skeletonized hammer; extended grip safety with locator pad; match-grade fit of all parts. Many options available. Introduced 1994. Made in U.S. by STI International.
Price: **$1,792.00**

THOMPSON/CENTER SUPER 14 CONTENDER
Caliber: 22 LR, 222 Rem., 223 Rem., 7-30 Waters, 30-30 Win., 357 Rem. Maximum, 44 Mag., single shot. **Barrel:** 14". **Weight:** 45 oz. **Length:** 17-1/4" overall. **Stocks:** T/C "Competitor Grip" (walnut and rubber). **Sights:** Fully adjustable target-type. **Features:** Break-open action with auto safety. Interchangeable barrels for both rimfire and centerfire calibers. Introduced 1978.
Price: Blued **$520.24**
Price: Stainless steel **$578.40**
Price: Extra barrels, blued **$251.06**
Price: Extra barrels, stainless steel **$278.68**

Thompson/Center Super 16 Contender
Same as the T/C Super 14 Contender except has 16-1/4" barrel. Rear sight can be mounted at mid-barrel position (10-3/4" radius) or moved to the rear (using scope mount position) for 14-3/4" radius. Overall length is 20-1/4". Comes with T/C Competitor Grip of walnut and rubber. Available in, 223 Rem., 45-70 Gov't. Also available with 16" vent rib barrel with internal choke, caliber 45 Colt/410 shotshell.

Price: Blue **$525.95**
Price: 45-70 Gov't., blue. **$531.52**
Price: Super 16 Vent Rib, blued **$559.70**
Price: Extra 16" barrel, blued **$245.61**
Price: Extra 45-70 barrel, blued **$251.08**
Price: Extra Super 16 vent rib barrel, blue **$278.73**

UNIQUE D.E.S. 32U TARGET PISTOL
Caliber: 32 S&W Long wadcutter. **Barrel:** 5.9". **Weight:** 40.2 oz. **Stocks:** Anatomically shaped, adjustable stippled French walnut. **Sights:** Blade front, micrometer click rear. **Features:** Trigger adjustable for weight and position; dry firing mechanism; slide stop catch. Optional sleeve weights. Introduced 1990. Imported from France by Nygord Precision Products.
Price: Right-hand, about. **$1,350.00**
Price: Left-hand, about. **$1,380.00**

UNIQUE D.E.S. 69U TARGET PISTOL
Caliber: 22 LR, 5-shot magazine. **Barrel:** 5.91". **Weight:** 35.3 oz. **Length:** 10.5" overall. **Stocks:** French walnut target-style with thumbrest and adjustable shelf; hand-checkered panels. **Sights:** Ramp front, micro. adjustable rear mounted on frame; 8.66" sight radius. **Features:** Meets U.I.T. standards. Comes with 260-gram barrel weight; 100, 150, 350-gram weights available. Fully adjustable match trigger; dry-firing safety device. Imported from France by Nygord Precision Products.
Price: Right-hand, about. **$1,250.00**
Price: Left-hand, about. **$1,290.00**

UNIQUE MODEL 96U TARGET PISTOL
Caliber: 22 LR, 5- or 6-shot magazine. **Barrel:** 5.9". **Weight:** 40.2 oz. **Length:** 11.2" overall. **Stocks:** French walnut. Target style with thumbrest and adjustable shelf. **Sights:** Blade front, micrometer rear mounted on frame. **Features:** Designed for Sport Pistol and Standard U.I.T. shooting. External hammer; fully adjustable and movable trigger; dry-firing device. Introduced 1997. Imported from France by Nygord Precision Products.
Price: **$1,350.00**

WALTHER GSP MATCH PISTOL
Caliber: 22 LR, 32 S&W Long (GSP-C), 5-shot magazine. **Barrel:** 4.22". **Weight:** 44.8 oz. (22 LR), 49.4 oz. (32). **Length:** 11.8" overall. **Stocks:** Walnut. **Sights:** Post front, match rear adjustable for windage and elevation. **Features:** Available with either 2.2-lb. (1000 gm) or 3-lb. (1360 gm) trigger. Spare magazine, barrel weight, tools supplied. Imported from Germany by Nygord Precision Products.
Price: GSP, with case. **$1,495.00**
Price: GSP-C, with case. **$1,595.00**

Includes models suitable for hunting and competitive courses of fire, both police and international.

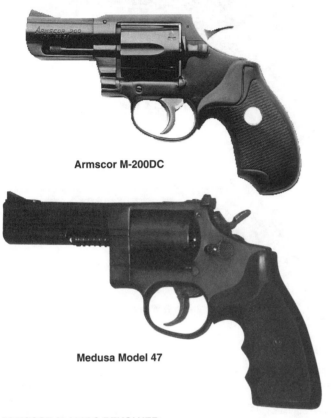

Armscor M-200DC

Ruger GP161

Medusa Model 47

ARMSCOR M-200DC REVOLVER
Caliber: 38 Spec., 6-shot cylinder. **Barrel:** 2-1/2", 4". **Weight:** 22 oz. (2-1/2" barrel). **Length:** 7-3/8" overall (2-1/2" barrel). **Stocks:** Checkered rubber. **Sights:** Blade front, fixed notch rear. **Features:** All-steel construction; floating firing pin, transfer bar ignition; shrouded ejector rod; blue finish. Reintroduced 1996. Imported from the Philippines by K.B.I., Inc.
Price: 2-1/2" $199.99
Price: 4" $205.00

ARMSPORT MODEL 4540 REVOLVER
Caliber: 38 Special. **Barrel:** 4". **Weight:** 32 oz **Length:** 9" overall. **Sights:** Fixed rear, blade front. **Features:** Ventilated rib; blued finish. Imported from Argentina by Armsport Inc.
Price: $140.00

E.A.A. STANDARD GRADE REVOLVERS
Caliber: 38 Spec., 6-shot; 357 magnum, 6-shot. **Barrel:** 2", 4". **Weight:** 38 oz. (22 rimfire, 4"). **Length:** 8.8" overall (4" bbl.). **Stocks:** Rubber with finger grooves. **Sights:** Blade front, fixed or adjustable on rimfires; fixed only on 32, 38. **Features:** Swing-out cylinder; hammer block safety; blue finish. Introduced 1991. Imported from Germany by European American Armory.
Price: 38 Special 2" $180.00
Price: 38 Special, 4" $199.00
Price: 357 Magnum, 2" $199.00
Price: 357 Magnum, 4" $233.00

MEDUSA MODEL 47 REVOLVER
Caliber: Most 9mm, 38 and 357 caliber cartridges; 6-shot cylinder. **Barrel:** 2-1/2", 3", 4", 5", 6"; fluted. **Weight:** 39 oz. **Length:** 10" overall (4" barrel). **Stocks:** Gripper-style rubber. **Sights:** Changeable front blades, fully adjustable rear. **Features:** Patented extractor allows gun to chamber, fire and extract over 25 different cartridges in the .355 to .357 range, without half-moon clips. Steel frame and cylinder; match quality barrel. Matte blue finish. Introduced 1996. Made in U.S. by Phillips & Rogers, Inc.
Price: $899.00

ROSSI MODEL 351/352 REVOLVERS
Caliber: 38 Special, 5-shot. **Barrel:** 2". **Weight:** 24 oz. **Length:** 6-1/2" overall. **Grips:** Rubber. **Sights:** Blade front, fixed rear. **Features:** Patented key-lock Taurus Security System; forged steel frame handles +P ammunition. Introduced 2001. Imported by BrazTech/Taurus.
Price: Model 351 (blued finish) $298.00
Price: Model 352 (stainless finish) $345.00

ROSSI MODEL 461/462 REVOLVERS
Caliber: 357 Magnum, 6-shot. **Barrel:** 2". **Weight:** 26 oz. **Length:** 6-1/2" overall. **Grips:** Rubber. **Sights:** Blade front, low-profile fixed rear. **Features:** Patented key-lock Taurus Security System; forged steel frame handles +P ammunition. Introduced 2001. Imported by BrazTech/Taurus.
Price: Model 461 (blued finish) $298.00
Price: Model 462 (stainless finish) $345.00

ROSSI MODEL 971/972 REVOLVERS
Caliber: 357 Magnum, 6-shot. **Barrel:** 4" or 6". **Weight:** NA. **Length:** 8-1/2" or 10-1/2" overall. **Grips:** Rubber. **Sights:** Red ramp front, adjustable rear. **Features:** Patented key-lock Taurus Security System; forged steel frame handles +P ammunition. Introduced 2001. Imported by BrazTech/Taurus.
Price: Model 971 (blued finish, 4" barrel) $345.00
Price: Model 972 (stainless steel finish, 6" barrel) $391.00

Rossi Model 851
Similar to the Model 971/972 except chambered for 38 Special. Blued finish, 4" barrel. Introduced 2001. From BrazTech/Taurus.
Price: $298.00

RUGER GP-100 REVOLVERS
Caliber: 38 Spec., 357 Mag., 6-shot. **Barrel:** 3", 3" full shroud, 4", 4" full shroud, 6", 6" full shroud. **Weight:** 3" barrel—35 oz., 3" full shroud—36 oz., 4" barrel—37 oz., 4" full shroud—38 oz. **Sights:** Fixed; adjustable on 4" full shroud and all 6" barrels. **Stocks:** Ruger Santoprene Cushioned Grip with Goncalo Alves inserts. **Features:** Uses action and frame incorporating improvements and features of both the Security-Six and Redhawk revolvers. Full length and short ejector shroud. Satin blue and stainless steel.
Price: GP-141 (357, 4" full shroud, adj. sights, blue) $475.00
Price: GP-160 (357, 6", adj. sights, blue) $475.00
Price: GP-161 (357, 6" full shroud, adj. sights, blue), 46 oz. ... $475.00
Price: GPF-331 (357, 3" full shroud) $465.00
Price: GPF-340 (357, 4") $465.00
Price: GPF-341 (357, 4" full shroud) $465.00
Price: KGP-141 (357, 4" full shroud, adj. sights, stainless) $515.00
Price: KGP-160 (357, 6", adj. sights, stainless), 43 oz. $515.00
Price: KGP-161 (357, 6" full shroud, adj. sights, stainless) 46 oz. $515.00
Price: KGPF-330 (357, 3", stainless) $499.00
Price: KGPF-331 (357, 3" full shroud, stainless) $499.00
Price: KGPF-340 (357, 4", stainless), KGPF-840 (38 Spec.) $499.00
Price: KGPF-341 (357, 4" full shroud, stainless) $499.00

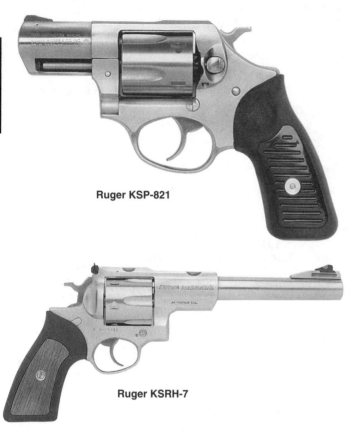

Ruger KSP-821

Ruger KSRH-7

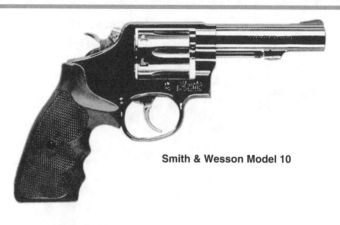

Smith & Wesson Model 10

Smith & Wesson Model 14

Ruger SP101 Double-Action-Only Revolver

Similar to the standard SP101 except is double-action-only with no single-action sear notch. Has spurless hammer for snag-free handling, floating firing pin and Ruger's patented transfer bar safety system. Available with 2-1/4" barrel in 357 Magnum. Weighs 25-1/2 oz., overall length 7.06". Natural brushed satin or high-polish stainless steel. Introduced 1993.

Price: KSP321XL (357 Mag.) **$458.00**

RUGER SP101 REVOLVERS

Caliber: 22 LR, 32 H&R Mag., 6-shot; 38 Spec. +P, 357 Mag., 5-shot. **Barrel:** 2-1/4", 3-1/16", 4". **Weight:** (38 & 357 mag models) 2-1/4"—25 oz.; 3-1/16"—27 oz. **Sights:** Adjustable on 22, 32, fixed on others. **Stocks:** Ruger Santoprene Cushioned Grip with Xenoy inserts. **Features:** Incorporates improvements and features found in the GP-100 revolvers into a compact, small frame, double-action revolver. Full-length ejector shroud. Stainless steel only. Introduced 1988.

Price: KSP-821X (2-1/2", 38 Spec.) **$458.00**
Price: KSP-831X (3-1/16", 38 Spec.) **$458.00**
Price: KSP-221X (2-1/4", 22 LR), 32 oz. **$458.00**
Price: KSP-240X (4", 22 LR), 33 oz. **$458.00**
Price: KSP-241X (4" heavy bbl., 22 LR), 34 oz. **$458.00**
Price: KSP-3231X (3-1/16", 32 H&R), 30 oz. **$458.00**
Price: KSP-321X (2-1/4", 357 Mag.). **$458.00**
Price: KSP331X (3-1/16", 357 Mag.) **$458.00**

RUGER REDHAWK

Caliber: 44 Rem. Mag., 45 Colt, 6-shot. **Barrel:** 5-1/2", 7-1/2". **Weight:** About 54 oz. (7-1/2" bbl.). **Length:** 13" overall (7-1/2" barrel). **Stocks:** Square butt Goncalo Alves. **Sights:** Interchangeable Patridge-type front, rear adjustable for windage and elevation. **Features:** Stainless steel, brushed satin finish, or blued ordnance steel. Has a 9-1/2" sight radius. Introduced 1979.

Price: Blued, 44 Mag., 5-1/2" RH-445, 7-1/2" RH-44 . . . . **$560.00**
Price: Blued, 44 Mag., 7-1/2" RH44R, with scope mount, rings . . **$595.00**
Price: Stainless, 44 Mag., 5-1/2", 7-1/2" KRH-445. . . . . **$615.00**

Price: Stainless, 44 Mag., 7-1/2", with scope mount, rings
KRH-44 . . . . **$615.00**
Price: Stainless, 45 Colt, 5-1/2", 7-1/2" KRH-455 . . . . **$615.00**
Price: Stainless, 45 Colt, 7-1/2", with scope mount KRH-45 . . . . **$615.00**

Ruger Super Redhawk Revolver

Similar to the standard Redhawk except has a heavy extended frame with the Ruger Integral Scope Mounting System on the wide topstrap. Also available in 454 Casull and new 480 Ruger. The wide hammer spur has been lowered for better scope clearance. Incorporates the mechanical design features and improvements of the GP-100. Choice of 7-1/2" or 9-1/2" barrel, both with ramp front sight base with Redhawk-style Interchangeable Insert sight blades, adjustable rear sight. Comes with Ruger "Cushioned Grip" panels of Santoprene with Goncalo Alves wood panels. Satin stainless steel. Introduced 1987.

Price: KSRH-7 (7-1/2"), KSRH-9 (9-1/2") **$650.00**
Price: KSRH-7454 (7-1/2") 454 Casull **$745.00**
New! **Price:** KSRH-7480 (7-1/2") 480 Ruger **$745.00**
New! **Price:** KSRH-9480 (9-1/2") 480 Ruger **$745.00**

Ruger Super Redhawk 454 Casull Revolver

Similar to the Ruger Super Redhawk except chambered for 454 Casull (also accepts 45 Colt cartridges). Unfluted cylinder, 7" barrel, weighs 53 ounces. Comes with 1" stainless scope rings. Introduced 2000.

Price: (Target gray stainless steel finish) **$745.00**

SMITH & WESSON MODEL 10 M&P HB REVOLVER

Caliber: 38 Spec., 6-shot. **Barrel:** 4". **Weight:** 33.5 oz. **Length:** 9-5/16" overall. **Stocks:** Uncle Mike's Combat soft rubber; square butt. **Sights:** Fixed; ramp front, square notch rear.

Price: Blue **$458.00**

SMITH & WESSON MODEL 14 FULL LUG REVOLVER

Caliber: 38 Spec., 6-shot. **Barrel:** 6", full lug. **Weight:** 47 oz. **Length:** 11-1/8" overall. **Stocks:** Hogue soft rubber. **Sights:** Pinned Patridge front, adjustable micrometer click rear. **Features:** Has .500" target hammer, .312" smooth combat trigger. Polished blue finish. Reintroduced 1991. Limited production.

Price: **$498.00**

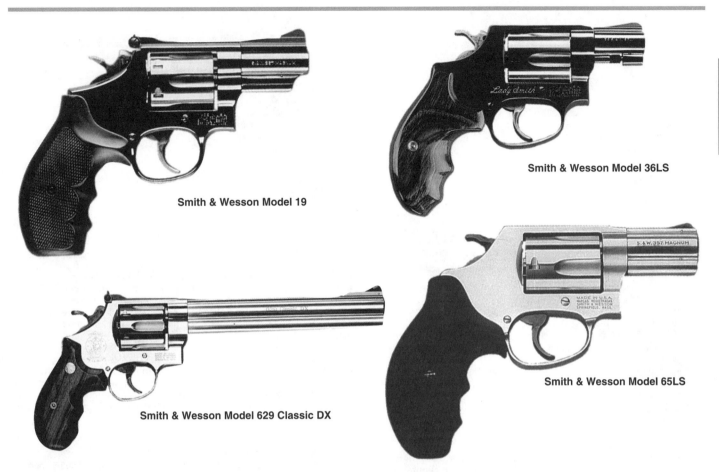

Smith & Wesson Model 19

Smith & Wesson Model 36LS

Smith & Wesson Model 629 Classic DX

Smith & Wesson Model 65LS

SMITH & WESSON MODEL 15 COMBAT MASTERPIECE
Caliber: 38 Spec., 6-shot. **Barrel:** 4". **Weight:** 32 oz. **Length:** 9-5/16" (4" bbl.). **Stocks:** Uncle Mike's Combat soft rubber. **Sights:** Serrated ramp front, micro-click rear adjustable for windage and elevation.
Price: Blued **$450.00**

SMITH & WESSON MODEL 19 COMBAT MAGNUM
Caliber: 357 Mag. and 38 Spec., 6-shot. **Barrel:** 4". **Weight:** 36 oz. **Length:** 9-9/16" (4" bbl.). **Stocks:** Uncle Mike's Combat soft rubber; wood optional. **Sights:** Red ramp front, micro-click rear adjustable for windage and elevation.
Price: 4" **$457.00**

SMITH & WESSON MODEL 629 REVOLVERS
Caliber: 44 Magnum, 6-shot. **Barrel:** 5", 6", 8-3/8". **Weight:** 47 oz. (6" bbl.). **Length:** 11-3/8" overall (6" bbl.). **Stocks:** Soft rubber; wood optional. **Sights:** 1/8" red ramp front, micro-click rear, adjustable for windage and elevation.
Price: Model 629 (stainless steel), 5" **$625.00**
Price: Model 629, 6" **$631.00**
Price: Model 629, 8-3/8" barrel. **$646.00**

Smith & Wesson Model 629 Classic Revolver
Similar to the standard Model 629 except has full-lug 5", 6-1/2" or 8-3/8" barrel; chamfered front of cylinder; interchangeable red ramp front sight with adjustable white outline rear; Hogue grips with S&W monogram; the frame is drilled and tapped for scope mounting. Factory accurizing and endurance packages. Overall length with 5" barrel is 10-1/2"; weighs 51 oz. Introduced 1990.
Price: Model 629 Classic (stainless), 5", 6-1/2" **$670.00**
Price: As above, 8-3/8". **$691.00**

Smith & Wesson Model 629 Classic DX Revolver
Similar to the Model 629 Classic except offered only with 6-1/2" or 8-3/8" full-lug barrel; comes with five front **sights:** red ramp; black Patridge; black Patridge with gold bead; black ramp; and black Patridge with white dot. Comes with Hogue combat-style and wood round butt grip. Introduced 1991.
Price: Model 629 Classic DX, 6-1/2" **$860.00**
Price: As above, 8-3/8". **$888.00**

SMITH & WESSON MODEL 36, 37 CHIEF'S SPECIAL & AIRWEIGHT
Caliber: 38 Spec.+P, 5-shot. **Barrel:** 1-7/8". **Weight:** 19-1/2 oz. (2" bbl.); 13-1/2 oz. (Airweight). **Length:** 6-1/2" (round butt). **Stocks:** Round butt soft rubber. **Sights:** Fixed, serrated ramp front, square notch rear.
Price: Blue, standard Model 36 . . . . **$406.00**
Price: Blue, Airweight Model 37 . . . . **$483.00**

Smith & Wesson Model 36LS, 60LS LadySmith
Similar to the standard Model 36. Available with 1-7/8" barrel, 38 Special. Comes with smooth, contoured rosewood grips with the S&W monogram. Has a speedloader cutout. Comes in a fitted carry/storage case. Introduced 1989.
Price: Model 36LS **$478.00**
Price: Model 60LS, as above except in stainless, 357 Magnum . **$539.00**

SMITH & WESSON MODEL 60 357 MAGNUM
Caliber: 357 Magnum, 5-shot. **Barrel:** 2-1/8" or 3". **Weight:** 24 oz. **Length:** 7-1/2 overall (3" barrel). **Stocks:** Uncle Mike's Combat. **Sights:** Fixed, serrated ramp front, square notch rear. **Features:** Stainless steel construction. Made in U.S. by Smith & Wesson.
Price: 2-1/8" barrel **$505.00**
Price: 3" barrel **$536.00**

SMITH & WESSON MODEL 65
Caliber: 357 Mag. and 38 Spec., 6-shot. **Barrel:** 3", 4". **Weight:** 34 oz. **Length:** 9-5/16" overall (4" bbl.). **Stocks:** Uncle Mike's Combat. **Sights:** 1/8" serrated ramp front, fixed square notch rear. **Features:** Heavy barrel. Stainless steel construction.
Price: **$501.00**

Smith & Wesson
Model 317 AirLite

Smith & Wesson Model 625

Smith & Wesson Model 586,
686 Distinguished Combat

SMITH & WESSON

MODEL 317 AIRLITE, 317 LADYSMITH REVOLVERS

Caliber: 22 LR, 8-shot. **Barrel:** 1-7/8" 3". **Weight:** 9.9 oz. **Length:** 6-3/16" overall. **Stocks:** Dymondwood Boot or Uncle Mike's Boot. **Sights:** Serrated ramp front, fixed notch rear. **Features:** Aluminum alloy, carbon and stainless steels, and titanium construction. Short spur hammer, smooth combat trigger. Clear Cote finish. Introduced 1997. Made in U.S. by Smith & Wesson.
Price: With Uncle Mike's Boot grip **$508.00**
Price: With DymondWood Boot grip, 3" barrel **$537.00**
Price: Model 317 LadySmith (DymondWood only, comes
with display case) **$568.00**

Smith & Wesson Model 637 Airweight Revolver

Similar to the Model 37 Airweight except has alloy frame, stainless steel barrel, cylinder and yoke; rated for 38 Spec. +P; Uncle Mike's Boot Grip. Weighs 15 oz. Introduced 1996. Made in U.S. by Smith & Wesson.
Price: **$459.00**

SMITH & WESSON MODEL 64 STAINLESS M&P

Caliber: 38 Spec., 6-shot. **Barrel:** 2", 3", 4". **Weight:** 34 oz. **Length:** 9-5/16" overall. **Stocks:** Soft rubber. **Sights:** Fixed, 1/8" serrated ramp front, square notch rear. **Features:** Satin finished stainless steel, square butt.
Price: 2" **$487.00**
Price: 3", 4" **$496.00**

SMITH & WESSON MODEL 65LS LADYSMITH

Caliber: 357 Magnum, 6-shot. **Barrel:** 3". **Weight:** 31 oz. **Length:** 7.94" overall. **Stocks:** Rosewood, round butt. **Sights:** Serrated ramp front, fixed notch rear. **Features:** Stainless steel with frosted finish. Smooth combat trigger, service hammer, shrouded ejector rod. Comes with case. Introduced 1992.
Price: **$539.00**

SMITH & WESSON MODEL 66 STAINLESS COMBAT MAGNUM

Caliber: 357 Mag. and 38 Spec., 6-shot. **Barrel:** 2-1/2", 4", 6". **Weight:** 36 oz. (4" barrel). **Length:** 9-9/16" overall. **Stocks:** Soft rubber. **Sights:** Red ramp front, micro-click rear adjustable for windage and elevation. **Features:** Satin finish stainless steel.

Price: 2-1/2" **$545.00**
Price: 4", 6". **$551.00**

SMITH & WESSON MODEL 67 COMBAT MASTERPIECE

Caliber: 38 Special, 6-shot. **Barrel:** 4". **Weight:** 32 oz. **Length:** 9-5/16" overall. **Stocks:** Soft rubber. **Sights:** Red ramp front, micro-click rear adjustable for windage and elevation. **Features:** Stainless steel with satin finish. Smooth combat trigger, semi-target hammer. Introduced 1994.
Price: **$546.00**

SMITH & WESSON MODEL 242 AIRLITE Ti REVOLVER

Caliber: 38 Special, 7-shot. **Barrel:** 2-1/2". **Weight:** 18.9 oz. **Length:** 7-3/8" overall. **Stocks:** Uncle Mike's Boot grip. **Sights:** Serrated ramp front, fixed notch rear. **Features:** Alloy frame, yoke and barrel shroud; titanium cylinder; stainless barrel insert. Medium L-frame size. Introduced 1999. Made in U.S. by Smith & Wesson.
Price: **$658.00**

SMITH & WESSON MODEL 296 AIRLITE Ti REVOLVER

Caliber: 44 Spec. **Barrel:** 2-1/2". **Weight:** 18.9 oz. **Length:** 7-3/8" overall. **Stocks:** Uncle Mike's Boot grip. **Sights:** Serrated ramp front, fixed notch rear. **Features:** Alloy frame, yoke and barrel shroud; titanium cylinder; stainless steel barrel insert. Medium, L-frame size. Introduced 1999. Made in U.S. by Smith & Wesson.
Price: **$718.00**

SMITH & WESSON MODEL 586,
686 DISTINGUISHED COMBAT MAGNUMS

Caliber: 357 Magnum. **Barrel:** 4", 6" (M 586); 2-1/2", 4", 6", 8-3/8" (M 686). **Weight:** 46 oz. (6"), 41 oz. (4"). **Stocks:** Soft rubber. **Sights:** Red ramp front, S&W micrometer click rear. Drilled and tapped for scope mount. **Features:** Uses L-frame, but takes all K-frame grips. Full-length ejector rod shroud. Smooth combat-type trigger, semi-target type hammer. Also available in stainless as Model 686. Introduced 1981.
Price: Model 586, blue, 4", from **$494.00**
Price: Model 586, blue, 6" **$499.00**
Price: Model 686, 6", ported barrel. **$564.00**
Price: Model 686, 8-3/8" **$550.00**
Price: Model 686, 2-1/2" **$514.00**

Smith & Wesson Model 686 Magnum PLUS Revolver

Similar to the Model 686 except has 7-shot cylinder, 2-1/2", 4" or 6" barrel. Weighs 34-1/2 oz., overall length 7-1/2" (2-1/2" barrel). Hogue rubber grips. Introduced 1996. Made in U.S. by Smith & Wesson.
Price: 2-1/2" barrel **$534.00**
Price: 4" barrel **$542.00**
Price: 6" barrel **$550.00**

SMITH & WESSON MODEL 625 REVOLVER

Caliber: 45 ACP, 6-shot. **Barrel:** 5". **Weight:** 46 oz. **Length:** 11.375" overall. **Stocks:** Soft rubber; wood optional. **Sights:** Patridge front on ramp, S&W micrometer click rear adjustable for windage and elevation. **Features:** Stainless steel construction with .400" semi-target hammer, .312" smooth combat trigger; full lug barrel. Introduced 1989.
Price: **$636.00**

Smith & Wesson Model 442

Smith & Wesson Model 649

SMITH & WESSON MODEL 640 CENTENNIAL

Caliber: 357 Mag., 5-shot. **Barrel:** 2-1/8". **Weight:** 25 oz. **Length:** 6-3/4" overall. **Stocks:** Uncle Mike's Boot Grip. **Sights:** Serrated ramp front, fixed notch rear. **Features:** Stainless steel. Fully concealed hammer, snag-proof smooth edges. Introduced 1995 in 357 Magnum.
Price: **$502.00**

SMITH & WESSON MODEL 617 FULL LUG REVOLVER

Caliber: 22 LR, 6- or 10-shot. **Barrel:** 4", 6", 8-3/8". **Weight:** 42 oz. (4" barrel). **Length:** NA. **Stocks:** Soft rubber. **Sights:** Patridge front, adjustable rear. Drilled and tapped for scope mount. **Features:** Stainless steel with satin finish; 4" has .312" smooth trigger, .375" semi-target hammer; 6" has either .312" combat or .400" serrated trigger, .375" semi-target or .500" target hammer; 8-3/8" with .400" serrated trigger, .500" target hammer. Introduced 1990.
Price: 4" **$534.00**
Price: 6", target hammer, target trigger **$524.00**
Price: 6", 10-shot **$566.00**
Price: 8-3/8", 10 shot **$578.00**

SMITH & WESSON MODEL 610 CLASSIC HUNTER REVOLVER

Caliber: 10mm, 6-shot cylinder. **Barrel:** 6-1/2" full lug. **Weight:** 52 oz. **Length:** 12" overall. **Stocks:** Hogue rubber combat. **Sights:** Interchangeable blade front, micro-click rear adjustable for windage and elevation. **Features:** Stainless steel construction; target hammer, target trigger; unfluted cylinder; drilled and tapped for scope mounting. Introduced 1998.
Price: **$684.00**

SMITH & WESSON MODEL 331, 332 AIRLITE Ti REVOLVERS

Caliber: 32 H&R Mag., 6-shot. **Barrel:** 1-7/8". **Weight:** 11.2 oz. (with wood grip). **Length:** 6-15/16" overall. **Stocks:** Uncle Mike's Boot or Dymondwood Boot. **Sights:** Black serrated ramp front, fixed notch rear. **Features:** Aluminum alloy frame, barrel shroud and yoke; titanium cylinder; stainless steel barrel liner. Matte finish. Introduced 1999. Made in U.S. by Smith & Wesson.
Price: Model 331 Chiefs **$682.00**
Price: Model 332 .... **$699.00**

SMITH & WESSON MODEL 337 CHIEFS SPECIAL AIRLITE Ti

Caliber: 38 Spec., 5-shot. **Barrel:** 1-7/8". **Weight:** 11.2 oz. (Dymondwood grips). **Length:** 6-5/16" overall. **Stocks:** Uncle Mike's Boot or Dymondwood Boot. **Sights:** Black serrated front, fixed notch rear. **Features:** Aluminum alloy frame, barrel shroud and yoke; titanium cylinder; stainless steel barrel liner. Matte finish. Introduced 1999. Made in U.S. by Smith & Wesson.
Price: **$682.00**

SMITH & WESSON MODEL 342 CENTENNIAL AIRLITE Ti

Caliber: 38 Spec., 5-shot. **Barrel:** 1-7/8". **Weight:** 11.3 oz. (Dymondwood stocks). **Length:** 6-15/16" overall. **Stocks:** Uncle Mike's Boot or Dymondwood Boot. **Sights:** Black serrated ramp front, fixed notch rear. **Features:** Aluminum alloy frame, barrel shroud and yoke; titanium cylinder; stainless steel barrel liner. Shrouded hammer. Matte finish. Introduced 1999. Made in U.S. by Smith & Wesson.
Price: **$699.00**

Smith & Wesson Model 442 Centennial Airweight

Similar to the Model 640 Centennial except has alloy frame giving weight of 15.8 oz. Chambered for 38 Special, 1-7/8" carbon steel barrel; carbon steel cylinder; concealed hammer; Uncle Mike's Boot grip. Fixed square notch rear sight, serrated ramp front. Introduced 1993.
Price: Blue **$459.00**

SMITH & WESSON MODEL 638 AIRWEIGHT BODYGUARD

Caliber: 38 Spec., 5-shot. **Barrel:** 1-7/8". **Weight:** 15 oz. **Length:** 6-15/16" overall. **Stocks:** Uncle Mike's Boot grip. **Sights:** Serrated ramp front, fixed notch rear. **Features:** Alloy frame, stainless cylinder and barrel; shrouded hammer. Introduced 1997. Made in U.S. by Smith & Wesson.
Price: With Uncle Mike's Boot grip **$492.00**

Smith & Wesson Model 642 Airweight Revolver

Similar to the Model 442 Centennial Airweight except has stainless steel barrel, cylinder and yoke with matte finish; Uncle Mike's Boot Grip; weighs 15.8 oz. Introduced 1996. Made in U.S. by Smith & Wesson.
Price: **$474.00**

Smith & Wesson Model 642LS LadySmith Revolver

Same as the Model 642 except has smooth combat wood grips, and comes with case; aluminum alloy frame, stainless cylinder, barrel and yoke; frosted matte finish. Weighs 15.8 oz. Introduced 1996. Made in U.S. by Smith & Wesson.
Price: **$505.00**

SMITH & WESSON MODEL 649 BODYGUARD REVOLVER

Caliber: 357 Mag., 5-shot. **Barrel:** 2-1/8". **Weight:** 20 oz. **Length:** 6-5/16" overall. **Stocks:** Uncle Mike's Combat. **Sights:** Black pinned ramp front, fixed notch rear. **Features:** Stainless steel construction; shrouded hammer; smooth combat trigger. Made in U.S. by Smith & Wesson.
Price: **$502.00**

SMITH & WESSON MODEL 657 REVOLVER

Caliber: 41 Mag., 6-shot. **Barrel:** 6". **Weight:** 48 oz. **Length:** 11-3/8" overall. **Stocks:** Soft rubber. **Sights:** Pinned 1/8" red ramp front, micro-click rear adjustable for windage and elevation. **Features:** Stainless steel construction.
Price: **$564.00**

SMITH & WESSON MODEL 696 REVOLVER

Caliber: 44 Spec., 5-shot. **Barrel:** 3". **Weight:** 35.5 oz. **Length:** 8-1/4" overall. **Stocks:** Uncle Mike's Combat. **Sights:** Red ramp front, click adjustable white outline rear. **Features:** Stainless steel construction; round butt frame; satin finish. Introduced 1997. Made in U.S. by Smith & Wesson.
Price: **$525.00**

TAURUS MODEL 65 REVOLVER

Caliber: 357 Mag., 6-shot. **Barrel:** 4". **Weight:** 38 oz. **Length:** 10-1/2" overall. **Stocks:** Soft rubber. **Sights:** Serrated front, notch rear. **Features:** Solid rib barrel; +P rated. Integral key-lock action. Imported by Taurus International.
Price: Blue **$345.00**
Price: Stainless. **$395.00**

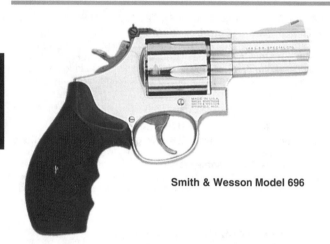

Smith & Wesson Model 696

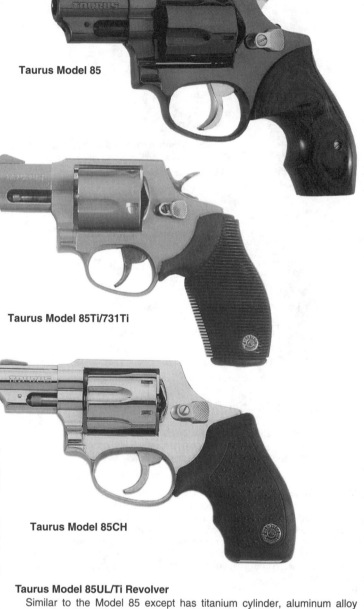

Taurus Model 85

Taurus Model 85Ti/731Ti

Taurus Model 85CH

Taurus Model 82

Taurus Model 66 Revolver

Same to the Model 65 except with 4" or 6" barrel, 7-shot cylinder, adjustable rear sight. Integral key-lock action. Imported by Taurus International.

Price: Blue $395.00
Price: Stainless....................................... $435.00

Taurus Model 66 Silhouette Revolver

Similar to the Model 66 except has a 12" barrel with scope mount, 7-shot cylinder, adjustable rear sight. Integral key-lock action, blue or matte stainless steel finish and rubber grips. Introduced 2001. Imported by Taurus International.

Price: .... $414.00 to $461.00

TAURUS MODEL 82 HEAVY BARREL REVOLVER

Caliber: 38 Spec., 6-shot. **Barrel:** 4", heavy. **Weight:** 34 oz. (4" bbl.). **Length:** 9-1/4" overall (4" bbl.). **Stocks:** Soft black rubber. **Sights:** Serrated ramp front, square notch rear. **Features:** Imported by Taurus International.

Price: Blue $325.00
Price: Polished, stainless $375.00

TAURUS MODEL 85 REVOLVER

Caliber: 38 Spec., 5-shot. **Barrel:** 2", 3". **Weight:** 21 oz. **Stocks:** Rubber, rosewood or mother-of-pearl. **Sights:** Ramp front, square notch rear. **Features:** Blue, matte, polished stainless steel, blue with gold accents, pearl and blue with gold accents; heavy barrel; rated for +P ammo. Introduced 1980. Imported by Taurus International.

Price: Blue, 2", 3" $345.00
Price: Stainless steel $395.00
Price: Blue, 2", ported barrel $360.00
Price: Stainless, 2", ported barrel..................... $405.00
Price: Blue, Ultra-Lite (17 oz.), 2" $375.00
Price: Stainless, Ultra-Lite (17 oz.), 2", ported barrel . . $425.00
Price: Blue with gold trim, ported, rosewood grips $380.00

Taurus Model 85UL/Ti Revolver

Similar to the Model 85 except has titanium cylinder, aluminum alloy frame, and ported aluminum barrel with stainless steel sleeve. Weight is 13.5 oz. International.

Price: $515.00

Taurus Model 85Ti Revolver

Similar to the 2" Model 85 except has titanium frame, cylinder and ported barrel with stainless steel liner; yoke detent and extended ejector rod. Weight is 15.4 oz. Comes with soft, ridged Ribber grips. Available in Bright and Matte Spectrum blue, Matte Spectrum gold, and Shadow Gray colors. Introduced 1999. Imported by Taurus International.

Price: Model 85Ti $530.00

Taurus Model 85CH Revolver

Same as the Model 85 except has 2" barrel only and concealed hammer. Double aciton only. Soft rubber boot grip. Introduced 1991. Imported by Taurus International.

Price: Blue $345.00
Price: Stainless..................................... $395.00
Price: Blue, ported barrel $360.00
Price: Stainless, ported barrel $405.00

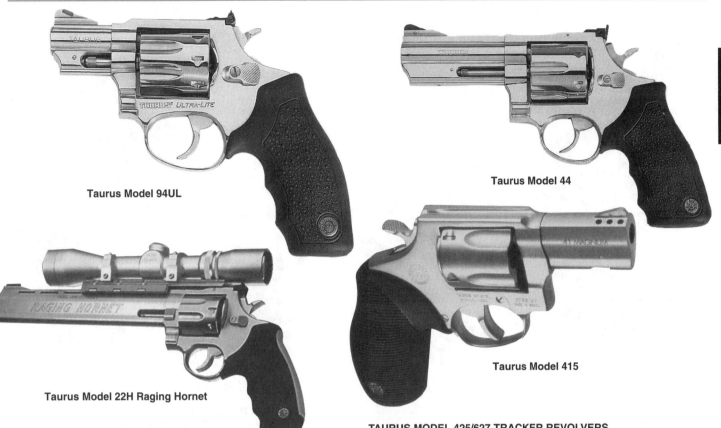

Taurus Model 94UL

Taurus Model 44

Taurus Model 22H Raging Hornet

Taurus Model 415

TAURUS MODEL 94 REVOLVER

Caliber: 22 LR, 9-shot cylinder. **Barrel:** 2", 4", 5". **Weight:** 25 oz. **Stocks:** Soft black rubber. **Sights:** Serrated ramp front, click-adjustable rear for windage and elevation. **Features:** Floating firing pin, color case-hardened hammer and trigger. Introduced 1989. Imported by Taurus International.

Price: Blue $325.00
Price: Stainless. $375.00
Price: Model 94 UL, blue, 2", fixed sight, weighs 14 oz. $365.00
Price: As above, stainless $410.00

TAURUS MODEL 22H RAGING HORNET REVOLVER

Caliber: 22 Hornet, 8-shot cylinder. **Barrel:** 10". **Weight:** 50 oz. **Length:** 6.5" overall. **Stocks:** Soft black rubber. **Sights:** Patridge front, micrometer click adjustable rear. **Features:** Ventilated rib; 1:10" twist rifling; comes with scope base; stainless steel construction with matte finish. Introduced 1999. Imported by Taurus International.

Price: $898.00

TAURUS MODEL 44 REVOLVER

Caliber: 44 Mag., 6-shot. **Barrel:** 4", 6-1/2", 8-3/8". **Weight:** 44-3/4 oz. (4" barrel). **Length:** NA. **Stocks:** Soft black rubber. **Sights:** Serrated ramp front, micro-click rear adjustable for windage and elevation. **Features:** Heavy solid rib on 4", vent rib on 6-1/2", 8-3/8". Compensated barrel. Blued model has color case-hardened hammer and trigger, integral key-lock action. Introduced 1994. Imported by Taurus International.

Price: Blue, 4". $500.00
Price: Blue, 6-1/2", 8-3/8" $525.00
Price: Stainless, 4" $565.00
Price: Stainless, 6-1/2", 8-3/8" $573.00

TAURUS MODEL 415 REVOLVER

Caliber: 41 Mag., 5-shot. **Barrel:** 2-1/2". **Weight:** 30 oz. **Length:** 7-1/8" overall. **Stocks:** Soft, ridged Ribber. **Sights:** Serrated front, notch rear. **Features:** Stainless steel construction; matte finish; ported barrel. Introduced 1999. Imported by Taurus International.

Price: $475.00

TAURUS MODEL 425/627 TRACKER REVOLVERS

Caliber: 357 Mag., 7-shot; 41 Mag., 5-shot. **Barrel:** 4" and 6". **Weight:** 24.3 oz. (titanium) to 40.0 oz. (6"). **Length:** 8-3/4" and 10-3/4" overall. **Grips:** Soft, ridged Ribber. **Sights:** Blade front, adjustable rear. **Features:** Stainless steel, Shadow Gray or Total Titanium; vent rib (steel models only); integral key-lock action. Imported by Taurus International.

Price: $500.00
Price: (Total Titanium). $690.00

TAURUS MODEL 445, 445CH REVOLVERS

Caliber: 44 Special, 5-shot. **Barrel:** 2". **Weight:** 28.25 oz. **Length:** 6-3/4" overall. **Stocks:** Soft black rubber. **Sights:** Serrated ramp front, notch rear. **Features:** Blue or stainless steel. Standard or concealed hammer. Introduced 1997. Imported by Taurus International.

Price: Blue $345.00
Price: Blue, ported $360.00
Price: Stainless. $395.00
Price: Stainless, ported $400.00
Price: M445CH, concealed hammer, blue, DAO $345.00
Price: M445CH, blue, ported $360.00
Price: M445CH, stainless $395.00
Price: M445CH, stainless, ported. $400.00
Price: M445CH, Ultra-Lite, stainless, ported $500.00

TAURUS MODEL 605 REVOLVER

Caliber: 357 Mag., 5-shot. **Barrel:** 2-1/4", 3". **Weight:** 24.5 oz. **Length:** NA. **Stocks:** Soft black rubber. **Sights:** Serrated ramp front, fixed notch rear. **Features:** Heavy, solid rib barrel; floating firing pin. Blue or stainless. Introduced 1995. Imported by Taurus International.

Price: Blue $345.00
Price: Stainless. $395.00
Price: Model 605CH (concealed hammer) 2-1/4", blue, DAO . . . $345.00
Price: Model 605CH, stainless, 2-1/4" $395.00
Price: Blue, 2-1/4", ported barrel $360.00
Price: Stainless, 2-1/4", ported barrel. $405.00
Price: Blue, 2-1/4", ported barrel, concealed hammer, DAO $360.00
Price: Stainless, 2-1/4", ported barrel, concealed hammer, DAO. $405.00

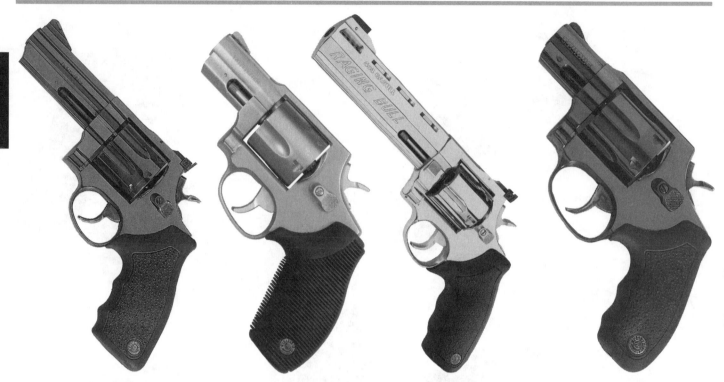

Taurus Model 608   Taurus Model 450   Taurus Model 454 Raging Bull   Taurus Model 817

TAURUS MODEL 608 REVOLVER

Caliber: 357 Mag., 8-shot. **Barrel:** 4", 6-1/2", 8-3/8". **Weight:** 44 oz. **Length:** 9-3/8" overall. **Grips:** Soft black rubber. **Sights:** Serrated ramp front, fully adjustable rear. **Features:** Built-in compensator, integral key-lock action. Available in blue or stainless. Introduced 1995. Imported by Taurus International.

Price: Blue, 4", solid rib **$445.00**
Price: Blue, 6-1/2", 8-3/8", vent rib **$465.00**
Price: Stainless, 4", solid rib **$510.00**
Price: Stainless, 6-1/2", 8-3/8", vent rib **$525.00**

TAURUS MODEL 650CIA REVOLVER

NEW! **Caliber:** 357 Magnum, 5-shot. **Barrel:** 2". **Weight:** NA. **Length:** NA. **Grips:** Rubber. **Sights:** Ramp front, square notch rear. **Features:** Double-action only; blue or matte stainless steel; rated for +P ammo; integral key-lock action. Introduced 2001. From Taurus International.
Price: . . . . **$375.00 to $422.00**

TAURUS MODEL 450 REVOLVER

Caliber: 45 Colt, 5-shot cylinder. **Barrel:** 2". **Weight:** 28 oz. **Length:** 6-5/8" overall. **Stocks:** Soft, ridged rubber. **Sights:** Serrated front, notch rear. **Features:** Stainless steel construction; ported barrel. Introduced 1999. Imported by Taurus International.
Price: **$470.00**
Price: Ultra-Lite (alloy frame) **$525.00**

TAURUS MODEL 444/454/480 RAGING BULL REVOLVERS

Caliber: 454 Casull, 5-shot (also fires 45 Colt). **Barrel:** 5", 6-1/2", 8-3/8". **Weight:** 53 oz. (6-1/2" barrel). **Length:** 12" overall (6-1/2" barrel). **Stocks:** Soft black rubber. **Sights:** Patridge front, micrometer click adjustable rear. **Features:** Ventilated rib; integral compensating system. Introduced 1997. Imported by Taurus International.

Price: 6-1/2", 8-3/8", blue **$785.00**
Price: 6-1/2", polished, stainless **$855.00**
Price: 5", 6-1/2", 8-3/8", matte stainless **$855.00**
Price: Model 444 (44 Mag.), blue, 6-1/2", 8-3/8", 6-shot **$575.00**
Price: Model 444, matte, stainless, 6-1/2", 8-3/8". **$630.00**
New! **Price:** Model 480 (480 Ruger), 5-shot **$855.00**

TAURUS MODEL 617 REVOLVER

Caliber: 357 Magnum, 7-shot. **Barrel:** 2". **Weight:** 29 oz. **Length:** 6-3/4" overall. **Stocks:** Soft black rubber. **Sights:** Serrated ramp front, notch rear. **Features:** Heavy, solid barrel rib, ejector shroud. Available with porting, concealed hammer. Introduced 1998. Imported by Taurus International.

Price: Blue, regular or concealed hammer **$375.00**
Price: Stainless, regular or concealed hammer **$420.00**
Price: Blue, ported **$395.00**
Price: Stainless, ported **$440.00**
Price: Blue, concealed hammer, ported **$395.00**
Price: Stainless, concealed hammer, ported **$440.00**

Taurus Model 415Ti, 445Ti, 450Ti, 617Ti Revolvers

Similar to the Model 617 except has titanium frame, cylinder, and ported barrel with stainless steel liner; yoke detent and extended ejector rod; +P rated; ridged Ribber grips. Available in Bright and Matte Spectrum Blue, Matte Spectrum Gold, and Shadow Gray. Introduced 1999. Imported by Taurus International.

Price: Model 617Ti, (357 Mag., 7-shot, 19.9 oz.) **$600.00**
Price: Model 415Ti (41 Mag., 5-shot, 20.9 oz.) **$600.00**
Price: Model 450Ti (45 Colt, 5-shot, 19.2 oz.) **$600.00**
Price: Model 445Ti (44 Spec., 5-shot, 19.8 oz.) **$600.00**

Taurus Model 617ULT Revolver

Similar to the Model 617 except has aluminum alloy and titanium components, matte stainless finish, integral key-lock action. Rated for +P ammo. Available ported or non-ported. Introduced 2001. Imported by Taurus International.
Price: (5-shot cylinder) . . . . **$530.00 to $545.00**

TAURUS MODEL 817 ULTRA-LITE REVOLVER

Caliber: 38 Spec., 7-shot. **Barrel:** 2". **Weight:** 21 oz. **Length:** 6-1/2" overall. **Grips:** Soft rubber. **Sights:** Serrated front, notch rear. **Features:** Compact alloy frame. Introduced 1999. Imported by Taurus International.
Price: Blue **$375.00**
Price: Blue, ported **$395.00**
Price: Matte, stainless **$420.00**
Price: Matte, stainless, ported **$440.00**

Taurus Model 941

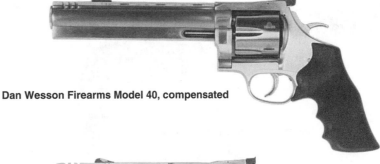

Dan Wesson Firearms Model 40, compensated

**Dan Wesson Firearms
Model 445 Supermag**

TAURUS MODEL 850CIA REVOLVER
Caliber: 38 Special, 5-shot. **Barrel:** 2". **Weight:** NA. **Length:** NA. **Grips:** Rubber. **Sights:** Ramp front, square notch rear. **Features:** Double-action only; blue or matte stainless steel; rated for +P ammo; integral key-lock action. Introduced 2001. From Taurus International.
Price: . . . .$375.00 to $422.00
Price: Total Titanium model $563.00

TAURUS MODEL 941 REVOLVER
Caliber: 22 WMR, 8-shot. **Barrel:** 2", 4", 5". **Weight:** 27.5 oz. (4" barrel). **Length:** NA. **Grips:** Soft black rubber. **Sights:** Serrated ramp front, rear adjustable for windage and elevation. **Features:** Solid rib heavy barrel with full-length ejector rod shroud. Blue or stainless steel. Introduced 1992. Imported by Taurus International.
Price: Blue $345.00
Price: Stainless. $395.00
Price: Model 941 Ultra Lite, blue, 2", fixed sight, weighs 8.5 oz. . . $375.00
Price: As above, stainless $419.00

TAURUS MODEL 970/971 TRACKER REVOLVERS
Caliber: 22 LR (Model 970), 22 WMR (Model 971); 7-shot. **Barrel:** 6". **Weight:** NA. **Length:** NA. **Grips:** Soft, black rubber. **Sights:** Blade front, adjustable rear. **Features:** Heavy barrel with ventilated rib; matte stainless finish. Introduced 2001. From Taurus International.
Price: $855.00

TAURUS MODEL 980/981 SILHOUETTE REVOLVERS
Caliber: 22 LR (Model 980), 22 WMR (Model 981); 7-shot. **Barrel:** 12". **Weight:** NA. **Length:** NA. **Grips:** Soft, black rubber. **Sights:** Blade front, adjustable rear. **Features:** Heavy barrel with ventilated rib and scope mount, matte stainless finish. Introduced 2001. From Taurus International.
Price: (Model 980) $397.00
Price: (Model 981) $414.00

DAN WESSON FIREARMS MODEL 722 SILHOUETTE REVOLVER
Caliber: 22 LR, 6-shot. **Barrel:** 10", vent heavy. **Weight:** 53 oz. **Stocks:** Combat style. **Sights:** Patridge-style front, .080" narrow notch rear. **Features:** Single action only. Satin brushed stainless finish. Reintroduced 1997. Made in U.S. by Dan Wesson Firearms.
Price: 722 VH10 (vent heavy 10" bbl.) $888.00
Price: 722 VH10 SRS1 (Super Ram Silhouette , Bo-Mar sights, front hood, trigger job). $1,164.00

DAN WESSON FIREARMS MODEL 3220/73220 TARGET REVOLVER
Caliber: 32-20, 6-shot. **Barrel:** 2.5", 4", 6", 8", 10" standard vent, vent heavy. **Weight:** 47 oz. (6" VH). **Length:** 11.25" overall. **Stocks:** Hogue Gripper rubber (walnut, exotic hardwoods optional). **Sights:** Red ramp interchangeable front, fully adjustable rear. **Features:** Bright blue (3220) or stainless (73220). Reintroduced 1997. Made in U.S. by Dan Wesson Firearms.
Price: 3220 VH2.5 (blued, 2.5" vent heavy bbl.). $643.00
Price: 73220 VH10 (stainless 10" vent heavy bbl.). $873.00

DAN WESSON FIREARMS MODEL 40/740 REVOLVERS
Caliber: 357 Maximum, 6-shot. **Barrel:** 4", 6", 8", 10". **Weight:** 72 oz. (8" bbl.). **Length:** 14.3" overall (8" bbl.). **Stocks:** Hogue Gripper rubber (walnut or exotic hardwood optional). **Sights:** 1/8" serrated front, fully adjustable rear. **Features:** Blue or stainless steel. Made in U.S. by Dan Wesson Firearms.
Price: Blue, 4". $702.00
Price: Blue, 6". $749.00
Price: Blue, 8". $795.00
Price: Blue, 10". $858.00
Price: Stainless, 4" $834.00
Price: Stainless, 6" $892.00
Price: Stainless, 8" slotted $1,024.00
Price: Stainless, 10". $998.00
Price: 4", 6", 8" Compensated, blue . . . . $749.00 to $885.00
Price: As above, stainless . . . . $893.00 to $1,061.00

DAN WESSON FIREARMS MODEL 22/722 REVOLVERS
Caliber: 22 LR, 22 WMR, 6-shot. **Barrel:** 2-1/2", 4", 6", 8" or 10"; interchangeable. **Weight:** 36 oz. (2-1/2"), 44 oz. (6"). **Length:** 9-1/4" overall (4" barrel). **Stocks:** Hogue Gripper rubber (walnut, exotic woods optional). **Sights:** 1/8" serrated, interchangeable front, white outline rear adjustable for windage and elevation. **Features:** Built on the same frame as the Wesson 357; smooth, wide trigger with over-travel adjustment, wide spur hammer, with short double-action travel. Available in blue or stainless steel. Reintroduced 1997. Contact Dan Wesson Firearms for complete price list.
Price: 22 VH2.5/722 VH2.5 (blued or stainless 2-1/2" bbl.) $551.00
Price: 22VH10/722 VH10 (blued or stainless 10" bbl.). $750.00

Dan Wesson 722M Small Frame Revolver
Similar to Model 22/722 except chambered for 22 WMR. Blued or stainless finish, 2-1/2", 4", 6", 8" or 10" barrels.
Price: Blued or stainless finish . . . . $643.00 to $873.00

Dan Wesson Firearms Model 414/7414 and 445/7445 SuperMag Revolvers
Similar size and weight as the Model 40 revolvers. Chambered for the 414 SuperMag or 445 SuperMag cartridge. Barrel lengths of 4", 6", 8", 10". Contact maker for complete price list. Reintroduced 1997. Made in the U.S. by Dan Wesson Firearms.
Price: 4", vent heavy, blue or stainless. $904.00
Price: 8", vent heavy, blue or stainless. $1,026.00
Price: 10", vent heavy, blue or stainless. $1,103.00
Price: Compensated models . . . . $965.00 to $1,149.00

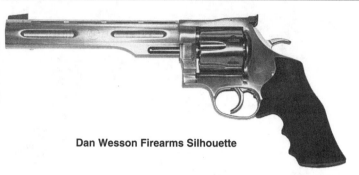

Dan Wesson Firearms Silhouette

Dan Wesson Firearms
Super Ram Silhouette

DAN WESSON FIREARMS MODEL 15/715 and 32/732 REVOLVERS

Caliber: 32-20, 32 H&R Mag. (Model 32), 357 Mag. (Model 15). **Barrel:** 2-1/2", 4", 6", 8" (M32), 2-1/2", 4", 6", 8", 10" (M15); vent heavy. **Weight:** 36 oz. (2-1/2" barrel). **Length:** 9-1/4" overall (4" barrel). **Stocks:** Checkered, interchangeable. **Sights:** 1/8" serrated front, fully adjustable rear. **Features:** New Generation Series. Interchangeable barrels; wide, smooth trigger, wide hammer spur; short double-action travel. Available in blue or stainless. Reintroduced 1997. Made in U.S. by Dan Wesson Firearms. Contact maker for full list of models.
Price: Model 15/715, 2-1/2" (blue or stainless)...............**$551.00**
Price: Model 15/715, 8" (blue or stainless)..................**$612.00**
Price: Model 15/715, compensated ....**$704.00 to $827.00**
Price: Model 32/732, 4" (blue or stainless).................**$674.00**
Price: Model 32/732, 8" (blue or stainless).................**$766.00**

DAN WESSON FIREARMS MODEL 41/741, 44/744 and 45/745 REVOLVERS

Caliber: 41 Mag., 44 Mag., 45 Colt, 6-shot. **Barrel:** 4", 6", 8", 10"; interchangeable; 4", 6", 8" Compensated. **Weight:** 48 oz. (4"). **Length:** 12" overall (6" bbl.) **Stocks:** Smooth. **Sights:** 1/8" serrated front, white outline rear adjustable for windage and elevation. **Features:** Available in blue or stainless steel. Smooth, wide trigger with adjustable over-travel; wide hammer spur. Available in Pistol Pac set also. Reintroduced 1997. Contact Dan Wesson Firearms for complete price list.
Price: 41 Mag., 4", vent heavy (blue or stainless) **$643.00**
Price: 44 Mag., 6", vent heavy (blue or stainless) **$689.00**
Price: 45 Colt, 8", vent heavy (blue or stainless) **$766.00**
Price: Compensated models (all calibers) ....**$812.00 to $934.00**

DAN WESSON FIREARMS MODEL 360/7360 REVOLVERS

Caliber: 357 Mag. **Barrel:** 4", 6", 8", 10"; vent heavy. **Weight:** 64 oz. (8" barrel). **Length:** NA. **Stocks:** Hogue rubber finger groove. **Sights:** Interchangeable ramp or Patridge front, fully adjustable rear. **Features:** New Generation Large Frame Series. Interchangeable barrels and grips; smooth trigger, wide hammer spur. Blue (360) or stainless (7360). Introduced 1999. Made in U.S. by Dan Wesson Firearms.
Price: 4" bbl., blue or stainless...........................**$735.00**
Price: 10" bbl., blue or stainless..........................**$873.00**
Price: Compensated models ....**$858.00 to $980.00**

DAN WESSON FIREARMS MODEL 460/7460 REVOLVERS

Caliber: 45 ACP, 45 Auto Rim, 45 Super, 45 Winchester Magnum and 460 Rowland. **Barrel:** 4", 6", 8", 10"; vent heavy. **Weight:** 49 oz. (4" barrel). **Length:** NA. **Stocks:** Hogue rubber finger groove; interchangeable. **Sights:** Interchangeable ramp or Patridge front, fully adjustable rear. **Features:** New Generation Large Frame Series. Shoots five cartridges (45 ACP, 45 Auto Rim, 45 Super, 45 Winchester Magnum and 460 Rowland; six half-moon clips for auto cartridges included). Interchangeable barrels and grips. Available with non-fluted cylinder and Slotted Lightweight barrel shroud. Introduced 1999. Made in U.S. by Dan Wesson Firearms.
Price: 4" bbl., blue or stainless...........................**$735.00**
Price: 10" bbl., blue or stainless..........................**$888.00**
Price: Compensated models ....**$919.00 to $1,042.00**

DAN WESSON FIREARMS STANDARD SILHOUETTE REVOLVERS

Caliber: 357 SuperMag/Maxi, 41 Mag., 414 SuperMag, 445 SuperMag. **Barrel:** 8", 10" **Weight:** 64 oz. (8" barrel). **Length:** 14.3" overall (8" barrel). **Stocks:** Hogue rubber finger groove; interchangeable. **Sights:** Patridge front, fully adjustable rear. **Features:** Interchangeable barrels and grips; fluted or non-fluted cylinder; satin brushed stainless finish. Introduced 1999. Made in U.S. by Dan Wesson Firearms.
Price: 357 SuperMag/Maxi, 8" **$1,057.00**
Price: 41 Mag., 10"....................................**$888.00**
Price: 414 SuperMag., 8" **$1,057.00**
Price: 445 SuperMag., 8" **$1,057.00**

Dan Wesson Firearms Super Ram Silhouette Revolver

Similar to the Standard Silhouette except has 10 land and groove Laser Coat barrel, Bo-Mar target sights with hooded front, and special laser engraving. Fluted or non-fluted cylinder. Introduced 1999. Made in U.S. by Dan Wesson Firearms.
Price: 357 SuperMag/Maxi, 414 SuperMag., 445 SuperMag., 8", blue or stainless **$1,364.00**
Price: 41 Magnum, 44 Magnum, 8", blue or stainless **$1,241.00**
Price: 41 Magnum, 44 Magnum, 10", blue or stainless **$1,333.00**

Both classic six-shooters and modern adaptations for hunting and sport.

American Frontier 1871-1872 Open-Top

American Frontier 1851 Mason

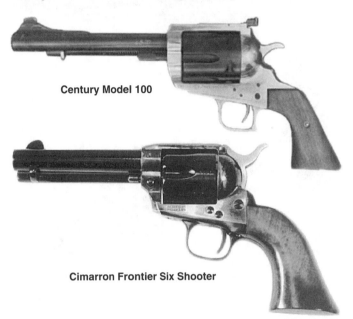

Century Model 100

Cimarron Frontier Six Shooter

AMERICAN FRONTIER 1851 NAVY CONVERSION
Caliber: 38, 44. **Barrel:** 5-1/2", 7-1/2", octagon. **Weight:** NA. **Length:** NA. **Stocks:** Varnished walnut, Navy size. **Sights:** Blade front, fixed rear. **Features:** Shoots metallic cartridge ammunition. Non-rebated cylinder; blued steel backstrap and trigger guard; color case-hardened hammer, trigger, ramrod, plunger; no ejector rod assembly. Introduced 1996.
Price: **$795.00**

AMERICAN FRONTIER 1871-1872 OPEN-TOP REVOLVERS
Caliber: 38, 44. **Barrel:** 5-1/2", 7-1/2", 8" round. **Weight:** NA. **Length:** NA. **Stocks:** Varnished walnut. **Sights:** Blade front, fixed rear. **Features:** Reproduction of the early cartridge conversions from percussion. Made for metallic cartridges. High polish blued steel, silver-plated brass backstrap and trigger guard, color case-hardened hammer; straight non-rebated cylinder with naval engagement engraving; stamped with original patent dates. Does not have conversion breechplate.
Price: **$795.00**

AMERICAN FRONTIER RICHARDS 1860 ARMY
Caliber: 38, 44. **Barrel:** 5-1/2", 7-1/2", round. **Weight:** NA. **Length:** NA. **Stocks:** Varnished walnut, Army size. **Sights:** Blade front, fixed rear. **Features:** Shoots metallic cartridge ammunition. Rebated cylinder; available with or without ejector assembly; high-polish blue including backstrap; silver-plated trigger guard; color case-hardened hammer and trigger. Introduced 1996.
Price: **$795.00**

American Frontier 1851 Navy Richards & Mason Conversion
Similar to the 1851 Navy Conversion except has Mason ejector assembly. Introduced 1996. Imported from Italy by American Frontier Firearms Mfg.
Price: **$695.00**

CABELA'S MILLENNIUM REVOLVER
Caliber: 45 Colt. **Barrel:** 4-3/4". **Weight:** NA. **Length:** 10" overall. **Grips:** Hardwood. **Sights:** Blade front, hammer notch rear. **Features:** Matte black finish; unpolished brass accents. Introduced 2001. From Cabela's.
Price: **$199.99**

CENTURY GUN DIST. MODEL 100 SINGLE-ACTION
Caliber: 30-30, 375 Win., 444 Marlin, 45-70, 50-70. **Barrel:** 6-1/2" (standard), 8", 10". **Weight:** 6 lbs. (loaded). **Length:** 15" overall (8" bbl.). **Stocks:** Smooth walnut. **Sights:** Ramp front, Millett adjustable square notch rear. **Features:** Highly polished high tensile strength manganese bronze frame; blue cylinder and barrel; coil spring trigger mechanism. Contact maker for full price information. Introduced 1975. Made in U.S. From Century Gun Dist., Inc.
Price: 6-1/2" barrel, 45-70 .... **$2,000.00**

CIMARRON LIGHTNING SA
Caliber: 38 Special. **Barrel:** 3-1/2", 4-3/4" or 5-1/2". **Weight:** NA. **Length:** NA. **Grips:** Checkered walnut. **Sights:** Blade front. **Features:** Replica of

the Colt 1877 Lightning DA. Similar to Cimarron Thunderer™, except smaller grip frame to fit smaller hands. Blue finish with color-case hardened frame. Introduced 2001. From Cimarron F.A. Co.
Price: **$389.00**

CIMARRON MODEL "P" JR.
Caliber: 38 Special. **Barrel:** 3-1/2" and 4-1/2". **Weight:** NA. **Length:** NA. **Grips:** Checkered walnut. **Sights:** Blade front. **Features:** Styled after 1873 Colt Peacemaker, except 20 percent smaller. Blue finish with color-case hardened frame; Cowboy Comp® action. Introduced 2001. From Cimarron F.A. Co.
Price: **$389.00**

CIMARRON U.S. CAVALRY MODEL SINGLE-ACTION
Caliber: 45 Colt. **Barrel:** 7-1/2". **Weight:** 42 oz. **Length:** 13-1/2" overall. **Stocks:** Walnut. **Sights:** Fixed. **Features:** Has "A.P. Casey" markings; "U.S." plus patent dates on frame, serial number on backstrap, trigger guard, frame and cylinder, "APC" cartouche on left grip; color case-hardened frame and hammer, rest charcoal blue. Exact copy of the original. Imported by Cimarron F.A. Co.
Price: **$499.00**

Cimarron Rough Rider Artillery Model Single-Action
Similar to the U.S. Cavalry model except has 5-1/2" barrel, weighs 39 oz., and is 11-1/2" overall. U.S. markings and cartouche, case-hardened frame and hammer; 45 Colt only.
Price: **$499.00**

CIMARRON 1872 OPEN TOP REVOLVER
Caliber: 38, 44 Special, 45 S&W Schofield. **Barrel:** 5-1/2" and 7-1/2". **Weight:** NA. **Length:** NA. **Grips:** Walnut. **Sights:** Blade front, fixed rear. **Features:** Replica of first cartridge-firing revolver. Blue, charcoal blue, nickel or Original® finish; Navy-style brass or steel Army-style frame. Introduced 2001 by Cimarron F.A. Co.
Price: **$469.00**

CIMARRON 1873 FRONTIER SIX SHOOTER
Caliber: 38 WCF, 357 Mag., 44 WCF, 44 Spec., 45 Colt. **Barrel:** 4-3/4", 5-1/2", 7-1/2". **Weight:** 39 oz. **Length:** 10" overall (4" barrel). **Stocks:** Walnut. **Sights:** Blade front, fixed or adjustable rear. **Features:** Uses "old model" blackpowder frame with "Bullseye" ejector or New Model frame. Imported by Cimarron F.A. Co.
Price: 4-3/4" barrel **$469.00**
Price: 5-1/2" barrel **$469.00**
Price: 7-1/2" barrel **$469.00**

Colt Cowboy

E.A.A. Bounty Hunter

Colt Single-Action Army

EMF Hartford

EMF 1894 Bisley

Cimarron Bisley Model Single-Action Revolvers
Similar to the 1873 Frontier Six Shooter except has special grip frame and trigger guard, knurled wide-spur hammer, curved trigger. Available in 357 Mag., 44 WCF, 45 Schofield, 45 Colt. Introduced 1999. Imported by Cimarron F.A. Co.
Price: **$499.00**

Cimarron Flat Top Single-Action Revolvers
Similar to the 1873 Frontier Six Shooter except has flat top strap with windage-adjustable rear sight, elevation-adjustable front sight. Available in 357 Mag., 44 WCF, 45 Schofield, 45 Colt; 4-3/4", 5-1/2", 7-1/2" barrel. Introduced 1999. Imported by Cimarron F.A. Co.
Price: **$479.00**

Cimarron Bisley Flat Top Revolver
Similar to the Flat Top revolver except has special grip frame and trigger guard, wide spur hammer, curved trigger. Introduced 1999. Imported by Cimarron F.A. Co.
Price: **$509.00**

CIMARRON THUNDERER REVOLVER
Caliber: 357 Mag., 44 WCF, 44 Spec., 45 Colt, 6-shot. **Barrel:** 3-1/2", 4-3/4", 5-1/2", 7-1/2", with ejector. **Weight:** 38 oz. (3-1/2" barrel). **Length:** NA. **Stocks:** Smooth walnut. **Sights:** Blade front, notch rear. **Features:** Thunderer grip; color case-hardened frame with balance blued. Introduced 1993. Imported by Cimarron F.A. Co.
Price: 3-1/2", 4-3/4", smooth grips **$489.00**
Price: As above, checkered grips **$524.00**
Price: 5-1/2", 7-1/2", smooth grips **$529.00**
Price: As above, checkered grips **$564.00**

CIMARRON 1872 OPEN-TOP REVOLVER
Caliber: 38 Spec., 38 Colt, 44 Spec., 44 Colt, 44 Russian, 45 Schofield. **Barrel:** 7-1/2". **Weight:** NA. **Length:** NA. **Stocks:** Smooth walnut. **Sights:** Blade front, fixed rear. **Features:** Replica of the original production. Color case-hardened frame, rest blued, including grip frame. Introduced 1999. Imported from Italy by Cimarron F.A. Co.
Price: **$579.00**

COLT COWBOY SINGLE-ACTION REVOLVER
Caliber: 45 Colt, 6-shot. **Barrel:** 5-1/2". **Weight:** 42 oz. **Stocks:** Black composition, first generation style. **Sights:** Blade front, notch rear. **Features:** Dimensional replica of Colt's original Peacemaker with medium-size color case-hardened frame; transfer bar safety system; half-cock loading. Introduced 1998. Made in U.S. by Colt's Mfg. Co.
Price: About **$670.00**

COLT SINGLE-ACTION ARMY REVOLVER
Caliber: 44-40, 45 Colt, 6-shot. **Barrel:** 4-3/4", 5-1/2", 7-1/2". **Weight:** 40 oz. (4-3/4" barrel). **Length:** 10-1/4" overall (4-3/4" barrel). **Stocks:** Black Eagle composite. **Sights:** Blade front, notch rear. **Features:** Available in full nickel finish with nickel grip medallions, or Royal Blue with color case-hardened frame, gold grip medallions. Reintroduced 1992.
Price: **$1,938.00**

E.A.A. BOUNTY HUNTER SA REVOLVERS
Caliber: 22 LR/22 WMR, 357 Mag., 44 Mag., 45 Colt, 6-shot. **Barrel:** 4-1/2", 7-1/2". **Weight:** 2.5 lbs. **Length:** 11" overall (4-5/8" barrel). **Stocks:** Smooth walnut. **Sights:** Blade front, grooved topstrap rear. **Features:** Transfer bar safety; three position hammer; hammer forged barrel. Introduced 1992. Imported by European American Armory.
Price: Blue or case-hardened **$280.00**
Price: Nickel **$298.00**
Price: 22LR/22WMR, blue **$187.20**
Price: As above, nickel **$204.36**

EMF HARTFORD SINGLE-ACTION REVOLVERS
Caliber: 357 Mag., 32-20, 38-40, 44-40, 44 Spec., 45 Colt. **Barrel:** 4-3/4", 5-1/2", 7-1/2". **Weight:** 45 oz. **Length:** 13" overall (7-1/2" barrel). **Stocks:** Smooth walnut. **Sights:** Blade front, fixed rear. **Features:** Identical to the original Colts with inspector cartouche on left grip, original patent dates and U.S. markings. All major parts serial numbered using original Colt-style lettering, numbering. Bullseye ejector head and color case-hardening on frame and hammer. Introduced 1990. From E.M.F.
Price: **$500.00**
Price: Cavalry or Artillery **$390.00**
Price: Nickel plated, add **$125.00**
Price: Casehardened New Model frame **$365.00**

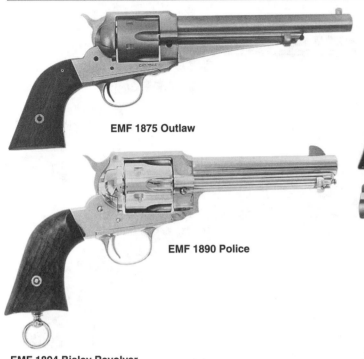

EMF 1875 Outlaw

Freedom Arms Premier

EMF 1890 Police

Freedom Arms Model 353

EMF 1894 Bisley Revolver

Similar to the Hartford single-action revolver except has special grip frame and trigger guard, wide spur hammer; available in 38-40 or 45 Colt, 4-3/4", 5-1/2" or 7-1/2" barrel. Introduced 1995. Imported by E.M.F.
Price: Casehardened/blue **$400.00**
Price: Nickel **$525.00**

EMF Hartford Pinkerton Single-Action Revolver

Same as the regular Hartford except has 4" barrel with ejector tube and birds head grip. Calibers: 357 Mag., 45 Colt. Introduced 1997. Imported by E.M.F.
Price: **$375.00**

Freedom Arms 83 475 Linebaugh

EMF Hartford Express Single-Action Revolver

Same as the regular Hartford model except uses grip of the Colt Lightning revolver. Barrel lengths of 4", 4-3/4", 5-1/2". Introduced 1997. Imported by E.M.F.
Price: **$375.00**

EMF 1875 OUTLAW REVOLVER

Caliber: 357 Mag., 44-40, 45 Colt. **Barrel:** 7-1/2". **Weight:** 46 oz. **Length:** 13-1/2" overall. **Stocks:** Smooth walnut. **Sights:** Blade front, fixed groove rear. **Features:** Authentic copy of 1875 Remington with firing pin in hammer; color case-hardened frame, blue cylinder, barrel, steel backstrap and brass trigger guard. Also available in nickel, factory engraved. Imported by E.M.F.
Price: All calibers **$575.00**
Price: Nickel **$735.00**

Freedom Arms Model 83

EMF 1890 Police Revolver

Similar to the 1875 Outlaw except has 5-1/2" barrel, weighs 40 oz., with 12-1/2" overall length. Has lanyard ring in butt. No web under barrel. Calibers 357, 44-40, 45 Colt. Imported by E.M.F.
Price: All calibers **$590.00**
Price: Nickel **$750.00**

FREEDOM ARMS MODEL 83 PREMIER GRADE REVOLVER

Caliber: 357 Mag., 41 Rem. Mag., 44 Rem. Mag., 454 Casull, 475 Linebaugh, 50 AE, 5-shot. **Barrel:** 4-3/4", 6", 7-1/2", 9" (357 Mag. only), 10" (except 475 Linebaugh). **Weight:** 52 oz. **Length:** 14" overall (7-1/2" bbl.). **Stocks:** Impregnated hardwood (Premier grade), or Pachmayr (Field Grade). **Sights:** Blade front, notch or adjustable rear. **Features:** All stainless steel construction; sliding bar safety system. Lifetime warranty. Made in U.S. by Freedom Arms, Inc.

Price: 454 Casull, 475 Linebaugh, 50 AE, adj. sights **$1,958.00**
Price: 454 Casull, fixed sight **$1,894.00**
Price: 357 Mag., 41 Rem. Mag., 44 Rem. Mag., adj. sights. . . . **$1,519.00**
Price: 44 Rem. Mag., fixed sight **$1,816.00**
Price: Extra cylinder **$264.00**

Freedom Arms Model 83 Field Grade Revolver

Made on the Model 83 frame. Weighs 52 oz. Field grade model has adjustable rear sight with replaceable front blade, matte finish, Pachmayr grips. All stainless steel. Introduced 1992. Made in U.S. by Freedom Arms Inc.
Price: 454 Casull, 475 Linebaugh, 50 AE, adj. sights **$1,519.00**
Price: 454 Casull, fixed sights **$1,484.00**
Price: 357 Mag., 41 Rem. Mag., 44 Rem. Mag., adj. sights. . . . **$1,442.00**
Price: Extra cylinder **$264.00**

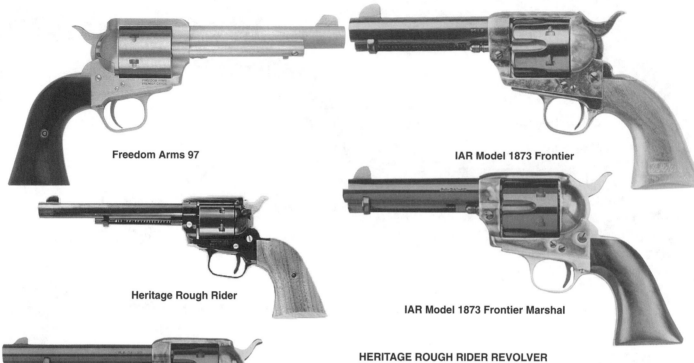

Freedom Arms 97

IAR Model 1873 Frontier

Heritage Rough Rider

IAR Model 1873 Frontier Marshal

IAR Model 1873 Six Shooter

Freedom Arms Model 83 Field Grade Varmint Class Revolver

Made on the Model 83 frame. Chambered for 22 LR with 5-shot cylinder; 5-1/8" or 7-1/2" barrel. Weighs 58 oz. (7-1/2" barrel). Brass bead front, adjustable rear express with shallow "V." All-stainless construction with matte finish, manual sliding-bar safety system, dual firing pins, lightened hammer, pre-set trigger stop. Made in U.S. by Freedom Arms.

Price: Varmint Class **$1,714.00**
Price: Extra fitted 22 WMR cylinder **$264.00**

FREEDOM ARMS MODEL 97 MID-FRAME REVOLVER

Caliber: 357 Mag., 6-shot cylinder; 45 Colt, 41 Rem. Mag., 5-shot. **Barrel:** 4-1/4", 5-1/2", 7-1/2". **Weight:** 41 oz. (5-1/2" barrel). **Length:** 10-3/4"overall (5-1/2" barrel). **Grips:** Impregnated hardwood or black Micarta optional. **Sights:** Blade on ramp front, fixed or fully adjustable rear. **Features:** Made of stainless steel; brushed finish; automatic transfer bar safety system. Introduced 1997. Made in U.S. by Freedom Arms.

Price: Adjustable sight **$1,576.00**
Price: 357 Mag., 45 Colt, fixed sight **$1,500.00**
Price: Extra cylinder **$264.00**

FREEDOM ARMS MODEL 252 VARMINT CLASS REVOLVER

Caliber: 22 LR, 5-shot. **Barrel:** 5.125", 7.5". **Weight:** 58 oz. (7.5" barrel). **Length:** NA. **Stocks:** Black and green laminated hardwood. **Sights:** Brass bead express front, express rear with shallow V-notch. **Features:** All stainless steel construction. Dual firing pins; lightened hammer; pre-set trigger stop. Built on Model 83 frame and accepts Model 83 Freedom Arms sights and/or scope mounts. Introduced 1991. Made in U.S. by Freedom Arms.

Price: **$1,527.00**
Price: Extra fitted 22 WMR cylinder **$264.00**

HERITAGE ROUGH RIDER REVOLVER

Caliber: 22 LR, 22 LR/22 WMR combo, 6-shot. **Barrel:** 2-3/4", 3-1/2", 4-3/4", 6-1/2", 9". **Weight:** 31 to 38 oz. **Length:** NA. **Grips:** Exotic hardwood, laminated wood or mother of pearl; bird's head models offered. **Sights:** Blade front, fixed rear. Adjustable sight on 6-1/2" only. **Features:** Hammer block safety. High polish blue or nickel finish. Introduced 1993. Made in U.S. by Heritage Mfg., Inc.

Price: . . . . **$184.95 to $239.95**

IAR MODEL 1873 SIX SHOOTER

Caliber: 22 LR/22 WMR combo. **Barrel:** 5-1/2". **Weight:** 36-1/2" oz. **Length:** 11-3/8" overall. **Stocks:** One-piece walnut. **Sights:** Blade front, notch rear. **Features:** A 3/4-scale reproduction. Color case-hardened frame, blued barrel. All-steel construction. Made by Uberti. Imported from Italy by IAR, Inc.

Price: **$360.00**

IAR MODEL 1873 FRONTIER REVOLVER

Caliber: 22 RL, 22 LR/22 WMR. **Barrel:** 4-3/4". **Weight:** 45 oz. **Length:** 10-1/2" overall. **Stocks:** One-piece walnut with inspector's cartouche. **Sights:** Blade front, notch rear. **Features:** Color case-hardened frame, blued barrel, black nickel-plated brass trigger guard and backstrap. Bright nickel and engraved versions available. Introduced 1997. Imported from Italy by IAR, Inc.

Price: **$395.00**
Price: Nickel-plated **$485.00**
Price: 22 LR/22WMR combo **$425.00**

IAR MODEL 1873 FRONTIER MARSHAL

Caliber: 357 Mag., 45 Colt. **Barrel:** 4-3/4", 5-1/2, 7-1/2". **Weight:** 39 oz. **Length:** 10-1/2" overall. **Stocks:** One-piece walnut. **Sights:** Blade front, notch rear. **Features:** Bright brass trigger guard and backstrap, color case-hardened frame, blued barrel and cylinder. Introduced 1998. Imported from Italy by IAR, Inc.

Price: **$395.00**

MAGNUM RESEARCH BFR SINGLE-ACTION REVOLVER

Caliber: 22 Hornet, 45 Colt +P, 454 Casull (Little Max, standard cylinder). **Barrel:** 7-1/2", 10". **Weight:** 4 lbs. **Length:** 11" overall with 7-1/2" barrel. **Stocks:** Checkered rubber. **Sights:** Orange blade on ramp front, fully adjustable rear. **Features:** Stainless steel construction. Optional exotic wood finger-groove grips available. Introduced 1997. Made in U.S. From Magnum Research, Inc.

Price: **$999.00**

HANDGUNS

Navy Arms Flat Top

Navy Arms 1873

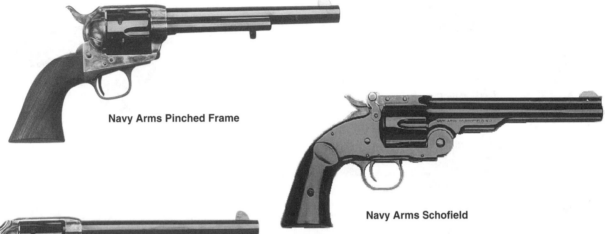

Navy Arms Pinched Frame

Navy Arms Schofield

Navy Arms Bisley

MAGNUM RESEARCH LITTLE MAX REVOLVER
Caliber: 22 Hornet, 45 Colt, 454 Casull, 50 A.E. **Barrel:** 6-1/2", 7-1/2", 10". **Weight:** 45 oz. **Length:** 13" overall (7-1/2" barrel). **Stocks:** Rubber. **Sights:** Ramp front, adjustable rear. **Features:** Single action; stainless steel construction. Announced 1998. Made in U.S. From Magnum Research.
Price: **$999.00**
Price: Maxine model (7-1/2", 10", 45 Colt/410, 45-70, 444 Marlin) **$999.00**

NAVY ARMS FLAT TOP TARGET MODEL REVOLVER
Caliber: 45 Colt, 6-shot cylinder. **Barrel:** 7-1/2". **Weight:** 40 oz. **Length:** 13-1/4" overall. **Stocks:** Smooth walnut. **Sights:** Spring-loaded German silver front, rear adjustable for windage. **Features:** Replica of Colt's Flat Top Frontier target revolver made from 1888 to 1896. Blue with color case-hardened frame. Introduced 1997. Imported by Navy Arms.
Price: **$435.00**

NAVY ARMS "PINCHED FRAME" SINGLE-ACTION REVOLVER
Caliber: 45 Colt, 6-shot. **Barrel:** 7-1/2". **Weight:** 37 oz. **Length:** 13" overall. **Stocks:** Smooth walnut **Sights:** German silver blade, notch rear. **Features:** Replica of Colt's original Peacemaker. Color case-hardened frame, hammer, rest charcoal blued. Introduced 1997. Imported by Navy Arms.
Price: **$415.00**

NAVY ARMS BISLEY MODEL SINGLE-ACTION REVOLVER
Caliber: 44-40 or 45 Colt, 6-shot cylinder. **Barrel:** 4-3/4", 5-1/2", 7-1/2". **Weight:** 40 oz. **Length:** 12-1/2" overall (7-1/2" barrel). **Stocks:** Smooth walnut. **Sights:** Blade front, notch rear. **Features:** Replica of Colt's Bisley Model. Polished blue finish, color case-hardened frame. Introduced 1997. Imported by Navy Arms.
Price: **$415.00**

NAVY ARMS 1872 OPEN TOP REVOLVER
Caliber: 38 Spec., 6-shot. **Barrel:** 5-1/2" or 7-1/2". **Weight:** 2 lbs., 12 oz. **Length:** 11" or 13". **Stocks:** Smooth walnut. **Sights:** Blade front, notch rear. **Features:** Replica of Colt's first production cartridge "six shooter." Polished blue finish with color case hardened frame, silver plated trigger guard and backstrap Introduced 2000. Imported by Navy Arms.
Price: **$390.00**

NAVY ARMS 1873 SINGLE-ACTION REVOLVER
Caliber: 357 Mag., 44-40, 45 Colt, 6-shot cylinder. **Barrel:** 4-3/4", 5-1/2", 7-1/2". **Weight:** 36 oz. **Length:** 10-3/4" overall (5-1/2" barrel). **Stocks:** Smooth walnut. **Sights:** Blade front, notch rear. **Features:** Blue with color case-hardened frame. Introduced 1991. Imported by Navy Arms.
Price: **$395.00**
Price: 1873 U.S. Cavalry Model (7-1/2", 45 Colt, arsenal markings) **$465.00**
Price: 1895 U.S. Artillery Model (as above, 5-1/2" barrel) **$465.00**

NAVY ARMS 1875 SCHOFIELD REVOLVER
Caliber: 44-40, 45 Colt, 6-shot cylinder. **Barrel:** 3-1/2", 5", 7". **Weight:** 39 oz. **Length:** 10-3/4" overall (5" barrel). **Stocks:** Smooth walnut. **Sights:** Blade front, notch rear. **Features:** Replica of Smith & Wesson Model 3 Schofield. Single-action, top-break with automatic ejection. Polished blue finish. Introduced 1994. Imported by Navy Arms.
Price: Hideout Model, 3-1/2" barrel **$695.00**
Price: Wells Fargo, 5" barrel. **$695.00**
Price: U.S. Cavalry model, 7" barrel, military markings **$695.00**

HANDGUNS

Navy Arms New Model Russian

North American Black Widow

North American Mini

Ruger Blackhawk

North American Mini-Master

NAVY ARMS NEW MODEL RUSSIAN REVOLVER

Caliber: 44 Russian, 6-shot cylinder. **Barrel:** 6-1/2". **Weight:** 40 oz. **Length:** 12" overall. **Stocks:** Smooth walnut. **Sights:** Blade front, notch rear. **Features:** Replica of the S&W Model 3 Russian Third Model revolver. Spur trigger guard, polished blue finish. Introduced 1999. Imported by Navy Arms.
Price: **$745.00**

NAVY ARMS 1851 NAVY CONVERSION REVOLVER

Caliber: 38 Spec., 38 Long Colt. **Barrel:** 5-1/2", 7-1/2". **Weight:** 44 oz. **Length:** 14" overall (7-1/2" barrel). **Stocks:** Smooth walnut. **Sights:** Bead front, notch rear. **Features:** Replica of Colt's cartridge conversion revolver. Polished blue finish with color case-hardened frame, silver plated trigger guard and backstrap. Introduced 1999. Imported by Navy Arms.
Price: **$365.00**

NAVY ARMS 1860 ARMY CONVERSION REVOLVER

Caliber: 38 Spec., 38 Long Colt. **Barrel:** 5-1/2", 7-1/2". **Weight:** 44 oz. **Length:** 13-1/2" overall (7-1/2" barrel). **Stocks:** Smooth walnut. **Sights:** Blade front, notch rear. **Features:** Replica of Colt's conversion revolver. Polished blue finish with color case-hardened frame, full-size 1860 Army grip with blued steel backstrap. Introduced 1999. Imported by Navy Arms.
Price: **$365.00**

NAVY ARMS 1861 NAVY CONVERSION REVOLVER

Caliber: 38 Spec., 38 Long Colt. **Barrel:** 5-1/2", 7-1/2". **Weight:** 44 oz. **Length:** 13-1/2" overall (7-1/2" barrel). **Stocks:** Smooth walnut. **Sights:** Blade front, notch rear. **Features:** Replica of Colt's cartridge conversion. Polished blue finish with color case-hardened frame, silver plated trigger guard and backstrap. Introduced 1999. Imported by Navy Arms.
Price: **$365.00**

NORTH AMERICAN MINI-REVOLVERS

Caliber: 22 Short, 22 LR, 22 WMR, 5-shot. **Barrel:** 1-1/8", 1-5/8". **Weight:** 4 to 6.6 oz. **Length:** 3-5/8" to 6-1/8" overall. **Stocks:** Laminated wood. **Sights:** Blade front, notch fixed rear. **Features:** All stainless steel construction. Polished satin and matte finish. Engraved models available. From North American Arms.
Price: 22 Short, 22 LR **$176.00**
Price: 22 WMR, 1-5/8" bbl. **$194.00**
Price: 22 WMR, 1-1/8" or 1-5/8" bbl. with extra 22 LR cylinder . . **$231.00**

NORTH AMERICAN MINI-MASTER

Caliber: 22 LR, 22 WMR, 5-shot cylinder. **Barrel:** 4". **Weight:** 10.7 oz. **Length:** 7.75" overall. **Stocks:** Checkered hard black rubber. **Sights:** Blade front, white outline rear adjustable for elevation, or fixed. **Features:** Heavy vent barrel; full-size grips. Non-fluted cylinder. Introduced 1989.
Price: Adjustable sight, 22 WMR or 22 LR **$299.00**
Price: As above with extra WMR/LR cylinder **$336.00**
Price: Fixed sight, 22 WMR or 22 LR **$281.00**
Price: As above with extra WMR/LR cylinder **$318.00**

North American Black Widow Revolver

Similar to the Mini-Master except has 2" heavy vent barrel. Built on the 22 WMR frame. Non-fluted cylinder, black rubber grips. Available with either Millett Low Profile fixed sights or Millett sight adjustable for elevation only. Overall length 5-7/8", weighs 8.8 oz. From North American Arms.
Price: Adjustable sight, 22 LR or 22 WMR **$269.00**
Price: As above with extra WMR/LR cylinder **$306.00**
Price: Fixed sight, 22 LR or 22 WMR **$251.00**
Price: As above with extra WMR/LR cylinder **$288.00**

RUGER NEW MODEL BLACKHAWK REVOLVER

Caliber: 30 Carbine, 357 Mag./38 Spec., 41 Mag., 45 Colt, 6-shot. **Barrel:** 4-5/8" or 5-1/2", either caliber; 7-1/2 (30 Carbine and 45 Colt). **Weight:** 42 oz. (6-1/2" bbl.). **Length:** 12-1/4" overall (5-1/2" bbl.). **Stocks:** American walnut. **Sights:** 1/8" ramp front, micro-click rear adjustable for windage and elevation. **Features:** Ruger transfer bar safety system, independent firing pin, hardened chrome-moly steel frame, music wire springs throughout. Comes with plastic lockable case and lock.

Ruger Bisley Vaquero

Ruger Bisley Single-Action

Ruger New Bearcat

Ruger Super Single-Six

Price: Blue 30 Carbine, 7-1/2" (BN31) **$415.00**
Price: Blue, 357 Mag., 4-5/8", 6-1/2" (BN34, BN36). **$415.00**
Price: As above, stainless (KBN34, KBN36) **$505.00**
Price: Blue, 357 Mag./9mm Convertible, 4-5/8", 6-1/2" (BN34X,
BN36X) **$465.00**
Price: Blue, 41 Mag., 4-5/8", 6-1/2" (BN41, BN42). **$415.00**
Price: Blue, 45 Colt, 4-5/8", 5-1/2", 7-1/2" (BN44, BN455,
BN45) **$415.00**
Price: Stainless, 45 Colt, 4-5/8", 7-1/2" (KBN44, KBN45) **$505.00**
Price: Blue, 45 Colt/45 ACP Convertible, 4-5/8", 5-1/2"
(BN44X, BN455X). **$465.00**

RUGER NEW MODEL SUPER BLACKHAWK

Caliber: 44 Mag., 6-shot. Also fires 44 Spec. **Barrel:** 4-5/8", 5-1/2", 7-1/2", 10-1/2" bull. **Weight:** 48 oz. (7-1/2" bbl.), 51 oz. (10-1/2" bbl.). **Length:** 13-3/8" overall (7-1/2" bbl.). **Stocks:** American walnut. **Sights:** 1/8" ramp front, micro-click rear adjustable for windage and elevation. **Features:** Ruger transfer bar safety system, fluted or un-fluted cylinder, steel grip and cylinder frame, round or square back trigger guard, wide serrated trigger and wide spur hammer. Comes with plastic lockable case and lock.
Price: Blue, 4-5/8", 5-1/2", 7-1/2" (S458N, S45N, S47N) **$489.00**
Price: Blue, 10-1/2" bull barrel (S411N) **$499.00**
Price: Stainless, 4-5/8", 5-1/2", 7-1/2" (KS458N, KS45N,
KS47N) **$510.00**
Price: Stainless, 10-1/2" bull barrel (KS411N) **$519.00**

RUGER VAQUERO SINGLE-ACTION REVOLVER

Caliber: 357 Mag., 44-40, 44 Mag., 45 Colt, 6-shot. **Barrel:** 4-5/8", 5-1/2", 7-1/2". **Weight:** 41 oz. **Length:** 13-1/8" overall (7-1/2" barrel). **Stocks:** Smooth rosewood with Ruger medallion. **Sights:** Blade front, fixed notch rear. **Features:** Uses Ruger's patented transfer bar safety system and loading gate interlock with classic styling. Blued model has color case-

hardened finish on the frame, the rest polished and blued. Stainless model has high-gloss polish. Introduced 1993. From Sturm, Ruger & Co.
Price: 357 Mag. BNV34 (4-5/8"), BNV35 (5-1/2"). **$510.00**
Price: 357 Mag. KBNV34 (4-5/8"), KBNV35 (5-1/2") stainless . . . **$510.00**
Price: BNV44 (4-5/8"), BNV445 (5-1/2"), BNV45 (7-1/2"), blue . . **$510.00**
Price: KBNV44 (4-5/8"), KBNV455 (5-1/2"), KBNV45 (7-1/2"),
stainless **$510.00**
Price: 45 Colt BNV455, all blue finish, 4-5/8" or 5-1/2" **$510.00**
Price: 45 Colt KBNV455, stainless, 5-1/2" **$510.00**

Ruger Bisley-Vaquero Single-Action Revolver

Similar to the Vaquero except has Bisley-style hammer, grip and trigger and is available in 357 Magnum, 44 Magnum and 45 Colt only, with 4-5/8" or 5-1/2" barrel. Has smooth rosewood grips with Ruger medallion. Roll-engraved, unfluted cylinder. Introduced 1997. From Sturm, Ruger & Co.
Price: Color case-hardened frame, blue grip frame, barrel and cylinder, RBNV-475, RBNV-455 . . . . **$510.00**
Price: High-gloss stainless steel, KRBNV-475, KRBNV-455 . . . . . **$529.00**
Price: For simulated ivory grips add. **$36.00**
Price: 44-40 BNV40 (4-5/8"), BNV405 (5-1/2"), BNV407 (7-1/2") . **$510.00**
Price: 44-40 KBNV40 (4-5/8"), KBNV405 (5-1/2"), KBNV407 (7-1/2") stainless **$510.00**

RUGER NEW BEARCAT SINGLE-ACTION

Caliber: 22 LR, 6-shot. **Barrel:** 4". **Weight:** 24 oz. **Length:** 8-7/8" overall. **Stocks:** Smooth rosewood with Ruger medallion. **Sights:** Blade front, fixed notch rear. **Features:** Reintroduction of the Ruger Bearcat with slightly lengthened frame, Ruger patented transfer bar safety system. Available in blue only. Introduced 1993. Comes with plastic lockable case and lock. From Sturm, Ruger & Co.
Price: SBC4, blue. **$359.00**

HANDGUNS

Uberti Cattleman

Uberti Russian

Uberti 1875 Army

Uberti 1890 Army

RUGER SINGLE-SIX AND SUPER SINGLE-SIX CONVERTIBLE

Caliber: 22 LR, 6-shot; 22 WMR in extra cylinder. **Barrel:** 4-5/8", 5-1/2", 6-1/2", 9-1/2" (6-groove). **Weight:** 35 oz. (6-1/2" bbl.). **Length:** 11-13/16" overall (6-1/2" bbl.). **Stocks:** Smooth American walnut. **Sights:** Improved Patridge front on ramp, fully adjustable rear protected by integral frame ribs (super single-six); or fixed sight single six). **Features:** Ruger transfer bar safety system, loading gate interlock, hardened chrome-moly steel frame, wide trigger, music wire springs throughout, independent firing pin.
Price: 4-5/8", 5-1/2", 6-1/2", 9-1/2" barrel, blue, adjustable sight NR4, NR6, NR9, NR5 . . . . **$369.00**
Price: 5-1/2", 6-1/2" bbl. only, stainless steel, adjustable sight KNR5, KNR6. . . . . **$449.00**
Price: 5-1/2", 6-1/2" barrel, blue fixed sights **$369.00**

Ruger Bisley Small Frame Revolver

Similar to the Single-Six except frame is styled after the classic Bisley "flat-top." Most mechanical parts are unchanged. Hammer is lower and smoothly curved with a deeply checkered spur. Trigger is strongly curved with a wide smooth surface. Longer grip frame designed with a hand-filling shape, and the trigger guard is a large oval. Adjustable dovetail rear sight; front sight base accepts interchangeable square blades of various heights and styles. Has an unfluted cylinder and roll engraving. Weighs 41 oz. Chambered for 22 LR, 6-1/2" barrel only. Comes with plastic lockable case and lock. Introduced 1985.
Price: RB-22AW **$402.00**

Ruger Bisley Single-Action Revolver

Similar to standard Blackhawk except the hammer is lower with a smoothly curved, deeply checkered wide spur. The trigger is strongly curved with a wide smooth surface. Longer grip frame has a hand-filling shape. Adjustable rear sight, ramp-style front. Has an unfluted cylinder and roll engraving, adjustable sights. Chambered for 357, 44 Mags. and 45 Colt; 7-1/2" barrel; overall length of 13"; weighs 48 oz. Comes with plastic lockable case and lock. Introduced 1985.
Price: RB-35W, 357Mag, R3-44W, 44Mag, RB-45W, 45 Colt . . . **$510.00**

TRISTAR/UBERTI REGULATOR REVOLVER

Caliber: 45 Colt. **Barrel:** 4-3/4", 5-1/2", 7-1/2". **Weight:** 32-38 oz. **Length:** 8-1/4" overall (4-3/4" bbl.) **Grips:** One-piece walnut. **Sights:** Blade front, notch rear. **Features:** Uberti replica of 1873 Colt Model "P" revolver. Color-case hardened steel frame, brass backstrap and trigger guard, hammer-block safety. Imported from Italy by Tristar Sporting Arms.
Price: Regulator **$335.00**
Price: Regulator Deluxe (blued backstrap, trigger guard) **$367.00**

UBERTI 1873 CATTLEMAN SINGLE-ACTION

Caliber: 22 LR/22 WMR, 38 Spec., 357 Mag., 44 Spec., 44-40, 45 Colt/45 ACP, 6-shot. **Barrel:** 4-3/4", 5-1/2", 7-1/2"; 44-40, 45 Colt also with 3", 3-1/2", 4". **Weight:** 38 oz. (5-1/2" bbl.). **Length:** 10-3/4" overall (5-1/2" bbl.). **Stocks:** One-piece smooth walnut. **Sights:** Blade front, groove rear; fully adjustable rear available. **Features:** Steel or brass backstrap, trigger guard; color case-hardened frame, blued barrel, cylinder. Imported from Italy by Uberti U.S.A.
Price: Steel backstrap, trigger guard, fixed sights **$435.00**
Price: Brass backstrap, trigger guard, fixed sights **$365.00**
Price: Bisley model. **$435.00**

Uberti 1873 Buckhorn Single-Action

A slightly larger version of the Cattleman revolver. Available in 44 Magnum or 44 Magnum/44-40 convertible, otherwise has same specs.
Price: Steel backstrap, trigger guard, fixed sights **$410.00**
Price: Convertible (two cylinders). **$475.00**

UBERTI 1875 SA ARMY OUTLAW REVOLVER

Caliber: 357 Mag., 44-40, 45 Colt, 45 Colt/45 ACP convertible, 6-shot. **Barrel:** 5-1/2", 7-1/2". **Weight:** 44 oz. **Length:** 13-3/4" overall. **Stocks:** Smooth walnut. **Sights:** Blade front, notch rear. **Features:** Replica of the 1875 Remington S.A. Army revolver. Brass trigger guard, color case-hardened frame, rest blued. Imported by Uberti U.S.A.
Price: **$435.00**
Price: 45 Colt/45 ACP convertible **$475.00**

UBERTI 1890 ARMY OUTLAW REVOLVER

Caliber: 357 Mag., 44-40, 45 Colt, 45 Colt/45 ACP convertible, 6-shot. **Barrel:** 5-1/2", 7-1/2". **Weight:** 37 oz. **Length:** 12-1/2" overall. **Stocks:** American walnut. **Sights:** Blade front, groove rear. **Features:** Replica of the 1890 Remington single-action. Brass trigger guard, rest is blued. Imported by Uberti U.S.A.
Price: **$435.00**
Price: 45 Colt/45 ACP convertible **$475.00**

UBERTI NEW MODEL RUSSIAN REVOLVER

Caliber: 44 Russian, 6-shot cylinder. **Barrel:** 6-1/2". **Weight:** 40 oz. **Length:** 12" overall. **Stocks:** Smooth walnut. **Sights:** Blade front, notch rear. **Features:** Repica of the S&W Model 3 Russian Third Model revolver. Spur trigger guard, polished blue finish. Introduced 1999. Imported by Uberti USA.
Price: **$775.00**

Uberti Schofield

Uberti Bisley

Uberti Bisley Flat Top

UBERTI 1875 SCHOFIELD REVOLVER

Caliber: 44-40, 45 Colt, 6-shot cylinder. **Barrel:** 5", 7". **Weight:** 39 oz. **Length:** 10-3/4" overall (5" barrel). **Stocks:** Smooth walnut. **Sights:** Blade front, notch rear. **Features:** Replica of Smith & Wesson Model 3 Schofield. Single-action, top-break with automatic ejection. Polished blue finish. Introduced 1994. Imported by Uberti USA.

Price: **$700.00**

UBERTI BISLEY MODEL SINGLE-ACTION REVOLVER

Caliber: 38-40, 357 Mag., 44 Spec., 44-40 or 45 Colt, 6-shot cylinder. **Barrel:** 4-3/4", 5-1/2", 7-1/2". **Weight:** 40 oz. **Length:** 12-1/2" overall (7-1/2" barrel). **Stocks:** Smooth walnut. **Sights:** Blade front, notch rear. **Features:** Replica of Colt's Bisley Model. Polished blue finish, color case-hardened frame. Introduced 1997. Imported by Uberti USA.

Price: **$435.00**

Uberti Bisley Model Flat Top Target Revolver

Similar to the standard Bisley model except with flat top strap, 7-1/2" barrel only, and a spring-loaded German silver front sight blade, standing leaf rear sight adjustable for windage. Polished blue finish, color case-hardened frame. Introduced 1998. Imported by Uberti USA.

Price: **$455.00**

U.S. FIRE-ARMS SINGLE ACTION ARMY REVOLVER

Caliber: 44 Russian, 38-40, 44-40, 45 Colt, 6-shot cylinder. **Barrel:** 4", 4-3/4", 5-1/2", 7-1/2", 10". **Weight:** 37 oz. **Length:** NA. **Grips:** Hard rubber. **Sights:** Blade front, notch rear. **Features:** Recreation of original guns; 3" and 4" have no ejector. Available with all-blue, blue with color case-hardening, or full nickel-plate finish. Made in U.S. by United States Fire-Arms Mfg. Co.

Price: 4" blue **$1,099.00**
Price: 4-3/4", blue/cased-colors **$1,199.00**
Price: 7-1/2", carbonal blue/case-colors **$1,425.00**
Price: 7-1/2" nickel **$1,349.00**

U.S. Fire-Arms Nettleton Cavalry Revolver

Similar to the Single Action Army, except in 45 Colt only, with 7-1/2" barrel, color case-hardened/blue finish, and has old-style hand numbering,

exact cartouche branding and correct inspector hand-stamp markings. Made in U.S. by United States Fire-Arms Mfg. Co.

Price: **$1,225.00**
Price: Artillery Model, 5-1/2" barrel **$1,225.00**

U.S. Fire-Arms Bird Head Model Revolver

Similar to the Single Action Army except has bird's-head grip and comes with 3-1/2", 4" or 4-3/4" barrel. Made in U.S. by United States Fire-Arms Mfg. Co.

Price: 3-1/2" or 4" blue/color-case hardening **$1,199.00**
Price: 4-3/4", nickel-plated **$1,299.00**

U.S. Fire-Arms Flattop Target Revolver

Similar to the Single Action Army except 4-3/4", 5-1/2" or 7-1/2" barrel, two-piece hard rubber stocks, flat top frame, adjustable rear sight. Made in U.S. by United States Fire-Arms Mfg. Co.

Price: 4-3/4", blue, polished hammer **$1,150.00**
Price: 4-3/4", blue, case-colored hammer **$1,150.00**
Price: 5-1/2", blue, case-colored hammer **$1,150.00**
Price: 5-1/2", nickel-plated **$1,299.00**
Price: 7-1/2", blue, polished hammer **$1,150.00**
Price: 7-1/2", blue, case-colored hammer **$1,150.00**

U.S. FIRE-ARMS BISLEY MODEL REVOLVER

Caliber: 4 Colt, 6-shot cylinder. **Barrel:** 4-3/4", 5-1/2", 7-1/2", 10". **Weight:** 38 oz. (5-1/2" barrel). **Length:** NA. **Grips:** Two-piece hard rubber. **Sights:** Blade front, notch rear. **Features:** Available in all-blue, blue with color case-hardening, or full nickel plate finish. Made in U.S. by United States Patent Fire-Arms Mfg. Co.

Price: 5-1/2", blue/case-colors **$1,350.00**
Price: 7-1/2", blue/case-colors **$1,350.00**
Price: 10", nickel **$1,435.00**

U.S. Fire-Arms "China Camp" Cowboy Action Revolver

Similar to Single Action Army revolver except available in Silver Steel finish only. Offered in 4-3/4", 5-1/2", 7-1/2" and 10" barrels. Made in U.S. by United States Fire-Arms Mfg. Co.

Price: **$995.00**

U.S. Fire-Arms "Buntline Special"

Similar to Single Action Army revolver except has 16" barrel, flip-up rear peep sight, 45 Colt only. Bone case frame, armory blue or nickel finish. Made in U.S. by United States Fire-Arms Mfg. Co.

Price: **$2,199.00**

U.S. Fire-Arms Omni-Potent Six Shooter

Similar to Single Action Army revolver except has bird's head grip with lanyard ring and hump in backstrap. Offered in 4-3/4", 5-1/2" and 7-1/2" barrels. Made in U.S. by United States Fire-Arms Mfg. Co.

Price: 3-1/2", 4" blue/color case hardening **$1,340.00**
Price: 4-3/4", nickel plated **$1,439.00**

Specially adapted single-shot and multi-barrel arms.

American Derringer Model 1

Bond Arms C2K Defender

AMERICAN DERRINGER MODEL 1

Caliber: 22 LR, 22 WMR, 30 Carbine, 30 Luger, 30-30 Win., 32 H&R Mag., 32-20, 380 ACP, 38 Super, 38 Spec., 38 Spec. shotshell, 38 Spec. +P, 9mm Para., 357 Mag., 357 Mag./45/410, 357 Maximum, 10mm, 40 S&W, 41 Mag., 38-40, 44-40 Win., 44 Spec., 44 Mag., 45 Colt, 45 Win. Mag., 45 ACP, 45 Colt/410, 45-70 single shot. **Barrel:** 3". **Weight:** 15-1/2 oz. (38 Spec.). **Length:** 4.82" overall. **Stocks:** Rosewood, Zebra wood. **Sights:** Blade front. **Features:** Made of stainless steel with high-polish or satin finish. Two-shot capacity. Manual hammer block safety. Introduced 1980. Available in almost any pistol caliber. Contact the factory for complete list of available calibers and prices. From American Derringer Corp.

Price: 22 LR **$320.00**
Price: 38 Spec. **$320.00**
Price: 357 Maximum. **$345.00**
Price: 357 Mag. **$335.00**
Price: 9mm, 380 . . . . **$320.00**
Price: 40 S&W **$335.00**
Price: 44 Spec. **$398.00**
Price: 44-40 Win. **$398.00**
Price: 45 Colt **$385.00**
Price: 30-30, 45 Win. Mag. **$460.00**
Price: 41, 44 Mags. **$470.00**
Price: 45-70, single shot. **$387.00**
Price: 45 Colt, 410, 2-1/2" **$385.00**
Price: 45 ACP, 10mm Auto. **$340.00**

American Derringer Model 4

Similar to the Model 1 except has 4.1" barrel, overall length of 6", and weighs 16-1/2 oz.; chambered for 357 Mag., 357 Maximum, 45-70, 3" 410-bore shotshells or 45 Colt or 44 Mag. Made of stainless steel. Manual hammer block safety. Introduced 1985.

Price: 3" 410/45 Colt. **$425.00**
Price: 45-70 . . . . **$560.00**
Price: 44 Mag. with oversize grips **$515.00**
Price: Alaskan Survival model (45-70 upper barrel, 410 or 45
Colt lower). **$475.00**

American Derringer Model 6

Similar to the Model 1 except has 6" barrel chambered for 3" 410 shotshells or 22 WMR, 357 Mag., 45 ACP, 45 Colt; rosewood stocks; 8.2" o.a.l. and weighs 21 oz. Shoots either round for each barrel. Manual hammer block safety. Introduced 1986.

Price: 22 WMR **$440.00**
Price: 357 Mag. **$440.00**
Price: 45 Colt/410. . . . . **$450.00**
Price: 45 ACP. **$440.00**

American Derringer Model 7 Ultra Lightweight

Similar to Model 1 except made of high strength aircraft aluminum. Weighs 7-1/2 oz., 4.82" o.a.l., rosewood stocks. Available in 22 LR, 22 WMR, 32 H&R Mag., 380 ACP, 38 Spec., 44 Spec. Introduced 1986.

Price: 22 LR, WMR. **$325.00**
Price: 38 Spec. **$325.00**

Price: 380 ACP. **$325.00**
Price: 32 H&R Mag/32 S&W Long **$325.00**
Price: 44 Spec. **$565.00**

American Derringer Model 10 Lightweight

Similar to the Model 1 except frame is of aluminum, giving weight of 10 oz. Stainless barrels. Available in 38 Spec., 45 Colt or 45 ACP only. Matte gray finish. Introduced 1989.

Price: 45 Colt **$385.00**
Price: 45 ACP **$330.00**
Price: 38 Spec. **$305.00**

American Derringer Lady Derringer

Same as the Model 1 except has tuned action, is fitted with scrimshawed synthetic ivory grips; chambered for 32 H&R Mag. and 38 Spec.; 357 Mag., 45 Colt, 45/410. Deluxe Grade is highly polished; Deluxe Engraved is engraved in a pattern similar to that used on 1880s derringers. All come in a French fitted jewelry box. Introduced 1991.

Price: 32 H&R Mag. **$375.00**
Price: 357 Mag. **$405.00**
Price: 38 Spec. **$360.00**
Price: 45 Colt, 45/410. . . . . **$435.00**

American Derringer Texas Commemorative

A Model 1 Derringer with solid brass frame, stainless steel barrel and rosewood grips. Available in 38 Spec., 44-40 Win., or 45 Colt. Introduced 1987.

Price: 38 Spec. **$365.00**
Price: 44-40 . . . . **$420.00**
Price: Brass frame, 45 Colt **$450.00**

AMERICAN DERRINGER DA 38 MODEL

Caliber: 22 LR, 9mm Para., 38 Spec., 357 Mag., 40 S&W. **Barrel:** 3". **Weight:** 14.5 oz. **Length:** 4.8" overall. **Stocks:** Rosewood, walnut or other hardwoods. **Sights:** Fixed. **Features:** Double-action only; two-shots. Manual safety. Made of satin-finished stainless steel and aluminum. Introduced 1989. From American Derringer Corp.

Price: 22 LR **$435.00**
Price: 38 Spec. **$460.00**
Price: 9mm Para. **$445.00**
Price: 357 Mag. **$450.00**
Price: 40 S&W **$475.00**

ANSCHUTZ MODEL 64P SPORT/TARGET PISTOL

Caliber: 22 LR, 22 WMR, 5-shot magazine. **Barrel:** 10". **Weight:** 3 lbs., 8 oz. **Length:** 18-1/2" overall. **Stock:** Choate Rynite. **Sights:** None furnished; grooved for scope mounting. **Features:** Right-hand bolt; polished blue finish. Introduced 1998. Imported from Germany by AcuSport.

Price: 22 LR **$455.95**
Price: 22 WMR **$479.95**

BOND ARMS TEXAS DEFENDER DERRINGER

Caliber: 9mm Para, 38 Spec./357 Mag., 40 S&W, 44 Spec./44 Mag., 45 Colt/410 shotshell. **Barrel:** 3", 3-1/2". **Weight:** 21 oz. **Length:** 5" overall. **Stocks:** Laminated black ash or rosewood. **Sights:** Blade front, fixed rear.

Davis Big Bore

Downsizer Single Shot

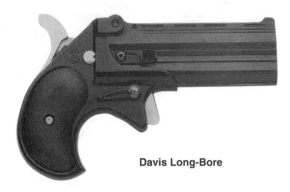

Davis Long-Bore

Gaucher GN1 Silhouette

IAR Model 1872 Derringer

Features: Interchangeable barrels; retracting firing pins; rebounding firing pins; cross-bolt safety; removable trigger guard; automatic extractor for rimmed calibers. Stainless steel construction with blasted/polished and ground combination finish. Introduced 1997. Made in U.S. by Bond Arms, Inc.
Price: **$349.00**
Price: Century 2000 Defender (410-bore, 3-1/2" barrels). **$369.00**

BROWN CLASSIC SINGLE SHOT PISTOL
Caliber: 17 Ackley Hornet through 45-70 Govt. **Barrel:** 15" airgauged match grade. **Weight:** About 3 lbs., 7 oz. **Stocks:** Walnut; thumbrest target style. **Sights:** None furnished; drilled and tapped for scope mounting. **Features:** Falling block action gives rigid barrel-receiver mating; hand-fitted and headspaced. Introduced 1998. Made in U.S. by E.A. Brown Mfg.
Price: **$499.00**

DAVIS BIG BORE DERRINGERS
Caliber: 22 WMR, 38 Spec., 9mm Para. **Barrel:** 2.75". **Weight:** 11.5 oz. **Length:** 4.65" overall. **Stocks:** Textured black synthetic. **Sights:** Blade front, fixed notch rear. **Features:** Alloy frame, steel-lined barrels, steel breech block. Plunger-type safety with integral hammer block. Chrome or black Teflon finish. Introduced 1992. Made in U.S. by Davis Industries.
Price: **$98.00**
Price: 9mm Para. **$104.00**

DAVIS LONG-BORE DERRINGERS
Caliber: 22 WMR, 38 Spec., 9mm Para. **Barrel:** 3.5". **Weight:** 13 oz. **Length:** 5.65" overall. **Stocks:** Textured black synthetic. **Sights:** Fixed. **Features:** Chrome or black Teflon finish. Larger than Davis D-Series models. Introduced 1995. Made in U.S. by Davis Industries.
Price: **$104.00**
Price: 9mm Para. **$110.00**
Price: Big-Bore models (same calibers, 3/4" shorter barrels). **$98.00**

DAVIS D-SERIES DERRINGERS
Caliber: 22 LR, 22 WMR, 25 ACP, 32 ACP. **Barrel:** 2.4". **Weight:** 9.5 oz. **Length:** 4" overall. **Stocks:** Laminated wood or pearl. **Sights:** Blade front, fixed notch rear. **Features:** Choice of black Teflon or chrome finish; spur trigger. Introduced 1986. Made in U.S. by Davis Industries.
Price: **$99.50**

DOWNSIZER WSP SINGLE SHOT PISTOL
Caliber: 357 Magnum, 45 ACP. **Barrel:** 2.10". **Weight:** 11 oz. **Length:** 3.25" overall. **Stocks:** Black polymer. **Sights:** None. **Features:** Single shot, tip-up barrel. Double action only. Stainless steel construction. Measures .900" thick. Introduced 1997. From Downsizer Corp.
Price: **$459.00**

GAUCHER GN1 SILHOUETTE PISTOL
Caliber: 22 LR, single shot. **Barrel:** 10". **Weight:** 2.4 lbs. **Length:** 15.5" overall. **Stocks:** European hardwood. **Sights:** Blade front, open adjustable rear. **Features:** Bolt action, adjustable trigger. Introduced 1990. Imported from France by Mandall Shooting Supplies.
Price: About **$525.00**
Price: Model GP Silhouette **$425.00**

IAR MODEL 1872 DERRINGER
Caliber: 22 Short. **Barrel:** 2-3/8". **Weight:** 7 oz. **Length:** 5-1/8" overall. **Stocks:** Smooth walnut. **Sights:** Blade front, notch rear. **Features:** Gold or nickel frame with blue barrel. Reintroduced 1996 using original Colt designs and tooling for the Colt Model 4 Derringer. Made in U.S. by IAR, Inc.
Price: **$99.00**
Price: Single cased gun **$125.00**
Price: Double cased set **$215.00**

IAR MODEL 1888 DOUBLE DERRINGER
Caliber: 38 Special. **Barrel:** 2-3/4". **Weight:** 16 oz. **Length:** NA. **Stocks:** Smooth walnut. **Sights:** Blade front, notch rear. **Features:** All steel construction. Blue barrel, color case-hardened frame. Uses original designs and tooling for the Uberti New Maverick Derringer. Introduced 1999. Made in U.S. by IAR, Inc.
Price: **$395.00**

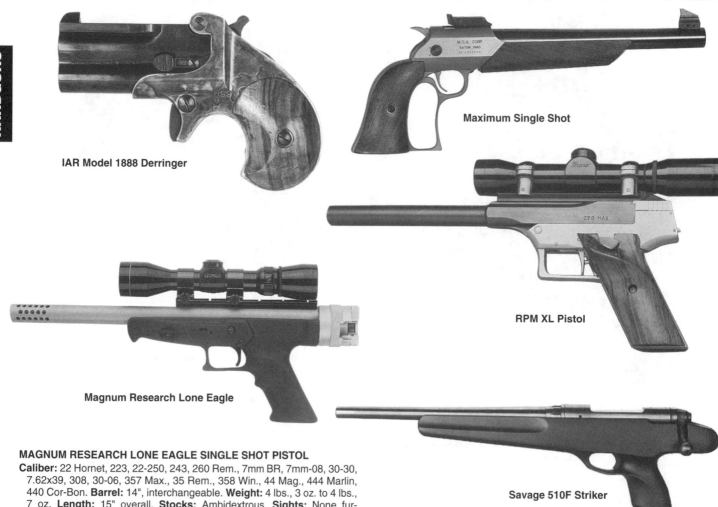

IAR Model 1888 Derringer

Maximum Single Shot

RPM XL Pistol

Magnum Research Lone Eagle

Savage 510F Striker

MAGNUM RESEARCH LONE EAGLE SINGLE SHOT PISTOL

Caliber: 22 Hornet, 223, 22-250, 243, 260 Rem., 7mm BR, 7mm-08, 30-30, 7.62x39, 308, 30-06, 357 Max., 35 Rem., 358 Win., 44 Mag., 444 Marlin, 440 Cor-Bon. **Barrel:** 14", interchangeable. **Weight:** 4 lbs., 3 oz. to 4 lbs., 7 oz. **Length:** 15" overall. **Stocks:** Ambidextrous. **Sights:** None furnished; drilled and tapped for scope mounting and open sights. Open sights optional. **Features:** Cannon-type rotating breech with spring-activated ejector. Ordnance steel with matte blue finish. Cross-bolt safety. External cocking lever on left side of gun. Muzzle brake optional. Introduced 1991. Available from Magnum Research, Inc.

Price: Complete pistol, black	$438.00
Price: Barreled action only, black	$319.00
Price: Complete pistol, chrome	$478.00
Price: Barreled action, chrome	$359.00
Price: Scope base	$14.00
Price: Adjustable open sights	$35.00

MAXIMUM SINGLE SHOT PISTOL

Caliber: 22 LR, 22 Hornet, 22 BR, 22 PPC, 223 Rem., 22-250, 6mm BR, 6mm PPC, 243, 250 Savage, 6.5mm-35M, 270 MAX, 270 Win., 7mm TCU, 7mm BR, 7mm-35, 7mm INT-R, 7mm-08, 7mm Rocket, 7mm Super-Mag., 30 Herrett, 30 Carbine, 30-30, 308 Win., 30x39, 32-20, 350 Rem. Mag., 357 Mag., 357 Maximum, 358 Win., 375 H&H, 44 Mag., 454 Casull. **Barrel:** 8-3/4", 10-1/2", 14". **Weight:** 61 oz. (10-1/2" bbl.); 78 oz. (14" bbl.). **Length:** 15", 18-1/2" overall (with 10-1/2" and 14" bbl., respectively). **Stocks:** Smooth walnut stocks and forend. Also available with 17" finger groove grip. **Sights:** Ramp front, fully adjustable open rear. **Features:** Falling block action; drilled and tapped for M.O.A. scope mounts; integral grip frame/receiver; adjustable trigger; Douglas barrel (interchangeable). Introduced 1983. Made in U.S. by M.O.A. Corp.

Price: Stainless receiver, blue barrel	$799.00
Price: Stainless receiver, stainless barrel	$883.00
Price: Extra blued barrel	$254.00
Price: Extra stainless barrel	$317.00
Price: Scope mount	$60.00

RPM XL SINGLE SHOT PISTOL

Caliber: 22 LR through 45-70. **Barrel:** 8", 10-3/4", 12", 14". **Weight:** About 60 oz. **Length:** NA. **Stocks:** Smooth Goncalo Alves with thumb and heel rests. **Sights:** Hooded front with interchangeable post, or Patridge; ISGW rear adjustable for windage and elevation. **Features:** Barrel drilled and tapped for scope mount. Visible cocking indicator. Spring-loaded barrel lock, positive hammer-block safety. Trigger adjustable for weight of pull and over-travel. Contact maker for complete price list. Made in U.S. by RPM.

Price: Hunter model (stainless frame, 5/16" underlug, latch lever and positive extractor)	$1,295.00
Price: Extra barrel, 8" through 10-3/4"	$387.50
Price: Extra barrel with positive extractor, add	$100.00
Price: Muzzle brake	$100.00

SAVAGE STRIKER BOLT-ACTION HUNTING HANDGUN

Caliber: 223, 22-250, 243, 206, 7mm-08, 308, 2-shot magazine. **Barrel:** 14". **Weight:** About 5 lbs. **Length:** 22-1/2" overall. **Stock:** Black composite ambidextrous mid-grip; grooved forend; "Dual Pillar" bedding. **Sights:** None furnished; drilled and tapped for scope mounting. **Features:** Short left-hand bolt with right-hand ejection; free-floated barrel; uses Savage Model 110 rifle scope rings/bases. Introduced 1998. Made in U.S. by Savage Arms, Inc.

Price: Model 510F (blued barrel and action)	$425.00
Price: Model 516FSS (stainless barrel and action)	$462.00
Price: Model 516FSAK (stainless, adjustable muzzle brake)	$512.00
Price: Super Striker	$512.00

T/C Encore

T/C Stainless Contender

Weatherby Mark V CFP

Savage Sport Striker Bolt-Action Hunting Handgun

Similar to the Striker, but chambered in 22 LR and 22 WMR. Detachable, 10-shot magazine (5-shot magazine for 22 WMR). Overall length 19", weighs 4 lbs. Ambidextrous fiberglass/graphite composite rear grip. Drilled and tapped, scope mount installed. Introduced 2000. Made in U.S. by Savage Arms Inc.

Price: Model 501F (blue finish, 22LR) **$201.00**
Price: Model 502F (blue finish, 22 WMR) **$221.00**

THOMPSON/CENTER ENCORE PISTOL

Caliber: 22-250, 223, 260 Rem., 7mm-08, 243, 308, 270, 30-06, 44 Mag., 454 Casull, 444 Marlin single shot. **Barrel:** 12", 15", tapered round. **Weight:** NA. **Length:** 21" overall with 12" barrel. **Stocks:** American walnut with finger grooves, walnut forend. **Sights:** Blade on ramp front, adjustable rear, or none. **Features:** Interchangeable barrels; action opens by squeezing the trigger guard; drilled and tapped for scope mounting; blue finish. Announced 1996. Made in U.S. by Thompson/Center Arms.

Price: **$554.06**
Price: Extra 12" barrels. **$240.68**
Price: Extra 15" barrels. **$248.14**
Price: 45 Colt/410 barrel, 12" **$263.24**
Price: 45 Colt/410 barrel, 15" **$280.39**

Thompson/Center Stainless Encore Pistol

Similar to the blued Encore except made of stainless steel and available wtih 15" barrel in 223, 22-250 7mm-08, 308. Comes with black rubber grip and forend. Made in U.S. by Thompson/Center Arms.

Price: **$620.99**

Thompson/Center Stainless Super 14

Same as the standard Super 14 and Super 16 except they are made of stainless steel with blued sights. Both models have black Rynite forend and finger-groove, ambidextrous grip with a built-in rubber recoil cushion that has a sealed-in air pocket. Receiver has a different cougar etching. Available in 22 LR Match, .223 Rem., 30-30 Win., 35 Rem. (Super 14), 45 Colt/410. Introduced 1993.

Price: **$578.40**
Price: 45 Colt/410, 14" **$613.94**

Thompson/Center Contender Shooter's Package

Package contains a 14" barrel without iron sights (10" for the 22 LR Match); Weaver-style base and rings; 2.5x-7x Recoil Proof pistol scope; and a soft carrying case. Calibers 22 LR, 223, 7-30 Waters, 30-30. Frame and barrel are blued; grip and forend are black composite. Introduced 1998. Made in U.S. by Thompson/Center Arms.

Price **$735.00**

THOMPSON/CENTER CONTENDER

Caliber: 7mm TCU, 30-30 Win., 22 LR, 22 WMR, 22 Hornet, 223 Rem., 270 Rem., 7-30 Waters, 32-20 Win., 357 Mag., 357 Rem. Max., 44 Mag., 10mm Auto, 445 SuperMag., 45/410, single shot. **Barrel:** 10", bull barrel and vent. rib. **Weight:** 43 oz. (10" bbl.). **Length:** 13-1/4" (10" bbl.). **Stock:** T/C "Competitor Grip." Right or left hand. **Sights:** Under-cut blade ramp front, rear adjustable for windage and elevation. **Features:** Break-open action with automatic safety. Single-action only. Interchangeable bbls., both caliber (rim & centerfire), and length. Drilled and tapped for scope. Engraved frame. See T/C catalog for exact barrel/caliber availability.

Price: Blued (rimfire cals.) **$509.03**
Price: Blued (centerfire cals.) **$509.03**
Price: Extra bbls. **$229.02**
Price: 45/410, internal choke bbl. **$235.11**

Thompson/Center Stainless Contender

Same as the standard Contender except made of stainless steel with blued sights, black Rynite forend and ambidextrous finger-groove grip with a built-in rubber recoil cushion that has a sealed-in air pocket. Receiver has a different cougar etching. Available with 10" bull barrel in 22 LR, 22 LR Match, 22 Hornet, 223 Rem., 30-30 Win., 357 Mag., 44 Mag., 45 Colt/410. Introduced 1993.

Price: **$566.59**
Price: 45 Colt/410. . . . . **$590.44**
Price: With 22 LR match chamber **$578.40**

UBERTI ROLLING BLOCK TARGET PISTOL

Caliber: 22 LR, 22 WMR, 22 Hornet, 357 Mag., 45 Colt, single shot. **Barrel:** 9-7/8", half-round, half-octagon. **Weight:** 44 oz. **Length:** 14" overall. **Stock:** Walnut grip and forend. **Sights:** Blade front, fully adjustable rear. **Features:** Replica of the 1871 rolling block target pistol. Brass trigger guard, color case-hardened frame, blue barrel. Imported by Uberti U.S.A.

Price: **$410.00**

WEATHERBY MARK V CFP PISTOL

Caliber: 22-250, 243, 7mm-08, 308. **Barrel:** 15" fluted stainless. **Weight:** NA. **Length:** NA. **Stock:** Brown laminate with ambidextrous rear grip. **Sights:** None furnished; drilled and tapped for scope mounting. **Features:** Uses Mark V lightweight receiver of chrome-moly steel, matte blue finish. Introduced 1998. Made in U.S. From Weatherby.

Price: **$1,049.00**

WEATHERBY MARK V ACCUMARK CFP PISTOL

Caliber: 223, 22-250, 243, 7mm-08, 308; 3-shot magazine. **Barrel:** 15"; 1:12" twist (223). **Weight:** 5 lbs. **Length:** 26-1/2" overall. **Stock:** Kevlar-fiberglass composite. **Sights:** None; drilled and tapped for scope mounting. **Features:** Molded-in aluminum bedding plate; fluted stainless steel barrel; fully adjustable trigger. Introduced 2000. From Weatherby.

Price: . . . . **NA**

HANDGUNS

Both classic arms and recent designs in American-style repeaters for sport and field shooting.

Armalite M15A2

Armalite AR-10A4

Auto-Ordnance 1927 A-1 Thompson

Barrett Model 82A-1

ARMALITE M15A2 CARBINE
Caliber: 223, 7-shot magazine. **Barrel:** 16" heavy chrome lined; 1:9" twist. **Weight:** 7 lbs. **Length:** 35-11/16" overall. **Stock:** Green or black composition. **Sights:** Standard A2. **Features:** Upper and lower receivers have push-type pivot pin; hard coat anodized; A2-style forward assist; M16A2-type raised fence around magazine release button. Made in U.S. by ArmaLite, Inc.
Price: Green $930.00
Price: Black $945.00

ARMALITE AR-10A4 SPECIAL PURPOSE RIFLE
Caliber: 308 Win., 10-shot magazine. **Barrel:** 20" chrome-lined, 1:12" twist. **Weight:** 9.6 lbs. **Length:** 41" overall **Stock:** Green or black composition. **Sights:** Detachable handle, front sight, or scope mount available; comes with international style flattop receiver with Picatinny rail. **Features:** Proprietary recoil check. Forged upper receiver with case deflector. Receivers are hard-coat anodized. Introduced 1995. Made in U.S. by ArmaLite, Inc.
Price: Green $1,378.00
Price: Black $1,393.00

AUTO-ORDNANCE 1927 A-1 THOMPSON
Caliber: 45 ACP. **Barrel:** 16-1/2". **Weight:** 13 lbs. **Length:** About 41" overall (Deluxe). **Stock:** Walnut stock and vertical forend. **Sights:** Blade front, open rear adjustable for windage. **Features:** Recreation of Thompson Model 1927. Semi-auto only. Deluxe model has finned barrel, adjustable rear sight and compensator; Standard model has plain barrel and military sight. From Auto-Ordnance Corp.
Price: Deluxe $950.00
Price: 1927A1C Lightweight model (9-1/2 lbs.) $950.00

Auto-Ordnance Thompson M1
Similar to the 1927 A-1 except is in the M-1 configuration with side cocking knob, horizontal forend, smooth unfinned barrel, sling swivels on butt and forend. Matte black finish. Introduced 1985.
Price: $950.00

Auto-Ordnance 1927A1 Commando
Similar to the 1927A1 except has Parkerized finish, black-finish wood butt, pistol grip, horizontal forend. Comes with black nylon sling. Introduced 1998. Made in U.S. by Auto-Ordnance Corp.
Price: $950.00

BARRETT MODEL 82A-1 SEMI-AUTOMATIC RIFLE
Caliber: 50 BMG, 10-shot detachable box magazine. **Barrel:** 29". **Weight:** 28.5 lbs. **Length:** 57" overall. **Stock:** Composition with energy-absorbing recoil pad. **Sights:** Scope optional. **Features:** Semi-automatic, recoil operated with recoiling barrel. Three-lug locking bolt; muzzle brake. Adjustable bipod. Introduced 1985. Made in U.S. by Barrett Firearms.
Price: From.. $7,200.00

Browning Mark II Safari

Bushmaster M17S

Bushmaster XM15 E2S

BROWNING BAR MARK II SAFARI SEMI-AUTO RIFLE

Caliber: 243, 25-06, 270, 30-06, 308. **Barrel:** 22" round tapered. **Weight:** 7-3/8 lbs. **Length:** 43" overall. **Stock:** French walnut pistol grip stock and forend, hand checkered. **Sights:** Gold bead on hooded ramp front, click adjustable rear, or no sights. **Features:** Has new bolt release lever; removable trigger assembly with larger trigger guard; redesigned gas and buffer systems. Detachable 4-round box magazine. Scroll-engraved receiver is tapped for scope mounting. BOSS barrel vibration modulator and muzzle brake system available only on models without sights. Mark II Safari introduced 1993. Imported from Belgium by Browning.

Price: Safari, with sights **$833.00**
Price: Safari, no sights **$815.00**
Price: Safari, 270 and 30-06, no sights, BOSS **$891.00**

Browning BAR MARK II Lightweight Semi-Auto

Similar to the Mark II Safari except has lighter alloy receiver and 20" barrel. Available in 243, 308, 270, 30-06, 7mm Rem. Mag., 300 Win. Mag., 338 Win. Mag. Weighs 7 lbs., 2 oz.; overall length 41". Has dovetailed, gold bead front sight on hooded ramp, open rear click adjustable for windage and elevation. Introduced 1997. Imported from Belgium by Browning.

Price: 243, 308, 270, 30-06 . . . . **$833.00**
Price: 7mm Rem. Mag., 300 Win. Mag., 338 Win. Mag **$909.00**

Browning BAR Mark II Safari Rifle in magnum calibers

Same as the standard caliber model, except weighs 8-3/8 lbs., 45" overall, 24" bbl., 3-round mag. Cals. 7mm Mag., 300 Win. Mag., 338 Win. Mag. BOSS barrel vibration modulator and muzzle brake system available only on models without sights. Introduced 1993.

Price: Safari, with sights **$909.00**
Price: Safari, no sights **$890.00**
Price: Safari, no sights, BOSS **$967.00**

Browning BAR High-Grade Auto Rifles

Similar to BAR Mark II Safari model except has grayed receiver with big-game scenes framed in gold with select walnut stock and forearm. Furnished with no sights. Introduced 2001.

Price: 270, 30-06 (whitetail and mule deer scenes) **$1,820.00**
Price: 7mm Rem. Mag., 300 Win. Mag. (moose and elk scenes)
. . . . **$1,876.00**

BROWNING BAR STALKER AUTO RIFLES

Caliber: 243, 308, 270, 30-06, 7mm Rem. Mag., 300 Win. Mag., 338 Win. Mag. **Barrel:** 20", 22" and 24". **Weight:** 6 lbs., 12 oz. (243) to 8 lbs., 2 oz. (magnum cals.) **Length:** 41" to 45" overall. **Stock:** Black composite stock and forearm. **Sights:** Hooded front and adjustable rear or none. **Features:** Optional BOSS (no sights); gas-operated action with seven-lug rotary bolt; dual action bars; 3- or 4-shot magazine (depending on caliber). Introduced 2001. Imported by Browning.

Price: BAR Stalker, open sights (243, 308, 270, 30-06) **$809.00**
Price: BAR Stalker, open sights (7mm, 300 Win. Mag.,
338 Win. Mag.) **$883.00**
Price: BAR Stalker, BOSS (7mm, 300 Win. Mag., 338 Win. Mag.) **$941.00**

BUSHMASTER M17S BULLPUP RIFLE

Caliber: 223, 10-shot magazine. **Barrel:** 21.5", chrome lined;1:9" twist. **Weight:** 8.2 lbs. **Length:** 30" overall. **Stock:** Fiberglass-filled nylon. **Sights:** Designed for optics—carrying handle incorporates scope mount rail for Weaver-type rings; also includes 25-meter open iron sights. **Features:** Gas-operated, short-stroke piston system; ambidextrous magazine release. Introduced 1993. Made in U.S. by Bushmaster Firearms, Inc./Quality Parts Co.
Price: **$625.00**

BUSHMASTER SHORTY XM15 E2S CARBINE

Caliber: 223,10-shot magazine. **Barrel:** 16", heavy; 1:9" twist. **Weight:** 7.2 lbs. **Length:** 34.75" overall. **Stock:** A2 type; fixed black composition. **Sights:** Fully adjustable M16A2 sight system. **Features:** Patterned after Colt M-16A2. Chrome-lined barrel with manganese phosphate finish. "Shorty" handguards. Has forged aluminum receivers with push-pin. Made in U.S. by Bushmaster Firearms Inc.
Price: **$780.00**

Bushmaster XM15 E2S Dissipator Carbine

Similar to the XM15 E2S Shorty carbine except has full-length "Dissipator" handguards. Weighs 7.6 lbs.; 34.75" overall; forged aluminum receivers with push-pin style takedown. Made in U.S. by Bushmaster Firearms, Inc.
Price **$790.00**

Calico Liberty 50

Carbon 15

Colt Match Target Lightweight

Heckler & Koch SLB 2000

Bushmaster XM15 E25 AK Shorty Carbine

Similar to the XM15 E2S Shorty except has 14.5" barrel with an AK muzzle brake permanently attached giving 16" barrel length. Weighs 7.3 lbs. Introduced 1999. Made in U.S. by Bushmaster Firearms, Inc.
Price: **$800.00**

CALICO LIBERTY 50, 100 CARBINES

Caliber: 9mm Para. **Barrel:** 16.1". **Weight:** 7 lbs. **Length:** 34.5" overall. **Stock:** Glass-filled, impact resistant polymer. **Sights:** Adjustable front post, fixed notch and aperture flip rear. **Features:** Helical feed magazine; ambidextrous, rotating sear/striker block safety; static cocking handle; retarded blowback action; aluminum alloy receiver. Introduced 1995. Made in U.S. by Calico.
Price: Liberty 50 .... **$860.00**
Price: Liberty 100 .... **$925.00**

CARBON 15 (TYPE 97) AUTO RIFLE

Caliber: 223. **Barrel:** 16". **Weight:** 3.9 lbs. **Length:** 35" overall. **Stock:** Carbon fiber butt and forend, rubberized pistol grip. **Sights:** None furnished; optics base. **Features:** Carbon fiber upper and lower receivers; stainless steel match-grade barrel; hard-chromed bolt and carrier; quick-detachable compensator. Made in U.S. by Professional Ordnance Inc.
Price: .... **$1,120.00 to $1,285.00**
Price: Type 20 (light-profile stainless barrel, compensator optional) **$1,550.00**

COLT MATCH TARGET RIFLE

Caliber: 223 Rem., 5-shot magazine. **Barrel:** 16.1" or 20". **Weight:** 7.1 to 8-1/2 lbs. **Length:** 34-1/2" to 39" overall. **Stock:** Composition stock, grip, forend. **Sights:** Post front, rear adjustable for windage and elevation. **Features:** 5-round detachable box magazine, flash suppressor, sling swivels. Forward bolt assist included. Introduced 1991. Made in U.S. by Colt's Manufacturing Co. Inc.
Price: Colt Light Rifle **$779.00**
Price: Match Target HBAR, from **$1,194.00**

DPMS PANTHER ARMS A-15 RIFLES

Caliber: 223 Rem., 7.62x39. **Barrel:** 16" to 24". **Weight:** 7-3/4 to 11-3/4 lbs. **Length:** 34-1/2 to 42-1/4" overall. **Stock:** Black Zytel® composite. **Sights:** Square front post, adjustable A2 rear. **Features:** Steel or stainless steel heavy or bull barrel; hard-coat anodized receiver; aluminum free-float tube handguard; many options. From DPMS Panther Arms.
Price: Panther Bull A-15 (20" stainless bull barrel) **$915.00**
Price: Panther Bull Twenty-Four (24" stainless bull barrel) **$945.00**
Price: Bulldog (20" stainless fluted barrel, flat top receiver) **$1,219.00**
Price: Panther Bull Sweet Sixteen (16" stainless bull barrel) **$885.00**
Price: DCM Panther (20" stainless heavy bbl., n.m. sights) **$1,099.00**
Price: Panther 7.62x39 (20" steel heavy barrel) **$849.00**

HECKLER & KOCH SLB 2000 RIFLE

Caliber: 30-06; 2-, 5- and 10-shot magazines. **Barrel:** 19.7". **Weight:** 8 lb. **Length:** 41.3". **Stock:** Oil-finished, checkered walnut. **Sights:** Ramp front, patridge rear. **Features:** Short-stroke, piston-actuated gas operation; modular steel and polymer construction; free-floating barrel; pistol grip angled for natural feel; interchangeable barrels in other calibers (available soon). Introduced 2001. From H&K.
Price: .... **NA**

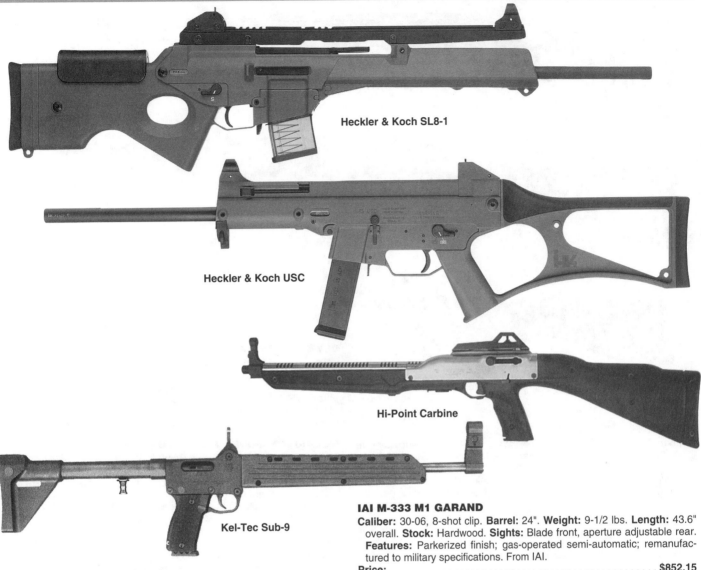

Heckler & Koch SL8-1

Heckler & Koch USC

Hi-Point Carbine

Kel-Tec Sub-9

HECKLER & KOCH SL8-1 RIFLE

Caliber: 223; 10-shot magazine. **Barrel:** 17.7". **Weight:** 8.6 lbs. **Length:** 38.6" overall. **Stock:** Polymer thumbhole. **Sights:** Blade front with integral hood; fully adjustable rear diopter. Picatinny rail. **Features:** Based on German military G36 rifle. Uses short-stroke piston-actuated gas operation; almost entirely constructed of carbon fiber-reinforced polymer. Free-floating heavy target barrel. Introduced 2000. From H&K.
Price: **$1,599.00**

HECKLER & KOCH USC CARBINE

Caliber: 45 ACP, 10-shot magazine. **Barrel:** 16". **Weight:** 8.6 lb. **Length:** 35.4" overall. **Stock:** Skeletonized polymer thumbhole. **Sights:** Blade front with integral hood, fully adjustable diopter. **Features:** Based on German UMP submachine gun. Blowback operation; almost entirely constructed of carbon fiber-reinforced polymer. Free-floating heavy target barrel. Introduced 2000. From H&K.
Price: **$1,199.00**

HI-POINT 9MM CARBINE

Caliber: 9mm Para., 40 S&W, 10-shot magazine. **Barrel:** 16-1/2" (17-1/2" for 40 S&W). **Weight:** 4-1/2 lbs. **Length:** 31-1/2" overall. **Stock:** Black polymer. **Sights:** Protected post front, aperture rear. Integral scope mount. **Features:** Grip-mounted magazine release. Black or chrome finish. Sling swivels. Introduced 1996. Made in U.S. by MKS Supply, Inc.
Price: Black or chrome, 9mm **$199.00**
Price: 40 S&W **$225.00**

IAI M-333 M1 GARAND

Caliber: 30-06, 8-shot clip. **Barrel:** 24". **Weight:** 9-1/2 lbs. **Length:** 43.6" overall. **Stock:** Hardwood. **Sights:** Blade front, aperture adjustable rear. **Features:** Parkerized finish; gas-operated semi-automatic; remanufactured to military specifications. From IAI.
Price: **$852.15**

IAI M-444 LIGHT SEMI-AUTOMATIC RIFLE

Caliber: 308. **Barrel:** 21". **Weight:** 10.4 lbs. **Length:** 40" overall. **Stock:** Synthetic. **Sights:** Blade front, rear adjustable. **Features:** Gas-operated; receiver machined from forged steel; muzzle brake; pistol grip. Imported from Imbel of Brazil by IAI.
Price: **$896.95**

IAI M-888 M1 CARBINE SEMI-AUTOMATIC RIFLE

Caliber: 30 Carbine. **Barrel:** 18". **Weight:** 5-1/2 lbs. **Length:** 35" overall. **Stock:** Walnut or birch. **Sights:** Blade front, adjustable rear. **Features:** Gas-operated; parkerized finish; manufactured to military specifications. From IAI.
Price: (birch stock, metal handguard). **$541.45**
Price: (walnut stock, metal handguard) **$572.95**
. . . . ($588.65 for wooden handguard)

KEL-TEC SUB-9 AUTO RIFLE

Caliber: 9mm Para or 40 S&W. **Barrel:** 16.1". **Weight:** 4.6 lbs. **Length:** 30" overall (extended), 15.9" (closed). **Stock:** Metal tube; grooved rubber butt pad. **Sights:** Hooded post front, flip-up rear. Interchangeable grip assemblies allow use of most double-column high capacity pistol magazines. **Features:** Barrel folds back over the butt for transport and storage. Introduced 1997. Made in U.S. by Kel-Tec CNC Industries, Inc.
Price: 9mm **$700.00**
Price: 40 S&W **$725.00**

RIFLES

Remington Model 7400

Ruger Deerfield 99/44 Carbine

Ruger PC4 Carbine

LES BAER CUSTOM ULTIMATE AR 223 RIFLES

Caliber: 223. **Barrel:** 18", 20", 22", 24". **Weight:** 7-3/4 to 9-3/4 lb. **Length:** NA. **Stock:** Black synthetic. **Sights:** None furnished; Picatinny-style flat top rail for scope mounting. **Features:** Forged receiver; Ultra single-stage trigger (Jewell two-stage trigger optional); titanium firing pin; Versa-Pod bipod; chromed National Match carrier; stainless steel, hand-lapped and cryo-treated barrel; guaranteed to shoot 1/2 or 3/4 MOA, depending on model. Made in U.S. by Les Bear Custom Inc.

Price: Super Varmint Model **$1,989.00**
Price: M4 Flattop Model **$2,195.00**
Price: IPSC Action Model **$2,195.00**

LR 300 SR LIGHT SPORT RIFLE

Caliber: 223. **Barrel:** 16-1/4"; 1:9" twist. **Weight:** 7.2 lbs. **Length:** 36" overall (extended stock), 26-1/4" (stock folded). **Stock:** Folding, tubular steel, with thumbhold-type grip. **Sights:** Trijicon post front, Trijicon rear. **Features:** Uses AR-15 type upper and lower receivers; flattop receiver with weaver base. Accepts all AR-15/M-16 magazines. Introduced 1996. Made in U.S. from Z-M Weapons.

Price: **$2,550.00**

OLYMPIC ARMS CAR-97 RIFLES

Caliber: 223, 7-shot; 9mm Para., 45 ACP, 40 S&W, 10mm, 10-shot. **Barrel:** 16". **Weight:** 7 lbs. **Length:** 34.75" overall. **Stock:** A2 stowaway grip, telescoping-look butt. **Sights:** Post front, fully adjustable aperature rear. **Features:** Based on AR-15 rifle. Post-ban version of the CAR-15. Made in U.S. by Olympic Arms, Inc.

Price: 223 . . . . **$780.00**
Price: 9mm Para., 45 ACP, 40 S&W, 10mm **$840.00**
Price: PCR Eliminator (223, full-length handguards) **$803.00**

OLYMPIC ARMS PCR-4 RIFLE

Caliber: 223, 10-shot magazine. **Barrel:** 20". **Weight:** 8 lbs., 5 oz. **Length:** 38.25" overall. **Stock:** A2 stowaway grip, trapdoor buttstock. **Sights:** Post front, A1 rear adjustable for windage. **Features:** Based on the AR-15 rifle. Barrel is button rifled with 1:9" twist. No bayonet lug. Introduced 1994. Made in U.S. by Olympic Arms, Inc.

Price: **$792.00**

OLYMPIC ARMS PCR-6 RIFLE

Caliber: 7.62x39mm (PCR-6), 10-shot magazine. **Barrel:** 16". **Weight:** 7 lbs. **Length:** 34" overall. **Stock:** A2 stowaway grip, trapdoor buttstock. **Sights:** Post front, A1 rear adjustable for windage. **Features:** Based on the CAR-15. No bayonet lug. Button-cut rifling. Introduced 1994. Made in U.S. by Olympic Arms, Inc.

Price: **$845.00**

REMINGTON MODEL 7400 AUTO RIFLE

Caliber: 243 Win., 270 Win., 280 Rem., 308 Win., 30-06, 4-shot magazine. **Barrel:** 22" round tapered. **Weight:** 7-1/2 lbs. **Length:** 42-5/8" overall. **Stock:** Walnut, deluxe cut checkered pistol grip and forend. Satin or high-gloss finish. **Sights:** Gold bead front sight on ramp; step rear sight with windage adjustable. **Features:** Redesigned and improved version of the Model 742. Positive cross-bolt safety. Receiver tapped for scope mount. Introduced 1981.

Price: About **$612.00**
Price: Carbine (18-1/2" bbl., 30-06 only) **$612.00**
Price: With black synthetic stock, matte black metal, rifle or carbine **$509.00**

ROCK RIVER ARMS STANDARD A2 RIFLE

Caliber: 45 ACP. **Barrel:** NA. **Weight:** 8.2 lbs. **Length:** NA. **Stock:** Thermoplastic. **Sights:** Standard AR-15 style sights. **Features:** Two-stage, national match trigger; optional muzzle brake. Made in U.S. From River Rock Arms.

Price: **$925.00**

RUGER DEERFIELD 99/44 CARBINE

Caliber: 44 Mag., 4-shot rotary magazine. **Barrel:** 18-1/2". **Weight:** 6-1/4 lbs. **Length:** 36-7/8" overall. **Stock:** Hardwood. **Sights:** Gold bead front, folding adjustable aperture rear. **Features:** Semi-automatic action; dual front-locking lugs lock directly into receiver; integral scope mount; push-button safety; includes 1" rings and gun lock. Introduced 2000. Made in U.S. by Sturm, Ruger & Co.

Price: **$649.00**

RUGER PC4, PC9 CARBINES

Caliber: 9mm Para., 40 cal., 10-shot magazine. **Barrel:** 16.25". **Weight:** 6 lbs., 4 oz. **Length:** 34.75" overall. **Stock:** Black DuPont (Zytel) with checkered grip and forend. **Sights:** Blade front, open adjustable rear; integral Ruger scope mounts. **Features:** Delayed blowback action; manual push-button cross bolt safety and internal firing pin block safety automatic slide lock. Introduced 1997. Made in U.S. by Sturm, Ruger & Co.

Price: PC9, PC4, (9mm, 40 cal.) **$575.00**

RIFLES

Ruger Mini 14/5R

Springfield M1A

Springfield National Match M1A

Springfield Super Match with Camo M1A

RUGER MINI-14/5 AUTOLOADING RIFLE

Caliber: 223 Rem., 5-shot detachable box magazine. **Barrel:** 18-1/2". Rifling twist 1:9". **Weight:** 6.4 lbs. **Length:** 37-1/4" overall. **Stock:** American hardwood, steel reinforced. **Sights:** Ramp front, fully adjustable rear. **Features:** Fixed piston gas-operated, positive primary extraction. New buffer system, redesigned ejector system. Ruger S100RH scope rings included.

Price: Mini-14/5R, Ranch Rifle, blued, scope rings $649.00
Price: K-Mini-14/5R, Ranch Rifle, stainless, scope rings $710.00
Price: Mini-14/5, blued, no scope rings $606.00
Price: K-Mini-14/5, stainless, no scope rings $664.00
Price: K-Mini-14/5P, stainless, synthetic stock $664.00
Price: K-Mini-14/5RP, Ranch Rifle, stainless, synthetic stock $710.00

Ruger Mini Thirty Rifle

Similar to the Mini-14 Ranch Rifle except modified to chamber the 7.62x39 Russian service round. Weight is about 6-7/8 lbs. Has 6-groove barrel with 1:10" twist, Ruger Integral Scope Mount bases and folding peep rear sight. Detachable 5-shot staggered box magazine. Blued finish. Introduced 1987.

Price: Blue, scope rings $649.00
Price: Stainless, scope rings $710.00

SPRINGFIELD, INC. M1A RIFLE

Caliber: 7.62mm NATO (308), 5- or 10-shot box magazine. **Barrel:** 25-1/16" with flash suppressor, 22" without suppressor. **Weight:** 8-3/4 lbs. **Length:** 44-1/4" overall. **Stock:** American walnut with walnut-colored heat-resistant fiberglass handguard. Matching walnut handguard available. Also available with fiberglass stock. **Sights:** Military, square blade front, full click-adjustable aperture rear. **Features:** Commercial equivalent of the U.S. M-14 service rifle with no provision for automatic firing. From Springfield, Inc.

Price: Standard M1A, black fiberglass stock $1,569.00
Price: Standard M1A, black fiberglass stock, stainless $1,629.00
Price: National Match, about $1,995.00
Price: Super Match (heavy premium barrel), about $2,449.00
Price: M21 Tactical Rifle (adj. cheekpiece), about $2,975.00

STONER SR-15 M-5 RIFLE

Caliber: 223. **Barrel:** 20". **Weight:** 7.6 lbs. **Length:** 38" overall. **Stock:** Black synthetic. **Sights:** Post front, fully adjustable rear (300-meter sight). **Features:** Modular weapon system; two-stage trigger. Black finish. Introduced 1998. Made in U.S. by Knight's Mfg.

Price: $1,595.00
Price: M-4 Carbine (16" barrel, 6.8 lbs) $1,495.00

STONER SR-25 CARBINE

Caliber: 7.62 NATO, 10-shot steel magazine. **Barrel:** 16" free-floating. **Weight:** 7-3/4 lbs. **Length:** 35.75" overall. **Stock:** Black synthetic. **Sights:** Integral Weaver-style rail. Scope rings, iron sights optional. **Features:** Shortened, non-slip handguard; removable carrying handle. Matte black finish. Introduced 1995. Made in U.S. by Knight's Mfg. Co.

Price: $2,995.00

Both classic arms and recent designs in American-style repeaters for sport and field shooting.

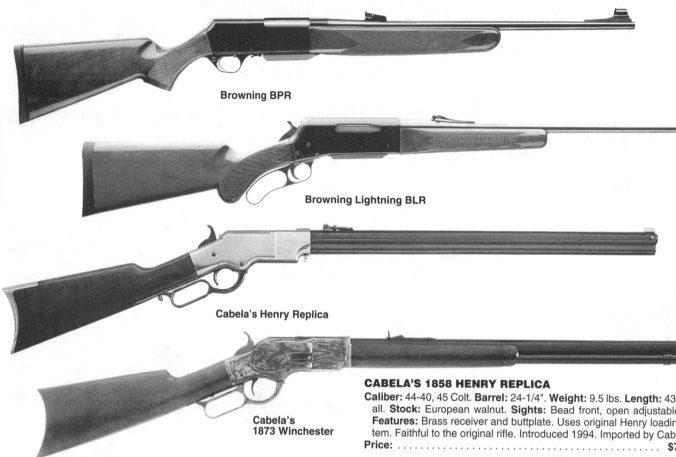

Browning BPR

Browning Lightning BLR

Cabela's Henry Replica

Cabela's 1873 Winchester

BROWNING BPR PUMP RIFLE

Caliber: 243, 308 (short action); 270, 30-06, 7mm Rem. Mag., 300 Win. Mag., 4-shot magazine (3 for magnums). **Barrel:** 22"; 24" for magnum calibers. **Weight:** 7 lbs., 3 oz. **Length:** 43" overall (22" barrel). **Stock:** Select walnut with full pistol grip, high gloss finish. **Sights:** Gold bead on hooded ramp front, open click adjustable rear. **Features:** Slide-action mechanism cams forend down away from the barrel. Seven-lug rotary bolt; cross-bolt safety behind trigger; removable magazine; alloy receiver. Introduced 1997. Imported from Belgium by Browning.

Price: Standard calibers **$718.00**
Price: Magnum calibers **$772.00**

BROWNING LIGHTNING BLR LEVER-ACTION RIFLE

Caliber: 22-250, 243, 7mm-08, 308 Win., 4-shot detachable magazine. **Barrel:** 20" round tapered. **Weight:** 6 lbs., 8 oz. **Length:** 39-1/2" overall. **Stock:** Walnut. Checkered grip and forend, high-gloss finish. **Sights:** Gold bead on ramp front; low profile square notch adjustable rear. **Features:** Wide, grooved trigger; half-cock hammer safety; fold-down hammer. Receiver tapped for scope mount. Recoil pad installed. Introduced 1996. Imported from Japan by Browning.

Price: **$649.00**

Browning Lightning BLR Long Action

Similar to the standard Lightning BLR except has long action to accept 30-06, 270, 7mm Rem. Mag. and 300 Win. Mag. Barrel lengths are 22" for 30-06 and 270, 24" for 7mm Rem. Mag. and 300 Win. Mag. Has six-lug rotary bolt; bolt and receiver are full-length fluted. Fold-down hammer at half-cock. Weighs about 7 lbs., overall length 42-7/8" (22" barrel). Introduced 1996.

Price: **$686.00**

CABELA'S 1858 HENRY REPLICA

Caliber: 44-40, 45 Colt. **Barrel:** 24-1/4". **Weight:** 9.5 lbs. **Length:** 43" overall. **Stock:** European walnut. **Sights:** Bead front, open adjustable rear. **Features:** Brass receiver and buttplate. Uses original Henry loading system. Faithful to the original rifle. Introduced 1994. Imported by Cabela's.

Price: **$749.99**

CABELA'S 1866 WINCHESTER REPLICA

Caliber: 44-40, 45 Colt. **Barrel:** 24-1/4". **Weight:** 9 lbs. **Length:** 43" overall. **Stock:** European walnut. **Sights:** Bead front, open adjustable rear. **Features:** Solid brass receiver, buttplate, forend cap. Octagonal barrel. Faithful to the original Winchester '66 rifle. Introduced 1994. Imported by Cabela's.

Price: **$619.99**

CABELA'S 1873 WINCHESTER REPLICA

Caliber: 44-40, 45 Colt. **Barrel:** 24-1/4", 30". **Weight:** 8.5 lbs. **Length:** 43-1/4" overall. **Stock:** European walnut. **Sights:** Bead front, open adjustable rear; globe front, tang rear. **Features:** Color case-hardened steel receiver. Faithful to the original Model 1873 rifle. Introduced 1994. Imported by Cabela's.

Price: Sporting model, 30" barrel, 44-40, 45 Colt **$749.99**
Price: Sporting model, 24" or 25" barrel **$729.99**

CIMARRON 1860 HENRY REPLICA

Caliber: 44 WCF, 13-shot magazine. **Barrel:** 24-1/4" (rifle), 22" (carbine). **Weight:** 9-1/2 lbs. **Length:** 43" overall (rifle). **Stock:** European walnut. **Sights:** Bead front, open adjustable rear. **Features:** Brass receiver and buttplate. Uses original Henry loading system. Faithful to the original rifle. Introduced 1991. Imported by Cimarron F.A. Co.

Price: **$1,029.00**

CIMARRON 1866 WINCHESTER REPLICAS

Caliber: 22 LR, 22 WMR, 38 Spec., 44 WCF. **Barrel:** 24-1/4" (rifle), 19" (carbine). **Weight:** 9 lbs. **Length:** 43" overall (rifle). **Stock:** European walnut. **Sights:** Bead front, open adjustable rear. **Features:** Solid brass receiver, buttplate, forend cap. Octagonal barrel. Faithful to the original Winchester '66 rifle. Introduced 1991. Imported by Cimarron F.A. Co.

Price: Rifle **$839.00**
Price: Carbine **$829.00**

Cimarron 1866 Winchester Replica

Cimarron Long Range 30"

Dixie 1873

IAR 1873
Revolver Carbine

CIMARRON 1873 SHORT RIFLE
Caliber: 22 LR, 22 WMR, 357 Mag., 44-40, 45 Colt. **Barrel:** 20" tapered octagon. **Weight:** 7.5 lbs. **Length:** 39" overall. **Stock:** Walnut. **Sights:** Bead front, adjustable semi-buckhorn rear. **Features:** Has half "button" magazine. Original-type markings, including caliber, on barrel and elevator and "Kings" patent. From Cimarron F.A. Co.
Price: **$799.00**

CIMARRON 1873 LONG RANGE RIFLE
Caliber: 22 LR, 22 WMR, 357 Mag., 38-40, 44-40, 45 Colt. **Barrel:** 30", octagonal. **Weight:** 8-1/2 lbs. **Length:** 48" overall. **Stock:** Walnut. **Sights:** Blade front, semi-buckhorn ramp rear. Tang sight optional. **Features:** Color case-hardened frame; choice of modern blue-black or charcoal blue for other parts. Barrel marked "Kings Improvement." From Cimarron F.A. Co.
Price: **$999.00**

Cimarron 1873 Sporting Rifle
Similar to the 1873 Long Range except has 24" barrel with half-magazine.
Price: **$949.00**
Price: 1873 Saddle Ring Carbine, 19" barrel **$949.00**

DIXIE ENGRAVED 1873 RIFLE
Caliber: 44-40, 11-shot magazine. **Barrel:** 20", round. **Weight:** 7-3/4 lbs. **Length:** 39" overall. **Stock:** Walnut. **Sights:** Blade front, adjustable rear. **Features:** Engraved and case-hardened frame. Duplicate of Winchester 1873. Made in Italy. From 21 Gun Works.
Price: **$1,295.00**
Price: Plain, blued carbine **$850.00**

E.M.F. 1860 HENRY RIFLE
Caliber: 44-40 or 45 Colt. **Barrel:** 24.25". **Weight:** About 9 lbs. **Length:** About 43.75" overall. **Stock:** Oil-stained American walnut. **Sights:** Blade front, rear adjustable for elevation. **Features:** Reproduction of the original Henry rifle with brass frame and buttplate, rest blued. From E.M.F.
Price: Brass frame **$850.00**
Price: Steel frame **$950.00**

E.M.F. 1866 YELLOWBOY LEVER ACTIONS
Caliber: 38 Spec., 44-40. **Barrel:** 19" (carbine), 24" (rifle). **Weight:** 9 lbs. **Length:** 43" overall (rifle). **Stock:** European walnut. **Sights:** Bead front, open adjustable rear. **Features:** Solid brass frame, blued barrel, lever, hammer, buttplate. Imported from Italy by E.M.F.

Price: Rifle **$690.00**
Price: Carbine. **$675.00**

E.M.F. HARTFORD MODEL 1892 LEVER-ACTION RIFLE
Caliber: 45 Colt. **Barrel:** 24", octagonal. **Weight:** 7-1/2 lbs. **Length:** 43" overall. **Stock:** European walnut. **Sights:** Blade front, open adjustable rear. **Features:** Color case-hardened frame, lever, trigger and hammer with blued barrel, or overall blue finish. Introduced 1998. Imported by E.M.F.
Price: Standard. **$590.00**

E.M.F. MODEL 1873 LEVER-ACTION RIFLE
Caliber: 32/20, 357 Mag., 38/40, 44-40, 44 Spec., 45 Colt. **Barrel:** 24". **Weight:** 8 lbs. **Length:** 43-1/4" overall. **Stock:** European walnut. **Sights:** Bead front, rear adjustable for windage and elevation. **Features:** Color case-hardened frame (blue on carbine). Imported by E.M.F.
Price: Rifle **$865.00**
Price: Carbine, 19" barrel **$865.00**

IAR MODEL 1873 REVOLVER CARBINE
Caliber: 357 Mag., 45 Colt. **Barrel:** 18". **Weight:** 4 lbs., 8 oz. **Length:** 34" overall. **Stock:** One-piece walnut. **Sights:** Blade front, notch rear. **Features:** Color case-hardened frame, blue barrel, backstrap and trigger-guard. Introduced 1998. Imported from Italy by IAR, Inc.
Price: Standard. **$490.00**

MARLIN MODEL 336C LEVER-ACTION CARBINE
Caliber: 30-30 or 35 Rem., 6-shot tubular magazine. **Barrel:** 20" Micro-Groove®. **Weight:** 7 lbs. **Length:** 38-1/2" overall. **Stock:** Checkered American black walnut, capped pistol grip with white line spacers. Mar-Shield® finish; rubber butt pad; swivel studs. **Sights:** Ramp front with Wide-Scan hood, semi-buckhorn folding rear adjustable for windage and elevation. **Features:** Hammer-block safety. Receiver tapped for scope mount, offset hammer spur; top of receiver sandblasted to prevent glare. Includes safety lock.
Price: **$502.00**

CENTERFIRE RIFLES — LEVER AND SLIDE

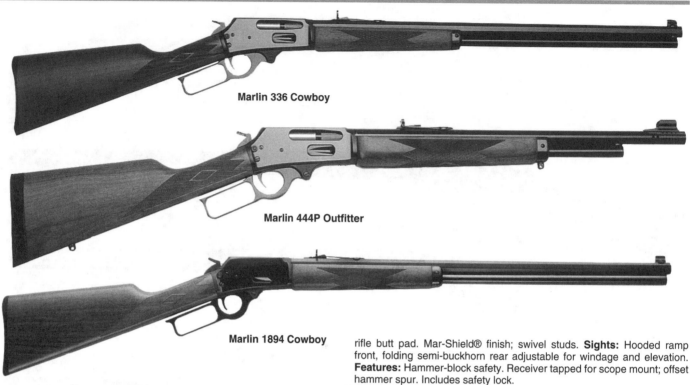

Marlin 336 Cowboy

Marlin 444P Outfitter

Marlin 1894 Cowboy

Marlin Model 336 Cowboy

Similar to the Model 336CS except chambered for 30-30 and 38-55 Win., 24" tapered octagon barrel with deep-cut Ballard-type rifling; straight-grip walnut stock with hard rubber buttplate; blued steel forend cap; weighs 7-1/2 lbs.; 42-1/2" overall. Introduced 1999. Includes safety lock. Made in U.S. by Marlin.

Price: **$697.00**

Marlin Model 336A Lever-Action Carbine

Same as the Marlin 336CS except has cut-checkered, walnut-finished Maine birch pistol grip stock with swivel studs, 30-30 only, 6-shot. Hammer-block safety. Adjustable rear sight, brass bead front. Includes safety lock.

Price: **$429.00**
Price: With 4x scope and mount. **$474.00**

Marlin Model 336CC Lever-Action Carbine

Same as the Marlin 336A except has Mossy Oak® Break-Up camouflage stock and forearm. 30-30 only, 6-shot; receiver tapped for scope mount or receiver sight. Introduced 2001. Includes safety lock. Made in U.S. by Marlin.

Price: **$478.00**

Marlin Model 336SS Lever-Action Carbine

Same as the 336C except receiver, barrel and other major parts are machined from stainless steel. 30-30 only, 6-shot; receiver tapped for scope. Includes safety lock.

Price: **$608.00**

Marlin Model 336W Lever-Action Rifle

Similar to the Model 336CS except has walnut-finished, cut-checkered Maine birch stock; blued steel barrel band has integral sling swivel; no front sight hood; comes with padded nylon sling; hard rubber butt plate. Introduced 1998. Includes safety lock. Made in U.S. by Marlin.

Price: **$434.00**
Price: With 4x scope and mount. **$481.00**

MARLIN MODEL 444 LEVER-ACTION SPORTER

Caliber: 444 Marlin, 5-shot tubular magazine. **Barrel:** 22" deep cut Ballard rifling. **Weight:** 7-1/2 lbs. **Length:** 40-1/2" overall. **Stock:** Checkered American black walnut, capped pistol grip with white line spacers, rubber

rifle butt pad. Mar-Shield® finish; swivel studs. **Sights:** Hooded ramp front, folding semi-buckhorn rear adjustable for windage and elevation. **Features:** Hammer-block safety. Receiver tapped for scope mount; offset hammer spur. Includes safety lock.

Price: **$599.00**

Marlin Model 444P Outfitter Lever-Action

Similar to the 444SS except has a ported 18-1/2" barrel with deep-cut Ballard-type rifling; weighs 6-3/4 lbs.; overall length 37". Available only in 444 Marlin. Introduced 1999. Includes safety lock. Made in U.S. by Marlin.

Price: **$612.00**

MARLIN MODEL 1894 LEVER-ACTION CARBINE

Caliber: 44 Spec./44 Mag., 10-shot tubular magazine. **Barrel:** 20" Ballard-type rifling. **Weight:** 6 lbs. **Length:** 37-1/2" overall. **Stock:** Checkered American black walnut, straight grip and forend. Mar-Shield® finish. Rubber rifle butt pad; swivel studs. **Sights:** Wide-Scan hooded ramp front, semi-buckhorn folding rear adjustable for windage and elevation. **Features:** Hammer-block safety. Receiver tapped for scope mount, offset hammer spur, solid top receiver sand blasted to prevent glare. Includes safety lock.

Price: **$526.00**

Marlin Model 1894C Carbine

Similar to the standard Model 1894S except chambered for 38 Spec./357 Mag. with full-length 9-shot magazine, 18-1/2" barrel, hammer-block safety, hooded front sight. Introduced 1983. Includes safety lock.

Price: **$526.00**

Marlin Model 1894P/1894CP Carbine

Similar to the Model 1894 except has ported 16-1/4" barrel with 8-shot magazine. Overal length 33-1/4", weighs 5-3/4 lbs. Includes safety lock. Made in U.S. by Marlin.

Price: Model 1894P (44 Spec./44 Mag.) **$546.00**
New! **Price:** Model 1894CP (38 Spec./357 Mag.). **$546.00**

MARLIN MODEL 1894 COWBOY, COWBOY II

Caliber: 357 Mag., 44 Mag., 45 Colt, 10-shot magazine. **Barrel:** 24" tapered octagon, deep cut rifling. **Weight:** 7-1/2 lbs. **Length:** 41-1/2" overall. **Stock:** Straight grip American black walnut with cut checkering, hard rubber buttplate, Mar-Shield® finish. **Sights:** Marble carbine front, adjustable Marble semi-buckhorn rear. **Features:** Squared finger lever; straight grip stock; blued steel forend tip. Designed for Cowboy Shooting events. Introduced 1996. Includes safety lock. Made in U.S. by Marlin.

Price: Cowboy I, 45 Colt. **$775.00**
Price: Cowboy II, 357 Mag., 44 Mag.. . . . . **$775.00**

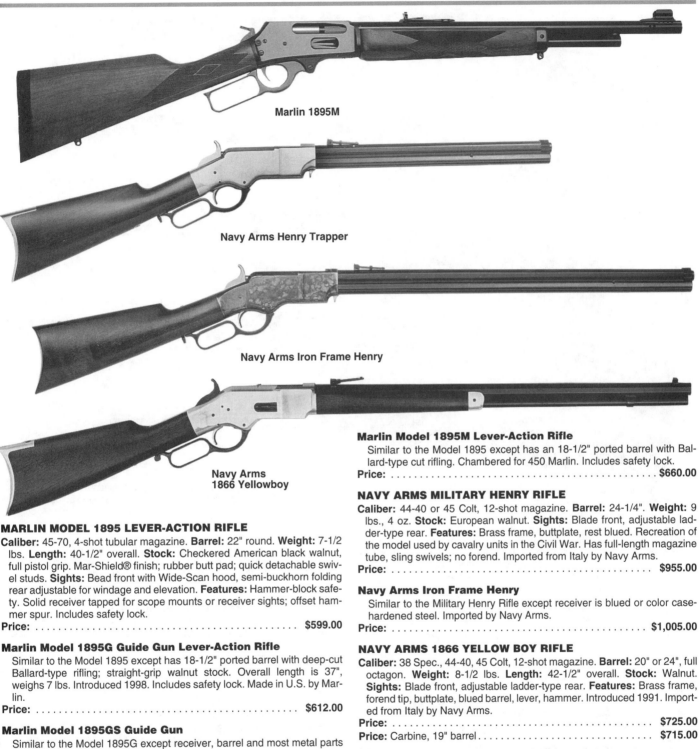

Marlin 1895M

Navy Arms Henry Trapper

Navy Arms Iron Frame Henry

Navy Arms 1866 Yellowboy

MARLIN MODEL 1895 LEVER-ACTION RIFLE

Caliber: 45-70, 4-shot tubular magazine. **Barrel:** 22" round. **Weight:** 7-1/2 lbs. **Length:** 40-1/2" overall. **Stock:** Checkered American black walnut, full pistol grip. Mar-Shield® finish; rubber butt pad; quick detachable swivel studs. **Sights:** Bead front with Wide-Scan hood, semi-buckhorn folding rear adjustable for windage and elevation. **Features:** Hammer-block safety. Solid receiver tapped for scope mounts or receiver sights; offset hammer spur. Includes safety lock.
Price: **$599.00**

Marlin Model 1895G Guide Gun Lever-Action Rifle

Similar to the Model 1895 except has 18-1/2" ported barrel with deep-cut Ballard-type rifling; straight-grip walnut stock. Overall length is 37", weighs 7 lbs. Introduced 1998. Includes safety lock. Made in U.S. by Marlin.
Price: **$612.00**

Marlin Model 1895GS Guide Gun

Similar to the Model 1895G except receiver, barrel and most metal parts are machined from stainless steel. Chambered for 45-70, 4-shot, 18-1/2" ported barrel. Overall length is 37", weighs 7 lbs. Introduced 2001. Includes safety lock. Made in U.S. by Marlin.
Price: **$719.00**

Marlin Model 1895 Cowboy Lever-Action Rifle

Similar to the Model 1895 except has 26" tapered octagon barrel with Ballard-type rifling, Marble carbine front sight and Marble adjustable semi-buckhorn rear sight. Receiver tapped for scope or receiver sight. Overall length is 44-1/2", weighs about 8 lbs. Introduced 2001. Includes safety lock. Made in U.S. by Marlin.
Price: **$775.00**

Marlin Model 1895M Lever-Action Rifle

Similar to the Model 1895 except has an 18-1/2" ported barrel with Ballard-type cut rifling. Chambered for 450 Marlin. Includes safety lock.
Price: **$660.00**

NAVY ARMS MILITARY HENRY RIFLE

Caliber: 44-40 or 45 Colt, 12-shot magazine. **Barrel:** 24-1/4". **Weight:** 9 lbs., 4 oz. **Stock:** European walnut. **Sights:** Blade front, adjustable ladder-type rear. **Features:** Brass frame, buttplate, rest blued. Recreation of the model used by cavalry units in the Civil War. Has full-length magazine tube, sling swivels; no forend. Imported from Italy by Navy Arms.
Price: **$955.00**

Navy Arms Iron Frame Henry

Similar to the Military Henry Rifle except receiver is blued or color case-hardened steel. Imported by Navy Arms.
Price: **$1,005.00**

NAVY ARMS 1866 YELLOW BOY RIFLE

Caliber: 38 Spec., 44-40, 45 Colt, 12-shot magazine. **Barrel:** 20" or 24", full octagon. **Weight:** 8-1/2 lbs. **Length:** 42-1/2" overall. **Stock:** Walnut. **Sights:** Blade front, adjustable ladder-type rear. **Features:** Brass frame, forend tip, buttplate, blued barrel, lever, hammer. Introduced 1991. Imported from Italy by Navy Arms.
Price: **$725.00**
Price: Carbine, 19" barrel **$715.00**

NAVY ARMS 1873 WINCHESTER-STYLE RIFLE

Caliber: 357 Mag., 44-40, 45 Colt, 12-shot magazine. **Barrel:** 24-1/4". **Weight:** 8-1/4 lbs. **Length:** 43" overall. **Stock:** European walnut. **Sights:** Blade front, buckhorn rear. **Features:** Color case-hardened frame, rest blued. Full-octagon barrel. Imported by Navy Arms.
Price: **$875.00**
Price: 1873 Carbine, 19" barrel **$800.00**
Price: 1873 Sporting Rifle (full oct. bbl., checkered walnut stock and forend) **$995.00**
Price: 1873 Border Model, 20" octagon barrel **$875.00**
Price: 1873 Deluxe Border Model **$995.00**

RIFLES

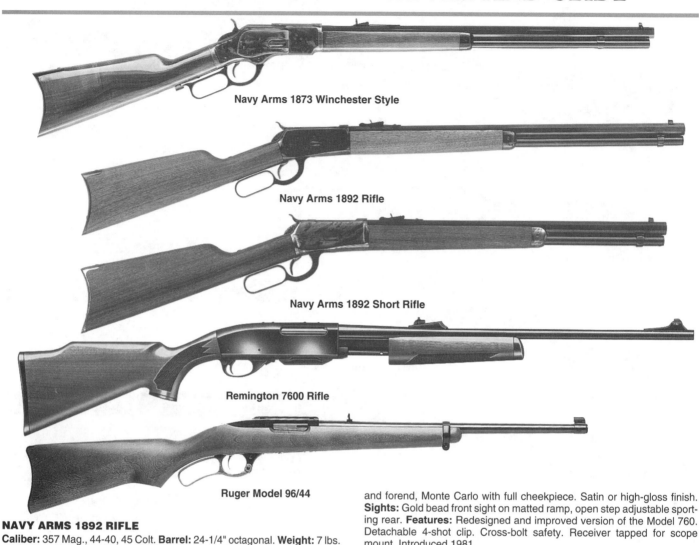

Navy Arms 1873 Winchester Style

Navy Arms 1892 Rifle

Navy Arms 1892 Short Rifle

Remington 7600 Rifle

Ruger Model 96/44

NAVY ARMS 1892 RIFLE

Caliber: 357 Mag., 44-40, 45 Colt. **Barrel:** 24-1/4" octagonal. **Weight:** 7 lbs. **Length:** 42" overall. **Stock:** American walnut. **Sights:** Blade front, semi-buckhorn rear. **Features:** Replica of Winchester's early Model 1892 with octagonal barrel, forend cap and crescent buttplate. Blued or color case-hardened receiver. Introduced 1998. Imported by Navy Arms.
Price: **$525.00**

Navy Arms 1892 Stainless Carbine

Similar to the 1892 Rifle except stainless steel, has 20" round barrel, weighs 5-3/4 lbs., and is 37-1/2" overall. Introduced 1998. Imported by Navy Arms.
Price: **$500.00**

Navy Arms 1892 Short Rifle

Similar to the 1892 Rifle except has 20" octagonal barrel, weighs 6-1/4 lbs., and is 37-3/4" overall. Replica of the rare, special order 1892 Winchester nicknamed the "Texas Special." Blued or color case-hardened receiver and furniture. Introduced 1998. Imported by Navy Arms.
Price: **$525.00**
Price: (stainless steel, 20" octagon barrel) **$565.00**

NAVY ARMS 1892 STAINLESS RIFLE

Caliber: 357 Mag., 44-40, 45 Colt. **Barrel:** 24-1/4" octagonal. **Weight:** 7 lbs. **Length:** 42". **Stock:** American walnut. **Sights:** Brass bead front, semi-buckhorn rear. **Features:** Designed for the Cowboy Action Shooter. Stainless steel barrel, receiver and furniture. Introduced 2000. Imported by Navy Arms.
Price: **$565.00**

REMINGTON MODEL 7600 PUMP ACTION

Caliber: 243, 270, 280, 30-06, 308. **Barrel:** 22" round tapered. **Weight:** 7-1/2 lbs. **Length:** 42-5/8" overall. **Stock:** Cut-checkered walnut pistol grip and forend, Monte Carlo with full cheekpiece. Satin or high-gloss finish. **Sights:** Gold bead front sight on matted ramp, open step adjustable sporting rear. **Features:** Redesigned and improved version of the Model 760. Detachable 4-shot clip. Cross-bolt safety. Receiver tapped for scope mount. Introduced 1981.
Price: **$576.00**
Price: Carbine (18-1/2" bbl., 30-06 only) **$576.00**
Price: With black synthetic stock, matte black metal, rifle or carbine **$473.00**

RUGER MODEL 96/44 LEVER-ACTION RIFLE

Caliber: 44 Mag., 4-shot rotary magazine. **Barrel:** 18-1/2". **Weight:** 5-7/8 lbs. **Length:** 37-5/16" overall. **Stock:** American hardwood. **Sights:** Gold bead front, folding leaf rear. **Features:** Solid chrome-moly steel receiver. Manual cross-bolt safety, visible cocking indicator; short-throw lever action; integral scope mount; blued finish; color case-hardened lever. Introduced 1996. Made In U.S. by Sturm, Ruger & Co.
Price: 96/44M, 44 Mag **$499.00**

TRADITIONS 1860 HENRY RIFLES

Caliber: 45 Colt. **Barrel:** 24-1/4" octagonal; 1:16" twist. **Weight:** 9.26 lbs. **Length:** 43-3/4" overall. **Stock:** Walnut. **Sights:** Blade front, adjustable folding rear. **Features:** Steel color-case hardened or brass receiver; 13-shot magazine. Introduced 2001. Imported from Uberti by Traditions.
Price: (steel color-case hardened receiver) **$869.00**
Price: (brass receiver) **$819.00**

TRADITIONS 1866 SPORTING YELLOWBOY RIFLES

Caliber: 45 Colt. **Barrel:** 24-1/4" octagonal; 1:16" twist. **Weight:** 8.16 lbs. **Length:** 43-3/4"overall. **Stock:** Walnut. **Sights:** Blade front, adjustable folding rear. **Features:** Brass receiver; blued or white barrel; 13-shot magazine. Introduced 2001. Imported from Uberti by Traditions.
Price: (blued barrel) **$669.00**
Price: (white barrel) **$749.00**

Winchester Model 94 Big Bore

Winchester 94 Traditional

Winchester Model 94 Trapper

TRADITIONS 1866 YELLOWBOY CARBINE

Similar to 1866 Sporting Yellowboy, except has 19" round, blued barrel with adjustable rear sight, 10-shot magazine. Weighs 7.35 lbs.; overall length 38-1/4". Introduced 2001. Imported from Uberti by Traditions.
Price: **$669.00**

TRADITIONS 1873 SPORTING RIFLES

Caliber: 45 Colt. **Barrel:** 24-1/4" octagonal; 1:16" twist. **Weight:** 8.16 lbs. **Length:** 43-3/4" overall. **Stock:** Walnut. **Sights:** Blade front, adjustable rear. **Features:** Blued barrel with color-case hardened receiver or white barrel and receiver; 13-shot magazine. Introduced 2001. Imported from Uberti by Traditions.
Price: (color-case hardened receiver and blued barrel) **$819.00**
Price: (white receiver and barrel) **$899.00**
Price: (Deluxe Sporting Rifle with checkered, high-grade walnut stock; adj. folding rear sight) **$969.00**

TRADITIONS 1873 SPORTING CARBINE

Similar to 1873 Sporting Rifle, except has 19" round, blued barrel with adjustable rear sight, 10-shot magazine. Weighs 7.38 lbs. Overall length 38-1/4". Introduced 2001. Imported from Uberti by Traditions.
Price: **$819.00**

TRISTAR/UBERTI 1873 SPORTING RIFLE

Caliber: 44-40, 45 Colt. **Barrel:** 24-1/4", 30", octagonal. **Weight:** 8.1 lbs. **Length:** 43-1/4" overall. **Stock:** Walnut. **Sights:** Blade front adjustable for windage, open rear adjustable for elevation. **Features:** Color case-hardened frame, blued barrel, hammer, lever, buttplate, brass elevator. Imported from Italy by Tristar Sporting Arms Ltd.
Price: 24-1/4" barrel **$919.00**
Price: 30" barrel **$964.00**

TRISTAR/UBERTI 1866 SPORTING RIFLE, CARBINE

Caliber: 22 LR, 22 WMR, 38 Spec., 44-40, 45 Colt. **Barrel:** 24-1/4", octagonal. **Weight:** 8.1 lbs. **Length:** 43-1/4" overall. **Stock:** Walnut. **Sights:** Blade front adjustable for windage, rear adjustable for elevation. **Features:** Frame, buttplate, forend cap of polished brass, balance charcoal blued. Imported by Tristar Sporting Arms Ltd.
Price: **$775.00**
Price: Yellowboy Carbine (19" round bbl.) **$735.00**

TRISTAR/UBERTI 1860 HENRY RIFLE

Caliber: 44-40, 45 Colt. **Barrel:** 24-1/4", half-octagon. **Weight:** 9.2 lbs. **Length:** 43-3/4" overall. **Stock:** American walnut. **Sights:** Blade front, rear adjustable for elevation. **Features:** Frame, elevator, magazine follower, buttplate are brass, balance blue. Imported by Tristar Sporting Arms Ltd. Arms, Inc.

Price: **$982.00**
Price: 1860 Henry White (polished steel finish) **$1,040.00**

TRISTAR/UBERTI 1860 HENRY TRAPPER CARBINE

Similar to the 1860 Henry Rifle except has 18-1/2" barrel, measures 37-3/4" overall, and weighs 8 lbs. Introduced 1999. Imported from Italy by Tristar Sporting Arms Ltd.
Price: Brass frame, blued barrel **$982.00**
Price: Henry Trapper White (brass frame, polished steel barrel) **$1,040.00**

VEKTOR H5 SLIDE-ACTION RIFLE

Caliber: 223 Rem., 5-shot magazine. **Barrel:** 18", 22". **Weight:** 9 lbs., 15 oz. **Length:** 42-1/2" overall (22" barrel). **Stock:** Walnut thumbhole. **Sights:** Comes with 1" 4x32 scope with low-light reticle. **Features:** Rotating bolt mechanism. Matte black finish. Introduced 1999. Imported from South Africa by Vektor USA.
Price: **$849.95**

WINCHESTER MODEL 94 TRADITIONAL BIG BORE

Caliber: 444 Marlin, 6-shot magazine. **Barrel:** 20". **Weight:** 6-1/2 lbs. **Length:** 38-5/8" overall. **Stock:** American walnut. Satin finish. **Sights:** Hooded ramp front, semi-buckhorn rear adjustable for windage and elevation. **Features:** All external metal parts have Winchester's deep blue finish. Rifling twist 1:12". Rubber recoil pad fitted to buttstock. Introduced 1983. From U.S. Repeating Arms Co., Inc.
Price: **$465.00**

Winchester Timber Carbine

Similar to the Model 94 Big Bore. Chambered for 444 Marlin; 18" barrel is ported; half-pistol grip stock with butt pad; checkered grip and forend. Introduced 1999. Made in U.S. by U.S. Repeating Arms Co., Inc.
Price: **$573.00**

WINCHESTER MODEL 94 TRADITIONAL-CW

Caliber: 30-30 Win., 6-shot; 44 Mag., 11-shot tubular magazine. **Barrel:** 20". **Weight:** 6-1/2 lbs. **Length:** 37-3/4" overall. **Stock:** Straight grip checkered walnut stock and forend. **Sights:** Hooded blade front, semi-buckhorn rear. Drilled and tapped for scope mount. Post front sight on Trapper model. **Features:** Solid frame, forged steel receiver; side ejection, exposed rebounding hammer with automatic trigger-activated transfer bar. Introduced 1984.
Price: 30-30 . . . . **$440.00**
Price: 44 Mag. **$463.00**
Price: Traditional (no checkering, 30-30 only) **$407.00**

Winchester Model 94 Trapper™

Similar to Model 94 Traditional except has 16" barrel, 5-shot magazine in 30-30, 9-shot in 357 Mag., 44 Magnum/44 Special, 45 Colt. Has stainless steel claw extractor, saddle ring, hammer spur extension, smooth walnut wood.
Price: 30-30 . . . . **$407.00**
Price: 44 Mag., 357 Mag., 45 Colt **$431.00**

Winchester Model 94 Trails End

Winchester Model 94 Legacy

Winchester Model 1895

Winchester Model 1886

Winchester Model 94 Trails End™

Similar to the Model 94 Walnut except chambered only for 357 Mag., 44-40, 44 Mag., 45 Colt; 11-shot magazine. Available with standard lever loop. Introduced 1997. From U.S. Repeating Arms Co., Inc.

Price: With standard lever loop. **$445.00**

Winchester Model 94 Legacy

Similar to the Model 94 Traditional-CW except has half-pistol grip walnut stock, checkered grip and forend. Chambered for 30-30, 357 Mag., 44 Mag., 45 Colt; 24" barrel. Introduced 1995. Made in U.S. by U.S. Repeating Arms Co., Inc.

Price: With 24" barrel **$457.00**

Winchester Model 94 Ranger

Similar to the Model 94 Traditional except has a hardwood stock, post-style front sight and hammer-spur extension.

Price: (20" barrel) **$355.00**

Winchester Model 94 Ranger Compact

Similar to the Model 94 Ranger except has 16" barrel and 12-1/2" length of pull, rubber recoil pad, post front sight. Introduced 1998. Made in U.S. by U.S. Repeating Arms Co., Inc.

Price: 357 Mag. **$378.00**
Price: 30-30 . . . . **$355.00**

WINCHESTER MODEL 1895 LEVER-ACTION RIFLE

Caliber: 405 Win, 4-shot magazine. **Barrel:** 24", round. **Weight:** 8 lbs. **Length:** 42" overall. **Stock:** American walnut. **Sights:** Gold bead front, buckhorn rear adjustable for elevation. **Features:** Recreation of the original Model 1895. Polished blue finish with Nimschke-style scroll engraving on receiver. Scalloped receiver, two-piece cocking lever, Schnabel forend, straight-grip stock. Introduced 1995. From U.S. Repeating Arms Co., Inc.

Price: Grade I. **$1,045.00**
Price: High Grade **$1,532.00**

WINCHESTER MODEL 1886 EXTRA LIGHT LEVER-ACTION RIFLE

Caliber: 45-70, 4-shot magazine. **Barrel:** 22", round tapered. **Weight:** 7-1/4 lbs. **Length:** 40-1/2" overall. **Stock:** Smooth walnut. **Sights:** Bead front, ramp-adjustable buckhorn-style rear. **Features:** Recreation of the Model 1886. Polished blue finish; crescent metal butt plate; metal forend cap; pistol grip stock. Reintroduced 1998. From U.S. Repeating Arms Co., Inc.

Price: Grade I **$1,152.00**
Price: High Grade **$1,440.00**

Includes models for a wide variety of sporting and competitive purposes and uses.

Anschutz 1733D

Arnold Arms Alaskan

Arnold Arms Safari

ANSCHUTZ 1743D BOLT-ACTION RIFLE

Caliber: 222 Rem., 3-shot magazine. **Barrel:** 19.7". **Weight:** 6.4 lbs. **Length:** 39" overall. **Stock:** European walnut. **Sights:** Hooded blade front, folding leaf rear. **Features:** Receiver grooved for scope mounting; single stage trigger; claw extractor; sling safety; sling swivels. Imported from Germany by AcuSport Corp.

Price: **$1,588.95**

ANSCHUTZ 1740 MONTE CARLO RIFLE

Caliber: 22 Hornet, 5-shot clip; 222 Rem., 3-shot clip. **Barrel:** 24". **Weight:** 6-1/2 lbs. **Length:** 43.25" overall. **Sights:** Hooded ramp front, folding leaf rear; drilled and tapped for scope mounting. **Features:** Uses match 54 action. Adjustable single stage trigger. Stock has roll-over Monte Carlo cheekpiece, slim forend with Schnabel tip, Wundhammer palm swell on grip, rosewood gripcap with white diamond insert. Skip-line checkering on grip and forend. Introduced 1997. Imported from Germany by AcuSport Corp.

Price: From **$1,439.00**
Price: Model 1730 Monte Carlo, as above except in
22 Hornet **$1,439.00**

Anschutz 1733D Rifle

Similar to the 1740 Monte Carlo except has full-length, walnut, Mannlicher-style stock with skip-line checkering, rosewood Schnabel tip, and is chambered for 22 Hornet. Weighs 6.4 lbs., overall length 39", barrel length 19.7". Imported from Germany by AcuSport Corp.

Price: **$1,588.95**

ARNOLD ARMS ALASKAN RIFLE

Caliber: 243 to 338 Magnum. **Barrel:** 22" to 26". **Weight:** NA. **Length:** NA. **Stock:** Synthetic; black, woodland or arctic camouflage. **Sights:** Optional; drilled and tapped for scope mounting. **Features:** Uses Apollo, Remington or Winchester action with controlled round feed or push feed; chrome-moly steel or stainless; one-piece bolt, handle, knob; cone head bolt and breech; three-position safety; fully adjustable trigger. Introduced 1996. Made in U.S. by Arnold Arms Co.

Price: From **$2,695.00**

Arnold Arms Alaskan Guide Rifle

Similar to the Alaskan rifle except chambered for 257 to 338 Magnum; choice of A-grade English walnut or synthetic stock; three-position safety; scope mount only. Introduced 1996. Made in U.S. by Arnold Arms Co.

Price: From **$3,249.00**

Arnold Arms Grand Alaskan Rifle

Similar to the Alaskan rifle except has AAA fancy select or exhibition-grade English walnut; barrel band swivel; comes with iron sights and scope mount; 24" to 26" barrel; 300 Magnum to 458 Win. Mag. Introduced 1996. Made in U.S. by Arnold Arms Co.

Price: From **$7,570.00**

Arnold Arms Alaskan Trophy Rifle

Similar to the Alaskan rifle except chambered for 300 Magnum to 458 Win. Mag.; 24" to 26" barrel; black synthetic or laminated stock; comes with barrel band on 375 H&H and larger; scope mount; iron sights. Introduced 1996. Made in U.S. by Arnold Arms Co.

Price: From **$3,249.00**

ARNOLD ARMS SAFARI RIFLE

Caliber: 243 to 458 Win. Mag. **Barrel:** 22" to 26". **Weight:** NA. **Length:** NA. **Stock:** Grade A and AA Fancy English walnut. **Sights:** Optional; drilled and tapped for scope mounting. **Features:** Uses Apollo, Remington or Winchester action with controlled or push round feed; one-piece bolt, handle, knob; cone head bolt and breech; three-position safety; fully adjustable trigger; chrome-moly steel in matte blue, polished, or bead blasted stainless. Introduced 1996. Made in U.S. by Arnold Arms Co.

Price: From **$6,495.00**

Arnold Arms African Trophy Rifle

Similar to the Safari rifle except has AAA Extra Fancy English walnut stock with wrap-around checkering; matte blue chrome-moly or polished or bead blasted stainless steel; scope mount standard or optional Express sights. Introduced 1996. Made in U.S. by Arnold Arms Co.

Price: Blued chrome-moly steel **$6,921.00**
Price: Stainless steel **$6,971.00**

Arnold Arms Grand African Rifle

Similar to the Safari rifle except has Exhibition Grade stock; polished blue chrome-moly steel or bead-blasted or Teflon-coated stainless; barrel band; scope mount, express sights; calibers 338 Magnum to 458 Win. Mag.; 24" to 26" barrel. Introduced 1996. Made in U.S. by Arnold Arms Co.

Price: Chrome-moly steel **$8,172.00**
Price: Stainless steel **$8,022.00**

Beretta Mato Deluxe

Barrett Model 95

Beretta Mato Synthetic

Blaser R93 Classic

BARRETT MODEL 95 BOLT-ACTION RIFLE

Caliber: 50 BMG, 5-shot magazine. **Barrel:** 29". **Weight:** 22 lbs. **Length:** 45" overall. **Stock:** Energy-absorbing recoil pad. **Sights:** Scope optional. **Features:** Bolt-action, bullpup design. Disassembles without tools; extendable bipod legs; match-grade barrel; high efficiency muzzle brake. Introduced 1995. Made in U.S. by Barrett Firearms Mfg., Inc.
Price: From **$4,950.00**

BERETTA MATO DELUXE BOLT-ACTION RIFLE

Caliber: 270, 280 Rem., 30-06, 7mm Rem. Mag., 300 Win. Mag., 338 Win. Mag., 375 H&H. **Barrel:** 23.6". **Weight:** 7.9 lbs. **Length:** 44.5" overall. **Stock:** XXX claro walnut with ebony forend tip, hand-rubbed oil finish. **Sights:** Bead on ramp front, open fully adjustable rear; drilled and tapped for scope mounting. **Features:** Mauser-style action with claw extractor; three-position safety; removable box magazine; 375 H&H has muzzle brake. Introduced 1998. From Beretta U.S.A.
Price: **$2,470.00**
Price: 375 H&H. **$2,795.00**

Beretta Mato Synthetic Bolt-Action Rifle

Similar to the Mato except has fiberglass/Kevlar/carbon fiber stock in classic American style with shadow line cheekpiece, aluminum bedding block and checkering. Introduced 1998. From Beretta U.S.A.
Price: **$1,117.00**
Price: 375 H&H. **$1,474.00**

BLASER R93 BOLT-ACTION RIFLE

Caliber: 22-250, 243, 6.5x55, 270, 7x57, 7mm-08, 308, 30-06, 257 Wea. Mag., 7mm Rem. Mag., 300 Win. Mag., 300 Wea. Mag., 338 Win Mag., 375 H&H, 416 Rem. Mag. **Barrel:** 22" (standard calibers), 26" (magnum). **Weight:** 7 lbs. **Length:** 40" overall (22" barrel). **Stock:** Two-piece European walnut. **Sights:** None furnished; drilled and tapped for scope mounting. **Features:** Straight pull-back bolt action with thumb-activated safety slide/cocking mechanism; interchangeable barrels and bolt heads. Introduced 1994. Imported from Germany by SIGARMS.
Price: R93 Classic **$3,680.00**
Price: R93 LX **$1,895.00**
Price: R93 Synthetic (black synthetic stock) **$1,595.00**
Price: R93 Safari Synthetic (416 Rem. Mag. only) **$1,855.00**
Price: R93 Grand Lux **$4,915.00**
Price: R93 Attaché **$5,390.00**

BRNO 98 BOLT-ACTION RIFLE

Caliber: 7x64, 243, 270, 308, 30-06, 300 Win. Mag., 9.3x62. **Barrrel:** 23.6". **Weight:** 7.2 lbs. **Length:** 40.9" overall. **Stock:** European walnut. **Sights:** Blade on ramp front, open adjustable rear. **Features:** Uses Mauser 98-type action; polished blue. Announced 1998. Imported from the Czech Republic by Euro-Imports.
Price: Standard calibers **$507.00**
Price: Magnum calibers **$547.00**
Price: With set trigger, standard calibers **$615.00**
Price: As above, magnum calibers. **$655.00**
Price: With full stock, set trigger, standard calibers **$703.00**
Price: As above, magnum calibers. **$743.00**

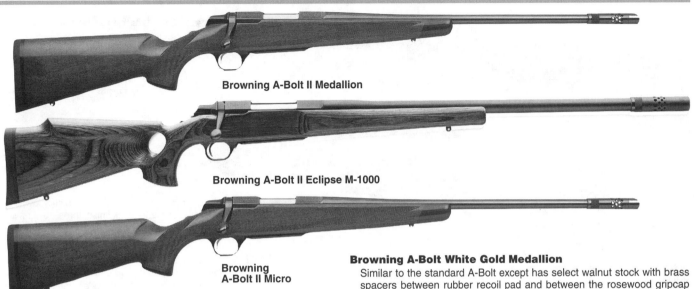

Browning A-Bolt II Medallion

Browning A-Bolt II Eclipse M-1000

Browning A-Bolt II Micro

BROWNING ACERA STRAIGHT-PULL RIFLE

Caliber: 30-06, 300 Win. Mag. **Barrel:** 22"; 24" for magnums. **Weight:** 6 lbs., 9 oz. **Length:** 41-1/4" overall. **Stock:** American walnut with high gloss finish. **Sights:** Blade on ramp front, open adjustable rear. **Features:** Straight-pull action; detachable box magazine; Teflon coated breechblock; drilled and tapped for scope mounting. Introduced 1999. Imported by Browning.

Price: 30-06, no sights $845.00
Price: 300 Win. Mag., no sights $877.00
Price: 30-06 with sights $869.00
Price: 300 Win. Mag., with sights $901.00
Price: 30-06, with BOSS $901.00
Price: 300 Win. Mag., with BOSS $933.00

BROWNING A-BOLT RIFLES

Caliber: 223, 22-250, 243, 7mm-08, 308, 25-06, 260, 270, 30-06, 260 Rem., 7mm Rem. Mag., 300 Win. Short Mag., 300 Win. Mag., 338 Win. Mag., 375 H&H Mag. **Barrel:** 22" medium sporter weight with recessed muzzle; 26" on mag. cals. **Weight:** 6-1/2 to 7-1/2 lbs. **Length:** 44-3/4" overall (magnum and standard); 41-3/4" (short action). **Stock:** Classic style American walnut; recoil pad standard on magnum calibers. **Features:** Short-throw (60") fluted bolt, three locking lugs, plunger-type ejector; adjustable trigger is grooved and gold-plated. Hinged floorplate, detachable box magazine (4 rounds std. cals., 3 for magnums). Slide tang safety. BOSS barrel vibration modulator and muzzle brake system not available in 375 H&H. Introduced 1985. Imported from Japan by Browning.

Price: Hunter, no sights $620.00
Price: Hunter, no sights, magnum calibers. $646.00
Price: For BOSS add $80.00

Browning A-Bolt Medallion

Similar to standard A-Bolt except has glossy stock finish, rosewood grip and forend caps, engraved receiver, high-polish blue, no sights.

Price: Short-action calibers. $730.00
Price: Long-action calibers $756.00
Price: Medallion, 375 H&H Mag., open sights $767.00
New! Price: 300 Win. Short Magnum $756.00
New! Price: 300 Rem. Ultra Mag., 338 Rem. Ultra Mag. $756.00
Price: For BOSS, add. $80.00

Browning A-Bolt Medallion Left-Hand

Same as the Medallion model A-Bolt except has left-hand action and is available in 270, 30-06, 7mm Rem. Mag., 300 Win. Mag. Introduced 1987.

Price: 270, 30-06 (no sights) $758.00
Price: 7mm Mag., 300 Win. Mag. (no sights) $784.00
Price: For BOSS, add. $80.00

Browning A-Bolt White Gold Medallion

Similar to the standard A-Bolt except has select walnut stock with brass spacers between rubber recoil pad and between the rosewood gripcap and forend tip; gold-filled barrel inscription; palm-swell pistol grip, Monte Carlo comb, 22 lpi checkering with double borders; engraved receiver flats. In 270, 30-06, 7mm Rem. Mag. and 300 Win. Mag. Introduced 1988.

Price: 270, 30-06 . . . . $1,046.00
Price: 7mm Rem. Mag, 300 Win. Mag. $1,072.00
Price: For BOSS, add. $76.00

Browning A-Bolt Custom Trophy Rifle

Similar to the A-Bolt Medallion except has select American walnut stock with recessed swivel studs, octagon barrel, skeleton pistol gripcap, gold highlights, shadowline cheekpiece. Calibers 270, 30-06, 7mm Rem. Mag., 300 Win. Mag. Introduced 1998. Imported from Japan by Browning.

Price: $1,360.00

Browning A-Bolt Eclipse Hunter

Similar to the A-Bolt II except has gray/black laminated, thumbhole stock, BOSS barrel vibration modulator and muzzle brake. Available in long and short action with heavy barrel. In 270 Win., 30-06, 7mm Rem. Mag. Introduced 1996. Imported from Japan by Browning.

Price: 270, 30-06, with BOSS. $1,017.00
Price: 7mm Rem. Mag, with BOSS $1,043.00

Browning A-Bolt Eclipse M-1000

Similar to the A-Bolt II Eclipse except has long action and heavy target barrel. Chambered only for 300 Win. Mag. Adjustable trigger, bench-style forend, 3-shot magazine; laminated thumbhold stock; BOSS system standard. Introduced 1997. Imported for Japan by Browning.

Price: $1,048.00

Browning A-Bolt Micro Hunter

Similar to the A-Bolt II Hunter except has 13-5/16" length of pull, 20" barrel, and comes in 260 Rem., 243, 308, 7mm-08, 223, 22-250, 22 Hornet. Weighs 6 lbs., 1 oz. Introduced 1999. Imported by Browning.

Price: (no sights) $614.00

Browning A-Bolt Classic Hunter

Similar to the A-Bolt unter except has low-luster bluing and walnut stock with Monte Carlo comb, pistol grip palm swell, double-border checkering. Available in 270, 30-06, 7mm Rem. Mag., 300 Win. Mag. Introduced 1999. Imported by Browning.

Price: 270, 30-06 . . . . $698.00
Price: 7mm Mag., 300 Mag. $724.00

Browning A-Bolt Stainless Stalker

Similar to the Hunter model A-Bolt except receiver and barrel are made of stainless steel; the rest of the exposed metal surfaces are finished with a durable matte silver-gray. Graphite-fiberglass composite textured stock. No sights are furnished. Available in 260, 243, 308, 7mm-08, 270, 280,30-06, 7mm Rem. Mag., 300 WSM, 300 Rem. Ultra Mag., 338 Win. Mag., 338 Rem. Ultra Mag., 375 H&H. Introduced 1987.

Charles Daly Superior

CZ 527

Price: Short-action calibers. **$813.00**
Price: Magnum calibers **$839.00**
New! Price: 300 Win. Short Magnum **$839.00**
New! Price: 300 Rem. Ultra Mag., 338 Rem. Ultra Mag. **$839.00**
Price: For BOSS, add **$80.00**
Price: Left-hand, 270, 30-06 . . . . **$838.00**
Price: Left-hand, 7mm, 300 Win. Mag., 338 Win. Mag. **$864.00**
Price: Left-hand, 375 H&H, with sights **$864.00**
Price: Left-hand, for BOSS, add **$80.00**
Price: Carbon-fiber barrel, 22-250 . . . . **$1,750.00**
Price: Carbon-fiber barrel, 300 Win. Mag. **$1,776.00**

Browning A-Bolt Composite Stalker

Similar to the A-Bolt Hunter except has black graphite-fiberglass stock with textured finish. Matte blue finish on all exposed metal surfaces. Available in 223, 22-250, 243, 7mm-08, 308, 30-06, 270, 280, 25-06, 7mm Rem. Mag., 300 WSM, 300 Win. Mag., 338 Win. Mag. BOSS barrel vibration modulator and muzzle brake system offered in all calibers. Introduced 1994.
Price: Standard calibers, no sights **$639.00**
Price: Magnum calibers, no sights **$665.00**
Price: For BOSS, add **$77.00**

CARBON ONE BOLT-ACTION RIFLE

Caliber: 22-250 to 375 H&H. **Barrel:** Up to 28". **Weight:** 5-1/2 to 7-1/4 lbs. **Length:** Varies. **Stock:** Synthetic or wood. **Sights:** None furnished. **Features:** Choice of Remington, Browning or Winchester action with free-floated Christensen graphite/epoxy/steel barrel, trigger pull tuned to 3 - 3-1/2 lbs. Made in U.S. by Christensen Arms.
Price: Carbon One Hunter Rifle, 6-1/2 to 7 lbs. **$1,499.00**
Price: Carbon One Custom, 5-1/2 to 6-1/2 lbs., Shilen trigger . . **$2,750.00**
Price: Carbon Ranger, 50 BMG, 5-shot repeater **$4,750.00**
Price: Carbon Ranger, 50 BMG, single shot **$3,950.00**

CHARLES DALY SUPERIOR BOLT-ACTION RIFLE

Caliber: 22 Hornet, 5-shot magazine. **Barrel:** 22.6". **Weight:** 6.6 lbs. **Length:** 41.25" overall. **Stock:** Walnut-finished hardwood with Monte Carlo comb and cheekpiece. **Sights:** Ramped blade front, fully adjustable open rear. **Features:** Receiver dovetailed for tip-off scope mount. Introduced 1996. Imported by K.B.I., Inc.
Price: **$364.95**

Charles Daly Empire Grade Rifle

Similar to the Superior except has oil-finished American walnut stock with 18 lpi hand checkering; black hardwood gripcap and forend tip; highly polished barreled action; jewelled bolt; recoil pad; swivel studs. Imported by K.B.I., Inc.
Price: **$469.95**

COLT LIGHT RIFLE BOLT ACTION

Caliber: 243, 7x57, 7mm-08, 308 (short action); 25-06, 270, 280, 7mm Rem., Mag., 30-06, 300 Win. Mag. **Barrel:** 24" **Weight:** 5.4 to 6 lbs.

Length: NA. **Stock:** Black synthetic. **Sights:** None furnished; low, medium, high scope mounts. **Features:** Matte black finish; three-position safety. Introduced 1999. Made in U.S. From Colt's Mfg., Inc.
Price: **$779.00**

COOPER MODEL 22 BOLT-ACTION RIFLE

Caliber: 22 BR, 22-250 Rem., 22-250 Ackley Imp., 243, 25-06, 25-06 Ackley Imp., 220 Swift, 257 Roberts, 257 Roberts Ackley Imp., 6mm Rem., 6mm PPC, 6mm BR, 7mm-08, single shot. **Barrel:** 24" stainless match grade. **Weight:** 7-3/4 to 8 lbs. **Stock:** AA Claro walnut, 20 lpi checkering. **Sights:** None furnished. **Features:** Uses three front locking lug system. Fully adjustable trigger. Many options available. Made in U.S. by Cooper Firearms.
Price: Classic **$1,295.00**
Price: Varminter **$1,199.00**
Price: Varmint Extreme **$1,895.00**
Price: Custom Classic **$2,195.00**
Price: Western Classic **$2,495.00**

COOPER MODEL 21, 38 BOLT-ACTION RIFLES

Caliber: 17 Rem., 17 Mach IV, 17 Javelina, 19-223 Calhoon, 20 VarTag, 22 PPC, Model 21, 6mm PPC, 221 Fireball, 222 Rem., 222 Rem. Mag., 223 Rem., 223 Ackley Imp., 6x45, 6x47, single shot; Model 38—17 Squirrel, 17 HeBee, 17 Ackley Hornet, 22 Hornet, 22 K Hornet, 218 Mashburn Bee, 218 Bee, 22 Squirrel, single shot. **Barrel:** 24" stainless match grade. **Weight:** 6-1/2 to 7-1/4 lbs. **Stock:** AA Claro walnut; 20 l.p.i. checkering. **Sights:** None furnished. **Features:** Uses three front locking lug system. Fully adjustable trigger. Many options available. Contact maker for details. Made in U.S. by Cooper Firearms.
Price: Classic **$1,050.00**
Price: Varminter **$995.00**
Price: Varmint Extreme **$1,795.00**
Price: Custom Classic **$1,995.00**
Price: Western Classic **$2,295.00**

COOPER ARMS MODEL 22 PRO VARMINT EXTREME

Caliber: 22-250, 220 Swift, 243, 25-06, 6mm PPC, 308, single shot. **Barrel:** 26"; stainless steel match grade, straight taper; free-floated. **Weight:** NA. **Length:** NA. **Stock:** AAA Claro walnut, oil finish, 22 lpi wrap-around borderless ribbon checkering, beaded cheekpiece, steel gripcap, flared varminter forend, Pachmayr pad. **Sights:** None furnished; drilled and tapped for scope mounting. **Features:** Uses a three front locking lug system. Available with sterling silver inlaid medallion, skeleton gripcap, and French walnut. Introduced 1995. Made in U.S. by Cooper Arms.
Price: **$1,795.00**
Price: Benchrest model with Jewell trigger **$2,195.00**
Price: Black Jack model (McMillan synthetic stock) **$1,795.00**

CZ 527 LUX BOLT-ACTION RIFLE

Caliber: 22 Hornet, 222 Rem., 223 Rem., detachable 5-shot magazine. **Barrel:** 23-1/2"; standard or heavy barrel. **Weight:** 6 lbs., 1 oz. **Length:** 42-1/2" overall. **Stock:** European walnut with Monte Carlo. **Sights:** Hooded front, open adjustable rear. **Features:** Improved mini-Mauser action with non-rotating claw extractor; single set trigger; grooved receiver. Imported from the Czech Republic by CZ-USA.
Price: **$540.00**
Price: Model FS, full-length stock, cheekpiece **$607.00**

RIFLES

CZ 550 Lux

CZ 550
American Classic

CZ 550
Magnum

Dakota 76
Classic

CZ 527 American Classic Bolt-Action Rifle

Similar to the CZ 527 Lux except has classic-style stock with 18 l.p.i. checkering; free-floating barrel; recessed target crown on barrel. No sights furnished. Introduced 1999. Imported from the Czech Republic by CZ-USA.
Price: 22 Hornet, 222 Rem., 223 Rem. **$540.00**

CZ 550 LUX BOLT-ACTION RIFLE

Caliber: 22-250, 243, 6.5x55, 7x57, 7x64, 308 Win., 9.3x62, 270 Win., 30-06. **Barrel:** 20.47". **Weight:** 7.5 lbs. **Length:** 44.68" overall. **Stock:** Turkish walnut in Bavarian style or FS (Mannlicher). **Sights:** Hooded front, adjustable rear. **Features:** Improved Mauser-style action with claw extractor, fixed ejector, square bridge dovetailed receiver; single set trigger. Imported from the Czech Republic by CZ-USA.
Price: Lux . . . . **$561.00 to $609.00**
Price: FS (full stock) **$645.00**

CZ 550 American Classic Bolt-Action Rifle

Similar to the CZ 550 Lux except has American classic-style stock with 18 l.p.i. checkering; free-floating barrel; recessed target crown. Has 25.6" barrel; weighs 7.48 lbs. No sights furnished. Introduced 1999. Imported from the Czech Republic by CZ-USA.
Price: . . . . **$576.00 to $609.00**

CZ 550 Medium Magnum Bolt-Action Rifle

Similar to the CZ 550 Lux except chambered for the 300 Win. Mag. and 7mm Rem. Mag.; 5-shot magazine. Adjustable iron sights, hammer-forged barrel, single-set trigger, Turkish walnut stock. Weighs 7.5 lbs. Introduced 2001. Imported from the Czech Republic by CZ USA.
Price: **$621.00**

CZ 550 Magnum Bolt-Action Rifle

Similar to the CZ 550 Lux except has long action for 300 Win. Mag., 375 H&H, 416 Rigby, 458 Win. Mag. Overall length is 46.45"; barrel length 25"; weighs 9.24 lbs. Comes with hooded front sight, express rear with one standing, two folding leaves. Imported from the Czech Republic by CZ-USA.
Price: 300 Win. Mag. **$717.00**

Price: 375 H&H. **$756.00**
Price: 416 Rigby **$796.00**
Price: 458 Win. Mag. **$744.00**

CZ 700 M1 SNIPER RIFLE

Caliber: 308 Winchester, 10-shot magazine. **Barrel:** 25.6". **Weight:** 11.9 lbs. **Length:** 45" overall. **Stock:** Laminated wood thumbhole with adjustable buttplate and cheekpiece. **Sights:** None furnished; permanently attached Weaver rail for scope mounting. **Features:** 60-degree bolt throw; oversized trigger guard and bolt handle for use with gloves; full-length equipment rail on forend; fully adjustable trigger. Introduced 2001. Imported from the Czech Republic by CZ USA.
Price: **$2,097.00**

DAKOTA 76 TRAVELER TAKEDOWN RIFLE

Caliber: 257 Roberts, 25-06, 7x57, 270, 280, 30-06, 338-06, 35 Whelen (standard length); 7mm Rem. Mag., 300 Win. Mag., 338 Win. Mag., 416 Taylor, 458 Win. Mag. (short magnums); 7mm, 300, 330, 375 Dakota Magnums. **Barrel:** 23". **Weight:** 7-1/2 lbs. **Length:** 43-1/2" overall. **Stock:** Medium fancy-grade walnut in classic style. Checkered grip and forend; solid butt pad. **Sights:** None furnished; drilled and tapped for scope mounts. **Features:** Threadless disassembly—no threads to wear or stretch, no interrupted cuts, and headspace remains constant. Uses modified Model 76 design with many features of the Model 70 Winchester. Left-hand model also available. Introduced 1989. Made in U.S. by Dakota Arms, Inc.
Price: Classic **$4,495.00**
Price: Safari **$5,495.00**
Price: Extra barrels. . . . . **$1,650.00 to $1,950.00**

DAKOTA 76 CLASSIC BOLT-ACTION RIFLE

Caliber: 257 Roberts, 270, 280, 30-06, 7mm Rem. Mag., 338 Win. Mag., 300 Win. Mag., 375 H&H, 458 Win. Mag. **Barrel:** 23". **Weight:** 7-1/2 lbs. **Length:** 43-1/2" overall. **Stock:** Medium fancy grade walnut in classic style. Checkered pistol grip and forend; solid butt pad. **Sights:** None furnished; drilled and tapped for scope mounts. **Features:** Has many features of the original Model 70 Winchester. One-piece rail trigger guard assembly; steel gripcap. Model 70-style trigger. Many options available. Left-hand rifle available at same price. Introduced 1988. From Dakota Arms, Inc.
Price: **$3,595.00**

Dakota 76 Safari

Dakota Longbow

Dakota 97 Lightweight Hunter

Dakota Hunter

DAKOTA 76 SAFARI BOLT-ACTION RIFLE

Caliber: 270 Win., 7x57, 280, 30-06, 7mm Dakota, 7mm Rem. Mag., 300 Dakota, 300 Win. Mag., 330 Dakota, 338 Win. Mag., 375 Dakota, 458 Win. Mag., 300 H&H, 375 H&H, 416 Rem. **Barrel:** 23". **Weight:** 8-1/2 lbs. **Length:** 43-1/2" overall. **Stock:** XXX fancy walnut with ebony forend tip; point-pattern with wrap-around forend checkering. **Sights:** Ramp front, standing leaf rear. **Features:** Has many features of the original Model 70 Winchester. Barrel band front swivel, inletted rear. Cheekpiece with shadow line. Steel gripcap. Introduced 1988. From Dakota Arms, Inc.
Price: Wood stock. **$4,595.00**

Dakota African Grade
Similar to the 76 Safari except chambered for 338 Lapua Mag., 404 Jeffery, 416 Rigby, 416 Dakota, 450 Dakota, 4-round magazine, select wood, two stock cross-bolts. Has 24" barrel, weight of 9-10 lbs. Ramp front sight, standing leaf rear. Introduced 1989.
Price: **$4,995.00**

DAKOTA LONGBOW TACTICAL E.R. RIFLE

Caliber: 300 Dakota Magnum, 330 Dakota Magnum, 338 Lapua Magnum. **Barrel:** 28", .950" at muzzle **Weight:** 13.7 lbs. **Length:** 50" to 52" overall. **Stock:** Ambidextrous McMillan A-2 fiberglass, black or olive green color; adjustable cheekpiece and buttplate. **Sights:** None furnished. Comes with Picatinny one-piece optical rail. **Features:** Uses the Dakota 76 action with controlled-round feed; three-position firing pin block safety, claw extractor; Model 70-style trigger. Comes with bipod, case tool kit. Introduced 1997. Made in U.S. by Dakota Arms, Inc.
Price: **$4,250.00**

DAKOTA 97 LIGHTWEIGHT HUNTER

Caliber: 22-250 to 330. **Barrel:** 22"-24". **Weight:** 6.1-6.5 lbs. **Length:** 43" overall. **Stock:** Fiberglass. **Sights:** Optional. **Features:** Matte blue finish, black stock. Right-hand action only. Introduced 1998. Made in U.S. by Dakota Arms, Inc.
Price: **$1,995.00**

DAKOTA LONG RANGE HUNTER RIFLE

Caliber: 25-06, 257 Roberts, 270 Win., 280 Rem., 7mm Rem. Mag., 7mm Dakota Mag., 30-06, 300 Win. Mag., 300 Dakota Mag., 338 Win. Mag., 330 Dakota Mag., 375 H&H Mag., 375 Dakota Mag. **Barrel:** 24", 26", match-quality; free-floating. **Weight:** 7.7 lbs. **Length:** 45" to 47" overall. **Stock:** H-S Precision black synthetic, with one-piece bedding block system. **Sights:** None furnished. Drilled and tapped for scope mounting. **Features:** Cylindrical machined receiver controlled round feed; Mauser-style extractor; three-position striker blocking safety; fully adjustable match trigger. Right-hand action only. Introduced 1997. Made in U.S. by Dakota Arms, Inc.
Price: **$1,995.00**

HARRIS GUNWORKS SIGNATURE CLASSIC SPORTER

Caliber: 22-250, 243, 6mm Rem., 7mm-08, 284, 308 (short action); 25-06, 270, 280 Rem., 30-06, 7mm Rem. Mag., 300 Win. Mag., 300 Wea. (long action); 338 Win. Mag., 340 Wea., 375 H&H (magnum action). **Barrel:** 22", 24", 26". **Weight:** 7 lbs. (short action). **Stock:** Fiberglass in green, beige, brown or black. Recoil pad and 1" swivels installed. Length of pull up to 14-1/4". **Sights:** None furnished. Comes with 1" rings and bases. **Features:** Uses right- or left-hand action with matte black finish. Trigger pull set at 3 lbs. Four-round magazine for standard calibers; three for magnums. Aluminum floorplate. Wood stock optional. Introduced 1987. From Harris Gunworks, Inc.
Price: **$2,700.00**

Harris Gunworks Alaskan

Harris Gunworks Signature Titanium Mountain

Harris Gunworks Signature Super Varminter

Harris Gunworks Talon Safari

Harris Gunworks Signature Classic Stainless Sporter

Similar to the Signature Classic Sporter except action is made of stainless steel. Same calibers, in addition to 416 Rem. Mag. Comes with fiberglass stock, right- or left-hand action in natural stainless, glass bead or black chrome sulfide finishes. Introduced 1990. From Harris Gunworks, Inc.

Price: **$2,900.00**

Harris Gunworks Signature Alaskan

Similar to the Classic Sporter except has match-grade barrel with single leaf rear sight, barrel band front, 1" detachable rings and mounts, steel floorplate, electroless nickel finish. Has wood Monte Carlo stock with cheekpiece, palm-swell grip, solid butt pad. Chambered for 270, 280 Rem., 30-06, 7mm Rem. Mag., 300 Win. Mag., 300 Wea., 358 Win., 340 Wea., 375 H&H. Introduced 1989.

Price: **$3,800.00**

Harris Gunworks Signature Titanium Mountain Rifle

Similar to the Classic Sporter except action made of titanium alloy, barrel of chrome-moly steel. Stock is of graphite reinforced fiberglass. Weight is 5-1/2 lbs. Chambered for 270, 280 Rem., 30-06, 7mm Rem. Mag., 300 Win. Mag. Fiberglass stock optional. Introduced 1989.

Price: **$3,300.00**
Price: With graphite-steel composite light weight barrel...... **$3,700.00**

Harris Gunworks Signature Varminter

Similar to the Signature Classic Sporter except has heavy contoured barrel, adjustable trigger, field bipod and special hand-bedded fiberglass stock. Chambered for 223, 22-250, 220 Swift, 243, 6mm Rem., 25-06, 7mm-08, 7mm BR, 308, 350 Rem. Mag. Comes with 1" rings and bases. Introduced 1989.

Price: **$2,700.00**

HARRIS GUNWORKS TALON SAFARI RIFLE

Caliber: 300 Win. Mag., 300 Wea. Mag., 300 Phoenix, 338 Win. Mag., 30/378, 338 Lapua, 300 H&H, 340 Wea. Mag., 375 H&H, 404 Jeffery, 416 Rem. Mag., 458 Win. Mag. (Safari Magnum); 378 Wea. Mag., 416 Rigby, 416 Wea. Mag., 460 Wea. Mag. (Safari Super Magnum). **Barrel:** 24". **Weight:** About 9-10 lbs. **Length:** 43" overall. **Stock:** Gunworks fiberglass Safari. **Sights:** Barrel band front ramp, multi-leaf express rear. **Features:** Uses Harris Gunworks Safari action. Has quick detachable 1" scope mounts, positive locking steel floorplate, barrel band sling swivel. Match-grade barrel. Matte black finish standard. Introduced 1989. From Harris Gunworks, Inc.

Price: Talon Safari Magnum........................... **$3,900.00**
Price: Talon Safari Super Magnum **$4,200.00**

HARRIS GUNWORKS TALON SPORTER RIFLE

Caliber: 22-250, 243, 6mm Rem., 6mm BR, 7mm BR, 7mm-08, 25-06, 270, 280 Rem., 284, 308, 30-06, 350 Rem. Mag. (long action); 7mm Rem. Mag., 7mm STW, 300 Win. Mag., 300 Wea. Mag., 300 H&H, 338 Win. Mag., 340 Wea. Mag., 375 H&H, 416 Rem. Mag. **Barrel:** 24" (standard). **Weight:** About 7-1/2 lbs. **Length:** NA. **Stock:** Choice of walnut or fiberglass. **Sights:** None furnished; comes with rings and bases. Open sights optional. **Features:** Uses pre-'64 Model 70-type action with cone breech, controlled feed, claw extractor and three-position safety. Barrel and action are of stainless steel; chrome-moly optional. Introduced 1991. From Harris Gunworks, Inc.

Price: **$2,900.00**

RIFLES

Howa Lightning

Howa M-1500 Hunter

Howa M-1500 PCS Police Counter Sniper

Howa M-1500 Varmint

L.A.R. Grizzly

HOWA LIGHTNING BOLT-ACTION RIFLE

Caliber: 223, 22-250, 243, 270, 308, 30-06, 7mm Rem. Mag., 300 Win. Mag., 338 Win. Mag. **Barrel:** 22", 24" magnum calibers. **Weight:** 7-1/2 lbs. **Length:** 42" overall (22" barrel). **Stock:** Black Bell & Carlson Carbelite composite with Monte Carlo comb; checkered grip and forend. **Sights:** None furnished. Drilled and tapped for scope mounting. **Features:** Sliding thumb safety; hinged floorplate; polished blue/black finish. Introduced 1993. From Legacy Sports International.

Price: Blue, standard calibers	$435.00
Price: Blue, magnum calibers	$455.00
Price: Stainless, standard calibers	$485.00
Price: Stainless, magnum calibers	$505.00

Howa M-1500 Hunter Bolt-Action Rifle

Similar to the Lightning model except has walnut-finished hardwood stock. Polished blue finish or stainless steel. Introduced 1999. From Legacy Sports International.

Price: Blue, standard calibers	$455.00
Price: Stainless, standard calibers	$505.00
Price: Blue, magnum calibers	$475.00
Price: Stainless, magnum calibers	$525.00

Howa M-1500 PCS Police Counter Sniper Rifle

Similar to the M-1500 Lightning except chambered only for 308 Win., 24" hammer-forged heavy barrel. Trigger is factory set at 4 lbs. Available in blue or stainless steel, polymer or hardwood stock. Introduced 1999. Imported from Japan by Legacy Sports International.

Price: Blue, polymer stock	$465.00
Price: Stainless, polymer stock	$525.00
Price: Blue, wood stock	$485.00
Price: Stainless, wood stock	$545.00

Howa M-1500 Varmint Rifle

Similar to the M-1500 Lightning except has heavy 24" hammer-forged barrel. Chambered for 223 and 22-250. Weighs 9.3 lbs.; overall length 44.5". Introduced 1999. Imported from Japan by Interarms/Howa.

Price: Blue, polymer stock	$465.00
Price: Stainless, polymer stock	$525.00
Price: Blue, wood stock	$485.00
Price: Stainless, wood stock	$545.00

KIMBER MODEL 84M BOLT-ACTION RIFLE

Caliber: 22-250, 243, 260 Rem., 7mm-08, 308, 5-shot magazine. **Barrel:** 22", 26". **Weight:** 5 lbs., 10 oz. to 7 lbs., 5 oz. **Length:** 41.25" overall (22" bbl.). **Stock:** Claro walnut, checkered with steel grip cap. **Sights:** None furnished; drilled and tapped for scope mount. **Features:** Mauser claw extractor; two-position wing safety; action bedded on aluminum pillars; free-floated barrel; match-grade trigger set at 3-1/2 - 4 lbs.; matte blue finish. Includes cable lock. Introduced 2001. Made in U.S. by Kimber Mfg. Inc.

Price: Classic (243, 260, 7mm-08, 308; 22" light sporter bbl.)	$895.00
Price: Varmint (22-250; 26" stainless heavy sporter bbl.)	$978.00

L.A.R. GRIZZLY 50 BIG BOAR RIFLE

Caliber: 50 BMG, single shot. **Barrel:** 36". **Weight:** 28.4 lbs. **Length:** 45.5" overall. **Stock:** Integral. Ventilated rubber recoil pad. **Sights:** None furnished; scope mount. **Features:** Bolt-action bullpup design; thumb safety. All-steel construction. Introduced 1994. Made in U.S. by L.A.R. Mfg., Inc.

Price:	$2,570.00

Magnum Research Tactical

Mountain Eagle Varmint

Raptor Bolt-Action

Remington 700 ADL Synthetic

Price: Model 20 (short action) **$2,500.00**
Price: Model 24 (long action) **$2,600.00**
Price: Model 28 (magnum action) **$2,900.00**
Price: Model 40 (300 Wea. Mag., 416 Rigby) **$2,900.00**
Price: Left-hand models, add **$100.00**

MAGNUM RESEARCH TACTICAL RIFLE

Caliber: 223 Rem., 22-250, 308 Win., 300 Win. Mag. **Barrel:** 26" Magnum Lite™ graphite. **Weight:** 8.3 lbs. **Length:** NA. **Stock:** H-S Precision™ tactical black synthetic. **Sights:** None furnished; drilled and tapped for scope mount. **Features:** Accurized Remington 700 action; adjustable trigger; adjustable comb height. Tuned to shoot 1/2" MOA or better. Introduced 2001. From Magnum Research Inc.
Price: **$2,400.00**

MOUNTAIN EAGLE RIFLE

Caliber: 222 Rem., 223 Rem. (Varmint); 270, 280, 30-06 (long action); 7mm Rem. Mag., 7mm STW, 300 Win. Mag., 338 Win. Mag., 300 Wea. Mag., 375 H&H, 416 Rem. Mag. (magnum action). **Barrel:** 24", 26" (Varmint); match-grade; fluted stainless on Varmint. Free floating. **Weight:** 7 lbs., 13 oz. **Length:** 44" overall (24" barrel). **Stock:** Kevlar-graphite with aluminum bedding block, high comb, recoil pad, swivel studs; made by H-S Precision. **Sights:** None furnished; accepts any Remington 700-type base. **Features:** Special Sako action with one-piece forged bolt, hinged steel floorplate, lengthened receiver ring; adjustable trigger. Krieger cut-rifled benchrest barrel. Introduced 1996. From Magnum Research, Inc.
Price: Right-hand **$1,499.00**
Price: Left-hand **$1,549.00**
Price: Varmint Edition **$1,629.00**
Price: 375 H&H, 416 Rem., add **$300.00**
Price: Magnum Lite (graphite barrel) **$2,295.00**

NEW ULTRA LIGHT ARMS BOLT-ACTION RIFLES

Caliber: 17 Rem. to 416 Rigby (numerous calibers available). **Barrel:** Douglas, length to order. **Weight:** 4-3/4 to 7-1/2 lbs. **Length:** Varies. **Stock:** Kevlar®/graphite composite, variety of finishes. **Sights:** None furnished; drilled and tapped for scope mount. **Features:** Timney trigger, hand-lapped action, button-rifled barrel, hand-bedded action, recoil pad, sling-swivel studs, optional Jewell Trigger. Made in U.S. by New Ultra Light Arms.

RAPTOR BOLT-ACTION RIFLE

Caliber: 270, 30-06, 243, 25-06, 308; 4-shot magazine. **Barrel:** 22". **Weight:** 7 lbs., 6 oz. **Length:** 42.5" overall. **Stock:** Black synthetic, fiberglass reinforced; checkered grip and forend; vented recoil pad; Monte Carlo cheekpiece. **Sights:** None furnished; drilled and tapped for scope mounts. **Features:** Rust-resistant "Taloncote" treated barreled action; pillar bedded; stainless bolt with three locking lugs; adjustable trigger. Announced 1997. Made in U.S. by Raptor Arms Co., Inc.
Price: **$249.00**

REMINGTON MODEL 700 CLASSIC RIFLE

Caliber: 7mm-08. **Barrel:** 24". **Weight:** About 7-1/4 lbs. **Length:** 44-1/2" overall. **Stock:** American walnut, 20 lpi checkering on pistol grip and forend. Classic styling. Satin finish. **Sights:** None furnished. Receiver drilled and tapped for scope mounting. **Features:** A "classic" version of the BDL with straight comb stock. Fitted with rubber recoil pad. Sling swivel studs installed. Hinged floorplate. Limited production in 2001 only.
Price: **$633.00**

REMINGTON MODEL 700 ADL DELUXE RIFLE

Caliber: 270, 308, 30-06 and 7mm Rem. Mag. **Barrel:** 22" or 24" round tapered. **Weight:** 7-1/4 to 7-1/2 lbs. **Length:** 41-5/8" to 44-1/2" overall. **Stock:** Walnut. Satin-finished pistol grip stock with fine-line cut checkering, Monte Carlo. **Sights:** Gold bead ramp front; removable, step-adjustable rear with windage screw. **Features:** Side safety, receiver tapped for scope mounts.
Price: From **$531.00**

Remington Model 700 ADL Synthetic

Similar to the 700 ADL except has a fiberglass-reinforced synthetic stock with straight comb, raised cheekpiece, positive checkering, and black rubber butt pad. Metal has matte finish. Available in 22-250, 223, 243, 270, 308, 30-06 with 22" barrel, 300 Win. Mag., 7mm Rem. Mag. with 24" barrel. Introduced 1996.
Price: From **$457.00**

Remington 700 BDL

Remington 700 BDL Left Hand

Remington 700 BDL SS DM

Remington 700 BDL SS DM-B

Remington Model 700 ADL Synthetic Youth

Similar to the Model 700 ADL Synthetic except has 1" shorter stock, 20" barrel. Chambered for 243, 308. Introduced 1998.

Price: **$484.00**

Remington Model 700 BDL Custom Deluxe Rifle

Same as the 700 ADL except chambered for 222, 223 (short action, 24" barrel), 22-250, 25-06. (short action, 22" barrel), 243, 270, 30-06; skip-line checkering; black forend tip and gripcap with white line spacers. Matted receiver top, fine-line engraving, quick-release floorplate. Hooded ramp front sight; quick detachable swivels. 7mm-08, .280.

Price: **$633.00**

Also available in 17 Rem., 7mm Rem. Mag., 7mm Rem. Ultra Mag., 7mm-08, 280, 300 Win. Mag. (long action, 24" barrel); 338 Win. Mag., (long action, 22" barrel); 300 Rem. Ultra Mag. 338 Rem. Ultra Mag. (26" barrel), 375 Rem. Ultra Mag. Overall length 44-1/2", weight about 7-1/2 lbs. 338 Rem Ultra Mag.

Price: **$660.00**

Remington Model 700 BDL Left Hand Custom Deluxe

Same as 700 BDL except mirror-image left-hand action, stock. Available in 270, 30-06, 7mm Rem. Mag., 300 Rem. Ultra Mag.

Price: **$660.00**

Price: 7mm Rem. Mag., 300 Rem. Ultra Mag. **$687.00**

Remington Model 700 BDL DM Rifle

Same as the 700 BDL except has detachable box magazine (4-shot, standard calibers, 3-shot for magnums). Has glossy stock finish, fine-line engraving, open sights, recoil pad, sling swivels. Available in 270, 30-06, 7mm Rem. Mag., 300 Win. Mag. Introduced 1995.

Price: From **$681.00**

Remington Model 700 BDL SS Rifle

Similar to the 700 BDL rifle except has hinged floorplate, 24" standard weight barrel in all calibers; magnum calibers have magnum-contour bar-

rel. No sights supplied, but comes drilled and tapped. Has corrosion-resistant follower and fire control, stainless BDL-style barreled action with fine matte finish. Synthetic stock has straight comb and cheekpiece, textured finish, positive checkering, plated swivel studs. Calibers—270, 30-06; magnums—7mm Rem. Mag., 300 Rem. Ultra Mag. (26" barrel) 300 Win. Mag., 338 Win. Mag., 338 Rem. Ultra Mag., 375 H&H. Weighs 7-3/8 - 7-1/2 lbs. Introduced 1993.

Price: From **$681.00**

Remington Model 700 BDL SS DM Rifle

Same as the 700 BDL SS except has detachable box magazine. Barrel, receiver and bolt made of #416 stainless steel; black synthetic stock, fine-line engraving. Available in 25-06, 260 Rem., 270, 280, 30-06, 7mm Rem. Mag., 7mm-08, 300 Win. Mag., 300 Wea. Mag. Introduced 1995.

Price: From **$756.00**

Remington Model 700 BDL SS DM-B

Same as the 700 BDL SS DM except has muzzle brake, fine-line engraving. Available only in 7mm STW, 300 Win. Mag. Introduced 1996.

Price: **$845.00**

Remington Model 700 Custom KS Mountain Rifle

Similar to the 700 BDL except custom finished with Kevlar reinforced resin synthetic stock. Available in both left- and right-hand versions. Chambered for 270 Win., 280 Rem., 30-06, 7mm Rem. Mag., 7mm STW, 300 Rem. Ultra Mag., 338 Rem. Ultra Mag., 300 Win. Mag., 300 Wea. Mag., 35 Whelen, 338 Win. Mag., 8mm Rem. Mag., 375 H&H, with 24" barrel (except 300 Rem. Ultra Mag., 26"). Weighs 6 lbs., 6 oz. Introduced 1986.

Price: .338 Ultra **$1,221.00**

Remington Model 700 LSS Mountain Rifle

Similar to Model 700 Custom KS Mountain Rifle except has stainless steel 22" barrel and two-tone laminated stock. Chambered in 260 Rem., 7mm-08, 270 Winchester and 30-06. Overall length 42-1/2", weighs 6-5/8 oz. Introduced 1999. From Remington Arms Co.

Price: **$744.00**

RIFLES

Remington 700 Safari KS

Remington 700 APR African Plains

Remington 700 VLS

Remington 700 Varmint Synthetic

Remington Model 700 Safari Grade

Similar to the 700 BDL except custom finished and tuned. In 8mm Rem. Mag., 375 H&H, 416 Rem. Mag. or 458 Win. Mag. calibers only with heavy barrel. Hand checkered, oil-finished stock in classic or Monte Carlo style with recoil pad installed. Classic available in right- and left-hand versions.
Price: From. **$1,225.00**
Price: Safari KS (Kevlar stock), from **$1,410.00**

Remington Model 700 AWR Alaskan Wilderness Rifle

Similar to the Model 700 BDL except has stainless barreled action with satin blue finish; special 24" Custom Shop barrel profile; matte gray stock of fiberglass and graphite, reinforced with DuPont Kevlar, straight comb with raised cheekpiece, magnum-grade black rubber recoil pad. Chambered for 7mm Rem. Mag., 7mm STW, 300 Rem. Ultra Mag., 300 Win. Mag., 300 Wea. Mag., 338 Rem. Ultra Mag., 338 Win. Mag., 375 H&H. Introduced 1994.
Price: From **$1,480.00**

Remington Model 700 APR African Plains Rifle

Similar to the Model 700 BDL except has magnum receiver and specially contoured 26" Custom Shop barrel with satin finish, laminated wood stock with raised cheekpiece, satin finish, black butt pad, 20 lpi cut checkering. Chambered for 7mm Rem. Mag., 300 Rem. Ultra Mag., 300 Win. Mag., 300 Wea. Mag., 338 Win. Mag., 338 Rem. Ultra Mag., 375 H&H. Introduced 1994.
Price: **$1,593.00**

Remington Model 700 EtronX Electronic Ignition Rifle

Similar to Model 700 VS SF except features battery-powered ignition system for near-zero lock time and electronic trigger mechanism. Requires ammunition with EtronX electrically fired primers. Aluminum-bedded 26" heavy, stainless steel, fluted barrel; overall length 45-7/8"; weight 8 lbs., 14 oz. Black, Kevlar-reinforced composite stock. Light-emitting diode display on grip top indicates fire or safe mode, loaded or unloaded chamber, battery condition. Introduced 2000. From Remington Arms Co.
Price: 220 Swift, 22-250 or 243 Win. **$1,999.00**

Remington Model 700 LSS Rifle

Similar to the 700 BDL except has stainless steel barreled action, gray laminated wood stock with Monte Carlo comb and cheekpiece. No sights furnished. Available in 7mm Rem. Mag., 300 Rem. Ultra Mag., 300 Win. Mag., and 338 Rem. Ultra Mag. in right-hand, and 270, 7mm Rem. Mag., 30-06, 300 Rem. Ultra Mag., 300 Win. Mag., 338 Rem. Ultra Mag. in left-hand model. Introduced 1996.
Price: From. **$771.00**

Remington Model 700 MTN DM Rifle

Similar to the 700 BDL except weighs 6-1/2 to 6-5/8 lbs., has a 22" tapered barrel. Redesigned pistol grip, straight comb, contoured cheekpiece, hand-rubbed oil stock finish, deep cut checkering, hinged floorplate and magazine follower, two-position thumb safety. Chambered for 260 Rem., 270 Win., 7mm-08, 25-06, 280 Rem., 30-06, 4-shot detachable box magazine. Overall length is 41-5/8"-42-1/2". Introduced 1995.
Price: About **$681.00**

Remington Model 700 Titanium

Similar to 700 BDL except has titanium receiver, spiral-cut fluted bolt, skeletonized bolt handle and carbon-fiber and Kevlar® stock with sling swivel studs. Barrel 22"; weighs 5-1/4 lbs. (short action) or 5-1/2 lbs. (long action). Satin stainless finish. Introduced 2001. From Remington Arms Co.
Price: **$1,199.00**

Remington Model 700 VLS Varmint Laminated Stock

Similar to the 700 BDL except has 26" heavy barrel without sights, brown laminated stock with beavertail forend, gripcap, rubber butt pad. Available in 223 Rem., 22-250, 6mm, 243, 308. Polished blue finish. Introduced 1995.
Price: From. **$675.00**

Remington Model 700 VS Varmint Synthetic Rifles

Similar to the 700 BDL Varmint Laminated except has composite stock reinforced with DuPont Kevlar, fiberglass and graphite. Has aluminum bedding block that runs the full length of the receiver. Free-floating 26" barrel. Metal has black matte finish; stock has textured black and gray finish and swivel studs. Available in 223, 22-250, 308. Right- and left-hand. Introduced 1992.
Price: From. **$759.00**

Remington 700 VS Composite

Remington 700 VF SF

Remington 700 Sendero SF

Remington Model Seven

Remington Model 700 VS Composite Rifle

Similar to the Model 700 VS Varmint Synthetic except has a composite varmint-weight barrel, weighs 7-1/8 lbs., and is available in right-hand in 22-250, 223, 308 Win. Introduced 1999.

Price: **$1,912.00**

Remington Model 700 VS SF Rifle

Similar to the Model 700 Varmint Synthetic except has satin-finish stainless barreled action with 26" fluted barrel, spherical concave muzzle crown. Chambered for 223, 220 Swift, 22-250. Introduced 1994.

Price: From **$916.00**

Remington Model 700 Sendero Rifle

Similar to the Model 700 Varmint Synthetic except has long action for magnum calibers. Has 26" heavy varmint barrel with spherical concave crown. Chambered for 25-06, 270, 7mm Rem. Mag., 300 Win. Mag. Introduced 1994.

Price: From **$759.00**

Remington Model 700 Sendero SF Rifle

Similar to the 700 Sendero except has stainless steel action and 26" fluted stainless barrel. Weighs 8-1/2 lbs. Chambered for 25-06, 7mm Rem. Mag., 300 Wea. Mag., 7mm STW, 300 Rem. Ultra Mag., 338 Rem. Ultra Mag., 300 Win. Mag. Introduced 1996.

Price: From **$943.00**

 ## REMINGTON MODEL 710 BOLT-ACTION RIFLE

Caliber: 270 Win., 30-06. **Barrel:** 22". **Weight:** 7-1/8 lbs. **Length:** 42-1/2" overall. **Stock:** Gray synthetic. **Sights:** Bushnell Sharpshooter 3-9x scope mounted and bore-sighted. **Features:** Unique action locks bolt directly into barrel; 60-degree bolt throw; 4-shot dual-stack magazine; key-operated Integrated Security System locks bolt open. Introduced 2001. Made in U.S. by Remington Arms Co.

Price: **$425.00**

REMINGTON MODEL SEVEN LSS BOLT-ACTION RIFLE

Caliber: 22-250, 243, 7mm-08. **Barrel:** 20". **Weight:** 6-1/2 lbs. **Length:** 39-1/4" overall. **Stock:** Brown laminated. Cut checkering. **Sights:** Ramp front, adjustable open rear. **Features:** Short-action design; silent side safety; free-floated barrel except for single pressure point at forend tip. Introduced 1983.

Price: **$727.00**

Remington Model Seven Custom KS

Similar to the Model Seven except has gray Kevlar reinforced stock with 1" black rubber recoil pad and swivel studs. Metal has black matte finish. No sights on 223, 260 Rem., 7mm-08, 308; 35 Rem. and 350 Rem. have iron sights.

Price: **$1,221.00**

Remington Model Seven LSS

Similar to Model Seven except has satin-finished, brown laminated stock, stainless steel 20" barrel and receiver. Overall length, 39-1/4", weighs 6-1/2 lbs. Chambered for 22-250, 243, 7mm-08 Rem. Introduced 2000.

Price: **$633.00**

Remington Model Seven LS

Similar to Model Seven except has satin-finished, brown laminated stock with 20" carbon steel barrel. Introduced 2000.

Price: **$633.00**

Remington Model Seven SS

Similar to the Model Seven except has stainless steel barreled action and black synthetic stock, 20" barrel. Chambered for 223, 243, 260 Rem., 7mm-08, 308. Introduced 1994.

Price: **$681.00**

Remington Model Seven Custom MS Rifle

Similar to the Model Seven except has full-length Mannlicher-style stock of laminated wood with straight comb, solid black recoil pad, black steel forend tip, cut checkering, gloss finish. Barrel length 20", weighs 6-3/4 lbs. Available in 222 Rem., 223, 22-250, 243, 6mm Rem., 260 Rem., 7mm-08 Rem., 308, 350 Rem. Mag. Calibers 250 Savage, 257 Roberts, 35 Rem. Polished blue finish. Introduced 1993. From Remington Custom Shop.

Price: From **$1,236.00**

RIFLES

Ruger 77/22 Hornet Varmint

Ruger M77 Mark II All-Weather

Ruger 77/44

Remington Model Seven Youth Rifle

Similar to the Model Seven except has hardwood stock with 12-3/16" length of pull and chambered for 223, 243, 260 Rem., 7mm-08. Introduced 1993.
Price: **$519.00**

Ruger M77RSI International Carbine

Same as the standard Model 77 except has 18" barrel, full-length International-style stock, with steel forend cap, loop-type steel sling swivels. Integral-base receiver, open sights, Ruger 1" steel rings. Improved front sight. Available in 243, 270, 308, 30-06. Weighs 7 lbs. Length overall is 38-3/8".
Price: M77RSIMKII.................................. **$735.00**

RUGER M77 MARK II EXPRESS RIFLE

Caliber: 270, 30-06, 7mm Rem. Mag., 300 Win. Mag., 338 Win. Mag., 4-shot magazine (3-shot Magnum calibers). **Barrel:** 22" (std. calibers) or 24" (Magnum calibers), with integral steel rib; barrel-mounted front swivel stud; hammer forged. **Weight:** 7.5 lbs. **Length:** 42.125" overall. **Stock:** Hand-checkered circassian walnut with steel gripcap, black rubber butt pad, swivel studs. **Sights:** Ramp front, V-notch two-leaf express rear adjustable for windage mounted on rib. **Features:** Mark II action with three-position safety, stainless steel bolt, steel trigger guard, hinged steel floorplate. Introduced 1991.
Price: M77RSEXPMKII............................. **$1,695.00**

RUGER 77/22 HORNET BOLT-ACTION RIFLE

Caliber: 22 Hornet, 6-shot rotary magazine. **Barrel:** 20". **Weight:** About 6 lbs. **Length:** 39-3/4" overall. **Stock:** Checkered American walnut, black rubber butt pad. **Sights:** Brass bead front, open adjustable rear; also available without sights. **Features:** Same basic features as the rimfire model except has slightly lengthened receiver. Uses Ruger rotary magazine. Three-position safety. Comes with 1" Ruger scope rings. Introduced 1994.
Price: 77/22RH (rings only) **$555.00**
Price: 77/22RSH (with sights)......................... **$575.00**
Price: K77/22VHZ Varmint, laminated stock, no sights **$599.00**

RUGER M77 MARK II RIFLE

Caliber: 223, 220 Swift, 22-250, 243, 6mm Rem., 257 Roberts, 25-06, 6.5x55 Swedish, 270, 7x57mm, 260 Rem., 280 Rem., 308, 30-06, 7mm Rem. Mag., 300 Win. Mag., 338 Win. Mag., 4-shot magazine. **Barrel:** 20", 22"; 24" (magnums). **Weight:** About 7 lbs. **Length:** 39-3/4" overall. **Stock:** Hand-checkered American walnut; swivel studs, rubber butt pad. **Sights:** None furnished. Receiver has Ruger integral scope mount base, comes with Ruger 1" rings. Some models have iron sights. **Features:** Short ac-

tion with new trigger and three-position safety. New trigger guard with re-designed floorplate latch. Left-hand model available. Introduced 1989.
Price: M77RMKII (no sights) **$649.00**
Price: M77RSMKII (open sights) **$725.00**
Price: M77LRMKII (left-hand, 270, 30-06, 7mm Rem. Mag.,300 Win. Mag.)
.... **$649.00**

Ruger M77 Mark II All-Weather Stainless Rifle

Similar to the wood-stock M77 Mark II except all metal parts are of stainless steel, and has an injection-moulded, glass-fiber-reinforced Du Pont Zytel stock. Also offered with laminated wood stock. Chambered for 223, 243, 270, 308, 30-06, 7mm Rem. Mag., 300 Win. Mag., 338 Win. Mag. Has the fixed-blade-type ejector, three-position safety, and new trigger guard with patented floorplate latch. Comes with integral Scope Base Receiver and 1" Ruger scope rings, built-in sling swivel loops. Introduced 1990.
Price: K77RFPMKII **$649.00**
Price: K77RLFPMKII Ultra-Light, synthetic stock, rings, no sights . **$649.00**
Price: K77LRBBZMKII, left-hand bolt, rings, no sights, laminated
stock **$699.00**
Price: K77RSFPMKII, synthetic stock, open sights **$725.00**
Price: K77RBZMKII, no sights, laminated wood stock, 223, 22/250, 243, 270, 280 Rem., 7mm Rem. Mag., 30-06, 308, 300 Win. Mag., 338 Win. Mag..................... **$699.00**
Price: K77RSBZMKII, open sights, laminated wood stock, 243, 270, 7mm Rem. Mag., 30-06, 300 Win. Mag., 338 Win. Mag. ... **$765.00**

Ruger M77RL Ultra Light

Similar to the standard M77 except weighs only 6 lbs., chambered for 223, 243, 308, 270, 30-06, 257 Roberts; barrel tapped for target scope blocks; has 20" Ultra Light barrel. Overall length 40". Ruger's steel 1" scope rings supplied. Introduced 1983.
Price: M77RLMKII **$699.00**

Ruger M77 Mark II Compact Rifles

Similar to the standard M77 except reduced in size with 16-1/2" barrel; weighs 5-3/4 lbs. Chambered for 223, 243, 260 Rem. and 308.
Price: M77CR MKII (blued finish, walnut stock) **$649.00**
Price: KM77CRBBZ MkII (stainless finish, black laminated stock). **$699.00**

RUGER M77 MARK II MAGNUM RIFLE

Caliber: 375 H&H, 4-shot magazine; 416 Rigby, 3-shot magazine. **Barrel:** 23", with integral steel rib; hammer forged. **Weight:** 9.25 lbs. (375); 9-3/4 lbs. (416, Rigby). **Length:** 40.5" overall. **Stock:** Circassian walnut with hand-cut checkering, swivel studs, steel gripcap, rubber butt pad. **Sights:** Ramp front, two leaf express on serrated integral steel rib. Rib also serves as base for front scope ring. **Features:** Uses an enlarged Mark II action with three-position safety, stainless bolt, steel trigger guard and hinged steel floorplate. Controlled feed. Introduced 1989.
Price: M77RSMMKII.................................. **$1,695.00**

Ruger M77VT Target

Sako TRG-S

Sako 75 Hunter

Sako 75 Deluxe

Sako 75 Stainless Hunter

RUGER 77/44 BOLT-ACTION RIFLE

Caliber: 44 Magnum, 4-shot magazine. **Barrel:** 18-1/2". **Weight:** 6 lbs. **Length:** 38-1/4" overall. **Stock:** American walnut with rubber butt pad and swivel studs or black polymer (stainless only). **Sights:** Gold bead front, folding leaf rear. Comes with Ruger 1" scope rings. **Features:** Uses same action as the Ruger 77/22. Short bolt stroke; rotary magazine; three-position safety. Introduced 1997. Made in U.S. by Sturm, Ruger & Co.
Price: Blue, walnut, 77/44RS **$580.00**
Price: Stainless, polymer, stock, K77/44RS **$580.00**

RUGER M77VT TARGET RIFLE

Caliber: 22-250, 220 Swift, 223, 243, 25-06, 308. **Barrel:** 26" heavy stainless steel with target gray finish. **Weight:** 9-3/4 lbs. **Length:** Approx. 44" overall. **Stock:** Laminated American hardwood with beavertail forend, steel swivel studs; no checkering or gripcap. **Sights:** Integral scope mount bases in receiver. **Features:** Ruger diagonal bedding system. Ruger steel 1" scope rings supplied. Fully adjustable trigger. Steel floorplate and trigger guard. New version introduced 1992.
Price: K77VTMKII **$779.00**

SAKO TRG-S BOLT-ACTION RIFLE

Caliber: 338 Lapua Mag., 30-378 Weatherby, 3-shot magazine. **Barrel:** 26". **Weight:** 7.75 lbs. **Length:** 45.5" overall. **Stock:** Reinforced polyurethane with Monte Carlo comb. **Sights:** None furnished. **Features:** Resistance-free bolt with 60-degree lift. Recoil pad adjustable for length. Free-floating barrel, detachable magazine, fully adjustable trigger. Matte blue metal. Introduced 1993. Imported from Finland by Beretta USA.
Price: **$875.00**

Sako TRG-42 BOLT-ACTION RIFLE

Similar to TRG-S except has 5-shot magazine, fully adjustable stock and competition trigger. Offered in 338 Lapua Mag. and 300 Win. Mag. Imported from Finland by Beretta USA.
Price: **$2,760.00**

SAKO 75 HUNTER BOLT-ACTION RIFLE

Caliber: 17 Rem., 222, 223, 22-250, 243, 7mm-08, 308 Win., 25-06, 270, 280, 30-06; 270 Wea. Mag., 7mm Rem. Mag., 7mm STW, 7mm Wea. Mag., 300 Win. Mag., 300 Wea. Mag., 338 Win. Mag., 340 Wea. Mag., 375 H&H, 416 Rem. Mag. **Barrel:** 22", standard calibers; 24", 26" magnum calibers. **Weight:** About 6 lbs. **Length:** NA. **Stock:** European walnut with matte lacquer finish. **Sights:** None furnished; dovetail scope mount rails. **Features:** New design with three locking lugs and a mechanical ejector; key locks firing pin and bolt; cold hammer-forged barrel is free-floating; two-position safety; hinged floorplate or detachable magazine that can be loaded from the top; short 70 degree bolt lift. Available in five action lengths. Introduced 1997. Imported from Finland by Beretta USA.
Price: Standard calibers **$1,115.00**
Price: Magnum Calibers **$1,145.00**

Sako 75 Stainless Synthetic Rifle

Similar to the 75 Hunter except all metal is of stainless steel, and the synthetic stock has soft composite panels moulded into the forend and pistol grip. Available in 22-250, 243, 308 Win., 25-06, 270, 30-06 with 22" barrel, 7mm Rem. Mag., 7mm STW, 300 Win. Mag., 338 Win. Mag. and 375 H&H Mag. with 24" barrel and 300 Wea. Mag., 300 Rem.Ultra Mag. with 26" barrel. Introduced 1997. Imported from Finland by Beretta USA.
Price: Standard calibers **$1,205.00**
Price: Magnum calibers **$1,235.00**

CENTERFIRE RIFLES — BOLT ACTION

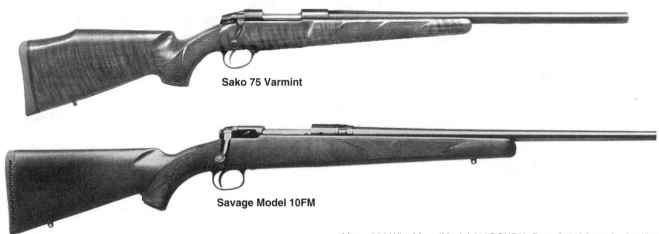

Sako 75 Varmint

Savage Model 10FM

Sako 75 Deluxe Rifle
Similar to the 75 Hunter except has select wood rosewood gripcap and forend tip. Available in 17 Rem., 222, 223, 25-06, 243, 7mm-08, 308, 25-06, 270, 280, 30-06; 270 Wea. Mag., 7mm Rem. Mag., 7mm STW, 7mm Wea. Mag., 300 Win. Mag., 300 Wea. Mag., 338 Win. Mag., 340 Wea. Mag., 375 H&H, 416 Rem. Mag. Introduced 1997. Imported from Finland by Beretta USA.
Price: Standard calibers **$1,615.00**
Price: Magnum calibers **$1,645.00**

Sako 75 Hunter Stainless Rifle
Similar to the Sako 75 Hunter except all metal is of stainless steel. Comes with walnut stock with matte lacquer finish, rubber butt pad. Introduced 1999. Imported from Finland by Beretta USA.
Price: 270, 30-06 . . . . **$1,205.00**
Price: 7mm Rem. Mag., 7mm STW, 300 Win. Mag.,
300 Wea. Mag., 338 Win. Mag. **$1,235.00**

Sako 75 Varmint Stainless Laminated Rifle
Similar to the Sako 75 Hunter except chambered only for 222, 223, 22-250, 22 PPC USA, 6mm PPC; has heavy 24" barrel with recessed crown; all metal is of stainless steel; has laminated wood stock with beavertail forend. Introduced 1999. Imported from Finland by Beretta USA.
Price: **$1,375.00**

Sako 75 Varmint Rifle
Similar to the Model 75 Hunter except chambered only for 17 Rem., 222 Rem., 223 Rem., 22-250 Rem., 22 PPC and 6mm PPC; 24" heavy barrel with recessed crown; beavertail forend. Introduced 1998. Imported from Finland by Beretta USA.
Price: **$1,280.00**

SAUER 202 BOLT-ACTION RIFLE
Caliber: Standard—243, 6.5x55, 270 Win., 308 Win., 30-06; magnum—7mm Rem. Mag., 300 Win. Mag., 300 Wea. Mag., 375 H&H. **Barrel:** 23.6" (standard), 26" (magnum). **Weight:** 7.7 lbs. **Length:** 44.3" overall (23.6" barrel). **Stock:** Select American Claro walnut with high-gloss epoxy finish, rosewood grip and forend caps; 22 lpi checkering. Synthetic also available. **Sights:** None furnished; drilled and tapped for scope mounting. **Features:** Short 60" bolt throw; detachable box magazine; six-lug bolt; quick-change barrel; tapered bore; adjustable two-stage trigger; firing pin cocking indicator. Introduced 1994. Imported from Germany by Sigarms, Inc.
Price: Standard calibers, right-hand **$1,035.00**
Price: Magnum calibers, right-hand **$1,106.00**
Price: Standard calibers, synthetic stock **$985.00**
Price: Magnum calibers, synthetic stock **$1,056.00**

SAVAGE MODEL 110GXP3, 110GCXP3 PACKAGE GUNS
Caliber: 223, 22-250, 243, 25-06, 270, 300 Sav., 30-06, 308, 7mm Rem. Mag., 7mm-08, 300 Win. Mag. (Model 110GXP3); 270, 30-06, 7mm Rem. Mag., 300 Win. Mag. (Model 110GCXP3). **Barrel:** 22" (standard calibers), 24" (magnum calibers). **Weight:** 7.25-7.5 lbs. **Length:** 43.5" overall (22" barrel). **Stock:** Monte Carlo-style hardwood with walnut finish, rubber butt pad, swivel studs. **Sights:** None furnished. **Features:** Model 110GXP3 has fixed, top-loading magazine, Model 110GCXP3 has detachable box magazine. Rifles come with a factory-mounted and bore-sighted 3-9x32 scope, rings and bases, quick-detachable swivels, sling. Left-hand models available in all calibers. Introduced 1991 (GXP3); 1994 (GCXP3). Made in U.S. by Savage Arms, Inc.
Price: Model 110GXP3, right- or left-hand **$513.00**
Price: Model 110GCXP3, right- or left-hand **$513.00**

Savage Model 111FXP3, 111FCXP3 Package Guns
Similar to the Model 110 Series Package Guns except with lightweight, black graphite/fiberglass composite stock with non-glare finish, positive checkering. Same calibers as Model 110 rifles, plus 338 Win. Mag. Model 111FXP3 has fixed top-loading magazine; Model 111FCXP3 has detachable box. Both come with mounted 3-9x32 scope, quick-detachable swivels, sling. Introduced 1994. Made in U.S. by Savage Arms, Inc.
Price: Model 111FXP3, right- or left-hand **$476.00**
Price: Model 111FCXP3, right- or left-hand **$525.00**

SAVAGE MODEL 110FM SIERRA ULTRA LIGHT WEIGHT RIFLE
Caliber: 243, 270, 308, 30-06. **Barrel:** 20". **Weight:** 6-1/4 lbs. **Length:** 41-1/2" overall. **Stock:** Graphite/fiberglass-filled composite. **Sights:** None furnished; drilled and tapped for scope mounting. **Features:** Comes with black nylon sling and quick-detachable swivels. Introduced 1996. Made in U.S. by Savage Arms, Inc.
Price: **$449.00**

Savage Model 10FM Sierra Ultra Light Rifle
Similar to the Model 110FM Sierra except has a true short action, chambered for 223, 243, 308; weighs 6 lbs. "Dual Pillar" bedding in black synthetic stock with silver medallion in gripcap. Comes with sling and quick-detachable swivels. Introduced 1998. Made in U.S. by Savage Arms, Inc.
Price: **$449.00**

SAVAGE MODEL 110FP TACTICAL RIFLE
Caliber: 223, 25-06, 308, 30-06, 300 Win. Mag., 7mm Rem. Mag., 4-shot magazine. **Barrel:** 24", heavy; recessed target muzzle. **Weight:** 8-1/2 lbs. **Length:** 45.5" overall. **Stock:** Black graphite/fiberglass composition; positive checkering. **Sights:** None furnished. Receiver drilled and tapped for scope mounting. **Features:** Pillar-bedded stock. Black matte finish on all metal parts. Double swivel studs on the forend for sling and/or bipod mount. Right or left-hand. Introduced 1990. From Savage Arms, Inc.
Price: Right- or left-hand **$476.00**

Savage Model 10FP Tactical Rifle
Similar to the Model 110FP except has true short action, chambered for 223, 308; black synthetic stock with "Dual Pillar" bedding. Introduced 1998. Made in U.S. by Savage Arms, Inc.
Price: **$476.00**
Price: Model 10FLP (left-hand) **$476.00**

RIFLES

Savage Model 10FP

Savage Model 11F

Savage Model 11G

Savage Model 10GY

Savage Model 114CE

SAVAGE MODEL 111 CLASSIC HUNTER RIFLES

Caliber: 223, 22-250, 243, 250 Sav., 25-06, 270, 300 Sav., 30-06, 308, 7mm Rem. Mag., 7mm-08, 300 Win. Mag., 338 Win. Mag. (Models 111G, GL, GNS, F, FL, FNS); 270, 30-06, 7mm Rem. Mag., 300 Win. Mag. (Models 111GC, GLC, FAK, FC, FLC). **Barrel:** 22", 24" (magnum calibers). **Weight:** 6.3 to 7 lbs. **Length:** 43.5" overall (22" barrel). **Stock:** Walnut-finished hardwood (M111G, GC); graphite/fiberglass filled composite. **Sights:** Ramp front, open fully adjustable rear; drilled and tapped for scope mounting. **Features:** Three-position top tang safety, double front locking lugs, free-floated button-rifled barrel. Comes with trigger lock, target, ear puffs. Introduced 1994. Made in U.S. by Savage Arms, Inc.

Price: Model 111FC (detachable magazine, composite stock, right- or left-hand) **$445.00**

Price: Model 111F (top-loading magazine, composite stock, right- or left-hand) **$419.00**

Price: Model 111FNS (as above, no sights, right-hand only) **$411.00**

Price: Model 111G (wood stock, top-loading magazine, right- or left-hand) **$395.00**

Price: Model 111GC (as above, detachable magazine), right- or left-hand **$433.00**

Price: Model 111GNS (wood stock, top-loading magzine, no sights, right-hand only) **$389.00**

Price: Model 111FAK Express (blued, composite stock, top loading magazine, Adjustable muzzle brake) . . . . **NA**

Savage Model 11 Hunter Rifles

Similar to the Model 111F except has true short action, chambered for 223, 22-250, 243, 308; black synthetic stock with "Dual Pillar" bedding,

positive checkering. Introduced 1998. Made in U.S. by Savage Arms, Inc.

Price: Model 11F **$419.00**
Price: Model 11FL (left-hand) **$419.00**
Price: Model 11FNS (right-hand, no sights) **$411.00**
Price: Model 11G (wood stock) **$395.00**
Price: Model 11GL (as above, left-hand) **$395.00**
Price: Model 11GNS (wood stock, no sights) **$389.00**

Savage Model 10GY, 110GY Rifle

Similar to the Model 111G except weighs 6.3 lbs., is 42-1/2" overall, and the stock is scaled for ladies, small-framed adults and youths. Chambered for 223, 243, 270, 308. Ramp front sight, open adjustable rear; drilled and tapped for scope mounts. Made in U.S. by Savage Arms, Inc.

Price: Model 110GY **$395.00**
Price: Model 10GY (short action, calibers 223, 243, 308) **$395.00**

SAVAGE MODEL 114C CLASSIC RIFLE

Caliber: 270, 30-06, 7mm Rem. Mag., 300 Win. Mag.; 4-shot detachable box magazine in standard calibers, 3-shot for magnums. **Barrel:** 22" for standard calibers, 24" for magnums. **Weight:** 7-1/8 lbs. **Length:** 45-1/2" overall. **Stock:** Oil-finished American walnut; checkered grip and forend. **Sights:** None furnished; drilled and tapped for scope mounting. **Features:** High polish blue on barrel, receiver and bolt handle; Savage logo laser-etched on bolt body; push-button magazine release. Introduced 1996. Made in U.S. by Savage Arms, Inc.

Price: **$556.00**

Savage Model 114CE Classic European

Similar to the Model 114C except the oil-finished walnut stock has a Schnabel forend tip, cheekpiece and skip-line checkering; bead on blade front sight, fully adjustable open rear; solid red butt pad. Chambered for 270, 30-06, 7mm Rem. Mag., 300 Win. Mag. Introduced 1996. Made in U.S. by Savage Arms, Inc.

Price: **$635.00**

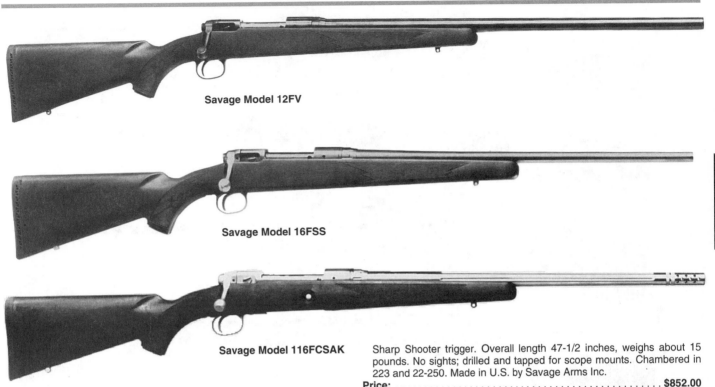

Savage Model 12FV

Savage Model 16FSS

Savage Model 116FCSAK

Savage Model 114U Ultra Rifle

Similar to the Model 114C except has high-luster blued finish, high-gloss walnut stock with custom cut checkering, ebony tip. No sights; drilled and tapped for scope. Chambered for 270, 30-06, 7mm Rem. Mag., 7mm STW and 300 Win.

Price: **$504.00**

SAVAGE MODEL 112 LONG RANGE RIFLES

Caliber: 22-250, 223, 5-shot magazine. **Barrel:** 26" heavy. **Weight:** 8.8 lbs. **Length:** 47.5" overall. **Stock:** Black graphite/fiberglass filled composite with positive checkering. **Sights:** None furnished; drilled and tapped for scope mounting. **Features:** Pillar-bedded stock. Blued barrel with recessed target-style muzzle. Double front swivel studs for attaching bipod. Introduced 1991. Made in U.S. by Savage Arms, Inc.

Price: Model 112FVSS (cals. 223, 22-250, 25-06, 7mm Rem. Mag., 300 Win. Mag., stainless barrel, bolt handle, trigger guard), right- or left-hand **$549.00**

Price: Model 112FVSS-S (as above, single shot) **$549.00**

Price: Model 112BVSS (heavy-prone laminated stock with high comb, Wundhammer swell, fluted stainless barrel, bolt handle, trigger guard) **$575.00**

Price: Model 112BVSS-S (as above, single shot) **$575.00**

Savage Model 12 Long Range Rifles

Similar to the Model 112 Long Range except with true short action, chambered for 223, 22-250, 308. Models 12FV, 12FVSS have black synthetic stocks with "Dual Pillar" bedding, positive checkering, swivel studs; model 12BVSS has brown laminated stock with beavertail forend, fluted stainless barrel. Introduced 1998. Made in U.S. by Savage Arms, Inc.

Price: Model 12FV (223, 22-250 only, blue) **$455.00**

Price: Model 12FVSS (blue action, fluted stainless barrel) **$549.00**

Price: Model 12FLVSS (as above, left-hand) **$549.00**

Price: Model 12FVSS-S (blue action, fluted stainless barrel, single shot) **$549.00**

Price: Model 12BVSS (laminated stock) **$575.00**

Price: Model 12BVSS-S (as above, single shot) **$575.00**

Savage Model 12VSS Varminter Rifle

Similar to other Model 12s except has blue/stainless steel action, fluted stainless barrel, Choate full pistol-grip, adjustable synthetic stock and Sharp Shooter trigger. Overall length 47-1/2 inches, weighs about 15 pounds. No sights; drilled and tapped for scope mounts. Chambered in 223 and 22-250. Made in U.S. by Savage Arms Inc.

Price: **$852.00**

SAVAGE MODEL 116SE SAFARI EXPRESS RIFLE

Caliber: 300 Win. Mag., 338 Win. Mag., 375 H&H, 458 Win. Mag. **Barrel:** 24". **Weight:** 8.5 lbs. **Length:** 45.5" overall. **Stock:** Classic-style select walnut with ebony forend tip, deluxe cut checkering. Two cross bolts; internally vented recoil pad. **Sights:** Bead on ramp front, three-leaf express rear. **Features:** Controlled-round feed design; adjustable muzzle brake; one-piece barrel band stud. Satin-finished stainless steel barreled action. Introduced 1994. Made in U.S. by Savage Arms, Inc.

Price: **$925.00**

SAVAGE MODEL 116 WEATHER WARRIORS

Caliber: 223, 243, 270, 30-06, 7mm Rem. Mag., 300 Win. Mag., 338 Win. Mag. (Model 116FSS); 270, 30-06, 7mm Rem. Mag., 300 Win. Mag. (Models 116FCSAK, 116FCS); 270, 30-06, 7mm Rem. Mag., 300 Win. Mag., 338 Win. Mag. (Models 116FSAK, 116FSK). **Barrel:** 22", 24" for 7mm Rem. Mag., 300 Win. Mag., 338 Win. Mag. (M116FSS only). **Weight:** 6.25 to 6.5 lbs. **Length:** 43.5" overall (22" barrel). **Stock:** Graphite/fiberglass filled composite. **Sights:** None furnished; drilled and tapped for scope mounting. **Features:** Stainless steel with matte finish; free-floated barrel; quick-detachable swivel studs; laser-etched bolt; scope bases and rings. Left-hand models available in all models, calibers at same price. Models 116FCS, 116FSS introduced 1991; Model 116FSK introduced 1993; Model 116FCSAK, 116FSAK introduced 1994. Made in U.S. by Savage Arms, Inc.

Price: Model 116FSS (top-loading magazine) **$528.00**

Price: Model 116FCS (detachable box magazine)............. **NA**

Price: Model 116FCSAK (as above with Savage Adjustable Muzzle Brake system) **$668.00**

Price: Model 116FSAK (top-loading magazine, Savage Adjustable Muzzle Brake system)................................ **$602.00**

Price: Model 116FSK Kodiak (as above with 22" Shock-Suppressor barrel) **$569.00**

Savage Model 16FSS Rifle

Similar to the Model 116FSS except has true short action, chambered for 223, 243, 308; 22" free-floated barrel; black graphite/fiberglass stock with "Dual Pillar" bedding. Introduced 1998. Made in U.S. by Savage Arms, Inc.

Price: **$528.00**

Price: Model 16FLSS (left-hand) **$528.00**

RIFLES

Sigarms SHR 970

Steyr Mannlicher SBS

Steyr SBS Forester

Steyr SBS Prohunter

Steyr Scout Rifle

SIGARMS SHR 970 SYNTHETIC RIFLE
Caliber: 270, 30-06. **Barrel:** 22". **Weight:** 7.2 lbs. **Length:** 41.9" overall. **Stock:** Textured black fiberglass or walnut. **Sights:** None furnished; drilled and tapped for scope mounting. **Features:** Quick takedown; interchangeable barrels; removable box magazine; cocking indicator; three-position safety. Introduced 1998. Imported by Sigarms, Inc.
Price: Synthetic stock **$499.00**
Price: Walnut stock **$550.00**

STEYR CLASSIC MANNLICHER SBS RIFLE
Caliber: 243, 25-06, 308, 6.5x55, 6.5x57, 270, 7x64 Brenneke, 7mm-08, 7.5x55, 30-06, 9.3x62, 6.5x68, 7mm Rem. Mag., 300 Win. Mag., 8x685, 4-shot magazine. **Barrel:** 23.6" standard; 26" magnum; 20" full stock standard calibers. **Weight:** 7 lbs. **Length:** 40.1" overall. **Stock:** Hand-checkered fancy European oiled walnut with standard forend. **Sights:** Ramp front adjustable for elevation, V-notch rear adjustable for windage. **Features:** Single adjustable trigger; 3-position roller safety with "safe-bolt" setting; drilled and tapped for Steyr factory scope mounts. Introduced 1997. Imported from Austria by GSI, Inc.
Price: Full-stock, standard calibers **$1,749.00**

STEYR SBS FORESTER RIFLE
Caliber: 243, 25-06, 270, 7mm-08, 308 Win., 30-06, 7mm Rem. Mag., 300 Win. Mag. Detachable 4-shot magazine. **Barrel:** 23.6", standard calibers; 25.6", magnum calibers. **Weight:** 7.5 lbs. **Length:** 44.5" overall (23.6" barrel). **Stock:** Oil-finished American walnut with Monte Carlo cheekpiece. Pachmayr 1" swivels. **Sights:** None furnished. Drilled and tapped for Browning A-Bolt mounts. **Features:** Steyr Safe Bolt systems, three-posi-

tion ambidextrous roller tang safety, for Safe, Loading Fire. Matte finish on barrel and receiver; adjustable trigger. Rotary cold-hammer forged barrel. Introduced 1997. Imported by GSI, Inc.
Price: Standard calibers **$799.00**
Price: Magnum calibers **$829.00**

Steyr SBS Prohunter Rifle
Similar to the SBS Forester except has ABS synthetic stock with adjustable butt spacers, straight comb without cheekpiece, palm swell, Pachmayr 1" swivels. Special 10-round magazine conversion kit available. Introduced 1997. Imported by GSI.
Price Standard calibers **$769.00**
Price Magnum calibers **$799.00**

STEYR SCOUT BOLT-ACTION RIFLE
Caliber: 308 Win., 5-shot magazine. **Barrel:** 19", fluted. **Weight:** NA. **Length:** NA. **Stock:** Gray Zytel. **Sights:** None furnished; comes with Leupold M8 2.5x28 IER scope on Picatinny optic rail with Steyr mounts. **Features:** Comes with luggage case, scout sling, two stock spacers, two magazines. Introduced 1998. From GSI.
Price: From **$1,969.00**

STEYR SSG BOLT-ACTION RIFLE
Caliber: 308 Win., detachable 5-shot rotary magazine. **Barrel:** 26" **Weight:** 8.5 lbs. **Length:** 44.5" overall. **Stock:** Black ABS Cycolac with spacers for length of pull adjustment. **Sights:** Hooded ramp front adjustable for elevation, V-notch rear adjustable for windage. **Features:** Sliding safety; NATO rail for bipod; 1" swivels; Parkerized finish; single or double-set triggers. Imported from Austria by GSI, Inc.
Price: SSG-PI, iron sights **$1,699.00**
Price: SSG-PII, heavy barrel, no sights **$1,699.00**
Price: SSG-PIIK, 20" heavy barrel, no sights **$1,699.00**
Price: SSG-PIV, 16.75" threaded heavy barrel with flash hider . **$2,659.00**

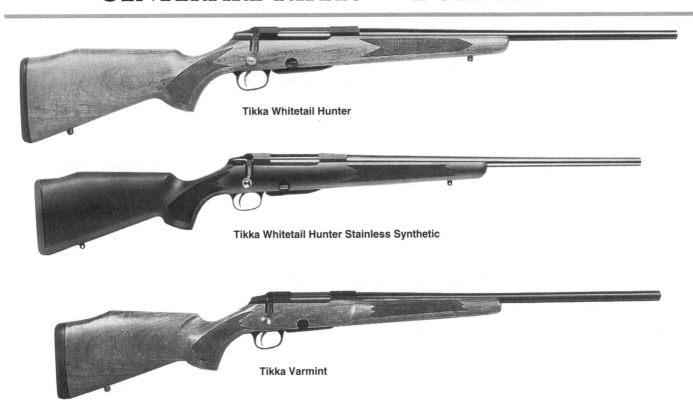

Tikka Whitetail Hunter

Tikka Whitetail Hunter Stainless Synthetic

Tikka Varmint

TIKKA WHITETAIL HUNTER BOLT-ACTION RIFLE

Caliber: 22-250, 223, 243, 7mm-08, 25-06, 270, 308, 30-06, 7mm Rem. Mag., 300 Win. Mag., 338 Win. Mag. **Barrel:** 22-1/2" (std. cals.), 24-1/2" (magnum cals.). **Weight:** 7-1/8 lbs. **Length:** 43" overall (std. cals.). **Stock:** European walnut with Monte Carlo comb, rubber butt pad, checkered grip and forend. **Sights:** None furnished. **Features:** Detachable four-shot magazine (standard calibers), three-shot in magnums. Receiver dovetailed for scope mounting. Reintroduced 1996. Imported from Finland by Beretta USA.
Price: Standard calibers $615.00
Price: Magnum calibers $645.00

Tikka Continental Varmint Rifle

Similar to the standard Tikka rifle except has 26" heavy barrel, extra-wide forend. Chambered for 17 Rem., 22-250, 223, 308. Reintroduced 1996. Made in Finland by Sako. Imported by Beretta USA.
Price: $720.00

Tikka Whitetail Hunter Deluxe Rifle

Similar to the Whitetail Hunter except has select walnut stock with rollover Monte Carlo comb, rosewood grip cap and forend tip. Has adjustable trigger, detachable magazine, free-floating barrel. Same calibers as the Hunter. Introduced 1999. Imported from Finland by Beretta USA.
Price: Standard calibers $745.00
Price: Magnum calibers $775.00

Tikka Whitetail Hunter Synthetic Rifle

Similar to the Whitetail Hunter except has black synthetic stock; calibers 223, 22-250, 243, 7mm-08, 25-06, 270 Win., 30-06, 7mm Rem. Mag., 300 Win. Mag., 338 Win. Mag. Introduced 1996. Imported from Finland by Beretta USA.
Price: Standard calibers $615.00
Price: Magnum calibers $645.00

Tikka Continental Long Range Hunting Rifle

Similar to the Whitetail Hunter except has 26" heavy barrel. Available in 25-06, 270 Win., 7mm Rem. Mag., 300 Win. Mag. Introduced 1996. Imported from Finland by Beretta USA.
Price: 25-06, 270 Win. $720.00
Price: 7mm Rem. Mag., 300 Win. Mag. $750.00

Tikka Whitetail Hunter Stainless Synthetic

Similar to the Whitetail Hunter except all metal is of stainless steel, and it has a black synthetic stock. Available in 22-250, 223, 243, 7mm-08, 25-06, 270, 308, 30-06, 7mm Rem. Mag., 300 Win. Mag., 338 Win. Mag. Introduced 1997. Imported from Finland by Beretta USA.
Price: Standard calibers $680.00
Price: Magnum calibers $710.00

VEKTOR BUSHVELD BOLT-ACTION RIFLE

Caliber: 243, 308, 7x57, 7x64 Brenneke, 270 Win., 30-06, 300 Win. Mag., 300 H&H, 9.3x62. **Barrel:** 22"-26". **Weight:** NA. **Length:** NA. **Stock:** Turkish walnut with wrap-around hand checkering. **Sights:** Blade on ramp front, fixed standing leaf rear. **Features:** Combines the best features of the Mauser 98 and Winchester 70 actions. Controlled-round feed; Mauser-type extractor; no cut-away through the bolt locking lug; M70-type three-position safety; Timney-type adjustable trigger. Introduced 1999. Imported from South Africa by Vektor USA.
Price: . . . . $1,595.00 to $1,695.00

VEKTOR MODEL 98 BOLT-ACTION RIFLE

Caliber: 243, 308, 7x57, 7x64 Brenneke, 270 Win., 30-06, 300 Win. Mag., 300 H&H, 375 H&H, 9.3x62. **Barrel:** 22"-26". **Weight:** NA. **Length:** NA. **Stock:** Turkish walnut with hand-checkered grip and forend. **Sights:** None furnished; drilled and tapped for scope mounting. **Features:** Bolt has guide rib; non-rotating, long extractor enhances positive feeding; polished blue finish. Updated Mauser 98 action. Introduced 1999. Imported from South Africa by Vektor USA.
Price: . . . . $1,149.00 to $1,249.00

WEATHERBY MARK V DELUXE BOLT-ACTION RIFLE

Caliber: All Weatherby calibers plus 22-250, 243, 25-06, 270 Win., 280 Rem., 7mm-08, 308 Win. **Barrel:** 26" round tapered. **Weight:** 8-1/2 to 10-1/2 lbs. **Length:** 46-5/8" to 46-3/4" overall. **Stock:** Walnut, Monte Carlo with cheekpiece; high luster finish; checkered pistol grip and forend; recoil pad. **Sights:** None furnished. **Features:** Cocking indicator; adjustable trigger; hinged floorplate, thumb safety; quick detachable sling swivels. Made in U.S. From Weatherby.
Price: 257, 270, 7mm. 300, 340 Wea. Mags., 26" barrel $1,649.00
Price: 416 Wea. Mag. with Accubrake, 26" barrel $1,999.00
Price: 460 Wea. Mag. with Accubrake, 26" barrel $2,349.00

CENTERFIRE RIFLES — BOLT ACTION

Weatherby Mark V Lazermark

Weatherby Mark V Euromark

Weatherby Mark V Stainless

Weatherby Mark V Synthetic

Weatherby Mark V Lazermark Rifle
Same as Mark V Deluxe except stock has extensive oak leaf pattern laser carving on pistol grip and forend. Introduced 1981.
Price: 257, 270, 7mm Wea. Mag., 300, 340, 26" **$1,849.00**
Price: 378 Wea. Mag., 26" **$2,179.00**
Price: 416 Wea. Mag., 26", Accubrake. **$2,179.00**
Price: 460 Wea. Mag., 26", Accubrake. **$2,559.00**

Weatherby Mark V Sporter Rifle
Same as the Mark V Deluxe without the embellishments. Metal has low-luster blue, stock is Claro walnut with high-gloss epoxy finish, Monte Carlo comb, recoil pad. Introduced 1993.
Price: 257, 270, 280, 7mm-08, 30-06, 308, 300, 340 Wea. Mags.,
26" **$1,049.00**
Price: 375 H&H, 24" **$1,099.00**
Price: 7mm Rem. Mag., 270 Wea. Mag., 7 mm Wea. Mag.,
300 Wea. Mag., 300 Win. Mag., 338 Win. Mag., 24" **$1,099.00**

Weatherby Mark V Euromark Rifle
Similar to the Mark V Deluxe except has raised-comb Monte Carlo stock with hand-rubbed oil finish, fine-line hand-cut checkering, ebony grip and forend tips. All metal has low-luster blue. Right-hand only. Uses Mark V action. Introduced 1995. Made in U.S. From Weatherby.
Price: 257, 270, 7mm, 300, 340 Wea. Mags., 26" barrel **$1,749.00**
Price: 7mm Rem. Mag., 300 Win. Mag., 338 Win. Mag.,
375 H&H, 24" barrel **$1,749.00**
Price: 378 Wea. Mag., 416 Wea. Mag., 28" barrel. **$2,049.00**

Weatherby Mark V Stainless Rifle
Similar to the Mark V Deluxe except made of 410-series stainless steel. Also available in 30-378 Wea. Mag. Has lightweight injection-moulded synthetic stock with raised Monte Carlo comb, checkered grip and forend, custom floorplate release. Right-hand only. Introduced 1995. Made in U.S. From Weatherby.
Price: 22-250, 243, 240 Wea. Mag., 25-06, 270, 280, 7mm-08, 30-06, 308,
7mm Rem. Mag., 300, 338 Win. Mags., 24" barrel **$979.00**
Price: Wea. Mags (257, 270, 7mm, 300, 340); 26" barrel **$1,029.00**
Wea. Mag.Price: 7mm Rem. Mag., 375 H&H, 24" barrel. **$1,029.00**
Price: 30-378 Wea. Mag., 28" barrel **$1,189.00**
Price: Stainless Carbine (as above with 20" barrel, 243 Win.,
7mm-08 Rem., 308 Win.), weighs 6 lbs.. . . . . **$979.00**

Weatherby Mark V SLS Stainless Laminate Sporter
Similar to the Mark V Stainless except all metalwork is 400 series stainless with a corrosion-resistant black oxide bead-blast matte finish. Action is hand-bedded in a laminated stock with a 1" recoil pad. Weighs 8-1/2 lbs. Introduced 1997. Made in U.S. From Weatherby.
Price: 257, 270, 7mm, 300, 340 Wea. Mags., 26" barrel **$1,339.00**
Price: 7mm Rem. Mag., 300 Win. Mag., 338 Win. Mag., 24" barrel
. . . . **$1,339.00**

Weatherby Mark V Eurosport Rifle
Similar to the Mark V Deluxe except has raised-comb Monte Carlo stock with hand-rubbed satin oil finish, low-luster blue metal. No gripcap or forend tip. Right-hand only. Introduced 1995. Made in U.S. From Weatherby.
Price: 257, 270, 7mm, 300, 340 Wea. Mags., 26" barrel **$1,099.00**
Price: 7mm Rem. Mag., 300, 338 Win. Mags., 24" barrel **$1,099.00**
Price: 375 H&H, 24" barrel. **$1,099.00**

Weatherby Mark V Synthetic
Similar to the Mark V Stainless except made of matte finished blued steel. Injection moulded synthetic stock. Weighs 6-1/2 lbs., 24" barrel. Available in 22-250, 240 Wea. Mag., 243, 25-06, 270, 7mm-08, 280, 30-06, 308. Introduced 1997. Made in U.S. From Weatherby.
Price: **$779.00**
Price: 257, 270, 7mm, 300, 340 Wea. Mags., 26" barrel **$829.00**
Price: 7mm STW, 7mm Rem. Mag., 300, 338 Win. Mags **$829.00**
Price: 375 H&H, 24" barrel. **$829.00**
Price: 30-378 Wea. Mag., 338-378 Wea.. . . . . **$979.00**

Weatherby Accumark

Wilderness Explorer

Winchester Model 70 Classic

WEATHERBY MARK V ACCUMARK RIFLE

Caliber: 257, 270, 7mm, 300, 340 Wea. Mags., 338-378 Wea. Mag., 30-378 Wea. Mag., 7mm STW, 7mm Rem. Mag., 300 Win. Mag. **Barrel:** 26". **Weight:** 8-1/2 lbs. **Length:** 46-5/8" overall. **Stock:** H-S Precision Pro-Series synthetic with aluminum bedding plate. **Sights:** None furnished. Drilled and tapped for scope mounting. **Features:** Uses Mark V action with heavy-contour stainless barrel with black oxidized flutes, muzzle diameter of .705". Introduced 1996. Made in U.S. From Weatherby.

Price: **$1,459.00**
Price: 30-378 Wea. Mag., 338-378 Wea. Mag., 28",
Accubrake. **$1,669.00**
Price: 223, 22-250, 243, 240 Wea. Mag., 25-06, 270,
280 Rem., 7mm-08, 30-06, 308; 24" **$1,399.00**
Price: Accumark Left-Hand 257, 270, 7mm, 300, 340 Wea.
Mag., 7mm Rem. Mag., 7mm STW, 300 Win. Mag. **$1,499.00**
Price: Accumark Left-Hand 30-378, 333-378 Wea. Mags. **$1,719.00**

Weatherby Mark V Accumark Ultra Lightweight Rifles

Similar to the Mark V Accumark except weighs 5-3/4 lbs.; free-floated 24" fluted barrel with recessed target crown; hand-laminated stock with CNC-machined aluminum bedding plate and faint gray "spider web" finish. Available in 257, 270, 7mm, 300 Wea. Mags., 243, 240 Wea. Mag., 25-06, 270 Win., 280 Rem., 7mm-08, 7mm Rem. Mag., 30-06, 338-06 A-Square, 308, 300 Win. Mag. Introduced 1998. Made in U.S. by Weatherby.

Price: . . . . **$1,349.00 to $1,399.00**
Price: Left-hand models **$1,459.00**

Weatherby Mark V SVM/SPM Rifles

Similar to the Mark V Accumark except has 26" fluted (SVM) or 24" fluted Krieger barrel, spiderweb-pattern tan laminated synthetic stock. SVM has a fully adjustable trigger. Chambered for 223, 22-250, 220 Swift (SVM only), 243, 7mm-08 and 308. Made in U.S. by Weatherby.

Price: SVM (Super VarmintMaster), repeater or single-shot . . . **$1,459.00**
New! Price: SPM (Super PredatorMaster) **$1,459.00**

Weatherby Mark V Fibermark Rifles

Similar to other Mark V models except has black Kevlar® and fiberglass composite stock and bead-blast blue or stainless finish. Chambered for 19 standard and magnum calibers. Introduced 1983; reintroduced 2001. Made in U.S. by Weatherby.

Price: Fibermark . . . . **$849.00 to $1,079.00**
Price: Fibermark Stainless . . . . **$1,079.00 to $1,289.00**

WEATHERBY MARK V DANGEROUS GAME RIFLE

Caliber: 375 H&H, 375 Wea. Mag., 378 Wea. Mag., 416 Rem. Mag., 416 Wea. Mag., 458 Win. Mag. and 460 Wea. Mag. **Barrel:** 24" or 26". **Weight:** 8-3/4 to 9-1/2 lbs. **Length:** 44-5/8" to 46-5/8" overall. **Stock:** Kevlar® and fiberglass composite. **Sights:** Barrel-band hooded front with large gold bead, adjustable ramp/shallow "V" rear. **Features:** Designed for dangerous-game hunting. Black oxide matte finish on all metalwork; Pachmayr Decelerator™ recoil pad, short-throw Mark V action. Introduced 2001. Made in U.S. by Weatherby.

Price: . . . . **$2,599.00 to $2,659.00**

WILDERNESS EXPLORER MULTI-CALIBER CARBINE

Caliber: 22 Hornet, 218 Bee, 44 Magnum, 50 A.E. (interchangeable). **Barrel:** 18", match grade. **Weight:** 5.5 lbs **Length:** 38-1/2" overall. **Stock:** Synthetic or wood. **Sights:** None furnished; comes with Weaver-style mount on barrel. **Features:** Quick-change barrel and bolt face for caliber switch. Removable box magazine; adjustable trigger with side safety; detachable swivel studs. Introduced 1997. Made in U.S. by Phillips & Rogers, Inc.

Price: **$995.00**

WINCHESTER MODEL 70 CLASSIC SPORTER LT

Caliber: 25-06, 270 Win., 30-06, 7mm STW, 7mm Rem. Mag., 300 Win. Mag., 338 Win. Mag., 3-shot magazine; 5-shot for 25-06, 270 Win., 30-06. **Barrel:** 24", 26" for magnums. **Weight:** 7-3/4 to 8 lbs. **Length:** 46-3/4" overall (26" bbl.). **Stock:** American walnut with cut checkering and satin finish. Classic style with straight comb. **Sights:** None furnished. Drilled and tapped for scope mounting. **Features:** Uses pre-64-type action with controlled round feeding. Three-position safety, stainless steel magazine follower; rubber butt pad; epoxy bedded receiver recoil lug. From U.S. Repeating Arms Co.

Price: 25-06, 270, 30-06. . . . . **$699.00**
Price: Other calibers. **$727.00**
Price: Left-hand, 270 or 30-06 . . . . **$733.00**
Price: Left-hand, 7mm Rem. Mag or 300 Win. Mag. **$761.00**

Winchester Model 70 Classic Stainless

Winchester Model 70 Classic Featherweight

Winchester Model 70 Classic Compact

Winchester Model 70 Classic Super Grade

Winchester Model 70 Classic Stainless Rifle

Same as the Model 70 Classic Sporter except has stainless steel barrel and pre-64-style action with controlled round feeding and matte gray finish, black composite stock impregnated with fiberglass and graphite, contoured rubber recoil pad. No sights (except 375 H&H). Available in 270 Win., 30-06, 7mm STW, 7mm Rem. Mag., 300 Win. Mag., 300 Ultra Mag., 338 Win. Mag., 375 H&H Mag. (24" barrel), 3- or 5-shot magazine. Weighs 7-1/2 lbs. Introduced 1994.

Price: 270, 30-06 . . . . **$768.00**
Price: 375 H&H Mag., with sights **$889.00**
Price: Other calibers **$798.00**

Winchester Model 70 Classic Featherweight

Same as the Model 70 Classic except has action bedded in a standard-grade walnut stock. Available in 22-250, 243, 6.5x55, 308, 7mm-08, 270 Win., 30-06. Drilled and tapped for scope mounts. Weighs 7 lbs. Introduced 1992.

Price: **$712.00**

Winchester Model 70 Classic Compact

Similar to the Classic Featherweight except scaled down for smaller shooters. Has 20" barrel, 12-1/2" length of pull. Pre-'64-type action. Available in 243, 308 or 7mm-08. Introduced 1998. Made in U.S. by U. S. Repeating Arms Co.

Price: **$712.00**

Winchester Model 70 Black Shadow

Similar to the Ranger except has black composite stock, matte blue barrel and action. Push-feed bolt design; hinged floorplate. Available in 270, 30-06, 7mm Rem. Mag., 300 Win. Mag. Made in U.S. by U.S. Repeating Arms Co.

Price: 270, 30-06 . . . . **$512.00**
Price: 7mm Rem. Mag., 300 Win. Mag. **$542.00**

Winchester Model 70 Coyote

Similar to the Model 70 Black Shadow except has laminated wood stock, 24" medium-heavy stainless steel barrel.

Price: Coyote (223, 22-250 or 243) **$679.00**

WINCHESTER MODEL 70 STEALTH RIFLE

Caliber: 223, 22-250, 308 Win. **Barrel:** 26". **Weight:** 10-3/4 lbs. **Length:** 46" overall. **Stock:** Kevlar/fiberglass/graphite Pillar Plus Accu-Block with full-length aluminum bedding block. **Sights:** None furnished. **Features:** Push-feed bolt design; matte finish. Introduced 1999. Made in U.S. by U.S. Repeating Arms Co.

Price: **$768.00**

WINCHESTER MODEL 70 CLASSIC SUPER GRADE

Caliber: 25-06, 270, 30-06, 5-shot magazine; 7mm Rem. Mag., 300 Win. Mag., 338 Win. Mag., 3-shot magazine. **Barrel:** 24", 26" for magnums. **Weight:** 7-3/4 lbs. to 8 lbs. **Length:** 44-1/2" overall (24" bbl.) **Stock:** Walnut with straight comb, sculptured cheekpiece, wrap-around cut checkering, tapered forend, solid rubber butt pad. **Sights:** None furnished; comes with scope bases and rings. **Features:** Controlled round feeding with stainless steel claw extractor, bolt guide rail, three-position safety; all steel bottom metal, hinged floorplate, stainless magazine follower. Introduced 1994. From U.S. Repeating Arms Co.

Price: 25-06, 270, 30-06 . . . . **$975.00**
Price: Other calibers **$1,003.00**

WINCHESTER MODEL 70 CLASSIC SAFARI EXPRESS

Caliber: 375 H&H Mag., 416 Rem. Mag., 458 Win. Mag., 3-shot magazine. **Barrel:** 24". **Weight:** 8-1/4 to 8-1/2 lbs. **Stock:** American walnut with Monte Carlo cheekpiece. Wrap-around checkering and finish. **Sights:** Hooded ramp front, open rear. **Features:** Controlled round feeding. Two steel cross bolts in stock for added strength. Front sling swivel stud mounted on barrel. Contoured rubber butt pad. From U.S. Repeating Arms Co.

Price: **$1,081.00**
Price: Left-hand, 375 H&H only **$1,117.00**

WINCHESTER MODEL 70 WSM RIFLES

Caliber: 300 WSM, 3-shot magazine. **Barrel:** 24". **Weight:** 7-1/4 to 7-3/4 lbs. **Length:** 44" overall. **Stock:** Checkered walnut, black synthetic or laminated wood. **Sights:** None. **Features:** Model 70 designed for the new 300 Winchester Short Magnum cartridge. Short-action receiver, three-position safety, knurled bolt handle. Introduced 2001. From U.S. Repeating Arms Co.

Price: Classic Featherweight WSM (checkered walnut stock
and forearm) **$740.00**
Price: Classic Stainless WSM (black syn. stock,
stainless steel bbl.) **$798.00**
Price: Classic Laminated WSM (laminated wood stock) **$761.00**

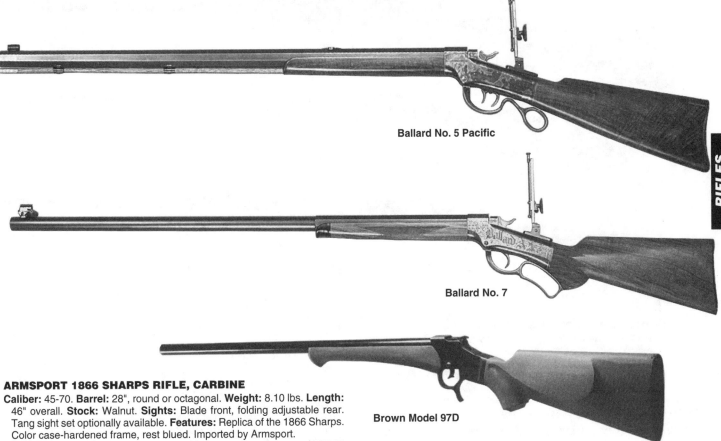

Ballard No. 5 Pacific

Ballard No. 7

Brown Model 97D

ARMSPORT 1866 SHARPS RIFLE, CARBINE

Caliber: 45-70. **Barrel:** 28", round or octagonal. **Weight:** 8.10 lbs. **Length:** 46" overall. **Stock:** Walnut. **Sights:** Blade front, folding adjustable rear. Tang sight set optionally available. **Features:** Replica of the 1866 Sharps. Color case-hardened frame, rest blued. Imported by Armsport.
Price: **$865.00**
Price: With octagonal barrel **$900.00**
Price: Carbine, 22" round barrel **$850.00**

BALLARD NO. 1 3/4 FAR WEST RIFLE

Caliber: 22 LR, 32-40, 38-55, 40-65, 40-70, 45-70, 45-110, 50-70, 50-90. **Barrel:** 30" std. or heavyweight. **Weight:** 10-1/2 lbs. (std.) or 11-3/4 lbs. (heavyweight bbl.) **Length:** NA. **Stock:** Walnut. **Sights:** Blade front, Rocky Mountain rear. **Features:** Single or double-set triggers, S-lever or ring-style lever; color case-hardened finish; hand polished and lapped Badger barrel. Made in U.S. by Ballard Rifle & Cartridge Co.
Price: **$2,050.00**

BALLARD NO. 4 PERFECTION RIFLE

Caliber: 22 LR, 32-40, 38-55, 40-65, 40-70, 45-70, 45-90, 45-110, 50-70, 50-90. **Barrel:** 30" or 32" octagon, standard or heavyweight. **Weight:** 10-1/2 lbs. (standard) or 11-3/4 lbs. (heavyweight bbl.). **Length:** NA. **Stock:** Smooth walnut. **Sights:** Blade front, Rocky Mountain rear. **Features:** Rifle or shotgun-style buttstock, straight grip action, single or double-set trigger, "S" or right lever, hand polished and lapped Badger barrel. Made in U.S. by Ballard Rifle & Cartridge Co.
Price: **$2,050.00**

BALLARD NO. 5 PACIFIC SINGLE-SHOT RIFLE

Caliber: 32-40, 38-55, 40-65, 40-90, 40-70 SS, 45-70 Govt., 45-110 SS, 50-70 Govt., 50-90 SS. **Barrel:** 30", or 32" octagonal. **Weight:** 10-1/2 lbs. **Length:** NA. **Stock:** High-grade walnut; rifle or shotgun style. **Sights:** Blade front, Rocky Mountain rear. **Features:** Standard or heavy barrel; double-set triggers; under-barrel wiping rod; ring lever. Introduced 1999. Made in U.S. by Ballard Rifle & Cartridge Co.
Price: **$2,575.00**

BALLARD NO. 7 LONG RANGE RIFLE

Caliber: 32-40, 38-55, 40-65, 40-70 SS, 45-70 Govt., 45-90, 45-110. **Barrel:** 32", 34" half-octagon. **Weight:** 11-3/4 lbs. **Length:** NA. **Stock:** Fancy walnut; checkered pistol grip shotgun butt, ebony forend cap. **Sights:** Globe front. **Features:** Designed for shooting up to 1000 yards. Standard or heavy barrel; single or double-set trigger; hard rubber or steel buttplate. Introduced 1999. Made in U.S. by Ballard Rifle & Cartridge Co.
Price: From **$2,950.00**

BALLARD NO. 8 UNION HILL RIFLE

Caliber: 22 LR, 32-40, 38-55, 40-65 Win., 40-70 SS. **Barrel:** 30" half-octagon. **Weight:** About 10-1/2 lbs. **Length:** NA. **Stock:** Fancy walnut; pistol grip butt with cheekpiece. **Sights:** Globe front. **Features:** Designed for 200-yard offhand shooting. Standard or heavy barrel; double-set triggers; full loop lever; hook Schuetzen buttplate. Introduced 1999. Made in U.S. by Ballard Rifle & Cartridge Co.
Price: From **$2,850.00**

BALLARD MODEL 1885 HIGH WALL SINGLE SHOT RIFLE

Caliber: 17 Bee, 22 Hornet, 218 Bee, 219 Don Wasp, 219 Zipper, 22 Hi-Power, 225 Win., 25-20 WCF, 25-35 WCF, 25 Krag, 7mmx57R, 30-30, 30-40 Krag, 303 British, 33 WCF, 348 WCF, 35 WCF, 35-30/30, 9.3x74R, 405 WCF, 50-110 WCF, 500 Express, 577 Express. **Barrel:** Lengths to 34". **Weight:** NA. **Length:** NA. **Stock:** Straight-grain American walnut. **Sights:** buckhorn or flat top rear, blade front. **Features:** Faithful copy of original Model 1885 High Wall; parts interchange with original rifles; variety of options available. Introduced 2000. Made in U.S. by Ballard Rifle & Cartridge LLC.
Price: From **$1,850.00**
Price: With single set trigger from **$2,050.00**

BARRETT MODEL 99 SINGLE SHOT RIFLE

Caliber: 50 BMG. **Barrel:** 33". **Weight:** 25 lbs. **Length:** 50.4" overall. **Stock:** Anodized aluminum with energy-absorbing recoil pad. **Sights:** None furnished; integral M1913 scope rail. **Features:** Bolt action; detachable bipod; match-grade barrel with high-efficiency muzzle brake. Introduced 1999. Made in U.S. by Barrett Firearms.
Price: From **$3,000.00**

RIFLES

Browning Model 1885 Traditional Hunter

Browning Model 1885 Low Wall

Cabela's Sharps

BROWN MODEL 97D SINGLE SHOT RIFLE

Caliber: 17 Ackley Hornet through 45-70 Govt. **Barrel:** Up to 26", air gauged match grade. **Weight:** About 5 lbs., 11 oz. **Stock:** Sporter style with pistol grip, cheekpiece and Schnabel forend. **Sights:** None furnished; drilled and tapped for scope mounting. **Features:** Falling block action gives rigid barrel-receiver matting; polished blue/black finish. Hand-fitted action. Many options. Made in U.S. by E. A.rthur Brown Co. Inc.
Price: From **$699.00**

BROWNING MODEL 1885 HIGH WALL SINGLE SHOT RIFLE

Caliber: 22-250, 30-06, 270, 7mm Rem. Mag., 454 Casull, 45-70. **Barrel:** 28". **Weight:** 8 lbs., 12 oz. **Length:** 43-1/2" overall. **Stock:** Walnut with straight grip, Schnabel forend. **Sights:** None furnished; drilled and tapped for scope mounting. **Features:** Replica of J.M. Browning's high-wall falling block rifle. Octagon barrel with recessed muzzle. Imported from Japan by Browning. Introduced 1985.
Price: **$1,027.00**

Browning Model 1885 BPCR Rifle

Similar to the 1885 High Wall rifle except the ejector system and shell deflector have been removed; chambered only for 40-65 and 45-70; color case-hardened full-tang receiver, lever, buttplate and gripcap; matte blue 30" part octagon, part round barrel. The Vernier tang sight has indexed elevation, is screw adjustable windage, and has three peep diameters. The hooded front sight has a built-in spirit level and comes with sight interchangeable inserts. Adjustable trigger. Overall length 46-1/8", weighs about 11 lbs. Introduced 1996. Imported from Japan by Browning.
Price: **$1,766.00**

Browning Model 1885 Low Wall Traditional Hunter

Similar to the Model 1885 Low Wall except chambered for 357 Mag., 44 Mag. and 45 Colt; steel crescent buttplate; 1/16" gold bead front sight, adjustable buckhorn rear, and tang-mounted peep sight with barrel-type elevation adjuster and knob-type windage adjustments. Barrel is drilled and tapped for a Browning scope base. Oil-finished select walnut stock with swivel studs. Introduced 1997. Imported for Japan by Browning.
Price: **$1,289.00**

Browning Model 1885 Low Wall Rifle

Similar to the Model 1885 High Wall except has trimmer receiver, thinner 24" octagonal barrel. Forend is mounted to the receiver. Adjustable trigger. Walnut pistol grip stock, trim Schnabel forend with high-gloss finish. Available in 22 Hornet and 260 Rem. Overall length 39-1/2", weighs 6 lbs., 11 oz. Rifling twist rates: 1:16" (22 Hornet); 1:9" (260). Polished blue finish. Introduced 1995. Imported from Japan by Browning.
Price: **$997.00**

BRNO ZBK 110 SINGLE SHOT RIFLE

Caliber: 222 Rem., 5.6x52R, 22 Hornet, 5.6x50 Mag., 6.5x57R, 7x57R, 8x57JRS. **Barrel:** 23.6". **Weight:** 5.9 lbs. **Length:** 40.1" overall. **Stock:** European walnut. **Sights:** None furnished; drilled and tapped for scope mounting. **Features:** Top tang opening lever; cross-bolt safety; polished blue finish. Announced 1998. Imported from The Czech Republic by Euro-Imports.
Price: Standard calibers **$223.00**
Price: 7x57R, 8x57JRS **$245.00**
Price: Lux model, standard calibers **$311.00**
Price: Lux model, 7x57R, 8x57JRS **$333.00**

CABELA'S SHARPS SPORTING RIFLE

Caliber: 45-70 or 45-120. **Barrel:** 32", tapered octagon. **Weight:** 9 lbs. **Length:** 47-1/4" overall. **Stock:** Checkered walnut. **Sights:** Blade front, open adjustable rear. **Features:** Color case-hardened receiver and hammer, rest blued. Introduced 1995. Imported by Cabela's.
Price: **$849.99**
Price: (Deluxe engraved Sharps) **$1,429.99**
Price: (Heavy target Sharps, 45-70 or 45-120) **$999.99**
Price: (Quigley Sharps, 45-70 or 45-120). **$1,299.99**

CIMARRON BILLY DIXON 1874 SHARPS SPORTING RIFLE

Caliber: 40-65, 45-70. **Barrel:** 32" tapered octagonal. **Weight:** NA. **Length:** NA. **Stock:** European walnut. **Sights:** Blade front, Creedmoor rear. **Features:** Color case-hardened frame, blued barrel. Hand-checkered grip and forend; hand-rubbed oil finish. Introduced 1999. Imported by Cimarron F.A. Co.
Price: **$1,295.00**

CIMARRON QUIGLEY MODEL 1874 SHARPS SPORTING RIFLE

Caliber: 45-70, 45-120. **Barrel:** 34" octagonal. **Weight:** NA. **Length:** NA. **Stock:** Checkered walnut. **Sights:** Blade front, adjustable rear. **Features:** Blued finish; double set triggers. From Cimarron F.A. Co.
Price: **$1,495.00**

CIMARRON SILHOUETTE MODEL 1874 SHARPS SPORTING RIFLE

Caliber: 45-70. **Barrel:** 32" octagonal. **Weight:** NA. **Length:** NA. **Stock:** Walnut. **Sights:** Blade front, adjustable rear. **Features:** Pistol-grip stock with shotgun-style butt plate; cut-rifled barrel. From Cimarron F.A. Co.
Price: **$1,095.00**

CIMARRON MODEL 1885 HIGH WALL RIFLE

Caliber: 38-55, 40-65, 45-70, 45-90. **Barrel:** 30" octagonal. **Weight:** NA. **Length:** NA. **Stock:** European walnut. **Sights:** Bead front, semi-buckhorn rear. **Features:** Replica of the Winchester 1885 High Wall rifle. Color case-hardened receiver and lever, blued barrel. Curved buttplate. Optional double set triggers. Introduced 1999. Imported by Cimarron F.A. Co.
Price: **$995.00**

Cumberland Mountain Plateau

Dakota Single Shot

Dixie 1874 Sharps Silhouette

H&R Ultra Hunter

CIMARRON CREEDMOOR ROLLING BLOCK RIFLE

Caliber: 40-65, 45-70. **Barrel:** 30" tapered octagon. **Weight:** NA. **Length:** NA. **Stock:** European walnut. **Sights:** Globe front, fully adjustable rear. **Features:** Color case-hardened receiver, blued barrel. Hand-checkered pistol grip and forend; hand-rubbed oil finish. Introduced 1999. Imported by Cimarron F.A. Co.
Price: **$1,295.00**

CUMBERLAND MOUNTAIN PLATEAU RIFLE

Caliber: 40-65, 45-70. **Barrel:** Up to 32"; round. **Weight:** About 10-1/2 lbs. (32" barrel). **Length:** 48" overall (32" barrel). **Stock:** American walnut. **Sights:** Marble's bead front, Marble's open rear. **Features:** Falling block action with underlever. Blued barrel and receiver. Stock has lacquer finish, crescent buttplate. Introduced 1995. Made in U.S. by Cumberland Mountain Arms, Inc.
Price: **$1,085.00**

DAKOTA MODEL 10 SINGLE SHOT RIFLE

Caliber: Most rimmed and rimless commercial calibers. **Barrel:** 23". **Weight:** 6 lbs. **Length:** 39-1/2" overall. **Stock:** Medium fancy grade walnut in classic style. Checkered grip and forend. **Sights:** None furnished. Drilled and tapped for scope mounting. **Features:** Falling block action with under-lever. Top tang safety. Removable trigger plate for conversion to single set trigger. Introduced 1990. Made in U.S. by Dakota Arms.
Price: **$3,595.00**
Price: Barreled action **$2,095.00**
Price: Action only **$1,850.00**
Price: Magnum calibers **$3,595.00**
Price: Magnum barreled action **$2,050.00**
Price: Magnum action only **$1,675.00**

DIXIE 1874 SHARPS BLACKPOWDER SILHOUETTE RIFLE

Caliber: 45-70. **Barrel:** 30"; tapered octagon; blued; 1:18" twist. **Weight:** 10 lbs., 3 oz. **Length:** 47-1/2" overall. **Stock:** Oiled walnut. **Sights:** Blade front, ladder-type hunting rear. **Features:** Replica of the Sharps #1 Sporter. Shotgun-style butt with checkered metal buttplate; color case-hard-

ened receiver, hammer, lever and buttplate. Tang is drilled and tapped for tang sight. Double-set triggers. Meets standards for NRA blackpowder cartridge matches. Introduced 1995. Imported from Italy by Dixie Gun Works.
Price: **$995.00**

Dixie 1874 Sharps Lightweight Hunter/Target Rifle

Same as the Dixie 1874 Sharps Blackpowder Silhouette model except has a straight-grip buttstock with military-style buttplate. Based on the 1874 military model. Introduced 1995. Imported from Italy by Dixie Gun Works.
Price: **$995.00**

E.M.F. 1874 METALLIC CARTRIDGE SHARPS RIFLE

Caliber: 45-70, 45/120. **Barrel:** 28", octagon. **Weight:** 10-3/4 lbs. **Length:** NA. **Stock:** Oiled walnut. **Sights:** Blade front, flip-up open rear. **Features:** Replica of the 1874 Sharps Sporting rifle. Color case-hardened lock; double-set trigger; blue finish. Imported by E.M.F.
Price: From **$700.00**
Price: With browned finish **$1,000.00**
Price: Military Carbine **$650.00**

HARRINGTON & RICHARDSON ULTRA VARMINT RIFLE

Caliber: 223, 243. **Barrel:** 24", heavy. **Weight:** About 7.5 lbs. **Length:** NA. **Stock:** Hand-checkered laminated birch with Monte Carlo comb. **Sights:** None furnished. Drilled and tapped for scope mounting. **Features:** Break-open action with side-lever release, positive ejection. Comes with scope mount. Blued receiver and barrel. Swivel studs. Introduced 1993. From H&R 1871, Inc.
Price: **$254.95**

Harrington & Richardson Ultra Hunter Rifle

Similar to the Ultra Varmint rifle except chambered for 25-06 with 26" barrel, or 308 Win. with 22" barrel. Stock and forend are of cinnamon-colored laminate; hand-checkered grip and forend. Introduced 1995. Made in U.S. by H&R 1871, LLC.
Price: **$268.95**
New! Price: 450 Marlin, 22" barrel **$268.95**

CENTERFIRE RIFLES — SINGLE SHOT

Model 1885 High Wall

Mossberg SSi-One Sporter

Navy Arms 1874 Sharps

Harrington & Richardson Ultra Comp Rifle

Similar to the Ultra Varmint except chambered for 270 or 30-06; has compensator to reduce recoil; camo-laminate stock and forend; blued, highly polished frame; scope mount. Made in U.S. by H&R 1871, LLC.
Price: **$303.95**

HARRIS GUNWORKS ANTIETAM SHARPS RIFLE

Caliber: 40-65, 45-75. **Barrel:** 30", 32", octagon or round, hand-lapped stainless or chrome-moly. **Weight:** 11.25 lbs. **Length:** 47" overall. **Stock:** Choice of straight grip, pistol grip or Creedmoor with Schnabel forend; pewter tip optional. Standard wood is A Fancy; higher grades available. **Sights:** Montana Vintage Arms #111 Low Profile Spirit Level front, #108 mid-range tang rear with windage adjustments. **Features:** Recreation of the 1874 Sharps sidehammer. Action is color case-hardened, barrel satin black. Chrome-moly barrel optionally blued. Optional sights include #112 Spirit Level Globe front with windage, #107 Long Range rear with windage. Introduced 1994. Made in U.S. by Harris Gunworks.
Price: $2,400.00

KRIEGHOFF HUBERTUS SINGLE-SHOT RIFLE

Caliber: 222, 243, 270, 308, 30-06, 5.6x50R Mag., 5.6x52R, 6x62R Freres, 6.5x57, 6.5x57R, 6.5x65R, 7x57, 7x57R, 7x64, 7x65R, 8x57JRS, 8x75RS, 270 Wea. Mag., 7mm Rem. Mag., 300 Win. Mag. **Barrel:** 23-1/2". **Weight:** 6-1/2 lbs. **Length:** NA. **Stock:** High-grade walnut. **Sights:** Blade front, open rear. **Features:** Break-loading with manual cocking lever on top tang; take-down; extractor; Schnabel forearm; many options. Imported from Germany by Krieghoff International Inc.
Price: Hubertus single shot, from **$5,850.00**
Price: Hubertus, magnum calibers **$6,850.00**

MODEL 1885 HIGH WALL RIFLE

Caliber: 30-40 Krag, 32-40, 38-55, 40-65 WCF, 45-70. **Barrel:** 26" (30-40), 28" all others. Douglas Premium #3 tapered octagon. **Weight:** NA. **Length:** NA. **Stock:** Premium American black walnut. **Sights:** Marble's standard ivory bead front, #66 long blade top rear with reversible notch and elevator. **Features:** Recreation of early octagon top, thick-wall High Wall with Coil spring action. Tang drilled, tapped for High Wall tang sight. Receiver, lever, hammer and breechblock color case-hardened. Introduced 1991. Available from Montana Armory, Inc.
Price: $1,095.00

MOSSBERG SSi-ONE SINGLE SHOT RIFLE

Caliber: 223 Rem., 22-250 Rem., 243 Win., 270 Win., 308 Rem., 30-06. **Barrel:** 24". **Weight:** 8 lbs. **Length:** 40". **Stock:** Satin-finished walnut, fluted and checkered; sling-swivel studs. **Sights:** None (scope base furnished). **Features:** Frame accepts interchangeable barrels, including 12-gauge, fully rifled slug barrel and 12 ga., 3-1/2" chambered barrel with Ulti-Full Turkey choke tube. Lever-opening, break-action design; single-stage trigger; ambidextrous, top-tang safety; internal eject/extract selector. Introduced 2000. From Mossberg.
Price: SSi-One Sporter (standard barrel) or 12 ga.,
3-1/2" chamber **$459.00**
Price: SSi-One Varmint (bull barrel, 22-250 Rem. only;
weighs 10 lbs.) **$480.00**
Price: SSi-One 12-gauge Slug (fully rifled barrel, no sights,
scope base) **$480.00**

NAVY ARMS 1874 SHARPS CAVALRY CARBINE

Caliber: 45-70. **Barrel:** 22". **Weight:** 7 lbs., 12 oz. **Length:** 39" overall. **Stock:** Walnut. **Sights:** Blade front, military ladder-type rear. **Features:** Replica of the 1874 Sharps miltary carbine. Color case-hardened receiver and furniture. Imported by Navy Arms.
Price: $1,000.00

NAVY ARMS 1874 SHARPS BUFFALO RIFLE

Caliber: 45-70, 45-90. **Barrel:** 28" heavy octagon. **Weight:** 10 lbs., 10 oz. **Length:** 46" overall. **Stock:** Walnut; checkered grip and forend. **Sights:** Blade front, ladder rear; tang sight optional. **Features:** Color case-hardened receiver, blued barrel; double-set triggers. Imported by Navy Arms.
Price: $1,160.00

Navy Arms Sharps Plains Rifle

Similar to the Sharps Buffalo rifle except 45-70 only, has 32" medium-weight barrel, weighs 9 lbs., 8 oz., and is 49" overall. Imported by Navy Arms.
Price: $1,125.00

Navy Arms Sharps Sporting Rifle

Same as the Navy Arms Sharps Plains Rifle except has pistol grip stock. Introduced 1997. Imported by Navy Arms.
Price: 45-70 only $1,160.00

RIFLES

Navy Arms 1885 High Wall

Navy Arms 1873 Springfield

Navy Arms #2 Creedmoor

Navy Arms No. 3 Long Range

New England Firearms Handi-Rifle

NAVY ARMS 1885 HIGH WALL RIFLE

Caliber: 45-70; others available on special order. **Barrel:** 28" round, 30" octagonal. **Weight:** 9.5 lbs. **Length:** 45-1/2" overall (30" barrel). **Stock:** Walnut. **Sights:** Blade front, vernier tang-mounted peep rear. **Features:** Replica of Winchester's High Wall designed by Browning. Color case-hardened receiver, blued barrel. Introduced 1998. Imported by Navy Arms.
Price: 28", round barrel, target sights **$900.00**
Price: 30" octagonal barrel, target sights **$975.00**

NAVY ARMS 1873 SPRINGFIELD CAVALRY CARBINE

Caliber: 45-70. **Barrel:** 22". **Weight:** 7 lbs. **Length:** 40-1/2" overall. **Stock:** Walnut. **Sights:** Blade front, military ladder rear. **Features:** Blued lockplate and barrel; color case-hardened breechblock; saddle ring with bar. Replica of 7th Cavalry gun. Imported by Navy Arms.
Price: **$930.00**

NAVY ARMS ROLLING BLOCK BUFFALO RIFLE

Caliber: 45-70. **Barrel:** 26", 30". **Stock:** Walnut. **Sights:** Blade front, adjustable rear. **Features:** Reproduction of classic rolling block action. Available with full-octagon or half-octagon-half-round barrel. Color case-hardened action, steel fittings. From Navy Arms.
Price: **$815.00**

NAVY ARMS NO. 2 CREEDMOOR TARGET RIFLE

Similar to the Navy Arms Rolling Block Buffalo Rifle except has 30" tapered octagon barrel, checkered full-pistol grip stock, blade front sight, open adjustable rear sight and Creedmoor tang sight. Imported by Navy Arms.
Price: **$995.00**

NAVY ARMS SHARPS NO. 3 LONG RANGE RIFLE

Caliber: 45-70, 45-90. **Barrel:** 34" octagon. **Weight:** 10 lbs., 12 oz. **Length:** 51-1/2". **Stock:** Deluxe walnut. **Sights:** Globe target front and match grade rear tang. **Features:** Shotgun buttplate, German silver forend cap, color case hardenend receiver. Imported by Navy Arms.
Price: **$1,860.00**

NEW ENGLAND FIREARMS HANDI-RIFLE

Caliber: 22 Hornet, 223, 243, 7x57, 7x64 Brenneke, 30-30, 270, 280 Rem., 308, 30-06, 357 Mag., 44 Mag., 45-70. **Barrel:** 22", 24"; 26" for 280 Rem. **Weight:** 7 lbs. **Stock:** Walnut-finished hardwood; black rubber recoil pad. **Sights:** Ramp front, folding rear (22 Hornet, 30-30, 45-70). Drilled and tapped for scope mount; 223, 243, 270, 280, 30-06 have no open sights, come with scope mounts. **Features:** Break-open action with side-lever release. The 223, 243, 270 and 30-06 have recoil pad and Monte Carlo stock for shooting with scope. Swivel studs on all models. Blue finish. Introduced 1989. From New England Firearms.
Price: **$219.95**
Price: 7x57, 7x64 Brenneke, 24" barrel **$219.95**
Price: 280 Rem., 26" barrel **$219.95**
Price: Synthetic Handi-Rifle (black polymer stock and forend, swivels, recoil pad) **$228.95**
Price: Handi-Rifle Youth (223, 243) **$219.95**

RIFLES

New England Firearms Super Light

New England Firearms Survivor

Remington No. 1 Mid-Range

Ruger No. 1B

New England Firearms Super Light Rifle

Similar to the Handi-Rifle except has new barrel taper, shorter 20" barrel with recessed muzzle and special lightweight synthetic stock and forend. No sights are furnished on the 223 and 243 versions, but have a factory-mounted scope base and offset hammer spur; Monte Carlo stock; 22 Hornet has ramp front, fully adjustable open rear. Overall length is 36", weight is 5.5 lbs. Introduced 1997. Made in U.S. by New England Firearms.
Price: 22 Hornet, 223 Rem. or 243 Win.. . . . . **$228.95**

NEW ENGLAND FIREARMS SURVIVOR RIFLE

Caliber: 223, 308 Win., single shot. **Barrel:** 22". **Weight:** 6 lbs. **Length:** 36" overall. **Stock:** Black polymer, thumbhole design. **Sights:** None furnished; scope mount provided. **Features:** Receiver drilled and tapped for scope mounting. Stock and forend have storage compartments for ammo, etc.; comes with integral swivels and black nylon sling. Introduced 1996. Made in U.S. by New England Firearms.
Price: Blue finish. **$227.95**

REMINGTON NO. 1 ROLLING BLOCK MID-RANGE SPORTER

Caliber: 45-70. **Barrel:** 30" round. **Weight:** 8-3/4 lbs. **Length:** 46-1/2" overall. **Stock:** American walnut with checkered pistol grip and forend. **Sights:** Beaded blade front, adjustable center-notch buckhorn rear. **Features:** Recreation of the original. Polished blue metal finish. Many options available. Introduced 1998. Made in U.S. by Remington.
Price: **$1,348.00**

RUGER NO. 1B SINGLE SHOT

Caliber: 218 Bee, 22 Hornet, 220 Swift, 22-250, 223, 243, 6mm Rem., 25-06, 257 Roberts, 270, 280, 30-06, 7mm Rem. Mag., 300 Win. Mag., 338 Win. Mag., 270 Wea., 300 Wea. **Barrel:** 26" round tapered with quarter-rib; with Ruger 1" rings. **Weight:** 8 lbs. **Length:** 43-3/8" overall. **Stock:** Walnut, two-piece, checkered pistol grip and semi-beavertail forend. **Sights:** None, 1" scope rings supplied for integral mounts. **Features:** Under-lever, hammerless falling block design has auto ejector, top tang safety.
Price: 1B. **$797.00**
Price: Barreled action **$575.00**
Price: K1-B-BBZ Stainless steel, laminated stock 25-06, 7MM mag, 7MM STW, 300 Win Mag. **$845.00**

Ruger No. 1A Light Sporter

Similar to the No. 1B Standard Rifle except has lightweight 22" barrel, Alexander Henry-style forend, adjustable folding leaf rear sight on quarter-rib, dovetailed ramp front with gold bead. Calibers 243, 30-06, 270 and 7x57. Weighs about 7-1/4 lbs.
Price: No. 1A **$797.00**
Price: Barreled action **$575.00**

Ruger No. 1V Varminter

Similar to the No. 1B Standard Rifle except has 24" heavy barrel. Semi-beavertail forend, barrel ribbed for target scope block, with 1" Ruger scope rings. Calibers 22-250, 220 Swift, 223, 25-06. Weight about 9 lbs.
Price: No. 1V **$797.00**
Price: Barreled action **$575.00**
Price: K1-V-BBZ stainless steel, laminated stock 22-250 . . . . . . **$845.00**

RIFLES

Ruger K1-B-BBZ

Ruger No. 1V Varminter

Ruger No. 1 RSI

Ruger No. 1H Tropical

**C. Sharps New Model
1875 Old Reliable**

Ruger No. 1 RSI International
Similar to the No. 1B Standard Rifle except has lightweight 20" barrel, full-length International-style forend with loop sling swivel, adjustable folding leaf rear sight on quarter-rib, ramp front with gold bead. Calibers 243, 30-06, 270 and 7x57. Weight is about 7-1/4 lbs.

Price: No. 1 RSI **$818.00**
Price: Barreled action **$575.00**

Ruger No. 1H Tropical Rifle
Similar to the No. 1B Standard Rifle except has Alexander Henry forend, adjustable folding leaf rear sight on quarter-rib, ramp front with dovetail gold bead, 24" heavy barrel. Calibers 375 H&H, 416 Rem. Mag. (weighs about 8-1/4 lbs.), 416 Rigby, and 458 Win. Mag. (weighs about 9 lbs.).

Price: No. 1H **$797.00**
Price: Barreled action **$575.00**

Ruger No. 1S Medium Sporter
Similar to the No. 1B Standard Rifle except has Alexander Henry-style forend, adjustable folding leaf rear sight on quarter-rib, ramp front sight base and dovetail-type gold bead front sight. Calibers 218 Bee, 7mm Rem. Mag., 338 Win. Mag., 300 Win. Mag. with 26" barrel, 45-70 with 22" barrel. Weighs about 7-1/2 lbs. In 45-70.

Price: No. 1S **$797.00**
Price: Barreled action **$575.00**

Ruger No. 1 Stainless Steel Rifles
Similar to No. 1 Standard except has stainless steel receiver and barrel, laminated hardwood stock. Calibers 25-06, 7mm Rem. Mag., 7mm STW, 300 Win. Mag. (Standard) or 22-250 (Varminter). Introduced 2000.

Price: No. 1 Stainless Standard (26" barrel, 8 lbs.) **$845.00**
Price: No. 1 Stainless Varminter (24" heavy barrel,
9 lbs.) **$845.00**

C. SHARPS ARMS NEW MODEL 1875 OLD RELIABLE RIFLE
Caliber: 22LR, 32-40 & 38-55 Ballard, 38-56 WCF, 40-65 WCF, 40-90 3-1/4", 40-90 2-5/8", 40-70 2-1/10", 40-70 2-1/4", 40-70 2-1/2", 40-50 1-11/16", 40-50 1-7/8", 45-90, 45-70, 45-100, 45-110, 45-120. Also available on special order only in 50-70, 50-90, 50-140. **Barrel:** 24", 26", 30" (standard), 32", 34" optional. **Weight:** 8-12 lbs. **Stock:** Walnut, straight grip, shotgun butt with checkered steel buttplate. **Sights:** Silver blade front, Rocky Mountain buckhorn rear. **Features:** Recreation of the 1875 Sharps rifle. Production guns will have case colored receiver. Available in Custom Sporting and Target versions upon request. Announced 1986. From C. Sharps Arms Co. and Montana Armory, Inc.

Price: 1875 Carbine (24" tapered round bbl.) **$810.00**
Price: 1875 Saddle Rifle (26" tapered oct. bbl.) **$910.00**
Price: 1875 Sporting Rifle (30" tapered oct. bbl.) **$975.00**
Price: 1875 Business Rifle (28" tapered round bbl.) **$860.00**

C. Sharps New Model 1874

C. Sharps New Model 1885

Thompson/Center Contender

C. Sharps Arms 1875 Classic Sharps

Similar to the New Model 1875 Sporting Rifle except has 26", 28" or 30" full octagon barrel, crescent buttplate with toe plate, Hartford-style forend with cast German silver nose cap. Blade front sight, Rocky Mountain buckhorn rear. Weighs 10 lbs. Introduced 1987. From C. Sharps Arms Co. and Montana Armory, Inc.

Price: **$1,185.00**

C. Sharps Arms New Model 1875 Target & Long Range

Similar to the New Model 1875 except available in all listed calibers except 22 LR; 34" tapered octagon barrel; globe with post front sight, Long Range Vernier tang sight with windage adjustments. Pistol grip stock with cheek rest; checkered steel buttplate. Introduced 1991. From C. Sharps Arms Co. and Montana Armory, Inc.

Price: **$1,535.00**

C. SHARPS ARMS NEW MODEL 1874 OLD RELIABLE

Caliber: 40-50, 40-70, 40-90, 45-70, 45-90, 45-100, 45-110, 45-120, 50-70, 50-90, 50-140. **Barrel:** 26", 28", 30" tapered octagon. **Weight:** About 10 lbs. **Length:** NA. **Stock:** American black walnut; shotgun butt with checkered steel buttplate; straight grip, heavy forend with Schnabel tip. **Sights:** Blade front, buckhorn rear. Drilled and tapped for tang sight. **Features:** Recreation of the Model 1874 Old Reliable Sharps Sporting Rifle. Double set triggers. Reintroduced 1991. Made in U.S. by C. Sharps Arms. Available from Montana Armory, Inc.

Price: **$1,175.00**

C. SHARPS ARMS NEW MODEL 1885 HIGHWALL RIFLE

Caliber: 22 LR, 22 Hornet, 219 Zipper, 25-35 WCF, 32-40 WCF, 38-55 WCF, 40-65, 30-40-Krag, 40-50 ST or BN, 40-70 ST or BN, 40-90 ST or BN, 45-70 2-1/10" ST, 45-90 2-4/10" ST, 45-100 2-6/10" ST, 45-110 2-7/8" ST, 45-120 3-1/4" ST. **Barrel:** 26", 28", 30", tapered full octagon. **Weight:** About 9 lbs., 4 oz. **Length:** 47" overall. **Stock:** Oil-finished American walnut; Schnabel-style forend. **Sights:** Blade front, buckhorn rear. Drilled and tapped for optional tang sight. **Features:** Single trigger; octagonal receiver top; checkered steel buttplate; color case-hardened receiver and buttplate, blued barrel. Many options available. Made in U.S. by C. Sharps Arms Co. Available from Montana Armory, Inc.

Price: From **$1,195.00**

SHARPS 1874 RIFLE

Caliber: 45-70. **Barrel:** 28", octagonal. **Weight:** 9-1/4 lbs. **Length:** 46" overall. **Stock:** Checkered walnut. **Sights:** Blade front, adjustable rear. **Features:** Double set triggers on rifle. Color case-hardened receiver and buttplate, blued barrel. Imported from Italy by E.M.F.

Price: Rifle or carbine **$950.00**

Price: Military rifle, carbine **$860.00**
Price: Sporting rifle **$860.00**

SHILOH SHARPS 1874 LONG RANGE EXPRESS

Caliber: 40-50 BN, 40-70 BN, 40-90 BN, 45-70 ST, 45-90 ST, 45-110 ST, 50-70 ST, 50-90 ST, 50-110 ST, 32-40, 38-55, 40-70 ST, 40-90 ST. **Barrel:** 34" tapered octagon. **Weight:** 10-1/2 lbs. **Length:** 51" overall. **Stock:** Oil-finished semi-fancy walnut with pistol grip, shotgun-style butt, traditional cheek rest, Schnabel forend. **Sights:** Globe front, sporting tang rear. **Features:** Recreation of the Model 1874 Sharps rifle. Double set triggers. Made in U.S. by Shiloh Rifle Mfg. Co.

Price: **$1,796.00**

Price: Sporting Rifle No. 1 (similar to above except with 30" bbl., blade front, buckhorn rear sight) **$1,706.00**

Price: Sporting Rifle No. 3 (similar to No. 1 except straight-grip stock, standard wood) **$1,504.00**

Price: 1874 Hartford model **$1,702.00**

Shiloh Sharps 1874 Montana Roughrider

Similar to the No. 1 Sporting Rifle except available with half-octagon or full-octagon barrel in 24", 26", 28", 30", 34" lengths; standard supreme or semi-fancy wood, shotgun, pistol grip or military-style butt. Weight about 8-1/2 lbs. Calibers 30-40, 30-30, 40-50x1-11/16"BN, 40-70x2-1/10" BN, 45-70x2-1/10"ST. Globe front and tang sight optional.

Price: Standard supreme **$1,504.00**
Price: Semi-fancy **$1,704.00**

Shiloh Sharps 1874 Business Rifle

Similar to No. 3 Rifle except has 28" heavy round barrel, military-style buttstock and steel buttplate. Weight about 9-1/2 lbs. Calibers 40-50 BN, 40-70 BN, 40-90 BN, 45-70 ST, 45-90 ST, 50-70 ST, 50-100 ST, 32-40, 38-55, 40-70 ST, 40-90 ST.

Price: **$1,604.00**

Price: 1874 Saddle Rifle (similar to Carbine except has 26" octagon barrel, semi-fancy shotgun butt) **$1,706.00**

THOMPSON/CENTER CONTENDER CARBINE

Caliber: 22 LR, 22 Hornet, 223 Rem., 7x30 Waters, 30-30 Win. **Barrel:** 21". **Weight:** 5 lbs., 2 oz. **Length:** 35" overall. **Stock:** Checkered American walnut with rubber butt pad. Also with Rynite stock and forend. **Sights:** Blade front, open adjustable rear. **Features:** Uses the T/C Contender action. Eleven interchangeable barrels available, all with sights, drilled and tapped for scope mounting. Introduced 1985. Offered as a complete Carbine only.

Price: Rifle calibers. **$571.38**
Price: Extra barrels, rifle calibers, each **$251.08**

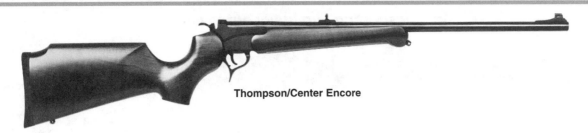

Thompson/Center Encore

THOMPSON/CENTER ENCORE RIFLE

Caliber: 22-250, 223, 243, 25-06, 270, 7mm-08, 308, 30-06, 7mm Rem. Mag., 300 Win. Mag. **Barrel:** 24", 26". **Weight:** 6 lbs., 12 oz. (24" barrel). **Length:** 38-1/2" (24" barrel). **Stock:** American walnut. Monte Carlo style; Schnabel forend or black composite. **Sights:** Ramp-style white bead front, fully adjustable leaf-type rear. **Features:** Interchangeable barrels; action opens by squeezing trigger guard; drilled and tapped for T/C scope mounts; polished blue finish. Introduced 1996. Made in U.S. by Thompson/Center Arms.

Price: **$582.29**
Price: Extra barrels. **$249.10**
Price: With black composite stock and forend **$582.29**

Thompson/Center Stainless Encore Rifle

Similar to the blued Encore except made of stainless steel with blued sights, and has black composite stock and forend. Available in 22-250, 223, 7mm-08, 30-06, 308. Introduced 1999. Made in U.S. by Thompson/Center Arms.

Price: **$650.42**

TRADITIONS 1874 SHARPS DELUXE RIFLE

Caliber: 45-70. **Barrel:** 32" octagonal; 1:18" twist. **Weight:** 11.67 lbs. **Length:** 48.8" overall. **Stock:** Checkered walnut with German silver nose cap and steel butt plate. **Sights:** Globe front, adjustable creedmore rear with 12 inserts. **Features:** Color-case hardened receiver; double-set triggers. Introduced 2001. Imported from Pedersoli by Traditions.

Price: **$969.00**

TRADITIONS 1874 SHARPS STANDARD RIFLE

Similar to 1874 Sharps Deluxe Rifle, except has blade front and adjustable buckhorn-style rear sight. Weighs 10.67 pounds. Introduced 2001. Imported from Pedersoli by Traditions.

Price: **$749.00**

TRADITIONS ROLLING BLOCK SPORTING RIFLE

Caliber: 45-70. **Barrel:** 30" octagonal; 1:18" twist. **Weight:** 11.67 lbs. **Length:** 46.7" overall. **Stock:** Walnut. **Sights:** Blade front, adjustable rear. **Features:** Antique silver, color-case hardened receiver, drilled and tapped for tang/globe sights; brass butt plate and trigger guard. Introduced 2001. Imported from Pedersoli by Traditions.

Price: **$749.00**

TRISTAR/UBERTI 1885 SINGLE SHOT

Caliber: 45-70. **Barrel:** 28". **Weight:** 8.75 lbs. **Length:** 44.5" overall. **Stock:** European walnut. **Sights:** Bead on blade front, open step-adjustable rear. **Features:** Recreation of the 1885 Winchester. Color case-hardened receiver and lever, blued barrel. Introduced 1998. Imported from Italy by Tristar Sporting Arms Ltd.

Price: **$765.00**

UBERTI BABY ROLLING BLOCK CARBINE

Caliber: 22 LR, 22 WMR, 22 Hornet, 357 Mag., single shot. **Barrel:** 22". **Weight:** 4.8 lbs. **Length:** 35-1/2" overall. **Stock:** Walnut stock and forend. **Sights:** Blade front, fully adjustable open rear. **Features:** Resembles Remington New Model No. 4 carbine. Brass trigger guard and buttplate; color case-hardened frame, blued barrel. Imported by Uberti USA Inc.

Price: **$490.00**
Price: Baby Rolling Block Rifle, 26" bbl. **$590.00**

WESSON & HARRINGTON BUFFALO CLASSIC RIFLE

Caliber: 45-70. **Barrel:** 32" heavy. **Weight:** 9 lbs. **Length:** 52" overall. **Stock:** American black walnut. **Sights:** None furnished; drilled and tapped for peep sight; barrel dovetailed for front sight. **Features:** Color case-hardened Handi-Rifle action with exposed hammer; color case-hardened crescent buttplate; 19th century checkering pattern. Introduced 1995. Made in U.S. by H&R 1871, Inc.

Price: About **$349.95**

Wesson & Harrington 38-55 Target Rifle

Similar to the Buffalo Classic rifle except chambered for 38-55 Win., has 28" barrel. The barrel and steel furniture, including steel trigger guard and forend spacer, are highly polished and blued. Color case-hardened receiver and buttplate. Barrel is dovetailed for a front sight, and drilled and tapped for receiver sight or scope mount. Introduced 1998. Made in U.S. by H&R 1871, Inc.

Price: **$389.95**

Designs for sporting and utility purposes worldwide.

RIFLES

Beretta Express SSO

Beretta Model 455 SxS

Charles Daly Superior

BERETTA EXPRESS SSO O/U DOUBLE RIFLES

Caliber: 375 H&H, 458 Win. Mag., 9.3x74R. **Barrel:** 25.5". **Weight:** 11 lbs. **Stock:** European walnut with hand-checkered grip and forend. **Sights:** Blade front on ramp, open V-notch rear. **Features:** Sidelock action with color case-hardened receiver (gold inlays on SSO6 Gold). Ejectors, double triggers, recoil pad. Introduced 1990. Imported from Italy by Beretta U.S.A.
Price: SSO6 . . . . **$21,000.00**
Price: SSO6 Gold **$23,500.00**

BERETTA MODEL 455 SxS EXPRESS RIFLE

Caliber: 375 H&H, 458 Win. Mag., 470 NE, 500 NE 3", 416 Rigby. **Barrel:** 23-1/2" or 25-1/2". **Weight:** 11 lbs. **Stock:** European walnut with hand-checkered grip and forend. **Sights:** Blade front, folding leaf V-notch rear. **Features:** Sidelock action with easily removable sideplates; color case-hardened finish (455), custom big game or floral motif engraving (455EELL). Double triggers, recoil pad. Introduced 1990. Imported from Italy by Beretta U.S.A.
Price: Model 455. . . . . **$36,000.00**
Price: Model 455EELL **$47,000.00**

BRNO 500 COMBINATION GUNS

Caliber/Gauge: 12 (2-3/4" chamber) over 5.6x52R, 5.6x50R, 222 Rem., 243, 6.x55, 308, 7x57R, 7x65R, 30-06. **Barrel:** 23.6". **Weight:** 7.6 lbs. **Length:** 40.5" overall. **Stock:** European walnut. **Sights:** Bead front, V-notch rear; grooved for scope mounting. **Features:** Boxlock action; double set trigger; blue finish with etched engraving. Announced 1998. Imported from The Czech Republic by Euro-Imports.
Price: **$1,023.00**
Price: O/U double rifle, 7x57R, 7x65R, 8x57JRS. **$1,125.00**

BRNO ZH 300 COMBINATION GUN

Caliber/Gauge: 22 Hornet, 5.6x50R Mag., 5.6x52R, 7x57R, 7x65R, 8x57JRS over 12, 16 (2-3/4" chamber). **Barrel:** 23.6". **Weight:** 7.9 lbs. **Length:** 40.5" overall. **Stock:** European walnut. **Sights:** Blade front, open adjustable rear. **Features:** Boxlock action; double triggers; automatic safety. Announced 1998. Imported from The Czech Republic by Euro-Imports.
Price: **$724.00**

BRNO ZH Double Rifles

Similar to the ZH 300 combination guns except with double rifle barrels. Available in 7x65R, 7x57R and 8x57JRS. Announced 1998. Imported from The Czech Republic by Euro-Imports.
Price: **$1,125.00**

CHARLES DALY SUPERIOR COMBINATION GUN

Caliber/Gauge: 12 ga. over 22 Hornet, 223 Rem., 22-250, 243 Win., 270 Win., 308 Win., 30-06. **Barrel:** 23.5", shotgun choked Imp. Cyl. **Weight:** About 7.5 lbs. **Stock:** Checkered walnut pistol grip buttstock and semi-beavertail forend. **Features:** Silvered, engraved receiver; chrome-moly steel barrels; double triggers; extractors; sling swivels; gold bead front sight. Introduced 1997. Imported from Italy by K.B.I. Inc.
Price: **$1,249.95**

Charles Daly Empire Combination Gun

Same as the Superior grade except has deluxe wood with European-style comb and cheekpiece; slim forend. Introduced 1997. Imported from Italy by K.B.I., Inc.
Price: **$1,789.95**

CZ 584 SOLO COMBINATION GUN

Caliber/Gauge: 7x57R; 12, 2-3/4" chamber. **Barrel:** 24.4". **Weight:** 7.37 lbs. **Length:** 45.25" overall. **Stock:** Circassian walnut. **Sights:** Blade front, open rear adjustable for windage. **Features:** Kersten-style double lump locking system; double-trigger Blitz-type mechanism with drop safety and adjustable set trigger for the rifle barrel; auto safety, dual extractors; receiver dovetailed for scope mounting. Imported from the Czech Republic by CZ-USA.
Price: **$850.00**

CZ 589 STOPPER OVER/UNDER GUN

Caliber: 458 Win. Magnum. **Barrels:** 21.7". **Weight:** 9.3 lbs. **Length:** 37.7" overall. **Stock:** Turkish walnut with sling swivels. **Sights:** Blade front, fixed rear. **Features:** Kersten-style action; Blitz-type double trigger; hammer-forged, blued barrels; satin-nickel, engraved receiver. Introduced 2001. Imported from the Czech Republic by CZ USA.
Price: **$2,999.00**
Price: Fully engraved model. **$3,999.00**

DRILLINGS, COMBINATION GUNS, DOUBLE GUNS

Hoenig Round Action

Krieghoff Classic Double Rifle

DAKOTA DOUBLE RIFLE

Caliber: 470 Nitro Express, 500 Nitro Express. **Barrel:** 25". **Weight:** NA. **Length:** NA. **Stock:** Exhibition-grade walnut. **Sights:** Express. **Features:** Round action; selective ejectors; recoil pad; Americase. From Dakota Arms Inc.
Price: **$25,000.00**

EAA/BAIKAL IZH-94 COMBINATION GUN

Caliber/Gauge: 12, 3" chamber; 222 Rem., 223, 5.6x50R, 5.6x55E, 7x57R, 7x65R, 7.62x39, 7.62x51, 308, 7.62x53R, 7.62x54R, 30-06. **Barrel:** 24", 26"; imp., mod. and full choke tubes. **Weight:** 7.28 lbs. **Stock:** Walnut; rubber butt pad. **Sights:** Express style. **Features:** Hammer-forged barrels with chrome-lined bores; machined receiver; single-selective or double triggers. Imported by European American Armory.
Price: Blued finish.. **$499.00**

GARBI EXPRESS DOUBLE RIFLE

Caliber: 7x65R, 9.3x74R, 375 H&H. **Barrel:** 24-3/4". **Weight:** 7-3/4 to 8-1/2 lbs. **Length:** 41-1/2" overall. **Stock:** Turkish walnut. **Sights:** Quarter-rib with express sight. **Features:** Side-by-side double; H&H-pattern sidelock ejector with reinforced action, chopper lump barrels of Boehler steel; double triggers; fine scroll and rosette engraving, or full coverage ornamental; coin-finished action. Introduced 1997. Imported from Spain by Wm. Larkin Moore.
Price: **$16,900.00**

HOENIG ROTARY ROUND ACTION DOUBLE RIFLE

Caliber: Most popular calibers from 225 Win. to 9.3x74R. **Barrel:** 22"-26". **Weight:** NA. **Length:** NA. **Stock:** English Walnut; to customer specs. **Sights:** Swivel hood front with button release (extra bead stored in trap door gripcap), express-style rear on quarter-rib adjustable for windage and elevation; scope mount. **Features:** Round action opens by rotating barrels, pulling forward. Has inertia extractor system; rotary safety blocks the strikers; single lever quick-detachable scope mount. Simple takedown without removing forend. Introduced 1997. Made in U.S. by George Hoenig.
Price: **$19,980.00**

KRIEGHOFF CLASSIC DOUBLE RIFLE

Caliber: 7x65R, 308 Win., 30-06, 30R Blaser, 8x57 JRS, 8x75RS, 9.3x74R. **Barrel:** 23.5". **Weight:** 7.3 to 8 lbs. **Length:** NA. **Stock:** High grade European walnut. Standard has conventional rounded cheekpiece, Bavaria has Bavarian-style cheekpiece. **Sights:** Bead front with removable, adjustable wedge (375 H&H and below), standing leaf rear on quarter-rib. **Features:** Boxlock action; double triggers; short opening angle for fast loading; quiet extractors; sliding, self-adjusting wedge for secure bolting; Purdey-style barrel extension; horizontal firing pin placement. Many options available. Introduced 1997. Imported from Germany by Krieghoff International.

Price: With small Arabesque engraving **$7,850.00**
Price: With engraved sideplates........................ **$9,800.00**
Price: For extra barrels................................ **$4,500.00**
Price: Extra 20-ga., 28" shotshell barrels **$3,200.00**

Krieghoff Classic Big Five Double Rifle

Similar to the standard Classic excpet available in 375 Flanged Mag. N.E., 500/416 N.E., 470 N.E., 500 N.E. 3". Has hinged front trigger, non-removable muzzle wedge (larger than 375-caliber), Universal Trigger System, Combi Cocking Device, steel trigger guard, specially weighted stock bolt for weight and balance. Many options available. Introduced 1997. Imported from Germany by Krieghoff International.
Price: **$9,450.00**
Price: With engraved sideplates........................ **$11,400.00**

LEBEAU - COURALLY EXPRESS RIFLE SxS

Caliber: 7x65R, 8x57JRS, 9.3x74R, 375 H&H, 470 N.E. **Barrel:** 24" to 26". **Weight:** 7-3/4 to 10-1/2 lbs. **Stock:** Fancy French walnut with cheekpiece. **Sights:** Bead on ramp front, standing left express rear on quarter-rib. **Features:** Holland & Holland-type sidelock with automatic ejectors; double triggers. Built to order only. Imported from Belgium by Wm. Larkin Moore.
Price: **$41,000.00**

MERKEL DRILLINGS

Caliber/Gauge: 12, 20, 3" chambers; 16, 2-3/4" chambers; 22 Hornet, 5.6x50R Mag., 5.6x52R, 222 Rem., 243 Win., 6.5x55, 6.5x57R, 7x57R, 7x65R, 308, 30-06, 8x57JRS, 9.3x74R, 375 H&H. **Barrel:** 25.6". **Weight:** 7.9 to 8.4 lbs. depending upon caliber. **Length:** NA. **Stock:** Oil-finished walnut with pistol grip; cheekpiece on 12-, 16-gauge. **Sights:** Blade front, fixed rear. **Features:** Double barrel locking lug with Greener cross-bolt; scroll-engraved, case-hardened receiver; automatic trigger safety; Blitz action; double triggers. Imported from Germany by GSI.
Price: Model 96K (manually cocked rifle system), from **$6,495.00**
Price: Model 96K Engraved (hunting series on receiver) **$7,995.00**

MERKEL OVER/UNDER DOUBLE RIFLES

Caliber: 22 Hornet, 5.6x50R Mag., 5.6x52R, 222 Rem., 243 Win., 6.5x55, 6.5x57R, 7x57R, 7x65R, 308, 30-06, 8x57JRS, 9.3x74R. **Barrel:** 25.6". **Weight:** About 7.7 lbs, depending upon caliber. **Length:** NA. **Stock:** Oil-finished walnut with pistol grip, cheekpiece. **Sights:** Blade front, fixed rear. **Features:** Kersten double cross-bolt lock; scroll-engraved, case-hardened receiver; Blitz action with double triggers. Imported from Germany by GSI.
Price: Model 221 E (silver-grayed receiver finish, hunting scene engraving).. **$10,895.00**

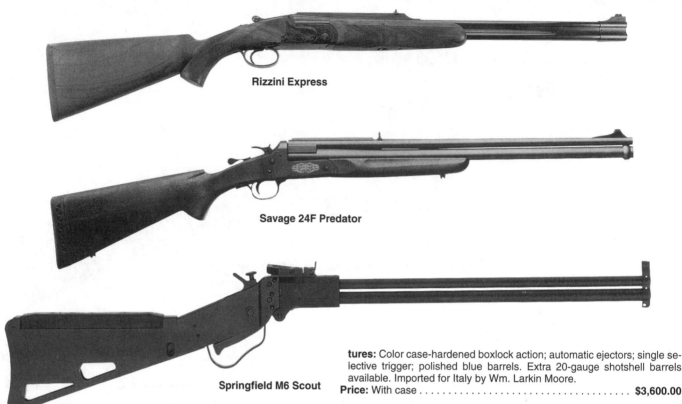

Rizzini Express

Savage 24F Predator

Springfield M6 Scout

MERKEL MODEL 160 SIDE-BY-SIDE DOUBLE RIFLE

Caliber: 22 Hornet, 5.6x50R Mag., 5.6x52R, 222 Rem., 243 Win., 6.5x55, 6.5x57R, 7x57R, 7x65R, 308, 30-06, 8x57JRS, 9.3x74R, 375 H&H. **Barrel:** 25.6". **Weight:** About 7.7 lbs, depending upon caliber. **Length:** NA. **Stock:** Oil-finished walnut with pistol grip, cheekpiece. **Sights:** Blade front on ramp, fixed rear. **Features:** Sidelock action. Double barrel locking lug with Greener cross-bolt; fine engraved hunting scenes on sideplates; Holland & Holland ejectors; double triggers. Imported from Germany by GSI.
Price: From. $13,295.00

Merkel Boxlock Double Rifles

Similar to the Model 160 double rifle except with Anson & Deely boxlock action with cocking indicators, double triggers, engraved color case-hardened receiver. Introduced 1995. Imported from Germany by GSI.
Price: Model 140-1, from $5,995.00
Price: Model 140-1.1 (engraved silver-gray receiver), from $6,995.00
Price: Model 150-1 (false sideplates, silver-gray receiver, Arabesque engraving), from $7,495.00
Price: Model 150-1.1 (as above with English Arabesque engraving), from $8,995.00

RIZZINI EXPRESS 90L DOUBLE RIFLE

Caliber: 30-06, 7x65R, 9.3x74R. **Barrel:** 24". **Weight:** 7-1/2 lbs. **Length:** 40" overall. **Stock:** Select European walnut with satin oil finish; English-style cheekpiece. **Sights:** Ramp front, quarter-rib with express sight. **Fea-**tures: Color case-hardened boxlock action; automatic ejectors; single selective trigger; polished blue barrels. Extra 20-gauge shotshell barrels available. Imported for Italy by Wm. Larkin Moore.
Price: With case $3,600.00

SAVAGE 24F PREDATOR O/U COMBINATION GUN

Caliber/Gauge: 22 Hornet, 223, 30-30 over 12 (24F-12) or 22 LR, 22 Hornet, 223, 30-30 over 20-ga. (24F-20); 3" chambers. **Action:** Takedown, low rebounding visible hammer. Single trigger, barrel selector spur on hammer. **Barrel:** 24" separated barrels; 12-ga. has Full, Mod., Imp. Cyl. choke tubes, 20-ga. has fixed Mod. choke. **Weight:** 8 lbs. **Length:** 40-1/2" overall. **Stock:** Black Rynite composition. **Sights:** Ramp front, rear open adjustable for elevation. Grooved for tip-off scope mount. **Features:** Removable butt cap for storage and accessories. Introduced 1989.
Price: 24F-12 . . . . $476.00
Price: 24F-20 . . . . $449.00

Savage 24F-12/410 Combination Gun

Similar to the 24F-12 except comes with "Four-Tenner" adaptor for shooting 410-bore shotshells. Rifle barrel chambered for 22 Hornet, 223 Rem., 30-30 Win. Introduced 1998. Made in U.S. by Savage Arms, Inc.
Price: $504.00

SPRINGFIELD, INC. M6 SCOUT RIFLE/SHOTGUN

Caliber/Gauge: 22 LR or 22 Hornet over 410-bore. **Barrel:** 18.25". **Weight:** 4 lbs. **Length:** 32" overall. **Stock:** Folding detachable with storage for 15 22 LR, four 410 shells. **Sights:** Blade front, military aperture for 22; V-notch for 410. **Features:** All-metal construction. Designed for quick disassembly and minimum maintenance. Folds for compact storage. Introduced 1982; reintroduced 1996. Imported from the Czech Republic by Springfield, Inc.
Price: Parkerized $185.00
Price: Stainless steel $219.00

Designs for hunting, utility and sporting purposes, including training for competition

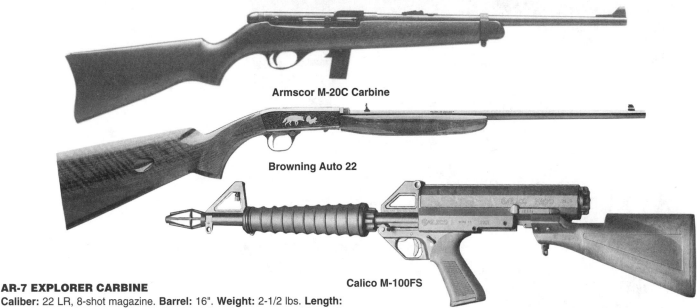

Armscor M-20C Carbine

Browning Auto 22

Calico M-100FS

AR-7 EXPLORER CARBINE

Caliber: 22 LR, 8-shot magazine. **Barrel:** 16". **Weight:** 2-1/2 lbs. **Length:** 34-1/2" / 16-1/2" stowed. **Stock:** Moulded Cycolac; snap-on rubber butt pad. **Sights:** Square blade front, aperture rear. **Features:** Takedown design stores barrel and action in hollow stock. Light enough to float. Reintroduced 1999. From AR-7 Industries, LLC.
Price: Black matte finish **$150.00**
Price: AR-20 Sporter (tubular stock, barrel shroud) **$200.00**
New! **Price:** AR-7 camo- or walnut-finish stock **$164.95**

ARMSCOR MODEL AK22 AUTO RIFLE

Caliber: 22 LR, 10-shot magazine. **Barrel:** 18.5". **Weight:** 7.5 lbs. **Length:** 38" overall. **Stock:** Plain mahogany. **Sights:** Adjustable post front, leaf rear adjustable for elevation. **Features:** Resembles the AK-47. Matte black finish. Introduced 1987. Imported from the Philippines by K.B.I., Inc.
Price: About **$219.95**

ARMSCOR M-1600 AUTO RIFLE

Caliber: 22 LR, 10-shot magazine. **Barrel:** 18.25". **Weight:** 6.2 lbs. **Length:** 38.5" overall. **Stock:** Black finished mahogany. **Sights:** Post front, aperture rear. **Features:** Resembles Colt AR-15. Matte black finish. Introduced 1987. Imported from the Philippines by K.B.I., Inc.
Price: About **$199.95**

ARMSCOR M-20C AUTO CARBINE

Caliber: 22 LR, 10-shot magazine. **Barrel:** 18.25". **Weight:** 6.5 lbs. **Length:** 38" overall. **Stock:** Walnut-finished mahogany. **Sights:** Hooded front, rear adjustable for elevation. **Features:** Receiver grooved for scope mounting. Blued finish. Introduced 1990. Imported from the Philippines by K.B.I., Inc.
Price: **$154.95**

BROWNING BUCK MARK SEMI-AUTO RIFLES

Caliber: 22 LR, 10-shot magazine. **Barrel:** 18" tapered (Sporter) or heavy bull (Target). **Weight:** 4 lbs., 2 oz. (Sporter) or 5 lbs., 4 oz. (Target). **Length:** 34" overall. **Stock:** Walnut stock and forearm with full pistol grip. **Sights:** Hi-Viz adjustable (Sporter). **Features:** A rifle version of the Buck Mark Pistol; straight blowback action; machined aluminum receiver with integral rail scope mount; recessed muzzle crown; manual thumb safety. Introduced 2001. From Browning.
Price: Sporter (adj. sights) **$518.00**
Price: Target (heavy bbl., no sights) **$518.00**

BROWNING SEMI-AUTO 22 RIFLE

Caliber: 22 LR, 11-shot. **Barrel:** 19-1/4". **Weight:** 5 lbs., 3 oz. **Length:** 37" overall. **Stock:** Checkered select walnut with pistol grip and semi-beavertail forend. **Sights:** Gold bead front, folding leaf rear. **Features:** Engraved receiver with polished blue finish; cross-bolt safety; tubular magazine in buttstock; easy takedown for carrying or storage. Imported from Japan by Browning.
Price: Grade I **$479.00**

Browning Semi-Auto 22, Grade VI

Same as the Grade I Auto-22 except available with either grayed or blued receiver with extensive engraving with gold-plated animals: right side pictures a fox and squirrel in a woodland scene; left side shows a beagle chasing a rabbit. On top is a portrait of the beagle. Stock and forend are of high-grade walnut with a double-bordered cut checkering design. Introduced 1987.
Price: Grade VI, blue or gray receiver **$1,028.00**

BRNO ZKM 611 AUTO RIFLE

Caliber: 22 WMR, 6- or 10-shot magazine. **Barrel:** 20.4". **Weight:** 5.9 lbs. **Length:** 38.9" overall. **Stock:** European walnut. **Sights:** Hooded blade front, open adjustable rear. **Features:** Removable box magazine; polished blue finish; cross-bolt safety; grooved receiver for scope mounting; easy takedown for storage. Imported from The Czech Republic by Euro-Imports.
Price: **$475.00**

CALICO M-100FS CARBINE

Caliber: 22 LR. **Barrel:** 16.25". **Weight:** 5 lbs. **Length:** 36" overall. **Stock:** Glass-filled, impact-resistant polymer. **Sights:** Adjustable post front, notch rear. **Features:** Has helical-feed magazine; aluminum receiver; ambidextrous safety. Made in U.S. by Calico.
Price: **$650.00**

CHARLES DALY FIELD GRADE AUTO RIFLE

Caliber: 22 LR, 10-shot magazine. **Barrel:** 20-3/4". **Weight:** 6.5 lbs. **Length:** 40-1/2" overall. **Stock:** Walnut-finished hardwood with Monte Carlo. **Sights:** Hooded front, adjustable open rear. **Features:** Receiver grooved for scope mounting; blue finish; shell deflector. Introduced 1998. Imported by K.B.I.
Price: **$124.00**
Price: Superior Grade (cut checkered stock, fully adjustable sight) **$199.00**

Charles Daly Empire Grade Auto Rifle

Similar to the Field Grade except has select California walnut stock with 24 l.p.i. hand checkering, contrasting forend and gripcaps, damascened bolt, high-polish blue. Introduced 1998. Imported by K.B.I.
Price: **$369.00**

Charles Daly Superior Grade

CZ 511 Auto

Henry U.S. Survival

Marlin Model 60

Marlin Model 60 SSK

Marlin Model 70PSS

CZ 511 AUTO RIFLE

Caliber: 22 LR, 8-shot magazine. **Barrel:** 22.2". **Weight:** 5.39 lbs. **Length:** 38.6" overall. **Stock:** Walnut with checkered pistol grip. **Sights:** Hooded front, adjustable rear. **Features:** Polished blue finish; detachable magazine; sling swivel studs. Imported from the Czech Republic by CZ-USA.
Price: $351.00

HENRY U.S. SURVIVAL RIFLE .22

Caliber: 22 LR, 8-shot magazine. **Barrel:** 16" steel lined. **Weight:** 2.5 lbs. **Stock:** ABS plastic. **Sights:** Blade front on ramp, aperture rear. **Features:** Takedown design stores barrel and action in hollow stock. Light enough to float. Silver, black or camo finish. Comes with two magazines. Introduced 1998. From Henry Repeating Arms Co.
Price: $165.00

MAGTECH MT 7022 AUTO RIFLE

Caliber: 22 LR, 10-shot magazine. **Barrel:** 18". **Weight:** 4.8 lbs. **Length:** 37" overall. **Stock:** Brazilian hardwood. **Sights:** Hooded blade front, fully adjustable open rear. **Features:** Cross-bolt safety; last-shot bolt hold-open; alloy receiver is drilled and tapped for scope mounting. Introduced 1998. Imported from Brazil by Magtech Ammunition Co.
Price: $100.00

MARLIN MODEL 60 AUTO RIFLE

Caliber: 22 LR, 14-shot tubular magazine. **Barrel:** 22" round tapered. **Weight:** About 5-1/2 lbs. **Length:** 40-1/2" overall. **Stock:** Press-check-ered, walnut-finished Maine birch with Monte Carlo, full pistol grip; Mar-Shield® finish. **Sights:** Ramp front, open adjustable rear. **Features:** Matted receiver is grooved for scope mount. Manual bolt hold-open; automatic last-shot bolt hold-open.
Price: $176.00
Price: With 4x scope. $183.00

Marlin Model 60SS Self-Loading Rifle

Same as the Model 60 except breech bolt, barrel and outer magazine tube are made of stainless steel; most other parts are either nickel-plated or coated to match the stainless finish. Monte Carlo stock is of black/gray Maine birch laminate, and has nickel-plated swivel studs, rubber butt pad. Introduced 1993.
Price: $281.00
Price: Model 60SSK (black fiberglass-filled stock) $244.00
Price: Model 60SB (walnut-finished birch stock) $223.00
Price: Model 60SB with 4x scope. $237.00

MARLIN 70PSS PAPOOSE STAINLESS RIFLE

Caliber: 22 LR, 7-shot magazine. **Barrel:** 16-1/4" stainless steel, Micro-Groove® rifling. **Weight:** 3-1/4 lbs. **Length:** 35-1/4" overall. **Stock:** Black fiberglass-filled synthetic with abbreviated forend, nickel-plated swivel studs, moulded-in checkering. **Sights:** Ramp front with orange post, cut-away Wide Scan® hood; adjustable open rear. Receiver grooved for scope mounting. **Features:** Takedown barrel; cross-bolt safety; manual bolt hold-open; last shot bolt hold-open; comes with padded carrying case. Introduced 1986. Made in U.S. by Marlin.
Price: $288.00

Marlin Model 922

Marlin 7000

Marlin 795

Remington 597

screw adjustable open rear. Receiver grooved for scope mount. Introduced 1997. Made in U.S. by Marlin Firearms Co.
Price: **$167.00**

REMINGTON MODEL 552 BDL DELUXE SPEEDMASTER RIFLE
Caliber: 22 S (20), L (17) or LR (15) tubular mag. **Barrel:** 21" round tapered. **Weight:** 5-3/4 lbs. **Length:** 40" overall. **Stock:** Walnut. Checkered grip and forend. **Sights:** Bead front, step open rear adjustable for windage and elevation. **Features:** Positive cross-bolt safety, receiver grooved for tip-off mount.
Price: **$365.00**

REMINGTON 597 AUTO RIFLE
Caliber: 22 LR, 10-shot clip. **Barrel:** 20". **Weight:** 5-1/2 lbs. **Length:** 40" overall. **Stock:** Gray synthetic. **Sights:** Bead front, fully adjustable rear. **Features:** Matte black finish, nickel-plated bolt. Receiver is grooved and drilled and tapped for scope mounts. Introduced 1997. Made in U.S. by Remington.
Price: **$163.00**
Price: Model 597 Magnum, 22 WMR, 8-shot clip **$321.00**
Price: Model 597 LSS (laminated stock, stainless) **$272.00**
Price: Model 597 Magnum LS (laminated stock) **$377.00**
Price: Model 597 SS (22 LR, stainless steel, black synthetic
    stock) **$217.00**
New! Price: Model 597 LS Heavy Barrel (22 LR, laminated stock) **$265.00**
New! Price: Model 597 Magnum LS Heavy Barrel
    (22 WMR, lam. stock) **$399.00**

MARLIN MODEL 922M AUTO RIFLE
Caliber: 22 WMR, 5-shot magazine. **Barrel:** 20.5". **Weight:** 6.5 lbs. **Length:** 39.75" overall. **Stock:** Now walnut finished hardwood, swivel studs, rubber butt pad. **Sights:** Ramp front with bead and removable Wide-Scan® hood, adjustable folding semi-buckhorn rear. **Features:** Action based on the centerfire Model 9 Carbine. Receiver drilled and tapped for scope mounting. Automatic last-shot bolt hold-open; magazine safety. Introduced 1993.
Price: **$454.00**

MARLIN MODEL 7000 AUTO RIFLE
Caliber: 22 LR, 10-shot magazine **Barrel:** 18" heavy target with 12-groove Micro-Groove® rifling, recessed muzzle. **Weight:** 5-1/2 lbs. **Length:** 37" overall. **Stock:** Black fiberglass-filled synthetic with Monte Carlo combo, swivel studs, moulded-in checkering. **Sights:** None furnished; comes with ring mounts. **Features:** Automatic last-shot bolt hold-open, manual bolt hold-open; cross-bolt safety; steel charging handle; blue finish, nickel-plated magazine. Introduced 1997. Made in U.S. by Marlin Firearms Co.
Price: **$236.00**

Marlin Model 795 Auto Rifle
Similar to the Model 7000 except has standard-weight 18" barrel with 16-groove Micro-Groove rifling. Comes with ramp front sight with brass bead,

RIFLES

Ruger 10/22 International

Savage Model 64FV

RUGER 10/22 AUTOLOADING CARBINE

Caliber: 22 LR, 10-shot rotary magazine. **Barrel:** 18-1/2" round tapered. **Weight:** 5 lbs. **Length:** 37-1/4" overall. **Stock:** American hardwood with pistol grip and barrel. band. **Sights:** Brass bead front, folding leaf rear adjustable for elevation. **Features:** Detachable rotary magazine fits flush into stock, cross-bolt safety, receiver tapped and grooved for scope blocks or tip-off mount. Scope base adaptor furnished with each rifle.
Price: Model 10/22 RB (blue) **$235.00**
Price: Model K10/22RB (bright finish stainless barrel) **$273.00**
Price: Model 10/22RP (blue, synthetic stock) **$235.00**

Ruger 10/22 International Carbine

Similar to the Ruger 10/22 Carbine except has full-length International stock of American hardwood, checkered grip and forend; comes with rubber butt pad, sling swivels. Reintroduced 1994.
Price: Blue (10/22RBI) **$275.00**
Price: Stainless (K10/22RBI) **$299.00**

Ruger 10/22 Deluxe Sporter

Same as 10/22 Carbine except walnut stock with hand checkered pistol grip and forend; straight buttplate, no barrel band, has sling swivels.
Price: Model 10/22 DSP **$299.00**

Ruger 10/22T Target Rifle

Similar to the 10/22 except has 20" heavy, hammer-forged barrel with tight chamber dimensions, improved trigger pull, laminated hardwood stock dimensioned for optical sights. No iron sights supplied. Introduced 1996. Made in U.S. by Sturm, Ruger & Co.
Price: 10/22T **$415.00**
Price: K10/22T, stainless steel **$465.00**
New! **Price:** K10/22TNZ, stainless steel 20" bbl. with cut-out pistol-grip laminated stock **$649.00**

Ruger K10/22RP All-Weather Rifle

Similar to the stainless K10/22/RP except has black composite stock of thermoplastic polyester resin reinforced with fiberglass; checkered grip and forend. Brushed satin, natural metal finish with clear hardcoat finish. Weighs 5 lbs., measures 36-3/4" overall. Introduced 1997. From Sturm, Ruger & Co.
Price: **$273.00**

RUGER 10/22 MAGNUM AUTOLOADING CARBINE

Caliber: 22 WMR, 9-shot rotary magazine. **Barrel:** 18-1/2". **Weight:** 6 lbs. **Length:** 37-1/4" overall. **Stock:** Birch. **Sights:** Gold bead front, folding rear. **Features:** All-steel receiver has integral Ruger scope bases for the included 1" rings. Introduced 1999. Made in U.S. by Sturm, Ruger & Co.
Price: **$450.00**

SAVAGE MODEL 64G AUTO RIFLE

Caliber: 22 LR, 10-shot magazine. **Barrel:** 20". **Weight:** 5-1/2 lbs. **Length:** 40" overall. **Stock:** Walnut-finished hardwood with Monte Carlo-type comb, checkered grip and forend. **Sights:** Bead front, open adjustable rear. Receiver grooved for scope mounting. **Features:** Thumb-operated rotating safety. Blue finish. Side ejection, bolt hold-open device. Introduced 1990. Made in Canada, from Savage Arms.
Price: **$134.00**
Price: Model 64F, black synthetic stock **$124.00**
Price: Model 64GXP Package Gun includes 4x15 scope and mounts **$140.00**
Price: Model 64FXP (black stock, 4x15 scope) **$128.00**

Savage Model 64FV Auto Rifle

Similar to the Model 64F except has heavy 21" barrel with recessed crown; no sights provided—comes with Weaver-style bases. Introduced 1998. Imported from Canada by Savage Arms, Inc.
Price: **$164.00**

THOMPSON/CENTER 22 LR CLASSIC RIFLE

Caliber: 22 LR, 8-shot magazine. **Barrel:** 22" match-grade. **Weight:** 5-1/2 pounds. **Length:** 39-1/2" overall. **Stock:** Satin-finished American walnut with Monte Carlo-type comb and pistol grip cap, swivel studs. **Sights:** Ramp-style front and fully adjustable rear, both with fiber optics. **Features:** All-steel receiver drilled and tapped for scope mounting; barrel threaded to receiver; thumb-operated safety; trigger-guard safety lock included.
Price: T/C 22 LR Classic (blue) **$335.55**

WINCHESTER MODEL 63 AUTO RIFLE

Caliber: 22 LR, 10-shot magazine. **Barrel:** 23". **Weight:** 6-1/4 lbs. **Length:** 39" overall. **Stock:** Walnut. **Sights:** Bead front, open adjustable rear. **Features:** Recreation of the original Model 63. Magazine tube loads through a port in the buttstock; forward cocking knob at front of forend; easy takedown for cleaning, storage; engraved receiver. Reintroduced 1997. From U.S. Repeating Arms Co.
Price: Grade I **$678.00**
Price: High grade, select walnut, cut checkering, engraved scenes with gold accents on receiver (made in 1997 only) **$1,083.00**

Classic and modern models for sport and utility, including training.

Browning BL-22

Henry Lever-Action 22

Henry Goldenboy 22

Henry Pump-Action 22

Marlin Model 39AS

BROWNING BL-22 LEVER-ACTION RIFLE
Caliber: 22 S (22), L (17) or LR (15), tubular magazine. **Barrel:** 20" round tapered. **Weight:** 5 lbs. **Length:** 36-3/4" overall. **Stock:** Walnut, two-piece straight grip Western style. **Sights:** Bead post front, folding-leaf rear. **Features:** Short throw lever, half-cock safety, receiver grooved for tip-off scope mounts, gold-colored trigger. Imported from Japan by Browning.
Price: Grade I **$415.00**
Price: Grade II (engraved receiver, checkered grip and forend) . **$471.00**
Price: Classic, Grade I (blued trigger, no checkering) **$415.00**
Price: Classic, Grade II (cut checkering, satin wood finish,
 polished blueing) **$471.00**

HENRY LEVER-ACTION 22
Caliber: 22 Long Rifle (15-shot). **Barrel:** 18-1/4" round. **Weight:** 5-1/2 lbs. **Length:** 34" overall. **Stock:** Walnut. **Sights:** Hooded blade front, open adjustable rear. **Features:** Polished blue finish; full-length tubular magazine; side ejection; receiver grooved for scope mounting. Introduced 1997. Made in U.S. by Henry Repeating Arms Co.
Price: **$239.95**
Price: Youth model (33" overall, 11-rounds 22 LR) **$229.95**

HENRY GOLDENBOY 22 LEVER-ACTION RIFLE
Caliber: 22 LR, 16-shot. **Barrel:** 20" octagonal. **Weight:** 6.25 lbs. **Length:** 38" overall. **Stock:** American walnut. **Sights:** Blade front, open rear. **Features:** Brasslite receiver, brass buttplate, blued barrel and lever. Introduced 1998. Made in U.S. from Henry Repeating Arms Co.
Price: **$379.95**

HENRY PUMP-ACTION 22 PUMP RIFLE
Caliber: 22 LR, 15-shot. **Barrel:** 18.25". **Weight:** 5.5 lbs. **Length:** NA. **Stock:** American walnut. **Sights:** Bead on ramp front, open adjustable rear. **Features:** Polished blue finish; receiver groved for scope mount; grooved slide handle; two barrel bands. Introduced 1998. Made in U.S. from Henry Repeating Arms Co.
Price: **$249.95**

MARLIN MODEL 39A GOLDEN LEVER-ACTION RIFLE
Caliber: 22 S (26), L (21), LR (19), tubular magazine. **Barrel:** 24" Micro-Groove®. **Weight:** 6-1/2 lbs. **Length:** 40" overall. **Stock:** Checkered American black walnut with white line spacers at pistol gripcap and buttplate; Mar-Shield® finish. Swivel studs; rubber butt pad. **Sights:** Bead ramp front with detachable Wide-Scan™ hood, folding rear semi-buckhorn adjustable for windage and elevation. **Features:** Hammer-block safety; rebounding hammer. Takedown action, receiver tapped for scope mount (supplied), offset hammer spur; gold-plated steel trigger.
Price: **$525.00**

Marlin Model 1897CB Cowboy

Remington Model 572

Ruger Model 96/22

Winchester 9422 Large Loop

Marlin Model 1897CB Cowboy Lever Action Rifle

Similar to the Model 39A except it has straight-grip stock with hard rubber buttplate; blued steel forend cap; 24" tapered octagon barrel with Micro-Groove® rifling; adjustable Marble semi-buckhorn rear sight, Marble carbine front with brass bead; overall length 40". Introduced 1999. Made in U.S. by Marlin.

Price: **$708.00**

REMINGTON 572 BDL DELUXE FIELDMASTER PUMP RIFLE

Caliber: 22 S (20), L (17) or LR (14), tubular magazine. **Barrel:** 21" round tapered. **Weight:** 5-1/2 lbs. **Length:** 40" overall. **Stock:** Walnut with checkered pistol grip and slide handle. **Sights:** Blade ramp front; sliding ramp rear adjustable for windage and elevation. **Features:** Cross-bolt safety; removing inner magazine tube converts rifle to single shot; receiver grooved for tip-off scope mount.

Price: **$379.00**

RUGER MODEL 96/22 LEVER-ACTION RIFLE

Caliber: 22 LR, 10-shot rotary magazine; 22 WMR, 9-shot rotary magazine. **Barrel:** 18-1/2". **Weight:** 5-1/4 lbs. **Length:** 37-1/4" overall. **Stock:** American hardwood. **Sights:** Gold bead front, folding leaf rear. **Features:** Cross-bolt safety, visible cocking indicator; short-throw lever action. Screw-on dovetail scope base. Introduced 1996. Made in U.S. by Sturm, Ruger & Co.

Price: 96/22 (22 LR) **$349.50**
Price: 96/22M (22 WMR) **$375.00**

TAURUS MODEL 62 PUMP RIFLE

Caliber: 22 LR, 12- or 13-shot. **Barrel:** 16-1/2" or 23" round. **Weight:** 4.6 to 5 lbs. **Length:** 39" overall. **Stock:** Walnut-finished hardwood, straight grip, grooved forend. **Sights:** Fixed front, adjustable rear. **Features:** Blue or stainless steel finish; bolt-mounted safety; tubular magzine; quick take-

down; integral security lock system. Imported from Brazil by Taurus International.

Price: (blued finish) **$280.00**
Price: (stainless steel finish) **$295.00**

Taurus Model 72 Pump Rifle

Same as Model 62 except chambered in 22 WMR; 16-1/2" bbl. holds 10 shots, 23" bbl. holds 11 shots. Introduced 2001. Imported from Brazil by Taurus International.

Price: (blued finish) **$295.00**
Price: (stainless steel finish) **$310.00**

WINCHESTER MODEL 9422 LEVER-ACTION RIFLES

Caliber: 22 LR, 22 WMR, tubular magazine. **Barrel:** 20-1/2". **Weight:** 6-1/4 lbs. **Length:** 37-1/8" overall. **Stock:** American walnut, two-piece, straight grip (Traditional) or semi-pistol grip (Legacy). **Sights:** Hooded ramp front, adjustable semi-buckhorn rear. **Features:** Side ejection, receiver grooved for scope mounting, takedown action. From U.S. Repeating Arms Co.

Price: Traditional, 22 LR 15-shot **$444.00**
Price: Traditional, 22WMR, 11-shot **$464.00**
Price: Legacy, 22 LR 15-shot **$473.00**
Price: Legacy 22 WMR, 11-shot **$496.00**

WINCHESTER MODEL 1886 EXTRA LIGHT GRADE I

Caliber: 45-70, 4-shot magazine. **Barrel:** 22". **Weight:** 7-1.4 lbs. **Length:** 40-1/2" overall. **Sights:** Blade front, buckhorn-style ramp-adjustable rear. **Features:** Round, tapered barrel; shotgun-style steel buttplate; half-magazine. Limited production. Introduced 2000. From U.S. Repeating Arms Co., Inc.

Price: **$1,152.00**
Price: High Grade (extra-fancy, checkered walnut stock, engraved elk and deer scenes) **$1,440.00**

Includes models for a variety of sports, utility and competitive shooting.

Anschutz 1518D Luxus

Anschutz 1710D

Charles Daly Field Grade

ANSCHUTZ 1416D/1516D CLASSIC RIFLES

Caliber: 22 LR (1416D), 5-shot clip; 22 WMR (1516D), 4-shot clip. **Barrel:** 22-1/2". **Weight:** 6 lbs. **Length:** 41" overall. **Stock:** European hardwood with walnut finish; classic style with straight comb, checkered pistol grip and forend. **Sights:** Hooded ramp front, folding leaf rear. **Features:** Uses Match 64 action. Adjustable single stage trigger. Receiver grooved for scope mounting. Imported from Germany by AcuSport Corp.

Price: 1416D, 22 LR	**$755.95**
Price: 1516D, 22 WMR	**$779.95**
Price: 1416D Classic left-hand	**$679.95**

Anschutz 1416D/1516D Walnut Luxus Rifles

Similar to the Classic models except have European walnut stocks with Monte Carlo cheekpiece, slim forend with Schnabel tip, cut checkering on grip and forend. Introduced 1997. Imported from Germany by AcuSport Corp.

Price: 1416D (22 LR)	**$755.95**
Price: 1516D (22 WMR)	**$779.95**

ANSCHUTZ 1518D LUXUS BOLT-ACTION RIFLE

Caliber: 22 WMR, 4-shot magazine. **Barrel:** 19-3/4". **Weight:** 5-1/2 lbs. **Length:** 37-1/2" overall. **Stock:** European walnut. **Sights:** Blade on ramp front, folding leaf rear. **Features:** Receiver grooved for scope mounting; single stage trigger; skip-line checkering; rosewood forend tip; sling swivels. Imported from Germany by AcuSport Corp.

Price: **$1,186.95**

ANSCHUTZ 1710D CUSTOM RIFLE

Caliber: 22 LR, 5-shot clip. **Barrel:** 24-1/4". **Weight:** 7-3/8 lbs. **Length:** 42-1/2" overall. **Stock:** Select European walnut. **Sights:** Hooded ramp front, folding leaf rear; drilled and tapped for scope mounting. **Features:** Match 54 action with adjustable single-stage trigger; roll-over Monte Carlo cheekpiece, slim forend with Schnabel tip, Wundhammer palm swell on pistol grip, rosewood gripcap with white diamond insert; skip-line checkering on grip and forend. Introduced 1988. Imported from Germany by AcuSport Corp.

Price: **$1,289.95**

CABANAS MASTER BOLT-ACTION RIFLE

Caliber: 177, round ball or pellet; single shot. **Barrel:** 19-1/2". **Weight:** 8 lbs. **Length:** 45-1/2" overall. **Stocks:** Walnut target-type with Monte Carlo. **Sights:** Blade front, fully adjustable rear. **Features:** Fires round ball or pellet with 22-cal. blank cartridge. Bolt action. Imported from Mexico by Mandall Shooting Supplies. Introduced 1984.

Price:	**$189.95**
Price: Varmint model (has 21-1/2" barrel, 4-1/2 lbs., 41" overall length, varmint-type stock)	**$119.95**

Cabanas Leyre Bolt-Action Rifle

Similar to Master model except 44" overall, has sport/target stock.

Price:	**$149.95**
Price: Model R83 (17" barrel, hardwood stock, 40" o.a.l.)	**$79.95**
Price: Mini 82 Youth (16-1/2" barrel, 33" overall length, 3-1/2 lbs.)	**$69.95**
Price: Pony Youth (16" barrel, 34" overall length, 3.2 lbs.)	**$69.95**

Cabanas Espronceda IV Bolt-Action Rifle

Similar to the Leyre model except has full sporter stock, 18-3/4" barrel, 40" overall length, weighs 5-1/2 lbs.

Price: **$134.95**

CABANAS LASER RIFLE

Caliber: 177. **Barrel:** 19". **Weight:** 6 lbs., 12 oz. **Length:** 42" overall. **Stock:** Target-type thumbhole. **Sights:** Blade front, open fully adjustable rear. **Features:** Fires round ball or pellets with 22 blank cartridge. Imported from Mexico by Mandall Shooting Supplies.

Price: **$159.95**

CHARLES DALY SUPERIOR BOLT-ACTION RIFLE

Caliber: 22 LR, 10-shot magazine. **Barrel:** 22-5/8". **Weight:** 6.7 lbs. **Length:** 41.25" overall. **Stock:** Walnut-finished mahogany. **Sights:** Bead front, rear adjustable for elevation. **Features:** Receiver grooved for scope mounting. Blued finish. Introduced 1998. Imported by K.B.I., Inc.

Price: **$189.95**

Charles Daly Field Grade Rifle

Similar to the Superior except has short walnut-finished hardwood stock for small shooters. Introduced 1998. Imported by K.B.I., Inc.

Price:	**$134.95**
Price: Field Youth (17.5" barrel)	**$144.95**

Charles Daly Superior Magnum Grade Rifle

Similar to the Superior except chambered for 22 WMR. Has 22.6" barrel, double lug bolt, checkered stock, weighs 6.5 lbs. Introduced 1987.

Price: About **$204.95**

Charles Daly Empire Magnum Grade Rifle

Similar to the Superior Magnum except has oil-finished American walnut stock with 18 lpi hand checkering; black hardwood gripcap and forend tip; highly polished barreled action; jewelled bolt; recoil pad; swivel studs. Imported from the Philippines by K.B.I., Inc.

Price: **$364.95**

Chipmunk Deluxe

CZ 452 American Classic

Kimber 22 Classic

Charles Daly Empire Grade Rifle

Similar to the Superior except has oil-finished American walnut stock with 18 lpi hand checkering; black hardwood gripcap and forend tip; highly polished barreled action; jewelled bolt; recoil pad; swivel studs. Imported by K.B.I., Inc.

Price: **$329.00**

CHARLES DALY TRUE YOUTH BOLT-ACTION RIFLE

Caliber: 22 LR, single shot. **Barrel:** 16-1/4". **Weight:** About 3 lbs. **Length:** 32" overall. **Stock:** Walnut-finished hardwood. **Sights:** Blade front, adjustable rear. **Features:** Scaled-down stock for small shooters. Blue finish. Introduced 1998. Imported by K.B.I., Inc.

Price: **$154.95**

CHIPMUNK SINGLE SHOT RIFLE

Caliber: 22 LR, 22 WMR, single shot. **Barrel:** 16-1/8". **Weight:** About 2-1/2 lbs. **Length:** 30" overall. **Stocks:** American walnut. **Sights:** Post on ramp front, peep rear adjustable for windage and elevation. **Features:** Drilled and tapped for scope mounting using special Chipmunk base ($13.95). Engraved model also available. Made in U.S. Introduced 1982. From Rogue Rifle Co., Inc.

Price: Standard.	**$194.25**
Price: Standard 22 WMR	**$209.95**
Price: Deluxe (better wood, checkering).	**$246.95**
Price: Deluxe 22 WMR	**$262.95**
Price: Laminated stock	**$209.95**
Price: Laminated stock, 22 WMR	**$225.95**
Price: Black-coated stock	**$183.95**
Price: Black-coated stock, 22 WMR	**$199.95**
Price: Bull barrel models of above, add	**$16.00**

CZ 452 M 2E LUX BOLT-ACTION RIFLE

Caliber: 22 LR, 22 WMR, 5-shot detachable magazine. **Barrel:** 24.8". **Weight:** 6.6 lbs. **Length:** 42.63" overall. **Stock:** Walnut with checkered pistol grip. **Sights:** Hooded front, fully adjustable tangent rear. **Features:** All-steel construction; adjustable trigger; polished blue finish. Imported from the Czech Republic by CZ-USA.

Price: 22 LR .	**$351.00**
Price: 22 WMR .	**$378.00**
Price: Synthetic stock, nickel finish, 22 LR.	**$344.00**

CZ 452 M 2E Varmint Rifle

Similar to the Lux model except has heavy 20.8" barrel; stock has beavertail forend; weighs 7 lbs.; no sights furnished. Available only in 22 LR. Imported from the Czech Republic by CZ-USA.

Price: **$369.00**

CZ 452 American Classic Bolt-Action Rifle

Similar to the CZ 452 M 2E Lux except has classic-style stock of Circassian walnut; 22.5" free-floating barrel with recessed target crown; receiver dovetail for scope mounting. No open sights furnished. Introduced 1999. Imported from the Czech Republic by CZ-USA.

Price: 22 LR .	**$351.00**
Price: 22 WMR .	**$378.00**

DAN WESSON COYOTE CLASSIC BOLT-ACTION RIMFIRE RIFLE

Caliber: 22 LR or 22 WMR. 5-shot magazine (10-shot optional magazine). **Barrel:** 22-3/4". **Weight:** NA. **Length:** NA. **Stock:** Laminated wood or exotic hardwood. **Sights:** Fully adjustable V-notch rear, brass bead ramp front. **Features:** Receiver drilled and tapped for scope mount; checkered pistol grip and fore end with DW medallion end cap; recessed target crown; sling swivel studs. Introduced 2001. From Dan Wesson Firearms.

Price: Coyote Classic, 22 LR or 22 WMR **$219.00**

DAN WESSON COYOTE TARGET BOLT-ACTION RIMFIRE RIFLE

Caliber: 22 LR or 22 WMR, 5-shot magazine (10-shot optional magazine). **Barrel:** 18-3/8" heavy. **Weight:** NA. **Length:** NA. **Stock:** Laminated wood or exotic hardwood. **Sights:** None furnished. **Features:** Receiver drilled and tapped for scope mount; target-crowned muzzle; high comb, smooth pistol grip and rubber butt plate. Introduced 2001. From Dan Wesson Firearms.

Price: Coyote Target, 22 LR or 22 WMR **$259.00**

HARRINGTON & RICHARDSON ULTRA HEAVY BARREL 22 MAG RIFLE

Caliber: 22 WMR, single shot. **Barrel:** 22" bull. **Weight:** NA. **Length:** NA. **Stock:** Cinnamon laminated wood with Monte Carlo cheekpiece. **Sights:** None furnished; scope mount rail included. **Features:** Hand-checkered stock and forend; deep-crown rifling; tuned trigger; trigger locking system; hammer extension. Introduced 2001. From H&R 1871 LLC.

Price: **$135.95**

KIMBER 22 CLASSIC BOLT-ACTION RIFLE

Caliber: 22 LR, 5-shot magazine. **Barrel:** 22" Kimber match grade; 11-degree target crown. **Weight:** About 6.5 lbs. **Length:** 40.5" overall. **Stock:** Classic style in Claro walnut with 18 l.p.i. hand-cut checkering; satin finish; steel gripcap; swivel studs. **Sights:** None furnished; Kimber sculpted bases available that accept all rotary dovetail rings. **Features:** All-new action with Mauser-style full-length claw extractor; two-position in M70-type safety; fully adjustable trigger set at 2 lbs.; pillar-bedded action with recoil lug, free-floated barrel. Introduced 1999. Made in U.S. by Kimber Mfg., Inc.

Price: **$950.00**

RIFLES

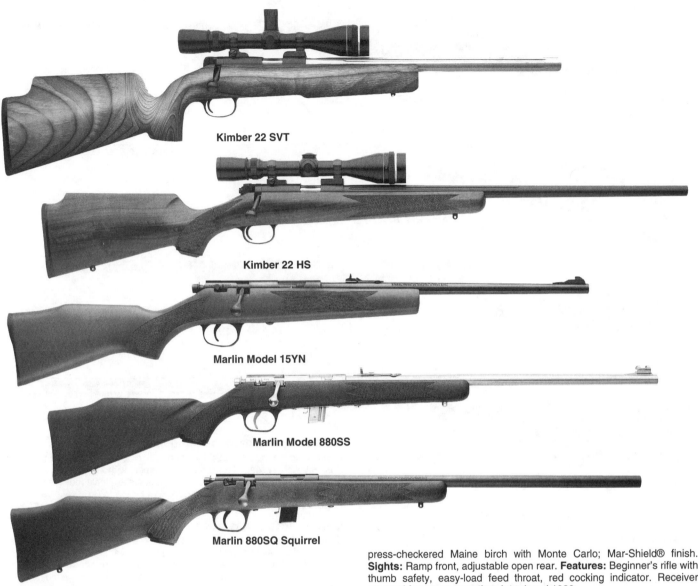

Kimber 22 SVT

Kimber 22 HS

Marlin Model 15YN

Marlin Model 880SS

Marlin 880SQ Squirrel

Kimber 22 SuperAmerica Bolt-Action Rifle

Similar to the 22 Classic except has AAA Claro walnut stock with wrap-around 22 l.p.i. hand-cut checkering, ebony forened tip, beaded cheekpiece. Introduced 1999. Made in U.S. by Kimber Mfg., Inc.

Price: **$1,560.00**

Kimber 22 SVT Bolt-Action Rilfe

Similar to the 22 Classic except has 18" stainless steel, fluted bull barrel, gray laminated, high-comb target-style stock with deep pistol grip, high comb, and beavertail forend with bipod stud. Weighs 7.5 lbs., overall length 36.5". Matte finish on action. Introduced 1999. Made in U.S. by Kimber Mfg., Inc.

Price: **$950.00**

Kimber 22 HS (Hunter Silhouette) Bolt-Action Rifle

Similar to the 22 Classic except has 24" medium sporter match-grade barrel with half-fluting; high comb, walnut, Monte Carlo target stock with 18 l.p.i. checkering; matte blue metal finish. Introduced 1999. Made in U.S. by Kimber Mfg., Inc.

Price: **$814.00**

MARLIN MODEL 15YN "LITTLE BUCKAROO"

Caliber: 22 S, L, LR, single shot. **Barrel:** 16-1/4" Micro-Groove®. **Weight:** 4-1/4 lbs. **Length:** 33-1/4" overall. **Stock:** One-piece walnut-finished, press-checkered Maine birch with Monte Carlo; Mar-Shield® finish. **Sights:** Ramp front, adjustable open rear. **Features:** Beginner's rifle with thumb safety, easy-load feed throat, red cocking indicator. Receiver grooved for scope mounting. Introduced 1989.

Price: **$197.00**

MARLIN MODEL 880SS BOLT-ACTION RIFLE

Caliber: 22 LR, 7-shot clip magazine. **Barrel:** 22" Micro-Groove®. **Weight:** 6 lbs. **Length:** 41" overall. **Stock:** Black fiberglass-filled synthetic with nickel-plated swivel studs and moulded-in checkering. **Sights:** Ramp front with orange post and cutaway Wide-Scan™ hood, adjustable semi-buck-horn folding rear. **Features:** Stainless steel barrel, receiver, front breech bolt and striker; receiver grooved for scope mounting. Introduced 1994. Made in U.S. by Marlin.

Price: **$297.00**

Marlin Model 81TS Bolt-Action Rifle

Same as the Marlin 880SS except blued steel, tubular magazine, holds 17 Long Rifle cartridges. Weighs 6 lbs.

Price: **$200.00**

Marlin Model 880SQ Squirrel Rifle

Similar to the Model 880SS except uses the heavy target barrel of Marlin's Model 2000L target rifle. Black synthetic stock with moulded-in checkering; double bedding screws; matte blue finish. Comes without sights, no dovetail or filler screws; receiver grooved for scope mount. Weighs 7 lbs. Introduced 1996. Made in U.S. by Marlin.

Price: **$312.00**

Marlin 25NC

Marlin 25MNC

Marlin 883SS

Marlin 83TS

Marlin Model 25N Bolt-Action Repeater

Similar to Marlin 880, except walnut-finished hardwood stock, adjustable open rear sight, ramp front.
Price: $199.00
Price: With 4x scope and mount.......................... $205.00

Marlin Model 25NC Bolt-Action Repeater

Same as the Model 25N except has a Mossy Oak® Break-Up camouflage stock. Made in U.S. by Marlin.
Price: $233.00

Marlin Model 25MN/25MNC Bolt-Action Rifles

Similar to the Model 25N except chambered for 22 WMR. Has 7-shot clip magazine, 22" Micro-Groove® barrel, checkered walnut-finished Maine birch stock. Introduced 1989.
Price: 25MN $227.00
New! Price: 25MNC (Mossy Oak® Break-Up camouflage stock). . $263.00

Marlin Model 882 Bolt-Action Rifle

Same as the Marlin 880 except 22 WMR cal. only with 7-shot clip magazine; weight about 6 lbs. Comes with swivel studs.
Price: $304.00
Price: Model 882L (laminated hardwood stock; weighs 6-1/4 lbs.) $322.00

Marlin Model 882SS Bolt-Action Rifle

Same as the Marlin Model 882 except has stainless steel front breech bolt, barrel, receiver and bolt knob. All other parts are either stainless steel or nickel-plated. Has black Monte Carlo stock of fiberglass-filled polycarbonate with moulded-in checkering, nickel-plated swivel studs. Introduced 1995. Made in U.S. by Marlin Firearms Co.
Price: $314.00

Marlin Model 882SSV Bolt-Action Rifle

Similar to the Model 882SS except has selected heavy 22" stainless steel barrel with recessed muzzle, and comes without sights; receiver is grooved for scope mount and 1" ring mounts are included. Weighs 7 lbs. Introduced 1997. Made in U.S. by Marlin Firearms Co.
Price: $309.00

MARLIN MODEL 883 BOLT-ACTION RIFLE

Caliber: 22 WMR. **Barrel:** 22"; 1:16" twist. **Weight:** 6 lbs. **Length:** 41" overall. **Stock:** Walnut Monte Carlo with sling swivel studs, rubber butt pad. **Sights:** Ramp front with brass bead, removable hood; adjustable semi-buckhorn folding rear. **Features:** Thumb safety; red cocking indicator; receiver grooved for scope mount. Made in U.S. by Marlin Firearms Co.
Price: $317.00

Marlin Model 883SS Bolt-Action Rifle

Same as the Model 883 except front breech bolt, striker knob, trigger stud, cartridge lifter stud and outer magazine tube are of stainless steel; other parts are nickel-plated. Has two-tone brown laminated Monte Carlo stock with swivel studs, rubber butt pad. Introduced 1993.
Price: $337.00

Marlin Model 83TS Bolt-Action Rifle

Same as the Model 883 except has a black Monte Carlo fiberglass-filled synthetic stock with sling swivel studs. Weighs 6 lbs., length 41" overall. Introduced 2001. Made in U.S. by Marlin Firearms Co.
Price: $244.00

NEW ENGLAND FIREARMS SPORTSTER™ SINGLE-SHOT RIFLES

Caliber: 22 LR, 22 WMR, single-shot. **Barrel:** 20". **Weight:** 5-1/2 lbs. **Length:** 36-1/4" overall. **Stock:** Black polymer. **Sights:** None furnished; scope mount included. **Features:** Break open, side-lever release; automatic ejection; recoil pad; sling swivel studs; trigger locking system. Introduced 2001. Made in U.S. by New England Firearms.
Price: $121.95
Price: Youth model (20" bbl., 33" overall, weighs 5-1/3 lbs.) $121.95

Ruger K77/22 Varmint

Ruger 77/22R

Sako Finnfire

NEW ULTRA LIGHT ARMS 20RF BOLT-ACTION RIFLE

Caliber: 22 LR, single shot or repeater. **Barrel:** Douglas, length to order. **Weight:** 5-1/4 lbs. **Length:** Varies. **Stock:** Kevlar®/graphite composite, variety of finishes. **Sights:** None furnished; drilled and tapped for scope mount. **Features:** Timney trigger, hand-lapped action, button-rifled barrel, hand-bedded action, recoil pad, sling-swivel studs, optional Jewell Trigger. Made in U.S. by New Ultra Light Arms.
Price: 20 RF single shot **$800.00**
Price: 20 RF repeater **$850.00**

ROSSI MATCHED PAIR SINGLE-SHOT RIFLE/SHOTGUN

Caliber: 22 LR or 22 WMR. **Barrel:** 18-1/2" or 23". **Weight:** NA. **Length:** NA. **Stock:** Hardwood (brown or black finish). **Sights:** Ramp front, fully adjustable rear. **Features:** Break-open breech with external hammer; transfer-bar manual safety; blued or stainless steel finish; sling-swivel studs; includes matched 410-, 20- or 12-gauge shotgun barrel with bead front sight. Introduced 2001. Imported by BrazTech/Taurus.
Price: 22 LR/410-, 20- or 12-gauge, blued finish,
brown hardwood stock **$140.00**
Price: 22 LR/410-gauge, stainless finish, black hardwood stock . . **$170.00**
Price: 22 WMR/12-gauge, blued finish, brown hardwood stock . . . **$140.00**

RUGER K77/22 VARMINT RIFLE

Caliber: 22 LR, 10-shot, 22 WMR, 9-shot detachable rotary magazine. **Barrel:** 24", heavy. **Weight:** 7.25 lbs. **Length:** 43.25" overall. **Stock:** Laminated hardwood with rubber butt pad, quick-detachable swivel studs. No checkering or gripcap. **Sights:** None furnished. Comes with Ruger 1" scope rings. **Features:** Made of stainless steel with target gray finish. Three-position safety, dual extractors. Stock has wide, flat forend. Introduced 1993.
Price: K77/22VBZ, 22 LR **$565.00**
Price: K77/22VMBZ, 22 WMR **$565.00**

RUGER 77/22 RIMFIRE BOLT-ACTION RIFLE

Caliber: 22 LR, 10-shot rotary magazine; 22 WMR, 9-shot rotary magazine. **Barrel:** 20". **Weight:** About 5-3/4 lbs. **Length:** 39-3/4" overall. **Stock:** Checkered American walnut or injection-moulded fiberglass-reinforced DuPont Zytel with Xenoy inserts in forend and grip, stainless sling swivels. **Sights:** Brass bead front, adjustable folding leaf rear or plain barrel with 1" Ruger rings. **Features:** Mauser-type action uses Ruger's 10-shot rotary magazine. Three-position safety, simplified bolt stop, patented bolt locking system. Uses the dual-screw barrel attachment system of the 10/22 rifle. Integral scope mounting system with 1" Ruger rings. Blued model introduced in 1983. Stainless steel model and blued model with the synthetic stock introduced in 1989.
Price: 77/22R (no sights, rings, walnut stock) **$525.00**
Price: 77/22RS (open sights, rings, walnut stock) **$535.00**
Price: K77/22RP (stainless, no sights, rings, synthetic stock) . . . **$525.00**
Price: K77/22RSP (stainless, open sights, rings, synthetic stock) . **$535.00**
Price: 77/22RM (22 WMR, blue, walnut stock) **$525.00**
Price: K77/22RSMP (22 WMR, stainless, open sights, rings,
synthetic stock) **$535.00**
Price: K77/22RMP (22 WMR, stainless, synthetic stock) **$525.00**
Price: 77/22RSM (22 WMR, blue, open sights, rings,
walnut stock) **$535.00**

SAKO FINNFIRE HUNTER BOLT-ACTION RIFLE

Caliber: 22 LR, 5-shot magazine. **Barrel:** 22". **Weight:** 5.75 lbs. **Length:** 39-1/2" overall. **Stock:** European walnut with checkered grip and forend. **Sights:** Hooded blade front, open adjustable rear. **Features:** Adjustable single-stage trigger; has 50-degree bolt lift. Introduced 1994. Imported from Finland by Beretta USA.
Price: **$874.00**
Price: Varmint (heavy barrel) **$924.00**

SAKO FINNFIRE SPORTER RIFLE

Caliber: 22 LR. **Barrel:** 22"; heavy, free-floating. **Weight:** NA. **Length:** NA. **Stock:** Match style of European walnut; adjustable cheekpiece and buttplate; stippled pistol grip and forend. **Sights:** None furnished; has 11mm integral dovetail scope mount. **Features:** Based on the Sako P94S action with two bolt locking lugs, 50-degree bolt lift and 30mm throw; adjustable trigger. Introduced 1999. Imported from Finland by Beretta USA.
Price: **$984.00**

SAVAGE MARK I-G BOLT-ACTION RIFLE

Caliber: 22 LR, single shot. **Barrel:** 20-3/4". **Weight:** 5-1/2 lbs. **Length:** 39-1/2" overall. **Stock:** Walnut-finished hardwood with Monte Carlo-type comb, checkered grip and forend. **Sights:** Bead front, open adjustable rear. Receiver grooved for scope mounting. **Features:** Thumb-operated rotating safety. Blue finish. Rifled or smooth bore. Introduced 1990. Made in Canada, from Savage Arms Inc.
Price: Mark I, rifled or smooth bore, right- or left-handed **$119.00**
Price: Mark I-GY (Youth), 19" barrel, 37" overall, 5 lbs. **$127.00**

RIFLES

Savage Mark II-FXP

Savage Model 93G

Winchester Model 52B

SAVAGE MARK II-G BOLT-ACTION RIFLE

Caliber: 22 LR, 10-shot magazine. **Barrel:** 20-1/2". **Weight:** 5-1/2 lbs. **Length:** 39-1/2" overall. **Stock:** Walnut-finished hardwood with Monte Carlo-type comb, checkered grip and forend. **Sights:** Bead front, open adjustable rear. Receiver grooved for scope mounting. **Features:** Thumb-operated rotating safety. Blue finish. Introduced 1990. Made in Canada, from Savage Arms, Inc.

Price: $140.00
Price: Mark II-GY (youth), 19" barrel, 37" overall, 5 lbs......... $140.00
Price: Mark II-GL, left-hand $140.00
Price: Mark II-GLY (youth) left-hand..................... $140.00
Price: Mark II-GXP Package Gun (comes with 4x15 scope), right- or left-handed $147.00
Price: Mark II-FXP (as above except with black synthetic stock) $133.00
Price: Mark II-F (as above, no scope) $127.00

Savage Mark II-LV Heavy Barrel Rifle

Similar to the Mark II-G except has heavy 21" barrel with recessed target-style crown; gray, laminated hardwood stock with cut checkering. No sights furnished, but has dovetailed receiver for scope mounting. Overall length is 39-3/4", weight is 6-1/2 lbs. Comes with 10-shot clip magazine. Introduced 1997. Imported from Canada by Savage Arms, Inc.

Price: $222.00
Price: Mark II-FV, with black graphite/polymer stock $194.00

Savage Mark II-FSS Stainless Rifle

Similar to the Mark II-G except has stainless steel barreled action and graphite/polymer filled stock; free-floated barrel. Weighs 5 lbs. Introduced 1997. Imported from Canada by Savage Arms, Inc.

Price: $169.00

Savage Model 93FVSS Magnum Rifle

Similar to the Model 93FSS Magnum except has 21" heavy barrel with recessed target-style crown; satin-finished stainless barreled action; black graphite/fiberglass stock. Drilled and tapped for scope mounting; comes with Weaver-style bases. Introduced 1998. Imported from Canada by Savage Arms, Inc.

Price: $222.00

SAVAGE MODEL 93G MAGNUM BOLT-ACTION RIFLE

Caliber: 22 WMR, 5-shot magazine. **Barrel:** 20-3/4". **Weight:** 5-3/4 lbs. **Length:** 39-1/2" overall. **Stock:** Walnut-finished hardwood with Monte Carlo-type comb, checkered grip and forend. **Sights:** Bead front, adjustable open rear. Receiver grooved for scope mount. **Features:** Thumb-operated rotary safety. Blue finish. Introduced 1994. Made in Canada, from Savage Arms.

Price: About $160.00
Price: Model 93F (as above with black graphite/fiberglass stock) $154.00

Savage Model 93FSS Magnum Rifle

Similar to the Model 93G except has stainless steel barreled action and black synthetic stock with positive checkering. Weighs 5-1/2 lbs. Introduced 1997. Imported from Canada by Savage Arms, Inc.

Price: $194.00

WINCHESTER MODEL 52B BOLT-ACTION RIFLE

Caliber: 22 Long Rifle, 5-shot magazine. **Barrel:** 24". **Weight:** 7 lbs. **Length:** 41-3/4" overall. **Stock:** Walnut with checkered grip and forend. **Sights:** None furnished; grooved receiver and drilled and tapped for scope mounting. **Features:** Has Micro Motion trigger adjustable for pull and over-travel; match chamber; detachable magazine. Reintroduced 1997. From U.S. Repeating Arms Co.

Price: $662.00

WINCHESTER MODEL 1885 LOW WALL RIMFIRE

Caliber: 22 LR, single-shot. **Barrel:** 24-1/2"; half-octagon. **Weight:** 8 lbs. **Length:** 41" overall. **Stock:** Walnut. **Sights:** Blade front, semi-buckhorn rear. **Features:** Drilled and tapped for scope mount or tang sight; target chamber. Limited production. From U.S. Repeating Arms Co.

Price: Grade I (2,400 made)............................ $828.00
Price: High Grade (1,100 made; engraved/gold inlaid squirrel and rabbit) $1,180.00

Includes models for classic American and ISU target competition and other sporting and competitive shooting.

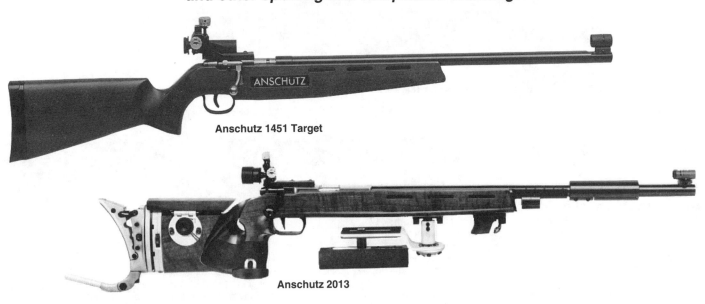

Anschutz 1451 Target

Anschutz 2013

ANSCHUTZ 1451R SPORTER TARGET RIFLE

Caliber: 22 LR, 5-shot magazine. **Barrel:** 22" heavy match. **Weight:** 6.4 lbs. **Length:** 39.75" overall. **Stock:** European hardwood with walnut finish. **Sights:** None furnished. Grooved receiver for scope mounting or Anschutz micrometer rear sight. **Features:** Sliding safety, two-stage trigger. Adjustable buttplate; forend slide rail to accept Anschutz accessories. Imported from Germany by AcuSport Corp.
Price: $549.00

ANSCHUTZ 1451 TARGET RIFLE

Caliber: 22 LR. **Barrel:** 22". **Weight:** About 6.5 lbs. **Length:** 40". **Sights:** Optional. Receiver grooved for scope mounting. **Features:** Designed for the beginning junior shooter with adjustable length of pull from 13.25" to 14.25" via removable butt spacers. Two-stage trigger factory set at 2.6 lbs. Introduced 1999. Imported from Germany by Gunsmithing, Inc.
Price: $347.00
Price: #6834 Match Sight Set $227.10

ANSCHUTZ 1808D-RT SUPER RUNNING TARGET RIFLE

Caliber: 22 LR, single shot. **Barrel:** 32-1/2". **Weight:** 9 lbs. **Length:** 50" overall. **Stock:** European walnut. Heavy beavertail forend; adjustable cheekpiece and buttplate. Stippled grip and forend. **Sights:** None furnished. Grooved for scope mounting. **Features:** Designed for Running Target competition. Nine-way adjustable single-stage trigger, slide safety. Introduced 1991. Imported from Germany by Accuracy International, Gunsmithing, Inc.
Price: Right-hand $1,364.10

ANSCHUTZ 1903 MATCH RIFLE

Caliber: 22 LR, single shot. **Barrel:** 25.5", .75" diameter. **Weight:** 10.1 lbs. **Length:** 43.75" overall. **Stock:** Walnut-finished hardwood with adjustable cheekpiece; stippled grip and forend. **Sights:** None furnished. **Features:** Uses Anschutz Match 64 action and #5098 two-stage trigger. A medium weight rifle for intermediate and advanced Junior Match competition. Introduced 1987. Imported from Germany by Accuracy International, Gunsmithing, Inc.
Price: Right-hand $720.40
Price: Left-hand $757.90

ANSCHUTZ 64-MSR SILHOUETTE RIFLE

Caliber: 22 LR, 5-shot magazine. **Barrel:** 21-1/2", medium heavy; 7/8" diameter. **Weight:** 8 lbs. **Length:** 39.5" overall. **Stock:** Walnut-finished hardwood, silhouette-type. **Sights:** None furnished. **Features:** Uses Match 64 action. Designed for metallic silhouette competition. Stock has stippled checkering, contoured thumb groove with Wundhammer swell.

Two-stage #5098 trigger. Slide safety locks sear and bolt. Introduced 1980. Imported from Germany by AcuSport Corp., Accuracy International, Gunsmithing, Inc.
Price: 64-MSR $704.30

ANSCHUTZ 2013 BENCHREST RIFLE

Caliber: 22 LR, single shot. **Barrel:** 19.6". **Weight:** About 10.3 lbs. **Length:** 37.75" to 42.5" overall. **Stock:** Benchrest style of European hardwood. Stock length adjustable via spacers and buttplate. **Sights:** None furnished. Receiver grooved for mounts. **Features:** Uses the Anschutz 2013 target action, #5018 two-stage adjustable target trigger factory set at 3.9 oz. Introduced 1994. Imported from Germany by Accuracy International, Gunsmithing, Inc.
Price: $1,757.20

Anschutz 2007 Match Rifle

Uses same action as the Model 2013, but has a lighter barrel. European walnut stock in right-hand, true left-hand or extra-short models. Sights optional. Available with 19.6" barrel with extension tube, or 26", both in stainless or blue. Introduced 1998. Imported from Germany by Gunsmithing, Inc., Accuracy International.
Price: Right-hand, blue, no sights $1,766.60
Price: Right-hand, blue, no sights, extra-short stock $1,756.60
Price: Left-hand, blue, no sights $1,856.80

ANSCHUTZ 1827 BIATHLON RIFLE

Caliber: 22 LR, 5-shot magazine. **Barrel:** 21-1/2". **Weight:** 8-1/2 lbs. with sights. **Length:** 42-1/2" overall. **Stock:** European walnut with cheekpiece, stippled pistol grip and forend. **Sights:** Optional globe front specially designed for Biathlon shooting, micrometer rear with hinged snow cap. **Features:** Uses Super Match 54 action and nine-way adjustable trigger; adjustable wooden buttplate, Biathlon butthook, adjustable hand-stop rail. Introduced 1982. Imported from Germany by Accuracy International, Gunsmithing, Inc.
Price: Right-hand, with sights, about . . . . $1,500.50 to $1,555.00

Anschutz 1827BT Fortner Biathlon Rifle

Similar to the Anschutz 1827 Biathlon rifle except uses Anschutz/Fortner system straight-pull bolt action, blued or stainless steel barrel. Introduced 1982. Imported from Germany by Accuracy International, Gunsmithing, Inc.
Price: Right-hand, with sights . . . . $1,908.00 to $2,210.00
Price: Left-hand, with sights . . . . $2,099.20 to $2,395.00
Price: Right-hand, sights, stainless barrel (Gunsmithing, Inc.) . . $2,045.20

Anschutz 54.18MS REP

Armalite AR-10 (T)

ANSCHUTZ SUPER MATCH SPECIAL MODEL 2013 RIFLE

Caliber: 22 LR, single shot. **Barrel:** 25.9". **Weight:** 13 lbs. **Length:** 41.7-42.9". **Stock:** A thumbhole version made of European walnut, both the cheekpiece and buttplate are highly adjustable. **Sights:** None furnished. **Features:** Developed by Anschütz for women to shoot in the sport rifle category. Stainless or blue. This top of the line rifle was introduced in 1997.

Price: Right-hand, blue, no sights, walnut $2,219.30
Price: Right-hand, stainless, no sights, walnut $2,345.30
Price: Left-hand, blue, no sights, walnut $2,319.50

ANSCHUTZ 2012 SPORT RIFLE

Caliber: 22 LR, 5-shot magazine. **Barrel:** 22.4" match; detachable muzzle tube. **Weight:** 7.9 lbs. **Length:** 40.9" overall. **Stock:** European walnut, thumbhole design. **Sights:** None furnished. **Features:** Uses Anschutz 54.18 barreled action with two-stage match trigger. Introduced 1997. Imported from Germany by Accuracy International, AcuSport Corp.

Price: . . . . $1,425.00 to $2,219.95

ANSCHUTZ 1911 PRONE MATCH RIFLE

Caliber: 22 LR, single shot. **Barrel:** 27-1/4". **Weight:** 11 lbs. **Length:** 46" overall. **Stock:** Walnut-finished European hardwood; American prone-style with adjustable cheekpiece, textured pistol grip, forend with swivel rail and adjustable rubber buttplate. **Sights:** None furnished. Receiver grooved for Anschutz sights (extra). **Features:** Two-stage #5018 trigger adjustable from 2.1 to 8.6 oz. Extremely fast lock time. Stainless or blue barrel. Imported from Germany by Accuracy International, Gunsmithing, Inc.

Price: Right-hand, no sights $1,714.20

ANSCHUTZ 1912 SPORT RIFLE

Caliber: 22 LR, single shot. **Barrel:** 25.9". **Weight:** About 11.4 lbs. **Length:** 41.7-42.9". **Stock:** European walnut or aluminum. **Sights:** None furnished. **Features:** Light weight sport rifle version. Still uses the 54 match action like the 1913 but weighs 1.5 pounds less. Stainless or blue barrel. Introduced 1997.

Price: Right-hand, blue, no sights, walnut $1,789.50
Price: Right-hand, blue, no sights, aluminum $2,129.80
Price: Right-hand, stainless, no sights, walnut $1,910.30
Price: Left-hand, blue, no sights, walnut $1,879.00

ANSCHUTZ 1913 SUPER MATCH RIFLE

Caliber: 22 LR, single shot. **Barrel:** 27.1". **Weight:** About 14.3 lbs. **Length:** 44.8-46". **Stock:** European walnut, color laminate, or aluminum. **Sights:** None furnished. **Features:** Two-stage #5018 trigger. Extremely fast lock time. Stainless or blue barrel.

Price: Right-hand, blue, no sights, walnut stock $2,262.90
Price: Right-hand, blue, no sights, color laminate stock $2,275.10
Price: Right-hand, blue, no sights, aluminum stock $2,262.90
Price: Left-hand, blue, no sights, walnut stock $2,382.20

Anschutz 1913 Super Match Rifle

Same as the Model 1911 except European walnut International-type stock with adjustable cheekpiece, or color laminate, both available with straight or lowered forend, adjustable aluminum hook buttplate, adjustable hand stop, weighs 15.5 lbs., 46" overall. Stainless or blue barrel. Imported from Germany by Accuracy International, Gunsmithing, Inc.

Price: Right-hand, blue, no sights, walnut stock. . . **$2,139.00 to $2,175.00**
Price: Right-hand, blue, no sights, color laminate stock. **$2,199.40**
Price: Right-hand, blue, no sights, walnut, lowered forend **$2,181.80**
Price: Right-hand, blue, no sights, color laminate, lowered forend **$2,242.20**
Price: Left-hand, blue, no sights, walnut stock. . . **$2,233.10 to $2,275.00**

Anschutz 54.18MS REP Deluxe Silhouette Rifle

Same basic action and trigger specifications as the Anschutz 1913 Super Match but with removable 5-shot clip magazine, 22.4" barrel extendable to 30" using optional extension and weight set. Weight id 8.1 lbs. Receiver drilled and tapped for scope mounting. Stock is Thumbhole silhouette version or standard silhouette version, both are European walnut. Introduced 1990. Imported from Germany by Accuracy International, Gunsmithing, Inc.

Price: Thumbhole stock **$1,461.40**
Price: Standard stock **$1,212.10**

Anschutz 1907 Standard Match Rifle

Same action as Model 1913 but with 7/8" diameter 26" barrel (stainless or blue). Length is 44.5" overall, weighs 10.5 lbs. Choice of stock configurations. Vented forend. Designed for prone and position shooting ISU requirements; suitable for NRA matches. Also available with walnut flat-forend stock for benchrest shooting. Imported from Germany by Accuracy International, Gunsmithing, Inc.

Price: Right-hand, blue, no sights, hardwood stock **$1,253.40 to $1,299.00**
Price: Right-hand, blue, no sights, colored laminated stock . . . . **$1,316.10 to $1,375.00**
Price: Right-hand, blue, no sights, walnut stock. **$1,521.10**
Price: Left-hand, blue barrel, no sights, walnut stock. **$1,584.60**

ARMALITE AR-10 (T) RIFLE

Caliber: 308, 10-shot magazine. **Barrel:** 24" target-weight Rock 5R custom. **Weight:** 10.4 lbs. **Length:** 43.5" overall. **Stock:** Green or black composition; N.M. fiberglass handguard tube. **Sights:** Detachable handle, front sight, or scope mount available. Comes with international-style flattop receiver with Picatinny rail. **Features:** National Match two-stage trigger. Forged upper receiver. Receivers hard-coat anodized. Introduced 1995. Made in U.S. by ArmaLite, Inc.

Price: Green $2,075.00
Price: Black $2,090.00
Price: AR-10 (T) Carbine, lighter 16" barrel, single stage trigger, weighs 8.8 lbs. Green $1,970.00
Price: Black $1,985.00

RIFLES

Bushmaster XM15 E2S Target

Bushmaster DCM

Colt Match Target HBAR

RIFLES

ARMALITE M15A4 (T) EAGLE EYE RIFLE

Caliber: 223, 7-shot magazine. **Barrel:** 24" heavy stainless; 1:8" twist. **Weight:** 9.2 lbs. **Length:** 42-3/8" overall. **Stock:** Green or black butt, N.M. fiberglass handguard tube. **Sights:** One-piece international-style flattop receiver with Weaver-type rail, including case deflector. **Features:** Detachable carry handle, front sight and scope mount (30mm or 1") available. Upper and lower receivers have push-type pivot pin, hard coat anodized. Made in U.S. by ArmaLite, Inc.
Price: Green **$1,378.00**
Price: Black **$1,393.00**

ARMALITE M15A4 ACTION MASTER RIFLE

Caliber: 223, 7-shot magazine. **Barrel:** 20" heavy stainless; 1:9" twist. **Weight:** 9 lbs. **Length:** 40-1/2" overall. **Stock:** Green or black plastic; N.M. fiberglass handguard tube. **Sights:** One-piece international-style flattop receiver with Weaver-type rail. **Features:** Detachable carry handle, front sight and scope mount available. National Match two-stage trigger group; Picatinny rail; upper and lower receivers have push-type pivot pin; hard coat anodized finish. Made in U.S. by ArmaLite, Inc.
Price: **$1,175.00**

BLASER R93 LONG RANGE RIFLE

Caliber: 308 Win., 10-shot detachable box magazine. **Barrel:** 24". **Weight:** 10.4 lbs. **Length:** 44" overall. **Stock:** Aluminum with synthetic lining. **Sights:** None furnished; accepts detachable scope mount. **Features:** Straight-pull bolt action with adjustable trigger; fully adjustable stock; quick takedown; corrosion resistant finish. Introduced 1998. Imported from Germany by Sigarms.
Price: **$2,360.00**

BUSHMASTER XM15 E2S TARGET MODEL RIFLE

Caliber: 223. **Barrel:** 20", 24", 26"; 1:9" twist; heavy. **Weight:** 8.3 lbs. **Length:** 38.25" overall (20" barrel). **Stock:** Black composition; A2 type. **Sights:** Adjustable post front, adjustable aperture rear. **Features:** Patterned after Colt M-16A2. Chrome-lined barrel with manganese phosphate exterior. Forged aluminum receivers with push-pin takedown. Made in U.S. by Bushmaster Firearms Co./Quality Parts Co.
Price: 20" match heavy barrel **$960.00**

Bushmaster DCM Competition Rifle

Similar to the XM15 E2S Target Model except has 20" extra-heavy (1" diameter) barrel with 1.8" twist for heavier competition bullets. Weighs about 12 lbs. with balance weights. Has special competition rear sight with interchangeable apertures, extra-fine 1/2- or 1/4-MOA windage and elevation adjustments; specially ground front sight post in choice of three widths. Full-length handguards over free-floater barrel tube. Introduced 1998. Made in U.S. by Bushmaster Firearms, Inc.
Price: **$1,525.00**

BUSHMASTER XM15 E2S V-MATCH RIFLE

Caliber: 223. **Barrel:** 20", 24", 26"; 1:9" twist; heavy. **Weight:** 8.1 lbs. **Length:** 38.25" overall (20" barrel). **Stock:** Black composition. A2 type. **Sights:** None furnished; upper receiver has integral scope mount base. **Features:** Chrome-lined .950" heavy barrel with counter-bored crown, manganese phosphate finish; free-floating aluminum handguard; forged aluminum receivers with push-pin takedown, hard anodized mil-spec finish. Competition trigger optional. Made in U.S. by Bushmaster Firearms, Inc.
Price: 20" Match heavy barrel **$1,025.00**
Price: 24" Match heavy barrel **$1,040.00**
Price: V-Match Carbine (16" barrel) **$1,015.00**

COLT MATCH TARGET MODEL RIFLE

Caliber: 223 Rem., 8-shot magazine. **Barrel:** 20". **Weight:** 7.5 lbs. **Length:** 39" overall. **Stock:** Composition stock, grip, forend. **Sights:** Post front, aperture rear adjustable for windage and elevation. **Features:** Five-round detachable box magazine, standard-weight barrel, sling swivels. Has forward bolt assist. Military matte black finish. Model introduced 1991.
Price: **$1,144.00**
Price: With compensator **$1,150.00**

Colt Accurized Rifle

Similar to the Colt Match Target Model except has 24" stainless steel heavy barrel with 1.9" rifling, flattop receiver with scope mount and 1" rings, weighs 9.25 lbs. Introduced 1998. Made in U.S. by Colt's Mfg. Co., Inc.
Price: **$1,424.00**

Colt Match Target HBAR Rifle

Similar to the Target Model except has heavy barrel, 800-meter rear sight adjustable for windage and elevation. Introduced 1991.
Price: **$1,194.00**

Colt Match Target Competition HBAR Rifle

Similar to the Sporter Target except has flat-top receiver with integral Weaver-type base for scope mounting. Counter-bored muzzle, 1:9" rifling twist. Introduced 1991.
Price: Model R6700 .... **$1,199.00**

Harris Gunworks Long Range

Harris Gunworks M-86

Marlin Model 2000L

Colt Match Target Competition HBAR II Rifle

Similar to the Match Target Competition HBAR except has 16:1" barrel, weighs 7.1 lbs., overall length 34.5"; 1:9" twist barrel. Introduced 1995.
Price: **$1,172.00**

E.A.A./HW 660 MATCH RIFLE

Caliber: 22 LR. **Barrel:** 26". **Weight:** 10.7 lbs. **Length:** 45.3" overall. **Stock:** Match-type walnut with adjustable cheekpiece and buttplate. **Sights:** Globe front, match aperture rear. **Features:** Adjustable match trigger; stippled pistol grip and forend; forend accessory rail. Introduced 1991. Imported from Germany by European American Armory.
Price: About **$999.00**
Price: With laminate stock **$1,159.00**

HARRIS GUNWORKS NATIONAL MATCH RIFLE

Caliber: 7mm-08, 308, 5-shot magazine. **Barrel:** 24", stainless steel. **Weight:** About 11 lbs. (std. bbl.). **Length:** 43" overall. **Stock:** Fiberglass with adjustable buttplate. **Sights:** Barrel band and Tompkins front; no rear sight furnished. **Features:** Gunworks repeating action with clip slot, Canjar trigger. Match-grade barrel. Available in right-hand only. Fiberglass stock, sight installation, special machining and triggers optional. Introduced 1989. From Harris Gunworks, Inc.
Price: **$3,500.00**

HARRIS GUNWORKS LONG RANGE RIFLE

Caliber: 300 Win. Mag., 7mm Rem. Mag., 300 Phoenix, 338 Lapua, single shot. **Barrel:** 26", stainless steel, match-grade. **Weight:** 14 lbs. **Length:** 46-1/2" overall. **Stock:** Fiberglass with adjustable buttplate and cheekpiece. Adjustable for length of pull, drop, cant and cast-off. **Sights:** Barrel band and Tompkins front; no rear sight furnished. **Features:** Uses Gunworks solid bottom single shot action and Canjar trigger. Barrel twist 1:12". Introduced 1989. From Harris Gunworks, Inc.
Price: **$3,620.00**

HARRIS GUNWORKS M-86 SNIPER RIFLE

Caliber: 308, 30-06, 4-shot magazine; 300 Win. Mag., 3-shot magazine. **Barrel:** 24", Gunworks match-grade in heavy contour. **Weight:** 11-1/4 lbs.

(308), 11-1/2 lbs. (30-06, 300). **Length:** 43-1/2" overall. **Stock:** Specially designed McHale fiberglass stock with textured grip and forend, recoil pad. **Sights:** None furnished. **Features:** Uses Gunworks repeating action. Comes with bipod. Matte black finish. Sling swivels. Introduced 1989. From Harris Gunworks, Inc.
Price: **$2,700.00**

HARRIS GUNWORKS M-89 SNIPER RIFLE

Caliber: 308 Win., 5-shot magazine. **Barrel:** 28" (with suppressor). **Weight:** 15 lbs., 4 oz. **Stock:** Fiberglass; adjustable for length; recoil pad. **Sights:** None furnished. Drilled and tapped for scope mounting. **Features:** Uses Gunworks repeating action. Comes with bipod. Introduced 1990. From Harris Gunworks, Inc.
Price: Standard (non-suppressed) **$3,200.00**

HARRIS GUNWORKS
COMBO M-87 SERIES 50-CALIBER RIFLES

Caliber: 50 BMG, single shot. **Barrel:** 29, with muzzle brake. **Weight:** About 21-1/2 lbs. **Length:** 53" overall. **Stock:** Gunworks fiberglass. **Sights:** None furnished. **Features:** Right-handed Gunworks stainless steel receiver, chrome-moly barrel with 1:15" twist. Introduced 1987. From Harris Gunworks, Inc.
Price: **$3,885.00**
Price: M87R 5-shot repeater **$4,000.00**
Price: M-87 (5-shot repeater) "Combo" **$4,300.00**
Price: M-92 Bullpup (shortened M-87 single shot with bullpup stock) **$4,770.00**
Price: M-93 (10-shot repeater with folding stock, detachable magazine). **$4,150.00**

MARLIN MODEL 2000L TARGET RIFLE

Caliber: 22 LR, single shot. **Barrel:** 22" heavy, Micro-Groove® rifling, match chamber, recessed muzzle. **Weight:** 8 lbs. **Length:** 41" overall. **Stock:** Laminated black/gray with ambidextrous pistol grip. **Sights:** Hooded front with ten aperture inserts, fully adjustable target rear peep. **Features:** Buttplate adjustable for length of pull, height and angle. Aluminum forend rail with stop and quick-detachable swivel. Two-stage target trigger; red cocking indicator. Five-shot adaptor kit available. Introduced 1991. From Marlin.
Price: **$711.00**

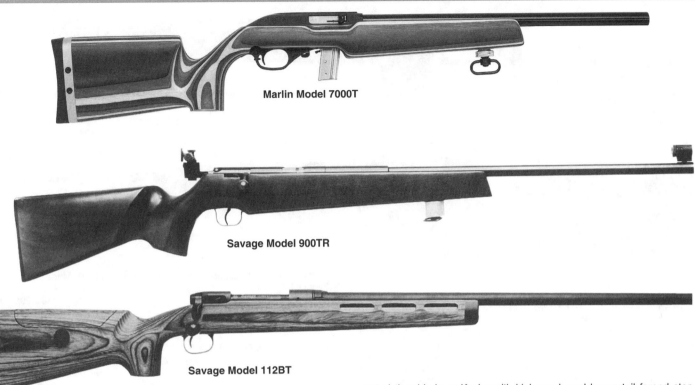

Marlin Model 7000T

Savage Model 900TR

Savage Model 112BT

MARLIN MODEL 7000T AUTO RIFLE

Caliber: 22 LR, 10-shot magazine. **Barrel:** 18" heavy target with Micro-Groove® rifling. **Weight:** 7-1/2 lbs. **Length:** 37" overall. **Stock:** Laminated red, white and blue hardwood with ambidextrous pistol grip, adjustable buttplate, aluminum forend rail. **Sights:** None furnished; grooved receiver for scope mounting. **Features:** Trigger stop; last-shot bolt hold-open; blue finish; scope mounts included. Introduced 1999. Made in U.S. by Marlin.
Price: $465.00

OLYMPIC ARMS PCR-SERVICEMATCH RIFLE

Caliber: 223, 10-shot magazine. **Barrel:** 20", broach-cut 416 stainless steel. **Weight:** About 10 lbs. **Length:** 39.5" overall. **Stock:** A2 stowaway grip and trapdoor buttstock. **Sights:** Post front, E2-NM fully adjustable aperture rear. **Features:** Based on the AR-15. Conforms to all DCM standards. Free-floating 1:8.5" or 1:10" barrel; crowned barrel; no bayonet lug. Introduced 1996. Made in U.S. by Olympic Arms, Inc.
Price: $1,062.00

OLYMPIC ARMS PCR-1 RIFLE

Caliber: 223, 10-shot magazine. **Barrel:** 20", 24"; 416 stainless steel. **Weight:** 10 lbs., 3 oz. **Length:** 38.25" overall with 20" barrel. **Stock:** A2 stowaway grip and trapdoor butt. **Sights:** None supplied; flattop upper receiver, cut-down front sight base. **Features:** Based on the AR-15 rifle. Broach-cut, free-floating barrel with 1:8.5" or 1:10" twist. No bayonet lug. Crowned barrel; fluting available. Introduced 1994. Made in U.S. by Olympic Arms, Inc.
Price: $1,038.00

Olympic Arms PCR-2, PCR-3 Rifles

Similar to the PCR-1 except has 16" barrel, weighs 8 lbs., 2 oz.; has post front sight, fully adjustable aperture rear. Model PCR-3 has flattop upper receiver, cut-down front sight base. Introduced 1994. Made in U.S. by Olympic Arms, Inc.
Price: $958.00

REMINGTON 40-XB RANGEMASTER TARGET CENTERFIRE

Caliber: 15 calibers from 220 Swift to 300 Win. Mag. **Barrel:** 27-1/4". **Weight:** 11-1/4 lbs. **Length:** 47" overall. **Stock:** American walnut, lami-

nated thumbhole or Kevlar with high comb and beavertail forend stop. Rubber non-slip buttplate. **Sights:** None. Scope blocks installed. **Features:** Adjustable trigger. Stainless barrel and action. Receiver drilled and tapped for sights.
Price: Standard single shot $1,565.00
Price: Repeater $1,684.00

REMINGTON 40-XBBR KS

Caliber: Five calibers from 22 BR to 308 Win. **Barrel:** 20" (light varmint class), 24" (heavy varmint class). **Weight:** 7-1/4 lbs. (light varmint class); 12 lbs. (heavy varmint class). **Length:** 38" (20" bbl.), 42" (24" bbl.). **Stock:** Kevlar. **Sights:** None. Supplied with scope blocks. **Features:** Unblued stainless steel barrel, trigger adjustable from 1-1/2 lbs. to 3-1/2 lbs. Special 2-oz. trigger at extra cost. Scope and mounts extra.
Price: With Kevlar stock $1,742.00

REMINGTON 40-XC TARGET RIFLE

Caliber: 7.62 NATO, 5-shot. **Barrel:** 24", stainless steel. **Weight:** 11 lbs. without sights. **Length:** 43-1/2" overall. **Stock:** Kevlar, with palm rail. **Sights:** None furnished. **Features:** Designed to meet the needs of competitive shooters. Stainless steel barrel and action.
Price: $1,742.00

SAKO TRG-22 BOLT-ACTION RIFLE

Caliber: 308 Win., 10-shot magazine. **Barrel:** 26". **Weight:** 10-1/4 lbs. **Length:** 45-1/4" overall. **Stock:** Reinforced polyurethane with fully adjustable cheekpiece and buttplate. **Sights:** None furnished. Optional quick-detachable, one-piece scope mount base, 1" or 30mm rings. **Features:** Resistance-free bolt, free-floating heavy stainless barrel, 60-degree bolt lift. Two-stage trigger is adjustable for length, pull, horizontal or vertical pitch. Introduced 2000. Imported from Finland by Beretta USA.
Price: $2,699.00
Price: Model TRG-42, as above except in 338 Lapua Mag or 300 Win. Mag. $3,099.00

SAVAGE MODEL 900TR TARGET RIFLE

Caliber: 22 LR, 5-shot magazine. **Barrel:** 25". **Weight:** 8 lbs. **Length:** 43-5/8". **Stock:** Target-type, walnut-finished hardwood. **Sights:** Target front with inserts, peep rear with 1/4-minute click adjustments. **Features:** Comes with shooting rail and hand stop. Introduced 1991. Made in Canada, from Savage Arms Inc.
Price: Right- or left-hand $440.00

Springfield, Inc. M1A Super Match

Springfield, Inc. M1A/M-21

SAVAGE MODEL 112BT COMPETITION GRADE RIFLE

Caliber: 223, 308, 5-shot magazine, 300 Win. Mag., single shot. **Barrel:** 26", heavy contour stainless with black finish; 1:9" twist (223), 1:10" (308). **Weight:** 10.8 lbs. **Length:** 47.5" overall. **Stock:** Laminated wood with straight comb, adjustable cheek rest, Wundhammer palm swell, ventilated forend. Recoil pad is adjustable for length of pull. **Sights:** None furnished; drilled and tapped for scope mounting and aperture target-style sights. Recessed target-style muzzle has .812" diameter section for universal target sight base. **Features:** Pillar-bedded stock, matte black alloy receiver. Bolt has black titanium nitride coating, large handle ball. Has alloy accessory rail on forend. Comes with safety gun lock, target and ear puffs. Introduced 1994. Made in U.S. by Savage Arms, Inc.
Price: **$1,028.00**
Price: 300 Win. Mag. (single shot 112BT-S) **$1,028.00**

SPRINGFIELD, INC. M1A SUPER MATCH

Caliber: 308 Win. **Barrel:** 22", heavy Douglas Premium. **Weight:** About 10 lbs. **Length:** 44.31" overall. **Stock:** Heavy walnut competition stock with longer pistol grip, contoured area behind the rear sight, thicker butt and forend, glass bedded. **Sights:** National Match front and rear. **Features:** Has figure-eight-style operating rod guide. Introduced 1987. From Springfield, Inc.
Price: About **$2,479.00**

Springfield, Inc. M1A/M-21 Tactical Model Rifle

Similar to the M1A Super Match except has special sniper stock with adjustable cheekpiece and rubber recoil pad. Weighs 11.2 lbs. From Springfield, Inc.
Price: **$2,975.00**

STONER SR-15 MATCH RIFLE

Caliber: 223. **Barrel:** 20". **Weight:** 7.9 lbs. **Length:** 38" overall. **Stock:** Black synthetic. **Sights:** None furnished; flat-top upper receiver for scope mounting. **Features:** Short Picatinny rail; two-stage match trigger. Introduced 1998. Made in U.S. by Knight's Mfg.Co.
Price: **$1,595.00**

STONER SR-25 MATCH RIFLE

Caliber: 7.62 NATO, 10-shot steel magazine, 5-shot optional. **Barrel:** 24" heavy match; 1:11.25" twist. **Weight:** 10.75 lbs. **Length:** 44" overall. **Stock:** Black synthetic AR-15A2 design. Full floating forend of Mil-spec synthetic attaches to upper receiver at a single point. **Sights:** None furnished. Has integral Weaver-style rail. Rings and iron sights optional. **Features:** Improved AR-15 trigger; AR-15-style seven-lug rotating bolt. Gas

block rail mounts detachable front sight. Introduced 1993. Made in U.S. by Knight's Mfg. Co.
Price: **$2,995.00**
Price: SR-25 Lightweight Match (20" medium match target contour barrel, 9.5 lbs., 40" overall) **$2,995.00**

TANNER 50 METER FREE RIFLE

Caliber: 22 LR, single shot. **Barrel:** 27.7". **Weight:** 13.9 lbs. **Length:** 44.4" overall. **Stock:** Seasoned walnut with palm rest, accessory rail, adjustable hook buttplate. **Sights:** Globe front with interchangeable inserts, Tanner micrometer-diopter rear with adjustable aperture. **Features:** Bolt action with externally adjustable set trigger. Supplied with 50-meter test target. Imported from Switzerland by Mandall Shooting Supplies. Introduced 1984.
Price: About **$3,900.00**

TANNER STANDARD UIT RIFLE

Caliber: 308, 7.5mm Swiss, 10-shot. **Barrel:** 25.9". **Weight:** 10.5 lbs. **Length:** 40.6" overall. **Stock:** Match style of seasoned nutwood with accessory rail; coarsely stippled pistol grip; high cheekpiece; vented forend. **Sights:** Globe front with interchangeable inserts, Tanner micrometer-diopter rear with adjustable aperture. **Features:** Two locking lug revolving bolt encloses case head. Trigger adjustable from 1/2 to 6-1/2 lbs.; match trigger optional. Comes with 300-meter test target. Imported from Switzerland by Mandall Shooting Supplies. Introduced 1984.
Price: About **$4,700.00**

TANNER 300 METER FREE RIFLE

Caliber: 308 Win., 7.5 Swiss, single shot. **Barrel:** 27.58". **Weight:** 15 lbs. **Length:** 45.3" overall. **Stock:** Seasoned walnut, thumbhole style, with accessory rail, palm rest, adjustable hook butt. **Sights:** Globe front with interchangeable inserts, Tanner-design micrometer-diopter rear with adjustable aperture. **Features:** Three-lug revolving-lock bolt design; adjustable set trigger; short firing pin travel; supplied with 300-meter test target. Imported from Switzerland by Mandall Shooting Supplies. Introduced 1984.
Price: About **$4,900.00**

TIKKA SPORTER RIFLE

Caliber: 223, 22-250, 308, detachable 5-shot magazine. **Barrel:** 23-1/2" heavy. **Weight:** 9 lbs. **Length:** 43-5/8" overall. **Stock:** European walnut with adjustable comb, adjustable buttplate; stippled grip and forend. **Sights:** None furnished; drilled and tapped for scope mounting. **Features:** Buttplate is adjustable for distance, angle, height and pitch; adjustable trigger; free-floating barrel. Introduced 1998. Imported from Finland by Beretta USA.
Price: **$939.00**

Includes a wide variety of sporting guns and guns suitable for various competitions.

Benelli Legacy

Benelli M1 Super 90 Camouflage

Benelli Super Black Eagle

BENELLI LEGACY SHOTGUN

Gauge: 12, 20, 3" chamber. **Barrel:** 26", 28" (Full, Mod., Imp. Cyl., Imp. Mod., Skeet choke tubes). Mid-bead sight. **Weight:** 7.1 to 7.6 lbs. **Length:** 49-5/8" overall (26" barrel). **Stock:** European walnut with high-gloss finish. Special competition stock comes with drop adjustment kit. **Features:** Uses the rotating bolt inertia recoil operating system with a two-piece steel/aluminum etched receiver (bright on lower, blue upper). Drop adjustment kit allows the stock to be custom fitted without modifying the stock. Black lower receiver finish, blued upper. Introduced 1998. Imported from Italy by Heckler & Koch, Inc.
Price: $1,350.00

Benelli Limited Edition Legacy

Similar to the Legacy model except receiver has gold-filled, etched game scenes and limited to 250 12 gauge (28" barrel) and 250 20 gauge (26" barrel) guns to commemorate the year 2000.
Price: $1,600.00

Benelli Sport Shotgun

Similar to the Legacy model except has matte blue receiver, two carbon fiber interchangeable ventilated ribs, adjustable butt pad, adjustable buttstock, and functions with ultra-light target loads. Walnut stock with satin finish. Introduced 1997. Imported from Italy by Benelli U.S.A.
Price: $1,340.00

BENELLI M1 FIELD AUTO SHOTGUN

Gauge: 12, 3" chamber. **Barrel:** 21", 24", 26", 28" (choke tubes). **Weight:** 7 lbs., 4 oz. **Stock:** High impact polymer; wood on 26", 28". **Sights:** Metal bead front. **Features:** Sporting version of the military & police gun. Uses the rotating Montefeltro bolt system. Ventilated rib; blue finish. Comes with set of five choke tubes. Imported from Italy by Benelli U.S.A.
Price: $920.00
Price: Wood stock version $935.00
Price: 24" rifled barrel, polymer stock.................... $1,000.00
Price: 24" rifled barrel, camo stock $1,100.00
Price: Synthetic stock, left-hand version (24", 26", 28" brls) $935.00
Price: Camo Stock, left-hand version (24", 26", 28" brls.) $1,025.00

Benelli Montefeltro 90 Shotgun

Similar to the M1 Super 90 except has checkered walnut stock with high-gloss finish. Uses the Montefeltro rotating bolt system with a simple inertia recoil design. Full, Imp. Mod, Mod., Imp. Cyl. choke tubes. Weighs 6.8-7.1 lbs. Finish is matte black. Introduced 1987.
Price: 24", 26", 28" $940.00
Price: Left-hand, 26", 28" $960.00

Benelli Montefeltro 20 gauge Shotgun

Similar to the 12 gauge Montefeltro except chambered for 3" 20 gauge, 24" or 26" barrel (choke tubes), weighs 5-1/2 lbs., has drop-adjustable walnut stock with satin or camo finish, blued receiver. Overall length 47.5". Introduced 1993. Imported from Italy by Benelli U.S.A.
Price: 26" barrels $940.00
Price: 26", camouflage finish $1,040.00
Price: Montefeltro Short Stock, 24" and 26" brls............. $975.00

BENELLI SUPER BLACK EAGLE SHOTGUN

Gauge: 12, 3-1/2" chamber. **Barrel:** 24", 26", 28" (Cyl. Imp. Cyl., Mod., Imp. Mod., Full choke tubes). **Weight:** 7 lbs., 5 oz. **Length:** 49-5/8" overall (28" barrel). **Stock:** European walnut with satin finish, or polymer. Adjustable for drop. **Sights:** Bead front. **Features:** Uses Montefeltro inertia recoil bolt system. Fires all 12 gauge shells from 2-3/4" to 3-1/2" magnums. Introduced 1991. Imported from Italy by Benelli U.S.A.
Price: With 26" and 28" barrel, wood stock $1,240.00
Price: With 24", 26" and 28" barrel, polymer stock........... $1,220.00
Price: Left-hand, 24", 26", 28", polymer stock $1,250.00
Price: Left-hand, 24", 26", 28", camo stock $1,330.00

Benelli Super Black Eagle Slug Gun

Similar to the Benelli Super Black Eagle except has 24" rifled barrel with 3" chamber, and drilled and tapped for scope. Uses the inertia recoil bolt system. Matte-finish receiver. Weight is 7.5 lbs., overall length 45.5". Wood or polymer stocks available. Introduced 1992. Imported from Italy by Benelli U.S.A.
Price: With wood stock.............................. $1,280.00
Price: With polymer stock............................. $1,270.00
Price: 26" barrels $1,390.00

Benelli Executive Series Shotguns

Similar to the Super Black Eagle except has grayed steel lower receiver, hand-engraved and gold inlaid (Grade III), and has highest grade of walnut stock with drop adjustment kit. Barrel lengths 26" or 28"; 3" chamber. Special order only. Introduced 1995. Imported from Italy by Benelli U.S.A.
Price: Grade I (engraved game scenes) $5,035.00
Price: Grade II (game scenes with scroll engraving) $5,720.00
Price: Grade III (full coverage, gold inlays) $6,670.00

Beretta Urika Gold Sporting

Beretta Urika Sporting

Beretta Urika Gold Trap

BERETTA AL391 URIKA AUTO SHOTGUNS

Gauge: 12, 20 gauge; 3" chamber. **Barrel:** 22", 24", 26", 28", 30"; five Mobilchoke choke tubes. **Weight:** 5.95 to 7.28 lbs. **Length:** Varies by model. **Stock:** Walnut, black or camo synthetic; shims, spacers and interchangeable recoil pads allow custom fit. **Features:** Self-compensating gas operation handles full range of loads; recoil reducer in receiver; enlarged trigger guard; reduced-weight receiver, barrel and forend; hard-chromed bore. Introduced 2000. Imported from Italy by Beretta USA.
Price: AL391 Urika (12 ga., 26", 28", 30" barrels) **$984.00**
Price: AL391 Urika (20 ga., 24", 26", 28" barrels) **$984.00**
Price: AL391 Urika Synthetic (12 ga., 24", 26", 28", 30" barrels) **$984.00**
Price: AL391 Urika Camo. (12 ga., Realtree Hardwoods
or Advantage Wetlands) **$1,083.00**

Beretta AL391 Urika Gold and Gold Sporting Auto Shotguns

Similar to AL391 Urika except features deluxe wood, jeweled bolt and carrier, gold-inlaid receiver with black or silver finish. Introduced 2000. Imported from Italy by Beretta USA.
Price: AL391 Urika Gold (12 or 20 ga., black receiver) **$1,180.00**
Price: AL391 Urika Gold (silver, lightweight receiver). **$1,217.00**
Price: AL391 Urika Gold Sporting (12 or 20, black receiver, engraving)
. . . . **$1,224.00**
Price: AL391 Urika Gold Sporting (12 ga., silver receiver, engraving)
. . . . **$1,260.00**

Beretta AL391 Urika Sporting Auto Shotguns

Similar to AL391 Urika except has competition sporting stock with rounded rubber recoil pad, wide ventilated rib with white front and mid-rib beads, satin-black receiver with silver markings. Available in 12 and 20 gauge. Introduced 2000. Imported from Italy by Beretta USA.
Price: AL391 Urika Sporting. **$1,027.00**

Beretta AL391 Urika Trap and Gold Trap Auto Shotguns

Similar to AL391 Urika except in 12 ga. only, has wide ventilated rib with white front and mid-rib beads, Monte Carlo stock and special trap recoil pad. Gold Trap features highly figured walnut stock and forend, gold-filled Beretta logo and signature on receiver. Introduced 2000. Imported from Italy by Beretta USA.
Price: AL391 Urika Trap **$1,027.00**
Price: AL391 Urika Gold Trap **$1,224.00**

Beretta AL391 Urika Parallel Target RL and SL Auto Shotguns

Similar to AL391 Urika except has parallel-comb, Monte Carlo stock with tighter grip radius to reduce trigger reach and stepped ventilated rib. SL model has same features but with 13.5" length of pull stock. Introduced 2000. Imported from Italy by Beretta USA.
Price: AL391 Urika Parallel Target RL **$1,027.00**
Price: AL391 Urika Parallel Target SL **$1,027.00**

Beretta AL391 Urika Youth Shotgun

Similar to AL391 except has a 24" or 26" barrel with 13.5" stock for youth and smaller shooters. Introduced 2000. From Beretta USA.
Price: **$960.00**

BERETTA ES100 NWTF SPECIAL AUTO SHOTGUN

Gauge: 12, 3" chamber. **Barrel:** 24", MC3 tubes and Briley extended Extra-Full Turkey. **Weight:** 7.3 lbs. **Stock:** Synthetic, checkered. **Sights:** Truglo fiber optic front and rear three-dot system. **Features:** Short recoil inertia operation. Mossy Oak Break-Up camouflage finish on stock and forend, black matte finish on all metal. Comes with camouflage sling. Introduced 1999. Imported from Italy by Beretta U.S.A.
Price: **$945.00**

Beretta ES 100 Auto Shotguns

Similar to the ES 100 MWTF model except offered with walnut, black synthetic or camouflage stock and fully rifled slug barrel model. Recoil-operated action. Imported from Italy by Beretta U.S.A.
Price: ES 100 Pintail (24", 26" or 28" bbl., black synthetic stock) . **$757.00**
Price: ES 100 Camouflage (28" bbl., Advantage Wetlands camo stock)
. . . . **$757.00**
Price: ES 100 Rifled Slug (24" rifled slug barrel, black syn. stock) **$899.00**
Price: ES 100 Rifled Slug Combo (24" rifled and 28" smoothbore bbls.)
. . . . **$1,047.00**

BROWNING GOLD HUNTER AUTO SHOTGUN

Gauge: 12, 3" or 3-1/2" chamber; 20, 3" chamber. **Barrel:** 12 ga.—26", 28", 30", Invector Plus choke tubes; 20 ga.—26", 30", Invector choke tubes. **Weight:** 7 lbs., 9 oz. (12 ga.), 6 lbs., 12 oz. (20 ga.). **Length:** 46-1/4" overall (20 ga., 26" barrel). **Stock:** 14"x1-1/2"x2-1/3"; select walnut with gloss finish; palm swell grip. **Features:** Self-regulating, self-cleaning gas system shoots all loads; lightweight receiver with special non-glare deep black finish; large reversible safety button; large rounded trigger guard, gold trigger. The 20 gauge has slightly smaller dimensions; 12 gauge have backbored barrels, Invector Plus tube system. Introduced 1994. Imported by Browning.
Price: 12 or 20 gauge, 3" chamber. **$894.00**
Price: 12 ga., 3-1/2" chamber. **$1,038.00**
Price: Extra barrels. . . . . **$336.00 to $415.00**

SHOTGUNS

Browning Gold Deer Hunter

Browning Gold Sporting Golden Clays

Browning Gold
Classic Stalker

Browning Gold Rifled Deer Hunter Auto Shotgun

Similar to the Gold Hunter except 12 or 20 gauge, 22" rifled barrel with cantilever scope mount, walnut stock with extra-thick recoil pad. Weighs 7 lbs., 12 oz., overall length 42-1/2". Sling swivel studs fitted on the magazine cap and butt. Introduced 1997. Imported by Browning.
Price: (12 gauge) **$887.00**
Price: With Mossy Oak Break-up camouflage **$1,046.00**
New! **Price:** 20 ga. (satin-finish walnut stock, 3" chamber) **$987.00**

Browning Gold Deer Stalker

Similar to the Gold Deer Hunter except has black composite stock and forend, fully rifled barrel, cantilever scope mount. Introduced 1999. Imported by Browning.
Price: (12 ga.) **$948.00**

Browning Gold Sporting Clays Auto

Similar to the Gold Hunter except 12 gauge only with 28" or 30" barrel; front Hi-Viz Pro-Comp and center bead on tapered ventilated rib; ported and back-bored Invector Plus barrel; 2-3/4" chamber; satin-finished stock with solid, radiused recoil pad with hard heel insert; non-glare black alloy receiver has "Sporting Clays" inscribed in gold. Introduced 1996. Imported from Japan by Browning.
Price: **$939.00**

Browning Gold Sporting Golden Clays

Similar to the Sporting Clays except has silvered receiver with gold engraving, high grade wood. Introduced 1999. Imported by Browning.
Price: **$1,457.00**

Browning Gold Ladies/Youth Sporting Clays Auto

Similar to the Gold Sporting Clays except has stock dimensions of 14-1/4"x1-3/4"x2" for women and younger shooters. Introduced 1999. Imported by Browning.
Price: **$902.00**

Browning Gold Micro Auto Shotgun

Similar to the Gold Hunter except has a 26" barrel, 13-7/8" pull length and smaller pistol grip for youths and other small shooters. Weighs 6 lbs., 10 oz. Introduced 2001. From Browning.
Price: **$894.00**

Browning Gold Stalker Auto Shotguns

Similar to the Gold Hunter except has black composite stock and forend. Choice of 3" or 3-1/2" chamber.
Price: 12 ga. with 3" chamber. **$856.00**
Price: With 3-1/2" chamber. **$1,002.00**

Browning Gold Mossy Oak® Shadow Grass Shotguns

Similar to the Gold Hunter except 12 gauge only, completely covered with Mossy Oak® Shadow Grass comouflage. Choice of 3" or 3-1/2" chamber and 26" or 28" barrel. Introduced 1999. Imported by Browning.
Price: 12 ga. 3" chamber **$967.00**
Price: 12 ga., 3-1/2" chamber. **$1,146.00**

Browning Gold Mossy Oak® Break-Up Shotguns

Similar to the Gold Hunter except 12 gauge only, completely covered with Mossy Oak® Break-Up camouflage. Imported by Browning.
Price: 3" chamber. **$967.00**
Price: 3-1/2" chamber. **$1,146.00**
New! **Price:** NWTF model, 3" chamber, 24" bbl. with Hi-Viz sight . **$998.00**
New! **Price:** NWTF model, 3-1/2" chamber, 24" bbl. with Hi-Viz sight **$1,177.00**
Price: Gold Rifled Deer (22" rifled bbl., Cantilever scope mount) **$1,046.00**

Browning Gold Classic Hunter Auto Shotgun

Similar to the Gold Hunter 3" except has semi-hump back receiver, magazine cut-off, adjustable comb, and satin-finish wood. Introduced 1999. Imported by Browning.
Price: 12 or 20 gauge. **$894.00**
Price: Classic High Grade (silvered, gold engraved receiver, high-grade wood) **$1,682.00**

Browning Gold Classic Stalker

Similar to the Gold Classic Hunter except has adjustable composite stock and forend. Introduced 1999. Imported by Browning.
Price: **$856.00**

Browning Gold Fusion™ Auto Shotgun

Similar to the Gold Hunter except is 1/2 lb. lighter, has a new-style vent rib, adjustable comb system, Hi-Viz Pro-Comp front sight and five choke tubes. Offered with 26", 28" or 30" barrel, 12 gauge, 3" chamber only. Includes hard case. Introduced 2001. Imported by Browning.
Price: **$985.00**

Browning NWTF Gold Turkey Stalker

Similar to the Gold Hunter except 12 ga., 3" chamber only, has 24" barrel with Hi-Viz front sight and National Wild Turkey Federation logo on stock. Imported by Browning.
Price: **$876.00**

Browning Gold Turkey/Waterfowl Camo Shotgun

Similar to the Gold Turkey/Waterfowl Hunter except 12 gauge only, 3" or 3-1/2" chamber, 24" barrel with extra-full turkey choke tube, Hi-Viz front sight. Completely covered with Mossy Oak Break-Up camouflage. Introduced 1999. Imported by Browning.
Price: **$929.00**
Price: Turkey/Waterfowl Stalker (black stock and metal) **$949.00**

SHOTGUNS — AUTOLOADERS

Browning Gold Waterfowl

Fabarm Gold Lion

Franchi AL48

 Browning Gold NWTF Turkey Series Camo Shotgun
Similar to the Gold Turkey/Waterfowl model except 10- or 12-gauge (3" or 3-1/2" chamber), 24" barrel with extra-full choke tube, Hi-Viz fiber-optic sights and complete gun coverage in Mossy Oak Break-Up camouflage with National Wild Turkey Federation logo on stock. Introduced 2001. From Browning.
Price: 10 gauge **$1,249.00**
Price: 12 gauge, 3-1/2" chamber **$1,177.00**
Price: 12 gauge, 3" chamber **$998.00**

 Browning Gold Upland Special Auto Shotgun
Similar to the Gold Classic Hunter except has straight-grip walnut stock, 12 or 20 gauge, 3" chamber. Introduced 2001. From Browning
Price: 12-gauge model (24" bbl., weighs 7 lbs.) **$894.00**
Price: 20-gauge model (26" bbl., weighs 6 lbs., 12 oz.) **$894.00**

BROWNING GOLD 10 AUTO SHOTGUN
Gauge: 10, 3-1/2" chamber, 5-shot magazine. **Barrel:** 26", 28", 30" (Imp. Cyl., Mod., Full standard Invector). **Weight:** 10 lbs. 7 oz. (28" barrel). **Stock:** 14-3/8"x1-1/2"x2-3/8". Select walnut with gloss finish, cut checkering, recoil pad. **Features:** Short-stroke, gas-operated action, cross-bolt safety. Forged steel receiver with polished blue finish. Introduced 1993. Imported by Browning.
Price: **$1,007.95**
Price: Extra barrel. **$293.00**

Browning Gold 10 Gauge Auto Combo
Similar to the Gold 10 except comes with 24" and 26" barrels with Imp. Cyl., Mod., Full Invector choke tubes. Introduced 1999. Imported by Browning.
Price: **$1,059.00**

 Browning Gold Light 10 Gauge Auto Shotgun
Similar to the Browning Gold 10, except has an alloy receiver that is 1 lb. lighter than standard model. Offered in 26" or 28" bbls. With Mossy Oak Break-Up or Shadow Grass coverage; 5-shot magazine. Weighs 9 lbs., 10 oz. (28" bbl.). Introduced 2001. Imported by Browning.
Price: **$1,224.00**
Price: Gold Light 10 Stalker (black composite stock and forearm)
. . . . **$1,155.00**

EAA/BAIKAL MP-153 AUTO SHOTGUN
Gauge: 12, 3-1/2" chamber. **Barrel:** 18-1/2", 20", 24", 26", 28"; imp., mod. and full choke tubes. **Weight:** 7.8 lbs. **Stock:** Walnut. **Features:** Gas-operated action with automatic gas-adjustment valve allows use of light and heavy loads interchangeably; 4-round magazine; rubber recoil pad. Introduced 2000. Imported by European American Armory.
Price: MP-153 (blued finish, walnut stock and forend). **$459.00**

FABARM GOLD LION MARK II AUTO SHOTGUN
Gauge: 12, 3" chamber. **Barrel:** 24", 26", 28", choke tubes. **Weight:** 7 lbs. **Length:** 45.5" overall. **Stock:** European walnut with gloss finish; olive wood grip cap. **Features:** TriBore barrel, reversible safety; gold-plated trigger and carrier release button; leather-covered rubber recoil pad. Introduced 1998. Imported from Italy by Heckler & Koch, Inc.
Price: **$849.00**

Fabarm Camo Lion Auto Shotgun
Similar to the Gold Lion except has 24", 26" or 28" ported TriBore barrel system with five choke tubes, and is completely covered with Wetlands camouflage pattern. Has red front sight bead and mid-rib bead. Introduced 1999. Imported from Italy by Heckler & Koch, Inc.
Price: **$979.00**

Fabarm Sporting Clays Extra Auto Shotgun
Similar to the Gold Lion except has 28" TriBore ported barrel with interchangeable colored front-sight beads, mid-rib bead, 10mm channeled vent rib, carbon-fiber finish, oil-finished walnut stock and forend with olive wood grip-cap. Stock dimensions are 14.58"x1.58"x2.44". Has distinctive gold-colored receiver logo. Available in 12 gauge only, 3" chamber. Introduced 1999. Imported from Italy by Heckler & Koch, Inc.
Price: **$1,249.00**

FRANCHI AL 48 SHOTGUN
Gauge: 12, 20 or 28, 2-3/4" chamber. **Barrel:** 24", 26", 28" (Franchoke cyl. imp. cyl., mod., choke tubes). **Weight:** 5.5 lbs. (20 gauge). **Length:** NA **Stock:** 14-1/4"x1-5/8"x2-1/2". Walnut with checkered grip and forend. **Features:** Recoil-operated action. Chrome-lined bore; cross-bolt safety. Imported from Italy by Benelli U.S.A.
Price: 12 ga. **$630.00**
Price: 20 ga. **$613.00**
Price: 28 ga. **$680.00**

Franchi AL 48 Deluxe Shotgun
Similar to AL 48 but with select walnut stock and forend and high-polish blue finish. Introduced 2000.
Price: (20 gauge, 26" barrel) **$710.00**
Price: (28 gauge, 26" barrel) **$680.00**

Franchi AL 48 Short Stock Shotgun
Similar to AL 48 but with stock shortened to 12-1/2 " length of pull.
Price: (20 gauge, 26" barrel) **$594.00**

FRANCHI VARIOPRESS 612 SHOTGUN
Gauge: 12, 3" chamber. **Barrel:** 24", 26", 28", Franchoke tubes. **Weight:** 7 lbs., 2 oz. **Length:** 47-1/2" overall. **Stock:** 14-1/4"x1-1/2"x2-1/2". European walnut. **Features:** Alloy frame with matte black finish; gas-operated with Variopress System; four-lug rotating bolt; loaded chamber indicator. Introduced 1996. Imported from Italy by Benelli U.S.A.
Price: **$595.00**
Price: Camo (Advantage camo) **$657.00**
Price: Synthetic (black synthetic stock, forend) **$579.00**
Price: (20 gauge, 24", 26", 28") **$595.00**
Price: Variopress 620 (Advantage camo). **$657.00**

SHOTGUNS — AUTOLOADERS

Remington Model 11-87 Premier

Remington Model 11-87 SPS Camo

Remington Model 11-87 SPS-T Turkey Camo

Franchi Variopress 612 Defense Shotgun

Similar to Variopress 612 except has 18-1/2 ",cylinder-bore barrel with black, synthetic stock. Available in 12 gauge, 3" chamber only. Weighs 6-1/2 pounds. Introduced 2000.
Price: **$520.00**

Franchi Variopress 612 Sporting Shotgun

Similar to Variopress 612 except has 30" ported barrel to reduce muzzle jump. Available in 12 gauge, 3" chamber only. Introduced 2000.
Price: **$900.00**

Franchi Variopress 620 Short Stock Shotgun

Similar to Variopress 620 but with stock shortened to 12-1/2 "length of pull for smaller shooters. Introduced 2000.
Price: (20 gauge, 26" barrel) **$605.00**

LUGER ULTRA LIGHT SEMI-AUTOMATIC SHOTGUNS

Gauge: 12, 3" and 3-1/2" chambers. **Barrel:** 26", 28"; imp. cyl., mod. and full choke tubes. **Weight:** 6-1/2 lbs. **Length:** 48" overall (28" barrel) **Stock:** Gloss-finish European walnut, checkered grip and forend. **Features:** Gas-operated action handles 2-3/4" and 3" loads; chrome-line barrel handles steel shot; blued finish. Introduced 2000. From Stoeger Industries.
Price: **$479.00**

REMINGTON MODEL 11-87 PREMIER SHOTGUN

Gauge: 12, 20, 3" chamber. **Barrel:** 26", 28", 30" Rem Choke tubes. Light Contour barrel. **Weight:** About 7-3/4 lbs. **Length:** 46" overall (26" bbl.). **Stock:** Walnut with satin or high-gloss finish; cut checkering; solid brown buttpad; no white spacers. **Sights:** Bradley-type white-faced front, metal bead middle. **Features:** Pressure compensating gas system allows shooting 2-3/4" or 3" loads interchangeably with no adjustments. Stainless magazine tube; redesigned feed latch, barrel support ring on operating bars; pinned forend. Introduced 1987.
Price: **$756.00**
Price: Left-hand **$809.00**
Price: Premier Cantilever Deer Barrel, sling, swivels, Monte Carlo stock **$836.00**

Remington Model 11-87 Special Purpose Magnum

Similar to the 11-87 Premier except has dull stock finish, Parkerized exposed metal surfaces. Bolt and carrier have dull blackened coloring.

Comes with 26" or 28" barrel with Rem Chokes, padded Cordura nylon sling and quick detachable swivels. Introduced 1987.
Price: **$756.00**
Price: With synthetic stock and forend (SPS). **$756.00**

Remington Model 11-87 SPS Special Purpose Synthetic Camo

Similar to the 11-87 Special Purpose Magnum except has synthetic stock and all metal (except bolt and trigger guard) and stock covered with Mossy Oak Break-Up camo finish. In 12 gauge only, 26", Rem Choke. Comes with camo sling, swivels. Introduced 1992.
Price: **$869.00**

Remington Model 11-87 SPS-T Turkey Camo

Similar to the 11-87 Special Purpose Magnum except with synthetic stock, 21" vent. rib barrel with Rem Choke tube. Completely covered with Mossy Oak Break-Up Brown camouflage. Bolt body, trigger guard and recoil pad are non-reflective black.
Price: **$869.00**
Price: Model 11-87 SPS-T RS/TG (TruGlo fiber optics sights) ... **$808.00**
Price: Model 11-87 SPS-T Camo CL/RD (Leupold/Gilmore red dot sight) **$1,193.00**

Remington Model 11-87 SPS-T Super Magnum Synthetic Camo

Similar to the 11-87 SPS-T Turkey Camo except has 23" vent rib barrel with Rem Choke tube, chambered for 12 ga., 3-1/2". Introduced 2001.
Price: **$935.00**

Remington Model 11-87 SPS-Deer Shotgun

Similar to the 11-87 Special Purpose Camo except has fully-rifled 21" barrel with rifle sights, black non-reflective, synthetic stock and forend, black carrying sling. Introduced 1993.
Price: **$789.00**
Price: With wood stock (Model 11-87 SP Deer gun) Rem choke, 21" barrel w/rifle sights **$736.00**

Remington Model 11-87 SPS Cantilever Shotgun

Similar to the 11-87 SPS except has fully rifled barrel; synthetic stock with Monte Carlo comb; cantilever scope mount deer barrel. Comes with sling and swivels. Introduced 1994.
Price: **$836.00**

SHOTGUNS — AUTOLOADERS

Remington Model 11-87 SC NP

Remington Model 1100 Youth Turkey Camo

Remington
Model 1100
Sporting 28

Remington Model 11-87 SC NP Shotgun

Similar to the Model 11-87 Sporting Clays except has low-luster nickel-plated receiver with fine-line engraving, and ported 28" or 30" Rem choke barrel with matte finish. Tournament-grade American walnut stock measures 14-3/16"x2-1/4"x1-1/2". Sporting Clays choke tubes have knurled extensions. Introduced 1997. Made in U.S. by Remington.
Price: **$948.00**

Remington Model 11-87 SP and SPS Super Magnum Shotguns

Similar to Model 11-87 Special Purpose Magnum except has 3-1/2" chamber. Available in flat-finish American walnut or black synthetic stock, 26" or 28" black-matte finished barrel and receiver; imp. cyl., modified and full Rem Choke tubes. Overall length 45-3/4", weighs 8 lbs., 2 oz. Introduced 2000. From Remington Arms Co.
Price: 11-87 SP Super Magnum (walnut stock) **$852.00**
Price: 11-87 SPS Super Magnum (synthetic stock) **$852.00**

Remington Model 11-87 Upland Special Shotgun

Similar to 11-87 Premier except has 23" ventilated rib barrel with straight-grip, English-style walnut stock. Available in 12 or 20 gauge. Overall length 43-1/2", weighs 7-1/4 lbs. (6-1/2 lbs. in 20 ga.). Comes with imp. cyl., modified and full choke tubes. Introduced 2000. From Remington Arms Co.
Price: 12 or 20 gauge **$756.00**

REMINGTON MODEL 1100 SYNTHETIC LT-20

Gauge: 20. **Barrel:** 26" Rem Chokes. **Weight:** 6-3/4 lbs. **Stock:** 14"x1-1/2"x2-1/2". Black synthetic, checkered pistol grip and forend. **Features:** Matted receiver top with scroll work on both sides of receiver.
Price: **$540.00**
Price: Youth Gun LT-20 (21" Rem Choke) **$540.00**

Remington Model 1100 Synthetic

12 gauge, and has black synthetic stock; vent. rib 28" barrel on 12 gauge, both with Mod. Rem Choke tube. Weighs about 7-1/2 lbs. Introduced 1996.
Price: **$540.00**

Remington Model 1100 Youth Synthetic Turkey Camo

Similar to the Model 1100 LT-20 except has 1" shorter stock, 21" vent rib barrel with Full Rem Choke tube; 3" chamber; synthetic stock and forend are covered with RealTree Advantage camo, and barrel and receiver have non-reflective, black matte finish. Introduced 1999.
Price: **$603.00**

Remington Model 1100 LT-20 Synthetic FR RS Shotgun

Similar to the Model 1100 LT-20 except has 21" fully rifled barrel with rifle sights, 2-3/4" chamber, and fiberglass-reinforced synthetic stock. Introduced 1997. Made in U.S. by Remington.
Price: **$573.00**

Remington Model 1100 Sporting 28

Similar to the 1100 LT-20 except in 28 gauge with 25" barrel; comes with Skeet, Imp. Cyl., Light Mod., Mod. Rem Choke tube. Semi-Fancy walnut with gloss finish, Sporting rubber butt pad. Made in U.S. by Remington. Introduced 1996.
Price: **$859.00**

Remington Model 1100 Sporting 20 Shotgun

Similar to the Model 1100 LT-20 except has tournament-grade American walnut stock with gloss finish and sporting-style recoil pad, 28" RemChoke barrel for Skeet, Imp. Cyl., Light Modified and Modified. Introduced 1998.
Price: **$859.00**

Remington Model 1100 Classic Trap Shotgun

Similar to Standard Model 1100 except 12 gauge with 30", low-profile barrel, semi-fancy American walnut stock and high-polish blued receiver with engraving and gold eagle inlay. Comes with singles, mid handicap and long handicap choke tubes. Overall length 50-1/2", weighs 8 lbs., 4 oz. Introduced 2000. From Remington Arms Co.
Price: **$885.00**

Remington Model 1100 Sporting 12 Shotgun

Similar to Model 1100 Sporting 20 Shotgun except in 12 gauge, has 28" ventilated barrel with semi-fancy American walnut stock, gold-plated trigger. Overall length 49", weighs 8 lbs. Introduced 2000. From Remington Arms Co.
Price: **$859.00**

Remington Model 1100 Synthetic FR CL Shotgun

Similar to the Model 1100 LT-20 except 12 gauge, has 21" fully rifled barrel with cantilever scope mount and fiberglass-reinforced synthetic stock with Monte Carlo comb. Introduced 1997. Made in U.S. by Remington.
Price: **$620.00**

REMINGTON MODEL SP-10 MAGNUM SHOTGUN

Gauge: 10, 3-1/2" chamber, 2-shot magazine. **Barrel:** 26", 30" (Full and Mod. Rem Chokes). **Weight:** 10-3/4 to 11 lbs. **Length:** 47-1/2" overall (26" barrel). **Stock:** Walnut with satin finish or black synthetic. Checkered grip and forend. **Sights:** Twin bead. **Features:** Stainless steel gas system with moving cylinder; 3/8" ventilated rib. Receiver and barrel have matte finish. Brown recoil pad. Comes with padded Cordura nylon sling. Introduced 1989.
Price: **$1,199.00**
Price: SP-10 Magnum Turkey Camo (23" vent rib barrel, Turkey Extra-Full Rem Choke tube) Mossy Oak Break-up **$1,319.00**

SHOTGUNS

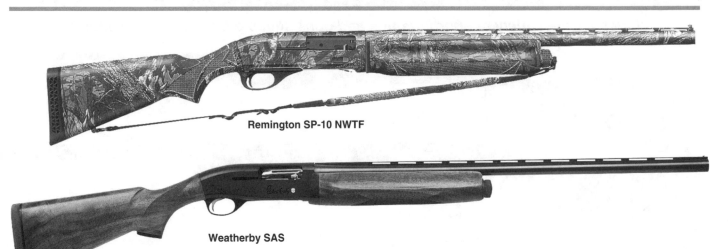

Remington SP-10 NWTF

Weatherby SAS

Remington Model SP-10 Magnum Camo Shotgun

Similar to the SP-10 Magnum except buttstock, forend, receiver, barrel and magazine cap are covered with Mossy Oak Break-Up camo finish; bolt body and trigger guard have matte black finish. Rem Choke tube, 26" vent. rib barrel with mid-rib bead and Bradley-style front sight, swivel studs and quick-detachable swivels, and a non-slip Cordura carrying sling in the same camo pattern. Introduced 1993.

Price: **$1,319.00**
Price: SP-10 Magnum Synthetic. **$1,199.00**

SARSILMAZ SEMI-AUTOMATIC SHOTGUN

Gauge: 12, 3" chamber. **Barrel:** 26" or 28"; fixed chokes. **Weight:** NA. **Length:** NA. **Stock:** Walnut or synthetic. **Features:** Handles 2-3/4" or 3" magnum loads. Introduced 2000. Imported from Turkey by Armsport Inc.

Price: With walnut stock **$969.95**
Price: With synthetic stock **$919.95**

TRADITIONS ALS 2100 SERIES SEMI-AUTOMATIC SHOTGUNS

Gauge: 12, 3" chamber; 20, 3" chamber. **Barrel:** 24", 26", 28" (Imp. Cyl., Mod. and Full choke tubes). **Weight:** 5 lbs., 10 oz. to 6 lbs., 5 oz. **Length:** 44" to 48" overall. **Stock:** Walnut or black composite. **Features:** Gas-operated; vent-rib barrelwith Beretta-style threaded muzzle. Introduced 2001 by Traditions.

Price: (12 or 20 ga., 26" or 28" barrel with walnut stock) **$469.00**
Price: (12 or 20 ga., 24" barrel Youth Model with walnut stock) . . . **$469.00**
Price: (12 or 20 ga., 26" or 28" barrel with composite stock) **$439.00**

TRADITIONS ALS 2100 TURKEY SEMI-AUTOMATIC SHOTGUN

Similar to ALS 2100 field models above, except chambered in 12 gauge, 3" only with 21" barrel and Mossy Oak® Break Up™ camo finish. Weighs 6 lbs., 1 oz.; 41" overall.

Price: **$509.00**

TRADITIONS ALS 2100 WATERFOWL SEMI-AUTOMATIC SHOTGUN

Similar to ALS 2100 field models above, except chambered in 12 gauge, 3" only with 28" barrel and Advantage® Wetlands™ camo finish. Weighs 6 lbs., 5 oz.; 48" overall.

Price: **$509.00**

TRISTAR PHANTOM AUTO SHOTGUNS

Gauge: 12, 3", 3-1/2" chamber. **Barrel:** 24", 26", 28" (Imp. Cyl., Mod., Full choke tubes). **Stock:** European walnut or black synthetic. **Features:** Gas-operated action; blued barrel; checkered pistol grip and forend; vent rib barrel. Introduced 1999. Imported by Tristar Sporting Arms Ltd.

Price: . . . . **$381.00 to $499.00**

WEATHERBY SAS AUTO SHOTGUN

Gauge: 12, 20, 2-3/4" or 3" chamber. **Barrel:** 26", 28" (20 ga.); 26", 28", 30" (12 ga.); Briley Multi-Choke tubes. **Weight:** 6-3/4 to 7-3/4 lbs. **Stock:** 14-1/4"x2-1/4"x1-1/2". Claro walnut; black, Shadow Grass or Mossy Oak Break-Up camo synthetic. **Features:** Alloy receiver with matte finish; gold-plated trigger; magazine cut-off. Introduced 1999. Imported by Weatherby.

Price: 12 or 20 ga. (walnut stock) **$945.00**
Price: 12 or 20 ga. (black synthetic stock) **$979.00**
Price: 12 ga. (camo stock) **$1,115.00**

WINCHESTER SUPER X2 AUTO SHOTGUN

Gauge: 12, 3", 3-1/2" chamber. **Barrel:** 24", 26", 28"; Invector Plus choke tubes. **Weight:** 7-1/4 to 7-1/2 lbs. **Stock:** 14-1/4"x1-3/4"x2". Walnut or black synthetic. **Features:** Gas-operated action shoots all loads without adjustment; vent. rib barrels; 4-shot magazine. Introduced 1999. Made in U.S. by U.S. Repeating Arms Co.

Price: Field, walnut or synthetic stock, 3" **$819.00**
Price: Magnum, 3-1/2", synthetic stock, 26" or 28" bbl. **$936.00**
Price: Camo Waterfowl, 3-1/2", Mossy Oak Shadow Grass. . . . **$1,080.00**
New! Price: NWTF Turkey, 3-1/2", black synthetic stock, 24" bbl. **$997.00**
New! Price: NWTF Turkey, 3-1/2", Mossy Oak Break-Up camo **$1,080.00**

Winchester Super X2 Sporting Clays Auto Shotgun

Similar to the Super X2 except has two gas pistons (one for target loads, one for heavy 3" loads), adjustable comb system and high-post rib. Back-bored barrel with Invector Plus choke tubes. Offered in 28" and 30" barrels. Introduced 2001. From U.S. Repeating Arms Co.

Price: Super X2 Sporting Clays **$1,206.00**

Winchester Super X2 Field 3" Auto Shotgun

Similar to the Super X2 except has a 3" chamber, walnut stock and fore-arm and high-profile rib. Back-bored barrel and Invector Plus choke tubes. Introduced 2001. From U.S. Repeating Arms Co.

Price: Super X2 Field 3", 26" or 28" bbl. **$819.00**

Includes a wide variety of sporting guns and guns suitable for competitive shooting.

Armscor M-30F Field

Benelli Nova Pump

Benelli Nova Pump Rifled Slug

Browning BPS 10 gauge

ARMSCOR M-30F FIELD PUMP SHOTGUN

Gauge: 12, 3" chamber. **Barrel:** 28" fixed Mod., or with Mod. and Full choke tubes. **Weight:** 7.6 lbs. **Stock:** Walnut-finished hardwood. **Features:** Double action slide bars; blued steel receiver; damascened bolt. Introduced 1996. Imported from the Philippines by K.B.I., Inc.
Price: With fixed choke **$239.00**
Price: With choke tubes **$269.00**

BENELLI NOVA PUMP SHOTGUN

Gauge: 12, 3-1/2" chamber. **Barrel:** 24", 26", 28"; chrome lined, vent rib; choke tubes. **Weight:** 8 lbs. **Length:** 47.5" overall. **Stock:** Black polymer. **Features:** Montefeltro rotating bolt design with dual action bars; magazine cut-0ff; synthetic trigger assembly. Four-shot magazine Introduced 1999. Imported from Italy by Benelli USA.
Price: With black stock **$390.00**
Price: With Camo finish **$456.00**

Benelli Nova Pump Slug Gun

Similar to the Nova except has 18.5" barrel with adjustable rifle-type or ghost ring sights; weighs 7.2 lbs.; black synthetic stock. Introduced 1999. Imported from Italy by Benelli USA.
Price: With rifle sights **$320.00**
Price: With ghost-ring sights **$355.00**

Benelli Nova Pump Rifled Slug Gun

Similar to Nova Pump Slug Gun except has 24" barrel and rifled bore; open rifle sights; synthetic stock; weighs 8.1 pounds.
Price: **$544.00**

BROWNING BPS PUMP SHOTGUN

Gauge: 10, 12, 3-1/2" chamber; 12 or 20, 3" chamber (2-3/4" in target guns), 28, 2-3/4" chamber, 5-shot magazine, 410 ga., 3" chamber. **Barrel:** 10 ga.— 24" Buck Special, 28", 30", 32" Invector; 12, 20 ga.—22", 24", 26", 28", 30", 32" (Imp. Cyl., mod. or full). 410 ga.—26" barrel. (Imp. Cyl.,

mod. and full choke tubes.) Also available with Invector choke tubes, 12 or 20 ga.; Upland Special has 22" barrel with Invector tubes. BPS 3" and 3-1/2" have back-bored barrel. **Weight:** 7 lbs., 8 oz. (28" barrel). **Length:** 48-3/4" overall (28" barrel). **Stock:** 14-1/4"x1-1/2"x2-1/2". Select walnut, semi-beavertail forend, full pistol grip stock. **Features:** All 12 gauge 3" guns except Buck Special and game guns have back-bored barrels with Invector Plus choke tubes. Bottom feeding and ejection, receiver top safety, high post vent. rib. Double action bars eliminate binding. Vent. rib barrels only. All 12 and 20 gauge guns with 3" chamber available with fully engraved receiver flats at no extra cost. Each gauge has its own unique game scene. Introduced 1977. Imported from Japan by Browning.
Price: 10 ga., Hunter, Invector **$552.00**
Price: 12 ga., 3-1/2" Magnum Hunter, Invector Plus **$552.00**
Price: 12 ga., 3-1/2" Magnum Stalker (black syn. stock) **$537.00**
Price: 12, 20 ga., Hunter, Invector Plus **$464.00**
Price: 12 ga. Deer Hunter (22" rifled bbl., cantilever mount) **$568.00**
Price: 28 ga., Hunter, Invector **$495.00**
Price: 410 ga., Hunter, Invector **$495.00**

Browning BPS 10 Gauge Shotguns

Chambered for the 10 gauge, 3-1/2" load. Offered in 24", 26" and 28" barrels. Offered with walnut, black composite (Stalker models) or camouflage stock and forend. Introduced 1999. Imported by Browning.
Price: Hunter (walnut). **$552.00**
Price: Stalker (composite) **$537.00**
Price: Mossy Oak® Shadow Grass or Break-Up Camo **$617.00**

Browning BPS 10 gauge Camo Pump

Similar to the BPS 10 gauge Hunter except completely covered with Mossy Oak Shadow Grass camouflage. Available with 24", 26", 28" barrel. Introduced 1999. Imported by Browning.
Price: **$602.00**

Browning BPS Waterfowl Camo Pump Shotgun

Similar to the BPS Hunter except completely covered with Mossy Oak Shadow Grass camouflage. Available in 12 gauge, with 24", 26" or 28" barrel, 3" chamber. Introduced 1999. Imported by Browning.
Price: **$514.00**

Fabarm Field Pump

Ithaca Model 37
Turkeyslayer

Browning BPS Game Gun Deer Hunter
Similar to the standard BPS except has newly designed receiver/magazine tube/barrel mounting system to eliminate play, heavy 20.5" barrel with rifle-type sights with adjustable rear, solid receiver scope mount, "rifle" stock dimensions for scope or open sights, sling swivel studs. Gloss or matte finished wood with checkering, polished blue metal. Introduced 1992.
Price: **$568.00**

Browning BPS Game Gun Turkey Special
Similar to the standard BPS except has satin-finished walnut stock and dull-finished barrel and receiver. Receiver is drilled and tapped for scope mounting. Rifle-style stock dimensions and swivel studs. Has Extra-Full Turkey choke tube. Introduced 1992.
Price: **$500.00**

Browning BPS Stalker Pump Shotgun
Same gun as the standard BPS except all exposed metal parts have a matte blued finish and the stock has a durable black finish with a black recoil pad. Available in 10 ga. (3-1/2") and 12 ga. with 3" or 3-1/2" chamber, 22", 28", 30" barrel with Invector choke system. Introduced 1987.
Price: 12 ga., 3" chamber, Invector Plus **$448.00**
Price: 10, 12 ga., 3-1/2" chamber........................ **$537.00**

Browning BPS NWTF Turkey Series Pump Shotgun
Similar to the BPS Stalker except has full coverage Mossy Oak® Break-Up camo finish on synthetic stock, forearm and exposed metal parts. Offered in 10 and 12 gauge, 3" or 3-1/2" chamber; 24" bbl. has extra-full choke tube and Hi-Viz fiber optic sights. Introduced 2001. From Browning.
Price: 10 ga., 3-1/2" chamber........................... **$637.00**
Price: 12 ga., 3-1/2" chamber........................... **$637.00**
Price: 12 ga., 3" chamber **$549.00**

Browning BPS Micro Pump Shotgun
Same as BPS Upland Special except 20 ga. only, 22" Invector barrel, stock has pistol grip with recoil pad. Length of pull is 13-1/4"; weighs 6 lbs., 12 oz. Introduced 1986.
Price: **$464.00**

EAA/BAIKAL MP-133 PUMP SHOTGUN
Gauge: 12, 3-1/2" chamber. **Barrel:** 18-1/2", 20", 24", 26", 28"; imp., mod. and full choke tubes. **Weight:** NA. **Stock:** Walnut; checkered grip and grooved forearm. **Features:** Hammer-forged, chrome-lined barrel with ventilated rib; machined steel parts; dual action bars; trigger-block safety; 4-shot magazine tube; handles 2-3/4" through 3-1/2" shells. Introduced 2000. Imported by European American Armory.
Price: MP-133 (blued finish, walnut stock and forend) **$279.00**

FABARM FIELD PUMP SHOTGUN
Gauge: 12, 3" chamber. **Barrel:** 28" (24" rifled slug barrel available). **Weight:** 6.6 lbs. **Length:** 48.25" overall. **Stock:** Polymer. **Features:** Similar to Fabarm FP6 Pump Shotgun. Alloy receiver; twin action bars; available in black or Mossy Oak Break-Up™ camo finish. Includes cyl., mod. and full choke tubes. Introduced 2001. Imported from Italy by Heckler & Koch Inc.
Price: Matte black finish **$399.00**
Price: Mossy Oak Break-Up™ finish **$469.00**

ITHACA MODEL 37 DELUXE PUMP SHOTGUN
Gauge: 12, 16, 20, 3" chamber. **Barrel:** 26", 28", 30" (12 gauge), 26", 28" (16 and 20 gauge), choke tubes. **Weight:** 7 lbs. **Stock:** Walnut with cut-checkered grip and forend. **Features:** Steel receiver; bottom ejection; brushed blue finish, vent rib barrels. Reintroduced 1996. Made in U.S. by Ithaca Gun Co.
Price: **$545.95**
Price: With straight English-style stock **$545.95**
Price: Model 37 New Classic (ringtail forend, sunburst recoil pad, hand-finished walnut stock, 26" or 28" barrel) **$695.95**

Ithaca Model 37 Waterfowler
Similar to the Model 37 Deluxe except in 12 gauge only with 28" barrel, special extended steel shot choke tube system. Complete coverage of Advantage Wetlands couflage. Introduced 1999. Made in U.S. by Ithaca Gun Co.
Price: **$595.00**

Ithaca Model 37 Turkeyslayer Pump Shotgun
Similar to the Model 37 Deluxe except has 22" barrel with rifle sights, extended ported choke tube and full-coverage, Realtree Advantage, Realtree All-Purpose Brown, All-Purpose Grey, or Xtra Brown camouflage finish. Introduced 1996. Made in U.S. by Ithaca Gun Co.
Price: 12 ga. only **$569.95**
Price: Youth Turkeyslayer (20 gauge, 6.5 lbs., shorter stock) **$569.95**

ITHACA MODEL 37 DEERSLAYER II PUMP SHOTGUN
Gauge: 12, 20, 3" chamber. **Barrel:** 20", 25", fully rifled. **Weight:** 7 lbs. **Stock:** Cut-checkered American walnut with Monte Carlo comb. **Sights:** Rifle-type. **Features:** Integral barrel and receiver. Bottom ejection. Brushed blue finish. Reintroduced 1997. Made in U.S. by Ithaca Gun Co.
Price: **$565.95**
Price: Smooth Bore Deluxe **$515.95**
Price: Rifled Deluxe **$515.95**

Ithaca Model 37 Hardwoods 20/2000 Deerslayer
Similar to the Model 37 Deerslayer II except has synthetic stock and forend, and has the Truglo Fibre Optic sight system. Drilled and tapped for scope mounting. Complete coverage of RealTree 20/2000 Hardwoods camouflage. Introduced 1999. Made in U.S. by Ithaca Gun Co.
Price: **$565.95**

Ithaca Model 37 Hardwoods 20/2000 Turkeyslayer
Similar to the Model 37 Turkeyslayer except has synthetic stock and forend, Extra-Full extended and ported choke tube, long forcing cone, and Truglo Fibre Optic sight system. Complete coverage of RealTree Hardwoods 20/2000 camouflage. Introduced 1999. Made in U.S. by Ithaca Gun Co.
Price: **$565.95**

MOSSBERG MODEL 835 ULTI-MAG PUMP
Gauge: 12, 3-1/2" chamber. **Barrel:** Ported 24" rifled bore, 24", 28", Accu-Mag choke tubes for steel or lead shot. **Weight:** 7-3/4 lbs. **Length:** 48-1/2" overall. **Stock:** 14"x1-1/2"x2-1/2". Dual Comb. Cut-checkered hardwood or camo synthetic; both have recoil pad. **Sights:** White bead front, brass mid-bead; Fiber Optic. **Features:** Shoots 2-3/4", 3" or 3-1/2" shells. Back-bored and ported barrel to reduce recoil, improve patterns. Ambidextrous thumb safety, twin extractors, dual slide bars. Mossberg Cablelock included. Introduced 1988.

Mossberg Model 835 Shadowgrass

Mossberg Model 500 Sporting

Mossberg Model 500 Trophy Slugster

Price: 28" vent. rib, hardwood stock **$370.00**
Price: Combo, 24" rifled bore, rifle sights, 24" vent. rib, Accu-Mag Ulti-Full choke tube, Woodlands camo finish **$572.00**
Price: RealTree Camo Turkey, 24" vent. rib, Accu-Mag Extra-Full tube, synthetic stock **$525.00**
Price: Mossy Oak Camo, 28" vent. rib, Accu-Mag tubes, synthetic stock **$583.00**
Price: OFM Camo, 28" vent. rib, Accu-Mag Mod. tube, synthetic stock **$407.00**

Mossberg Model 835 Synthetic Stock
Similar to the Model 835, except with 28" ported barrel with Accu-Mag Mod. choke tube, Parkerized finish, black synthetic stock and forend. Introduced 1998. Made in U.S. by Mossberg.
Price: **$370.00**

MOSSBERG MODEL 500 SPORTING PUMP
Gauge: 12, 20, 410, 3" chamber. **Barrel:** 18-1/2" to 28" with fixed or Accu-Choke, plain or vent. rib. **Weight:** 6-1/4 lbs. (410), 7-1/4 lbs. (12). **Length:** 48" overall (28" barrel). **Stock:** 14"x1-1/2"x2-1/2". Walnut-stained hardwood. Cut-checkered grip and forend. **Sights:** White bead front, brass mid-bead; Fiber Optic. **Features:** Ambidextrous thumb safety, twin extractors, disconnecting safety, dual action bars. Quiet Carry forend. Many barrels are ported. Mossberg Cablelock included. From Mossberg.
Price: From about **$301.00**
Price: Sporting Combos (field barrel and Slugster barrel), from . . **$403.00**

Mossberg Model 500 Bantam Pump
Same as the Model 500 Sporting Pump except 12 (new for 2001) or 20 gauge, 22" vent. rib Accu-Choke barrel with choke tube set; has 1" shorter stock, reduced length from pistol grip to trigger, reduced forend reach. Introduced 1992.
Price: **$301.00**
Price: With full Woodlands camouflage finish (20 ga. only) **$384.00**

Mossberg Model 500 Camo Pump
Same as the Model 500 Sporting Pump except 12 gauge only and entire gun is covered with special camouflage finish. Receiver drilled and tapped for scope mounting. Comes with quick detachable swivel studs, swivels, camouflage sling, Mossberg Cablelock.
Price: From about **$370.00**

Mossberg Model 500 Persuader/Cruiser Shotguns
Similar to Mossberg Model 500 except has 18-1/2" or 20" barrel with cylinder bore choke, synthetic stock and blue or parkerized finish. Available in 12, 20 and 410 gauge with bead or ghost ring sights, 6- or 8-shot magazines. From Mossberg.
Price: 12 gauge, 20" barrel, 8-shot, bead sight. **$308.00**
Price: 20 or 410 gauge, 18-1/2" barrel, 6-shot, bead sight **$329.00**
Price: 12 gauge, parkerized finish, 6-shot, 18-1/2" barrel, ghost ring sights **$437.00**
Price: Home Security 410 (410 gauge, 18-1/2" barrel with spreader choke) **$335.00**

Mossberg Model 590 Special Purpose Shotguns
Similar to Model 500 except has parkerized or Marinecote finish, 9-shot magazine and black synthetic stock (some models feature Speed Feed). Available in 12 gauge only with 20", cylinder bore barrel. Weighs 7-1/4 lbs. From Mossberg.
Price: Bead sight, heat shield over barrel **$389.00**
Price: Ghost ring sight, Speed Feed stock. **$546.00**

MOSSBERG MODEL 500 SLUGSTER
Gauge: 12, 20, 3" chamber. **Barrel:** 24", ported rifled bore. Integral scope mount. **Weight:** 7-1/4 lbs. **Length:** 44" overall. **Stock:** 14" pull, 1-3/8" drop at heel. Walnut; Dual Comb design for proper eye positioning with or without scoped barrels. Recoil pad and swivel studs. **Features:** Ambidextrous thumb safety, twin extractors, dual slide bars. Comes with scope mount. Mossberg Cablelock included. Introduced 1988.
Price: Rifled bore, with integral scope mount, Dual-Comb stock, 12 or 20 . . . . **$398.00**
Price: Fiber Optic, rifle sights **$398.00**
Price: Rifled bore, rifle sights **$367.00**
Price: 20 ga., Standard or Bantam, from **$367.00**

REMINGTON MODEL 870 WINGMASTER
Gauge: 12, 3" chamber. **Barrel:** 26", 28", 30" (Rem Chokes). Light Contour barrel. **Weight:** 7-1/4 lbs. **Length:** 46-1/2" overall (26" bbl.). **Stock:** 14"x2-1/2"x1". American walnut with satin or high-gloss finish, cut-checkered pistol grip and forend. Rubber butt pad. **Sights:** Ivory bead front, metal mid-bead. **Features:** Double action bars; cross-bolt safety; blue finish. Introduced 1986.
Price: **$569.00**
Price: 870 Wingmaster Super Magnum **$649.00**

Remington 870 Wingmaster

Remington Model 870 Express Super Magnum

Remington Model 870 50th Anniversary Classic Trap Shotgun

Similar to Model 870 TC Wingmaster except has 30" ventilated rib with singles, mid handicap and long handicap choke tubes, semi-fancy American walnut stock and high-polish blued receiver with engraving and gold shield inlay. From Remington Arms Co.

Price: **$775.00**

Remington Model 870 Marine Magnum

Similar to the 870 Wingmaster except all metal is plated with electroless nickel and has black synthetic stock and forend. Has 18" plain barrel (Cyl.), bead front sight, 7-shot magazine. Introduced 1992.

Price: **$545.00**

Remington Model 870 Wingmaster LW 20 ga.

Similar to the Model 870 Wingmaster except in 28 gauge and 410-bore only, 25" vent rib barrel with Rem Choke tubes, high-gloss wood finish. 26" & 28" barrels-20 ga.

Price: 20 gauge **$569.00**
Price: 410-bore.. **$596.00**
Price: 28 gauge **$649.00**

Remington Model 870 Express

Similar to the 870 Wingmaster except has a walnut-toned hardwood stock with solid, black recoil pad and pressed checkering on grip and forend. Outside metal surfaces have a black oxide finish. Comes with 26" or 28" vent. rib barrel with a Mod. Rem Choke tube. Introduced 1987.

Price: 12 or 20 .... **$329.00**
Price: Express Combo, 12 ga., 26" vent rib with Mod. Rem Choke and 20" fully rifled barrel with rifle sights **$436.00**
Price: Express 20 ga., 26" or 28" with Mod. Rem Choke tubes .. **$329.00**
Price: Express L-H (left-hand), 12 ga., 28" vent rib with Mod. Rem Choke tube.. **$356.00**
Price: Express Synthetic, 12-ga, 26" or 28" **$329.00**
Price: Express Combo (20 ga.) with extra Deer rifled barrel **$436.00**

Remington Model 870 Express Super Magnum

Similar to the 870 Express except has 28" vent. rib barrel with 3-1/2" chamber, vented recoil pad. Introduced 1998.

Price: **$369.00**
Price: Super Magnum Synthetic........................... **$376.00**
Price: Super Magnum Turkey Camo (Turkey Extra Full Rem Choke, full-coverage RealTree Advantage camo) **$500.00**
Price: Super Magnum Combo (26" with Mod. Rem Choke and 20" fully rifled deer barrel with 3" chamber and rifle sights; wood stock) **$516.00**
Price: Super Magnum Synthetic Turkey (black) **$389.00**

Remington Model 870 Wingmaster Super Magnum Shotgun

Similar to Model 870 Express Super Magnum except has high-polish blued finish, 28" ventilated barrel with imp. cyl., modified and full choke tubes, checkered high-gloss walnut stock. Overall length 48", weighs 7-1/2 lbs. Introduced 2000.

Price: **$649.00**

Remington Model 870 Express Youth Gun

Same as the Model 870 Express except comes with 13" length of pull, 21" barrel with Mod. Rem Choke tube. Hardwood stock with low-luster finish. Introduced 1991.

Price: 20 ga. Express Youth (1" shorter stock), from **$329.00**
Price: 20 ga. Youth Deer 20" FR/RS **$363.00**

Remington Model 870 Express Rifle-Sighted Deer Gun

Same as the Model 870 Express except comes with 20" barrel with fixed Imp. Cyl. choke, open iron sights, Monte Carlo stock. Introduced 1991.

Price: **$329.00**
Price: With fully rifled barrel **$363.00**
Price: Express Synthetic Deer (black synthetic stock, black matte metal) **$369.00**

Remington Model 870 Express Turkey

Same as the Model 870 Express except comes with 3" chamber, 21" vent. rib turkey barrel and Extra-Full Rem Choke Turkey tube; 12 ga. only. Introduced 1991.

Price: **$343.00**
Price: Express Turkey Camo stock has RealTree Advantage camo, matte black metal...................................... **$396.00**
Price: Express Youth Turkey camo (as above with 1" shorter length of pull).. **$396.00**

Remington Model 870 Express Synthetic HD Home Defense

Similar to the 870 Express with 18" barrel except has synthetic stock and forend. Introduced 1994.

Price: **$316.00**

Remington Model 870 SPS Super Slug Deer Gun

Similar to the Model 870 Express Synthetic except has 23" rifled, modified contour barrel with cantilever scope mount. Comes with black synthetic stock and forend with swivel studs, black Cordura nylon sling. Introduced 1999. Fully rifled centilever barrel.

Price: **$555.00**

Remington Model 870 SPS-T Synthetic Camo Shotgun

Chambered for 12 ga., 3" shells, has Mossy Oak Break-Up® synthetic stock and metal treatment, Tru-Glo fiber optic sights. Introduced 2001.

Price: **$569.00**

Remington Model 870 SPS Super Magnum Camo

Has synthetic stock and all metal (except bolt and trigger guard) and stock covered with Mossy Oak Break-Up camo finish In 12 gauge 3-1/2", 26" vent. rib, Rem Choke. Comes with camo sling, swivels.

Price: **$569.00**
Price: Model 870 SPS-T Super Magnum Camo (3-1/2" chamber). **$569.00**
Price: Model 870 SPS-T RS/TG (TruGlo fiber optics sights) **$544.00**
New! Price: Model 870 SPS-T Super Magnum Synthetic Camo (3-1/2" chamber, cantilever mount) **$895.00**
Price: Model 870 SPS-T Super Mag Camo CL/RD (Leupold/Gilmore dot sight)........................... **$889.00**

Winchester 1300 Black Shadow Field Gun

Winchester NWTF Turkey

Winchester 9410

Price: With cantilever scope mount **$400.00**
Price: Combo (22" rifled and 28" smoothbore bbls.) **$433.00**
Price: Compact (20 ga., 22" rifled barrel, shorter stock). **$371.00**

SARSILMAZ PUMP SHOTGUN

Gauge: 12, 3" chamber. **Barrel:** 26" or 28". **Weight:** NA. **Length:** NA. Stocks: Oil-finished hardwood. **Features:** Includes extra pistol-grip stock. Introduced 2000. Imported from Turkey by Armsport Inc.
Price: With pistol-grip stock **$299.95**
Price: With metal stock. **$349.95**

WINCHESTER MODEL 1300 WALNUT FIELD PUMP

Gauge: 12, 20, 3" chamber, 5-shot capacity. **Barrel:** 26", 28", vent. rib, with Full, Mod., Imp. Cyl. Winchoke tubes. **Weight:** 6-3/8 lbs. **Length:** 42-5/8" overall. **Stock:** American walnut, with deep cut checkering on pistol grip, traditional ribbed forend; high luster finish. **Sights:** Metal bead front. **Features:** Twin action slide bars; front-locking rotary bolt; roll-engraved receiver; blued, highly polished metal; cross-bolt safety with red indicator. Introduced 1984. From U.S. Repeating Arms Co., Inc.
Price: **$396.00**

Winchester Model 1300 Upland Pump Gun

Similar to the Model 1300 Walnut except has straight-grip stock, 24" barrel. Introduced 1999. Made in U.S. by U.S. Repeating Arms Co.
Price: **$396.00**

Winchester Model 1300 Black Shadow Field Gun

Similar to the Model 1300 Walnut except has black composite stock and forend, matte black finish. Has vent. rib 26" or 28" barrel, 3" chamber, comes with Mod. Winchoke tube. Introduced 1995. From U.S. Repeating Arms Co., Inc.
Price: 12 or 20 gauge **$335.00**

Winchester Model 1300 Deer Black Shadow Gun

Similar to the Model 1300 Black Shadow Turkey Gun except has ramp-type front sight, fully adjustable rear, drilled and tapped for scope mounting. Black composite stock and forend, matte black metal. Smoothbore 22" barrel with one Imp. Cyl. WinChoke tube; 12 gauge only, 3" chamber. Weighs 6-3/4 lbs. Introduced 1994. From U.S. Repeating Arms Co., Inc.
Price: **$334.00**
Price: With rifled barrel **$359.00**

WINCHESTER MODEL 1300 RANGER PUMP GUN

Gauge: 12, 20, 3" chamber, 5-shot magazine. **Barrel:** 28" vent. rib with Full, Mod., Imp. Cyl. Winchoke tubes. **Weight:** 7 to 7-1/4 lbs. **Length:** 48-5/8" to 50-5/8" overall. **Stock:** Walnut-finished hardwood with ribbed forend. **Sights:** Metal bead front. **Features:** Cross-bolt safety, black rubber recoil pad, twin action slide bars, front-locking rotating bolt. From U.S. Repeating Arms Co., Inc.
Price: Vent. rib barrel, Winchoke **$349.00**
Price: Model 1300 Compact, 24" vent. rib **$348.00**

Winchester Model 1300 NWTF Black Shadow Turkey Gun

Similar to the Model 1300 Deer Black Shadow except black composite stock has "Team NWTF" decal. Matte black metal. Drilled and tapped for scope mounting. In 12 gauge, 3" chamber, 22" vent. rib barrel; comes with one Extra-Full Winchoke tube. Introduced 2001. From U.S. Repeating Arms Co., Inc.
Price: **$346.00**

Winchester Model 1300 NWTF camouflage guns

Similar to the Black Shadow deer and turkey guns except has full stock, forearm and metal coverage with Trebark® Superflauge. "Team NWTF" decal on stock; includes special offer on National Wild Turkey Federation membership. In 12 ga., 3" chamber only with TruGlo® sights on 22" bbl. Introduced 2001. From U.S. Repeating Arms Co.
Price: NWTF Buck & Tom Superflauge™ gun (rifled and X-Full tubes)
. . . . **$499.00**
Price: NWTF Turkey Superflauge™ gun (X-Full choke tube, vent rib)
. . . . **$522.00**

WINCHESTER MODEL 9410 LEVER-ACTION SHOTGUN

Gauge: 410, 2-1/2" chamber. **Barrel:** 24" (Cyl. bore). **Weight:** 6-3/4 lbs. **Length:** 42-1/8" overall. **Stock:** Checkered walnut straight-grip; checkered walnut forearm. **Sights:** Adjustable "V" rear, TRUGLO® front. **Features:** A Model 94 rifle action (smoothbore) chambered for 410 shotgun. Angle Controlled Eject extractor/ejector; 9-shot tubular magazine; 13-1/2" length of pull. Introduced 2001. From U.S. Repeating Arms Co.
Price: 9410 Lever-Action Shotgun **$531.00**

Includes a variety of game guns and guns for competitive shooting.

Beretta 682 Gold Skeet

Beretta 682 Gold Sporting

APOLLO TR AND TT SHOTGUNS

Gauge: 12, 20, 410, 3" chambers; 28 2-3/4" chambers. **Barrel:** 26", 28", 30", 32". **Weight:** 6 to 7-1/4 lbs. **Length:** NA. **Stock:** Oil-finished European walnut. **Features:** Boxlock action; hard-chromed bores; automatic ejectors; single selective trigger; choke tubes (12 and 20 ga. only). Introduced 2000. From Sigarms.
Price: Apollo TR 30 Field (color casehardened side plates). . . . **$2,240.00**
Price: Apollo TR 40 Gold (gold overlays on game scenes) **$2,675.00**
Price: Apollo TT 25 Competition (wide vent. rib with mid-bead). **$1,995.00**

BERETTA DT 10 TRIDENT SHOTGUNS

Gauge: 12, 2-3/4", 3" chambers. **Barrel:** 28", 30", 32", 34"; competition-style vent rib; fixed or Optima Choke tubes. **Weight:** 7.9 to 9 lbs. **Length:** NA. **Stock:** High-grade walnut stock with oil finish; hand-checkered grip and forend; adjustable stocks available. **Features:** Detachable, adjustable trigger group; raised and thickened receiver; forend iron has replaceable nut to guarantee wood-to-metal fit; Optima Bore to improve shot pattern and reduce felt recoil. Introduced 2000. Imported from Italy by Beretta USA.
Price: DT 10 Trident Trap (selective, lockable single trigger; adjustable stock). **$9,450.00**
Price: DT 10 Trident Trap Combo (single and o/u barrels) . . . **$11,995.00**
New! **Price:** DT 10 Trident Trap Bottom Single Combo (adj. point of impact rib on single bbl.) **$12,270.00**
Price: DT 10 Trident Skeet (skeet stock with rounded recoil pad, tapered rib). **$9,450.00**
Price: DT 10 Trident Sporting (sporting clays stock with rounded recoil pad) **$9,240.00**

BERETTA SERIES S682 GOLD SKEET, TRAP OVER/UNDERS

Gauge: 12, 2-3/4" chambers. **Barrel:** Skeet—28"; trap—30" and 32", Imp. Mod. & Full and Mobilchoke; trap mono shotguns—32" and 34" Mobilchoke; trap top single guns—32" and 34" Full and Mobilchoke; trap combo sets—from 30" O/U, to 32" O/U, 34" top single. **Stock:** Close-grained walnut, hand checkered. **Sights:** White Bradley bead front sight and center bead. **Features:** Receiver has Greystone gunmetal gray finish with gold accents. Trap Monte Carlo stock has deluxe trap recoil pad. Various grades available; contact Beretta USA for details. Imported from Italy by Beretta USA
Price: S682 Gold Skeet **$2,850.00**
Price: S682 Gold Skeet, adjustable stock **$3,515.00**
Price: S682 Gold Trap **$3,100.00**
Price: S682 Gold Trap Top Combo **$4,085.00**
Price: S682 Gold Trap with adjustable stock **$3,625.00**
Price: S686 Silver Pigeon Trap **$1,850.00**
Price: S686 Silver Pigeon Trap Top Mono. **$1,850.00**

Price: S686 Silver Pigeon Skeet (28") **$1,760.00**
Price: S687 EELL Diamond Pigeon Trap. **$4,815.00**
Price: S687 EELL Diamond Pigeon Skeet **$4,790.00**
Price: S687 EELL Diamond Pigeon Skeet, adjustable stock . . . **$5,810.00**
Price: S687 EELL Diamond Pigeon Trap Top Mono. . . . . **$5,055.00 to $5,105.00**
Price: ASE Gold Skeet. **$12,060.00**
Price: ASE Gold Trap. **$12,145.00**
Price: ASE Gold Trap Combo **$16,055.00**

Beretta S682 Gold E Trap O/U

Similar to other S682 Gold models except has a select walnut stock in International style with interchangeable rubber recoil pad and beavertail forend, flat top rib with white front sight, gold non-selective single trigger. Introduced 2001. Imported from Italy by Beretta U.S.A.
Price: Gold E Trap, adj. stock **$4,320.00**
Price: Gold E Skeet, adj. stock. **$4,320.00**
Price: Gold E Trap Combo Top (O/U and single bbls.) **$5,305.00**

BERETTA MODEL S686 WHITEWING O/U

Gauge: 12, 3" chambers. **Barrel:** 26", 28", Mobilchoke tubes (Imp. Cyl., Mod., Full). **Weight:** 6.7 lbs. **Length:** 45.7" overall (28" barrels). **Stock:** 14.5"x2.2"x1.4". American walnut; radiused black buttplate. **Features:** Matte chrome finish on receiver, matte blue barrels; hard-chrome bores; low-profile receiver with dual conical locking lugs; single selective trigger, ejectors. Introduced 1999. Imported from Italy by Beretta U.S.A.
Price: **$1,295.00**

BERETTA S686 ONYX SPORTING O/U SHOTGUN

Gauge: 12, 3" chambers. **Barrel:** 28", 30" (Mobilchoke tubes). **Weight:** 7.7 lbs. **Stock:** Checkered American walnut. **Features:** Intended for the beginning Sporting Clays shooter. Has wide, vented 12.5mm target rib, radiused recoil pad. Polished black finish on receiver and barrels. Introduced 1993. Imported from Italy by Beretta U.S.A.
Price: **$1,583.00**
New! **Price:** With X-Tra Wood (highly figured) **$1,737.00**

BERETTA ULTRALIGHT OVER/UNDER

Gauge: 12, 2-3/4" chambers. **Barrel:** 26", 28", Mobilchoke choke tubes. **Weight:** About 5 lbs., 13 oz. **Stock:** Select American walnut with checkered grip and forend. **Features:** Low-profile aluminum alloy receiver with titanium breech face insert. Electroless nickel receiver with game scene engraving. Single selective trigger; automatic safety. Introduced 1992. Imported from Italy by Beretta U.S.A.
Price: **$1,795.00**

Beretta Ultralight Deluxe Over/Under Shotgun

Similar to the Ultralight except has matte electroless nickel finish receiver with gold game scene engraving; matte oil-finished, select walnut stock and forend. Introduced 1999. Imported from Italy by Beretta U.S.A.
Price: **$1,985.00**

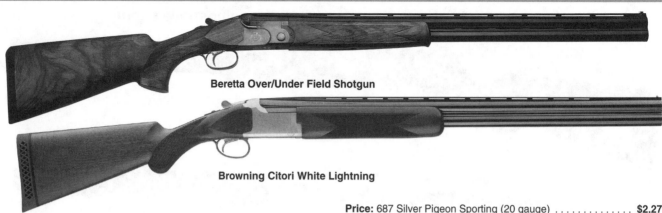

Beretta Over/Under Field Shotgun

Browning Citori White Lightning

BERETTA OVER/UNDER FIELD SHOTGUNS

Gauge: 12, 20, 28, and 410 bore, 2-3/4", 3" and 3-1/2" chambers. **Barrel:** 26" and 28" (Mobilchoke tubes). **Stock:** Close-grained walnut. **Features:** Highly-figured, American walnut stocks and forends, and a unique, weather-resistant finish on barrels. The S686 Onyx bears a gold P. Beretta signature on each side of the receiver. Silver designates standard 686, 687 models with silver receivers; 686 Silver Pigeon has enhanced engraving pattern, Schnabel forend; 686 Silver Essential has matte chrome finish; Gold indicates higher grade 686EL, 687EL models with full sideplates; Diamond is for 687EELL models with highest grade wood, engraving. Case provided with Gold and Diamond grades. Silver Gold, Diamond grades introduced 1994. Imported from Italy by Beretta U.S.A.

Price: S686 Onyx	**$1,565.00**
Price: S686 Silver Pigeon two-bbl. set	**$2,560.00**
Price: S686 Silver Pigeon	**$1,869.00**
Price: S687 Silver Pigeon	**$2,255.00**
Price: S687 Silver Pigeon II (deep relief game scene engraving, oil finish wood, 12 ga. only)	**$2,134.00**
Price: S687EL Gold Pigeon (gold inlays, sideplates)	**$4,099.00**
Price: S687EL Gold Pigeon, 410, 26"; 28 ga., 28"	**$4,273.00**
New! **Price:** S687 EL Gold Pigeon II (deep relief engraving)	**$4,513.00**
New! **Price:** S687 EL Gold Pigeon II Sporting (d.r. engraving)	**$4,554.00**
Price: S687EELL Diamond Pigeon (engraved sideplates)	**$5,540.00**
Price: S687EELL Diamond Pigeon Combo, 20 and 28 ga., 26".	**$6,180.00**

BERETTA MODEL SO5, SO6, SO9 SHOTGUNS

Gauge: 12, 2-3/4" chambers. **Barrel:** To customer specs. **Stock:** To customer specs. **Features:** SO5—Trap, Skeet and Sporting Clays models SO5; SO6—SO6 and SO6 EELL are field models. SO6 has a case-hardened or silver receiver with contour hand engraving. SO6 EELL has hand-engraved receiver in a fine floral or "fine English" pattern or game scene, with bas-relief chisel work and gold inlays. SO6 and SO6 EELL are available with sidelocks removable by hand. Imported from Italy by Beretta U.S.A.

Price: SO5 Trap, Skeet, Sporting	**$13,000.00**
Price: SO6 Trap, Skeet, Sporting	**$17,500.00**
Price: SO6 EELL Field, custom specs	**$28,000.00**
Price: SO9 (12, 20, 28, 410, 26", 28", 30", any choke)	**$31,000.00**

BERETTA SPORTING CLAYS SHOTGUNS

Gauge: 12 and 20, 2-3/4" and 3" chambers. **Barrel:** 28", 30", 32" Mobilchoke. **Stock:** Close-grained walnut. **Features:** Equipped with Beretta Mobilchoke flush-mounted screw-in choke tube system. Dual-purpose O/U for hunting and Sporting Clays.12 or 20 gauge, 28", 30" Mobilchoke tubes (four, Skeet, Imp. Cyl., Mod., Full). Wide 12.5mm top rib with 2.5mm center groove; 686 Silver Pigeon has silver receiver with scroll engraving; 687 Silver Pigeon Sporting has silver receiver, highly figured walnut; 687 EL Pigeon Sporting has game scene engraving with gold inlaid animals on full sideplate. Introduced 1994. Imported from Italy by Beretta USA.

Price: 682 Gold Sporting, 28", 30", 31" (with case)	**$3,100.00**
Price: 682 Gold Sporting, 28", 30", ported, adj. l.o.p.	**$3,230.00**
Price: 686 Silver Pigeon Sporting	**$1,931.00**
Price: 686 Silver Pigeon Sporting (20 gauge)	**$1,931.00**
New! **Price:** 686 E Sporting (enhanced styling, 5 choke tubes)	**$2,008.00**
687 Silver Pigeon Sporting	**$2,270.00**
Price: 687 Silver Pigeon Sporting (20 gauge)	**$2,270.00**
Price: 687 Diamond Pigeon EELL Sporter (hand engraved sideplates, deluxe wood)	**$5,515.00**
Price: ASE Gold Sporting Clay	**$12,145.00**

Beretta S687EL Gold Pigeon Sporting O/U

Similar to the S687 Silver Pigeon Sporting except has sideplates with gold inlay game scene, vent. side and top ribs, bright orange front sight. Stock and forend are of high grade walnut with fine-line checkering. Available in 12 gauge only with 28" or 30" barrels and Mobilchoke tubes. Weight is 6 lbs., 13 oz. Introduced 1993. Imported from Italy by Beretta USA.

Price:	**$4,015.00**

BRNO ZH 300 OVER/UNDER SHOTGUN

Gauge: 12, 2-3/4" chambers. **Barrel:** 26", 27-1/2", 29" (Skeet, Imp. Cyl., Mod., Full). **Weight:** 7 lbs. **Length:** 44.4" overall. **Stock:** European walnut. **Features:** Double triggers; automatic safety; polished blue finish engraved receiver. Announced 1998. Imported from the Czech Republic by Euro-Imports.

Price: ZH 301, field	**$594.00**
Price: ZH 302, Skeet	**$608.00**
Price: ZH 303, 12 ga. trap	**$608.00**
Price: ZH 321, 16 ga.	**$595.00**

BRNO 501.2 OVER/UNDER SHOTGUN

Gauge: 12, 2-3/4" chambers. **Barrel:** 27.5" (Full & Mod.). **Weight:** 7 lbs. **Length:** 44" overall. **Stock:** European walnut. **Features:** Boxlock action with double triggers, ejectors; automatic safety; hand-cut checkering. Announced 1998. Imported from The Czech Republic by Euro-Imports.

Price:	**$850.00**

BROWNING CITORI O/U SHOTGUNS

Gauge: 12, 20, 28 and 410. **Barrel:** 26", 28" in 28 and 410. Offered with Invector choke tubes. All 12 and 20 gauge models have back-bored barrels and Invector Plus choke system. **Weight:** 6 lbs., 8 oz. (26" 410) to 7 lbs., 13 oz. (30" 12 ga.). **Length:** 43" overall (26" bbl.). **Stock:** Dense walnut, hand checkered, full pistol grip, beavertail forend. Field-type recoil pad on 12 ga. field guns and trap and Skeet models. **Sights:** Medium raised beads, German nickel silver. **Features:** Barrel selector integral with safety, automatic ejectors, three-piece takedown. Imported from Japan by Browning. Contact Browning for complete list of models and prices.

Price: Grade I, Hunter, Invector, 12 and 20	**$1,486.00**
Price: Grade I, Lightning, 28 and 410, Invector	**$1,594.00**
Price: Grade III, Lightning, 28 and 410, Invector	**$2,570.00**
Price: Grade VI, 28 and 410 Lightning, Invector	**$3,780.00**
Price: Grade I, Lightning, Invector Plus, 12, 20	**$1,534.00**
Price: Grade I, Hunting, 28", 30" only, 3-1/2", Invector Plus	**$1,489.00**
Price: Grade III, Lightning, Invector, 12, 20	**$2,300.00**
Price: Grade VI, Lightning, Invector, 12, 20	**$3,510.00**
Price: Gran Lightning, 26", 28", Invector, 12, 20	**$2,184.00**
Price: Gran Lightning, 28, 410	**$2,302.00**
Price: Micro Lightning, 20 ga., 24" bbl., 6 lbs., 4 oz.	**$1,591.00**
Price: White Lightning (silver nitride receiver w/engraving, 12 or 20 ga., 26", 28")	**$1,583.00**
Price: White Lightning, 28 or 410 gauge	**$1,654.00**
Price: Citori Satin Hunter (12 ga., satin-finished wood, matte-finished barrels and receiver) 3-1/2" chambers	**$1,535.00**

SHOTGUNS

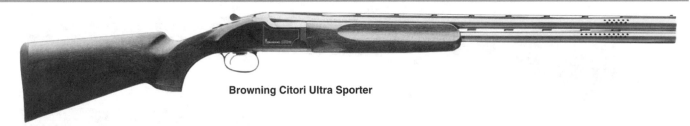

Browning Citori Ultra Sporter

Browning Superlight Citori Over/Under

Similar to the standard Citori except available in 12, 20 with 24", 26" or 28" Invector barrels, 28 or 410 with 26" barrels choked Imp. Cyl. & Mod. or 28" choked Mod. & Full. Has straight grip stock, Schnabel forend tip. Superlight 12 weighs 6 lbs., 9 oz. (26" barrels); Superlight 20, 5 lbs., 12 oz. (26" barrels). Introduced 1982.

Price: Grade I, 28 or 410, Invector **$1,666.00**
Price: Grade III, Invector, 12. . . . . **$2,300.00**
Price: Grade VI, Invector, 12 or 20, gray or blue **$3,510.00**
Price: Grade VI, 28 or 410, Invector, gray or blue **$3,780.00**
Price: Grade I Invector, 12 or 20 . . . . **$1,580.00**
Price: Grade I Invector, White Upland Special (24" bbls.),
12 or 20 . . . . **$1,583.00**
Price: Citori Superlight Feather (12 ga., alloy receiver,
6 lbs. 4 oz.) **$1,756.00**

Browning Citori XT Trap Over/Under

Similar to the Citori Special Trap except has engraved silver nitride receiver with gold highlights, vented side barrel rib. Available in 12 gauge with 30" or 32" barrels, Invector-Plus choke tubes. Introduced 1999. Imported by Browning.

Price: **$1,834.00**
Price: With adjustable-comb stock **$2,054.00**

Browning Micro Citori Lightning

Similar to the standard Citori 20 ga. Lightning except scaled down for smaller shooter. Comes with 24" Invector Plus back-bored barrels, 13-3/4" length of pull. Weighs about 6 lbs., 3 oz. Introduced 1991.

Price: Grade I **$1,486.00**

Browning Citori Lightning Feather O/U

Similar to the 12 gauge Citori Grade I except has 2-3/4" chambers, rounded pistol grip, Lightning-style forend, and lighweight alloy receiver. Weighs 6 lbs. 15 oz. with 26" barrels (12 ga.); 6 lbs., 2 oz. (20 ga., 26" bbl.). Silvered, engraved receiver. Introduced 1999. Imported by Browning.

Price: 12 or 20 ga., 26" or 28" barrels **$1,693.00**
Price: Lightning Feather Combo (20 and 28 ga. bbls., 27" each) **$2,751.00**

Browning Citori Sporting Hunter

Similar to the Citori Hunting I except has Sporting Clays stock dimensions, a Superposed-style forend, and Sporting Clays butt pad. Available in 12 gauge with 3" chambers, back-bored 26", 28" and 30", all with Invector Plus choke tube system. Introduced 1998. Imported from Japan by Browning.

Price: 12 gauge, 3-1/2" **$1,709.00**
Price: 12, 20 gauge, 3" **$1,607.00**

Browning Citori Ultra XS Skeet

Similar to other Citori Ultra models except features a semi-beavertail forearm with deep finger grooves, ported barrels and triple system. Adjustable comb is optional. Introduced 2000.

Price: 12 ga., 28" or 30" barrel **$2,162.00**
New! **Price:** 20 ga., 28" or 30" barrel **$2,162.00**
Price: Adjustable comb model, 12 or 20 ga. **$2,380.00**

Browning Citori Ultra XS Trap

Similar to other Citori Ultra models except offered in 12 ga. only with 30" or 32" ported barrel, high-post rib, ventilated side ribs, Triple Trigger System™ and silver nitride receiver. Includes full, modified and imp. cyl. choke tubes. From Browning.

Price: 30" or 32" barrel **$2,022.00**
Price: Adjustable-comb model **$2,265.00**

Browning Citori Ultra XS Sporting

Similar to other Citori Ultra XS models except offered in 12, 20, 28 and 410 gauge. Silver nitride receiver, Schnabel forearm, ventilated side rib. Imported by Browning.

Price: 410 or 28 ga. **$2,268.00**
Price: 12 or 20 ga. **$2,196.00**

Browning Citori Feather XS Shotguns

Similar to the standard Citori except has lightweight alloy receiver, silver nitrade Nitex receiver, Schnabel forearm, ventilated side rib and Hi-Viz Comp fiber optics sight. Available in 12, 20, 28 and 410 gauges. Introduced 2000.

Price: 28" or 30" barrel . . . . **$2,266.00 to $2,338.00**

Browning Citori High Grade Shotguns

Similar to standard Citori except has full sideplates with engraved hunting scenes and gold inlays, high-grade, hand-oiled walnut stock and forearm. Introduced 2000. From Browning.

Price: Citori Privilege (fully embellished sideplates), 12 or 20 ga.
. . . . **$5,376.00**
Price: Citori BG VI Lightning (gold inlays of ducks and pheasants)
. . . . from **$3,340.00**
Price: Citori BG III Superlight (scroll engraving on grayed receiver,
gold inlays) **$2,190.00**
Price: Citori 425 Golden Clays (engraving of game bird-clay bird transition,
gold accents), 12 or 20 ga. **$3,977.00**

Browning Nitra Citori XS Sporting Clays

Similar to the Citori Grade I except has silver nitride receiver with gold accents, stock dimensions of 14-3/4"x1-1/2"x2-1/4" with satin finish, right-hand palm swell, Schnabel forend. Comes with Modified, Imp. Cyl. and Skeet Invector-Plus choke tubes. Back-bored barrels; vented side ribs. Introduced 1999. Imported by Browning.

Price: 12, 20 ga. **$2,011.00**
Price: 28 ga., 410-bore. **$2,077.00**

Browning Special Sporting Clays

Similar to the Citori Ultra Sporter except has full pistol grip stock with palm swell, gloss finish, 28", 30" or 32" barrels with back-bored Invector Plus chokes (ported or non-ported); high post tapered rib. Also available as 28" and 30" two-barrel set. Introduced 1989.

Price: With ported barrels. **$1,636.00**
Price: As above, adjustable comb **$1,856.00**

Browning Lightning Sporting Clays

Similar to the Citori Lightning with rounded pistol grip and classic forend. Has high post tapered rib or lower hunting-style rib with 30" back-bored Invector Plus barrels, ported or non-ported, 3" chambers. Gloss stock finish, radiused recoil pad. Has "Lightning Sporting Clays Edition" engraved and gold filled on receiver. Introduced 1989.

Price: Low-rib, ported **$1,691.00**
Price: High-rib, ported **$1,770.00**

BROWNING LIGHT SPORTING 802 ES O/U

Gauge: 12, 2-3/4" chambers. **Barrel:** 28", back-bored Invector Plus. Comes with flush-mounted Imp. Cyl. and Skeet; 2" extended Imp. Cyl. and Mod.; and 4" extended Imp. Cyl. and Mod. tubes. **Weight:** 7 lbs., 5 oz. **Length:** 45" overall. **Stock:** 14-3/8" x 1/8" x 1-9/16" x 1-3/4". Select walnut with radiused solid recoil pad, Schnabel-type forend. **Features:** Trigger adjustable for length of pull; narrow 6.2mm ventilated rib; ventilated barrel side rib; blued receiver. Introduced 1996. Imported from Japan from Browning.
Price: **$2,063.00**

SHOTGUNS

SHOTGUNS — OVER/UNDERS

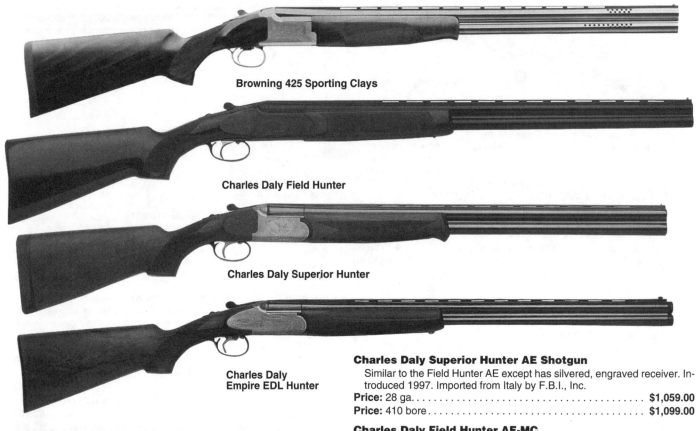

Browning 425 Sporting Clays

Charles Daly Field Hunter

Charles Daly Superior Hunter

Charles Daly
Empire EDL Hunter

BROWNING 425 SPORTING CLAYS

Gauge: 12, 20, 2-3/4" chambers. **Barrel:** 12 ga.—28", 30", 32" (Invector Plus tubes), back-bored; 20 ga.—28", 30" (Invector Plus tubes). **Weight:** 7 lbs., 13 oz. (12 ga., 28"). **Stock:** 14-13/16" (1/8")x1-7/16"x2-3/16" (12 ga.). Select walnut with gloss finish, cut checkering, Schnabel forend. **Features:** Grayed receiver with engraving, blued barrels. Barrels are ported on 12 gauge guns. Has low 10mm wide vent rib. Comes with three interchangeable trigger shoes to adjust length of pull. Introduced in U.S. 1993. Imported by Browning.

Price: Grade I, 12, 20 ga., Invector Plus. **$2,006.00**
Price: Golden Clays, 12, 20 ga., Invector Plus. **$3,977.00**

CHARLES DALY SUPERIOR TRAP AE MC

Gauge: 12, 2-3/4" chambers. **Barrel:** 30" choke tubes. **Weight:** About 7 lbs. **Stock:** Checkered walnut; pistol grip, semi-beavertail forend. **Features:** Silver engraved receiver, chrome moly steel barrels; gold single selective trigger; automatic safety, automatic ejectors; red bead front sight, metal bead center; recoil pad. Introduced 1997. Imported from Italy by K.B.I., Inc.

Price: **$1,219.00**

CHARLES DALY FIELD HUNTER OVER/UNDER SHOTGUN

Gauge: 12, 20, 28 and 410 bore (3" chambers, 28 ga. has 2-3/4"). **Barrel:** 28" Mod & Full, 26" Imp. Cyl. & Mod (410 is Full & Full). **Weight:** About 7 lbs. **Length:** NA. **Stock:** Checkered walnut pistol grip and forend. **Features:** Blued engraved receiver, chrome moly steel barrels; gold single selective trigger; automatic safety; extractors; gold bead front sight. Introduced 1997. Imported from Italy by K.B.I., Inc.

Price: 12 or 20 ga. **$749.00**
Price: 28 ga. **$809.00**
Price: 410 bore **$849.00**

Charles Daly Field Hunter AE Shotgun

Similar to the Field Hunter except 28 gauge and 410-bore only; 26" (Imp. Cyl. & Mod., 28 gauge), 26" (Full & Full, 410); automatic; ejectors. Introduced 1997. Imported from Italy by K.B.I., Inc.

Price: 28 . . . . **$889.00**
Price: 410 . . . . **$929.00**

Charles Daly Superior Hunter AE Shotgun

Similar to the Field Hunter AE except has silvered, engraved receiver. Introduced 1997. Imported from Italy by F.B.I., Inc.

Price: 28 ga. **$1,059.00**
Price: 410 bore **$1,099.00**

Charles Daly Field Hunter AE-MC

Similar to the Field Hunter except in 12 or 20 only, 26" or 28" barrels with five multichoke tubes; automatic ejectors. Introduced 1997. Imported from Italy by K.B.I., Inc.

Price: 12 or 20 . . . . **$979.95**

Charles Daly Superior Sporting O/U

Similar to the Field Hunter AE-MC except 28" or 30" barrels; silvered, engraved receiver; five choke tubes; ported barrels; red bead front sight. Introduced 1997. Imported from Italy by K.B.I., Inc.

Price: **$1,259.95**

CHARLES DALY EMPIRE TRAP AE MC

Gauge: 12, 2-3/4" chambers. **Barrel:** 30" choke tubes. **Weight:** About 7 lbs. **Stock:** Checkered walnut; pistol grip, semi-beavertail forend. **Features:** Silvered, engraved, reinforced receiver; chrome moly steel barrels; gold single selective trigger; automatic safety, automatic ejector; red bead front sight, metal bead center; recoil pad. Introduced 1997. Imported from Italy by K.B.I., Inc.

Price: **$1,539.95**

CHARLES DALY DIAMOND REGENT GTX DL HUNTER O/U

Gauge: 12, 20, 410, 3" chambers, 28, 2-3/4" chambers. **Barrel:** 26", 28", 30" (choke tubes), 26" (Imp. Cyl. & Mod. in 28, 26" (Full & Full) in 410. **Weight:** About 7 lbs. **Stock:** Extra select fancy European walnut with 24" hand checkering, hand rubbed oil finish. **Features:** Boss-type action with internal side lumps. Deep cut hand-engraved scrollwork and game scene set in full sideplates. GTX detachable single selective trigger system with coil springs; chrome moly steel barrels; automatic safety; automatic ejectors, white bead front sight, metal bead center sight. Introduced 1997. Imported from Italy by K.B.I., Inc.

Price: 12 or 20 . . . . **$22,299.00**
Price: 28 . . . . **$22,369.00**
Price: 410 . . . . **$22,419.00**
Price: Diamond Regent GTX EDL Hunter (as above with engraved scroll and birds, 10 gold inlays), 12 or 20 . . . . **$26,249.00**
Price: As above, 28 . . . . **$26,499.00**
Price: As above, 410 . . . . **$26,549.00**

SHOTGUNS

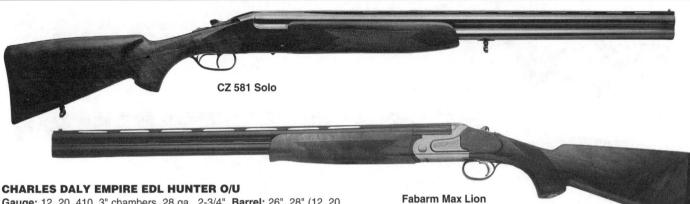

CZ 581 Solo

Fabarm Max Lion

CHARLES DALY EMPIRE EDL HUNTER O/U

Gauge: 12, 20, 410, 3" chambers, 28 ga., 2-3/4". **Barrel:** 26", 28" (12, 20, choke tubes), 26" (Imp. Cyl. & Mod., 28 ga.), 26" (Full & Full, 410). **Weight:** About 7 lbs. Stocks: Checkered walnut pistol grip buttstock, semi-beavertail forend; recoil pad. **Features:** Silvered, engraved receiver; chrome moly barrels; gold single selective trigger; automatic safety; automatic ejectors; red bead front sight, metal bead middle sight. Introduced 1997. Imported from Italy by K.B.I., Inc.

Price: Empire EDL (dummy sideplates) 12 or 20 . . . . **$1,559.95**
Price: Empire EDL, 28 . . . . **$1,559.95**
Price: Empire EDL, 410 . . . . **$1,599.95**

Charles Daly Empire Sporting O/U

Similar to the Empire EDL Hunter except 12 or 20 gauge only, 28", 30" barrels with choke tubes; ported barrels; special stock dimensions. Introduced 1997. Imported from Italy by K.B.I., Inc.

Price: **$1,499.95**

CHARLES DALY DIAMOND GTX SPORTING O/U SHOTGUN

Gauge: 12, 20, 3" chambers. **Barrel:** 28", 30" with choke tubes. **Weight:** About 8.5 lbs. **Stock:** Checkered deluxe walnut; Sporting clays dimensions. Pistol grip; semi-beavertail forend; hand rubbed oil finish. **Features:** Chromed, hand-engraved receiver; chrome moly steel barrels; GTX detachable single selective trigger system with coil springs, automatic safety; automatic ejectors; red bead front sight; ported barrels. Introduced 1997. Imported from Italy by K.B.I., Inc.

Price: **$5,804.95**

CHARLES DALY DIAMOND GTX TRAP AE-MC O/U SHOTGUN

Gauge: 12, 2-3/4" chambers. **Barrel:** 30" (Full & Full). **Weight:** About 8.5 lbs. **Stock:** Checkered deluxe walnut; pistol grip; trap dimensions; semi-beavertail forend; hand-rubbed oil finish. **Features:** Silvered, hand-engraved receiver; chrome moly steel barrels; GTX detachable single selective trigger system with coil springs, automatic safety, automatic-ejectors; red bead front sight, metal bead middle; recoil pad. Introduced 1997. Imported from Italy by K.B.I., Inc.

Price: **$5,804.95**

CHARLES DALY DIAMOND GTX DL HUNTER O/U

Gauge: 12, 20, 410, 3" chambers, 28, 2-3/4" chambers. **Barrel:** 26, 28", choke tubes in 12 and 20 ga., 26" (Imp. Cyl. & Mod.), 26" (Full & Full) in 410-bore. **Weight:** About 8.5 lbs. **Stock:** Select fancy European walnut stock, with 24 lpi hand checkering; hand-rubbed oil finish. **Features:** Boss-type action with internal side lugs, hand-engraved scrollwork and game scene. GTX detachable single selective trigger system with coil springs; chrome moly steel barrels, automatic safety, automatic ejectors; red bead front sight, recoil pad. Introduced 1997. Imported from Italy by K.B.I., Inc.

Price: 12 or 20 . . . . **$12,399.00**
Price: 28 . . . . **$12,489.00**
Price: 410 . . . . **$12,529.00**
Price: GTX EDL Hunter (with gold inlays), 12, 20 . . . . **$15,999.00**
Price: As above, 28 . . . . **$16,179.00**
Price: As above, 410 . . . . **$16,219.00**

CZ 581 SOLO OVER/UNDER SHOTGUN

Gauge: 12, 2-3/4" chambers. **Barrel:** 27.6" (Mod. & Full). **Weight:** 7.37 lbs. **Length:** 44.5" overall. **Stock:** Circassian walnut. **Features:** Automatic ejectors; double triggers; Kersten-style double lump locking system. Imported from the Czech Republic by CZ-USA.

Price: **$799.00**

EAA/BAIKAL MP-233 OVER/UNDER SHOTGUN

Gauge: 12, 3" chambers. **Barrel:** 26", 28", 30"; imp., mod. and full choke tubes. **Weight:** 7.28 lbs. **Stock:** Walnut; checkered forearm and grip. **Features:** Hammer-forged barrels; chrome-lined bores; removable trigger assembly (optional single selective trigger or double trigger); ejectors. Introduced 2000. Imported by European American Armory.

Price: MP-233. . . . . **$879.00**

EAA/BAIKAL IZH-27 OVER/UNDER SHOTGUN

Gauge: 12 (3" chambers), 16 (2-3/4" chambers), 20 (3" chambers), 28 (2-3/4" chambers), 410 (3"). **Barrel:** 26-1/2", 28-1/2" (imp., mod. and full choke tubes for 12 and 20 gauges; improved cylinder and modified for 16 and 28 gauges; improved modified and full for 410; 16 also offered in mod. and full). **Weight:** NA. **Stock:** Walnut, checkered forearm and grip. Imported by European American Armory.

Price: IZH-27 (12, 16 and 20 gauge) **$459.00**
Price: IZH-27 (28 and 410 gauge) **$499.00**

FABARM MAX LION OVER/UNDER SHOTGUNS

Gauge: 12, 3" chambers, 20, 3" chambers. **Barrel:** 26", 28", 30" (12 ga.); 26", 28" (20 ga.), choke tubes. **Weight:** 7.4 lbs. **Length:** 47.5" overall (26" barrel). **Stock:** European walnut; leather-covered recoil pad. **Features:** TriBore barrel, boxlock action with single selective trigger, manual safety, automatic ejectors; chrome-lined barrels; adjustable trigger. Silvered, engraved receiver. Comes with locking, fitted luggage case. Introduced 1998. Imported from Italy by Heckler & Koch, Inc.

Price: 12 or 20 . . . . **$1,899.00**

FABARM ULTRA MAG LION O/U SHOTGUN

Gauge: 12, 3-1/2" chambers. **Barrel:** 28" (Cyl., Imp. Cyl., Mod., Imp. Mod., Full, SS-Mod., SS-Full choke tubes). **Weight:** 7.9 lbs. **Length:** 50" overall. **Stock:** Black-colored walnut. **Features:** TriBore barrel, matte finished metal surfaces; single selective trigger; non-auto ejectors; leather-covered recoil pad. Comes with locking hard plastic case. Introduced 1998. Imported from Italy by Heckler & Koch, Inc.

Price: **$1,229.00**

Fabarm Ultra Camo Mag Lion O/U Shotgun

Similar to the Ultra Mag Lion except completely covered with Wetlands camouflage pattern, has the ported TriBore barrel system, and a mid-rib bead. Chambered for 3-1/2" shells. Stock and forend are walnut. Introduced 1999. Imported from Italy by Heckler & Koch, Inc.

Price: **$1,299.00**

FABARM SILVER LION OVER/UNDER SHOTGUNS

Gauge: 12, 3" chambers, 20, 3" chambers. **Barrel:** 26", 28", 30" (12 ga.); 26", 28" (20 ga.), choke tubes. **Weight:** 7.2 lbs. **Length:** 47.5" overall (26" barrels). **Stock:** Walnut; leather-covered recoil pad. **Features:** TriBore barrel, boxlock action with single selective trigger; silvered receiver with engraving; automatic ejectors. Comes with locking hard plastic case. Introduced 1998. Imported from Italy by Heckler & Koch, Inc.

Price: 12 or 20 . . . . **$1,299.00**

SHOTGUNS

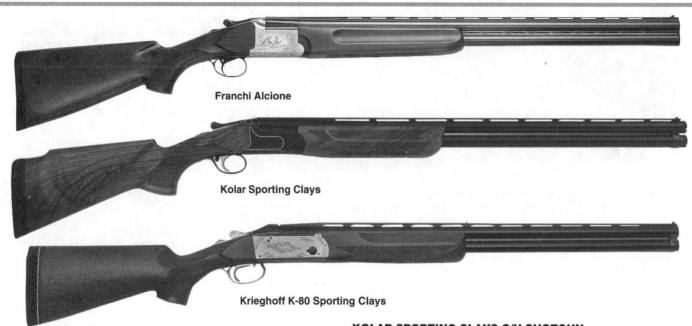

Franchi Alcione

Kolar Sporting Clays

Krieghoff K-80 Sporting Clays

Fabarm Silver Lion Cub Model O/U

Similar to the Silver Lion except has 12.5" length of pull, is in 20 gauge only (3-1/2" chambers), and comes with 24" TriBore barrel system. Weight is 6 lbs. Introduced 1999. Imported from Italy by Heckler & Koch, Inc.

Price: **$1,299.00**

FABARM CAMO TURKEY MAG O/U SHOTGUN

Gauge: 12, 3-1/2" chambers. **Barrel:** 20" TriBore (Ultra-Full ported tubes). **Weight:** 7.5 lbs. **Length:** 46" overall. **Stock:** 14.5"x1.5"x2.29". Walnut. **Sights:** Front bar, Picatinny rail scope base. **Features:** Completely covered with Xtra Brown camouflage finish. Unported barrels. Introduced 1999. Imported from Italy by Heckler & Koch, Inc.

Price: **$1,339.00**

FABARM SPORTING CLAYS COMPETITION EXTRA O/U

Gauge: 12, 20, 3" chambers. **Barrel:** 12 ga. has 30", 20 ga. has 28"; ported TriBore barrel system with five tubes. **Weight:** 7 to 7.8 lbs. **Length:** 49.6" overall (20 ga.). **Stock:** 14.50"x1.38"x2.17" (20 ga.); deluxe walnut; leather-covered recoil pad. **Features:** Single selective trigger, auto ejectors; 10mm channeled rib; carbon fiber finish. Introduced 1999. Imported from Italy by Heckler & Koch, Inc.

Price: **$1,749.00**

FRANCHI ALCIONE FIELD OVER/UNDER SHOTGUN

Gauge: 12, 3" chambers. **Barrel:** 26", 28"; Franchoke tubes. **Weight:** 7.5 lbs. **Length:** 43" overall with 26" barrels. **Stock:** European walnut. **Features:** Boxlock action with ejectors; barrel selector is mounted on the trigger; silvered, engraved receiver; vent center rib; automatic safety. Imported from Italy by Benelli USA. Hard case included.

Price: **$993.00**

Price: (20 gauge barrel set) **$336.00**

Franchi Alcione Sport O/U Shotgun

Similar to the Alcione except has 2-3/4" chambers, elongated forcing cones and porting for Sporting Clays shooting. 10mm vent rib, tightly curved pistol grip, manual safety, removeable sideplates. Imported from Italy by Benelli USA.

Price: **$1,300.00**

Franchi Alcione Light Field (LF) Shotgun

Similar to Alcione Field except features alloy frame, weighs 6.8 pounds (12 gauge) or 6.7 pounds (20 gauge). Both frames accept either the 2-3/4 "-chamber 12 gauge or 3"-chamber 20 gauge barrel sets.

Price: **$1,100.00**

KOLAR SPORTING CLAYS O/U SHOTGUN

Gauge: 12, 2-3/4" chambers. **Barrel:** 28", 30", 32"; extended choke tubes. **Stock:** 14-5/8"x2-1/2"x1-7/8"x1-3/8". French walnut. **Features:** Single selective trigger, detachable, adjustable for length; overbored barrels with long forcing cones; flat tramline rib; matte blue finish. Made in U.S. by Kolar.

Price: Standard. **$7,250.00**
Price: Elite **$10,050.00**
Price: Elite Gold **$11,545.00**
Price: Legend **$13,045.00**
Price: Custom Gold **$24,750.00**

Kolar AAA Competition Trap Over/Under Shotgun

Similar to the Sporting Clays gun except has 32" O/U /34" Unsingle or 30" O/U /34" Unsingle barrels as an over/under, unsingle, or combination set. Stock dimensions are 14-1/2"x2-1/2"x1-1/2"; American or French walnut; step parallel rib standard. Contact maker for full listings. Made in U.S. by Kolar.

Price: Over/under, choke tubes, Standard **$7,025.00**
Price: Unsingle, choke tubes, Standard **$7,775.00**
Price: Combo (30"/34", 32"/34"), Standard. **$10,170.00**

Kolar AAA Competition Skeet Over/Under Shotgun

Similar to the Sporting Clays gun except has 28" or 30" barrels with Kolarite AAA sub gauge tubes; stock of American or French walnut with matte finish; flat tramline rib; under barrel adjustable for point of impact. Many options available. Contact maker for complete listing. Made in U.S. by Kolar.

Price: Standard, choke tubes **$8,645.00**
Price: Standard, choke tubes, two-barrel set **$10,710.00**

KRIEGHOFF K-80 SPORTING CLAYS O/U

Gauge: 12. **Barrel:** 28", 30" or 32" with choke tubes. **Weight:** About 8 lbs. **Stock:** #3 Sporting stock designed for gun-down shooting. **Features:** Choice of standard or lightweight receiver with satin nickel finish and classic scroll engraving. Selective mechanical trigger adjustable for position. Choice of tapered flat or 8mm parallel flat barrel rib. Free-floating barrels. Aluminum case. Imported from Germany by Krieghoff International, Inc.

Price: Standard grade with five choke tubes, from **$8,150.00**

KRIEGHOFF K-80 SKEET SHOTGUN

Gauge: 12, 2-3/4" chambers. **Barrel:** 28" (Skeet & Skeet, optional Tula or choke tubes). **Weight:** About 7-3/4 lbs. **Stock:** American Skeet or straight Skeet stocks, with palm-swell grips. Walnut. **Features:** Satin gray receiver finish. Selective mechanical trigger adjustable for position. Choice of ventilated 8mm parallel flat rib or ventilated 8-12mm tapered flat rib. Introduced 1980. Imported from Germany by Krieghoff International, Inc.

SHOTGUNS

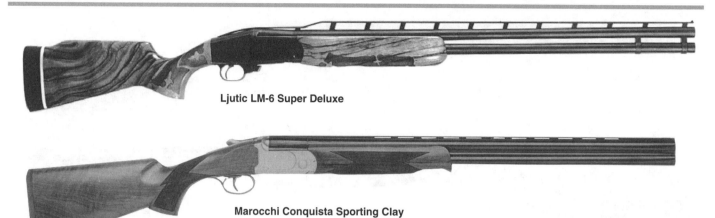

Ljutic LM-6 Super Deluxe

Marocchi Conquista Sporting Clay

Price: Standard, Skeet chokes......................... **$6,900.00**
Price: As above, Tula chokes.......................... **$7,825.00**
Price: Lightweight model (weighs 7 lbs.), Standard **$6,900.00**
Price: Two-Barrel Set (tube concept), 12 ga., Standard..... **$11,840.00**
Price: Skeet Special (28", tapered flat rib, Skeet & Skeet choke
tubes) **$7,575.00**

Krieghoff K-80 Four-Barrel Skeet Set

Similar to the Standard Skeet except comes with barrels for 12, 20, 28, 410. Comes with fitted aluminum case.
Price: Standard grade............................... **$16,950.00**

Krieghoff K-80 International Skeet

Similar to the Standard Skeet except has 1/2" ventilated Broadway-style rib, special Tula chokes with gas release holes at muzzle. International Skeet stock. Comes in fitted aluminum case.
Price: Standard grade............................... **$7,825.00**

KRIEGHOFF K-80 O/U TRAP SHOTGUN

Gauge: 12, 2-3/4" chambers. **Barrel:** 30", 32" (Imp. Mod. & Full or choke tubes). **Weight:** About 8-1/2 lbs. **Stock:** Four stock dimensions or adjustable stock available; all have palm swell grips. Checkered European walnut. **Features:** Satin nickel receiver. Selective mechanical trigger, adjustable for position. Ventilated step rib. Introduced 1980. Imported from Germany by Krieghoff International, Inc.
Price: K-80 O/U (30", 32", Imp. Mod. & Full), from.......... **$7,375.00**
Price: K-80 Unsingle (32", 34", Full), Standard, from........ **$7,950.00**
Price: K-80 Combo (two-barrel set), Standard, from **$10,475.00**

Krieghoff K-20 O/U Shotguns

Similar to the K-80 except built on a 20-gauge frame. Designed for skeet, sporting clays and field use. Offered in 20, 28 and 410 gauge, 28" and 30" barrels. Imported from Germany by Krieghoff International Inc.
Price: K-20, 20 gauge, from............................ **$8,150.00**
Price: K-20, 28 gauge, from........................... **$8,425.00**
Price: K-20, 410 gauge, from.......................... **$8,425.00**

LEBEAU - COURALLY BOSS-VEREES O/U

Gauge: 12, 20, 2-3/4" chambers. **Barrel:** 25" to 32". **Weight:** To customer specifications. **Stock:** Exhibition-quality French walnut. **Features:** Boss-type sidelock with automatic ejectors; single or double triggers; chopper lump barrels. A custom gun built to customer specifications. Imported from Belgium by Wm. Larkin Moore.
Price: From..................................... **$65,000.00**

LJUTIC LM-6 SUPER DELUXE O/U SHOTGUN

Gauge: 12. **Barrel:** 28" to 34", choked to customer specs for live birds, trap, International Trap. **Weight:** To customer specs. **Stock:** To customer specs. Oil finish, hand checkered. **Features:** Custom-made gun. Hollow-milled rib, pull or release trigger, pushbutton opener in front of trigger guard. From Ljutic Industries.

Price: Super Deluxe LM-6 O/U....................... **$17,995.00**
Price: Over/Under Combo (interchangeable single barrel, two trigger guards, one for single trigger, one for doubles) **$24,995.00**
Price: Extra over/under barrel sets, 29"-32"............... **$5,995.00**

LUGER CLASSIC O/U SHOTGUNS

Gauge: 12, 3" and 3-1/2" chambers. **Barrel:** 26", 28", 30"; imp. cyl. mod. and full choke tubes. **Weight:** 7-1/2 lbs. **Length:** 45" overall (28" barrel) **Stock:** Select-grade European walnut, hand-checkered grip and forend. **Features:** Gold, single selective trigger; automatic ejectors. Introduced 2000. From Stoeger Industries.
Price: Classic (26", 28" or 30" barrel; 3-1/2" chambers)....... **$919.00**
Price: Classic Sporting (30" barrel; 3" chambers) **$964.00**

MAROCCHI CONQUISTA SPORTING CLAYS O/U SHOTGUNS

Gauge: 12, 2-3/4" chambers. **Barrel:** 28", 30", 32" (ContreChoke tubes); 10mm concave vent. rib. **Weight:** About 8 lbs. **Stock:** 14-1/2"-14-7/8"x2-3/16"x1-7/16"; American walnut with checkered grip and forend; Sporting Clays butt pad. **Sights:** 16mm luminescent front. **Features:** Has lower monoblock and frame profile. Fast lock time. Ergonomically-shaped trigger is adjustable for pull length. Automatic selective ejectors. Coin-finished receiver, blued barrels. Comes with five choke tubes, hard case. Also available as true left-hand model—opening lever operates from left to right; stock has left-hand cast. Introduced 1994. Imported from Italy by Precision Sales International.
Price: Grade I, right-hand............................ **$1,995.00**
Price: Grade I, left-hand............................. **$2,120.00**
Price: Grade II, right-hand **$2,330.00**
Price: Grade II, left-hand **$2,685.00**
Price: Grade III, right-hand, from **$3,599.00**
Price: Grade III, left-hand, from **$3,995.00**

Marocchi Lady Sport O/U Shotgun

Ergonomically designed specifically for women shooters. Similar to the Conquista Sporting Clays model except has 28" or 30" barrels with five Contrechoke tubes, stock dimensions of 13-7/8"-14-1/4"x1-11/32"x2-9/32"; weighs about 7-1/2 lbs. Also available as left-hand model—opening lever operates from left to right; stock has left-hand cast. Also available with colored graphics finish on frame and opening lever. Introduced 1995. Imported from Italy by Precision Sales International.
Price: Grade I, right-hand............................ **$2,120.00**
Price: Left-hand, add (all grades)........................ **$101.00**
Price: Lady Sport Spectrum (colored receiver panel)......... **$2,199.00**
Price: Lady Sport Spectrum, left-hand **$2,300.00**

Marocchi Conquista Trap Over/Under Shotgun

Similar to the Conquista Sporting Clays model except has 30" or 32" barrels choked Full & Full, stock dimensions of 14-1/2"-14-7/8"x1-11/16"x1-9/32"; weighs about 8-1/4 lbs. Introduced 1994. Imported from Italy by Precision Sales International.
Price: Grade I, right-hand............................ **$1,995.00**
Price: Grade II, right-hand **$2,330.00**
Price: Grade III, right-hand, from **$3,599.00**

SHOTGUNS — OVER/UNDERS

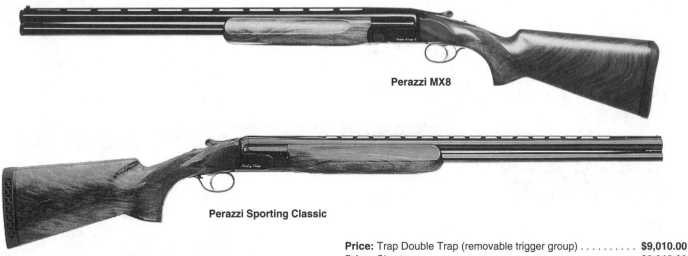

Perazzi MX8

Perazzi Sporting Classic

Marocchi Conquista Skeet Over/Under Shotgun

Similar to the Conquista Sporting Clays except has 28" (Skeet & Skeet) barrels, stock dimensions of 14-3/8"-14-3/4"x2-3/16"x1-1/2". Weighs about 7-3/4 lbs. Introduced 1994. Imported from Italy by Precision Sales International.

Price: Grade I, right-hand **$1,995.00**
Price: Grade II, right-hand **$2,330.00**
Price: Grade III, right-hand, from **$3,599.00**

MAROCCHI CLASSIC DOUBLES
MODEL 92 SPORTING CLAYS O/U SHOTGUN

Gauge: 12, 3" chambers. **Barrel:** 30"; back-bored, ported (ContreChoke Plus tubes); 10 mm concave ventilated middle rib. **Weight:** 8 lbs. 2 oz. **Stock:** 14-1/4"-14-5/8"x 2-1/8"x1-3/8"; American walnut with checkered grip and forend; Sporting Clays butt pad. **Features:** Low profile frame; fast lock time; automatic selective ejectors; blued receiver and barrels. Comes with three choke tubes. Ergonomically shaped trigger adjustable for pull length without tools. Barrels are back-bored and ported. Introduced 1996. Imported from Italy by Precision Sales International.

Price: **$1,598.00**

MERKEL MODEL 2001EL O/U SHOTGUN

Gauge: 12, 20, 3" chambers, 28, 2-3/4" chambers. **Barrel:** 12—28"; 20, 28 ga.—26-3/4". **Weight:** About 7 lbs. (12 ga.). **Stock:** Oil-finished walnut; English or pistol grip. **Features:** Self-cocking Blitz boxlock action with cocking indicators; Kersten double cross-bolt lock; silver-grayed receiver with engraved hunting scenes; coil spring ejectors; single selective or double triggers. Imported from Germany by GSI, Inc.

Price: 12, 20 . . . . **$6,495.00**
Price: 28 ga. **$6,495.00**
Price: Model 2000EL (scroll engraving, 12 or 20) **$5,195.00**

Merkel Model 303EL O/U Shotgun

Similar to the Model 2001 EL except has Holland & Holland-style sidelock action with cocking indicators; English-style Arabesque engraving. Available in 12, 20 gauge. Imported from Germany by GSI, Inc.

Price: **$19,995.00**

Merkel Model 2002 EL O/U Shotgun

Similar to the Model 2001 EL except has dummy sideplates, Arabesque engraving with hunting scenes; 12, 20 gauge. Imported from Germany by GSI, Inc.

Price: **$9,995.00**

PERAZZI MX8 OVER/UNDER SHOTGUNS

Gauge: 12, 2-3/4" chambers. **Barrel:** 28-3/8" (Imp. Mod. & Extra Full), 29-1/2" (choke tubes). **Weight:** 7 lbs., 12 oz. **Stock:** Special specifications. **Features:** Has single selective trigger; flat 7/16"x5/16" vent. rib. Many options available. Imported from Italy by Perazzi U.S.A., Inc.

Price: Sporting **$9,980.00**

Price: Trap Double Trap (removable trigger group) **$9,010.00**
Price: Skeet **$9,010.00**
Price: SC3 grade (variety of engraving patterns) . . . . . Starting at **$15,300**
Price: SCO grade (more intricate engraving, gold inlays)
. . . . Starting at **$26,000**

PERAZZI MX12 HUNTING OVER/UNDER

Gauge: 12, 2-3/4" chambers. **Barrel:** 26-3/4", 27-1/2", 28-3/8", 29-1/2" (Mod. & Full); choke tubes available in 27-5/8", 29-1/2" only (MX12C). **Weight:** 7 lbs., 4 oz. **Stock:** To customer specs; Interchangeable. **Features:** Single selective trigger; coil springs used in action; Schnabel forend tip. Imported from Italy by Perazzi U.S.A., Inc.

Price: From **$9,010.00**
Price: MX12C (with choke tubes), from **$9,460.00**

Perazzi MX20 Hunting Over/Under

Similar to the MX12 except 20 ga. frame size. Non-removable trigger group. Available in 20, 28, 410 with 2-3/4" or 3" chambers. 26" standard, and choked Mod. & Full. Weight is 6 lbs., 6 oz.

Price: From **$9,010.00**
Price: MX20C (as above, 20 ga. only, choke tubes), from **$9,460.00**

PERAZZI MX8/MX8 SPECIAL TRAP, SKEET

Gauge: 12, 2-3/4" chambers. **Barrel:** Trap—29-1/2" (Imp. Mod. & Extra Full), 31-1/2" (Full & Extra Full). Choke tubes optional. Skeet—27-5/8" (Skeet & Skeet). **Weight:** About 8-1/2 lbs. (Trap); 7 lbs., 15 oz. (Skeet). **Stock:** Interchangeable and custom made to customer specs. **Features:** Has detachable and interchangeable trigger group with flat V springs. Flat 7/16" ventilated rib. Many options available. Imported from Italy by Perazzi U.S.A., Inc.

Price: From **$8,840.00**
Price: MX8 Special (adj. four-position trigger), from **$9,350.00**
Price: MX8 Special Combo (o/u and single barrel sets), from . **$12,340.00**

Perazzi MX8 Special Skeet Over/Under

Similar to the MX8 Skeet except has adjustable four-position trigger, Skeet stock dimensions.

Price: From **$9,350.00**

Perazzi MX8/20 Over/Under Shotgun

Similar to the MX8 except has smaller frame and has a removable trigger mechanism. Available in trap, Skeet, sporting or game models with fixed chokes or choke tubes. Stock is made to customer specifications. Introduced 1993.

Price: From **$9,790.00**

PERAZZI MX10 OVER/UNDER SHOTGUN

Gauge: 12, 2-3/4" chambers. **Barrel:** 29.5", 31.5" (fixed chokes). **Weight:** NA. **Stock:** Walnut; cheekpiece adjustable for elevation and cast. **Features:** Adjustable rib; vent. side rib. Externally selective trigger. Available in single barrel, combo, over/under trap, Skeet, pigeon and sporting models. Introduced 1993. Imported from Italy by Perazzi U.S.A., Inc.

Price: From **$11,030.00**

Perazzi MX8 Special Combo Single Barrel

Perazzi MX28

Piotti Boss

Rizzini S790 Emel

PERAZZI MX28, MX410 GAME O/U SHOTGUNS
Gauge: 28, 2-3/4" chambers, 410, 3" chambers. **Barrel:** 26" (Imp. Cyl. & Full). **Weight:** NA. **Stock:** To customer specifications. **Features:** Made on scaled-down frames proportioned to the gauge. Introduced 1993. Imported from Italy by Perazzi U.S.A., Inc.
Price: From $17,670.00

PIOTTI BOSS OVER/UNDER SHOTGUN
Gauge: 12, 20. **Barrel:** 26" to 32", chokes as specified. **Weight:** 6.5 to 8 lbs. **Stock:** Dimensions to customer specs. Best quality figured walnut. **Features:** Essentially a custom-made gun with many options. Introduced 1993. Imported from Italy by Wm. Larkin Moore.
Price: From $34,000.00

REMINGTON MODEL 300 IDEAL O/U SHOTGUN
Gauge: 12, 3" chambers. **Barrel:** 26", 28", 30" (imp. cyl., mod. and full Rem Choke tubes). **Weight:** 7 lbs. 6 oz. to 7 lbs. 14 oz. **Length:** 42-3/4" overall (26" brl.) **Stock:** Satin-finished American walnut; checkered forearm and grip; rubber recoil pad. **Features:** Low-profile rib; mid-bead and ivory front bead; fine-line engraved receiver with high-polish blued finish; automatic ejectors. Introduced 2000. From Remington Arms Co.
Price: $1,999.00

RIZZINI S790 EMEL OVER/UNDER SHOTGUN
Gauge: 20, 28, 410. **Barrel:** 26", 27.5" (Imp. Cyl. & Imp. Mod.). **Weight:** About 6 lbs. **Stock:** 14"x1-1/2"x2-1/8". Extra-fancy select walnut. **Features:** Boxlock action with profuse engraving; automatic ejectors; single selective trigger; silvered receiver. Comes with Nizzoli leather case. Introduced 1996. Imported from Italy by Wm. Larkin Moore & Co.
Price: From $7,800.00

Rizzini S792 EMEL Over/Under Shotgun
Similar to the S790 EMEL except has dummy sideplates with extensive engraving coverage. Comes with Nizzoli leather case. Introduced 1996. Imported from Italy by Wm. Larkin Moore & Co.
Price: From $7,300.00

RIZZINI UPLAND EL OVER/UNDER SHOTGUN
Gauge: 12, 16, 20, 28, 410. **Barrel:** 26", 27-1/2", Mod. & Full, Imp. Cyl. & Imp. Mod. choke tubes. **Weight:** About 6.6 lbs. **Stock:** 14-1/2"x1-1/2"x2-1/4". **Features:** Boxlock action; single selective trigger; ejectors; profuse engraving on silvered receiver. Comes with fitted case. Introduced 1996. Imported from Italy by Wm. Larkin Moore & Co.
Price: From $2,800.00

Rizzini Artemis Over/Under Shotgun
Same as the Upland EL model except has dummy sideplates with extensive game scene engraving. Fancy European walnut stock. Comes with fitted case. Introduced 1996. Imported from Italy by Wm. Larkin Moore & Co.
Price: From $1,700.00

RIZZINI S782 EMEL OVER/UNDER SHOTGUN
Gauge: 12, 2-3/4" chambers. **Barrel:** 26", 27.5" (Imp. Cyl. & Imp. Mod.). **Weight:** About 6.75 lbs. **Stock:** 14-1/2"x1-1/2"x2-1/4". Extra fancy select walnut. **Features:** Boxlock action with dummy sideplates; extensive engraving with gold inlaid game birds; silvered receiver; automatic ejectors; single selective trigger. Comes with Nizzoli leather case. Introduced 1996. Imported from Italy by Wm. Larkin Moore & Co.
Price: From $9,200.00

ROTTWEIL PARAGON OVER/UNDER
Gauge: 12, 2-3/4" chambers. **Barrel:** 28", 30", five choke tubes. **Weight:** 7 lbs. **Stock:** 14-1/2"x1-1/2"x2-1/2"; European walnut. **Features:** Boxlock action. Detachable trigger assembly; ejectors can be deactivated; convertible top lever for right- or left-hand use; trigger adjustable for position. Imported from Germany by Dynamit Nobel-RWS, Inc.
Price: $5,995.00

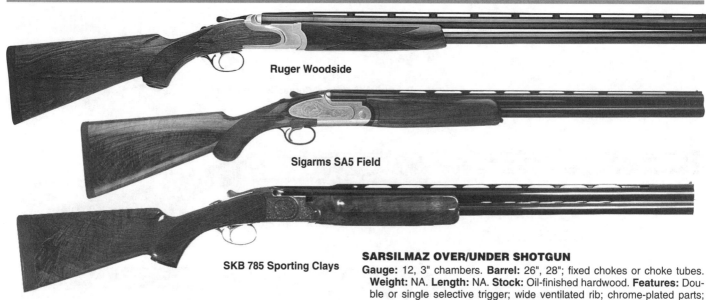

Ruger Woodside

Sigarms SA5 Field

SKB 785 Sporting Clays

RUGER WOODSIDE OVER/UNDER SHOTGUN

Gauge: 12, 3" chambers. **Barrel:** 26", 28", 30" (Full, Mod., Imp. Cyl. and two Skeet tubes). **Weight:** 7-1/2 to 8 lbs. **Stock:** 14-1/8"x1-1/2"x2-1/2". Select Circassian walnut; pistol grip or straight English grip. **Features:** Has a newly patented Ruger cocking mechanism for easier, smoother opening. Buttstock extends forward into action as two side panels. Single selective mechanical trigger, selective automatic ejectors; serrated free-floating rib; back-bored barrels with stainless steel choke tubes. Blued barrels, stainless steel receiver. Engraved action available. Introduced 1995. Made in U.S. by Sturm, Ruger & Co.

Price: **$1,889.00**
Price: Woodside Sporting Clays (30" barrels) **$1,889.00**

RUGER RED LABEL O/U SHOTGUN

Gauge: 12, 20, 3" chambers; 28 2-3/4" chambers. **Barrel:** 26", 28" (Skeet [two], Imp. Cyl., Full, Mod. screw-in choke tubes). Proved for steel shot. **Weight:** About 7 lbs. (20 ga.); 7-1/2 lbs. (12 ga.). **Length:** 43" overall (26" barrels). **Stock:** 14"x1-1/2"x2-1/2". Straight grain American walnut or black synthetic. Checkered pistol grip and forend, rubber butt pad. **Features:** Stainless steel receiver. Single selective mechanical trigger, selective automatic ejectors; serrated free-floating vent. rib. Comes with two Skeet, one Imp. Cyl., one Mod., one Full choke tube and wrench. Made in U.S. by Sturm, Ruger & Co.

Price: Red Label with pistol grip stock **$1,399.00**
Price: English Field with straight-grip stock **$1,399.00**
Price: All-Weather Red Label with black synthetic stock **$1,399.00**
Price: Factory engraved All-Weather models . . . . **$1,575.00 to $1,650.00**

Ruger Engraved Red Label O/U Shotguns

Similar to Red Label except has scroll engraved receiver with 24-carat gold game bird (pheasant in 12 gauge, grouse in 20 gauge, woodcock in 28 gauge, duck on All-Weather 12 gauge). Introduced 2000.

Price: Engraved Red Label (12 gauge, 30" barrel). **$1,650.00**
Price: Engraved Red Label (12, 20 and 28 gauge in 26"
and 28" barrels) **$1,575.00**
Price: Engraved Red Label, All-Weather (synthetic stock,
12 gauge only; 26" and 28" brls.) **$1,575.00**
Price: Engraved Red Label, All-Weather (synthetic stock,
12 gauge only, 30" barrel) **$1,650.00**

Ruger Sporting Clays O/U Shotgun

Similar to the Red Label except 30" back-bored barrels, stainless steel choke tubes. Weighs 7.75 lbs., overall length 47". Stock dimensions of 14-1/8"x1-1/2"x2-1/2". Free-floating serrated vent. rib with brass front and mid-rib beads. No barrel side spacers. Comes with two Skeet, one Imp. Cyl., one Mod. + Full choke tubes. 12 ga. introduced 1992, 20 ga. introduced 1994.

Price: 12 or 20 . . . . **$1,475.00**
Price: All-Weather with black synthetic stock **$1,475.00**

SARSILMAZ OVER/UNDER SHOTGUN

Gauge: 12, 3" chambers. **Barrel:** 26", 28"; fixed chokes or choke tubes. **Weight:** NA. **Length:** NA. **Stock:** Oil-finished hardwood. **Features:** Double or single selective trigger; wide ventilated rib; chrome-plated parts; blued finish. Introduced 2000. Imported from Turkey by Armsport Inc.

Price: Double triggers; mod. and full or imp. cyl. and mod. fixed
chokes **$499.95**
Price: Single selective trigger; imp. cyl. and mod. or mod.
and full fixed chokes **$575.00**
Price: Single selective trigger; five choke tubes and wrench **$695.00**

SIGARMS SA5 OVER/UNDER SHOTGUN

Gauge: 12, 20, 3" chamber. **Barrel:** 26-1/2", 27" (Full, Imp. Mod., Mod., Imp. Cyl., Cyl. choke tubes). **Weight:** 6.9 lbs. (12 gauge), 5.9 lbs. (20 gauge). **Stock:** 14-1/2" x 1-1/2" x 2-1/2". Select grade walnut; checkered 20 l.p.i. at grip and forend. **Features:** Single selective trigger, automatic ejectors; hand-engraved detachable sideplated; matte nickel receiver, rest blued; tapered bolt lock-up. Introduced 1997. Imported by Sigarms, Inc.

Price: Field, 12 gauge **$2,670.00**
Price: Sporting Clays **$2,800.00**
Price: Field 20 gauge **$2,670.00**

SKB Model 505 Shotguns

Similar to the Model 585 except blued receiver, standard bore diameter, standard Inter-Choke system on 12, 20, 28, different receiver engraving. Imported from Japan by G.U. Inc.

Price: Field, 12 (26", 28"), 20 (26", 28") **$1,189.00**
Price: Sporting Clays, 12 (28", 30") **$1,299.00**

SKB MODEL 785 OVER/UNDER SHOTGUN

Gauge: 12, 20, 3"; 28, 2-3/4"; 410, 3". **Barrel:** 26", 28", 30", 32" (Inter-Choke tubes). **Weight:** 6 lbs., 10 oz. to 8 lbs. **Stock:** 14-1/8"x1-1/2"x2-3/16" (Field). Hand-checkered American black walnut with high-gloss finish; semi-beavertail forend. Target stocks available in standard or Monte Carlo styles. **Sights:** Metal bead front (Field), target style on Skeet, trap, Sporting Clays models. **Features:** Boxlock action with Greener-style cross bolt; single selective chrome-plated trigger, chrome-plated selective ejectors; manual safety. Chrome-plated, over-size, back-bored barrels with lengthened forcing cones. Introduced 1995. Imported from Japan by G.U. Inc.

Price: Field, 12 or 20 . . . . **$2,119.00**
Price: Field, 28 or 410 . . . . **$2,199.00**
Price: Field set, 12 and 20 . . . . **$3,079.00**
Price: Field set, 20 and 28 or 28 and 410 . . . . **$3,179.00**
Price: Sporting Clays, 12 or 20. . . . . **$2,269.00**
Price: Sporting Clays, 28 . . . . **$2,349.00**
Price: Sporting Clays set, 12 and 20 . . . . **$3,249.00**
Price: Skeet, 12 or 20. . . . . **$2,199.00**
Price: Skeet, 28 or 410. . . . . **$2,239.00**
Price: Skeet, three-barrel set, 20, 28, 410 . . . . **$4,439.00**
Price: Trap, standard or Monte Carlo. **$2,199.00**
Price: Trap combo, standard or Monte Carlo. **$3,079.00**

SHOTGUNS — OVER/UNDERS

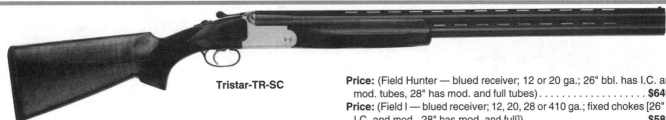

Tristar-TR-SC

SKB MODEL 585 OVER/UNDER SHOTGUN

Gauge: 12 or 20, 3"; 28, 2-3/4"; 410, 3". **Barrel:** 12 ga.—26", 28", 30", 32", 34" (Inter-Choke tubes); 20 ga.—26", 28" (Inter-Choke tube); 28—26", 28" (Inter-Choke tubes); 410—26", 28" (Inter-Choke tubes). Ventilated side ribs. **Weight:** 6.6 to 8.5 lbs. **Length:** 43" to 51-3/8" overall. **Stock:** 14-1/8"x1-1/2"x2-3/16". Hand checkered walnut with high-gloss finish. Target stocks available in standard and Monte Carlo. **Sights:** Metal bead front (field), target style on Skeet, trap, Sporting Clays. **Features:** Boxlock action; silver nitride finish with Field or Target pattern engraving; manual safety, automatic ejectors, single selective trigger. All 12 gauge barrels are back-bored, have lengthened forcing cones and longer choke tube system. Sporting Clays models in 12 gauge with 28" or 30" barrels available with optional 3/8" step-up target-style rib, matte finish, nickel center bead, white front bead. Introduced 1992. Imported from Japan by G.U., Inc.

Price: Field **$1,499.00**
Price: Two-barrel Field Set, 12 & 20. . . . . **$2,399.00**
Price: Two-barrel Field Set, 20 & 28 or 28 & 410 . . . . **$2,469.00**
Price: Trap, Skeet. **$1,619.00**
Price: Two-barrel trap combo **$2,419.00**
Price: Sporting Clays model . . . . **$1,679.00 to $1,729.00**
Price: Skeet Set (20, 28, 410) **$3,779.00**

SKB Model 585 Gold Package
Similar to the Model 585 Field except has gold-plated trigger, two gold-plated game inlays, and Schnabel forend. Silver or blue receiver. Introduced 1998. Imported from Japan by G.U. Inc.

Price: 12, 20 ga. **$1,689.00**
Price: 28, 410 . . . . **$1,749.00**

STOEGER/IGA CONDOR I OVER/UNDER SHOTGUN

Gauge: 12, 20, 3" chambers. **Barrel:** 26" (Imp. Cyl. & Mod. choke tubes), 28" (Mod. & Full choke tubes). **Weight:** 6-3/4 to 7 lbs. **Stock:** 14-1/2"x1-1/2"x2-1/2". Oil-finished hardwood with checkered pistol grip and forend. **Features:** Manual safety, single trigger, extractors only, ventilated top rib. Introduced 1983. Imported from Brazil by Stoeger Industries.

Price: With choke tubes **$559.00**
Price: Condor Supreme (same as Condor I with single trigger, choke tubes, but with auto. ejectors), 12 or 20 ga., 26", 28" . . . **$674.00**

Stoeger/IGA Condor Waterfowl O/U
Similar to the Condor I except has Advantage camouflage on the barrels, stock and forend; all other metal has matte black finish. Comes only with 30" choke tube barrels, 3" chambers, automatic ejectors, single trigger and manual safety. Designed for steel shot. Introduced 1997. Imported from Brazil by Stoeger.

Price: **$729.00**

Stoeger/IGA Turkey Model O/U
Similar to the Condor I model except has Advantage camouflage on the barrels stock and forend. All exposed metal and recoil pad are matte black. Has 26" (Full & Full) barrels, single trigger, manual safety, 3" chambers. Introduced 1997. Imported from Brazil by Stoeger.

Price: **$729.00**

TRADITIONS CLASSIC SERIES O/U SHOTGUNS

Gauge: 12, 3"; 20, 3"; 16, 2-3/4"; 28, 2-3/4"; 410, 3". **Barrel:** 26" and 28". **Weight:** 6 lbs., 5 oz. to 7 lbs., 6 oz. **Length:** 43" to 45". **Stock:** Walnut. **Features:** Single-selective trigger; chrome-lined barrels with screw-in choke tubes; extractors (Field Hunter and Field I models) or automatic ejectors (Field II and Field III models); rubber butt pad; top tang safety. Imported from Fausti of Italy by Traditions.

Price: (Field Hunter — blued receiver; 12 or 20 ga.; 26" bbl. has I.C. and mod. tubes, 28" has mod. and full tubes) **$649.00**
Price: (Field I — blued receiver; 12, 20, 28 or 410 ga.; fixed chokes [26" has I.C. and mod., 28" has mod. and full]) **$589.00**
Price: (Field II — coin-finish receiver; 12, 16, 20, 28 or 410 ga.; gold trigger; choke tubes) . . . . **$759.00 ($799.00 for 16 ga.)**
Price: (Field III — coin-finish receiver; gold engraving and trigger; 12 ga.; 26" or 28" bbl.; choke tubes) **$979.00**
Price: (Upland II — blued receiver; 12 or 20 ga.; English-style straight walnut stock; choke tubes) **$799.00**
Price: (Upland III — blued receiver with gold engraving; 20 ga.; high-grade pistol grip walnut stock; choke tubes) **$1,019.00**
Price: (Sporting Clay II — silver receiver; 12 ga.; ported barrels with skeet, i.c., mod. and full extended tubes) **$919.00**

TRADITIONS MAG 350 SERIES O/U SHOTGUNS

Gauge: 12, 3-1/2". **Barrels:** 24", 26" and 28". **Weight:** 7 lbs. to 7 lbs., 4 oz. **Length:** 41" to 45" overall. **Stock:** Walnut or composite with Mossy Oak® Break-Up™ or Advantage® Wetlands ™ camouflage. **Features:** Black matte, engraved receiver; vent rib; automatic ejectors; single-selective trigger; three screw-in choke tubes; rubber recoil pad; top tang safety. Imported from Fausti of Italy by Traditions.

Price: (Mag Hunter II — 28" black matte barrels, walnut stock, includes I.C., Mod. and Full tubes) **$769.00**
Price: (Turkey II — 24" or 26" camo barrels, Break-Up camo stock, includes Mod., Full and X-Full tubes) **$849.00**
Price: (Waterfowl II — 28" camo barrels, Advantage Wetlands camo stock, includes I.C., Mod. and Full tubes) **$849.00**

Tristar Silver II Shotgun
Similar to the Silver I except 26" barrel (Imp. Cyl., Mod., Full choke tubes, 12 and 20 ga.), 28" (Imp. Cyl., Mod., Full choke tubes, 12 ga. only), 26" (Imp. Cyl. & Mod. fixed chokes, 28 and 410), automatic selective ejectors. Weight is about 6 lbs., 15 oz. (12 ga., 26").

Price: **$566.00**

TRISTAR SILVER SPORTING O/U

Gauge: 12, 2-3/4" chambers, 20 3" chambers. **Barrel:** 28", 30" (Skeet, Imp. Cyl., Mod., Full choke tubes). **Weight:** 7-3/8 lbs. **Length:** 45-1/2" overall. **Stock:** 14-3/8"x1-1/2"x2-3/8". Figured walnut, cut checkering; Sporting Clays quick-mount buttpad. **Sights:** Target bead front. **Features:** Boxlock action with single selective mechanical trigger; automatic selective ejectors; special broadway channeled rib; vented barrel rib; chrome bores. Chrome-nickel finish on frame, with engraving. Introduced 1990. Imported from Italy by Tristar Sporting Arms Ltd.

Price: **$765.00**

TRISTAR-TR-SC "EMILIO RIZZINI" OVER/UNDER

Gauge: 12, 20, 2-3/4" chambers. **Barrel:** 28", 30" (Imp. Cyl., Mod., Full choke tubes). **Weight:** 7-1/2 lbs. **Length:** 46" overall (28" barrel). **Stock:** 1-1/2"x2-3/8"x14-3/8". Semi-fancy walnut; pistol grip with palm swell; semi-beavertail forend; black Sporting Clays recoil pad. **Features:** Silvered boxlock action with Four Locks locking system, auto ejectors, single selective (inertia) trigger, auto safety. Hard chrome bores. Vent. 10mm rib with target-style front and mid-rib beads, vent. spacer rib. Introduced 1998. Imported from Italy by Tristar Sporting Arms, Ltd.

Price: Sporting Clay model **$996.00**
Price: 20 ga. **$1,073.00**

Tristar TR-Royal Emillio Rizzini Over/Under
Similar to the TR-SC except has special parallel stock dimensions (1-1/2"x1-5/8"x14-3/8") to give low felt recoil; Rhino ported, extended choke tubes; solid barrel spacer; has "TR-Royal" gold engraved on the silvered receiver. Available in 12 gauge (28", 30") 20 and 28 gauge (28" only). Introduced 1999. Imported from Italy by Tristar Sporting Arms, Ltd.

Price: 12 ga. **$1,340.00**
Price: 20, 28 ga. **$1,258.00**

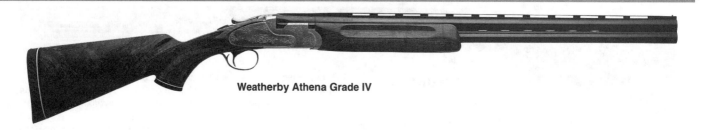

Weatherby Athena Grade IV

Tristar-TR-L "Emilio Rizzini" Over/Under

Similar to the TR-SC except has stock dimensions designed for female shooters (1-1/2" x 3" x 13-1/2"). Standard grade walnut. Introduced 1998. Imported from Italy by Tristar Sporting Arms, Ltd.

Price: **$1,014.00**

TRISTAR-TR-I, II "EMILIO RIZZINI" OVER/UNDERS

Gauge: 12, 20, 3" chambers (TR-I); 12, 16, 20, 28, 410 3" chambers (except 28, 2-3/4"). **Barrel:** 12 ga., 26" (Imp. Cyl. & Mod.), 28" (Mod. & Full); 20 ga., 26" (Imp. Cyl. & Mod.), fixed chokes. **Weight:** 7-1/2 lbs. **Stock:** 1-1/2"x2-3/8"x14-3/8". Walnut with palm swell pistol grip, hand checkering, semi-beavertail forend, black recoil pad. **Features:** Boxlock action with blued finish, Four Locks locking system, gold single selective (inertia) trigger system, automatic safety, extractors. Introduced 1998. Imported from Italy by Tristar Sporting Arms, Ltd.

Price: TR-I **$687.00**
Price: TR-II (automatic ejectors, choke tubes) 12, 16 ga. **$879.00**
Price: 20, 28 ga., 410 .... **$924.00**

Tristar-TR-MAG "Emilio Rizzini" Over/Under

Similar to the TR-I except 12 gauge, 3-1/2" chambers; choke tubes; 24" or 28" barrels with three choke tubes; extractors; auto safety. Matte blue finish on all metal, non-reflective wood finish. Introduced 1998. Imported from Italy by Tristar Sporting Arms, Ltd.

Price: **$764.00**
Price: Mossy Oak® Break-Up camo. **$942.00**
Price: Mossy Oak® Shadow Grass camo **$942.00**
Price: 10 ga., Mossy Oak® camo patterns. **$1,132.10**

TRISTAR TR-CLASS SL EMILIO RIZZINI O/U

Gauge: 12, 2-3/4" chambers. **Barrel:** 28", 30", (Imp. Cyl., Mod., Full choke tubes). **Weight:** 7-1/2-7-3/4 lbs. **Stock:** 1-1/2"x1-3/8"x14-1/4". Fancy walnut with palm swell, hand checkering, semi-beavertail forend, black recoil pad, gloss finish. **Features:** Boxlock action with silvered, engraved sideplates; Four Lock locking system; automatic ejectors; hard chrome bores; vent tapered 7mm rib with target-style front bead. hand-fitted gun. Introduced 1999. Imported from Italy by Tristar Sporting Arms, Ltd.

Price: **$1,775.00**

TRISTAR WS/OU 12 SHOTGUN

Gauge: 12, 3-1/2" chambers. **Barrel:** 28" or 30" (Imp. Cyl., Mod., Full choke tubes). **Weight:** 6 lbs., 15 oz. **Length:** 46" overall. **Stock:** 14-1/8"x1-1/8"x2-3/8". European walnut with cut checkering, black vented recoil pad, matte finish. **Features:** Boxlock action with single selective trigger, automatic selective ejectors; chrome bores. Matte metal finish. Imported by Tristar Sporting Arms Ltd.

Price: **$610.00**

VERONA LX501 HUNTING O/U SHOTGUNS

Gauge: 12, 20, (3" chambers), 28, 410 (2-3/4"). **Barrel:** 28"; 12, 20 ga. have Interchoke tubes, 28 ga. and 410 have fixed Full & Mod. **Weight:** 6-7 lbs. **Stock:** Matte-finished walnut with machine-cut checkering. **Features:** Gold-plated single-selective trigger; ejectors; engraved, blued receiver; non-automatic safety; coil spring-operated firing pins. Introduced 1999. Imported from Italy by B.C. Outdoors.

Price: 12 and 20 ga. **$720.00**
Price: 28 ga. and 410 .... **$755.00**

Verona LX692 Gold Hunting Over/Under Shotguns

Similar to tthe Verona LX501 except has engraved, silvered receiver with false sideplates showing gold-inlaid bird hunting scenes on three sides; Schnabel forend tip; hand-cut checkering; black rubber butt pad. Available in 12 and 20 gauge only, with five InterChoke tubes. Introduced 1999. Imported from Italy by B.C. Outdoors.

Price: **$1,295.00**

Verona LX680 Sporting Over/Under Shotguns

Similar to the Verona LX501 except has engraved, silvered receiver; ventilated middle rib; beavertail forend; hand-cut checkering; available in 12 or 20 gauge only with 2-3/4" chambers. Introduced 1999. Imported from Italy by B.C. Outdoors.

Price: **$1,020.00**

Verona LX680 Skeet/Sporting, Trap O/U Shotguns

Similar to the Verona LX501 except with Skeet or trap stock dimensions; beavertail forend; palm swell on pistol grip; ventilated center barrel rib. Introduced 1999. Imported from Italy by B.C. Outdoors.

Price: **$1,130.00**
Price: Gold Competition (false sideplates with gold-inlaid hunting scenes) **$1,500.00**

Verona LX692 Gold Sporting Over/Under Shotguns

Similar to the Verona LX680 except with false sideplates that have gold-inlaid bird hunting scenes on three sides; red high-visibility front sight. Introduced 1999. Imported from Italy by B.C. Outdoors.

Price: **$1,365.00**

WEATHERBY ATHENA GRADE IV O/U SHOTGUNS

Gauge: 12, 20, 3" chambers. Action: Boxlock (simulated sidelock) top lever break-open. Selective auto ejectors, single selective trigger (selector inside trigger guard). **Barrel:** 26", 28", IMC Multi-Choke tubes. **Weight:** 12 ga., 7-3/8 lbs.; 20 ga. 6-7/8 lbs. **Stock:** American walnut, checkered pistol grip and forend (14-1/4"x1-1/2"x2-1/2"). **Features:** Mechanically operated trigger. Top tang safety, Greener cross bolt, fully engraved receiver, recoil pad installed. IMC models furnished with three interchangeable flush-fitting choke tubes. Imported from Japan by Weatherby. Introduced 1982.

Price: 12 ga., IMC, 26", 28" **$2,499.00**
Price: 20 ga., IMC, 26", 28" **$2,499.00**

Weatherby Athena Grade V Classic Field O/U

Similar to the Athena Grade IV except has rounded pistol grip, slender forend, oil-finished Claro walnut stock with fine-line checkering, Old English recoil pad. Sideplate receiver has rose and scroll engraving. Available in 12 gauge, 26", 28", 20 gauge, 26", 28", all with 3" chambers. Introduced 1993.

Price: **$2,919.00**

Weatherby Athena III Classic Field O/U

Has Grade III Claro walnut with oil finish, rounded pistol grip, slender forend; silver nitride/gray receiver has rose and scroll engraving with gold-overlay upland game scenes. Introduced 1999. Imported from Japan by Weatherby.

Price: 12, 20, 28 ga. **$2,089.00**

WEATHERBY ORION GRADE III FIELD O/U SHOTGUNS

Gauge: 12, 20, 3" chambers. **Barrel:** 26", 28", IMC Multi-Choke tubes. **Weight:** 6-1/2 to 9 lbs. **Stock:** 14-1/4"x1-1/2"x2-1/2". American walnut, checkered grip and forend. **Features:** Selective automatic ejectors, single selective inertia trigger. Top tang safety, Greener cross bolt. Has silver-gray receiver with engraving and gold duck/pheasant. Imported from Japan by Weatherby.

Price: Orion III, Field, 12, IMC, 26", 28" **$1,879.00**
Price: Orion III, Field, 20, IMC, 26", 28" **$1,879.00**

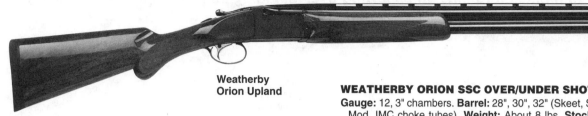

Weatherby Orion Upland

Weatherby Orion Grade III Classic Field O/U

Similar to the Orion III Field except the stock has a rounded pistol grip, satin oil finish, slender forend, Old English recoil pad. Introduced 1993. Imported from Japan by Weatherby.
Price: **$1,879.00**

Weatherby Orion III English Field O/U

Similar to the Orion III Classic Field except has straight grip English-style stock. Available in 12 gauge (28"), 20 gauge (26", 28") with IMC Multi-Choke tubes. Silver/gray nitride receiver is engraved and has gold-plate overlay. Introduced 1997. Imported from Japan by Weatherby.
Price: **$1,959.00**

Weatherby Orion Grade II Classic Field O/U

Similar to the Orion III Classic Field except stock has high-gloss finish, and the bird on the receiver is not gold. Available in 12 gauge, 26", 28", 30" barrels, 20 gauge, 26" 28", both with 3" chambers, 28 gauge, 26", 2-3/4" chambers. All have IMC choke tubes. Imported from Japan by Weatherby.
Price: **$1,559.00**

Weatherby Orion Grade I Field O/U

Similar to the Orion Grade III Field except has blued receiver with engraving, and the bird is not gold. Available in 12 gauge, 26", 28", 30", 20 gauge, 20", 28", both with 3" chambers and IMC choke tubes. Imported from Japan by Weatherby.
Price: **$1,509.00**

Weatherby Orion Upland O/U

Similar to the Orion Grade I. Plain blued receiver, gold W on the trigger guard; rounded pistol grip, slender forend of Claro walnut with high-gloss finish; black butt pad. Available in 12 and 20 gauge with 26" and 28" barrels. Introduced 1999. Imported from Japan by Weatherby.
Price: **$1,249.00**

WEATHERBY ORION SSC OVER/UNDER SHOTGUN

Gauge: 12, 3" chambers. **Barrel:** 28", 30", 32" (Skeet, SC1, Imp. Cyl., SC2, Mod. IMC choke tubes). **Weight:** About 8 lbs. **Stock:** 14-3/4"x2-1/4"x1-1/2". Claro walnut with satin oil finish; Schnabel forend tip; Sporter-style pistol grip; Pachmayr Decelerator recoil pad. **Features:** Designed for Sporting Clays competition. Has lengthened forcing cones and back-boring; ported barrels with 12mm grooved rib with mid-bead sight; mechanical trigger is adjustable for length of pull. Introduced 1998. Imported from Japan by Weatherby.
Price: SSC (Super Sporting Clays) **$1,979.00**

Weatherby Orion Grade II Classic Sporting O/U

Similar to the Orion II Classic Field except in 12 gauge only with (3" chambers), 28", 30" barrels with Skeet, SC1, SC2 Imp. Cyl., Mod. chokes. Weighs 7.5-8 lbs. Competition center vent rib; middle barrel and enlarged front beads. Rounded grip; high gloss stock. Radiused heel recoil pad. Receiver finished in silver nitride with acid-etched, gold-plate clay pigeon monogram. Barrels have lengthened forcing cones. Introduced 1993. Imported by Weatherby.
Price: **$1,719.00**

Weatherby Orion Grade II Sporting

Similar to the Orion II Classic Sporting except has traditional pistol grip with diamond inlay, and standard full-size forend. Available in 12 gauge only, 28", 30" barrels with Skeet, Imp. Cyl., SC2, Mod. Has lengthened forcing cones, back-boring, stepped competition rib, radius heel recoil pad, hand-engraved, silver/nitride receiver. Introduced 1992. Imported by Weatherby.
Price: **$1,719.00**

WINCHESTER SUPREME O/U SHOTGUNS

Gauge: 12, 2-3/4", 3" chambers. **Barrel:** 28", 30", Invector Plus choke tubes. **Weight:** 7 lbs. 6 oz. to 7 lbs. 12. oz. **Length:** 45" overall (28" barrel). **Stock:** Checkered walnut stock. **Features:** Chrome-plated chambers; back-bored barrels; tang barrel selector/safety; deep-blued finish. Introduced 2000. From U.S. Repeating Arms. Co.
Price: Supreme Field (26" or 28" barrel, 6mm ventilated rib) . . **$1,383.00**
Price: Supreme Sporting (28" or 30" barrel, 10mm rib,
    adj. trigger) **$1,551.00**

SHOTGUNS

Variety of models for utility and sporting use, including some competitive shooting.

Beretta Model 470
Silver Hawk

Charles Daly Field Hunter

ARRIETA SIDELOCK DOUBLE SHOTGUNS

Gauge: 12, 16, 20, 28, 410. **Barrel:** Length and chokes to customer specs. **Weight:** To customer specs. **Stock:** 14-1/2"x1-1/2"x2-1/2 (standard dimensions), or to customer specs. Straight English with checkered butt (standard), or pistol grip. Select European walnut with oil finish. **Features:** Essentially a custom gun with myriad options. Holland & Holland-pattern hand-detachable sidelocks, selective automatic ejectors, double triggers (hinged front) standard. Some have self-opening action. Finish and engraving to customer specs. Imported from Spain by Wingshooting Adventures.

Price: Model 557, auto ejectors, from	**$2,750.00**
Price: Model 570, auto ejectors, from	**$3,380.00**
Price: Model 578, auto ejectors, from	**$3,740.00**
Price: Model 600 Imperial, self-opening, from	**$4,990.00**
Price: Model 601 Imperial Tiro, self-opening, from	**$5,750.00**
Price: Model 801, from	**$7,950.00**
Price: Model 802, from	**$7,950.00**
Price: Model 803, from	**$5,850.00**
Price: Model 871, auto ejectors, from	**$4,290.00**
Price: Model 872, self-opening, from	**$9,790.00**
Price: Model 873, self-opening, from	**$6,850.00**
Price: Model 874, self-opening, from	**$7,950.00**
Price: Model 875, self-opening, from	**$12,950.00**

BERETTA MODEL 470 SILVER HAWK SHOTGUN

Gauge: 12, 20, 3" chambers. **Barrel:** 26" (Imp. Cyl. & Imp. Mod.), 28" (Mod. & Full). **Weight:** 5.9 lbs. (20 gauge). **Stock:** Select European walnut, straight English grip. **Features:** Boxlock action with single selective trigger; selector provides automatic ejection or extraction; silver-chrome action and forend iron with fine engraving; top lever highlighted with gold inlaid hawk's head. Comes with ABS case. Introduced 1997. Imported from Italy by Beretta U.S.A.

Price: 12 ga.	**$3,630.00**
Price: 20 ga.	**$3,755.00**

CHARLES DALY SUPERIOR HUNTER DOUBLE SHOTGUN

Gauge: 12, 20, 3" chambers, 28, 2-3/4" chambers. **Barrel:** 28" (Mod. & Full) 26" (Imp. Cyl. & Mod.). **Weight:** About 7 lbs. **Stock:** Checkered walnut pistol grip buttstock, splinter forend. **Features:** Silvered, engraved receiver; chrome-lined barrels; gold single trigger; automatic safety; extractors; gold bead front sight. Introduced 1997. Imported from Italy by K.B.I., Inc.

Price:	**$1,179.95**
Price: 28 ga., 26"	**$1,094.95**

Charles Daly Empire Hunter Double Shotgun

Similar to the Superior Hunter except has deluxe wood, game scene engraving, automatic ejectors. Introduced 1997. Imported from Italy by K.B.I., Inc.

Price: 12 or 20	**$1,595.95**

CHARLES DALY DIAMOND REGENT DL DOUBLE SHOTGUN

Gauge: 12, 20, 410, 3" chambers, 28, 2-3/4" chambers. **Barrel:** 28" (Mod. & Full), 26" (Imp. Cyl. & Mod.), 26" (Full & Full, 410). **Weight:** About 5-7 lbs. **Stock:** Special select fancy European walnut, English-style butt, splinter forend; hand-checkered; hand-rubbed oil finish. **Features:** Drop-forged action with gas escape valves; demiblock barrels of chrome-nickel steel with concave rib; selective automatic-ejectors; hand-detachable, double-safety H&H sidelocks with demi-relief hand engraving; H&H pattern easy-opening feature; hinged trigger; coin finished action. Introduced 1997. Imported from Spain by K.B.I., Inc.

Price: 12 or 20	**$19,999.00**
Price: 28	**$20,499.00**
Price: 410	**$20,499.00**

CHARLES DALY FIELD HUNTER DOUBLE SHOTGUN

Gauge: 10, 12, 20, 28, 410 (3" chambers; 28 has 2-3/4"). **Barrel:** 32" (Mod. & Mod.), 28, 30" (Mod. & Full), 26" (Imp. Cyl. & Mod.) 410 (Full & Full). **Weight:** 6 lbs. to 11.4 lbs. **Stock:** Checkered walnut pistol grip and forend. **Features:** Silvered, engraved receiver; gold single selective trigger in 10-, 12, and 20 ga.; double triggers in 28 and 410; automatic safety; gold bead front sight. Introduced 1997. Imported from Spain by K.B.I., Inc.

Price: 10 ga.	**$984.95**
Price: 12 or 20 ga.	**$809.95**
Price: 28 ga.	**$854.95**
Price: 410-bore	**$854.95**
Price: As above, 12 or 20 AE. MC	**$939.95**

CHARLES DALY DIAMOND DL DOUBLE SHOTGUN

Gauge: 12, 20, 410, 3" chambers, 28, 2-3/4" chambers. **Barrel:** 28" (Mod. & Full), 26" (Imp. Cyl. & Mod.), 26" (Full & Full, 410). **Weight:** About 5-7 lbs. **Stock:** Select fancy European walnut, English-style butt, beavertail forend; hand-checkered, hand-rubbed oil finish. **Features:** Drop-forged action with gas escape valves; demiblock barrels with concave rib; selective automatic ejectors; hand-detachable double safety sidelocks with hand-engraved rose and scrollwork. Hinged front trigger. Color case-hardened receiver. Introduced 1997. Imported from Spain by K.B.I., Inc.

Price: 12 or 20	**$6,959.95**
Price: 28	**$7,274.95**
Price: 410	**$7,274.95**

DAKOTA PREMIER GRADE SHOTGUNS

Gauge: 12, 16, 20, 28, 410. **Barrel:** 27". **Weight:** NA. **Length:** NA. **Stock:** Exhibition-grade English walnut, hand-rubbed oil finish with straight grip and splinter forend. **Features:** French grey finish; 50 percent coverage engraving; double triggers; selective ejectors. Finished to customer specifications. Made in U.S. by Dakota Arms.

Price: 12, 16, 20 gauge	**$13,950.00**
Price: 28 and 410 gauge	**$15,345.00**

Dakota The Dakota Legend Shotguns

Similar to Premier Grade except has special selection English walnut, full-coverage scroll engraving, oak and leather case. Made in U.S. by Dakota Arms.

Price: 12, 16, 20 gauge	**$18,000.00**
Price: 28 and 410 gauge	**$19,800.00**

SHOTGUNS

SHOTGUNS — SIDE BY SIDES

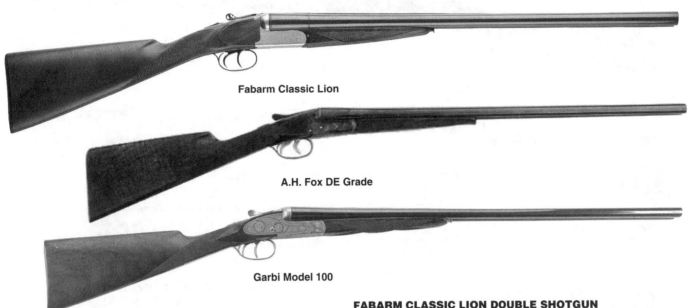

Fabarm Classic Lion

A.H. Fox DE Grade

Garbi Model 100

EAA/BAIKAL BOUNTY HUNTER IZH-43K SHOTGUN

Gauge: 12 (2-3/4", 3" chambers), 20 (3" chambers), 28 (2-3/4" chambers), 410 (3" chambers). **Barrel:** 18-1/2", 20", 24", 26", 28", three choke tubes. **Weight:** 7.28 lbs. Overall **length:** NA. **Stock:** Walnut, checkered forearm and grip. **Features:** Machined receiver; hammer-forged barrels with chrome-line bores; external hammers; double triggers (single, selective trigger available); rifle barrel inserts optional. Imported by European American Armory.
Price: IZH-43K (12 gauge) $439.00
Price: IZH-43K (20, 28 and 410 gauge) $469.00

EAA/BAIKAL IZH-43 BOUNTY HUNTER SHOTGUNS

Gauge: 12 (2-3/4", 3" chambers), 16 (2-3/4" chambers), 20 (2-3/4" and 3" chambers). **Barrel:** 20", 24", 26", 28"; imp., mod. and full choke tubes. **Weight:** NA. **Stock:** Hardwood or walnut; checkered forend and grip. **Features:** Hammer forged barrel; internal hammers; extractors; engraved receiver; automatic tang safety; non-glare rib. Imported by European American Armory.
Price: IZH-43 Bounty Hunter (12 gauge, 2-3/4" chambers, 20" brl., dbl. triggers, hardwood stock) $299.00
Price: IZH-43 Bounty Hunter (12 or 20 gauge, 2-3/4" chambers, 20" brl., dbl. triggers, walnut stock) $359.00

EAA/BAIKAL MP-213 SHOTGUN

Gauge: 12, 3" chambers. **Barrel:** 24", 26", 28"; imp., mod. and full choke tubes. **Weight:** 7.28 lbs. **Stock:** Walnut, checkered forearm and grip; rubber butt pad. **Features:** Hammer-forged barrels; chrome-lined bores; machined receiver; double trigger (each trigger fires both barrels independently); ejectors. Introduced 2000. Imported by European American Armory.
Price: IZH-213 . . . . $899.00

EAA/BAIKAL BOUNTY HUNTER MP-213 COACH GUN

Gauge: 12, 2-3/4" chambers. **Barrel:** 20", imp., mod. and full choke tubes. **Weight:** 7 lbs. **Stock:** Walnut, checkered forend and grip. **Features:** Selective double trigger with removable assembly (single trigger and varied pull weights available); ejectors; engraved receiver. Imported by European American Armory.
Price: MP-213 . . . . $899.00

E.M.F. HARTFORD MODEL COWBOY SHOTGUN

Gauge: 12. **Barrel:** 20". **Weight:** NA. **Length:** NA. **Stock:** Checkered walnut. **Sights:** Center bead. **Features:** Exposed hammers; color-case hardened receiver; blued barrel. Introduced 2001. Imported from Spain by E.M.F. Co. Inc.
Price: $625.00

FABARM CLASSIC LION DOUBLE SHOTGUN

Gauge: 12, 3" chambers. **Barrel:** 26" (Cyl., Imp. Cyl., Mod., Imp. Mod., Full choke tubes). **Weight:** 7.2 lbs. **Length:** 47.6" overall. **Stock:** English-style oil-finished European walnut. **Features:** Boxlock action with double triggers, automatic ejectors, automatic safety. Introduced 1998. Imported from Italy by Heckler & Koch, Inc.
Price: Grade I $1,499.00
Price: Grade II $2,249.00

A.H. FOX SIDE-BY-SIDE SHOTGUNS

Gauge: 16, 20, 28, 410. **Barrel:** Length and chokes to customer specifications. Rust-blued Chromox or Krupp steel. **Weight:** 5-1/2 to 6-3/4 lbs. **Stock:** Dimensions to customer specifications. Hand-checkered Turkish Circassian walnut with hand-rubbed oil finish. Straight, semi or full pistol grip; splinter, Schnabel or beavertail forend; traditional pad, hard rubber buttplate or skeleton butt. **Features:** Boxlock action with automatic ejectors; double or Fox single selective trigger. Scalloped, rebated and color case-hardened receiver; hand finished and hand-engraved. Grades differ in engraving, inlays, grade of wood, amount of hand finishing. Add $1,500 for 28 or 410-bore. Introduced 1993. Made in U.S. by Connecticut Shotgun Mfg.
Price: CE Grade $11,000.00
Price: XE Grade $12,500.00
Price: DE Grade $15,000.00
Price: FE Grade $20,000.00
Price: Exhibition Grade $30,000.00
Price: 28/410 CE Grade $12,500.00
Price: 28/410 XE Grade $14,000.00
Price: 28/410 DE Grade $16,500.00
Price: 28/410 FE Grade $21,500.00
Price: 28/410 Exhibition Grade $30,000.00

GARBI MODEL 100 DOUBLE

Gauge: 12, 16, 20, 28. **Barrel:** 26", 28", choked to customer specs. **Weight:** 5-1/2 to 7-1/2 lbs. **Stock:** 14-1/2"x2-1/4"x1-1/2". European walnut. Straight grip, checkered butt, classic forend. **Features:** Sidelock action, automatic ejectors, double triggers standard. Color case-hardened action, coin finish optional. Single trigger; beavertail forend, etc. optional. Five other models are available. Imported from Spain by Wm. Larkin Moore.
Price: From $3,700.00

Garbi Model 200 Side-by-Side

Similar to the Garbi Model 100 except has heavy-duty locks, magnum proofed. Very fine Continental-style floral and scroll engraving, well figured walnut stock. Other mechanical features remain the same. Imported from Spain by Wm. Larkin Moore.
Price: $10,000.00

SHOTGUNS

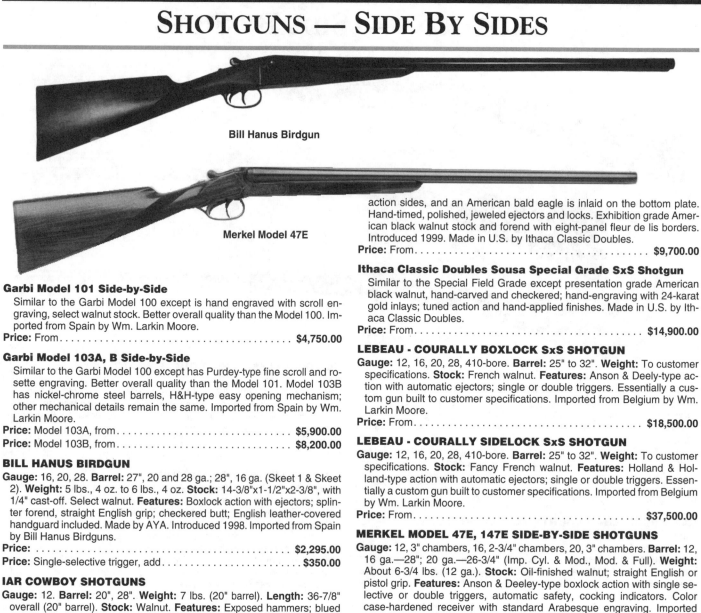

Bill Hanus Birdgun

Merkel Model 47E

Garbi Model 101 Side-by-Side

Similar to the Garbi Model 100 except is hand engraved with scroll engraving, select walnut stock. Better overall quality than the Model 100. Imported from Spain by Wm. Larkin Moore.
Price: From. **$4,750.00**

Garbi Model 103A, B Side-by-Side

Similar to the Garbi Model 100 except has Purdey-type fine scroll and rosette engraving. Better overall quality than the Model 101. Model 103B has nickel-chrome steel barrels, H&H-type easy opening mechanism; other mechanical details remain the same. Imported from Spain by Wm. Larkin Moore.
Price: Model 103A, from. **$5,900.00**
Price: Model 103B, from. **$8,200.00**

BILL HANUS BIRDGUN

Gauge: 16, 20, 28. **Barrel:** 27", 20 and 28 ga.; 28", 16 ga. (Skeet 1 & Skeet 2). **Weight:** 5 lbs., 4 oz. to 6 lbs., 4 oz. **Stock:** 14-3/8"x1-1/2"x2-3/8", with 1/4" cast-off. Select walnut. **Features:** Boxlock action with ejectors; splinter forend, straight English grip; checkered butt; English leather-covered handguard included. Made by AYA. Introduced 1998. Imported from Spain by Bill Hanus Birdguns.
Price: **$2,295.00**
Price: Single-selective trigger, add. **$350.00**

IAR COWBOY SHOTGUNS

Gauge: 12. **Barrel:** 20", 28". **Weight:** 7 lbs. (20" barrel). **Length:** 36-7/8" overall (20" barrel). **Stock:** Walnut. **Features:** Exposed hammers; blued or brown barrels; double triggers. Introduced 1997. Imported from Italy by IAR, Inc.
Price: Gentry model, 20" or 28", engraved, bright-finished locks, blue barrels **$1,895.00**
Price: Cowboy model, 20" or 28", no engraving on color case-hardened locks, brown patina barrels. **$1,895.00**

ITHACA CLASSIC DOUBLES SPECIAL FIELD GRADE SxS

Gauge: 20, 28, 2-3/4" chambers, 410, 3". **Barrel:** 26", 28", 30", fixed chokes. **Weight:** 5 lbs., 14 oz. (20 gauge). **Stock:** 14-1/2"x2-1/4"x1-3/8". High-grade American black walnut, hand-rubbed oil finish; splinter or beavertail forend, straight or pistol grip. **Features:** Double triggers, ejectors; color case-hardened, engraved action body with matted top surfaces. Introduced 1999. Made in U.S. by Ithaca Classic Doubles.
Price: From. **$3,150.00**

Ithaca Classic Doubles Grade 4E Classic SxS Shotgun

Similar to the Special Field Grade except has gold-plated triggers, jeweled barrel flats and hand-turned locks. Feather crotch and flame-grained black walnut is hand-checkered 28 lpi with fleur de lis pattern. Action body is engraved with three game scenes and bank note scroll, and color case-hardened. Introduced 1999. Made in U.S. by Ithaca Classic Doubles.
Price: From. **$4,900.00**

Ithaca Classic Doubles Grade 7E Classic SxS Shotgun

Similar to the Special Field Grade except engraved with bank note scroll and flat 24k gold game scenes: gold setter and gold pointer on opposite action sides, and an American bald eagle is inlaid on the bottom plate. Hand-timed, polished, jeweled ejectors and locks. Exhibition grade American black walnut stock and forend with eight-panel fleur de lis borders. Introduced 1999. Made in U.S. by Ithaca Classic Doubles.
Price: From. **$9,700.00**

Ithaca Classic Doubles Sousa Special Grade SxS Shotgun

Similar to the Special Field Grade except presentation grade American black walnut, hand-carved and checkered; hand-engraving with 24-karat gold inlays; tuned action and hand-applied finishes. Made in U.S. by Ithaca Classic Doubles.
Price: From. **$14,900.00**

LEBEAU - COURALLY BOXLOCK SxS SHOTGUN

Gauge: 12, 16, 20, 28, 410-bore. **Barrel:** 25" to 32". **Weight:** To customer specifications. **Stock:** French walnut. **Features:** Anson & Deely-type action with automatic ejectors; single or double triggers. Essentially a custom gun built to customer specifications. Imported from Belgium by Wm. Larkin Moore.
Price: From. **$18,500.00**

LEBEAU - COURALLY SIDELOCK SxS SHOTGUN

Gauge: 12, 16, 20, 28, 410-bore. **Barrel:** 25" to 32". **Weight:** To customer specifications. **Stock:** Fancy French walnut. **Features:** Holland & Holland-type action with automatic ejectors; single or double triggers. Essentially a custom gun built to customer specifications. Imported from Belgium by Wm. Larkin Moore.
Price: From. **$37,500.00**

MERKEL MODEL 47E, 147E SIDE-BY-SIDE SHOTGUNS

Gauge: 12, 3" chambers, 16, 2-3/4" chambers, 20, 3" chambers. **Barrel:** 12, 16 ga.—28"; 20 ga.—26-3/4" (Imp. Cyl. & Mod., Mod. & Full). **Weight:** About 6-3/4 lbs. (12 ga.). **Stock:** Oil-finished walnut; straight English or pistol grip. **Features:** Anson & Deeley-type boxlock action with single selective or double triggers, automatic safety, cocking indicators. Color case-hardened receiver with standard Arabesque engraving. Imported from Germany by GSI.
Price: Model 47E (H&H ejectors) **$2,795.00**
Price: Model 147E (as above with ejectors) **$3,395.00**

Merkel Model 47SL, 147SL Side-by-Sides

Similar to the Model 122 except with Holland & Holland-style sidelock action with cocking indicators, ejectors. Silver-grayed receiver and sideplates have Arabesque engraving, engraved border and screws (Model 47S), or fine hunting scene engraving (Model 147S). Imported from Germany by GSI.
Price: Model 47SL **$5,395.00**
Price: Model 147SL **$6,995.00**
Price: Model 247SL (English-style engraving, large scrolls) . . . **$6,995.00**
Price: Model 447SL (English-style engraving, small scrolls) . . . **$8,995.00**

Merkel Model 280EL and 360EL Shotguns

Similar to Model 47E except has smaller frame. Greener cross bolt with double under-barrel locking lugs, fine engraved hunting scenes on silver-grayed receiver, luxury-grade wood, Anson and Deely box-lock action. Holland & Holland ejectors, single-selective or double triggers. Introduced 2000. From Merkel.
Price: Model 280EL (28 gauge, 28" barrel, imp. cyl. and mod. chokes) 4 mod. chokes) **$4,995.00**
Price: Model 360EL (410 gauge, 28" barrel, mod. and full chokes). **$4,995.00**
Price: Model 280/360EL two-barrel set (28 and 410 gauge as above) **$7,495.00**

SHOTGUNS

SHOTGUNS — SIDE BY SIDES

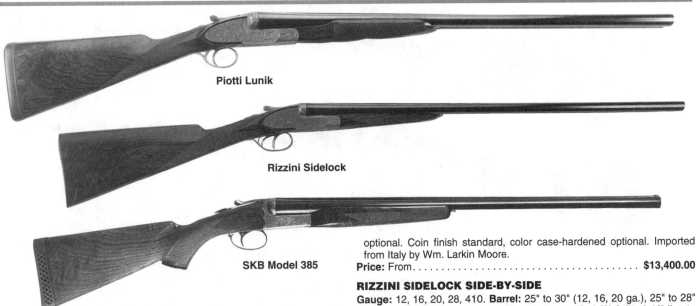

Piotti Lunik

Rizzini Sidelock

SKB Model 385

Merkel Model 280SL and 360SL Shotguns

Similar to Model 280EL and 360EL except has sidelock action, double triggers, English-style Arabesque engraving. Introduced 2000. From Merkel.
Price: Model 280SL (28 gauge, 28" barrel, imp. cyl. and
mod. chokes) **$7,495.00**
Price: Model 360SL (410 gauge, 28" barrel, mod. and
full chokes) **$7,495.00**
Price: Model 280/360SL two-barrel set **$10,995.00**

PIOTTI KING NO. 1 SIDE-BY-SIDE

Gauge: 12, 16, 20, 28, 410. **Barrel:** 25" to 30" (12 ga.), 25" to 28" (16, 20, 28, 410). To customer specs. Chokes as specified. **Weight:** 6-1/2 lbs. to 8 lbs. (12 ga. to customer specs.). **Stock:** Dimensions to customer specs. Finely figured walnut; straight grip with checkered butt with classic splinter forend and hand-rubbed oil finish standard. Pistol grip, beavertail forend. **Features:** Holland & Holland pattern sidelock action, automatic ejectors. Double trigger; non-selective single trigger optional. Coin finish standard; color case-hardened optional. Top rib; level, file-cut; concave, ventilated optional. Very fine, full coverage scroll engraving with small floral bouquets. Imported from Italy by Wm. Larkin Moore.
Price: From **$20,900.00**

Piotti King Extra Side-by-Side

Similar to the Piotti King No. 1 except with upgraded engraving. Choice of any type of engraving, including bulino game scene engraving and game scene engraving with gold inlays. Engraved and signed by a master engraver. Other mechanical specifications remain the same. Imported from Italy by Wm. Larkin Moore.
Price: From **$25,900.00**

Piotti Lunik Side-by-Side

Similar to the Piotti King No. 1 in overall quality. Has Renaissance-style large scroll engraving in relief. Best quality Holland & Holland-pattern sidelock ejector double with chopper lump (demi-bloc) barrels. Other mechanical specifications remain the same. Imported from Italy by Wm. Larkin Moore.
Price: From **$21,900.00**

PIOTTI PIUMA SIDE-BY-SIDE

Gauge: 12, 16, 20, 28, 410. **Barrel:** 25" to 30" (12 ga.), 25" to 28" (16, 20, 28, 410). **Weight:** 5-1/2 to 6-1/4 lbs. (20 ga.). **Stock:** Dimensions to customer specs. Straight grip stock with walnut checkered butt, classic splinter forend, hand-rubbed oil finish are standard; pistol grip, beavertail forend, satin luster finish optional. **Features:** Anson & Deeley boxlock ejector double with chopper lump barrels. Level, file-cut rib, light scroll and rosette engraving, scalloped frame. Double triggers; single non-selective

optional. Coin finish standard, color case-hardened optional. Imported from Italy by Wm. Larkin Moore.
Price: From **$13,400.00**

RIZZINI SIDELOCK SIDE-BY-SIDE

Gauge: 12, 16, 20, 28, 410. **Barrel:** 25" to 30" (12, 16, 20 ga.), 25" to 28" (28, 410). To customer specs. Chokes as specified. **Weight:** 6-1/2 lbs. to 8 lbs. (12 ga. to customer specs). **Stock:** Dimensions to customer specs. Finely figured walnut; straight grip with checkered butt with classic splinter forend and hand-rubbed oil finish standard. Pistol grip, beavertail forend. **Features:** Sidelock action, auto ejectors. Double triggers or non-selective single trigger standard. Coin finish standard. Imported from Italy by Wm. Larkin Moore.
Price: 12, 20 ga., from **$52,000.00**
Price: 28, 410 bore, from **$60,000.00**

SKB Model 385 Sporting Clays

Similar to the Field Model 385 except 12 gauge only; 28" barrel with choke tubes; raised ventilated rib with metal middle bead and white front. Stock dimensions 14-1/4"x1-7/16"x1-7/8". Introduced 1998. Imported from Japan by G.U. Inc.
Price: **$2,159.00**
Price: Sporting Clays set, 20, 28 ga. **$3,059.00**

SKB MODEL 385 SIDE-BY-SIDE

Gauge: 12, 20, 3" chambers; 28, 2-3/4" chambers. **Barrel:** 26" (Imp. Cyl., Mod., Skeet choke tubes). **Weight:** 6-3/4 lbs. **Length:** 42-1/2" overall. **Stock:** 14-1/8"x1-1/2"x2-1/2" American walnut with straight or pistol grip stock, semi-beavertail forend. **Features:** Boxlock action. Silver nitrided receiver with engraving; solid barrel rib; single selective trigger, selective automatic ejectors, automatic safety. Introduced 1996. Imported from Japan by G.U. Inc.
Price: **$2,049.00**
Price: Field Set, 20, 28 ga., 26" or 28", English or pistol grip . . . **$2,929.00**

SKB Model 485 Side-by-Side

Similar to the Model 385 except has dummy sideplates, raised ventilated rib with metal middle bead and white front, extensive upland game scene engraving, semi-fancy American walnut English or pistol grip stock. Imported from Japan by G.U. Inc.
Price: **$2,769.00**
Price: Field set, 20, 28 ga., 26" **$2,769.00**

STOEGER/IGA UPLANDER SIDE-BY-SIDE SHOTGUN

Gauge: 12, 20, 28, 2-3/4" chambers; 410, 3" chambers. **Barrel:** 26" (Full & Full, 410 only, Imp. Cyl. & Mod.), 28" (Mod. & Full). **Weight:** 6-3/4 lbs. to 7 lbs. **Stock:** 14-1/2"x1-1/2"x2-1/2". Oil-finished hardwood. Checkered pistol grip and forend. **Features:** Automatic safety, extractors only, solid matted barrel rib. Double triggers only. Introduced 1983. Imported from Brazil by Stoeger Industries.
Price: **$437.00**
Price: With choke tubes **$477.00**
Price: Coach Gun, 12, 20, 410, 20" bbls. **$415.00**
Price: Coach Gun, nickel finish, black stock. **$464.00**
Price: Coach Gun, engraved stock. **$479.00**

SHOTGUNS — SIDE BY SIDES

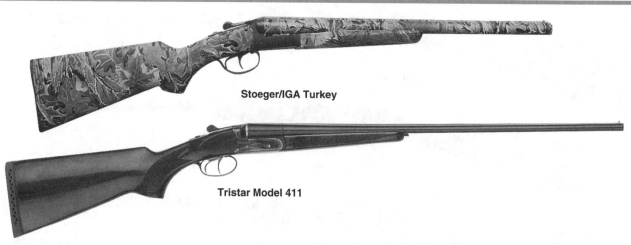

Stoeger/IGA Turkey

Tristar Model 411

Stoeger/IGA Ladies Side-by-Side
Similar to the Uplander except in 20 ga. only with 24" barrels (Imp. Cyl. & Mod. choke tubes), 13" length of pull, ventilated rubber recoil pad. Has extractors, double triggers, automatic safety. Introduced 1996. Imported from Brazil by Stoeger.
Price: **$489.00**

Stoeger/IGA Turkey Side-by-Side
Similar to the Uplander Model except has Advantage camouflage on stock, forend and barrels; 12 gauge only with 3" chambers, and has 24" choke tube barrels. Overall length 40". Introduced 1997. Imported from Brazil by Stoeger.
Price: **$559.00**

Stoeger/IGA English Stock Side-by-Side
Similar to the Uplander except in 410 or 20 ga. only with 24" barrels, straight English stock and beavertail forend. Has automatic safety, extractors, double triggers. Intro 1996. Imported from Brazil by Stoeger.
Price: 410 ga (mod. and mod. chokes). **$437.00**
Price: 20 ga (imp. cyl and mod. choke tubes) **$477.00**

Stoeger/IGA Youth Side-by-Side
Similar to the Uplander except in 410-bore with 24" barrels (Mod.), or 20 ga. (imp. cyl. and mod.), 13" length of pull, ventilated recoil pad. Has double triggers, extractors, auto safety. Intro 1996. Imported from Brazil by Stoeger.
Price: 410 gauge **$449.00**
Price: 20 gauge **$449.00**

Stoeger/IGA Coach and Deluxe Coach Gun
Similar to the Uplander except 12, 20 or 410 gauges, 20" barrels, choked Imp. Cyl. & Mod., 3" chambers; hardwood pistol grip stock with checkering; double triggers; extractors. Introduced 1997. Imported form Brazil by Stoeger.
Price: Coach Gun **$415.00**
Price: Deluxe Coach Gun (engraved stagecoach on stock). **$415.00**

Stoeger/IGA Uplander Shotgun
Gauge: 12, 20, 410 (3" chambers); 28 (2-3/4" chambers). **Barrel:** 24", 26", 28". **Weight:** 6-3/4 lbs. **Length:** 40" to 44" overall. **Stock:** Brazilian hardwood; checkered grip and forearm. **Feautures:** Automatic safety; extractors; handles steel shot. Introduced 1997. Imported from Brazil by Stoeger.
Price: With chokes tubes **$477.00**

Stoeger/IGA Deluxe Uplander Supreme Shotgun
Similar to the Uplander except with semi-fancy American walnut with thin black Pachmayr rubber recoil pad, matte lacquer finish. Choke tubes and 3" chambers standard 12 and 20 gauge; 28 gauge has 26", 3" chokes, fixed Mod. & Full. Double gold plated triggers; extractors. Introduced 1997. Imported from Brazil by Stoeger.
Price: 12, 20 . . . . **$599.00**

TRADITIONS ELITE SERIES SIDE-BY-SIDE SHOTGUNS
Gauge: 12, 3"; 20, 3"; 28, 2-3/4"; 410, 3". **Barrel:** 26". **Weight:** 5 lbs., 12 oz. to 6-1/2 lbs. **Length:** 43" overall. **Stock:** Walnut. **Features:** Chrome-lined barrels; fixed chokes (Elite Field III ST, Field I DT and Field I ST) or choke tubes (Elite Hunter ST); extractors (Hunter ST and Field I models) or automatic ejectors (Field III ST); top tang safety. Imported from Fausti of Italy by Traditions.
Price: (Elite Field I DT — 12, 20, 28 or 410 ga.; I.C. and Mod. fixed chokes [F and F on 410]; double triggers) . . . . **$759.00 to $819.00**
Price: (Elite Field I ST — 12, 20, 28 or 410 ga.; same as DT but with single trigger) . . . . **$889.00 to $949.00**
Price: (Elite Field III ST — 28 or 410 ga.; gold-engraved receiver; high-grade walnut stock) **$1,999.00**
Price: (Elite Hunter ST — 12 or 20 ga.; blued receiver; I.C. and Mod. choke tubes) **$949.00**

TRISTAR ROTA MODEL 411 SIDE-BY-SIDE
Gauge: 12, 16, 20, 410, 3" chambers; 28, 2-3/4". **Barrel:** 12 ga., 26", 28"; 16, 20, 28 ga., 410-bore, 26"; 12 and 20 ga. have three choke tubes, 16, 28 (Imp. Cyl. & Mod.), 410 (Mod. & Full) fixed chokes. **Weight:** 6-6-3/4 lbs. **Stock:** 14-3/8" l.o.p. Standard walnut with pistol grip, splinter-style forend; hand checkered. **Features:** Engraved, color case-hardened boxlock action; double triggers, extractors; solid barrel rib. Introduced 1998. Imported from Italy by Tristar Sporting Arms, Ltd.
Price: **$745.00**

Tristar Rota Model 411D Side-by-Side
Similar to the Model 411 except has automatic ejectors, straight English-style stock, single trigger. Solid barrel rib with matted surface; chrome bores; color case-hardened frame; splinter forend. Introduced 1999. Imported from Italy by Tristar Sporting Arms, Ltd.
Price: **$1,110.00**

Tristar Rota Model 411R Coach Gun Side-by-Side
Similar to the Model 411 except in 12 or 20 gauge only with 20" barrels and fixed chokes (Cyl. & Cyl.). Has double triggers, extractors, choke tubes. Introduced 1999. Imported from Italy by Tristar Sporting Arms, Ltd.
Price: **$745.00**

Tristar Rota Model 411F Side-by-Side
Similar to the Model 411 except has silver, engraved receiver, ejectors, IC, M and F choke tubes, English-style stock. Imported from Italy by Tristar Sporting Arms Ltd.
Price: **$1,602.00**

Variety of designs for utility and sporting purposes, as well as for competitive shooting.

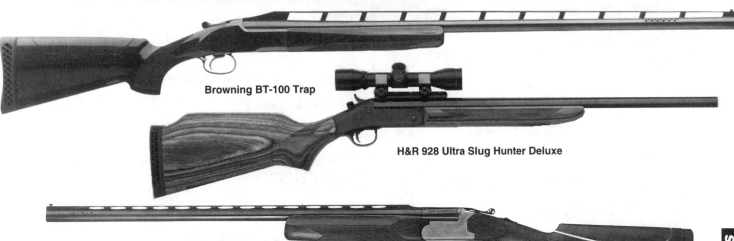

Browning BT-100 Trap

H&R 928 Ultra Slug Hunter Deluxe

Fabarm Monotrap

BERETTA DT 10 TRIDENT TRAP TOP SINGLE SHOTGUN

Gauge: 12, 3" chamber. **Barrel:** 34"; five Optima Choke tubes (full, full, imp. modified, mod. and imp. cyl.). **Weight:** 8.8 lbs. **Length:** NA. **Stock:** High-grade walnut; adjustable. **Features:** Detachable, adjustable trigger group; Optima Bore for improved shot pattern and reduced recoil; slim Optima Choke tubes; raised and thickened receiver for long life. Introduced 2000. Imported from Italy by Beretta USA.
Price: **$9,450.00**

BRNO ZBK 100 SINGLE BARREL SHOTGUN

Gauge: 12 or 20. **Barrel:** 27.5". **Weight:** 5.5 lbs. **Length:** 44" overall. **Stock:** Beech. **Features:** Polished blue finish; sling swivels. Announced 1998. Imported from The Czech Republic by Euro-Imports.
Price: **$185.00**

BROWNING BT-99 TRAP SHOTGUN

Gauge: 12, 2-3/4" chamber. **Barrel:** 32" or 34"; Invector choke system (full choke tube only included); High Post Rib; back-bored. **Weight:** 8 lbs., 10 oz. (34" bbl.). **Length:** 50-1/2" overall (34" bbl.). **Stock:** Conventional or adjustable-comb. **Features:** Re-introduction of the BT-99 Trap Shotgun. Full beavertail forearm; checkered walnut stock; ejector; rubber butt pad. Re-introduced 2001. Imported by Browning.
Price: Conventional stock, 32" or 34" barrel................ **$1,216.00**
Price: Adj.-comb stock, 32" or 34" barrel **$1,449.00**

BROWNING BT-100 TRAP SHOTGUN

Gauge: 12, 2-3/4" chamber. **Barrel:** 32", 34" (Invector Plus); back-bored; also with fixed Full choke. **Weight:** 8 lbs., 10 oz. (34" bbl.). **Length:** 48-1/2" overall (32" barrel). **Stock:** 14-3/8"x1-9/16"x1-7/16x2" (Monte Carlo); 14-3/8"x1-3/4"x1-1/4"x2-1/8" (thumbhole). Walnut with high gloss finish; cut checkering. Wedge-shaped forend with finger groove. **Features:** Available in stainless steel or blue. Has drop-out trigger adjustable for weight of pull from 3-1/2 to 5-1/2 lbs., and for three length positions; Ejector-Selector allows ejection or extraction of shells. Available with adjustable comb stock and thumbhole style. Introduced 1995. Imported from Japan by Browning.
Price: Grade I, blue, Monte Carlo, Invector Plus **$2,222.00**
Price: Grade I, blue, adj. comb, Invector Plus **$2,455.00**
Price: Stainless steel, Monte Carlo, Invector Plus **$2,688.00**
Price: Stainless steel, adj. comb, Invector Plus **$2,923.00**

EAA/BAIKAL IZH-18 SINGLE BARREL SHOTGUN

Gauge: 12 (2-3/4" and 3" chambers), 20 (2-3/4" and 3"), 16 (2-3/4"), 410 (3"). **Barrel:** 26-1/2", 28-1/2"; modified or full choke (12 and 20 gauge); full only (16 gauge), improved cylinder (20 gauge) and full or improved modified (410). **Weight:** NA. **Stock:** Walnut-stained hardwood; rubber recoil pad. **Features:** Hammer-forged steel barrel; machined receiver; cross-block safety; cocking lever with external cocking indicator; optional automatic ejector; screw-in chokes and rifle barrel. Imported by European American Armory.
Price: IZH-18 (12, 16, 20 or 410) **$95.00**
Price: IZH-18 (20 gauge with imp. cyl. or 410 with imp. mod.).... **$109.00**

EAA/BAIKAL IZH-18MAX SINGLE BARREL SHOTGUN

Gauge: 12, 3"; 20, 3"; 410, 3". **Barrel:** 24" (410), 26" (410 or 20 ga.) or 28" (12 ga.). **Weight:** 6.4 to 6.6 lbs. **Length:** NA. **Stock:** Walnut. **Features:** Polished nickel receiver; ventilated rib; I.C., Mod. and Full choke tubes; titanium-coated trigger; internal hammer; selectable ejector/extractor; rubber butt pad; decocking system. Imported by European American Armory.
Price: (12 or 20 ga., choke tubes) **$169.00**
Price: (410 ga., full choke only) **$189.00**

FABARM MONOTRAP SHOTGUN

Caliber: 12; 2-3/4" chamber. **Barrel:** 30", 34". **Weight:** 6.7 to 6.9 lbs. **Length:** 48.5" overall (30" bbl.) **Stock:** Walnut; adjustable comb competition-style. **Sights:** Red front sight bar, mid-rib bead. **Features:** Built on 20-gauge receiver for quick handling. Silver receiver with blued barrel; special trap rib (micrometer adjustable); includes three choke tubes (M, IM, F). Introduced 2000.
Price: **$1,799.00**

HARRINGTON & RICHARDSON NWTF SHOTGUNS

Gauge: 12, 3-1/2" chamber, fixed full choke; 20, 3" chamber, fixed modified choke. **Barrel:** 24" (12 ga.) or 22" (20 ga.) **Weight:** 5 to 6 lbs. **Length:** NA. **Stock:** Straight-grip camo laminate with recoil pad and sling swivel studs. **Sights:** Bead front. **Features:** Break-open single-shot action with side lever release; hand-checkered stock and forearm; includes trigger lock. Purchase supports National Wild Turkey Federation; NWTF logo on receiver.
Price: 12 ga. **$176.95**
Price: 20 ga. youth gun (12-1/2" length of pull, weighs 5 lbs.) **$169.95**

HARRINGTON & RICHARDSON SB2-980 ULTRA SLUG

Gauge: 12, 20, 3" chamber. **Barrel:** 22" (20 ga. Youth) 24", fully rifled. **Weight:** 9 lbs. **Length:** NA. **Stock:** Walnut-stained hardwood. **Sights:** None furnished; comes with scope mount. **Features:** Uses the H&R 10 gauge action with heavy-wall barrel. Monte Carlo stock has sling swivels; comes with black nylon sling. Introduced 1995. Made in U.S. by H&R 1871, LLC.
Price: **$209.95**

Harrington & Richardson Model 928 Ultra Slug Hunter Deluxe

Similar to the SB2-980 Ultra Slug except uses 12 gauge action and 12 gauge barrel blank bored to 20 gauge, then fully rifled with 1:35" twist. Has hand-checkered camo laminate Monte Carlo stock and forend. Comes with Weaver-style scope base, offset hammer extension, ventilated recoil pad, sling swivels and nylon sling. Introduced 1997. Made in U.S. by H&R 1871 LLC.
Price: **$255.95**

Krieghoff KS-5 Trap

Ljutic Mono Gun

Marlin 25MG Garden

HARRINGTON & RICHARDSON TAMER SHOTGUN

Gauge: 410, 3" chamber. **Barrel:** 20" (Full). **Weight:** 5-6 lbs. **Length:** 33" overall. **Stock:** Thumbhole grip of high density black polymer. **Features:** Uses H&R Topper action with matte electroless nickel finish. Stock holds four spare shotshells. Introduced 1994. From H&R 1871, LLC.

Price: $124.95

HARRINGTON & RICHARDSON TOPPER MODEL 098

Gauge: 12, 16, 20, 28 (2-3/4"), 410, 3" chamber. **Barrel:** 12 ga.—28" (Mod., Full); 16 ga.— 28" (Mod.); 20 ga.—26" (Mod.); 28 ga.—26" (Mod.); 410 bore—26" (Full). **Weight:** 5-6 lbs. **Stock:** Black-finish hardwood with full pistol grip; semi-beavertail forend. **Sights:** Gold bead front. **Features:** Break-open action with side-lever release, automatic ejector. Satin nickel frame, blued barrel. Reintroduced 1992. From H&R 1871, LLC.

Price: $116.95
Price: Topper Junior 098 (as above except 22" barrel, 20 ga. (Mod.), 410-bore (Full), 12-1/2" length of pull) $122.95

Harrington & Richardson Topper Deluxe Model 098

Similar to the standard Topper 098 except 12 gauge only with 3-1/2" chamber, 28" barrel with choke tube (comes with Mod. tube, others optional). Satin nickel frame, blued barrel, black-finished wood. Introduced 1992. From H&R 1871, LLC.

Price: $136.95

Harrington & Richardson Topper Junior Classic Shotgun

Similar to the Topper Junior 098 except available in 20 gauge (3", Mod.), 410-bore (Full) with 3" chamber; 28 gauge, 2-3/4" chamber (Mod.); all have 22" barrel. Stock is American black walnut with cut-checkered pistol grip and forend. Ventilated rubber recoil pad with white line spacers. Blued barrel, blued frame. Introduced 1992. From H&R 1871, LLC.

Price: $150.95

Harrington & Richardson Topper Deluxe Rifled Slug Gun

Similar to the 12 gauge Topper Model 098 except has fully rifled and ported barrel, ramp front sight and fully adjustable rear. Barrel twist is 1:35". Nickel-plated frame, blued barrel, black-finished stock and forend. Introduced 1995. Made in U.S. by H&R 1871, Inc.

Price: $169.95

KRIEGHOFF K-80 SINGLE BARREL TRAP GUN

Gauge: 12, 2-3/4" chamber. **Barrel:** 32" or 34" Unsingle; 34" Top Single. Fixed Full or choke tubes. **Weight:** About 8-3/4 lbs. **Stock:** Four stock dimensions or adjustable stock available. All hand-checkered European walnut. **Features:** Satin nickel finish with K-80 logo. Selective mechanical trigger adjustable for finger position. Tapered step vent. rib. Adjustable point of impact on Unsingle.

Price: Standard grade full Unsingle, from $7,950.00
Price: Standard grade full Top Single combo (special order), from $9,975.00
Price: RT (removable trigger) option, add $1,000.00

KRIEGHOFF KS-5 TRAP GUN

Gauge: 12, 2-3/4" chamber. **Barrel:** 32", 34"; Full choke or choke tubes. **Weight:** About 8-1/2 lbs. **Stock:** Choice of high Monte Carlo (1-1/2"), low Monte Carlo (1-3/8") or factory adjustable stock. European walnut. **Features:** Ventilated tapered step rib. Adjustable trigger or optional release trigger. Satin gray electroless nickel receiver. Comes with fitted aluminum case. Introduced 1988. Imported from Germany by Krieghoff International, Inc.

Price: Fixed choke, cased $3,695.00
Price: With choke tubes $4,120.00

Krieghoff KS-5 Special

Same as the KS-5 except the barrel has a fully adjustable rib and adjustable stock. Rib allows shooter to adjust point of impact from 50%/50% to nearly 90%/10%. Introduced 1990.

Price: $4,695.00

LJUTIC MONO GUN SINGLE BARREL

Gauge: 12 only. **Barrel:** 34", choked to customer specs; hollow-milled rib, 35-1/2" sight plane. **Weight:** Approx. 9 lbs. **Stock:** To customer specs. Oil finish, hand checkered. **Features:** Totally custom made. Pull or release trigger; removable trigger guard contains trigger and hammer mechanism; Ljutic pushbutton opener on front of trigger guard. From Ljutic Industries.

Price: With standard, medium or Olympic rib, custom 32"-34" bbls., and fixed choke. $5,795.00
Price: As above with screw-in choke barrel $6,095.00
Price: Stainless steel mono gun...................... $6,795.00

Ljutic LTX PRO 3 Deluxe Mono Gun

Deluxe light weight version of the Mono Gun with high quality wood, upgrade checkering, special rib height, screw in chokes, ported and cased.

Price: $8,995.00
Price: Stainless steel model......................... $9,995.00

MARLIN MODEL 25MG GARDEN GUN SHOTGUN

Gauge: 22 WMR shotshell, 7-shot magazine. **Barrel:** 22" smoothbore. **Weight:** 6 lbs. **Length:** 41" overall. **Stock:** Press-checkered hardwood. **Sights:** High-visibility bead front. **Features:** Bolt action; thumb safety; red cocking indicator. Introduced 1999. Made in U.S. by Marlin.

Price: $231.00

MARLIN MODEL 512P SLUGMASTER SHOTGUN

Gauge: 12, 3" chamber; 2-shot detachable box magazine. **Barrel:** 21", rifled (1:28" twist). **Weight:** 8 lbs. **Length:** 41-3/4" overall. **Stock:** Black fiberglass-filled synthetic stock with moulded-in checkering, swivel studs; ventilated recoil pad; padded black nylon sling. **Sights:** Ramp front with brass bead and removable Wide-Scan hood and fiber-optic inserts, adjustable fiber-optic rear. Drilled and tapped for scope mounting. **Features:** Uses Model 55 action with thumb safety. Designed for shooting saboted slugs. Comes with special Weaver scope mount. Introduced 1997. Made in U.S. by Marlin Firearms Co.

Price: $388.00

SHOTGUNS — BOLT ACTIONS & SINGLE SHOTS

Marlin 512P Slugmaster

Mossberg 695

**New England
Firearms
Camo Turkey**

MOSSBERG MODEL 695 SLUGSTER

Gauge: 12, 3" chamber. **Barrel:** 22"; fully rifled, ported. **Weight:** 7-1/2 lbs. **Stock:** Black synthetic, with swivel studs and rubber recoil pad. **Sights:** Blade front, folding rifle-style leaf rear; Fiber Optic. Comes with Weaver-style scope bases. **Features:** Matte metal finish; rotating thumb safety; detachable 2-shot magazine. Mossberg Cablelock. Made in U.S. by Mossberg. Introduced 1996.

Price: **$345.00**
Price: With Fiber Optic rifle sights **$367.00**
Price: With woodlands camo stock, Fiber Optic sights. **$397.00**

MOSSBERG SSi-ONE 12 GAUGE SLUG SHOTGUN

Gauge: 12, 3" chamber. **Barrel:** 24", fully rifled. **Weight:** 8 pounds. **Length:** 40" overall. **Stock:** Walnut, fluted and cut checkered; sling-swivel studs; drilled and tapped for scope base. **Sights:** None (scope base supplied). **Features:** Frame accepts interchangeable rifle barrels (see Mossberg SSi-One rifle listing); lever-opening, break-action design; ambidextrous, top-tang safety; internal eject/extract selector. Introduced 2000. From Mossberg.

Price: **$480.00**

Mossberg SSi-One Turkey Shotgun

Similar to SSi-One 12 gauge Slug Shotgun, but chambered for 12 ga., 3-1/2" loads. Includes Accu-Mag Turkey Tube. Introduced 2001. From Mossberg.

Price: **$459.00**

NEW ENGLAND FIREARMS CAMO TURKEY SHOTGUNS

Gauge: 10, 3-1/2 "; 12, 20, 3" chamber. **Barrel:** 24"; extra-full, screw-in choke tube (10 ga.); fixed full choke (12, 20). **Weight:** NA. **Stock:** American hardwood, green and black camouflage finish with sling swivels and ventilated recoil pad. **Sights:** Bead front. **Features:** Matte metal finish; stock counterweight to reduce recoil; patented transfer bar system for hammer-down safety; includes camo sling and trigger lock. Accepts other factory-fitted barrels. Introduced 2000. From New England Firearms.

Price: 10, 12 ga. **$205.95**
Price: 20 ga. youth model (22" bbl.) **$128.95**

NEW ENGLAND FIREARMS TRACKER SLUG GUN

Gauge: 12, 20, 3" chamber. **Barrel:** 24" (Cyl.). **Weight:** 5-1/4 lbs. **Length:** 40" overall. **Stock:** Walnut-finished hardwood with full pistol grip, recoil pad. **Sights:** Blade front, fully adjustable rifle-type rear. **Features:** Break-open action with side-lever release; blued barrel, color case-hardened frame. Introduced 1992. From New England Firearms.

Price: Tracker **$142.95**
Price: Tracker II (as above except fully rifled bore) **$150.95**

NEW ENGLAND FIREARMS SPECIAL PURPOSE SHOTGUNS

Gauge: 10, 3-1/2" chamber. **Barrel:** 28" (Full), 32" (Mod.). **Weight:** 9.5 lbs. **Length:** 44" overall (28" barrel). **Stock:** American hardwood with walnut or matte camo finish; ventilated rubber recoil pad. **Sights:** Bead front. **Features:** Break-open action with side-lever release; ejector. Matte finish on metal. Introduced 1992. From New England Firearms.

Price: Walnut-finish wood sling and swivels. **$168.95**
Price: Camo finish, sling and swivels **$183.95**
Price: Camo finish, 32", sling and swivels **$197.95**
Price: Black matte finish, 24", Turkey Full choke tube,
sling and swivels. **$199.95**

NEW ENGLAND FIREARMS SURVIVOR

Gauge: 12, 20, 410/45 Colt, 3" chamber. **Barrel:** 22" (Mod.); 20" (410/45 Colt, rifled barrel, choke tube). **Weight:** 6 lbs. **Length:** 36 overall. **Stock:** Black polymer with thumbhole/pistol grip, sling swivels; beavertail forend. **Sights:** Bead front. **Features:** Buttplate removes to expose storage for extra ammunition; forend also holds extra ammunition. Black or nickel finish. Introduced 1993. From New England Firearms.

Price: Black **$129.95**
Price: Nickel **$150.95**
Price: 410/45 Colt, black **$164.95**
Price: 410/45 Colt, nickel **$178.95**

NEW ENGLAND FIREARMS STANDARD PARDNER

Gauge: 12, 20, 410, 3" chamber; 16, 28, 2-3/4" chamber. **Barrel:** 12 ga.—28" (Full, Mod.), 32" (Full); 16 ga.—28" (Full); 20 ga.—26" (Full, Mod.); 28 ga.—26" (Mod.); 410-bore—26" (Full). **Weight:** 5-6 lbs. **Length:** 43" overall (28" barrel). **Stock:** Walnut-finished hardwood with full pistol grip. **Sights:** Bead front. **Features:** Transfer bar ignition; break-open action with side-lever release. Introduced 1987. From New England Firearms.

Price: **$106.95**
Price: Youth model (12, 20, 28 ga., 410, 22" barrel, recoil pad). . **$114.95**
Price: 12 ga., 32" (Full). **$119.95**

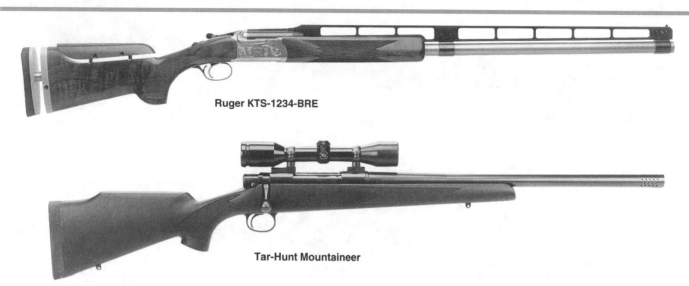

Ruger KTS-1234-BRE

Tar-Hunt Mountaineer

RUGER KTS-1234-BRE TRAP MODEL SINGLE-BARREL SHOTGUN

Gauge: 12, 2-3/4" chamber. **Barrel:** 34". **Weight:** 9 lbs. **Length:** 50 -1/2" overall. **Stock:** Select walnut checkered; adjustable pull length 13 -15". **Features:** Fully adjustable rib for pattern position; adjustable stock comb cast for right- or left-handed shooters; straight grooves the length of barrel to keep wad from rotating for pattern improvement. Full and modified choke tubes supplied. Gold inlaid eagle and Ruger name on receiver. Introduced 2000. From Sturm Ruger & Co.
Price: **$2,850.00**

ROSSI MODEL 12-G SHOTGUN

Gauge: 12, 20, 2-3/4" chamber; 410, 3" chamber. **Barrel:** 28". **Weight:** 5 lbs. **Length:** NA. **Stock:** Stained hardwood. **Features:** Spur hammer; intregral safety; ejector; spur hammer. Imported from Brazil by BrazTech/Taurus.
Price: **$99.00**
Price: Youth (shorter stock, 22" barrel) **$99.00**

ROSSI MATCHED PAIR SINGLE-SHOT SHOTGUN/RIFLE

NEW!
Gauge: 410, 20 or 12. **Barrel:** 22" (410 or 20 ga.), 28" (12 ga.). **Weight:** NA. **Length:** NA. **Stock:** Hardwood (brown or black finish). **Sights:** bead front. **Features:** Break-open breech with external hammer; transfer-bar manual safety; blued or stainless steel finish; sling-swivel studs; includes matched 22 LR or 22 WMR barrel with fully adjustable rear sight. Introduced 2001. Imported by BrazTech/Taurus.
Price: 22 LR/410-, 20- or 12-gauge, blued finish, brown hardwood stock
. . . . **$140.00**
Price: 22 LR/410-gauge, stainless finish, black hardwood stock . . **$170.00**
Price: 22 WMR/12-gauge, blued finish, brown hardwood stock . . . **$140.00**

SAVAGE MODEL 210F MASTER SHOT SLUG GUN

Gauge: 12, 3" chamber; 2-shot magazine. **Barrel:** 24" 1:35" rifling twist. **Weight:** 7-1/2 lbs. **Length:** 43.5" overall. **Stock:** Glass-filled polymer with positive checkering. **Features:** Based on the Savage Model 110 action; 60 bolt lift; controlled round feed; comes with scope mount. Introduced 1996. Made in U.S. by Savage Arms.
Price: **$402.00**

Savage Model 210FT Master Shot Shotgun

Similar to the Model 210F except has smoothbore barrel threaded for Winchoke-style choke tubes (comes with one Full tube); Advantage camo pattern covers the stock; pillar-bedded synthetic stock; bead front sight, U-notch rear. Introduced 1997. Made in U.S. by Savage Arms, Inc.
Price: **$466.00**

SNAKE CHARMER II SHOTGUN

Gauge: 410, 3" chamber. **Barrel:** 18-1/4". **Weight:** About 3-1/2 lbs. **Length:** 28-5/8" overall. **Stock:** ABS grade impact resistant plastic. **Fea-**tures: Thumbhole-type stock holds four extra rounds. Stainless steel barrel and frame. Reintroduced 1989. From Sporting Arms Mfg., Inc.
Price: **$149.00**
Price: Snake Charmer II Field Gun (as above except has conventional wood buttstock with 14" length of pull, 24" barrel 410 or 28 ga.) . **$160.00**
Price: New Generation Snake Charmer (as above except with black carbon steel bbl.) **$139.00**

TAR-HUNT RSG-12 PROFESSIONAL RIFLED SLUG GUN

Gauge: 12, 2-3/4" chamber, 1-shot magazine. **Barrel:** 21-1/2"; fully rifled, with muzzle brake. **Weight:** 7-3/4 lbs. **Length:** 41-1/2" overall. **Stock:** Matte black McMillan fiberglass with Pachmayr Decelerator pad. **Sights:** None furnished; comes with Leupold windage bases only. **Features:** Uses rifle-style action with two locking lugs; two-position safety; Shaw barrel; single-stage, trigger; muzzle brake. Many options available. Right- and left-hand models at same prices. Introduced 1991. Made in U.S. by Tar-Hunt Custom Rifles, Inc.
Price: Professional model, right- or left-hand **$1,695.00**
Price: Millennium/10th Anniversary models (limited to 25 guns):
NP-3 nickel/Teflon metal finish, black McMillan
Fibergrain stock, Jewell adj. trigger **$2,300.00**

Tar-Hunt RSG-20 Mountaineer Slug Gun

Similar to the RSG-12 Professional except chambered for 20 gauge (2-3/4") shells; 21" Shaw rifled barrel, with muzzle brake; two-lug bolt; one-shot blind magazine; matte black finish; McMillan fiberglass stock with Pachmayr Decelerator pad; receiver drilled and tapped for Rem. 700 bases. Weighs 6-1/2 lbs. Introduced 1997. Made in U.S. by Tar-Hunt Custom Rifles, Inc.
Price: **$1,695.00**

THOMPSON/CENTER ENCORE RIFLED SLUG GUN

Gauge: 20, 3" chamber. **Barrel:** 26", fully rifled. **Weight:** About 7 pounds. **Length:** 40-1/2" overall. **Stock:** Walnut with walnut forearm. **Sights:** Steel, click-adjustable rear and ramp-style front, both with fiber optics. **Features:** Encore system features a variety of rifle, shotgun and muzzle-loading rifle barrels interchangeable with the same frame. Break-open design operates by pulling up and back on trigger guard spur. Composite stock and forearm available. Introduced 2000.
Price: **$612.48**

WESSON & HARRINGTON LONG TOM CLASSIC SHOTGUN

Gauge: 12, 3" chamber. **Barrel:** 32", (Full). **Weight:** 7-1/2 lbs. **Length:** 46" overall. **Stock:** 14"x1-3/4"x2-5/8". American black walnut with hand-checkered grip and forend. **Features:** Color case-hardened receiver and crescent steel buttplate, blued barrel. Receiver engraved with the National Wild Turkey Federation logo. Introduced 1998. Made in U.S. by H&R 1871, Inc.
Price: **$349.95**

Designs for utility, suitable for and adaptable to competitions and other sporting purposes.

Benelli M1 Tactical

Fabarm Tactical

Mossberg M500 Persuader

BENELLI M3 CONVERTIBLE SHOTGUN

Gauge: 12, 3" chamber, 5-shot magazine. **Barrel:** 19-3/4" (Cyl.). **Weight:** 7 lbs., 8 oz. **Length:** 41" overall. **Stock:** High-impact polymer with sling loop in side of butt; rubberized pistol grip on stock. **Sights:** Post front, buckhorn rear adjustable for windage. Ghost ring system available. **Features:** Combination pump/auto action. Alloy receiver with inertia recoil rotating locking lug bolt; matte finish; automatic shell release lever. Introduced 1989. Imported by Benelli USA.
Price: With standard stock, open rifle sights. **$1,060.00**
Price: With ghost ring sight system, standard stock. **$1,100.00**
Price: With ghost ring sights, pistol grip stock **$1,120.00**

BENELLI M1 TACTICAL SHOTGUN

Gauge: 12, 3", 5-shot magazine. **Barrel:** 18.5", choke tubes. **Weight:** 6.5 lbs. **Length:** 39.75" overall. **Stock:** Black polymer. **Sights:** Rifle type with Ghost Ring system, tritium night sights optional. **Features:** Semi-auto intertia recoil action. Cross-bolt safety; bolt release button; matte-finish metal. Introduced 1993. Imported from Italy by Benelli USA.
Price: With rifle sights, standard stock **$890.00**
Price: With ghost ring rifle sights, standard stock. **$960.00**
Price: With ghost ring sights, pistol grip stock **$970.00**
Price: With rifle sights, pistol grip stock **$910.00**

Benelli M1 Practical

Similar to M1 Field Shotgun, but with Picatinny receiver rail for scope mounting, nine-round magazine, 26" compensated barrel and ghost-ring sights. Designed for IPSC competition.
Price: **$1,200.00**

BENELLI M4 SUPER 90 JOINT SERVICE COMBAT SHOTGUN

Gauge: 12, 3" chamber. **Barrel:** 18.5". **Weight:** 8.4 pounds. **Length:** 39.8 inches. **Stock:** Synthetic, modular. **Sights:** Ghost-ring style, rear adjustable for windage and elevation using cartridge rim. **Features:** Auto-regulating, gas-operated (ARGO) action. Integral, Picatinny rail on receiver for sight mounting. Black matte finish. Improved cylinder. Can be reconfigured without tools with three buttstocks and two barrels. Introduced 2000. Imported from Italy by Benelli USA.
Price: . . . . **NA**

BERETTA MODEL 1201FP GHOST RING AUTO SHOTGUN

Gauge: 12, 3" chamber. **Barrel:** 18" (Cyl.). **Weight:** 6.3 lbs. **Stock:** Special strengthened technopolymer, matte black finish. **Stock:** Fixed rifle type. **Features:** Has 5-shot magazine. Adjustable Ghost Ring rear sight, tritium front. Introduced 1988. Imported from Italy by Beretta U.S.A.
Price: **$860.00**

CROSSFIRE SHOTGUN/RIFLE

Gauge/Caliber: 12, 2-3/4" **Chamber:** 4-shot/223 Rem. (5-shot). **Barrel:** 20" (shotgun), 18" (rifle). **Weight:** About 8.6 lbs. **Length:** 40" overall. **Stock:** Composite. **Sights:** Meprolight night sights. Integral Weaver-style scope rail. **Features:** Combination pump-action shotgun, rifle; single selector, single trigger; dual action bars for both upper and lower actions; ambidextrous selector and safety. Introduced 1997. Made in U.S. From Hesco.
Price: About **$1,895.00**
Price: With camo finish. **$1,995.00**

FABARM FP6 PUMP SHOTGUN

Gauge: 12, 3" chamber. **Barrel:** 20" (Cyl.); accepts choke tubes. **Weight:** 6.6 lbs. **Length:** 41.25" overall. **Stock:** Black polymer with textured grip, grooved slide handle. **Sights:** Blade front. **Features:** Twin action bars; anodized finish; free carrier for smooth reloading. Introduced 1998. Imported from Italy by Heckler & Koch, Inc.
Price: (Carbon fiber finish) **$499.00**
Price: With flip-up front sight, Picatinny rail with rear sight, oversize safety button **$499.00**

FABARM TACTICAL SEMI-AUTOMATIC SHOTGUN

Gauge: 12, 3" chamber. **Barrel:** 20". **Weight:** 6.6 lbs. **Length:** 41.2" overall. **Stock:** Polymer or folding. **Sights:** Ghost ring (tritium night sights optional). **Features:** Gas operated; matte receiver; twin forged action bars; oversized bolt handle and safety button; Picatinny rail; includes cylinder bore choke tube. Introduced 2001. Imported from Italy by Heckler & Koch Inc.
Price: . . . . **NA**

MOSSBERG MODEL 500 PERSUADER SECURITY SHOTGUNS

Gauge: 12, 20, 410, 3" chamber. **Barrel:** 18-1/2", 20" (Cyl.). **Weight:** 7 lbs. **Stock:** Walnut-finished hardwood or black synthetic. **Sights:** Metal bead front. **Features:** Available in 6- or 8-shot models. Top-mounted safety, double action slide bars, swivel studs, rubber recoil pad. Blue, Parkerized, Marinecote finishes. Mossberg Cablelock included. From Mossberg.
Price: 12 or 20 ga., 18-1/2", blue, wood or synthetic stock, 6-shot **$329.00**
Price: Cruiser, 12 or 20 ga., 18-1/2", blue, pistol grip, heat shield **$333.00**
Price: As above, 410-bore **$322.00**

Tactical Response TR-870

Winchester Model 1300 Defender

Mossberg Model 500, 590 Mariner Pump

Similar to the Model 500 or 590 Security except all metal parts finished with Marinecote metal finish to resist rust and corrosion. Synthetic field stock; pistol grip kit included. Mossberg Cablelock included.
Price: 6-shot, 18-1/2" barrel **$468.00**
Price: 9-shot, 20" barrel **$484.00**

Mossberg Model HS410 Shotgun

Similar to the Model 500 Security pump except chambered for 20 gauge or 410 with 3" chamber; has pistol grip forend, thick recoil pad, muzzle brake and has special spreader choke on the 18.5" barrel. Overall length is 37.5", weight is 6.25 lbs. Blue finish; synthetic field stock. Mossberg Cablelock and video included. Introduced 1990.
Price: HS 410 .... **$335.00**

Mossberg Model 500, 590 Ghost-Ring Shotguns

Similar to the Model 500 Security except has adjustable blade front, adjustable Ghost-Ring rear sight with protective "ears." Model 500 has 18.5" (Cyl.) barrel, 6-shot capacity; Model 590 has 20" (Cyl.) barrel, 9-shot capacity. Both have synthetic field stock. Mossberg Cablelock included. Introduced 1990. From Mossberg.
Price: 500 parkerized **$437.00**
Price: 590 parkerized **$445.00**
Price: Parkerized Speedfeed stock .... **$546.00 to $634.00**

MOSSBERG MODEL 590 SHOTGUN

Gauge: 12, 3" chamber. **Barrel:** 20" (Cyl.). **Weight:** 7-1/4 lbs. **Stock:** Synthetic field or Speedfeed. **Sights:** Metal bead front. **Features:** Top-mounted safety, double slide action bars. Comes with heat shield, bayonet lug, swivel studs, rubber recoil pad. Blue, Parkerized or Marinecote finish. Mossberg Cablelock included. From Mossberg.
Price: Blue, synthetic stock **$389.00**
Price: Parkerized, synthetic stock **$445.00**
Price: Parkerized, Speedfeed stock **$485.00**

Mossberg 590DA Double-Action Pump Shotgun

Similar to Model 590 except trigger requires a long stroke for each shot, duplicating the trigger pull of double-action-only pistols and revolvers. Available in 12 gauge only with black synthetic stock and parkerized finish with 14" (law enforcement only), 18-1/2 "and 20" barrels. Six-shot magazine tube (nine-shot for 20" barrel). Front bead or ghost ring sights. Weighs 7 pounds (18 1/2" barrel). Introduced 2000. From Mossberg.
Price: Bead sight, 6-shot magazine **$510.00**
Price: Ghost ring sights, 6-shot magazine **$558.00**
Price: Bead sight, 9-shot magazine **$541.00**
Price: Ghost ring sights, 9-shot magazine **$597.00**

TACTICAL RESPONSE TR-870 STANDARD MODEL SHOTGUN

Gauge: 12, 3" chamber, 7-shot magazine. **Barrel:** 18" (Cyl.). **Weight:** 9 lbs. **Length:** 38" overall. **Stock:** Fiberglass-filled polypropolene with non-snag recoil absorbing butt pad. Nylon tactical forend houses flashlight. **Sights:** Trak-Lock ghost ring sight system. Front sight has tritium insert. **Features:** Highly modified Remington 870P with Parkerized finish. Comes with nylon three-way adjustable sling, high visibility non-binding follower, high performance magazine spring, Jumbo Head safety, and Side Saddle extended 6-shot shell carrier on left side of receiver. Introduced 1991. From Scatter-gun Technologies, Inc.
Price: Standard model **$815.00**
Price: FBI model **$770.00**
Price: Patrol model **$595.00**
Price: Border Patrol model **$605.00**
Price: K-9 model (Rem. 11-87 action) **$995.00**
Price: Urban Sniper, Rem. 11-87 action **$1,290.00**
Price: Louis Awerbuck model **$705.00**
Price: Practical Turkey model **$725.00**
Price: Expert model **$1,350.00**
Price: Professional model **$815.00**
Price: Entry model **$840.00**
Price: Compact model **$635.00**
Price: SWAT model **$1,195.00**

TRISTAR PHANTOM HP AUTO SHOTGUN

Gauge: 12, 3" chamber. **Barrel:** 19"; threaded for external choke tubes. **Stock:** Black synthetic. **Sights:** Bead front. **Features:** Gas-operated action; blue/black finish; five-shot extended magazine tube. Imported by Tristar Sporting Arms Ltd.
Price: .... **NA**

WINCHESTER MODEL 1300 DEFENDER PUMP GUNS

Gauge: 12, 20, 3" chamber, 5- or 8-shot capacity. **Barrel:** 18" (Cyl.). **Weight:** 6-3/4 lbs. **Length:** 38-5/8" overall. **Stock:** Walnut-finished hardwood stock and ribbed forend, synthetic or pistol grip. **Sights:** Metal bead front or TRUGLO® fiber-optic. **Features:** Cross-bolt safety, front-locking rotary bolt, twin action slide bars. Black rubber butt pad. From U.S. Repeating Arms Co.
Price: 8-Shot (black synthetic stock, TRUGLO® sight) **$326.00**
Price: 8-Shot Pistol Grip (pistol grip synthetic stock) **$326.00**

Winchester Model 1300 Stainless Marine Pump Gun

Same as the Defender 8-Shot except has bright chrome finish, stainless steel barrel, bead front sight. Phosphate coated receiver for corrosion resistance.
Price: **$518.00**

Winchester Model 1300 Camp Defender®

Same as the Defender 8-Shot except has hardwood stock and forearm, fully adjustable open sights and 22" barrel with WinChoke® choke tube system (cylinder choke tube included). Weighs 6-7/8 lbs. Introduced 2001. From U.S. Repeating Arms Co.
Price: Camp Defender® **$373.00**

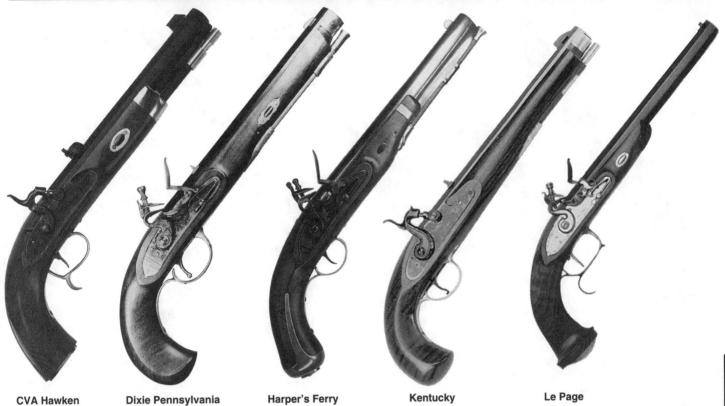

CVA Hawken　　Dixie Pennsylvania　　Harper's Ferry　　Kentucky　　Le Page

CVA HAWKEN PISTOL

Caliber: 50. **Barrel:** 9-3/4"; 15/16" flats. **Weight:** 50 oz. **Length:** 16-1/2" overall. **Stocks:** Select hardwood. **Sights:** Beaded blade front, fully adjustable open rear. **Features:** Color case-hardened lock, polished brass wedge plate, instep, ramrod thimble, trigger guard, grip cap. Imported by CVA.

Price: **$167.95**
Price: Kit **$127.95**

DIXIE PENNSYLVANIA PISTOL

Caliber: 44 (.430" round ball). **Barrel:** 10", (7/8" octagon). **Weight:** 2-1/2 labs. **Stocks:** Walnut-stained hardwood. **Sights:** Blade front, open rear drift-adjustable for windage; brass. **Features:** Available in flint only. Brass trigger guard, thimbles, instep, wedge plates; high-luster blue barrel. Imported from Italy by Dixie Gun Works.

Price: Finished **$195.00**
Price: Kit **$185.00**

FRENCH-STYLE DUELING PISTOL

Caliber: 44. **Barrel:** 10". **Weight:** 35 oz. **Length:** 15-3/4" overall. **Stocks:** Carved walnut. **Sights:** Fixed. **Features:** Comes with velvet-lined case and accessories. Imported by Mandall Shooting Supplies.

Price: **$295.00**

HARPER'S FERRY 1806 PISTOL

Caliber: 58 (.570" round ball). **Barrel:** 10". **Weight:** 40 oz. **Length:** 16" overall. **Stocks:** Walnut. **Sights:** Fixed. **Features:** Case-hardened lock, brass-mounted browned barrel. Replica of the first U.S. Gov't.-made flintlock pistol. Imported by Navy Arms, Dixie Gun Works.

Price: . . . . **$275.00 to $405.00**
Price: Kit (Dixie) **$249.00**

KENTUCKY FLINTLOCK PISTOL

Caliber: 44, 45. **Barrel:** 10-1/8". **Weight:** 32 oz. **Length:** 15-1/2" overall. **Stocks:** Walnut. **Sights:** Fixed. **Features:** Specifications, including caliber, weight and length may vary with importer. Case-hardened lock, blued barrel; available also as brass barrel flint Model 1821. Imported by Navy Arms, The Armoury.

Price: . . . . **$145.00 to $235.00**
Price: In kit form, from . . . . **$90.00 to $112.00**
Price: Single cased set (Navy Arms) **$360.00**
Price: Double cased set (Navy Arms) **$590.00**

Kentucky Percussion Pistol

Similar to flint version but percussion lock. Imported by The Armoury, Navy Arms, CVA (50-cal.).

Price: . . . . **$129.95 to $225.00**
Price: Blued steel barrel (CVA) **$167.95**
Price: Kit form (CVA) **$119.95**
Price: Steel barrel (Armoury) **$179.00**
Price: Single cased set (Navy Arms) **$355.00**
Price: Double cased set (Navy Arms) **$600.00**

LE PAGE PERCUSSION DUELING PISTOL

Caliber: 44. **Barrel:** 10", rifled. **Weight:** 40 oz. **Length:** 16" overall. **Stocks:** Walnut, fluted butt. **Sights:** Blade front, notch rear. **Features:** Double-set triggers. Blued barrel; trigger guard and buttcap are polished silver. Imported by Dixie Gun Works.

Price: **$259.95**

LYMAN PLAINS PISTOL

Caliber: 50 or 54. **Barrel:** 8"; 1:30" twist, both calibers. **Weight:** 50 oz. **Length:** 15" overall. **Stocks:** Walnut half-stock. **Sights:** Blade front, square notch rear adjustable for windage. **Features:** Polished brass trigger guard and ramrod tip, color case-hardened coil spring lock, spring-loaded trigger, stainless steel nipple, blackened iron furniture. Hooked patent breech, detachable belt hook. Introduced 1981. From Lyman Products.

Price: Finished **$229.95**
Price: Kit **$184.95**

PEDERSOLI MANG TARGET PISTOL

Caliber: 38. **Barrel:** 10.5", octagonal; 1:15" twist. **Weight:** 2.5 lbs. **Length:** 17.25" overall. **Stocks:** Walnut with fluted grip. **Sights:** Blade front, open rear adjustable for windage. **Features:** Browned barrel, polished breech plug, rest color case-hardened. Imported from Italy by Dixie Gun Works.

Price: **$786.00**

Lyman Plains Pistol   Pedersoli Mang   Queen Anne   Traditions Pioneer   Traditions William Parker

QUEEN ANNE FLINTLOCK PISTOL

Caliber: 50 (.490" round ball). **Barrel:** 7-1/2", smoothbore. **Stocks:** Walnut. **Sights:** None. **Features:** Browned steel barrel, fluted brass trigger guard, brass mask on butt. Lockplate left in the white. Made by Pedersoli in Italy. Introduced 1983. Imported by Dixie Gun Works.

Price: $225.00
Price: Kit $175.00

THOMPSON/CENTER ENCORE 209x50 MAGNUM PISTOL

Caliber: 50. **Barrel:** 15"; 1:20" twist. **Weight:** About 4 lbs. **Grips:** American walnut grip and forend. **Sights:** Click-adjustable, steel rear, ramp front. **Features:** Uses 209 shotgun primer for closed-breech ignition; accepts charges up to 110 grains of FFg black powder or two, 50-grain Pyrodex pellets. Introduced 2000.

Price: $569.47

TRADITIONS BUCKHUNTER PRO IN-LINE PISTOL

Caliber: 50. **Barrel:** 9-1/2", round. **Weight:** 48 oz. **Length:** 14" overall. **Stocks:** Smooth walnut or black epoxy-coated hardwood grip and forend. **Sights:** Beaded blade front, folding adjustable rear. **Features:** Thumb safety; removable stainless steel breech plug; adjustable trigger, barrel drilled and tapped for scope mounting. From Traditions.

Price: With walnut grip $229.00
Price: Nickel with black grip $239.00
Price: With walnut grip and 12-1/2" barrel $239.00
Price: Nickel with black grip, muzzle brake and 14-3/4"
 fluted barrel.. $284.00

TRADITIONS KENTUCKY PISTOL

Caliber: 50. **Barrel:** 10"; octagon with 7/8" flats; 1:20" twist. **Weight:** 40 oz. **Length:** 15" overall. **Stocks:** Stained beech. **Sights:** Blade front, fixed rear. **Features:** Birds-head grip; brass thimbles; color case-hardened lock. Percussion only. Introduced 1995. From Traditions.

Price: Finished $139.00
Price: Kit....................................... $109.00

TRADITIONS PIONEER PISTOL

Caliber: 45. **Barrel:** 9-5/8"; 13/16" flats, 1:16" twist. **Weight:** 31 oz. **Length:** 15" overall. **Stocks:** Beech. **Sights:** Blade front, fixed rear. **Features:** V-type mainspring. Single trigger. German silver furniture, blackened hardware. From Traditions.

Traditions Buckhunter Pro

Price: $139.00
Price: Kit....................................... $119.00

TRADITIONS TRAPPER PISTOL

Caliber: 50. **Barrel:** 9-3/4"; 7/8" flats; 1:20" twist. **Weight:** 2-3/4 lbs. **Length:** 16" overall. **Stocks:** Beech. **Sights:** Blade front, adjustable rear. **Features:** Double-set triggers; brass buttcap, trigger guard, wedge plate, forend tip, thimble. From Traditions.

Price: Percussion................................... $189.00
Price: Flintlock.................................... $209.00
Price: Kit... $149.00

TRADITIONS VEST-POCKET DERRINGER

Caliber: 31. **Barrel:** 2-1/4"; brass. **Weight:** 8 oz. **Length:** 4-3/4" overall. **Stocks:** Simulated ivory. **Sights:** Beed front. **Features:** Replica of river-boat gamblers' derringer; authentic spur trigger. From Traditions.

Price: $109.00

TRADITIONS WILLIAM PARKER PISTOL

Caliber: 50. **Barrel:** 10-3/8"; 15/16" flats; polished steel. **Weight:** 37 oz. **Length:** 17-1/2" overall. **Stocks:** Walnut with checkered grip. **Sights:** Brass blade front, fixed rear. **Features:** Replica dueling pistol with 1:20" twist, hooked breech. Brass wedge plate, trigger guard, cap guard; separate ramrod. Double-set triggers. Polished steel barrel, lock. Imported by Traditions.

Price: $269.00

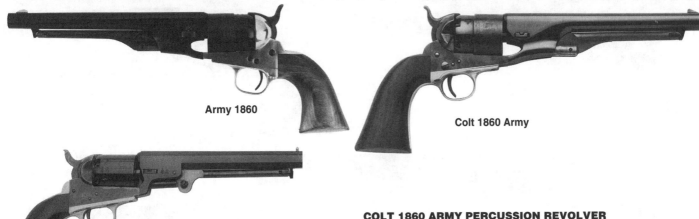

Army 1860

Colt 1860 Army

Baby Dragoon 1848

ARMY 1851 PERCUSSION REVOLVER

Caliber: 44, 6-shot. **Barrel:** 7-1/2". **Weight:** 45 oz. **Length:** 13" overall. **Stocks:** Walnut finish. **Sights:** Fixed. **Features:** 44-caliber version of the 1851 Navy. Imported by The Armoury, Armsport.
Price: **$129.00**

ARMY 1860 PERCUSSION REVOLVER

Caliber: 44, 6-shot. **Barrel:** 8". **Weight:** 40 oz. **Length:** 13-5/8" overall. **Stocks:** Walnut. **Sights:** Fixed. **Features:** Engraved Navy scene on cylinder; brass trigger guard; case-hardened frame, loading lever and hammer. Some importers supply pistol cut for detachable shoulder stock, have accessory stock available. Imported by Cabela's (1860 Lawman), E.M.F., Navy Arms, The Armoury, Cimarron, Dixie Gun Works (half-fluted cylinder, not roll engraved), Euroarms of America (brass or steel model), Armsport, Traditions (brass or steel), Uberti U.S.A. Inc., United States Patent Fire-Arms.
Price: About .... **$92.95 to $395.00**
Price: Hartford model, steel frame, German silver trim,
  cartouches (E.M.F.) **$215.00**
Price: Single cased set (Navy Arms) **$300.00**
Price: Double cased set (Navy Arms)..................... **$490.00**
Price: 1861 Navy: Same as Army except 36-cal., 7-1/2" bbl., weighs 41 oz., cut for shoulder stock; round cylinder (fluted available), from Cabela's, CVA (brass frame, 44-cal.), United States Patent Fire-Arms
.... **$99.95 to $385.00**
Price: Steel frame kit (E.M.F., Euroarms).......... **$125.00 to $216.25**
Price: Colt Army Police, fluted cyl., 5-1/2", 36-cal. (Cabela's) ... **$124.95**
Price: With nickeled frame, barrel and backstrap, gold-tone fluted cylinder, trigger and hammer, simulated ivory grips (Traditions) **$199.00**

BABY DRAGOON 1848, 1849 POCKET, WELLS FARGO

Caliber: 31. **Barrel:** 3", 4", 5", 6"; seven-groove; RH twist. **Weight:** About 21 oz. **Stocks:** Varnished walnut. **Sights:** Brass pin front, hammer notch rear. **Features:** No loading lever on Baby Dragoon or Wells Fargo models. Unfluted cylinder with stagecoach holdup scene; cupped cylinder pin; no grease grooves; one safety pin on cylinder and slot in hammer face; straight (flat) mainspring. From Armsport, Cimarron F.A. Co., Dixie Gun Works, Uberti U.S.A. Inc.
Price: 6" barrel, with loading lever (Dixie Gun Works) **$254.95**
Price: 4" (Uberti USA Inc.) **$335.00**

CABELA'S STARR PERCUSSION REVOLVERS

Caliber: 44. **Barrel:** 6", 8". **Weight:** N/A. **Length:** N/A. **Grips:** Walnut. **Sights:** Blade front. **Features:** Replicas of government-contract revolvers made by Ebenezer T. Starr. Knurled knob allows quick removal and replacement of cylinder. Introduced 2000. From Cabela's.
Price: Starr 1858 Army double action, 6" barrel. **$349.99**
Price: Starr 1863 Army single action, 8" barrel **$349.99**

COLT 1860 ARMY PERCUSSION REVOLVER

Caliber: 44. **Barrel:** 8", 7-groove, left-hand twist. **Weight:** 42 oz. **Stocks:** One-piece walnut. **Sights:** German silver front sight, hammer notch rear. **Features:** Steel backstrap cut for shoulder stock; brass trigger guard. Cylinder has Navy scene. Color case-hardened frame, hammer, loading lever. Reproduction of original gun with all original markings. From Colt Blackpowder Arms Co.
Price: **$449.95**

COLT 1848 BABY DRAGOON REVOLVER

Caliber: 31, 5-shot. **Barrel:** 4". **Weight:** About 21 oz. **Stocks:** Smooth walnut. **Sights:** Brass pin front, hammer notch rear. **Features:** Color case-hardened frame; no loading lever; square-back trigger guard; round bolt cuts; octagonal barrel; engraved cylinder scene. Imported by Colt Blackpowder Arms Co.
Price: **$429.95**

Colt 1860 "Cavalry Model" Percussion Revolver

Similar to the 1860 Army except has fluted cylinder. Color case-hardened frame, hammer, loading lever and plunger; blued barrel, backstrap and cylinder, brass trigger guard. Has four-screw frame cut for optional shoulder stock. From Colt Blackpowder Arms Co.
Price: **$399.95**

COLT 1851 NAVY PERCUSSION REVOLVER

Caliber: 36. **Barrel:** 7-1/2", octagonal; 7-groove left-hand twist. **Weight:** 40-1/2 oz. **Stocks:** One-piece oiled American walnut. **Sights:** Brass pin front, hammer notch rear. **Features:** Faithful reproduction of the original gun. Color case-hardened frame, loading lever, plunger, hammer and latch. Blue cylinder, trigger, barrel, screws, wedge. Silver-plated brass backstrap and square-back trigger guard. From Colt Blackpowder Arms Co.
Price: **$449.95**

COLT 1861 NAVY PERCUSSION REVOLVER

Caliber: 36. **Barrel:** 7-1/2". **Weight:** 42 oz. **Length:** 13-1/8" overall. **Stocks:** One-piece walnut. **Sights:** Blade front, hammer notch rear. **Features:** Color case-hardened frame, loading lever, plunger; blued barrel, backstrap, trigger guard; roll-engraved cylinder and barrel. From Colt Blackpowder Arms Co.
Price: **$449.95**

COLT 1849 POCKET DRAGOON REVOLVER

Caliber: 31. **Barrel:** 4". **Weight:** 24 oz. **Length:** 9-1/2" overall. **Stocks:** One-piece walnut. **Sights:** Fixed. Brass pin front, hammer notch rear. **Features:** Color case-hardened frame. No loading lever. Unfluted cylinder with engraved scene. Exact reproduction of original. From Colt Blackpowder Arms Co.
Price: **$429.95**

COLT 1862 POCKET POLICE "TRAPPER MODEL" REVOLVER

Caliber: 36. **Barrel:** 3-1/2". **Weight:** 20 oz. **Length:** 8-1/2" overall. **Stocks:** One-piece walnut. **Sights:** Blade front, hammer notch rear. **Features:** Has separate 4-5/8" brass ramrod. Color case-hardened frame and hammer; silver-plated backstrap and trigger guard; blued semi-fluted cylinder, blued barrel. From Colt Blackpowder Arms Co.
Price: **$429.95**

BLACKPOWDER

BLACKPOWDER REVOLVERS

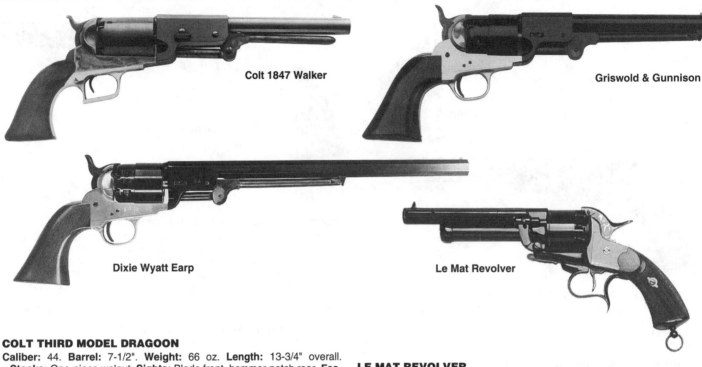

Colt 1847 Walker

Griswold & Gunnison

Dixie Wyatt Earp

Le Mat Revolver

COLT THIRD MODEL DRAGOON

Caliber: 44. **Barrel:** 7-1/2". **Weight:** 66 oz. **Length:** 13-3/4" overall. **Stocks:** One-piece walnut. **Sights:** Blade front, hammer notch rear. **Features:** Color case-hardened frame, hammer, lever and plunger; round trigger guard; flat mainspring; hammer roller; rectangular bolt cuts. From Colt Blackpowder Arms Co.
Price: Three-screw frame with brass grip straps **$499.95**
Price: First Dragoon (oval bolt cuts in cylinder, square-back trigger guard) **$499.95**
Price: Second Dragoon (rectangular bolt cuts in cylinder, square-back trigger guard) **$499.95**

Colt Walker 150th Anniversary Revolver

Similar to the standard Walker except has original-type "A Company No. 1" markings embellished in gold. Serial numbers begin with 221, a continuation of A Company numbers. Imported by Colt Blackpowder Arms Co.
Price: **$699.95**

COLT 1847 WALKER PERCUSSION REVOLVER

Caliber: 44. **Barrel:** 9", 7-groove; right-hand twist. **Weight:** 73 oz. **Stocks:** One-piece walnut. **Sights:** German silver front sight, hammer notch rear. **Features:** Made in U.S. Faithful reproduction of the original gun, including markings. Color case-hardened frame, hammer, loading lever and plunger. Blue steel backstrap, brass square-back trigger guard. Blue barrel, cylinder, trigger and wedge. From Colt Blackpowder Arms Co.
Price: **$499.95**

DIXIE WYATT EARP REVOLVER

Caliber: 44. **Barrel:** 12", octagon. **Weight:** 46 oz. **Length:** 18" overall. **Stocks:** Two-piece walnut. **Sights:** Fixed. **Features:** Highly polished brass frame, backstrap and trigger guard; blued barrel and cylinder; case-hardened hammer, trigger and loading lever. Navy-size shoulder stock ($45) will fit with minor fitting. From Dixie Gun Works.
Price: **$150.00**

GRISWOLD & GUNNISON PERCUSSION REVOLVER

Caliber: 36 or 44, 6-shot. **Barrel:** 7-1/2". **Weight:** 44 oz. (36-cal.). **Length:** 13" overall. **Stocks:** Walnut. **Sights:** Fixed. **Features:** Replica of famous Confederate pistol. Brass frame, backstrap and trigger guard; case-hardened loading lever; rebated cylinder (44-cal. only). Rounded Dragoon-type barrel. Imported by Navy Arms as Reb Model 1860.
Price: **$115.00**
Price: Kit **$90.00**
Price: Single cased set **$235.00**
Price: Double cased set **$365.00**

LE MAT REVOLVER

Caliber: 44/65. **Barrel:** 6-3/4" (revolver); 4-7/8" (single shot). **Weight:** 3 lbs., 7 oz. **Stocks:** Hand-checkered walnut. **Sights:** Post front, hammer notch rear. **Features:** Exact reproduction with all-steel construction; 44-cal. 9-shot cylinder, 65-cal. single barrel; color case-hardened hammer with selector; spur trigger guard; ring at butt; lever-type barrel release. From Navy Arms.
Price: Cavalry model (lanyard ring, spur trigger guard) **$595.00**
Price: Army model (round trigger guard, pin-type barrel release) **$595.00**
Price: Naval-style (thumb selector on hammer) **$595.00**
Price: Engraved 18th Georgia cased set **$795.00**
Price: Engraved Beauregard cased set **$1,000.00**

NAVY ARMS NEW MODEL POCKET REVOLVER

Caliber: 31, 5-shot. **Barrel:** 3-1/2", octagon. **Weight:** 15 oz. **Length:** 7-3/4". **Stocks:** Two-piece walnut. **Sights:** Fixed. **Features:** Replica of the Remington New Model Pocket. Available with polishd brass frame or nickel plated finish. Introduced 2000. Imported by Navy Arms.
Price: Brass frame **$165.00**
Price: Nickel plated **$175.00**

NAVY ARMS DELUXE 1858 REMINGTON-STYLE REVOLVER

Caliber: 44. **Barrel:** 6". **Weight:** 3 lbs. **Length:** 11-3/4". **Stocks:** Smooth walnut. **Sights:** Blade front, notch rear. **Features:** Replica of the famous percussion double action revolver. Polished blue finish. Introduced 1999. Imported by Navy Arms.
Price: **$355.00**

NAVY ARMS STARR SINGLE ACTION MODEL 1863 ARMY REVOLVER

Caliber: 44. **Barrel:** 8". **Weight:** 3 lbs. **Length:** 13-3/4". **Stocks:** Smooth walnut. **Sights:** Blade front, notch rear. **Features:** Replica of the third most popular revolver used by Union forces during the Civil War. Polished blue finish. Introduced 1999. Imported by Navy Arms.
Price: **$355.00**

NAVY ARMS STARR DOUBLE ACTION MODEL 1858 ARMY REVOLVER

Caliber: 44. **Barrel:** 8". **Weight:** 2 lbs., 13 oz. **Stocks:** Smooth walnut. **Sights:** Dovetailed blade front. **Features:** First exact reproduction—correct in size and weight to the original, with progressive rifling; highly polished with blue finish. From Navy Arms.
Price: Deluxe model **$415.00**

BLACKPOWDER

BLACKPOWDER REVOLVERS

Uberti 1858

Rogers & Spencer

North American Companion

Ruger Old Army

Pocket Police 1862

NAVY MODEL 1851 PERCUSSION REVOLVER
Caliber: 36, 44, 6-shot. **Barrel:** 7-1/2". **Weight:** 44 oz. **Length:** 13" overall. **Stocks:** Walnut finish. **Sights:** Post front, hammer notch rear. **Features:** Brass backstrap and trigger guard; some have 1st Model squareback trigger guard, engraved cylinder with navy battle scene; case-hardened frame, hammer, loading lever. Imported by The Armoury, Cabela's, Cimarron F.A. Co., Navy Arms, E.M.F., Dixie Gun Works, Euroarms of America, Armsport, CVA (44-cal. only), Traditions (44 only), Uberti U.S.A. Inc., United States Patent Fire-Arms.

Price: Brass frame	**$99.95 to $385.00**
Price: Steel frame	**$130.00 to $285.00**
Price: Kit form	**$110.00 to $123.95**
Price: Engraved model (Dixie Gun Works)	**$159.95**
Price: Single cased set, steel frame (Navy Arms)	**$280.00**
Price: Double cased set, steel frame (Navy Arms)	**$455.00**
Price: Confederate Navy (Cabela's)	**$89.99**
Price: Hartford model, steel frame, German silver trim, cartouche (E.M.F.)	**$190.00**

NEW MODEL 1858 ARMY PERCUSSION REVOLVER
Caliber: 36 or 44, 6-shot. **Barrel:** 6-1/2" or 8". **Weight:** 38 oz. **Length:** 13-1/2" overall. **Stocks:** Walnut. **Sights:** Blade front, groove-in-frame rear. **Features:** Replica of Remington Model 1858. Also available from some importers as Army Model Belt Revolver in 36-cal., a shortened and lightened version of the 44. Target Model (Uberti U.S.A. Inc., Navy Arms) has fully adjustable target rear sight, target front, 36 or 44. Imported by Cabela's, Cimarron F.A. Co., CVA (as 1858 Army, brass frame, 44 only), Dixie Gun Works, Navy Arms, The Armoury, E.M.F., Euroarms of America (engraved, stainless and plain), Armsport, Traditions (44 only), Uberti U.S.A. Inc.

Price: Steel frame, about	**$99.95 to $280.00**
Price: Steel frame kit (Euroarms, Navy Arms)	**$115.95 to $150.00**
Price: Single cased set (Navy Arms)	**$290.00**
Price: Double cased set (Navy Arms)	**$480.00**
Price: Stainless steel Model 1858 (Euroarms, Uberti U.S.A. Inc., Cabela's, Navy Arms, Armsport, Traditions)	**$169.95 to $380.00**
Price: Target Model, adjustable rear sight (Cabela's, Euroarms, Uberti U.S.A. Inc., Stone Mountain Arms)	**$95.95 to $399.00**
Price: Brass frame (CVA, Cabela's, Traditions, Navy Arms)	**$79.95 to $159.95**
Price: As above, kit (Dixie Gun Works, Navy Arms)	**$145.00 to $188.95**

Price: Buffalo model, 44-cal. (Cabela's)	**$119.99**
Price: Hartford model, steel frame, German silver trim, cartouche (E.M.F.)	**$215.00**

NORTH AMERICAN COMPANION PERCUSSION REVOLVER
Caliber: 22. **Barrel:** 1-1/8". **Weight:** 5.1 oz. **Length:** 4-5/10" overall. **Stocks:** Laminated wood. **Sights:** Blade front, notch fixed rear. **Features:** All stainless steel construction. Uses standard #11 percussion caps. Comes with bullets, powder measure, bullet seater, leather clip holster, gun rug. Long Rifle or Magnum frame size. Introduced 1996. Made in U.S. by North American Arms.

Price: Long Rifle frame	**$191.00**

North American Magnum Companion Percussion Revolver
Similar to the Companion except has larger frame. Weighs 7.2 oz., has 1-5/8" barrel, measures 5-7/16" overall. Comes with bullets, powder measure, bullet seater, leather clip holster, gun rag. Introduced 1996. Made in U.S. by North American Arms.

Price:	**$209.00**

POCKET POLICE 1862 PERCUSSION REVOLVER
Caliber: 36, 5-shot. **Barrel:** 4-1/2", 5-1/2", 6-1/2", 7-1/2". **Weight:** 26 oz. **Length:** 12" overall (6-1/2" bbl.). **Stocks:** Walnut. **Sights:** Fixed. **Features:** Round tapered barrel; half-fluted and rebated cylinder; case-hardened frame, loading lever and hammer; silver or brass trigger guard and backstrap. Imported by Dixie Gun Works, Navy Arms (5-1/2" only), Uberti U.S.A. Inc. (5-1/2", 6-1/2" only), United States Patent Fire-Arms and Cimarron F.A. Co.

Price: About	**$139.95 to $335.00**
Price: Single cased set with accessories (Navy Arms)	**$365.00**
Price: Hartford model, steel frame, German silver trim, cartouche (E.M.F.)	**$215.00**

ROGERS & SPENCER PERCUSSION REVOLVER
Caliber: 44. **Barrel:** 7-1/2". **Weight:** 47 oz. **Length:** 13-3/4" overall. **Stocks:** Walnut. **Sights:** Cone front, integral groove in frame for rear. **Features:** Accurate reproduction of a Civil War design. Solid frame; extra large nipple cut-out on rear of cylinder; loading lever and cylinder easily removed for cleaning. From Dixie Gun Works, Euroarms of America (standard blue, engraved, burnished, target models), Navy Arms.

Price:	**$160.00 to $299.95**
Price: Nickel-plated	**$215.00**
Price: Engraved (Euroarms)	**$287.00**

BLACKPOWDER REVOLVERS

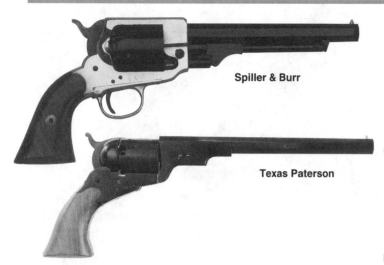

Spiller & Burr

Texas Paterson

Walker

Price: Kit version. . . . . **$245.00 to $252.00**
Price: Target version (Euroarms) . . . . **$239.00 to $270.00**
Price: Burnished London Gray (Euroarms) . . . . **$245.00 to $270.00**

RUGER OLD ARMY PERCUSSION REVOLVER

Caliber: 45, 6-shot. Uses .457" dia. lead bullets. **Barrel:** 7-1/2" (6-groove; 16" twist). **Weight:** 46 oz. **Length:** 13-3/4" overall. **Stocks:** Smooth walnut. **Sights:** Ramp front, rear adjustable for windage and elevation; or fixed (groove). **Features:** Stainless steel; standard size nipples, chrome-moly steel cylinder and frame, same lockwork as in original Super Blackhawk. Also available in stainless steel. Includes hard case and lock. Made in USA. From Sturm, Ruger & Co.
Price: Stainless steel (Model KBP-7) **$510.00**
Price: Blued steel (Model BP-7) **$478.00**
Price: Blued steel, fixed sight (BP-7F) **$478.00**
Price: Stainless steel, fixed sight (KBP-7F) **$510.00**

SHERIFF MODEL 1851 PERCUSSION REVOLVER

Caliber: 36, 44, 6-shot. **Barrel:** 5". **Weight:** 40 oz. **Length:** 10-1/2" overall. **Stocks:** Walnut. **Sights:** Fixed. **Features:** Brass backstrap and trigger guard; engraved navy scene; case-hardened frame, hammer, loading lever. Imported by E.M.F.
Price: Steel frame. **$172.00**
Price: Brass frame **$140.00**

SPILLER & BURR REVOLVER

Caliber: 36 (.375" round ball). **Barrel:** 7", octagon. **Weight:** 2-1/2 lbs. **Length:** 12-1/2" overall. **Stocks:** Two-piece walnut. **Sights:** Fixed. **Features:** Reproduction of the C.S.A. revolver. Brass frame and trigger guard. Also available as a kit. From Dixie Gun Works, Navy Arms.
Price: **$145.00**
Price: Kit form (Dixie) **$149.95**
Price: Single cased set (Navy Arms) **$270.00**
Price: Double cased set (Navy Arms). **$430.00**

TEXAS PATERSON 1836 REVOLVER

Caliber: 36 (.375" round ball). **Barrel:** 7-1/2". **Weight:** 42 oz. **Stocks:** One-piece walnut. **Sights:** Fixed. **Features:** Copy of Sam Colt's first commercially-made revolving pistol. Has no loading lever but comes with loading tool. From Cimarron F.A. Co., Dixie Gun Works, Navy Arms, Uberti U.S.A. Inc.
Price: About . . . . **$310.00 to $395.00**
Price: With loading lever (Uberti U.S.A. Inc.) **$450.00**
Price: Engraved (Navy Arms). **$485.00**

Uberti 1861 Navy Percussion Revolver

Similar to Colt 1851 Navy except has round 7-1/2" barrel, rounded trigger guard, German silver blade front sight, "creeping" loading lever. Available with fluted or round cylinder. Imported by Uberti U.S.A. Inc.
Price: Steel backstrap, trigger guard, cut for stock. **$300.00**

1ST U.S. MODEL DRAGOON

Caliber: 44. **Barrel:** 7-1/2", part round, part octagon. **Weight:** 64 oz. **Stocks:** One-piece walnut. **Sights:** German silver blade front, hammer notch rear. **Features:** First model has oval bolt cuts in cylinder, square-back flared trigger guard, V-type mainspring, short trigger. Ranger and Indian scene roll-engraved on cylinder. Color case-hardened frame, loading lever, plunger and hammer; blue barrel, cylinder, trigger and wedge. Available with old-time charcoal blue or standard blue-black finish. Polished brass backstrap and trigger guard. From Cimarron F.A. Co., Uberti U.S.A. Inc., United States Patent Fire-Arms, Navy Arms.
Price: . . . . **$325.00 to $435.00**

2nd U.S. Model Dragoon Revolver

Similar to the 1st Model except distinguished by rectangular bolt cuts in the cylinder. From Cimarron F.A. Co., Uberti U.S.A. Inc., United States Patent Fire-Arms, Navy Arms.
Price: . . . . **$325.00 to $435.00**

3rd U.S. Model Dragoon Revolver

Similar to the 2nd Model except for oval trigger guard, long trigger, modifications to the loading lever and latch. Imported by Cimarron F.A. Co., Uberti U.S.A. Inc., United States Patent Fire-Arms.
Price: Military model (frame cut for shoulder stock,
steel backstrap) . . . . **$330.00 to $435.00**
Price: Civilian (brass backstrap, trigger guard) **$325.00**

1862 POCKET NAVY PERCUSSION REVOLVER

Caliber: 36, 5-shot. **Barrel:** 5-1/2", 6-1/2", octagonal, 7-groove, LH twist. **Weight:** 27 oz. (5-1/2" barrel). **Length:** 10-1/2" overall (5-1/2" bbl.). **Stocks:** One-piece varnished walnut. **Sights:** Brass pin front, hammer notch rear. **Features:** Rebated cylinder, hinged loading lever, brass or silver-plated backstrap and trigger guard, color-cased frame, hammer, loading lever, plunger and latch, rest blued. Has original-type markings. From Cimarron F.A. Co. and Uberti U.S.A. Inc.
Price: With brass backstrap, trigger guard **$310.00**

1861 Navy Percussion Revolver

Similar to Colt 1851 Navy except has round 7-1/2" barrel, rounded trigger guard, German silver blade front sight, "creeping" loading lever. Fluted or round cylinder. Imported by Cimarron F.A. Co., Uberti U.S.A. Inc.
Price: Steel backstrap, trigger guard, cut for stock. **$300.00**

U.S. PATENT FIRE-ARMS 1862 POCKET NAVY

Caliber: 36. **Barrel:** 4-1/2", 5-1/2", 6-1/2". **Weight:** 27 oz. (5-1/2" barrel). **Length:** 10-1/2" overall (5-1/2" barrel). **Stocks:** Smooth walnut. **Sights:** Brass pin front, hammer notch rear. **Features:** Blued barrel and cylinder, color case-hardened frame, hammer, lever; silver-plated backstrap and trigger guard. Imported from Italy; available from United States Patent Fire-Arms Mfg. Co.
Price: **$335.00**

WALKER 1847 PERCUSSION REVOLVER

Caliber: 44, 6-shot. **Barrel:** 9". **Weight:** 84 oz. **Length:** 15-1/2" overall. **Stocks:** Walnut. **Sights:** Fixed. **Features:** Case-hardened frame, loading lever and hammer; iron backstrap; brass trigger guard; engraved cylinder. Imported by Cabela's, Cimarron F.A. Co., Navy Arms, Dixie Gun Works, Uberti U.S.A. Inc., E.M.F., Cimarron, Traditions, United States Patent Fire-Arms.
Price: About . . . . **$225.00 to $445.00**
Price: Single cased set (Navy Arms) **$405.00**
Price: Deluxe Walker with French fitted case (Navy Arms) **$540.00**
Price: Hartford model, steel frame, German silver trim,
cartouche (E.M.F.) **$295.00**

Cabela's Blue Ridge

Cabela's Traditional Hawken

Cook & Brother

ARMOURY R140 HAWKEN RIFLE

Caliber: 45, 50 or 54.**Barrel:** 29". **Weight:** 8-3/4 to 9 lbs. **Length:** 45-3/4" overall. **Stock:** Walnut, with cheekpiece. **Sights:** Dovetail front, fully adjustable rear. **Features:** Octagon barrel, removable breech plug; double set triggers; blued barrel, brass stock fittings, color case-hardened percussion lock. From Armsport, The Armoury.
Price: . . . . **$225.00 to $245.00**

AUSTIN & HALLECK MODEL 420 LR IN-LINE RIFLE

Caliber: 50. **Barrel:** 26", 1" octagon to 3/4" round; 1:28" twist. **Weight:** 7-7/8 lbs. **Length:** 47-1/2" overall. **Stock:** Lightly figured maple in Classic or Monte Carlo style. **Sights:** Ramp front, fully adjustable rear. **Features:** Blue or electroless nickel finish; in-line percussion action with removable weather shroud; Timney adjustable target trigger with sear block safety. Introduced 1998. Made in U.S. by Austin & Halleck.
Price: Blue **$459.00**
Price: Stainless steel **$549.00**
Price: Blue, hand-select highly figured stock **$775.00**
Price: Blue, exhibition-grade Monte Carlo stock. **$1,322.00**
Price: Stainless steel, exhibition-grade Monte Carlo stock. **$1,422.00**

Austin & Halleck Model 320 LR In-Line Rifle

Similar to the Model 420 LR except has black resin synthetic stock with checkered grip and forend. Introduced 1998. Made in U.S. by Austin & Halleck.
Price: Blue **$380.00**
Price: Stainless steel **$447.00**

AUSTIN & HALLECK MOUNTAIN RIFLE

Caliber: 50. **Barrel:** 32"; 1:28" or 1:66" twist; 1" flats. **Weight:** 7-1/2 lbs. **Length:** 49" overall. **Stock:** Curly maple. **Sights:** Silver blade front, buckhorn rear. **Features:** Available in percussion or flintlock; double throw adjustable set triggers; rust brown finish. Made in U.S. by Austin & Halleck.
Price: Flintlock **$539.00**
Price: Percussion **$578.00**
Price: Percussion, fancy wood **$592.00**
Price: Percussion, select wood. **$660.00**

BOSTONIAN PERCUSSION RIFLE

Caliber: 45. **Barrel:** 30", octagonal. **Weight:** 7-1/4 lbs. **Length:** 46" overall. **Stock:** Walnut. **Sights:** Blade front, fixed notch rear. **Features:** Color case-hardened lock, brass trigger guard, buttplate, patchbox. Imported from Italy by E.M.F.
Price: **$285.00**

CABELA'S TRADITIONAL HAWKEN

Caliber: 50, 54. **Barrel:** 29". **Weight:** About 9 lbs. **Stock:** Walnut. **Sights:** Blade front, open adjustable rear. **Features:** Flintlock or percussion. Adjustable double-set triggers. Polished brass furniture, color case-hardened lock. Imported by Cabela's.
Price: Percussion, right-hand **$189.99**
Price: Percussion, left-hand **$199.99**
Price: Flintlock, right-hand **$224.99**

CABELA'S BLUE RIDGE RIFLE

Caliber: 32, 36, 45, 50. **Barrel:** 39", octagonal. **Weight:** About 7-3/4 lbs. **Length:** 55" overall. **Stock:** American black walnut. **Sights:** Blade front, rear drift adjustable for windage. **Features:** Color case-hardened lockplate and cock/hammer, brass trigger guard and buttplate, double set, double-phased triggers. From Cabela's.
Price: Percussion **$379.99**
Price: Flintlock **$399.99**

CABELA'S KODIAK EXPRESS DOUBLE RIFLE

Caliber: 50, 54, 58, 72. **Barrel:** Length n/a; 1:48" twist. **Weight:** 9.3 lbs. **Length:** 45-1/4" overall. **Stock:** European walnut, oil finish. **Sights:** Fully adjustable double folding-leaf rear, ramp front. **Features:** Percussion. Barrels regulated to point of aim at 75 yards; polished and engraved lock, top tang and trigger guard. From Cabela's.
Price: 50, 54, 58 calibers **$649.99**
Price: 72 caliber **$679.99**

CABELA'S PINE RIDGE LR IN-LINE RIFLE

Caliber: 50. **Barrel:** 26" blued or stainless steel. **Weight:** About 7 lbs. **Length:** N/A. **Stock:** Black synthetic. **Sights:** Fiber-optic blade front, fully adjustable rear. **Features:** No. 209 Flame-Thrower ignition system; adjustable trigger; handles up to 150 grains of blackpowder or Pyrodex. From Cabela's.
Price: (blued barrel) **$229.99**
Price: (stainless steel barrel) **$269.99**

Cabela's Sporterized Hawken Hunter Rifle

Similar to the Traditional Hawken except has more modern stock style with rubber recoil pad, blued furniture, sling swivels. Percussion only, in 50- or 54-caliber.
Price: Carbine or rifle, right-hand **$219.99**

COLT MODEL 1861 MUSKET

Caliber: 58. **Barrel:** 40". **Weight:** 9 lbs., 3 oz. **Length:** 56" overall. **Stock:** Oil-finished walnut. **Sight:** Blade front, adjustable folding leaf rear. **Features:** Made to original specifications and has authentic Civil War Colt markings. Bright-finished metal, blued nipple and rear sight. Bayonet and accessories available. From Colt Blackpowder Arms Co.
Price: **$799.95**

BLACKPOWDER MUSKETS & RIFLES

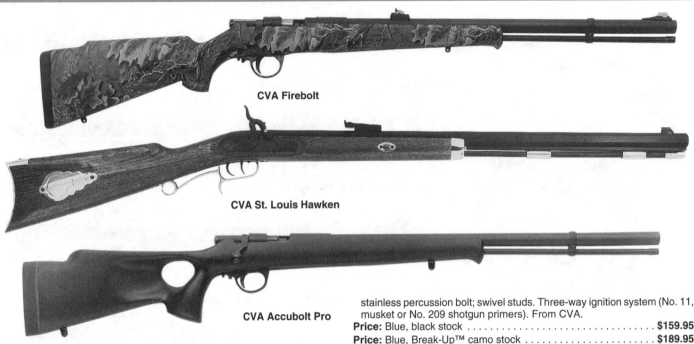

CVA Firebolt

CVA St. Louis Hawken

CVA Accubolt Pro

COOK & BROTHER CONFEDERATE CARBINE

Caliber: 58. **Barrel:** 24". **Weight:** 7-1/2 lbs. **Length:** 40-1/2" overall. **Stock:** Select walnut. **Features:** Recreation of the 1861 New Orleans-made artillery carbine. Color case-hardened lock, browned barrel. Buttplate, trigger guard, barrel bands, sling swivels and nosecap of polished brass. From Euroarms of America.
Price: $447.00
Price: Cook & Brother rifle (33" barrel) $480.00

CUMBERLAND MOUNTAIN BLACKPOWDER RIFLE

Caliber: 50. **Barrel:** 26", round. **Weight:** 9-1/2 lbs. **Length:** 43" overall. **Stock:** American walnut. **Sights:** Bead front, open rear adjustable for windage. **Features:** Falling block action fires with shotshell primer. Blued receiver and barrel. Introduced 1993. Made in U.S. by Cumberland Mountain Arms, Inc.
Price: $931.50

CVA COLORADO MUSKET MAG 100 RIFLE

Caliber: 50, 54 **Barrel:** 26"; 1:32" twist. **Weight:** 7-1/2 lbs. **Length:** 42" overall. **Stock:** Synthetic; black, Hardwoods or X-Tra Brown camo. **Sights:** Illuminator front and rear. **Features:** Sidelock action uses musket caps for ignition. Introduced 1999. From CVA.
Price: With black stock $184.95
Price: With camo stock $219.95

CVA YOUTH HUNTER RIFLE

Caliber: 50. **Barrel:** 24"; 1:48" twist, octagonal. **Weight:** 5-1/2 lbs. **Length:** 38" overall. **Stock:** Stained hardwood. **Sights:** Bead front, Williams adjustable rear. **Features:** Oversize trigger guard; wooden ramrod. Introduced 1999. From CVA.
Price: $135.95

CVA BOBCAT RIFLE

Caliber: 50 or 54. **Barrel:** 26"; 1:48" twist. **Weight:** 6-1/2 lbs. **Length:** 42" overall. **Stock:** Dura-Grip synthetic or wood. **Sights:** Blade front, open rear. **Features:** Oversize trigger guard; wood ramrod; matte black finish. Introduced 1995. From CVA.
Price: (wood stock, 50 cal. only) $127.95
Price: (black synthetic stock, 50 or 54 cal.) $104.95

CVA ECLIPSE 209 MAGNUM IN-LINE RIFLE

Caliber: 50. **Barrel:** 24" round; 1:32" rifling. **Weight:** 7 lbs. **Length:** 42" overall. **Stock:** Black or Mossy Oak® Break-Up™ camo synthetic. **Sights:** Illuminator Fiber Optic Sight System; drilled and tapped for scope mounting. **Features:** In-line action uses modern trigger with automatic safety;

stainless percussion bolt; swivel studs. Three-way ignition system (No. 11, musket or No. 209 shotgun primers). From CVA.
Price: Blue, black stock $159.95
Price: Blue, Break-Up™ camo stock $189.95

CVA Stag Horn 209 Magnum Rifle

Similar to the Eclipse except has light-gathering Solar Sights, manual safety, black synthetic stock and ramrod. Weighs 6 lbs. From CVA.
Price: 50 cal. $129.95

CVA MOUNTAIN RIFLE

Caliber: 50. **Barrel:** 32"; 1:66" rifling. **Weight:** 8-1/2 lbs. **Length:** NA. **Stock:** American hard maple. **Sights:** Blade front, buckhorn rear. **Features:** Browned steel furniture; German silver wedge plates; patchbox. Made in U.S. From CVA.
Price: $399.95

CVA ST. LOUIS HAWKEN RIFLE

Caliber: 50, 54. **Barrel:** 28", octagon; 15/16" across flats; 1:48" twist. **Weight:** 8 lbs. **Length:** 44" overall. **Stock:** Select hardwood. **Sights:** Beaded blade front, fully adjustable open rear. **Features:** Fully adjustable double-set triggers; synthetic ramrod (kits have wood); brass patchbox, wedge plates, nosecap, thimbles, trigger guard and buttplate; blued barrel; color case-hardened, engraved lockplate. V-type mainspring. Button breech. Introduced 1981. From CVA.
Price: St. Louis Hawken, finished (50-, 54-cal.) $207.95
Price: Left-hand, percussion $264.95
Price: Flintlock, 50-cal. only $264.95
Price: Percussion kit (50-cal., blued, wood ramrod) $191.95

CVA HunterBolt 209 Magnum Rifle

Similar to the Firebolt except has 24" barrel and black or Mossy Oak® Break-Up™ synthetic stock. Three-way ignition system. Weighs 6 lbs. From CVA.
Price: 45 or 50 cal. .... $199.95 to $254.95

CVA FIREBOLT MUSKETMAG BOLT-ACTION IN-LINE RIFLES

Caliber: 45 or 50. **Barrel:** 26". **Weight:** 7 lbs. **Length:** 44". **Stock:** Rubber-coated black or Mossy Oak® Break-Up™ camo synthetic. **Sights:** CVA Illuminator Fiber Optic Sight System. **Features:** Bolt-action, in-line ignition system handles up to 150 grains blackpowder or Pyrodex; Nickel or matte blue barrel; removable breech plug; trigger-block safety. Introduced 1997. Three-way ignition system. From CVA.
Price: Nickel finish, black stock, 50 cal. $279.95
Price: Nickel finish, black stock, 45 cal. $289.95
Price: Nickel finish, Break-Up™ stock, 45 cal. $329.95
Price: Matte blue finish, Break-Up™ camo stock, 50 cal. $299.95
Price: Matte blue finish, black stock, 50 cal. $259.95
Price: Matte blue finish, Break-Up™ stock, 45 cal. $309.95

BLACKPOWDER

Dixie English Matchlock

Dixie Inline Carbine

Dixie 1859 Sharps

Dixie Model 1816

DIXIE ENGLISH MATCHLOCK MUSKET

Caliber: 72. **Barrel:** 44". **Weight:** 8 lbs. **Length:** 57.75" overall. **Stock:** Walnut with satin oil finish. **Sights:** Blade front, open rear adjustable for windage. **Features:** Replica of circa 1600-1680 English matchlock. Getz barrel with 11" octagonal area at rear, rest is round with cannon-type muzzle. All steel finished in the white. Imported by Dixie Gun Works.
Price: $895.00

DIXIE EARLY AMERICAN JAEGER RIFLE

Caliber: 54. **Barrel:** 27-1/2" octagonal; 1:24" twist. **Weight:** 8-1/4 lbs. **Length:** 43-1/2" overall. **Stock:** American walnut; sliding wooden patchbox on on butt. **Sights:** Notch rear, blade front. **Features:** Flintlock or percussion. Browned steel furniture. Introduced 2000. Imported from Italy by Dixie Gun Works.
Price: Flintlock or percussion $695.00

DIXIE DELUXE CUB RIFLE

Caliber: 40. **Barrel:** 28". **Weight:** 6-1/2 lbs. **Stock:** Walnut. **Sights:** Fixed.**Features:** Short rifle for small game and beginning shooters. Brass patchbox and furniture. Flint or percussion. From Dixie Gun Works.
Price: Finished $415.00
Price: Kit $375.00
Price: Super Cub (50-caliber) $367.00

DIXIE 1863 SPRINGFIELD MUSKET

Caliber: 58 (.570" patched ball or .575" Minie). **Barrel:** 50", rifled. **Stock:** Walnut stained. **Sights:** Blade front, adjustable ladder-type rear. **Features:** Bright-finish lock, barrel, furniture. Reproduction of the last of the regulation muzzleloaders. Imported from Japan by Dixie Gun Works.
Price: Finished $595.00
Price: Kit $525.00

DIXIE INLINE CARBINE

Caliber: 50, 54. **Barrel:** 24"; 1:32" twist. **Weight:** 6.5 lbs. **Length:** 41" overall. **Stock:** Walnut-finished hardwood with Monte Carlo comb. **Sights:** Ramp front with red insert, open fully adjustable rear. **Features:** Sliding "bolt" fully encloses cap and nipple. Fully adjustable trigger, automatic safety. Aluminum ramrod. Imported from Italy by Dixie Gun Works.
Price: $349.95

DIXIE PEDERSOLI 1857 MAUSER RIFLE

Caliber: 54. **Barrel:** 39-3/8". **Weight:** N/A. **Length:** 52" overall. **Stock:** European walnut with oil finish, sling swivels. **Sights:** Fully adjustable rear, lug front. **Features:** Percussion (musket caps). Armory bright finish with color case-hardened lock and barrel tang, engraved lockplate, steel ramrod. Introduced 2000. Imported from Italy by Dixie Gun Works.
Price: $895.00

DIXIE PEDERSOLI 1766 CHARLEVILLE MUSKET

Caliber: 69. **Barrel:** 44-3/4". **Weight:** 10-1/2 lbs. **Length:** 57-1/2" overall. **Stock:** European walnut with oil finish. **Sights:** Fixed rear, lug front. **Features:** Smoothbore flintlock. Armory bright finish with steel furniture and ramrod. Introduced 2000. Imported from Italy by Dixie Gun Works.
Price: $795.00

DIXIE SHARPS NEW MODEL 1859 MILITARY RIFLE

Caliber: 54. **Barrel:** 30", 6-groove; 1:48" twist. **Weight:** 9 lbs. **Length:** 45-1/2" overall. **Stock:** Oiled walnut. **Sights:** Blade front, ladder-style rear. **Features:** Blued barrel, color case-hardened barrel bands, receiver, hammer, nosecap, lever, patchbox cover and buttplate. Introduced 1995. Imported from Italy by Dixie Gun Works.
Price: $895.00

DIXIE U.S. MODEL 1816 FLINTLOCK MUSKET

Caliber: 69. **Barrel:** 42", smoothbore. **Weight:** 9.75 lbs. **Length:** 56.5" overall. **Stock:** Walnut with oil finish. **Sights:** Blade front. **Features:** All metal finished "National Armory Bright"; three barrel bands with springs; steel ramrod with button-shaped head. Imported by Dixie Gun Works.
Price: $725.00

DIXIE U.S. MODEL 1861 SPRINGFIELD

Caliber: 58. **Barrel:** 40". **Weight:** About 8 lbs. **Length:** 55-13/16" overall. **Stock:** Oil-finished walnut. **Sights:** Blade front, step adjustable rear. **Features:** Exact recreation of original rifle. Sling swivels attached to trigger guard bow and middle barrel band. Lockplate marked "1861" with eagle motif and "U.S. Springfield" in front of hammer; "U.S." stamped on top of buttplate. From Dixie Gun Works.
Price: $595.00
Price: From Stone Mountain Arms $599.00
Price: Kit $525.00

BLACKPOWDER MUSKETS & RIFLES

Dixie U.S. Model 1861

Euroarms Volunteer

Euroarms 1861

Gonic Model 93 Thumbhole

Harper's Ferry 1803

E.M.F. 1863 SHARPS MILITARY CARBINE
Caliber: 54. **Barrel:** 22", round. **Weight:** 8 lbs. **Length:** 39" overall. **Stock:** Oiled walnut. **Sights:** Blade front, military ladder-type rear. **Features:** Color or case-hardened lock, rest blued. Imported by E.M.F.
Price: **$600.00**

EUROARMS VOLUNTEER TARGET RIFLE
Caliber: .451. **Barrel:** 33" (two-band), 36" (three-band). **Weight:** 11 lbs. (two-band). **Length:** 48.75" overall (two-band). **Stock:** European walnut with checkered wrist and forend. **Sights:** Hooded bead front, adjustable rear with interchangeable leaves. **Features:** Alexander Henry-type rifling with 1:20" twist. Color case-hardened hammer and lockplate, brass trigger guard and nosecap, rest blued. Imported by Euroarms of America.
Price: Two-band **$720.00**
Price: Three-band. **$773.00**

EUROARMS 1861 SPRINGFIELD RIFLE
Caliber: 58. **Barrel:** 40". **Weight:** About 10 lbs. **Length:** 55.5" overall. **Stock:** European walnut. **Sights:** Blade front, three-leaf military rear. **Features:** Reproduction of the original three-band rifle. Lockplate marked "1861" with eagle and "U.S. Springfield." Metal left in the white. Imported by Euroarms of America.
Price: **$530.00**

GONIC MODEL 93 M/L RIFLE
Caliber: 45, 50. **Barrel:** 26"; 1:24" twist. **Weight:** 6-1/2 to 7 lbs. **Length:** 43" overall. **Stock:** American hardwood with black finish. **Sights:** Adjustable or aperture rear, hooded post front. **Features:** Adjustable trigger with side safety; unbreakable ram rod; comes with A. Z. scope bases installed. Introduced 1993. Made in U.S. by Gonic Arms, Inc.
Price: Model 93 Standard (blued barrel) **$720.00**
Price: Model 93 Standard (stainless brl., 50 cal. only) **$782.00**

Gonic Model 93 Deluxe M/L Rifle
Similar to the Model 93 except has classic-style walnut or gray laminated wood stock. Introduced 1998. Made in U.S. by Gonic Arms, Inc.
Price: Blue barrel, sights, scope base, choice of stock **$902.00**
Price: Stainless barrel, sights, scope base, choice of stock
(50 cal. only). **$964.00**

Gonic Model 93 Mountain Thumbhole M/L Rifles
Similar to the Model 93 except has high-grade walnut or gray laminate stock with extensive hand-checkered panels, Monte Carlo cheekpiece and beavertail forend; integral muzzle brake. Introduced 1998. Made in U.S. by Gonic Arms, Inc.
Price: Blue or stainless. **$2,625.00**

HARPER'S FERRY 1803 FLINTLOCK RIFLE
Caliber: 54 or 58. **Barrel:** 35". **Weight:** 9 lbs. **Length:** 59-1/2" overall. **Stock:** Walnut with cheekpiece. **Sights:** Brass blade front, fixed steel rear. **Features:** Brass trigger guard, sideplate, buttplate; steel patchbox. Imported by Euroarms of America, Navy Arms (54-cal. only), Cabela's.
Price: . . . . **$495.95 to $729.00**
Price: 54-cal. (Navy Arms) **$625.00**
Price: 54-caliber (Cabela's) **$599.99**

BLACKPOWDER MUSKETS & RIFLES

J.P. Murray

Kentucky Flintlock

Knight Bighorn In/Line

HAWKEN RIFLE
Caliber: 45, 50, 54 or 58. **Barrel:** 28", blued, 6-groove rifling. **Weight:** 8-3/4 lbs. **Length:** 44" overall. **Stock:** Walnut with cheekpiece. **Sights:** Blade front, fully adjustable rear. **Features:** Coil mainspring, double-set triggers, polished brass furniture. From Armsport, Navy Arms, E.M.F.
Price: .... **$220.00 to $345.00**

J.P. MURRAY 1862-1864 CAVALRY CARBINE
Caliber: 58 (.577" Minie). **Barrel:** 23". **Weight:** 7 lbs., 9 oz. **Length:** 39" overall. **Stock:** Walnut. **Sights:** Blade front, rear drift adjustable for windage. **Features:** Browned barrel, color case-hardened lock, blued swivel and band springs, polished brass buttplate, trigger guard, barrel bands. From Navy Arms, Euroarms of America.
Price: .... **$405.00 to $453.00**

J.P. HENRY TRADE RIFLE
Caliber: 54. **Barrel:** 34"; 1" flats. **Weight:** 8-1/2 lbs. **Length:** 45" overall. **Stock:** Premium curly maple. **Sights:** Silver blade front, fixed buckhorn rear. **Features:** Brass buttplate, side plate, trigger guard and nosecap; browned barrel and lock; L&R Large English percussion lock; single trigger. Made in U.S. by J.P. Gunstocks, Inc.
Price: **$965.50**

KENTUCKIAN RIFLE
Caliber: 44. **Barrel:** 35". **Weight:** 7 lbs. (Rifle), 5-1/2 lbs. (Carbine). **Length:** 51" overall (Rifle), 43" (Carbine). **Stock:** Walnut stain. **Sights:** Brass blade front, steel V-ramp rear. **Features:** Octagon barrel, case-hardened and engraved lockplates. Brass furniture. Imported by Dixie Gun Works.
Price: Flintlock **$269.95**
Price: Percussion **$259.95**

KENTUCKY FLINTLOCK RIFLE
Caliber: 44, 45, or 50. **Barrel:** 35". **Weight:** 7 lbs. **Length:** 50" overall. **Stock:** Walnut stained, brass fittings. **Sights:** Fixed. **Features:** Available in carbine model also, 28" bbl. Some variations in detail, finish. Kits also available from some importers. Imported by Navy Arms, The Armoury.
Price: About .... **$217.95 to $345.00**
Price: Flintlock, 45 or 50-cal. (Navy Arms) **$435.00**

Kentucky Percussion Rifle
Similar to flintlock except percussion lock. Finish and features vary with importer. Imported by Navy Arms, The Armoury, CVA.

Price: About **$259.95**
Price: 45- or 50-cal. (Navy Arms) **$425.00**
Price: Kit, 50-cal. (CVA) **$189.95**

KNIGHT 50 CALIBER DISC IN-LINE RIFLE
Caliber: 50. **Barrel:** 24", 26". **Weight:** 7 lbs., 14 oz. **Length:** 43" overall (24" barrel). **Stock:** Checkered synthetic with palm swell grip, rubber recoil pad, swivel studs; black, Advantage or Mossy Oak Break-Up camouflage. **Sights:** Bead on ramp front, fully adjustable open rear. **Features:** Bolt-action in-line system uses #209 shotshell primer for ignition; primer is held in plastic drop-in Primer Disc. Available in blued or stainless steel. Made in U.S. by Knight Rifles (Modern Muzzleloading).
Price: .... **$459.95 to $615.95**

Knight Master Hunter II DISC In-Line Rifle
Similar to Knight 50 caliber DISC rifle except features premier, wood laminated two-tone stock, gold-plated trigger and engraved trigger guard, jeweled bolt and fluted, air-gauged Green Mountain 26" barrel. Length 45" overall, weighs 7 lbs., 7 oz. Includes black composite thumbhole stock. Introduced 2000. Made in U.S. by Knight Rifles (Modern Muzzleloading).
Price: **$1,099.95**

Knight 45 Super DISC In-Line Rifle
Similar to the 50 caliber DISC rifle except in 45 caliber to fire saboted bullets and up to 150 grains of blackpowder or equivalent at up to 2,600 fps. Fluted 26" Green Mountain barrel in blue or stainless finish; thumbhole or standard synthetic stock in black, Advantage Timber HD or Mossy Oak Break-Up camouflage. Weighs 8 lbs., 3 oz. Made in U.S. by Knight Rifles (Modern Muzzleloading).

KNIGHT BIGHORN IN-LINE RIFLE
Caliber: 50. **Barrel:** 22", 26"; 1:28" twist. **Weight:** About 7 lbs. **Length:** 41" overall (22" barrel). **Stock:** Synthetic; black Advantage or Mossy Oak Break-Up camouflage. Black rubber recoil pad. **Sights:** Fully adjustable Tru-Glo fiber optic. **Features:** Patented double safety system; adjustable trigger; comes with #11 Red Hot Nipple and 209 shotshell primer conversion kit. Available in blue or stainless steel. Made in U.S. by Knight Rifles.
Price: (right- or left-hand model) .... **$349.95 to $478.95**

KNIGHT AMERICAN KNIGHT M/L RIFLE
Caliber: 50. **Barrel:** 22"; 1:28" twist. **Weight:** 6 lbs. **Length:** 41" overall. **Stock:** Black composite. **Sights:** Bead on ramp front, open fully adjustable rear. **Features:** Double safety system; one-piece removable hammer assembly; drilled and tapped for scope mounting. Introduced 1998. Made in U.S. by Knight Rifles.
Price: **$199.95**

BLACKPOWDER

Knight Wolverine II

London Armory 1861

Lyman Cougar In/Line

Lyman Trade

BLACKPOWDER

KNIGHT WOLVERINE II RIFLE

Caliber: 50, 54. **Barrel:** 22". **Weight:** 6 lbs., 7 oz. **Stock:** Black, Advantage Timber HD, Mossy Oak Break-Up camo. **Sights:** Fully adjustable Tru-Glo fiber optic. **Features:** Blued or stainless finish; patented double safety system; removable breech plug; Sure-Fire in-line percussion ignition system; can be converted to use 209 shotshell primers. Handles up to 150 grains of blackpowder. Introduced 2000. Made in U.S. by Knight Rifles.
Price: From **$277.95**
Price: Wolverine II stainless, from **$341.95**
Price: Wolverine II thumbhole, from **$312.95**
Price: Youth model value pack, blued, 50-cal. only **$299.95**

LONDON ARMORY 2-BAND 1858 ENFIELD

Caliber: .577" Minie, .575" round ball. **Barrel:** 33". **Weight:** 10 lbs. **Length:** 49" overall. **Stock:** Walnut. **Sights:** Folding leaf rear adjustable for elevation. **Features:** Blued barrel, color case-hardened lock and hammer, polished brass buttplate, trigger guard, nosecap. From Navy Arms, Euroarms of America, Dixie Gun Works.
Price: . . . . **$385.00 to $531.00**

LONDON ARMORY 1861 ENFIELD MUSKETOON

Caliber: 58, Minie ball. **Barrel:** 24", round. **Weight:** 7 - 7-1/2 lbs. **Length:** 40-1/2" overall. **Stock:** Walnut, with sling swivels. **Sights:** Blade front, graduated military-leaf rear. **Features:** Brass trigger guard, nosecap, buttplate; blued barrel, bands, lockplate, swivels. Imported by Euroarms of America, Navy Arms.
Price: . . . . **$300.00 to $427.00**
Price: Kit. . . . . **$365.00 to $373.00**

LONDON ARMORY 3-BAND 1853 ENFIELD

Caliber: 58 (.577" Minie, .575" round ball, .580" maxi ball). **Barrel:** 39". **Weight:** 9-1/2 lbs. **Length:** 54" overall. **Stock:** European walnut. **Sights:** Inverted "V" front, traditional Enfield folding ladder rear. **Features:** Recreation of the famed London Armory Company Pattern 1853 Enfield Musket. One-piece walnut stock, brass buttplate, trigger guard and nosecap. Lockplate marked "London Armoury Co." and with a British crown. Blued Baddeley barrel bands. From Dixie Gun Works, Euroarms of America, Navy Arms.
Price: About . . . . **$350.00 to $495.00**
Price: Assembled kit (Dixie, Euroarms of America) . . **$425.00 to $431.00**

LYMAN COUGAR IN-LINE RIFLE

Caliber: 50 or 54. **Barrel:** 22"; 1:24" twist. **Weight:** NA. **Length:** NA. **Stock:** Smooth walnut; swivel studs. **Sights:** Bead on ramp front, folding adjustable rear. Drilled and tapped for Lyman 57WTR receiver sight and Weaver scope bases. **Features:** Blued barrel and receiver. Has bolt safety notch and trigger safety. Rubber recoil pad. Delrin ramrod. Introduced 1996. From Lyman.
Price: **$249.95**
Price: Stainless steel **$299.95**

LYMAN TRADE RIFLE

Caliber: 50, 54. **Barrel:** 28" octagon; 1:48" twist. **Weight:** 8-3/4 lbs. **Length:** 45" overall. **Stock:** European walnut. **Sights:** Blade front, open rear adjustable for windage or optional fixed sights. **Features:** Fast twist rifling for conical bullets. Polished brass furniture with blue steel parts, stainless steel nipple. Hook breech, single trigger, coil spring percussion lock. Steel barrel rib and ramrod ferrules. Introduced 1980. From Lyman.
Price: Percussion **$299.95**
Price: Flintlock **$324.95**

Lyman Deerstalker

Lyman Great Plains

Markesbery Black Bear

Markesbery KM Colorado

LYMAN DEERSTALKER RIFLE

Caliber: 50, 54. **Barrel:** 24", octagonal; 1:48" rifling. **Weight:** 7-1/2 lbs. **Stock:** Walnut with black rubber buttpad. **Sights:** Lyman #37MA beaded front, fully adjustable fold-down Lyman #16A rear. **Features:** Stock has less drop for quick sighting. All metal parts are blackened, with color case-hardened lock; single trigger. Comes with sling and swivels. Available in flint or percussion. Introduced 1990. From Lyman.

Price: 50- or 54-cal., percussion	$304.95
Price: 50- or 54-cal., flintlock	$334.95
Price: 50- or 54-cal., percussion, left-hand	$319.95
Price: 50-cal., flintlock, left-hand	$349.95
Price: Stainless steel	$384.95

LYMAN GREAT PLAINS RIFLE

Caliber: 50- or 54-cal. **Barrel:** 32"; 1:60" twist. **Weight:** 9 lbs. **Stock:** Walnut. **Sights:** Steel blade front, buckhorn rear adjustable for windage and elevation and fixed notch primitive sight included. **Features:** Blued steel furniture. Stainless steel nipple. Coil spring lock, Hawken-style trigger guard and double-set triggers. Round thimbles recessed and sweated into rib. Steel wedge plates and toe plate. Introduced 1979. From Lyman.

Price: Percussion	$434.95
Price: Flintlock	$459.95
Price: Percussion kit	$349.95
Price: Flintlock kit	$374.95
Price: Left-hand percussion	$444.95
Price: Left-hand flintlock	$469.95

Lyman Great Plains Hunter Rifle

Similar to the Great Plains model except has 1:32" twist shallow-groove barrel and comes drilled and tapped for the Lyman 57GPR peep sight.

Price:	$434.95 to $459.95

MARKESBERY KM BLACK BEAR M/L RIFLE

Caliber: 36, 45, 50, 54. **Barrel:** 24"; 1:26" twist. **Weight:** 6-1/2 lbs. **Length:** 38-1/2" overall. **Stock:** Two-piece American hardwood, walnut, black laminate, green laminate, black composition, X-Tra or Mossy Oak Break-Up camouflage. **Sights:** Bead front, open fully adjustable rear. **Features:** Interchangeable barrels; exposed hammer; Outer-Line Magnum ignition system uses small rifle primer or standard No. 11 cap and nipple. Blue, black matte, or stainless. Made in U.S. by Markesbery Muzzle Loaders.

Price: American hardwood walnut, blue finish	$536.63
Price: American hardwood walnut, stainless	$553.09
Price: Black laminate, blue finish	$539.67
Price: Camouflage stock, blue finish	$556.46
Price: Black composite, blue finish	$532.65

MARKESBERY KM COLORADO ROCKY MOUNTAIN M/L RIFLE

Caliber: 36, 45, 50, 54. **Barrel:** 24"; 1:26" twist. **Weight:** 6-1/2 lbs. **Length:** 38-1/2" overall. **Stock:** American hardwood walnut, green or black laminate. **Sights:** Firesight bead on ramp front, fully adjustable open rear. **Features:** Replicates Reed/Watson rifle of 1851. Straight grip stock with or without two barrel bands, rubber recoil pad, large-spur hammer. Made in U.S. by Markesbery Muzzle Loaders, Inc.

Price: American hardwood walnut, blue finish	$545.92
Price: Black or green laminate, blue finish	$548.30
Price: American hardwood walnut, stainless	$563.17
Price: Black or green laminate, stainless	$566.34

Markesbery KM Grizzly Bear

Markesbery KM Brown Bear

Mississippi 1841

Navy Arms 1763

Markesbery KM Brown Bear M/L Rifle

Similar to the KM Black Bear except has one-piece thumbhole stock with Monte Carlo comb. Stock available in Crotch Walnut composite, green or black laminate, black composite or X-Tra or Mossy Oak Break-Up camouflage. Contact maker for complete price listing. Made in U.S. by Markesbery Muzzle Loaders, Inc.

Price: Black composite, blue finish **$658.83**
Price: Crotch Walnut composite, stainless **$676.11**
Price: Green laminate, stainless **$680.07**

Markesbery KM Grizzly Bear M/L Rifle

Similar to the KM Black Bear except has thumbhole buttstock with Monte Carlo comb. Stock available in Crotch Walnut composite, green or black laminate, black composite or X-Tra or Mossy Oak Break-Up camouflage. Contact maker for complete price listing. Made in U.S. by Markesbery Muzzle Loaders, Inc.

Price: Black composite, blue finish **$642.96**
Price: Crotch Walnut composite, stainless **$660.98**
Price: Camouflage composite, blue finish **$666.67**

Markesbery KM Polar Bear M/L Rifle

Similar to the KM Black Bear except has one-piece stock with Monte Carlo comb. Stock available in American Hardwood walnut, green or black laminate, black composite, or X-Tra or Mossy Oak Break-Up camouflage. Has interchangeable barrel system, Outer-Line ignition system, cross-bolt double safety. Available in 36, 45, 50, 54 caliber. Contact maker for full price listing. Made in U.S. by Markesbery Muzzle Loaders, Inc.

Price: American Hardwood walnut , blue finish **$539.01**
Price: Black composite, blue finish **$536.63**
Price: Black laminate, blue finish **$541.17**
Price: Camouflage, stainless **$573.94**

MDM BUCKWACKA IN-LINE RIFLES

Caliber: 45, 50. **Barrel:** 23", 25". **Weight:** 7 to 7-3/4 lbs. **Length:** N/A. **Stock:** Black, walnut, laminated and camouflage finishes. **Sights:** Williams Fire Sight blade front, Williams fully adjustable rear with ghost-ring peep aperture. **Features:** Break-open action; Incinerating Ignition System incorporates 209 shotshell primer directly into breech plug; 50-caliber models handle up to 150 grains of Pyrodex; synthetic ramrod; transfer bar safety; stainless or blued finish. Made in U.S. by Millennium Designed Muzzleloaders Ltd.

Price: 50 cal., blued finish **$309.95**
Price: 50 cal., stainless. **$339.95**
Price: Camouflage stock . . . . **$359.95 to $389.95**

MDM M2K In-Line Rifle

Similar to Buckwacka except has adjustable trigger and double-safety mechanism designed to prevent misfires. Made in U.S. by Millennium Designed Muzzleloaders Ltd.

Price: . . . . **$529.00 to $549.00**

Mississippi 1841 Percussion Rifle

Similar to Zouave rifle but patterned after U.S. Model 1841. Imported by Dixie Gun Works, Euroarms of America, Navy Arms.

Price: About . . . . **$430.00 to $500.00**

NAVY ARMS 1763 CHARLEVILLE

Caliber: 69. **Barrel:** 44-5/8". **Weight:** 8 lbs., 12 oz. **Length:** 59-3/8" overall. **Stock:** Walnut. **Sights:** Brass blade front. **Features:** Replica of the French musket used by American troops during the Revolution. Imported by Navy Arms.

Price: **$1,020.00**

BLACKPOWDER MUSKETS & RIFLES

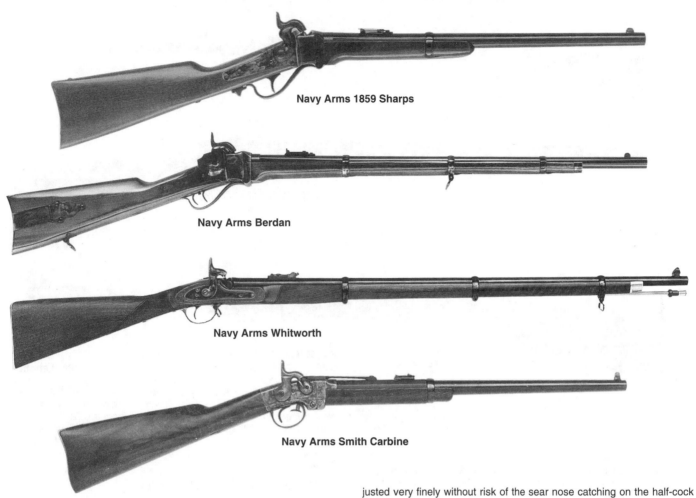

Navy Arms 1859 Sharps

Navy Arms Berdan

Navy Arms Whitworth

Navy Arms Smith Carbine

NAVY ARMS PARKER-HALE VOLUNTEER RIFLE

Caliber: .451. **Barrel:** 32". **Weight:** 9-1/2 lbs. **Length:** 49" overall. **Stock:** Walnut, checkered wrist and forend. **Sights:** Globe front, adjustable ladder-type rear. **Features:** Recreation of the type of gun issued to volunteer regiments during the 1860s. Rigby-pattern rifling, patent breech, detented lock. Stock is glass bedded for accuracy. Imported by Navy Arms.
Price: **$905.00**

NAVY ARMS 1859 SHARPS CAVALRY CARBINE

Caliber: 54. **Barrel:** 22". **Weight:** 7-3/4 lbs. **Length:** 39" overall. **Stock:** Walnut. **Sights:** Blade front, military ladder-type rear. **Features:** Color case-hardened action, blued barrel. Has saddle ring. Introduced 1991. Imported from Navy Arms.
Price: **$1,000.00**

NAVY ARMS BERDAN 1859 SHARPS RIFLE

Caliber: 54. **Barrel:** 30". **Weight:** 8 lbs., 8 oz. **Length:** 46-3/4" overall. **Stock:** Walnut. **Sights:** Blade front, folding military ladder-type rear. **Features:** Replica of the Union sniper rifle used by Berdan's 1st and 2nd Sharpshooter regiments. Color case-hardened receiver, patchbox, furniture. Double-set triggers. Imported by Navy Arms.
Price: **$1,165.00**
Price: 1859 Sharps Infantry Rifle (three-band). **$1,100.00**

NAVY ARMS PARKER-HALE WHITWORTH MILITARY TARGET RIFLE

Caliber: 45. **Barrel:** 36". **Weight:** 9-1/4 lbs. **Length:** 52-1/2" overall. **Stock:** Walnut. Checkered at wrist and forend. **Sights:** Hooded post front, open step-adjustable rear. **Features:** Faithful reproduction of the Whitworth rifle, only bored for 45-cal. Trigger has a detented lock, capable of being ad-justed very finely without risk of the sear nose catching on the half-cock bent and damaging both parts. Introduced 1978. Imported by Navy Arms.
Price: **$930.00**

NAVY ARMS SMITH CARBINE

Caliber: 50. **Barrel:** 21-1/2". **Weight:** 7-3/4 lbs. **Length:** 39" overall. **Stock:** American walnut. **Sights:** Brass blade front, folding ladder-type rear. **Features:** Replica of the breech-loading Civil War carbine. Color case-hardened receiver, rest blued. Cavalry model has saddle ring and bar, Artillery model has sling swivels. Imported by Navy Arms.
Price: Cavalry model **$635.00**
Price: Artillery model **$635.00**

NAVY ARMS 1863 C.S. RICHMOND RIFLE

Caliber: 58. **Barrel:** 40". **Weight:** 10 lbs. **Length:** NA. **Stocks:** Walnut. **Sights:** Blade front, adjustable rear. **Features:** Copy of the three-band rifle musket made at Richmond Armory for the Confederacy. All steel polished bright. Imported by Navy Arms.
Price: **$590.00**

NAVY ARMS 1861 SPRINGFIELD RIFLE

Caliber: 58. **Barrel:** 40" **Weight:** 10 lbs., 4 oz. **Length:** 56" overall. **Stock:** Walnut. **Sights:** Blade front, military leaf rear. **Features:** Steel barrel, lock and all furniture have polished bright finish. Has 1855-style hammer. Imported by Navy Arms.
Price: **$590.00**

NAVY ARMS 1863 SPRINGFIELD

Caliber: 58, uses .575 Minie. **Barrel:** 40", rifled. **Weight:** 9-1/2 lbs. **Length:** 56" overall. **Stock:** Walnut. **Sights:** Open rear adjustable for elevation. **Features:** Full-size, three-band musket. Polished bright metal, including lock. From Navy Arms.
Price: Finished rifle. **$590.00**

BLACKPOWDER MUSKETS & RIFLES

Navy Arms 1863

Pacific Model 1837 Zephyr

Peifer TS-93

OCTOBER COUNTRY GREAT AMERICAN SPORTING RIFLE
Caliber: 62, 66, 69, 72. **Barrel:** 28" or 36"; tapered octagon 1-1/4" to 1"; 1:104" twist. **Weight:** 9 lbs. (28" bbl.) **Length:** 48" overall. **Stock:** Walnut (optional maple with ebony nosecap). **Sights:** Silver blade front, adjustable shallow "V" rear (optional three-blade express or A.O. ghost ring). **Features:** Hooked, patent Manton-style breech plug; iron furniture; bedded barrel; blue finish. Made in U.S. by October Country Muzzleloading Inc.
Price: **$1,695.00**

OCTOBER COUNTRY LIGHT AMERICAN SPORTING RIFLE
Caliber: 62. **Barrel:** 28" or 36"; tapered octagon 1-1/8" to 1"; 1:104" twist. **Weight:** 8 lbs. **Length:** 48" overall. **Stock:** Walnut (optional maple with ebony nosecap). **Sights:** Blade front, adjustable shallow "V" rear (optional three-blade express or A.O. ghost ring). **Features:** English-style hooked breach with side bar; L&R lock; iron furniture; bedded barrel; hot blue finish. Made in U.S. by October Country Muzzleloading Inc.
Price: **$1,595.00**

OCTOBER COUNTRY HEAVY RIFLE
Caliber: 8 bore or 4 bore. **Barrel:** 30"; tapered octagon 1-1/2" to 1-1/4" (8 bore) or 1-3/4" to 1-1/2" (4 bore); 1:144" twist. **Weight:** 14 lbs. (8 bore) or 18 lbs. (4 bore). **Length:** 50" overall. **Stock:** Checkered English walnut. **Sights:** Blade front, three-blade express rear. **Features:** English-style hooked breech; L&R lock; iron furniture; bedded barrel; hot blue finish. Made in U.S. by October Country Muzzleloading Inc.
Price: **$2,995.00**

OCTOBER COUNTRY DOUBLE RIFLE
Caliber: 8 bore. **Barrel:** 30" round; 1:144" twist. **Weight:** 14 lbs. **Length:** 50". **Stock:** Checkered English walnut. **Sights:** Blade front, three-blade express rear. **Features:** English-style hooked breech; L& R lock; iron furniture; bedded barrel; hot blue finish. Made in U.S. by October Country Muzzleloaders Inc.
Price: **$4,995.00**

PACIFIC RIFLE MODEL 1837 ZEPHYR
Caliber: 62. **Barrel:** 30", tapered octagon. **Weight:** 7-3/4 lbs. **Length:** NA. **Stock:** Oil-finished fancy walnut. **Sights:** German silver blade front, semi-buckhorn rear. Options available. **Features:** Improved underhammer action. First production rifle to offer Forsyth rifle, with narrow lands and shallow rifling with 1:144" pitch for high-velocity round balls. Metal finish is slow rust brown with nitre blue accents. Optional sights, finishes and integral muzzle brake available. Introduced 1995. Made in U.S. by Pacific Rifle Co.
Price: From **$995.00**

Pacific Rifle Big Bore, African Rifles
Similar to the 1837 Zephyr except in 72-caliber and 8-bore. The 72-caliber is available in standard form with 28" barrel, or as the African with flat buttplate, checkered upgraded wood; weight is 9 lbs. The 8-bore African has dual-cap ignition, 24" barrel, weighs 12 lbs., checkered English walnut, engraving, gold inlays. Introduced 1998. Made in U.S. by Pacific Rifle Co.
Price: 72-caliber, from **$1,150.00**
Price: 8-bore from. **$2,500.00**

PEIFER MODEL TS-93 RIFLE
Caliber: 45, 50. **Barrel:** 24" Douglas premium; 1:20" twist in 45; 1:28" in 50. **Weight:** 7 lbs. **Length:** 43-1/4" overall. **Stock:** Bell & Carlson solid composite, with recoil pad, swivel studs. **Sights:** Williams bead front on ramp, fully adjustable open rear. Drilled and tapped for Weaver scope mounts with dovetail for rear peep. **Features:** In-line ignition uses #209 shotshell primer; extremely fast lock time; fully enclosed breech; adjustable trigger; automatic safety; removable primer holder. Blue or stainless. Made in U.S. by Peifer Rifle Co. Introduced 1996.
Price: Blue, black stock **$730.00**
Price: Blue, wood or camouflage composite stock, or stainless with black composite stock **$803.00**
Price: Stainless, wood or camouflage composite stock **$876.00**

PRAIRIE RIVER ARMS PRA CLASSIC RIFLE
Caliber: 50, 54. **Barrel:** 26"; 1:28" twist. **Weight:** 7-1/2 lbs. **Length:** 40-1/2" overall. **Stock:** Hardwood or black all-weather. **Sights:** Blade front, open adjustable rear. **Features:** Patented internal percussion ignition system. Drilled and tapped for scope mount. Introduced 1995. Made in U.S. by Prairie River Arms, Ltd.
Price: 4140 alloy barrel, hardwood stock **$375.00**
Price: As above, stainless barrel **$425.00**
Price: 4140 alloy barrel, black all-weather stock **$390.00**
Price: As above, stainless barrel **$440.00**

BLACKPOWDER MUSKETS & RIFLES

Remington Model 700 ML

C.S. Richmond 1863

Ruger K77/50RSBBZ

Second Model Brown Bess

BLACKPOWDER

PRAIRIE RIVER ARMS PRA BULLPUP RIFLE

Caliber: 50, 54. **Barrel:** 28"; 1:28" twist. **Weight:** 7-1/2 lbs. **Length:** 31-1/2" overall. **Stock:** Hardwood or black all-weather. **Sights:** Blade front, open adjustable rear. **Features:** Bullpup design thumbhole stock. Patented internal percussion ignition system. Left-hand model available. Dovetailed for scope mount. Introduced 1995. Made in U.S. by Prairie River Arms, Ltd.

Price: 4140 alloy barrel, hardwood stock **$375.00**
Price: As above, black stock. **$390.00**
Price: Stainless barrel, hardwood stock **$425.00**
Price: As above, black stock. **$440.00**

REMINGTON MODEL 700 ML, MLS RIFLES

Caliber: 50, 54. **Barrel:** 24"; 1:28" twist. **Weight:** 7-3/4 lbs. **Length:** 44-1/2" overall. **Stock:** Black fiberglass-reinforced synthetic with checkered grip and forend; magnum-style buttpad. **Sights:** Ramped bead front, open fully adjustable rear. Drilled and tapped for scope mounts. **Features:** Uses the Remington 700 bolt action, stock design, safety and trigger mechanisms; removable stainelss steel breech plug, No. 11 nipple; solid aluminum ramrod. Comes with cleaning tools and accessories.

Price: ML, blued, 50-caliber only **$396.00**
Price: MLS, stainless, 50- or 54-caliber **$496.00**
Price: ML, blued, Mossy Oak Break-Up camo stock **$439.00**
Price: MLS, stainless, Mossy Oak Break-Up camo stock. **$532.00**
Price: ML Youth (12-3/8" length of pull, 21" barrel) **$396.00**

C.S. RICHMOND 1863 MUSKET

Caliber: 58. **Barrel:** 40". **Weight:** 11 lbs. **Length:** 56-1/4" overall. **Stock:** European walnut with oil finish. **Sights:** Blade front, adjustable folding leaf rear. **Features:** Reproduction of the three-band Civil War musket. Sling swivels attached to trigger guard and middle barrel band. Lockplate marked "1863" and "C.S. Richmond." All metal left in the white. Brass buttplate and forend cap. Imported by Euroarms of America, Navy Arms.
Price: . . . . **NA**

RUGER 77/50 IN-LINE PERCUSSION RIFLE

Caliber: 50. **Barrel:** 22"; 1:28" twist. **Weight:** 6-1/2 lbs. **Length:** 41-1/2" overall. **Stock:** Birch with rubber buttpad and swivel studs. **Sights:** Gold bead front, folding leaf rear. Comes with Ruger scope mounts. **Features:** Shares design features with the Ruger 77/22 rifle. Stainless steel bolt and nipple/breech plug; uses #11 caps; three-position safety; blued steel ramrod. Introduced 1997. Made in U.S. by Sturm, Ruger & Co.

Price: 77/50RS **$434.00**
Price: 77/50RSO Officer's (straight-grip checkered walnut stock, blued) **$555.00**
Price: K77/50RSBBZ (stainless steel, black laminated stock) **$601.00**
Price: K77/50RSP All-Weather (stainless steel, synthetic stock) . . **$580.00**

SECOND MODEL BROWN BESS MUSKET

Caliber: 75, uses .735" round ball. **Barrel:** 42", smoothbore. **Weight:** 9-1/2 lbs. **Length:** 59" overall. **Stock:** Walnut (Navy); walnut-stained hardwood (Dixie). **Sights:** Fixed. **Features:** Polished barrel and lock with brass trigger guard and buttplate. Bayonet and scabbard available. From Navy Arms, Dixie Gun Works, Cabela's.

Price: Finished . . . . **$475.00 to $850.00**
Price: Kit (Dixie Gun Works, Navy Arms) . . . . **$575.00 to $625.00**
Price: Carbine (Navy Arms) **$835.00**

THOMPSON/CENTER BLACK MOUNTAIN MAGNUM RIFLE

Caliber: 50, 54. **Barrel:** 26"; 1:28" twist. **Weight:** 7 lbs. **Length:** 4-3/4" overall. **Stock:** American Walnut or black composite. **Sights:** Ramp front with Tru-Glo fiber optic inseat, click adjustable open rear with Tru-Glo fiber optic inserts. **Features:** Side lock percussion with breeech designed for Pyrodex Pellets, loose blackpowder and Pyrodex. blued steel. Uses QLA muzzle system. Introduced 1999. Made in U.S. by Thompson/Center Arms.

Price: Blue, composite stock, 50-cal. **$353.52**
Price: Blue, walnut stock, 50- or 54-cal. (westraner) **$387.16**

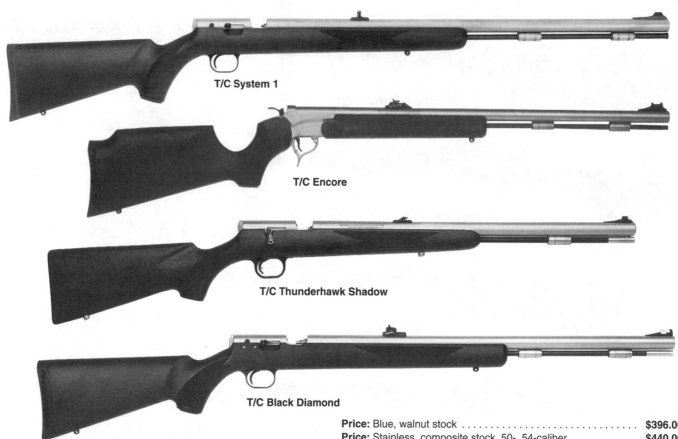

T/C System 1

T/C Encore

T/C Thunderhawk Shadow

T/C Black Diamond

THOMPSON/CENTER FIRE STORM RIFLE

Caliber: 50. **Barrel:** 26"; 1:28" twist. **Weight:** 7 lbs. **Length:** 41-3/4" overall. **Stock:** Black synthetic with rubber recoil pad, swivel studs. **Sights:** Click-adjustable steel rear and ramp-style front, both with fiber optic inserts. **Features:** Side hammer lock is the first designed for up to three 50-grain Pyrodex pellets; patented Pyrodex Pyramid breech directs ignition fire 360 degrees around base of pellet; uses 209 shotgun primers; Quick Load Accurizor Muzzle System; aluminum ramrod. Introduced 2000. Made in U.S. by Thompson/Center Arms.
Price: Blue finish, percussion model. $391.00
Price: Blue finish, flintlock model with 1:48" twist for round balls, conicals. $391.00

THOMPSON/CENTER PENNSYLVANIA HUNTER RIFLE

Caliber: 50. **Barrel:** 28", octagonal. **Weight:** About 7-1/2 lbs. **Length:** 48" overall. **Stock:** Black walnut. **Sights:** Open, adjustable. **Features:** Rifled 1:66" for round-ball shooting. Available in flintlock only. From Thompson/Center.
Price: $417.00

Thompson/Center Pennsylvania Hunter Carbine

Similar to the Pennsylvania Hunter except has 21" barrel, weighs 6.5 lbs., and has an overall length of 38". Designed for shooting patched round balls. Available in flintlock only. Introduced 1992. From Thompson/Center.
Price: $438.00

THOMPSON/CENTER SYSTEM 1 IN-LINE RIFLE

Caliber: 32, 50, 54, 58; 12-gauge. **Barrel:** 26" round; 1:38" twist. **Weight:** About 7-1/2lbs. **Length:** 44" overall. **Stock:** American black walnut or composite. **Sights:** Ramp front with white bead, adjustable leaf rear. **Features:** In-line ignition. Interchangeable barrels; removable breech plug allows cleaning from the breech; fully adjustable trigger; sliding thumb safety; QLA muzzle system; rubber recoil pad; sling swivel studs. Introduced 1997. Made in U.S. by Thompson/Center Arms.

Price: Blue, walnut stock $396.00
Price: Stainless, composite stock, 50-, 54-caliber $440.00
Price: Stainless, camo composite stock, 50-caliber $479.00
Price: Extra barrels, blue $176.00
Price: Extra barrels, stainless, 50-, 54-caliber $220.00

THOMPSON/CENTER ENCORE 209x50 MAGNUM

Caliber: 50. **Barrel:** 26"; interchangeable with centerfire calibers. **Weight:** 7 lbs. **Length:** 40-1/2" overall. **Stock:** American walnut butt and forend, or black composite. **Sights:** Tru-Glo Fiber Optic front, Tru-Glo Fiber Optic rear. **Features:** Blue or stainless steel. Uses the stock, frame and forend of the Encore centerfire pistol; break-open design using trigger guard spur; stainless steel universal breech plug; uses #209 shotshell primers. Introduced 1998. Made in U.S. by Thompson/Center Arms.
Price: $590.03
Price: Blue, walnut stock and forend $590.03
Price: Blue, composite stock and forend $590.03
Price: Stainless, composite stock and forend. $665.91

THOMPSON/CENTER THUNDERHAWK SHADOW

Caliber: 50, 54. **Barrel:** 24"; 1:38" twist. **Weight:** 7 lbs. **Length:** 41-3/4" overall. **Stock:** American walnut or black composite with rubber recoil pad. **Sights:** Bead on ramp front, adjustable leaf rear. **Features:** Uses modern in-line ignition system, adjustable trigger. Knurled striker handle indicators for Safe and Fire. Black wood ramrod, Drilled and tapped for T/C scope mounts. Introduced 1996. From Thompson/Center Arms.
Price: Blued $294.00

THOMPSON/CENTER BLACK DIAMOND RIFLE

Caliber: 50. **Barrel:** 22-1/2" with QLA; 1:28" twist. **Weight:** 6 lbs., 9 oz. **Length:** 41-1/2" overall. **Stock:** Black Rynite with moulded-in checkering and grip cap, or walnut. **Sights:** Tru-Glo Fiber Optic ramp-style front, Tru-Glo Fiber Optic open rear. **Features:** In-line ignition system for musket cap, No. 11 cap, or 209 shotshell primer; removable universal breech plug; stainless steel construction. Introduced 1998. Made in U.S. by Thompson/Center Arms.
Price: $312.87
Price: With walnut stock $353.32

BLACKPOWDER MUSKETS & RIFLES

T/C Hawken

Traditions Buckhunter Pro In-Line

Traditions Buckhunter

THOMPSON/CENTER HAWKEN RIFLE

Caliber: 45, 50 or 54. **Barrel:** 28" octagon, hooked breech. **Stock:** American walnut. **Sights:** Blade front, rear adjustable for windage and elevation. **Features:** Solid brass furniture, double-set triggers, button rifled barrel, coil-type mainspring. From Thompson/Center Arms.
Price: Percussion model (45-, 50- or 54-cal.) **$489.35**
Price: Flintlock model (50-cal.) **$501.14**

TRADITIONS BUCKHUNTER IN-LINE RIFLES

Caliber: 50, 54. **Barrel:** 24", round; 1:32" (50); 1:48" (54) twist. **Weight:** About 7 lbs. **Length:** 41" overall. **Stock:** All-Weather black composite. **Sights:** blade front, click adjustable rear. Drilled and tapped for scope mounting. **Features:** Removable breech plug; PVC ramrod; sling swivels. Introduced 1995. From Traditions.
Price: (blued barrel) **$149.00**
Price: (C-Nickel barrel, 50 caliber only) **$159.00**
Price: With RS Redi-Pak (powder measure, powder flask, two fast loaders, 5-in-1 loader, capper, ball starter, ball puller, cleaning jag, nipple wrench, bullets); 50 caliber only. **$199.00**

TRADITIONS BUCKHUNTER PRO MAGNUM IN-LINE RIFLES

Caliber: 50 (1:32" twist); 54 (1:48" twist). **Barrel:** 24" tapered round. **Weight:** 7 lbs., 4 oz. **Length:** 43" overall. **Stock:** Composite in black or Mossy Oak Break-Up™ camouflage. **Sights:** Fiber-optic ramp front, fully adjustable rear. Drilled and tapped for scope mounting. **Features:** In-line percussion ignition system that allows use of 209 shotgun primers, musket caps or No. 11 percussion caps; adjustable trigger; manual thumb safety; removable stainless steel breech plug. From Traditions.
Price: (24" blued barrel) **$169.00**
Price (24" C-Nickel barrel) **$189.00**
Price (24" C-Nickel barrel, Mossy Oak Break-Up™ stock) **$219.00**

TRADITIONS BUCKSKINNER CARBINE

Caliber: 50. **Barrel:** 21"; 15/16" flats, half octagon, half round; 1:20" or 1:66" twist. **Weight:** 6 lbs. **Length:** 37" overall. **Stock:** Beech or black laminated. **Sights:** Beaded blade front, fiber optic open rear click adjustable for windage and elevation or fiber optics. **Features:** Uses V-type mainspring, single trigger. Non-glare hardware; sling swivels. From Traditions.
Price: Flintlock **$219.00**
Price: Flintlock, laminated stock **$299.00**

TRADITIONS DEERHUNTER RIFLE SERIES

Caliber: 32, 50 or 54. **Barrel:** 24", octagonal; 15/16" flats; 1:48" or 1:66" twist. **Weight:** 6 lbs. **Length:** 40" overall. **Stock:** Stained hardwood or All-Weather composite with rubber buttpad, sling swivels. **Sights:** Lite Optic blade front, adjustable rear fiber optics. **Features:** Flint or percussion with color case-hardened lock. Hooked breech, oversized trigger guard, blackened furniture, PVC ramrod. All-Weather has composite stock and C-Nickel barrel. Drilled and tapped for scope mounting. Imported by Traditions, Inc.
Price: Percussion, 50; blued barrel; 1:48" twist **$159.00**
Price: Flintlock, 50-caliber only; 1:66" twist **$189.00**
Price: Flintlock, All-Weather, 50-cal. **$179.00**
New! **Price:** Flintlock, left-handed hardwood, 50-cal. **$189.00**
Price: Percussion, All-Weather, 50 or 54 cal. **$159.00**
Price: Percussion; 32 cal. **$169.00**

TRADITIONS E-BOLT 209 BOLT-ACTION RIFLES

Caliber: 50. **Barrel:** 22" blued or C-Nickel finish; 1:28" twist. **Weight:** 6 lbs., 7 oz. **Length:** 41" overall. **Stock:** Black or Advantage Timber® composite. **Sights:** Lite Optic blade front, adjustable rear. **Features:** Thumb safety; quick-release bolt; covered breech; one-piece breech plug takes 209 shotshell primers; accepts 150 grains of Pyrodex pellets; receiver drilled and tapped for scope; sling swivel studs and rubber butt pad. Introduced 2001. From Traditions.
Price: (Black composite stock with 22" blued barrel) **$169.00**
Price: (Black composite stock with 22" C-Nickel barrel) **$179.00**
Price: (Advantage Timber® stock with 22"C-Nickel barrel) **$229.00**
Price: (Redi-Pak with black stock/blued barrel and powder flask, capper, ball starter, other supplies) **$219.00**
Price: (Redi-Pak with Advantage Timber® stock/C-Nickel barrel and powder flask, capper, ball starter, other supplies) **$279.00**

TRADITIONS HAWKEN WOODSMAN RIFLE

Caliber: 50 and 54. **Barrel:** 28"; 15/16" flats. **Weight:** 7 lbs., 11 oz. **Length:** 44-1/2" overall. **Stock:** Walnut-stained hardwood. **Sights:** Beaded blade front, hunting-style open rear adjustable for windage and elevation. **Features:** Percussion only. Brass patchbox and furniture. Double triggers. From Traditions.
Price: 50 or 54 . . . . **$249.00**
Price: 50-cal., left-hand **$239.00**
Price: 50-caliber, flintlock **$249.00**

TRADITIONS KENTUCKY RIFLE

Caliber: 50. **Barrel:** 33-1/2"; 7/8" flats; 1:66" twist. **Weight:** 7 lbs. **Length:** 49" overall. **Stock:** Beech; inletted toe plate. **Sights:** Blade front, fixed rear. **Features:** Full-length, two-piece stock; brass furniture; color case-hardened lock. Introduced 1995. From Traditions.
Price: Finished **$229.00**
Price: Kit **$179.00**

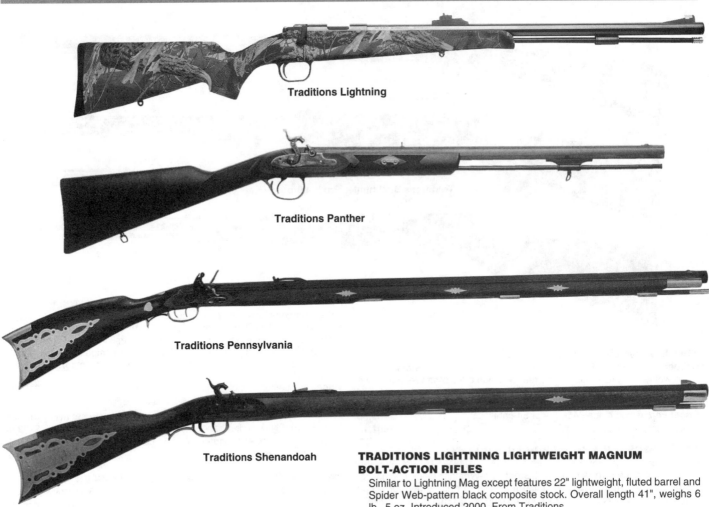

Traditions Lightning

Traditions Panther

Traditions Pennsylvania

Traditions Shenandoah

TRADITIONS LIGHTNING MAG BOLT-ACTION MUZZLELOADER

Caliber: 50, 54. **Barrel:** 24" round; blued, stainless, C-Nickel or Ultra Coat. **Weight:** 6-1/2 to 7 lbs. 10 oz. **Length:** 43" overall. **Stock:** All-Weather composite, Advantage, or Break-Up camouflage. **Sights:** Fiber Optic blade front, fully adjustable open rear. **Features:** Field-removable stainless steel bolt; silent thumb safety; adjustable trigger; drilled and tapped for scope mounting. Lightning Fire Magnum System allows use of No. 11, musket caps or 209 shotgun primers. Introduced 1997. Imported by Traditions.

Price: All-Weather composite stock, blue finish $199.00
Price: All-Weather composite stock, blue finish, muzzle brake . . . $229.00
Price: All-Weather composite, stainless steel. $279.00
Price: Camouflage composite, stainless steel $309.00
Price: Camouflage composite $229.00
Price: Composite, with muzzle brake, stainless, fluted barrel $329.00

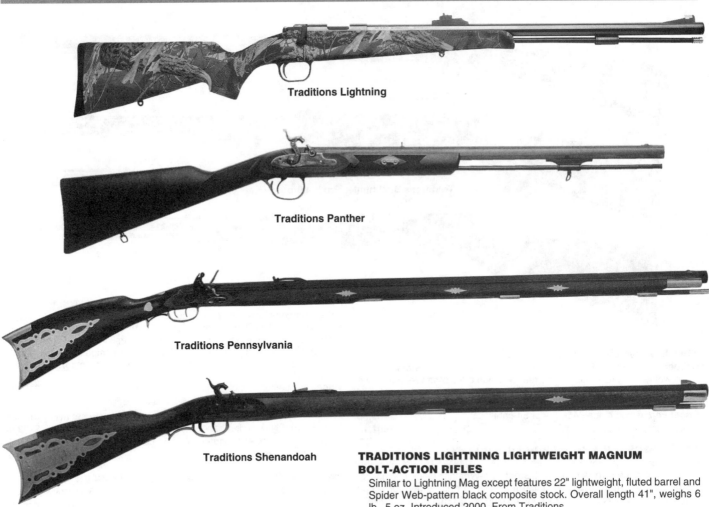 **NEW!**

TRADITIONS LIGHTNING 45 LD BOLT-ACTION RIFLES

Similar to Lightning Mag, but chambered for 45 caliber with a 26" fluted blued or C-Nickel barrel; 1:20" twist. Black or Advantage Timber® stock; fiber optic blade front and adjustable rear sights. Accepts 150 grains of Pyrodex. Weighs 7 lbs., 2 oz. Overall length 45". Introduced 2001. From Traditions.

Price: (black stock with blued barrel) $229.00
Price: (black stock with C-Nickel barrel). $239.00
Price: (Advantage Timber® stock with C-Nickel barrel) $289.00

TRADITIONS LIGHTNING LIGHTWEIGHT MAGNUM BOLT-ACTION RIFLES

Similar to Lightning Mag except features 22" lightweight, fluted barrel and Spider Web-pattern black composite stock. Overall length 41", weighs 6 lb., 5 oz. Introduced 2000. From Traditions.

Price: Blued finish. $239.00
Price: C-Nickel finish. $249.00
Price: Stainless $279.00
Price: Stainless, camo stock $289.00

TRADITIONS MAGNUM PLAINS RIFLE

Similar to Thunder Magnum except has 28" blued, octagonal barrel, double-set triggers and adj. steel fiber optics sights.
Price: $359.00

TRADITIONS PANTHER SIDELOCK RIFLE

Similar to Deerhunter rifle, but has blade front and windage-adjustable-only rear sight, black composite stock.
Price: $119.00

TRADITIONS PENNSYLVANIA RIFLE

Caliber: 50. **Barrel:** 40-1/4"; 7/8" flats; 1:66" twist, octagon. **Weight:** 9 lbs. **Length:** 57-1/2" overall. **Stock:** Walnut. **Sights:** Blade front, adjustable rear. **Features:** Brass patchbox and ornamentation. Double-set triggers. From Traditions.

Price: Flintlock $479.00
Price: Percussion $469.00

TRADITIONS SHENANDOAH RIFLE

Caliber: 50. **Barrel:** 33-1/2" octagon; 1:66" twist. **Weight:** 7 lbs., 3 oz. **Length:** 49-1/2" overall. **Stock:** Walnut. **Sights:** Blade front, buckhorn rear. **Features:** V-type mainspring; double-set trigger; solid brass buttplate, patchbox, nosecap, thimbles, trigger guard. Introduced 1996. From Traditions.

Price: Flintlock $369.00
Price: Percussion $349.00

BLACKPOWDER

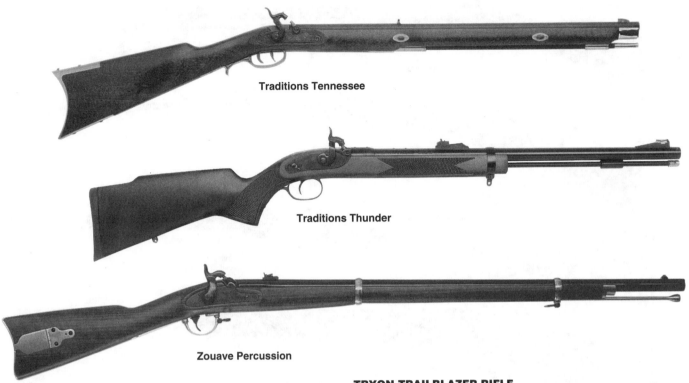

Traditions Tennessee

Traditions Thunder

Zouave Percussion

TRADITIONS TENNESSEE RIFLE

Caliber: 50. **Barrel:** 24", octagon; 15/16" flats; 1:66" twist. **Weight:** 6 lbs. **Length:** 40-1/2" overall. **Stock:** Stained beech. **Sights:** Blade front, fixed rear. **Features:** One-piece stock has inletted brass furniture, cheekpiece; double-set trigger; V-type mainspring. Flint or percussion. Introduced 1995. From Traditions.
Price: Flintlock $289.00
Price: Percussion $269.00

TRADITIONS THUNDER MAGNUM RIFLE

Caliber: 50. **Barrel:** 24"; 1:32" twist. **Weight:** 7 lbs., 9 oz. **Length:** 42-1/2" overall. **Stock:** Hardwood or composite. **Sights:** Fiber optic front, adjustable rear. **Features:** Sidelock action with thumb-activated safety. Takes 150 grains of Pyrodex pellets and musket caps. Introduced 1999. From Traditions.
Price: Hardwood $349.00
Price: All-weather hardwood, C-Nickel $359.00

TRADITIONS TRACKER 209 IN-LINE RIFLES

Caliber: 50. **Barrel:** 22" blued or C-Nickel finish; 1:28" twist. **Weight:** 6 lbs., 4 oz. **Length:** 41" overall. **Stock:** Black or Advantage Timber® composite. **Sights:** Lite Optic blade front, adjustable rear. **Features:** Thumb safety; adjustable trigger; rubber butt pad and sling swivel studs; takes 150 grains of Pyrodex pellets; one-piece breech system takes 209 shotshell primers. Drilled and tapped for scope. Introduced 2001. From Traditions.
Price: (Black composite stock with 22" blued barrel) $119.00
Price: (Black composite stock with 22" C-Nickel barrel) $129.00
Price: (Advantage Timber® stock with 22" C-Nickel barrel) $179.00
Price: (Redi-Pak with black stock and blued barrel, powder flask, capper, ball starter and other access.) $169.00

TRYON TRAILBLAZER RIFLE

Caliber: 50, 54. **Barrel:** 28", 30". **Weight:** 9 lbs. **Length:** 48" overall. **Stock:** European walnut with cheekpiece. **Sights:** Blade front, semi-buckhorn rear. **Features:** Reproduction of a rifle made by George Tryon about 1820. Double-set triggers, back action lock, hooked breech with long tang. From Armsport.
Price: About $825.00

WHITE MODEL 97 WHITETAIL HUNTER RIFLE

Caliber: 45, 50. **Barrel:** 22", 1:24" twist (50 cal.). **Weight:** 7.6 lbs. **Length:** 39-7/8" overall. **Stock:** Black laminated wood or black composite with swivel studs. **Sights:** Marble fully adjustable, steel rear with white diamond; red-bead front with high-visibility inserts. **Features:** In-line ignition with FlashFire one-piece nipple and breech plug that uses standard or magnum No. 11 caps; fully adjustable trigger; double safety system; aluminum ramrod; drilled and tapped for scope. Includes hard gun case. Introduced 2000. Made in U.S. by Muzzleloading Technologies Inc.
Price: Laminated wood stock $549.95
Price: Black composite stock $549.95

White Model 98 Elite Hunter Rifle

Similar to Model 97 but features 24" barrel with longer action for extended sight radius. Overall length 43-5/16", weighs 8.2 lbs. Choice of black laminated or black hardwood stock. From Muzzleloading Technologies Inc.
Price: Black laminated stock (45 or 50 cal.) $699.95
Price: Black hardwood stock (45 or 50 cal.) $699.95

ZOUAVE PERCUSSION RIFLE

Caliber: 58, 59. **Barrel:** 32-1/2". **Weight:** 9-1/2 lbs. **Length:** 48-1/2" overall. **Stock:** Walnut finish, brass patchbox and buttplate. **Sights:** Fixed front, rear adjustable for elevation. **Features:** Color case-hardened lockplate, blued barrel. From Navy Arms, Dixie Gun Works, E.M.F., Cabela's.
Price: About . . . . $325.00 to $465.00

CVA NWTF Gobbler

Dixie Magnum

Knight TK2000

Traditions
Buckhunters Pro

CABELA'S BLACKPOWDER SHOTGUNS

Gauge: 10, 12, 20. **Barrel:** 10-ga., 30"; 12-ga., 28-1/2" (Extra-Full, Mod., Imp. Cyl. choke tubes); 20-ga., 27-1/2" (Imp. Cyl. & Mod. fixed chokes). **Weight:** 6-1/2 to 7 lbs. **Length:** 45" overall (28-1/2" barrel). **Stock:** American walnut with checkered grip; 12- and 20-gauge have straight stock, 10-gauge has pistol grip. **Features:** Blued barrels, engraved, color case-hardened locks and hammers, brass ramrod tip. From Cabela's.
Price: 10-gauge **$499.99**
Price: 12-gauge **$449.99**
Price: 20-gauge **$429.99**

CVA NWTF GOBBLER SERIES SHOTGUN

NEW!

Gauge: 12. **Barrel:** 28". **Weight:** 6 lbs. **Length:** 46" overall. **Stock:** Hardwood. **Sights:** Bead front. **Features:** National Wild Turkey Federation logo engraved on lock plate; full-color laser engraving of a flying wild turkey on the stock; portion of sales goes to NWTF. Limited edition introduced 2001. From CVA.
Price: **$367.95**

CVA TRAPPER PERCUSSION SHOTGUN

Gauge: 12. **Barrel:** 28". **Weight:** 6 lbs. **Length:** 46" overall. **Stock:** English-style checkered straight grip of walnut-finished hardwood. **Sights:** Brass bead front. **Features:** Single-blued barrel; color case-hardened lockplate and hammer; screw adjustable sear engagements, V-type mainspring; brass wedge plates; color case-hardened and engraved trigger guard and tang. From CVA.
Price: Finished **$287.95**

DIXIE MAGNUM PERCUSSION SHOTGUN

Gauge: 10, 12, 20. **Barrel:** 30" (Imp. Cyl. & Mod.) in 10-gauge; 28" in 12-gauge. **Weight:** 6-1/4 lbs. **Length:** 45" overall. **Stock:** Hand-checkered walnut, 14" pull. **Features:** Double triggers; light hand engraving; case-hardened locks in 12-gauge, polished steel in 10-gauge; sling swivels. From Dixie Gun Works.
Price: Upland **$449.00**
Price: 12-ga. kit. **$375.00**

Price: 20-ga. **$495.00**
Price: 10-ga. **$495.00**
Price: 10-ga. kit **$395.00**

KNIGHT TK2000 MUZZLELOADING SHOTGUN

Gauge: 12. **Barrel:** 26", extra-full choke tube. **Weight:** 7 lbs., 9 oz. **Length:** 45" overall. **Stock:** Synthetic black or Advantage Timber HD; recoil pad; swivel studs. **Sights:** Fully adjustable rear, blade front with fiber optics. **Features:** Receiver drilled and tapped for scope mount; in-line ignition; adjustable trigger; removable breech plug; double safety system; imp. cyl. choke tube available. Introduced 2000. Made in U.S. by Knight Rifles.
Price: . . . . **$349.95 to $399.95**

NAVY ARMS STEEL SHOT MAGNUM SHOTGUN

Gauge: 10. **Barrel:** 28" (Cyl. & Cyl.). **Weight:** 7 lbs., 9 oz. **Length:** 45-1/2" overall. **Stock:** Walnut, with cheekpiece. **Features:** Designed specifically for steel shot. Engraved, polished locks; sling swivels; blued barrels. Imported by Navy Arms.
Price: **$605.00**

NAVY ARMS T&T SHOTGUN

Gauge: 12. **Barrel:** 28" (Full & Full). **Weight:** 7-1/2 lbs. **Stock:** Walnut. **Sights:** Bead front. **Features:** Color case-hardened locks, double triggers, blued steel furniture. From Navy Arms.
Price: **$580.00**

TRADITIONS BUCKHUNTER PRO SHOTGUN

Gauge: 12. **Barrel:** 24", choke tube. **Weight:** 6 lbs., 4 oz. **Length:** 43" overall. **Stock:** Composite matte black, Break-Up or Advantage camouflage. **Features:** In-line action with removable stainless steel breech plug; thumb safety; adjustable trigger; rubber buttpad. Introduced 1996. From Traditions.
Price: **$248.00**
Price: With Advantage, Shadow Branch, or Break-Up
camouflage stock **$292.00**

THOMPSON/CENTER BLACK MOUNTAIN MAGNUM SHOTGUN

Gauge: 12. **Barrel:** 27" screw-in Turkey choke tube. **Weight:** 7 lbs. **Length:** 41-3/4" overall. **Stock:** Black composite. **Sights:** Bead front. **Features:** Sidelock percussion action. Polished blue finish. Introduced in 1999. Made in U.S. by Thompson/Center Arms.
Price: **$387.16**

BLACKPOWDER

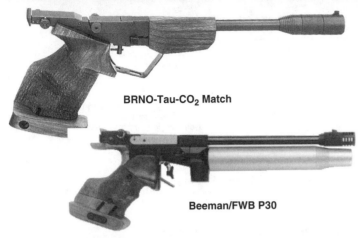

BRNO-Tau-CO₂ Match

Beeman/FWB P30

Benjamin Sheridan CO₂

Crosman Model 1377

BEEMAN P1 MAGNUM AIR PISTOL

Caliber: 177, 5mm, single shot. **Barrel:** 8.4". **Weight:** 2.5 lbs. **Length:** 11" overall. **Power:** Top lever cocking; spring-piston. **Stocks:** Checkered walnut. **Sights:** Blade front, square notch rear with click micrometer adjustments for windage and elevation. Grooved for scope mounting. **Features:** Dual power for 177 and 20-cal.: low setting gives 350-400 fps; high setting 500-600 fps. Rearward expanding mainspring simulates firearm recoil. All Colt 45 auto grips fit gun. Dry-firing feature for practice. Optional wooden shoulder stock. Introduced 1985. Imported by Beeman.
Price: 177, 5mm... $415.00

Beeman P2 Match Air Pistol

Similar to the Beeman P1 Magnum except shoots only 177 pellets; completely recoilless single-stroke pnuematic action. Weighs 2.2 lbs. Choice of thumbrest match grips or standard style. Introduced 1990.
Price: 177, 5mm, standard grip............................. $385.00
Price: 177, match grip.................................... $455.00

BEEMAN P3 AIR PISTOL

Caliber: 177 pellet, single shot. **Barrel:** N/A. **Weight:** 1.7 lbs. **Length:** 9.6" overall. **Power:** Single-stroke pneumatic; overlever barrel cocking. **Grips:** Reinforced polymer. **Sights:** Adjustable rear, blade front. **Features:** Velocity 410 fps. Polymer frame; automatic safety; two-stage trigger; built-in muzzle brake. Introduced 1999 by Beeman.
Price: $159.00

BEEMAN/FEINWERKBAU 65 MKII AIR PISTOL

Caliber: 177, single shot. **Barrel:** 6.1", removable bbl. wgt. available. **Weight:** 42 oz. **Length:** 13.3" overall. **Power:** Spring, sidelever cocking. **Stocks:** Walnut, stippled thumbrest; adjustable or fixed. **Sights:** Front, interchangeable post element system, open rear, click adjustable for windage and elevation and for sighting notch width. Scope mount available. **Features:** New shorter barrel for better balance and control. Cocking effort 9 lbs. Two-stage trigger, four adjustments. Quiet firing, 525 fps. Programs instantly for recoil or recoilless operation. Permanently lubricated. Steel piston ring. Imported by Beeman.
Price: Right-hand.. $1,070.00

BEEMAN/FEINWERKBAU 103 PISTOL

Caliber: 177, single shot. **Barrel:** 10.1", 12-groove rifling. **Weight:** 2.5 lbs. **Length:** 16.5" overall. **Power:** Single-stroke pneumatic, underlever cocking. **Stocks:** Stippled walnut with adjustable palm shelf. **Sights:** Blade front, open rear adjustable for windage and elevation. Notch size adjustable for width. Interchangeable front blades. **Features:** Velocity 510 fps. Fully adjustable trigger. Cocking effort of 2 lbs. Imported by Beeman.
Price: Right-hand.. $1,195.00
Price: Left-hand... $1,235.00

BEEMAN/FWB P30 MATCH AIR PISTOL

Caliber: 177, single shot. **Barrel:** 10-5/16", with muzzlebrake. **Weight:** 2.4 lbs. **Length:** 16.5" overall. **Power:** Pre-charged pneumatic. **Stocks:** Stippled walnut; adjustable match type. **Sights:** Undercut blade front, fully adjustable match rear. **Features:** Velocity to 525 fps; up to 200 shots per CO2 cartridge. Fully adjustable trigger; built-in muzzlebrake. Introduced 1995. Imported from Germany by Beeman.
Price: Right-hand.. $1,275.00
Price: Left-hand... $1,350.00

BEEMAN/FWB C55 CO2 RAPID FIRE PISTOL

Caliber: 177, single shot or 5-shot magazine. **Barrel:** 7.3". **Weight:** 2.5 lbs. **Length:** 15" overall. **Power:** Special CO2 cylinder. **Stocks:** Anatomical, adjustable. **Sights:** Interchangeable front, fully adjustable open micro-click rear with adjustable notch size. **Features:** Velocity 510 fps. Has 11.75" sight radius. Built-in muzzlebrake. Introduced 1993. Imported by Beeman Precision Airguns.
Price: Right-hand.. $1,460.00
Price: Left-hand... $1,520.00

BEEMAN HW70A AIR PISTOL

Caliber: 177, single shot. **Barrel:** 6-1/4", rifled. **Weight:** 38 oz. **Length:** 12-3/4" overall. **Power:** Spring, barrel cocking. **Stocks:** Plastic, with thumbrest. **Sights:** Hooded post front, square notch rear adjustable for windage and elevation. Comes with scope base. **Features:** Adjustable trigger, 31-lb. cocking effort, 440 fps MV; automatic barrel safety. Imported by Beeman.
Price: $185.00
Price: HW70S, black grip, silver finish................... $210.00

BEEMAN/WEBLEY TEMPEST AIR PISTOL

Caliber: 177, 22, single shot. **Barrel:** 6-7/8". **Weight:** 32 oz. **Length:** 8.9" overall. **Power:** Spring-piston, break barrel. **Stocks:** Checkered black plastic with thumbrest. **Sights:** Blade front, adjustable rear. **Features:** Velocity to 500 fps (177), 400 fps (22). Aluminum frame; black epoxy finish; manual safety. Imported from England by Beeman.
Price: $180.00

Beeman/Webley Hurricane Air Pistol

Similar to the Tempest except has extended frame in the rear for a click-adjustable rear sight; hooded front sight; comes with scope mount. Imported from England by Beeman.
Price: $225.00

BENJAMIN SHERIDAN CO2 PELLET PISTOLS

Caliber: 177, 20, 22, single shot. **Barrel:** 6-3/8", rifled brass. **Weight:** 29 oz. **Length:** 9.8" overall. **Power:** 12-gram CO2 cylinder. **Stocks:** Walnut. **Sights:** High ramp front, fully adjustable notch rear. **Features:** Velocity to 500 fps. Turn-bolt action with cross-bolt safety. Gives about 40 shots per CO2 cylinder. Black or nickel finish. Made in U.S. by Benjamin Sheridan Co.
Price: Black finish, EB17 (177), EB20 (20), about.......... $115.23

BENJAMIN SHERIDAN PNEUMATIC PELLET PISTOLS

Caliber: 177, 20, 22, single shot. **Barrel:** 9-3/8", rifled brass. **Weight:** 38 oz. **Length:** 13-1/8" overall. **Power:** Underlever pnuematic, hand pumped. **Stocks:** Walnut stocks and pump handle. **Sights:** High ramp front, fully adjustable notch rear. **Features:** Velocity to 525 fps (variable). Bolt action with cross-bolt safety. Choice of black or nickel finish. Made in U.S. by Benjamin Sheridan Co.
Price: Black finish, HB17 (177), HB20 (20), HB22 (22), about........... $129.50

BERETTA 92 FS/CO2 AIR PISTOLS

Caliber: 177 pellet, 8-shot magazine. **Barrel:** 4.9". **Weight:** 44.4 oz. **Length:** 8.2" (10.2" with compensator). **Power:** CO2 cartridge. **Grips:** plastic or wood. **Sights:** Adjustable rear, blade front. **Features:** Velocity 375 fps. Replica of Beretta 92 FS pistol. Single- and double-action trigger; ambidextrous safety; black or nickel-plated finish. Made by Umarex for Beretta USA.
Price: Starting at $200.00

BRNO TAU-7 CO2 MATCH PISTOL

Caliber: 177. **Barrel:** 10.24". **Weight:** 37 oz. **Length:** 15.75" overall. **Power:** 12.5-gram CO2 cartridge. **Stocks:** Stippled hardwood with adjustable palm rest. **Sights:** Blade front, open fully adjustable rear. **Features:** Comes with extra seals and counterweight. Blue finish. Imported by Great Lakes Airguns.
Price: About $299.50

BSA 240 MAGNUM AIR PISTOL

Caliber: 177, 22, single shot. **Barrel:** 6". **Weight:** 2 lbs. **Length:** 9" overall. **Power:** Spring-air, top-lever cocking. **Stocks:** Walnut. **Sights:** Blade front, micrometer adjustable rear. **Features:** Velocity 510 fps (177), 420 fps (22); crossbolt safety. Combat autoloader styling. Imported from U.K. by Precision Sales International, Inc.
Price: $259.99

AIRGUNS

Daisy/Power Line 717

COLT GOVERNMENT 1911 A1 AIR PISTOL
Caliber: 177, 8-shot cylinder magazine. **Barrel:** 5", rifled. **Weight:** 38 oz. **Length:** 8-1/2" overall. **Power:** CO2 cylinder. **Stocks:** Checkered black plastic or smooth wood. **Sights:** Post front, adjustable rear. **Features:** Velocity to 393 fps. Quick-loading cylinder magazine; single and double action; black or silver finish. Introduced 1998. Imported by Colt's Mfg. Co., Inc.
Price: Black finish. $199.00
Price: Silver finish. $209.00

CROSMAN BLACK VENOM PISTOL
Caliber: 177 pellets, BB, 17-shot magazine; darts, single shot. **Barrel:** 4.75" smoothbore. **Weight:** 16 oz. **Length:** 10.8" overall. **Power:** Spring. **Stocks:** Checkered. **Sights:** Blade front, adjustable rear. **Features:** Velocity to 270 fps (BBs), 250 fps (pellets). Spring-fed magazine; cross-bolt safety. Introduced 1996. Made in U.S. by Crosman Corp.
Price: About $20.00

CROSMAN BLACK FANG PISTOL
Caliber: 177 BB, 17-shot magazine. **Barrel:** 4.75" smoothbore. **Weight:** 10 oz. **Length:** 10.8" overall. **Power:** Spring. **Stocks:** Checkered. **Sights:** Blade front, fixed notch rear. **Features:** Velocity to 250 fps. Spring-fed magazine; cross-bolt safety. Introduced 1996. Made in U.S. by Crosman Corp.
Price: About $16.00

CROSMAN MODEL 1322, 1377 AIR PISTOLS
Caliber: 177 (M1377), 22 (M1322), single shot. **Barrel:** 8", rifled steel. **Weight:** 39 oz. **Length:** 13-5/8". **Power:** Hand pumped. **Sights:** Blade front, rear adjustable for windage and elevation. **Features:** Bolt action moulded plastic grip, hand size pump forearm. Cross-bolt safety. From Crosman.
Price: About $60.00

CROSMAN AUTO AIR II PISTOL
Caliber: BB, 17-shot magazine, 177 pellet, single shot. **Barrel:** 8-5/8" steel, smoothbore. **Weight:** 13 oz. **Length:** 10-3/4" overall. **Power:** CO2 Powerlet. **Stocks:** Grooved plastic. **Sights:** Blade front, adjustable rear; highlighted system. **Features:** Velocity to 480 fps (BBs), 430 fps (pellets). Semi-automatic action with BBs, single shot with pellets. Silvered finish. Introduced 1991. From Crosman.
Price: About $38.00

CROSMAN MODEL 357 SERIES AIR PISTOL
Caliber: 177 10-shot pellet clips. **Barrel:** 4" (Model 3574GT), 6" (Model 3576GT). **Weight:** 32 oz. (6"). **Length:** 11-3/8" overall (357-6). **Power:** CO2 Powerlet. **Stocks:** Grip, wrap-around style. **Sights:** Ramp front, fully adjustable rear. **Features:** Average 430 fps (Model 3574GT). Break-open barrel for easy loading. Single or double action. Vent. rib barrel. Wide, smooth trigger. Two cylinders come with each gun. Black finish. From Crosman.
Price: 4" or 6", about $65.00

CROSMAN MODEL 1008 REPEAT AIR
Caliber: 177, 8-shot pellet clip. **Barrel:** 4.25", rifled steel. **Weight:** 17 oz. **Length:** 8.625" overall. **Power:** CO2 Powerlet. **Stocks:** Checkered black plastic. **Sights:** Post front, adjustable rear. **Features:** Velocity about 430 fps. Break-open barrel for easy loading; single or double semi-automatic action; two 8-shot clips included. Optional carrying case available. Introduced 1992. From Crosman.
Price: About $60.00
Price: With case, about $70.00
Price: Model 1008SB (silver and black finish), about $60.00

DAISY MODEL 2003 PELLET PISTOL
Caliber: 177 pellet, 35-shot clip. **Barrel:** Rifled steel. **Weight:** 2.2 lbs. **Length:** 11.7" overall. **Power:** CO2. **Stocks:** Checkered plastic. **Sights:** Blade front, open rear. **Features:** Velocity to 400 fps. Crossbolt trigger-block safety. Made in U.S. by Daisy Mfg. Co.
Price: About $67.95

DAISY MODEL 454 AIR PISTOL
Caliber: 177 BB, 20-shot clip. **Barrel:** Smoothbore steel. **Weight:** 1.6 lbs. **Length:** 10.4" overall. **Power:** CO2. **Stocks:** Moulded black, ribbed composition. **Sights:** Blade front, fixed rear. **Features:** Velocity to 420 fps. Semi-automatic action; cross-bolt safety; black finish. Introduced 1998. Made in U.S. by Dairy Mfg. Co.
Price: $61.95

DAISY/POWERLINE 717 PELLET PISTOL
Caliber: 177, single shot. **Barrel:** 9.61". **Weight:** 2.25 lbs. **Length:** 13-1/2" overall. **Stocks:** Moulded wood-grain plastic, with thumbrest. **Sights:** Blade and ramp front, micro-adjustable notch rear. **Features:** Single pump pneumatic pistol. Rifled steel barrel. Cross-bolt trigger block. Muzzle velocity 385 fps. From Daisy Mfg. Co. Introduced 1979.
Price: About $71.95

Daisy/PowerLine 747 Pistol
Similar to the 717 pistol except has a 12-groove rifled steel barrel by Lothar Walther, and adjustable trigger pull weight. Velocity of 360 fps. Manual cross-bolt safety.
Price: About $140.00

DAISY/POWERLINE 1140 PELLET PISTOL
Caliber: 177, single shot. **Barrel:** Rifled steel. **Weight:** 1.3 lbs. **Length:** 11.7" overall. **Power:** Single-stroke barrel cocking. **Stocks:** Checkered resin. **Sights:** Hooded post front, open adjustable rear. **Features:** Velocity to 325 fps. Made of black lightweight engineering resin. Introduced 1995. From Daisy.
Price: About $38.95

DAISY/POWERLINE 44 REVOLVER
Caliber: 177 pellets, 6-shot. **Barrel:** 6", rifled steel; interchangeable 4" and 8". **Weight:** 2.7 lbs. **Length:** 13.1" overall. **Power:** CO2. **Stocks:** Moulded plastic with checkering. **Sights:** Blade on ramp front, fully adjustable notch rear. **Features:** Velocity up to 400 fps. Replica of 44 Magnum revolver. Has swingout cylinder and interchangeable barrels. Introduced 1987. From Daisy Mfg. Co.
Price: $59.95

DAISY/POWERLINE 1270 CO2 AIR PISTOL
Caliber: BB, 60-shot magazine. **Barrel:** Smoothbore steel. **Weight:** 17 oz. **Length:** 11.1" overall. **Power:** CO2 pump action. **Stocks:** Moulded black polymer. **Sights:** Blade on ramp front, adjustable rear. **Features:** Velocity to 420 fps. Crossbolt trigger block safety; plated finish. Introduced 1997. Made in U.S. by Daisy Mfg. Co.
Price: About $39.95

EAA/BAIKAL IZH-46 TARGET AIR PISTOL
Caliber: 177, single shot. **Barrel:** 11.02". **Weight:** 2.87 lbs. **Length:** 16.54" overall. **Power:** Underlever single-stroke pneumatic. **Grips:** Adjustable wooden target. **Sights:** Micrometer fully adjustable rear, blade front. **Features:** Velocity about 420 fps. Hammer-forged, rifled barrel. Imported from Russia by European American Armory.
Price: $309.00

EAA/BAIKAL MP-654K AIR PISTOL
Caliber: 177 BB, detachable 13-shot magazine. **Barrel:** 3.75". **Weight:** 1.6 lbs. **Length:** 6.34". **Power:** CO2 cartridge. **Grips:** Black checkered plastic. **Sights:** Notch rear, blade front. **Features:** Velocity about 380 fps. Double-action trigger; slide safety; metal slide and frame. Replica of Makarov pistol. Imported from Russia by European American Armory.
Price: $119.00

EAA/BAIKAL MP-651K AIR PISTOL/RIFLE
Caliber: 177 pellet (8-shot magazine); 177 BB (23-shot). **Barrel:** 5.9" (17.25" with rifle attachment). **Weight:** 1.54 lbs. (3.3 lbs. with rifle attachment). **Length:** 9.4" (31.3" with rifle attachment) **Power:** CO2 cartridge, semi-automatic. **Stock:** Plastic. **Sights:** Notch rear/blade front (pistol); periscopic sighting system (rifle). **Features:** Velocity 328 fps. Unique pistol/rifle combination allows the pistol to be inserted into the rifle shell. Imported from Russia by European American Armory.
Price: $99.00

"GAT" AIR PISTOL
Caliber: 177, single shot. **Barrel:** 7-1/2" cocked, 9-1/2" extended. **Weight:** 22 oz. **Power:** Spring-piston. **Stocks:** Cast checkered metal. **Sights:** Fixed. **Features:** Shoots pellets, corks or darts. Matte black finish. Imported from England by Stone Enterprises, Inc.
Price: $24.95

HAMMERLI 480 MATCH AIR PISTOL
Caliber: 177, single shot. **Barrel:** 9.8". **Weight:** 37 oz. **Length:** 16.5" overall. **Power:** Air or CO2. **Stocks:** Walnut with 7-degree rake adjustment. Stippled grip area. **Sights:** Undercut blade front, fully adjustable open match rear. **Features:** Under-barrel cannister charges with air or CO2 for power supply; gives 320 shots per filling. Trigger adjustable for position. Introduced 1994. Imported from Switzerland by Hammerli Pistols U.S.A.
Price: $1,325.00

AIRGUNS

Marksman 2005 Laserhawk

Hammerli 480K2 Match Air Pistol
Similar to the 480 except has a short, detachable aluminum air cylinder for use only with compressed air; can be filled while on the gun or off; special adjustable barrel weights. Muzzle velocity of 470 fps, gives about 180 shots. Has stippled black composition grip with adjustable palm shelf and rake angle. Comes with air pressure gauge. Introduced 1996. Imported from Switzerland by SIGARMS, Inc.
Price: **$1,112.50**

MARKSMAN 1010 REPEATER PISTOL
Caliber: 177, 18-shot BB repeater. **Barrel:** 2-1/2", smoothbore. **Weight:** 24 oz. **Length:** 8-1/4" overall. **Power:** Spring. **Features:** Velocity to 200 fps. Thumb safety. Black finish. Uses BBs, darts, bolts or pellets. Repeats with BBs only. From Marksman Products.
Price: Matte black finish **$26.00**
Price: Model 2000 (as above except silver-chrome finish). **$27.00**

MARKSMAN 2005 LASERHAWK SPECIAL EDITION AIR PISTOL
Caliber: 177, 24-shot magazine. **Barrel:** 3.8", smoothbore. **Weight:** 22 oz. **Length:** 10.3" overall. **Power:** Spring-air. **Stocks:** Checkered. **Sights:** Fixed fiber optic front sight. **Features:** Velocity to 300 fps with Hyper-Velocity pellets. Square trigger guard with skeletonized trigger; extended barrel for greater velocity and accuracy. Shoots BBs, pellets, darts or bolts. Made in the U.S. From Marksman Products.
Price: **$32.00**

MORINI 162E MATCH AIR PISTOL
Caliber: 177, single shot. **Barrel:** 9.4". **Weight:** 32 oz. **Length:** 16.1" overall. **Power:** Scuba air. **Stocks:** Adjustable match type. **Sights:** Interchangeable blade front, fully adjustable match-type rear. **Features:** Power mechanism shuts down when pressure drops to a pre-set level. Adjustable electronic trigger. Introduced 1995. Imported from Switzerland by Nygord Precision Products.
Price: **$995.00**

PARDINI K58 MATCH AIR PISTOL
Caliber: 177, single shot. **Barrel:** 9.0". **Weight:** 37.7 oz. **Length:** 15.5" overall. **Power:** Pre-charged compressed air; single-stroke cocking. **Stocks:** Adjustable match type; stippled walnut. **Sights:** Interchangeable post front, fully adjustable match rear. **Features:** Fully adjustable trigger. Introduced 1995. Imported from Italy by Nygord Precision Products.
Price: **$750.00**
Price: K2 model, precharged air pistol, introduced in 1998 . . . . **$895.00**

RWS 9B/9N AIR PISTOLS
Caliber: 177, single shot. **Barrel:** N/A. **Weight:** N/A. **Length:** N/A. **Grips:** Plastic with thumbrest. **Sights:** Adjustable. **Features:** Spring-piston powered; 550 fps. Black or nickel finish. Introduced 2001. Imported from Germany by Dynamit Nobel-RWS.
Price: . . . . **NA**

RWS C-225 AIR PISTOLS
Caliber: 177, 8-shot rotary magazine. **Barrel:** 4", 6". **Weight:** NA. **Length:** NA. **Power:** CO2. **Stocks:** Checkered black plastic. **Sights:** Post front, rear adjustable for windage. **Features:** Velocity to 385 fps. Semi-automatic fire; decocking lever. Imported from Germany by Dynamit Nobel-RWS.
Price: 4", blue. **$210.00**
Price: 4", nickel. **$220.00**
Price: 6", blue. **$220.00**

STEYR LP 5CP MATCH AIR PISTOL
Caliber: 177, 5-shot magazine. **Barrel:** NA. **Weight:** 40.7 oz. **Length:** 15.2" overall. **Power:** Pre-charged air cylinder. **Stocks:** Adjustable match type. **Sights:** Interchangeable blade front, fully adjustable match rear. **Features:** Adjustable sight radius; fully adjustable trigger. Has barrel compensator. Introduced 1995. Imported from Austria by Nygord Precision Products.
Price: **$1,150.00**

STEYR LP10P MATCH PISTOL
Caliber: 177, single shot. **Barrel:** 9". **Weight:** 38.7 oz. **Length:** 15.3" overall. **Power:** Scuba air. **Stocks:** Fully adjustable Morini match with palm shelf; stippled walnut. **Sights:** Interchangeable blade in 4mm, 4.5mm or 5mm widths, fully adjustable open rear with interchangeable 3.5mm or 4mm leaves. **Features:** Velocity about 500 fps. Adjustable trigger, adjustable sight radius from 12.4" to 13.2". With compensator. Imported from Austria by Nygord Precision Products.
Price: **$1,125.00**

TECH FORCE SS2 OLYMPIC COMPETITION AIR PISTOL
Caliber: 177 pellet, single shot. **Barrel:** 7.4". **Weight:** 2.8 lbs. **Length:** 16.5" overall. **Power:** Spring piston, sidelever. **Grips:** Hardwood. **Sights:** Extended adjustable rear, blade front accepts inserts. **Features:** Velocity 520 fps. Recoilless design; adjustments allow duplication of a firearm's feel. Match-grade, adjustable trigger; includes carrying case. Imported from China by Compasseco Inc.
Price: **$295.00**

TECH FORCE 35 AIR PISTOL
Caliber: 177 pellet, single shot. **Barrel:** N/A. **Weight:** 2.86 lbs. **Length:** 14.9" overall. **Power:** Spring piston, underlever. **Grips:** Hardwood. **Sights:** Micrometer adjustable rear, blade front. **Features:** Velocity 400 fps. Grooved for scope mount; trigger safety. Imported from China by Compasseco Inc.
Price: **$49.95**

Tech Force 8 Air Pistol
Similar to Tech Force 35, but with break-barrel action, ambidextrous polymer grips. From Compasseco Inc.
Price: **$59.95**

Tech Force S2-1 Air Pistol
Similar to Tech Force 8, but more basic grips and sights for plinking. From Compasseco Inc.
Price: **$29.95**

WALTHER CP88 PELLET PISTOL
Caliber: 177, 8-shot rotary magazine. **Barrel:** 4", 6". **Weight:** 37 oz. (4" barrel) **Length:** 7" (4" barrel). **Power:** CO2. **Stocks:** Checkered plastic. **Sights:** Blade front, fully adjustable rear. **Features:** Faithfully replicates size, weight and trigger pull of the 9mm Walther P88 compact pistol. Has SA/DA trigger mechanism; ambidextrous safety, levers. Comes with two magazines, 500 pellets, one CO2 cartridge. Introduced 1997. Imported from Germany by Interarms.
Price: Blue **$179.00**
Price: Nickel **$189.00**

WALTHER LP201 MATCH PISTOL
Caliber: 177, single shot. **Barrel:** 8.66". **Weight:** NA. **Length:** 15.1" overall. **Power:** Scuba air. **Stocks:** Orthopaedic target type. **Sights:** Undercut blade front, open match rear fully adjustable for windage and elevation. **Features:** Adjustable velocity; matte finish. Introduced 1995. Imported from Germany by Nygord Precision Products.
Price: **$1,095.00**

Walther CP88 Competition Pellet Pistol
Similar to the standard CP88 except has 6" match-grade barrel, muzzle weight, wood or plastic stocks. Weighs 41 oz., has overall length of 9". Introduced 1997. Imported from Germany by Interarms.
Price: Blue, plastic grips. **$170.00**
Price: Nickel, plastic grips **$195.00**
Price: Blue, wood grips. **$205.00**
Price: Nickel, wood grips **$232.00**

WALTHER CP99 AIR PISTOL
Caliber: 177 pellet, 8-shot rotary magazine. **Barrel:** 3". **Weight:** 26 oz. **Length:** 7.1" overall. **Power:** CO2 cartridge. **Grip:** Polymer. **Sights:** Drift-adjustable rear, blade front. **Features:** Velocity 320 fps. Replica of Walther P99 pistol. Trigger allows single and double action; ambidextrous magazine release; interchangeable backstraps to fit variety of hand sizes. Introduced 2000. From Walther USA.
Price: . . . . **NA**

WALTHER PPK/S AIR PISTOL
Caliber: 177 BB. **Barrel:** N/A. **Weight:** 20 oz. **Length:** 6.3" overall. **Power:** CO2 cartridge. **Grip:** Plastic. **Sights:** Fixed rear, blade front. **Features:** Replica of Walther PPK pistol. Blow back system moves slide when fired; trigger allows single and double action. Introduced 2000. From Walther USA.
Price: . . . . **NA**

AIRGUNS

Anschutz 2002

AIRROW MODEL A-8SRB STEALTH AIR GUN
Caliber: 177, 22, 25, 38, 9-shot. **Barrel:** 19.7"; rifled. **Weight:** 6 lbs. **Length:** 34" overall. **Power:** CO2 or compressed air; variable power. **Stock:** Telescoping CAR-15-type. **Sights:** Variable 3.5-10x scope. **Features:** Velocity 1100 fps in all calibers. Pneumatic air trigger. All aircraft aluminum and stainless steel construction. Mil-spec materials and finishes. Introduced 1992. From Swivel Machine Works, Inc.
Price: About **$2,599.00**

AIRROW MODEL A-8S1P STEALTH AIR GUN
Caliber: #2512 16" arrow. **Barrel:** 16". **Weight:** 4.4 lbs. **Length:** 30.1" overall. **Power:** CO2 or compressed air; variable power. **Stock:** Telescoping CAR-15-type. **Sights:** Scope rings only. **Features:** Velocity to 650 fps with 260-grain arrow. Pneumatic air trigger. All aircraft aluminum and stainless steel construction. Mil-spec materials and finishes. Waterproof case. Introduced 1991. From Swivel Machine Works, Inc.
Price: About **$1,699.00**

ARS/KING HUNTING MASTER AIR RIFLE
Caliber: 22, 5-shot repeater. **Barrel:** 22-3/4". **Weight:** 7-3/4 lbs. **Length:** 42" overall. **Power:** Pre-compressed air from 3000 psi diving tank. **Stock:** Indonesian walnut with checkered grip and forend; rubber buttpad. **Sights:** Blade front, fully adjustable open rear. Receiver grooved for scope mounting. **Features:** Velocity over 1000 fps with 32-grain pellet. High and low power switch for hunting or target velocities. Side lever cocks action and inserts pellet. Rotary magazine. Imported from Korea by Air Rifle Specialists.
Price: **$580.00**
Price: Hunting Master 900 (9mm, limited production) **$1,000.00**

ARS/Magnum 6 Air Rifle
Similar to the King Hunting Master except is 6-shot repeater with 23-3/4" barrel, weighs 8-1/4 lbs. Stock is walnut-stained hardwood with checkered grip and forend; rubber buttpad. Velocity of 1000+ fps with 32-grain pellet. Imported from Korea by Air Rifle Specialists.
Price: **$500.00**

ARS HUNTING MASTER AR6 AIR RIFLE
Caliber: 22, 6-shot repeater. **Barrel:** 25-1/2". **Weight:** 7 lbs. **Length:** 41-1/4" overall. **Power:** Pre-compressed air from 3000 psi diving tank. **Stock:** Indonesian walnut with checkered grip; rubber buttpad. **Sights:** Blade front, adjustable peep rear. **Features:** Velocity over 1000 fps with 32-grain pellet. Receiver grooved for scope mounting. Has 6-shot rotary magazine. Imported from Air Rifle Specialists.
Price: **$580.00**

ARS/CAREER 707 AIR RIFLE
Caliber: 22, 6-shot repeater; variable power. **Barrel:** 23". **Weight:** 7.75 lbs. **Length:** 40.5" overall. **Power:** Pre-compressed air; variable power. **Stock:** Indonesian walnut with checkered grip, gloss finish. **Sights:** Hooded post front with interchangeable inserts, fully adjustable diopter rear. **Features:** Velocity to 1000 fps. Lever-action with straight feed magazine; pressure gauge in lower front air reservoir; scope mounting rail included. Introduced 1996. Imported from the Philippines by Air Rifle Specialists.
Price: **$580.00**

ARS/FARCO FP SURVIVAL AIR RIFLE
Caliber: 22, 25, single shot. **Barrel:** 22-3/4". **Weight:** 5-3/4 lbs. **Length:** 42-3/4" overall. **Power:** Multi-pump foot pump. **Stock:** Philippine hardwood. **Sights:** Blade front, fixed rear. **Features:** Velocity to 850 fps (22 or 25). Receiver grooved for scope mounting. Imported from the Philippines by Air Rifle Specialists.
Price: **$295.00**

ARS/FARCO CO2 AIR SHOTGUN
Caliber: 51 (28-gauge). **Barrel:** 30". **Weight:** 7 lbs. **Length:** 48-1/2" overall. **Power:** 10-oz. refillable CO2 tank. **Stock:** Hardwood. **Sights:** Blade front, fixed rear. **Features:** Gives over 100 ft. lbs. energy for taking small game. Imported from the Philippines by Air Rifle Specialists.
Price: **$460.00**

ARS/Farco CO2 Stainless Steel Air Rifle
Similar to the ARS/Farco CO2 shotgun except in 22- or 25-caliber with 21-1/2" barrel; weighs 6-3/4 lbs., 42-1/2" overall; Philippine hardwood stock with stippled grip and forend; blade front sight, adjustable rear, grooved for scope mount. Uses 10-oz. refillable CO2 cylinder. Made of stainless steel. Imported from the Philippines by Air Rifle Specialists.
Price: Including CO2 cylinder **$460.00**

ARS/QB77 DELUXE AIR RIFLE
Caliber: 177, 22, single shot. **Barrel:** 21-1/2". **Weight:** 5-1/2 lbs. **Length:** 40" overall. **Power:** Two 12-oz. CO2 cylinders. **Stock:** Walnut-stained hardwood. **Sights:** Blade front, adjustable rear. **Features:** Velocity to 625 fps (22), 725 fps (177). Receiver grooved for scope mounting. Comes with bulk-fill valve. Imported by Air Rifle Specialists.
Price: **$195.00**

ANSCHUTZ 2002 MATCH AIR RIFLE
Caliber: 177, single shot. **Barrel:** 25.2". **Weight:** 10.4 lbs. **Length:** 44.5" overall. **Stock:** European walnut, blonde hardwood or colored laminated hardwood; stippled grip and forend. Also available with flat-forend walnut stock for benchrest shooting and aluminum. **Sights:** Optional sight set #6834. **Features:** Muzzle velocity 575 fps. Balance, weight match the 1907 ISU smallbore rifle. Uses #5021 match trigger. Recoil and vibration free. Fully adjustable cheekpiece and buttplate; accessory rail under forend. Available in Pneumatic and Compressed Air versions. Introduced 1988. Imported from Germany by Gunsmithing, Inc., Accuracy International, Champion's Choice.
Price: Right-hand, blonde hardwood stock, with sights **$1,275.00**
Price: Right-hand, walnut stock **$1,275.00**
Price: Right-hand, color laminate stock **$1,300.00**
Price: Right-hand, aluminum stock, butt plate **$1,495.00**
Price: Left-hand, color laminate stock **$1,595.00**
Price: Model 2002D-RT Running Target, right-hand, no sights **$1,248.90**
Price: #6834 Sight Set **$227.10**

BEEMAN BEARCUB AIR RIFLE
Caliber: 177, single shot. **Barrel:** 13". **Weight:** 7.2 lbs. **Length:** 37.8" overall. **Power:** Spring-piston, barrel cocking. **Stock:** Stained hardwood. **Sights:** Hooded post front, open fully adjustable rear. **Features:** Velocity to 915 fps. Polished blue finish; receiver dovetailed for scope mounting. Imported from England by Beeman Precision Airguns.
Price: **$325.00**

BEEMAN CROW MAGNUM AIR RIFLE
Caliber: 20, 22, 25, single shot. **Barrel:** 16"; 10-groove rifling. **Weight:** 8.5 lbs. **Length:** 46" overall. **Power:** Gas-spring; adjustable power to 32 foot pounds muzzle energy. Barrel-cocking. **Stock:** Classic-style hardwood; hand checkered. **Sights:** For scope use only; built-in base and 1" rings included. **Features:** Adjustable two-stage trigger. Automatic safety. Also available in 22-caliber on special order. Introduced 1992. Imported by Beeman.
Price: **$1,220.00**

BEEMAN KODIAK AIR RIFLE
Caliber: 25, single shot. **Barrel:** 17.6". **Weight:** 9 lbs. **Length:** 45.6" overall. **Power:** Spring-piston, barrel cocking. **Stock:** Stained hardwood. **Sights:** Blade front, open fully adjustable rear. **Features:** Velocity to 820 fps. Up to 30 foot pounds muzzle energy. Introduced 1993. Imported by Beeman.
Price: **$625.00**

BEEMAN MAKO AIR RIFLE
Caliber: 177, single shot. **Barrel:** 20", with compensator. **Weight:** 7.3 lbs. **Length:** 38.5" overall. **Power:** Pre-charged pneumatic. **Stock:** Stained beech; Monte Carlo cheekpiece; checkered grip. **Sights:** None furnished. **Features:** Velocity to 930 fps. Gives over 50 shots per charge. Manual safety; brass trigger blade; vented rubber butt pad. Requires scuba tank for air. Introduced 1994. Imported from England by Beeman.
Price: **$1,000.00**
Price: Mako FT (thumbhole stock) **$1,350.00**

BEEMAN R1 AIR RIFLE
Caliber: 177, 20 or 22, single shot. **Barrel:** 19.6", 12-groove rifling. **Weight:** 8.5 lbs. **Length:** 45.2" overall. **Power:** Spring-piston, barrel cocking. **Stock:** Walnut-stained beech; cut-checkered pistol grip; Monte Carlo comb and cheekpiece; rubber buttpad. **Sights:** Tunnel front with interchangeable inserts, open rear click-adjustable for windage and elevation. Grooved for scope mounting. **Features:** Velocity of 940-1000 fps (177), 860 fps (20), 800 fps (22). Non-drying nylon piston and breech seals. Adjustable metal trigger. Milled steel safety. Right- or left-hand stock. Available with adjustable cheekpiece and buttplate at extra cost. Custom and Super Laser versions available. Imported by Beeman.
Price: Right-hand, 177, 20, 22 . . . . **$540.00**
Price: Left-hand, 177, 20, 22 . . . . **$575.00**

BEEMAN R6 AIR RIFLE
Caliber: 177, single shot. **Barrel:** NA. **Weight:** 7.1 lbs. **Length:** 41.8" overall. **Power:** Spring-piston, barrel cocking. **Stock:** Stained hardwood. **Sights:** Tunnel post front, open fully adjustable rear. **Features:** Velocity to 815 fps. Two-stage Rekord adjustable trigger; receiver dovetailed for scope mounting; automatic safety. Introduced 1996. Imported from Germany by Beeman Precision Airguns.
Price: **$285.00**

AIRGUNS

AIRGUNS—LONG GUNS

BEEMAN R1 LASER MK II AIR RIFLE

Caliber: 177, 20, 22, 25, single shot. **Barrel:** 16.1" or 19.6". **Weight:** 8.4 lbs. **Length:** 41.7" overall. **Power:** Spring-piston, barrel cocking. **Stock:** Laminated wood with high cheekpiece, ventilated recoil pad. **Sights:** Tunnel front with interchangeable inserts, open adjustable rear; receiver grooved for scope mounting. **Features:** Velocity to 1150 fps (177). Special powerplant components. Built from the Beeman R1 rifle by Beeman.

Price: **$895.00**

BEEMAN R7 AIR RIFLE

Caliber: 177, 20, single shot. **Barrel:** 17". **Weight:** 6.1 lbs. **Length:** 40.2" overall. **Power:** Spring piston. **Stock:** Stained beech. **Sights:** Hooded front, fully adjustable micrometer click open rear. **Features:** Velocity to 700 fps (177), 620 fps (20). Receiver grooved for scope mounting; double-jointed cocking lever; fully adjustable trigger; checkered grip. Imported by Beeman.

Price: **$280.00**

BEEMAN R9 AIR RIFLE

Caliber: 177, 20, single shot. **Barrel:** NA. **Weight:** 7.3 lbs. **Length:** 43" overall. **Power:** Spring-piston, barrel cocking. **Stock:** Stained hardwood. **Sights:** Tunnel post front, fully adjustable open rear. **Features:** Velocity to 1000 fps (177), 800 fps (20). Adjustable Rekord trigger; automatic safety; receiver dovetailed for scope mounting. Introduced 1996. Imported from Germany by Beeman Precision Airguns.

Price: **$320.00**

Beeman R9 Deluxe Air Rifle

Same as the R9 except has an extended forend stock, checkered pistol grip, grip cap, carved Monte Carlo cheekpiece. Globe front sight with inserts. Introduced 1997. Imported by Beeman.

Price: **$370.00**

BEEMAN R11 AIR RIFLE

Caliber: 177, single shot. **Barrel:** 19.6". **Weight:** 8.8 lbs. **Length:** 47" overall. **Power:** Spring-piston, barrel cocking. **Stock:** Walnut-stained beech; adjustable buttplate and cheekpiece. **Sights:** None furnished. Has dovetail for scope mounting. **Features:** Velocity 910-940 fps. All-steel barrel sleeve. Imported by Beeman.

Price: **$530.00**

BEEMAN SUPER 12 AIR RIFLE

Caliber: 22, 25, 12-shot magazine. **Barrel:** 19", 12-groove rifling. **Weight:** 7.8 lbs. **Length:** 41.7" overall. **Power:** Pre-charged pneumatic; external air reservoir. **Stock:** European walnut. **Sights:** None furnished; drilled and tapped for scope mounting; scope mount included. **Features:** Velocity to 850 fps (25-caliber). Adjustable power setting gives 30-70 shots per 400 cc air bottle. Requires scuba tank for air. Introduced 1995. Imported by Beeman.

Price: **$1,675.00**

BEEMAN S1 MAGNUM AIR RIFLE

Caliber: 177, single shot. **Barrel:** 19". **Weight:** 7.1 lbs. **Length:** 45.5" overall. **Power:** Spring-piston, barrel cocking. **Stock:** Stained beech with Monte Carlo cheekpiece; checkered grip. **Sights:** Hooded post front, fully adjustable micrometer click rear. **Features:** Velocity to 900 fps. Automatic safety; receiver grooved for scope mounting; two-stage adjustable trigger; curved rubber buttpad. Introduced 1995. Imported by Beeman.

Price: **$210.00**

BEEMAN RX-1 GAS-SPRING MAGNUM AIR RIFLE

Caliber: 177, 20, 22, 25, single shot. **Barrel:** 19.6", 12-groove rifling. **Weight:** 8.8 lbs. **Power:** Gas-spring piston air; single stroke barrel cocking. **Stock:** Walnut-finished hardwood, hand checkered, with cheekpiece. Adjustable cheekpiece and buttplate. **Sights:** Tunnel front, click-adjustable rear. **Features:** Velocity adjustable to about 1200 fps. Uses special sealed chamber of air as a mainspring. Gas-spring cannot take a set. Introduced 1990. Imported by Beeman.

Price: 177, 20, 22 or 25 regular, right-hand **$590.00**
Price: 177, 20, 22, 25, left-hand **$625.00**

BEEMAN R1 CARBINE

Caliber: 177, 20, 22, 25, single shot. **Barrel:** 16.1". **Weight:** 8.6 lbs. **Length:** 41.7" overall. **Power:** Spring-piston, barrel cocking. **Stock:** Stained beech; Monte Carlo comb and checkpiece; cut checkered pistol grip; rubber buttpad. **Sights:** Tunnel front with interchangeable inserts, open adjustable rear; receiver grooved for scope mounting. **Features:** Velocity up to 1000 fps (177). Non-drying nylon piston and breech seals. Adjustable metal trigger. Machined steel receiver end cap and safety. Right- or left-hand stock. Imported by Beeman.

Price: 177, 20, 22, 25, right-hand. **$540.00**
Price: As above, left-hand **$575.00**
Price: R1-AW (synthetic stock, nickel plating) **$650.00**

BEEMAN/FEINWERKBAU 300-S SERIES MATCH RIFLE

Caliber: 177, single shot. **Barrel:** 19.9", fixed solid with receiver. **Weight:** Approx. 10 lbs. with optional bbl. sleeve. **Length:** 42.8" overall. **Power:** Spring-piston, single stroke sidelever. **Stock:** Match model—walnut, deep forend, adjustable buttplate. **Sights:** Globe front with interchangeable inserts. Click micro. adjustable match aperture rear. Front and rear sights move as a single unit. **Features:** Recoilless, vibration free. Five-way adjustable match trigger. Grooved for scope mounts. Permanent lubrication, steel piston ring. Cocking effort 9 lbs. Optional 10-oz. barrel sleeve. Available from Beeman.

Price: Right-hand **$1,235.00**
Price: Left-hand **$1,370.00**

BEEMAN/FEINWERKBAU 603 AIR RIFLE

Caliber: 177, single shot. **Barrel:** 16.6". **Weight:** 10.8 lbs. **Length:** 43" overall. **Power:** Single stroke pneumatic. **Stock:** Special laminated hardwoods and hard rubber for stability. Multi-colored stock also available. **Sights:** Tunnel front with interchangeable inserts, click micrometer match aperture rear. **Features:** Velocity to 570 fps. Recoilless action; double supported barrel; special, short rifled area frees pellet form barrel faster so shooter's motion has minimum effect on accuracy. Fully adjustable match trigger with separately adjustable trigger and trigger slack weight. Trigger and sights blocked when loading latch is open. Introduced 1997. Imported by Beeman.

Price: Right-hand **$1,625.00**
Price: Left-hand **$1,775.00**

BEEMAN/FEINWERKBAU 300-S MINI-MATCH

Caliber: 177, single shot. **Barrel:** 17-1/8". **Weight:** 8.8 lbs. **Length:** 40" overall. **Power:** Spring-piston, single stroke sidelever cocking. **Stock:** Walnut. Stippled grip, adjustable buttplate. Scaled-down for youthful or slightly built shooters. **Sights:** Globe front with interchangeable inserts, micro. adjustable rear. Front and rear sights move as a single unit. **Features:** Recoilless, vibration free. Grooved for scope mounts. Steel piston ring. Cocking effort about 9-1/2 lbs. Barrel sleeve optional. Left-hand model available. Introduced 1978. Imported by Beeman.

Price: Right-hand **$1,270.00**
Price: Left-hand **$1,370.00**

BEEMAN/FEINWERKBAU P70 AIR RIFLE

Caliber: 177, single shot. **Barrel:** 16.6". **Weight:** 10.6 lbs. **Length:** 42.6" overall. **Power:** Precharged pneumatic. **Stock:** Laminated hardwoods and hard rubber for stability. Multi-colored stock also available. **Sights:** Tunnel front with interchangeable inserts, click micormeter match aperture rear. **Features:** Velocity to 570 fps. Recoilless action; double supported barrel; special short rifled area frees pellet from barrel faster so shooter's motion has minimum effect on accuracy. Fully adjustable match trigger with separately adjustable trigger and trigger slack weight. Trigger and sights blocked when loading latch is open. Introduced 1997. Imported by Beeman.

Price: P70, pre-charged, right-hand **$1,545.00**
Price: P70, pre-charged, left-hand **$1,640.00**
Price: P70, pre-charged, right-hand, multi **$1,645.00**
Price: P70, pre-charged, left-hand, multi **$1,745.00**

BEEMAN/HW 97 AIR RIFLE

Caliber: 177, 20, single shot. **Barrel:** 17.75". **Weight:** 9.2 lbs. **Length:** 44.1" overall. **Power:** Spring-piston, underlever cocking. **Stock:** Walnut-stained beech; rubber buttpad. **Sights:** None. Receiver grooved for scope mounting. **Features:** Velocity 830 fps (177). Fixed barrel with fully opening, direct loading breech. Adjustable trigger. Introduced 1994. Imported by Beeman Precision Airguns.

Price: Right-hand only **$530.00**

BENJAMIN SHERIDAN PNEUMATIC (PUMP-UP) AIR RIFLES

Caliber: 177 or 22, single shot. **Barrel:** 19-3/8", rifled brass. **Weight:** 5-1/2 lbs. **Length:** 36-1/4" overall. **Power:** Underlever pneumatic, hand pumped. **Stock:** American walnut stock and forend. **Sights:** High ramp front, fully adjustable notch rear. **Features:** Variable velocity to 800 fps. Bolt action with ambidextrous push-pull safety. Black or nickel finish. Introduced 1991. Made in the U.S. by Benjamin Sheridan Co.

Price: Black finish, Model 397 (177), Model 392 (22), about **$140.00**
Price: Nickel finish, Model S397 (177), Model S392 (22), about **$150.00**

BENJAMIN SHERIDAN W.F. AIR RIFLE

Caliber: 177 single-shot. **Barrel:** 19-3/8", rifled brass. **Weight:** 5 lbs. **Length:** 36-1/2" overall. Power 12-gram CO2 cylinder. Stocks: American walnut with buttplate. **Sights:** High ramp front, fully adjustable notch rear. **Features:** Velocity to 680 fps (177). Bolt action with ambidextrous push-pull safety. Gives about 40 shots per cylinder. Black finish. Introduced 1991. Made in the U.S. by Benjamin Sheridan Co.

Price: Black finish, Model G397 (177) **$140.00**

BRNO TAU-200 AIR RIFLE

Caliber: 177, single shot. **Barrel:** 19", rifled. **Weight:** 7-1/2 lbs. **Length:** 42" overall. **Power:** 6-oz. CO2 cartridge. **Stock:** Wood match style with adjustable comb and buttplate. **Sights:** Globe front with interchangeable inserts, fully adjustable open rear. **Features:** Adjustable trigger. Comes with extra seals, large CO2 bottle, counterweight. Introduced 1993. Imported by Great Lakes Airguns. Available in Standard Universal, Deluxe Universal, International and Target Sporter versions.

Price: Standard Universal (ambidex. stock with buttstock extender, adj. cheekpiece).. . . . . **$349.50**
Price: Deluxe Universal (as above but with micro-adj. aperture sight) **$449.50**
Price: International (like Deluxe Universal but with right- or left-hand stock) **$454.50**
Price: Target Sporter (like Std. Universal but with 4X scope, no sights) **$412.50**

BSA MAGNUM SUPERSTAR™ MK2 MAGNUM AIR RIFLE, CARBINE

Caliber: 177, 22, 25, single shot. **Barrel:** 18". **Weight:** 8 lbs., 8 oz. **Length:** 43" overall. **Power:** Spring-air, underlever cocking. **Stock:** Oil-finished hardwood; Monte Carlo with cheekpiece, checkered at grip; recoil pad. **Sights:** Ramp front, micrometer adjustable rear. Maxi-Grip scope rail. **Features:** Velocity 1020 fps (177), 800 fps (22), 675 fps (25). Patented rotating breech design. Maxi-Grip scope rail protects optics from recoil; automatic anti-beartrap plus manual safety. Imported from U.K. by Precision Sales International, Inc.

Price: **$479.99**
Price: MKII Carbine (14" barrel, 39-1/2" overall) **$479.99**

BRNO TAU-200 Sporter

BSA MAGNUM SUPERSPORT™ AIR RIFLE

Caliber: 177, 22, 25, single shot. **Barrel:** 18". **Weight:** 6 lbs., 8 oz. **Length:** 41" overall. **Power:** Spring-air, barrel cocking. **Stock:** Oil-finished hardwood; Monte Carlo with cheekpiece, recoil pad. **Sights:** Ramp front, micrometer adjustable rear. Maxi-Grip scope rail. **Features:** Velocity 1020 fps (177), 800 fps (22), 675 fps (25). Patented Maxi-Grip scope rail protects optics from recoil; automatic anti-beartrap plus manual tang safety. Muzzle brake standard. Imported for U.K. by Precision Sales International, Inc.
Price: $279.99
Price: Carbine, 14" barrel, muzzle brake $299.99

BSA MAGNUM GOLDSTAR MAGNUM AIR RIFLE

Caliber: 177, 22, 10-shot repeater. **Barrel:** 18". **Weight:** 8 lbs., 8 oz. **Length:** 42.5" overall. **Power:** Spring-air, underlever cocking. **Stock:** Oil-finished hardwood; Monte Carlo with cheekpiece, checkered at grip; recoil pad. **Sights:** Ramp front, micrometer adjustable rear; comes with Maxi-Grip scope rail. **Features:** Velocity 1020 fps (177), 800 fps (22). Patented 10-shot indexing magazine; Maxi-Grip scope rail protects optics from recoil; automatic anti-beartrap plus manual safety; muzzlebrake standard. Imported from U.K. by Precision Sales International, Inc.
Price: $699.99

BSA MAGNUM SUPERTEN AIR RIFLE

Caliber: 177, 22 10-shot repeater. **Barrel:** 17-1/2". **Weight:** 7 lbs., 8 oz. **Length:** 37" overall. **Power:** Precharged pneumatic via buddy bottle. **Stock:** Oil-finished hardwood; Monte Carlo with cheekpiece, cut checkering at grip; adjustable recoil pad. **Sights:** No sights; intended for scope use. **Features:** Velocity 1300+ fps (177), 1000+ fps (22). Patented 10-shot indexing magazine, bolt-action loading. Left-hand version also available. Imported from U.K. by Precision Sales International, Inc.
Price: $879.99
Price: Left-hand $1,069.00

BSA METEOR MK6 AIR RIFLE

Caliber: 177, 22, single shot. **Barrel:** 18". **Weight:** 6 lbs. **Length:** 41" overall. **Power:** Spring-air, barrel cocking. **Stock:** Oil-finished hardwood. **Sights:** Ramp front, micrometer adjustable rear. **Features:** Velocity 650 fps (177), 500 fps (22). Automatic anti-beartrap; manual tang safety. Receiver grooved for scope mounting. Imported from U.K. by Precision Sales International, Inc.
Price: Rifle $199.99
Price: Carbine $219.99

COPPERHEAD BLACK SERPENT RIFLE

Caliber: 177 pellets, 5-shot, on BB, 195-shot magazine. **Barrel:** 19-1/2" smoothbore steel. **Weight:** 2 lbs., 14 oz. **Length:** 35-7/8" overall. **Power:** Pneumatic, single pump. **Stock:** Textured plastic. **Sights:** Blade front, open adjustable rear. **Features:** Velocity to 405 fps. Introduced 1996. Made in U.S. by Crosman Corp.
Price: About $48.00

NEW! CROSMAN CHALLENGER 2000 AIR RIFLE

Caliber: 177, single shot. **Barrel:** N/A. **Weight:** 6.95 lbs. **Power:** CO2 Powerlet. **Length:** 36 1/4" overall. **Stock:** Black synthetic with adjustable buttplate and cheekpiece. **Sights:** Hooded front, micrometer-adjustable aperture rear. **Features:** Up to 485 fps. Two-stage trigger; accessory rail on forearm. Designed for competition shooting. Introduced 2001. Made in U.S. by Crosman Corp.
Price: $299.00

CROSMAN MODEL 66 POWERMASTER

Caliber: 177 (single shot pellet) or BB, 200-shot reservoir. **Barrel:** 20", rifled steel. **Weight:** 3 lbs. **Length:** 38-1/2" overall. **Power:** Pneumatic; hand pumped. **Stock:** Wood-grained ABS plastic; checkered pistol grip and forend. **Sights:** Ramp front, fully adjustable open rear. **Features:** Velocity about 645 fps. Bolt action, cross-bolt safety. Introduced 1983. From Crosman.
Price: About $60.00
Price: Model 664X (as above, with 4x scope) $70.00
Price: Model 664SB (as above with silver and black finish), about $75.00
Price: Model 664GT (black and gold finish, 4x scope) about $73.00

CROSMAN MODEL 760 PUMPMASTER

Caliber: 177 pellets (single shot) or BB (200-shot reservoir). **Barrel:** 19-1/2", rifled steel. **Weight:** 2 lbs., 12 oz. **Length:** 33.5" overall. **Power:** Pneumatic, hand pumped. **Stock:** Walnut-finished ABS plastic stock and forend. **Features:** Velocity to 590 fps (BBs, 10 pumps). Short stroke, power determined by number of strokes. Post front sight and adjustable rear sight. Cross-bolt safety. Introduced 1966. From Crosman.
Price: About $40.00
Price: Model 760SB (silver and black finish), about $55.00

CROSMAN MODEL 782 BLACK DIAMOND AIR RIFLE

Caliber: 177 pellets (5-shot clip) or BB (195-shot reservoir). **Barrel:** 18", rifled steel. **Weight:** 3 lbs. **Power:** CO2 Powerlet. **Stock:** Wood-grained ABS plastic; checkered grip and forend. **Sights:** Blade front, open adjustable rear. **Features:** Velocity up to 595 fps (pellets), 650 fps (BB). Black finish with white diamonds. Introduced 1990. From Crosman.
Price: About $63.00

CROSMAN MODEL 795 SPRING MASTER RIFLE

Caliber: 177, single shot. **Barrel:** Rifled steel. **Weight:** 4 lbs., 8 oz. **Length:** 42" overall. **Power:** Spring-piston. **Stock:** Black synthetic. **Sights:** Hooded front, fully adjustable rear. **Features:** Velocity about 550 fps. Introduced 1995. From Crosman.
Price: About $90.00

CROSMAN MODEL 1077 REPEATAIR RIFLE

Caliber: 177 pellets, 12-shot clip. **Barrel:** 20.3", rifled steel. **Weight:** 3 lbs., 11 oz. **Length:** 38.8" overall. **Power:** CO2 Powerlet. **Stock:** Textured synthetic or American walnut. **Sights:** Blade front, fully adjustable rear. **Features:** Velocity 590 fps. Removable 12-shot clip. True semi-automatic action. Introduced 1993. From Crosman.
Price: About $75.00
Price: 1077W (walnut stock) $110.00

CROSMAN 2264 X AIR RIFLE

Caliber: 22, single shot. **Barrel:** 24". **Weight:** 5 lbs., 12 oz. **Length:** 39.75" overall. **Power:** C02 Powerlet. **Stock:** Hardwood. **Sights:** Blade front, adjustable rear; includes 4x32 scope, rings and base included. **Features:** About 600 fps. Scoped version of 2260 rifle. Introduced 2001. Made in U.S. by Crosman Corp.
Price: $159.95

CROSMAN 2260 AIR RIFLE

Caliber: 22, single shot. **Barrel:** 24". **Weight:** 4 lbs., 12 oz. **Length:** 39.75" overall. **Power:** CO2 Powerlet. **Stock:** Hardwood. **Sights:** Blade front, adjustable rear open or peep. **Features:** About 600 fps. Made in U.S. by Crosman Corp.
Price: .... NA

CROSMAN MODEL 2289 RIFLE

Caliber: .22, single shot. **Barrel:** 14.625", rifled steel. **Weight:** 3 lbs. 3 oz. **Length:** 31" overall. **Power:** Hand pumped, pneumatic. **Stock:** Composition, skeletal type. **Sights:** Blade front, rear adjustable for windage and elevation. **Features:** Velocity to 575 fps. Detachable stock. Metal parts blued. From Crosman.
Price: About $73.00

CROSMAN MODEL 2100 CLASSIC AIR RIFLE

Caliber: 177 pellets (single shot) or BB (200-shot BB reservoir). **Barrel:** 21", rifled. **Weight:** 4 lbs., 13 oz. **Length:** 39-3/4" overall. **Power:** Pump-up, pneumatic. **Stock:** Wood-grained checkered ABS plastic. **Features:** Three pumps give about 450 fps, 10 pumps about 755 fps (BBs). Cross-bolt safety; concealed reservoir holds over 200 BBs. From Crosman.
Price: About $75.00
Price: Model 2104GT (black and gold finish, 4x scope), about $95.00
Price: Model 2100W (walnut stock, pellets only), about $120.00

CROSMAN MODEL 2200 MAGNUM AIR RIFLE

Caliber: 22, single shot. **Barrel:** 19", rifled steel. **Weight:** 4 lbs., 12 oz. **Length:** 39" overall. **Stock:** Full-size, wood-grained ABS plastic with checkered grip and forend or American walnut. **Sights:** Ramp front, open step-adjustable rear. **Features:** Variable pump power—three pumps give 395 fps, six pumps 530 fps, 10 pumps 595 fps (average). Full-size adult air rifle. Has white line spacers at pistol grip and buttplate. Introduced 1978. From Crosman.
Price: About $75.00
Price: 2200W, about $120.00

DAISY MODEL 840

Caliber: 177 pellet single shot; or BB 350-shot. **Barrel:** 19", smoothbore, steel. **Weight:** 2.7 lbs. **Length:** 36.8" overall. **Power:** Pneumatic, single pump. **Stock:** Moulded wood-grain stock and forend. **Sights:** Ramp front, open, adjustable rear. **Features:** Muzzle velocity 335 fps (BB), 300 fps (pellet). Steel buttplate; straight pull bolt action; cross-bolt safety. Forend forms pump lever. Introduced 1978. From Daisy Mfg. Co.
Price: About $32.95

DAISY/POWERLINE 853

Caliber: 177 pellets. **Barrel:** 20.9"; 12-groove rifling, high-grade solid steel by Lothar Waltherô, precision crowned; bore size for precision match pellets. **Weight:** 5.08 lbs. **Length:** 38.9" overall. **Stock:** Full-length, select American hardwood, stained and finished; black buttplate with white spacers. **Sights:** Globe front with four aperture inserts; precision micrometer adjustable rear peep sight mounted on a standard 3/8" dovetail receiver mount. **Features:** Single shot. From Daisy Mfg. Co.
Price: About $225.00

DAISY/POWERLINE 856 PUMP-UP AIRGUN

Caliber: 177 pellets (single shot) or BB (100-shot reservoir). **Barrel:** Rifled steel with shroud. **Weight:** 2.7 lbs. **Length:** 37.4" overall. **Power:** Pneumatic pump-up. **Stock:** Moulded wood-grain with Monte Carlo cheekpiece. **Sights:** Ramp and blade front, open rear adjustable for elevation. **Features:** Velocity from 315 fps (two pumps) to 650 fps (10 pumps). Shoots BBs or pellets. Heavy die-cast metal receiver. Cross-bolt trigger-block safety. Introduced 1984. From Daisy Mfg. Co.
Price: About $39.95

DAISY MODEL 990 DUAL-POWER AIR RIFLE

Caliber: 177 pellets (single shot) or BB (100-shot magazine). **Barrel:** Rifled steel. **Weight:** 4.1 lbs. **Length:** 37.4" overall. **Power:** Pneumatic pump-up and 12-gram CO_2. **Stock:** Moulded woodgrain. **Sights:** Ramp and blade front, adjustable open rear. **Features:** Velocity to 650 fps (BB), 630 fps (pellet). Choice of pump or CO2 power. Shoots BBs or pellets. Heavy die-cast receiver dovetailed for scope mount. Cross-bolt trigger block safety. Introduced 1993. From Daisy Mfg. Co.
Price: About $58.95

DAISY 1938 RED RYDER 60th ANNIVERSARY CLASSIC

Caliber: BB, 650-shot repeating action. **Barrel:** Smoothbore steel with shroud. **Weight:** 2.2 lbs. **Length:** 35.4" overall. **Stock:** Walnut stock burned with Red Ryder lariat signature. **Sights:** Post front, adjustable V-slot rear. **Features:** Walnut forend. Saddle ring with leather thong. Lever cocking. Gravity feed. Controlled velocity. One of Daisy's most popular guns. From Daisy Mfg. Co.
Price: About $39.95

DAISY/POWERLINE 1170 PELLET RIFLE

Caliber: 177, single shot. **Barrel:** Rifled steel. **Weight:** 5.5 lbs. **Length:** 42.5" overall. **Power:** Spring-air, barrel cocking. **Stock:** Hardwood. **Sights:** Hooded post front, micrometer adjustable open rear. **Features:** Velocity to 800 fps. Monte Carlo comb. Introduced 1995. From Daisy Mfg. Co.
Price: About $129.95
Price: Model 131 (velocity to 600 fps) $117.95
Price: Model 1150 (black copolymer stock, velocity to 600 fps). $77.95

DAISY/POWERLINE EAGLE 7856 PUMP-UP AIRGUN

Caliber: 177 (pellets), BB, 100-shot BB magazine. **Barrel:** Rifled steel with shroud. **Weight:** 3.3 lbs. **Length:** 37.4" overall. **Power:** Pneumatic pump-up. **Stock:** Moulded wood-grain plastic. **Sights:** Ramp and blade front, open rear adjustable for elevation. **Features:** Velocity from 315 fps (two pumps) to 650 fps (10 pumps). Finger grooved forend. Cross-bolt trigger-block safety. Introduced 1985. From Daisy Mfg. Co.
Price: With 4x scope, about $49.95

DAISY/POWERLINE 880

Caliber: 177 pellet or BB, 50-shot BB magazine, single shot for pellets. **Barrel:** Rifled steel. **Weight:** 3.7 lbs. **Length:** 37.6" overall. **Power:** Multi-pump pneumatic. **Stock:** Moulded wood grain; Monte Carlo comb. **Sights:** Hooded front, adjustable rear. **Features:** Velocity to 685 fps. (BB). Variable power (velocity and range) increase with pump strokes; resin receiver with dovetail scope mount. Introduced 1997. Made in U.S. by Daisy Mfg. Co.
Price: About $50.95
Price: Model 4880 with Glo-Point fiber optic sight $57.95

DAISY/POWERLINE 1000 AIR RIFLE

Caliber: 177, single shot. **Barrel:** NA. **Weight:** 6.15 lbs. **Length:** 43" overall. **Power:** Spring-air, barrel cocking. **Stock:** Stained hardwood. **Sights:** Hooded blade front on ramp, fully adjustable micrometer rear. **Features:** Velocity to 1000 fps. Blued finish; trigger block safety. Introduced 1997. From Daisy Mfg. Co.
Price: About $208.95

DAISY/YOUTHLINE MODEL 105 AIR RIFLE

Caliber: BB, 400-shot magazine. **Barrel:** 13-1/2". **Weight:** 1.6 lbs. **Length:** 29.8" overall. **Power:** Spring. **Stock:** Moulded woodgrain. **Sights:** Blade on ramp front, fixed rear. **Features:** Velocity to 275 fps. Blue finish. Cross-bolt trigger block safety. Made in U.S. by Daisy Mfg. Co.
Price: $28.95

DAISY/YOUTHLINE MODEL 95 AIR RIFLE

Caliber: BB, 700-shot magazine. **Barrel:** 18". **Weight:** 2.4 lbs. **Length:** 35.2" overall. **Power:** Spring. **Stock:** Stained hardwood. **Sights:** Blade on ramp front, open adjust-able rear. **Features:** Velocity to 325 fps. Cross-bolt trigger block safety. Made in U.S. by Daisy Mfg. Co.
Price: $38.95

EAA/BAIKAL IZH-32BK AIR RIFLE

Caliber: 177 pellet, single shot. **Barrel:** 11.68". **Weight:** 12.13 lbs. **Length:** 47.24" overall. **Power:** Single-stroke pneumatic. **Stock:** Walnut with full pistol grip, adjustable cheek piece and butt stock. **Sights:** None; integral rail for scope mount. **Features:** Velocity 541 fps. Side-cocking mechanism; hammer-forged, rifled barrel; five-way adjustable trigger. Designed for 10-meter running target competition. Introduced 2000. Imported from Russia by European American Armory.
Price: $1,099.00

EAA/BAIKAL IZH-61 AIR RIFLE

Caliber: 177 pellet, 5-shot magazine. **Barrel:** 17.75". **Weight:** 6.39 lbs. **Length:** 30.98" overall. **Power:** Spring piston, side-cocking lever. **Stock:** Black plastic. **Sights:** Adjustable rear, fully hooded front. **Features:** Velocity 490 fps. Futuristic design with adjustable stock. Imported from Russia by European American Armory.
Price: $99.00

EAA/BAIKAL MP-512 AIR RIFLE

Caliber: 177 or 22 pellet, single shot. **Barrel:** 17.7". **Weight:** 6.17 lbs. **Length:** 41.34" overall. **Power:** Spring-piston, single stroke. **Stock:** Black synthetic. **Sights:** Adjustable rear, hooded front. **Features:** Velocity 490 fps. Hammer-forged, rifled barrel; automatic safety; scope mount rail. Introduced 2000. Imported from Russia by European American Armory.
Price: 177 caliber $50.00
Price: 22 caliber $63.00

EAA/BAIKAL MP-532 AIR RIFLE

Caliber: 177 pellet, single shot. **Barrel:** 15.75". **Weight:** 9.26 lbs. **Length:** 46.06" overall. **Power:** Single-stroke pneumatic. **Stock:** One- or two-piece competition-style stock with adjustable butt pad, pistol grip. **Sights:** Fully adjustable rear, hooded front. **Features:** Velocity 460 fps. Five-way adjustable trigger. Introduced 2000. Imported from Russia by European American Armory.
Price: $599.00

HAMMERLI AR 50 AIR RIFLE

Caliber: 177. **Barrel:** 19.8". **Weight:** 10 lbs. **Length:** 43.2" overall. **Power:** Compressed air. **Stock:** Anatomically-shaped universal and right-hand; match style; multi-colored laminated wood. **Sights:** Interchangeable element tunnel front, fully adjustable Hammerli peep rear. **Features:** Vibration-free firing release; fully adjustable match trigger and trigger stop; stainless air tank, built-in pressure gauge. Gives 270 shots per filling. Introduced 1998. Imported from Switzerland by Sigarms, Inc.
Price: . . . . $1,062.50 to $1,400.00

HAMMERLI MODEL 450 MATCH AIR RIFLE

Caliber: 177, single shot. **Barrel:** 19.5". **Weight:** 9.8 lbs. **Length:** 43.3" overall. **Power:** Pneumatic. **Stock:** Match style with stippled grip, rubber buttpad. Beach or walnut. **Sights:** Match tunnel front, Hammerli diopter rear. **Features:** Velocity about 560 fps. Removable sights; forend sling rail; adjustable trigger; adjustable comb. Introduced 1994. Imported from Switzerland by Sigarms, Inc.
Price: Beech stock $1,355.00
Price: Walnut stock. $1,395.00

MARKSMAN BB BUDDY AIR RIFLE

Caliber: 177, 20-shot magazine. **Barrel:** 10.5" smoothbore. **Weight:** 1.6 lbs. **Length:** 33" overall. **Power:** Spring-air. **Stock:** Moulded composition. **Sights:** Blade on ramp front, adjustable V-slot rear. **Features:** Velocity 275 fps. Positive feed; automatic safety. Youth-sized lightweight design. Introduced 1998. Made in U.S. From Marksman Products.
Price: $27.95

MARKSMAN 1798 COMPETITION TRAINER AIR RIFLE

Caliber: 177, single shot. **Barrel:** 15", rifled. **Weight:** 4.7 lbs. **Power:** Spring-air, barrel cocking. **Stock:** Synthetic. **Sights:** Laserhawk fiber optic front, match-style diopter rear. **Features:** Velocity about 495 fps. Automatic safety. Introduced 1998. Made in U.S. From Marksman Products.
Price: $70.00

MARKSMAN 1745 BB REPEATER AIR RIFLE

Caliber: 177 BB or pellet, 18-shot BB reservoir. **Barrel:** 15-1/2", rifled. **Weight:** 4.75 lbs. **Length:** 36" overall. **Power:** Spring-air. **Stock:** Moulded composition with ambidextrous Monte Carlo cheekpiece and rubber recoil pad. **Sights:** Hooded front, adjustable rear. **Features:** Velocity about 450 fps. Break-barrel action; automatic safety. Uses BBs, pellets, darts or bolts. Introduced 1997. Made in the U.S. From Marksman Products.
Price: $58.00
Price: Model 1745S (same as above except comes with #1804 4x20 scope). $73.00

MARKSMAN 1790 BIATHLON TRAINER

Caliber: 177, single shot. **Barrel:** 15", rifled. **Weight:** 4.7 lbs. **Power:** Spring-air, barrel cocking. **Stock:** Synthetic. **Sights:** Hooded front, match-style diopter rear. **Features:** Velocity of 450 fps. Endorsed by the U.S. Shooting Team. Introduced 1989. From Marksman Products.
Price: $70.00

AIRGUNS

AIRGUNS—LONG GUNS

MARKSMAN 2015 LASERHAWK™ BB REPEATER AIR RIFLE
Caliber: 177 BB, 20-shot magazine. **Barrel:** 10.5" smoothbore. **Weight:** 1.6 lbs. **Length:** Adjustable to 33", 34" or 35" overall. **Power:** Spring-air. **Stock:** Moulded composition. **Sights:** Fixed fiber optic front sight, adjustable elevation V-slot rear. **Features:** Velocity about 275 fps. Positive feed; automatic safety. Adjustable stock. Introduced 1997. Made in the U.S. From Marksman Products.
Price: $33.00

RWS/DIANA MODEL 24 AIR RIFLE
Caliber: 177, 22, single shot. **Barrel:** 17", rifled. **Weight:** 6 lbs. **Length:** 42" overall. **Power:** Spring-air, barrel cocking. **Stock:** Beech. **Sights:** Hooded front, adjustable rear. **Features:** Velocity of 700 fps (177). Easy cocking effort; blue finish. Imported from Germany by Dynamit Nobel-RWS, Inc.
Price: $215.00
Price: Model 24C $215.00

RWS/Diana Model 34 Air Rifle
Similar to the Model 24 except has 19" barrel, weighs 7.5 lbs. Gives velocity of 1000 fps (177), 800 fps (22). Adjustable trigger, synthetic seals. Comes with scope rail.
Price: 177 or 22 .... $290.00
Price: Model 34N (nickel-plated metal, black epoxy-coated wood stock) ... $350.00
Price: Model 34BC (matte black metal, black stock, 4x32 scope, mounts) .. $510.00

RWS/DIANA MODEL 36 AIR RIFLE
Caliber: 177, 22, single shot. **Barrel:** 19", rifled. **Weight:** 8 lbs. **Length:** 45" overall. **Power:** Spring-air, barrel cocking. **Stock:** Beech. **Sights:** Hooded front (interchangeable inserts available), adjustable rear. **Features:** Velocity of 1000 fps (177-cal.). Comes with scope mount; two-stage adjustable trigger. Imported from Germany by Dynamit Nobel-RWS, Inc.
Price: $435.00
Price: Model 36 Carbine (same as Model 36 rifle except has 15" barrel) ... $435.00

RWS/DIANA MODEL 52 AIR RIFLE
Caliber: 177, 22, single shot. **Barrel:** 17", rifled. **Weight:** 8-1/2 lbs. **Length:** 43" overall. **Power:** Spring-air, sidelever cocking. **Stock:** Beech, with Monte Carlo, cheekpiece, checkered grip and forend. **Sights:** Ramp front, adjustable rear. **Features:** Velocity of 1100 fps (177). Blue finish. Solid rubber buttpad. Imported from Germany by Dynamit Nobel-RWS, Inc.
Price: $565.00
Price: Model 52 Deluxe (select walnut stock, rosewood grip and forend caps, palm swell grip) $810.00
Price: Model 48B (as above except matte black metal, black stock) $535.00
Price: Model 48 (same as Model 52 except no Monte Carlo, cheekpiece or checkering) $510.00

RWS/DIANA MODEL 45 AIR RIFLE
Caliber: 177, single shot. **Weight:** 8 lbs. **Length:** 45" overall. **Power:** Spring-air, barrel cocking. **Stock:** Walnut-finished hardwood with rubber recoil pad. **Sights:** Globe front with interchangeable inserts, micro. click open rear with four-way blade. **Features:** Velocity of 820 fps. Dovetail base for either micrometer peep sight or scope mounting. Automatic safety. Imported from Germany by Dynamit Nobel-RWS, Inc.
Price: $350.00

RWS/DIANA MODEL 46 AIR RIFLE
Caliber: 177, 22, single shot. **Barrel:** 18". **Weight:** 8.2 lbs. **Length:** 45" overall. **Stock:** Hardwood Monte Carlo. **Sights:** Blade front, adjustable rear. **Features:** Underlever cocking spring-air (950 fps in 177, 780 fps in 22); extended scope rail, automatic safety, rubber buttpad, adjustable trigger. Imported from Germany by Dynamit Nobel-RWS Inc.
Price: .... $430.00 to $470.00

RWS/DIANA MODEL 54 AIR RIFLE
Caliber: 177, 22, single shot. **Barrel:** 17". **Weight:** 9 lbs. **Length:** 43" overall. **Power:** Spring-air, sidelever cocking. **Stock:** Walnut with Monte Carlo cheekpiece, checkered grip and forend. **Sights:** Ramp front, fully adjustable rear. **Features:** Velocity to 1000 fps (177), 900 fps (22). Totally recoilless system; floating action absorbs recoil. Imported from Germany by Dynamit Nobel-RWS, Inc.
Price: $785.00

RWS/DIANA MODEL 93/94 AIR RIFLES
Caliber: 177, 22, single shot. **Barrel:** N/A. **Weight:** N/A. **Length:** N/A. **Stock:** Beechwood; Monte Carlo. **Sights:** Hooded front, fully adjustable rear. **Features:** Break-barrel, spring-air; receiver grooved for scope; adjustable trigger; lifetime warranty. Imported from Spain by Dynamit Nobel-RWS Inc.
Price: Model 93 (manual safety, 850 fps in 177) $180.00
Price: Model 94 (auto safety, 1,000 fps in 177) $225.00

RWS/DIANA MODEL 350 MAGNUM AIR RIFLE
Caliber: 177, single shot. **Barrel:** 19-1/2". **Weight:** 8 lbs. **Length:** 48". **Stock:** Beechwood; Monte Carlo. **Sights:** Hooded front, fully adjustable rear. **Features:** Break-barrel, spring-air; 1,250 fps. Imported from Germany by Dynamit Nobel-RWS Inc.
Price: Model 350 ....$600.00

RWS/DIANA MODEL 707/EXCALIBRE AIR RIFLES
Caliber: 22, 25, 9mm, 8-shot lever-action repeater or side-loading single shot. **Barrel:** 23". **Weight:** 7 to 9 1/4 lbs. **Length:** 40" to 42" overall. **Stock:** Checkered walnut.

Sights: Hooded post front, fully adjustable rear (Excalibre has no sights, integral scope grooves). **Features:** Pre-charged pneumatic stores compressed air from SCUBA tank or optional hand pump in reservoir for 18 to 30 shots at full power (adjustable power to 1,200 fps in 22 cal.); pressure gauge; adjustable trigger (9mm and Excalibre). Imported from Germany by Dynamit Nobel-RWS Inc.
Price: 707 (22, 25, 9 mm) $730.00
Price: 707 Carbine (22) $730.00
Price: Excalibre (22, 25) $840.00

SAVAGE MODEL 1000G AIR RIFLE
Caliber: 177 pellet, single shot. **Barrel:** 18". **Weight:** 7.25 lbs. **Length:** 45.3" overall. **Power:** Spring piston, break-barrel action. **Stock:** Walnut-finished hardwood with recoil pad. **Sights:** Adjustable rear notch, hooded front post. **Features:** Velocity 1,000 fps. Also available with 2.5-power scope. Introduced 2000. From Savage Arms.
Price: $181.00

SAVAGE MODEL 600F AIR RIFLE
Caliber: 177 pellet, 25-shot tubular magazine. **Barrel:** 18" polymer-coated steel. **Weight:** 6 lbs. **Length:** 40" overall. **Power:** spring piston, break-barrel action. **Stock:** Black polymer stock with lacquer finish. **Sights:** Adjustable rear notch, hooded front post. **Features:** Velocity 600 fps. Repeating action. Also available with 2.5-power scope. Introduced 2000. From Savage Arms.
Price: $126.00

SAVAGE MODEL 560F AIR RIFLE
Caliber: 177 pellet, single shot. **Barrel:** 18" polymer-coated steel. **Weight:** 5.5 lbs. **Length:** 39" overall. **Power:** Spring piston, break-barrel action. **Stock:** Metallic-black finished polymer stock. **Sights:** Adjustable notch rear, post front. **Features:** Velocity 560 fps. Introduced 2000. From Savage Arms.
Price: $92.00

TECH FORCE BS4 OLYMPIC COMPETITION AIR RIFLE
Caliber: 177 pellet, single shot. **Barrel:** N/A. **Weight:** 10.8 lbs. **Length:** 43.3" overall. **Power:** Spring piston, sidelever action. **Stock:** Wood with semi-pistol grip, adjustable butt plate. **Sights:** Micro-adjustable competition rear, hooded front. **Features:** Velocity 640 fps. Recoilless action; adjustable trigger. Includes carrying case. Imported from China by Compasseco Inc.
Price: $595.00
Price: Optional diopter rear sight. $79.95

TECH FORCE 6 AIR RIFLE
Caliber: 177 pellet, single shot. **Barrel:** 14". **Weight:** 6 lbs. **Length:** 35.5" overall. **Power:** Sspring piston, sidelever action. **Stock:** Paratrooper-style folding, full pistol grip. **Sights:** Adjustable rear, hooded front. **Features:** Velocity 800 fps. All-metal construction; grooved for scope mounting. Imported from China by Compasseco Inc.
Price: $69.95

Tech Force 51 Air Rifle
Similar to Tech Force 6, but with break-barrel cocking mechanism and folding stock fitted with recoil pad. Overall length, 36". Weighs 6 lbs. From Compasseco Inc.
Price: $69.95

TECH FORCE 25 AIR RIFLE
Caliber: 177, 22 pellet; single shot. **Barrel:** N/A. **Weight:** 7.5 lbs. **Length:** 46.2" overall. **Power:** Spring piston, break-action barrel. **Stock:** Oil-finished wood; Monte Carlo stock with recoil pad. **Sights:** Adjustable rear, hooded front with insert. **Features:** Velocity 1,000 fps (177); grooved receiver and scope stop for scope mounting; adjustable trigger; trigger safety. Imported from China by Compasseco Inc.
Price: 177 or 22 caliber $125.00
Price: Includes rifle and Tech Force 96 red dot point sight $164.95

TECH FORCE 36 AIR RIFLE
Caliber: 177 pellet, single shot. **Barrel:** N/A. **Weight:** 7.4 lbs. **Length:** 43" overall. **Power:** Spring piston, underlever cocking. **Stock:** Monte Carlo hardwood stock; recoil pad. **Sights:** Adjustable rear, hooded front. **Features:** Velocity 900 fps; grooved receiver and scope stop for scope mounting; auto-reset safety. Imported from China by Compasseco Inc.
Price: $89.95

WHISCOMBE JW SERIES AIR RIFLES
Caliber: 177, 20, 22, 25, single shot. **Barrel:** 15", Lothar Walther. Polygonal rifling. **Weight:** 9 lbs., 8 oz. **Length:** 39" overall. **Power:** Dual spring-piston, multi-stroke; underlever cocking. **Stock:** Walnut with adjustable buttplate and cheekpiece. **Sights:** None furnished; grooved scope rail. **Features:** Velocity 660-1000 (JW80) fps (22-caliber, fixed barrel) depending upon model. Interchangeable barrels; automatic safety; muzzle weight; semi-floating action; twin opposed pistons with counterwound springs; adjustable trigger. All models include H.O.T. System (Harmonic Optimization Tunable System). Introduced 1995. Imported from England by Pelaire Products.
Price: JW50, MKII fixed barrel only $1,895.00
Price: JW60, MKII fixed barrel only $1,895.00
Price: JW70, MKII fixed barrel only $1,950.00
Price: JW80, MKII $1,995.00

CH4D Heavyduty Champion

Frame: Cast iron
Frame Type: O-frame
Die Thread: 7/8-14 or 1-14
Avg. Rounds Per Hour: NA
Ram Stroke: 3-1/4"
Weight: 26 lbs.
Features: 1.185" diameter ram with 16 square inches of bearing surface; ram drilled to allow passage of spent primers; solid steel handle; toggle that slightly breaks over the top dead center. Includes universal primer arm with large and small punches. From CH Tool & Die/4D Custom Die.
Price: **$220.00**

CH4D No. 444 4-Station "H" Press

Frame: Aluminum alloy
Frame Type: H-frame
Die Thread: 7/8-14
Avg. Rounds Per Hour: 200
Ram Stroke: 3-3/4"
Weight: 12 lbs.
Features: Two 7/8" solid steel shaft "H" supports; platen rides on permanently lubed bronze bushings; loads smallest pistol to largest magnum rifle cases and has strength to full-length resize. Includes four rams, large and small primer arm and primer catcher. From CH Tool & Die/4D Custom Die, Co.
Price: **$195.00**

CH4D No. 444-X Pistol Champ

Frame: Aluminum alloy
Frame Type: H-frame
Die Thread: 7/8-14
Avg. Rounds Per Hour: 200
Ram Stroke: 3-3/4"
Weight: 12 lbs.
Features: Tungsten carbide sizing die; Speed Seater seating die with tapered entrance to automatically align bullet on case mouth; automatic primer feed for large or small primers; push-button powder measure with easily changed bushings for 215 powder/load combinations; taper crimp die. Conversion kit for caliber changeover available. From CH Tool & Die/4D Custom Die, Co.
Price: .... **$292.00-$316.50**

FORSTER Co-Ax Press B-2

Frame: Cast iron
Frame Type: Modified O-frame
Die Thread: 7/8-14
Avg. Rounds Per Hour: 120
Ram Stroke: 4"
Weight: 18 lbs.
Features: Snap in/snap out die change; spent primer catcher with drop tube threaded into carrier below shellholder; automatic, handle-activated, cammed shellholder with opposing spring-loaded jaws to contact extractor groove; floating guide rods for alignment and reduced friction; no torque on the head due to design of linkage and pivots; shellholder jaws that float with die permitting case to center in the die; right- or left-hand operation; priming device for seating to factory specifications. "S" shellholder jaws included. From Forster Products.
Price: **$298.00**
Price: Extra shellholder jaws **$26.00**

HOLLYWOOD Senior Press

Frame: Ductile iron
Frame Type: O-frame
Die Thread: 7/8-14
Avg. Rounds Per Hour: 50-100
Ram Stroke: 6-1/2"
Weight: 50 lbs.
Features: Leverage and bearing surfaces ample for reloading cartridges or swaging bullets. Precision ground one-piece 2-1/2" pillar with base; operating

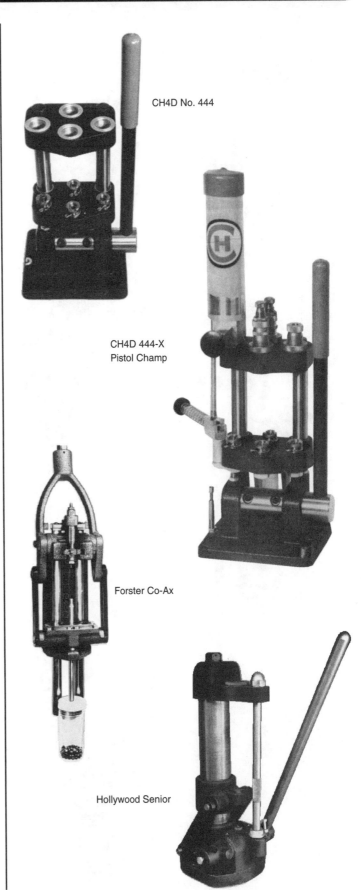

CH4D No. 444

CH4D 444-X
Pistol Champ

Forster Co-Ax

Hollywood Senior

ACCESSORIES

METALLIC CARTRIDGE PRESSES

Hollywood Senior Turret

Hornady Lock-N-Load Classic

Lee Hand Press

Lee Challenger

handle of 3/4" steel and 15" long; 5/8" steel tie-down rod fro added strength when swaging; heavy steel toggle and camming arms held by 1/2" steel pins in reamed holes. The 1-1/2" steel die bushing takes standard threaded dies; removed, it allows use of Hollywood shotshell dies. From Hollywood Engineering.
Price: $500.00

HOLLYWOOD Senior Turret Press
Frame: Ductile iron
Frame Type: H-frame
Die Thread: 7/8-14
Avg. Rounds Per Hour: 50-100
Ram Stroke: 6-1/2"
Weight: 50 lbs.
Features: Same features as Senior press except has three-position turret head; holes in turret may be tapped 1-1/2" or 7/8" or four of each. Height, 15". Comes complete with one turret indexing handle; one 1-1/2" to 7/8" die hole bushing; one 5/8" tie down bar for swaging. From Hollywood Engineering.
Price: $600.00

HORNADY Lock-N-Load Classic
Frame: Die cast heat-treated aluminum alloy
Frame Type: O-frame
Die Thread: 7/8-14
Avg. Rounds Per Hour: NA
Ram Stroke: 3-5/8"
Weight: 14 lbs.
Features: Features Lock-N-Load bushing system that allows instant die changeovers. Solid steel linkage arms that rotate on steel pins; 30° angled frame design for improved visibility and accessibility; primer arm automatically moves in and out of ram for primer pickup and solid seating; two primer arms for large and small primers; long offset handle for increased leverage and unobstructed reloading; lifetime warranty. Comes as a package with primer catcher, PPS automatic primer feed and three Lock-N-Load die bushings. Dies and shellholder available separately or as a kit with primer catcher, positive priming system, automatic primer feed, three die bushings and reloading accessories. From Hornady Mfg. Co.
Price: Press and Three Die Bushings $99.95
Price: Classic Reloading Kit...............................$259.95

LEE Hand Press
Frame: ASTM 380 aluminum
Frame Type: NA
Die Thread: 7/8-14
Avg. Rounds Per Hour: 100
Ram Stroke: 3-1/4"
Weight: 1 lb., 8 oz.
Features: Small and lightweight for portability; compound linkage for handling up to 375 H&H and case forming. Dies and shellholder not included. From Lee Precision, Inc.
Price: $22.98

LEE Challenger Press
Frame: ASTM 380 aluminum
Frame Type: O-frame
Die Thread: 7/8-14
Avg. Rounds Per Hour: 100
Ram Stroke: 3-1/2"
Weight: 4 lbs., 1 oz.
Features: Larger than average opening with 30° offset for maximum hand clearance; steel connecting pins; spent primer catcher; handle adjustable for start and stop positions; handle repositions for left- or right-hand use; shortened handle travel to prevent springing the frame from alignment. Dies and shellholders not included. From Lee Precision, Inc.
Price: $45.00

METALLIC CARTRIDGE PRESSES

LEE Loader

Kit consists of reloading dies to be used with mallet or soft hammer. Neck sizes only. Comes with powder charge cup. From Lee Precision, Inc.
Price: **$19.98**

LEE Reloader Press

Frame: ASTM 380 aluminum
Frame Type: C-frame
Die Thread: 7/8-14
Avg. Rounds Per Hour: 100
Ram Stroke: 3"
Weight: 1 lb., 12 oz.
Features: Balanced lever to prevent pinching fingers; unlimited hand clearance; left- or right-hand use. Dies and shellholders not included. From Lee Precision, Inc.
Price: **$24.98**

LEE Turret Press

Frame: ASTM 380 aluminum
Frame Type: O-frame
Die Thread: 7/8-14
Avg. Rounds Per Hour: 300
Ram Stroke: 3"
Weight: 7 lbs., 2 oz.
Features: Replaceable turret lifts out by rotating 30˚; T-primer arm reverses for large or small primers; built-in primer catcher; adjustable handle for right- or left-hand use or changing angle of down stroke; accessory mounting hole for Lee Auto-Disk powder measure. Optional Auto-Index rotates die turret to next station for semi-progressive use. Safety override prevents overstressing should turret not turn. From Lee Precision, Inc.
Price: **$69.98**
Price: With Auto-Index **$83.98**
Price: Four-Hole Turret with Auto-Index **$85.98**

LYMAN 310 Tool

Frame: Stainless steel
Frame Type: NA
Die Thread: 7/8-14
Avg. Rounds Per Hour: NA
Ram Stroke: NA
Weight: 10 oz.
Features: Compact, portable reloading tool for pistol or rifle cartridges. Adapter allows loading rimmed or rimless cases. Die set includes neck resizing/decapping die, primer seating chamber; neck expanding die; bullet seating die; and case head adapter. From Lyman Products Corp.
Price: Dies **$34.95**
Price: Press **$34.95**
Price: Carrying pouch...................................... **$9.95**

LYMAN AccuPress

Frame: Die cast
Frame Type: C-frame
Die Thread: 7/8-14
Avg. Rounds Per Hour: 75
Ram Stroke: 3.4"
Weight: 4 lbs.
Features: Reversible, contoured handle for bench mount or hand-held use; for rifle or pistol; compound leverage; Delta frame design. Accepts all standard powder measures. From Lyman Products Corp.
Price: **$32.00**

Lee Reloader

Lee Turret

Lyman 310

METALLIC CARTRIDGE PRESSES

Turret handle disconnector

Lyman T-Mag II

Lyman Crusher II

Ponsness/Warren
Metal-Matic P-200

LYMAN Crusher II

Frame: Cast iron
Frame Type: O-frame
Die Thread: 7/8-14
Avg. Rounds Per Hour: 75
Ram Stroke: 3-7/8"
Weight: 19 lbs.
Features: Reloads both pistol and rifle cartridges; 1" diameter ram; 4-1/2" press opening for loading magnum cartridges; direct torque design; right- or left-hand use. New base design with 14 square inches of flat mounting surface with three bolt holes. Comes with priming arm and primer catcher. Dies and shellholders not included. From Lyman Products Corp.
Price: **$108.00**

LYMAN T-Mag II

Frame: Cast iron with silver metalflake powder finish
Frame Type: Turret
Die Thread: 7/8-14
Avg. Rounds Per Hour: 125
Ram Stroke: 3-13/16"
Weight: 18 lbs.
Features: Reengineered and upgraded with new turret system for ease of indexing and tool-free turret removal for caliber changeover; new flat machined base for bench mounting; new nickel-plated non-rust handle and links; and new silver hammertone powder coat finish for durability. Right- or left-hand operation; handles all rifle or pistol dies. Comes with priming arm and primer catcher. Dies and shellholders not included. From Lyman Products Corp.
Price: **$149.95**
Price: Extra turret **$34.95**

PONSNESS/WARREN Metal-Matic P-200

Frame: Die cast aluminum
Frame Type: Unconventional
Die Thread: 7/8-14
Avg. Rounds Per Hour: 200+
Weight: 18 lbs.
Features: Designed for straight-wall cartridges; die head with 10 tapped holes for holding dies and accessories for two calibers at one time; removable spent primer box; pivoting arm moves case from station to station. Comes with large and small primer tool. Optional accessories include primer feed, extra die head, primer speed feeder, powder measure extension and dust cover. Dies, powder measure and shellholder not included. From Ponsness/Warren.
Price: **$215.00**
Price: Extra die head. **$44.95**
Price: Powder measure extension **$29.95**
Price: Primer feed **$44.95**
Price: Primer speed feed. **$14.50**
Price: Dust cover. **$21.95**

RCBS Partner

Frame: Aluminum
Frame Type: O-frame
Die Thread: 7/8-14
Avg. Rounds Per Hour: 50-60
Ram Stroke: 3-5/8"
Weight: 5 lbs.
Features: Designed for the beginning reloader. Comes with primer arm equipped with interchangeable primer plugs and sleeves for seating large and small primers. Shellholder and dies not included. Available in kit form (see Metallic Presses—Accessories). From RCBS.
Price: **$61.95**

METALLIC CARTRIDGE PRESSES

RCBS AmmoMaster Single

Frame: Aluminum base; cast iron top plate connected by three steel posts.
Frame Type: NA
Die Thread: 1-1/4"-12 bushing; 7/8-14 threads
Avg. Rounds Per Hour: 50-60
Ram Stroke: 5-1/4"
Weight: 19 lbs.
Features: Single-stage press convertible to progressive. Will form cases or swage bullets. Case detection system to disengage powder measure when no case is present in powder charging station; five-station shellplate; Uniflow Powder measure with clear powder measure adaptor to make bridged powders visible and correctable. 50-cal. conversion kit allows reloading 50 BMG. Kit includes top plate to accommodate either 1-3/8" x 12 or 1-1/2" x 12 reloading dies. Piggyback die plate for quick caliber change-overs available. Reloading dies not included. From RCBS.
Price: **$206.95**
Price: 50 conversion kit **$96.95**
Price: Piggyback/AmmoMaster die plate **$25.95**
Price: Piggyback/AmmoMaster shellplate **$25.95**
Price: Press cover **$10.95**

RCBS Reloader Special-5

Frame: Aluminum
Frame Type: 30˚ offset O-frame
Die Thread: 1-1/4"-12 bushing; 7/8-14 threads
Avg. Rounds Per Hour: 50-60
Ram Stroke: 3-1/16"
Weight: 7.5 lbs.
Features: Single-stage press convertible to progressive with RCBS Piggyback II. Primes cases during resizing operation. Will accept RCBS shotshell dies. From RCBS.
Price: **$112.95**

RCBS Rock Chucker

Frame: Cast iron
Frame Type: O-frame
Die Thread: 1-1/4"-12 bushing; 7/8-14 threads
Avg. Rounds Per Hour: 50-60
Ram Stroke: 3-1/16"
Weight: 17 lbs.
Features: Designed for heavy-duty reloading, case forming and bullet swaging. Provides 4" of ram-bearing surface to support 1" ram and ensure alignment; ductile iron toggle blocks; hardened steel pins. Comes standard with Universal Primer Arm and primer catcher. Can be converted from single-stage to progressive with Piggyback II conversion unit. From RCBS.
Price: **$141.95**

REDDING Turret Press

Frame: Cast iron
Frame Type: Turret
Die Thread: 7/8-14
Avg. Rounds Per Hour: NA
Ram Stroke: 3.4"
Weight: 23 lbs., 2 oz.
Features: Strength to reload pistol and magnum rifle, case form and bullet swage; linkage pins heat-treated, precision ground and in double shear; hollow ram to collect spent primers; removable turret head for caliber changes; progressive linkage for increased power as ram nears die; slight frame tilt for comfortable operation; rear turret support for stability and precise alignment; six-station turret head; priming arm for both large and small primers. Also available in kit form with shellholder, primer catcher and one die set. From Redding Reloading Equipment.
Price: **$298.50**
Price: Kit **$336.00**

RCBS Partner

RCBS AmmoMaster Single

RCBS Reloader Special-5

RCBS Rock Chucker

REDDING Boss

Frame: Cast iron
Frame Type: O-frame
Die Thread: 7/8-14
Avg. Rounds Per Hour: NA
Ram Stroke: 3.4"
Weight: 11 lbs., 8 oz.
Features: 36° frame offset for visibility and accessibility; primer arm positioned at bottom ram travel; positive ram travel stop machined to hit exactly top-dead-center. Also available in kit form with shellholder and set of Redding A dies. From Redding Reloading Equipment.
Price:.. **$135.00**
Price: Kit **$172.00**

REDDING Ultramag

Frame: Cast iron
Frame Type: Non-conventional
Die Thread: 7/8-14
Avg. Rounds Per Hour: NA
Ram Stroke: 4-1/8"
Weight: 23 lbs., 6 oz.
Features: Unique compound leverage system connected to top of press for tons of ram pressure; large 4-3/4" frame opening for loading outsized cartridges; hollow ram for spent primers. Kit available with shellholder and one set Redding A dies. From Redding Reloading Equipment.
Price:.. **$298.50**
Price: Kit **$336.00**

ROCK CRUSHER Press

Frame: Cast iron
Frame Type: O-frame
Die Thread: 2-3/4"-12 with bushing reduced to 1-1/2"-12
Avg. Rounds Per Hour: 50
Ram Stroke: 6"
Weight: 67 lbs.
Features: Designed to load and form ammunition from 50 BMG up to 23x115 Soviet. Frame opening of 8-1/2"x3-1/2"; 1-1/2"x12"; bushing can be removed and bushings of any size substituted; ram pressure can exceed 10,000 lbs. with normal body weight; 40mm diameter ram. Angle block for bench mounting and reduction bushing for RCBS dies available. Accessories for Rock Crusher include powder measure, dies, shellholder, bullet puller, priming tool, case gauge and other accessories found elsewhere in this catalog. From The Old Western Scrounger.
Price:.. **$795.00**
Price: Angle block **$57.95**
Price: Reduction bushing **$21.00**
Price: Shellholder **$47.25**
Price: Priming tool, 50 BMG, 20 Lahti **$65.10**

PROGRESSIVE PRESSES

DILLON AT 500

Frame: Aluminum alloy
Frame Type: NA
Die Thread: 7/8-14
Avg. Rounds Per Hour: 200-300
Ram Stroke: 3-7/8"
Weight: NA
Features: Four stations; removable tool head to hold dies in alignment and allow caliber changes without die adjustment; manual indexing; capacity to be upgraded to progressive RL 550B. Comes with universal shellplate to accept 223, 22-250, 243, 30-06, 9mm, 38/357, 40 S&W, 45 ACP. Dies not included. From Dillon Precision Products.
Price: **$193.95**

Redding Model 25

Rock Crusher

Redding Boss

Redding Ultramag

DILLON RL 550B

Frame: Aluminum alloy
Frame Type: NA
Die Thread: 7/8-14
Avg. Rounds Per Hour: 500-600
Ram Stroke: 3-7/8"
Weight: 25 lbs.
Features: Four stations; removable tool head to hold dies in alignment and allow caliber changes without die adjustment; auto priming system that emits audible warning when primer tube is low; a 100-primer capacity magazine contained in DOM steel tube for protection; new auto powder measure system with simple mechanical connection between measure and loading platform for positive powder bar return; a separate station for crimping with star-indexing system; 220 ejected-round capacity bin; 3/4-lb. capacity powder measure. Height above bench, 35"; requires 3/4" bench overhang. Will reload 120 different rifle and pistol calibers. Comes with one caliber conversion kit. Dies not included. From Dillon Precision Products, Inc.
Price: **$325.95**

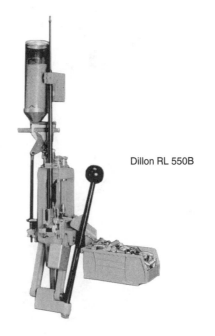

Dillon RL 550B

DILLON RL 1050

Frame: Ductile iron
Frame Type: Platform type
Die Thread: 7/8-14
Avg. Rounds Per Hour: 1000-1200
Ram Stroke: 2-5/16"
Weight: 62 lbs.
Features: Eight stations; auto case feed; primer pocket swager for military cartridge cases; auto indexing; removable tool head; auto prime system with 100-primer capacity; low primer supply alarm; positive powder bar return; auto powder measure; 515 ejected round bin capacity; 500-600 case feed capacity; 3/4-lb. capacity powder measure. Loads all pistol rounds as well as 30 M1 Carbine, 223, and 7.62x39 rifle rounds. Height above the bench, 43". Dies not included. From Dillon Precision Products, Inc.
Price: **$1,199.95**

DILLON Super 1050

Similar to RL1050, but has lengthened frame and short-stroke crank to accommodate long calibers.
Price: **$1,299.95**

DILLON Square Deal B

Frame: Zinc alloy
Frame Type: NA
Die Thread: None (unique Dillon design)
Avg. Rounds Per Hour: 400-500
Ram Stroke: 2-5/16"
Weight: 17 lbs.
Features: Four stations; auto indexing; removable tool head; auto prime system with 100-primer capacity; low primer supply alarm; auto powder measure; positive powder bar return; 170 ejected round capacity bin; 3/4-lb. capacity powder measure. Height above the bench, 34". Comes complete with factory adjusted carbide die set. From Dillon Precision Products, Inc.
Price: **$252.95**

DILLON XL 650

Frame: Aluminum alloy
Frame Type: NA
Die Thread: 7/8-14
Avg. Rounds Per Hour: 800-1000
Ram Stroke: 4-9/16"
Weight: 46 lbs.
Features: Five stations; auto indexing; auto case feed; removable tool head;

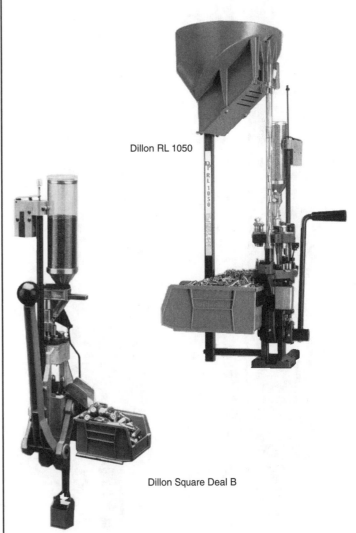

Dillon RL 1050

Dillon Square Deal B

METALLIC CARTRIDGE PRESSES

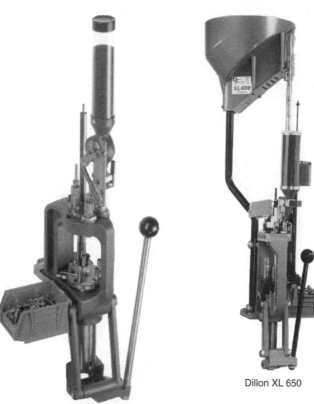

Hornady Lock-N-Load AP

Dillon XL 650

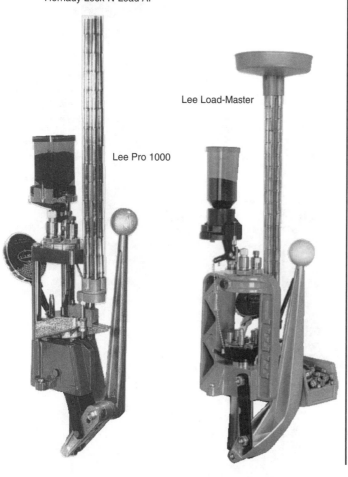

Lee Load-Master

Lee Pro 1000

auto prime system with 100-primer capacity; low primer supply alarm; auto powder measure; positive powder bar return; 220 ejected round capacity bin; 3/4-lb. capacity powder measure. 500-600 case feed capacity with optional auto case feed. Loads all pistol/rifle calibers less than 3-1/2" in length. Height above the bench, 44"; 3/4" bench overhang required. From Dillon Precision Products, Inc.

Price: Less dies **$443.95**

HORNADY Lock-N-Load AP
Frame: Die cast heat-treated aluminum alloy
Frame Type: O-frame
Die Thread: 7/8-14
Avg. Rounds Per Hour: NA
Ram Stroke: 3-3/4"
Weight: 26 lbs.
Features: Features Lock-N-Load bushing system that allows instant die changeovers; five-station die platform with option of seating and crimping separately or adding taper-crimp die; auto prime with large and small primer tubes with 100-primer capacity and protective housing; brass kicker to eject loaded rounds into 80-round capacity cartridge catcher; offset operating handle for leverage and unobstructed operation; 2" diameter ram driven by heavy-duty cast linkage arms rotating on steel pins. Comes with five Lock-N-Load die bushings, shellplate, deluxe powder measure, auto powder drop, and auto primer feed and shut-off, brass kicker and primer catcher. Lifetime warranty. From Hornady Mfg. Co.

Price: **$367.65**

LEE Load-Master
Frame: ASTM 380 aluminum
Frame Type: O-frame
Die Thread: 7/8-14
Avg. Rounds Per Hour: 600
Ram Stroke: 3-1/4"
Weight: 8 lbs., 4 oz.
Features: Available in kit form only. A 1-3/4" diameter hard chrome ram for handling largest magnum cases; loads rifle or pistol rounds; five station press to factory crimp and post size; auto indexing with wedge lock mechanism to hold one ton; auto priming; removable turrets; four-tube case feeder with optional case collator and bullet feeder (late 1995); loaded round ejector with chute to optional loaded round catcher; quick change shellplate; primer catcher. Dies and shellholder for one caliber included. From Lee Precision, Inc.

Price: Rifle **$320.00**
Price: Pistol **$330.00**
Price: Extra turret **$10.98**
Price: Adjustable charge bar **$9.98**

LEE Pro 1000
Frame: ASTM 380 aluminum and steel
Frame Type: O-frame
Die Thread: 7/8-14
Avg. Rounds Per Hour: 600
Ram Stroke: 3-1/4"
Weight: 8 lbs., 7 oz.
Features: Optional transparent large/small or rifle case feeder; deluxe auto-disk case-activated powder measure; case sensor for primer feed. Comes complete with carbide die set (steel dies for rifle) for one caliber. Optional accessories include: case feeder for large/small pistol cases or rifle cases; shell plate carrier with auto prime, case ejector, auto-index and spare parts; case collator for case feeder. From Lee Precision, Inc.

Price: **$199.98**

PONSNESS/WARREN Metallic II
Frame: Die cast aluminum
Frame Type: H-frame
Die Thread: 7/8-14
Avg. Rounds Per Hour: 150+
Ram Stroke: NA

ACCESSORIES

Weight: 32 lbs.

Features: Die head with five tapped 7/8-14 holes for dies, powder measure or other accessories; pivoting die arm moves case from station to station; depriming tube for removal of spent primers; auto primer feed; interchangeable die head. Optional accessories include additional die heads, powder measure extension tube to accommodate any standard powder measure, primer speed feeder to feed press primer tube without disassembly. Comes with small and large primer seating tools. Dies, powder measure and shellholder not included. From Ponsness/Warren.

Price: **$375.00**
Price: Extra die head **$56.95**
Price: Primer speed feeder **$14.50**
Price: Powder measure extension **$29.95**
Price: Dust cover **$27.95**

RCBS AmmoMaster

RCBS AmmoMaster-Auto

Frame: Aluminum base; cast iron top plate connected by three steel posts
Frame Type: NA
Die Thread: 1-1/4-12 bushing; 7/8-14 threads
Avg. Rounds Per Hour: 400-500
Ram Stroke: 5-1/4"
Weight: 19 lbs.
Features: Progressive press convertible to single-stage. Features include: 1-1/2" solid ram; automatic indexing, priming, powder charging and loaded round ejection. Case detection system disengages powder measure when no case is present in powder charging station. Comes with five-station shellplate and Uniflow powder measure with clear powder measure adaptor to make bridged powders visible and correctable. Piggyback die plate for quick caliber change-over available. Reloading dies not included. From RCBS.

Price: **$394.95**
Price: Piggyback/AmmoMaster die plate **$22.95**
Price: Piggyback/AmmoMaster shellplate **$27.95**
Price: Press cover **$10.95**

RCBS Pro 2000™

Frame: Cast iron
Frame Type: H-Frame
Die Thread: 7/8 x 14
Avg. Rounds Per Hour: NA
Ram Stroke: NA
Weight: NA
Features: Five-station manual indexing; full-length sizing; removable die plate; fast caliber conversion. Uses APS Priming System. From RCBS.
Price: **$468.95**

STAR Universal Pistol Press

Frame: Cast iron with aluminum base
Frame Type: Unconventional
Die Thread: 11/16-24 or 7/8-14
Avg. Rounds Per Hour: 300
Ram Stroke: NA
Weight: 27 lbs.
Features: Four or five-station press depending on need to taper crimp; handles all popular handgun calibers from 32 Long to 45 Colt. Comes completely assembled and adjusted with carbide dies (except 30 Carbine) and shellholder to load one caliber. Prices slightly higher for 9mm and 30 Carbine. From Star Machine Works.

Price: With taper crimp **$1,055.00**
Price: Without taper crimp **$1,025.00**
Price: Extra tool head, taper crimp **$425.00**
Price: Extra tool head, w/o taper crimp **$395.00**

Fully-automated Star Universal

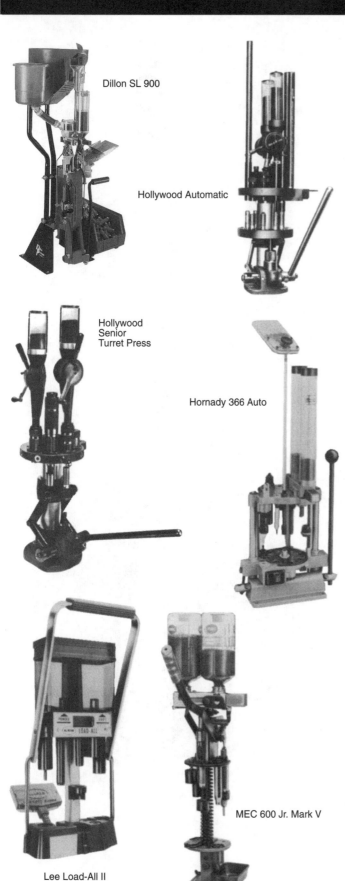

Dillon SL 900

Hollywood Automatic

Hollywood Senior Turret Press

Hornady 366 Auto

Lee Load-All II

MEC 600 Jr. Mark V

DILLON SL 900

Press Type: Progressive
Avg. Rounds Per Hour: 700-900
Weight: 51 lbs.
Features: 12-ga. only; factory adjusted to load AA hulls; extra large 25-pound capacity shot hopper; fully-adjustable case-activated shot system; hardened steel starter crimp die; dual-action final crimp and taper die; tilt-out wad guide; auto prime; auto index; strong mount machine stand. From Dillon Precision Products.
Price: **$819.95**

HOLLYWOOD Automatic Shotshell Press

Press Type: Progressive
Avg. Rounds Per Hour: 1,800
Weight: 100 lbs.
Features: Ductile iron frame; fully automated press with shell pickup and ejector; comes completely set up for one gauge; one starter crimp; one finish crimp; wad guide for plastic wads; decap and powder dispenser unit; one wrench for inside die lock screw; one medium and one large spanner wrench for spanner nuts; one shellholder; powder and shot measures. Available for 10, 12, 20, 28 or 410. From Hollywood Engineering.
Price: **$3,600.00**

HOLLYWOOD Senior Turret Press

Press Type: Turret
Avg. Rounds Per Hour: 200
Weight: 50 lbs.
Features: Multi-stage press constructed of ductile iron comes completely equipped to reload one gauge; one starter crimp; one finish crimp; wad guide for plastic wads; decap and powder dispenser unit; one wrench for inside die lock screw; one medium and one large spanner wrench for spanner nuts; one shellholder; powder and shot measures. Available for 10, 12, 16, 20, 28 or 410. From Hollywood Engineering.
Price: Press only **$700.00**
Price: Dies **$195.00**

HORNADY 366 Auto

Press Type: Progressive
Avg. Rounds Per Hour: NA
Weight: 25 lbs.
Features: Heavy-duty die cast and machined steel body and components; auto primer feed system; large capacity shot and powder tubes; adjustable for right- or left-hand use; automatic charge bar with shutoff; swing-out wad guide; primer catcher at base of press; interchangeable shot and powder bushings; life-time warranty. Available for 12, 20, 28 2-3/4 and 410 2-1/2. From Hornady Mfg. Co.
Price: **$434.95**
Price: Die set, 12, 20, 28 . . . .**$196.86**
Price: Magnum conversion dies, 12, 20 . . . .**$43.25**

LEE Load-All II

Press Type: Single stage
Avg. Rounds Per Hour: 100
Weight: 3 lbs., 3 oz.
Features: Loads steel or lead shot; built-in primer catcher at base with door in front for emptying; recesses at each station for shell positioning; optional primer feed. Comes with safety charge bar with 24 shot and powder bushings. Available for 12-, 16- or 20-gauge. From Lee Precision, Inc.
Price: **$49.98**

MEC 600 Jr. Mark V

Press Type: Single stage
Avg. Rounds Per Hour: 200
Weight: 10 lbs.
Features: Spindex crimp starter for shell alignment during crimping; a cam-action crimp die; Pro-Check to keep charge bar properly positioned; adjustable for three shells. Available in 10, 12, 16, 20, 28 gauges and 410 bore. Die set not included. From Mayville Engineering Company, Inc.
Price: **$84.95**
Price: Die set **$59.38**

ACCESSORIES

SHOTSHELL RELOADING PRESSES

MEC 650

Press Type: Progressive
Avg. Rounds Per Hour: 400
Weight: NA
Features: Six-station press; does not resize except as separate operation; auto primer feed standard; three crimping stations for starting, closing and tapering crimp. Die sets not available. Available in 12, 16, 20, 28 and 410. From Mayville Engineering Company, Inc.
Price: $179.95

MEC 8567 Grabber

Press Type: Progressive
Avg. Rounds Per Hour: 400
Weight: 15 lbs.
Features: Ten-station press; auto primer feed; auto-cycle charging; three-stage crimp; power ring resizer returns base to factory specs; resizes high and low base shells; optional kits to reload three shells and steel shot. Available in 12, 16, 20, 28 gauge and 410 bore. From Mayville Engineering Company, Inc.
Price: $239.95
Price: 3" kit, 12-ga. $60.00
Price: 3" kit, 20-ga. $16.95
Price: Steel shot kit. $22.95

MEC 9000 Grabber

Press Type: Progressive
Avg. Rounds Per Hour: 400
Weight: 18 lbs.
Features: All same features as the MEC Grabber, but with auto-indexing and auto-eject. Finished shells automatically ejected from shell carrier to drop chute for boxing. Available in 12, 16, 20, 28 and 410. From Mayville Engineering Company, Inc.
Price: $269.95
Price: 3" kit, 12-ga. $60.00
Price: 3" kit, 20-ga. $16.95
Price: Steel shot kit. $22.95

MEC 9000 Hustler

Press Type: Progressive
Avg. Rounds Per Hour: 400
Weight: 23 lbs.
Features: Same features as 9000G with addition of foot pedal-operated hydraulic system for complete automation. Operates on standard 110V household current. Comes with bushing-type charge bar and three bushings. Available in 12, 16, 20, 28 gauge and 410 bore. From Mayville Engineering Company, Inc.
Price: $669.95
Price: Steel shot kit. $22.95

MEC Sizemaster

Press Type: Single stage
Avg. Rounds Per Hour: 150
Weight: 13 lbs.
Features: Power ring eight-fingered collet resizer returns base to factory specs; handles brass or steel, high or low base heads; auto primer feed; adjustable for three shells. Available in 10, 12, 16, 20, 28 gauges and 410 bore. From Mayville Engineering Company, Inc.
Price: $129.95
Price: Die set, 12, 16, 20, 28, 410 .... $88.67
Price: Die set, 10-ga. $104.06
Price: Steel shot kit. $12.95
Price: Steel shot kit, 12-ga. 3-1/2" $70.27

MEC Steelmaster

Press Type: Single stage
Avg. Rounds Per Hour: 150
Weight: 13 lbs.
Features: Same features as Sizemaster except can load steel shot. Press is available for 3-1/2" 10-ga. and 12-ga. 2-3/4" ,3" or 3-1/2". For loading lead shot, die sets available in 10, 12, 16, 20, 28 and 410. From Mayville Engineering Company, Inc.
Price: $139.95
Price: 12 ga. 3-1/2" $154.95

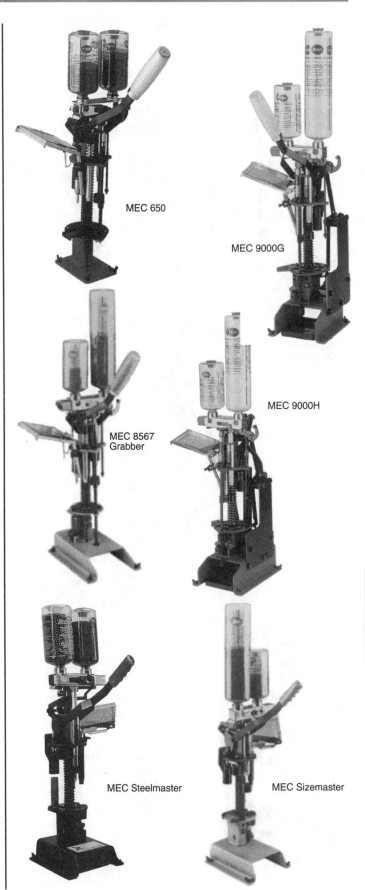

MEC 650

MEC 9000G

MEC 8567 Grabber

MEC 9000H

MEC Steelmaster

MEC Sizemaster

SHOTSHELL RELOADING PRESSES

Ponsness/Warren
Hydro-Multispeed

Ponsness/Warren
Du-O-Matic 375C

Ponsness/Warren
L/S-1000

Ponsness/Warren
Platinum 2000

Ponsness/Warren
Size-O-Matic
900 Elite

PONSNESS/WARREN Du-O-Matic 375C
Press Type: Progressive
Avg. Rounds Per Hour: NA
Weight: 31 lbs.
Features: Steel or lead shot reloader; large shot and powder reservoirs; bushing access plug for dropping in shot buffer or buckshot; positive lock charging ring to prevent accidental flow of powder; double-post construction for greater leverage; removable spent primer box; spring-loaded ball check for centering size die at each station; tip-out wad guide; two-gauge capacity tool head. Available in 10 (extra charge), 12, 16, 20, 28 and 410 with case lengths of 2-1/2, 2-3/4, 3 and 3-1/2 inches. From Ponsness/ Warren.
    Price: 12-, 20-, and 28-ga., 2-3/4" and 410, 2-1/2" $289.00
    Price: 12-ga. 3-1/2"; 3" 12, 20, 410. . . . .$305.00
    Price: 12, 20 2-3/4". $383.95
    Price: 10-ga. press. $315.00

PONSNESS/WARREN Hydro-Multispeed
Hydraulic system developed for the Ponsness/Warren L/S-1000. Also usable for the 950, 900 and 800 series presses. Three reloading speed settings operated with variable foot pedal control. Features stop/reverse at any station; automatic shutdown with pedal control release; fully adjustable hydraulic cylinder rod to prevent racking or bending of machine; quick disconnect hoses for ease of installation. Comes preassembled with step-by-step instructions. From Ponsness/Warren.
    Price: $879.00
    Price: Cylinder kit. $399.95

PONSNESS/WARREN L/S-1000
Frame: Die cast aluminum
Avg. Rounds Per Hour: NA
Weight: 55 lbs.
Features: Fully progressive press to reload steel, bismuth or lead shot. Equipped with new Uni-Drop shot measuring and dispensing system which allows the use of all makes of shot in any size. Shells automatically resized and deprimed with new Auto-Size and De-Primer system. Loaded rounds drop out of shellholders when completed. Each shell pre-crimped and final crimped with Tru-Crimp system. Available in 10-gauge 3-1/2 or 12-gauge 2-3/4" and 3". 12-gauge 3-1/2" conversion kit also available. 20-gauge 2-3/4 and 3 special order only. From Ponsness/Warren.
    Price: 12 ga. $849.00
    Price: 10 ga. $895.00
    Price: Conversion kit $199.00

PONSNESS/WARREN Size-O-Matic 900 Elite
Press Type: Progressive
Avg. Rounds Per Hour: 500-800
Weight: 49 lbs.
Features: Progressive eight-station press; frame of die cast aluminum; center post design index system ensures positive indexing; timing factory set, drilled and pinned. Automatic features include index, deprime, reprime, powder and shot drop, crimp start, tapered final crimp, finished shell ejection. Available in 12, 20, 28 and 410. 16-ga. special order. Kit includes the new shellholders, seating port, resize/primer knockout assembly and new crimp assembly. From Ponsness/Warren.
    Price: $749.00
    Price: Conversion tooling, 12, 20, 28, 410. . . . .$189.00

PONSNESS/WARREN Platinum 2000
Press Type: Progressive
Avg. Rounds Per Hour: 500-800
Weight: 52 lbs.
Features: Progressive eight-station press is similar to the 900 and 950 except has die removal system that allows removal of any die component during the reloading cycle. Comes standard with 25-lb. shot tube, 19" powder tube, brass adjustable priming feed allows adjustment of primer seating depth. From Ponsness/Warren.
    Price. $889.00

Maker and Model	Magn.	Field at 100 Yds. (feet)	Eye Relief (in.)	Length (in.)	Tube Dia. (in.)	W & E Adjustments	Weight (ozs.)	Price	Other Data
ADCO									
Magnum 50 mm[5]	0	—	—	4.1	45 mm	Int.	6.8	$269.00	[1]Multi-Color Dot system changes from red to green. [2]For airguns, paint-ball, rimfires. Uses common lithium water battery. [3]Comes with standard dovetail mount. [4].75" dovetail mount; poly body; adj. intensity diode. [5]10 MOA dot; black or nickel. [6]Square format; with mount battery. From ADCO Sales.
MIRAGE Ranger 1"	0	—	—	5.2	1	Int.	3.9	159.00	
MIRAGE Ranger 30mm	0	—	—	5.5	30mm	Int.	5	159.00	
MIRAGE Competitor	0	—	—	5.5	30mm	Int.	5.5	229.00	
IMP Sight[2]	0	—	—	4.5	—	Int.	1.3	17.95	
Square Shooter 2[3]	0	—	—	5	—	Int.	5	99.00	
MIRAGE Eclipse[1]	0	—	—	5.5	30mm	Int.	5.5	229.00	
Champ Red Dot	0	—	—	4.5	—	Int.	2	33.95	
Vantage 1"	0	—	—	3.9	1	Int.	3.9	129.00	
Vantage 30mm	0	—	—	4.2	30mm	Int.	4.9	132.00	
Vision 2000[6]	0	60	—	4.7	—	Int.	6.2	79.00	
e-dot ESB[1]	0	—	—	4.12	1	Int.	3.7	139.00	
e-dot E1B	0	—	—	4.12	1	Int.	3.7	119.00	
e-dot ECB	0	—	—	3.8	30mm	Int.	6.4	119.00	
e-dot E30B	0	—	—	4.3	30mm	Int.	4.6	119.00	
AIMPOINT									
Comp	0	—	—	4.6	30mm	Int.	4.3	331.00	Illuminates red dot in field of view. Noparallax (dot does not need to be centered). Unlimited field of view and eye relief. On/off, adj. intensity. Dot covers 3" @100 yds. [1]Comes with 30mm rings, battery, lense cloth. [2]Requires 1" rings. Black finish. AP Comp avail. in black, blue, SS, camo. [3]Black finish (AP 5000-B) ; avail. with regular 3-min. or 10-min. Mag Dot as B2 or S2. [4]Band pass reflection coating for compatibility with night vision equipment; U.S. Army contract model; with anti-reflex coated lenses (Comp ML), $359.00. From Aimpoint U.S.A.
Comp M[4]	0	—	—	5	30mm	Int.	6.1	409.00	
Series 5000[3]	0	—	—	6	30mm	Int.	6	297.00	
Series 3000 Universal[2]	0	—	—	6.25	1	Int.	6	232.00	
Series 5000/2x[1]	2	—	—	7	30mm	Int.	9	388.00	
ARMSON O.E.G.									
Standard	0	—	—	5.125	1	Int.	4.3	202.00	Shown red dot aiming point. No batteries needed. Standard model fits 1" ring mounts (not incl.). Other O.E.G. models for shotguns and rifles can be special ordered. [1]Daylight Only Sight with .375" dovetail mount for 22s. Does not contain tritium. From Trijicon, Inc.
22 DOS[1]	0	—	—	3.75	—	Int.	3	127.00	
22 Day/Night	0	—	—	3.75	—	Int.	3	169.00	
M16/AR-15	0	—	—	5.125	—	Int.	5.5	226.00	
ARTEMIS 2000									
4x32	4	34.4	3.15	10.7	1	Int.	17.5	215.00	Click-stop windage and elevation adjustments; constantly centered reticle; rubber eyepiece ring; nitrogen filled. Imported from the Czech Republic by CZ-USA.
6x42	6	23	3.15	13.7	1	Int.	17.5	317.00	
7x50	7	18.7	3.15	13.9	1	Int.	17.5	329.00	
1.5-6x42	1.5-6	40-12.8	2.95	12.4	30mm	Int.	19.4	522.00	
2-8x42	2-8	31-9.5	2.95	13.1	30mm	Int.	21.1	525.00	
3-9x42	3-9	24.6-8.5	2.95	12.4	30mm	Int.	19.4	466.00	
3-12x50	3-12	20.6-6.2	2.95	14	30mm	Int.	22.9	574.00	
BEC									
EuroLux									
EL2510x56	2.5-10	39.4-11.5	3.25-2	15.1	30mm	Int.	25.4	249.90	Black matte finish. Multi-coated lenses; 1/4-MOA click adjustments (1/2-MOA on EL4x25, AR4x22WA); fog and water-proof. [1]For AR-15;bullet drop compensator; q.d. mount. [2]Rubber armored. Imported by BEC Inc. Partial listing shown. Contact BEC for complete details. [3]All Goldlabel scopes feature lighted reticles and finger-adjustable windage and elevation adjustments. [4]Bullet-drop compensator system for Mini-14 and AR-15 rifles.
EL39x42	3-9	34.1-13.2	3.5-3	12.3	30mm	Int.	17.7	99.80	
EL28x36	2-8	44.9-11.5	3.8-3	12.2	30mm	Int.	15.9	149.50	
ELA39x40RB[2]	3-9	39-13	3	12.7	30mm	Int.	14.3	95.95	
EL6x42	6	21	3	12.6	30mm	Int.	14.8	69.00	
EL4x42	4	29	3	12.6	30mm	Int.	14.8	59.60	
EL4x36	4	29	3	12	30mm	Int.	14	49.90	
EL4x25	4	26	3	7	30mm	Int.	7.6	37.00	
AR4x22WA[1]	4	24	3	7	34mm	Int.	13.6	109.97	
Goldlabel[3]									
GLI 624x50	6-24	16-4	3.5-3	15.3	1	Int.	22.5	139.00	
GLI 416x50	4-16	25-6	3.5-3	13.5	1	Int.	21.8	135.00	
GLI 39x40R[2]	3-9	39-13	3.5-3	12.7	28mm	Int.	18.5	99.00	
GLC 5x42BD[4]	5	24	3.5	8.7	1	Int.	16.5	79.00	
BEEMAN									
Rifle Scopes									
5045[1]	4-12	26.9-9	3	13.2	1	Int.	15	275.00	All scopes have 5 point reticle, all glass fully coated lenses. [1]Parallel adjustable. [2]Reticle lighted by ambient light. [3]Available with lighted Electro-Dot reticle. Imported by Beeman.
5046[1]	6-24	18-4.5	3	16.9	1	Int.	20.2	395.00	
5050[1]	4	26	3.5	11.7	1	Int.	11	80.00	
5055[1]	3-9	38-13	3.5	10.75	1	Int.	11.2	90.00	
5060[1]	4-12	30-10	3	12.5	1	Int.	16.2	210.00	
5065[1]	6-18	17-6	3	14.7	1	Int.	17.3	265.00	
5066RL[2]	2-7	58-15	3	11.4	1	Int.	17	380.00	
5047L[2]	4	25	3.5	7	1	Int.	13.7	NA	
Pistol Scopes									
5021	2	19	10-24	9.1	1	Int.	7.4	85.50	
5020	1.5	14	11-16	8.3	.75	Int.	3.6	NA	
BSA									
Catseye[1]									
CE1545x32	1.5-4.5	78-23	4	11.25	1	Int.	12	91.95	[1]Waterproof, fogproof; multi-coated lenses; finger-adjustable knobs. [2]Waterproof, fogproof; matte black finish. [3]With 4" sunshade; target knobs; 1/8-MOA click adjustments. [4]Adjustable for parallax; with sunshades; target knobs, 1/8-MOA adjustments. Imported by BSA. [5]Illuminated reticle model; also available in 3-10x, 3.5-10x, and 3-9x. [6]Red dot sights also available in 42mm and 50mm versions. [7]Includes Universal Bow Mount. [8]Five other models offered. From BSA.
CE310x44	3-10	39-12	3.25	12.75	1	Int.	16	151.95	
CE3510x50	3.5-10	30-10.5	3.25	13.25	1	Int.	17.25	171.95	
CE416x50	4-16	25-6	3	15.25	1	Int.	22	191.95	
CE624x50	6-24	16-3	3	16	1	Int.	23	222.95	
CE1545x32IR	1.5-4.5	78-23	5	11.25	1	Int.	12	121.95	
Deer Hunter[2]									

Maker and Model	Magn.	Field at 100 Yds. (feet)	Eye Relief (in.)	Length (in.)	Tube Dia. (in.)	W & E Adjustments	Weight (ozs.)	Price	Other Data
DH25x20	2.5	72	6	7.5	1	Int.	7.5	59.95	
DH4x32	4	32	3	12	1	Int.	12.5	49.95	
DH39x32	3-9	39-13	3	12	1	Int.	11	69.95	
DH39x40	3-9	39-13	3	13	1	Int.	12.1	89.95	
DH39x50	3-9	41-15	3	12.75	1	Int.	13	109.95	
DH2510x44	2.5-10	42-12	3	13	1	Int.	12.5	99.95	
DH1545x32	1.5-4.5	78-23	5	11.25	1	Int.	12	79.95	
Contender[3]									
CT24x40TS	24	6	3	15	1	Int.	18	129.95	
CT36x40TS	36	3	3	15.25	1	Int.	19	139.95	
CT312x40TS	3-12	28-7	3	13	1	Int.	17.5	119.95	
CT416x40TS	4-16	21-5	3	13.5	1	Int.	18	129.95	
CT624x40TS	6-24	16-4	3	15.5	1	Int.	20	144.95	
CT832x40TS	8-32	11-3	3	15.5	1	Int.	20	169.95	
CT24x50TS	24	6	3	15	1	Int.	22	149.95	
CT36x50TS	36	3	3	15.25	1	Int.	23	159.95	
CT312x50TS	3-12	28-7	3	13.75	1	Int.	21	129.95	
CT416x50TS	4-16	21-5	3	15.25	1	Int.	22	149.95	
CT624x50TS	6-24	16-4	3	16	1	Int.	23	169.95	
CT832x50TS	8-32	11-3	3	16.5	1	Int.	24	189.95	
Pistol									
P52x20	2	N/A	N/A	N/A	N/A	Int.	N/A	79.95	
P54x28	4	N/A	N/A	N/A	N/A	Int.	N/A	89.95	
Platinum[4]									
PT24x44TS	24	4.5	3	16.25	1	Int.	17.9	189.55	
PT36x44TS	36	3	3	14.9	1	Int.	17.9	199.95	
PT624x44TS	6-24	15-4.5	3	15.25	1	Int.	18.5	219.95	
PT832x44TS	8-32	11-3.5	3	17.25	1	Int.	19.5	239.95	
PT1050x60TS	10-50	7-2	3	18	1	Int.	22	399.95	
.22 Special									
S25x20WR	2.5	58	3	8	1	Int.	7	39.95	
S4x32WR	4	26	3	10.75	1	Int.	9	49.95	
Air Rifle									
AR4x32	4	33	3	13	1	Int.	14	69.95	
AR27x32	2-7	48	3	12.25	1	Int.	14	79.95	
AR312x44	3-12	36	3	12.25	1	Int.	15	109.95	
Red Dot									
RD30[6]	0	—	—	3.8	30mm	Int.	5	59.95	
PB30[6]	0	—	—	3.8	30mm	Int.	4.5	79.95	
Bow30[7]	0	—	—	N/A	30mm	Int.	5	89.95	
BigCat[8]	3.5-10	30-11	5	9.7	1	Int.	16.8	219.95	

BURRIS

Mr. T Black Diamond Titanium									
2.5-10x50[A]	2.5-10	4.25-4.75		13.6	30mm	Int.	29	2,129.00	
Black Diamond									
3-12x50[3,4,6]	3.2-11.9	34-12	3.5-4	13.8	30mm	Int.	25	880.00	
6-24x50	6-24	18-6	3.5-4	16.2	30mm	Int.	25	954.00	
Fullfield & Fullfield II									
2.5x[9]	2.5	55	3.5-3.75	10.25	1	Int.	9	308.00	
4x[1,2,3]	3.75	36	3.5-3.75	11.25	1	Int.	11.5	314.00	
6x[1,3]	5.8	23	3.5-3.75	13	1	Int.	12	343.00	
1.75-5x[1,2,9,10]	1.7-4.6	66-25	3.5-3.75	10.875	1	Int.	13	374.00	
2-7x[1,2,3]	2.5-6.8	47-18	3.5-3.75	12	1	Int.	14	399.00	
3-9x40[1,2,3,10]	3.3-8.7	38-15	3.5-3.75	12.625	1	Int.	15	356.00	
3-9x50	3-9	35-15	3.5-3.75	13	1	Int.	18	427.00	
3.5-10x50mm[3,5,10]	3.7-9.7	29.5-11	3.5-3.75	14	1	Int.	19	496.00	
4-12x[1,4,8,11]	4.4-11.8	27-10	3.5-3.75	15	1	Int.	18	500.00	
6-18x[1,3,4,6,7,8]	6.5-17.6	16.7	3.5-3.75	15.8	1	Int.	18.5	527.00	
Compact Scopes									
1x XER[3]	1	51	4.5-20	8.8	1	Int.	7.9	290.00	
4x[4,5]	3.6	24	3.75-5	8.25	1	Int.	7.8	270.00	
6x[1,4]	5.5	17	3.75-5	9	1	Int.	8.2	287.00	
6x HBR[1,5,8]	6	13	4.5	11.25	1	Int.	13	451.00	
1-4x XER[3]	1-3.8	53-15	4.25-30	8.8	1	Int.	10.3	377.00	
3-9x[4,5]	3.6-8.8	25-11	3.75-5	12.625	1	Int.	11.5	368.00	
4-12x[1,4,6]	4.5-11.6	19-8	3.75-4	15	1	Int.	15	500.00	
Signature Series									
1.5-6x[2,3,5,9,10]	1.7-5.8	70-20	3.5-4	10.8	1	Int.	13	484.00	
6x[3]	6	20	3.5-4	12.125	1	Int.	14	413.00	
2-8x[3,5,11]	2.1-7.7	53-17	3.5-4	11.75	1	Int.	14	558.00	
3-9x[3,5,10,13]	3.3-8.8	36-14	3.5-4	12.875	1	Int.	15.5	571.00	
2.50-10x[3,5,10]	2.7-9.5	37-10.5	3.5-4	14	1	Int.	19	635.00	
3-12x[3,10]	3.3-11.7	34-9	3.5-4	14.25	1	Int.	21	691.00	
4-16x[1,3,5,6,8,10]	4.3-15.7	33-9	3.5-4	15.4	1	Int.	23.7	723.00	
6-24x[1,3,5,6,8,10,13]	6.6-23.8	17-6	3.5-4	16	1	Int.	22.7	742.00	
8-32x[8,10,12]	8.6-31.4	13-3.8	3.5-4	17	1	Int.	24	798.00	
Speeddot 135[13]									
Red Dot	1	—	—	4.85	35mm	Int.	5	291.00	
Handgun									
1.50-4x LER[1,5,10]	1.6-3.	16-11	11-25	10.25	1	Int.	11	363.00	
2-7x LER[3,4,5,10]	2-6.5	21-7	7-27	9.5	1	Int.	12.6	401.00	

[A]Available in Carbon Black, Titanium Gray and Autumn Gold finishes.
Black Diamond & Fullfield: All scopes avail. with Plex reticle. Steel-on-steel click adjustments. [1]Dot reticle on some models. [2]Post crosshair reticle extra. [3]Matte satin finish. [4]Available with parallax adjustment (standard on 10x, 12x, 4-12x, 6-12x, 6-18x, 6x HBR and 3-12x Signature). [5]Silver matte finish extra. [6]Target knobs extra, standard on silhouette models. LER and XER with P.A., 6x HBR. [7]Sunshade avail. [8]Avail. with Fine Plex reticle. [9]Available with Heavy Plex reticle. [10]Available with Posi-Lock. [11]Available with Peep Plex reticle. [12]Also avail. for rimfires, airguns. [13]Selected models available with camo finish.
Signature Series: LER=Long Eye Relief; IER=Intermediate Eye Relief; XER=Extra Eye Relief.
Speeddot 135: [13]Waterproof, fogproof, coated lenses, 11 brightness settings; 3-MOA or 11-MOA dot size; includes Weaver-style rings and battery. **Partial listing shown.** Contact Burris for complete details.

Plex Fine Plex

Heavy Plex & Electro-Dot Plex Peep Plex Ballistic Mil-Dot

Target Dot Mil-Dot

ACCESSORIES

Maker and Model	Magn.	Field at 100 Yds. (feet)	Eye Relief (in.)	Length (in.)	Tube Dia. (in.)	W & E Adjustments	Weight (ozs.)	Price	Other Data
3-9x LER[4,5,10]	3.4-8.4	12-5	22-14	11	1	Int.	14	453.00	
2x LER[4,5,6]	1.7	21	10-24	8.75	1	Int.	6.8	265.00	
4x LER[1,4,5,6,10]	3.7	11	10-22	9.625	1	Int.	9	296.00	
10x LER[1,4,6]	9.5	4	8-12	13.5	1	Int.	14	460.00	
Scout Scope									
1xXER[3,9]	1.5	32	4-24	9	1	Int.	7.0	290.00	
2.75x[3,9]	2.7	15	7-14	9.375	1	Int.	7.0	319.00	

BUSHNELL (Bausch & Lomb Elite rifle scopes now sold under Bushnell name)

Elite 4200 RainGuard									(Bushnell Elite)
42-6244A[1]	6-24	18-6	3	16.9	1	Int.	20.2	729.95	[1]Adj. objective, sunshade; also in matte and with 1/4-MOA dot or Mil Dot
42-2104G[2]	2.5-10	41.5-10.8	3	13.5	1	Int.	16	642.95	reticle. [2]Also in matte and silver finish. [3]Only in matte finish. [4]Also in matte
42-1636M[3]	1.5-6	61.8-16.1	3	12.8	1	Int.	15.4	608.95	and silver finish. [5]Adjustable objective. [6]50mm objective; also in matte
42-3640A	36	3	3	15	1	Int.	17.6	955.95	finish. [7]Also in silver finish. **Partial listings shown. Contact Bushnell**
42-4165M[5]	4-16	26-7	3	15.6	1	Int.	22	834.95	**Performance Optics for details.**
Elite 3200 RainGuard									
32-5155M	5-15	21-7	3	15.9	1	Int.	19	528.95	
32-4124A[1]	4-12	26.9-9	3	13.2	1	Int.	15	469.95	
32-3940G[4]	3-9	33.8-11.5	3	12.6	1	Int.	13	351.95	
32-2732M	2-7	44.6-12.7	3	11.6	1	Int.	12	342.95	
32-3950G[6]	3-9	31.5-10.5	3	15.7	1	Int.	19	428.95	
32-3955E	3-9	31.5-10.5	3	15.6	30mm	Int.	22	640.95	
Elite 3200 Handgun									
32-2632M[7]	2-6	10-4	20	9	1	Int.	10	444.95	
32-2632G	2-6	10-4	20	9	1	Int.	10	444.95	
Scopechief									(Bushnell)
70-3104M[4]	3.5-10	43-15	3.5	13	1	Int.	17	294.95	[1]Wide Angle. [2]Also silver finish. [3]Also silver finish. [4]Matte finish. [5]Also
70-4145A[12]	4-14	31-9	3.5	14.1	1	Int.	23	408.95	silver finish. [7]Adj. obj. [8]Variable intensity; fits Weaver-style base.
Trophy									[9]Blackpowder scope; extended eye relief, Circle-X reticle. [10]50mm objec-
73-15001	1.75-5	68-23	3.5	10.8	1	Int.	12.3	262.95	tive. [11]With Circle-X reticle, matte finish. [12]Matte finish, adjustable objec-
73-4124[1]	4-12	32-11	3	12.5	1	Int.	16.1	285.95	tive.
73-3940[2]	3-9	42-14	3	11.7	1	Int.	13.2	159.95	
73-6184[7]	6-18	17.3-6	3	14.8	1	Int.	17.9	360.95	
Turkey & Brush									
73-1421[11]	1.75-4	73-30	3.5	10.8	32mm	Int.	10.9	171.95	
HOLOsight Model[8]	1	—	—	6	—	Int.	8.7	444.95	
Trophy Handgun									
73-0232[2]	2	20	9-26	8.7	1	Int.	7.7	218.95	
73-2632[3]	2-6	21-7	9-26	9.1	1	Int.	10.9	287.95	
Banner									
71-1545	1.5-4.5	67-23	3.5	10.5	1	Int.	10.5	116.95	
71-3944[9]	3-9	36-13	4	11.5	1	Int.	12.5	125.95	
71-3950[10]	3-9	26-10	3	16	1	Int.	19	186.95	
71-4124[7]	4-12	29-11	3	12	1	Int.	15	157.95	
71-4228	4	26.5	3	11.75	1	Int.	10	81.95	
71-6185[10]	6-18	17-6	3	16	1	Int.	18	209.95	
Sportsman									
79-0004	4	31	4	11.7	1	Int.	11.2	98.95	
79-0039	3-9	38-13	3.5	10.75	1	Int.	11.2	116.95	
79-0412[7]	4-12	27-9	3.2	13.1	1	Int.	14.6	141.95	
79-1393[6]	3-9	35-12	3.5	11.75	1	Int.	10	68.95	
79-1545	1.5-4.5	69-24	3	10.7	1	Int.	8.6	86.95	
79-1548[11]	1.5-4.5	71-25	3.5	10.4	1	Int.	11.8	104.95	
79-2538[11]	2.5	45	3	11	1	Int.	10	76.95	
79-1403	4	29	4	11.75	1	Int.	9.2	57.95	
79-6184	6-18	19.1-6.8	3	14.5	1	Int.	15.9	170.95	
79-3940M	3-9	42-14	3	12.7	1	Int.	12.5	95.95	

HOLOSIGHT RETICLES

MOA Dot   Standard

SCOPE RETICLES

CP2   Multi   Euro   Circle-X

C-MORE SYSTEMS

Classic AR[1]	4	225	3	7.2	35mm	Int.	14.6	249.00	[1]All Weaver and Picatinny-style rail mounts. [2]Flattop mount for A3-style
SSE[2]	6	159	3.3	12.8	30mm	Int.	22.8	499.00	receivers. [3]Most popular auto pistols. [4]Mounts to any flat surface, custom
Tactical Elite[2]	10	159	3.38	13	30mm	Int.	22.6	539.00	mounts, shotgun ribs; Glock adapter plate for direct slide mounting. From
Compact 1-5x20[3]	1-5	301-62	3.45	9.5	30mm	Int.	14.2	549.00	C-More Systems, Inc. For click-smooth models of red-dot sights, add
Red Dots									$50.00.
Railway[1]	1	—	—	4.8	—	Int.	5	249.00	
AR Scout	1	—	—	11	—	Int.	7.5	368.00	
Serendipity[3]	1	—	—	5.3	—	Int.	3.75	249.00	
Slide Ride[4]	1	—	—	4.8	—	Int.	3	249.00	
Colt Tactical[2]	1	—	—	8	—	Int.	12	444.00	

DOCTER OPTIC

Fixed Power									Matte black and matte silver finish available. All lenses multi-coated. Illu-
4x32	4	31	3	10.7	26mm	Int.	10	898.00	minated reticle avail., choice of reticles. [1]Rail mount, aspherical lenses
6x42	6	20	3	12.8	26mm	Int.	12.7	1,004.00	avail. Aspherical lens model, **$1,375.00.** Imported from Germany by
8x56[1]	8	15	3	14.7	26mm	Int.	15.6	1,240.00	Docter Optic Technologies, Inc.
Variables									
1-4x24	1-4	79.7-31.3	3	10.8	30mm	Int.	13	1,300.00	
1.2-5x32	1.2-5	65-25	3	11.6	30mm	Int.	15.4	1,345.00	
1.5-6x42	1.5-6	41.3-20.6	3	12.7	30mm	Int.	16.8	1,378.00	
2.5-10x48	2.5-10	36.6-12.4	3	13.7	30mm	Int.	18.6	1,378.00	
2-12x56	3-12	44.2-13.8	3	14.8	30mm	Int.	20.3	1,425.00	
3-10x40	3-10	34.4-11.7	3	13	1	Int.	18	795.00	

ACCESSORIES

Maker and Model	Magn.	Field at 100 Yds. (feet)	Eye Relief (in.)	Length (in.)	Tube Dia. (in.)	W & E Adjustments	Weight (ozs.)	Price	Other Data
EUROPTIK SUPREME									
4x36K	4	39	3.5	11.6	26mm	Int.	14	795.00	[1]Military scope with adjustable parallax. Fixed powers have 26mm tubes,
6x42K	6	21	3.5	13	26mm	Int.	15	875.00	variables have 30mm tubes. Some models avail. with steel tubes. All
8x56K	8	18	3.5	14.4	26mm	Int.	20	925.00	lenses multi-coated. Dust and water tight. From Europtik.
1.5-6x42K	1.5-6	61.7-23	3.5	12.6	30mm	Int.	17	1,095.00	
2-8x42K	2-8	52-17	3.5	13.3	30mm	Int.	17	1,150.00	
2.5-10x56K	2.5-10	40-13.6	3.5	15	30mm	Int.	21	1,295.00	
3-12x56 Super	3-12	10.8-34.7	3.5-2.5	15.2	30mm	Int.	24	1,495.00	
4-16x56 Super	4-16	9.8-3.9	3.1	18	30mm	Int.	26	1,575.00	
3-9x40 Micro	3-9	3.2-12.1	2.7	13	1	Int.	14	1,450.00	
2.5-10x46 Micro	2.5-10	13.7-33.4	2.7	14	30mm	Int.	20	1,395.00	
4-16x56 EDP[1]	4-16	22.3-7.5	3.1	18	30mm	Int.	29	1,995.00	
7-12x50 Target	7-12	8.8-5.5	3.5	15	30mm	Int.	21	1,495.00	
KAHLES									
4x36	4	34.5	3.15	11.2	1	Int.	12.7	555.00	Aluminum tube. Multi-coated, waterproof. [1]Also available with illuminated
6x42	6	23	3.15	12.4	1	Int.	14.4	694.00	reticle. Imported from Austria by Swarovski Optik.
8x50[1]	8	17.3	3.15	13	1	Int.	16.5	749.00	
1.1-4x24	1.1-4	108-31.8	3.5	10.8	30mm	Int.	12.7	722.00	
1.5-6x42[1]	1.5-6	72-21.3	3.5	12.0	30mm	Int.	15.8	832.00	
2.5-10x50[1]	2.5-10	43.5-12.9	3.5	12.8	30mm	Int.	15.8	1,353.00	
3-9x42	3-9	43-16	3.5	12	1	Int.	13	621.06	
3-9x42AH	3-9	43-15	3.5	12.36	1	Int.	12.7	665.00	
3-12x56[1]	3-12	30-11	3.5	15.4	30mm	Int.	18	1,377.72	

No. 4A	No. 7A	Plex	Illuminated No. 4N	Illuminated Plex N	TD Smith

Maker and Model	Magn.	Field at 100 Yds. (feet)	Eye Relief (in.)	Length (in.)	Tube Dia. (in.)	W & E Adjustments	Weight (ozs.)	Price	Other Data
KILHAM									
Hutson Handgunner II	1.7	8	—	5.5	.875	Int.	5.1	119.95	Unlimited eye relief; internal click adjustments; crosshair reticle. Fits
Hutson Handgunner	3	8	10-12	6	.875	Int.	5.3	119.95	Thompson/Center rail mounts, for S&W K, N, Ruger Blackhawk, Super, Super Single-Six, Contender.
LEICA									
Ultravid 1.75-6x32	1.75-6	47-18	4.8-3.7	11.25	30mm	Int.	14	749.00	Aluminum tube with hard anodized matte black finish with titanium
Ultravid 3.5-10x42	3.5-10	29.5-10.7	4.6-3.6	12.62	30mm	Int.	16	849.00	accents; finger-adjustable windage and elevation with 1/4-MOA clicks.
Ultravid 4.5-14x42	4.5-14	20.5-7.4	5-3.7	12.28	30mm	Int.	18	949.00	Made in U.S. From Leica.

Leicaplex Standard	Leica Dot	Standard Dot	Crosshair	Euro	Post & Plex

Maker and Model	Magn.	Field at 100 Yds. (feet)	Eye Relief (in.)	Length (in.)	Tube Dia. (in.)	W & E Adjustments	Weight (ozs.)	Price	Other Data
LEUPOLD									
Vari-X III 3.5x10 Tactical	3.5-10	29.5-10.7	3.6-4.6	12.5	1	Int.	13.5	801.80	Constantly centered reticles, choice of Duplex, tapered CPC, Leupold
M8-2X EER[1]	1.7	21.2	12-24	7.9	1	Int.	6	312.50	Dot, Crosshair and Dot. CPC and Dot reticles extra. [1]2x and 4x scopes
M8-2X EER Silver[1]	1.7	21.2	12-24	7.9	1	Int.	6	337.50	have from 12"-24" of eye relief and are suitable for handguns, top ejection
M8-2.5x28 IER Scout	2.3	22	9.3	10.1	1	Int.	7.5	408.90	arms and muzzleloaders. [2]3x9 Compact, 6x Compact, 12x, 3x9, and
M8-4X EER[1]	3.7	9	12-24	8.4	1	Int.	7	425.00	6.5x20 come with adjustable objective. Sunshade available for all adjust-
M8-4X EER Silver[1]	3.7	9	12-24	8.4	1	Int.	7	425.00	able objective scopes, **$23.20-$41.10**. [3]Silver finish about $25.00 extra.
Vari-X 2.5-8 EER	2.5-8	13-4.3	11.7-12	9.7	1	Int.	10.9	608.90	[4]Long Range scopes have side focus parallax adjustment, additional
M8-4X Compact	3.6	25.5	4.5	9.2	1	Int.	7.5	382.10	windage and elevation travel. Partial listing shown. **Contact Leupold for**
Vari-X 2-7x Compact	2.5-6.6	41.7-16.5	5-3.7	9.9	1	Int.	8.5	478.60	**complete details.**
Vari-X 3-9x Compact	3.2-8.6	34-13.5	4-3	11-11.3	1	Int.	11	519.60	*Models available with illuminated reticle for additional cost.
M8-4X	4	24	4	10.7	1	Int.	9.3	385.70	
M8-6X36mm	5.9	17.7	4.3	11.4	1	Int.	10	410.70	
M8-6x 42mm	6	17	4.5	12	1	Int.	11.3	510.70	
*M8-6x42 A.O. Tactical	6	17	4.2	12.1	1	Int.	11.3	628.60	
M8-12x A.O. Varmint	11.6	9.1	4.2	13	1	Int.	13.5	571.40	
Vari-X 3-9x Compact EFR A.O.	3.8-8.6	34-13.5	4-3	11	1	Int.	11	550.00	
Vari-X-II 1x4	1.6-4.2	70.5-28.5	4.3-3.8	9.2	1	Int.	9	396.40	
Vari-X-II 2x7	2.5-6.6	42.5-17.8	4.9-3.8	11	1	Int.	10.5	428.60	
Vari-X-II 3x9[1,3]	3.3-8.6	32.3-14	4.1-3.7	12.3	1	Int.	13.5	432.10	
Vari-X-II 3-9x50mm	3.3-8.6	32.3-14	4.7-3.7	12	1	Int.	13.6	510.70	
Vari-X II 3-9x40 Tactical	3-9	32.3-14	4.7-3.7	12.2	1	Int.	13	535.70	
Vari-X-II 4-12 A.O. Matte	4.4-11.6	22.8-11	5-3.3	12.3	1	Int.	13.5	594.60	
*Vari-X-III 1.5-5x20	1.5-4.5	66-23	5.3-3.7	9.4	1	Int.	9.5	635.70	
Vari-X-III 1.75-6x32	1.9-5.6	47-18	4.8-3.7	9.8	1	Int.	11	683.90	
Vari-X-III 2.5x8	2.6-7.8	37-13.5	4.7-3.7	11.3	1	Int.	11.5	678.60	
Vari-X-III 3.5-10x40 Long Range M3[4]	3.9-9.7	29.8-11	4-3.5	13.5	30mm	Int.	19.5	1,157.10	
Vari-X-III 3.5-10x50	3.3-9.7	29.5-10.7	4.6-3.6	12.4	1	Int.	13	796.40	*Models available with illuminated reticle for additional cost.

Duplex	CPC	Post & Duplex
Leupold Dot	**Dot**	

SCOPES / HUNTING, TARGET & VARMINT

Maker and Model	Magn.	Field at 100 Yds. (feet)	Eye Relief (in.)	Length (in.)	Tube Dia. (in.)	W & E Adjustments	Weight (ozs.)	Price	Other Data
Vari-X-III 4.5-14x40 A.O.	4.7-13.7	20.8-7.4	5-3.7	12.4	1	Int.	14.5	780.40	
*Vari-X-III 4.5-14x50 A.O.	4.7-13.7	20.8-7.4	5-3.7	12.4	1	Int.	14.5	903.60	
Vari-X III 4.5-14x 50 Long Range Tactical[4]	4.9-14.3	19-6	5-3.7	12.1	30mm	Int.	17.5	1,082.10	
Vari-X-III 6.5-20 A.O.	6.5-19.2	14.2-5.5	5.3-3.6	14.2	1	Int.	17.5	823.20	
Vari-X-III 6.5x20xTarget EFR A.O.	6.5-19.2	—	5.3-3.6	14.2	1	Int.	16.5	919.60	
Vari-X III 6.5-20x 50 Long Range Target[4]	6.8-19.2	14.7-5.4	4.9-3.7	14.3	30mm	Int.	19	1,166.10	
Vari-X III 8.5-25x40 A.O. Target	8.5-25	10.86-4.2	5.3	14.3	1	Int.	17.5	900.00	
Vari-X III 8.5-25x 50 Long Range Target[4]	8.3-24.2	11.4-4.3	4.4-3.6	14.3	30mm	Int.	19	1,260.70	
Mark 4 M1-10x40	10	11.1	3.6	13.125	30mm	Int.	21	1,807.10	
Mark 4 M1-16x40	16	6.6	4.1	12.875	30mm	Int.	22	1,807.10	
Mark 4 M3-10x40	10	11.1	3.6	13.125	30mm	Int.	21	1,807.10	
Vari-X III 6.5x20[2] A.O.	6.5-19.2	14.2-5.5	5.3-3.6	14.2	1	Int.	16	823.20	
BR-D 24x40 A.O. Target	24	4.7	3.2	13.6	1	Int.	15.3	1,035.70	
BR-D 36x-40 A.O. Target	36	3.2	3.4	14.1	1	Int.	15.6	1,083.90	
LPS 1.5-6x42	1.5-6	58.7-15.7	4	11.2	30mm	Int.	16	1,476.80	
LPS 3.5-14x52 A.O.	3.5-14	28-7.2	4	13.1	30mm	Int.	22	1,569.60	
Rimfire									
Vari-X 2-7x RF Special	3.6	25.5	4.5	9.2	1	Int.	7.5	478.60	
Shotgun									
M8 4x33	3.7	9	12-24	8.4	1	Int.	6	410.70	
Vari-X II 1x4	1.6-4.2	70.5-28.5	4.3-3.8	9.2	1	Int.	9	421.40	
Vari-X-II 2x7	2.5-6.6	42.5-17.8	4.9-3.8	11	1	Int.	9	453.60	

German #1   German #2   Turkey Reticle

3/4-Mil. Dot   Crosshair

LYMAN

Super TargetSpot[1]	10, 12, 15, 20, 25, 30	5.5	2	24.3	.75	Int.	27.5	685.00	

Made under license from Lyman to Lyman's orig. specs. Blue steel. Three-point suspension rear mount with .25-min. click adj. Data listed are for 20x model. [1]Price approximate. Made in U.S. by Parsons Optical Mfg. Co.

McMILLAN

Vision Master 2.5-10x	2.5-10	14.2-4.4	4.3-3.3	13.3	30mm	Int.	17	1,250.00	
Vision Master Model 1[1]	2.5-10	14.2-4.4	4.3-3.3	13.3	30mm	Int.	17	1,250.00	

42mm obj. lens; .25-MOA clicks; nitrogen filled; fogproof; waterproof; etched duplex-type reticle. [1]Tactical Scope with external adj. knobs, military reticle; 60+ min. adj.

MEOPTA

Artemis									
4x32A[1]	4	34	3.15	11	1	Int.	14.7	194.00	
6x42A[1]	6	23	3.15	13.6	1	Int.	18.2	267.00	
7x50A[1]	7	18	3.15	14.1	1	Int.	19	278.00	

Steel tubes are waterproof, dustproof, and shockproof; nitrogen fille.d Anti-reflective coatings, protective rubber eye piece, clear caps. Made in Czech Replublic by Meopta. [1]Range finder reticles available. Partial listing shown.

MEPROLIGHT

Meprolight Reflex Sights 14-21 5.5 MOA 1x30[1]	1	—	—	4.4	30mm	Int.	5.2	335.00	

[1]Also available with 4.2 MOA dot. Uses tritium and fiber optics-no batteries required. From Hesco, Inc.

MILLETT

Buck 3-9x44	3-9	38-14	3.25-4	13	1	Int.	16.2	549.00	
SP-1 Compact[1] Red Dot	1	36.65	—	4.1	1	Int.	3.2	149.95	
SP-2 Compact[2] Red Dot	1	58	—	4.5	30mm	Int.	4.3	149.95	
MultiDot SP[3]	1	50	—	4.8	30mm	Int.	5.3	289.95	
30mm Wide View[4]	1	60	—	5.5	30mm	Int.	5	289.95	

[1]3-MOA dot. [2]5-MOA dot. [3]3-, 5-, 8-, 10-MOA dots. [4]10-MOA dot. All have click adjustments; waterproof, shockproof; 11 dot intensity settings. All avail. in matte/black or silver finish. From Millett Sights.

MIRADOR

RXW 4x40[1]	4	37	3.8	12.4	1	Int.	12	179.95	
RXW 1.5-5x20[1]	1.5-5	46-17.4	4.3	11.1	1	Int.	10	188.95	
RXW 3-9x40	3-9	43-14.5	3.1	12.9	1	Int.	13.4	251.95	

[1]Wide angle scope. Multi-coated objective lens. Nitrogen filled; waterproof; shockproof. From Mirador Optical Corp.

NIGHTFORCE

2.5-10x50	2.5-10	31.4-9.4	3.3	13.9	30mm	Int.	28	847.87	
3.5-15x56	3.5-15	24.5-6.9	3	15.8	30mm	Int.	32	507.78	
5.5-22x56	5.5-22	15.7-4.4	3	19.4	30mm	Int.	38.5	965.53	
8-32x56	8-32	9.4-3.1	3	16.6	30mm	Int.	36	997.90	
12-42x56	12-42	6.7-2.3	3	17	30mm	Int.	36	1,053.64	

Lighted reticles with eleven intensity levels. Most scopes have choice of reticles. From Lightforce U.S.A.

NIKON

Monarch UCC									
4x40[2]	4	26.7	3.5	11.7	1	Int.	11.7	330.95	
1.5-4.5x20[3]	1.5-4.5	67.8-22.5	3.7-3.2	10.1	1	Int.	9.5	364.95	
2-7x32	2-7	46.7-13.7	3.9-3.3	11.3	1	Int.	11.3	426.95	
3-9x40[1]	3-9	33.8-11.3	3.6-3.2	12.5	1	Int.	12.5	430.95	
3.5-10x50	3.5-10	25.5-8.9	3.9-3.8	13.7	1	Int.	15.5	644.95	

Super multi-coated lenses and blackening of all internal metal parts for maximum light gathering capability; positive .25-MOA; fogproof; waterproof; shockproof; luster and matte finish. [1]Also available in matte silver finish. [2]Available in silver matte finish. [3]Available with TurkeyPro or Nikoplex reticle. [4]Silver Shadow finish; black matte **$296.95**. Partial listing shown. From Nikon, Inc.

ACCESSORIES

Maker and Model	Magn.	Field at 100 Yds. (feet)	Eye Relief (in.)	Length (in.)	Tube Dia. (in.)	W & E Adjustments	Weight (ozs.)	Price	Other Data
4-12x40 A.O.	4-12	25.7-8.6	3.6-3.2	14	1	Int.	16.6	552.95	
6.5-20x44	6.5-19.4	16.2-5.4	3.5-3.1	14.8	1	Int.	19.6	684.95	
2x20 EER	2	22	26.4	8.1	1	Int.	6.3	248.95	
Buckmasters									
4x40	4	30.4	3.3	12.7	1	Int.	11.8	244.95	
3-9x40[4]	3.3-8.6	33.8-11.3	3.5-3.4	12.7	1	Int.	13.4	324.95	
3-9x50	3.3-8.6	33.8-11.3	3.5-3.4	12.9	1	Int.	18.2	452.95	

NORINCO

Maker and Model	Magn.	Field at 100 Yds. (feet)	Eye Relief (in.)	Length (in.)	Tube Dia. (in.)	W & E Adjustments	Weight (ozs.)	Price	Other Data
N2520	2.5	44.1	4	—	1	Int.	—	52.28	Partial listing shown. Some with Ruby Lens coating, blue/black and matte finish. Imported by Nic Max, Inc.
N420	4	29.3	3.7	—	1	Int.	—	52.70	
N640	6	20	3.1	—	1	Int.	—	67.88	
N154520	1.5-4.5	63.9-23.6	4.1-3.2	—		Int.	—	80.14	
N251042	2.5-10	27-11	3.5-2.8	—	1	Int.	—	206.60	
N3956	3-9	35.1-6.3	3.7-2.6	—	1	Int.	—	231.88	
N31256	3-12	26-10	3.5-2.8	—	1	Int.	—	290.92	
NC2836M	2-8	50.8-14.8	3.6-2.7	—	1	Int.	—	255.60	

PARSONS

Maker and Model	Magn.	Field at 100 Yds. (feet)	Eye Relief (in.)	Length (in.)	Tube Dia. (in.)	W & E Adjustments	Weight (ozs.)	Price	Other Data
Parsons Long Scope	6	10	2	28-34+	.75	Ext.	13	475.00-525.00	Adjustable for parallax, focus. Micrometer rear mount with .25-min. click adjustments. Price is approximate. Made in U.S. by Parsons Optical Mfg. Co.

PENTAX

Maker and Model	Magn.	Field at 100 Yds. (feet)	Eye Relief (in.)	Length (in.)	Tube Dia. (in.)	W & E Adjustments	Weight (ozs.)	Price
Lightseeker 1.75-6x[1]	1.75-6	71-20	3.5-4	10.8	1	Int.	13	526.00
Lightseeker 2-8x[2]	2-8	53-17	3.5-4	11.7	1	Int.	14	560.00
Lightseeker 3-9x[3,4,10,11]	3-9	36-14	3.5-4	12.7	1	Int.	15	594.00
Lightseeker 3.5-10x[5]	3.5-10	29.5-11	3.5-4	14	1	Int.	19.5	630.00
Lightseeker 4-16x[6,9]	4-16	33-9	3.5-4	15.4	1	Int.	22.7	796.00
Lightseeker 6-24x[7,12]	6-24	18-5.5	3.5-4	16	1	Int.	23.7	856.00
Lightseeker 8.5-32x[8]	8.5-32	13-3.8	3.5-4	17.2	1	Int.	24	944.00
Shotgun								
Lightseeker 2.5x[13]	2.5	55	3.5-4	10	1	Int.	9	350.00
Lightseeker Zero-X SG Plus	0	51	4.5-15	8.9	1	Int.	7.9	372.00
Lightseeker Zero-X/V Still-Target	0-4	53.8-15	3.5-7	8.9	1	Int.	10.3	476.00
Lightseeker Zero X/V	0-4	53.8-15	3.5-7	8.9	1	Int.	10.3	454.00

[1]Glossy finish; Matte finish, Heavy Plex or Penta-Plex, **$546.00**. [2]Glossy finish; Matte finish, **$594.00**. [3]Glossy finish; Matte finish, **$628.00**; Heavy Plex, add **$20.00**. [4]Matte finish; Mil-Dot, **$798.00**. [5]Glossy finish; Matte finish, **$652.00**; Heavy Plex, add **$10.00**. [6]Glossy finish; Matte finish, **$816.00**; with Heavy Plex, **$830.00**; with Mil-Dot, **$978.00**. [7]Matte finish; with Mil-Dot, **$1,018.00**. [8]Matte finish; with Mil-Dot, **$1098.00**. [9]Lightseeker II, Matte finish, **$844.00**. [10]Lightseeker II, Glossy finish, **$636.00**. [11]Lightseeker II, Matte finish, **$660.00**. [12]Lightseeker II, Matte finish, **$878.00**. [13]Matte finish; Advantage finish, Break-up Mossy Oak finish, Treestand Mossy Oak finish, **$364.00**. From Pentax Corp.

Heavy Plex   **Fine Plex**   **Penta-Plex**

RWS

Maker and Model	Magn.	Field at 100 Yds. (feet)	Eye Relief (in.)	Length (in.)	Tube Dia. (in.)	W & E Adjustments	Weight (ozs.)	Price
300	4	36	3.5	11.75	1	Int.	13.2	170.00
400[1]	2-7	55-16	3.5	11.75	1	Int.	13.2	190.00
450	3-9	43-14	3.5	12	1	Int.	14.3	215.00
500	4	36	3.5	12.25	1	Int.	13.9	225.00
550	2-7	55-16	3.5	12.75	1	Int.	14.3	235.00
600	3-9	43-14	3.5	13	1	Int.	16.5	260.00

SCHMIDT & BENDER

Maker and Model	Magn.	Field at 100 Yds. (feet)	Eye Relief (in.)	Length (in.)	Tube Dia. (in.)	W & E Adjustments	Weight (ozs.)	Price
Fixed								
4x36	4	30	3.25	11	1	Int.	14	760.00
6x42	6	21	3.25	13	1	Int.	17	835.00
8x56	8	16.5	3.25	14	1	Int.	22	960.00
10x42	10	10.5	3.25	13	1	Int.	18	955.00
Variables								
1.25-4x20[5]	1.25-4	96-16	3.75	10	30mm	Int.	15.5	995.00
1.5-6x42[1,5]	1.5-6	60-19.5	3.70	12	30mm	Int.	19.7	1,125.00
2.5-10x56[1,5]	2.5-10	37.5-12	3.90	14	30mm	Int.	24.6	1,390.00
3-12x42[2]	3-12	34.5-11.5	3.90	13.5	30mm	Int.	19	1,290.00
3-12x50[1,5]	3-12	33.3-12.6	3.90	13.5	30mm	Int.	22.9	1,360.00
4-16x50 Varmint[4,6]	4-16	22.5-7.5	3.90	14	30mm	Int.	26	1,525.00
Police/Marksman II								
3-12x50[7]	3-12	33.3-12.6	3.74	13.9	34mm	Int.	18.5	1,555.00

All scopes have 30-yr. warranty, click adjustments, centered reticles, rotation indicators. [1]Glass reticle; aluminum. Available in aluminum with mounting rail. [2]Aluminum only. [3]Aluminum tube. Choice of two bullet drop compensators, choice of two sunshades, two range finding reticles. From Schmidt & Bender, Inc. [4]Parallax adjustment in third turret; extremely fine crosshairs. [5]Available with illuminated reticle that glows red; third turret houses on/off switch, dimmer and battery. 64-16x50/Long Range. [7]Also with Long Eye Relief. From Schmidt & Bender, Inc. Available with illuminated crosshairs and parallax adjustment.

Reticle No. 6   **Reticle No. 7**   **P3 Mil-Dot**

SHEPHERD

Maker and Model	Magn.	Field at 100 Yds. (feet)	Eye Relief (in.)	Length (in.)	Tube Dia. (in.)	W & E Adjustments	Weight (ozs.)	Price
310-Pl[1]	3-10	41.5-15	3-3.5	12.8	1	Int.	17	549.00
6x18x40 Varminter	6-18	5.5 (16x)	3-3.5	16.25	40mm	Int.	20.8	625.00

[1]Also avail. as 310-P1, 310-P2, 310-P3, 310-PIA, 310-PE1, 310-P22, 310-P22 Mag., 310-PE, $549.00. All have patented Dual Reticle system with range finder bullet drop compensation; multi-coated lenses, waterproof, shock-proof, nitrogen filled, matte finish. From Shepherd Scope, Ltd.

SIGHTRON

Maker and Model	Magn.	Field at 100 Yds. (feet)	Eye Relief (in.)	Length (in.)	Tube Dia. (in.)	W & E Adjustments	Weight (ozs.)	Price
Variables								
SII 1.56x42	1.5-6	50-15	3.8-4	11.69	1	Int.	15.35	259.95
SII 2.5-7x32SG[8]	2.5-7	26-7	4.3	10.9	1	Int.	8.46	199.95
SII 2.58x42	2.5-8	36-12	3.6-4.2	11.89	1	Int.	12.82	233.95
SII 39x42[4,6,7]	3-9	34-12	3.6-4.2	12.00	1	Int.	13.22	246.95
SII 312x42[6]	3-12	32-9	3.6-4.2	11.89	1	Int.	12.99	261.95
SII 3.510x42	3.5-10	32-11	3.6	11.89	1	Int.	13.16	261.95
SII 4.514x42[1]	4.5-14	22-7.9	3.6	13.88	1	Int.	16.07	340.95
Target								
SII6x42HBR	6	20	4	12.48	1	Int.	12.3	259.95
SII 24x44	24	4.1	4.33	13.30	1	Int.	15.87	279.95
SII 416x42[1,4,5,6,7]	4-16	26-7	3.6	13.62	1	Int.	16	317.95
SII 624-42[1,4,5,7]	6-24	16-5	3.6	14.6	1	Int.	18.7	334.95
SII1040x42	10-40	8.9-4	3.6	16.1	1	Int.	19	399.95

[1]Adjustable objective. [2,3]MOA dot; also with 5 or 10 MOA dot. [3]Variable 3, 5, 10 MOA dot; black finish; also stainless. [4]Satin black; also stainless. Electronic Red Dot scopes come with ring mount, front and rear extension tubes, polarizing filter, battery, haze filter caps, wrench. Rifle, pistol, shotgun scopes have aluminum tubes, Exac Trak adjustments. Lifetime warranty. From Sightron, Inc. 53" sun shade. [6]Mil Dot or Plex reticle. [7]Dot or Plex reticle. [8]Double Diamond reticle.

ACCESSORIES

SCOPES / HUNTING, TARGET & VARMINT

Maker and Model	Magn.	Field at 100 Yds. (feet)	Eye Relief (in.)	Length (in.)	Tube Dia. (in.)	W & E Adjustments	Weight (ozs.)	Price	Other Data
Compact									
SII 4x32	4	25	4.5	9.69	1	Int.	9.34	123.95	
SII2.5-10x32	2.5-10	41-10.5	3.75-3.5	10.9	1	Int.	10.39	233.95	
Shotgun									
SII 2.5x20SG	2.5	41	4.3	10.28	1	Int.	8.46	133.95	
Pistol									
SII 1x28P[4]	1	30	9-24	9.49	1	Int.	8.46	135.95	
SII 2x28P[4]	2	16-10	9-24	9.49	1	Int.	8.28	135.95	

SIMMONS

Maker and Model	Magn.	Field at 100 Yds. (feet)	Eye Relief (in.)	Length (in.)	Tube Dia. (in.)	W & E Adjustments	Weight (ozs.)	Price
AETEC								
2100[8]	2.8-10	44-14	5	11.9	1	Int.	15.5	234.99
2104[16]	3.8-12	33-11	4	13.5	1	Int.	20	259.99
44Mag								
M-1044[3]	3-10	34-10.5	3	12.75	1	Int.	15.5	179.99
M-1045[3]	4-12	29.5-9.5	3	13.2	1	Int.	18.25	278.99
M-1047[3]	6.5-20	14-.5	2.6-3.4	12.8	1	Int.	19.5	224.99
1048[3,20] (3)	6.5-20	16-5.5	2.6-3.4	14.5	1	Int.	20	259.99
M-1050DM[3,19]	3.8-12	26-9	3	13.08	1	Int.	16.75	269.99
8-Point								
4-12x40mmAO[3]	4-12	29-10	3-2 7/8	13.5	1	Int.	15.75	129.99
4x32mm[3]	4	28.75	3	11.625	1	Int.	14.25	44.99
3-9x32mm[3]	3-9	37.5-13	3-2 7/8	11.875	1	Int.	11.5	60.99
3-9x40mm[18]	3-9	37-13	3-2 7/8	12.25	1	Int.	12.25	84.99-94.99
3-9x50mm[3]	3-9	32-11.75	3-2 7/8	13	1	Int.	15.25	97.99
Prohunter								
7700	2-7	53-16.25	3	11.5	1	Int.	12.5	124.99
7710[2]	3-9	36-13	3	12.6	1	Int.	13.5	139.99
7716	4-12	26-9	3	12.6	1	Int.	16.75	159.99
7721	6-18	18.5-6	3	13.75	1	Int.	16	179.99
7740[3]	6	21.75	3	12.5	1	Int.	12	120.99
Prohunter Handgun								
7732[18]	2	22	9-17	8.75	1	Int.	7	139.99
7738[18]	4	15	11.8-17.6	8.5	1	Int.	8	149.99
Whitetail Classic								
WTC 11[4]	1.5-5	75-23	3.4-3.2	9.3	1	Int.	9.7	184.99
WTC 12[4]	2.5-8	45-14	3.2-3	11.3	1	Int.	13	199.99
WTC 13[4]	3.5-10	30-10.5	3.2-3	12.4	1	Int.	13.5	209.99
WTC 15[4]	3.5-10	29.5-11.5	3.2	12.75	1	Int.	13.5	289.99
WTC 45[4]	4.5-14	22.5-8.6	3.2	13.2	1	Int.	14	265.99
Whitetail Expedition								
1.5-6x32mm[3]	1.5-6	72-19	3	11.16	1	Int.	15	289.99
3-9x42mm[3]	3-9	40-13.5	3	13.2	1	Int.	17.5	309.99
4-12x42mm[3]	4-12	29-9.6	3	13.46	1	Int.	21.25	334.99
6-18x42mm[3]	6-18	18.3-6.5	3	15.35	1	Int.	22.5	364.99
Pro50								
8800[10]	4-12	27-9	3.5	13.2	1	Int.	18.25	219.99
8810[10]	6-18	17-5.8	3.6	13.2	1	Int.	18.25	239.99
Shotgun								
21004	4	16	5.5	8.8	1	Int.	9.1	84.99
21005	2.5	24	6	7.4	1	Int.	7	59.99
7789D	2	31	5.5	8.8	1	Int.	8.75	99.99
7790D	4	17	5.5	8.5	1	Int.	8.75	114.99
7791D	1.5-5	76-23.5	3.4	9.5	1	Int.	10.75	138.99
Rimfire								
1031[18]	4	23.5	3	7.25	1	Int.	8.25	79.99
1022[7]	4	29.5	3	11.75	1	Int.	11	69.99
1022T	3-9	42-14	3.5	11.5	1	Int.	12	166.99
1039[18]	3-9	38-13	3.3-2.9	11.6	1	Int.	13	84.99
Blackpowder								
BP0420M[17]	4	19.5	4	7.5	1	Int.	8.3	114.99
BP2732M[12]	2-7	57.7-16.6	3	11.6	1	Int.	12.4	135.99
Red Dot								
51004[21]	1	—	—	4.8	25mm	Int.	4.7	59.99
51112[22]	1	—	—	5.25	30mm	Int.	6	99.99
Pro Air Gun								
21608 A.O.	4	25	3.5	12	1	Int.	11.3	109.99
21613 A.O.	4-12	25-9	3.1-2.9	13.1	1	Int.	15.8	199.99
21619 A.O.	6-18	18-7	2.9-2.7	13.8	1	Int.	18.2	209.99

[1]Matte; also polished finish. [2]Silver; also black matte or polished. [3]Black matte finish. [4]Granite finish. [5]Camouflage. [6]Black polish. [7]With ring mounts. [8]Silver; black polish avail. [10]50mm obj.; black matte. [11]Black or silver matte. [12]75-yd. parallax; black or silver matte. [13]TV view. [14]Adj. obj. [15]Silver matte. [16]Adj. objective; 4" sunshade; black matte. [17]Octagon body; rings included; black matte or silver finish. [18]Black matte finish; also available in silver. [19]Smart reticle. [20]Target turrets. [21]With dovetail rings. [23]With 3V lithium battery, extension tube, polarizing filter, Weaver rings. **Only selected models shown.** Contact Simmons Outdoor Corp. for complete details.

SPRINGFIELD ARMORY

Maker and Model	Magn.	Field at 100 Yds. (feet)	Eye Relief (in.)	Length (in.)	Tube Dia. (in.)	W & E Adjustments	Weight (ozs.)	Price
6x40 Government Model 7.62mm[1]	6	—	3.5	13	1	Int.	14.7	379.00
4-14x70 Tactical Government Model[2]	4-14	—	3.5	14.25	1	Int.	15.8	395.00
4-14x56 1st Gen. Government Model[3]	4-14	—	3.5	14.75	30mm	Int.	23	480.00
10x56 Mil Dot Government Model[4]	10	—	3.5	14.75	30mm	Int.	28	672.00
6-20x56 Mil Dot Government Model	6-20	—	3.5	18.25	30mm	Int.	33	783.00

[1]Range finding reticle with automatic bullet drop compensator for 308 match ammo to 700 yds. [2]Range finding reticle with automatic bullet drop compensator for 223 match ammo to 700 yds. [3]Also avail. as 2nd Gen. with target knobs and adj. obj., **$549.00**; as 3rd Gen. with illuminated reticle, **$749.00**; as Mil Dot model with illuminated Target Tracking reticle, target knobs, adj. obj., **$698.00**. [4]Unlimited range finding, target knobs, adj. obj., illuminated Target Tracking green reticle. All scopes have matte black finish, internal bubble level, 1/4-MOA clicks. From Springfield, Inc.

ACCESSORIES

SCOPES / HUNTING, TARGET & VARMINT

Maker and Model	Magn.	Field at 100 Yds. (feet)	Eye Relief (in.)	Length (in.)	Tube Dia. (in.)	W & E Adjustments	Weight (ozs.)	Price	Other Data
STEINER									Waterproof, fogproof, nitrogen filled. [1]Heavy-Duplex, Duplex or European #4 reticle. Aluminum tubes; matte black finish. From Pioneer Research.
Hunting Z									
1.5-5x20[1]	1.5-5	32-12	4.3	9.6	30mm	Int.	11.7	1,399.00	
2.5-8x36[1]	2.5-8	40-15	4	11.6	30mm	Int.	13.4	1,599.00	
3.5-10x50[1]	3.5-10	77-25	4	12.4	30mm	Int.	16.9	1,799.00	
SWAROVSKI OPTIK									[1]Aluminum tubes; special order for steel. [2]Also with 56mm obj., **$1,398.89**. [3]Also available with illuminated reticle. [4]Aluminum only. Partial listing shown. Imported from Austria by Swarovski Optik.
PF Series									
8x50[1,3]	8	17	3.15	13.9	30mm	Int.	21.5	987.78	
8x56[1,3]	8	17	3.15	14.29	30mm	Int.	24	1,054.44	
PH Series									
1.25-4x24[1]	1.25-4	98.4-31.2	3.15	10.63	30mm	Int.	16.2	1,087.78	
1.5-6x42[1]	1.5-6	65.4-21	3.15	12.99	30mm	Int.	20.8	1,221.11	
2.5-10x42[1,2]	2.5-10	39.6-12.6	3.15	13.23	30mm	Int.	19.8	1,376.67	
3-12x50[1]	3-12	33-10.5	3.15	14.33	30mm	Int.	22.4	1,421.11	
4-16x50	4-16	30-8.5	3.15	14.22	30mm	Int.	22.3	1,476.67	
6-24x50	6-24	18.6-5.4	3.15	15.4	30mm	Int.	23.6	1,687.78	
A-Line Series									
3-9x36AV[4]	3-9	39-13.5	3.35	11.8	1	Int.	11.7	743.33	
3-10x42AV[4]	3-10	33-11.7	3.35	12.44	1	Int.	12.7	821.11	
4-12x50AV[4]	4-12	29.1-9.9	3.35	13.5	1	Int.	13.9	843.33	

No. 1   No. 1A   No. 2   No. 4   No. 4A   No. 7A

Maker and Model	Magn.	Field at 100 Yds. (feet)	Eye Relief (in.)	Length (in.)	Tube Dia. (in.)	W & E Adjustments	Weight (ozs.)	Price	Other Data
SWIFT									All Swift scopes, with the exception of the 4x15, have Quadraplex reticles and are fogproof and waterproof. The 4x15 has crosshair reticle and is non-waterproof. [1]Available in regular matte black or silver finish. [2]Comes with ring mounts, wrench, lens caps, extension tubes, filter, battery. [3]Regular and matte black finish. [4]Speed Focus scopes. Partial listing shown. From Swift Instruments.
600 4x15	4	17	2.8	10.6	.75	Int.	3.5	15.00	
601 3-7x20	3-7	25-12	3-2.9	11	.75	Int.	5.6	35.00	
650 4x32	4	26	4	12	1	Int.	9.1	75.00	
653 4x40WA[1]	4	35	4	12.2	1	Int.	12.6	125.00	
654 3-9x32	3-9	35-12	3.4-2.9	12	1	Int.	9.8	125.00	
656 3-9x40WA[1]	3-9	40-14	3.4-2.8	12.6	1	Int.	12.3	140.00	
657 6x40	6	28	4	12.6	1	Int.	10.4	125.00	
658 2-7x40WA[3]	2-7	55-18	3.3-3	11.6	1	Int.	12.5	160.00	
659 3.5-10x44WA	3.5-10	34-12	3-2.8	12.8	1	Int.	13.5	230.00	
665 1.5-4.5x21	1.5-4.5	69-24.5	3.5-3	10.9	1	Int.	9.6	125.00	
665M 1.5-4.5x21	1.5-4.5	69-24.5	3.5-3	10.9	1	Int.	9.6	125.00	
666M Shotgun 1x20	1	113	3.2	7.5	1	Int.	9.6	130.00	
667 Fire-Fly[2]	1	40	—	5.4	30mm	Int.	5	220.00	
668M 4x32	4	25	4	10	1	Int.	8.9	120.00	
669M 6-18x44	6-18	18-6.5	2.8	14.5	1	Int.	17.6	220.00	
Premier[4]									
649R 4-12x50WA[3]	4-12	29.5-9.5	3.2-3	13.8	1	Int.	17.8	245.00	
671M 3-9x50WA	3-9	35-12	3.24-3.12	15.5	1	Int.	18.2	250.00	
672M 6-18x50WA	6-18	19.4-6.7	3.25-3	15.8	1	Int.	20.9	260.00	
673M 2.5-10x50WA	2.5-10	33-9	4-3.5	11.8	30mm	Int.	18.9	295.00	
674M 3-5x40WA	3-9	40-14.2	3.6-2.9	12	1	Int.	13.1	170.00	
676 4-12x40WA[1]	4-12	29.3-10.5	3.15-2.9	12.4	1	Int.	15.4	180.00	
Pistol									
679M 1.25-4x28	1.25-4	23-9	23-15	9.3	1	Int.	8.2	250.00	
Pistol Scopes									
661 4x32	4	90	10-22	9.2	1	Int.	9.5	130.00	
663 2x20[1]	2	18.3	9-21	7.2	1	Int.	8.4	130.00	
TASCO									[1]Water, fog & shockproof; fully coated optics; .25-min. click stops; haze filter caps; 30-day/limited lifetime warranty. [2]30/30 range finding reticle. [3]Fits most popular auto pistols, MP5, AR-15/M16. [4]1/3 greater zoom range. [5]Trajectory compensating scopes, Opti-Centered® stadia reticle. [6]Black gloss or stainless. [7]True one-power scope. [8]Coated optics; crosshair reticle; ring mounts included to fit most 22, 10mm receivers. [9]Red dot; also with switchable red/green dot (EZ02, **$42.05**). [10]Also matte aluminum finish. [11]11-position rheostat, 10-MOA dot; built-in dovetail-style mount. Also with crosshair reticle. [12]Also 30/30 reticle. [13]Also in stainless finish. [14]Black matte or stainless finish. [15]Also with stainless finish. [16]Also in matte black. [17]Available with 5-min., or 10-min. dot. [18]Red dot device; can be used on rifles, shotguns, handguns; 3.5 or 7 MOA dot. Available with 10, 15, 20-min. dot. [19]20mm; also 32mm. [20]20mm; black matte; also stainless steel; also 32mm. [21]Pro-Shot reticle. [22]Has 4, 8, 12, 16MOA dots (switchable). [23]Available with BDC. **Contact Tasco for details on complete line.**
Mag IV									
W312x40[1,2,4]	3-12	35-9	3	12.25	1	Int.	12	89.99	
W416x40[1,2,4,13,14]	4-16	26-7	3	14.25	1	Int.	15.6	124.99	
W416x50	4-16	31-8	4	13.5	1	Int.	16	124.99	
DW520x50[23]	5-20	24-6	4	13.5	1	Int.	16	189.99	
Golden Antler									
DMGA4x32TV	4	32	3	13	1	Int.	12.7	34.99	
DMGA39x32TV[1]	3-9	39-13	3	—	1	Int.	12.2	49.99	
DMGA39x40TV	3-9	39-13	3	12.5	1	Int.	13	69.99	
Silver Antler									
DMSA4x40	4	32	3	12	1	Int.	12.5	39.99	
DMSA39x32	3-9	39-13	3	13.25	1	Int.	12.2	49.99	
DMSA39x40WA[10]	3-9	41-15	3	12.75	1	Int.	13	69.99	
Pronghorn									
PH4x32	4	32	3	12	1	Int.	12.5	29.99	
PH39x32	3-9	39-13	3	12	1	Int.	11	34.99	
PH39x40	3-9	39-13	3	13	1	Int.	12.1	44.99	
Bantam									
S1.5-45x20A[19,21]	1.5-4.5	69.5-23	4	10.25	1	Int.	10	54.99	
S1.54x32A[21]	1.5-4.5	69.5-23	4	11.25	1	Int.	12	54.99	
S2.5x20A[20,21]	2.5	22	6	7.5	1	Int.	7.5	44.99	
SA2.5x32A	2.5	32	6	8.5	1	Int.	8.5	44.99	
Airgun									
AG4x32N	4	30	3	—	1	Int.	12.25	84.99	
Rimfire									
RF4x15[8]	4	22.5	2.5	11	.75	Int.	4	6.99	
RF4x20WA	4	23	2.5	10.5	.75	Int.	3.8	9.99	
RF4x32[16]	4	31	3	12.25	1	Int.	12.6	29.99	

ACCESSORIES

Maker and Model	Magn.	Field at 100 Yds. (feet)	Eye Relief (in.)	Length (in.)	Tube Dia. (in.)	W & E Adjustments	Weight (ozs.)	Price	Other Data
RF37x20	3-7	24-11	2.5	11.5	.75	Int.	5.7	19.99	
Propoint									
PDP2[10, 17]	1	40	Unltd.	5	30mm	Int.	5	109.99	
PDP3[10, 17]	1	52	Unltd.	5	30mm	Int.	5	129.99	
PDP3CMP	1	68	Unltd.	4.75	33mm	Int.	—	144.99	
PDP5CMP[22]	1	82	Unltd.	4	47mm	Int.	8	204.99	
Optima 2000									
OPP2000-3.5[3, 20]	1	—	—	1.5	—	Int.	1/2	249.99	
OPP2000-7[3, 20]	1	—	—	1.5	—	Int.	1.2	249.99	
Pistol Scopes									
PX20[10]	2	21	10-23	8	1	Int.	6.5	69.99	
P1.254x28[10]	1.25-4	23-9	15-23	9.25	1	Int.	8.2	109.99	
Tactical & Target									
TAC840x56M	8-40	11.5-2.6	3	16	30mm	Int.	31.5	734.99	
EZ01	1	35	—	4.75	1	Int.	2.5	19.99	
World Class Plus									
WCP4x44	4	32	3.25	12.75	1	Int.	13.5	249.55	
WCP3.510x50[18]	3.5-10	30-10.5	3.75	13	1	Int.	17.1	159.99	
WCP39x44[1,16]	3-9	39-14	3.5	12.75	1	Int.	15.8	154.99	
WCP416x40	4-16	26-7	3	14.25	1	Int.	16.8	244.99	
WCP624x40	6-24	17.4	3	15.5	1	Int.	17.5	254.99	

THOMPSON/CENTER RECOIL PROOF SERIES

Maker and Model	Magn.	Field at 100 Yds. (feet)	Eye Relief (in.)	Length (in.)	Tube Dia. (in.)	W & E Adjustments	Weight (ozs.)	Price	Other Data
Pistol Scopes									[1]Black finish; silver optional. [2]Black; lighted reticle. From Thompson/Center Arms.
8315[2]	2.5-7	15-5	8-21, 8-11	9.25	1	Int.	9.2	308.99	
8326[4]	2.5-7	15-5	8-21, 8-11	9.25	1	Int.	10.5	360.49	
Muzzleloader Scopes									
8658	1	60	3.8	9.125	1	Int.	10.2	125.99	
8662	4	16	3	8.8	1	Int.	9.1	125.99	

TRIJICON

Maker and Model	Magn.	Field at 100 Yds. (feet)	Eye Relief (in.)	Length (in.)	Tube Dia. (in.)	W & E Adjustments	Weight (ozs.)	Price	Other Data
ReflexII 1x24	1	—	—	4.25	1	Int.	4.6	379.00	[1]Advanced Combat Optical Gunsight for AR-15, M16, with intergral mount. Other mounts available. All models feature tritium and fiber optics dual lighting system that requires no batteries. From Trijicon, Inc.
TA44 1.5x16[1]	1.5	43.8	2.4	4.1	—	Int.	3.5	695.00	
TA45 1.5x24[1]	1.5	28.9	3.6	5.6	—	Int.	3.9	675.00	
TA47 2x20[1]	2	33.1	2.1	4.5	—	Int.	3.8	695.00	
TA50 3x24[1]	3	28.9	1.4	4.8	—	Int.	3.9	695.00	
TA11 3.5x35[1]	3.5	28.9	2.4	8	—	Int.	14	1,295.00	
TAO1 4x32[1]	4	36.8	1.5	5.8	—	Int.	9.9	895.00	
Variable AccuPoint									
3-9x40	3-9	—	3.2-3.6	12.2	1	Int.	12.8	699.00	
1.25-4x24	1.25-4	61.6-20.5	3.4-4.8	10.2	1	Int.	11.4	599.00	

ULTRA DOT

Maker and Model	Magn.	Field at 100 Yds. (feet)	Eye Relief (in.)	Length (in.)	Tube Dia. (in.)	W & E Adjustments	Weight (ozs.)	Price	Other Data
Micro-Dot Scopes[1]									[1]Brightness-adjustable fiber optic red dot reticle. Waterproof, nitrogen-filled one-piece tube. Tinted see-through lens covers and battery included. [2]Parallax adjustable. [3]Ultra Dot sights include rings, battery, polarized filter, and 5-year warranty. All models available in black or satin finish. [4]Illuminated red dot has eleven brightness settings. Shock-proof aluminum tube. From Ultra Dot Distribution.
1.5-4.5x20 Rifle	1.5-4.5	80-26	3	9.8	1	Int.	10.5	297.00	
2-7x32	2-7	54-18	3	11	1	Int.	12.1	308.00	
3-9x40	3-9	40-14	3	12.2	1	Int.	13.3	327.00	
4x-12x56[2]	4-12	30-10	3	14.3	1	Int.	18.3	417.00	
Ultra-Dot Sights[3]									
Ultra-Dot 25[4]	1	—	—	5.1	1	Int.	3.9	159.00	
Ultra-Dot 30[4]	1	—	—	5.1	30mm	Int.	4	179.00	

UNERTL

Maker and Model	Magn.	Field at 100 Yds. (feet)	Eye Relief (in.)	Length (in.)	Tube Dia. (in.)	W & E Adjustments	Weight (ozs.)	Price	Other Data
1" Target	6, 8, 10	16-10	2	21.5	.75	Ext.	21	358.00	[1]Dural .25-MOA click mounts. Hard coated lenses. Non-rotating objective lens focusing. [2].25-MOA click mounts. [3]With target mounts. [4]With calibrated head. [5]Same as 1" Target but without objective lens focusing. [6]With new Posa mounts. [7]Range focus unit near rear of tube. Price is with Posa or standard mounts. Magnum clamp. From Unertl.
1.25: Target[1]	8, 10, 12, 14	12-16	2	25	.75	Ext.	21	466.00	
1.5" Target	10, 12, 14, 16, 18, 20	11.5-3.2	2.25	25.5	.75	Ext.	31	487.00	
2" Target[2]	10, 12, 14, 16, 18, 24, 30, 32, 36,	8	2.25	26.25	1	Ext.	44	642.00	
Varmint, 1.25"[3]	6, 8, 10, 12, 8, 10, 12,	1-7	2.50	19.50	.875	Ext.	26	466.00	
Ultra Varmint, 2"[4]	15	12.6-7	2.25	24	1	Ext.	34	630.00	
Small Game[5]	3, 4, 6	25-17	2.25	18	.75	Ext.	16	284.00	
Programmer 200[7]	10, 12, 14, 16, 18, 20, 24, 30, 36	11.3-4	—	26.5	1	Ext.	45	805.00	
BV-20[8]	2	8	4.4	17.875	1	Ext.	21.25	595.00	
Tube Sight	—	—	—	17	—	Ext.	—	262.50	

U.S. OPTICS

Maker and Model	Magn.	Field at 100 Yds. (feet)	Eye Relief (in.)	Length (in.)	Tube Dia. (in.)	W & E Adjustments	Weight (ozs.)	Price	Other Data
SN-1/TAR Fixed Power System									Prices shown are estimates; scopes built to order; choice of reticles; choice of front or rear focal plane; extra-heavy MIL-SPEC construction; extra-long turrets; individual w&e rebound springs; up to 100mm dia. objectives; up to 50mm tubes; all lenses multi-coated. Other magnifications available. [1]Modular components allow a variety of fixed or variable magnifications, night vision, etc. Made in U.S. by U.S. Optics.
16.2x	15	8.6	4.3	16.5	30mm	Int.	27	1,700.00	
22.4x	20	5.8	3.8	18	30mm	Int.	29	1,800.00	
26x	24	5	3.4	18	30mm	Int.	31	1,900.00	
31x	30	4.6	3.5	18	30mm	Int.	32	2,100.00	
37x	36	4	3.6	18	30mm	Int.	32	2,300.00	
48x	50	3	3.8	18	30mm	Int.	32	2,500.00	
Variables									
SN-2	4-22	26.8-5.8	5.4-3.8	18	30mm	Int.	24	1,762.00	
SN-3	1.6-8	—	4.4-4.8	18.4	30mm	Int.	36	1,435.00	

ACCESSORIES

Maker and Model	Magn.	Field at 100 Yds. (feet)	Eye Relief (in.)	Length (in.)	Tube Dia. (in.)	W & E Adjustments	Weight (ozs.)	Price	Other Data
SN-4	1-4	116-31.2	4.6-4.9	18	30mm	Int.	35	1,065.00	
Fixed Power									
SN-6	8, 10, 17, 22	14-8.5	3.8-4.8	9.2	30mm	Int.	18	1,195.00	
SN-8 Modular[1]	4, 10, 20, 40	32	3.3	7.5	30mm	Int.	11.1	890.00- 4,000.00	

WEAVER

Riflescopes

Maker and Model	Magn.	Field at 100 Yds. (feet)	Eye Relief (in.)	Length (in.)	Tube Dia. (in.)	W & E Adjustments	Weight (ozs.)	Price
K2.5[1]	2.5	35	3.7	9.5	1	Int.	7.3	179.99
K4[1-2]	3.7	26.5	3.3	11.3	1	Int.	10	194.99
K6[1]	5.7	18.5	3.3	11.4	1	Int.	10	194.99
KT15[1]	14.6	7.5	3.2	12.9	1	Int.	14.7	374.99
V3[1-2]	1.1-2.8	88-32	3.9-3.7	9.2	1	Int.	8.5	299.99
V9[1-2]	2.8-8.7	33-11	3.5-3.4	12.1	1	Int.	11.1	249.99- 299.99
V9x50[1-2]	3-9	29.4-9.9	3.6-3	13.1	1	Int.	14.5	319.99
V10[1-2-3]	2.2-9.6	38.5-9.5	3.4-3.3	12.2	1	Int.	11.2	259.99- 269.99
V10-50[1-2-3]	2.3-9.7	40.2-9.2	2.9-2.8	13.75	1	Int.	15.2	365.99
V16 MDX[2-3]	3.8-15.5	26.8-6.8	3.1	13.9	1	Int.	16.5	434.99
V16 MFC[2-3]	3.8-15.5	26.8-6.8	3.1	13.9	1	Int.	16.5	434.99
V16 MDT[2-3]	3.8-15.5	26.8-6.8	3.1	13.9	1	Int.	16.5	434.99
V24 Varmint[2]	6-24	15.3-4	3.15	14.3	1	Int.	17.5	509.99
Handgun								
H2[1-3]	2	21	4-29	8.5	1	Int.	6.7	212.99- 224.99
H4[1-3]	4	18	11.5-18	8.5	1	Int.	6.7	234.99
VH4[1-3]	1.5-4	13.6-5.8	11-17	8.6	1	Int.	8.1	289.99
VH8[1-2-3]	2.5-8	8.5-3.7	12.16	9.3	1	Int.	8.3	299.99
Rimfire								
R4[2-3]	3.9	29	3.9	9.7	1	Int.	8.8	159.99
RV7[2]	2.5-7	37-13	3.7-3.3	10.75	1	Int.	10.7	184.99- 189.99
Grand Slam								
6-20x40mm Varminter Reticle[2]	6-20X	16.5-5.25	2.75-3	14.48	1	Int.	17.75	499.99
6-20x40mm Fine Crosshairs with a Dot[2]	6-20X	16.5-5.25	2.75-3	14.48	1	Int.	17.75	499.99
1.5-5x32mm[2]	1.5-5X	71-21	3.25	10.5	1	Int.	10.5	429.99
4.75x40mm[2]	4.75X	14.75	3.25	11	1	Int.	10.75	359.99
3-10x40mm[2]	3-10X	35-11.33	3.5-3	12.08	1	Int.	12.08	379.99
3.5-10x50mm[2]	3.5-10X	30.5-10.8	3.5-3	12.96	1	Int.	16.25	459.99
4.5-14x40mm	4.5-14X	22.5-10.5	3.5-3	14.48	1	Int.	17.5	499.99
T-Series								
T-6[4]	614	14	3.58	12.75	1	Int.	14.9	424.95
T-36[3-4]	36	3	3	15.1	1	Int.	16.7	794.99

[1]Gloss black, [2]Matte black, [3]Silver, [4]Satin, [5]Silver and black (slightly higher in price). [6]Field of view measured at 18" eye relief..25 MOA click adjustments, except T-Series which vary from .125 to .25 clicks. One-piece tubes with multi-coated lenses. All scopes are shock-proof, water-proof, and fogproof. Dual-X reticle available in all except V24 which has a fine X-hair and ot; T-Series in which certain models are available in fine X-hair and dots; Qwik-Point red dot scopes which are available in fixed 4 or 12 MOA, or variable 4-8-12 MOA. V16 also available with fine X-hair, dot or Dual-X reticle. T-Series scopes have Micro-Trac® adjustments. From Weaver Products.

ZEISS

ZM/Z

Maker and Model	Magn.	Field at 100 Yds. (feet)	Eye Relief (in.)	Length (in.)	Tube Dia. (in.)	W & E Adjustments	Weight (ozs.)	Price
6x42MC	6	22.9	3.2	12.7	1	Int.	13.4	749.00
8x56MC	8	18	3.2	13.8	1	Int.	17.6	829.00
1.25-4x24MC	1.25-4	105-33	3.2	11.46	30mm	Int.	17.3	779.00
1.5-6x42MC	1.5-6	65.5-22.9	3.2	12.4	30mm	Int.	18.5	899.00
2.5-10x48MC[1]	2.5-10	33-11.7	3.2	14.5	30mm	Int.	24	1,029.00
3-12x56MC[1]	3-12	27.6-9.9	3.2	15.3	30mm	Int.	25.8	1,099.00
Conquest								
3-9x36MC	3-9	34-11	4	13.15	1	Int.	15	499.00
VM/V								
1.1-4x24 VariPoint T[2]	1.1-4	120-34	3.5	11.8	30mm	Int.	15.8	1,799.00
1.5-6x42T*	1.5-6	65.5-22.9	3.2	12.4	30mm	Int.	18.5	1,349.00
2.5-10x50T*[1]	2.5-10	47.1-13	3.5	12.5	30mm	Int.	16.25	1,549.00
3-12x56T*	3-12	37.5-10.5	3.5	13.5	30mm	Int.	19.5	1,599.00
3-9x42T*	3-9	42-15	3.74	13.3	1	Int.	15.3	1,249.00
5-15x42T*	5-15	25.7-8.5	3.74	13.3	1	Int.	15.4	1,499.00

[1]Also avail. with illuminated reticle. [2]Illuminated Vari-point reticle. Black matte finish. All scopes have .25-min. click-stop adjustments. Choice of Z-Plex or fine crosshair reticles. Rubber armored objective bell, rubber eyepiece ring. Lenses have T-Star coating for highest light transmission. VM/V scopes avail. with rail mount. Partial listing shown. From Carl Zeiss Optical, Inc.

Hunting scopes in general are furnished with a choice of reticle—crosshairs, post with crosshairs, tapered or blunt post, or dot crosshairs, etc. The great majority of target and varmint scopes have medium or fine crosshairs but post or dot reticles may be ordered. W—Windage E—Elevation MOA—Minute of Angle or 1" (approx.) at 100 yards.

LASER SIGHTS

Lasergrips LG-206

Alpec Mini Shot

Laser Devices ULS 2001 with TLS 8R light

Maker and Model	Wavelength (nm)	Beam Color	Lens	Operating Temp. (degrees F.)	Weight (ozs.)	Price	Other Data
ALPEC							[1]Range 1000 yards. [2]Range 300 yards. Mini Shot II range 500 yards, output 650mm, **$129.95**. [3]Range 300 yards; Laser Shot II 500 yards; Super Laser Shot 1000 yards. Black or stainless finish aluminum; removable pressure or push-button switch. Mounts for most handguns, many rifles and shotguns. From Alpec Team, Inc.
Power Shot[1]	635	Red	Glass	NA	2.5	$199.95	
Mini Shot[2]	670	Red	Glass	NA	2.5	99.95	
Laser Shot[3]	670	Red	Glass	NA	3.0	99.95	
BEAMSHOT							[1]Black or silver finish; adj. for windage and elevation; 300-yd. range; also M1000/S (500-yd. range), M1000/u (800-yd.). [2]Black finish; 300-, 500-, 800-yd. models. All come with removable touch pad switch, 5" cable. Mounts to fit virtually any firearm. From Quarton USA Co.
1000[1]	670	Red	Glass	—	3.8	NA	
3000[2]	635/670	Red	Glass	—	2	NA	
1001/u	635	Red	Glass	—	3.8	NA	
780	780	Red	Glass	—	3.8	NA	
BSA							[1]Comes with mounts for 22/air rifle and Weaver-style bases.
LS650[1]	N/A	Red	N/A	N/A	N/A	49.95	
LASERAIM							[1]Red dot/laser combo; 300-yd. range: LA3xHD Hotdot has 500-yd. range **$249.00**; 4 MOA dot size, laser gives 2" dot size at 100 yds. [2]30mm obj. lens: 4 MOA dot at 100 yds: fits Weaver base. [3]300-yd range; 2" dot at 100 yds.; rechargeable Nicad battery [4]1.5-mile range; 1" dot at 100 yds.; 20+ hrs. batt. life. [5]1.5-mile range; 1" dot at 100 yds; rechargeable Nicad battery (comes with in-field charger); [6]Black or satin finish. With mount, **$169.00**. [7]Laser projects 2" dot at 100 yds.: with rotary switch; with Hotdot **$237.00**; with Hotdot touch switch **$357.00**. [8]For Glock 17-27; G1 Hotdot **$299.00**; price installed. [10]Fits std. Weaver base, no rings required; 6-MOA dot; seven brightness settings. All have w&e adj.; black or satin silver finish. From Laseraim Technologies, Inc.
LA10 Hotdot[4]	—	—	—	—	NA	199.00	
Lasers							
MA-35RB Mini Aimer[7]	—	—	—	—	1.0	129.00	
G1 Laser[8]	—	—	—	—	2.0	229.00	
LASER DEVICES							[1]For S&W P99 semi-auto pistols; also BA-2, 5 oz., **$339.00**. [2]For revolvers. [3]For HK, Walther P99. [4]For semi-autos. [5]For rifles; also FA-4/ULS, 2.5 oz., **$325.00**. [6]For HK sub guns. [7]For military rifles. [8]For shotguns. [9]For SIG-Pro pistol. [10]Universal, semi-autos. [11]For AR-15 variants. All avail. with Magnum Power Point (650nM) or daytime-visible Super Power Point (632nM) diode. Infrared diodes avail. for law enforcement. From Laser Devices, Inc.
BA-1[1]	632	Red	Glass	—	2.4	372.00	
BA-3[2]	632	Red	Glass	—	3.3	332.50	
BA-5[3]	632	Red	Glass	—	3.2	372.00	
Duty-Grade[4]	632	Red	Glass	—	3.5	372.00	
FA-4[5]	632	Red	Glass	—	2.6	358.00	
LasTac[1]	632	Red	Glass	—	5.5	298.00 to 477.00	
MP-5[6]	632	Red	Glass	—	2.2	495.00	
MR-2[7]	632	Red	Glass	—	6.3	485.00	
SA-2[8]	632	Red	Glass	—	3.0	360.00	
SIG-Pro[9]	632	Red	Glass	—	2.6	372.00	
ULS-2001[10]	632	Red	Glass	—	4.5	210.95	
Universal AR-2A	632	Red	Glass	—	4.5	445.00	
LASERGRIPS							Replaces existing grips with built-in laser high in the right grip panel. Integrated pressure sensitive pad in grip activates the laser. Also has master on/off switch. [1]For Colt 1911/Commander. [2]For all Glock models. Option on/off switch. Requires factory installation. [3]For S&W K, L, N frames, round or square butt (LG-207); [4]For Taurus small-frame revolvers. [5]For Ruger SP-101. [6]For SIG Sauer P226. From Crimson Trace Corp. [7]For Beretta 92/96. [8]For Ruger MK II. [9]For S&W J-frame. [10]For Sig Sauer P228/229. [11]For Colt 1911 full size, wraparound. [12]For Beretta 92/96, wraparound. [13]For Colt 1911 compact, wraparound. [14]For S&W J-frame, rubber.
LG-201[1]	633	Red-Orange	Glass	NA	—	299.00	
LG-206[3]	633	Red-Orange	Glass	NA	—	229.00	
LG-085[4]	633	Red-Orange	Glass	NA	—	229.00	
LG-101[5]	633	Red-Orange	Glass	NA	—	229.00	
LG-226[6]	633	Red-Orange	Glass	NA	—	229.00	
GLS-630[2]	633	Red-Orange	Glass	NA	—	595.00	
LG202[7]	633	Red-Orange	Glass	NA	—	299.00	
LG203[8]	633	Red-Orange	Glass	NA	—	299.00	
LG205[9]	633	Red-Orange	Glass	NA	—	299.00	
LG229[10]	633	Red-Orange	Glass	NA	—	299.00	
LG301[11]	633	Red-Orange	Glass	NA	—	329.00	
LG302[12]	633	Red-Orange	Glass	NA	—	329.00	
LG304[13]	633	Red-Orange	Glass	NA	—	329.00	
LG305[14]	633	Red-Orange	Glass	NA	—	299.00	
LASERLYTE							[1]Dot/circle or dot/crosshair projection; black or stainless. [2]Also 635/645mm model. From TacStar Laserlyte.
LLX-0006-140/090[1]	635/645	Red	—	—	1.4	159.95	
WPL-0004-140/090[2]	670	Red	—	—	1.2	109.95	
TPL-0004-140/090[2]	670	Red	—	—	1.2	109.95	
T7S-0004-140[2]	670	Red	—	—	0.8	109.95	
LASERMAX							Replaces the recoil spring guide rod; includes a customized takedown lever that serves as the laser's instant on/off switch. For Glock, Smith & Wesson, Sigarms, Beretta and select Taurus models. Installs in most pistols without gunsmithing. Battery life 1/2 hour to 2 hours in continuous use. From LaserMax.
LMS-1000 Internal Guide Rod	635	Red-Orange	Glass	40-120	.25	389.00	
NIGHT STALKER							Waterproof; LCD panel displays power remaining; programmable blink rate; constant or memory on. From Wilcox Industries Corp.
S0 Smart	635	Red	NA	NA	2.46	515.00	

Maker, Model, Type	Adjust.	Scopes	Price
AIMTECH			
Handguns			
AMT Auto Mag II .22 Mag.	No	Weaver rail	$56.99
Astra .44 Mag Revolver	No	Weaver rail	63.25
Beretta/Taurus 92/99	No	Weaver rail	63.25
Browning Buckmark/Challenger II	No	Weaver rail	56.99
Browning Hi-Power	No	Weaver rail	63.25
Glock 17, 17L, 19, 23, 24 etc. no rail	No	Weaver rail	63.25
Glock 20, 21 no rail	No	Weaver rail	63.25
Glock 9mm and .40 with access. rail	No	Weaver rail	74.95
Govt. 45 Auto/.38 Super	No	Weaver rail	63.25
Hi-Standard (Mitchell version) 107	No	Weaver rail	63.25
H&K USP 9mm/40 rail mount	No	Weaver rail	74.95
Rossi 85/851/951 Revolvers	No	Weaver rail	63.25
Ruger Mk I, Mk II	No	Weaver rail	49.95
Ruger P85/P89	No	Weaver rail	63.25
S&W K, L, N frames	No	Weaver rail	63.25
S&W K. L, N with tapped top strap*	No	Weaver rail	69.95
S&W Model 41 Target 22	No	Weaver rail	63.25
S&W Model 52 Target 38	No	Weaver rail	63.25
S&W Model 99 Walther frame rail mount	No	Weaver rail	74.95
S&W 2nd Gen. 59/459/659 etc.	No	Weaver rail	56.99
S&W 3rd Gen. full size 5906 etc.	No	Weaver rail	69.95
S&W 422, 622, 2206	No	Weaver rail	56.99
S&W 645/745	No	Weaver rail	56.99
S&W Sigma	No	Weaver rail	64.95
Taurus PT908	No	Weaver rail	63.25
Taurus 44 6.5" bbl.	No	Weaver rail	69.95
Walther 99	No	Weaver rail	74.95
Shotguns			
Benelli M-1 Super 90**	No	Weaver rail	44.95
Benelli Montefeltro	No	Weaver rail	44.95
Benelli Nova**	No	Weaver rail	69.95
Benelli Super Black Eagle**	No	Weaver rail	49.95
Browning A-5 12-ga.	No	Weaver rail	40.95
Browning BPS 12-ga.	No	Weaver rail	40.95
Browning Gold Hunter 12-ga.	No	Weaver rail	44.95
Browning Gold Hunter 20-ga.	No	Weaver rail	49.95
Browning Gold Hunter 10-ga.	No	Weaver rail	49.95
Beretta 303 12-ga.	No	Weaver rail	44.95
Beretta 390 12-ga.**	No	Weaver rail	44.95
Beretta Pintail	No	Weaver rail	44.95
H&K Fabarms Gold/SilverLion	no	Weaver rail	49.95
Ithaca 37/87 12-ga.**	No	Weaver rail	40.95
Ithaca 37/87 20-ga.**	No	Weaver rail	40.95
Mossberg 500/Maverick 12-ga.**	No	Weaver rail	40.95
Mossberg 500/Maverick 20-ga.**	No	Weaver rail	40.95
Mossberg 835 3.5" Ulti-Mag**	No	Weaver rail	40.95
Mossberg 5500/9200	No	Weaver rail	40.95
Remington 1100/1187 12-ga.**	No	Weaver rail	40.95
Remington 1100/1187 12-ga. LH	No	Weaver rail	40.95
Remington 1100/1187 20-ga.**	No	Weaver rail	40.95
Remington 1100/1187 20-ga. LH	No	Weaver rail	40.95
Remington 870 12-ga.**	No	Weaver rail	40.95
Remington 870 12-ga. LH	No	Weaver rail	40.95
Remington 870 20-ga.**	No	Weaver rail	40.95
Remington 870 20-ga. LH	No	Weaver rail	40.95
Remington 870 Express Magnum**	No	Weaver rail	40.95
Remington SP-10 10-ga.**	No	Weaver rail	49.95
Winchester 1300 12-ga.**	No	Weaver rail	40.95
Winchester 1400 12-ga.**	No	Weaver rail	40.95
Winchester Super X2	No	Weaver rail	44.95
Rifles			
AR-15/M16	No	Weaver rail	21.95
Browning A-Bolt	No	Weaver rail	21.95
Browning BAR	No	Weaver rail	21.95
Browning BLR	No	Weaver rail	21.95
CVA Apollo	No	Weaver rail	21.95
Marlin 336	No	Weaver rail	21.95
Mauser Mark X	No	Weaver rail	21.95
Modern Muzzleloading	No	Weaver rail	21.95
Remington 700 Short Action	No	Weaver rail	21.95
Remington 700 Long Action	No	Weaver rail	21.95
Remington 7400/7600	No	Weaver rail	21.95
Ruger 10/22	No	Weaver rail	21.95
Ruger Mini 14 Scout Rail***	No	Weaver rail	89.50
Savage 110, 111, 113, 114, 115, 116	No	Weaver rail	21.95
Thompson Center Thunderhawk	No	Weaver rail	21.95
Traditions Buckhunter	No	Weaver rail	21.95
White W Series	No	Weaver rail	21.95
White G Series	No	Weaver rail	21.95
White WG Series	No	Weaver rail	21.95
Winchester Model 70	No	Weaver rail	21.95
Winchester 94 AE	No	Weaver rail	21.95

Maker, Model, Type	Adjust.	Scopes	Price
AIMTECH (cont.)			
All mounts no-gunsmithing, iron sight usable. Rifle mounts are solid see-through bases. All mounts accommodate standard Weaver-style rings of all makers. From Aimtech division, L&S Technologies, Inc. *3-blade sight mount combination. **These models available exclusively in Realtree or Advantage camo patterns. ***Replacement handguard and mounting rail.			
A.R.M.S.			
M16A1,A2,AR-15	No	Weaver rail	$59.95
Multibase	No	Weaver rail	59.95
#19 ACOG Throw Lever Mt.	No	Weaver rail	150.00
#19 Weaver/STANAG Throw Lever Rail	No	Weaver rail	140.00
STANAG Rings	No	30mm	75.00
Throw Lever Rings	No	Weaver rail	99.00
Ring Inserts	No	1", 30mm	29.00
#22M68 Aimpoint Comp	No	Weaver rail	89.00
Ring Throw Lever			
#38 Std. Swan Sleeve[1]	No	—	180.00
#39 A2 Plus Mod. Mt.	No	#39T rail	125.00
[1]Avail. in three lengths. From A.R.M.S., Inc.			
ARMSON			
AR-15[1]	No	1"	45.00
Mini-14[2]	No	1"	66.00
H&K[3]	No	1"	82.00
[1]Fastens with one nut. [2]Models 181, 182, 183, 184, etc. [3]Claw mount. From Trijicon, Inc.			
ARMSPORT			
100 Series [1]	No	1" rings, Low, med., high	10.75
104 22-cal.	No	1"	10.75
201 See-Thru	No	1"	13.00
1-Piece Base[2]	No	—	5.50
2-Piece Base[2]	No	—	2.75
[1]Weaver-type ring. [2]Weaver-type base; most popular rifles. Made in U.S. From Armsport.			
AO			
AO/Lever Scout Scope	No	Weaver rail	50.00
No gunsmithing required for lever-action rifles with 8" Weaver-style rails; surrounds barrel shank; 6" long; low profile. AO Sight Systems Inc.			
B-SQUARE			
Pistols (centerfire)			
Beretta 92, 96/Taurus 99	No	Weaver rail	66.95
Colt M1911	E only	Weaver rail	66.95
Desert Eagle	No	Weaver rail	66.95
Glock	No	Weaver rail	66.95
H&K USP, 9mm and 40 S&W	No	Weaver rail	66.95
Ruger P85/89	E only	Weaver rail	66.95
SIG Sauer P226	E only	Weaver rail	66.95
Pistols (rimfire)			
Browning Buck Mark	No	Weaver rail	29.95
Colt 22	No	Weaver rail	33.95
Ruger Mk I/II, bull or taper	No	Weaver rail	29.95-49.95
Smith & Wesson 41, 2206	No	Weaver rail	36.95-49.95
Revolvers			
Colt Anaconda/Python	No	Weaver rail	29.95-74.95
Ruger Single-Six	No	Weaver rail	64.95
Ruger GP-100	No	Weaver rail	64.95
Ruger Blackhawk, Super	No	Weaver rail	64.95
Ruger Redhawk, Super	No	Weaver rail	64.95
Smith & Wesson K, L, N	No	Weaver rail	36.95-74.95
Taurus 66, 669, 607, 608	No	Weaver rail	64.95
Rifles (sporting)			
Browning BAR, A-Bolt	No	Weaver rail	45.90
Marlin MR7	No	Weaver rail	45.90
Mauser 98 Large Ring	No	Weaver rail	45.90
Mauser 91/93/95/96 Small Ring	No	Weaver rail	45.90
Remington 700, 740, 742, 760	No	Weaver rail	45.90
Remington 7400, 7600	No	Weaver rail	45.90
Remington Seven	No	Weaver rail	45.90
Rossi 62, 59 and 92	No	Weaver rail	44.95
Ruger Mini-14	W&E	Weaver rail	66.95
Ruger 96/22	No	Weaver rail	45.90
Ruger M77 (short and long)	No	Weaver rail	62.95
Ruger 10/22 (reg. and See-Thru)	No	Weaver rail	45.90
Savage 110-116, 10-16	No	Weaver rail	45.90
Modern Military (rings incl.)			
AK-47/MAC 90	No	Weaver rail	66.95
Colt AR-15	No	Weaver rail	66.95-81.95
FN/FAL/LAR (See-Thru rings)	No	Weaver rail	99.95

SCOPE RINGS & BASES

Maker, Model, Type	Adjust.	Scopes	Price
B-SQUARE (cont.)			
Classic Military (rings incl.)			
FN 49	No	Weaver rail	66.95
Hakim	No	Weaver rail	66.95
Mauser 38, 94, 96, 98	E only	Weaver rail	66.95
Mosin-Nagant (all)	E only	Weaver rail	66.95
Air Rifles			
RWS, Diana, BSA, Gamo	W&E	11mm rail	49.95-59.95
Weihrauch, Anschutz, Beeman, Webley	W&E	11mm rail	59.95-69.95
Shotguns/Slug Guns			
Benelli Super 90 (See-Thru)	No	Weaver rail	52.95
Browning BPS, A-5 9 (See-Thru)	No	Weaver rail	52.95
Browning Gold 10/12/20-ga. (See-Thru)	No	Weaver rail	52.95
Ithaca 37, 87	No	Weaver rail	52.95
Mossberg 500/Mav. 88	No	Weaver rail	52.95
Mossberg 835/Mav. 91	No	Weaver rail	52.95
Remington 870/1100/11-87	No	Weaver rail	52.95
Remington SP10	No	Weaver rail	52.95
Winchester 1200-1500	No	Weaver rail	52.95

Prices shown for anodized black finish; add $10 for stainless finish. Partial listing of mounts shown here. Contact B-Square for complete listing and details.

Maker, Model, Type	Adjust.	Scopes	Price
BEEMAN			
Two-Piece, Med.	No	1"	31.50
Deluxe Two-Piece, High	No	1"	33.00
Deluxe Two-Piece	No	30mm	41.00
Deluxe One-Piece	No	1"	50.00
Dampa Mount	No	1"	120.00

All grooved receivers and scope bases on all known air rifles and 22-cal. rimfire rifles (1/2" to 5/8"—6mm to 15mm).

Maker, Model, Type	Adjust.	Scopes	Price
BOCK			
Swing ALK[1]	W&E	1", 26mm, 30mm	349.00
Safari KEMEL[2]	W&E	1", 26mm, 30mm	149.00
Claw KEMKA[3]	W&E	1", 26mm, 30mm	224.00
ProHunter Fixed[4]	No	1", 26mm, 30mm	95.00

[1]Q.D.: pivots right for removal. For Steyr-Mannlicher, Win. 70, Rem. 700, Mauser 98, Dakota, Sako, Sauer 80, 90. Magnum has extra-wide rings, same price. [2]Heavy-duty claw-type reversible for front or rear removal. For Steyr-Mannlicher rifles. [3]True claw mount for bolt-action rifles. Also in extended model. For Steyr-Mannlicher, Win. 70, Rem. 700. Also avail. as Gunsmith Bases—bases not drilled or contoured—same price. [4]Extra-wide rings. Imported from Germany by GSI, Inc.

Maker, Model, Type	Adjust.	Scopes	Price
BURRIS			
Supreme (SU) One-Piece (T)[1]	W only	1" split rings, 3 heights	1-piece base - 23.00-27.00
Trumount (TU) Two-Piece (T)	W only	1" split rings, 3 heights	2-piece base - 21.00-30.00
Trumount (TU) Two-Piece Ext.	W only	1" split rings	26.00
Browning 22-cal. Auto Mount[2]	No	1" split rings	20.00
1" 22-cal. Ring Mounts[3]	No	1" split rings	1"rings - 24.00-41.00
L.E.R. (LU) Mount Bases[4]	W only	1" split rings	24.00-52.00
L.E.R. No Drill-No Tap Bases[4,7,8]	W only	1" split rings	48.00-52.00
Extension Rings[5]	No	1" scopes	28.00-46.00
Ruger Ring Mount[6,9]	W only	1" split rings	50.00-68.00
Std. 1" Rings[9]	—	Low, medium, high heights	29.00-43.00
Zee Rings[9]	—	Fit Weaver bases; medium and high heights	29.00-44.00
Signature Rings	No	30mm split rings	68.00
Rimfire/Airgun Rings	W only	1" split rings, med. & high	24.00-41.00
Double Dovetail (DD) Bases	No	30mm Signature	23.00-26.00

[1]Most popular rifles. Universal rings, mounts fit Burris, Universal, Redfield, Leupold and Browning bases. Comparable prices. [2]Browning Standard 22 Auto rifle. [3]Grooved receivers. [4]Universal dovetail; accepts Burris, Universal, Redfield, Leupold rings. For Dan Wesson, S&W, Virginian, Ruger Blackhawk, Win. 94. [5]Medium standard front, extension rear, per pair. Low standard front, extension rear per pair. [6]Compact scopes, scopes with 2" bell for M77R. [7]Selected rings and bases available with matte Safari or silver finish. [8]For S&W K, L, N frames, Colt Python, Dan Wesson with 6" or longer barrels. [9]Also in 30mm.

Maker, Model, Type	Adjust.	Scopes	Price
CATCO			
Enfield Drop-In	No	1"	39.95

Uses Weaver-style rings (not incl.). No gunsmithing required. See-Thru design. From CATCO.

Maker, Model, Type	Adjust.	Scopes	Price
CLEAR VIEW			
Universal Rings, Mod. 101[1]	No	1" split rings	21.95
Standard Model[2]	No	1" split rings	21.95
Broad View[3]	No	1"	21.95
22 Model[4]	No	3/4", 7/8", 1"	13.95
SM-94 Winchester[5]	No	1" split rings	23.95
94 EJ[6]	No	1" split rings	21.95

[1]Most rifles by using Weaver-type base; allows use of iron sights. [2]Most popular rifles; allows use of iron sights. [3]Most popular rifles; low profile, wide field of view. [4]22 rifles with grooved receiver. [5]Side mount. [6]For Win. A.E. From Clear View Mfg.

Maker, Model, Type	Adjust.	Scopes	Price
CONETROL			
Huntur[1]	W only	1", split rings, 3 heights	99.96
Gunnur[2]	W only	1", split rings, 3 heights	119.88
Custom[3]	W only	1", split rings, 3 heights	149.88
One-Piece Side Mount Base[4]	W only	1", 26mm, 26.5mm solid or split rings, 3 heights	NA
DapTar Bases[5]	W only	1", 26mm, 26.5mm solid or split rings, 3 heights	NA
Pistol Bases, 2- or 3-ring[6]	W only		NA
Fluted Bases[7]	W only	Standard Conetrol rings	119.88
Metric Rings[8]	W only	26mm, 26.5mm, 30mm	99.96-149.88

[1]All popular rifles, including metric-drilled foreign guns. Price shown for base, two rings. Matte finish. [2]Gunnur grade has mirror-finished rings to match scopes. Satin-finish base to match guns. Price shown for base, two rings. [3]Custom grade has mirror-finished rings and mirror-finished, streamlined base. Price shown for base, two rings. [4]Win. 94, Krag, older split-bridge Mannlicher-Schoenauer, Mini-14, etc. Prices same as above. [5]For all popular guns with integral mounting provision, including Sako. BSA Ithacagun, Ruger, Tikka, H&K, BRNO—$39.96-$59.94—and many others. Also for grooved-receiver rimfires and air rifles. Prices same as above. [6]For XP-100, T/C Contender, Colt SAA, Ruger Blackhawk, S&W and others. [7]Sculptured two-piece bases as found on fine custom rifles. Price shown is for base alone. Also available unfinished—$79.92, or finished but unblued—$99.96. [8]26mm, 26.5mm, and 30mm rings made in projectionless style, in three heights. Three-ring mount for T/C Contender and other pistols in Conetrol's three grades. Any Conetrol mount available in stainless or Teflon for double regular cost of grade.

Maker, Model, Type	Adjust.	Scopes	Price
CUSTOM QUALITY			
Custom See-Thru	No	Up to 44mm	29.95
Dovetail 101-1 See-Thru	No	1"	29.95
Removable Rings	No	1"	29.95
Solid Dovetail	No	1", 30mm vertically split	29.95
Dovetail 22 See-Thru	No	1"	29.95

Mounts for many popular rifles. From Custom Quality Products, Inc.

Maker, Model, Type	Adjust.	Scopes	Price
EAW			
Quick-Loc Mount	W&E	1", 26mm	253.00
	W&E	30mm	271.00
Magnum Fixed Mount	W&E	1", 26mm	198.00
	W&E	30mm	215.00

Fit most popular rifles. Avail. in 4 heights, 4 extensions. Reliable return to zero. Stress-free mounting. Imported by New England Custom Gun Svc.

Maker, Model, Type	Adjust.	Scopes	Price
EXCEL INDUSTRIES, INC.			
Titanium Weaver-Style Rings	No	1" and 30mm, low and high	179.00
Steel Weaver-Style Rings	No	1" and 30mm, low and high	149.00
Flashlight Mounts - Titanium and Steel	No	1" and 30mm, low and high	89.50/75.00

Maker, Model, Type	Adjust.	Scopes	Price
GENTRY			
Feather-Light Rings and Bases	No	1", 30mm	90.00-125.00

Bases for Rem. Seven, 700, Mauser 98, Browning A-Bolt, Weatherby Mk. V, Win. 70, HVA, Dakota. Two-piece base for Rem. Seven, chrome moly or stainless. Rings in matte or regular blue, or stainless gray; four heights. From David Gentry.

Maker, Model, Type	Adjust.	Scopes	Price
GRIFFIN & HOWE			
Topmount[1]	No	1", 30mm	625.00
Sidemount[2]	No	1", 30mm	255.00
Garand Mount[3]	No	1"	255.00

[1]Quick-detachable, double-lever mount with 1" rings, installed; with 30mm rings $875.00. [2]Quick-detachable, double-lever mount with 1" rings; with 30mm rings $375.00; installed, 1" rings. $405.00; installed, 30mm rings $525.00. [3]Price installed, with 1" rings $405.00. From Griffin & Howe.

SCOPE RINGS & BASES

Maker, Model, Type	Adjust.	Scopes	Price
G. G. & G.			
Remington 700 Rail	No	Weaver base	135.00
Sniper Grade Rings	No	30mm	159.95
M16/AR15 F.I.R.E. Std.[1]	No	Weaver rail	75.00
M16/AR15 F.I.R.E. Scout	No	Weaver rail	82.95
Aimpoint Standard Ring	No	—	164.95
Aimpoint Cantilever Ring	No	Weaver rail	212.00

[1]For M16/A3, AR15 flat top receivers; also in extended length. [2]For Aimpoint 5000 and Comp; quick detachable; spare battery compartment. [3]Low profile; quick release. From G. G. & G.

Maker, Model, Type	Adjust.	Scopes	Price
IRONSIGHTER			
Ironsighter See-Through Mounts[1]	No	1" split rings	29.40-64.20
Ironsighter S-94	No	1" split rings	45.28
Ironsighter AR-15/M-16[8]	No	1", 30mm	70.10
Ironsighter 22-Cal.Rimfire[2]	No	1"	18.45
Model #570[9]	No	1" split rings	29.40
Model #573[9]	No	30mm split rings	45.28
Model #727[3]	No	.875" split rings	18.45
Blackpowder Mount[7]	No		34.20-78.25

[1]Most popular rifles. Rings have oval holes to permit use of iron sights. [2]For 1" dia. scopes. [3]For .875 dia. scopes. [4]For 1" dia. extended eye relief scopes. [6]732—Ruger 77/22 R&RS, No. 1, Ranch Rifle; 778 fits Ruger 77R, RS. Both 733, 778 fit Ruger Integral bases. [7,8]Fits most popular blackpowder rifles; two-piece (CVA, Knight, Marlin and Austin & Halleck) and one-piece integral (T/C). [8]Model 716 with 1" #540 rings; Model 717 with 30mm #530 rings. [9]Fits Weaver-style bases. Some models in stainless finish. From Ironsighter Co.

Maker, Model, Type	Adjust.	Scopes	Price
K MOUNT By KENPATABLE			
Shotgun Mount	No	1", laser or red dot device	49.95
SKS[1]	No	1"	39.95

Wrap-around design; no gunsmithing required. Models for Browning BPS, A-5 12-ga., Sweet 16, 20, Rem. 870/1100 (LTW, and L.H.), S&W 916, Mossberg 500, Ithaca 37 & 51 12-ga., S&W 1000/3000, Win. 1400. [1]Requires simple modification to gun. From KenPatable Ent.

Maker, Model, Type	Adjust.	Scopes	Price
KRIS MOUNTS			
Side-Saddle[1]	No	1",26mm split rings	12.98
Two-Piece (T)[2]	No	1", 26mm split rings	8.98
One Piece (T)[3]	No	1", 26mm split rings	12.98

[1]One-piece mount for Win. 94. [2]Most popular rifles and Ruger. [3]Blackhawk revolver. Mounts have oval hole to permit use of iron sights.

Maker, Model, Type	Adjust.	Scopes	Price
KWIK-SITE			
KS-See-Thru[1]	No	1"	27.95-57.95
AA-22 See-Thru[2]	No	1"	21.95
KS-W94[3]	No	1"	42.95
KS-WEV (Weaver-style rings)	No	1"	19.95
KS-WEV-HIGH	No	1"	19.95
KS-T22 1"[4]	No	1"	17.95
KS-FL Flashlite[5]	No	Mini or C cell flashlight	37.95
KS-T88[6]	No	1"	21.95
KS-T89	No	30mm	21.95
KSN 22 See-Thru	No	1", 7/8"	17.95
KSN-T22	No	1", 7/8"	17.95
KSN-M-16 See-Thru (for M16 + AR-15)	No	1"	49.95
KS-202[1]	No	1"	27.97
KS-203	No	30mm	42.95
KSBP[7]	No	Integral	76.95
KSB Base Set	—	—	5.95
Combo Bases & Rings	No	1"	21.95

Bases interchangeable with Weaver bases. [1]Most rifles. Allows use of iron sights. [2]22-cal. rifles with grooved receivers. Allows use of iron sights. [3]Model 94, 94 Big Bore. No drilling or tapping. Also in adjustable model **$57.95**. [4]Non-See-Thru model for grooved receivers. [5]Allows C-cell or, Mini Mag Lites to be mounted atop See-Thru mounts. [6]Fits any Redfield, Tasco, Weaver or Universal-style Kwik-Site dovetail base. [7]Blackpowder mount with integral rings and sights. [8]Shotgun side mount. Bright blue, black matte or satin finish. Standard, high heights.

Maker, Model, Type	Adjust.	Scopes	Price
LASER AIM	No	Laser Aim	19.99-69.00

Mounts Laser Aim above or below barrel. Avail. for most popular handguns, rifles, shotguns, including militaries. From Laser Aim Technologies, Inc.

Maker, Model, Type	Adjust.	Scopes	Price
LEUPOLD			
STD Bases[1]	W only	One- or two-piece bases	24.60
STD Rings[2]	—	1" super low, low, medium, high	32.40
DD RBH Handgun Mounts[2]	No	—	59.40
Dual Dovetail Bases[3]	No	—	24.60
Dual Dovetail Rings[8]	—	1", low, med, high	32.40
Ring Mounts[4,5,6]	No	7/8", 1"	81.00
22 Rimfire[8]	No	7/8", 1"	60.00

Maker, Model, Type	Adjust.	Scopes	Price
LEOPOLD (cont.)			
Gunmaker Base[7]	W only	1"	16.50
Quick Release Rings	—	1", low, med., high	33.00-71.00
Quick Release Bases[9]	No	1", one- or two-piece	71.40

[1]Base and two rings; Casull, Ruger, S&W, T/C; add $5.00 for silver finish. [2]Rem. 700, Win. 70-type actions. For Ruger No. 1, 77, 77/22; interchangeable with Ruger units. For dovetailed rimfire rifles. Sako; high, medium, low.[7] Must be drilled, tapped for each action. [8]13mm dovetail receiver. [9]BSA Monarch, Rem. 40x, 700, 721, 725, Ruger M77, S&W 1500, Weatherby Mark V, Vanguard, Win. M70.

Maker, Model, Type	Adjust.	Scopes	Price
MARLIN			
One-Piece QD (T)	No	1" split rings	10.10

Most Marlin lever actions.

Maker, Model, Type	Adjust.	Scopes	Price
MILLETT			
Black Onyx Smooth	—	1", low, medium, high	31.15
Chaparral Engraved	—	engraved	46.15
One-Piece Bases[6]	Yes	1"	23.95
Universal Two-Piece Bases			
700 Series	W only	Two-piece bases	25.15
FN Series	W only	Two-piece bases	25.15
70 Series[1]	W only	1", two-piece bases	25.15
Angle-Loc Rings[2]	W only	1", low, medium, high	32.20-47.20
Ruger 77 Rings[3]	—	1"	47.20
Shotgun Rings[4]	—	1"	28.29
Handgun Bases, Rings[5]	—	1"	34.60-69.15
30mm Rings[7]	—	30mm	37.75-42.95
Extension Rings[8]	—	1"	35.65
See-Thru Mounts[9]	No	1"	27.95-32.95
Shotgun Mounts[10]	No	1"	49.95
Timber Mount	No	1"	78.00

BRNO, Rem. 40x, 700, 722, 725, 7400 Ruger 77 (round top), Marlin, Weatherby, FN Mauser, FN Brownings, Colt 57, Interarms Mark X, Parker-Hale, Savage 110, Sako (round receiver), many others. [1]Fits Win. M70 70XTR, 670, Browning BBR, BAR, BLR, A-Bolt, Rem. 7400/7600, Four, Six, Marlin 336, Win. 94 A. E., Sav. 110. [2]To fit Weaver-type bases. [3]Engraved. Smooth **$34.60**. [4]For Rem. 870, 1100; smooth. [5]Two- and three-ring sets for Colt Python, Trooper, Diamondback, Peacekeeper, Dan Wesson, Ruger Redhawk, Super Redhawk. [6]Turn-in bases and Weaver-style for most popular rifles and T/C Contender, XP-100 pistols. [7]Both Weaver and turn-in styles; three heights. [8]Med. or high; ext. front—std. rear, ext. rear—std. front, ext. front—ext. rear; **$40.90** for double extension. [9]Many popular rifles, Knight MK-85, T/C Hawken, Renegade, Mossberg 500 Slugster, 835 slug. [10]For Rem. 879/1100, Win. 1200, 1300/1400, 1500, Mossberg 500. Some models available in nickel at extra cost. [11]For T/C Hawken and Renegade; See-Thru with adj. open sight inside. From Millett Sights.

Maker, Model, Type	Adjust.	Scopes	Price
MMC			
AK[1]	No	—	39.95
FN FAL/LAR[2]	No	—	59.95

[1]Fits all AK derivative receivers; Weaver-style base; low-profile scope position. [2]Fits all FAL versions; Weaver-style base. From MMC.

Maker, Model, Type	Adjust.	Scopes	Price
RAM-LINE			
Mini-14 Mount	Yes	1"	24.97

No drilling or tapping. Uses std. dovetail rings. Has built-in shell deflector. Made of solid black polymer. From Ram-Line, Inc.

Maker, Model, Type	Adjust.	Scopes	Price
REDFIELD			
JR-SR (T)[1]. One/two-piece bases.	W only	3/4", 1", 26mm, 30mm	JR-15.99-46.99 SR-15.99-33.49
Ring (T)[2]	No	3/4" and 1"	27.95-29.95
Widefield See-Thru Mounts	No	1"	15.95
Ruger Rings[4]	No	1", med., high	30.49-36.49
Ruger 30mm[5]	No	1"	37.99-40.99
Midline Ext. Rings	No	1"	24.95

[1]Low, med. & high, split rings. Reversible extension front rings for 1". 2-piece bases for Sako. Colt Sauer bases **$39.95**. Med. Top Access JR rings nickel-plated, **$28.95**. SR two-piece ABN mount nickel-plated **$22.95**. [2]Split rings for grooved 22s; 30mm, black matte **$42.95**. [3]Used with MP scopes for S&W K, L or N frame, XP-100, T/C Contender, Ruger receivers. [4]For Ruger Model 77 rifles, medium and high; medium only for M77/22. [5]For Model 77. Also in matte finish **$45.95**. [6]Aluminun 22 groove mount **$14.95**; base and medium rings **$18.95**. [7]Fits American or Weaver-style base. Non-Gunsmithing mount system. For many popular shotguns, rifles, handguns and blackpowder rifles. Uses existing screw holes.

Maker, Model, Type	Adjust.	Scopes	Price
S&K			
Insta-Mount (T) Bases and Rings[1]	W only	Uses S&K rings only	47.00-117.00
Conventional Rings and Bases[2]	W only	1" split rings	From 65.00
Sculptured Bases, Rings[2]	W only	1", 26mm, 30mm	From 65.00
Smooth Contoured Rings[3]	Yes	1", 26mm, 30mm	90.00-120.00

[1]1903, A3, M1 Carbine, Lee Enfield #1. Mk.III, #4, #5, M1917, M98 Mauser, AR-15, AR-180, M-14, M-1, Ger. K-43, Mini-14, M1-A, Krag, AKM, Win. 94, SKS Type 56, Daewoo, H&K. [2]Most popular rifles already drilled and tapped and Sako, Tikka dovetails. [3]No projections; weigh 1/2-oz. each; matte or gloss finish. Horizontally and vertically split rings, matte or high gloss.

ACCESSORIES

SCOPE RINGS & BASES

Maker, Model, Type	Adjust.	Scopes	Price
SAKO			
QD Dovetail	W only	1"	70.00-155.00
Sako, or any rifle using Sako action, 3 heights available. Stoeger, importer.			
SPRINGFIELD, INC.			
M1A Third Generation	No	1" or 30mm	123.00
M1A Standard	N0	1" or 30mm	77.00
M6 Scout Mount	No	—	29.00
Weaver-style bases. From Springfield, Inc.			
TALBOT			
QD Bases	No	—	180.00-190.00
Rings	No	1", 30mm	50.00-70.00
Blue or stainless steel; standard or extended bases; rings in three heights. For most popular rifles. From Talbot QD Mounts.			
TASCO			
World Class			
Aluminum Ringsets	Yes	1", 30mm	12.00-17.00
See-Thru	No	1"	19.00
Shotgun Bases	Yes	—	34.00
From Tasco.			
THOMPSON/CENTER			
Duo-Ring Mount[1]	No	1"	61.99-62.99
Weaver-Style Bases	No	—	10.28-33.36
Weaver-Style Rings[3]	No	1"	27.74-42.13
Weaver-Style See-Thru Rings[4]	No	1"	27.74
[1]Attaches directly to T/C Contender bbl., no drilling/tapping; also for T/C M/L rifles, needs base adapter; blue or stainless. [3]Medium and high; blue or silver finish. [4]For T.C FireHawk, ThunderHawk; blue; silver $29.80. From Thompson/Center.			
UNERTL			
1/4 Click[1]	Yes	3/4", 1" target scopes	Per set 186.00
[1]Unertl target or varmint scopes. Posa or standard mounts, less bases. From Unertl.			
WARNE			
Premier Series (all steel)			
T.P.A. (Permanently Attached)	No	1", 4 heights	87.75
		30mm, 2 heights	98.55
Sako	No	1", 4 heights	87.75
		30mm, 3 heights	98.55
Premier Series Rings fit Premier Series Bases			
Premier Series (all-steel Q.D. rings)			
Premier Series (all-steel)	No	1", 4 heights	125.00
Quick detachable lever		26mm, 2 heights	129.95
		30mm, 3 heights	136.70
BRNO 19mm	No	1", 3 heights	125.00
		30mm, 2 heights	136.70
BRNO 16mm	No	1", 2 heights	125.00
Ruger	No	1", 4 heights	125.00
		30mm, 3 heights	136.70
Ruger M77	No	1", 3 heights	125.00
		30mm, 2 heights	136.70
Sako Medium & Long Action	No	1", 4 heights	125.00
		30mm, 3 heights	136.70
Sako Short Action	No	1", 3 heights	125.00
All-Steel One-Piece Base, ea.			38.50
All-Steel Two-Piece Base, ea.			14.00
Maxima Series (fits all Weaver-style bases)			
Permanently Attached[1]	No	1", 3 heights	34.55
		30mm, 3 heights	50.00
Adjustable Double Lever[2]	No	1", 3 heights	72.60
		30mm, 3 heights	80.75
Thumb Knob	No	1", 3 heights	59.95
		30mm, 3 heights	68.25
Stainless-Steel Two-Piece Base, ea.			15.25
Vertically split rings with dovetail clamp, precise return to zero. Fit most popular rifles, handguns. Regular blue, matte blue, silver finish. [1]All-Steel, non-Q.D. rings. [2]All-steel, Q.D. rings. From Warne Mfg. Co.			
WEAVER			
Detachable Mounts			
Top Mount	No	7/8", 1", 30mm, 33mm	24.95-38.95
Side Mount	No	1", 1" long	14.95-34.95
Tip-Off Rings	No	7/8", 1"	24.95-32.95
Pivot Mounts	No	1"	38.95
Complete Mount Systems			
Pistol	No	1"	75.00-105.00

Maker, Model, Type	Adjust.	Scopes	Price
WEAVER (cont.)			
Rifle	No	1"	32.95
SKS Mount System	No	1"	49.95
Pro-View (no base required)	No	1"	13.95-15.95
Converta-Mount, 12-ga. (Rem. 870, Moss. 500)	No	1", 30mm	74.95
See-Thru Mounts			
Detachable	No	1"	27.00-32.00
System (no base required)	No	1"	15.00-35.00
Tip-Off	No	1"	15.00
Nearly all modern rifles, pistols, and shotguns. Detachable rings in standard, See-Thru, and extension styles, in Low, Medium, High or X-High heights; gloss (blued), silver and matte finishes to match scopes. Extension rings are only available in 1" High style and See-Thru X-tensions only in gloss finish. Tip-Off rings only for 3/8" grooved receivers or 3/8"grooved adaptor bases; no base required. See-Thru & Pro-View mounts for most modern big bore rifles, some in silver. No Drill & Tap Pistol systems in gloss or silver for: Colt Python, Trooper, 357, Officer's Model; Ruger Single-Six, Security-Six (gloss finish only); Blackhawk, Super Blackhawk, Blackhawk SRM 357, Redhawk, Mini-14 Series (not Ranch), Ruger 22 Auto Pistols, Mark II; Smith & Wesson I- and current K-frames with adj. rear sights. Converta-Mount Systems in Standard and See-Under for: Mossberg 500 (12- and 20-ga.); Remington 870, 11-87 (12- and 20-ga. lightweight); Winchester 1200, 1300, 1400, 1500. Converta Brackets, Bases, Rings also avail. for Beretta A303 and A390; Browning A-5, BPS Pump; Ithaca 37, 87. From Weaver.			
WEIGAND			
Browning Buck Mark[1]	No	—	29.95
Colt 22 Automatic[1]	No	—	19.95
Integra Mounts[2]	No	—	39.95-69.00
S&W Revolver[3]	No	—	29.95
Ruger 10/22[4]	No	—	14.95-39.95
Ruger Revolver[5]	No	—	29.95
Taurus Revolver[4]	No	—	29.95-65.00
T/C Encore Monster Mount	No	—	69.00
T/C Contender Monster Mount	No	—	69.00
Lightweight Rings	No	1", 30mm	29.95-39.95
1911, P-9 Scopemounts			
SM3[6]	No	Weaver rail	99.95
SRS 1911-2[7]	No	30mm	59.95
APCMNT[8]	No	—	69.95
[1]No gunsmithing. [2] S&W K, L, N frames; Taurus vent rib models; Colt Anaconda/Python; Ruger Redhawk; Ruger 10/22. [3]K, L, N frames. [4]Three models. [5] Redhawk, Blackhawk, GP-100. [6]3rd Gen.; drill and tap; without slots $59.95. [7]Ringless design, silver only. [8]For Aimpoint Comp. Red Dot scope, silver only. From Weigand Combat Handguns, Inc.			
WIDEVIEW			
Premium 94 Angle Eject and side mount	No	1"	18.70
Premium See-Thru	No	1"	18.70
22 See-Thru	No	3/4", 1"	13.60
Universal Ring Angle Cut	No	1"	18.70
Universal Ring Straight Cut	No	1"	18.70
Solid Mounts			
Lo Ring Solid[1]	No	1"	13.60
Hi Ring Solid[1]	No	1"	13.60
SR Rings	—	1", 30mm	13.60
22 Grooved Receiver	No	1"	13.60
Blackpowder Mounts[2]	No	1"	18.70-37.40
High, extra-high ring mounts with base	No	up to 60mm	18.70
Desert Eagle Pistol Mount	No	1", 30mm	34.95-44.95
[1]For Weaver-type base. Models for many popular rifles. Low ring, high ring and grooved receiver types. [2]No drilling, tapping, for T/C Renegade, Hawken, CVA, Knight Traditions guns. From Wideview Scope Mount Corp.			
WILLIAMS			
Side Mount with HCO Rings[1]	No	1", split or extension rings	74.35
Side Mount, Offset Rings[2]	No	Same	61.45
Sight-Thru Mounts[3]	No	1", 7/8" sleeves	19.50
Streamline Mounts	No	1" (bases form rings)	26.50
[1]Most rifles, Br. S.M.L.E. (round rec.) $14.41 extra. [2]Most rifles including Win. 94 Big Bore. [3]Many modern rifles, including CVA Apollo, others with 1" octagon barrels.			
YORK			
M-1 Garand	Yes	1"	39.95
Centers scope over the action. No drilling, tapping or gunsmithing. Uses standard dovetail rings. From York M-1 Conversions.			

NOTES

(S)—Side Mount; (T)—Top Mount; 22mm=.866"; 25.4mm=1.024"; 26.5mm=1.045"; 30mm=1.81".

ACCESSORIES

Sporting Leaf and Open Sights

ERA EXPRESS SIGHTS A wide variety of open sights and bases for custom installation. Partial listing shown. From New England Custom Gun Service.
Price: One-leaf express **$66.00**
Price: Two-leaf express **$71.50**
Price: Three-leaf express **$77.00**
Price: Bases for above **$27.50**
Price: Standing rear sight, straight **$13.25**
Price: Base for above **$16.50**
ERA PROFESSIONAL EXPRESS SIGHTS Standing or folding leaf sights are securely locked to the base with the ERA Magnum Clamp, but can be loosened for sighting in. Base can be attached with two socket-head cap screws or soldered. Finished and blued. Barrel diameters from .600″ to .930″.
Price: Standing leaf **$54.00**
Price: One-leaf express **$96.00**
Price: Two-leaf express **$101.00**
Price: Three-leaf express **$109.00**
ERA MASTERPIECE REAR SIGHT Adjustable for windage and elevation, and adjusted and locked with a small screwdriver. Comes with 8-36 socket-head cap screw and wrench. Barrel diameters from .600″ to .930″.
Price: **$75.00**
G.G. & G. SAME PLANE APERTURE M-16/AR-15 A2-style dual aperture rear sight with both large and small apertures centered on the same plane.
Price: **$45.00**

Williams Ruger Fire Sight

LYMAN No.16 Middle sight for barrel dovetail slot mounting. Folds flat when scope or peep sight is used. Sight notch plate adjustable for elevation. White triangle for quick aiming. 3 heights: A-.400″ to.500″, B-.345″ to .445″, C-.500″ to .600″.
Price: **$12.25**
MARBLE FALSE BASE #76, #77, #78 New screw-on base for most rifles replaces factory base. 3/8″ dovetail slot permits installation of any folding rear sight. Can be had in sweat-on models also.
Price: **$8.00**
MARBLE FOLDING LEAF Flat-top or semi-buckhorn style. Folds down when scope or peep sights are used. Reversible plate gives choice of "U" or "V" notch. Adjustable for elevation.
Price: **$16.00**
Price: Also available with both windage and elevation adjustment **$18.00**
MARBLE SPORTING REAR With white enamel diamond, gives choice of two "U" and two "V" notches or different sizes. Adjustment in height by means of double step elevator and sliding notch piece. For all rifles; screw or dovetail installation.
Price: . . . . **$16.00-$17.00**
MARBLE #20 UNIVERSAL New screw or sweat-on base. Both have .100″ elevation adjustment. In five base sizes. Three styles of U-notch, square notch, peep. Adjustable for windage and elevation.
Price: Screw-on **$23.00**
Price: Sweat-on **$21.00**
MILLETT SPORTING & BLACKPOWDER RIFLE Open click adjustable rear fits 3/8″ dovetail cut in barrel. Choice of white outline, target black or open express V rear blades. Also available is a replacement screw-on sight with express V, .562″ hole centers. Dovetail fronts in white or blaze orange in seven heights (.157″-.540″).
Price: Dovetail or screw-on rear **$55.60**
Price: Front sight **$12.34**
MILLETT SCOPE-SITE Open, adjustable or fixed rear sights dovetail into a base integral with the top scope-mounting ring. Blaze orange front ramp sight is integral with the front ring half. Rear sights have white outline aperture. Provides fast, short-radius, Patridge-type open sights on the top of the scope. Can be used with all Millett rings, Weaver-style bases, Ruger 77 (also fits Redhawk), Ruger Ranch Rifle, No. 1, No. 3, Rem. 870, 1100; Burris, Leupold and Redfield bases.
Price: Scope-Site top only, windage only **$31.15**
Price: As above, fully adjustable **$66.10**
Price: Scope-Site Hi-Turret, fully adjustable, low, medium, high **$66.10**
WICHITA MULTI RANGE SIGHT SYSTEM Designed for silhouette shooting. System allows you to adjust the rear sight to four repeatable range settings, once it is pre-set. Sight clicks to any of the settings by turning a serrated wheel. Front sight is adjustable for weather and light conditions with one adjustment. Specify gun when ordering.
Price: Rear sight **$120.00**
Price: Front sight **$90.00**
WILLIAMS DOVETAIL OPEN SIGHT (WDOS) Open rear sight with windage and elevation adjustment. Furnished with "U" notch or choice of blades. Slips into dovetail and locks with gib lock. Heights from .281″ to .531″.
Price: With blade **$15.86**
Price: Less Blade **$9.92**

WILLIAMS GUIDE OPEN SIGHT (WGOS) Open rear sight with windage and elevation adjustment. Bases to fit most military and commercial barrels. Choice of square "U" or "V" notch blade, 3/16″, 1/4″, 5/16″, or 3/8″ high.
Price: Less blade **$16.34**
Price: Extra blades, each **$6.37**
WILLIAMS WGOS OCTAGON Open rear sight for 1″ octagon barrels. Installs with two 6-48 screws and uses same hole spacing as most T/C muzzleloading rifles. Four heights, choice of square, U, V, B blade.
Price: **$21.80**
WILLIAMS WSKS, WAK47 Replaces original military-type rear sight. Adjustable for windage and elevation. No drilling or tapping. Peep aperture or open. For SKS carbines, AK-47.
Price: Aperture **$24.67**
Price: Open **$22.61**
WILLIAMS WM-96 Fits Mauser 96-type military rifles, replaces original rear sight with open blade or aperture. Fully adjustable for windage and elevation. No drilling; tapping.
Price: Aperture **$24.67**
Price: Open **$22.61**
WILLIAMS FIRE RIFLE SETS Replacement front and rear fiber optic sights, red bead front, two green elements in the fully adjustable rear. Made of CNC-machined metal.
Price: For Ruger 10/22 . . . . **$34.95**
Price: For most Marlin and Win. (3/8″ dovetail) **$29.95**
Price: For Remington (newer style sight base) **$24.95**

Aperture and Micrometer Receiver Sights

Ashley Ghost Ring

AO GHOST RING HUNTING SIGHT Fully adjustable for windage and elevation. Available for most rifles, including blackpowder guns. Minimum gunsmithing required for most installations; matches most mounting holes. From AO Sight Systems, Inc.
Price: **$90.00**
AO AR-15/M-16 APERTURE Drop-in replacement of factory sights. Both apertures are on the same plane. Large ghost ring has .230″ inside diameter; small ghost ring has .100″ inside diameter. From AO Sight Systems, Inc.
Price: **$30.00**
BEEMAN/FEINWERKBAU 5454 MATCH APERTURE SIGHT Small size, new-design sight uses constant-pressure flat springs to eliminate point of impact shifts.
Price: **$350.00**
BEEMAN SPORT APERTURE SIGHT Positive click micrometer adjustments. Standard units with flush surface screwdriver adjustments. Deluxe version has target knobs. For air rifles with grooved receivers.
Price: Standard **$40.00**
Price: Deluxe **$50.00**

Williams Fire Sight Peep Set

EAW RECEIVER SIGHT A fully adjustable aperture sight that locks securely into the EAW quick-detachable scope mount rear base. Made by New England Custom Gun Service.
Price: **$95.00**
G.G.&G. MAD IRIS Multiple Aperture Device is a four sight, rotating aperture disk with small and large apertures on the same plane. Mounts on M-16/AR-15 flat top receiver. Fully adjustable.
Price: **$141.95**
Price: A2 IRIS, two apertures, full windage adjustments **$124.95**

METALLIC SIGHTS

LYMAN NO. 2 TANG SIGHT Designed for the Winchester Model 94. Has high index marks on aperture post; comes with both .093" quick sighting aperture, .040" large disk aperture, and replacement mounting screws.
Price:...**$69.95**
Price: For Marlin lever actions **$71.56**

Lyman No. 57 GPR

LYMAN No. 57 1/4-minute clicks. Stayset knobs. Quick release slide, adjustable zero scales. Made for almost all modern rifles.
Price:...**$62.50**
Price: No. 57SME, 57SMET (for White Systems Model 91 and Whitetail rifles) **$62.50**
LYMAN 57GPR Designed especially for the Lyman Great Plains Rifle. Mounts directly onto the tang of the rifle and has 1/4-minute micrometer click adjustments.
Price:...**$62.50**
LYMAN No. 66 Fits close to the rear of flat-sided receivers, furnished with Stayset knobs. Quick release slide, 1/4-min. adjustments. For most lever or slide action or flat-sided automatic rifles.
Price:...**$62.50**
Price: No. 66MK (for all current versions of the Knight MK-85 in-line rifle with flat-sided receiver) **$62.50**
Price: No. 66 SKS fits Russian and Chinese SKS rifles; large and small apertures **$62.50**
LYMAN No. 66U Light weight, designed for most modern shotguns with a flat-sided, round-top receiver. 1/4-minute clicks. Requires drilling, tapping. Not for Browning A-5, Rem. M11.
Price:...**$71.50**
LYMAN 90MJT RECEIVER SIGHT Mounts on standard Lyman and Williams FP bases. Has 1/4-minute audible micrometer click adjustments, target knobs with direction indicators. Adjustable zero scales, quick release slide. Large 7/8" diameter aperture disk.
Price: Right- or left-hand **$72.50**
MARBLE PEEP TANG SIGHT All-steel construction. Micrometer-like click adjustments for windage and elevation. For most popular old and new lever-action rifles.
Price:...**$125.00**
MILLETT PEEP RIFLE SIGHTS Fully adjustable, heat-treated nickel steel peep aperture receiver sight for the Mini-14. Has fine windage and elevation adjustments; replaces original.
Price: Rear sight, Mini-14 ....**$49.00**
Price: Front sight, Mini-14 ....**$18.75**
Price: Front and rear combo with hood...................**$64.00**
WILLIAMS FIRE SIGHT PEEP SETS Combines the Fire Sight front bead with Williams fully adjustable metallic peep rear.
Price: For SKS **$39.95**
Price: For Ruger 10/22 ....**$39.95**
Price: For Marlin or Winchester lever actions............**$73.95**
WILLIAMS FP Internal click adjustments. Positive locks. For virtually all rifles, T/C Contender, Heckler & Koch HK-91, Ruger Mini-14, plus Win., Rem. and Ithaca shotguns.
Price: From **$59.95**
Price: With Target Knobs **$71.20**
Price: With Square Notched Blade **$63.03**
Price: With Target Knobs & Square Notched Blade **$74.45**
Price: FP-GR (for dovetail-grooved receivers, 22s and air guns)...........**$59.95**
Price: FP-94BBSE (for Win. 94 Big Bore A.E.; uses top rear scope mount holes)..**$59.95**
WILLIAMS TARGET FP Similar to the FP series but developed for most bolt-action rimfire rifles. Target FP High adjustable from 1.250" to 1.750" above centerline of bore; Target FP Low adjustable from .750" to 1.250". Attaching bases for Rem. 540X, 541-S, 580, 581, 582 (#540); Rem. 510, 511, 512, 513-T, 521-T (#510); Win. 75 (#75); Savage/Anschutz 64 and Mark 12 (#64). Some rifles require drilling, tapping.
Price: High or Low.....................................**$77.15**
Price: Base only **$12.98**
Price: FP-T/C Scout rifle, from **$59.95**
Price: FP-94BBSE (for Win. 94 Big Bore A.E.; uses top rear scope mount holes)..**$59.95**
WILLIAMS 5-D SIGHT Low cost sight for shotguns, 22s and the more popular big game rifles. Adjustment for windage and elevation. Fits most guns without drilling and tapping. Also for British SMLE, Winchester M94 Side Eject.
Price: From **$31.47**
Price: With Shotgun Aperture **$31.47**
WILLIAMS GUIDE (WGRS) Receiver sight for 30 M1 Carbine, M1903A3 Springfield, Savage 24s, Savage-Anschutz and Weatherby XXII. Utilizes military dovetail; no drilling. Double-dovetail windage adjustment, sliding dovetail adjustment for elevation.
Price:...**$30.85**
Price: WGRS-CVA (for rifles with octagon barrels, receivers) **$30.85**

Front Sights

ASHLEY AR-15/M-16 FRONT SIGHTS Drop-in replacement sight post. Double faced so it can be rotated 180 degrees for 2.5 MOA elevation adjustment. Available in .080" width with .030" white stripe, or .100" with .040" stripe. From Ashley Outdoors, Inc.
Price:...**$30.00**
Price: Tritium Dot Express **$60.00**
ERA FRONT SIGHTS European-type front sights inserted from the front. Various heights available. From New England Custom Gun Service.
Price: 1/16" silver bead................................**$11.50**
Price: 3/32" silver bead................................**$16.00**
Price: Sourdough bead **$14.50**
Price: Tritium night sight **$44.00**
Price: Folding night sight with ivory bead **$39.50**
LYMAN HUNTING SIGHTS Made with gold or white beads 1/16" to 3/32" wide and in varying heights for most military and commercial rifles. Dovetail bases.
Price:...**$8.75**
MARBLE STANDARD Ivory, red, or gold bead. For all American-made rifles, 1/16" wide bead with semi-flat face which does not reflect light. Specify type of rifle when ordering.
Price:...**$10.00**
MARBLE CONTOURED Has 3/8" dovetail base, .090" deep, is 5/8" long. Uses standard 1/16" or 3/32" bead, ivory, red, or gold. Specify rifle type.
Price:...**$11.50**
WILLIAMS RISER BLOCKS For adding .250" height to front sights when using a receiver sight. Two widths available: .250" for Williams Streamlined Ramp or .340" on all standard ramps having this base width. Uses standard 3/8" dovetail.
Price:...**$5.46**

Globe Target Front Sights

LYMAN 20 MJT TARGET FRONT Has 7/8" diameter, one-piece steel globe with 3/8" dovetail base. Height is .700" from bottom of dovetail to center of aperture; height on 20 LJT is .750". Comes with seven Anschutz-size steel inserts—two posts and five apertures .126" through .177".
Price: 20 MJT or 20 LJT **$31.50**
LYMAN No. 17A TARGET Includes seven interchangeable inserts: four apertures, one transparent amber and two posts .50" and .100" in width.
Price:...**$26.00**
Price: Insert set **$9.00**

Lyman 17AEU

LYMAN 17AEU Similar to the Lyman 17A except has a special dovetail design to mount easily onto European muzzleloaders such as CVA, Traditions and Investarm. All steel, comes with eight inserts.
Price:...**$26.00**
LYMAN No. 93 MATCH Has 7/8" diameter, fits any rifle with a standard dovetail mounting block. Comes with seven target inserts and accepts most Anschutz accessories. Hooked locking bolt and nut allows quick removal, installation. Base available in .860" (European) and .562" (American) hole spacing.
Price:...**$41.25**
WILLIAMS TARGET GLOBE FRONT Adapts to many rifles. Mounts to the base with a knurled locking screw. Height is .545" from center, not including base. Comes with inserts.
Price:...**$30.85**
Price: Dovetail base (low) .220" **$17.00**
Price: Dovetail base (high) .465".......................**$17.00**
Price: Screw-on base, .300" height, .300" radius **$15.45**
Price: Screw-on base, .450" height, .350" radius **$15.45**
Price: Screw-on base, .215" height, .400" radius **$15.45**

Ramp Sights

ERA MASTERPIECE Banded ramps; 21 sizes; hand-detachable beads and hood; beads inserted from the front. Various heights available. From New England Custom Gun Service.
Price: Banded ramp **$54.00**
Price: Hood...**$10.50**

Price: 1/16″ silver bead $11.50
Price: 3/32″ silver bead $16.00
Price: Sourdough bead $14.50
Price: Tritium night sight $47.00
Price: Folding night sight with ivory bead $39.50

LYMAN NO. 18 SCREW-ON RAMP Used with 8-40 screws but may also be brazed on. Heights from .10″ to .350″. Ramp without sight.
Price: $13.75

MARBLE FRONT RAMPS Available in polished or dull matte finish or serrated style. Standard 3/8x.090″ dovetail slot. Made for MR-width (.340″) front sights. Can be used as screw-on or sweat-on. Heights: .100″, .150″, .300″.
Price: Polished or matte $14.00
Price: Serrated $10.00

WILLIAMS SHORTY RAMP Companion to "Streamlined" ramp, about 1/2″ shorter. Screw-on or sweat-on. It is furnished in 1/8″, 3/16″, 9/32″, and 3/8″ heights without hood only. Also for shotguns.
Price: $15.90
Price: With dovetail lock $18.55

WILLIAMS STREAMLINED RAMP Available in screw-on or sweat-on models. Furnished in 9/16″, 7/16″, 3/8″, 5/16″, 3/16″ heights.
Price: $17.35
Price: Sight hood $3.95

WILLIAMS STREAMLINED FRONT SIGHTS Narrow (.250″ width) for Williams Streamlined ramps and others with 1/4″ top width; medium (.340″ width) for all standard factory ramps. Available with white, gold or flourescent beads, 1/16″ or 3/32″.
Price: .... $8.93 to $9.25

Handgun Sights

AO EXPRESS SIGHTS Low-profile, snag-free express-type sights. Shallow V rear with white vertical line, white dot front. All-steel, matte black finish. Rear is available in different heights. Made for most pistols, many with double set-screws. From AO Sight Systems, Inc.
Price: Standard Set, front and rear $60.00
Price: Big Dot Set, front and rear $60.00
Price: Tritium Set, Standard or Big Dot $90.00

BO-MAR DELUXE BMCS Gives 3/8″ windage and elevation adjustment at 50 yards on Colt Gov't 45; sight radius under 7″. For GM and Commander models only. Uses existing dovetail slot. Has shield-type rear blade.
Price: $65.95
Price: BMCS-2 (for GM and 9mm) $68.95
Price: Flat bottom $65.95
Price: BMGC (for Colt Gold Cup), angled serrated blade, rear $68.95
Price: BMGC front sight $12.95
Price: BMCZ-75 (for CZ-75, TZ-75, P-9 and most clones). Works with factory front $68.95

BO-MAR FRONT SIGHTS Dovetail style for S&W 4506, 4516, 1076; undercut style (.250″, .280″, 5/16″ high); Fast Draw style (.210″, .250″, .230″ high).
Price $12.95

BO-MAR BMU XP-100/T/C CONTENDER No gunsmithing required; has .080″ notch.
Price: $77.00

BO-MAR BMML For muzzleloaders; has .062″ notch, flat bottom.
Price: $65.95
Price: With 3/8″ dovetail $65.95

BO-MAR RUGER "P" ADJUSTABLE SIGHT Replaces factory front and rear sights.
Price: Rear sight $65.95
Price: Front sight $12.00

BO-MAR BMR Fully adjustable rear sight for Ruger MKI, MKII Bull barrel autos.
Price: Rear $65.95
Price: Undercut front sight $12.00

BO-MAR GLOCK Fully adjustable, all-steel replacement sights. Sight fits factory dovetail. Longer sight radius. Uses Novak Glock .275″ high, .135″ wide front, or similar.
Price: Rear sight $68.95
Price: Front sight $20.95

BO-MAR LOW PROFILE RIB & ACCURACY TUNER Streamlined rib with front and rear sights; 7 1/8″ sight radius. Brings sight line closer to the bore than standard or extended sight and ramp. Weight 5 oz. Made for Colt Gov't 45, Super 38, and Gold Cup 45 and 38.
Price: $140.00

BO-MAR COMBAT RIB For S&W Model 19 revolver with 4″ barrel. Sight radius 5 3/4″, weight 5 1/2 oz.
Price: $127.00

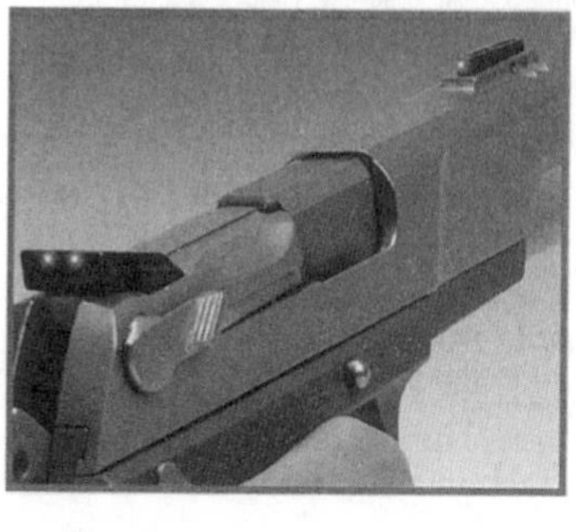

Williams Fire Sight Set

BO-MAR WINGED RIB For S&W 4″ and 6″ length barrels—K-38, M10, HB 14 and 19. Weight for the 6″ model is about 7 1/4 oz.
Price: $140.00

BO-MAR COVER-UP RIB Adjustable rear sight, winged front guards. Fits right over revolver's original front sight. For S&W 4″ M-10HB, M-13, M-58, M-64 & 65, Ruger 4″ models SDA-34, SDA-84, SS-34, SS-84, GF-34, GF-84.
Price: $130.00

C-MORE SIGHTS Replacement front sight blades offered in two types and five styles. Made of Du Pont Acetal, they come in a set of five high-contrast colors: blue, green, pink, red and yellow. Easy to install. Patridge style for Colt Python (all barrels), Ruger Super Blackhawk (7 1/2″), Ruger Blackhawk (4 5/8″); ramp style for Python (all barrels), Blackhawk (4 5/8″), Super Blackhawk (7 1/2″ and 10 1/2″). From C-More Systems.
Price: Per set $19.95

G.G. & G. GHOST RINGS Replaces the factory rear sight without gunsmithing. Black phosphate finish. Available for Colt M1911 and Commander, Beretta M92F, Glock, S&W, SIG Sauer.
Price: $65.00

JP GHOST RING Replacement bead front, ghost ring rear for Glock and M1911 pistols. From JP Enterprises.
Price: $79.95
Price: Bo-Mar replacement leaf with JP dovetail front bead $99.95

MMC TACTICAL ADJUSTABLE SIGHTS Low-profile, snag free design. Twenty-two click positions for elevation, drift adjustable for windage. Machined from 4140 steel and heat treated to 40 RC. Tritium and non-tritium. Ten different configurations and colors. Three different finishes. For 1911s, all Glock, HK USP, S&W, Browning Hi-Power.
Price: Sight set, tritium $144.92
Price: Sight set, white outline or white dot $99.90
Price: Sight set, black $93.90

MEPROLIGHT TRITIUM NIGHT SIGHTS Replacement sight assemblies for use in low-light conditions. Available for rifles, shotguns, handguns and bows. **TRU-DOT** models carry a 12-year warranty on the useable illumination, while non-**TRU-DOT** have a 5-year warranty. Contact Hesco, Inc. for complete list of available models.
Price: Kahr K9, K40, fixed, **TRU-DOT** $100.00
Price: Ruger P85, P89, P94, adjustable, **TRU-DOT** $156.00
Price: Ruger Mini-14R sights $140.00
Price: SIG Sauer P220, P225, P226, P228, adjustable, **TRU-DOT** $156.00
Price: Smith&Wesson autos, fixed or adjustable, **TRU-DOT** $100.00
Price: Taurus PT92, PT100, adjustable, **TRU-DOT** $156.00
Price: Walther P-99, fixed, **TRU-DOT** $100.00
Price: Shotgun bead $32.00
Price: Beretta M92, Cougar, Brigadier, fixed, **TRU-DOT** $100.00
Price: Browning Hi-Power, adjustable, **TRU-DOT** $156.00
Price: Colt M1911 Govt., adjustable, **TRU-DOT** $156.00

MILLETT SERIES 100 REAR SIGHTS All-steel highly visible, click adjustable. Blades in white outline, target black, silhouette, 3-dot, and tritium bars. Fit most popular revolvers and autos.
Price: .... $49.30 to $80.00

MILLETT BAR-DOT-BAR TRITIUM NIGHT SIGHTS Replacement front and rear combos fit most automatics. Horizontal tritium bars on rear, dot front sight.
Price: $145.00

MILLETT 3-DOT SYSTEM SIGHTS The 3-Dot System sights use a single white dot on the front blade and two dots flanking the rear notch. Fronts available in Dual-Crimp and Wide Stake-On styles, as well as special applications. Adjustable rear sight available for most popular auto pistols and revolvers.
Price: Front, from $16.00
Price: Adjustable rear $55.60

MILLETT REVOLVER FRONT SIGHTS All-steel replacement front sights with either white or orange bar. Easy to install. For Ruger GP-100, Redhawk, Security-Six, Police-Six, Speed-Six, Colt Trooper, Diamondback, King Cobra, Peacemaker, Python, Dan Wesson 22 and 15-2.
Price: .... $13.60 to $16.00

MILLETT DUAL-CRIMP FRONT SIGHT Replacement front sight for automatic pistols. Dual-Crimp uses an all-steel two-point hollow rivet system. Available in eight heights and four styles. Has a skirted base that covers the front sight pad. Easily installed with the Millett Installation Tool Set. Available in Blaze Orange Bar, White Bar, Serrated Ramp, Plain Post.
Price: $16.00

MILLETT STAKE-ON FRONT SIGHT Replacement front sight for automatic pistols. Stake-On sights have skirted base that covers the front sight pad. Easily installed with the Millet Installation Tool Set. Available in seven heights and four styles—Blaze Orange Bar, White Bar, Serrated Ramp, Plain Post.
Price: $16.00

OMEGA OUTLINE SIGHT BLADES Replacement rear sight blades for Colt and Ruger single action guns and the Interarms Virginian Dragoon. Standard Outline available in gold or white notch outline on blue metal. From Omega Sales, Inc.
Price: $8.95

OMEGA MAVERICK SIGHT BLADES Replacement "peep-sight" blades for Colt, Ruger SAs, Virginian Dragoon. Three models available—No. 1, Plain; No. 2, Single Bar; No. 3, Double Bar Rangefinder. From Omega Sales, Inc.
Price: Each $6.95

PACHMAYR ACCU-SET Low-profile, fully adjustable rear sight to be used with existing front sight. Available with target, white outline or 3-dot blade. Blue finish. Uses factory dovetail and locking screw. For Browning, Colt, Glock, SIG Sauer, S&W and Ruger autos. From Pachmayr.
Price: .... NA

ACCESSORIES

METALLIC SIGHTS

P-T TRITIUM NIGHT SIGHTS Self-luminous tritium sights for most popular handguns, Colt AR-15, H&K rifles and shotguns. Replacement handgun sight sets available in 3-Dot style (green/green, green/yellow, green/orange) with bold outlines around inserts; Bar-Dot available in green/green with or without white outline rear sight. Functional life exceeds 15 years. From Innovative Weaponry, Inc.
Price: Handgun sight sets $99.95
Price: Rifle sight sets $99.95
Price: Rifle, front only $49.95
Price: Shotgun, front only $49.95
TRIJICON NIGHT SIGHTS Three-dot night sight system uses tritium lamps in the front and rear sights. Tritium "lamps" are mounted in silicone rubber inside a metal cylinder. A polished crystal sapphire provides protection and clarity. Inlaid white outlines provide 3-dot aiming in daylight also. Available for most popular handguns. From Trijicon, Inc.
Price: . . . . $50.00 to $175.00

Wichita Series 70/80

WICHITA SERIES 70/80 SIGHT Provides click windage and elevation adjustments with precise repeatability of settings. Sight blade is grooved and angled back at the top to reduce glare. Available in Low Mount Combat or Low Mount Target styles for Colt 45s and their copies, S&W 645, Hi-Power, CZ 75 and others.
Price: Rear sight, target or combat $75.00
Price: Front sight, Patridge or ramp $15.00
WICHITA GRAND MASTER DELUXE RIBS Ventilated rib has wings machined into it for better sight acquisition and is relieved for Mag-Na-Porting. Milled to accept Weaver see-thru-style rings. Made of stainless or blued steel; front and rear sights blued. Has Wichita Multi-Range rear sight system, adjustable front sight. Made for revolvers with 6" barrel.
Price: Model 301S, 301B (adj. sight K frames with custom bbl. of 1" to 1.032" dia. L and N frame with 1.062" to 1.100" dia. bbl.) $189.00
Price: Model 303S, 303B (adj. sight K, L, N frames with factory barrel) $189.00
WILLIAMS FIRE SIGHT SETS Red fiber optic metallic sight replaces the original. Rear sight has two green fiber optic elements. Made of CNC-machined aluminum. Fits all Glocks, Ruger P-Series (except P-85), S&W 910, Colt Gov't. Model Series 80, Ruger GP 100 and Redhawk, and SIG Sauer (front only).
Price: Front and rear set $39.95
Price: SIG Sauer front $19.95

Shotgun Sights

ACCURA-SITE For shooting shotgun slugs. Three models to fit most shotguns—"A" for vent. rib barrels, "B" for solid ribs, "C" for plain barrels. Rear sight has windage and elevation provisions. Easily removed and replaced. Includes front and rear sights. From All's, The Jim Tembeils Co.
Price: . . . .$27.95 to $34.95
FIRE FLY EM-109 SL SHOTGUN SIGHT Made of aircraft-grade aluminum, this 1/4-oz. "channel" sight has a thick, sturdy hollowed post between the side rails to give a Patridge sight picture. All shooting is done with both eyes open, allowing the shooter to concentrate on the target, not the sights. The hole in the sight post gives reduced-light shooting capability and allows for fast, precise aiming. For sport or combat shooting. Model EM-109 fits all vent. rib and double barrel shotguns and muzzleloaders with octagon barrel. Model MOC-110 fits all plain barrel shotguns without screw-in chokes. From JAS, Inc.
Price: $35.00
LYMAN Three sights of over-sized ivory beads. No. 10 Front (press fit) for double barrel or ribbed single barrel guns..$4.50; No. 10D Front (screw fit) for non-ribbed single barrel guns (comes with wrench)...$5.50; No. 11 Middle (press fit) for double and ribbed single barrel guns...$4.75.
MMC M&P COMBAT SHOTGUN SIGHT SET A durable, protected ghost ring aperture, combat sight made of steel. Fully adjustable for windage and elevation.
Price: M&P Sight Set (front and rear) $73.45
Price: As above, installed $83.95
MMC TACTICAL GHOST RING SIGHT Click adjustable for elevation with 30 MOA total adjustment in 3 MOA increments. Click windage adjustment. Machined from 4140 steel, heat treated to 40 RC. Front sight available in banded tactical or serrated ramp. Front and rear sights available with or without tritium. Available in three different finishes.

Price: Rear Ghost Ring with tritium. $119.95
Price: Rear Ghost Ring without tritium $99.95
Price: Front Banded Tactical with tritium. $59.95
Price: Front Banded Tactical without tritium $39.95
Price: Front serrated ramp $24.95
MARBLE SHOTGUN BEAD SIGHTS No. 214—Ivory front bead, 11/64", tapered shank...**$4.40**; No. 223—Ivory rear bead, .080", tapered shank...**$4.40**; No. 217—Ivory front bead, 11/64", threaded shank...**$4.75**; No. 223-T—Ivory rear bead, .080", threaded shank...**$5.95**. Reamers, taps and wrenches available from Marble Arms.
MILLETT SHURSHOT SHOTGUN SIGHT A sight system for shotguns with ventilated rib. Rear sight attaches to the rib, front sight replaces the front bead. Front has an orange face, rear has two orange bars. For 870, 1100 or other models.
Price: Rear $13.15
Price: Adjustable front and rear set. $31.00
Price: Front $12.95
POLY-CHOKE Replacement front shotgun sights in four styles—Xpert, Poly Bead, Xpert Mid Rib sights, and Bev-L-Block. Xpert Front available in 3x56, 6x48 thread, 3/32" or 5/32" shank length, gold, ivory...**$4.70**; or Sun Spot orange bead...**$5.95**; Poly Bead is standard replacement 1/8" bead, 6x48...**$2.95**; Xpert Mid Rib in tapered carrier (ivory only) …**$5.95**, or 3x56 threaded shank (gold only)...**$2.95**; Hi and Lo Blok sights with 6x48 thread, gold or ivory...**$5.25**. From Marble Arms.
SLUG SIGHTS Made of non-marring black nylon, front and rear sights stretch over and lock onto the barrel. Sights are low profile with blaze orange front blade. Adjustable for windage and elevation. For plain-barrel (non-ribbed) guns in 12-, 16- and 20-gauge, and for shotguns with 5/16" and 3/8" ventilated ribs. From Innovision Ent.
Price: $11.95
WILLIAMS GUIDE BEAD SIGHT Fits all shotguns, 1/8" ivory, red or gold bead. Screws into existing sight hole. Various thread sizes and shank lengths.
Price: $4.77
WILLIAMS SLUGGER SIGHTS Removable aluminum sights attach to the shotgun rib. High profile front, fully adjustable rear. Fits 1/4", 5/16" or 3/8" (special) ribs.
Price: $34.95
WILLIAMS FIRE SIGHTS Fiber optic light gathering front sights in red or yellow, glow with natural light. Fit 1/4", 5/16" or 3/8" vent. ribs, most popular shotguns.
Price: $13.95

Sight Attachments

MERIT ADJUSTABLE APERTURES Eleven clicks give 12 different apertures. No. 3 Disc and Master, primarily target types, 0.22" to .125"; No. 4, 1/2" dia. hunting type, .025" to .155". Available for all popular sights. The Master, with flexible rubber light shield, is particularly adapted to extension, scope height, and tang sights. All models have internal click springs; are hand fitted to minimum tolerance.
Price: No. 3 Master Disk $66.00
Price: No. 3 Target Disc (Plain Face) $56.00
Price: No. 4 Hunting Disc $48.00
MERIT LENS DISC Similar to Merit Iris Shutter (Model 3 or Master) but incorporates provision for mounting prescription lens integrally. Lens may be obtained locally from your optician. Sight disc is 7/16" wide (Model 3), or 3/4" wide (Master).
Price: No. 3 Target Lens Disk $68.00
Price: No. 3 Master Lens Disk. $78.00

Merit Optical Attachment

MERIT OPTICAL ATTACHMENT For iron sight shooting with handgun or rifle. Instantly attached by rubber suction cup to prescription or shooting glasses. Swings aside. Aperture adjustable from .020" to .156".
Price: $65.00
WILLIAMS APERTURES Standard thread, fits most sights. Regular series 3/8" to 1/2" O.D., .050" to .125" hole. "Twilight" series has white reflector ring.
Price: Regular series. $4.97
Price: Twilight series $6.79
Price: Wide open 5/16" aperture for shotguns fits 5-D or Foolproof sights (specify model) $8.77

SPOTTING SCOPES

Swift M700T Scout

Nikon
Fieldscope 78mm

BAUSCH & LOMB DISCOVERER 15x to 60x zoom, 60mm objective. Constant focus throughout range. Field at 1000 yds. 38 ft (60x), 150 ft. (15x). Comes with lens caps. Length 17 1/2"; weight 48.5 oz.
Price: **$391.95**

BAUSCH & LOMB ELITE 15x to 45x zoom, 60mm objective. Field at 1000 yds., 125-65 ft. Length is 12.2"; weight, 26.5 oz. Waterproof, armored. Tripod mount. Comes with black case.
Price: **$766.95**

BAUSCH & LOMB ELITE ZOOM 20x-60x, 70mm objective. Roof prism. Field at 1000 yds. 90-50 ft. Length is 16"; weight 40 oz. Waterproof, armored. Tripod mount. Comes with black case.
Price: **$921.95**

BAUSCH & LOMB 80MM ELITE 20x-60x zoom, 80mm objective. Field of view at 1000 yds. (zoom). Weight 51 oz. (20x, 30x), 54 oz. (zoom); length 17". Interchangeable bayonet-style eyepieces. Built-in peep sight.
Price: With EDPrime Glass **$1,212.95**

BURRIS 18-45x SIGNATURE SPOTTER 60mm objective, 18x-45x, constant focus, Field at 1000 yds. 112-63 ft.; weighs 29oz.; length 12.6". Camera adapters available.
Price: **$819.00**

BURRIS LANDMARK SPOTTER 15-45x, 60mm objective. Straight type. Field at 100 yds. 146-72 ft. Length 12.7"; weight 24 oz. Rubber armor coating, multi-coated lenses, 22mm eye relief. Recessed focus adjustment. Nitrogen filled. .
Price: 30x 60mm **$644.00**

BUSHNELL TROPHY 63mm objective, 20x-60x zoom. Field at 1000 yds. 90ft. (20x), 45 ft. (60x). Length 12.7"; weight 20 oz. Black rubber armored, waterproof. Case included.
Price: **$421.95**

BUSHNELL COMPACT TROPHY 50mm objective, 20x-50x zoom. Field at 1000 yds. 92 ft. (20x), 52 ft. (50x). Length 12.2"; weight 17 oz. Black rubber armored, waterproof. Case included.
Price: **$337.95**

BUSHNELL BANNER SENTRY 18x-36x zoom, 50mm objective. Field at 1000 yds. 115-75 ft. Length 14.5", weight 31 oz. Black rubber armored. Built-in peep sight. Comes with tripod and hardcase.
Price: **$180.95**
Price: With 45 field eyepiece, includes tripod **$202.95**

BUSHNELL SPACEMASTER 20x-45x zoom. Long eye relief. Rubber armored, prismatic. 60mm objective. Field at 1000 yds. 90-58 ft. Minimum focus 20 ft. Length 12.7"; weight 43 oz.
Price: With tripod, carrying case and 20x-45x LER eyepiece. **$560.95**

BUSHNELL SPORTVIEW 12x-36x zoom, 50mm objective. Field at 100 yds. 160 ft. (12x), 90 ft. (36x). Length 14.6"; weight 25 oz.
Price: With tripod and carrying case **$159.95**

BUSHNELL X-TRA WIDE® 15-45x zoom, 60mm objective. Field at 1000 yds. 160-87 ft. Length 13"; weight 35 oz.
Price: **$640.95**

HERMES 1 70mm objective, 16x, 25x, 40x. Field at 1000 meters 160 ft. (16x), 75ft. (40x). Length 12.2"; weight 33 oz. From CZ-USA.
Price: Body **$359.00**
Price: 25x eyepiece **$86.00**
Price: 40x eyepiece **$128.00**

KOWA TSN SERIES Offset 45 or straight body. 77mm objective, 20x WA, 25x, 25x LER, 30x WA, 40x, 60x, 77x and 20-60x zoom. Field at 1000 yds. 179 ft. (20xWA), 52 ft. (60x). Available with flourite lens.
Price: TSN-1 (without eyepiece) 45 offset scope **$696.00**
Price: TSN-2 (without eyepiece) Straight scope **$660.00**
Price: 20x W.A. (wide angle) eyepiece **$230.00**
Price: 25x eyepiece **$143.00**
Price: 25x LER (long eye relief) eyepiece **$214.00**

Price: 30x W.A. (wide angle) eyepiece **$266.00**
Price: 40x eyepiece **$159.00**
Price: 60x W.A. (wide angle) eyepiece **$230.00**
Price: 77x eyepiece **$235.00**
Price: 20-60x zoom eyepiece **$302.00**

KOWA TS-610 SERIES Offset 45 or straight body. 60mm objective, 20x WA, 25x, 25x LER, 27x WA, 40x and 20-60x zoom. Field at 1000 yds. 162 ft. (20x WA), 51 ft. (60x). Available with ED lens.
Price: TS-611 (without eyepiece) 45 offset scope **$510.00**
Price: TS-612 (without eyepiece) Straight scope **$462.00**
Price: 20x W.A. (wide angle) eyepiece **$111.00**
Price: 25x eyepiece **$95.00**
Price: 25x LER (long eye relief) eyepiece **$214.00**
Price: 27x W.A. (wide angle) eyepiece **$166.00**
Price: 40x eyepiece **$98.00**
Price: 20-60x zoom eyepiece **$207.00**

KOWA TS-9 SERIES Offset 45, straight or rubber armored (straight only). 50mm objective, 15x, 20x and 11-33x zoom. Field at 1000 yds. 188 ft. (15x), 99 ft. (33x).
Price: TS-9B (without eyepiece) 45 offset scope. **$223.00**
Price: TS-9C (without eyepiece) straight scope **$176.00**
Price: TS-9R (without eyepiece) straight rubber armored scope/black. **$197.00**
Price: 15x eyepiece **$38.00**
Price: 20x eyepiece **$36.00**
Price: 11-33x zoom eyepiece **$122.00**

LEUPOLD 12-40x60 VARIABLE 60mm objective, 12-40x. Field at 100 yds. 17.5-5.3 ft.; eye relief 1.2" (20x). Overall length 11.5", weight 32 oz. Rubber armored.
Price: **$1,217.90**

LEUPOLD 25x50 COMPACT 50mm objective, 25x. Field at 100 yds. 8.3 ft.; eye relief 1"; length overall 9.4"; weight 20.5 oz.
Price: Armored model **$848.20**
Price: Packer Tripod **$96.40**

MEOPTA HA 70 (Hermes I) Spotting scope 70mm objective, 16x, 25xWA, 40x, 50x or 20-45x. Length 12.2"; weight 32.5 oz.
Price: .... **NA**

MIRADOR TTB SERIES Draw tube armored spotting scopes. Available with 75mm or 80mm objective. Zoom model (28x-62x, 80mm) is 11 7/8" (closed), weighs 50 oz. Field at 1000 yds. 70-42 ft. Comes with lens covers.
Price: 28-62x80mm **$1,133.95**
Price: 32x80mm **$971.95**
Price: 26-58x75mm **$989.95**
Price: 30x75mm **$827.95**

MIRADOR SSD SPOTTING SCOPES 60mm objective, 15x, 20x, 22x, 25x, 40x, 60x, 20-60x; field at 1000 yds. 37 ft.; length 10 1/4"; weight 33 oz.
Price: 25x **$575.95**
Price: 22x Wide Angle **$593.95**
Price: 20-60x Zoom **$746.95**
Price: As above, with tripod, case. **$944.95**

MIRADOR SIA SPOTTING SCOPES Similar to the SSD scopes except with 45° eyepiece. Length 12 1/4"; weight 39 oz.
Price: 25x **$809.95**
Price: 22x Wide Angle **$827.95**
Price: 20-60x Zoom **$980.95**

MIRADOR SSR SPOTTING SCOPES 50mm or 60mm objective. Similar to SSD except rubber armored in black or camouflage. Length 11 1/8"; weight 31 oz.
Price: Black, 20x **$521.95**
Price: Black, 18x Wide Angle **$539.95**
Price: Black, 16-48x Zoom **$692.95**
Price: Black, 20x, 60mm, EER **$692.95**
Price: Black, 22x Wide Angle, 60mm **$701.95**
Price: Black, 20-60x Zoom **$854.95**

MIRADOR SSF FIELD SCOPES Fixed or variable power, choice of 50mm, 60mm, 75mm objective lens. Length 9 3/4"; weight 20 oz. (15-32x50).
Price: 20x50mm **$359.95**
Price: 25x60mm **$440.95**
Price: 30x75mm **$584.95**
Price: 15-32x50mm Zoom **$548.95**
Price: 18-40x60mm Zoom **$629.95**
Price: 22-47x75mm Zoom **$773.95**

MIRADOR SRA MULTI ANGLE SCOPES Similar to SSF Series except eyepiece head rotates for viewing from any angle.
Price: 20x50mm **$503.95**
Price: 25x60mm **$647.95**

SPOTTING SCOPES

Price: 30x75mm $764.95
Price: 15-32x50mm Zoom $692.95
Price: 18-40x60mm Zoom $836.95
Price: 22-47x75mm Zoom $953.95

MIRADOR SIB FIELD SCOPES Short-tube, 45° scopes with porro prism design. 50mm and 60mm objective. Length 10 1/4"; weight 18.5 oz. (15-32x50mm); field at 1000 yds. 129-81 ft.
Price: 20x50mm $386.95
Price: 25x60mm $449.95
Price: 15-32x50mm Zoom $575.95
Price: 18-40x60mm Zoom $638.95

NIKON FIELDSCOPES 60mm and 78mm lens. Field at 1000 yds. 105 ft. (60mm, 20x), 126 ft. (78mm, 25x). Length 12.8" (straight 60mm), 12.6" (straight 78mm); weight 34.5-47.5 oz. Eyepieces available separately.
Price: 60mm straight body $690.95
Price: 60mm angled body $796.95
Price: 60mm straight ED body $1,200.95
Price: 60mm angled ED body $1,314.95
Price: 78mm straight ED body $2,038.95
Price: 78mm angled ED body $2,170.95
Price: Eyepieces (15x to 60x) .... **$146.95** to **$324.95**
Price: 20-45x eyepiece (25-56x for 78mm) $318.95

NIKON SPOTTING SCOPE 60mm objective, 20x fixed power or 15-45x zoom. Field at 1000 yds. 145 ft. (20x). Gray rubber armored. Straight or angled eyepiece. Weighs 44.2 oz., length 12.1" (20x).
Price: 20x60 fixed (with eyepiece) $368.95
Price: 15-45x zoom (with case, tripod, eyepiece) $578.95

PENTAX PF-80ED spotting scope 80mm objective lenses available in 18x, 24x, 36x, 48x, 72x and 20-60x. Length 15.6", weight 11.9 to 19.2 oz.
Price: $1,320.00

SIGHTRON SII 2050X63 63mm objective lens, 20x-50x zoom. Field at 1000 yds 91.9 ft. (20x), 52.5 ft. (50x). Length 14"; weight 30.8 oz. Black rubber finish. Also available with 80mm objective lens.
Price: 63mm or 80mm $339.95

SIMMONS 1280 50mm objective, 15-45x zoom. Black matte finish. Ocular focus. Peep finder sight. Waterproof. FOV 95-51 ft. @ 1000 yards. Wgt. 33.5 oz., length 12".
Price: With tripod $267.99

SIMMONS 1281 60mm objective, 20-60x zoom. Black matte finish. Ocular focus. Peep finder sight. Waterproof. FOV 78-43 ft. @ 1000 yards. Wgt. 34.5 oz. Length 12".
Price: With tripod $295.99

SIMMONS 77206 PROHUNTER 50mm objectives, 25x fixed power. Field at 1000 yds. 113 ft.; length 10.25"; weighs 33.25 oz. Black rubber armored.
Price: With tripod case $160.60

SIMMONS 41200 REDLINE 50mm objective, 15x-45x zoom. Field at 1000 yds. 104-41 ft.; length 16.75"; weighs 32.75 oz.
Price: With hard case and tripod $99.99
Price: 20-60x, Model 41201 .... $129.99

STEINER FIELD TELESCOPE 24x, 80mm objective. Field at 1000 yds. 105 ft. Weight 44 oz. Tripod mounts. Rubber armored.
Price: $1,299.00

SWAROVSKI CT EXTENDIBLE SCOPES 75mm or 85mm objective, 20-60x zoom, or fixed 15x, 22x, 30x, 32x eyepieces. Field at 1000 yds. 135 ft. (15x), 99 ft. (32x); 99 ft. (20x), 5.2 ft. (60x) for zoom. Length 12.4" (closed), 17.2" (open) for the CT75; 9.7"/17.2" for CT85. Weight 40.6 oz. (CT75), 49.4 oz. (CT85). Green rubber armored.
Price: CT75 body $765.56
Price: CT85 body $1,094.44
Price: 20-60x eyepiece $343.33
Price: 15x, 22x eyepiece $232.22
Price: 30x eyepiece $265.55

SWAROVSKI AT-80/ST-80 SPOTTING SCOPES 80mm objective, 20-60x zoom, or fixed 15x, 22x, 30x, 32x eyepieces. Field at 1000 yds. 135 ft. (15x), 99 ft. (32x); 99 ft. (20x), 52.5 ft. (60x) for zoom. Length 16" (AT-80), 15.6" (ST-80); weight 51.8 oz. Available with HD (high density) glass.
Price: AT-80 (angled) body $1,094.44
Price: ST-80 (straight) body $1,094.44
Price: With HD glass $1,555.00
Price: 20-60x eyepiece $343.33
Price: 15x, 22x eyepiece $232.22
Price: 30x eyepiece $265.55

SWIFT LYNX M836 15x-45x zoom, 60mm objective. Weight 7 lbs., length 14". Has 45° eyepiece, sunshade.
Price: $315.00

SWIFT NIGHTHAWK M849U 80mm objective, 20x-60x zoom, or fixed 19, 25x, 31x, 50x, 75x eyepieces. Has rubber armored body, 1.8x optical finder, retractable lens hood, 45° eyepiece. Field at 1000 yds. 60 ft. (28x), 41 ft. (75x). Length 13.4 oz.; weight 39 oz.
Price: Body only $870.00
Price: 20-68x eyepiece $370.00
Price: Fixed eyepieces .... **$130.00** to **$240.00**
Price: Model 849 (straight) body $795.00

SWIFT NIGHTHAWK M850U 65mm objective, 16x-48x zoom, or fixed 19x, 20x, 25x, 40x, 60x eyepieces. Rubber armored with a 1.8x optical finder, retractable lens hood. Field at 1000 yds. 83 ft. (22x), 52 ft. (60x). Length 12.3"; weight 30 oz. Has 45° eyepiece.
Price: Body only $650.00
Price: 16x-48x eyepiece $370.00
Price: Fixed eyepieces .... **$130.00** to **$240.00**
Price: Model 850 (straight) body $575.00

SWIFT LEOPARD M837 50mm objective, 25x. Length 9 11/16" to 10 1/2". Weight with tripod 28 oz. Rubber armored. Comes with tripod.
Price: $160.00

SWIFT TELEMASTER M841 60mm objective. 15x to 60x variable power. Field at 1000 yds. 160 feet (15x) to 40 feet (60x). Weight 3.25 lbs.; length 18" overall.
Price: $399.50

SWIFT PANTHER M844 15x-45x zoom or 22x WA, 15x, 20x, 40x. 60mm objective. Field at 1000 yds. 141 ft. (15x), 68 ft. (40x), 95-58 ft. (20x-45x).
Price: Body only $380.00
Price: 15x-45x zoom eyepiece $120.00
Price: 20x-45x zoom (long eye relief) eyepiece $140.00
Price: 15x, 20x, 40x eyepiece $65.00
Price: 22x WA eyepiece $80.00

SWIFT M700T 12x-36x, 50mm objective. Field of view at 100 yds. 16 ft. (12x), 9 ft. (36x). Length 14"; weight with tripod 3.22 lbs.
Price: $225.00

SWIFT SEARCHER M839 60mm objective, 20x, 40x. Field at 1000 yds. 118 ft. (30x), 59 ft. (40x). Length 12.6"; weight 3 lbs. Rotating eyepiece head for straight or 45° viewing.
Price: $580.00
Price: 30x, 50x eyepieces, each $67.00

TASCO 29TZBWP WATERPROOF SPOTTER 60mm objective lens, 20x-60x zoom. Field at 100 yds. 7 ft., 4 in. to 3 ft., 8 in. Black rubber armored. Comes with tripod, hard case.
Price: $356.50

TASCO WC28TZ WORLD CLASS SPOTTING SCOPE 50mm objective, 12-36x zoom. Field at 100 yds. World Class. 13-3.8 ft. Comes with tripod and case.
Price: $220.00

TASCO CW5001 COMPACT ZOOM 50mm objective, 12x-36x zoom. Field at 100 yds. 16 ft., 9 in. Includes photo adapter tube, tripod with panhead lever, case.
Price: $280.00

TASCO 3700WP WATERPROOF SPOTTER 50mm objective, 18x-36x zoom. Field at 100 yds. 12ft., 6 in. to 7 ft., 9 in. Black rubber armored. Comes with tripod, hard case.
Price: $288.60

TASCO 3700, 3701 SPOTTING SCOPE 50mm objective. 18x-36x zoom. Field at 100 yds. 12 ft., 6 in. to 7 ft., 9 in. Black rubber armored.
Price: Model 3700 (black, with tripod, case) $237.00
Price: Model 3701 (as above, brown camo) $237.00

TASCO 21EB ZOOM 50mm objective lens, 15x-45x zoom. Field at 100 yds. 11 ft. (15x). Weight 22 oz.; length 18.3" overall. Comes with panhead lever tripod.
Price: $119.00

TASCO 22EB ZOOM 60mm objective lens, 20x-60x zoom. Field at 100 yds. 7 ft., 2 in. (20x). Weight 28 oz.; length 21.5" overall. Comes with micro-adjustable tripod.
Price: $183.00

UNERTL "FORTY-FIVE" 54mm objective. 20x (single fixed power). Field at 100 yds. 10',10"; eye relief 1"; focusing range infinity to 33 ft. Weight about 32 oz.; overall length 153/4". With lens covers.
Price: With multi-layer lens coating $662.00
Price: With mono-layer magnesium coating $572.00

UNERTL STRAIGHT PRISMATIC 63.5mm objective, 24x. Field at 100 yds., 7 ft. Relative brightness, 6.96. Eye relief 1/2". Weight 40 oz.; length closed 19". Push-pull and screw-focus eyepiece. 16x and 32x eyepieces **$125.00** each.
Price: $515.00

UNERTL 20x STRAIGHT PRISMATIC 54mm objective, 20x. Field at 100 yds. 8.5 ft. Relative brightness 6.1. Eye relief 1/2". Weight 36 oz.; length closed 13 1/2". Complete with lens covers.
Price: $477.00

UNERTL TEAM SCOPE 100mm objective. 15x, 24x, 32x eyepieces. Field at 100 yds. 13 to 7.5 ft. Relative brightness, 39.06 to 9.79. Eye relief 2" to 11/2". Weight 13 lbs.; length 29 7/8" overall. Metal tripod, yoke and wood carrying case furnished (total weight 80 lbs.).
Price: $2,810.00

WEAVER 20x50 50mm objective. Field of view 124 ft. at 100 yds. Eye relief .85"; weighs 21 oz.; overall length 10". Waterproof, armored.
Price: $368.99

WEAVER 15-40x60 ZOOM 60mm objective. 15x-40x zoom. Field at 100 yds. 119 ft. (15x), 66 ft. (60x). Overall length 12.5", weighs 26 oz. Waterproof, armored.
Price: $551.99

ACCESSORIES

CHOKES & BRAKES

Briley Screw-In Chokes

Installation of these choke tubes requires that all traces of the original choking be removed, the barrel threaded internally with square threads and then the tubes are custom fitted to the specific barrel diameter. The tubes are thin and, therefore, made of stainless steel. Cost of installation for single-barrel guns (pumps, autos), lead shot, 12-gauge, **$149.00**, 20-gauge **$159.00**; steel shot **$179.00** and **$189.00**, all with three chokes; un-single target guns run **$219.00**; over/unders and side-by-sides, lead shot, 12-gauge, **$369.00**, 20-gauge **$389.00**; steel shot **$469.00** and **$489.00**, all with five chokes. For 10-gauge auto or pump with two steel shot chokes, **$189.00**; over/unders, side-by-sides with three steel shot chokes, **$349.00**. For 16-gauge auto or pump, three lead shot chokes, **$179.00**; over/unders, side-by-sides with five lead shot chokes, **$449.00**. The 28 and 410-bore run **$179.00** for autos and pumps with three lead shot chokes, **$449.00** for over/unders and side-by-sides with five lead shot chokes.

Cutts Compensator

The Cutts Compensator is one of the oldest variable choke devices available. Manufactured by Lyman Gunsight Corporation, it is available with a steel body. A series of vents allows gas to escape upward and downward. For the 12-ga. Comp body, six fixed-choke tubes are available: the Spreader—popular with Skeet shooters; Improved Cylinder; Modified; Full; Superfull, and Magnum Full. Full, Modified and Spreader tubes are available for 12 or 20. Cutts Compensator, complete with wrench, adaptor and any single tube **$87.50**. All single choke tubes **$26.00** each. No factory installation available.

Dayson Automatic Brake System

This system fits most single barrel shotguns threaded for choke tubes, and cuts away 30 grooves on the exterior of a standard one-piece wad as it exits the muzzle. This slows the wad, allowing shot and wad to separate faster, reducing shot distortion and tightening patterns. The A.B.S. Choke Tube is claimed to reduce recoil by about 25 percent, and with the Muzzle Brake up to 60 percent. Ventilated Choke Tubes available from .685″ to .725″, in .005″ increments. Model I Ventilated Choke Tube for use with A.B.S. Muzzle Brake, **$49.95**; for use without Muzzle Brake, **$52.95**; A.B.S. Muzzle Brake, from **$69.95**. Contact Dayson Arms for more data.

Gentry Quiet Muzzle Brake

Developed by gunmaker David Gentry, the "Quiet Muzzle Brake" is said to reduce recoil by up to 85 percent with no loss of accuracy or velocity. There is no increase in noise level because the noise and gases are directed away from the shooter. The barrel is threaded for installation and the unit is blued to match the barrel finish. Price, installed, is **$150.00**. Add **$15.00** for stainless steel, **$45.00** for knurled cap to protect threads. Shipping extra.

JP Muzzle Brake

JP Muzzle Brake

Designed for single shot handguns, AR-15, Ruger Mini-14, Ruger Mini Thirty and other sporting rifles, the JP Muzzle Brake redirects high pressure gases against a large frontal surface which applies forward thrust to the gun. All gases are directed up, rearward and to the sides. Priced at **$79.95** (AR-15 or sporting rifles), **$89.95** (bull barrel and SKS, AK models), **$89.95** (Ruger Minis), Dual Chamber model **$79.95**. From JP Enterprises, Inc.

KDF Slim Line Muzzle Brake

This threaded muzzle brake has 30 pressure ports that direct combustion gases in all directions to reduce felt recoil up to a claimed 80 percent without affecting accuracy or ballistics. It is said to reduce felt recoil of a 30-06 to that of a 243. Price, installed, is **$179.00**. From KDF, Inc.

Laseraim

Simple, no-gunsmithing compensator reduces felt recoil and muzzle flip by up to 30 percent. Machined from single piece of Stainless Steel (Beretta/Taurus model made of aircraft aluminum). In black and polished finish. For Colt Government/Commander and Beretta/Taurus full-size pistols. Weighs 1 ounce. **$49.00**. From Laseraim Arms Inc.

Mag-Na-Port

Electrical Discharge Machining works on any firearm except those having non-conductive shrouded barrels. EDM is a metal erosion technique using carbon electrodes that control the area to be processed. The Mag-Na-Port venting process utilizes small trapezoidal openings to direct powder gases upward and outward to reduce recoil. No effect is had on bluing or nickeling outside the Mag-Na-Port area so no refinishing is needed. Rifle-style porting on single shot or large caliber handguns with barrels 7 1/2″ or longer is **$110.00**; Dual Trapezoidal porting on most handguns with minimum barrel length of 3″, **$100.00**; standard revolver porting **$78.50**; porting through the slide and barrel for semi-autos, **$115.00**; traditional rifle porting, **$125.00**. Prices do not include shipping, handling and insurance. From Mag-Na-Port International.

Mag-Na-Brake

A screw-on brake under 2″ long with progressive integrated exhaust chambers to neutralize expanding gases. Gases dissipate with an opposite twist to prevent the brake from unscrewing, and with a 5-degree forward angle to minimize sound pressure level. Available in blue, satin blue, bright or satin stainless. Standard and Light Contour installation cost **$179.00** for bolt-action rifles, many single action and single shot handguns. A knurled thread protector supplied at extra cost. Also available in Varmint style with exhaust chambers covering 220 degrees for prone-position shooters. From Mag-Na-Port International.

Poly-Choke

Marble Arms Corp., manufacturer of the Poly-Choke adjustable shotgun choke, now offers two models in 12-, 16-, 20-, and 28-gauge—the Ventilated and Standard style chokes. Each provides nine choke settings including Xtra-Full and Slug. The Ventilated model reduces 20 percent of a shotgun's recoil, the company claims, and is priced at **$135.00**. The Standard Model is **$125.00**. Postage not included. Contact Marble Arms for more data.

Pro-port

A compound ellipsoid muzzle venting process similar to Mag-Na-Porting, only exclusively applied to shotguns. Like Mag-Na-Porting, this system reduces felt recoil, muzzle jump, and shooter fatigue. Very helpful for trap doubles shooters. Pro-Port is a patented process and installation is available in both the U.S. and Canada. Cost for the Pro-Port process is **$129.50** for over/unders (both barrels); **$99.50** for only the top or bottom barrel; and **$78.50** for single-barrel shotguns. Optional pigeon porting costs **$25.00** extra per barrel. Prices do not include shipping and handling. From Pro-port Ltd.

Que Industries Adjustable Muzzle Brake

The Que Brake allows for fine-tuning of a rifle's accuracy by rotating the brake to one of 100 indexed stops. Mounts in minutes without barrel modification with heat-activated tensioning ring. The slotted exhaust ports reduce recoil by venting gases sideways, away from rifle. **$189.50**. From Que Industries.

SSK Arrestor muzzle brakes

SSK Arrestor Brake

This is a true muzzle brake with an expansion chamber. It takes up about 1″ of barrel and reduces velocity accordingly. Some Arrestors are added to a barrel, increasing its length. Said to reduce the felt recoil of a 458 to that approaching a 30-06. Can be set up to give zero muzzle rise in any caliber, and can be added to most guns. For handgun or rifle. Prices start at **$95.00**. Contact SSK Industries for full data.

PERIODICAL PUBLICATIONS

AAFTA News (M)
5911 Cherokee Ave., Tampa, FL 33604. Official newsletter of the American Airgun Field Target Assn.

Action Pursuit Games Magazine (M)
CFW Enterprises, Inc., 4201 W. Vanowen Pl., Burbank, CA 91505 818-845-2656. $4.99 single copy U.S., $5.50 Canada. Editor: Dan Reeves. World's leading magazine of paintball sports.

Air Gunner Magazine
4 The Courtyard, Denmark St., Wokingham, Berkshire RG11 2AZ, England/011-44-734-771677. $U.S. $44 for 1 yr. Leading monthly airgun magazine in U.K.

Airgun Ads
Box 33, Hamilton, MT 59840/406-363-3805; Fax: 406-363-4117. $35 1 yr. (for first mailing; $20 for second mailing; $35 for Canada and foreign orders.) Monthly tabloid with extensive For Sale and Wanted airgun listings.

The Airgun Letter
Gapp, Inc., 4614 Woodland Rd., Ellicott City, MD 21042-6329/410-730-5496; Fax: 410-730-9544; e-mail: staff@airgnltr.net; http://www.airgunletter.com. $21 U.S., $24 Canada, $27 Mexico and $33 other foreign orders, 1 yr. Monthly newsletter for airgun users and collectors.

Airgun World
4 The Courtyard, Denmark St., Wokingham, Berkshire RG40 2AZ, England/011-44-734-771677. Call for subscription rates. Oldest monthly airgun magazine in the U.K., now a sister publication to *Air Gunner*.

Alaska Magazine
Morris Communications, 735 Broad Street, Augusta, GA 30901/706-722-6060. Hunting, Fishing and Life on the Last Frontier articles of Alaska and western Canada.

American Firearms Industry
Nat'l. Assn. of Federally Licensed Firearms Dealers, 2455 E. Sunrise Blvd., Suite 916, Ft. Lauderdale, FL 33304. $35.00 yr. For firearms retailers, distributors and manufacturers.

American Guardian
NRA, 11250 Waples Mill Rd., Fairfax, VA 22030. Publications division. $15.00 1 yr. Magazine features personal protection; home-self-defense; family recreation shooting; women's issues; etc.

American Gunsmith
Belvoir Publications, Inc., 75 Holly Hill Lane, Greenwich, CT 06836-2626/203-661-6111. $49.00 (12 issues). Technical journal of firearms repair and maintenance.

American Handgunner*
Publisher's Development Corp., 591 Camino de la Reina, Suite 200, San Diego, CA 92108/800-537-3006 $16.95 yr. Articles for handgun enthusiasts, competitors, police and hunters.

American Hunter (M)
National Rifle Assn., 11250 Waples Mill Rd., Fairfax, VA 22030 (Same address for both.) Publications Div. $35.00 yr. Wide scope of hunting articles.

American Rifleman (M)
National Rifle Assn., 11250 Waples Mill Rd., Fairfax, VA 22030 (Same address for both). Publications Div. $35.00 yr. Firearms articles of all kinds.

American Single Shot Rifle News* (M)
Membership Secy. Tim Mather, 1180 Easthill SE, N. Canton, Ohio. Annual dues $20 for 6 issues. Official journal of the American Single Shot Rifle Assn.

American Survival Guide
McMullen Angus Publishing, Inc., 774 S. Placentia Ave., Placentia, CA 92670-6846. 12 issues $19.95/714-572-2255; FAX: 714-572-1864.

Armes & Tir*
c/o FABECO, 38, rue de Trévise 75009 Paris, France. Articles for hunters, collectors, and shooters. French text.

Arms Collecting (Q)
Museum Restoration Service, P.O. Box 70, Alexandria Bay, NY 13607-0070. $22.00 yr.; $62.00 3 yrs.; $112.00 5 yrs.

Australian Shooter *(formerly Australian Shooters Journal)*
Sporting Shooters' Assn. of Australia, Inc., P.O. Box 2066, Kent Town SA 5071, Australia. $60.00 yr. locally; $65.00 yr. overseas surface mail. Hunting and shooting articles.

The Backwoodsman Magazine
P.O. Box 627, Westcliffe, CO 81252. $16.00 for 6 issues per yr.; $30.00 for 2 yrs.; sample copy $2.75. Subjects include muzzle-loading, woodslore, primitive survival, trapping, homesteading, blackpowder cartridge guns, 19th century how-to.

Black Powder Cartridge News (Q)
SPG, Inc., P.O. Box 761, Livingston, MT 59047/Phone/Fax: 406-222-8416. $17 yr. (4 issues) ($6 extra 1st class mailing). For the blackpowder cartridge enthusiast.

Blackpowder Hunting (M)
Intl. Blackpowder Hunting Assn., P.O. Box 1180Z, Glenrock, WY 82637/307-436-9817. $20.00 1 yr., $36.00 2 yrs. How-to and where-to features by experts on hunting; shooting; ballistics; traditional and modern blackpowder rifles, shotguns, pistols and cartridges.

Black Powder Times
P.O. Box 234, Lake Stevens, WA 98258. $20.00 yr.; add $5 per year for Canada, $10 per year other foreign. Tabloid newspaper for blackpowder activities; test reports.

Blade Magazine
Krause Publications, 700 East State St., Iola, WI 54990-0001. $25.98 for 12 issues. Foreign price (including Canada-Mexico) $50.00. A magazine for all enthusiasts of handmade, factory and antique knives.

Caliber
GFI-Verlag, Theodor-Heuss Ring 62, 50668 K"ln, Germany. For hunters, target shooters and reloaders.

The Caller (Q) (M)
National Wild Turkey Federation, P.O. Box 530, Edgefield, SC 29824. Tabloid newspaper for members; 4 issues per yr. (membership fee $25.00)

Cartridge Journal (M)
Robert Mellichamp, 907 Shirkmere, Houston, TX 77008/713-869-0558. Dues $12 for U.S. and Canadian members (includes the newsletter); 6 issues.

The Cast Bullet*(M)
Official journal of The Cast Bullet Assn. Director of Membership, 203 E. 2nd St., Muscatine, IA 52761. Annual membership dues $14, includes 6 issues.

COLTELLI, che Passione (Q)
Casella postale N.519, 20101 Milano, Italy/Fax:02-48402857. $15 1 yr., $27 2 yrs. Covers all types of knives—collecting, combat, historical. Italian text.

Combat Handguns*
Harris Publications, Inc., 1115 Broadway, New York, NY 10010.

Deer & Deer Hunting Magazine
Krause Publications, 700 E. State St., Iola, WI 54990-0001. $19.95 yr. (9 issues). For the serious deer hunter. Website: www.krause.com

The Derringer Peanut (M)
The National Association of Derringer Collectors, P.O. Box 20572, San Jose, CA 95160. A newsletter dedicated to developing the best derringer information. Write for details.

Deutsches Waffen Journal
Journal-Verlag Schwend GmbH, Postfach 100340, D-74503 Schwäbisch Hall, Germany/0791-404-500; FAX:0791-404-505 and 404-424. DM102 p. yr. (interior); DM125.30 (abroad), postage included. Antique and modern arms and equipment. German text.

Double Gun Journal
P.O. Box 550, East Jordan, MI 49727/800-447-1658. $35 for 4 issues.

Ducks Unlimited, Inc. (M)
1 Waterfowl Way, Memphis, TN 38120

The Engraver (M) (Q)
P.O. Box 4365, Estes Park, CO 80517/970-586-2388; Fax: 970-586-0394. Mike Dubber, editor. The journal of firearms engraving.

The Field
King's Reach Tower, Stamford St., London SE1 9LS England. £36.40 U.K. 1 yr.; 49.90 (overseas, surface mail) yr.; £82.00 (overseas, air mail) yr. Hunting and shooting articles, and all country sports.

Field & Stream
Times Mirror Magazines, Two Park Ave., New York, NY 10016/212-779-5000. Monthly shooting column. Articles on hunting and fishing. Website: www.timesmirror.com

Field Tests
Belvoir Publications, Inc., 75 Holly Hill Lane; P.O. Box 2626, Greenwich, CT 06836-2626/203-661-6111; 800-829-3361 (subscription line). U.S. & Canada $29 1 yr., $58 2 yrs.; all other countries $45 1 yr., $90 2 yrs. (air).

Fur-Fish-Game
A.R. Harding Pub. Co., 2878 E. Main St., Columbus, OH 43209. $15.95 yr. Practical guidance regarding trapping, fishing and hunting.

The Gottlieb-Tartaro Report
Second Amendment Foundation, James Madison Bldg., 12500 NE 10th Pl., Bellevue, WA 98005/206-454-7012;Fax:206-451-3959. $30 for 12 issues. An insiders guide for gun owners.

Gray's Sporting Journal
Gray's Sporting Journal, P.O. Box 1207, Augusta, GA 30903. $36.95 per yr. for 6 issues. Hunting and fishing journals. Expeditions and Guides Book (Annual Travel Guide).

Gun List†
700 E. State St., Iola, WI 54990. $36.98 yr. (26 issues); $65.98 2 yrs. (52 issues). Indexed market publication for firearms collectors and active shooters; guns, supplies and services. Website: www.krause.com

Gun News Digest (Q)
Second Amendment Fdn., P.O. Box 488, Station C, Buffalo, NY 14209/716-885-6408;Fax:716-884-4471. $10 U.S.; $20 foreign.

The Gun Report
World Wide Gun Report, Inc., Box 38, Aledo, IL 61231-0038. $33.00 yr. For the antique and collectable gun dealer and collector.

Gunmaker (M) (Q)
ACGG, P.O. Box 812, Burlington, IA 52601-0812. The journal of custom gunmaking.

The Gunrunner
Div. of Kexco Publ. Co. Ltd., Box 565G, Lethbridge, Alb., Canada T1J 3Z4. $23.00 yr., sample $2.00. Monthly newspaper, listing everything from antiques to artillery.

Gun Show Calendar (Q)
700 E. State St., Iola, WI 54990. $14.95 yr. (4 issues). Gun shows listed; chronologically and by state. Website: www.krause.com

Gun Tests
11 Commerce Blvd., Palm Coast, FL 32142. The consumer resource for the serious shooter. Write for information.

Gun Trade News
Bruce Publishing Ltd., P.O. Box 82, Wantage, Ozon OX12 7A8, England/44-1-235-771770; Fax: 44-1-235-771848. Britain's only "trade only" magazine exclusive to the gun trade.

Gun Week†
Second Amendment Foundation, P.O. Box 488, Station C, Buffalo, NY 14209. $35.00 yr. U.S. and possessions; $45.00 yr. other countries. Tabloid paper on guns, hunting, shooting and collecting (36 issues).

Gun World
Y-Visionary Publishing, LP 265 South Anita Drive, Ste. 120, Orange, CA 92868. $21.97 yr.; $34.97 2 yrs. For the hunting, reloading and shooting enthusiast.

Guns & Ammo
EMAP USA, 6420 Wilshire Blvd., Los Angeles, CA 90048/213-782-2780. $23.94 yr. Guns, shooting, and technical articles.

Guns
Publishers Development Corporation, P.O. Box 85201, San Diego, CA 92138/800-537-3006. $19.95 yr. In-depth articles on a wide range of guns, shooting equipment and related accessories for gun collectors, hunters and shooters.

Guns Review
Ravenhill Publishing Co. Ltd., Box 35, Standard House, Bonhill St., London EC 2A 4DA, England. £20.00 sterling (approx. U.S. $38 USA & Canada) yr. For collectors and shooters.

H.A.C.S. Newsletter (M)
Harry Moon, Pres., P.O. Box 50117, South Slope RPO, Burnaby BC, V5J 5G3, Canada/604-438-0950; Fax:604-277-3646. $25 p. yr. U.S. and Canada. Official newsletter of The Historical Arms Collectors of B.C. (Canada).

Handgunner*
Richard A.J. Munday, Seychelles house, Brightlingsen, Essex CO7 ONN, England/012063-305201. £18.00 (sterling).

Handguns
EMAP USA, 6420 Wilshire Blvd., Los Angeles, CA 90048/323-782-2868. $23/94 yr. For the handgunning and shooting enthusiast. Website: www.petersenco.com

Handloader*
Wolfe Publishing Co., 6471 Airpark Dr., Prescott, AZ 86301/520-445-7810;Fax:520-778-5124. $22.00 yr. The journal of ammunition reloading.

INSIGHTS*
NRA, 11250 Waples Mill Rd., Fairfax, VA 22030. Editor, John E. Robbins. $15.00 yr., which includes NRA junior membership; $10.00 for adult subscriptions (12 issues). Plenty of details for the young hunter and target shooter; emphasizes gun safety, marksmanship training, hunting skills.

International Arms & Militaria Collector (Q)
Arms & Militaria Press, P.O. Box 80, Labrador, Qld. 4215, Australia. A$39.50 yr. (U.S. & Canada), 2 yrs. A$77.50; A$37.50 (others), 1 yr., 2 yrs. $73.50 all air express mail; surface mail is less. Editor: Ian D. Skennerton.

International Shooting Sport*/UIT Journal
International Shooting Union (UIT), Bavariaring 21, D-80336 Munich, Germany. Europe: (Deutsche Mark) DM44.00 yr., 2 yrs. DM83.00; outside Europe: DM50.00 yr., 2 yrs. DM95.00 (air mail postage included.) For international sport shooting.

Internationales Waffen-Magazin
Habegger-Verlag Zürich, Postfach 9230, CH-8036 Zürich, Switzerland. SF 105.00 (approx. U.S. $73.00) surface mail for 10 issues. Modern and antique arms, self-defense. German text; English summary of contents.

The Journal of the Arms & Armour Society (M)
A. Dove, P.O. Box 10232, London, SW19 2ZD England. £15.00 surface mail; £20.00 airmail sterling only yr. Articles for the historian and collector.

Journal of the Historical Breechloading Smallarms Assn.
Published annually. P.O. Box 12778, London, SE1 6XB, England. $21.00 yr. Articles for the collector plus mailings of short articles on specific arms, reprints, newsletters, etc.

Knife World
Knife World Publications, P.O. Box 3395, Knoxville, TN 37927. $15.00 yr.; $25.00 2 yrs. Published monthly for knife enthusiasts and collectors. Articles on custom and factory knives; other knife-related interests, monthly column on knife identification, military knives.

Man At Arms*
P.O. Box 460, Lincoln, RI 02865. $27.00 yr., $52.00 2 yrs. plus $8.00 for foreign subscribers. The N.R.A. magazine of arms collecting-investing, with excellent articles for the collector of antique arms and militaria.

---

*Published bi-monthly
† Published weekly
‡Published three times per month. All others are published monthly.

M=Membership requirements; write for details.
Q=Published Quarterly.

REFERENCE

The Mannlicher Collector (Q)(M)
Mannlicher Collectors Assn., Inc., P.O. Box 7144, Salem Oregon 97303. $20/ yr. subscription included in membership.

MAN/MAGNUM
S.A. Man (Pty) Ltd., P.O. Box 35204, Northway, Durban 4065, Republic of South Africa. SA Rand 200.00 for 12 issues. Africa's only publication on hunting, shooting, firearms, bushcraft, knives, etc.

The Marlin Collector (M)
R.W. Paterson, 407 Lincoln Bldg., 44 Main St., Champaign, IL 61820.

Muzzle Blasts (M)
National Muzzle Loading Rifle Assn., P.O. Box 67, Friendship, IN 47021/812-667-5131. $35.00 yr. annual membership. For the blackpowder shooter.

Muzzleloader Magazine*
Scurlock Publishing Co., Inc., Dept. Gun, Route 5, Box 347-M, Texarkana, TX 75501. $18.00 U.S.; $22.50 U.S./yr. for foreign subscribers. The publication for blackpowder shooters.

National Defense (M)*
American Defense Preparedness Assn., Two Colonial Place, Suite 400, 2101 Wilson Blvd., Arlington, VA 22201-3061/703-522-1820; FAX: 703-522-1885. $35.00 yr. Articles on both military and civil defense field, including weapons, materials technology, management.

National Knife Magazine (M)
Natl. Knife Coll. Assn., 7201 Shallowford Rd., P.O. Box 21070, Chattanooga, TN 37424-0070. Membership $35 yr.; $65.00 International yr.

National Rifle Assn. Journal (British) (Q)
Natl. Rifle Assn. (BR.), Bisley Camp, Brookwood, Woking, Surrey, England. GU24, OPB. £24.00 Sterling including postage.

National Wildlife*
Natl. Wildlife Fed., 1400 16th St. NW, Washington, DC 20036, $16.00 yr. (6 issues); *International Wildlife*, 6 issues, $16.00 yr. Both, $22.00 yr., includes all membership benefits. Write attn.: Membership Services Dept., for more information.

New Zealand GUNS*
Waitekauri Publishing, P.O. 45, Waikino 3060, New Zealand. $NZ90.00 (6 issues) yr. Covers the hunting and firearms scene in New Zealand.

New Zealand Wildlife (Q)
New Zealand Deerstalkers Assoc., Inc., P.O. Box 6514, Wellington, N.Z. $30.00 (N.Z.). Hunting, shooting and firearms/game research articles.

North American Hunter* (M)
P.O. Box 3401, Minnetonka, MN 55343/612-936-9333; e-mail: huntingclub@pclink.com. $18.00 yr. (7 issues). Articles on all types of North American hunting.

Outdoor Life
Times Mirror Magazines, Two Park Ave., New York, NY 10016. $16.95/yr. Extensive coverage of hunting and shooting. Shooting column by Jim Carmichel. Website: www.timesmirror.com

La Passion des Courteaux (Q)
Phenix Editions, 25 rue Mademoiselle, 75015 Paris, France. French text.

Paintball Games International Magazine
Aceville Publications, Castle House, 97 High St., Colchester, Essex, England CO1 1TH/011-44-206-564840. Write for subscription rates. Leading magazine in the U.K. covering competitive paintball activities.

Paintball News
PBN Publishing, P.O. Box 1608, 24 Henniker St., Hillsboro, NH 03244/603-464-6080. $35 U.S. 1 yr. Bi-weekly. Newspaper covering the sport of paintball, new product reviews and industry features.

Paintball Sports (Q)
Paintball Publications, Inc., 540 Main St., Mount Kisco, NY 10549/941-241-7400. $24.75 U.S. 1 yr., $32.75 foreign. Covering the competitive paintball scene.

Performance Shooter
Belvoir Publications, Inc., 75 Holly Hill Lane, Greenwich, CT 06836-2626/203-661-6111. $45.00 yr. (12 issues). Techniques and technology for improved rifle and pistol accuracy.

Petersen's HUNTING Magazine
EMAP USA, 6420 Wilshire Blvd., Los Angeles, CA 90048. $19.94 yr.; Canada $29.34 yr.; foreign countries $29.94 yr. Hunting articles for all game; test reports.

P.I. Magazine
America's Private Investigation Journal, 755 Bronx Dr., Toledo, OH 43609. Chuck Klein, firearms editor with column about handguns.

Pirsch
BLV Verlagsgesellschaft mbH, Postfach 400320, 80703 Munich, Germany/089-12704-0;Fax:089-12705-354. German text.

Point Blank
Citizens Committee for the Right to Keep and Bear Arms (sent to contributors), Liberty Park, 12500 NE 10th Pl., Bellevue, WA 98005

POINTBLANK (M)
Natl. Firearms Assn., Box 4384 Stn. C, Calgary, AB T2T 5N2, Canada. Official publication of the NFA.

The Police Marksman*
6000 E. Shirley Lane, Montgomery, AL 36117. $17.95 yr. For law enforcement personnel.

Police Times (M)
3801 Biscayne Blvd., Miami, FL 33137/305-573-0070.

Popular Mechanics
Hearst Corp., 224 W. 57th St., New York, NY 10019. Firearms, camping, outdoor oriented articles.

Precision Shooting
Precision Shooting, Inc., 222 McKee St., Manchester, CT 06040. $32.00 yr. U.S. Journal of the International Benchrest Shooters, and target shooting in general. Also considerable coverage of varmint shooting, as well as big bore, small bore, schuetzen, lead bullet, wildcats and precision reloading.

Rifle*
Wolfe Publishing Co., 6471 Airpark Dr., Prescott, AZ 86301/520-445-7810; Fax: 520-778-5124. $19.00 yr. The sporting firearms journal.

Rifle's Hunting Annual
Wolfe Publishing Co., 6471 Airpark Dr., Prescott, AZ 86301/520-445-7810; Fax: 520-778-5124. $4.99 Annual. Dedicated to the finest pursuit of the hunt.

Rod & Rifle Magazine
Lithographic Serv. Ltd., P.O. Box 38-138, Wellington, New Zealand. $50.00 yr. (6 issues). Hunting, shooting and fishing articles.

Safari* (M)
Safari Magazine, 4800 W. Gates Pass Rd., Tucson, AZ 85745/602-620-1220. $55.00 (6 times). The journal of big game hunting, published by Safari Club International. Also publish *Safari Times*, a monthly newspaper, included in price of $55.00 national membership.

Second Amendment Reporter
Second Amendment Foundation, James Madison Bldg., 12500 NE 10th Pl., Bellevue, WA 98005. $15.00 yr. (non-contributors).

Shooter's News
23146 Lorain Rd., Box 349, North Olmsted, OH 44070/216-979-5258;Fax:216-979-5259. $29 U.S. 1 yr., $54 2 yrs.; $52 foreign surface. A journal dedicated to precision riflery.

Shooting Industry
Publisher's Dev. Corp., 591 Camino de la Reina, Suite 200, San Diego, CA 92108. $50.00 yr. To the trade. $25.00.

Shooting Sports USA
National Rifle Assn. of America, 11250 Waples Mill Road, Fairfax, VA 22030. Annual subscriptions for NRA members are $5 for classified shooters and $10 for non-classified shooters. Non-NRA member subscriptions are $15. Covering events, techniques and personalities in competitive shooting.

Shooting Sportsman*
P.O. Box 11282, Des Moines, IA 50340/800-666-4955 (for subscriptions). Editorial: P.O. Box 1357, Camden, ME 04843. $19.95 for six issues. The magazine of wingshooting and fine guns.

The Shooting Times & Country Magazine (England)†
IPC Magazines Ltd., King's Reach Tower, Stamford St, 1 London SE1 9LS, England/0171-261-6180;Fax:0171-261-7179. £65 (approx. $98.00) yr.; £79 yr. overseas (52 issues). Game shooting, wild fowling, hunting, game fishing and firearms articles. Britain's best selling field sports magazine.

Shooting Times
Primedia, News Plaza, P.O. Box 1790, Peoria, IL 61656/309-682-6626. $16.97 yr. Guns, shooting, reloading; articles on every gun activity.

The Shotgun News‡
Primedia, News Plaza, P.O. Box 1790, Peoria, IL 61656/800-495-8362. $28.95 yr.; foreign subscription call for rates. Sample copy $4.00. Gun ads of all kinds.

SHOT Business
Flintlock Ridge Office Center, 11 Mile Hill Rd., Newtown, CT 06470-2359/203-426-1320; FAX: 203-426-1087. For the shooting, hunting and outdoor trade retailer.

Shotgun Sports
P.O. Box 6810, Auburn, CA 95604/916-889-2220; FAX:916-889-9106. $31.00 yr. Trapshooting how-to's, shotshell reloading, shotgun patterning, shotgun tests and evaluations, Sporting Clays action, waterfowl/upland hunting. Call 1-800-676-8920 for a free sample copy.

The Sixgunner (M)
Handgun Hunters International, P.O. Box 357, MAG, Bloomingdale, OH 43910

The Skeet Shooting Review
National Skeet Shooting Assn., 5931 Roft Rd., San Antonio, TX 78253. $20.00 yr. (Assn. membership includes mag.) Competition results, personality profiles of top Skeet shooters, how-to articles, technical, reloading information.

Soldier of Fortune
Subscription Dept., P.O. Box 348, Mt. Morris, IL 61054. $29.95 yr.; $39.95 Canada; $50.95 foreign.

Sporting Clays Magazine
Patch Communications, 5211 South Washington Ave., Titusville, FL 32780/407-268-5010; FAX: 407-267-7216. $29.95 yr. (12 issues). Official publication of the National Sporting Clays Association.

Sporting Goods Business
Miller Freeman, Inc., One Penn Plaza, 10th Fl., New York, NY 10119-0004. Trade journal.

Sporting Goods Dealer
Two Park Ave., New York, NY 10016. $100.00 yr. Sporting goods trade journal.

Sporting Gun
Bretton Court, Bretton, Peterborough PE3 8DZ, England. £27.00 (approx. U.S. $36.00), airmail £35.50 yr. For the game and clay enthusiasts.

Sports Afield
11650 Riverside Drive, North Hollywood, CA 91602-1066/818-904-9981.

The Squirrel Hunter
P.O. Box 368, Chireno, TX 75937. $14.00 yr. Articles about squirrel hunting.

Stott's Creek Calendar
Stott's Creek Printers, 2526 S 475 W, Morgantown, IN 46160/317-878-5489. 1 yr (3 issues) $11.50; 2 yrs. (6 issues) $20.00. Lists all gun shows everywhere in convenient calendar form; call for information.

Super Outdoors
2695 Aiken Road, Shelbyville, KY 40065/502-722-9463; 800-404-6064; Fax: 502-722-8093. Mark Edwards, publisher. Contact for details.

TACARMI
Via E. De Amicis, 25; 20123 Milano, Italy. $100.00 yr. approx. Antique and modern guns. (Italian text.)

Territorial Dispatch—1800s Historical Publication (M)
National Assn. of Buckskinners, 4701 Marion St., Suite 324, Livestock Exchange Bldg., Denver, CO 80216. Michael A. Nester & Barbara Wyckoff, editors. 303-297-9671.

Trap & Field
1000 Waterway Blvd., Indianapolis, IN 46202. $25.00 yr. Official publ. Amateur Trapshooting Assn. Scores, averages, trapshooting articles.

Turkey Call* (M)
Natl. Wild Turkey Federation, Inc., P.O. Box 530, Edgefield, SC 29824. $25.00 with membership (6 issues per yr.)

Turkey & Turkey Hunting*
Krause Publications, 700 E. State St., Iola, WI 54990-0001. $13.95 (6 issue p. yr.). Magazine with leading-edge articles on all aspects of wild turkey behavior, biology and the successful ways to hunt better with that info. Learn the proper techniques to calling, the right equipment, and more.

The U.S. Handgunner* (M)
U.S. Revolver Assn., 40 Larchmont Ave., Taunton, MA 02780. $10.00 yr. General handgun and competition articles. Bi-monthly sent to members.

U.S. Airgun Magazine
P.O. Box 2021, Benton, AR 72018/800-247-4867; Fax: 501-316-8549. 10 issues a yr. Cover the sport from hunting, 10-meter, field target and collecting. Write for details.

The Varmint Hunter Magazine (Q)
The Varmint Hunters Assn., Box 759, Pierre, SD 57501/800-528-4868. $24.00 yr.

Waffenmarkt-Intern
GFI-Verlag, Theodor-Heuss Ring 62, 50668 K"ln, Germany. Only for gunsmiths, licensed firearms dealers and their suppliers in Germany, Austria and Switzerland.

Wild Sheep (M) (Q)
Foundation for North American Wild Sheep, 720 Allen Ave., Cody, WY 82414. Website: http://www.iwc.net/non/fnaws/fnaws.htm; e-mail: fnaws@wyoming.com. Official journal of the foundation.

Wisconsin Outdoor Journal
Krause Publications, 700 E. State St., Iola, WI 54990-0001. $17.97 yr. (8 issues). For Wisconsin's avid hunters and fishermen, with features from all over that state with regional reports, legislative updates, etc. Website: www.krause.com

Women & Guns
P.O. Box 488, Sta. C, Buffalo, NY 14209. $24.00 U.S.; $72.00 foreign (12 issues). Only magazine edited by and for women gun owners.

World War II*
Cowles History Group, 741 Miller Dr. SE, Suite D-2, Leesburg, VA 20175-8920. Annual subscriptions $19.95 U.S.; $25.95 Canada; 43.95 foreign. The title says it—WWII; good articles, ads, etc.

---

*Published bi-monthly
† Published weekly
‡Published three times per month. All others are published monthly.

M=Membership requirements; write for details.
Q=Published Quarterly.

IMPORTANT NOTICE TO BOOK BUYERS

Books listed here may be bought from Ray Riling Arms Books Co., 6844 Gorsten St., P.O. Box 18925, Philadelphia, PA 19119, Phone 215/438-2456; FAX: 215-438-5395. E-Mail: sales@rayrilingarms-books.com. Joe Riling is the researcher and compiler of "The Arms Library" and a seller of gun books for over 32 years. The Riling stock includes books classic and modern, many hard-to-find items, and many not obtainable elsewhere. These pages list a portion of the current stock. They offer prompt, complete service, with delayed shipments occurring only on out-of-print or out-of-stock books.

Visit our web site at **www.rayrilingarmsbooks.com** and order all of your favorite titles on line from our secure site.

NOTICE FOR ALL CUSTOMERS: Remittance in U.S. funds must accompany all orders. For your convenience we now accept VISA, Master-Card & American Express. For shipments in the U.S. add $7.00 for the 1st book and $2.00 for each additional book for postage and insurance. Mini-mum order $10.00. International Orders add $13.00 for the 1st book and $5.00 for each additional book. All International orders are shipped at the buyer's risk unless an additional $5 for insurance is included. USPS does not offer insurance to all countries unless shipped Air-Mail please e-mail or call for pricing.

Payments in excess of order or for "Backorders" are credited or fully re-funded at request. Books "As-Ordered" are not returnable except by permis-sion and a handling charge on these of 10% or $2.00 per book which ever is greater is deducted from refund or credit. Only Pennsylvania customers must include current sales tax.

A full variety of arms books also available from Rutgers Book Center, 127 Raritan Ave., Highland Park, NJ 08904/908-545-4344; FAX: 908-545-6686 or I.D.S.A. Books, 1324 Stratford Drive, Piqua, OH 45356/937-773-4203; FAX: 937-778-1922.

BALLISTICS AND HANDLOADING

ABC's of Reloading, 6th Edition, by C. Rodney James and the editors of Hand-loader's Digest, DBI Books, a division of Krause Publications, Iola, WI, 1997. 288 pp., illus. Paper covers. $21.95
The definitive guide to every facet of cartridge and shotshell reloading.

Accurate Arms Loading Guide Number 2, by Accurate Arms. McEwen, TN: Accu-rate Arms Company, Inc., 2000. Paper Covers. $18.95
Includes new data on smokeless powders XMR4064 and XMP5744 as well as a special section on Cowboy Action Shooting. The new manual includes 50 new pages of data. An appendix includes nominal rotor charge weights, bullet diameters.

The American Cartridge, by Charles Suydam, Borden Publishing Co. Alhambra, CA, 1986. 184 pp., illus. $24.95
An illustrated study of the rimfire cartridge in the United States.

Ammo and Ballistics, by Robert W. Forker, Safari Press, Inc., Huntington Beach, CA., 1999. 252 pp., illustrated. Paper covers. $18.95
Ballistic data on 125 calibers and 1,400 loads out to 500 yards.

Ammunition: Grenades and Projectile Munitions, by Ian V. Hogg, Stackpole Books, Mechanicsburg, PA, 1998. 144 pp., illus. $22.95
Concise guide to modern ammunition. International coverage with detailed specifications and illustrations.

Barnes Reloading Manual #2, Barnes Bullets, American Fork, UT, 1999. 668 pp., illus. $24.95
Features data and trajectories on the new weight X, XBT and Solids in calibers from .22 to .50 BMG.

Big Bore Rifles And Cartridges, Wolfe Publishing Co., Prescott, AZ, 1991. Paper covers. $26.00
This book covers cartridges from 8mm to .600 Nitro with loading tables.

Black Powder Guide, 2nd Edition, by George C. Nonte, Jr., Stoeger Publishing Co., So. Hackensack, NJ, 1991. 288 pp., illus. Paper covers. $14.95
How-to instructions for selection, repair and maintenance of muzzleloaders, making your own bullets, restoring and refinishing, shooting techniques.

Blackpowder Loading Manual, 3rd Edition, by Sam Fadala, DBI Books, a division of Krause Publications, Iola, WI, 1995. 368 pp., illus. Paper covers. $20.95
Revised and expanded edition of this landmark blackpowder loading book. Covers hundreds of loads for most of the popular blackpowder rifles, handguns and shotguns.

Cartridges of the World, 9th Edition, by Frank Barnes, Krause Publications, Iola, WI, 2000. 512 pp., illus. Paper covers. $27.95
Completely revised edition of the general purpose reference work for which collectors, police, scientists and laymen reach first for answers to cartridge identification questions.

Cartridge Reloading Tools of the Past, by R.H. Chamberlain and Tom Quigley, Tom Quigley, Castle Rock, WA, 1998. 167 pp., illustrated. Paper covers. $25.00
A detailed treatment of the extensive Winchester and Ideal line of handloading tools and bullet molds, plus Remington, Marlin, Ballard, Browning, Maynard, and many others.

Cast Bullets for the Black Powder Rifle, by Paul A. Matthews, Wolfe Publishing Co., Prescott, AZ, 1996. 133 pp., illus. Paper covers. $22.50
The tools and techniques used to make your cast bullet shooting a success.

Complete Blackpowder Handbook, 3rd Edition, by Sam Fadala, DBI Books, a di-vision of Krause Publications, Iola, WI, 1997. 400 pp., illus. Paper covers. $21.95
Expanded and completely rewritten edition of the definitive book on the subject of blackpowder.

Complete Reloading Guide, by Robert & John Traister, Stoeger Publishing Co., Wayne, NJ, 1997. 608 pp., illus. Paper covers. $34.95
Perhaps the finest, most comprehensive work ever published on the subject of reloading.

Complete Reloading Manual, One Book / One Caliber. California: Load Books USA, 2000. $7.95 Each
Containing unabridged information from U. S. Bullet and Powder Makers. With thousands of proven and tested loads, plus dozens of various bullet designs and different powders. Spiral bound. Available in all Calibers.

Early Loading Tools & Bullet Molds, Pioneer Press, 1988. 88 pages, illustrated. Softcover. $7.50

European Sporting Cartridges: Volume 1, by Brad Dixon, Seattle, WA: Armory Publications, 1997. 1st edition. 250 pp., Illus. $60.00
Photographs and drawings of over 550 centerfire cartridge case types in 1,300 illustrations produced in Germany and Austria from 1875-1995.

European Sporting Cartridges: Volume 2, by Brad Dixon, Seattle, WA: Armory Publications, 2000. 1st edition. 240 pages. $60.00
An illustrated history of centerfire hunting and target cartridges produced in Czechoslovakia, Switzerland, Norway, Sweden, Finland, Russia, Italy, Denmark, Belguim from 1875 to 1998. Adds 50 specimens to volume 1, Germany-Austria. Also, illustrates 40 small arms magazine experiments during the late 19th Century, and includes the English-Language export ammunition catalogue of Kovo (Povaszke Strojarne), Prague, Czeck. from the 1930's.

Game Loads and Practical Ballistics for the American Hunter, by Bob Hagel, Wolfe Publishing Co., Prescott, AZ, 1992. 310 pp., illus. $27.90
Hagel's knowledge gained as a hunter, guide and gun enthusiast is gathered in this informative text.

German 7.9MM Military Ammunition 1888-1945, by Daniel Kent, Ann Arbor, MI: Kent, 1990. 153 pp., plus appendix. illus., b&w photos. $35.00

Handbook for Shooters and Reloaders, by P.O. Ackley, Salt Lake City, UT, 1998, (Vol. I), 567 pp., illus. Includes a separate exterior ballistics chart. $21.95 (Vol. II), a new printing with specific new material. 495 pp., illus. $20.95

Handgun Muzzle Flash Tests: How Police Cartridges Compare, by Robert Olsen, Paladin Press, Boulder, CO.Fully illustrated. 133 pages. Softcover. $20.00
Tests dozens of pistols and revolvers for the brightness of muzzle flash, a critical factor in the safety of law enforcement personnel.

Handgun Stopping Power; The Definitive Study, by Marshall & Sandow. Boulder, CO: Paladin Press, 1992. 240 pages. $45.00
Offers accurate predictions of the stopping power of specific loads in calibers from .380 Auto to .45 ACP, as well as such specialty rounds as the Glaser Safety Slug, Federal Hydra-Shok, MagSafe, etc. This is the definitive methodology for predicting the stopping power of handgun loads, the first to take into account what really happens when a bullet meets a man.

Handloader's Digest, 17th Edition, edited by Bob Bell. DBI Books, a division of Krause Publications, Iola, WI, 1997. 480 pp., illustrated. Paper covers. $27.95
Top writers in the field contribute helpful information on techniques and components. Greatly expanded and fully indexed catalog of all currently available tools, accessories and components for metallic, blackpowder cartridge, shotgun reloading and swaging.

Handloader's Manual of Cartridge Conversions, by John J. Donnelly, Stoeger Publishing Co., So. Hackensack, NJ, 1986. Unpaginated. $39.95
From 14 Jones to 70-150 Winchester in English and American cartridges, and from 4.85 U.K. to 15.2x28R Gevelot in metric cartridges. Over 900 cartridges described in detail.

Hatcher's Notebook, by S. Julian Hatcher, Stackpole Books, Harrisburg, PA, 1992. 488 pp., illus. $39.95
A reference work for shooters, gunsmiths, ballisticians, historians, hunters and collectors.

REFERENCE

History and Development of Small Arms Ammunition; Volume 2 Centerfire: Primitive, and Martial Long Arms. by George A. Hoyem. Oceanside, CA: Armory Publications, 1991. 303 pages, illustrated. $60.00

Covers the blackpowder military centerfire rifle, carbine, machine gun and volley gun ammunition used in 28 nations and dominions, together with the firearms that chambered them.

History and Development of Small Arms Ammunition; Volume 4, American Military Rifle Cartridges. Oceanside, CA: Armory Publications, 1998. 244pp., illus. $60.00

Carries on what Vol. 2 began with American military rifle cartridges. Now the sporting rifle cartridges are at last organized by their originators-235 individual case types designed by eight makers of single shot rifles and four of magazine rifles from .50-140 Winchester Express to .22-15-60 Stevens. plus experimentals from .70-150 to .32-80. American Civil War enthusiasts and European collectors will find over 150 primitives in Appendix A to add to those in Volumes One and Two. There are 16 pages in full color of 54 box labels for Sharps, Remington and Ballard cartridges. There are large photographs with descriptions of 15 Maynard, Sharps, Winchester, Browning, Freund, Remington-Hepburn, Farrow and other single shot rifles, some of them rare one of a kind specimens.

Hodgdon Powder Data Manual #27, Hodgdon Powder Co., Shawnee Mission, KS, 1999. 800 pp. $27.95

Reloading data for rifle and pistol loads.

Hodgdon Shotshell Data Manual, Hodgdon Powder Co., Shawnee Mission, KS, 1999. 208 pp. $19.95

Contains hundreds of loads for lead shot, buck shot, slugs, bismuth shot and steel shot plus articles on ballistics, patterning, special reloads and much more.

Home Guide to Cartridge Conversions, by Maj. George C. Nonte Jr., The Gun Room Press, Highland Park, NJ, 1976. 404 pp., illus. $24.95

Revised and updated version of Nonte's definitive work on the alteration of cartridge cases for use in guns for which they were not intended.

Hornady Handbook of Cartridge Reloading, 5th Edition, Vol. I and II, Edited by Larry Steadman, Hornady Mfg. Co., Grand Island, NE, 2000., illus. $49.95

2 Volumes; Volume 1, 773 pp.; Volume 2, 717 pp. New edition of this famous reloading handbook covers rifle and handgun reloading data and ballistic tables. Latest loads, ballistic information, etc.

How-To's for the Black Powder Cartridge Rifle Shooter, by Paul A. Matthews, Wolfe Publishing Co., Prescott, AZ, 1995. 45 pp. Paper covers. $22.50

Covers lube recipes, good bore cleaners and over-powder wads. Tips include compressing powder charges, combating wind resistance, improving ignition and much more.

The Illustrated Reference of Cartridge Dimensions, edited by Dave Scovill, Wolfe Publishing Co., Prescott, AZ, 1994. 343 pp., illus. Paper covers. $19.00

A comprehensive volume with over 300 cartridges. Standard and metric dimensions have been taken from SAAMI drawings and/or fired cartridges.

Kynock, by Dale J. Hedlund, Armory Publications, Seattle, WA, 2000. 130 pages, illus. 9" x 12" with four color dust jacket. $59.95

A comprehensive review of Kynoch shotgun cartridges covering over 50 brand names and case types, and over 250 Kynoch shotgun cartridge headstamps. Additional information on Kynoch metallic ammunition including the identity of the mysterious .434 Seelun.

Lee Modern Reloading, by Richard Lee, 350 pp. of charts and data and 85 illustrations. 512 pp. $24.95

Bullet casting, lubricating and author's formula for calculating proper charges for cast bullets. Includes virtually all current load data published by the powder suppliers. Exclusive source of volume measured loads.

Loading the Black Powder Rifle Cartridge, by Paul A Matthews, Wolfe Publishing Co., Prescott, AZ, 1993. 121 pp., illus. Paper covers. $22.50

Author Matthews brings the blackpowder cartridge shooter valuable information on the basics, including cartridge care, lubes and moulds, powder charges and developing and testing loads in his usual authoritative style.

Loading the Peacemaker—Colt's Model P, by Dave Scovill, Wolfe Publishing Co., Prescott, AZ, 1996. 227 pp., illus. $24.95

A comprehensive work about the history, maintenance and repair of the most famous revolver ever made, including the most extensive load data ever published.

Lyman Cast Bullet Handbook, 3rd Edition, edited by C. Kenneth Ramage, Lyman Publications, Middlefield, CT, 1980. 416 pp., illus. Paper covers. $19.95

Information on more than 5000 tested cast bullet loads and 19 pages of trajectory and wind drift tables for cast bullets.

Lyman Black Powder Handbook, edited by C. Kenneth Ramage, Lyman Products for Shooters, Middlefield, CT, 1975. 239 pp., illus. Paper covers. $14.95

Comprehensive load information for the modern blackpowder shooter.

Lyman Pistol & Revolver Handbook, 2nd Edition, edited by Thomas J. Griffin, Lyman Publications, Middlefield, CT, 1996. 287 pp., illus. Paper covers. $18.95

The most up-to-date loading data available including the hottest new calibers, like 40 S&W, 9x21, 9mm Makarov, 9x25 Dillon and 454 Casull.

Lyman Reloading Handbook No. 47, edited by Edward A. Matunas, Lyman Publications, Middlefield, CT, 1992. 480 pp., illus. Paper covers. $24.95

A comprehensive reloading manual complete with "How to Reload" information. Expanded data section with all the newest rifle and pistol calibers.

Lyman Shotshell Handbook, 4th Edition, edited by Edward A. Matunas, Lyman Products Co., Middlefield, CT, 1996. 330 pp., illus. Paper covers. $24.95

Has 9000 loads, including slugs and buckshot, plus feature articles and a full color I.D. section.

Lyman's Guide to Big Game Cartridges & Rifles, by Edward Matunas, Lyman Publishing Corporation, Middlefield, CT, 1994. 287 pp., illus. Paper covers. $17.95

A selection guide to cartridges and rifles for big game—antelope to elephant.

Making Loading Dies and Bullet Molds, by Harold Hoffman, H & P Publishing, San Angelo, TX, 1993. 230 pp., illus. Paper covers. $24.95

A good book for learning tool and die making.

Metallic Cartridge Reloading, 3rd Edition, by M.L. McPherson, DBI Books, a division of Krause Publications, Iola, WI., 1996. 352 pp., illus. Paper covers. $21.95

A true reloading manual with over 10,000 loads for all popular metallic cartridges and a wealth of invaluable technical data provided by a recognized expert.

Military Rifle and Machine Gun Cartridges, by Jean Huon, Alexandria, VA: Ironside International, 1995. 1st edition. 378 pages, over 1,000 photos. $34.95

Superb reference text.

Modern Combat Ammunition, by Duncan Long, Paladin Press, Boulder, CO, 1997, soft cover, photos, illus., 216 pp. $34.00

Now, Paladin's leading weapons author presents his exhaustive evaluation of the stopping power of modern rifle, pistol, shotgun and machine gun rounds based on actual case studies of shooting incidents. He looks at the hot new cartridges that promise to dominate well into the next century .40 S&W, 10mm auto, sub-sonic 9mm's - as well as the trusted standbys. Find out how to make your own exotic tracers, fléchette and sabot rounds, caseless ammo and fragmenting bullets.

Modern Exterior Ballistics, by Robert L. McCoy, Schiffer Publishing Co., Atglen, PA, 1999. 128 pp. $95.00

Advanced students of exterior ballistics and flight dynamics will find this comprehensive textbook on the subject a useful addition to their libraries.

Modern Handloading, by Maj. Geo. C. Nonte, Winchester Press, Piscataway, NJ, 1972. 416 pp., illus. $15.00

Covers all aspects of metallic and shotshell ammunition loading, plus more loads than any book in print.

Modern Reloading, by Richard Lee, Inland Press, 1996. 510 pp., illus. $24.98

The how-to's of rifle, pistol and shotgun reloading plus load data for rifle and pistol calibers.

Modern Sporting Rifle Cartridges, by Wayne van Zwoll, Stoeger Publishing Co., Wayne, NJ, 1998. 310 pp., illustrated. Paper covers. $21.95

Illustrated with hundreds of photos and backed up by dozens of tables and schematic drawings, this four-part book tells the story of how rifle bullets and cartridges were developed and, in some cases, discarded.

Modern Practical Ballistics, by Art Pejsa, Pejsa Ballistics, Minneapolis, MN, 1990. 150 pp., illus. $29.95

Covers all aspects of ballistics and new, simplified methods. Clear examples illustrate new, easy but very accurate formulas.

Mr. Single Shot's Cartridge Handbook, by Frank de Haas, Mark de Haas, Orange City, IA, 1996. 116 pp., illus. Paper covers. $21.50

This book covers most of the cartridges, both commercial and wildcat, that the author has known and used.

Nick Harvey's Practical Reloading Manual, by Nick Harvey, Australian Print Group, Maryborough, Victoria, Australia, 1995. 235 pp., illus. Paper covers. $24.95

Contains data for rifle and handgun including many popular wildcat and improved cartridges. Tools, powders, components and techniques for assembling optimum reloads with particular application to North America.

Nosler Reloading Manual #4, edited by Gail Root, Nosler Bullets, Inc., Bend, OR, 1996. 516 pp., illus. $26.99

Combines information on their Ballistic Tip, Partition and Handgun bullets with traditional powders and new powders never before used, plus trajectory information from 100 to 500 yards.

The Paper Jacket, by Paul Matthews, Wolfe Publishing Co., Prescott, AZ, 1991. Paper covers. $13.50

Up-to-date and accurate information about paper-patched bullets.

Reloading Tools, Sights and Telescopes for S/S Rifles, by Gerald O. Kelver, Brighton, CO, 1982. 163 pp., illus. Softcover. $15.00

A listing of most of the famous makers of reloading tools, sights and telescopes with a brief description of the products they manufactured.

Reloading for Shotgunners, 4th Edition, by Kurt D. Fackler and M.L. McPherson, DBI Books, a division of Krause Publications, Iola, WI, 1997. 320 pp., illus. Paper covers. $19.95

Expanded reloading tables with over 11,000 loads. Bushing charts for every major press and component maker. All new presentation on all aspects of shotshell reloading by two of the top experts in the field.

The Rimfire Cartridge in the United States and Canada, Illustrated history of rimfire cartridges, manufacturers, and the products made from 1857-1984. by John L. Barber, Thomas Publications, Gettysburg, PA 2000. 1st edition. Profusely illustrated. 221 pages. $50.00

The author has written an encyclopedia of rimfire cartridges from the .22 to the massive 1.00 in. Gatling. Fourteen chapters, six appendices and an excellent bibliography make up a reference volume that all cartridge collectors should aquire.

Sierra 50th Anniversary, 4th Edition Rifle Manual, edited by Ken Ramage, Sierra Bullets, Santa Fe Springs, CA, 1997. 800 pp., illus. $26.99

New cartridge introductions, etc.

Sierra 50th Anniversary, 4th Edition Handgun Manual, edited by Ken Ramage, Sierra Bullets, Santa Fe, CA, 1997. 700 pp., illus. $21.99

Histories, reloading recommendations, bullets, powders and sections on the reloading process, etc.

Sixgun Cartridges and Loads, by Elmer Keith, The Gun Room Press, Highland Park, NJ, 1986. 151 pp., illus. $24.95

A manual covering the selection, uses and loading of the most suitable and popular revolver cartridges. Originally published in 1936. Reprint.

Speer Reloading Manual No. 13, edited by members of the Speer research staff, Omark Industries, Lewiston, ID, 1999. 621 pp., illustrated. $24.95

With thirteen new sections containing the latest technical information and reloading trends for both novice and expert in this latest edition. More than 9,300 loads are listed, including new propellant powders from Accurate Arms, Alliant, Hodgdon and Vihtavuori.

Street Stoppers, The Latest Handgun Stopping Power Street Results, by Marshall & Lanow. Boulder, CO, Paladin Press, 1996. 374 pages, illus. Softcover. $42.95

Street Stoppers is the long-awaited sequel to Handgun Stopping Power. It provides the latest results of real-life shootings in all of the major handgun calibers, plus more than 25 thought-provoking chapters that are vital to anyone interested in firearms, would ballistics, and combat shooting. This book also covers the street results of the hottest new caliber to hit the shooting world in years, the .40 Smith & Wesson. Updated street results of the latest exotic ammunition including Remington Golden Saber and CCI-Speer Gold Dot, plus the venerable offerings from MagSafe, Glaser, Cor-Bon and others. A fascinating look at the development of Hydra-Shok ammunition is included.

Understanding Ballistics, Revised 2nd Edition by Robert A. Rinker, Mulberry House Publishing Co., Corydon, IN, 2000. 430 pp., illus Paper covers. New, Revised and Expanded. 2nd Edition. $24.95

Explains basic to advanced firearm ballistics in understandable terms.

Why Not Load Your Own?, by Col. T. Whelen, Gun Room Press, Highland Park, NJ 1996, 4th ed., rev. 237 pp., illus. $20.00

A basic reference on handloading, describing each step, materials and equipment. Includes loads for popular cartridges.

Wildcat Cartridges Volumes 1 & 2 Combination, by the editors of Handloaders magazine, Wolfe Publishing Co., Prescott, AZ, 1997. 350 pp., illus. Paper covers. $39.95

A profile of the most popular information on wildcat cartridges that appeared in the Handloader magazine.

COLLECTORS

A Glossary of the Construction, Decoration and Use of Arms and Armor in All Countries and in All Times. By George Cameron Stone., Dover Publishing, New York 1999. Softcover. $39.95

An exhaustive study of arms and armor in all countries through recorded history - from the stone age up to the second world war. With over 4500 Black & White Illustrations. This Dover edition is an unabridged republication of the work originally published in 1934 by the Southworth Press, Portland MA. A new Introduction has been specially prepared for this edition.

Accoutrements of the United States Infantry, Riflemen, and Dragoons 1834-1839. by R.T. Huntington, Historical Arms Series No. 20. Canada: Museum Restoration. 58 pp. illus. Softcover. $8.95

Although the 1841 edition of the U.S. Ordnance Manual provides ample information on the equipment that was in use during the 1840s, it is evident that the patterns of equipment that it describes were not introduced until 1838 or 1839. This guide is intended to fill this gap in our knowledge by providing an overview of what we now know about the accoutrements that were issued to the regular infantryman, rifleman, and dragoon, in the 1830's with excursions into earlier and later years.

Age of the Gunfighter; Men and Weapons on the Frontier 1840-1900, by Joseph G. Rosa, University of Oklahoma Press, Norman, OK, 1999. 192 pp., illustrated. Paper covers. $21.95

Stories of gunfighters and their encounters and detailed descriptions of virtually every firearm used in the old West.

Air Guns, by Eldon G. Wolff, Duckett's Publishing Co., Tempe, AZ, 1997. 204 pp., illus Paper covers. $35.00

Historical reference covering many makers, European and American guns, canes and more.

Allied and Enemy Aircraft: May 1918; Not to be Taken from the Front Lines, Historical Arms Series No. 27. Canada: Museum Restoration. Softcover. $8.95

The basis for this title is a very rare identification manual published by the French government in 1918 that illustrated 60 aircraft with three or more views: French, English American, German, Italian, and Belgian, which might have been seen over the trenches ofFrance. Each is describe in a text translated from the original French. This is probably the most complete collection of illustrations of WW1 aircraft which has survived.

American Beauty; The Prewar Colt National Match Government Model Pistol, by Timothy J. Mullin, Collector Grade Publications, Cobourg, Ontario, Canada. 72 pp., illustrated. $34.95

Includes over 150 serial numbers, and 20 spectacular color photos of factory engraved guns and other authenticated upgrades, including rare "double-carved" ivory grips.

The American Military Saddle, 1776-1945, by R. Stephen Dorsey & Kenneth L. McPheeters, Collector's Library, Eugene, OR, 1999. 400 pp., illustrated. $59.95

The most complete coverage of the subject ever writteen on the American Military Saddle. Nearly 1000 actual photos and official drawings, from the major public and private collections in the U.S. and Great Britain.

American Police Collectibles; Dark Lanterns and Other Curious Devices, by Matthew G. Forte, Turn of the Century Publishers, Upper Montclair, NJ, 1999. 248 pp., illustrated. $24.95

For collectors of police memorabilia (handcuffs, police dark lanterns, mechanical and chain nippers, rattles, billy clubs and nightsticks) and police historians.

Ammunition; Small Arms, Grenades, and Projected Munitions, by Greenhill Publishing. 144 pp., Illustrated. $22.95 The best concise guide to modern ammunition available today. Covers ammo for small arms, grenades, and projected munitions. 144 pp., Illustrated. As NEW – Hardcover.

Antique Guns, the Collector's Guide, 2nd Edition, edited by John Traister, Stoeger Publishing Co., So. Hackensack, NJ, 1994. 320 pp., illus. Paper covers. $19.95

Covers a vast spectrum of pre-1900 firearms: those manufactured by U.S. gunmakers as well as Canadian, French, German, Belgian, Spanish and other foreign firms.

Arming the Glorious Cause; Weapons of the Second War for Independence, by James B. Whisker, Daniel D. Hartzler and Larry W. Tantz, Old Bedford Village Press, Bedford, PA., 1998. 175 pp., illustrated. $45.00

A photographic study of Confederate weapons.

Arms & Accoutrements of the Mounted Police 1873-1973, by Roger F. Phillips and Donald J. Klancher, Museum Restoration Service, Ont., Canada, 1982. 224 pp., illus. $49.95

A definitive history of the revolvers, rifles, machine guns, cannons, ammunition, swords, etc. used by the NWMP, the RNWMP and the RCMP during the first 100 years of the Force.

Arms and Armor In Antiquity and The Middle Ages. By Charles Boutell, Combined Books Inc., PA 1996. 296 pp., w/ b/w illus. Also a descriptive Notice of Modern Weapons. Translated from the French of M.P. Lacombe, and with a preface, notes, and one additional chapter on Arms and Armour in England. $14.95

Arms and Armor in the Art Institute of Chicago. By Waltler J. Karcheski, Bulfinch, New York 1999. 128 pp., 103 color photos, 12 black & white illustrations. $50.00

The George F. Harding Collection of arms and armor is the most visited installation at the Art Institute of Chicago - a testament to the enduring appeal of swords, muskets and the other paraphernalia of medieval and early modern war. Organized both chronologically and by type of weapon, this book captures the best of this astonishing collection in 115 striking photographs - most in color - accompanied by illuminating text. Here are intricately filigreed breastplates and ivory-handled crossbows, samurai katana and Toledo-steel scimitars, elaborately decorated maces and beautifully carved flintlocks - a treat for anyone who has ever been beguiled by arms, armor and the age of chivalry.

Arms and Armor in Colonial America 1526-1783. by Harold Peterson, Dover Publishing, New York, 2000. 350 pages with over 300 illustrations, index, bibliography & appendix. Softcover. $29.95

Over 200 years of firearms, ammunition, equipment & edged weapons.

Arms and Armor: The Cleveland Museum of Art. By Stephen N. Fliegel, Abrams, New York, 1998. 172 color photos, 17 halftones. 181 pages. $49.50

Intense look at the culture of the warrior and hunter, with an intriguing discussion of the decorative arts found on weapons and armor, set against the background of political and social history. Also provides information on the evolution of armor, together with manufacture and decoration, and weapons as technology and art.

Arms and Equipment of the Civil War, by Jack Coggins, Barnes & Noble, Rockleight, N.J., 1999. 160 pp., illustrated. $12.98

This unique encyclopedia provides a new perspective on the war. It provides lively explanations of how ingenious new weapons spelled victory or defeat for both sides. Aided by more than 500 illustrations and on-the-scene comments by Union and Confederate soldiers.

Arms Makers of Colonial America, by James B. Whisker, Selinsgrove, PA:, 1992: Susquehanna University Press. 1st edition. 217 pages, illustrated. $45.00

A comprehensively documented historial survey of the broad spectrum of arms makers in America who were active before 1783.

Arms Makers of Maryland, by Daniel D. Hartzler, George Shumway, York, PA, 1975. 200 pp., illus. $50.00

A thorough study of the gunsmiths of Maryland who worked during the late 18th and early 19th centuries.

Arms Makers of Pennsylvania, by James B. Whisker, Selinsgrove, PA, Susquehanna Univ. Press, 1990. 1st edition. 218 pages, illustrated in black and white and color. $45.00

Concentrates primarily on the cottage industry gunsmiths & gun makers who worked in the Keystone State from it's early years through 1900.

Arms Makers of Western Pennsylvania, by James B. Whisker, Old Bedford Village Press. 1st edition. This deluxe hard bound edition has 176 pages, $45.00

Printed on fine coated paper, with many large photographs, and detailed text describing the period, lives, tools, and artistry of the Arms Makers of Western Pennsylvania.

Arsenal Of Freedom: The Springfield Armory 1890-1948, by Lt. Col. William Brophy, Andrew Mowbray, Inc., Lincoln, RI,1997. 20 pgs. of photos. 400 pages. As new - Softcover. $29.95

A year by year account drawn from offical records. Packed with reports, charts, tables, line drawings, and 20 page photo section.

Artistic Ingredients of the Longrifle, by George Shumway Publisher, 1989 102 pp., with 94 illus. $20.00

After a brief review of Pennsylvania-German folk art and architecture, to establish the artistic enviroment in which the longrifle was made, the author demonstrates that the sophisticated rococo decoration on many of the finer longrifles is comparable to the best rococo work of Philadelphia cabinet makers and silversmiths.

The Art of Gun Engraving, by Claude Gaier and Pietro Sabatti, Knickerbocker Press, N.Y., 1999. 160 pp., illustrated. $34.95

The richness and detail lavished on early firearms represents a craftmanship nearly vanished. Beginning with crossbows in the 100's, hunting scenes, portraits, or mythological themes are intricately depicted within a few square inches of etched metal. The full-color photos contained herein recaptures this lost art with exquisite detail.

THE ARMS LIBRARY

Astra Automatic Pistols, by Leonardo M. Antaris, FIRAC Publishing Co., Sterling, CO, 1989. 248 pp., illus. $55.00
Charts, tables, serial ranges, etc. The definitive work on Astra pistols.

Basic Documents on U.S. Martial Arms, commentary by Col. B. R. Lewis, reissue by Ray Riling, Phila., PA, 1956 and 1960. *Rifle Musket Model 1855.*
The first issue rifle of musket caliber, a muzzle loader equipped with the Maynard Primer, 32 pp. *Rifle Musket Model 1863.* The typical Union muzzle-loader of the Civil War, 26 pp. *Breech-Loading Rifle Musket Model 1866.* The first of our 50-caliber breechloading rifles, 12 pp. *Remington Navy Rifle Model 1870.* A commercial type breech-loader made at Springfield, 16 pp. *Lee Straight Pull Navy Rifle Model 1895.* A magazine cartridge arm of 6mm caliber. 23 pp. *Breech-Loading Arms* (five models) 27 pp. *Ward-Burton Rifle Musket 1871*-16 pp. Each $10.00.

Battle Weapons of the American Revolution, by George C. Neuman, Scurlock Publishing Co., Texarkana, TX, 2001. 400 pp. Illus. Softcovers. $34.95
The most extensive photographic collection of Revolutionary War weapons ever in one volume. More than 1,600 photos of over 500 muskets, rifles, swords, bayonets, knives and other arms used by both sides in America's War for Independence.

The Bedford County Rifle and Its Makers, by George Shumway. 40pp. illustrated, Softcover. $10.00
The authors study of the graceful and distinctive muzzle-loading rifles made in Bedford County, Pennsylvania. Stands as a milestone on the long path to the understanding of America's longrifles.

Behold the Longrifle Again, by James B. Whisker, Old Bedford Village Press, Bedford, PA, 1997. 176 pp., illus. $45.00
Excellent reference work for the collector profusely illustrated with photographs of some of the finest Kentucky rifles showing front and back profiles and overall view.

The Belgian Rattlesnake; The Lewis Automatic Machine Gun, by William M. Easterly, Collector Grade Publications, Cobourg, Ontario, Canada, 1998. 584 pp., illustrated. $79.95
The most complete account ever published on the life and times of Colonel Isaac Newton Lewis and his crowning invention, the Lewis Automatic machine gun.

Beretta Automatic Pistols, by J.B. Wood, Stackpole Books, Harrisburg, PA, 1985. 192 pp., illus. $24.95
Only English-language book devoted to the Beretta line. Includes all important models.

The Big Guns, Civil War Siege, Seacoast, and Naval Cannon, by Edwin Olmstead, Wayne E. Stark, and Spencer C. Tucker, Museum Restoration Service, Bloomfield, Ontario, Canada, 1997. 360 pp., illustrated. $80.00
This book is designed to identify and record the heavy guns available to both sides by the end of the Civil War.

Birmingham Gunmakers, by Douglas Tate, Safari Press, Inc., Huntington Beach, CA, 1997. 300 pp., illus. $50.00
An invaluable work for anybody interested in the fine sporting arms crafted in this famous British gunmakers' city.

Blue Book of Gun Values, 22nd Edition, edited by S.P. Fjestad, Blue Book Publications, Inc. Minneapolis, MN 2001. $34.95
This new 22nd Edition simply contains more firearms values and information than any other single publication. Expanded to over 1,600 pages featuring over 100,000 firearms prices, the new Blue Book of Gun Values also contains over million words of text – no other book is even close! Most of the information contained in this publication is simply not available anywhere else, for any price!

Blue Book of Modern Black Powder Values, by Dennis Adler, Blue Book Publications, Inc. Minneapolis, MN 2000. 200 pp., illustrated. 41 color photos. Softcover. $14.95
This new title contains more up-to-date black powder values and related information than any other single publication. With 120 pages, this new book will keep you up to date on modern black powder models and prices, including most makes & models introduced this year! .

The Blunderbuss 1500-1900, by James D. Forman, Historical Arms Series No. 32. Canada: Museum Restoration, 1994. An excellent and authoritative booklet giving tons of information on the Blunderbuss, a very neglected subject. 40 pages, illustrated. Softcover. $8.95

Boarders Away I: With Steel-Edged Weapons & Polearms, by William Gilkerson, Andrew Mowbray, Inc. Publishers, Lincoln, RI, 1993. 331 pages. $48.00
Contains the essential 24 page chapter 'War at Sea' which sets the historical and practical context for the arms discussed. Includeds chapters on, Early Naval Weapons, Boarding Axes, Cutlasses, Officers Fighting Swords and Dirks, and weapons at hand of Random Mayhem.

Boarders Away, Volume II: Firearms of the Age of Fighting Sail, by William Gilkerson, Andrew Mowbray, Inc. Publishers, Lincoln, RI, 1993. 331 pp., illus. $65.00
Covers the pistols, muskets, combustibles and small cannon used aboard American and European fighting ships, 1626-1826.

The Book of Colt Firearms, by R. L. Wilson, Blue Book Publications, Inc, Minneapolis, MN, 1993. 616 pp., illus. $158.00
A complete Colt library in a single volume. In over 1,250.000 words, over 1,250 black and white and 67 color photographs, this mammoth work tells the Colt story from 1832 throught the present.

Boothroyd's Revised Directory Of British Gunmakers, by Geoffrey Boothroyd, Long Beach, CA: Safari Press, 2000. Revised edition. 412pp, photos. $39.95
Over a 30 year period Geoffrey Boothroyd has accumulated information on just about every sporting gun maker that ever has existed in the British Isles from 1850 onward. In this magnificent reference work he has placed all the gun makers he has found over the years (over 1000 entries) in an alphabetical listing with as much information as he has been able to unearth. One of the best reference sources on all British makers (including Wales, Scotland and Ireland)

in which you can find data on the most obscure as well as the most famous. Contains starting date of the business, addresses, proprietors, what they made and how long they operated with other interesting details for the collector of fine British guns.

Boston's Gun Bible, by Boston T. Party, Ignacio, CO: Javelin Press, August 2000. Expanded Edition.Softcover. $28.00
This mammoth guide for gun owners everywhere is a completely updated and expanded edition (more than 500 new pages!) of Boston T. Party's classic Boston on Guns and Courage. Pulling no punches, Boston gives new advice on which shoulder weapons and handguns to buy and why before exploring such topics as why you should consider not getting a concealed carry permit, what guns and gear will likely be outlawed next, how to spend within your budget, why you should go to a quality defensive shooting academy now, which guns and gadgets are inferior and why, how to stay off illegal government gun registration lists, how to spot an undercover agent trying to entrap law-abiding gun owners and much more.

Breech-Loading Carbines of the United States Civil War Period, by Brig. Gen. John Pitman, Armory Publications, Tacoma, WA, 1987. 94 pp., illus. $29.95
The first in a series of previously unpublished manuscripts originated by the late Brigadier General John Putnam. Exploded drawings showing parts actual size follow each sectioned illustration.

The Breech-Loading Single-Shot Rifle, by Major Ned H. Roberts and Kenneth L. Waters, Wolfe Publishing Co., Prescott, AZ, 1995. 333 pp., illus. $28.50
A comprehensive and complete history of the evolution of the Schutzen and single-shot rifle.

The Bren Gun Saga, by Thomas B. Dugelby, Collector Grade Publications, Cobourg, Ontario, Canada, 1999, revised and expanded edition. 406 pp., illustrated. $65.95
A modern, definitive book on the Bren in this revised expanded edition, which in terms of numbers of pages and illustrations is nearly twice the size of the original.

British Board of Ordnance Small Arms Contractors 1689-1840, by De Witt Bailey, Rhyl, England: W. S. Curtis, 2000. 150 pp. $18.00
Thirty years of research in the Archives of the Ordnance Board in London has identified more than 600 of these suppliers. The names of many can be found marking the regulation firearms of the period. In the study, the contractors are identified both alphabetically and under a combination of their date period together with their specialist trade.

The British Enfield Rifles, Volume 1, The SMLE Mk I and Mk III Rifles, by Charles R. Stratton, North Cape Pub. Tustin, CA, 1997. 150 pp., illus. Paper covers. $16.95
A systematic and thorough examination on a part-by-part basis of the famous British battle rifle that endured for nearly 70 years as the British Army's number one battle rifle.

British Enfield Rifles, Volume 2, No.4 and No.5 Rifles, by Charles R. Stratton, North Cape Publications, Tustin, CA, 1999. 150 pp., illustrated. Paper covers. $16.95
The historical background for the development of both rifles describing each variation and an explanation of all the "marks", "numbers" and codes found on most parts.

British Enfield Rifles, Volume 4, The Pattern 1914 and U. S. Model 1917 Rifles, by Charles R. Stratton, North Cape Publications, Tustin, CA, 2000. Paper covers. $16.95
One of the lease know American and British collectible military rifles is analyzed on a part by part basis. All markings and codes, refurbishment procedures and WW 2 upgrade are included as are the varios sniper rifle versions.

The British Falling Block Breechloading Rifle from 1865, by Jonathan Kirton, Tom Rowe Books, Maynardsville, TN, 2nd edition, 1997. 380 pp., illus. $70.00
Expanded 2nd edition of a comprehensive work on the British falling block rifle.

British Gun Engraving, by Douglas Tate, Safari Press, Inc., Huntington Beach, CA, 1999. 240 pp., illustrated. Limited, signed and numbered edition, in a slipcase. $80.00
A historic and photographic record of the last two centuries.

British Service Rifles and Carbines 1888-1900, by Alan M. Petrillo, Excaliber Publications, Latham, NY, 1994. 72 pp., illus, Paper covers. $11.95
A complete review of the Lee-Metford and Lee-Enfield rifles and carbines.

British Single Shot Rifles, Volume 1, Alexander Henry, by Wal Winfer, Tom Rowe, Maynardsville, TN, 1998, 200 pp., illus. $50.00
Detailed Study of the single shot rifles made by Henry. Illustrated with hundreds of photographs and drawings.

British Single Shot Rifles Volume 2, George Gibbs, by Wal Winfer, Tom Rowe, Maynardsville, TN, 1998. 177 pp., illus. $50.00
Detailed study of the Farquharson as made by Gibbs. Hundreds of photos.

British Single Shot Rifles, Volume 3, Jeffery, by Wal Winfer, Rowe Publications, Rochester, N.Y., 1999. 260 pp., illustrated. $60.00
The Farquharsen as made by Jeffery and his competitors, Holland & Holland, Bland, Westley, Manton, etc. Large section on the development of nitro cartridges including the .600.

British Single Shot Rifles, Vol. 4; Westley Richards, by Wal Winfer, Rowe Publications, Rochester, N.Y., 2000. 265 pages, illustrated, photos. $60.00
In his 4th volume Winfer covers a detailed study of the Westley Richards single shot rifles, including Monkey Tails, Improved Martini, 1872,1873, 1878,1881, 1897 Falling Blocks. He also covers Westley Richards Cartridges, History and Reloading information.

THE ARMS LIBRARY

British Small Arms Ammunition, 1864-1938 (Other than .303 inch), by Peter Labbett, Armory Publications, Seattle, WA. 1993, 358 pages, illus. Four-color dust jacket. $79.00

A study of British military rifle, handgun, machine gun, and aiming tube ammunition through 1 inch from 1864 to 1938. Photo-illustrated including the firearms that chambered the cartridges.

The British Soldier's Firearms from Smoothbore to Rifled Arms, 1850-1864, by Dr. C.H. Roads, R&R Books, Livonia, NY, 1994. 332 pp., illus. $49.00

A reprint of the classic text covering the development of British military hand and shoulder firearms in the crucial years between 1850 and 1864.

British Sporting Guns & Rifles, compiled by George Hoyem, Armory Publications, Coeur d'Alene, ID, 1997. 1024 pp., illus. In two volumes. $250.00

Eighteen old sporting firearms trade catalogs and a rare book reproduced with their color covers in a limited, signed and numbered edition.

Browning Dates of Manufacture, compiled by George Madis, Art and Reference House, Brownsboro, TX, 1989. 48 pp. $10.00

Gives the date codes and product codes for all models from 1824 to the present.

Browning Sporting Arms of Distinction 1903-1992, by Matt Eastman, Matt Eastman Publications, Fitzgerald, GA, 1995. 450 pp., illus. $49.95

The most recognized publication on Browning sporting arms; covers all models.

Buffalo Bill's Wild West: An American Legend, by R.L. Wilson and Greg Martine, Random House, N.Y., 1999. 3,167 pp., illustrated. $60.00

Over 225 color plates and 160 black-and-white illustrations, with in-depth text and captions, the colorful arms, posters, photos, costumes, saddles, accoutrement are brought to life.

Bullard Arms, by G. Scott Jamieson, The Boston Mills Press, Ontario, Canada, 1989. 244 pp., illus. $35.00

The story of a mechanical genius whose rifles and cartridges were the equal to any made in America in the 1880s.

Burning Powder, compiled by Major D.B. Wesson, Wolfe Publishing Company, Prescott, AZ, 1992. 110 pp. Soft cover. $10.95

A rare booklet from 1932 for Smith & Wesson collectors.

The Burnside Breech Loading Carbines, by Edward A. Hull, Andrew Mowbray, Inc., Lincoln, RI, 1986. 95 pp., illus. $16.00

No. 1 in the "Man at Arms Monograph Series." A model-by-model historical/technical examination of one of the most widely used cavalry weapons of the American Civil War based upon important and previously unpublished research.

Camouflage Uniforms of European and NATO Armies; 1945 to the Present, by J. F. Borsarello, Atglen, PA: Schiffer Publications. Over 290 color and b/w photographs, 120 pages. Softcover. $29.95

This full-color book covers nearly all of the NATO, and other European armies' camouflaged uniforms, and not only shows and explains the many patterns, but also their efficacy of design. Described and illustrated are the variety of materials tested in over forty different armies, and includes the history of obsolete trial tests from 1945 to the present time. More than two hundred patterns have been manufactured since World War II using various landscapes and seasonal colors for their look. The Vietnam and Gulf Wars, African or South American events, as well as recent Yugoslavian independence wars have been used as experimental terrains to test a variety of patterns. This book provides a superb reference for the historian, reenactor, designer, and modeler.

Camouflage Uniforms of the Waffen-SS A Photographic Reference, by Michael Beaver, Schiffer Publishing, Atglen, PA. Over 1,000 color and b/w photographs and illustrations, 296 pages. $69.95

Finally a book that unveils the shroud of mystery surrounding Waffen-SS camouflage clothing. Illustrated here, both in full color and in contemporary black and white photographs, this unparalleled look at Waffen-SS combat troops and their camouflage clothing will benefit both the historian and collector.

Canadian Gunsmiths from 1608: A Checklist of Tradesmen, by John Belton, Historical Arms Series No. 29. Canada: Museum Restoration, 1992. 40 pp., 17 illustrations. Softcover. $8.95

This Checklist is a greatly expanded version of HAS No. 14, listing the names, occupation, location, and dates of more than 1,500 men and women who worked as gunmakers, gunsmiths, armorers, gun merchants, gun patent holders, and a few other gun related trades. A collection of contemporary gunsmiths' letterhead have been provided to add color and depth to the study.

Cap Guns, by James Dundas, Schiffer Publishing, Atglen, PA, 1996. 160 pp., illus. Paper covers. $29.95

Over 600 full-color photos of cap guns and gun accessories with a current value guide.

Carbines of the Civil War, by John D. McAulay, Pioneer Press, Union City, TN, 1981. 123 pp., illus. Paper covers. $12.95

A guide for the student and collector of the colorful arms used by the Federal cavalry.

Carbines of the U.S. Cavalry 1861-1905, by John D. McAulay, Andrew Mowbray Publishers, Lincoln, RI, 1996. $35.00

Covers the crucial use of carbines from the beginning of the Civil War to the end of the cavalry carbine era in 1905.

Cartridge Carbines of the British Army, by Alan M. Petrillo, Excalibur Publications, Latham, NY, 1998. 72 pp., illustrated. Paper covers. $11.95

Begins with the Snider-Enfield which was the first regulation cartridge carbine introduced in 1866 and ends with the .303 caliber No.5, Mark 1 Enfield.

Cartridge Catalogues, compiled by George Hoyem, Armory Publications, Coeur d'Alene, ID., 1997. 504 pp., illus. $125.00

Fourteen old ammunition makers' and designers' catalogs reproduced with their color covers in a limited, signed and numbered edition. Completely revised edition of the general purpose reference work for which collectors, police,

scientists and laymen reach first for answers to cartridge identification questions. Available October, 1996.

Cartridge Reloading Tools of the Past, by R.H. Chamberlain and Tom Quigley, Tom Quigley, Castle Rock, WA, 1998. 167 pp., illustrated. Paper covers. $25.00

A detailed treatment of the extensive Winchester and Ideal lines of handloading tools and bulletmolds plus Remington, Marlin, Ballard, Browning and many others.

Cartridges for Collectors, by Fred Datig, Pioneer Press, Union City, TN, 1999. In three volumes of 176 pp. each. Vol.1 (Centerfire); Vol.2 (Rimfire and Misc.) types; Vol.3 (Additional Rimfire, Centerfire, and Plastic.). All illustrations are shown in full-scale drawings. Volume 1, softcover only, $19.95. Volumes 2 & 3, Hardcover $19.95

Civil War Arms Makers and Their Contracts, edited by Stuart C. Mowbray and Jennifer Heroux, Andrew Mowbray Publishing, Lincoln, RI, 1998. 595 pp. $39.50

A facsimile reprint of the Report by the Commissioner of Ordnance and Ordnance Stores, 1862.

Civil War Arms Purchases and Deliveries, edited by Stuart C. Mowbray, Andrew Mowbray Publishing, Lincoln, RI, 1998. 300pp., illus. $39.50

A facsimile reprint of the master list of Civil War weapons purchases and deliveries including Small Arms, Cannon, Ordnance and Projectiles.

Civil War Breech Loading Rifles, by John D. McAulay, Andrew Mowbray, Inc., Lincoln, RI, 1991. 144 pp., illus. Paper covers. $15.00

All the major breech-loading rifles of the Civil War and most, if not all, of the obscure types are detailed, illustrated and set in their historical context.

Civil War Cartridge Boxes of the Union Infantryman, by Paul Johnson, Andrew Mowbray, Inc., Lincoln, RI, 1998. 352 pp., illustrated. $45.00

There were four patterns of infantry cartridge boxes used by Union forces during the Civil War. The author describes the development and subsequent pattern changes to these cartridge boxes.

Civil War Commanders, by Dean Thomas, Thomas Publications, Gettysburg, PA. 1998. 72 pages, illustrated, photos. Paper Covers. $9.95

138 photographs and capsule biographies of Union and Confederate officers. A convenient personalities reference guide.

Civil War Firearms, by Joseph G. Bilby, Combined Books, Conshohocken, PA, 1996. 252 pp., illus. $34.95

A unique work combining background data on each firearm including its battlefield use, and a guide to collecting and firing surviving relics and modern reproductions.

Civil War Guns, by William B. Edwards, Thomas Publications, Gettysburg, PA, 1997. 444 pp., illus. $40.00

The complete story of Federal and Confederate small arms; design, manufacture, identifications, procurement issue, employment, effectiveness, and postwar disposal by the recognized expert.

Civil War Infantryman: In Camp, On the March, and In Battle, by Dean Thomas, Thomas Publications, Gettysburg, PA. 1998. 72 pages, illustrated, Softcovers. $12.95

Uses first-hand accounts to shed some light on the "common soldier" of the Civil War from enlistment to muster-out, including camp, marching, rations, equipment, fighting, and more.

Civil War Pistols, by John D. McAulay, Andrew Mowbray Inc., Lincoln, RI, 1992. 166 pp., illus. $38.50

A survey of the handguns used during the American Civil War.

Civil War Sharps Carbines and Rifles, by Earl J. Coates and John D. McAulay, Thomas Publications, Gettysburg, PA, 1996. 108 pp., illus. Paper covers. $12.95

Traces the history and development of the firearms including short histories of specific serial numbers and the soldiers who received them.

Civil War Small Arms of the U.S. Navy and Marine Corps, by John D. McAulay, Mowbray Publishing, Lincoln, RI, 1999. 186 pp., illustrated. $39.00

The first reliable and comprehensive guide to the firearms and edged weapons of the Civil War Navy and Marine Corps.

The W.F. Cody Buffalo Bill Collector's Guide with Values, by James W. Wojtowicz, Collector Books, Paducah, KY, 1998. 271 pp., illustrated. $24.95

A profusion of colorful collectibles including lithographs, programs, photographs, books, medals, sheet music, guns, etc. and today's values.

Col. Burton's Spiller & Burr Revolver, by Matthew W. Norman, Mercer University Press, Macon, GA, 1997. 152 pp., illus. $22.95

A remarkable archival research project on the arm together with a comprehensive story of the establishment and running of the factory.

Collector's Guide to Colt .45 Service Pistols Models of 1911 and 1911A1, Enlarged and revised edition. Clawson Publications, Fort Wayne, IN, 1998. 130 pp., illustrated. $45.00

From 1911 to the end of production in 1945 with complete military identification including all contractors.

A Collector's Guide to United States Combat Shotguns, by Bruce N. Canfield, Andrew Mowbray Inc., Lincoln, RI, 1992. 184 pp., illus. Paper covers. $24.00

This book provides full coverage of combat shotguns, from the earliest examples right up to the Gulf War and beyond.

A Collector's Guide to Winchester in the Service, by Bruce N. Canfield, Andrew Mowbray, Inc., Lincoln, RI, 1991. 192 pp., illus. Paper covers. $22.00

The firearms produced by Winchester for the national defense. From Hotchkiss to the M14, each firearm is examined and illustrated.

A Collector's Guide to the '03 Springfield, by Bruce N. Canfield, Andrew Mowbray Inc., Lincoln, RI, 1989. 160 pp., illus. Paper covers. $22.00

A comprehensive guide follows the '03 through its unparalleled tenure of service. Covers all of the interesting variations, modifications and accessories of this highly collectible military rifle.

THE ARMS LIBRARY

Collector's Illustrated Encyclopedia of the American Revolution, by George C. Neumann and Frank J. Kravic, Rebel Publishing Co., Inc., Texarkana, TX, 1989. 286 pp., illus. $36.95
A showcase of more than 2,300 artifacts made, worn, and used by those who fought in the War for Independence.

Colonial Frontier Guns, by T.M. Hamilton, Pioneer Press, Union City, TN, 1988. 176 pp., illus. Paper covers. $17.50
A complete study of early flint muskets of this country.

Colt: An American Legend, by R.L. Wilson, Artabras, New York, 1997. 406 pages, fully illustrated, most in color. $60.00
A reprint of the commemorative album celebrates 150 years of the guns of Samuel Colt and the manufacturing empire he built, with expert discussion of every model ever produced, the innovations of each model and variants, updated model and serial number charts and magnificent photographic showcases of the weapons.

The Colt Armory, by Ellsworth Grant, Man-at-Arms Bookshelf, Lincoln, RI, 1996. 232 pp., illus. $35.00
A history of Colt's Manufacturing Company.

Colt Blackpowder Reproductions & Replica: A Collector's and Shooter's Guide, by Dennis Miller, Blue Book Publications, Minneapolis, MN, 1999. 288 pp., illustrated. Paper covers. $29.95
The first book on this important subject, and a must for the investor, collector, and shooter.

Colt Heritage, by R.L. Wilson, Simon & Schuster, 1979. 358 pp., illus. $75.00
The official history of Colt firearms 1836 to the present.

Colt Memorabilia Price Guide, by John Ogle, Krause Publications, Iola, WI, 1998. 256 pp., illus. Paper covers. $29.95
The first book ever compiled about the vast array of non-gun merchandise produced by Sam Colt's companies, and other companies using the Colt name.

The Colt Model 1905 Automatic Pistol, by John Potocki, Andrew Mowbray Publishing, Lincoln, RI, 1998. 191 pp., illus. $28.00
Covers all aspects of the Colt Model 1905 Automatic Pistol, from its invention by the legendary John Browning to its numerous production variations.

Colt Peacemaker British Model, by Keith Cochran, Cochran Publishing Co., Rapid City, SD, 1989. 160 pp., illus. $35.00
Covers those revolvers Colt squeezed in while completing a large order of revolvers for the U.S. Cavalry in early 1874, to those magnificent cased target revolvers used in the pistol competitions at Bisley Commons in the 1890s.

Colt Peacemaker Encyclopedia, by Keith Cochran, Keith Cochran, Rapid City, SD, 1986. 434 pp., illus. $65.00
A must book for the Peacemaker collector.

Colt Peacemaker Encyclopedia, Volume 2, by Keith Cochran, Cochran Publishing Co., SD, 1992. 416 pp., illus. $60.00
Included in this volume are extensive notes on engraved, inscribed, historical and noted revolvers, as well as those revolvers used by outlaws, lawmen, movie and television stars.

Colt Percussion Accoutrements 1834-1873, by Robin Rapley, Robin Rapley, Newport Beach, CA, 1994. 432 pp., illus. Paper covers. $39.95
The complete collector's guide to the identification of Colt percussion accoutrements; including Colt conversions and their values.

Colt Pocket Hammerless Pistols, by Dr. John W. Brunner, Phillips Publications, Williamstown, NJ, 1998. 212 pp., illustrated. $59.95
You will never again have to locate a .25, .32 or .380 with this well illustrated, definitive reference guide at hand.

Colt Revolvers and the Tower of London, by Joseph G. Rosa, Royal Armouries of the Tower of London, London, England, 1988. 72 pp., illus. Soft covers. $15.00
Details the story of Colt in London through the early cartridge period.

Colt Rifles and Muskets from 1847-1870, by Herbert Houze, Krause Publications, Iola, WI, 1996. 192 pp., illus. $34.95
Discover previously unknown Colt models along with an extensive list of production figures for all models.

Colt's SAA Post War Models, by George Garton, The Gun Room Press, Highland Park, NJ, 1995. 166 pp., illus. $39.95
Complete facts on the post-war Single Action Army revolvers. Information on calibers, production numbers and variations taken from factory records.

Colt Single Action Army Revolvers: The Legend, the Romance and the Rivals, by "Doc" O'Meara, Krause Publications, Iola, WI, 2000. 160 pp., illustrated with 250 photos in b&w and a 16 page color section. $34.95
Production figures, serial numbers by year, and rarities.

Colt Single Action Army Revolvers and Alterations, by C. Kenneth Moore, Mowbray Publishers, Lincoln, RI, 1999. 112 pp., illustrated. $35.00
A comprehensive history of the revolvers that collectors call "Artillery Models." These are the most historical of all S.A.A. Colts, and this new book covers all the details.

Colt Single Action Army Revolvers and the London Agency, by C. Kenneth Moore, Andrew Mowbray Publishers, Lincoln, RI, 1990. 144 pp., illus. $35.00
Drawing on vast documentary sources, this work chronicles the relationship between the London Agency and the Hartford home office.

The Colt U.S. General Officers' Pistols, by Horace Greeley IV, Andrew Mowbray Inc., Lincoln, RI, 1990. 199 pp., illus. $38.00
These unique weapons, issued as a badge of rank to General Officers in the U.S. Army from WWII onward, remain highly personal artifacts of the military leaders who carried them. Includes serial numbers and dates of issue.

Colts from the William M. Locke Collection, by Frank Sellers, Andrew Mowbray Publishers, Lincoln, RI, 1996. 192 pp., illus. $55.00
This important book illustrates all of the famous Locke Colts, with captions by arms authority Frank Sellers.

Colt's Dates of Manufacture 1837-1978, by R.L. Wilson, published by Maurie Albert, Coburg, Australia; N.A. distributor I.D.S.A. Books, Hamilton, OH, 1983. 61 pp. $6.00
An invaluable pocket guide to the dates of manufacture of Colt firearms up to 1978.

Colt's 100th Anniversary Firearms Manual 1836-1936: A Century of Achievement, Wolfe Publishing Co., Prescott, AZ, 1992. 100 pp., illus. Paper covers. $12.95
Originally published by the Colt Patent Firearms Co., this booklet covers the history, manufacturing procedures and the guns of the first 100 years of the genius of Samuel Colt.

Colt's Pocket '49: Its Evolution Including the Baby Dragoon and Wells Fargo, by Robert Jordan and Darrow Watt, privately printed, Loma Mar, CA 2000. 304 pages, with 984 color photos, illus. Beautifully bound in a deep blue leather like case. $125.00
Detailed information on all models and covers engaving, cases, accoutrements, holsters, fakes, and much more. Included is a summary booklet containing information such as serial numbers, production ranges & identifing photos. This book is a masterpiece on its subject.

Complete Guide to all United States Military Medals 1939 to Present, by Colonel Frank C. Foster, Medals of America Press, Fountain Inn, SC, 2000. 121 pp,.illustrated, photos. $29.95
Complete criteria for every Army, Navy, Marines, Air Force, Coast Guard, and Merchant Marine awards since 1939. All decorations, service medals, and ribbons shown in full-color and accompanied by dates and campaigns as well as detailed descriptions on proper wear and display.

Complete Guide to the M1 Garand and the M1 Carbine, by Bruce N. Canfield, 2nd printing, Andrew Mowbray Inc., Lincoln, RI, 1999. 296 pp., illus. $39.50
Expanded and updated coverage of both the M1 Garand and the M1 Carbine, with more than twice as much information as the author's previous book on this topic.

The Complete Guide to U.S. Infantry Weapons of the First War, by Bruce Canfield, Andrew Mowbray, Publisher, Lincoln, RI, 2000. 304 pp., illus. $39.95
The definitive study of the U.S. Infantry weapons used in WW1.

The Complete Guide to U.S. Infantry Weapons of World War Two, by Bruce Canfield, Andrew Mowbray, Publisher, Lincoln, RI, 1995. 303 pp., illus. $39.95
A definitive work on the weapons used by the United States Armed Forces in WWII.

A Concise Guide to the Artillery at Gettysburg, by Gregory Coco, Thomas Publications, Gettysburg, PA, 1998. 96 pp., illus. Paper Covers. $10.00
Coco's tenth book on Gettysburg is a beginner's guide to artillery and its use at the battle. It covers the artillery batteries describing the types of cannons, shells, fuses, etc.using interesting narrative and human interest stories.

Cooey Firearms, Made in Canada 1919-1979, by John A. Belton, Museum Restoration, Canada, 1998. 36pp., with 46 illus. Paper Covers. $8.95
More than 6 million rifles and at least 67 models, were made by this small Canadian riflemaker. They have been identified from the first 'Cooey Canuck' through the last variations made by the 'Winchester-Cooey'. Each is descibed and most are illustrated in this first book on The Cooey.

Cowboy Collectibles and Western Memorabilia, by Bob Bell and Edward Vebell, Schiffer Publishing, Atglen, PA, 1992. 160 pp., illus. Paper covers. $29.95
The exciting era of the cowboy and the wild west collectibles including rifles, pistols, gun rigs, etc.

Cowboy Culture: The Last Frontier of American Antiques, by Michael Friedman, Schiffer Publishing, Ltd., West Chester, PA, 1992. 300 pp., illustrated.
Covers the artful aspects of the old west, the antiques and collectibles. Illustrated with clear color plates of over 1,000 items such as spurs, boots, guns, saddles etc.

Cowboy and Gunfighter Collectible, by Bill Mackin, Mountain Press Publishing Co., Missoula, MT, 1995. 178 pp., illus. Paper covers. $25.00
A photographic encyclopedia with price guide and makers' index.

Cowboys and the Trappings of the Old West, by William Manns and Elizabeth Clair Flood, Zon International Publishing Co., Santa Fe, NM, 1997, 1st edition. 224 pp., illustrated. $45.00
A pictorial celebration of the cowboys dress and trappings.

Cowboy Hero Cap Pistols, by Rudy D'Angelo, Antique Trader Books, Dubuque, IA, 1998. 196 pp., illus. Paper covers. $34.95
Aimed at collectors of cap pistols created and named for famous film and television cowboy heros, this in-depth guide hits all the marks. Current values are given.

Custom Firearms Engraving, by Tom Turpin, Krause Publications, Iola, WI, 1999. 208 pp., illustrated. $49.95
Over 200 four-color photos with more than 75 master engravers profiled. Engravers Directory with addresses in the U.S. and abroad.

The Decorations, Medals, Ribbons, Badges and Insignia of the United States Army; World War 2 to Present, by Col. Frank C. Foster, Medals of America Press, Fountain Inn, SC. 2001. 145 pages, illustrated. $29.95
The most complete guide to United States Army medals, ribbons, rank, insignia nad patches from WWII to the present day. Each medal and insignia shown in full color. Includes listing of respective criteria and campaigns.

The Decorations, Medals, Ribbons, Badges and Insignia of the United States Navy; World War 2 to Present, by James G. Thompson, Medals of America Press, Fountain Inn, SC. 2000. 123 pages, illustrated. $29.95
The most complete guide to United States Army medals, ribbons, rank, insignia nad patches from WWII to the present day. Each medal and insignia shown in full color. Includes listing of respective criteria and campaigns.

The Derringer in America, Volume 1, The Percussion Period, by R.L. Wilson and L.D. Eberhart, Andrew Mowbray Inc., Lincoln, RI, 1985. 271 pp., illus. $48.00
A long awaited book on the American percussion deringer.

The Derringer in America, Volume 2, The Cartridge Period, by L.D. Eberhart and R.L. Wilson, Andrew Mowbray Inc., Publishers, Lincoln, RI, 1993. 284 pp., illus. $65.00
Comprehensive coverage of cartridge deringers organized alphabetically by maker. Includes all types of deringers known by the authors to have been offered to the American market.

The Devil's Paintbrush: Sir Hiram Maxim's Gun, by Dolf Goldsmith, 3rd Edition, expanded and revised, Collector Grade Publications, Toronto, Canada, 2000. 384 pp., illus. $79.95
The classic work on the world's first true automatic machine gun.

Dr. Josephus Requa Civil War Dentist and the Billinghurst-Requa Volley Gun, by John M. Hyson, Jr., & Margaret Requa DeFrancisco, Museum Restoration Service, Bloomfield, Ont., Canada, 1999. 36 pp. Paper covers. $8.95
The story of the inventor of the first practical rapid-fire gun to be used during the American Civil War.

The Duck Stamp Story, by Eric Jay Dolin and Bob Dumaine, Krause Publications, Iola, WI, 2000. 208 pp., illustrated with color throughout. Paper covers. $29.95; Hardbound. $49.95.
Detailed information on the value and rarity of every federal duck stamp. Outstanding art and illustrations.

The Dutch Luger (Parabellum) A Complete History, by Bas J. Martens and Guus de Vries, Ironside International Publishers, Inc., Alexandria, VA, 1995. 268 pp., illus. $49.95.
The history of the Luger in the Netherlands. An extensive description of the Dutch pistol and trials and the different models of the Luger in the Dutch service.

The Eagle on U.S. Firearms, by John W. Jordan, Pioneer Press, Union City, TN, 1992. 140 pp., illus. Paper covers. $17.50.
Stylized eagles have been stamped on government owned or manufactured firearms in the U.S. since the beginning of our country. This book lists and illustrates these various eagles in an informative and refreshing manner.

Encyclopedia of Rifles & Handguns; A Comprehensive Guide to Firearms, edited by Sean Connolly, Chartwell Books, Inc., Edison, NJ., 1996. 160 pp., illustrated. $26.00.
A lavishly illustrated book providing a comprehensive history of military and civilian personal firepower.

Eprouvettes: A Comprehensive Study of Early Devices for the Testing of Gunpowder, by R.T.W. Kempers, Royal Armouries Museum, Leeds, England, 1999. 352 pp., illustrated with 240 black & white and 28 color plates. $125.00.
The first comprehensive study of eprouvettes ever attempted in a single volume.

European Firearms in Swedish Castles, by Kaa Wennberg, Bohuslaningens Boktryckeri AB, Uddevalla, Sweden, 1986. 156 pp., illus. $50.00.
The famous collection of Count Keller, the Ettersburg Castle collection, and others. English text.

European Sporting Cartridges, Part 1, by W.B. Dixon, Armory Publications, Inc., Coeur d'Alene, ID, 1997. 250 pp., illus. $63.00
Photographs and drawings of over 550 centerfire cartridge case types in 1,300 illustrations produced in German and Austria from 1875 to 1995.

European Sporting Cartridges, Part 2, by W.B. Dixon, Armory Publications, Inc., Coeur d'Alene, ID, 2000. 240 pp., illus. $63.00
An illustrated history of centerfire hunting and target cartridges produced in Czechoslovakia, Switzerland, Norway, Sweden, Finland, Russia, Italy, Denmark, Belguim from 1875 to 1998. Adds 50 specimens to volume 1 (Germany-Austria). Also, illustrates 40 small arms magazine experiments during the late 19th Century, and includes the English-Language export ammunition catalogue of Kovo (Povazske Strojarne), Prague, Czeck. from the, 1930's.

Fifteen Years in the Hawken Lode, by John D. Baird, The Gun Room Press, Highland Park, NJ, 1976. 120 pp., illus. $24.95.
A collection of thoughts and observations gained from many years of intensive study of the guns from the shop of the Hawken brothers.

'51 Colt Navies, by Nathan L. Swayze, The Gun Room Press, Highland Park, NJ, 1993. 243 pp., illus. $59.95.
The Model 1851 Colt Navy, its variations and markings.

Fighting Iron, by Art Gogan, Andrew Mowbray, Inc., Lincoln, R.I., 1999. 176 pp., illustrated. $28.00.
It doesn't matter whether you collect guns, swords, bayonets or accountrement—sooner or later you realize that it all comes down to the metal. If you don't understand the metal you don't understand your collection.

Fine Colts, The Dr. Joseph A. Murphy Collection, by R.L. Wilson, Sheffield Marketing Associates, Inc., Doylestown, PA, 1999. 258 pp., illustrated. Limited edition signed and numbered. $99.00.
This lavish new work covers exquisite, deluxe and rare Colt arms from Paterson and other percussion revolvers to the cartridge period and up through modern times.

Firearms, by Derek Avery, Desert Publications, El Dorado, AR, 1999. 95 pp., illustrated. $9.95.
The firearms included in this book are by necessity only a selection, but nevertheless one that represents the best and most famous weapons seen since the Second World War.

Firearms and Tackle Memorabilia, by John Delph, Schiffer Publishing, Ltd., West Chester, PA, 1991. 124 pp., illus. $39.95.
A collector's guide to signs and posters, calendars, trade cards, boxes, envelopes, and other highly sought after memorabilia. With a value guide.

Firearms of the American West 1803-1865, Volume 1, by Louis A. Garavaglia and Charles Worman, University of Colorado Press, Niwot, CO, 1998. 402 pp., illustrated. $59.95.
Traces the development and uses of firearms on the frontier during this period.

Firearms of the American West 1866-1894, by Louis A. Garavaglia and Charles G. Worman, University of Colorado Press, Niwot, CO, 1998. 416 pp., illus. $59.95.
A monumental work that offers both technical information on all of the important firearms used in the West during this period and a highly entertaining history of how they were used, who used them, and why.

Firearms from Europe, by David Noe, Larry W. Yantz, Dr. James B. Whisker, Rowe Publications, Rochester, N.Y., 1999. 192 pp., illustrated. $45.00.
A history and description of firearms imported during the American Civil War by the United States of America and the Confederate States of America.

Firepower from Abroad, by Wiley Sword, Andrew Mowbray Publishing, Lincoln, R.I., 2000. 120 pp., illustrated. $23.00.
The Confederate Enfield and the LeMat revolver and how they reached the Confederate market.

Flayderman's Guide to Antique American Firearms and Their Values, 7th Edition, edited by Norm Flayderman, DBI books, a division of Krause Publications, Iola, WI, 1998. 656 pp., illus. Paper covers. $32.95.
A completely updated and new edition with more than 3,600 models and variants extensively described with all marks and specifications necessary for quick identification.

The FN-FAL Rifle, et al, by Duncan Long, Paladin Press, Boulder, CO, 1999. 144 pp., illustrated. Paper covers. $18.95.
Detailed descriptions of the basic models produced by Fabrique Nationale and the myriad variants that evolved as a result of the firearms universal acceptance.

The .45-70 Springfield, by Joe Poyer and Craig Riesch, North Cape Publications, Tustin, CA, 1996. 150 pp., illus. Paper covers. $16.95.
A revised and expanded second edition of a best-selling reference work organized by serial number and date of production to aid the collector in identifying popular "Trapdoor" rifles and carbines.

The French 1935 Pistols, by Eugene Medlin and Colin Doane, Eugene Medlin, El Paso, TX, 1995. 172 pp., illus. Paper covers. $25.95.
The development and identification of successive models, fakes and variants, holsters and accessories, and serial numbers by dates of production.

Freund & Bro. Pioneer Gunmakers to the West, by F.J. Pablo Balentine, Graphic Publishers, Newport Beach, CA, 1997. 380 pp., illustrated $69.95.
The story of Frank W. and George Freund, skilled German gunsmiths who plied their trade on the Western American frontier during the final three decades of the nineteenth century.

From the Kingdom of Lilliput: The Miniature Firearms of David Kucer, by K. Corey Keeble and **The Making of Miniatures,** by David Kucer, Museum Restoration Service, Ontario, Canada, 1994. 51 pp., illus, $25.00.
An overview of the subject of miniatures in general combined with an outline by the artist himself on the way he makes a miniature firearm.

Frontier Pistols and Revolvers, by Dominique Venner, Book Sales Inc., Edison, N.J., 1998. 144 pp., illus. $19.95.
Colt, Smith & Wesson, Remington and other early-brand revolvers which tamed the American frontier are shown amid vintage photographs, etchings and paintings to evoke the wild West.

The Fusil de Tulole in New France, 1691-1741, by Russel Bouchard, Museum Restorations Service, Bloomfield, Ontario, Canada, 1997. 36 pp., illus. Paper covers. $8.95
The development of the company and the identification of their arms.

Game Guns & Rifles: Percussion to Hammerless Ejector in Britain, by Richard Akehurst, Trafalgar Square, N. Pomfret, VT, 1993. 192 pp., illus. $39.95.
Long considered a classic this important reprint covers the period of British gunmaking between 1830-1900.

The Gas Trap Garand, by Billy Pyle, Collector Grade Publications, Cobourg, Ontario, Canada, 1999 316 pp., illustrated. $59.95.
The in-depth story of the rarest Garands of them all, the initial 80 Model Shop rifles made under the personal supervision of John Garand himself in 1934 and 1935, and the first 50,000 plus production "gas trap" M1's manufactured at Springfield Armory between August, 1937 and August, 1940.

George Schreyer, Sr. and Jr., Gunmakers of Hanover, Pennsylvania, by George Shumway, George Shumway Publishers, York, PA, 1990. 160pp., illus. $50.00.
This monograph is a detailed photographic study of almost all known surviving long rifles and smoothbore guns made by highly regarded gunsmiths George Schreyer, Sr. and Jr.

The German Assault Rifle 1935-1945, by Peter R. Senich, Paladin Press, Boulder, CO, 1987. 328 pp., illus. $60.00.
A complete review of machine carbines, machine pistols and assault rifles employed by Hitler's Wehrmacht during WWII.

The German K98k Rifle, 1934-1945: The Backbone of the Wehrmacht, by Richard D. Law, Collector Grade Publications, Toronto, Canada, 1993. 336 pp., illus. $69.95.
The most comprehensive study ever published on the 14,000,000 bolt-action K98k rifles produced in Germany between 1934 and 1945.

German Machine Guns, by Daniel D. Musgrave, revised edition, Ironside International Publishers, Inc. Alexandria, VA, 1992. 586 pp., 650 illus. $49.95.
The most definitive book ever written on German machineguns. Covers the introduction and development of machineguns in Germany from 1899 to the rearmament period after WWII.

German Military Rifles and Machine Pistols, 1871-1945, by Hans Dieter Gotz, Schiffer Publishing Co., West Chester, PA, 1990. 245 pp., illus. $35.00.
This book portrays in words and pictures the development of the modern German weapons and their ammunition including the scarcely known experimental types.

The German MP40 Maschinenpistole, by Frank Iannamico, Moose Lake Publishing, Harmony, ME, 1999. 185 pp., illustrated. Paper covers. $19.95.
The history, development and use of this famous gun of World War 2.

THE ARMS LIBRARY

German 7.9mm Military Ammunition, by Daniel W. Kent, Daniel W. Kent, Ann Arbor, MI, 1991. 244 pp., illus. $35.00.
The long-awaited revised edition of a classic among books devoted to ammunition.

The Golden Age of Remington, by Robert W.D. Ball, Krause publications, Iola, WI, 1995. 194 pp., illus. $29.95.
For Remington collectors or firearms historians, this book provides a pictorial history of Remington through World War I. Includes value guide.

The Government Models, by William H.D. Goddard, Andrew Mowbray Publishing, Lincoln, RI, 1998. 296 pp., illustrated. $58.50.
The most authoritative source on the development of the Colt model of 1911.

Grasshoppers and Butterflies, by Adrian B. Caruana, Museum Restoration Service, Alexandria, Bay, N.Y., 1999. 32 pp., illustrated. Paper covers. $8.95.
No.39 in the Historical Arms Series. The light 3 pounders of Pattison and Townsend.

The Greener Story, by Graham Greener, Quiller Press, London, England, 2000. 256 pp., illustrated with 32 pages of color photos. $64.50.
W.W. Greener, his family history, inventions, guns, patents, and more.

A Guide to American Trade Catalogs 1744-1900, by Lawrence B. Romaine, Dover Publications, New York, NY. 422 pp., illus. Paper covers. $12.95

A Guide to Ballard Breechloaders, by George J. Layman, Pioneer Press, Union City, TN, 1997. 261 pp., illus. Paper covers. $19.95
Documents the saga of this fine rifle from the first models made by Ball & Williams of Worchester, to its production by the Marlin Firearms Co, to the cessation of 19th century manufacture in 1891, and finally to the modern reproductions made in the 1990's.

A Guide to the Maynard Breechloader, by George J. Layman, George J. Layman, Ayer, MA, 1993. 125 pp., illus. Paper covers. $11.95.
The first book dedicated entirely to the Maynard family of breech-loading firearms. Coverage of the arms is given from the 1850s through the 1880s.

A Guide to U. S. Army Dress Helmets 1872-1904, by Kasal and Moore, North Cape Publications, 2000. 88 pp., illus. Paper covers. $15.95
This thorough study provides a complete description of the Model 1872 & 1881 dress helmets worn by the U.S. Army. Including all componets from bodies to plates to plumes & shoulder cords and tells how to differentiate the originals from reproductions. Extensively illustrated with photographs, '8 pages in full color' of complete helmets and their components.

Gun Collecting, by Geoffrey Boothroyd, Sportsman's Press, London, 1989. 208 pp., illus. $29.95.
The most comprehensive list of 19th century British gunmakers and gunsmiths ever published.

Gunmakers of London 1350-1850, by Howard L. Blackmore, George Shumway Publisher, York, PA, 1986. 222 pp., illus. $35.00.
A listing of all the known workmen of gun making in the first 500 years, plus a history of the guilds, cutlers, armourers, founders, blacksmiths, etc. 260 gunmarks are illustrated.

Gunmakers of London Supplement 1350-1850, by Howard L. Blackmore, Museum Restoration Service, Alexandria Bay, NY, 1999. 156 pp., illustrated. $60.00.
Begins with an introductory chapter on "foreighn" gunmakers followed by records of all the new information found about previously unidentified armourers, gunmakers and gunsmiths.

The Guns that Won the West: Firearms of the American Frontier, 1865-1898, by John Walter, Stackpole Books, Inc., Mechanicsburg, PA.,1999. 256 pp., illustrated. $34.95.
Here is the story of the wide range of firearms from pistols to rifles used by plainsmen and settlers, gamblers, native Americans and the U.S. Army.

Gunsmiths of Illinois, by Curtis L. Johnson, George Shumway Publishers, York, PA, 1995. 160 pp., illus. $50.00.
Genealogical information is provided for nearly one thousand gunsmiths. Contains hundreds of illustrations of rifles and other guns, of handmade origin, from Illinois.

The Gunsmiths of Manhattan, 1625-1900: A Checklist of Tradesmen, by Michael H. Lewis, Museum Restoration Service, Bloomfield, Ont., Canada, 1991. 40 pp., illus. Paper covers. $8.95.
This listing of more than 700 men in the arms trade in New York City prior to about the end of the 19th century will provide a guide for identification and further research.

The Guns of Dagenham: Lanchester, Patchett, Sterling, by Peter Laidler and David Howroyd, Collector Grade Publications, Inc., Cobourg, Ont., Canada, 1995. 310 pp., illus. $39.95.
An in-depth history of the small arms made by the Sterling Company of Dagenham, Essex, England, from 1940 until Sterling was purchased by British Aerospace in 1989 and closed.

Guns of the Western Indian War, by R. Stephen Dorsey, Collector's Library, Eugene, OR, 1997. 220 pp., illus. Paper covers. $30.00.
The full story of the guns and ammunition that made western history in the turbulent period of 1865-1890.

Gun Powder Cans & Kegs, by Ted & David Bacyk and Tom Rowe, Rowe Publications, Rochester, NY, 1999. 150 pp., illus. $65.00.
The first book devoted to powder tins and kegs. All cans and kegs in full color. With a price guide and rarity scale.

The Guns of Remington: Historic Firearms Spanning Two Centuries, compiled by Howard M. Madaus, Biplane Productions, Publisher, in cooperation with Buffalo Bill Historical Center, Cody, WY, 1998. 352 pp., illustrated with over 800 color photos. $79.95.
A complete catalog of the firearms in the exhibition, "It Never Failed Me: The Arms & Art of Remington Arms Company" at the Buffalo Bill Historical Center, Cody, Wyoming.

Gun Tools, Their History and Identification by James B. Shaffer, Lee A. Rutledge and R. Stephen Dorsey, Collector's Library, Eugene, OR, 1992. 375 pp., illus. $30.00.
Written history of foreign and domestic gun tools from the flintlock period to WWII.

Gun Tools, Their History and Identifications, Volume 2, by Stephen Dorsey and James B. Shaffer, Collectors' Library, Eugene, OR, 1997. 396 pp., illus. Paper covers. $30.00.
Gun tools from the Royal Armouries Museum in England, Pattern Room, Royal Ordnance Reference Collection in Nottingham and from major private collections.

Gunsmiths of the Carolinas 1660-1870, by Daniel D. Hartzler and James B. Whisker, Old Bedford Village Press, Bedford, PA, 1998. 176 pp., illustrated. $40.00.
This deluxe hard bound edition of 176 pages is printed on fine coated paper, with about 90 pages of large photographs of fine longrifles from the Carolinas, and about 90 pages of detailed research on the gunsmiths who created the highly prized and highly collectable longrifles. Dedicated to serious students of original Kentucky rifles, who may seldom encounter fine longrifles from the Carolinas.

Gunsmiths of Maryland, by Daniel D. Hartzler and James B. Whisker, Old Bedford Village Press, Bedford, PA, 1998. 208 pp., illustrated. $45.00.
Covers firelock Colonial period through the breech-loading patent models. Featuring longrifles.

Gunsmiths of Virginia, by Daniel D. Hartzler and James B. Whisker, Old Bedford Village Press, Bedford, PA, 1992. 206 pp., illustrated. $45.00.
A photographic study of American longrifles.

Gunsmiths of West Virginia, by Daniel D. Hartzler and James B. Whisker, Old Bedford Village Press, Bedford, PA, 1998. 176 pp., illustrated. $40.00.
A photographic study of American longrifles.

Gunsmiths of York County, Pennsylvania, by Daniel D. Hartzler and James B. Whisker, Old Bedford Village Press, Bedford, PA, 1998. 160 pp., illustrated. $40.00.
160 pages of photographs and research notes on the longrifles and gunsmiths of York County, Pennsylvania. Many longrifle collectors and gun builders have noticed that York County style rifles tend to be more formal in artistic decoration than some other schools of style. Patriotic themes, and folk art were popular design elements.

Hall's Military Breechloaders, by Peter A. Schmidt, Andrew Mowbray Publishers, Lincoln, RI, 1996. 232 pp., illus. $55.00.
The whole story behind these bold and innovative firearms.

The Handgun, by Geoffrey Boothroyd, David and Charles, North Pomfret, VT, 1989. 566 pp., illus. $60.00.
Every chapter deals with an important period in handgun history from the 14th century to the present.

Handgun of Military Rifle Marks 1866-1950, by Richard A. Hoffman and Noel P. Schott, Mapleleaf Militaria Publishing, St. Louis, MO, 1999, second edition. 60 pp., illustrated. Paper covers. $20.00.
An illustrated guide to identifying military rifle and marks.

Handguns & Rifles: The Finest Weapons from Around the World, by Ian Hogg, Random House Value Publishing, Inc., N.Y., 1999. 128 pp., illustrated. $18.98.
The serious gun collector will welcome this fully illustrated examination of international handguns and rifles. Each entry covers the history of the weapon, what purpose it serves, and its advantages and disadvantages.

The Hawken Rifle: Its Place in History, by Charles E. Hanson, Jr., The Fur Press, Chadron, NE, 1979. 104 pp., illus. Paper covers. $15.00.
A definitive work on this famous rifle.

Hawken Rifles, The Mountain Man's Choice, by John D. Baird, The Gun Room Press, Highland Park, NJ, 1976. 95 pp., illus. $29.95.
Covers the rifles developed for the Western fur trade. Numerous specimens are described and shown in photographs.

High Standard: A Collector's Guide to the Hamden & Hartford Target Pistols, by Tom Dance, Andrew Mowbray, Inc., Lincoln, RI, 1991. 192 pp., illus. Paper covers. $24.00.
From Citation to Supermatic, all of the production models and specials made from 1951 to 1984 are covered according to model number or series.

Historic Pistols: The American Martial Flintlock 1760-1845, by Samuel E. Smith & Edwin W. Bitter, The Gun Room Press, Highland Park, NJ, 1986. 353 pp., illus. $45.00.
Covers over 70 makers and 163 models of American martial arms.

Historical Hartford Hardware, by William W. Dalrymple, Colt Collector Press, Rapid City, SD, 1976. 42 pp., illus. Paper covers. $10.00.
Historically associated Colt revolvers.

The History and Development of Small Arms Ammunition, Volume 2, by George A. Hoyem, Armory Publications, Oceanside, CA, 1991. 303 pp., illus. $65.00.
Covers the blackpowder military centerfire rifle, carbine, machine gun and volley gun ammunition used in 28 nations and dominions, together with the firearms that chambered them.

The History and Development of Small Arms Ammunition, Volume 4, by George A. Hoyem, Armory Publications, Seattle, WA, 1998. 200 pp., illustrated $65.00.
A comprehensive book on American black powder and early smokeless rifle cartridges.

The History of Colt Firearms, by Dean Boorman, Lyons Press, New York, NY, 2001. 144 pp., illus. $29.95
Discover the fascinating story of the world's most famous revolver, complete with more than 150 stunning full-color photographs.

THE ARMS LIBRARY

History of Modern U.S. Military Small Arms Ammunition. Volume 1, 1880-1939, revised by F.W. Hackley, W.H. Woodin and E.L. Scranton, Thomas Publications, Gettysburg, PA, 1998. 328 pp., illus. $49.95.

This revised edition incorporates all publicly available information concerning military small arms ammunition for the period 1880 through 1939 in a single volume.

History of Modern U.S. Military Small Arms Ammunition. Volume 2, 1940-1945 by F.W. Hackley, W.H. Woodin and E.L. Scranton. Gun Room Press, Highland Park, NJ. 300 + pages, illustrated. $39.95

Based on decades of original research conducted at the National Archives, numerous military, public and private museums and libraries, as well as individual collections, this edition incorporates all publicly available information concerning military small arms ammunition for the period 1940 through 1945.

The History of Winchester Rifles, by Dean Boorman, Lyons Press, New York, NY, 2001. 144 pp., illus. $29.95

A captivating and wonderfully photographed history of one of the most legendary names in gun lore. 150 full-color photos.

The History of Winchester Firearms 1866-1992, sixth edition, updated, expanded, and revised by Thomas Henshaw, New Win Publishing, Clinton, NJ, 1993. 280 pp., illus. $27.95.

This classic is the standard reference for all collectors and others seeking the facts about any Winchester firearm, old or new.

History of Winchester Repeating Arms Company, by Herbert G. Houze, Krause Publications, Iola, WI, 1994. 800 pp., illus. $50.00.

The complete Winchester history from 1856-1981.

Honour Bound: The Chauchat Machine Rifle, by Gerard Demaison and Yves Buffetaut, Collector Grade Publications, Inc., Cobourg, Ont., Canada, 1995. $39.95.

The story of the CSRG (Chauchat) machine rifle, the most manufactured automatic weapon of World War One.

Hopkins & Allen Revolvers & Pistols, by Charles E. Carder, Avil Onze Publishing, Delphos, OH, 1998, illustrated. Paper covers. $24.95.

Covers over 165 photos, graphics and patent drawings.

How to Buy and Sell Used Guns, by John Traister, Stoeger Publishing Co., So. Hackensack, NJ, 1984. 192 pp., illus. Paper covers. $10.95.

A new guide to buying and selling guns.

Hunting Weapons From the Middle Ages to the Twentieth Century, by Howard L. Blackmore, Dover Publications, Meneola, NY, 2000. 480 pp., illustrated. Paper covers. $16.95.

Dealing mainly with the different classes of weapons used in sport—swords, spears, crossbows, guns, and rifles—from the Middle Ages until the present day.

Identification Manual on the .303 British Service Cartridge, No. 1-Ball Ammunition, by B.A. Temple, I.D.S.A. Books, Piqua, OH, 1986. 84 pp., 57 illus. $12.50

Identification Manual on the .303 British Service Cartridge, No. 2-Blank Ammunition, by B.A. Temple, I.D.S.A. Books, Piqua, OH, 1986. 95 pp., 59 illus. $12.50

Identification Manual on the .303 British Service Cartridge, No. 3-Special Purpose Ammunition, by B.A. Temple, I.D.S.A. Books, Piqua, OH, 1987. 82 pp., 49 illus. $12.50

Identification Manual on the .303 British Service Cartridge, No. 4-Dummy Cartridges Henry 1869-c.1900, by B.A. Temple, I.D.S.A. Books, Piqua, OH, 1988. 84 pp., 70 illus. $12.50

Identification Manual on the .303 British Service Cartridge, No. 5-Dummy Cartridges (2), by B.A. Temple, I.D.S.A. Books, Piqua, OH, 1994. 78 pp. $12.50

The Illustrated Book of Guns, by David Miller, Salamander Books, N.Y., N.Y., 2000. 304 pp., illustrated in color. $34.95.

An illustrated directory of over 1,000 military and sporting firearms.

The Illustrated Encyclopedia of Civil War Collectibles, by Chuck Lawliss, Henry Holt and Co., New York, NY, 1997. 316 pp., illus. Paper covers. $22.95.

A comprehensive guide to Union and Confederate arms, equipment, uniforms, and other memorabilia.

Illustrations of United States Military Arms 1776-1903 and Their Inspector's Marks, compiled by Turner Kirkland, Pioneer Press, Union City, TN, 1988. 37 pp., illus. Paper covers. $7.00.

Reprinted from the 1949 Bannerman catalog. Valuable information for both the advanced and beginning collector.

Indian War Cartridge Pouches, Boxes and Carbine Boots, by R. Stephen Dorsey, Collector's Library, Eugene, OR, 1993. 156 pp., illus. Paper Covers. $20.00.

The key reference work to the cartridge pouches, boxes, carbine sockets and boots of the Indian War period 1865-1890.

An Introduction to the Civil War Small Arms, by Earl J. Coates and Dean S. Thomas, Thomas Publishing Co., Gettysburg, PA, 1990. 96 pp., illus. Paper covers. $10.00.

The small arms carried by the individual soldier during the Civil War.

Japanese Rifles of World War Two, by Duncan O. McCollum, Excalibur Publications, Latham, NY, 1996. 64 pp., illus. Paper covers. $18.95.

A sweeping view of the rifles and carbines that made up Japan's arsenal during the conflict.

Kalashnikov Arms, compiled by Alexei Nedelin, Design Military Parade, Ltd., Moscow, Russia, 1997. 240 pp., illus. $49.95.

Weapons versions stored in the St. Petersburg Military Historical Museum of Artillery, Engineer Troops and Communications and in the Izhmash JSC.

Kalashnikov "Machine Pistols, Assault Rifles, and Machine Guns, 1945 to the Present", by John Walter, Paladin Press, Boulder, CO, 1999, hardcover, photos, illus., 146 pp $22.95

This exhaustive work published by Greenhill Military Manuals features a gun-by-gun directory of Kalashnikov variants. Technical specifications and illustrations are provided throughout, along with details of sights, bayonets, markings and ammunition. A must for the serious collector and historian.

The Kentucky Pistol, by Roy Chandler and James Whisker, Old Bedford Village Press, Bedford, PA, 1997. 225 pp., illus. $60.00

A photographic study of Kentucky pistols from famous collections.

The Kentucky Rifle, by Captain John G.W. Dillin, George Shumway Publisher, York, PA, 1993. 221 pp., illus. $50.00.

This well-known book was the first attempt to tell the story of the American longrifle. This edition retains the original text and illustrations with supplemental footnotes provided by Dr. George Shumway.

Know Your Broomhandle Mausers, by R.J. Berger, Blacksmith Corp., Southport, CT, 1985. 96 pp., illus. Paper covers. $12.95.

An interesting story on the big Mauser pistol and its variations.

Krag Rifles, by William S. Brophy, The Gun Room Press, Highland Park, NJ, 1980. 200 pp., illus. $35.00.

The first comprehensive work detailing the evolution and various models, both military and civilian.

The Krieghoff Parabellum, by Randall Gibson, Midland, TX, 1988. 279 pp., illus. $40.00.

A comprehensive text pertaining to the Lugers manufactured by H. Krieghoff Waffenfabrik.

Las Pistolas Espanolas Tipo "Mauser," by Artemio Mortera Perez, Quiron Ediciones, Valladolid, Spain, 1998. 71 pp., illustrated. Paper covers. $34.95.

This book covers in detail Spanish machine pistols and C96 copies made in Spain. Covers all Astra "Mauser" pistol series and the complete line of Beistegui C96 type pistols. Spanish text.

Law Enforcement Memorabilia Price and Identification Guide, by Monty McCord, DBI Books a division of Krause Publications, Inc. Iola, WI, 1999. 208 pp., illustrated. Paper covers. $19.95.

An invaluable reference to the growing wave of law enforcement collectors. Hundreds of items are covered from miniature vehicles to clothes, patches, and restraints.

Legendary Sporting Guns, by Eric Joly, Abbeville Press, New York, N.Y., 1999. 228 pp., illustrated. $65.00.

A survey of hunting through the ages and relates how many different types of firearms were created and refined for use afield.

Legends and Reality of the AK, by Val Shilin and Charlie Cutshaw, Paladen Press, Boulder, CO, 2000. 192 pp., illustrated. Paper covers. $35.00.

A behind-the-scenes look at history, design and impact of the Kalashnikov family of weapons.

LeMat, the Man, the Gun, by Valmore J. Forgett and Alain F. and Marie-Antoinette Serpette, Navy Arms Co., Ridgefield, NJ, 1996. 218 pp., illus. $49.95.

The first definitive study of the Confederate revolvers invention, development and delivery by Francois Alexandre LeMat.

Les Pistolets Automatiques Francaise 1890-1990, by Jean Huon, Combined Books, Inc., Conshohocken, PA, 1997. 160 pp., illus. French text. $34.95

French automatic pistols from the earliest experiments through the World Wars and Indo-China to modern security forces.

Levine's Guide to Knives And Their Values, 4th Edition, by Bernard Levine, DBI Books, a division of Krause Publications, Iola, WI, 1997. 512 pp., illus. Paper covers. $27.95

All the basic tools for identifying, valuing and collecting folding and fixed blade knives.

The Light 6-Pounder Battalion Gun of 1776, by Adrian Caruana, Museum Restoration Service, Bloomfield, Ontario, Canada, 2001. 76 pp., illus. Paper covers. $8.95

The London Gun Trade, 1850-1920, by Joyce E. Gooding, Museum Restoration Service, Bloomfield, Ontario, Canada, 2001. 48 pp., illus. Paper covers. $8.95

Names, dates and locations of London gunmakers working between 1850 and 1920 are listed. Compiled from the original Kelly's Post Office Directories of the City of London.

The London Gunmakers and the English Duelling Pistol, 1770-1830, by Keith R. Dill, Museum Restoration Service, Bloomfield, Ontario, Canada, 1997. 36 pp., illus. Paper covers. $8.95

Ten gunmakers made London one of the major gunmaking centers of the world. This book examines how the design and construction of their pistols contributed to that reputation and how these characteristics may be used to date flintlock arms.

Longrifles of North Carolina, by John Bivens, George Shumway Publisher, York, PA, 1988. 256 pp., illus. $50.00.

Covers art and evolution of the rifle, immigration and trade movements. Committee of Safety gunsmiths, characteristics of the North Carolina rifle.

Longrifles of Pennsylvania, Volume 1, Jefferson, Clarion & Elk Counties, by Russel H. Harringer, George Shumway Publisher, York, PA, 1984. 200 pp., illus. $50.00.

First in series that will treat in great detail the longrifles and gunsmiths of Pennsylvania.

The Luger Handbook, by Aarron Davis, Krause Publications, Iola, WI, 1997. 112 pp., illus. Paper covers. $9.95.

Quick reference to classify Luger models and variations with complete details including proofmarks.

Lugers at Random, by Charles Kenyon, Jr., Handgun Press, Glenview, IL, 1990. 420 pp., illus. $59.95.

A new printing of this classic, comprehensive reference for all Luger collectors.

The Luger Story, by John Walter, Stackpole Books, Mechanicsburg, PA, 2001. 256 pp., illus. Paper Covers $29.95.

The standard history of the world's most famous handgun.

M1 Carbine, by Larry Ruth, Gun room Press, Highland Park, NJ, 1987. 291 pp., illus. Paper $19.95.
The origin, development, manufacture and use of this famous carbine of World War II.

The M1 Carbine: Owner's Guide, by Scott A. Duff, Scott A. Duff, Export, PA, 1997. 126 pp., illus. Paper covers. $19.95.
This book answers the questions M1 owners most often ask concerning maintenance activities not encounted by military users.

The M1 Garand: Owner's Guide, by Scott A. Duff, Scott A. Duff, Export, PA, 1998. 132 pp., illus. Paper covers. $19.95.
This book answers the questions M1 owners most often ask concerning maintenance activities not encounted by military users.

The M1 Garand Serial Numbers and Data Sheets, by Scott A. Duff, Export, PA, 1995. 101 pp., illus. Paper covers. $11.95.
Provides the reader with serial numbers related to dates of manufacture and a large sampling of data sheets to aid in identification or restoration.

The M1 Garand 1936 to 1957, by Joe Poyer and Craig Riesch, North Cape Publications, Tustin, CA, 1996. 216 pp., illus. Paper covers. $19.95.
Describes the entire range of M1 Garand production in text and quick-scan charts.

The M1 Garand: Post World War, by Scott A. Duff, Scott A. Duff, Export, PA, 1990. 139 pp., illus. Soft covers. $19.95.
A detailed account of the activities at Springfield Armory through this period. International Harvester, H&R, Korean War production and quantities delivered. Serial numbers.

The M1 Garand: World War 2, by Scott A. Duff, Scott A. Duff, Export, PA, 1993. 210 pp., illus. Paper covers. $39.95.
The most comprehensive study available to the collector and historian on the M1 Garand of World War II.

Maine Made Guns and Their Makers, by Dwight B. Demeritt Jr., Maine State Museum, Augusta, ME, 1998. 209 pp., illustrated. $55.00.
An authoritative, biographical study of Maine gunsmiths.

Marlin Firearms: A History of the Guns and the Company That Made Them, by Lt. Col. William S. Brophy, USAR, Ret., Stackpole Books, Harrisburg, PA, 1989. 672 pp., illus. $75.00.
The definitive book on the Marlin Firearms Co. and their products.

Martini-Henry .450 Rifles & Carbines, by Dennis Lewis, Excalibur Publications, Latham, NY, 1996. 72 pp., illus. Paper covers. $11.95.
The stories of the rifles and carbines that were the mainstay of the British soldier through the Victorian wars.

Mauser Bolt Rifles, by Ludwig Olson, F. Brownell & Son, Inc., Montezuma, IA, 1999. 364 pp., illus. $59.95.
The most complete, detailed, authoritative and comprehensive work ever done on Mauser bolt rifles. Completely revised deluxe 3rd edition.

Mauser Military Rifles of the World, 2nd Edition, by Robert Ball, Krause Publications, Iola, WI, 2000. 304 pp., illustrated with 1,000 b&w photos and a 48 page color section. $44.95.
This 2nd edition brings more than 100 new photos of these historic rifles and the wars in which they were carried.

Mauser Smallbores Sporting, Target and Training Rifles, by Jon Speed, Collector Grade Publications, Cobourg, Ontario, Canada 1998. 349 pp., illustrated. $67.50.
A history of all the smallbore sporting, target and training rifles produced by the legendary Mauser-Werke of Obendorf Am Neckar.

Military Holsters of World War 2, by Eugene J. Bender, Rowe Publications, Rochester, NY, 1998. 200 pp., illustrated. $45.00.
A revised edition with a new price guide of the most definitive book on this subject.

Military Pistols of Japan, by Fred L. Honeycutt, Jr., Julin Books, Palm Beach Gardens, FL, 1997. 168 pp., illus. $42.00.
Covers every aspect of military pistol production in Japan through WWII.

The Military Remington Rolling Block Rifle, by George Layman, Pioneer Press, TN, 1998. 146 pp., illus. Paper covers. $24.95.
A standard reference for those with an interest in the Remington rolling block family of firearms.

Military Rifles of Japan, 5th Edition, by F.L. Honeycutt, Julin Books, Lake Park, FL, 1999. 208 pp., illus. $42.00.
A new revised and updated edition. Includes the early Murata-period markings, etc.

Military Small Arms Data Book, by Ian V. Hogg, Stackpole Books, Mechanicsburg, PA, 1999. $44.95. 336 pp., illustrated.
Data on more than 1,500 weapons. Covers a vast range of weapons from pistols to anti-tank rifles. Essential data, 1870-2000, in one volume.

Modern Beretta Firearms, by Gene Gangarosa, Jr., Stoeger Publishing Co., So. Hackensack, NJ, 1994. 288 pp., illus. Paper covers. $16.95.
Traces all models of modern Beretta pistols, rifles, machine guns and combat shotguns.

Modern Gun Values, The Gun Digest Book of, 10th Edition, by the Editors of Gun Digest, DBI Books, a division of Krause Publications, Iola, WI., 1996. 560 pp. illus. Paper covers. $21.95.
Greatly updated and expanded edition describing and valuing over 7,000 firearms manufactured from 1900 to 1996. The standard for valuing modern firearms.

Modern Gun Identification & Value Guide, 13th Edition, by Russell and Steve Quertermous, Collector Books, Paducah, KY, 1998. 504 pp., illus. Paper covers. $14.95.
Features current values for over 2,500 models of rifles, shotguns and handguns, with over 1,800 illustrations.

More Single Shot Rifles, by James C. Grant, The Gun Room Press, Highland Park, NJ, 1976. 324 pp., illus. $35.00.
Details the guns made by Frank Wesson, Milt Farrow, Holden, Borchardt, Stevens, Remington, Winchester, Ballard and Peabody-Martini.

Mortimer, the Gunmakers, 1753-1923, by H. Lee Munson, Andrew Mowbray Inc., Lincoln, RI, 1992. 320 pp., illus. $65.00.
Seen through a single, dominant, English gunmaking dynasty this fascinating study provides a window into the classical era of firearms artistry.

The Mosin-Nagant Rifle, by Terence W. Lapin, North Cape Publications, Tustin, CA, 1998. 30 pp., illustrated. Paper covers. $19.95.
The first ever complete book on the Mosin-Nagant rifle written in English. Covers every variation.

The Navy Luger, by Joachim Gortz and John Walter, Handgun Press, Glenview, IL, 1988. 128 pp., illus. $24.95.
The 9mm Pistole 1904 and the Imperial German Navy. A concise illustrated history.

The New World of Russian Small Arms and Ammunition, by Charlie Cutshaw, Paladin Press, Boulder, CO, 1998. 160 pp., illustrated. $42.95.
Detailed descriptions, specifications and first-class illustrations of the AN-94, PSS silent pistol, Bizon SMG, Saifa-12 tactical shotgun, the GP-25 grenade launcher and more cutting edge Russian weapons.

The Number 5 Jungle Carbine, by Alan M. Petrillo, Excalibur Publications, Latham, NY, 1994. 32 pp., illus. Paper covers. $7.95.
A comprehensive treatment of the rifle that collectors have come to call the "Jungle Carbine"—the Lee-Enfield Number 5, Mark 1.

The '03 Era: When Smokeless Revolutionized U.S. Riflery, by Clark S. Campbell, Collector Grade Publications, Inc., Ontario, Canada, 1994. 334 pp., illus. $44.50.
A much-expanded version of Campbell's *The '03 Springfields*, representing forty years of in-depth research into "all things '03."

Observations on Colt's Second Contract, November 2, 1847, by G. Maxwell Longfield and David T. Basnett, Museum Restoration Service, Bloomfield, Ontario, Canada, 1997. 36 pp., illus. Paper covers. $6.95.
This study traces the history and the construction of the Second Model Colt Dragoon supplied in 1848 to the U.S. Cavalry.

Official Guide to Gunmarks, 3rd Edition, by Robert H. Balderson, House of Collectibles, New York, NY, 1996. 367 pp., illus. Paper covers. $15.00.
Identifies manufacturers' marks that appear on American and foreign pistols, rifles and shotguns.

Official Price Guide to Gun Collecting, by R.L. Wilson, Ballantine/House of Collectibles, New York, NY, 1998. 450 pp., illus. Paper covers. $21.50.
Covers more than 30,000 prices from Colt revolvers to Winchester rifles and shotguns to German Lugers and British sporting rifles and game guns.

Official Price Guide to Military Collectibles, 6th Edition, by Richard J. Austin, Random House, Inc., New York, NY, 1998. 200 pp., illus. Paper cover. $20.00.
Covers weapons and other collectibles from wars of the distant and recent past. More than 4,000 prices are listed. Illustrated with 400 black & white photos plus a full-color insert.

The Official Soviet SVD Manual, by Major James F. Gebhardt (Ret.) Paladin Press, Boulder, CO, 1999. 112 pp., illustrated. Paper covers. $15.00.
Operating instructions for the 7.62mm Dragunov, the first Russian rifle developed from scratch specifically for sniping.

Old Gunsights: A Collector's Guide, 1850 to 2000, by Nicholas Stroebel, Krause Publications, Iola, WI, 1998. 320 pp., illus. Paper covers. $29.95
An in-depth and comprehensive examination of old gunsights and the rifles on which they were used to get accurate feel for prices in this expanding market.

Old Rifle scopes, by Nicholas Stroebel, Krause Publications, Iola, WI, 2000. 400 pp., illustrated. Paper covers. $31.95.
This comprehensive collector's guide takes aim at more than 120 scope makers and 60 mount makers and features photos and current market values for 300 scopes and mounts manufactured from 1950-1985.

The P-08 Parabellum Luger Automatic Pistol, edited by J. David McFarland, Desert Publications, Cornville, AZ, 1982. 20 pp., illus. Paper covers. $11.95.
Covers every facet of the Luger, plus a listing of all known Luger models.

Packing Iron, by Richard C. Rattenbury, Zon International Publishing, Millwood, NY, 1993. 216 pp., illus. $45.00.
The best book yet produced on pistol holsters and rifle scabbards. Over 300 variations of holster and scabbards are illustrated in large, clear plates.

Parabellum: A Technical History of Swiss Lugers, by Vittorio Bobba, Priuli & Verlucca, Editori, Torino, Italy, 1996. Italian and English text. Illustrated. $100.00.

Patents for Inventions, Class 119 (Small Arms), 1855-1930. British Patent Office, Armory Publications, Oceanside, CA, 1993. 7 volume set. $250.00.
Contains 7980 abridged patent descriptions and their sectioned line drawings, plus a 37-page alphabetical index of the patentees.

Pattern Dates for British Ordnance Small Arms, 1718-1783, by DeWitt Bailey, Thomas Publications, Gettysburg, PA, 1997. 116 pp., illus. Paper covers. $20.00
The weapons discussed in this work are those carried by troops sent to North America between 1737 and 1783, or shipped to them as replacement arms while in America.

The Pitman Notes on U.S. Martial Small Arms and Ammunition, 1776-1933, Volume 2, Revolvers and Automatic Pistols, by Brig. Gen. John Pitman, Thomas Publications, Gettysburg, PA, 1990. 192 pp., illus. $29.95.
A most important primary source of information on United States military small arms and ammunition.

The Plains Rifle, by Charles Hanson, Gun Room Press, Highland Park, NJ, 1989. 169 pp., illus. $35.00.
All rifles that were made with the plainsman in mind, including pistols.

THE ARMS LIBRARY

Powder and Ball Small Arms, by Martin Pegler, Windrow & Green, London, 1998. 128 pp., illus. $39.95.

Part of the new "Live Firing Classic Weapons" series featuring full color photos of experienced shooters dressed in authentic costumes handling, loading and firing historic weapons.

The Powder Flask Book, by Ray Riling, R&R Books, Livonia, NY, 1993. 514 pp., illus. $69.95.

The complete book on flasks of the 19th century. Exactly scaled pictures of 1,600 flasks are illustrated.

Proud Promise: French Autoloading Rifles, 1898-1979, by Jean Huon, Collector Grade Publications, Inc., Cobourg, Ont., Canada, 1995. 216 pp., illus. $39.95.

The author has finally set the record straight about the importance of French contributions to modern arms design.

E. C. Prudhomme's Gun Engraving Review, by E. C. Prudhomme, R&R Books, Livonia, NY, 1994. 164 pp., illus. $60.00.

As a source for engravers and collectors, this book is an indispensable guide to styles and techniques of the world's foremost engravers.

Purdey Gun and Rifle Makers: The Definitive History, by Donald Dallas, Quiller Press, London, 2000. 245 pp., illus. Color throughout. $100.00

A limited edition of 3,000 copies. Signed and Numbered. With a PURDEY book plate.

Reloading Tools, Sights and Telescopes for Single Shot Rifles, by Gerald O. Kelver, Brighton, CO, 1982. 163 pp., illus. Paper covers. $13.95.

A listing of most of the famous makers of reloading tools, sights and telescopes with a brief description of the products they manufactured.

The Remington-Lee Rifle, by Eugene F. Myszkowski, Excalibur Publications, Latham, NY, 1995. 100 pp., illus. Paper covers. $22.50.

Features detailed descriptions, including serial number ranges, of each model from the first Lee Magazine Rifle produced for the U.S. Navy to the last Remington-Lee Small Bores shipped to the Cuban Rural Guard.

Revolvers of the British Services 1854-1954, by W.H.J. Chamberlain and A.W.F. Taylerson, Museum Restoration Service, Ottawa, Canada, 1989. 80 pp., illus. $27.50.

Covers the types issued among many of the United Kingdom's naval, land or air services.

Rhode Island Arms Makers & Gunsmiths, by William O. Archibald, Andrew Mowbray, Inc., Lincoln, RI, 1990. 108 pp., illus. $16.50.

A serious and informative study of an important area of American arms making.

Rifles of the World, by Oliver Achard, Chartwell Books, Inc., Edison, NJ, 141 pp., illus. $24.95.

A unique insight into the world of long guns, not just rifles, but also shotguns, carbines and all the usual multi-barreled guns that once were so popular with European hunters, especially in Germany and Austria.

The Rock Island '03, by C.S. Ferris, C.S. Ferris, Arvada, CO, 1993. 58 pp., illus. Paper covers. $12.50.

A monograph of interest to the collector or historian concentrating on the U.S. M1903 rifle made by the less publicized of our two producing facilities.

Round Ball to Rimfire, Vol. 1, by Dean Thomas, Thomas Publications, Gettysburg, PA, 1997. 144 pp., illus. $40.00.

The first of a two-volume set of the most complete history and guide for all small arms ammunition used in the Civil War. The information includes data from research and development to the arsenals that created it.

Ruger and his Guns, by R.L. Wilson, Simon & Schuster, New York, NY, 1996. 358 pp., illus. $65.00.

A history of the man, the company and their firearms.

Russell M. Catron and His Pistols, by Warren H. Buxton, Ucross Books, Los Alamos, NM, 1998. 224 pp., illustrated. Paper covers. $49.50.

An unknown American firearms inventor and manufacturer of the mid twentieth century. Military, commerical, ammunition.

The SAFN-49 and The FAL, by Joe Poyer and Dr. Richard Feirman, North Cape Publications, Tustin, CA, 1998. 160 pp., illus. Paper covers. $14.95.

The first complete overview of the SAFN-49 battle rifle, from its pre-World War 2 beginnings to its military service in countries as diverse as the Belgian Congo and Argentina. The FAL was "light" version of the SAFN-49 and it became the Free World's most adopted battle rifle.

Sam Colt's Own Record 1847, by John Parsons, Wolfe Publishing Co., Prescott, AZ, 1992. 167 pp., illus. $24.50.

Chronologically presented, the correspondence published here completes the account of the manufacture, in 1847, of the Walker Model Colt revolver.

J. P. Sauer & Sohn, Sauer "Dein Waffenkamerad" Volume 2, by Cate & Krause, Walsworth Publishing, Chattanooga, TN, 2000. 440 pp., illus. $79.00.

A historical study of Sauer automatic pistols. This new volume includes a great deal of new knowledge that has surfaced about the firm J.P. Sauer. You will find new photos, documentation, serial number ranges and historial facts which will expand the knowledge and interest in the oldest and best of the German firearms companies.

Scottish Firearms, by Claude Blair and Robert Woosnam-Savage, Museum Restoration Service, Bloomfield, Ont., Canada, 1995. 52 pp., illus. Paper covers. $8.95.

This revision of the first book devoted entirely to Scottish firearms is supplemented by a register of surviving Scottish long guns.

The Scottish Pistol, by Martin Kelvin. Fairleigh Dickinson University Press, Dist. By Associated University Presses, Cranbury, NJ, 1997. 256 pp., illus. $49.50.

The Scottish pistol, its history, manufacture and design.

Sharps Firearms, by Frank Seller, Frank M. Seller, Denver, CO, 1998. 358 pp., illus. $55.00.

Traces the development of Sharps firearms with full range of guns made including all martial variations.

Simeon North: First Official Pistol Maker of the United States, by S. North and R. North, The Gun Room Press, Highland Park, NJ, 1972. 207 pp., illus. $15.95.

Reprint of the rare first edition.

The SKS Carbine, by Steve Kehaya and Joe Poyer, North Cape Publications, Tustin, CA, 1997. 150 pp., illus. Paper covers. $16.95.

The first comprehensive examination of a major historical firearm used through the Vietnam conflict to the diamond fields of Angola.

The SKS Type 45 Carbines, by Duncan Long, Desert Publications, El Dorado, AZ, 1992. 110 pp., illus. Paper covers. $19.95

Covers the history and practical aspects of operating, maintaining and modifying this abundantly available rifle.

Smith & Wesson 1857-1945, by Robert J. Neal and Roy G. Jinks, R&R Books, Livonia, NY, 1996. 434 pp., illus. $50.00.

The bible for all existing and aspiring Smith & Wesson collectors.

Sniper Variations of the German K98k Rifle, by Richard D. Law, Collector Grade Publications, Ontario, Canada, 1997. 240 pp., illus. $47.50.

Volume 2 of "Backbone of the Wehrmacht" the author's in-depth study of the German K98k rifle. This volume concentrates on the telescopic-sighted rifle of choice for most German snipers during World War 2.

Southern Derringers of the Mississippi Valley, by Turner Kirkland, Pioneer Press, Tenn., 1971. 80 pp., illus., paper covers. $4.00.

A guide for the collector, and a much-needed study.

Soviet Russian Postwar Military Pistols and Cartridges, by Fred A. Datig, Handgun Press, Glenview, IL, 1988. 152 pp., illus. $29.95.

Thoroughly researched, this definitive sourcebook covers the development and adoption of the Makarov, Stechkin and the new PSM pistols. Also included in this source book is coverage on Russian clandestine weapons and pistol cartridges.

Soviet Russian Tokarev "TT" Pistols and Cartridges 1929-1953, by Fred Datig, Graphic Publishers, Santa Ana, CA, 1993. 168 pp., illus. $39.95.

Details of rare arms and their accessories are shown in hundreds of photos. It also contains a complete bibliography and index.

Soviet Small-Arms and Ammunition, by David Bolotin, Handgun Press, Glenview, IL, 1996. 264 pp., illus. $49.95.

An authoritative and complete book on Soviet small arms.

Sporting Collectibles, by Jim and Vivian Karsnitz, Schiffer Publishing Ltd., West Chester, PA, 1992. 160 pp., illus. Paper covers. $29.95.

The fascinating world of hunting related collectibles presented in an informative text.

The Springfield 1903 Rifles, by Lt. Col. William S. Brophy, USAR, Ret., Stackpole Books Inc., Harrisburg, PA, 1985. 608 pp., illus. $75.00.

The illustrated, documented story of the design, development, and production of all the models, appendages, and accessories.

Springfield Armory Shoulder Weapons 1795-1968, by Robert W.D. Ball, Antique Trader Books, Dubuque, IA, 1998. 264 pp., illus. $34.95.

This book documents the 255 basic models of rifles, including test and trial rifles, produced by the Springfield Armory. It features the entire history of rifles and carbines manufactured at the Armory, the development of each weapon with specific operating characteristics and procedures.

Springfield Model 1903 Service Rifle Production and Alteration, 1905-1910, by C.S. Ferris and John Beard, Arvada, CO, 1995. 66 pp., illus. Paper covers. $12.50.

A highly recommended work for any serious student of the Springfield Model 1903 rifle.

Springfield Shoulder Arms 1795-1865, by Claud E. Fuller, S. & S. Firearms, Glendale, NY, 1996. 76 pp., illus. Paper covers. $17.95.

Exact reprint of the scarce 1930 edition of one of the most definitive works on Springfield flintlock and percussion muskets ever published.

Standard Catalog of Firearms, 11th Edition, by Ned Schwing, Krause Publications, Iola, WI, 2001. 1328 Pages, illustrated. 6,000+ b&w photos plus a 16-page color section. Paper covers. $32.95.

This is the largest, most comprehensive and best-selling firearm book of all time! And this year's edition is a blockbuster for both shooters and firearm collectors. More than 12,000 firearms are listed and priced in up to six grades of condition. That's almost 80,000 prices! Gun enthusiasts will love the new full-color section of photos highlighting the finest firearms sold at auction this past year –including the new record for an American historical firearm: $684,000!

Standard Catalog of Winchester, 1st Edition, edited by David D. Kowalski, Krause Publications, Iola, WI, 2000. 704 pp., illustrated with 2,000 B&W photos and 75 color photos. Paper covers. $39.95.

This book identifies and values more than 5,000 collectibles, including firearms, cartridges shotshells, fishing tackle, sporting goods and tools manufactured by Winchester Repeating Arms Co.

Steel Canvas: The Art of American Arms, by R.L. Wilson, Random House, NY, 1995, 384 pp., illus. $65.00.

Presented here for the first time is the breathtaking panorama of America's extraordinary engravers and embellishers of arms, from the 1700s to modern times.

Stevens Pistols & Pocket Rifles, by K.L. Cope, Museum Restoration Service, Alexandria Bay, NY, 1992. 114 pp., illus. $24.50.

This is the story of the guns and the man who designed them and the company which he founded to make them.

A Study of Colt Conversions and Other Percussion Revolvers, by R. Bruce McDowell, Krause Publications, Iola, WI, 1997. 464 pp., illus. $39.95.

The ultimate reference detailing Colt revolvers that have been converted from percussion to cartridge.

THE ARMS LIBRARY

The Sumptuous Flaske, by Herbert G. Houze, Andrew Mowbray, Inc., Lincoln, RI, 1989. 158 pp., illus. Soft covers. $35.00.

Catalog of a recent show at the Buffalo Bill Historical Center bringing together some of the finest European and American powder flasks of the 16th to 19th centuries.

The Swedish Mauser Rifles, by Steve Kehaya and Joe Poyer, North Cape Publications, Tustin, CA, 1999. 267 pp., illustrated. Paper covers. $19.95.

Every known variation of the Swedish Mauser carbine and rifle is described including all match and target rifles and all sniper fersions. Includes serial number and production data.

Televisions Cowboys, Gunfighters & Cap Pistols, by Rudy A. D'Angelo, Antique Trader Books, Norfolk, VA, 1999. 287 pp., illustrated in color and black and white. Paper covers. $31.95.

Over 850 beautifully photographed color and black and white images of cap guns, actors, and the characters they portrayed in the "Golden Age of TV Westerns." With accurate descriptions and current values.

Thompson: The American Legend, by Tracie L. Hill, Collector Grade Publications, Ontario, Canada, 1996. 584 pp., illus. $85.00.

The story of the first American submachine gun. All models are featured and discussed.

Toys That Shoot and Other Neat Stuff, by James Dundas, Schiffer Books, Atglen, PA, 1999. 112 pp., illustrated. Paper covers. $24.95.

Shooting toys from the twentieth century, especially 1920's to 1960's, in over 420 color photographs of BB guns, cap shooters, marble shooters, squirt guns and more. Complete with a price guide.

The Trapdoor Springfield, by M.D. Waite and B.D. Ernst, The Gun Room Press, Highland Park, NJ, 1983. 250 pp., illus. $39.95.

The first comprehensive book on the famous standard military rifle of the 1873-92 period.

Treasures of the Moscow Kremlin: Arsenal of the Russian Tsars, A Royal Armories and the Moscow Kremlin exhibition. HM Tower of London 13, June 1998 to 11 September, 1998. BAS Printers, Over Wallop, Hampshire, England. xxii plus 192 pp. over 180 color illustrations. Text in English and Russian. $65.00.

For this exhibition catalog each of the 94 objects on display are photographed and described in detail to provide a most informative record of this important exhibition.

U.S. Breech-Loading Rifles and Carbines, Cal. 45, by Gen. John Pitman, Thomas Publications, Gettysburg, PA, 1992. 192 pp., illus. $29.95.

The third volume in the Pitman Notes on U.S. Martial Small Arms and Ammunition, 1776-1933. This book centers on the "Trapdoor Springfield" models.

U.S. Handguns of World War 2: The Secondary Pistols and Revolvers, by Charles W. Pate, Andrew Mowbray, Inc., Lincoln, RI, 1998. 515 pp., illus. $39.00.

This indispensable new book covers all of the American military handguns of World War 2 except for the M1911A1 Colt automatic.

United States Martial Flintlocks, by Robert M. Reilly, Mowbray Publishing Co., Lincoln, RI, 1997. 264 pp., illus. $40.00.

A comprehensive history of American flintlock longarms and handguns (mostly military) c. 1775 to c. 1840.

U.S. Martial Single Shot Pistols, by Daniel D. Hartzler and James B. Whisker, Old Bedford Village Pess, Bedford, PA, 1998. 128 pp., illus. $45.00.

A photographic chronicle of military and semi-martial pistols supplied to the U.S. Government and the several States.

U.S. Military Arms Dates of Manufacture from 1795, by George Madis, David Madis, Dallas, TX, 1989. 64 pp. Soft covers. $6.00.

Lists all U.S. military arms of collector interest alphabetically, covering about 250 models.

U.S. Military Small Arms 1816-1865, by Robert M. Reilly, The Gun Room Press, Highland Park, NJ, 1983. 270 pp., illus. $39.95.

Covers every known type of primary and secondary martial firearms used by Federal forces.

U.S. M1 Carbines: Wartime Production, by Craig Riesch, North Cape Publications, Tustin, CA, 1994. 72 pp., illus. Paper covers. $16.95.

Presents only verifiable and accurate information. Each part of the M1 Carbine is discussed fully in its own section; including markings and finishes.

U.S. Naval Handguns, 1808-1911, by Fredrick R. Winter, Andrew Mowbray Publishers, Lincoln, RI, 1990. 128 pp., illus. $26.00.

The story of U.S. Naval Handguns spans an entire century—included are sections on each of the important naval handguns within the period.

Walther: A German Legend, by Manfred Kersten, Safari Press, Inc., Huntington Beach, CA, 2000. 400 pp., illustrated. $85.00.

This comprehensive book covers, in rich detail, all aspects of the company and its guns, including an illustrious and rich history, the WW2 years, all the pistols (models 1 through 9), the P-38, P-88, the long guns, .22 rifles, centerfires, Wehrmacht guns, and even a gun that could shoot around a corner.

Walther Pistols: Models 1 Through P99, Factory Variations and Copies, by Dieter H. Marschall, Ucross Books, Los Alamos, NM. 2000. 140 pages, with 140 b & w illustrations, index. Paper Covers. $19.95.

This is the English translation, revised and updated, of the highly successful and widely acclaimed German language edition. This book provides the collector with a reference guide and overview of the entire line of the Walther military, police, and self-defense pistols from the very first to the very latest. Models 1-9, PP, PPK, MP, AP, HP, P.38, P1, P4, P38K, P5, P88, P99 and the Manurhin models. Variations, where issued, serial ranges, calibers, marks, proofs, logos, and design aspects in an astonishing quantity and variety are crammed into this very well researched and highly regarded work.

The Walther Handgun Story: A Collector's and Shooter's Guide, by Gene Gangarosa, Steiger Publications, 1999. 300., illustrated. Paper covers. $21.95.

Covers the entire history of the Walther empire. Illustrated with over 250 photos.

Walther P-38 Pistol, by Maj. George Nonte, Desert Publications, Cornville, AZ, 1982. 100 pp., illus. Paper covers. $11.95.

Complete volume on one of the most famous handguns to come out of WWII. All models covered.

Walther Models PP & PPK, 1929-1945 – Volume 1, by James L. Rankin, Coral Gables, FL, 1974. 142 pp., illus. $40.00.

Complete coverage on the subject as to finish, proofmarks and Nazi Party inscriptions.

Walther Volume II, Engraved, Presentation and Standard Models, by James L. Rankin, J.L. Rankin, Coral Gables, FL, 1977. 112 pp., illus. $40.00.

The new Walther book on embellished versions and standard models. Has 88 photographs, including many color plates.

Walther, Volume III, 1908-1980, by James L. Rankin, Coral Gables, FL, 1981. 226 pp., illus. $40.00.

Covers all models of Walther handguns from 1908 to date, includes holsters, grips and magazines.

Winchester: An American Legend, by R.L. Wilson, Random House, New York, NY, 1991. 403 pp., illus. $65.00.

The official history of Winchester firearms from 1849 to the present.

Winchester Bolt Action Military & Sporting Rifles 1877 to 1937, by Herbert G. Houze, Andrew Mowbray Publishing, Lincoln, RI, 1998. 295 pp., illus. $45.00.

Winchester was the first American arms maker to commercially manufacture a bolt action repeating rifle, and this book tells the exciting story of these Winchester bolt actions.

The Winchester Book, by George Madis, David Madis Gun Book Distributor, Dallas, TX, 1986. 650 pp., illus. $49.50.

A new, revised 25th anniversary edition of this classic book on Winchester firearms. Complete serial ranges have been added.

Winchester Dates of Manufacture 1849-1984, by George Madis, Art & Reference House, Brownsboro, TX, 1984. 59 pp. $9.95.

A most useful work, compiled from records of the Winchester factory.

Winchester Engraving, by R.L. Wilson, Beinfeld Books, Springs, CA, 1989. 500 pp., illus. $135.00.

A classic reference work of value to all arms collectors.

The Winchester Handbook, by George Madis, Art & Reference House, Lancaster, TX, 1982. 287 pp., illus. $24.95.

The complete line of Winchester guns, with dates of manufacture, serial numbers, etc.

The Winchester-Lee Rifle, by Eugene Myszkowski, Excalibur Publications, Tucson, AZ 2000. 96 pp., illustrated. Paper Covers. $22.95.

The development of the Lee Straight Pull, the cartridge and the approval for military use. Covers details of the inventor and memorabilia of Winchester-Lee related material.

Winchester Lever Action Repeating Firearms, Vol. 1, The Models of 1866, 1873 and 1876, by Arthur Pirkle, North Cape Publications, Tustin, CA, 1995. 112 pp., illus. Paper covers. $19.95.

Complete, part-by-part description, including dimensions, finishes, markings and variations throughout the production run of these fine, collectible guns.

Winchester Lever Action Repeating Rifles, Vol. 2, The Models of 1886 and 1892, by Arthur Pirkle, North Cape Publications, Tustin, CA, 1996. 150 pp., illus. Paper covers. $19.95.

Describes each model on a part-by-part basis by serial number range complete with finishes, markings and changes.

Winchester Lever Action Repeating Rifles, Volume 3, The Model of 1894, by Arthur Pirkle, North Cape Publications, Tustin, CA, 1998. 150 pp., illus. Paper covers. $19.95.

The first book ever to provide a detailed description of the Model 1894 rifle and carbine.

The Winchester Lever Legacy, by Clyde "Snooky" Williamson, Buffalo Press, Zachary, LA, 1988. 664 pp., illustrated. $75.00

A book on reloading for the different calibers of the Winchester lever action rifle.

The Winchester Model 94: The First 100 Years, by Robert C. Renneberg, Krause Publications, Iola, WI, 1991. 208 pp., illus. $34.95.

Covers the design and evolution from the early years up to the many different editions that exist today.

Winchester Rarities, by Webster, Krause Publications, Iola, WI, 2000. 208 pp., with over 800 color photos, illus. $49.95.

This book details the rarest of the rare; the one-of-a-kind items and the advertising pieces from years gone by. With nearly 800 full color photos and detailed pricing provided by experts in the field, this book gives collectors and enthusiasts everything they need.

Winchester Shotguns and Shotshells, by Ronald W. Stadt, Krause Publications, Iola, WI, 1995. 256 pp., illus. $34.95.

The definitive book on collectible Winchester shotguns and shotshells manufactured through 1961.

The Winchester Single-Shot- Volume 1; A History and Analysis, by John Campbell, Andrew Mowbray, Inc., Lincoln RI, 1995. 272 pp., illus. $55.00.

Covers every important aspect of this highly-collectible firearm.

The Winchester Single-Shot- Volume 2; Old Secrets and New Discoveries, by John Campbell, Andrew Mowbray, Inc., Lincoln RI, 2000. 280 pp., illus. $55.00.

An exciting follow-up to the classic first volume.

REFERENCE

Winchester Slide-Action Rifles, Volume 1: Model 1890 & 1906, by Ned Schwing, Krause Publications, Iola, WI, 1992. 352 pp., illus. $39.95.

First book length treatment of models 1890 & 1906 with over 50 charts and tables showing significant new information about caliber style and rarity.

Winchester Slide-Action Rifles, Volume 2: Model 61 & Model 62, by Ned Schwing, Krause Publications, Iola, WI, 1993. 256 pp., illus. $34.95.

A complete historic look into the Model 61 and the Model 62. These favorite slide-action guns receive a thorough presentation which takes you to the factory to explore receivers, barrels, markings, stocks, stampings and engraving in complete detail.

Winchester's North West Mounted Police Carbines and other Model 1876 Data, by Lewis E. Yearout, The author, Great Falls, MT, 1999. 224 pp., illustrated. Paper covers. $38.00

An impressive accumulation of the facts on the Model 1876, with particular empasis on those purchased for the North West Mounted Police.

Worldwide Webley and the Harrington and Richardson Connection, by Stephen Cuthbertson, Ballista Publishing and Distributing Ltd., Gabriola Island, Canada, 1999. 259 pp., illus. $50.00

A masterpiece of scholarship. Over 350 photographs plus 75 original documents, patent drawings, and advertisements accompany the text.

EDGED WEAPONS

101 Patented Knife Designs, by Will Hannah, Krause Publications, Iola, WI, 1998. 380 pp., illustrated. Paper covers. $49.95.

Spans 130 years of specs and designs. Indexed by patent number, name, and date with complete descriptions, detailed drawings. Actual reproductions of U.S. Patent Office's approved application.

The American Eagle Pommel Sword: The Early Years 1794-1830, by Andrew Mowbray, Manrat Arms Publications, Lincoln, RI, 1997. 244 pp., illus. $65.00.

The standard guide to the most popular style of American sword.

American Knives; The First History and Collector's Guide, by Harold L. Peterson, The Gun Room Press, Highland Park, NJ, 1980. 178 pp., illus. $24.95.

A reprint of this 1958 classic. Covers all types of American knives.

American Military Bayonets of the 20th Century, by Gary M. Cunningham, Scott A. Duff Publications, Export, PA, 1997. 116 pp., illus. Paper covers. $19.95.

A guide for collectors, including notes on makers, markings, finishes, variations, scabbards, and production data.

American Premium Guide to Knives and Razors, 5th edition, by Jim Sargent, Krause Publications, Iola, WI, 1999. 496 pp., illustrated. Paper covers. $24.95.

Updates current values for thousands of the most popular and collectible pocket knives and razors.

American Primitive Knives 1770-1870, by G.B. Minnes, Museum Restoration Service, Ottawa, Canada, 1983. 112 pp., illus. $24.95.

Origins of the knives, outstanding specimens, structural details, etc.

American Socket Bayonets and Scabbards, by Robert M. Reilly, 2nd printing, Andrew Mowbray, Inc., Lincoln, RI, 1998. 208 pp., illustrated. $45.00.

Full coverage of the socket bayonet in America, from Colonial times through the post-Civil War.

The American Sword, 1775-1945, by Harold L. Peterson, Ray Riling Arms Books, Co., Phila., PA, 2001. 286 pp. plus 60 pp. of illus. $49.95.

1977 reprint of a survey of swords worn by U.S. uniformed forces, plus the rare "American Silver Mounted Swords, (1700-1815)."

American Swords and Makers Marks; A Photographic Guide for Collectors, by Donald Furr, Paragon Agency, Orange, CA, 1999. 253 pp., illus. $64.95

An indepth guide for collectors and dealers of American swords. This new reference book contains over 525 photos of Silverhilts, Cavalry sabres, Eaglehead, Presentation swords, Regalia, Militia, Enlisted & Officers swords of both the U.S. & Confederacy. 8 page color section. Profusely illus & price guide.

American Swords and Sword Makers, by Richard H. Bezdek, Paladin Press, Boulder, CO, 1994. 648 pp., illus. $79.95.

The long-awaited definitive reference volume to American swords, sword makers and sword dealers from Colonial times to the present.

American Swords & Sword Makers Volume 2, by Richard H. Bezdek, Paladin Press, Boulder, CO, 1999. 376 pp., illus. $69.95.

More than 400 stunning photographs of rare, unusual and one-of-a-kind swords from the top collections in the country

American Swords from the Philip Medicus Collection, edited by Stuart C. Mowbray, with photographs and an introduction by Norm Flayderman, Andrew Mowbray Publishers, Lincoln, RI, 1998. 272 pp., with 604 swords illustrated. $55.00.

Covers all areas of American sword collecting.

The Ames Sword Company, 1829-1935, by John D. Hamilton, Andrew Mowbray Publisher, Lincoln, RI, 1995. 255 pp., illus. $45.00.

An exhaustively researched and comprehensive history of America's foremost sword manufacturer and arms supplier during the Civil War.

Antlers & Iron II, by Krause Publications, Iola, WI, 1999. 40 Pages, illustrated with a 100 photos. Paper covers. $12.00.

Lays out actual plans so you can build your mountain man folding knife using ordinary hand tools. Step-by-step instructions, with photos, for layout, design, antler slotting and springs.

The Art of Throwing Weapons, by James W. Madden, Paladin Press, Boulder, CO, 1993. 102 pp., illus. $14.00.

This comprehensive manual covers everything from the history and development of the five most common throwing weapons--spears, knives, tomahawks, shurikens and boomerangs--to their selection or manufacture, grip, distances, throwing motions and advanced combat methods.

Battle Blades: A Professional's Guide to Combat Fighting Knives, by Greg Walker; Foreword by Al Mar, Paladin Press, Boulder, CO, 1993. 168 pp., illus. $40.95.

The author evaluates daggers, Bowies, switchblades and utility blades according to their design, performance, reliability and cost.

The Bayonet in New France, 1665-1760, by Erik Goldstein, Museum Restoration Service, Bloomfield, Ontario, Canada, 1997. 36 pp., illus. Paper covers. $8.95.

Traces bayonets from the recently developed plug bayonet, through the regulation socket bayonets which saw service in North America.

Bayonets, Knives & Scabbards; United States Army Weapons Report 1917 Thru 1945, edited by Frank Trzaska, Knife Books, Deptford, NJ, 1999. 80 pp., illustrated. Paper covers. $15.95.

Follows the United States edged weapons from the close of World War 1 through the end of World War 2. Manufacturers involved, dates, numbers produced, problems encountered, and production data.

The Book of the Sword, by Richard F. Burton, Dover Publications, New York, NY, 1987. 199 pp., illus. Paper covers. $12.95.

Traces the swords origin from its birth as a charged and sharpened stick through diverse stages of development.

Borders Away, Volume 1: With Steel, by William Gilkerson, Andrew Mowbray, Inc., Lincoln, RI, 1991. 184 pp., illus. $48.00.

A comprehensive study of naval armament under fighting sail. This first voume covers axes, pikes and fighting blades in use between 1626-1826.

Borders Away, Volume 2: Firearms of the Age of Fighting Sail, by William Gilkerson, Andrew Mowbray, Inc., Lincoln, RI, 1999. 331 pp., illus. $65.00.

Completing a two volume set, this impressive work covers the pistols, muskets, combustibles, and small cannon once employed aboard American and European fightng ships. 200 photos, 16 color plates.

Bowies, Big Knives, and the Best of Battle Blades, by Bill Bagwell, Paladin Press, Boulder, CO. 2001. 184 pp., illus. Paper covers. $30.00

This book binds the timeless observations and invaluable advice of master bladesmith and blade combat expert Bill Bagwell under one cover for the first time. As the outspoken author of Soldier of Fortune's "Battle Blades" column from 1984 to 1988, Bagwell was considered both outrageous and revolutionary in his advocacy of carrying fighting knives as long as 10 inches and his firm belief that the Bowie was the most effective and efficient fighting knife ever developed. Here, you'llfind all of Bagwell's classic SOF columns, plus all-new material linking his early insights with his latest conclusions. Must reading for serious knife fans.

British & Commonwealth Bayonets, by Ian D. Skennerton and Robert Richardson, I.D.S.A. Books, Piqua, OH, 1986. 404 pp., 1300 illus. $40.00.

British and Commonwealth Military Knives, by Ron Flook, Airlife, Shrewsbury, 1999. 256 pp., illus. 49.95

First major reference on Knives issued to British & Commonwealth Forces from 1850 to the present. Over 500 Knives illustrated and described .

Civil War Knives, by Marc Newman, Paladin Press, Boulder, CO, 1999. 120 pp., illustrated. $44.95.

The author delves into the blade designs used at Gettysburg, Vicksburg, Antitam, Chancellorsville, and Bull Run. Photos of rare and common examples of cut-down swords, poignards, ornate clip-point knives, exquisite presentation knives and more.

Collecting the Edged Weapons of Imperial Germany, by Thomas M. Johnson and Thomas T. Wittmann, Johnson Reference Books, Fredericksburg, VA, 1989. 363 pp., illus. $39.50

An in-depth study of the many ornate military, civilian, and government daggers and swords of the Imperial era.

Collecting Indian Knives, 1st Edition, by Lar Hothem, Krause Publications, Iola, WI, 1992. 152 pp., illustrated. Paper covers. $14.95.

Maps the sharp-edged weapons and ceremonial knives used and crafted by Native Americans from every region. Historic photos and accurate values help you complete your quest for a definitive guide on identification.

Collecting Indian Knives, 2nd Edition, by Lar Hothem, Krause Publications, Iola, WI, 2000. 176 pp., illustrated. Paper covers. $19.95.

Expanded and updated with new photos and information, this 2nd edition will be a must have for anyone who collects or wants to learn about chipped Indian artifacts in the knife family. With an emphasis on prehistoric times, the book is loaded with photos, values and identification guidelines to help identify blades as to general time-period and, in many cases, help date sites where such artifacts are found. Includes information about different regional materials and basic styles, how knives were made and for what they were probably used.

Collector's Guide to Ames U.S. Contract Military Edged Weapons: 1832-1906, by Ron G. Hickox, Pioneer Press, Union City, IN, 1993. 70 pp., illus. Paper covers. $17.50.

While this book deals primarily with edged weapons made by the Ames Manufacturing Company, this guide refers to other manufactureres of United States swords.

A Collector's Guide to Swords, Daggers & Cutlasses, by Gerald Weland, Chartwell Press, London, 1999. 128 pp., illustrated in color. $24.95

An informative overview of edged weapons from medieval through 19th century. Explains the military and technological background and distinguishing features of the most sought-after pieces. Includes lists of leading museums and weapons collections plus a comprehensive bibliography and index.

Collector's Handbook of World War 2 German Daggers, by LtC. Thomas M. Johnson, Johnson Reference Books, Fredericksburg, VA, 2nd edition, 1991. 252 pp., illus. Paper covers. $25.00.

Concise pocket reference guide to Third Reich daggers and accoutrements in a convenient format. With value guide.

THE ARMS LIBRARY

Collins Machetes and Bowies 1845-1965, by Daniel E. Henry, Krause Publications, Iola, WI, 1996. 232 pp., illus. Paper covers. $19.95.

A comprehensive history of Collins machetes and bowies including more than 1200 blade instruments and accessories.

The Complete Bladesmith: Forging Your Way to Perfection, by Jim Hrisoulas, Paladin Press, Boulder, CO, 1987. 192 pp., illus. $42.95.

Novice as well as experienced bladesmith will benefit from this definitive guide to smithing world-class blades.

The Complete Book of Pocketknife Repair, by Ben Kelly, Jr., Krause Publications, Iola, WI, 1995. 130 pp., illus. Paper covers. $10.95.

Everything you need to know about repairing knives can be found in this step-by-step guide to knife repair.

Confederate Edged Weapons, by W.A. Albaugh, R&R Books, Lavonia, NY, 1994. 198 pp., illus. $40.00.

The master reference to edged weapons of the Confederate forces. Features precise line drawings and an extensive text.

The Connoisseur's Book of Japanese Swords, by Nagayama, Kodauska International, Tokyo, Japan, 1997. 348pp., illustrated. $69.95

Translated by Kenji Mishina. A comprehensive guide to the appreciation and appraisal of the blades of Japanese swords. The most informative guide to the blades of Japanese swords ever to appear in English.

Daggers and Bayonets a History, by Logan Thompson, Paladin Press, Boulder, CO, 1999. 128 pp., illustrated. $40.00.

This authoritative history of military daggers and bayonets examines all patterns of daggers in detail, from the utilitarian Saxon scamasax used at Hastings to lavishly decorated Cinquedas, Landsknecht and Holbein daggers of the late high Renaissance.

Daggers and Fighting Knives of the Western World: From the Stone Age till 1900, by Harold Peterson, Dover Publishing, Mineola, NY, 2001. 96 pages, plus 32 pages of matte stock. Over 100 illustrations. Softcover. $9.95

The only full-scale reference book devoted entirely to the subject of fighting knives: flint knives, daggers of all sorts, scramasaxes, hauswehren, dirks and more. 108 plates, bibliography and Index.

Eickhorn Edged Weapons Exports, Vol. 1: Latin America, by A.M. de Quesada, Jr. and Ron G. Hicock, Pioneer Press, Union City, TN, 1996. 120 pp., illus. Paper covers. $15.00.

This research studies the various Eickhorn edged weapons and accessories manufactured for various countries outside of Germany.

Encyclopedia of Native American Bows, Arrows & Quivers, Volume 1, by Steve Allely and Jim Hamm, The Lyons Press, N.Y., 1999. 137 pp., illustrated. $29.95.

Beautifully detailed full-page pen-and-ink drawings give dimensions, decorations, and construction details on more than a hundred historic bows, scores of arrows, and more than a dozen quivers from over thirty tribes.

Exploring the Dress Daggers of the German Army, by Thomas T. Wittmann, Johnson Reference Books, Fredericksburg, VA, 1995. 350 pp., illus. $59.95.

The first in-depth analysis of the dress daggers worn by the German Army.

Exploring the Dress Daggers of the German Luftwaffe, by Thomas T. Wittmann, Johnson Reference Books, Fredericksburg, VA, 1998. 350 pp., illus. $59.95.

Examines the dress daggers and swords of the German Luftwaffe. The designs covered include the long DLV patterns, the Glider Pilot designs of the NSFK and DLV, 1st and 2nd model Luftwaffe patterns, the Luftwaffe sword and the General OFficer Dengen. Many are pictured for the first time in color.

Exploring The Dress Daggers Of The German Navy, by Thomas T. Wittmann, Johnson Reference Books, Fredericksburg, VA, 2000. 560 pp., illus. $79.95.

Explores the dress daggers and swords of the Imperial, Weimar, and Third Reich eras, from 1844-1945. Provides detailed information, as well as many superb black and white and color photographs of individual edged weapons. Many are pictured for the first time in full color.

The First Commando Knives, by Prof. Kelly Yeaton and Col. Rex Applegate, Phillips Publications, Williamstown, NJ, 1996. 115 pp., illus. Paper covers. $12.95.

Here is the full story of the Shanghai origins of the world's best known dagger.

German Clamshells and Other Bayonets, by G. Walker and R.J. Weinard, Johnson Reference Books, Fredericksburg, VA, 1994. 157 pp., illus. $22.95.

Includes unusual bayonets, many of which are shown for the first time. Current market values are listed.

German Military Fighting Knives 1914-1945, by Gordon A. Hughes, Johnson Reference Books, Fredericksburg, VA, 1994. 64 pp., illus. Paper covers. $24.50.

Documents the different types of German military fighting knives used during WWI and WWII. Makers' proofmarks are shown as well as details of blade inscriptions, etc.

German Swords and Sword Makers: Edged Weapons Makers from the 14th to the 20th Centuries, by Richard H. Bezdek, Paladin Press, Boulder, CO, 2000. 248 pp., illustrated. $59.95.

This book contains the most informations ever published on German swords and edged weapons makers from the Middle Ages to the present.

A Guide to Military Dress Daggers, Volume 1, by Kurt Glemser, Johnson Reference Books, Fredericksburg, VA, 1991. 160 pp., illus. Softcover. $26.50.

Very informative guide to dress daggers of foreign countries, to include an excellent chapter on DDR daggers. There is also a section on reproduction Third Reich period daggers. Provides, for the first time, identification of many of the war-time foreign dress daggers. There is also a section on Damascus blades. Good photographic work. Mr. Glemser is certainly to be congratulated on this book on such a neglected area of militaria.

A Guide to Military Dress Daggers, Volume 2, by Kurt Glemser, Johnson Reference Books, Fredericksburg, VA, 1993. 160 pp., illus. $32.50.

As in the first volume, reproduction daggers are covered in depth (Third Reich, East German, Italian, Polish and Hungarian). American Navy dirks are featured for the first time. Bulgarian Youth daggers, Croatioan daggers and Imperial German Navy dagger scabbards all have chapters devoted to them. Continues research initiated in Volume I on such subjects as dress daggers, Solingen export daggers, East German daggers and Damascus Smith Max Dinger.

A Guide to Military Dress Daggers, Volume 3, by Kurt Glemser, Johnson Reference Books, Fredericksburg, VA, 1996. 260 pp., illus. $39.50.

Includes studies of Swedish daggers, Italian Cadet daggers, Rumanian daggers, Austrian daggers, Dress daggers of the Kingdom of Yugoslavia, Czechoslovakian daggers, Paul Dinger Damastschmied, Swiss Army daggers, Polish daggers (1952-1994), and Hungarian Presentation daggers.

A Guide to Military Dress Daggers, Volume 4, by Kurt Glemser, Johnson Reference Books, Fredericksburg, VA, 2001. 252 pp., illus. $49.50.

Several chapters dealing with presentation daggers to include a previously unknown series of East German daggers. Other chapters cover: Daggers in wear; Czech & Slovak daggers; Turkish daggers; swiss Army daggers; Solingen Export daggers; Miniature daggers; Youth knives.

The Halberd and other European Polearms 1300-1650, by George Snook, Museum Restoration Service, Bloomfield, Ontario, Canada, 1998. 40 pp., illus. Paper covers. $8.95

A comprehensive introduction to the history, use, and identification of the staff weapons of Europe.

The Hand Forged Knife, Krause Publications, Iola, WI. 136 pp., illus., $12.95.

Explains the techniques for forging, hardening and tempering knives and other stainless steel tools.

Historic American Swords, by Howard R. Crouch, SCS Publications, 2000. 174 pp., photos, illus. $39.95

Includes a history of each sword, sword types and terminology, the role of the U.S. Ordnance Department, makers- U.S. and Confederate, A nomenclature of the sword, details of design, production and use.

How to Make Folding Knives, by Ron Lake, Frank Centofante and Wayne Clay, Krause Publications, Iola, WI, 1995. 193 pp., illus. Paper covers. $13.95.

With step-by-step instructions, learn how to make your own folding knife from three top custom makers.

How to Make Knives, by Richard W. Barney and Robert W. Loveless, Krause Publications, Iola, WI, 1995. 182 pp., illus. Paper covers. $13.95.

Complete instructions from two premier knife makers on making high-quality, handmade knives.

How to Make Multi-Blade Folding Knives, by Eugene Shadley & Terry Davis, Krause Publications, Iola, WI, 1997. 192 pp., illus. Paper covers. $19.95.

This step-by-step instructional guide teaches knifemakers how to craft these complex folding knives.

How to Make a Tactical Folder, by Bob Tetzuola, Krause Publications, Iola, WI, 2000. 160 pp., illustrated. Paper covers. $16.95.

Step-by-step instructions and outstanding photography guide the knifemaker from start to finish.

The Modern Swordsman, by Fred Hutchinson, Paladin Press, Boulder, CO, 1999. 80 pp., illustrated. Paper covers. $22.00

Realistic training for serious self-defense.

The Wonder of Knifemaking, by Wayne Goddard, Krause Publications, Iola, WI, 2000. 160 pp., illustrated with 150 b&w photos and a 16 page color section. Paper covers. $19.95.

Tips for Knifemakers of all skill levels. Heat treating and steel selection.

KA-BAR: The Next Generation of the Ultimate Fighting Knife, by Greg Walker, Paladin Press, Boulder, CO, 2001. 88 pp., illus. Soft covers. $16.00.

The KA-BAR Fighting/Utility Knife is the most widely recognized and popular combat knife ever to be produced in the United States. Since its introduction on 23 November 1942, the KA-BAR has performed brilliantly on the battlefields of Europe, the South Pacific, Korea, Southeast Asia, Central America and the Middle East, earning its moniker as the "ultimate fighting knife." In this book, Greg Walker gives readers an inside view of the exacting design criteria, cutting-edge materials, extensivefactory tests and exhaustive real-life field tests that went into the historic redesign of the blade, handguard, handle, pommel, and sheath of the ultimate fighting knife of the future. The new knife excelled at these rigorous tests, earning the right tobe called a KA-BAR.

Knife and Tomahawk Throwing: The Art of the Experts, by Harry K. McEvoy, Charles E. Tuttle, Rutland, VT, 1989. 150 pp., illus. Soft covers. $8.95.

The first book to employ side-by-side the fascinating art and science of knives and tomahawks.

Knife Talk, The Art and Science of Knifemaking, by Ed. Fowler, Krause Publications, Iola, WI, 1998. 158 pp., illus. Paper covers. $14.95.

Valuable how-to advice on knife design and construction plus 20 years of memorable articles from the pages of "Blade" Magazine.

Knifemakers of Old San Francisco, by Bernard Levine, 2nd edition, Paladin Press, Boulder, CO, 1998. 150 pp., illus. $39.95.

The definitive history of the knives and knife-makers of 19th century San Francisco.

Knifemaking, The Gun Digest Book of, by Jack Lewis and Roger Combs, DBI Books, a division of Krause Publications, Iola, WI, 1989. 256 pp., illus. Paper covers. $16.95.

All the ins and outs from the world of knifemaking in a brand new book.

Knives, 5th Edition, The Gun Digest Book of, edited by Jack Lewis and Roger Combs, DBI Books, a division of Krause Publications, Iola, WI, 1997. 256 pp., illus. Paper covers. $19.95.

Covers practically every aspect of the knife world.

THE ARMS LIBRARY

Knives 2002, 22st Annual Edition, edited by Joe Kertzman, Krause Publications, Iola, WI, 2001. 320 pp., illustrated. Paper covers. $22.95.

More than 1,200 photos and listings of new knives plus articles from top writers in the field.

Les Baionnettes Reglementaires Francises de 1840 a 1918 'The Bayonets; Military Issue 1840-1918, by French Assoc.of Bayonet Collectors, 2000. 77 pp. illus. $24.95

Profusely illustrated. By far the most comprehenive guide to French military bayonets done for this period. Includes hundreds of illustrations. 77 large 8 1/4 x ll 1/2 inch pages. French Text. Color photos are magnificent!

Living on the Edge; Logos of the Loveless Legend, by Al Williams, Krause Publications, Iola, WI, 1995. 128 pp.,illustrated with full color. $19.95

Also included is an original 32-page section written entirely in the Japanese language for his Japanese customers and fans who have an insatiable appetite for everything Loveless.

The Master Bladesmith: Advanced Studies in Steel, by Jim Hrisoulas, Paladin Press, Boulder, CO, 1990. 296 pp., illus. $49.95.

The author reveals the forging secrets that for centuries have been protected by guilds.

Medieval Swordsmanship, Illustrated Methods and Techniques, by John Clements, Paladin Press, Boulder, CO, 1998. 344 pp., illustrated. $40.00.

The most comprehensive and historically accurate view ever written of the lost fighting arts of Medieval knights.

Military Knives: A Reference Book, by Frank Trzaska (editor), Knife Books, Deptford, NJ, 2001. 255 pp., illustrated. Softcover. $17.95

A collection of your favorite Military Knive articles fron the pages of Knife World Magazine. 67 articles ranging from the Indian Wars to the present day modern military knives.

Modern Combat Blades, by Duncan Long, Paladin Press, Boulder, CO, 1993. 128 pp., illus. $30.00.

Long discusses the pros and cons of bowies, bayonets, commando daggers, kukris, switchblades, butterfly knives, belt-buckle blades and many more.

On Damascus Steel, by Dr. Leo S. Figiel, Atlantis Arts Press, Atlantis, FL, 1991. 145 pp., illus. $65.00.

The historic, technical and artistic aspects of Oriental and mechanical Damascus. Persian and Indian sword blades, from 1600-1800, which have never been published, are illustrated.

The Pattern-Welded Blade: Artistry in Iron, by Jim Hrisoulas, Paladin Press, Boulder, CO, 1994. 120 pp., illus. $44.95.

Reveals the secrets of this craft—from the welding of the starting billet to the final assembly of the complete blade.

Randall Made Knives, by Robert L. Gaddis, Paladin Press, Boulder, CO, 2000. 292 pp., illus. $59.95.

Plots the designs of all 24 of Randall's unique knives. This step-by-step book, seven years in the making, is worth every penny and moment of your time.

The Razor Anthology, by Krause Publications, Iola, WI. 1998. 246 pp., illustrated. Paper covers. $14.95.

Razor Anthology is a cut above the rest. Razor aficionados will find this collection of articles about razors both informative and interesting.

Razor Edge, by John Juranitch, Krause Publications, Iola, WI. 1998. 132 pp., illustrated. Paper covers. $15.00.

Reveals step-by-step instructions for sharpening everything from arrowheads, to blades, to fish hooks.

Renaissance Swordsmanship, by John Clements, Paladin Press, Boulder, CO, 1997. 152 pp., illus. Paper covers. $25.00.

The illustrated use of rapiers and cut-and-thrust swords.

Rice's Trowel Bayonet, reprinted by Ray Riling Arms Books, Co., Phila., PA, 1968. 8 pp., illus. Paper covers. $3.00.

A facsimile reprint of a rare circular originally published by the U.S. government in 1875 for the information of U.S. troops.

The Scottish Dirk, by James D. Forman, Museum Restoration Service, Bloomfield, Ont., Canada, 1991. 60 pp., illus. Paper covers. $8.95.

More than 100 dirks are illustrated with a text that sets the dirk and Sgian Dubh in their socio-historic content following design changes through more than 300 years of evolution.

Scottish Swords from the Battlefield at Culloden, by Lord Archibald Campbell, The Mowbray Co., Providence, RI, 1973. 63 pp., illus. $15.00.

A modern reprint of an exceedingly rare 1894 privately printed edition.

Seitengewehr: History of the German Bayonet, 1919-1945, by George T. Wheeler, Johnson Reference Books, Fredericksburg, VA, 2000. 320 pp., illus. $44.95.

Provides complete information on Weimar and Third Reich bayonets, as well astheir accompanying knots and frogs. Illustrates re-issued German and foreign bayonets utilized by both the Reichswehr and the Wehrmacht, and details the progression ofnewly manufactured bayonets produced after Hitler's rise to power. Photos illustrate rarely seen bayonets worn by the Polizei, Reichsbahn, Postschutz, Hitler Jugend, and other civil and political organiztions. German modified bayonets from other countries are pictured and described. Book contains an up-to-date price guide including current valuations of various Imperial, Weimar, and Third Reich bayonets.

Silver Mounted Swords: The Lattimer Family Collection; Featuring Silver Hilts Through the Golden Age, by Daniel Hartzler, Rowe Publications, New York, 2000. 300 pages, with over 1000 illustrations and 1350 photo's. Oversize 9x12.

The Worlds Largest Silver Hilt Collection. $75.00

Small Arms Identification Series, No. 6-British Service Sword & Lance Patterns, by Ian Skennerton, I.D.S.A. Books, Piqua, OH, 1994. 48 pp. $9.50.

Small Arms Series, No. 2. The British Spike Bayonet, by Ian Skennerton, I.D.S.A. Books, Piqua, OH, 1982. 32 pp., 30 illus. $9.00.

The Socket in the British Army 1667-1783, by Erik Goldstein, Andrew Mowbray, Inc., Lincoln, RI, 2001. 136 pp., illus. $23.00.

The spectacle of English "redcoats" on the attack, relentlessly descending upon enemy lines with fixed bayonets, is one of the most chilling images from European history and the American Revolution. The bayonets covered in this book stood side by side with the famous "Brown Bess" as symbols of English military power throughout the world. Drawing upon new information from archaeological digs and archival records, the author explains how to identify each type of bayonet and shows which bayonets were used where and with which guns. No student of military history or weapons development can afford to do without this useful new book.

Socket Bayonets of the Great Powers, by Robert W. Shuey, Excalibur Publications, Tucson, AZ, 2000 96 pp., illus. Paper covers $22.95

With 175 illustrations the author brings together in one place, many of the standard socket arrnagements used by some of the " Great Powers". With an illustrated glossary of blade shape and socket design.

Spyderco Story: The New Shape of Sharp, by Kenneth T. Delavigne, Paladin Press, Boulder, CO, 1998. 312 pp., illus. $69.95.

Discover the history and inner workings of the company whose design innovations have redefined the shape of the modern folding knife and taken high-performance cutting to a new level.

Standard Knife Collectors Guide, 3rd Edition, by Roy Ritchie, Krause Publications, Iola, WI. 1999. 688 pp, 28 page color section., illustrated. Paper covers. $12.95.

Tap into the latest knife history developments with this updated guide accurately reflects current values for collector pocket-and fixed-blade knives.

Swords and Sword Makers of the War of 1812, by Richard Bezdek, Paladin Press, Boulder, CO, 1997. 104 pp., illus. $49.95.

The complete history of the men and companies that made swords during and before the war. Includes examples of cavalry and artillery sabers.

Swords from Public Collections in the Commonwealth of Pennsylvania, edited by Bruce S. Bazelon, Andrew Mowbray Inc., Lincoln, RI, 1987. 127 pp., illus. Paper covers. $12.00.

Contains new information regarding swordmakers of the Philadelphia area.

Swords And Sabers of the Armory at Springfield, by Burton A. Kellerstedt, Burton A. Kellerstedt, New Britain, CT, 1998. 121 pp, illus. Softcover. $29.95

The basic and most important reference for it's subject, and one that is unlikely to be surpassed for comprehensiveness and accuracy.

Swords and Blades of the American Revolution, by George C. Neumann, Rebel Publishing Co., Inc., Texarkana, TX, 1991. 288 pp., illus. $36.95.

The encyclopedia of bladed weapons—swords, bayonets, spontoons, halberds, pikes, knives, daggers, axes—used by both sides, on land and sea, in America's struggle for independence.

Swords of Imperial Japan, 1868-1945, by Jim Dawson, Published by the Author. 160 Pages, illustrated with 263 b&w photos. Paper covers. $29.95.

Details the military, civilian, diplomatic and civil, police and colonial swords and the post-Samurai era as well as the swords of Manchukuo, the Japanese independent territory.

Tactical Folding Knife; A Study of the Anatomy and Construction of the Liner-Locked Folder, by Terzuola, Krause Publications, Iola, WI. 2000. 160 Pages, 200 b&w photos, illustrated. Paper covers. $16.00

Step-by-step instructions and outstanding photography guide the knifemaker from start to finish. Knifemaker Bob Terzuola has been called the father of the tactical folding knife. This book details everything from the basic definition of a tactical folder to the final polishing as the knife is finished.

U.S. Military Knives, Bayonets and Machetes Price Guide, 4th ed. by Frank Trzaska (editor), Knife Books, Deptford, NJ, 2001. 80 pp., illustrated. Softcover. $7.95

This volume follows in the tradition of the previous three versions of using major works on the subject as a reference to keep the price low to you.

Wayne Goddard's $50 Knife Shop, by Wayne Goddard, Krause Publications, Iola, WI. 2000. 160 Pages, illus. Soft covers. $19.95

This new book expands on information from Goddard's popular column in Blade magazine to show knifemakers of all skill levels how to create helpful gadgets and supply their shop on a shoestring.

Wonder of Knifemaking, by Wayne Goddard, Krause Publications, Iola, WI. 2000. 160 Pages, illus. Soft covers. $19.95

Master bladesmith Wayne Goddard draws on his decades of experience to answer questions of knifemakers at all levels. As a columnist for Blade magazine, Goddard has been answering real questions from real knifemakers for the past eight years. Now, all the details are compiled in one place as a handy reference for every knifemaker, amateur or professional.

The Working Folding Knife, by Steven Dick, Stoeger Publishing Co., Wayne, NJ, 1998. 280 pp., illus. Paper covers. $21.95

From the classic American Barlow to exotic folders like the spanish Navaja this book has it all.

GENERAL

Action Shooting: Cowboy Style, by John Taffin, Krause Publications, Iola, WI, 1999. 320 pp., illustrated. $39.95.

Details on the guns and ammunition. Explanations of the rules used for many events. The essential cowboy wardrobe.

Advanced Muzzleloader's Guide, by Toby Bridges, Stoeger Publishing Co., So. Hackensack, NJ, 1985. 256 pp., illus. Paper covers. $14.95.

The complete guide to muzzle-loading rifles, pistols and shotguns—flintlock and percussion.

THE ARMS LIBRARY

Aids to Musketry for Officers & NCOs, by Capt. B.J. Friend, Excalibur Publications, Latham, NY, 1996. 40 pp., illus. Paper covers. $7.95.

A facsimile edition of a pre-WWI British manual filled with useful information for training the common soldier.

Air Gun Digest, 3rd Edition, by J.I. Galan, DBI Books, a division of Krause Publications, Iola, WI, 1995. 258 pp., illus. Paper covers. $19.95

Everything from A to Z on air gun history, trends and technology.

American and Imported Arms, Ammunition and Shooting Accessories, Catalog No. 18 of the Shooter's Bible, Stoeger, Inc., reprinted by Fayette Arsenal, Fayetteville, NC, 1988. 142 pp., illus. Paper covers. $10.95.

A facsimile reprint of the 1932 Stoeger's Shooter's Bible.

America's Great Gunmakers, by Wayne van Zwoll, Stoeger Publishing Co., So. Hackensack, NJ, 1992. 288 pp., illus. Paper covers. $16.95.

This book traces in great detail the evolution of guns and ammunition in America and the men who formed the companies that produced them.

Ammunition: Small Arms, Grenades and Projected Munitions, by Ian V. Hogg, Greenhill Books, London, England, 1998. 144 pp., illustrated. $22.95.

The best concise guide to modern ammunition. Wide-ranging and international coverage. Detailed specifications and illustrations.

Armed and Female, by Paxton Quigley, E.P. Dutton, New York, NY, 1989. 237 pp., illus. $16.95.

The first complete book on one of the hottest subjects in the media today, the arming of the American woman.

Arming the Glorious Cause: Weapons of the Second War for Independence, by James B. Whisker, Daniel D. Hartzler and Larry W. Yantz, R & R Books, Livonia, NY, 1998. 175 pp., illustrated. $45.00.

A photographic study of Confederate weapons.

Arms and Armour in Antiquity and the Middle Ages, by Charles Boutell, Stackpole Books, Mechanicsburg, PA, 1996. 352 pp., illus. $22.95.

Detailed descriptions of arms and armor, the development of tactics and the outcome of specific battles.

Arms & Armor in the Art Institute of Chicago, by Walter J. Karcheski, Jr., Bulfinch Press, Boston, MA, 1995. 128 pp., illus. $35.00.

Now, for the first time, the Art Institute of Chicago's arms and armor collection is presented in the visual delight of 103 color illustrations.

Arms for the Nation: Springfield Longarms, edited by David C. Clark, Scott A. Duff, Export, PA, 1994. 73 pp., illus. Paper covers. $9.95.

A brief history of the Springfield Armory and the arms made there.

Arsenal of Freedom, The Springfield Armory, 1890-1948: A Year-by-Year Account Drawn from Official Records, compiled and edited by Lt. Col. William S. Brophy, USAR Ret., Andrew Mowbray, Inc., Lincoln, RI, 1991. 400 pp., illus. Soft covers. $29.95.

A "must buy" for all students of American military weapons, equipment and accoutrements.

Assault Pistols, Rifles and Submachine Guns, by Duncan Long, Paladin Press, Boulder, CO, 1997, 8 1/2 x 11, soft cover, photos, illus. 152 pp. $21.95

This book offers up-to-date, practical information on how to operate and field-strip modern military, police and civilian combat weapons. Covers new developments and trends such as the use of fiber optics, liquid-recoil systems and lessening of barrel length are covered. Troubleshooting procedures, ballistic tables and a list of manufacturers and distributors are also included.

Assault Weapons, 5ᵗʰ Edition, The Gun Digest Book of, edited by Jack Lewis and David E. Steele, DBI Books, a division of Krause Publications, Iola, WI, 2000. 256 pp., illustrated. Paper covers. $21.95.

This is the latest word on true assault weaponry in use today by international military and law enforcement organizations.

The Belgian Rattlesnake: The Lewis Automatic Machine Gun, by William M. Easterly, Collector Grade Publications, Inc., Cobourg, Ont. Canada, 1998. 542 pp., illus. $79.95.

A social and technical biography of the Lewis automatic machine gun and its inventors.

The Big Guns: Civil War Siege, Seacoast, and Naval Cannon, by Edwin Olmstead, Wayne E. Stark and Spencer C. Tucker, Museum Restoration Service, Bloomfield, Ontario, Canada, 1997. 360 pp., illus. $80.00.

This book is designed to identify and record the heavy guns available to both sides during the Civil War.

Blackpowder Loading Manual, 3rd Edition, by Sam Fadala, DBI Books, a division of Krause Publications, Iola, WI, 1995. 368 pp., illus. Paper covers. $20.95.

Revised and expanded edition of this landmark blackpowder loading book. Covers hundreds of loads for most of the popular blackpowder rifles, handguns and shotguns.

Bolt Action Rifles, 3rd Edition, by Frank de Haas, DBI Books, a division of Krause Publications, Iola, WI, 1995. 528 pp., illus. Paper covers. $24.95.

A revised edition of the most definitive work on all major bolt-action rifle designs.

The Book of the Crossbow, by Sir Ralph Payne-Gallwey, Dover Publications, Mineola, NY, 1996. 416 pp., illus. Paper covers. $14.95.

Unabridged republication of the scarce 1907 London edition of the book on one of the most devastating hand weapons of the Middle Ages.

Bows and Arrows of the Native Americans, by Jim Hamm, Lyons & Burford Publishers, New York, NY, 1991. 156 pp., illus. $19.95.

A complete step-by-step guide to wooden bows, sinew-backed bows, composite bows, strings, arrows and quivers.

British Small Arms of World War 2, by Ian D. Skennerton, I.D.S.A. Books, Piqua, OH, 1988. 110 pp., 37 illus. $25.00.

"Carbine," the Story of David Marshall Williams, by Ross E. Beard, Jr. Phillips Publications, Williamstown, NJ, 1999. 225 pp., illus. $29.95.

The story of the firearms genius, David Marshall "Carbine" Williams. From prison to the pinnacles of fame, the tale of this North Carolinian is inspiring. The author details many of Williams' firearms inventions and developments.

Combat Handgunnery, 4th Edition, The Gun Digest Book of, by Chuck Taylor, DBI Books, a division of Krause Publications, Iola, WI, 1997. 256 pp., illus. Paper covers. $18.95.

This edition looks at real world combat handgunnery from three different perspectives—military, police and civilian.

The Complete Blackpowder Handbook, 3rd Edition, by Sam Fadala, DBI Books, a division of Krause Publications, Iola, WI, 1997. 400 pp., illus. Paper covers. $21.95.

Expanded and completely rewritten edition of the definitive book on the subject of blackpowder.

The Complete Guide to Game Care and Cookery, 3rd Edition, by Sam Fadala, DBI Books, a division of Krause Publications, Iola, WI, 1994. 320 pp., illus. Paper covers. $18.95.

Over 500 photos illustrating the care of wild game in the field and at home with a separate recipe section providing over 400 tested recipes.

The Complete .50-caliber Sniper Course, by Dean Michaelis, Paladin Press, Boulder, CO, 2000. 576 pp., illustrated. $60.00

The history from German Mauser T-Gewehr of World War 1 to the Soviet PTRD and beyond. Includes the author's Program of Instruction for Special Operations Hard-Target Interdiction Course.

Complete Guide to Guns & Shooting, by John Malloy, DBI Books, a division of Krause Publications, Iola, WI, 1995. 256 pp., illus. Paper covers. $18.95.

What every shooter and gun owner should know about firearms, ammunition, shooting techniques, safety, collecting and much more.

Cowboy Action Shooting, by Charly Gullett, Wolfe Publishing Co., Prescott, AZ, 1995. 400 pp., illus. Paper covers. $24.50.

The fast growing of the shooting sports is comprehensively covered in this text—the guns, loads, tactics and the fun and flavor of this Old West era competition.

Crossbows, edited by Roger Combs, DBI Books, a division of Krause Publications, Iola, WI, 1986. 192 pp., illus. Paper covers. $15.95.

Complete, up-to-date coverage of the hottest bow going—and the most controversial.

Custom Firearms Engraving, by Tom Turpin, Krause Publications, Iola, WI, 1999. 208 pp., illustrated. $49.95.

Provides a broad and comprehensive look at the world of firearms engraving. The exquisite styles of more than 75 master engravers are shown on beautiful examples of handguns, rifles, shotguns, and other firearms, as well as knives.

Dead On, by Tony Noblitt and Warren Gabrilska, Paladin Press, Boulder, CO, 1998. 176 pp., illustrated. Paper covers. $22.00

The long-range marksman's guide to extreme accuracy.

Death from Above: The German FG42 Paratrooper Rifle, by Thomas B. Dugelby and R. Blake Stevens, Collector Grade Publications, Toronto, Canada, 1990. 147 pp., illus. $39.95.

The first comprehensive study of all seven models of the FG42.

Early American Flintlocks, by Daniel D. Hartzler and James B. Whisker, Bedford Valley Press, Bedford, PA 2000. 192 pp., Illustrated.

Covers early Colonial Guns, New England Guns, Pennsylvania Guns and Souther Guns.

Encyclopedia of Modern Firearms, Vol. 1, compiled and publ. by Bob Brownell, Montezuma, IA, 1959. 1057 pp. plus index, illus. $70.00. Dist. By Bob Brownell, Montezuma, IA 50171.

Massive accumulation of basic information of nearly all modern arms pertaining to "parts and assembly." Replete with arms photographs, exploded drawings, manufacturers' lists of parts, etc.

Encyclopedia of Native American Bows, Arrows and Quivers, by Steve Allely and Jim Hamm, The Lyons Press, N.Y., 1999. 160 pp., illustrated. $29.95.

A landmark book for anyone interested in archery history, or Native Americans.

The Exercise of Armes, by Jacob de Gheyn, edited and with an introduction by Bas Kist, Dover Publications, Inc., Mineola, NY, 1999. 144 pp., illustrated. Paper covers. $12.95.

Republications of all 117 engravings from the 1607 classic military manual. A meticulously accurate portrait of uniforms and weapons of the 17ᵗʰ century Netherlands.

Exploded Long Gun Drawings, The Gun Digest Book of, edited by Harold A. Murtz, DBI Books, a division of Krause Publications, Iola, WI, 512 pp., illus. Paper covers. $20.95.

Containing almost 500 rifle and shotgun exploded drawings.

Fighting Iron; A Metals Handbook for Arms Collectors, by Art Gogan, Mowbray Publishers, Inc., Lincoln, RI, 1999. 176 pp., illustrated. $28.00.

A guide that is easy to use, explains things in simple English and covers all of the different historical periods that we are interested in.

The Fighting Submachine Gun, Machine Pistol, and Shotgun, a Hands-On Evaluation, by Timothy J. Mullin, Paladin Press, Boulder, CO, 1999. 224 pp., illustrated. Paper covers. $35.00.

An invaluable reference for military, police and civilian shooters who may someday need to know how a specific weapon actually performs when the targets are shooting back and the margin of errors is measured in lives lost.

Fireworks: A Gunsight Anthology, by Jeff Cooper, Paladin Press, Boulder, CO, 1998. 192 pp., illus. Paper cover. $27.00

A collection of wild, hilarious, shocking and always meaningful tales from the remarkable life of an American firearms legend.

Frank Pachmayr: The Story of America's Master Gunsmith and his Guns, by John Lachuk, Safari Press, Huntington Beach, CA, 1996. 254 pp., illus. First edition, limited, signed and slipcased. $85.00; Second printing trade edition. $50.00.

The colorful and historically significant biography of Frank A. Pachmayr, America's own gunsmith emeritus.

From a Stranger's Doorstep to the Kremlin Gate, by Mikhail Kalashnikov, Ironside International Publishers, Inc., Alexandria, VA, 1999. 460 pp., illustrated. $34.95.

A biography of the most influential rifle designer of the 20th century. His AK-47 assault rifle has become the most widely used (and copied) assault rifle of this century.

The Frontier Rifleman, by H.B. LaCrosse Jr., Pioneer Press, Union City, TN, 1989. 183 pp., illus. Soft covers. $17.50.

The Frontier rifleman's clothing and equipment during the era of the American Revolution, 1760-1800.

The Gatling Gun: 19th Century Machine Gun to 21st Century Vulcan, by Joseph Berk, Paladin Press, Boulder, CO, 1991. 136 pp., illus. $34.95.

Here is the fascinating on-going story of a truly timeless weapon, from its beginnings during the Civil War to its current role as a state-of-the-art modern combat system.

German Artillery of World War Two, by Ian V. Hogg, Stackpole Books, Mechanicsburg, PA, 1997. 304 pp., illus. $44.95.

Complete details of German artillery use in WWII.

Grand Old Lady of No Man's Land: The Vickers Machine Gun, by Dolf L. Goldsmith, Collector Grade Publications, Cobourg, Canada, 1994. 600 pp., illus. $79.95.

Goldsmith brings his years of experience as a U.S. Army armourer, machine gun collector and shooter to bear on the Vickers, in a book sure to become a classic in its field.

The Grenade Recognition Manual, Volume 1, U.S. Grenades & Accessories, by Darryl W. Lynn, Service Publications, Ottawa, Canada, 1998. 112 pp., illus. Paper covers. $29.95.

This new book examines the hand grenades of the United States beginning with the hand grenades of the U.S. Civil War and continues through to the present.

The Grenade Recognition Manual, Vol. 2, British and Commonwealth Grenades and Accessories, by Darryl W. Lynn, Printed by the Author, Ottawa, Canada, 2001. 201 pp., illustrated with over 200 photos and drawings. Paper covers. $29.95.

Covers British, Australian, and Canadian Grenades. It has the complete British Numbered series, most of the L series as well as the Australian and Canadian grenades in use. Also covers Launchers, fuzes and lighters, launching cartridges, fillings, and markings.

Gun Digest Treasury, 7th Edition, edited by Harold A. Murtz, DBI Books, a division of Krause Publications, Iola, WI, 1994. 320 pp., illus. Paper covers. $17.95.

A collection of some of the most interesting articles which have appeared in Gun Digest over its first 45 years.

Gun Digest 2002, 56th Edition, edited by Ken Ramage, DBI Books a division of Krause Publications, Iola, WI, 2001. 544 pp., illustrated. Paper covers. $24.95.

This all new 56th edition continues the editorial excellence, quality, content and comprehensive cataloguing that firearms enthusiasts have come to know and expect. The most read gun book in the world for the last half century.

Gun Engraving, by C. Austyn, Safari Press Publication, Huntington Beach, CA, 1998. 128 pp., plus 24 pages of color photos. $50.00.

A well-illustrated book on fine English and European gun engravers. Includes a fantastic pictorial section that lists types of engravings and prices.

Gun Notes, Volume 1, by Elmer Keith, Safari Press, Huntington Beach, CA, 1995. 219 pp., illustrated Limited Edition, Slipcased. $75.00

A collection of Elmer Keith's most interesting columns and feature stories that appeared in "Guns & Ammo" magazine from 1961 to the late 1970's.

Gun Notes, Volume 2, by Elmer Keith, Safari Press, Huntington Beach, CA, 1997. 292 pp., illus. Limited 1st edition, numbered and signed by Keith's son. Slipcased. $75.00. Trade edition. $35.00.

Covers articles from Keith's monthly column in "Guns & Ammo" magazine during the period from 1971 through Keith's passing in 1982.

Gun Talk, edited by Dave Moreton, Winchester Press, Piscataway, NJ, 1973. 256 pp., illus. $9.95.

A treasury of original writing by the top gun writers and editors in America. Practical advice about every aspect of the shooting sports.

The Gun That Made the Twenties Roar, by Wm. J. Helmer, rev. and enlarged by George C. Nonte, Jr., The Gun Room Press, Highland Park, NJ, 1977. Over 300 pp., illus. $24.95.

Historical account of John T. Thompson and his invention, the infamous "Tommy Gun."

Gun Trader's Guide, 23rd Edition, published by Stoeger Publishing Co., Wayne, NJ, 1999. 592 pp., illus. Paper covers. $23.95.

Complete specifications and current prices for used guns. Prices of over 5,000 handguns, rifles and shotguns both foreign and domestic.

Gun Writers of Yesteryear, compiled by James Foral, Wolfe Publishing Co., Prescott, AZ, 1993. 449 pp. $35.00.

Here, from the pre-American rifleman days of 1898-1920, are collected some 80 articles by 34 writers from eight magazines.

The Gunfighter, Man or Myth? by Joseph G. Rosa, Oklahoma Press, Norman, OK, 1969. 229 pp., illus. (including weapons). Paper covers. $14.95.

A well-documented work on gunfights and gunfighters of the West and elsewhere. Great treat for all gunfighter buffs.

Gunfitting: The Quest for Perfection, by Michael Yardley, Safari Press, Huntington Beach, CA, 1995. 128 pp., illus. $24.95.

The author, a very experienced shooting instructor, examines gun stocks and gunfitting in depth.

Guns Illustrated 2002, 3rd Edition, edited by Ken Ramage, DBI Books a division of Krause Publications, Iola, WI, 1999. 352 pp., illustrated. Paper covers. $22.95.

Highly informative, technical articles on a wide range of shooting topics by some of the top writers in the industry. A catalog section lists more than 3,000 firearms currently manufactured in or imported to the U.S.

Guns & Shooting: A Selected Bibliography, by Ray Riling, Ray Riling Arms Books Co., Phila., PA, 1982. 434 pp., illus. Limited, numbered edition. $75.

A limited edition of this superb bibliographical work, the only modern listing of books devoted to guns and shooting.

Guns, Bullets, and Gunfighters, by Jim Cirillo, Paladin Press, Boulder, CO, 1996. 119 pp., illus. Paper covers. $16.00.

Lessons and tales from a modern-day gunfighter.

Guns, Loads, and Hunting Tips, by Bob Hagel, Wolfe Publishing Co., Prescott, AZ, 1986. 509 pp., illus. $19.95.

A large hardcover book packed with shooting, hunting and handloading wisdom.

Handgun Digest, 3rd Edition, edited by Chris Christian, DBI Books, a division of Krause Publications, Iola, WI, 1995. 256 pp., illus. Paper covers. $18.95.

Full coverage of all aspects of handguns and handgunning from a highly readable and knowledgeable author.

Hidden in Plain Sight, "A Practical Guide to Concealed Handgun Carry" (Revised 2nd Edition), by Trey Bloodworth and Mike Raley, Paladin Press, Boulder, CO, 1997, 5 1/2 x 8 1/2, softcover, photos, 176 pp. $20.00

Concerned with how to comfortably, discreetly and safely exercise the privileges granted by a CCW permit? This invaluable guide offers the latest advice on what to look for when choosing a CCW, how to dress for comfortable, effective concealed carry, traditional and more unconventional carry modes, accessory holsters, customized clothing and accessories, accessibility data based on draw-time comparisons and new holsters on the market. Includes 40 new manufacturer listings.

HK Assault Rifle Systems, by Duncan Long, Paladin Press, Boulder, CO, 1995. 110 pp., illus. Paper covers. $27.95.

The little known history behind this fascinating family of weapons tracing its beginnings from the ashes of World War Two to the present time.

The Hunter's Table, by Terry Libby/Recipes of Chef Richard Blondin, Countrysport Press, Selma, AL, 1999. 230 pp. $30.00.

The Countrysport book of wild game guisine.

I Remember Skeeter, compiled by Sally Jim Skelton, Wolfe Publishing Co., Prescott, AZ, 1998. 401 pp., illus. Paper covers. $19.95.

A collection of some of the beloved storyteller's famous works interspersed with anecdotes and tales from the people who knew best.

In The Line of Fire, "A Working Cop's Guide to Pistol Craft", by Michael E. Conti, Paladin Press, Boulder, CO, 1997, soft cover, photos, illus., 184 pp. $30.00

As a working cop, you want to end your patrol in the same condition you began: alive and uninjured. Improve your odds by reading and mastering the information in this book on pistol selection, stopping power, combat reloading, stoppages, carrying devices, stances, grips and Conti's "secrets" to accurate shooting.

Joe Rychertinik Reflects on Guns, Hunting, and Days Gone By, by Joe Rychertinik, Precision Shooting, Inc., Manchester, CT, 1999. 281 pp., illustrated. Paper covers. $16.95.

Thirty articles by a master story-teller.

Kill or Get Killed, by Col. Rex Applegate, Paladin Press, Boulder, CO, 1996. 400 pp., illus. $39.95.

The best and longest-selling book on close combat in history.

Larrey: Surgeon to Napoleon's Imperial Guard, by Robert G. Richardson, Quiller Press, London, 2000. 269 pp., illus. B & W photos, maps and drawings. $23.95

Not a book for the squeamish, but one full of interest, splendidly researched, bringing both the character of the Napoleonic wars and Larrey himself vividly to life. Authenticity of detail is preserved throughout.

The Long-Range War: Sniping in Vietnam, by Peter R. Senich, Paladin Press, Boulder, CO, 1994. 280 pp., illus. $49.95.

The most complete report on Vietnam-era sniping ever documented.

Manual for H&R Reising Submachine Gun and Semi-Auto Rifle, edited by George P. Dillman, Desert Publications, El Dorado, AZ, 1994. 81 pp., illus. Paper covers. $12.95.

A reprint of the Harrington & Richardson 1943 factory manual and the rare military manual on the H&R submachine gun and semi-auto rifle.

The Manufacture of Gunflints, by Sydney B.J. Skertchly, facsimile reprint with new introduction by Seymour de Lotbiniere, Museum Restoration Service, Ontario, Canada, 1984. 90 pp., illus. $24.50.

Limited edition reprinting of the very scarce London edition of 1879.

Master Tips, by J. Winokur, Potshot Press, Pacific Palisades, CA, 1985. 96 pp., illus. Paper covers. $11.95.

Basics of practical shooting.

The Military and Police Sniper, by Mike R. Lau, Precision Shooting, Inc., Manchester, CT, 1998. 352 pp., illustrated. Paper covers. $44.95.

Advanced precision shooting for combat and law enforcement.

Military Rifle & Machine Gun Cartridges, by Jean Huon, Paladin Press, Boulder, CO, 1990. 392 pp., illus. $34.95.

Describes the primary types of military cartridges and their principal loadings, as well as their characteristics, origin and use.

Military Small Arms of the 20th Century, 7th Edition, by Ian V. Hogg and John Weeks, DBI Books, a division of Krause Publications, Iola, WI, 2000. 416 pp., illustrated. Paper covers. $24.95.

Cover small arms of 46 countries. Over 800 photographs and illustrations.

Modern Custom Guns, Walnut, Steel, and Uncommon Artistry, by Tom Turpin, Krause Publications, Iola, WI, 1997. 206 pp., illus. $49.95.

From exquisite engraving to breathtaking exotic woods, the mystique of today's custom guns is expertly detailed in word and awe-inspiring color photos of rifles, shotguns and handguns.

Modern Guns Identification & Values, 13th Edition, by Russell & Steve Quertermous, Collector Books, Paducah, KY, 1999. 516 pp., illus. Paper covers. $12.95.

A standard reference for over 20 years. Over 1,800 illustrations of over 2,500 models with their current values.

Modern Law Enforcement Weapons & Tactics, 2nd Edition, by Tom Ferguson, DBI Books, a division of Krause Publications, Iola, WI, 1991. 256 pp., illus. Paper covers. $18.95.

An in-depth look at the weapons and equipment used by law enforcement agencies of today.

Modern Machine Guns, by John Walter, Stackpole Books, Inc. Mechanicsburg, PA, 2000. 144 pp., with 146 illustrations. $22.95.

A compact and authoritative guide to post-war machine-guns. A gun-by-gun directory identifying individual variants and types including detailed evaluations and technical data.

Modern Sporting Guns, by Christopher Austyn, Safari Press, Huntington Beach, CA, 1994. 128 pp., illus. $40.00.

A discussion of the "best" English guns; round action, over-and-under, boxlocks, hammer guns, bolt action and double rifles as well as accessories.

The More Complete Cannoneer, by M.C. Switlik, Museum & Collectors Specialties Co., Monroe, MI, 1990. 199 pp., illus. $19.95.

Compiled agreeably to the regulations for the U.S. War Department, 1861, and containing current observations on the use of antique cannons.

The MP-40 Machine Gun, Desert Publications, El Dorado, AZ, 1995. 32 pp., illus. Paper covers. $11.95.

A reprint of the hard-to-find operating and maintenance manual for one of the most famous machine guns of World War II.

Naval Percussion Locks and Primers, by Lt. J. A. Dahlgren, Museum Restoration Service, Bloomfield, Canada, 1996. 140 pp., illus. $35.00

First published as an Ordnance Memoranda in 1853, this is the finest existing study of percussion locks and primers origin and development.

The Official Soviet AKM Manual, translated by Maj. James F. Gebhardt (Ret.), Paladin Press, Boulder, CO, 1999. 120 pp., illustrated. Paper covers. $18.00.

This official military manual, available in English for the first time, was originally published by the Soviet Ministry of Defence. Covers the history, function, maintenance, assembly and disassembly, etc. of the 7.62mm AKM assault rifle.

The One-Round War: U.S.M.C. Scout-Snipers in Vietnam, by Peter Senich, Paladin Press, Boulder, CO, 1996. 384 pp., illus. Paper covers $59.95.

Sniping in Vietnam focusing specifically on the Marine Corps program.

Pin Shooting: A Complete Guide, by Mitchell A. Ota, Wolfe Publishing Co., Prescott, AZ, 1992. 145 pp., illus. Paper covers. $14.95.

Traces the sport from its humble origins to today's thoroughly enjoyable social event, including the mammoth eight-day Second Chance Pin Shoot in Michigan.

Powder and Ball Small Arms, by Martin Pegler, Windrow & Greene Publishing, London, 1998. 128 pp., illustrated with 200 color photos. $39.95.

Part of the new "Live Firing Classic Weapons" series. Full-color photos of experienced shooters dressed in authentic costumes handling, loading and firing historic weapons.

Principles of Personal Defense, by Jeff Cooper, Paladin Press, Boulder, CO, 1999. 56 pp., illustrated. Paper covers. $14.00.

This revised edition of Jeff Cooper's classic on personal defense offers great new illustrations and a new preface while retaining the timeliness theory of individual defense behavior presented in the original book.

E.C. Prudhomme, Master Gun Engraver, A Retrospective Exhibition: 1946-1973, intro. by John T. Amber, The R. W. Norton Art Gallery, Shreveport, LA, 1973. 32 pp., illus. Paper covers. $9.95.

Examples of master gun engravings by Jack Prudhomme.

The Quotable Hunter, edited by Jay Cassell and Peter Fiduccia, The lyons Press, N.Y., 1999. 224 pp., illustrated. $20.00.

This collection of more than three hundred memorable quotes from hunters through the ages captures the essence of the sport, with all its joys idiosyncrasies, and challenges.

A Rifleman Went to War, by H. W. McBride, Lancer Militaria, Mt. Ida, AR, 1987. 398 pp., illus. $29.95.

The classic account of practical marksmanship on the battlefields of World War I.

Sharpshooting for Sport and War, by W.W. Greener, Wolfe Publishing Co., Prescott, AZ, 1995. 192 pp., illus. $30.00.

This classic reprint explores the *first* expanding bullet; service rifles; shooting positions; trajectories; recoil; external ballistics; and other valuable information.

The Shooter's Bible 2002, No. 93, edited by William S. Jarrett, Stoeger Publishing Co., Wayne, NJ, 2001. 576 pp., illustrated. Paper covers. $23.95.

Over 3,000 firearms currently offered by major American and foreign gunmakers. Represented are handguns, rifles, shotguns and black powder arms with complete specifications and retail prices.

Shooting To Live, by Capt. W. E. Fairbairn & Capt. E. A. Sykes, Paladin Press, Boulder, CO, 1997, 4 1/2 x 7, soft cover, illus., 112 pp. $14.00

Shooting to Live is the product of Fairbairn's and Sykes' practical experience with the handgun. Hundreds of incidents provided the basis for the first true book on life-or-death shootouts with the pistol. Shooting to Live teaches all concepts, considerations and applications of combat pistol craft.

Shooting Sixguns of the Old West, by Mike Venturino, MLV Enterprises, Livingston, MT, 1997. 221 pp., illus. Paper covers. $26.50.

A comprehensive look at the guns of the early West: Colts, Smith & Wesson and Remingtons, plus blackpowder and reloading specs.

Sniper Training, FM 23-10, Reprint of the U.S. Army field manual of August, 1994, Paladin Press, Boulder, CO, 1995. 352pp., illus. Paper covers. $30.00

The most up-to-date U.S. military sniping information and doctrine.

Sniping in France, by Major H. Hesketh-Prichard, Lancer Militaria, Mt. Ida, AR, 1993. 224 pp., illus. $24.95.

The author was a well-known British adventurer and big game hunter. He was called upon in the early days of "The Great War" to develop a program to offset an initial German advantage in sniping. How the British forces came to overcome this advantage.

Special Warfare: Special Weapons, by Kevin Dockery, Emperor's Press, Chicago, IL, 1997. 192 pp., illus. $29.95.

The arms and equipment of the UDT and SEALS from 1943 to the present.

Sporting Collectibles, by Dr. Stephen R. Irwin, Stoeger Publishing Co., Wayne, NJ, 1997. 256 pp., illus. Paper covers. $19.95.

A must book for serious collectors and admirers of sporting collectibles.

The Sporting Craftsmen: A Complete Guide to Contemporary Makers of Custom-Built Sporting Equipment, by Art Carter, Countrysport Press, Traverse City, MI, 1994. 240 pp., illus. $35.00.

Profiles leading makers of centerfire rifles; muzzleloading rifles; bamboo fly rods; fly reels; flies; waterfowl calls; decoys; handmade knives; and traditional longbows and recurves.

Sporting Rifle Takedown & Reassembly Guide, 2nd Edition, by J.B. Wood, DBI Books, a division of Krause Publications, Iola, WI, 1997. 480 pp., illus. $19.95.

An updated edition of the reference guide for anyone who wants to properly care for their sporting rifle. (Available September 1997)

2001 Standard Catalog of Firearms, the Collector's Price & Reference Guide, 11th Edition, by Ned Schwing, Krause Publications, Iola, WI, 2000. 1,248 pp., illus. Paper covers. $32.95.

Packed with more than 80,000 real world prices with more than 5,000 photos. Easy to use master index listing every firearm model.

The Street Smart Gun Book, by John Farnam, Police Bookshelf, Concord, NH, 1986. 45 pp., illus. Paper covers. $11.95.

Weapon selection, defensive shooting techniques, and gunfight-winning tactics from one of the world's leading authorities.

Stress Fire, Vol. 1: Stress Fighting for Police, by Massad Ayoob, Police Bookshelf, Concord, NH, 1984. 149 pp., illus. Paper covers. $9.95.

Gunfighting for police, advanced tactics and techniques.

Survival Guns, by Mel Tappan, Desert Publications, El Dorado, AZ, 1993. 456 pp., illus. Paper covers. $21.95.

Discusses in a frank and forthright manner which handguns, rifles and shotguns to buy for personal defense and securing food, and the ones to avoid.

The Tactical Advantage, by Gabriel Suarez, Paladin Press, Boulder, CO, 1998. 216 pp., illustrated. Paper covers. $22.00.

Learn combat tactics that have been tested in the world's toughest schools.

Tactical Marksman, by Dave M. Lauch, Paladin Press, Boulder, CO, 1996. 165 pp., illus. Paper covers. $35.00.

A complete training manual for police and practical shooters.

Thompson Guns 1921-1945, Anubis Press, Houston, TX, 1980. 215 pp., illus. Paper covers. $15.95.

Facsimile reprinting of five complete manuals on the Thompson submachine gun.

To Ride, Shoot Straight, and Speak the Truth, by Jeff Cooper, Paladin Press, Boulder, CO, 1997, 5 1/2 x 8 1/2, soft-cover, illus., 384 pp. $32.00

Combat mind-set, proper sighting, tactical residential architecture, nuclear war - these are some of the many subjects explored by Jeff Cooper in this illustrated anthology. The author discusses various arms, fighting skills and the importance of knowing how to defend oneself, and one's honor, in our rapidly changing world.

Trailriders Guide to Cowboy Action Shooting, by James W. Barnard, Pioneer Press, Union City, TN, 1998. 134 pp., plus 91 photos, drawings and charts. Paper covers. $24.95.

Covers the complete spectrum of this shooting discipline, from how to dress to authentic leather goods, which guns are legal, calibers, loads and ballistics.

The Ultimate Sniper, by Major John L. Plaster, Paladin Press, Boulder, CO, 1994. 464 pp., illus. Paper covers. $42.95.

An advanced training manual for military and police snipers.

Unrepentant Sinner, by Col. Charles Askins, Paladin Press, Boulder, CO, 2000. 322 pp., illustrated. $29.95.

The autobiography of Colonel Charles Askins.

U.S. Marine Corp Rifle and Pistol Marksmanship, 1935, reprinting of a government publication, Lancer Militaria, Mt. Ida, AR, 1991. 99 pp., illus. Paper covers. $11.95.

The old corps method of precision shooting.

U.S. Marine Corps Scout/Sniper Training Manual, Lancer Militaria, Mt. Ida, AR, 1989. Soft covers. $19.95.

Reprint of the original sniper training manual used by the Marksmanship Training Unit of the Marine Corps Development and Education Command in Quantico, Virginia.

U.S. Marine Corps Scout-Sniper, World War II and Korea, by Peter R. Senich, Paladin Press, Boulder, CO, 1994. 236 pp., illus. $44.95.

The most thorough and accurate account ever printed on the training, equipment and combat experiences of the U.S. Marine Corps Scout-Snipers.

REFERENCE

U.S. Marine Corps Sniping, Lancer Militaria, Mt. Ida, AR, 1989. Irregular pagination. Soft covers. $17.95.
> A reprint of the official Marine Corps FMFM1-3B.

Weapons of the Waffen-SS, by Bruce Quarrie, Sterling Publishing Co., Inc., 1991. 168 pp., illus. $24.95.
> An in-depth look at the weapons that made Hitler's Waffen-SS the fearsome fighting machine it was.

Weatherby: The Man, The Gun, The Legend, by Grits and Tom Gresham, Cane River Publishing Co., Natchitoches, LA, 1992. 290 pp., illus. $24.95.
> A fascinating look at the life of the man who changed the course of firearms development in America.

The Winchester Era, by David Madis, Art & Reference House, Brownsville, TX, 1984. 100 pp., illus. $19.95.
> Story of the Winchester company, management, employees, etc.

Winchester Repeating Arms Company by Herbert Houze, Krause Publications, Iola, WI. 512 pp., illus. $50.00.

With British Snipers to the Reich, by Capt. C. Shore, Lander Militaria, Mt. Ida, AR, 1988. 420 pp., illus. $29.95.
> One of the greatest books ever written on the art of combat sniping.

The World's Machine Pistols and Submachine Guns - Vol. 2a 1964 to 1980, by Nelson & Musgrave, Ironside International, Alexandria, VA, 2000. 673 pages, illustrated. $59.99.
> Containing data, history and photographs of over 200 weapons. With a special section covering shoulder stocked automatic pistols, 100 additional photos.

The World's Submachine Guns - Vol. 1 1918 to 1963, by Nelson & Musgrave, Ironside International, Alexandria, VA, 2001. 673 pages, illustrated. $59.99.
> A revised edition covering much new material that has come to light since the book was originally printed in 1963.

The World's Sniping Rifles, by Ian V. Hogg, Paladin Press, Boulder, CO, 1998. 144 pp., illustrated. $22.95.
> A detailed manual with descriptions and illustrations of more than 50 high-precision rifles from 14 countries and a complete analysis of sights and systems.

GUNSMITHING

Accurizing the Factory Rifle, by M.L. McPherson, Precision Shooting, Inc., Manchester, CT, 1999. 335 pp., illustrated. Paper covers. $44.95.
> A long-awaiting book, which bridges the gap between the rudimentary (mounting sling swivels, scope blocks and that general level of accomplishment) and the advanced (precision chambering, barrel fluting, and that general level of accomplishment) books that are currently available today.

Advanced Rebarreling of the Sporting Rifle, by Willis H. Fowler, Jr., Willis H. Fowler, Jr., Anchorage, AK, 1994. 127 pp., illus. Paper covers. $32.50.
> A manual outlining a superior method of fitting barrels and doing chamber work on the sporting rifle.

The Art of Engraving, by James B. Meek, F. Brownell & Son, Montezuma, IA, 1973. 196 pp., illus. $38.95.
> A complete, authoritative, imaginative and detailed study in training for gun engraving. The first book of its kind—and a great one.

Artistry in Arms, The R. W. Norton Gallery, Shreveport, LA, 1970. 42 pp., illus. Paper covers. $9.95.
> The art of gunsmithing and engraving.

Barrels & Actions, by Harold Hoffman, H&P Publishers, San Angelo, TX, 1990. 309 pp., illus. Spiral bound. $29.95.
> A manual on barrel making.

Black Powder Hobby Gunsmithing, by Sam Fadala and Dale Storey, DBI Books, a division of Krause Publications, Iola, WI., 1994. 256 pp., illus. Paper covers. $18.95.
> A how-to guide for gunsmithing blackpowder pistols, rifles and shotguns from two men at the top of their respective fields.

Checkering and Carving of Gun Stocks, by Monte Kennedy, Stackpole Books, Harrisburg, PA, 1962. 175 pp., illus. $39.95.
> Revised, enlarged cloth-bound edition of a much sought-after, dependable work.

The Complete Metal Finishing Book, by Harold Hoffman, H&P Publishers, San Angelo, TX, 1992. 364 pp., illus. Paper covers. $29.95.
> Instructions for the different metal finishing operations that the normal craftsman or shop will use. Primarily firearm related.

Exploded Handgun Drawings, The Gun Digest Book of, edited by Harold A. Murtz, DBI Books, a division of Krause Publications, Iola, WI. 1992. 512 pp., illus. Paper covers. $20.95.
> Exploded or isometric drawings for 494 of the most popular handguns.

Exploded Long Gun Drawings, The Gun Digest Book of, edited by Harold A. Murtz, DBI Books, a division of Krause Publications, Iola, WI. 512 pp., illus. Paper covers. $20.95.
> Containing almost 500 rifle and shotgun exploded drawings. An invaluable aid to both professionals and hobbyists.

The Finishing of Gun Stocks, by Harold Hoffman, H&P Publishers, San Angelo, TX, 1994. 98 pp., illus. Paper covers. $17.95.
> Covers different types of finishing methods and finishes.

Firearms Assembly/Disassembly, Part I: Automatic Pistols, 2nd Revised Edition, The Gun Digest Book of, by J.B. Wood, DBI Books, a division of Krause Publications, Iola, WI, 1999. 480 pp., illus. Paper covers. $24.95.
> Covers 58 popular autoloading pistols plus nearly 200 variants of those models integrated into the text and completely cross-referenced in the index.

Firearms Assembly/Disassembly Part II: Revolvers, Revised Edition, The Gun Digest Book of, by J.B. Wood, DBI Books, a division of Krause Publications, Iola, WI, 1990. 480 pp., illus. Paper covers. $19.95.
> Covers 49 popular revolvers plus 130 variants. The most comprehensive and professional presentation available to either hobbyist or gunsmith.

Firearms Assembly/Disassembly Part III: Rimfire Rifles, Revised Edition, The Gun Digest Book of, by J. B. Wood, DBI Books, a division of Krause Publications, Iola, WI., 1994. 480 pp., illus. Paper covers. $19.95.
> Greatly expanded edition covering 65 popular rimfire rifles plus over 100 variants all completely cross-referenced in the index.

Firearms Assembly/Disassembly Part IV: Centerfire Rifles, Revised Edition, The Gun Digest Book of, by J.B. Wood, DBI Books, a division of Krause Publications, Iola, WI, 1991. 480 pp., illus. Paper covers. $19.95.
> Covers 54 popular centerfire rifles plus 300 variants. The most comprehensive and professional presentation available to either hobbyist or gunsmith.

Firearms Assembly/Disassembly, Part V: Shotguns, Revised Edition, The Gun Digest Book of, by J.B. Wood, DBI Books, a division of Krause Publications, Iola, WI, 1992. 480 pp., illus. Paper covers. $19.95.
> Covers 46 popular shotguns plus over 250 variants with step-by-step instructions on how to dismantle and reassemble each. The most comprehensive and professional presentation available to either hobbyist or gunsmith.

Firearms Assembly/Disassembly Part VI: Law Enforcement Weapons, The Gun Digest Book of, by J.B. Wood, DBI Books, a division of Krause Publications, Iola, WI, 1981. 288 pp., illus. Paper covers. $16.95.
> Step-by-step instructions on how to completely dismantle and reassemble the most commonly used firearms found in law enforcement arsenals.

Firearms Assembly 3: The NRA Guide to Rifle and Shotguns, NRA Books, Wash., DC, 1980. 264 pp., illus. Paper covers. $13.95.
> Text and illustrations explaining the takedown of 125 rifles and shotguns, domestic and foreign.

Firearms Assembly 4: The NRA Guide to Pistols and Revolvers, NRA Books, Wash., DC, 1980. 253 pp., illus. Paper covers. $13.95.
> Text and illustrations explaining the takedown of 124 pistol and revolver models, domestic and foreign.

Firearms Bluing and Browning, By R.H. Angier, Stackpole Books, Harrisburg, PA. 151 pp., illus. $19.95.
> A world master gunsmith reveals his secrets of building, repairing and renewing a gun, quite literally, lock, stock and barrel. A useful, concise text on chemical coloring methods for the gunsmith and mechanic.

Firearms Disassembly—With Exploded Views, by John A. Karns & John E. Traister, Stoeger Publishing Co., S. Hackensack, NJ, 1995. 320 pp., illus. Paper covers. $19.95.
> Provides the do's and don'ts of firearms disassembly. Enables owners and gunsmiths to disassemble firearms in a professional manner.

Guns and Gunmaking Tools of Southern Appalachia, by John Rice Irwin, Schiffer Publishing Ltd., 1983. 118 pp., illus. Paper covers. $9.95.
> The story of the Kentucky rifle.

Gunsmithing: Pistols & Revolvers, by Patrick Sweeney, DBI Books, a division of Krause Publications, Iola, WI, 1998. 352 pp., illus. Paper covers. $24.95.
> Do-it-Yourself projects, diagnosis and repair for pistols and revolvers.

Gunsmithing: Rifles, by Patrick Sweeney, Krause Publications, Iola, WI, 1999. 352 pp., illustrated. Paper covers. $24.95.
> Tips for lever-action rifles. Building a custom Ruger 10/22. Building a better hunting rifle.

Gunsmithing Tips and Projects, a collection of the best articles from the *Handloader* and *Rifle* magazines, by various authors, Wolfe Publishing Co., Prescott, AZ, 1992. 443 pp., illus. Paper covers. $25.00.
> Includes such subjects as shop, stocks, actions, tuning, triggers, barrels, customizing, etc.

Gunsmith Kinks, by F.R. (Bob) Brownell, F. Brownell & Son, Montezuma, IA, 1st ed., 1969. 496 pp., well illus. $22.98.
> A widely useful accumulation of shop kinks, short cuts, techniques and pertinent comments by practicing gunsmiths from all over the world.

Gunsmith Kinks 2, by Bob Brownell, F. Brownell & Son, Publishers, Montezuma, IA, 1983. 496 pp., illus. $22.95.
> A collection of gunsmithing knowledge, shop kinks, new and old techniques, shortcuts and general know-how straight from those who do them best—the gunsmiths.

Gunsmith Kinks 3, edited by Frank Brownell, Brownells Inc., Montezuma, IA, 1993. 504 pp., illus. $24.95.
> Tricks, knacks and "kinks" by professional gunsmiths and gun tinkerers. Hundreds of valuable ideas are given in this volume.

Gunsmith Kinks 4, edited by Frank Brownell, Brownells Inc., Montezuma, IA, 2001. 564 pp., illus. $27.75
> 332 detailed illustrations. 560+ pages with 706 separate subject headings and over 5000 cross-indexed entries. An incredible gold mine of information.

Gunsmithing, by Roy F. Dunlap, Stackpole Books, Harrisburg, PA, 1990. 742 pp., illus. $34.95.
> A manual of firearm design, construction, alteration and remodeling. For amateur and professional gunsmiths and users of modern firearms.

Gunsmithing at Home: Lock, Stock and Barrel, by John Traister, Stoeger Publishing Co., Wayne, NJ, 1997. 320 pp., illus. Paper covers. $19.95.
> A complete step-by-step fully illustrated guide to the art of gunsmithing.

The Gunsmith's Manual, by J.P. Stelle and Wm. B. Harrison, The Gun Room Press, Highland Park, NJ, 1982. 376 pp., illus. $19.95.
> For the gunsmith in all branches of the trade.

REFERENCE

THE ARMS LIBRARY

Home Gunsmithing the Colt Single Action Revolvers, by Loren W. Smith, Ray Riling Arms Books, Co., Phila., PA, 2001. 119 pp., illus. $29.95.

Affords the Colt Single Action owner detailed, pertinent information on the operating and servicing of this famous and historic handgun.

How to Convert Military Rifles, Williams Gun Sight Co., Davision, MI, new and enlarged seventh edition, 1997. 76 pp., illus. Paper covers. $13.95.

This latest edition updated the changes that have occured over the past thirty years. Tips, instructions and illustratons on how to convert popular military rifles as the Enfield, Mauser 96 nad SKS just to name a few are presented.

Mauser M98 & M96, by R.A. Walsh, Wolfe Publishing Co., Prescott, AR, 1998. 123 pp., illustrated. Paper covers. $32.50.

How to build your own favorite custom Mauser rifle from two of the best bolt action rifle designs ever produced—the military Mauser Model 1898 and Model 1896 bolt rifles.

Mr. Single Shot's Gunsmithing-Idea-Book, by Frank de Haas, Mark de Haas, Orange City, IA, 1996. 168 pp., illus. Paper covers. $21.50.

Offers easy to follow, step-by-step instructions for a wide variety of gunsmithing procedures all reinforced by plenty of photos.

Pistolsmithing, by George C. Nonte, Jr., Stackpole Books, Harrisburg, PA, 1974. 560 pp., illus. $34.95.

A single source reference to handgun maintenance, repair, and modification at home, unequaled in value.

Practical Gunsmithing, by the editors of American Gunsmith, DBI Books, a division of Krause Publications, Iola, WI, 1996. 256 pp., illus. Paper covers. $19.95.

A book intended primarily for home gunsmithing, but one that will be extremely helpful to professionals as well.

Professional Stockmaking, by D. Wesbrook, Wolfe Publishing Co., Prescott AZ, 1995. 308 pp., illus. $54.00.

A step-by-step how-to with complete photographic support for every detail of the art of working wood into riflestocks.

Recreating the American Longrifle, by William Buchele, et al, George Shumway Publisher, York, Pa, 5th edition, 1999. 175 pp., illustrated. $40.00.

Includes full size plans for building a Kentucky rifle.

Riflesmithing, The Gun Digest Book of, by Jack Mitchell, DBI Books, a division of Krause Publications, Iola, WI, 1982. 256 pp., illus. Paper covers. $16.95.

The art and science of rifle gunsmithing. Covers tools, techniques, designs, finishing wood and metal, custom alterations.

Shotgun Gunsmithing, The Gun Digest Book of, by Ralph Walker, DBI Books, a division of Krause Publications, Iola, WI, 1983. 256 pp., illus. Paper covers. $16.95.

The principles and practices of repairing, individualizing and accurizing modern shotguns by one of the world's premier shotgun gunsmiths.

Sporting Rifle Take Down & Reassembly Guide, 2nd Edition, by J.B. Wood, Krause Publications, Iola, WI, 1997. 480 pp., illus. Paper covers. $19.95.

Hunters and shooting enthusiasts must have this reference featuring 52 of the most popular and widely used sporting centerfire and rimfire rifles.

The Story of Pope's Barrels, by Ray M. Smith, R&R Books, Livonia, NY, 1993. 203 pp., illus. $39.00.

A reissue of a 1960 book whose author knew Pope personally. It will be of special interest to Schuetzen rifle fans, since Pope's greatest days were at the height of the Schuetzen-era before WWI.

Survival Gunsmithing, by J.B. Wood, Desert Publications, Cornville, AZ, 1986. 92 pp., illus. Paper covers. $11.95.

A guide to repair and maintenance of the most popular rifles, shotguns and handguns.

The Tactical 1911, by Dave Lauck, Paladin Press, Boulder, CO, 1998. 137 pp., illus. Paper covers. $20.00.

Here is the only book you will ever need to teach you how to select, modify, employ and maintain your Colt.

HANDGUNS

Advanced Master Handgunning, by Charles Stephens, Paladin Press, Boulder, CO., 1994. 72 pp., illus. Paper covers. $14.00.

Secrets and surefire techniques for winning handgun competitions.

American Beauty: The Prewar Colt National Match Government Model Pistol, by Timothy Mullin, Collector Grade Publications, Canada, 1999. 72 pp., 69 illus. $34.95

69 illustrations, 20 in full color photos of factory engraved guns and other authenticated upgrades, including rare 'double-carved' ivory grips.

Axis Pistols: WORLD WAR TWO 50 YEARS COMMEMORATIVE ISSUE, by Jan C. Stills, Walsworth Publishing, 1989. 360 pages, illus. $59.95

The Ayoob Files: The Book, by Massad Ayoob, Police Bookshelf, Concord, NH, 1995. 223 pp., illus. Paper covers. $14.95.

The best of Massad Ayoob's acclaimed series in American Handgunner magazine.

Big Bore Sixguns, by John Taffin, Krause Publications, Iola, WI, 1997. 336 pp., illus. $39.95.

The author takes aim on the entire range of big bores from .357 Magnums to .500 Maximums, single actions and cap-and-ball sixguns to custom touches for big bores..

The Browning High Power Automatic Pistol (Expanded Edition), by Blake R. Stevens, Collector Grade Publications, Canada, 1996. 310 pages, with 313 illus. $49.95

An in-depth chronicle of seventy years of High Power history, from John M Browning's original 16-shot prototypes to the present. Profusely illustrated with rare original photos and drawings from the FN Archive to describe virtually every sporting and military version of the High Power. The numerous modifications made to the basic design over the years are, for the first time, accurately arranged in chronological order, thus permitting the dating of any High Power to within a few years of its production. Full details on the WWII Canadian-made Inglis Browning High Power pistol. The Expanded Edition contains 30 new pages on the interesting Argentine full-auto High Power, the latest FN 'MK3' and BDA9 pistols, plus FN's revolutionary P90 5.7x28mm Personal Defence Weapon, and more!

Browning Hi-Power Pistols, Desert Publications, Cornville, AZ, 1982. 20 pp., illus. Paper covers. $11.95.

Covers all facets of the various military and civilian models of the Browning Hi-Power pistol.

Canadian Military Handguns 1855-1985, by Clive M. Law, Museum Restoration Service, Bloomfield, Ont. Canada, 1994. 130pp., illus. $40.00.

A long-awaited and important history for arms historians and pistol collectors.

The Colt .45 Auto Pistol, compiled from U.S. War Dept. Technical Manuals, and reprinted by Desert Publications, Cornville, AZ, 1978. 80 pp., illus. Paper covers. $11.95.

Covers every facet of this famous pistol from mechanical training, manual of arms, disassembly, repair and replacement of parts.

Colt Automatic Pistols, by Donald B. Bady, Pioneer Press, Union City, TN, 1999. 368 pp., illustrated. Softcover. $19.95.

A revised and enlarged edition of a key work on a fascinating subject. Complete information on every Colt automatic pistol.

Combat Handgunnery, 4th Edition, by Chuck Taylor, DBI Books, a division of Krause Publications, Iola, WI, 1997. 256 pp., illus. Paper covers. $18.95.

This all-new edition looks at real world combat handgunnery from three different perspectives—military, police and civilian. Available, October, 1996.

Combat Revolvers, by Duncan Long, Paladin Press, Boulder, CO, 1999, 8 1/2 x 11, soft cover, 115 photos, 152 pp. $21.95

This is an uncompromising look at modern combat revolvers. All the major foreign and domestic guns are covered: the Colt Python, S&W Model 29, Ruger GP 100 and hundreds more. Know the gun that you may one day stake your life on.

The Complete Book of Combat Handgunning, by Chuck Taylor, Desert Publications, Cornville, AZ, 1982. 168 pp., illus. Paper covers. $20.00.

Covers virtually every aspect of combat handgunning.

Complete Guide to Compact Handguns, by Gene Gangarosa, Jr., Stoeger Publishing Co., Wayne, NJ, 1997. 228 pp., illus. Paper covers. $22.95.

Includes hundreds of compact firearms, along with text results conducted by the author.

Complete Guide to Service Handguns, by Gene Gangarosa, Jr., Stoeger Publishing Co., Wayne, NJ, 1998. 320 pp., illus. Paper covers. $22.95.

The author explores the revolvers and pistols that are used around the globe by military, law enforcement and civilians.

The Custom Government Model Pistol, by Layne Simpson, Wolfe Publishing Co., Prescott, AZ, 1994. 639 pp., illus. Paper covers. $24.50.

The book about one of the world's greatest firearms and the things pistolsmiths do to make it even greater.

The CZ-75 Family: The Ultimate Combat Handgun, by J.M. Ramos, Paladin Press, Boulder, CO, 1990. 100 pp., illus. Soft covers. $25.00.

An in-depth discussion of the early-and-late model CZ-75s, as well as the many newest additions to the Czech pistol family.

Encyclopedia of Pistols & Revolvers, by A.E. Hartnik, Knickerbocker Press, New York, NY, 1997. 272 pp., illus. $19.95.

A comprehensive encyclopedia specially written for collectors and owners of pistols and revolvers.

Experiments of a Handgunner, by Walter Roper, Wolfe Publishing Co., Prescott, AZ, 1989. 202 pp., illus. $37.00.

A limited edition reprint. A listing of experiments with functioning parts of handguns, with targets, stocks, rests, handloading, etc.

The Farnam Method of Defensive Handgunning, by John S. Farnam, Police Bookshelf, 1999. 191 pp., illus. Paper covers. $25.00

A book intended to not only educate the new shooter, but also to serve as a guide and textbook for his and his instructor's training courses.

Fast and Fancy Revolver Shooting, by Ed. McGivern, Anniversary Edition, Winchester Press, Piscataway, NJ, 1984. 484 pp., illus. $18.95.

A fascinating volume, packed with handgun lore and solid information by the acknowledged dean of revolver shooters.

.45 ACP Super Guns, by J.M. Ramos, Paladin Press, Boulder, CO, 1991. 144 pp., illus. Paper covers. $24.00.

Modified .45 automatic pistols for competition, hunting and personal defense.

The .45, The Gun Digest Book of, by Dean A. Grennell, DBI Books, a division of Krause Publications, Iola, WI, 1989. 256 pp., illus. Paper covers. $17.95.

Definitive work on one of America's favorite calibers.

Glock: The New Wave in Combat Handguns, by Peter Alan Kasler, Paladin Press, Boulder, CO, 1993. 304 pp., illus. $27.00.

Kasler debunks the myths that surround what is the most innovative handgun to be introduced in some time.

Glock's Handguns, by Duncan Long, Desert Publications, El Dorado, AR, 1996. 180 pp., illus. Paper covers. $18.95.

An outstanding volume on one of the world's newest and most successful firearms of the century.

Hand Cannons: The World's Most Powerful Handguns, by Duncan Long, Paladin Press, Boulder, CO, 1995. 208 pp., illus. Paper covers. $22.00.

Long describes and evaluates each powerful gun according to their features.

The Handgun, by Geoffrey Boothroyd, Safari Press, Inc., Huntington Beach, CA, 1999. 566 pp., illustrated. $50.00.

A very detailed history of the handgun. Now revised and a completely new chapter written to take account of developments since the 1970 edition.

Handguns 2002, 13th Edition, edited by Harold A. Murtz, DBI Books a division of Krause Publications, Iola, WI, 1999. 352 pp., illustrated. Paper covers. $22.95.

Top writers in the handgun industry give you a complete report on new handgun developments, testfire reports on the newest introductions and previews on what's ahead.

Handgun Digest, 3rd Edition, edited by Chris Christian, DBI Books, a division of Krause Publications, Iola, WI, 1995. 256 pp., illus. Paper covers. $18.95.

Full coverage of all aspects of handguns and handgunning from a highly readable and knowledgeable author.

Handgun Reloading, The Gun Digest Book of, by Dean A. Grennell and Wiley M. Clapp, DBI Books, a division of Krause Publications, Iola, WI, 1987. 256 pp., illus. Paper covers. $16.95.

Detailed discussions of all aspects of reloading for handguns, from basic to complex. New loading data.

Handgun Stopping Power "The Definitive Study", by Evan P. Marshall & Edwin J. Sanow, Paladin Press, Boulder, CO, 1997, soft cover, photos, 240 pp. $45.00

Dramatic first-hand accounts of the results of handgun rounds fired into criminals by cops, storeowners, cabbies and others are the heart and soul of this long-awaited book. This is the definitive methodology for predicting the stopping power of handgun loads, the first to take into account what really happens when a bullet meets a man.

Heckler & Koch's Handguns, by Duncan Long, Desert Publications, El Dorado, AR, 1996. 142 pp., illus. Paper covers. $19.95.

Traces the history and the evolution of H&K's pistols from the company's beginning at the end of WWII to the present.

Hidden in Plain Sight, by Trey Bloodworth & Mike Raley, Professional Press, Chapel Hill, NC, 1995. Paper covers. $19.95.

A practical guide to concealed handgun carry.

High Standard Automatic Pistols 1932-1950, by Charles E. Petty, The Gunroom Press, Highland Park, NJ, 1989. 124 pp., illus. $19.95.

A definitive source of information for the collector of High Standard arms.

Hi-Standard Pistols and Revolvers, 1951-1984, by James Spacek, James Spacek, Chesire, CT, 1998. 128 pp., illustrated. Paper covers. $12.50.

Technical details, marketing features and instruction/parts manual of every model High Standard pistol and revolver made between 1951 and 1984. Most accurate serial number information available.

The Hi-Standard Pistol Guide, by Burr Leyson, Duckett's Sporting Books, Tempe AZ, 1995. 128 pp., illus. Paper covers. $22.00.

Complete information on selection, care and repair, ammunition, parts, and accessories.

How to Become a Master Handgunner: The Mechanics of X-Count Shooting, by Charles Stephens, Paladin Press, Boulder, CO, 1993. 64 pp., illus. Paper covers. $14.00.

Offers a simple formula for success to the handgunner who strives to master the technique of shooting accurately.

Hunting for Handgunners, by Larry Kelly and J.D. Jones, DBI Books, a division of Krause Publications, Iola, WI, 1990. 256 pp., illus. Paper covers. $16.95.

Covers the entire spectrum of hunting with handguns in an amusing, easy-flowing manner that combines entertainment with solid information.

Illustrated Encyclopedia of Handguns, by A.B. Zhuk, Stackpole Books, Mechanicsburg, PA, 1994. 256 pp., illus. Cloth cover, $49.95

Identifies more than 2,000 military and commercial pistols and revolvers with details of more than 100 popular handgun cartridges.

The Inglis Diamond: The Canadian High Power Pistol, by Clive M. Law, Collector Grade Publications, Canada, 2001. 312 pp., illustrated. $49.95

This definitive work on Canada's first and indeed only mass produced handgun, in production for a very brief span of time and consequently made in relatively few numbers, the venerable Inglis-made Browning High Power covers the pistol's initial history, the story of Chinese and British adoption, use post-war by Holland, Australia, Greece, Belgium, New Zealand, Peru, Brasil and other countries. All new information on the famous light-weights and the Inglis Diamond variations. Completely researched through official archives in a dozen countries. Many of the bewildering variety of markings have never been satisfactorily explained until now. Also included are many photos of holsters and accessories.

Instinct Combat Shooting, by Chuck Klein, The Goose Creek, IN, 1989. 49 pp., illus. Paper covers. $12.00.

Defensive handgunning for police.

Know Your Czechoslovakian Pistols, by R.J. Berger, Blacksmith Corp., Chino Valley, AZ, 1989. 96 pp., illus. Soft covers. $12.95.

A comprehensive reference which presents the fascinating story of Czech pistols.

Know Your 45 Auto Pistols—Models 1911 & A1, by E.J. Hoffschmidt, Blacksmith Corp., Southport, CT, 1974. 58 pp., illus. Paper covers. $12.95.

A concise history of the gun with a wide variety of types and copies.

Know Your Walther P38 Pistols, by E.J. Hoffschmidt, Blacksmith Corp., Southport, CT, 1974. 77 pp., illus. Paper covers. $12.95.

Covers the Walther models Armee, M.P., H.P., P.38—history and variations.

Know Your Walther PP & PPK Pistols, by E.J. Hoffschmidt, Blacksmith Corp., Southport, CT, 1975. 87 pp., illus. Paper covers. $12.95.

A concise history of the guns with a guide to the variety and types.

La Connaissance du Luger, Tome 1, by Gerard Henrotin, H & L Publishing, Belguim, 1996. 144 pages, illustrated. $45.00.

(The Knowledge of Luger, Volume 1, translated.) B&W and Color photo's. French text.

The Luger Handbook, by Aarron Davis, Krause Publications, Iola, WI, 1997. 112 pp., illus. Paper covers. $9.95.

Now you can identify any of the legendary Luger variations using a simple decision tree. Each model and variation includes pricing information, proof marks and detailed attributes in a handy, user-friendly format. Plus, it's fully indexed. Instantly identify that Luger!

Lugers of Ralph Shattuck, by Ralph Shattuck, Peoria, AZ, 2000. 49 pages, illus. Hardcover. $29.95.

49 pages, illustrated with maps and full color photos of here to now never before shown photos of some of the rarest lugers ever. Written by one of the world's renowned collectors. A MUST have book for any Luger collector.

Lugers at Random (Revised Format Edition), by Charles Kenyon, Jr., Handgun Press, Glenview, IL, 2000. 420 pp., illus. $59.95.

A new printing of this classic, comprehensive reference for all Luger collectors.

The Luger Story, by John Walter, Stackpole Books, Mechanicsburg, PA, 2001. 256 pp., illus. Paper Covers. $29.95.

The standard history of the world's most famous handgun.

The Mauser Self-Loading Pistol, by Belford & Dunlap, Borden Publ. Co., Alhambra, CA. Over 200 pp., 300 illus., large format. $29.95.

The long-awaited book on the "Broom Handles," covering their inception in 1894 to the end of production. Complete and in detail: pocket pistols, Chinese and Spanish copies, etc.

9mm Handguns, 2nd Edition, The Gun Digest Book of, edited by Steve Comus, DBI Books, a division of Krause Publications, Iola, WI, 1993. 256 pp., illus. Paper covers. $18.95.

Covers the 9mm cartridge and the guns that have been made for it in greater depth than any other work available.

9mm Parabellum; The History & Development of the World's 9mm Pistols & Ammunition, by Klaus-Peter Konig and Martin Hugo, Schiffer Publishing Ltd., Atglen, PA, 1993. 304 pp., illus. $39.95.

Detailed history of 9mm weapons from Belguim, Italy, Germany, Israel, France, USA, Czechoslovakia, Hungary, Poland, Brazil, Finland and Spain.

The Official 9mm Markarov Pistol Manual, translated into English by Major James Gebhardt, U.S. Army (Ret.), Desert Publications, El Dorado, AR, 1996. 84 pp., illus. Paper covers. $12.95.

The information found in this book will be of enormous benefit and interest to the owner or a prospective owner of one of these pistols.

The Official Soviet 7.62mm Handgun Manual, by Translation by Maj. James F. Gebhardt Ret.), Paladin Press, Boulder, CO, 1997, soft cover, illus., 104 pp. $20.00

This Soviet military manual, now available in English for the first time, covers instructions for use and maintenance of two side arms, the Nagant 7.62mm revolver, used by the Russian tsarist armed forces and later the Soviet armed forces, and the Tokarev7.62mm semi-auto pistol, which replaced the Nagant.

P-38 Automatic Pistol, by Gene Gangarosa, Jr., Stoeger Publishing Co., S. Hackensack, NJ, 1993. 272 pp., illus. Paper covers. $16.95

This book traces the origins and development of the P-38, including the momentous political forces of the World War II era that caused its near demise and, later, its rebirth.

The P-38 Pistol: The Walther Pistols, 1930-1945. Volume 1. by Warren Buxton, Ucross Books, Los Alamos, MN 1999. $68.50

A limited run reprint of this scarce and sought-after work on the P-38 Pistol. 328 pp. with 160 illustrations.

The P-38 Pistol: The Contract Pistols, 1940-1945. Volume 2. by Warren Buxton, Ucross Books, Los Alamos, MN 1999. 256 pp. with 237 illustrations. $68.50

The P-38 Pistol: Postwar Distributions, 1945-1990. Volume 3. by Warren Buxton, Ucross Books, Los Alamos, MN 1999. $68.50

Plus an addendum to Volumes 1 & 2. 272 pp. with 342 illustrations.

PARABELLUM - A Technical History of Swiss Lugers, by V. Bobba, Italy.1998. 224pp, profuse color photos, large format. $100.00.

The is the most beautifully illustrated and well-documented book on the Swiss Lugers yet produced. This splendidly produced book features magnificent images while giving an incredible amount of detail on the Swiss Luger. In-depth coverage of key issues include: the production process, pistol accessories, charts with serial numbers, production figures, variations, markings, patent drawings, etc. Covers the Swiss Luger story from 1894 when the first Bergmann-Schmeisser models were tested till the commercial model 1965. Shows every imaginable production variation in amazing detail and full color! A must for all Luger collectors. This work has been produced in an extremely attractive package using quality materials throughout and housed in a protective slipcase.

Pistols and Revolvers, by Jean-Noel Mouret, Barns and Noble, Rockleigh, N.J., 1999. 141 pp., illustrated. $12.98.

Here in glorious display is the master guidebook to flintlocks, minatures, the Sig P-210 limited edition, the Springfield Trophy Master with Aimpoint 5000 telescopic sight, every major classic and contemporary handgun, complete with their technical data.

Report of Board on Tests of Revolvers and Automatic Pistols, From the Annual Report of the Chief of Ordnance, 1907. Reprinted by J.C. Tillinghast, Marlow, NH, 1969. 34 pp., 7 plates, paper covers. $9.95.

A comparison of handguns, including Luger, Savage, Colt, Webley-Fosbery and other makes.

REFERENCE

THE ARMS LIBRARY

Ruger Automatic Pistols and Single Action Revolvers, by Hugo A. Lueders, edited by Don Findley, Blacksmith Corp., Chino Valley, AZ, 1993. 79 pp., illus. Paper covers. $14.95.

The definitive work on Ruger automatic pistols and single action revolvers.

The Ruger "P" Family of Handguns, by Duncan Long, Desert Publications, El Dorado, AZ, 1993. 128 pp., illus. Paper covers. $14.95.

A full-fledged documentary on a remarkable series of Sturm Ruger handguns.

The Ruger .22 Automatic Pistol, Standard/Mark I/Mark II Series, by Duncan Long, Paladin Press, Boulder, CO, 1989. 168 pp., illus. Paper covers. $16.00.

The definitive book about the pistol that has served more than 1 million owners so well.

The Semiautomatic Pistols in Police Service and Self Defense, by Massad Ayoob, Police Bookshelf, Concord, NH, 1990. 25 pp., illus. Soft covers. $9.95.

First quantitative, documented look at actual police experience with 9mm and 45 police service automatics.

The Sharpshooter—How to Stand and Shoot Handgun Metallic Silhouettes, by Charles Stephens, Yucca Tree Press, Las Cruces, NM, 1993. 86 pp., illus. Paper covers. $10.00.

A narration of some of the author's early experiences in silhouette shooting, plus how-to information.

Shooting Colt Single Actions, by Mike Venturino, Livingston, MT, 1997. 205 pp., illus. Paper covers. $25.00

A definitive work on the famous Colt SAA and the ammunition it shoots.

Sig/Sauer Handguns, by Duncan Long, Desert Publications, El Dorado, AZ, 1995. 150 pp., illus. Paper covers. $16.95.

The history of Sig/Sauer handguns, including Sig, Sig-Hammerli and Sig/Sauer variants.

Sixgun Cartridges and Loads, by Elmer Keith, reprint edition by The Gun Room Press, Highland Park, NJ, 1984. 151 pp., illus. $24.95.

A manual covering the selection, use and loading of the most suitable and popular revolver cartridges.

Sixguns, by Elmer Keith, Wolfe Publishing Company, Prescott, AZ, 1992. 336 pp. Paper covers. $29.95. Hardcover $35.00

The history, selection, repair, care, loading, and use of this historic frontiersman's friend—the one-hand firearm.

Smith & Wesson's Automatics, by Larry Combs, Desert Publications, El Dorado, AZ, 1994. 143 pp., illus. Paper covers. $19.95.

A must for every S&W auto owner or prospective owner.

Spanish Handguns: The History of Spanish Pistols and Revolvers, by Gene Gangarosa, Jr., Stoeger Publishing Co., Accokeek, MD, 2001. 320 pp., illustrated. B & W photos. Paper covers. $21.95

Street Stoppers: The Latest Handgun Stopping Power Street Results, by Evan P. Marshall & Edwin J. Sandow, Paladin Press, Boulder, CO, 1997. 392 pp., illus. Paper covers. $42.95.

Compilation of the results of real-life shooting incidents involving every major handgun caliber.

The Tactical 1911, by Dave Lauck, Paladin Press, Boulder, CO, 1999. 152 pp., illustrated. Paper covers. $22.00.

The cop's and SWAT operator's guide to employment and maintenance.

The Tactical Pistol, by Gabriel Suarez with a foreword by Jeff Cooper, Paladin Press, Boulder, CO, 1996. 216 pp., illus. Paper covers. $25.00.

Advanced gunfighting concepts and techniques.

The Thompson/Center Contender Pistol, by Charles Tephens, Paladin Press, Boulder, CO, 1997. 58 pp., illus. Paper covers. $14.00.

How to tune and time, load and shoot accurately with the Contender pistol.

The .380 Enfield No. 2 Revolver, by Mark Stamps and Ian Skennerton, I.D.S.A. Books, Piqua, OH, 1993. 124 pp., 80 illus. Paper covers. $19.95.

The Truth AboUt Handguns, by Duane Thomas, Paladin Press, Boulder, CO, 1997. 136 pp., illus. Paper covers. $18.00.

Exploding the myths, hype, and misinformation about handguns.

Walther Pistols: Models 1 Through P99, Factory Variations and Copies, by Dieter H. Marschall, Ucross Books, Los Alamos, NM. 2000. 140 pages, with 140 b & w illustrations, index. Paper Covers. $19.95.

This is the English translation, revised and updated, of the highly successful and widely acclaimed German language edition. This book provides the collector with a reference guide and overview of the entire line of the Walther military, police, and self-defense pistols from the very first to the very latest. Models 1-9, PP, PPK, MP, AP, HP, P.38, P1, P4, P38K, P5, P88, P99 and the Manurhin models. Variations, where issued, serial ranges, calibers, marks, proofs, logos, and design aspects in an astonishing quantity and variety are crammed into this very well researched and highly regarded work.

U.S. Handguns of World War 2, The Secondary Pistols and Revolvers, by Charles W. Pate, Mowbray Publishers, Lincoln, RI, 1997. 368 pp., illus. $39.00.

This indispensable new book covers all of the American military handguns of W.W.2 except for the M1911A1.

HUNTING

NORTH AMERICA

Advanced Black Powder Hunting, by Toby Bridges, Stoeger Publishing Co., Wayne, NJ, 1998. 288 pp., illus. Paper covers. $21.95.

The first modern day publication to be filled from cover to cover with guns, loads, projectiles, accessories and the techniques to get the most from today's front loading guns.

Advanced Strategies for Trophy Whitetails, by David Morris, Safari Press, Inc., Huntington Beach, CA, 1999. 399 pp., illustrated. $29.95.

This book is a must-have for any serious trophy hunter.

After the Hunt With Lovett Williams, by Lovett Williams, Krause Publications, Iola, WI, 1996. 256 pp., illus. Paper covers. $15.95.

The author carefully instructs you on how to prepare your trophy turkey for a trip to the taxidermist. Plus help on planning a grand slam hunt.

Aggressive Whitetail Hunting, by Greg Miller, Krause Publications, Iola, WI, 1995. 208 pp., illus. Paper covers. $14.95.

Learn how to hunt trophy bucks in public forests, private farmlands and exclusive hunting grounds from one of America's foremost hunters.

All About Bears, by Duncan Gilchrist, Stoneydale Press Publishing Co., Stevensville, MT, 1989. 176 pp., illus. $19.95.

Covers all kinds of bears—black, grizzly, Alaskan brown, polar and leans on a lifetime of hunting and guiding experiences to explore proper hunting techniques.

American Duck Shooting, by George Bird Grinnell, Stackpole Books, Harrisburg, PA, 1991. 640 pp., illus. Paper covers. $19.95.

First published in 1901 at the height of the author's career. Describes 50 species of waterfowl, and discusses hunting methods common at the turn of the century.

American Hunting and Fishing Books, 1800-1970, Volume 1, by Morris Heller, Nimrod and Piscator Press, Mesilla, NM, 1997. 220 pp., illus. A limited, numbered edition. $125.00.

An up-to-date, profusely illustrated, annotated bibliography on American hunting and fishing books and booklets.

The American Wild Turkey, Hunting Tactics and Techniques, by John McDaniel, The Lyons Press, New York, NY, 2000. 240 pp., illustrated. $29.95.

Loaded with turkey hunting anectdotes gleaned from a lifetime of experience.

American Wingshooting: A Twentieth Century Pictorial Saga, by Ben O. Williams, Willow Creek Press, Minocqua, WI, 2000. 160 pp., illustrated with 180 color photographs. $35.00.

A beautifully photographed celebration of upland bird hunting now and how as it once existed.

The Art of Super-Accurate Hunting with Scoped Rifles, by Don Judd, Wolfe Publishing Co., Prescott, AZ, 1996. 99 pp., illus. Paper covers. $14.95.

The philosophy of super-accurate hunting and the rewards of making your shot a trophy.

As I Look Back; Musings of a Birdhunter, by Robert Branen, Safari Press, Inc., Huntington Beach, CA, 1999. Limited, signed and numbered edition. $60.00.

The author shares his recollections of bird hunting around the world.

Autumn Passages, Compiled by the editors of Ducks Unlimited Magazine, Willow Creek Press, Minocqua, WI, 1997. 320 pp. $27.50.

An exceptional collection of duck hunting stories.

Awesome Antlers of North America, by Odie Sudbeck, HTW Publications, Seneca, KS, 1993. 150 pp., illus. $35.00.

500 world-class bucks in color and black and white. This book starts up where the Boone & Crockett recordbook leaves off.

Backtracking, by I.T. Taylor, Safari Press, Inc., Huntington Beach, CA, 1998. 201 pp., illustrated. $24.95.

Reminiscences of a hunter's life in rural America.

Bare November Days, by George Bird Evans et al, Countrysport Press, Traverse City, MI, 1992. 136 pp., illus. $39.50.

A new, original anthology, a tribute to ruffed grouse, king of upland birds.

Bear Attacks, by K. Etling, Safari Press, Long Beach, CA, 1998. 574 pp., illus. In 2 volumes. $75.00.

Classic tales of dangerous North American bears.

The Bear Hunter's Century, by Paul Schullery, Stackpole Books, Harrisburg, PA, 1989. 240 pp., illus. $19.95.

Thrilling tales of the bygone days of wilderness hunting.

The Best of Babcock, by Havilah Babcock, selected and with an introduction by Hugh Grey, The Gunnerman Press, Auburn Hills, MI, 1985. 262 pp., illus. $19.95.

A treasury of memorable pieces, 21 of which have never before appeared in book form.

The Best of Nash Buckingham, by Nash Buckingham, selected, edited and annotated by George Bird Evans, Winchester Press, Piscataway, NJ, 1973. 320 pp., illus. $35.00.

Thirty pieces that represent the very cream of Nash's output on his whole range of outdoor interests—upland shooting, duck hunting, even fishing.

Better on a Rising Tide, by Tom Kelly, Lyons & Burford Publishers, New York, NY, 1995. 184 pp. $22.95.

Tales of wild turkeys, turkey hunting and Southern folk.

Big Bucks the Benoit Way, by Bryce Towsley, Krause Publications Iola, WI, 1998. 208 pp., illus. $24.95.

Secrets from America's first family of whitetail hunting.

Big December Canvasbacks, by Worth Mathewson, Sand Lake Press, Amity, OR, 1997. 171 pp., illus. By David Hagenbaumer. Limited, signed and numbered edition. $29.95.

Duck hunting stories.

Big Game Hunting, by Duncan Gilchrist, Outdoor Expeditions, books and videos, Corvallis, MT, 1999. 192 pp., illustrated. $14.95

Designed to be a warehouse of hunting information covering the major North American big game species.

Big Woods, by William Faulkner, wilderness adventures, Gallatin Gateway, MT, 1998. 208 pp., illus. Slipcased. $60.00.

A collection of Faulkner's best hunting stories that belongs in the library of every sportsman.

REFERENCE

Birdhunter, by Richard S. Grozik, Safari Press, Huntington Beach, CA, 1998. 180 pp., illus. Limited, numbered and signed edition. Slipcased. $60.00.
    An entertaining salute to the closeness between man and his dog, man and his gun, and man and the great outdoors.

Bird Dog Days, Wingshooting Ways, by Archibald Rutledge, edited by Jim Casada, Wilderness Adventure Press, Gallatin Gateway, MT, 1998. 200 pp., illus. $35.00.
    One of the most popular and enduring outdoor writers of this century, the poet laureate of South Carolina.

Birds on the Horizon, by Stuart Williams, Countrysport Press, Traverse City, MI, 1993. 288 pp., illus. $49.50.
    Wingshooting adventures around the world.

Blacktail Trophy Tactics, by Boyd Iverson, Stoneydale Press, Stevensville, MI, 1992. 166 pp., illus. Paper covers. $14.95.
    A comprehensive analysis of blacktail deer habits, describing a deer's and man's use of scents, still hunting, tree techniques, etc.

Boone & Crockett Club's 23rd Big Game Awards, 1995-1997, Boone & Crockett Club, Missoula, MT, 1999. 600 pp., illustrated with black & white photographs plus a 16 page color section. $39.95.
    A complete listing of the 3,511 trophies accepted in the 23rd Awards Entry Period.

Bowhunter's Handbook, Expert Strategies and Techniques, by M.R. James with Fred Asbell, Dave Holt, Dwight Schuh & Dave Samuel, DBI Books, a division of Krause Publications, Iola, WI, 1997. 256 pp., illus. Paper covers. $19.95.
    Tips from the top on taking your bowhunting skills to the next level.

The Buffalo Harvest, by Frank Mayer as told to Charles Roth, Pioneer Press, Union City, TN, 1995. 96 pp., illus. Paper covers. $8.50.
    The story of a hide hunter during his buffalo hunting days on the plains.

Bugling for Elk, by Dwight Schuh, Stoneydale Press Publishing Co., Stevensville, MT, 1983. 162 pp., illus. $18.95.
    A complete guide to early season elk hunting.

Call of the Quail: A Tribute to the Gentleman Game Bird, by Michael McIntosh, et al., Countrysport Press, Traverse City, MI, 1990. 175 pp., illus. $35.00.
    A new anthology on quail hunting.

Calling All Elk, by Jim Zumbo, Cody, WY, 1989. 169 pp., illus. Paper covers. $14.95.
    The only book on the subject of elk hunting that covers every aspect of elk vocalization.

Campfires and Game Trails: Hunting North American Big Game, by Craig Boddington, Winchester Press, Piscataway, NJ, 1985. 295 pp., illus. $23.95.
    How to hunt North America's big game species.

Come October, by Gene Hill et al, Countrysport Press, Inc., Traverse City, MI, 1991. 176 pp., illus. $39.50.
    A new and all-original anthology on the woodcock and woodcock hunting.

The Complete Book of Grouse Hunting, by Frank Woolner, The Lyons Press, New York, NY, 2000. 192 pp., illustrated Paper covers. $24.95.
    The history, habits, and habitat of one of America's great game birds—and the methods used to hunt it.

The Complete Book of Mule Deer Hunting, by Walt Prothero, The Lyons Press, New York, NY, 2000. 192 pp., illustrated. Paper covers. $24.95.
    Field-tested practical advice on how to bag the trophy buck of a lifetime.

The Complete Book of Wild Turkey Hunting, by John Trout Jr., The Lyons Press, New York, NY, 2000. 192 pp., illustrated. Paper covers. $24.95.
    An illustrated guide to hunting for one of America's most popular game birds.

The Complete Book of Woodcock Hunting, by Frank Woolner, The Lyons Press, New York, NY, 2000. 192 pp., illustrated. Paper covers. $24.95.
    A thorough, practical guide to the American woodcock and to woodcock hunting.

The Complete Guide to Bird Dog Training, by John R. Falk, Lyons & Burford, New York, NY, 1994. 288 pp., illus. $22.95.
    The latest on live-game field training techniques using released quail and recall pens. A new chapter on the services available for entering field trials and other bird dog competitions.

The Complete Guide to Game Care & Cookery, 3rd Edition, by Sam Fadala, DBI Books, a division of Krause Publications, Iola, WI, 1994. 320 pp., illus. Paper covers. $18.95.
    Over 500 photos illustrating the care of wild game in the field and at home with a separate recipe section providing over 400 tested recipes.

The Complete Smoothbore Hunter, by Brook Elliot, Winchester Press, Piscataway, NJ, 1986. 240 pp., illus. $16.95.
    Advice and information on guns and gunning for all varieties of game.

The Complete Venison Cookbook from Field to Table, by Jim & Ann Casada, Krause Publications, Iola, WI, 1996. 208 pp., Comb-bound. $12.95.
    More than 200 kitchen tested recipes make this book the answer to a table full of hungry hunters or guests.

Coveys and Singles: The Handbook of Quail Hunting, by Robert Gooch, A.S. Barnes, San Diego, CA, 1981. 196 pp., illus. $11.95.
    The story of the quail in North America.

Coyote Hunting, by Phil Simonski, Stoneydale Press, Stevensville, MT, 1994. 126 pp., illus. Paper covers. $12.95.
    Probably the most thorough "How-to-do-it" book on coyote hunting ever written.

Dabblers & Divers: A Duck Hunter's Book, compiled by the editors of Ducks Unlimited Magazine, Willow Creek Press, Minocqua, WI, 1997. 160 pp., illus. $39.95.
    A word-and-photographic portrayal of waterfowl hunter's singular intimacy with, and passion for, watery haunts and wildfowl.

Dancers in the Sunset Sky, by Robert F. Jones, The Lyons Press, New York, NY, 1997. 192 pp., illus. $22.95.
    The musings of a bird hunter.

Deer & Deer Hunting, by Al Hofacker, Krause Publications, Iola, WI, 1993. 208 pp., illus. $34.95.
    Coffee-table volume packed full of how-to-information that will guide hunts for years to come.

Deer and Deer Hunting: The Serious Hunter's Guide, by Dr. Robert Wegner, Stackpole Books, Harrisburg, PA, 1984. 384 pp., illus. Paper covers. $18.95.
    In-depth information from the editor of "Deer & Deer Hunting" magazine. Major bibliography of English language books on deer and deer hunting from 1838-1984.

Deer and Deer Hunting Book 2, by Dr. Robert Wegner, Stackpole Books, Harrisburg, PA, 1987. 400 pp., illus. Paper covers. $18.95.
    Strategies and tactics for the advanced hunter.

Deer and Deer Hunting, Book 3, by Dr. Robert Wegner, Stackpole Books, Harrisburg, PA, 1990. 368 pp., illus. $18.95.
    This comprehensive volume covers natural history, deer hunting lore, profiles of deer hunters, and discussion of important issues facing deer hunters today.

The Deer Hunters: The Tactics, Lore, Legacy and Allure of American Deer Hunting, Edited by Patrick Durkin, Krause Publications, Iola, WI, 1997. 208 pp., illus. $29.95.
    More than twenty years of research from America's top whitetail hunters, researchers, and photographers have gone in to the making of this book.

Deer Hunting, by R. Smith, Stackpole Books, Harrisburg, PA, 1978. 224 pp., illus. Paper covers. $14.95.
    A professional guide leads the hunt for North America's most popular big game animal.

Doves and Dove Shooting, by Byron W. Dalrymple, New Win Publishing, Inc., Hampton, NJ, 1992. 256 pp., illus. $17.95.
    The author reveals in this classic book his penchant for observing, hunting, and photographing this elegantly fashioned bird.

Dove Hunting, by Charley Dickey, Galahad Books, NY, 1976. 112 pp., illus. $10.00.
    This indispensable guide for hunters deals with equipment, techniques, types of dove shooting, hunting dogs, etc.

Dreaming the Lion, by Thomas McIntyre, Countrysport Press, Traverse City, MI, 1994. 309 pp., illus. $35.00.
    Reflections on hunting, fishing and a search for the wild. Twenty-three stories by *Sports Afield* editor, Tom McIntyre.

Duck Decoys and How to Rig Them, by Ralf Coykendall, revised by Ralf Coykendall, Jr., Nick Lyons Books, New York, NY, 1990. 137 pp., illus. Paper covers. $14.95.
    Sage and practical advice on the art of decoying ducks and geese.

The Duck Hunter's Handbook, by Bob Hinman, revised, expanded, updated edition, Winchester Press, Piscataway, NJ, 1985. 288 pp., illus. $15.95.
    The duck hunting book that has it all.

Eastern Upland Shooting, by Dr. Charles C. Norris, Countrysport Press, Traverse City, MI, 1990. 424 pp., illus. $49.00.
    A new printing of this 1946 classic with a new, original Foreword by the author's friend and hunting companion, renowned author George Bird Evans.

Elk and Elk Hunting, by Hart Wixom, Stackpole Books, Harrisburg, PA, 1986. 288 pp., illus. $34.95.
    Your practical guide to fundamentals and fine points of elk hunting.

Elk Hunting in the Northern Rockies, by Ed. Wolff, Stoneydale Press, Stevensville, MT, 1984. 162 pp., illus. $18.95.
    Helpful information about hunting the premier elk country of the northern Rocky Mountain states—Wyoming, Montana and Idaho.

Elk Hunting with the Experts, by Bob Robb, Stoneydale Press, Stevensville, MT, 1992. 176 pp., illus. Paper covers. $15.95.
    A complete guide to elk hunting in North America by America's top elk hunting expert.

Elk Rifles, Cartridges and Hunting Tactics, by Wayne van Zwoll, Larsen's Outdoor Publishing, Lakeland, FL, 1992. 414 pp., illus. $24.95.
    The definitive work on which rifles and cartridges are proper for hunting elk plus the tactics for hunting them.

Encyclopedia of Deer, by G. Kenneth Whitehead, Safari Press, Huntington, CA, 1993. 704 pp., illus. $130.00.
    This massive tome will be the reference work on deer for well into the next century.

A Fall of Woodcock, by Tom Huggler, Countrysport Press, Selman, AL, 1997. 256 pp., illus. $39.00.
    A book devoted to the woodcock and to those who await his return to their favorite converts each autumn.

Firelight, by Burton L. Spiller, Gunnerman Press, Auburn Hills, MI, 1990. 196 pp., illus. $19.95.
    Enjoyable tales of the outdoors and stalwart companions.

Following the Flight, by Charles S. Potter, Countrysport Books, Selma, AL, 1999. 130 pp., illustrated. $25.00.
    The great waterfowl passage and the experiences of a young man who has lived their migration come to life in the pages of this book.

Fresh Looks at Deer Hunting, by Byron W. Dalrymple, New Win Publishing, Inc., Hampton, NJ, 1993. 288 pp., illus. $24.95.
    Tips and techniques abound throughout the pages of this latest work by Mr. Dalrymple whose name is synonymous with hunting proficiency.

From the Peace to the Fraser, by Prentis N. Gray, Boone and Crockett Club, Missoula, MT, 1995. 400 pp., illus. $49.95.
    Newly discovered North American hunting and exploration journals from 1900 to 1930.

Fur Trapping In North America, by Steven Geary, Winchester Press, Piscataway, NJ, 1985. 160 pp., illus. Paper covers. $19.95.
A comprehensive guide to techniques and equipment, together with fascinating facts about fur bearers.

Getting the Most Out of Modern Waterfowling, by John O. Cartier, St. Martin's Press, NY, 1974. 396 pp., illus. $29.95.
The most comprehensive, up-to-date book on waterfowling imaginable.

Getting a Stand, by Miles Gilbert, Pioneer Press, Union City, TN, 1993. 204 pp., illus. Paper covers. $13.95.
An anthology of 18 short personal experiences by buffalo hunters of the late 1800s, specifically from 1870-1882.

The Gordon MacQuarrie Sporting Treasury. Introduction and commentary by Zack Taylor. Countrysport Press, Selman, AL, 1999. $29.50.
Hunting and fishing masterpieces you can read over and over.

Gordon MacQuarrie Trilogy: Stories of the Old Duck Hunters, by Gordon Mac-Quarrie, Willow Creek Press, Minocqua, WI, 1994. $49.00.
A slip-cased three volume set of masterpieces by one of America's finest outdoor writers.

The Grand Passage: A Chronicle of North American Waterfowling, by Gene Hill, et al., Countrysport Press, Traverse City, MI, 1990. 175 pp., illus. $35.00.
A new original anthology by renowned sporting authors on our world of waterfowling.

Greatest Elk; The Complete Historical and Illustrated Record of North America's Biggest Elk, by R. Selner, Safari Press, Huntington Beach, CA, 2000. 209 pages, profuse color illus. $39.95.
Here is the book all elk hunters have been waiting for! This oversized book holds the stories and statistics of the biggest bulls ever killed in North America. Stunning, full-color photographs highlight over 40 world-class heads, including the old world records!

Grouse and Woodcock, A Gunner's Guide, by Don Johnson, Krause Publications, Iola, WI, 1995. 256 pp., illus. Paper covers. $14.95.
Find out what you need in guns, ammo, equipment, dogs and terrain.

Grouse of North America, by Tom Huggler, NorthWord Press, Inc., Minocqua, WI, 1990. 160 pp., illus. $29.95.
A cross-continental hunting guide.

Grouse Hunter's Guide, by Dennis Walrod, Stackpole Books, Harrisburg, PA, 1985. 192 pp., illus. $19.95.
Solid facts, observations, and insights on how to hunt the ruffed grouse.

Gunning for Sea Ducks, by George Howard Gillelan, Tidewater Publishers, Centreville, MD, 1988. 144 pp., illus. $14.95.
A book that introduces you to a practically untouched arena of waterfowling.

Heartland Trophy Whitetails, by Odie Sudbeck, HTW Publications, Seneca, KS, 1992. 130 pp., illus. $35.00.
A completely revised and expanded edition which includes over 500 photos of Boone & Crockett class whitetail, major mulies and unusual racks.

The Heck with Moose Hunting, by Jim Zumbo, Wapiti Valley Publishing Co., Cody, WY, 1996. 199 pp., illus. $17.95.
Jim's hunts around the continent including encounters with moose, caribou, sheep, antelope and mountain goats.

High Pressure Elk Hunting, by Mike Lapinski, Stoneydale Press Publishing Co., Stevensville, MT, 1996. 192 pp., illus. $19.95.
The secrets of hunting educated elk revealed.

Hill Country, by Gene Hill, Countrysport Press, Traverse City, MI, 1996. 180 pp., illus. $25.00.
Stories about hunting, fishing, dogs and guns.

Home from the Hill, by Fred Webb, Safari Press, Huntington Beach, CA, 1997. 283 pp., illus. Limited edition, signed and numbered. In a slipcase. $50.00.
The story of a big-game guide in the Canadian wilderness.

Horns in the High Country, by Andy Russell, Alfred A. Knopf, NY, 1973. 259 pp., illus. Paper covers. $12.95.
A many-sided view of wild sheep and their natural world.

How to Hunt, by Dave Bowring, Winchester Press, Piscataway, NJ, 1982. 208 pp., illus. Hardcover $15.00.
A basic guide to hunting big game, small game, upland birds, and waterfowl.

Hunt Alaska Now: Self-Guiding for Trophy Moose & Caribou, by Dennis W. Confer, Wily Ventures, Anchorage, AK, 1997. 309 pp., illus. Paper covers. $26.95.
How to plan affordable, successfull, safe hunts you can do yourself.

The Hunters and the Hunted, by George Laycock, Outdoor Life Books, New York, NY, 1990. 280 pp., illus. $34.95.
The pursuit of game in America from Indian times to the present.

A Hunter's Fireside Book, by Gene Hill, Winchester Press, Piscataway, NJ, 1972. 192 pp., illus. $17.95.
An outdoor book that will appeal to every person who spends time in the field—or who wishes he could.

A Hunter's Road, by Jim Fergus, Henry Holt & Co., NY, 1992. 290 pp. $22.50
A journey with gun and dog across the American uplands.

Hunt High for Rocky Mountain Goats, Bighorn Sheep, Chamois & Tahr, by Duncan Gilchrist, Stoneydale Press, Stevensville, MT, 1992. 192 pp., illus. Paper covers. $19.95.
The source book for hunting mountain goats.

The Hunter's Shooting Guide, by Jack O'Connor, Outdoor Life Books, New York, NY, 1982. 176 pp., illus. Paper covers. $9.95.
A classic covering rifles, cartridges, shooting techniques for shotguns/rifles/handguns.

The Hunter's World, by Charles F. Waterman, Winchester Press, Piscataway, NJ, 1983. 250 pp., illus. $29.95.
A classic. One of the most beautiful hunting books that has ever been produced.

Hunting Adventure of Me and Joe, by Walt Prothero, Safari Press, Huntington Beach, CA, 1995. 220 pp., illus. $22.50.
A collection of the author's best and favorite stories.

Hunting America's Game Animals and Birds, by Robert Elman and George Peper, Winchester Press, Piscataway, NJ, 1975. 368 pp., illus. $16.95.
A how-to, where-to, when-to guide—by 40 top experts—covering the continent's big, small, upland game and waterfowl.

Hunting Ducks and Geese, by Steven Smith, Stackpole Books, Harrisburg, PA, 1984. 160 pp., illus. $19.95.
Hard facts, good bets, and serious advice from a duck hunter you can trust.

Hunting for Handguns, by Larry Kelly and J.D. Jones, DBI Books, a division of Krause Publications, Iola, WI, 1990. 256 pp., illus. Soft covers. $16.95.
A definitive work on an increasingly popular sport.

Hunting in Many Lands, edited by Theodore Roosevelt and George Bird Grinnell, et al., Boone & Crockett Club, Dumphries, VA, 1990. 447 pp., illus. $40.00.
A limited edition reprinting of the original Boone & Crockett Club 1895 printing.

Hunting Mature Bucks, by Larry L. Weishuhn, Krause Publications, Iola, WI, 1995. 256 pp., illus. Paper covers. $14.95.
One of North America's top white-tailed deer authorities shares his expertise on hunting those big, smart and elusive bucks.

Hunting Open-Country Mule Deer, by Dwight Schuh, Sage Press, Nampa, ID, 1989. 150 pp., illus. $18.95.
A guide taking Western bucks with rifle and bow.

Hunting Predators for Hides and Profits, by Wilf E. Pyle, Stoeger Publishing Co., So. Hackensack, NJ, 1985. 224 pp., illus. Paper covers. $11.95.
The author takes the hunter through every step of the hunting/marketing process.

Hunting the American Wild Turkey, by Dave Harbour, Stackpole Books, Harrisburg, PA, 1975. 256 pp., illus. $24.95.
The techniques and tactics of hunting North America's largest, and most popular, woodland game bird.

Hunting the Rockies, Home of the Giants, by Kirk Darner, Marceline, MO, 1996. 291 pp., illus. $25.00.
Understand how and where to hunt Western game in the Rockies.

Hunting the Sun, by Ted Nelson Lundrigan, Countrysport Press, Selma, AL, 1997. 240 pp., illus. $30.00.
One of the best books on grouse and woodcock ever published.

Hunting Trips in North America, by F.C. Selous, Wolfe Publishing Co., Prescott, AZ, 1988. 395 pp., illus. $52.00.
A limited edition reprint. Coverage of caribou, moose and other big game hunting in virgin wilds.

Hunting Trophy Deer, by John Wootters, The Lyons Press, New York, NY, 1997. 272 pp., illus. $24.95.
A revised edition of the definitive manual for identifying, scouting, and successfully hunting a deer of a lifetime.

Hunting Trophy Whitetails, by David Morris, Stoneydale Press, Stevensville, MT, 1993. 483 pp., illus. $29.95.
This is one of the best whitetail books published in the last two decades. The author is the former editor of *North American Whitetail* magazine.

Hunting Upland Birds, by Charles F. Waterman, Countrysport Press, Selma, AL, 1997. 220 pp., illus. $30.00.
Originally published a quarter of a century ago, this classic has been newly updated with the latest information for today's wingshooter.

Hunting Western Deer, by Jim and Wes Brown, Stoneydale Press, Stevensville, MT, 1994. 174 pp., illus. Paper covers. $14.95.
A pair of expert Oregon hunters provide insight into hunting mule deer and blacktail deer in the western states.

Hunting Wild Turkeys in the West, by John Higley, Stoneydale Press, Stevensville, MT, 1992. 154 pp., illus. Paper covers. $12.95.
Covers the basics of calling, locating and hunting turkeys in the western states.

Hunting with the Twenty-two, by Charles Singer Landis, R&R Books, Livonia, NY, 1994. 429 pp., illus. $35.00.
A miscellany of articles touching on the hunting and shooting of small game.

I Don't Want to Shoot an Elephant, by Havilah Babcock, The Gunnerman Press, Auburn Hills, MI, 1985. 184 pp., illus. $19.95.
Eighteen delightful stories that will enthrall the upland gunner for many pleasurable hours.

In Search of the Buffalo, by Charles G. Anderson, Pioneer Press, Union City, TN, 1996. 144 pp., illus. Paper covers. $13.95.
The primary study of the life of J. Wright Mooar, one of the few hunters fortunate enough to kill a white buffalo.

In Search of the Wild Turkey, by Bob Gooch, Great Lakes Living Press, Ltd., Waukegan, IL, 1978. 182 pp., illus. $9.95.
A state-by-state guide to wild turkey hot spots, with tips on gear and methods for bagging your bird.

In the Turkey Woods, by Jerome B. Robinson, The Lyons Press, N.Y., 1998. 207 pp., illustrated. $24.95.
Practical expert advice on all aspects of turkey hunting—from calls to decoys to guns.

Indian Hunts and Indian Hunters of the Old West, by Dr. Frank C. Hibben, Safari Press, Long Beach, CA, 1989. 228 pp., illus. $24.95.
Tales of some of the most famous American Indian hunters of the Old West as told to the author by an old Navajo hunter.

Jack O'Connor's Gun Book, by Jack O'Connor, Wolfe Publishing Company, Prescott, AZ, 1992. 208 pp. Hardcover. $26.00.
  Jack O'Connor imparts a cross-section of his knowledge on guns and hunting. Brings back some of his writings that have here-to-fore been lost.

Jaybirds Go to Hell on Friday, by Havilah Babcock, The Gunnerman Press, Auburn Hills, MI, 1985. 149 pp., illus. $19.95.
  Sixteen jewels that reestablish the lost art of good old-fashioned yarn telling.

Last Casts and Stolen Hunts, edited by Jim Casada and Chuck Wechsler, Countrysport Press, Traverse City, MI, 1994. 270 pp., illus. $29.95.
  The world's best hunting and fishing stories by writers such as Zane Grey, Jim Corbett, Jack O'Connor, Archibald Rutledge and others.

A Listening Walk...and Other Stories, by Gene Hill, Winchester Press, Piscataway, NJ, 1985. 208 pp., illus. $17.95.
  Vintage Hill. Over 60 stories.

Longbows in the Far North, by E. Donnall Thomas, Jr. Stackpole Books, Mechanicsburg, PA, 1994. 200 pp., illus. $18.95.
  An archer's adventures in Alaska and Siberia.

Mammoth Monarchs of North America, by Odie Sudbeck, HTW Publications, Seneca, KA, 1995. 288 pp., illus. $35.00.
  This book reveals eye-opening big buck secrets.

Matching the Gun to the Game, by Clair Rees, Winchester Press, Piscataway, NJ, 1982. 272 pp., illus. $17.95.
  Covers selection and use of handguns, blackpowder firearms for hunting, matching rifle type to the hunter, calibers for multiple use, tailoring factory loads to the game.

Measuring and Scoring North American Big Game Trophies, 2nd Edition, by Wm. H. Nesbitt and Philip L. Wright, The Boone & Crockett Club, Missoula, MT, 1999. 150 pp., illustrated. $34.95.
  The definitive manual for anyone wanting to learn the Club's world-famous big game measuring system.

Meditation on Hunting, by Jose Ortego y Gasset, Wilderness Adventures Press, Bozeman, MT, 1996. 140 pp., illus. In a slipcase. $60.00.
  The classic work on the philosophy of hunting.

Montana—Land of Giant Rams, by Duncan Gilchrist, Stoneydale Press Publishing Co., Stevensville, MT, 1990. 208 pp., illus. $19.95.
  Latest information on Montana bighorn sheep and why so many Montana bighorn rams are growing to trophy size.

Montana—Land of Giant Rams, Volume 2, by Duncan Gilchrist, Outdoor Expeditions and Books, Corvallis, MT, 1992. 208 pp., illus. $34.95.
  The reader will find stories of how many of the top-scoring trophies were taken.

Montana—Land of Giant Rams, Volume 3, by Duncan Gilchrist, Outdoor Expeditions, books and videos, Corvallis, MT, 1999. 224 pp., illus. Paper covers. $19.95.
  All new sheep information including over 70 photos. Learn about how Montana became the "Land of Giant Rams" and what the prospects of the future as we enter a new millenium.

More Grouse Feathers, by Burton L. Spiller, Crown Publ., NY, 1972. 238 pp., illus. $25.00.
  Facsimile of the original Derrydale Press issue of 1938. Guns and dogs, the habits and shooting of grouse, woodcock, ducks, etc. Illus. by Lynn Bogue Hunt.

More Tracks: 78 Years of Mountains, People & Happiness, by Howard Copenhaver, Stoneydale Press, Stevensville, MT, 1992. 150 pp., illus. $18.95.
  A collection of stories by one of the back country's best storytellers about the people who shared with Howard his great adventure in the high places and wild Montana country.

Moss, Mallards and Mules, by Robert Brister, Countrysport Books, Selma, AL, 1998. 216 pp., illustrated by David Maass. $30.00.
  Twenty-seven short stories on hunting and fishing on the Gulf Coast.

Mostly Huntin', by Bill Jordan, Everett Publishing Co., Bossier City, LA, 1987. 254 pp., illus. $21.95.
  Jordan's hunting adventures in North America, Africa, Australia, South America and Mexico.

Mostly Tailfeathers, by Gene Hill, Winchester Press, Piscataway, NJ, 1975. 192 pp., illus. $17.95.
  An interesting, general book about bird hunting.

"Mr. Buck": The Autobiography of Nash Buckingham, by Nash Buckingham, Countrysport Press, Traverse City, MI, 1990. 288 pp., illus. $40.00.
  A lifetime of shooting, hunting, dogs, guns, and Nash's reflections on the sporting life, along with previously unknown pictures and stories written especially for this book.

Mule Deer: Hunting Today's Trophies, by Tom Carpenter and Jim Van Norman, Krause Publications, Iola, WI, 1998. 256 pp., illustrated. Paper covers. $19.95.
  A tribute to both the deer and the people who hunt them. Includes info on where to look for big deer, prime mule deer habitat and effective weapons for the hunt.

Murry Burnham's Hunting Secrets, by Murry Burnham with Russell Tinsley, Winchester Press, Piscataway, NJ, 1984. 244 pp., illus. $17.95.
  One of the great hunters of our time gives the reasons for his success in the field.

My Health is Better in November, by Havilah Babcock, University of S. Carolina Press, Columbia, SC, 1985. 284 pp., illus. $24.95.
  Adventures in the field set in the plantation country and backwater streams of SC.

North American Big Game Animals, by Byron W. Dalrymple and Erwin Bauer, Outdoor Life Books/Stackpole Books, Harrisburg, PA, 1985. 258 pp., illus. $29.95.
  Complete illustrated natural histories. Habitat, movements, breeding, birth and development, signs, and hunting.

North American Elk: Ecology and Management, edited by Jack Ward Thomas and Dale E. Toweill, Stackpole Books, Harrisburg, PA, 1982. 576 pp., illus. $39.95.
  The definitive, exhaustive, classic work on the North American elk.

The North American Waterfowler, by Paul S. Bernsen, Superior Publ. Co., Seattle, WA, 1972. 206 pp. Paper covers. $9.95.
  The complete inside and outside story of duck and goose shooting. Big and colorful, illustrations by Les Kouba.

Of Bears and Man, by Mike Cramond, University of Oklahoma Press, Norman, OK, 1986. 433 pp., illus. $29.95.
  The author's lifetime association with bears of North America. Interviews with survivors of bear attacks.

The Old Man and the Boy, by Robert Ruark, Henry Holt & Co., New York, NY, 303 pp., illus. $24.95.
  A timeless classic, telling the story of a remarkable friendship between a young boy and his grandfather as they hunt and fish together.

The Old Man's Boy Grows Older, by Robert Ruark, Henry Holt & Co., Inc., New York, NY, 1993. 300 pp., illus. $24.95.
  The heartwarming sequel to the best-selling *The Old Man and the Boy*.

Old Wildfowling Tales, Volume 2, edited by Worth Mathewson, Sand Lake Press, Amity, OR, 1996. 240 pp. $21.95.
  A collection of duck and geese hunting stories based around accounts from the past.

One Man, One Rifle, One Land; Hunting all Species of Big Game in North America, by J.Y. Jones, Safari Press, Huntington Beach, CA, 2000. 400 pp., illustrated. $59.95.
  Journey with J.Y. Jones as he hunts each of the big-game animals of North America—from the polar bear of the high Artic to the jaguar of the low-lands of Mexico—with just one rifle.

161 Waterfowling Secrets, edited by Matt Young, Willow Creek Press, Minocqua, WI, 1997. 78 pp., Paper covers. $10.95.
  Time-honored, field-tested waterfowling tips and advice.

The Only Good Bear is a Dead Bear, by Jeanette Hortick Prodgers, Falcon Press, Helena, MT, 1986. 204 pp. Paper covers. $12.50.
  A collection of the West's best bear stories.

Outdoor Pastimes of an American Hunter, by Theodore Roosevelt, Stackpole Books, Mechanicsburg, PA, 1994. 480 pp., illus. Paper covers. $18.95.
  Stories of hunting big game in the West and notes about animals pursued and observed.

The Outlaw Gunner, by Harry M. Walsh, Tidewater Publishers, Cambridge, MD, 1973. 178 pp. illus. $22.95.
  A colorful story of market gunning in both its legal and illegal phases.

Passing a Good Time, by Gene Hill, Countrysport Press, Traverse City, MI, 1996. 200 pp., illus. $25.00.
  Filled with insights and observations of guns, dogs and fly rods that make Gene Hill a master essayist.

Pear Flat Philosophies, by Larry Weishuhn, Safari Press, Huntington Beach, CA, 1995. 234 pp., illus. $24.95.
  The author describes his more lighthearted adventures and funny anecdotes while out hunting.

Pheasant Days, by Chris Dorsey, Voyageur Press, Stillwater, MN, 1992. 233 pp., illus. $24.95.
  The definitive resource on ringnecks. Includes everything from basic hunting techniques to the life cycle of the bird.

Pheasant Hunter's Harvest, by Steve Grooms, Lyons & Burford Publishers, New York, NY, 1990. 180 pp. $22.95.
  A celebration of pheasant, pheasant dogs and pheasant hunting. Practical advice from a passionate hunter.

Pheasant Tales, by Gene Hill et al, Countrysport Press, Traverse City, MI, 1996. 202 pp., illus. $39.00.
  Charley Waterman, Michael McIntosh and Phil Bourjaily join the author to tell some of the stories that illustrate why the pheasant is America's favorite game bird.

Pheasants of the Mind, by Datus Proper, Wilderness Adventures Press, Bozeman, MT, 1994. 154 pp., illus. $25.00.
  No single title sums up the life of the solitary pheasant hunter like this masterful work.

Portraits of Elk Hunting, by Jim Zumbo, Safari Press, Huntington Beach, CA, 2001. 222 pp. illustrated. $39.95
  Zumbo has captured in photos as well as in words the essence, charisma, and wonderful components of elk hunting: back-country wilderness camps, sweaty guides, happy hunters, favorite companions, elk woods, and, of course, the majestic elk. Join Zumbo in the uniqueness of the pursuit of the magnificent and noble elk.

Predator Calling with Gerry Blair, by Gerry Blair, Krause Publications, Iola, WI, 1996. 208 pp., illus. Paper covers. $14.95.
  Time-tested secrets lure predators closer to your camera or gun.

Proven Whitetail Tactics, by Greg Miller, Krause Publications, Iola, WI, 1997. 224 pp., illus. Paper covers. $19.95.
  Proven tactics for scouting, calling and still-hunting whitetail.

Quail Hunting in America, by Tom Huggler, Stackpole Books, Harrisburg, PA, 1987. 288 pp., illus. $22.95.
  Tactics for finding and taking bobwhite, valleys, Gambel's Mountain, scaled-blue, and Mearn's quail by season and habitat.

Quest for Dall Rams, by Duncan Gilchrist, Duncan Gilchrist Outdoor Expeditions and Books, Corvallis, MT, 1997. 224 pp., illus. Limited numbered edition. $34.95.
  The most complete book of Dall sheep ever written. Covers information on Alaska and provinces with Dall sheep and explains hunting techniques, equipment, etc.

REFERENCE

THE ARMS LIBRARY

Quest for Giant Bighorns, by Duncan Gilchrist, Outdoor Expeditions and Books, Corvallis, MT, 1994. 224 pp., illus. Paper covers. $19.95.
How some of the most successful sheep hunters hunt and how some of the best bighorns were taken.

Radical Elk Hunting Strategies, by Mike Lapinski, Stoneydale Press Publishing Co., Stevensville, MT, 1988. 161 pp., illus. $18.95.
Secrets of calling elk in close.

Rattling, Calling & Decoying Whitetails, by Gary Clancy, Edited by Patrick Durkin, Krause Publications, Iola, WI, 2000. 208 pp., illustrated. Paper covers. $19.95.
How to consistently coax big bucks into range.

Records of North American Big Game 11th Edition, with hunting chapters by Craig Boddington, Tom McIntyre and Jim Zumbo, The Boone and Crockett Club, Missoula, MT, 1999. 700 pp., featuring a 32 page color section. $49.95.
Listing over 17,150, of the top trophy big game animals ever recorded. Over 4,000 new listings are featured in this latest edition.

Records of North American Big Game 1932, by Prentis N. Grey, Boone and Crockett Club, Dumfries, VA, 1988. 178 pp., illus. $79.95.
A reprint of the book that started the Club's record keeping for native North American big game.

Records of North American Caribou and Moose, Craig Boddington et al, The Boone & Crockett Club, Missoula, MT, 1997. 250 pp., illus. $24.95.
More than 1,800 caribou listings and more than 1,500 moose listings, organized by the state or Canadian province where they were taken.

Records of North American Elk and Mule Deer, 2nd Edition, edited by Jack and Susan Reneau, Boone & Crockett Club, Missoula, MT, 1996. 360 pp., illus. Paper cover, $18.95; hardcover, $24.95.
Updated and expanded edition featuring more than 150 trophy, field and historical photos of the finest elk and mule deer trophies ever recorded.

Records of North American Sheep, Rocky Mountain Goats and Pronghorn edited by Jack and Susan Reneau, Boone & Crockett Club, Missoula, MT, 1996. 400 pp., illus. Paper cover, $18.95; hardcover, $24.95.
The first B&C Club records book featuring all 3941 accepted wild sheep, Rocky Mountain goats and pronghorn trophies.

Return of Royalty; Wild Sheep of North America, by Dr. Dale E. Toweill and Dr. Valerius Geist, Boone and Crockett Club, Missoula, MT, 1999. 224 pp., illustrated. $59.95.
A celebration of the return of the wild sheep to many of its historical ranges.

The Rifles, the Cartridges, and the Game, by Clay Harvey, Stackpole Books, Harrisburg, PA, 1991. 254 pp., illus. $32.95.
Engaging reading combines with exciting photos to present the hunt with an intense level of awareness and respect.

Ringneck; A Tribute to Pheasants and Pheasant Hunting, by Steve Grooms, Russ Sewell and Dave Nomsen, The Lyons Press, New York, NY, 2000. 120 pp., illustrated. $40.00.
A glorious full-color coffee-table tribute to the pheasant and those who hunt them.

Ringneck! Pheasants & Pheasant Hunting, by Ted Janes, Crown Publ., NY, 1975. 120 pp., illus. $15.95.
A thorough study of one of our more popular game birds.

Rub-Line Secrets, by Greg Miller, edited by Patrick Durkin, Krause Publications, Iola, WI, 1999. 208 pp., illustrated. Paper covers. $19.95.
Based on nearly 30 years experience. Proven tactics for finding, analyzing and hunting big bucks' rub-lines.

Ruffed Grouse, edited by Sally Atwater and Judith Schnell, Stackpole Books, Harrisburg, PA, 1989. 370 pp., illus. $59.95.
Everything you ever wanted to know about the ruffed grouse. More than 25 wildlife professionals provided in-depth information on every aspect of this popular game bird's life. Lavishly illustrated with over 300 full-color photos.

The Russell Annabel Adventure Series, by Russell Annabel, Safari Press, Huntington Beach, CA: Vol. 2, Adventure is My Business, 1951-1955. $35.00, Vol. 3, Adventure is in My Blood, 1957-1964. $35.00, Vol. 4, High Road to Adventure, 1964-1970. $35.00, Vol. 5, The Way We Were, 1970-1979. $35.00.
A complete collection of previously unpublished magazine articles in book form by this gifted outdoor writer.

The Season, by Tom Kelly, Lyons & Burford, New York, NY, 1997. 160 pp., illus. $22.95.
The delight and challenges of a turkey hunter's Spring season.

Secret Strategies from North America's Top Whitetail Hunters, compiled by Nick Sisley, Krause Publications, Iola, WI, 1995. 256 pp., illus. Paper covers. $14.95.
Bow and gun hunters share their success stories.

Secrets of the Turkey Pros, by Glenn Sapir, North American Hunting Club, Minnetonka, MN, 1999. 176 pp., illustrated. $19.95.
This work written by a seasoned turkey hunter draws on the collective knowledge and experience on some of the most renowned names in the world of wild turkey.

Sheep Hunting in Alaska—The Dall Sheep Hunter's Guide, by Tony Russ, Outdoor Expeditions and Books, Corvallis, MT, 1994. 160 pp., illus. Paper covers. $19.95.
A how-to guide for the Dall sheep hunter.

Shorebirds: The Birds, The Hunters, The Decoys, by John M. Levinson & Somers G. Headley, Tidewater Publishers, Centreville, MD, 1991. 160 pp., illus. $49.95.
A thorough study of shorebirds and the decoys used to hunt them. Photographs of more than 200 of the decoys created by prominent carvers are shown.

Shots at Big Game, by Craig Boddington, Stackpole Books, Harrisburg, PA, 1989. 198 pp., illus. $24.95.
How to shoot a rifle accurately under hunting conditions.

Some Bears Kill!: True-Life Tales of Terror, by Larry Kanuit, Safari Press, Huntington Beach, CA, 1997. 313 pp., illus. $24.95.
A collection of 38 stories as told by the victims, and in the case of fatality, recounted by the author from institutional records, episodes involve all three species of North American bears.

Southern Deer & Deer Hunting, by Larry Weishuhn and Bill Bynum, Krause Publications, Iola, WI, 1995. 256 pp., illus. Paper covers. $14.95.
Mount a trophy southern whitetail on your wall with this firsthand account of stalking big bucks below the Mason-Dixon line.

Spring Gobbler Fever, by Michael Hanback, Krause Publications, Iola, WI, 1996. 256 pp., illus. Paper covers. $15.95.
Your complete guide to spring turkey hunting.

Spirit of the Wilderness, Compiled by Theodore J. Holsten, Jr., Susan C. Reneau and Jack Reneau, the Boone & Crockett Club, Missoula, MT, 1997 300 pp., illus. $29.95.
Stalking wild sheep, tracking a trophy cougar, hiking the back country of British Columbia, fishing for striped bass and coming face-to-face with a grizzly bear are some of the adventures found in this book.

Stand Hunting for Whitetails, by Richard P. Smith, Krause Publications, Iola, WI, 1996. 256 pp., illus. Paper covers. $14.95.
The author explains the tricks and strategies for successful stand hunting.

The Sultan of Spring: A Hunter's Odyssey Through the World of the Wild Turkey, by Bob Saile, The Lyons Press, New York, NY, 1998. 176 pp., illus. $22.95.
A literary salute to the magic and mysticism of spring turkey hunting.

Taking Big Bucks, by Ed Wolff, Stoneydale Press, Stevensville, MT, 1987. 169 pp., illus. $18.95.
Solving the whitetail riddle.

Taking More Birds, by Dan Carlisle and Dolph Adams, Lyons & Burford Publishers, New York, NY, 1993. 160 pp., illus. Paper covers. $15.95.
A practical handbook for success at Sporting Clays and wing shooting.

Tales of Quails 'n Such, by Havilah Babcock, University of S. Carolina Press, Columbia, SC, 1985. 237 pp. $19.95.
A group of hunting stories, told in informal style, on field experiences in the South in quest of small game.

Tears and Laughter, by Gene Hill, Countrysport Press, Traverse City, MI, 1996. 176 pp., illus. $25.00.
In twenty-six stories, Gene Hill explores the ancient and honored bond between man and dog.

Tenth Legion, by Tom Kelly, the Lyons Press, New York, NY, 1998. 128 pp., illus. $21.95.
The classic work on that frustrating, yet wonderful sport of turkey hunting.

They Left Their Tracks, by Howard Coperhaver, Stoneydale Press Publishing Co., Stevensville, MT, 1990. 190 pp., illus. $18.95.
Recollections of 60 years as an outfitter in the Bob Marshall Wilderness.

Timberdoodle, by Frank Woolner, Nick Lyons Books, N. Y., NY, 1987. 168 pp., illus. $18.95.
The classic guide to woodcock and woodcock hunting.

Timberdoodle Tales: Adventures of a Minnesota Woodcock Hunter, by T. Waters, Safari Press, Huntington Beach, CA, 1997. 220 pp., illus. $35.00.
The life history and hunt of the American woodcock by the author. A fresh appreciation of this captivating bird and the ethics of its hunt.

To Heck with Moose Hunting, by Jim Zumbo, Wapiti Publishing Co., Cody, WY, 1996. 199 pp., illus. $17.95.
Jim's hunts around the continent and even an African adventure.

Trail and Campfire, edited by George Bird Grinnel and Theodore Roosevelt, The Boone and Crockett Club, Dumfries, VA, 1989. 357 pp., illus. $39.50.
Reprint of the Boone and Crockett Club's 3rd book published in 1897.

Trailing a Bear, by Robert S. Munger, The Munger Foundation, Albion, MI, 1997. 352 pp., illus. Paper covers. $19.95.
An exciting and humorous account of hunting with legendary archer Fred Bear.

The Trickiest Thing in Feathers, by Corey Ford; compiled and edited by Laurie Morrow and illustrated by Christopher Smith, Wilderness Adventures, Gallatin Gateway, MT, 1998. 208 pp., illus. $29.95.
Here is a collection of Corey Ford's best wing-shooting stories, many of them previously unpublished.

Trophy Mule Deer: Finding & Evaluating Your Trophy, by Lance Stapleton, Outdoor Experiences Unlimited, Salem, OR, 1993. 290 pp., illus. Paper covers. $24.95.
The most comprehensive reference book on mule deer.

Turkey Hunter's Digest, Revised Edition, by Dwain Bland, DBI Books, a division of Krause Publications, Iola, WI, 1994. 256 pp., illus. Paper covers. $17.95.
A no-nonsense approach to hunting all five sub-species of the North American wild turkey that make up the Royal Grand Slam.

The Upland Equation: A Modern Bird-Hunter's Code, by Charles Fergus, Lyons & Burford Publishers, New York, NY, 1996. 86 pp. $18.00
A book that deserves space in every sportsman's library. Observations based on firsthand experience.

Upland Tales, by Worth Mathewson (Ed.), Sand Lake Press, Amity, OR, 1996. 271 pp., illus. $29.95.
A collection of articles on grouse, snipe and quail.

A Varmint Hunter's Odyssey, by Steve Hanson with a guest chapter by Mike Johnson, Precision Shooting, Inc. Manchester, CT, 1999. 279 pp., illustrated. Paper covers. $37.95.
A new classic by a writer who eats, drinks and sleeps varmint hunting and varmint rifles.

Varmint and Small Game Rifles and Cartridges, by various authors, Wolfe Publishing Co., Prescott, AZ, 1993. 228 pp., illus. Paper covers. $26.00.
This is a collection of reprints of articles originally appearing in Wolfe's *Rifle* and *Handloader* magazines from 1966 through 1990.

Waterfowler's World, by Bill Buckley, Ducks Unlimited, Inc., Memphis, TN, 1999. 192 pp., illustrated in color. $37.50.
An unprecedented pictorial book on waterfowl and waterfowlers.

Waterfowling Horizons: Shooting Ducks and Geese in the 21st Century, by Chris and Jason Smith, Wilderness Adventures, Gallatin Gateway, MT, 1998. 320 pp., illus. $49.95.
A compendium of the very latest in everything for the duck and goose hunter today.

Waterfowling These Past 50 Years, Especially Brant, by David Hagerbaumer, Sand Lake Press, Amity, OR, 1999. 182 pp., illustrated. $35.00.
This is the compilation of David Hagerbaumer's experiences as a waterfowler since the end of WW2.

Wegner's Bibliography on Dear and Deer Hunting, by Robert Wegner, St. Hubert's Press, Deforest, WI, 1993. 333 pp., 16 full-page illustrations. $45.00.
A comprehensive annotated compilation of books in English pertaining to deer and their hunting 1413-1991.

Western Hunting Guide, by Mike Lapinski, Stoneydale Press Publishing Co., Stevensville, MT, 1989. 168 pp., illus. $18.95.
A complete where-to-go and how-to-do-it guide to Western hunting.

When the Duck Were Plenty, by Ed Muderlak, Safari Press, Inc., Huntington Beach, CA, 2000. 300 pp., illustrated. Limited edition, numbered, signed, slipcased. $49.95.
The golden age of waterfowling and duck hunting from 1840 till 1920. An anthology.

Whispering Wings of Autumn, by Gene Hill and Steve Smith, Wilderness Adventures Press, Bozeman, MT, 1994. 150 pp., illus. $29.00.
Hill and Smith, masters of hunting literature, treat the reader to the best stories of grouse and woodcock hunting.

Whitetail: Behavior Through the Seasons, by Charles J. Alsheimer, Krause Publications, Iola, WI, 1996. 208 pp., illus. $34.95.
In-depth coverage of whitetail behavior presented through striking portraits of the whitetail in every season.

Whitetail: The Ultimate Challenge, by Charles J. Alsheimer, Krause Publications, Iola, WI, 1995. 228 pp., illus. Paper covers. $14.95.
Learn deer hunting's most intriguing secrets—fooling deer using decoys, scents and calls—from America's premier authority.

Whitetails by the Moon, by Charles J. Alsheimer, edited by Patrick Durkin, Krause Publications, Iola, WI, 1999. 208 pp., illustrated. Paper covers. $19.95.
Predict peak times to hunt whitetails. Learn what triggers the rut.

Wildfowler's Season, by Chris Dorsey, Lyons & Burford Publishers, New York, NY, 1998. 224 pp., illus. $37.95.
Modern methods for a classic sport.

Wildfowling Tales, by William C. Hazelton, Wilderness Adventures Press, Belgrade, MT, 1999. 117 pp., illustrated with etchings by Brett Smith. In a slipcase. $50.00.
Tales from the great ducking resorts of the Continent.

Wildfowling Tales 1888-1913, Volume One, edited by Worth Mathewson, Sand Lake Press, Amity, OR, 1998. 186 pp., illustrated by David Hagerbaumer. $22.50.
A collection of some of the best accounts from our literary heritage.

Windward Crossings: A Treasury of Original Waterfowling Tales, by Chuck Petrie et al, Willow Creek Press, Minocqua, WI, 1999. 144 pp., 48 color art and etching reproductions. $35.00.
An illustrated, modern anthology of previously unpublished waterfowl hunting (fiction and creative non fiction) stories by America's finest outdoor journalists.

Wings of Thunder: New Grouse Hunting Revisited, by Steven Mulak, Countrysport Books, Selma, AL, 1998. 168 pp. illustrated. $30.00.
The author examines every aspect of New England grouse hunting as it is today - the bird and its habits, the hunter and his dog, guns and loads, shooting and hunting techniques, practice on clay targets, clothing and equipment.

Wings for the Heart, by Jerry A. Lewis, West River Press, Corvallis, MT, 1991. 324 pp., illus. Paper covers. $14.95.
A delightful book on hunting Montana's upland birds and waterfowl.

Wisconsin Hunting, by Brian Lovett, Krause Publications, Iola, WI, 1997. 208 pp., illus. Paper covers. $16.95.
A comprehensive guide to Wisconsin's public hunting lands.

The Woodchuck Hunter, by Paul C. Estey, R&R Books, Livonia, NY, 1994. 135 pp., illus. $25.00.
This book contains information on woodchuck equipment, the rifle, telescopic sights and includes interesting stories.

Woodcock Shooting, by Steve Smith, Stackpole Books, Inc., Harrisburg, PA, 1988. 142 pp., illus. $16.95.
A definitive book on woodcock hunting and the characteristics of a good woodcock dog.

World Record Whitetails, by Gordon Whittington, Safari Press, Inc., Huntington Beach, CA, 1998. 246 pp. with over 100 photos in color and black-and-white. $32.95.
The first and only complete chronicle of all the bucks that have ever held the title "World record whitetail."

The Working Retrievers, Tom Quinn, The Lyons Press, New York, NY, 1998. 257 pp., illus. $40.00.
The author covers every aspect of the training of dogs for hunting and field trials - from the beginning to the most advanced levels - for Labradors, Chesapeakes, Goldens and others.

World Record Whitetails, by Gordon Whittington, Safari Press Books, Inc., Huntington Beach, CA, 1998. 246 pp., illustrated. $39.95.
The first and only complete chronicle of all the bucks that have ever held the title "World Record Whitetail." Covers the greatest trophies ever recorded in their categories, typical, non-typical, gun, bow, and muzzleloader.

AFRICA/ASIA/ELSEWHERE

A Hunter's Wanderings in Africa, by Frederick Courteney Selous, Wolfe Publishing Co., Prescott, Arizona, 1986. 504 pp., illustrated plus folding map. $29.95.
A reprinting of the 1920 London edition. A narrative of nine years spent amongst the game of the far interior of South Africa.

The Adventurous Life of a Vagabond Hunter, by Sten Cedergren, Safari Press, Inc., Huntington Beach, CA, 2000. 300 pp., illustrated. Limited edition, numbered, signed, and slipcased. $70.00.
An unusual story in the safari business by a remarkable character.

Africa's Greatest Hunter; The Lost Writings of Frederick C. Selous, edited by Dr. james A. Casada, Safari Press, Huntington Beach, CA, 1999. $50.00.
All the stories in this volume relate to the continent that fascinated Selous his entire life. With many previously unpublished photos.

African Adventures, by J.F. Burger, Safari Press, Huntington Beach, CA, 1993. 222 pp., illus. $35.00.
The reader shares adventures on the trail of the lion, the elephant and buffalo.

The African Adventures: A Return to the Silent Places, by Peter Hathaway Capstick, St. Martin's Press, New York, NY, 1992. 220 pp., illus. $22.95.
This book brings to life four turn-of-the-century adventurers and the savage frontier they braved. Frederick Selous, Constatine "Iodine" Ionides, Johnny Boyes and Jim Sutherland.

African Camp-fire Nights, by J.E. Burger, Safari Press, Huntington Beach, CA, 1993. 192 pp., illus. $32.50.
In this book the author writes of the men who made hunting their life's profession.

African Game Trails, by Theodore Roosevelt, Peter Capstick, Series Editor, St. Martin's Press, New York, NY 1988. 583 pp., illus. $24.95.
The famed safari of the noted sportsman, conservationist, and President.

African Hunter, by James Mellon, Safari Press, Huntington Beach, CA, 1996. 522 pp., illus. Paper Covers, $75.00.
Regarded as the most comprehensive title ever published on African hunting.

African Hunting and Adventure, by William Charles Baldwin, Books of Zimbabwe, Bulawayo, 1981. 451 pp., illus. $75.00.
Facsimile reprint of the scarce 1863 London edition. African hunting and adventure from Natal to the Zambezi.

African Jungle Memories, by J.F. Burger, Safari Press, Huntington Beach, CA, 1993. 192 pp., illus. $32.50.
A book of reminiscences in which the reader is taken on many exciting adventures on the trail of the buffalo, lion, elephant and leopard.

African Rifles & Cartridges, by John Taylor, The Gun Room Press, Highland Park, NJ, 1977. 431 pp., illus. $35.00.
Experiences and opinions of a professional ivory hunter in Africa describing his knowledge of numerous arms and cartridges for big game. A reprint.

African Safaris, by Major G.H. Anderson, Safari Press, Long Beach, CA, 1997. 173 pp., illus. $35.00.
A reprinting of one of the rarest books on African hunting, with a foreword by Tony Sanchez.

African Twilight, by Robert F. Jones, Wilderness Adventure Press, Bozeman, MT, 1994. 208 pp., illus. $36.00.
Details the hunt, danger and changing face of Africa over a span of three decades.

A Man Called Lion: The Life and Times of John Howard "Pondoro" Taylor, by P.H. Capstick, Safari Press, Huntington Beach, CA, 1994. 240 pp., illus. $24.95.
With the help of Brian Marsh, an old Taylor acquaintance, Peter Capstick has accumulated over ten years of research into the life of this mysterious man.

An Annotated Bibliography of African Big Game Hunting Books, 1785 to 1950, by Kenneth P. Czech, Land's Edge Press, St. Cloud, MN 2000. $50.00
This bibliography features over 600 big game hunting titles describing the regions the authors hunted, species of game bagged, and physical descriptions of the books (pages, maps, plates, bindings, etc.) It also features a suite of 16 colored plates depicting decorated bindings from some of the books. Limited to 700 numbered, signed copies.

Argali: High-Mountain Hunting, by Ricardo Medem, Safari Press, Huntington Beach, CA, 1995. 304 pp., illus. Limited, signed edition. $150.00.
Medem describes hunting seven different countries in the pursuit of sheep and other mountain game.

Baron in Africa; The Remarkable Adventures of Werner von Alvensleben, by Brian Marsh, Safari Press, Huntington Beach, CA, 2001. 288 pp., illus. $35.00.
Follow his career as he hunts lion, goes after large kudu, kills a full-grown buffalo with a spear, and hunts for elephant and ivory in some of the densest brush in Africa. The adventure and the experience were what counted to this fascinating character, not the money or fame; indeed, in the end he left Mozambique with barely more than the clothes on his back. This is a must-read adventure story on one of the most interesting characters to have come out of Africa after World War II. Foreword by Ian Player.

The Big Five; Hunting Adventures in Today's Africa, by Dr. S. Lloyd Newberry, Safari Press, Huntington Beach, CA, 2001. 214 pp., illus. Limited edition, numbered, signed and slipcased. $70.00.
Many books have been written about the old Africa and its fabled Big Five, but almost nothing exits in print that describes hunting the Big Five as its exists today.

Big Game and Big Game Rifles, by John "Pondoro" Taylor, Safari Press, Huntington Beach, CA, 1999. 215 pp., illus. $24.95.

Covers rifles and calibers for elephant, rhino, hippo, buffalo, and lion.

Big Game Hunting Around the World, by Bert Klineburger and Vernon W. Hurst, Exposition Press, Jericho, NY, 1969. 376 pp., illus. $30.00.

The first book that takes you on a safari all over the world.

Big Game Hunting in North-Eastern Rhodesia, by Owen Letcher, St. Martin's Press, New York, NY, 1986. 272 pp., illus. $24.95.

A classic reprint and one of the very few books to concentrate on this fascinating area, a region that today is still very much safari country.

Big Game Shooting in Cooch Behar, the Duars and Assam, by The Maharajah of Cooch Behar, Wolfe Publishing Co., Prescott, AZ, 1993. 461 pp., illus. $49.50.

A reprinting of the book that has become legendary. This is the Maharajah's personal diary of killing 365 tigers.

Buffalo, Elephant, and Bongo, by Dr. Reinald von Meurers, Safari Press, Huntington Beach, CA, 1999. Limited edition signed and in a slipcase. $75.00.

Alone in the Savannas and Rain Forests of the Cameroon.

Campfire Lies of a Canadian Guide, by Fred Webb, Safari Press, Inc., Huntington Beach, CA, 2000. 250 pp., illustrated. Limited edition, numbered, signed and slip-cased. $50.00.

Forty years in the life of a guide in the North Country.

Cottar: The Exception was the Rule, by Pat Cottar, Trophy Room Books, Agoura, CA, 1999. 350 pp., illustrated. Limited, numbered and signed edition. $135.00

The remarkable big game hunting stories of one of Kenya's most remarkable pioneers.

A Country Boy in Africa, by George Hoffman, Trophy Room Books, Agoura, CA, 1998. 267 pp., illustrated with over 100 photos. Limited, numbered edition signed by the author. $85.00

In addition to the author's long and successful hunting career, he is known for developing a most effective big game cartridge, the .416 Hoffman.

Death and Double Rifles, by Mark Sullivan, Nitro Express Safaris, Phoenix, AZ, 2000. 295 pages, illus. $85.00

Sullivan has captured every thrilling detail of hunting dangerous game in this lavishly illustrated book. Full of color pictures of African hunts & rifles.

Death in a Lonely Land, by Peter Capstick, St. Martin's Press, New York, NY, 1990. 284 pp., illus. $22.95

Twenty-three stories of hunting as only the master can tell them.

Death in the Dark Continent, by Peter Capstick, St. Martin's Press, New York, NY, 1983. 238 pp., illus. $22.95

A book that brings to life the suspense, fear and exhilaration of stalking ferocious killers under primitive, savage conditions, with the ever present threat of death.

Death in the Long Grass, by Peter Hathaway Capstick, St. Martin's Press, New York, NY, 1977. 297 pp., illus. $22.95

A big game hunter's adventures in the African bush.

Death in the Silent Places, by Peter Capstick, St. Martin's Press, New York, NY, 1981. 243 pp., illus. $23.95

The author recalls the extraordinary careers of legendary hunters such as Corbett, Karamojo Bell, Stigand and others.

Duck Hunting in Australia, by Dick Eussen, Australia Outdoor Publishers Pty Ltd., Victoria, Australia, 1994. 106 pp., illus. Paper covers. $17.95

Covers the many aspects of duck hunting from hides to hunting methods.

East Africa and its Big Game, by Captain Sir John C. Willowghby, Wolfe Publishing Co., Prescott, AZ, 1990. 312 pp., illus. $52.00

A deluxe limited edition reprint of the very scarce 1889 edition of a narrative of a sporting trip from Zanzibar to the borders of the Masai.

Elephant Hunting in East Equatorial Africa, by A. Neumann, St. Martin's Press, New York, NY, 1994. 455 pp., illus. $26.95

This is a reprint of one of the rarest elephant hunting titles ever.

Elephants of Africa, by Dr. Anthony Hall-Martin, New Holland Publishers, London, England, 1987. 120 pp., illus. $45.00

A superbly illustrated overview of the African elephant with reproductions of paintings by the internationally acclaimed wildlife artist Paul Bosman.

Encounters with Lions, by Jan Hemsing, Trophy Room books, Agoura, CA, 1995. 302 pp., illus $75.00.

Some stories fierce, fatal, frightening and even humorous of when man and lion meet.

Fourteen Years in the African Bush, by A. Marsh, Safari Press Publication, Huntington Beach, CA, 1998. 312 pp., illus. Limited signed, numbered, slipcased. $70.00

An account of a Kenyan game warden. A graphic and well-written story.

From Sailor to Professional Hunter: The Autobiography of John Northcote, Trophy Room Books, Agoura, CA, 1997. 400 pp., illus. Limited edition, signed and numbered. $125.00

Only a handfull of men can boast of having a fifty-year professional hunting career throughout Africa as John Northcote has had.

Gone are the Days; Jungle Hunting for Tiger and other Game in India and Nepal 1953-1969, by Peter Byrne, Safari Press, Inc., Huntington Beach, CA, 2001. 225 pp., illus. Limited signed, numbered, slipcased. $70.00

Great Hunters: Their Trophy Rooms and Collections, Volume 1, compiled and published by Safari Press, Inc., Huntington Beach, CA, 1997. 172 pp., illustrated in color. $60.00

A rare glimpse into the trophy rooms of top international hunters. A few of these trophy rooms are museums.

Great Hunters: Their Trophy Rooms & Collections, Volume 2, compiled and published by Safari Press, Inc., Huntington Beach, CA, 1998. 224 pp., illustrated with 260 full-color photographs. $60.00

Volume two of the world's finest, best produced series of books on trophy rooms and game collections. 46 sportsmen sharing sights you'll never forget on this guided tour.

Great Hunters: Their Trophy Rooms & Collections, Volume 3, compiled and published by Safari Press, Inc., Huntington Beach, CA, 2000. 204 pp., illustrated with 260 full-color photographs. $60.00

At last, the long-awaited third volume in the best photographic series ever published of trophy room collections is finally available. Unbelievable as it may sound, this book tops all previous volumes. Besides some of the greatest North American trophy rooms ever seen, an extra effort was made to include European collections. Believe it or not, volume 3 includes the Sandringham Castle big-game collection, home of Queen Elizabeth II! Also included is the complete Don Cox African and Asian collection as displayed at his alma mater. This stupendous gallery contains the trophy collections of Prince D' Arenberg, Umberto D'Entreves, George and Edward Keller, Paul Roberts, Joe Bishop, and James Clark to name but a few. Whether it be castles, palaces, mansions, or museums, the finest of the finest in trophy room designs and collection unequaled anywhere will be found in this book. As before, each trophy room is accompanied by an informative text explaining the collection and giving you insights into the hunters who went to such great efforts to create their trophy rooms. All professionally photographed in the highest quality possible.

Heart of an African Hunter, by Peter F. Flack, Safari Press, Inc., Huntington Beach, CA, 1999. Limited, numbered, slipcased edition. $70.00

Stories on the Big Five and Tiny Ten.

Horned Death, by John F. Burger, Safari Press, Huntington Beach, CA, 1992. 343 pp.illus. $35.00

The classic work on hunting the African buffalo.

Horn of the Hunter, by Robert Ruark, Safari Press, Long Beach, CA, 1987. 315 pp., illus. $35.00

Ruark's most sought-after title on African hunting, here in reprint.

Horned Giants, by Capt. John Brandt, Safari Press, Inc., Huntington Beach, CA, 1999. 288 pp., illustrated. Limited edition, numbered, signed and slipcased. $80.00

Hunting Eurasian wild cattle.

Hunter, by J.A. Hunter, Safari Press Publications, Huntington Beach, CA, 1999. 263 pp., illus. $24.95

Hunter's best known book on African big-game hunting. Internationally recognized as being one of the all-time African hunting classics.

A Hunter's Africa, by Gordon Cundill, Trophy Room Books, Agoura, CA, 1998. 298 pp., over 125 photographic illustrations. Limited numbered edition signed by the author. $125.00

A good look by the author at the African safari experience - elephant, lion, spiral-horned antelope, firearms, people and events, as well as the clients that make it worthwhile.

A Hunter's Wanderings in Africa, by Frederick Courteney Selous, Wolfe Publishing Co., Prescott, Arizona, 1986. 504 pp., illustrated plus folding map. $29.95

A reprinting of the 1920 London edition. A narrative of nine years spent amongst the game of the far interior of South Africa.

Hunter's Tracks, by J.A. Hunter, Safari Press Publications, Huntington Beach, CA, 1999. 240 pp., illustrated. $24.95

This is the exciting story of John Hunter's efforts to capture the shady headman of a gang of ivory poachers and smugglers. The story is interwoven with the tale of one of East Africa's most grandiose safaris taken with an Indian maharaja.

Hunting Adventures Worldwide, by Jack Atcheson, Jack Atcheson & Sons, Butte, MT, 1995. 256 pp., illus. $29.95

The author chronicles the richest adventures of a lifetime spent in quest of big game across the world – including Africa, North America and Asia.

Hunting in Ethiopia, An Anthology, by Tony Sanchez-Arino, Safari Press, Huntington Beach, CA, 1996. 350 pp., illus. Limited, signed and numbered edition. $135.00

The finest selection of hunting stories ever compiled on hunting in this great game country.

The Hunting Instinct, by Phillip D. Rowter, Safari Press, Inc., Huntington Beach, CA, 1999. Limited edition signed and numbered and in a slipcase. $50.00

Safari chronicles from the Republic of South Africa and Namibia 1990-1998.

Hunting in Kenya, by Tony Sanchez-Arino, Safari Press, Inc., Huntington Beach, CA, 2000. 350 pp., illustrated. Limited, signed and numbered edition in a slipcase. $135.00

The finest selection of hunting stories ever compiled on hunting in this great game country make up this anthology.

Hunting in Many Lands, by Theodore Roosevelt and George Bird Grinnel, The Boone and Crockett Club, Dumfries, VA, 1987. 447 pp., illus. $40.00

Limited edition reprint of this 1895 classic work on hunting in Africa, India, Mongolia, etc.

Hunting in the Sudan, An Anthology, compiled by Tony Sanchez-Arino, Safari Press, Huntington Beach, CA, 1992. 350 pp., illus. Limited, signed and numbered edition in a slipcase. $125.00

The finest selection of hunting stories ever compiled on hunting in this great game country.

Hunting, Settling and Remembering, by Philip H. Percival, Trophy Room Books, Agoura, CA, 1997. 230 pp., illus. Limited, numbered and signed edition. $85.00

If Philip Percival is to come alive again, it will be through this, the first edition of his easy, intricate and magical book illustrated with some of the best historical big game hunting photos ever taken.

THE ARMS LIBRARY

Hunting the Dangerous Game of Africa, by John Kingsley-Heath, Sycamore Island Books, Boulder, CO, 1998. 477 pp., illustrated. $95.00

Written by one of the most respected, successful, and ethical P.H.'s to trek the sunlit plains of Botswana, Kenya, Uganda, Tanganyika, Somaliland, Eritrea, Ethiopia, and Mozambique. Filled with some of the most gripping and terrifying tales ever to come out of Africa.

In the Salt, by Lou Hallamore, Trophy Room Books, Agoura, CA, 1999. 227 pp., illustrated in black & white and full color. Limited, numbered and signed edition. $125.00

A book about people, animals and the big game hunt, about being outwitted and out maneuvered. It is about knowing that sooner or later your luck will change and your trophy will be "in the salt."

International Hunter 1945-1999, Hunting's Greatest Era, by Bert klineburger, Sportsmen on Film, Kerrville, TX, 1999. 400 pp., illustrated. A limited, numbered and signed edition. $125.00

The most important book of the greatest hunting era by the world's preeminent International hunter.

Jaguar Hunting in the Mato Grosso and Bolivia, by T. Almedia, Safari Press, Long Beach, CA, 1989. 256 pp., illus. $35.00

Not since Sacha Siemel has there been a book on jaguar hunting like this one.

Jim Corbett, Master of the Jungle, by Tim Werling, Safari Press, Huntington Beach, CA, 1998. 215 pp., illus. $30.00

A biography of India's most famous hunter of man-eating tigers and leopards.

King of the Wa-Kikuyu, by John Boyes, St. Martin Press, New York, NY, 1993. 240 pp., illus. $19.95

In the 19th and 20th centuries, Africa drew to it a large number of great hunters, explorers, adventurers and rogues. Many have become legendary, but John Boyes (1874-1951) was the most legendary of them all.

Last Horizons: Hunting, Fishing and Shooting on Five Continents, by Peter Capstick, St. Martin's Press, New York, NY, 1989. 288 pp., illus. $19.95

The first in a two volume collection of hunting, fishing and shooting tales from the selected pages of The American Hunter, Guns & Ammo and Outdoor Life.

Last of the Few: Forty-Two Years of African Hunting, by Tony Sanchez-Arino, Safari Press, Huntington Beach, CA, 1996. 250 pp., illus. $39.95

The story of the author's career with all the highlights that come from pursuing the unusual and dangerous animals that are native to Africa.

Last of the Ivory Hunters, by John Taylor, Safari Press, Long Beach, CA, 1990. 354 pp., illus. $29.95

Reprint of the classic book "Pondoro" by one of the most famous elephant hunters of all time.

Legends of the Field: More Early Hunters in Africa, by W.R. Foran, Trophy Room Press, Agoura, CA, 1997. 319 pp., illus. Limited edition. $100.00

This book contains the biographies of some very famous hunters: William Cotton Oswell, F.C. Selous, Sir Samuel Baker, Arthur Neumann, Jim Sutherland, W.D.M. Bell and others.

The Lost Classics, by Robert Ruark, Safari Press, Huntington Beach, CA, 1996. 260 pp., illus. $35.00

The magazine stories that Ruark wrote in the 1950s and 1960s finally in print in book form.

The Lost Wilderness; True Accounts of Hunters and Animals in East Africa, by Mohamed Ismail & Alice Pianfetti, Safari Press, Inc., Huntington Beach, CA, 2000. 216 pp., photos, illustrated. Limited edition signed and numbered and slipcased. $60.00

The Magic of Big Games, by Terry Wieland, Countrysport Books, Selma, AL, 1998. 200 pp., illus. $39.00

Original essays on hunting big game around the world.

Mahonhboh, by Ron Thomson, Hartbeesport, South Africa, 1997. 312 pp., illustrated. Limited signed and numbered edition. $50.00

Elephants and elephant hunting in South Central Africa.

The Man-Eaters of Tsavo, by Lt. Colonel J.H. Patterson, Peter Capstick, series editor, St. Martin's Press, New York, NY, 1986, 5th printing. 346 pp., illus. $22.95

The classic man-eating story of the lions that halted construction of a railway line and reportedly killed one hundred people, told by the man who risked his life to successfully shoot them.

McElroy Hunts Asia, by C.J. McElroy, Safari Press, Inc., Huntington Beach, CA, 1989. 272 pp., illustrated. $50.00

From the founder of SCI comes a book on hunting the great continent of Asia for big game: tiger, bear, sheep and ibex. Includes the story of the all-time record Altai Argali as well as several markhor hunts in Pakistan.

Memoirs of an African Hunter, by Terry Irwin, Safari Press Publications, Huntington Beach, CA, 1998. 421 pp., illustrated. Limited numbered, signed and slipcased. $125.00

A narrative of a professional hunter's experiences in Africa.

Memoirs of a Sheep Hunter, by Rashid Jamsheed, Safari Press, Inc., Huntington Beach, CA, 1996. 330 pp., illustrated. $70.00

The author reveals his exciting accounts of obtaining world-record heads from his native Iran, and his eventual move to the U.S. where he procured a grand-slam of North American sheep.

Months of the Sun; Forty Years of Elephant Hunting in the Zambezi Valley, by Ian Nyschens, Safari Press, Huntington Beach, CA, 1998. 420 pp., illus. $60.00

The author has shot equally as many elephants as Walter Bell, and under much more difficult circumstances. His book will rank, or surpass, the best elephant-ivory hunting books published this century.

Mundjamba: The Life Story of an African Hunter, by Hugo Seia, Trophy Room Books, Agoura, CA, 1996. 400 pp., illus. Limited, numbered and signed by the author. $125.00

An autobiography of one of the most respected and appreciated professional African hunters.

My Last Kambaku, by Leo Kroger, Safari Press, Huntington Beach, CA, 1997. 272 pp., illus. Limited edition signed and numbered and slipcased. $60.00

One of the most engaging hunting memoirs ever published.

The Nature of the Game, by Ben Hoskyns, Quiller Press, Ltd., London, England, 1994. 160 pp., illus. $37.50

The first complete guide to British, European and North American game.

On Target, by Christian Le Noel, Trophy Room Books, Agoura, CA, 1999. 275 pp., illustrated. Limited, numbered and signed edition. $85.00

History and hunting in Central Africa.

One Long Safari, by Peter Hay, Trophy Room Books, Agoura, CA, 1998. 350 pp., with over 200 photographic illustrations and 7 maps. Limited numbered edition signed by the author. $100.00

Contains hunts for leopards, sitatunga, hippo, rhino, snakes and, of course, the general African big game bag.

Optics for the Hunter, by John Barsness, Safari Press, Inc., Huntington Beach, CA, 1999. 236 pp., illustrated. $24.95

An evaluation of binoculars, scopes, range finders, spotting scopes for use in the field.

Out in the Midday Shade, by William York, Safari Press, Inc., Huntington Beach, CA, 1999. Limited, signed and numbered edition in a slipcase. $70.00

Memoirs of an African Hunter 1949-1968.

The Path of a Hunter, by Gilles Tre-Hardy, Trophy Room Books, Agoura, CA, 1997. 318 pp., illus. Limited Edition, signed and numbered. $85.00

A most unusual hunting autobiography with much about elephant hunting in Africa.

The Perfect Shot; Shot Placement for African Big Game, by Kevin "Doctari" Robertson, Safari Press, Inc., Huntington Beach, CA, 1999. 230 pp., illustrated. $65.00

The most comprehensive work ever undertaken to show the anatomical features for all classes of African game. Includes caliber and bullet selection, rifle selection, trophy handling.

Peter Capstick's Africa: A Return to the Long Grass, by Peter Hathaway Capstick, St. Martin's Press, N. Y., NY, 1987. 213 pp., illus. $35.00

A first-person adventure in which the author returns to the long grass for his own dangerous and very personal excursion.

Pondoro, by John Taylor, Safari Press, Inc., Huntington Beach, CA, 1999. 354 pp., illustrated. $29.95

The author is considered one of the best storytellers in the hunting book world, and Pondoro is highly entertaining. A classic African big-game hunting title.

The Quotable Hunter, by Jay Cassell and Peter Fiduccia, The Lyons Press, N.Y., 1999. 288 pp., illustrated. $20.00

This collection of more than three hundred quotes from hunters through the ages captures the essence of the sport, with all its joys, idosyncrasies, and challenges.

The Recollections of an Elephant Hunter 1864-1875, by William Finaughty, Books of Zimbabwe, Bulawayo, Zimbabwe, 1980. 244 pp., illus. $85.00

Reprint of the scarce 1916 privately published edition. The early game hunting exploits of William Finaughty in Matabeleland and Nashonaland.

Records of Big Game, XXV (25th) Edition, Rowland Ward, distributed by Safari Press, Inc., Huntington Beach, CA, 1999. 1,000 pp., illustrated. Limited edition. $150.00

Covers big game records of Africa, Asia, Europe, and the America's.

Robert Ruark's Africa, by Robert Ruark, edited by Michael McIntosh, Countrysport Press, Selma, AL, 1999. 256 pp illustrated with 19 original etchings by Bruce Langton. $32.00

These previously uncollected works of Robert Ruark make this a classic big-game hunting book.

Safari: A Chronicle of Adventure, by Bartle Bull, Viking/Penguin, London, England, 1989. 383 pp., illus. $40.00

The thrilling history of the African safari, highlighting some of Africa's best-known personalities.

Safari: A Dangerous Affair, by Walt Prothero, Safari Press, Huntington Beach, CA, 2000. 275 pp., illustrated. Limited edition, numbered, signed and slipcased. $60.00

True accounts of hunters and animals of Africa.

Safari Rifles: Double, Magazine Rifles and Cartridges for African Hunting, by Craig Boddington, Safari Press, Huntington Beach, CA, 1990. 416 pp., illus. $37.50

A wealth of knowledge on the safari rifle. Historical and present double-rifle makers, ballistics for the large bores, and much, much more.

Safari: The Last Adventure, by Peter Capstick, St. Martin's Press, New York, NY, 1984. 291 pp., illus. $22.95

A modern comprehensive guide to the African Safari.

Safari Guide - A Guide To Planning Your Hunting Safari, by Richard Conrad, Safari Press, Huntington Beach, CA, 314pp, photos, illustrated. $29.95

Dozens of books have been published in the last decade on tales of African hunting. But few, if any, give a comprehensive country-by-country and animal-by-animal comparison or a guide on how to plan your (first) safari.

Sands of Silence, by Peter H. Capstick, Saint Martin's Press, New York, NY, 1991. 224 pp., illus. $35.00

Join the author on safari in Nambia for his latest big-game hunting adventures.

Shoot Straight And Stay Alive: A Lifetime of Hunting Experiences, by Fred Bartlett, Safari Press, Huntington Beach, CA, 2000. 256 pp., illus. $35.00

Bartlett grew up on a remote farm in Kenya where he started hunting at an early age. After serving in WWII, he returned to Kenya to farm. After a few years, he decided to join the Kenya Game Department as a game control officer, which required him to shoot buffalo and elephant at very close range. He had a fine reputation as a buffalo hunter and was considered to be one of the quickest shots with a double rifle.

Solo Safari, by T. Cacek, Safari Press, Huntington Beach, CA, 1995. 270 pp., illus. $30.00

Here is the story of Terry Cacek who hunted elephant, buffalo, leopard and plains game in Zimbabwe and Botswana on his own.

Spiral-Horn Dreams, by Terry Wieland, Trophy Room Books, Agoura, CA, 1996. 362 pp., illus. Limited, numbered and signed by the author. $85.00

Everyone who goes to hunt in Africa is looking for something; this is for those who go to hunt the spiral-horned antelope—the bongo, myala, mountain nyala, greater and lesser kudu, etc.

Sport Hunting on Six Continents, by Ken Wilson, Sportsmen of Film, Kerrville, TX, 1999. 300 pp., illustrated. $69.95

Hunting around the world....from Alaska to Australia...from the Americas, to Africa, Asia, and Europe.

Tales of the African Frontier, by J.A. Hunter, Safari Press Publications, Huntington Beach, CA, 1999. 308 pp., illus. $24.95

The early days of East Africa is the subject of this powerful John Hunter book.

Trophy Hunter in Africa, by Elgin Gates, Safari Press, Huntington Beach, CA, 1994. 315 pp., illus. $40.00

This is the story of one man's adventure in Africa's wildlife paradise.

Uganda Safaris, by Brian Herne, Winchester Press, Piscataway, NJ, 1979. 236 pp., illus. $24.95

The chronicle of a professional hunter's adventures in Africa.

Under the African Sun, by Dr. Frank Hibben, Safari Press, Inc., Huntington Beach, CA, 1999. Limited edition signed, numbered and in a slipcase. $85.00

Forty-eight years of hunting the African continent.

Under the Shadow of Man Eaters, by Jerry Jaleel, The Jim Corbett Foundation, Edmonton, Alberta, Canada, 1997. 152 pp., illus. A limited, numbered and signed edition. Paper covers. $35.00

The life and legend of Jim Corbett of Kumaon.

Use Enough Gun, by Robert Ruark, Safari Press, Huntington Beach, CA, 1997. 333 pp., illus. $35.00

Robert Ruark on big game hunting.

Warrior: The Legend of Col. Richard Meinertzhagen, by Peter H. Capstick, St. Martins Press, New York, NY, 1998. 320 pp., illus. $23.95

A stirring and vivid biography of the famous British colonial officer Richard Meinertzhagen, whose exploits earned him fame and notoriety as one of the most daring and ruthless men to serve during the glory days of the British Empire.

The Waterfowler's World, by Bill Buckley, Willow Creek Press, Minocqua, WI, 1999. 176 pp., 225 color photographs. $37.50

Waterfowl hunting from Canadian prairies, across the U.S. heartland, to the wilds of Mexico, from the Atlantic to the Pacific coasts and the Gulf of Mexico.

Where Lions Roar: Ten More Years of African Hunting, by Craig Boddington, Safari Press, Huntington Beach, CA, 1997. 250 pp $35.00

The story of Boddington's hunts in the Dark Continent during the last ten years.

White Hunter, by J.A. Hunter, Safari Press Publications, Huntington Beach, CA, 1999. 282 pp., illustrated. $24.95

This book is a seldom-seen account of John Hunter's adventures in pre-WW2 Africa.

A White Hunters Life, by Angus MacLagan, an African Heritage Book, published by Amwell Press, Clinton, NJ, 1983. 283 pp., illus. Limited, signed, and numbered deluxe edition, in slipcase. $100.00

True to life, a sometimes harsh yet intriguing story.

Wild Sports of Southern Africa, by William Cornwallis Harris, New Holland Press, London, England, 1987. 376 pp., illus. $36.00

Originally published in 1863, describes the author's travels in Southern Africa.

Wind, Dust and Snow, by Robert M. Anderson, Safari Press, Inc., Huntington Beach, CA, 1997. 240 pp., illustrated. $65.00

A complete chronology of modern exploratory and pioneering Asian sheep-hunting expeditions from 1960 until 1996, with wonderful background history and previously untold stories.

With a Gun in Good Country, by Ian Manning, Trophy Room Books, Agoura, CA, 1996. Limited, numbered and signed by the author. $85.00

A book written about that splendid period before the poaching onslaught which almost closed Zambia and continues to the granting of her independence. It then goes on to recount Manning's experiences in Botswana, Congo, and briefly in South Africa.

RIFLES

The Accurate Rifle, by Warren Page, Claymore Publishing, Ohio, 1997. 254 pages, illustrated. Revised edition. Paper Covers. $17.95

Provides hunters & shooter alike with detailed practical information on the whole range of subjects affecting rifle accuracy, he explains techniques in ammo, sights & shooting methods. With a 1996 equipment update from Dave Brennan.

The Accurate Varmint Rifle, by Boyd Mace, Precision Shooting, Inc., Whitehall, NY, 1991. 184 pp., illus. $15.00

A long overdue and long needed work on what factors go into the selection of components for and the subsequent assembly of...the accurate varmint rifle.

The AK-47 Assault Rifle, Desert Publications, Cornville, AZ, 1981. 150 pp., illus. Paper covers. $13.95

Complete and practical technical information on the only weapon in history to be produced in an estimated 30,000,000 units.

American Hunting Rifles: Their Application in the Field for Practical Shooting, by Craig Boddington, Safari Press, Huntington Beach, CA, 1996. 446 pp., illus. First edition, limited, signed and slipcased. $85.00. Second printing trade edition. $35.00

Covers all the hunting rifles and calibers that are needed for North America's diverse game.

The AR-15/M16, A Practical Guide, by Duncan Long. Paladin Press, Boulder, CO, 1985. 168 pp., illus. Paper covers. $22.00

The definitive book on the rifle that has been the inspiration for so many modern assault rifles.

The Art of Shooting With the Rifle, by Col. Sir H. St. John Halford, Excalibur Publications, Latham, NY, 1996. 96 pp., illus. Paper covers. $12.95

A facsimile edition of the 1888 book by a respected rifleman providing a wealth of detailed information.

The Art of the Rifle, by Jeff Cooper, Paladin Press, Boulder, CO, 1997. 104 pp., illus. $29.95

Everything you need to know about the rifle whether you use it for security, meat or target shooting.

Australian Military Rifles & Bayonets, 200 Years of, by Ian Skennerton, I.D.S.A. Books, Piqua, OH, 1988. 124 pp., 198 illus. Paper covers. $19.50

Australian Service Machine Guns, 100 Years of, by Ian Skennerton, I.D.S.A. Books, Piqua, OH, 1989. 122 pp., 150 illus. Paper covers. $19.50

The Big Game Rifle, by Jack O'Connor, Safari Press, Huntington Beach, CA, 1994. 370 pp., illus. $37.50

An outstanding description of every detail of construction, purpose and use of the big game rifle.

Big Game Rifles and Cartridges, by Elmer Keith, reprint edition by The Gun Room Press, Highland Park, NJ, 1984. 161 pp., illus. $17.95

Reprint of Elmer Keith's first book, a most original and accurate work on big game rifles and cartridges.

Black Magic: The Ultra Accurate AR-15, by John Feamster, Precision Shooting, Manchester, CT, 1998. 300 pp., illustrated. $29.95

The author has compiled his experiences pushing the accuracy envelope of the AR-15 to its maximum potential. A wealth of advice on AR-15 loads, modifications and accessories for everything from NRA Highpower and Service Rifle competitions to benchrest and varmint shooting.

The Black Rifle, M16 Retrospective, R. Blake Stevens and Edward C. Ezell, Collector Grade Publications, Toronto, Canada, 1987. 400 pp., illus. $59.95

The complete story of the M16 rifle and its development.

Bolt Action Rifles, 3rd Edition, by Frank de Haas, DBI Books, a division of Krause Publications, Iola, WI, 1995. 528 pp., illus. Paper covers. $24.95

A revised edition of the most definitive work on all major bolt-action rifle designs.

The Book of the Garand, by Maj. Gen. J.S. Hatcher, The Gun Room Press, Highland Park, NJ, 1977. 292 pp., illus. $26.95

A new printing of the standard reference work on the U.S. Army M1 rifle.

The Book of the Twenty-Two: The All American Caliber, by Sam Fadala, Stoeger Publishing Co., So. Hackensack, NJ, 1989. 288 pp., illus. Soft covers. $16.95

The All American Caliber from BB caps up to the powerful 226 Barnes. It's about ammo history, plinking, target shooting, and the quest for the one-hole group.

British Military Martini, Treatise on the, Vol. 1, by B.A. Temple and Ian Skennerton, I.D.S.A. Books, Piqua, OH, 1983. 256 pp., 114 illus. $40.00

British Military Martini, Treatise on the, Vol. 2, by B.A. Temple and Ian Skennerton, I.D.S.A. Books, Piqua, OH, 1989. 213 pp., 135 illus. $40.00

British .22RF Training Rifles, by Dennis Lewis and Robert Washburn, Excalibur Publications, Latham, NY, 1993. 64 pp., illus. Paper covers. $10.95

The story of Britain's training rifles from the early Aiming Tube models to the post-WWII trainers.

Classic Sporting Rifles, by Christopher Austyn, Safari Press, Huntington Beach, CA, 1997. 128 pp., illus. $50.00

As the head of the gun department at Christie's Auction House the author examines the "best" rifles built over the last 150 years.

The Complete AR15/M16 Sourcebook, by Duncan Long, Paladin Press, Boulder, CO, 1993. 232 pp., illus. Paper covers. $35.00

The latest development of the AR15/M16 and the many spin-offs now available, selective-fire conversion systems for the 1990s, the vast selection of new accessories.

The Competitive AR15: The Mouse That Roared, by Glenn Zediker, Zediker Publishing, Oxford, MS, 1999. 286 pp., illustrated. Paper covers. $29.95

A thorough and detailed study of the newest precision rifle sensation.

Complete Book of U.S. Sniping, by Peter R. Senich, Paladin Press, Boulder, CO, 1997, 8 1/2 x 11, hardcover, photos, 288 pp. $52.95

Trace American sniping materiel from its infancy to today's sophisticated systems with this volume, compiled from Senich's early books, Limited War Sniping and The Pictorial History of U.S. Sniping. Almost 400 photos, plus information gleaned from official documents and military archives, pack this informative work.

Complete Guide To The M1 Garand and The M1 Carbine, by Bruce Canfield, Andrew Mowbray, Inc., Lincoln, RI, 1999. 296 pp., illustrated. $39.50

Covers all of the manufacturers of components, parts, variations and markings. Learn which parts are proper for which guns. The total story behind these guns, from their invention through WWII, Korea, Vietnam and beyond! 300+ photos show you features, markings, overall views and action shots. Thirty-three tables and charts give instant reference to serial numbers, markings, dates of issue and proper configurations. Special sections on Sniper guns, National Match Rifles, exotic variations, and more!

The Complete M1 Garand, by Jim Thompson, Paladin Press, Boulder, CO, 1998. 160 pp., illustrated. Paper cover. $25.00
A guide for the shooter and collector, heavily illustrated.

Exploded Long Gun Drawings, The Gun Digest Book of, edited by Harold A. Murtz, DBI Books, a division of Krause Publications, Iola, WI, 512 pp., illus. Paper covers. $20.95
Containing almost 500 rifle and shotgun exploded drawings. An invaluable aid to both professionals and hobbyists.

The FAL Rifle, by R. Blake Stevens and Jean van Rutten, Collector Grade Publications, Cobourg, Canada, 1993. 848 pp., illus. $129.95
Originally published in three volumes, this classic edition covers North American, UK and Commonwealth and the metric FAL's.

The Fighting Rifle, by Chuck Taylor, Paladin Press, Boulder, CO, 1983. 184 pp., illus. Paper covers. $25.00
The difference between assault and battle rifles and auto and light machine guns.

Firearms Assembly/Disassembly Part III: Rimfire Rifles, Revised Edition, The Gun Digest Book of, by J. B. Wood, DBI Books, a division of Krause Publications, Iola, WI., 1994. 480 pp., illus. Paper covers. $19.95
Covers 65 popular rimfires plus over 100 variants, all cross-referenced in the index.

Firearms Assembly/Disassembly Part IV: Centerfire Rifles, Revised Edition, The Gun Digest Book of, by J.B. Wood, DBI Books, a division of Krause Publications, Iola, WI, 1991. 480 pp., illus. Paper covers. $19.95
Covers 54 popular centerfire rifles plus 300 variants. The most comprehensive and professional presentation available to either hobbyist or gunsmith.

The FN-FAL Rifle, et al, by Duncan Long, Delta Press, El Dorado, AR, 1998. 148 pp., illustrated. Paper covers. $18.95
A comprehensive study of one of the classic assault weapons of all times. Detailed descriptions of the basic models plus the myriad of variants that evolved as a result of its universal acceptance.

Forty Years with the .45-70, second edition, revised and expanded, by Paul A. Matthews, Wolfe Publishing Co., Prescott, AZ, 1997. 184 pp., illus. Paper covers. $14.95
This book is pure gun lore-lore of the .45-70. It not only contains a history of the cartridge, but also years of the author's personal experiences.

F.N.-F.A.L. Auto Rifles, Desert Publications, Cornville, AZ, 1981. 130 pp., illus. Paper covers. $16.95
A definitive study of one of the free world's finest combat rifles.

German Sniper 1914-1945, by Peter R. Senich, Paladin Press, Boulder, CO, 1997 8 1/2 x 11, hardcover, photos, 468 pp. $69.95
The complete story of Germany's sniping arms development through both World Wars. Presents more than 600 photos of Mauser 98's, Selbstladegewehr 41s and 43s, optical sights by Goerz, Zeiss, etc., plus German snipers in action. An exceptional hardcover collector's edition for serious military historians everywhere.

Hints and Advice on Rifle-Shooting, by Private R. McVittie with new introductory material by W.S. Curtis, W.S. Curtis Publishers, Ltd., Clwyd, England, 1993. 32 pp. Paper covers. $10.00
A reprint of the original 1886 London edition.

How-To's for the Black Powder Cartridge Rifle Shooter, by Paul A. Matthews, Wolfe Publishing Co., Prescott, AZ, 1996. 136 pp., illus. Paper covers. $22.50
Practices and procedures used in the reloading and shooting of blackpowder cartridges.

Hunting with the .22, by C.S. Landis, R&R Books, Livonia, NY, 1995. 429 pp., illus. $35.00
A reprinting of the classical work on .22 rifles.

The Hunting Rifle, by Townsend Whelen, Wolfe Publishing Co., Prescott, Arizona, 1984. 463 pp., illustrated. $24.95
A thoroughly dependable coverage on the materiel and marksmanhip with relation to the sportsman's rifle for big game.

Illustrated Handbook of Rifle Shooting, by A.L. Russell, Museum Restoration Service, Alexandria Bay, NY, 1992. 194 pp., illus. $24.50
A new printing of the 1869 edition by one of the leading military marksman of the day.

Know Your M1 Garand, by E. J. Hoffschmidt, Blacksmith Corp., Southport, CT, 1975, 84 pp., illus. Paper covers. $15.95
Facts about America's most famous infantry weapon. Covers test and experimental models, Japanese and Italian copies, National Match models.

Know Your Ruger 10/22 Carbine, by William E. Workman, Blacksmith Corp., Chino Valley, AZ, 1991. 96 pp., illus. Paper covers. $12.95
The story and facts about the most popular 22 autoloader ever made.

The Lee Enfield No. 1 Rifles, by Alan M. Petrillo, Excaliber Publications, Latham, NY, 1992. 64 pp., illus. Paper covers. $10.95
Highlights the SMLE rifles from the Mark 1-VI.

The Lee Enfield Number 4 Rifles, by Alan M. Petrillo, Excalibur Publications, Latham, NY, 1992. 64 pp., illus. Paper covers. $10.95
A pocket-sized, bare-bones reference devoted entirely to the .303 World War II and Korean War vintage service rifle.

Legendary Sporting Rifles, by Sam Fadala, Stoeger Publishing Co., So. Hackensack, NJ, 1992. 288 pp., illus. Paper covers. $16.95
Covers a vast span of time and technology beginning with the Kentucky Long-rifle.

The Li'l M1 .30 Cal. Carbine, by Duncan Long, Desert Publications, El Dorado, AZ, 1995. 203 pp., illus. Paper covers. $14.95
Traces the history of this little giant from its original creation.

Make It Accurate: Get the Maximum Performance from Your Hunting Rifle, by Craig Boddington, Safari Press Publications, Huntington Beach, CA, 1999. 224 pp., illustrated. $24.95
Tips on how to select the rifle, cartridge, and scope best suited to your needs. A must-have for any hunter who wants to improve his shot.

Mauser Smallbore Sporting, Target and Training Rifles, by Jon Speed, Collector Grade Publications, Inc., Cobourg, Ont., Canada, 1998. 372 pp., illustrated. $67.50
The history of all the smallbore sporting, target and training rifles produced by the legendary Mauser-Werke of Obendorf am Neckar.

Mauser: Original-Oberndorf Sporting Rifles, by Jon Speed, Collector Grade Publications, Inc., Cobourg, Ont., Canada, 1997. 508 pp., illustrated. $89.95
The most exhaustive study ever published of the design origins and manufacturing history of the original Oberndorf Mauser Sporter.

M14/M14A1 Rifles and Rifle Markmanship, Desert Publications, El Dorado, AZ, 1995. 236 pp., illus. Paper covers. $18.95
Contains a detailed description of the M14 and M14A1 rifles and their general characteristics, procedures for disassembly and assembly, operating and functioning of the rifles, etc.

The M14 Owner's Guide and Match Conditioning Instructions, by Scott A. Duff and John M. Miller, Scott A. Duff Publications, Export, PA, 1996. 180 pp., illus. Paper covers. $19.95
Traces the history and development from the T44 through the adoption and production of the M14 rifle.

The M-14 Rifle, facsimile reprint of FM 23-8, Desert Publications, Cornville, AZ, 50 pp., illus. Paper $11.95
Well illustrated and informative reprint covering the M-14 and M-14E2.

The M14-Type Rifle: A Shooter's and Collector's Guide, by Joe Poyer, North Cape Publications, Tustin, CA, 1997. 82 pp., illus. Paper covers. $18.95
Covers the history and development, commercial copies, cleaning and maintenance instructions, and targeting and shooting.

The M16/AR15 Rifle, by Joe Poyer, North Cape Publications, Tustin, CA, 1998. 150 pp., illustrated. Paper covers. $19.95
From its inception as the first American assault battle rifle to the firing lines of the National Matches, the M16/AR15 rifle in all its various models and guises has made a significant impact on the American rifleman.

Military Bolt Action Rifles, 1841-1918, by Donald B. Webster, Museum Restoration Service, Alexander Bay, NY, 1993. 150 pp., illus. $34.50
A photographic survey of the principal rifles and carbines of the European and Asiatic powers of the last half of the 19th century and the first years of the 20th century.

The Mini-14, by Duncan Long, Paladin Press, Boulder, CO, 1987. 120 pp., illus. Paper covers. $17.00
History of the Mini-14, the factory-produced models, specifications, accessories, suppliers, and much more.

Mr. Single Shot's Book of Rifle Plans, by Frank de Haas, Mark de Haas, Orange City, IA, 1996. 85 pp., illus. Paper covers. $22.50
Contains complete and detailed drawings, plans and instructions on how to build four different and unique breech-loading single shot rifles of the author's own proven design.

M1 Carbine Owner's Manual, M1, M2 & M3 .30 Caliber Carbines, Firepower Publications, Cornville, AZ, 1984. 102 pp., illus. Paper covers. $16.95
The complete book for the owner of an M1 Carbine.

The M1 Garand Serial Numbers & Data Sheets, by Scott A. Duff, Scott A. Duff, Export, PA, 1995. 101 pp. Paper covers. $11.95
This pocket reference book includes serial number tables and data sheets on the Springfield Armory, Gas Trap Rifles, Gas Port Rifles, Winchester Repeating Arms, International Harvester and H&R Arms Co. and more.

The M1 Garand: Post World War, by Scott A. Duff, Scott A. Duff, Export, PA, 1990. 139 pp., illus. Soft covers. $19.95
A detailed account of the activities at Springfield Armory through this period. International Harvester, H&R, Korean War production and quantities delivered. Serial numbers.

The M1 Garand: World War 2, by Scott A. Duff, Scott A. Duff, Export, PA, 1993. 210 pp., illus. Paper covers. $39.95
The most comprehensive study available to the collector and historian on the M1 Garand of World War II.

Modern Sniper Rifles, by Duncan Long, Paladin Press, Boulder, CO, 1997, 8 1/2 x 11, soft cover, photos, illus., 120 pp. $20.00
Noted weapons expert Duncan Long describes the .22 LR, single-shot, bolt-action, semiautomatic and large-caliber rifles that can be used for sniping purposes, including the U.S. M21, Ruger Mini-14, AUG and HK-94SG1. These and other models are evaluated on the basis of their features, accuracy, reliability and handiness in the field. The author also looks at the best scopes, ammunition and accessories.

More Single Shot Rifles and Actions, by Frank de Haas, Mark de Haas, Orange City, IA, 1996. 146 pp., illus. Paper covers. $22.50
Covers 45 different single shot rifles. Includes the history plus photos, drawings and personal comments.

The Muzzle-Loading Rifle...Then and Now, by Walter M. Cline, National Muzzle Loading Rifle Association, Friendship, IN, 1991. 161 pp., illus. $32.00
This extensive compilation of the muzzleloading rifle exhibits accumulative preserved data concerning the development of the "hallowed old arms of the Southern highlands."

THE ARMS LIBRARY

The No. 4 (T) Sniper Rifle: An Armourer's Perspective, by Peter Laidler with Ian Skennerton, I.D.S.A. Books, Piqua, OH, 1993. 125 pp., 75 illus. Paper covers. $19.95

Notes on Rifle-Shooting, by Henry William Heaton, reprinted with a new introduction by W.S. Curtis, W.S. Curtis Publishers, Ltd., Clwyd, England, 1993. 89 pp. $19.95

A reprint of the 1864 London edition. Captain Heaton was one of the great rifle shots from the earliest days of the Volunteer Movement.

The Official SKS Manual, Translation by Major James F. Gebhardt (Ret.), Paladin Press, Boulder, CO, 1997. 96 pp., illus. Paper covers. $16.00

This Soviet military manual covering the widely distributed SKS is now available in English.

The Pennsylvania Rifle, by Samuel E. Dyke, Sutter House, Lititz, PA, 1975. 61 pp., illus. Paper covers. $10.00

History and development, from the hunting rifle of the Germans who settled the area. Contains a full listing of all known Lancaster, PA, gunsmiths from 1729 through 1815.

Police Rifles, by Richard Fairburn, Paladin Press, Boulder, CO, 1994. 248 pp., illus. Paper covers. $35.00

Selecting the right rifle for street patrol and special tactical situations.

The Poor Man's Sniper Rifle, by D. Boone, Paladin Press, Boulder, CO, 1995. 152 pp., illus. Paper covers. $18.95

Here is a complete plan for converting readily available surplus military rifles to high-performance sniper weapons.

A Potpourri of Single Shot Rifles and Actions, by Frank de Haas, Mark de Haas, Ridgeway, MO, 1993. 153 pp., illus. Paper covers. $22.50

The author's 6th book on non-bolt-action single shots. Covers more than 40 single-shot rifles in historical and technical detail.

Precision Shooting with the M1 Garand, by Roy Baumgardner, Precision Shooting, Inc., Manchester, CT, 1999. 142 pp., illustrated. Paper covers. $12.95

Starts off with the ever popular ten-article series on accurizing the M1 that originally appeared in Precision Shooting in the 1993-95 era. There follows nine more Baumgardner authored articles on the M1 Garand and finally a 1999 updating chapter.

Purdey Gun and Rifle Makers: The Definitive History, by Donald Dallas, Quiller Press, London, 2000. 245 pp., illus. Color throughout. $100.00

A limited edition of 3,000 copies. Signed and Numbered. With a PURDEY book plate.

The Remington 700, by John F. Lacy, Taylor Publishing Co., Dallas, TX, 1990. 208 pp., illus. $44.95

Covers the different models, limited editions, chamberings, proofmarks, serial numbers, military models, and much more.

The Revolving Rifles, by Edsall James, Pioneer Press, Union City, TN, 1975. 23 pp., illus. Paper covers. $5.00

Valuable information on revolving cylinder rifles, from the earliest matchlock forms to the latest models of Colt and Remington.

Rifle Guide, by Sam Fadala, Stoeger Publishing Co., S. Hackensack, NJ, 1993. 288 pp., illus. Paper covers. $16.95

This comprehensive, fact-filled book beckons to both the seasoned rifleman as well as the novice shooter.

The Rifle: Its Development for Big-Game Hunting, by S.R. Truesdell, Safari Press, Huntington Beach, CA, 1992. 274 pp., illus. $35.00

The full story of the development of the big-game rifle from 1834-1946.

Riflesmithing, The Gun Digest Book of, by Jack Mitchell, DBI Books, a division of Krause Publications, Iola, WI, 1982. 256 pp., illus. Paper covers. $16.95

Covers tools, techniques, designs, finishing wood and metal, custom alterations.

Rifles of the World, 2nd Edition, edited by John Walter, DBI Books, a division of Krause Publications, Iola, WI, 1998. 384 pp., illus. $24.95

The definitive guide to the world's centerfire and rimfire rifles.

Ned H. Roberts and the Schuetzen Rifle, edited by Gerald O. Kelver, Brighton, CO, 1982. 99 pp., illus. $13.95

A compilation of the writings of Major Ned H. Roberts which appeared in various gun magazines.

Schuetzen Rifles, History and Loading, by Gerald O. Kelver, Gerald O. Kelver, Publisher, Brighton, CO, 1972. Illus. $13.95

Reference work on these rifles, their bullets, loading, telescopic sights, accuracy, etc. A limited, numbered ed.

Shooting the Blackpowder Cartridge Rifle, by Paul A. Matthews, Wolfe Publishing Co., Prescott, AZ, 1994. 129 pp., illus. Paper covers. $22.50

A general discourse on shooting the blackpowder cartridge rifle and the procedure required to make a particular rifle perform.

Shooting Lever Guns of the Old West, by Mike Venturino, MLV Enterprises, Livingston, MT, 1999. 300 pp., illustrated. Paper covers. $27.95

Shooting the lever action type repeating rifles of our American west.

Single Shot Rifles and Actions, by Frank de Haas, Orange City, IA, 1990. 352 pp., illus. Soft covers. $27.00

The definitive book on over 60 single shot rifles and actions.

Sixty Years of Rifles, by Paul A. Matthews, Wolfe Publishing Co., Prescott, AZ, 1991. 224 pp., illus. $19.50

About rifles and the author's experience and love affair with shooting and hunting.

S.L.R.—Australia's F.N. F.A.L. by Ian Skennerton and David Balmer, I.D.S.A. Books, Piqua, OH, 1989. 124 pp., 100 illus. Paper covers. $19.50

Small Arms Identification Series, No. 2—.303 Rifle, No. 4 Marks I, & I*, Marks 1/2, 1/3 & 2, by Ian Skennerton, I.D.S.A. Books, Piqua, OH, 1994. 48 pp. $9.50

Small Arms Identification Series, No. 3—9mm Austen Mk I & 9mm Owen Mk I Sub-Machine Guns, by Ian Skennerton, I.D.S.A. Books, Piqua, OH, 1994. 48 pp. $9.50

Small Arms Identification Series, No. 4—.303 Rifle, No. 5 Mk I, by Ian Skennerton, I.D.S.A. Books, Piqua, OH, 1994. 48 pp. $9.50

Small Arms Identification Series, No. 5—.303-in. Bren Light Machine Gun, by Ian Skennerton, I.D.S.A. Books, Piqua, OH, 1994. 48 pp. $9.50

Small Arms Series, No. 1 DeLisle's Commando Carbine, by Ian Skennerton, I.D.S.A. Books, Piqua, OH, 1981. 32 pp., 24 illus. $9.00

Small Arms Identification Series, No. 1—.303 Rifle, No. 1 S.M.L.E. Marks III and III*, by Ian Skennerton, I.D.S.A. Books, Piqua, OH, 1981. 48 pp. $9.50

Sporting Rifle Takedown & Reassembly Guide, 2nd Edition, by J.B. Wood, DBI Books, a division of Krause Publications, Iola, WI, 1997. 480 pp., illus. $19.95

An updated edition of the reference guide for anyone who wants to properly care for their sporting rifle. (Available September 1997)

The Springfield Rifle M1903, M1903A1, M1903A3, M1903A4, Desert Publications, Cornville, AZ, 1982. 100 pp., illus. Paper covers. $12.00

Covers every aspect of disassembly and assembly, inspection, repair and maintenance.

Still More Single Shot Rifles, by James J. Grant, Pioneer Press, Union City, TN, 1995. 211 pp., illus. $29.95

This is Volume Four in a series of Single-Shot Rifles by America's foremost authority. It gives more in-depth information on those single-shot rifles which were presented in the first three books.

The Sturm, Ruger 10/22 Rifle and .44 Magnum Carbine, by Duncan Long, Paladin Press, Boulder, CO, 1988. 108 pp., illus. Paper covers. $15.00

An in-depth look at both weapons detailing the elegant simplicity of the Ruger design. Offers specifications, troubleshooting procedures and ammunition recommendations.

The Tactical Rifle, by Gabriel Suarez, Paladin Press, Boulder, CO, 1999. 264 pp., illustrated. Paper covers. $25.00

The precision tool for urban police operations.

Target Rifle in Australia, by J.E. Corcoran, R&R, Livonia, NY, 1996. 160 pp., illus. $40.00

A most interesting study of the evolution of these rifles from 1860 - 1900. British rifles from the percussion period through the early smokeless era are discussed.

To the Dreams of Youth: The .22 Caliber Single Shot Winchester Rifle, by Herbert Houze, Krause Publications, Iola, WI, 1993. 192 pp., illus. $34.95

A thoroughly researched history of the 22-caliber Winchester single shot rifle, including interesting photographs.

The Ultimate in Rifle Accuracy, by Glenn Newick, Stoeger Publishing Co., Wayne, N.J., 1999. 205 pp., illustrated. Paper covers. $11.95

This handbook contains the information you need to extract the best performance from your rifle.

U.S. Marine Corps AR15/M16 A2 Manual, reprinted by Desert Publications, El Dorado, AZ, 1993. 262 pp., illus. Paper covers. $16.95

A reprint of TM05538C-23&P/2, August, 1987. The A-2 manual for the Colt AR15/M16.

U.S. Rifle M14—From John Garand to the M21, by R. Blake Stevens, Collector Grade Publications, Inc., Toronto, Canada, revised second edition, 1991. 350 pp., illus. $49.50

A classic, in-depth examination of the development, manufacture and fielding of the last wood-and-metal ("lock, stock, and barrel") battle rifle to be issued to U.S. troops.

War Baby!: The U.S. Caliber 30 Carbine, Volume I, by Larry Ruth, Collector Grade Publications, Toronto, Canada, 1992. 512 pp., illus. $69.95

Volume 1 of the in-depth story of the phenomenally popular U.S. caliber 30 carbine. Concentrates on design and production of the military 30 carbine during World War II.

War Baby Comes Home: The U.S. Caliber 30 Carbine, Volume 2, by Larry Ruth, Collector Grade Publications, Toronto, Canada, 1993. 386 pp., illus. $49.95

The triumphant competion of Larry Ruth's two-volume in-depth series on the most popular U.S. military small arm in history.

The Winchester Model 52, Perfection in Design, by Herbert G. Houze, Krause Publications, Iola, WI, 1997. 192 pp., illus. $34.95

This book covers the complete story of this technically superior gun.

The Winchester Model 94: The First 100 Years, by Robert C. Renneberg, Krause Publications, Iola, WI, 1991. 208 pp., illus. $34.95

Covers the design and evolution from the early years up to today.

Winchester Slide-Action Rifles, Volume I: Model 1890 and Model 1906 by Ned Schwing, Krause Publications, Iola, WI. 352 pp., illus. $39.95

Traces the history through word and picture in this chronolgy of the Model 1890 and 1906.

Winchester Slide-Action Rifles, Volume II: Model 61 & Model 62 by Ned Schwing, Krause Publications, Iola, WI. 256 pp., illus. $34.95

Historical look complete with markings, stampings and engraving.

SHOTGUNS

Advanced Combat Shotgun: The Stress Fire Concept, by Massad Ayoob, Police Bookshelf, Concord, NH, 1993. 197 pp., illus. Paper covers. $9.95

Advanced combat shotgun fighting for police.

THE ARMS LIBRARY

Best Guns, by Michael McIntosh, Countrysport Press, Selma, AL, 1999, revised edition. 418 pp. $39.00

Combines the best shotguns ever made in America with information on British and Continental makers.

The Better Shot, by Ken Davies, Quiller Press, London, England, 1992. 136 pp., illus. $39.95

Step-by-step shotgun technique with Holland and Holland.

The Big Shots; Edwardian Shooting Parties, by Jonathan Ruffer, Quiller Press, London, England, 1997 160pp. B & W illus. $24.95

A book about Edwardian shooting parties, now a former pastime and enjoyed by the selected few, who recall the hunting of pheasants. Foreword by HRH The Prince of Wales.

The British Shotgun, Volume 1, 1850-1870, by I.M. Crudington and D.J. Baker, Barrie & Jenkins, London, England, 1979. 256 pp., illus. $65.00

An attempt to trace, as accurately as is now possible, the evolution of the shotgun during its formative years in Great Britain.

Boothroyd on British Shotguns, by Geoffrey Boothroyd, Sand Lake Press, Amity, OR, 1996. 221 pp., illus. plus a 32 page reproduction of the 1914 Webley & Scott catalog. A limited, numbered edition. $34.95

Based on articles by the author that appeared in the British Publication *Shooting Times & Country Magazine.*

Boss & Co. Builders of the Best Guns Only, by Donald Dallas, Quiller Press, London, 1995. 262 pp., illustrated. $79.95

Large four colour plates, b/w photos, bibliography. The definitive history authorized by Boss & Co.

The British Over-and-Under Shotgun, by Geoffrey and Susan Boothroyd, Sand Lake Press, Amity, OR, 1996. 137 pp., illus. $34.95

Historical outline of the development of the O/U shotgun with individual chapters devoted to the twenty-two British makers.

The Browning Superposed: John M. Browning's Last Legacy, by Ned Schwing, Krause Publications, Iola, WI, 1996. 496 pp., illus. $49.95

An exclusive story of the man, the company and the best-selling over-and-under shotgun in North America.

Clay Target Handbook, by Jerry Meyer, Lyons & Buford, Publisher, New York, NY, 1993. 182 pp., illus. $22.95

Contains in-depth, how-to-do-it information on trap, skeet, sporting clays, international trap, international skeet and clay target games played around the country.

Clay Target Shooting, by Paul Bentley, A&C Black, London, England, 1987. 144 pp., illus. $25.00

Practical book on clay target shooting written by a very successful international competitor, providing valuable professional advice and instruction for shooters of all disciplines.

Cogswell & Harrison; Two Centuries of Gunmaking, by G. Cooley & J. Newton, Safari Press, Long Beach, CA, 2000. 128pp, 30 color photos, 100 b&w photos. $39.95

The authors have gathered a wealth of fascinating historical and technical material that will make the book indispensable, not only to many thousands of "Coggie" owners worldwide, but also to anyone interested in the general history of British gunmaking.

A Collector's Guide to United States Combat Shotguns, by Bruce N. Canfield, Andrew Mowbray Inc., Publishers, Lincoln, RI, 1993. 184 pp., illus. Paper covers. $24.00

Full coverage of the combat shotgun, from the earliest examples to the Gulf War and beyond.

Combat Shotgun and Submachine Gun, "A Special Weapons Analysis" by Chuck Taylor, Paladin Press, Boulder, CO, 1997, soft cover, photos, 176 pp. $25.00

From one of America's top shooting instructors comes an analysis of two controversial, misunderstood and misemployed small arms. Hundreds of photos detail field-testing of both, basic and advanced training drills, tactical rules, gun accessories and modifications. Loading procedures, carrying and fighting positions and malfunction clearance drills are included to promote weapon effectiveness.

Cradock on Shotguns, by Chris Cradock, Banford Press, London, England, 1989. 200 pp., illus. $45.00

A definitive work on the shotgun by a British expert on shotguns.

The Defensive Shotgun, by Louis Awerbuck, S.W.A.T. Publications, Cornville, AZ, 1989. 77 pp., illus. Soft covers. $14.95

Cuts through the myths concerning the shotgun and its attendant ballistic effects.

The Double Shotgun, by Don Zutz, Winchester Press, Piscataway, NJ, 1985. 304 pp., illus. $22.95

Revised, updated, expanded edition of the history and development of the world's classic sporting firearms.

The Ducks Unlimited Guide to Shotgunning, by Don Zutz, Willow Creek Press, Minocqua, WI, 2000. 166 pg. Illustrated. $24.50

This book covers everything from the grand old guns of yesterday to todays best shotguns and loads, from the basic shotgun fit and function to expert advice on ballistics, chocks, and shooting techniques.

Finding the Extra Target, by Coach John R. Linn & Stephen A. Blumenthal, Shotgun Sports, Inc., Auburn, CA, 1989. 126 pp., illus. Paper covers. $14.95

The ultimate training guide for all the clay target sports.

Fine Gunmaking: Double Shotguns, by Steven Dodd Hughes, Krause Publications Iola, WI, 1998. 167 pp., illustrated. $34.95

An in-depth look at the creation of fine shotguns.

Firearms Assembly/Disassembly, Part V: Shotguns, Revised Edition, The Gun Digest Book of, by J.B. Wood, DBI Books, a division of Krause Publications, Iola, WI, 1992. 480 pp., illus. Paper covers. $19.95

Covers 46 popular shotguns plus over 250 variants. The most comprehensive and professional presentation available to either hobbyist or gunsmith.

A.H. Fox "The Finest Gun in the World", revised and enlarged edition, by Michael McIntosh, Countrysport, Inc., New Albany, OH, 1995. 408 pp., illus. $49.00

The first detailed history of one of America's finest shotguns.

Game Shooting, by Robert Churchill, Countrysport Press, Selma, AL, 1998. 258 pp., illus. $30.00

The basis for every shotgun instructional technique devised and the foundation for all wingshooting and the game of sporting clays.

The Golden Age of Shotgunning, by Bob Hinman, Wolfe Publishing Co., Inc., Prescott, AZ, 1982. $22.50

A valuable history of the late 1800s detailing that fabulous period of development in shotguns, shotshells and shotgunning.

The Greener Story, by Graham Greener, Safari Press, Long Beach, CA, 2000. 231pp, color and b&w illustrations. $69.95

The history of the Greener Gunmakers and their guns

Grand Old Shotguns, by Don Zutz, Shotgun Sports Magazine, Auburn, CA, 1995. 136 pp., illus. Paper covers. $19.95

A study of the great smoothbores, their history and how and why they were discontinued. Find out the most sought-after and which were the best shooters.

Gun Digest Book of Sporting Clays, 2nd Edition, edited by Harold A. Murtz, Krause Publications, Iola, WI, 1999. 256 pp., illus. Paper covers. $21.95

A concise Gun Digest book that covers guns, ammo, chokes, targets and course layouts so you'll stay a step ahead.

The Gun Review Book, by Michael McIntosh, Countrysport Press, Selman, AL, 1999. Paper covers. $19.95

Compiled here for the first time are McIntosh's popular gun reviews from *Shooting Sportsman; The Magazine of Wingshooting* and *Fine Shotguns.* The author traces the history of gunmakes, then examines, analyzes, and critique the fine shotguns of England, Continental Europe and the United States.

Hartman on Skeet, by Barney Hartman, Stackpole Books, Harrisburg, PA, 1973. 143 pp., illus. $19.95

A definitive book on Skeet shooting by a pro.

The Heyday of the Shotgun, by David Baker, Safari Press, Inc., Huntington Beach, CA, 2000. 160 pp., illustrated. $39.95

The art of the gunmaker at the turn of the last century when British craftsmen brought forth the finest guns ever made.

The Italian Gun, by Steve Smith & Laurie Morrow, wilderness Adventures, Gallatin Gateway, MT, 1997. 325 pp., illus. $49.95

The first book ever written entirely in English for American enthusiasts who own, aspire to own, or simply admire Italian guns.

The Ithaca Featherlight Repeater; the Best Gun Going, by Walter C. Snyder, Southern Pines, NC, 1998. 300 pp., illus. $89.95

Describes the complete history of each model of the legendary Ithaca Model 37 and Model 87 Repeaters from their conception in 1930 throught 1997.

The Ithaca Gun Company from the Beginning, by Walter C. Snyder, Cook & Uline Publishing Co., Southern Pines, NC, 2nd Edition, 1999. 384 pp., illustrated in color and black and white. $90.00

The entire family of Ithaca Gun Company products is described along with new historical information and the serial number/date of manufacturing listing has been improved.

L.C. Smith Shotguns, by Lt. Col. William S. Brophy, The Gun Room Press, Highland Park, NJ, 1979. 244 pp., illus. $35.00

The first work on this very important American gun and manufacturing company.

The Little Trapshooting Book, by Frank Little, Shotgun Sports Magazine, Auburn, CA, 1994. 168 pp., illus. Paper covers. $19.95

Packed with know-how from one of the greatest trapshooters of all time.

Lock, Stock, and Barrel, by C. Adams & R. Braden, Safari Press, Huntington Beach, CA, 1996. 254 pp., illus. $24.95

The process of making a best grade English gun from a lump of steel and a walnut tree trunk to the ultimate product plus practical advise on consistent field shooting with a double gun.

Mental Training for the Shotgun Sports, by Michael J. Keyes, Shotgun Sports, Auburn, CA, 1996. 160 pp., illus. Paper covers. $24.95

The most comprehensive book ever published on what it takes to shoot winning scores at trap, Skeet and Sporting Clays.

The Model 12, 1912-1964, by Dave Riffle, Dave Riffle, Ft. Meyers, FL, 1995. 274 pp., illus. $49.95

The story of the greatest hammerless repeating shotgun ever built.

More Shotguns and Shooting, by Michael McIntosh, Countrysport Books, Selma, AL, 1998 256 pp., illustrated. $30.00

From specifics of shotguns to shooting your way out of a slump, it's McIntosh at his best.

Mossberg: More Gun for the Money, by Victor & Cheryl Havlin, Blue Book Publications, Minneapolis, MN, 1995. 204 pages, illustrated. $24.95

The History of O.F. Mossberg & Sons, Inc.

Mossberg's Shotguns, by Duncan Long, Delta Press, El Dorado, AR, 2000. 120 pp., illustrated. $24.95

This book contains a brief history of the company and it's founder, full coverage of the pump and semiautomatic shotguns, rare products and a care and maintenance section.

REFERENCE

The Mysteries of Shotgun Patterns, by George G. Oberfell and Charles E. Thompson, Oklahoma State University Press, Stillwater, OK, 1982. 164 pp., illus. Paper covers. $25.00

Shotgun ballistics for the hunter in non-technical language.

The Parker Gun, by Larry Baer, Gun Room Press, Highland Park, NJ, 1993. 195 pages, illustrated with B & W and Color photos. $35.00

Covers in detail, production of all models on this classic gun. Many fine specimens from great collections are illustrated.

Parker Guns "The Old Reliable", by Ed Muderiak, Safari Press, Inc., Huntington Beach, CA, 1997. 325 pp., illus. $40.00

A look at the small beginnings, the golden years, and the ultimate decline of the most famous of all American shotgun manufacturers.

The Parker Story; Volumes 1 & 2, by Bill Mullins, "etal". The Double Gun Journal, East Jordan, MI, 2000. 1,025 pages of text and 1,500 color and monochrome illustrations. Hardbound in a gold-embossed cover. $295.00

The most complete and attractive "last word" on America's preeminent double gun maker. Includes tables showing the number of guns made by gauge, barrel length and special features for each grade.

Positive Shooting, by Michael Yardley, Safari Press, Huntington Beach, CA, 1995. 160 pp., illus. $30.00

This book will provide the shooter with a sound foundation from which to develop an effective, personal technique that can dramatically improve shooting performance.

Purdey Gun and Rifle Makers: The Definitive History, by Donald Dallas, Quiller Press, London 2000. 245 pages, illus. $100.00

245 Colour plates, b/w photos, ills, bibliography. The definitive history. A limited edition of 3,000 copies. Signed and Numbered. With a PURDEY book plate.

Recognizing Side by Side Shotguns, by Charles Carder, Anvil Onze Publishing, 2000. 225 pp., illus. Paper Covers. $5.95

A graphic description of the visible features of side by side breech loading shotguns.

Reloading for Shotgunners, 4th Edition, by Kurt D. Fackler and M.L. McPherson, DBI Books, a division of Krause Publications, Iola, WI, 1997. 320 pp., illus. Paper covers. $19.95

Expanded reloading tables with over 11,000 loads. Bushing charts for every major press and component maker. All new presentation on all aspects of shotshell reloading by two of the top experts in the field. (Available October 1997.)

Remington Double Shotguns, by Charles G. Semer, Denver, CO, 1997. 617 pp., illus. $60.00

This book deals with the entire production and all grades of double shotguns made by Remington during the period of their production 1873-1910.

75 Years with the Shotgun, by C.T. (Buck) Buckman, Valley Publ., Fresno, CA, 1974. 141 pp., illus. $10.00

An expert hunter and trapshooter shares experiences of a lifetime.

The Shotgun in Combat, by Tony Lesce, Desert Publications, Cornville, AZ, 1979. 148 pp., illus. Paper covers. $14.00

A history of the shotgun and its use in combat.

Shotgun Digest, 4th Edition, edited by Jack Lewis, DBI Books, a division of Krause Publications, Iola, WI, 1993. 256 pp., illus. Paper covers. $17.95

A look at what's happening with shotguns and shotgunning today.

The Shotgun Encyclopedia, by John Taylor, Safari Press, Inc., Huntington Beach, CA, 2000. 260 pp., illustrated. $34.95

A comprehensive reference work on all aspects of shotguns and shotgun shooting.

Shotgun Gunsmithing, The Gun Digest Book of, by Ralph Walker, DBI Books, a division of Krause Publications, Iola, WI, 1983. 256 pp., illus. Paper covers. $16.95

The principles and practices of repairing, individualizing and accurizing modern shotguns by one of the world's premier shotgun gunsmiths.

The Shotgun: History and Development, by Geoffrey Boothroyd, Safari Press, Huntington Beach, CA, 1995. 240 pp., illus. $35.00

The first volume in a series that traces the development of the British shotgun from the 17th century onward.

The Shotgun Handbook, by Mike George, The Croswood Press, London, England, 1999. 128 pp., illus. $35.00

For all shotgun enthusiasts, this detailed guide ranges from design and selection of a gun to adjustment, cleaning, and maintenance.

Shotgun Stuff, by Don Zutz, Shotgun Sports, Inc., Auburn, CA, 1991. 172 pp., illus. Paper covers. $19.95

This book gives shotgunners all the "stuff" they need to achieve better performance and get more enjoyment from their favorite smoothbore.

Shotgunner's Notebook: The Advice and Reflections of a Wingshooter, by Gene Hill, Countrysport Press, Traverse City, MI, 1990. 192 pp., illus. $25.00

Covers the shooting, the guns and the miscellany of the sport.

Shotgunning: The Art and the Science, by Bob Brister, Winchester Press, Piscataway, NJ, 1976. 321 pp., illus. $18.95

Hundreds of specific tips and truly novel techniques to improve the field and target shooting of every shotgunner.

Shotgunning Trends in Transition, by Don Zutz, Wolfe Publishing Co., Prescott, AZ, 1990. 314 pp., illus. $29.50

This book updates American shotgunning from post WWII to present.

Shotguns and Cartridges for Game and Clays, by Gough Thomas, edited by Nigel Brown, A & C Black, Ltd., Cambs, England, 1989. 256 pp., illus. Soft covers. $24.95

Gough Thomas' well-known and respected book for game and clay pigeon shooters in a thoroughly up-dated edition.

Shotguns and Gunsmiths: The Vintage Years, by Geoffrey Boothroyd, Safari Press, Huntington Beach, CA, 1995. 240 pp., illus. $35.00

A fascinating insight into the lives and skilled work of gunsmiths who helped develop the British shotgun during the Victorian and Edwardian eras.

Shotguns and Shooting, by Michael McIntosh, Countrysport Press, New Albany, OH, 1995. 258 pp., illus. $30.00

The art of guns and gunmaking, this book is a celebration no lover of fine doubles should miss.

Shotguns for Wingshooting, by John Barsness, DBI Books, a division of Krause Publications, Inc., Iola, WI, 1999. 208 pp., illustrated. $49.95

Detailed information on all styles of shotgun. How to select the correct ammunition for specific hunting applications.

Side by Sides of the World for Y2K, by Charles Carder, Anvil Onze Publishing, 2000. 221 pp., illus. Paper Covers. $25.95

This book lists more than 1600 names & features side by sides shotguns from all over the world, in alphabetical order. 500 + illustrations.

Sidelocks & Boxlocks, by Geoffrey Boothroyd, Sand Lake Press, Amity, OR, 1991. 271 pp., illus. $24.95

The story of the classic British shotgun.

Spanish Best: The Fine Shotguns of Spain, by Terry Wieland, Countrysport, Inc., Traverse City, MI, 1994. 264 pp., illus. $45.00

A practical source of information for owners of Spanish shotguns and a guide for those considering buying a used shotgun.

The Sporting Clay Handbook, by Jerry Meyer, Lyons and Burford Publishers, New York, NY, 1990. 140 pp., illus. Soft covers. $17.95

Introduction to the fastest growing, and most exciting, gun game in America.

Streetsweepers, "The Complete Book of Combat Shotguns", by Duncan Long, Paladin Press, Boulder, CO,1997, soft cover, 63 photos, illus., appendices, 160 pp. $24.95

Streetsweepers is the newest, most comprehensive book out on combat shotguns, covering single- and double-barreled, slide-action, semi-auto and rotary cylinder shotguns, plus a chapter on grenade launchers you can mount on your weapon and info about shotgun models not yet on the market. Noted gun writer Duncan Long also advises on which ammo to use, accessories and combat shotgun tactics.

The Tactical Shotgun, by Gabriel Suzrez, Paladin Press, Boulder, CO, 1996. 232 pp., illus. Paper covers. $25.00

The best techniques and tactics for employing the shotgun in personal combat.

Taking More Birds, by Dan Carlisle & Dolph Adams, Lyons & Burford, New York, NY, 1993. 120 pp., illus. $19.95

A practical guide to greater success at sporting clays and wing shooting.

Tip Up Shotguns from Hopkins and Allen, by Charles Carder, Anvil Onze Publishing, 2000. 81 pp., illus. Paper Covers. $13.95

All the descriptive material and graphics used in this book have been reproduced from original Hopkins & Allen Arms Company catalogs, except the patent drawings.

Trap & Skeet Shooting, 3rd Edition, by Chris Christian, DBI Books, a division of Krause Publications, Iola, WI, 1994. 288 pp., illus. Paper covers. $17.95

A detailed look at the contemporary world of Trap, Skeet and Sporting Clays.

Trapshooting is a Game of Opposites, by Dick Bennett, Shotgun Sports, Inc., Auburn, CA, 1996. 129 pp., illus. Paper covers. $19.95

Discover everything you need to know about shooting trap like the pros.

Turkey Hunter's Digest, Revised Edition, by Dwain Bland, DBI Books, a division of Krause Publications, Iola, WI, 1994. 256 pp., illus. Paper covers. $17.95

Presents no-nonsense approach to hunting all five sub-species of the North American wild turkey.

U.S. Shotguns, All Types, reprint of TM9-285, Desert Publications, Cornville, AZ, 1987. 257 pp., illus. Paper covers. $9.95

Covers operation, assembly and disassembly of nine shotguns used by the U.S. armed forces.

U.S. Winchester Trench and Riot Guns and Other U.S. Military Combat Shotguns, by Joe Poyer, North Cape Publications, Tustin, CA, 1992. 124 pp., illus. Paper covers. $15.95

A detailed history of the use of military shotguns, and the acquisition procedures used by the U.S. Army's Ordnance Department in both World Wars.

The Winchester Model Twelve, by George Madis, David Madis, Dallas, TX, 1984. 176 pp., illus. $24.95

A definitive work on this famous American shotgun.

The Winchester Model 42, by Ned Schwing, Krause Pub., Iola, WI, 1990. 160 pp., illus. $34.95

Behind-the-scenes story of the model 42's invention and its early development. Production totals and manufacturing dates; reference work.

Winchester Shotguns and Shotshells, by Ron Stadt, Krause Pub., Iola, WI. 288 pp., illus. $34.95.

Must-have for Winchester collectors of shotguns manufactured through 1961.

Winchester's Finest, the Model 21, by Ned Schwing, Krause Publications, Iola, WI, 1990. 360 pp., illus. $49.95

The classic beauty and the interesting history of the Model 21 Winchester shotgun.

The World's Fighting Shotguns, by Thomas F. Swearengen, T.B.N. Enterprises, Alexandria, VA, 1979. 500 pp., illus. $39.95

The complete military and police reference work from the shotgun's inception to date, with up-to-date developments.

REFERENCE

ARMS ASSOCIATIONS

UNITED STATES

ALABAMA
Alabama Gun Collectors Assn.
Secretary, P.O. Box 70965, Tuscaloosa, AL 35407

ALASKA
Alaska Gun Collectors Assn., Inc.
C.W. Floyd, Pres., 5240 Little Tree, Anchorage, AK 99507

ARIZONA
Arizona Arms Assn.
Don DeBusk, President, 4837 Bryce Ave., Glendale, AZ 85301

CALIFORNIA
California Cartridge Collectors Assn.
Rick Montgomery, 1729 Christina, Stockton, CA 95204/209-463-7216 evs.
California Waterfowl Assn.
4630 Northgate Blvd., #150, Sacramento, CA 95834
Greater Calif. Arms & Collectors Assn.
Donald L. Bullock, 8291 Carburton St., Long Beach, CA 90808-3302
Los Angeles Gun Ctg. Collectors Assn.
F.H. Ruffra, 20810 Amie Ave., Apt. #9, Torrance, CA 90503
Stock Gun Players Assn.
6038 Appian Way, Long Beach, CA, 90803

COLORADO
Colorado Gun Collectors Assn.
L.E.(Bud) Greenwald, 2553 S. Quitman St., Denver, CO 80219/303-935-3850
Rocky Mountain Cartridge Collectors Assn.
John Roth, P.O. Box 757, Conifer, CO 80433

CONNECTICUT
Ye Connecticut Gun Guild, Inc.
Dick Fraser, P.O. Box 425, Windsor, CT 06095

FLORIDA
Unified Sportsmen of Florida
P.O. Box 6565, Tallahassee, FL 32314

GEORGIA
Georgia Arms Collectors Assn., Inc.
Michael Kindberg, President, P.O. Box 277, Alpharetta, GA 30239-0277

ILLINOIS
Illinois State Rifle Assn.
P.O. Box 637, Chatsworth, IL 60921
Mississippi Valley Gun & Cartridge Coll. Assn.
Bob Filbert, P.O. Box 61, Port Byron, IL 61275/309-523-2593
Sauk Trail Gun Collectors
Gordell M. Matson, P.O. Box 1113, Milan, IL 61264
Wabash Valley Gun Collectors Assn., Inc.
Roger L. Dorsett, 2601 Willow Rd., Urbana, IL 61801/217-384-7302

INDIANA
Indiana State Rifle & Pistol Assn.
Thos. Glancy, P.O. Box 552, Chesterton, IN 46304
Southern Indiana Gun Collectors Assn., Inc.
Sheila McClary, 309 W. Monroe St., Boonville, IN 47601/812-897-3742

IOWA
Beaver Creek Plainsmen Inc.
Steve Murphy, Secy., P.O. Box 298, Bondurant, IA 50035
Central States Gun Collectors Assn.
Dennis Greischar, Box 841, Mason City, IA 50402-0841

KANSAS
Kansas Cartridge Collectors Assn.
Bob Linder, Box 84, Plainville, KS 67663

KENTUCKY
Kentuckiana Arms Collectors Assn.
Charles Billips, President, Box 1776, Louisville, KY 40201
Kentucky Gun Collectors Assn., Inc.
Ruth Johnson, Box 64, Owensboro, KY 42302/502-729-4197

LOUISIANA
Washitaw River Renegades
Sandra Rushing, P.O. Box 256, Main St., Grayson, LA 71435

MARYLAND
Baltimore Antique Arms Assn.
Mr. Cillo, 1034 Main St., Darlington, MD 21304

MASSACHUSETTS
Bay Colony Weapons Collectors, Inc.
John Brandt, Box 111, Hingham, MA 02043
Massachusetts Arms Collectors
Bruce E. Skinner, P.O. Box 31, No. Carver, MA 02355/508-866-5259

MICHIGAN
Association for the Study and Research of .22 Caliber Rimfire Cartridges
George Kass, 4512 Nakoma Dr., Okemos, MI 48864

MINNESOTA
Sioux Empire Cartridge Collectors Assn.
Bob Cameron, 14597 Glendale Ave. SE, Prior Lake, MN 55372

MISSISSIPPI
Mississippi Gun Collectors Assn.
Jack E. Swinney, P.O. Box 16323, Hattiesburg, MS 39402

MISSOURI
Greater St. Louis Cartridge Collectors Assn.
Don MacChesney, 634 Scottsdale Rd., Kirkwood, MO 63122-1109
Mineral Belt Gun Collectors Assn.
D.F. Saunders, 1110 Cleveland Ave., Monett, MO 65708
Missouri Valley Arms Collectors Assn., Inc.
L.P Brammer II, Membership Secy., P.O. Box 33033, Kansas City, MO 64114

MONTANA
Montana Arms Collectors Assn.
Dean E. Yearout, Sr., Exec. Secy., 1516 21st Ave. S., Great Falls, MT 59405
Weapons Collectors Society of Montana
R.G. Schipf, Ex. Secy., 3100 Bancroft St., Missoula, MT 59801/406-728-2995

NEBRASKA
Nebraska Cartridge Collectors Club
Gary Muckel, P.O. Box 84442, Lincoln, NE 68501

NEW HAMPSHIRE
New Hampshire Arms Collectors, Inc.
James Stamatelos, Secy., P.O. Box 5, Cambridge, MA 02139

NEW JERSEY
Englishtown Benchrest Shooters Assn.
Michael Toth, 64 Cooke Ave., Carteret, NJ 07008
Jersey Shore Antique Arms Collectors
Joe Sisia, P.O. Box 100, Bayville, NJ 08721-0100
New Jersey Arms Collectors Club, Inc.
Angus Laidlaw, Vice President, 230 Valley Rd., Montclair, NJ 07042/201-746-0939; e-mail: acclaidlaw@juno.com

NEW YORK
Iroquois Arms Collectors Assn.
Bonnie Robinson, Show Secy., P.O. Box 142, Ransomville, NY 14131/716-791-4096
Mid-State Arms Coll. & Shooters Club
Jack Ackerman, 24 S. Mountain Terr., Binghamton, NY 13903

NORTH CAROLINA
North Carolina Gun Collectors Assn.
Jerry Ledford, 3231-7th St. Dr. NE, Hickory, NC 28601

OHIO
Ohio Gun Collectors Assn.
P.O. Box 9007, Maumee, OH 43537-9007/419-897-0861; Fax:419-897-0860
Shotshell Historical and Collectors Society
Madeline Bruemmer, 3886 Dawley Rd., Ravenna, OH 44266
The Stark Gun Collectors, Inc.
William I. Gann, 5666 Waynesburg Dr., Waynesburg, OH 44688

OREGON
Oregon Arms Collectors Assn., Inc.
Phil Bailey, P.O. Box 13000-A, Portland, OR 97213-0017/503-281-6864; off.:503-281-0918
Oregon Cartridge Collectors Assn.
Boyd Northrup, P.O. Box 285, Rhododendron, OR 97049

PENNSYLVANIA
Presque Isle Gun Collectors Assn.
James Welch, 156 E. 37 St., Erie, PA 16504

SOUTH CAROLINA
Belton Gun Club, Inc.
Attn. Secretary, P.O. Box 126, Belton, SC 29627/864-369-6767

Gun Owners of South Carolina
Membership Div.: William Strozier, Secretary, P.O. Box 70, Johns Island, SC 29457-0070/803-762-3240; Fax:803-795-0711; e-mail:76053.222@compuserve.com

SOUTH DAKOTA
Dakota Territory Gun Coll. Assn., Inc.
Curt Carter, Castlewood, SD 57223

TENNESSEE
Smoky Mountain Gun Coll. Assn., Inc.
Hugh W. Yabro, President, P.O. Box 23225, Knoxville, TN 37933
Tennessee Gun Collectors Assn., Inc.
M.H. Parks, 3556 Pleasant Valley Rd., Nashville, TN 37204-3419

TEXAS
Houston Gun Collectors Assn., Inc.
P.O. Box 741429, Houston, TX 77274-1429
Texas Cartridge Collectors Assn., Inc.
Robert Mellichamp, Memb. Contact, 907 Shirkmere, Houston, TX 77008/713-869-0558
Texas Gun Collectors Assn.
Bob Eder, Pres., P.O. Box 12067, El Paso, TX 79913/915-584-8183
Texas State Rifle Assn.
1131 Rockingham Dr., Suite 101, Richardson, TX 75080-4326

VIRGINIA
Virginia Gun Collectors Assn., Inc.
Addison Hurst, Secy., 38802 Charlestown Height, Waterford, VA 20197/540-882-3543

WASHINGTON
Association of Cartridge Collectors on the Pacific Northwest
Robert Jardin, 14214 Meadowlark Drive KPN, Gig Harbor, WA 98329
Washington Arms Collectors, Inc.
Joyce Boss, P.O. Box 389, Renton, WA, 98057-0389/206-255-8410

WISCONSIN
Great Lakes Arms Collectors Assn., Inc.
Edward C. Warnke, 2913 Woodridge Lane, Waukesha, WI 53188
Wisconsin Gun Collectors Assn., Inc.
Lulita Zellmer, P.O. Box 181, Sussex, WI 53089

WYOMING
Wyoming Weapons Collectors
P.O. Box 284, Laramie, WY 82073/307-745-4652 or 745-9530

NATIONAL ORGANIZATIONS

Amateur Trapshooting Assn.
David D. Bopp, Exec. Director, 601 W. National Rd., Vandalia, OH 45377/937-898-4638; Fax:937-898-5472
American Airgun Field Target Assn.
5911 Cherokee Ave., Tampa, FL 33604
American Coon Hunters Assn.
Opal Johnston, P.O. Cadet, Route 1, Box 492, Old Mines, MO 63630
American Custom Gunmakers Guild
Jan Billeb, Exec. Director, P.O. Box 812, Burlington, IA 52601-0812/319-752-6114 (Phone or Fax)
American Defense Preparedness Assn.
Two Colonial Place, 2101 Wilson Blvd., Suite 400, Arlington, VA 22201-3061
American Paintball League
P.O. Box 3561, Johnson City, TN 37602/800-541-9169
American Pistolsmiths Guild
Alex B. Hamilton, Pres., 1449 Blue Crest Lane, San Antonio, TX 78232/210-494-3063
American Police Pistol & Rifle Assn.
3801 Biscayne Blvd., Miami, FL 33137
American Single Shot Rifle Assn.
Gary Staup, Secy., 709 Carolyn Dr., Delphos, OH 45833/419-692-3866. Website: www.assra.com
American Society of Arms Collectors
George E. Weatherly, P.O. Box 2567, Waxahachie, TX 75165
American Tactical Shooting Assn.(A.T.S.A.)
c/o Skip Gochenour, 2600 N. Third St., Harrisburg, PA 17110/717-233-0402; Fax:717-233-5340
Association of Firearm and Tool Mark Examiners
Lannie G. Emanuel, Secy., Southwest Institute of Forensic Sciences, P.O. Box 35728, Dallas, TX 75235/214-920-5979; Fax:214-920-5928; Membership Secy., Ann D. Jones, VA Div. of Forensic Science, P.O. Box 999, Richmond, VA 23208/804-786-4706; Fax:804-371-8328
Boone & Crockett Club
250 Station Dr., Missoula, MT 59801-2753
Browning Collectors Assn.
Secretary:Scherrie L. Brennac, 2749 Keith Dr., Villa Ridge, MO 63089/314-742-0571
The Cast Bullet Assn., Inc.
Ralland J. Fortier, Editor, 4103 Foxcraft Dr., Traverse City, MI 49684
Citizens Committee for the Right to Keep and Bear Arms
Natl. Hq., Liberty Park, 12500 NE Tenth Pl., Bellevue, WA 98005
Colt Collectors Assn.
25000 Highland Way, Los Gatos, CA 95030/408-353-2658.
Ducks Unlimited, Inc.
Natl. Headquarters, One Waterfowl Way, Memphis, TN 38120/901-758-3937
Fifty Caliber Shooters Assn.
PO Box 111, Monroe UT 84754-0111
Firearms Coalition/Neal Knox Associates
Box 6537, Silver Spring, MD 20906/301-871-3006
Firearms Engravers Guild of America
Rex C. Pedersen, Secy., 511 N. Rath Ave., Lundington, MI 49431/616-845-7695(Phone and Fax)
Foundation for North American Wild Sheep
720 Allen Ave., Cody, WY 82414-3402/web site: http://iigi.com/os/non/fnaws/fnaws.htm; e-mail: fnaws@wyoming.com
Freedom Arms Collectors Assn.
P.O. Box 160302, Miami, FL 33116-0302

ARMS ASSOCIATIONS

Garand Collectors Assn.
P.O. Box 181, Richmond, KY
40475

**Golden Eagle Collectors Assn.
(G.E.C.A.)**
Chris Showler, 11144 Slate Creek
Rd., Grass Valley, CA 95945

Gun Owners of America
8001 Forbes Place, Suite 102,
Springfield, VA
22151/703-321-8585

Handgun Hunters International
J.D. Jones, Director, P.O. Box 357
MAG, Bloomingdale, OH 43910

**Harrington & Richardson Gun
Coll. Assn.**
George L. Cardet, 330 S.W. 27th
Ave., Suite 603, Miami, FL 33135

High Standard Collectors' Assn.
John J. Stimson, Jr., Pres., 540 W.
92nd St., Indianapolis, IN 46260

**Hopkins & Allen Arms & Memo-
rabilia Society (HAAMS)**
P.O. Box 187, 1309 Pamela Circle,
Delphos, OH 45833

**International Ammunition Associ-
ation, Inc.**
C.R. Punnett, Secy., 8 Hillock
Lane, Chadds Ford, PA
19317/610-358-1285;Fax:610-3
58-1560

International Benchrest Shooters
Joan Borden, RR1, Box 250BB,
Springville, PA
18844/717-965-2366

**International Blackpowder Hunt-
ing Assn.**
P.O. Box 1180, Glenrock, WY
82637/307-436-9817

**IHMSA (Intl. Handgun Metallic
Silhouette Assn.)**
PO Box 368, Burlington, IA 52601
Website: www.ihmsa.cor

**International Society of Mauser
Arms Collectors**
Michael Kindberg, Pres., P.O. Box
277, Alpharetta, GA 30239-0277

**Jews for the Preservation of Fire-
arms Ownership (JPFO) 501(c)(3)**
2872 S. Wentworth Ave., Milwaukee, WI 53207/414-769-0760;
Fax:414-483-8435

The Mannlicher Collectors Assn.
Membership Office: P.O.
Box1249, The Dalles, Oregon
97058

**Marlin Firearms Collectors
Assn., Ltd.**
Dick Paterson, Secy., 407 Lincoln
Bldg., 44 Main St., Champaign, IL
61820

Merwin Hulbert Association,
2503 Kentwood Ct., High Point,
NC 27265

**Miniature Arms Collectors/Mak-
ers Society, Ltd.**
Ralph Koebbeman, Pres., 4910
Kilburn Ave., Rockford, IL
61101/815-964-2569

**M1 Carbine Collectors Assn.
(M1-CCA)**
623 Apaloosa Ln., Gardnerville,
NV 89410-7840

**National Association of Buckskin-
ners (NAB)**
Territorial Dispatch—1800s Historical Publication, 4701 Marion
St., Suite 324, Livestock Exchange
Bldg., Denver, CO
80216/303-297-9671

**The National Association of Der-
ringer Collectors**
P.O. Box 20572, San Jose, CA
95160

**National Assn. of Federally
Licensed Firearms Dealers**
Andrew Molchan, 2455 E. Sun-
rise, Ft. Lauderdale, FL 33304

**National Association to Keep and
Bear Arms**
P.O. Box 78336, Seattle, WA
98178

**National Automatic Pistol Collec-
tors Assn.**
Tom Knox, P.O. Box 15738, Tower
Grove Station, St. Louis, MO
63163

**National Bench Rest Shooters
Assn., Inc.**
Pat Ferrell, 2835 Guilford Lane,
Oklahoma City, OK
73120-4404/405-842-9585; Fax:
405-842-9575

**National Muzzle Loading Rifle
Assn.**
Box 67, Friendship, IN 47021 /
812-667-5131. Website:
www.nmlra@nmlra.org

**National Professional Paintball
League (NPPL)**
540 Main St., Mount Kisco, NY
10549/914-241-7400

**National Reloading
Manufacturers Assn.**
One Centerpointe Dr., Suite 300,
Lake Oswego, OR 97035

National Rifle Assn. of America
11250 Waples Mill Rd., Fairfax, VA
22030 / 703-267-1000. Website:
www.nra.org

**National Shooting Sports Foun-
dation, Inc.**
Robert T. Delfay, President, Flintlock Ridge Office Center, 11 Mile
Hill Rd., Newtown, CT
06470-2359/203-426-1320; FAX:
203-426-1087

National Skeet Shooting Assn.
Dan Snyuder, Director, 5931 Roft
Road, San Antonio, TX
78253-9261/800-877-5338.
Website: nssa-nsca.com

**National Sporting Clays Associa-
tion**
Ann Myers, Director, 5931 Roft
Road, San Antonio, TX
78253-9261/800-877-5338.
Website: nssa-nsca.com

**National Wild Turkey
Federation, Inc.**
P.O. Box 530, 770 Augusta Rd.,
Edgefield, SC 29824

North American Hunting Club
P.O. Box 3401, Minnetonka, MN
55343/612-936-9333; Fax:
612-936-9755

**North American Paintball Refer-
ees Association (NAPRA)**
584 Cestaric Dr., Milpitas, CA
95035

North-South Skirmish Assn., Inc.
Stevan F. Meserve, Exec. Secretary, 507 N. Brighton Court, Sterling, VA 20164-3919

Remington Society of America
Gordon Fosburg, Secretary, 11900
North Brinton Road, Lake, MI
48623

**Rocky Mountain Elk
Foundation**
P.O. Box 8249, Missoula, MT
59807-8249/406-523-4500;Fax:
406-523-4581
Website: www.rmef.org

Ruger Collector's Assn., Inc.
P.O. Box 240, Greens Farms, CT
06436

Safari Club International
4800 W. Gates Pass Rd., Tucson,
AZ 85745/520-620-1220

Sako Collectors Assn., Inc.
Jim Lutes, 202 N. Locust, Whitewater, KS 67154

Second Amendment Foundation
James Madison Building, 12500
NE 10th Pl., Bellevue, WA 98005

**Single Action Shooting Society
(SASS)**
23255-A La Palma Avenue, Yorba
Linda, CA 92887/714-6941800;
FAX: 714-694-1815/email:
sasseot@aol.com Website:
www.sassnet.com

**Smith & Wesson
Collectors Assn.**
Cally Pletl, Admin. Asst.,PO Box
444, Afton, NY 13730

**The Society of American Bayonet
Collectors**
P.O. Box 234, East Islip, NY
11730-0234

**Southern California Schuetzen
Society**
Dean Lillard, 34657 Ave. E.,
Yucaipa, CA 92399

**Sporting Arms and Ammunition
Manufacturers' Institute (SAAMI)**
Flintlock Ridge Office Center, 11
Mile Hill Rd., Newtown, CT
06470-2359/203-426-4358; FAX:
203-426-1087

Sporting Clays of America (SCA)
Ron L. Blosser, Pres., 9257 Buckeye Rd., Sugar Grove, OH
43155-9632/614-746-8334; Fax:
614-746-8605

The Thompson/Center Assn.
Joe Wright, President, Box 792,
Northboro, MA
01532/508-845-6960

**U.S. Practical Shooting
Assn./IPSC**
Dave Thomas, P.O. Box 811,
Sedro Woolley, WA
98284/360-855-2245

U.S. Revolver Assn.
Brian J. Barer, 40 Larchmont Ave.,
Taunton, MA
02780/508-824-4836

U.S. Shooting Team
U.S. Olympic Shooting Center,
One Olympic Plaza, Colorado
Springs, CO 80909/719-578-4670

The Varmint Hunters Assn., Inc.
Box 759, Pierre, SD 57501/Mem-
ber Services 800-528-4868

Weatherby Collectors Assn., Inc.
P.O. Box 888, Ozark, MO 65721

The Wildcatters
P.O. Box 170, Greenville, WI
54942

**Winchester Arms Collectors
Assn.**
P.O. Box 230, Brownsboro, TX
75756/903-852-4027

**The Women's Shooting Sports
Foundation (WSSF)**
4620 Edison Avenue, Ste. C, Colorado Springs, CO
80915/719-638-1299; FAX:
719-638-1271/email:
wssf@worldnet.att.net

ARGENTINA
**Asociacion Argentina de Colec-
cionistas de Armes y Municiones**
Castilla de Correos No. 28, Suc-
cursal I B, 1401 Buenos Aires,
Republica Argentina

AUSTRALIA
**Antique & Historical Arms Col-
lectors of Australia**
P.O. Box 5654, GCMC Queensland
9726, Australia

**The Arms Collector's Guild of
Queensland Inc.**
Ian Skennerton, P.O. Box 433,
Ashmore City 4214, Queensland,
Australia

**Australian Cartridge
Collectors Assn., Inc.**
Bob Bennett, 126 Landscape Dr.,
E. Doncaster 3109, Victoria, Ausr-
talia

**Sporting Shooters Assn. of Aus-
tralia, Inc.**
P.O. Box 2066, Kent Town, SA
5071, Australia

CANADA

ALBERTA
Canadian Historical Arms Society
P.O. Box 901, Edmonton, Alb.,
Canada T5J 2L8

National Firearms Assn.
Natl. Hq: P.O. Box 1779, Edmonton, Alb., Canada T5J 2P1

BRITISH COLUMBIA
**The Historical Arms
Collectors of B.C.
(Canada)**
Harry Moon, Pres., P.O. Box
50117, South Slope RPO, Burn-
aby, BC V5J 5G3, Can-
ada/604-438-0950;
Fax:604-277-3646

ONTARIO
**Association of Canadian Car-
tridge Collectors**
Monica Wright, RR 1, Millgrove,
ON, LOR IVO, Canada

Tri-County Antique Arms Fair
P.O. Box 122, RR #1, North Lancaster, Ont., Canada K0C 1Z0

EUROPE

BELGIUM
**European Catridge Research
Assn.**
Graham Irving, 21 Rue Schaltin,
4900 Spa, Bel-
gium/32.87.77.43.40;
Fax:32.87.77.27.51

CZECHOSLOVAKIA
**Spolecnost Pro Studium Naboju
(Czech Cartridge Research Assn.)**
JUDr. Jaroslav Bubak, Pod
Homolko 1439, 26601 Beroun 2,
Czech Republic

DENMARK
**Aquila Dansk Jagtpatron Historic
Forening (Danish Historical Cartridge Collectors Club)**
Steen Elgaard Møller, Ulriksdalsvej
7, 4840 Nr. Alslev, Denmark
10045-53846218;Fax:00455384
6209

ENGLAND
Arms and Armour Society
Hon. Secretary A. Dove, P.O. Box
10232, London, 5W19 2ZD,
England

Dutch Paintball Federation
Aceville Publ., Castle House 97
High Street, Colchester, Essex C01
1TH, England/011-44-206-564840

**European Paintball Sports Foun-
dation**
c/o Aceville Publ., Castle House 97
High St., Colchester, Essex, C01
1TH, England

**Historical Breechloading Small-
arms Assn.**
D.J. Penn M.A., Secy., P.O. Box
12778, London SE1 6BX, England.
Journal and newsletter are $23 a
yr., including airmail.

National Rifle Assn.
(Great Britain) Bisley Camp,
Brookwood, Woking Surrey GU24
OPB, England/01483.797777; Fax:
014730686275

United Kingdom Cartridge Club
Ian Southgate, 20 Millfield, Elmley
Castle, Nr. Pershore, Worcester-
shire, WR10 3HR, England

FRANCE
STAC-Western Co.
3 Ave. Paul Doumer (N.311);
78360 Montesson,
France/01.30.53-43-65; Fax:
01.30.53.19.10

GERMANY
**Bund Deutscher Sportschützen
e.v. (BDS)**
Borsigallee 10, 53125 Bonn 1,
Germany

Deutscher Schützenbund
Lahnstrasse 120, 65195 Wies-
baden, Germany

SPAIN
**Asociacion Espanola de Collec-
cionistas de Cartuchos (A.E.C.C.)**
Secretary: Apdo. Correos No.
1086, 2880-Alcala de Henares
(Madrid), Spain. President: Apdo.
Correos No. 682, 50080 Zaragoza,
Spain

SWEDEN
**Scandinavian Ammunition
Research Assn.**
Box 107, 77622 Hedemora, Swe-
den

NEW ZEALAND
**New Zealand Cartridge Collectors
Club**
Terry Castle, 70 Tiraumea Dr.,
Pakuranga, Auckland, New
Zealand

New Zealand Deerstalkers Assn.
P.O. Box 6514 TE ARO, Wellington, New Zealand

SOUTH AFRICA
**Historical Firearms Soc. of South
Africa**
P.O. Box 145, 7725 Newlands,
Republic of South Africa

**Republic of South Africa Car-
tridge Collectors Assn.**
Arno Klee, 20 Eugene St., Malan-
shof Randburg, Gauteng 2194,
Republic of South Africa

**S.A.A.C.A.
(Southern Africa Arms and
Ammunition Assn.)**
Gauteng Office:
P.O. Box 7597, Weltevreden Park,
1715, Republic of South
Africa/011-679-1151; Fax:
011-679-1131;
e-mail:
saaaca@iafrica.com.

Kwa-Zulu Natal office:
P.O. Box 4065, Northway, Kwa-
zulu-Natal 4065, Republic of
South Africa

**SAGA
(S.A. Gunowners' Assn.)**
P.O. Box 35203, Northway, Kwa-
zulu-Natal 4065, Republic of
South Africa

2002
GUN DIGEST
DIRECTORY OF THE
ARMS TRADE

The **Product Directory** contains 85 product categories. The **Arms Trade Directory** alphabetically lists the manufacturers with their addresses, phone numbers, FAX numbers and Internet addresses, if available.

DIRECTORY OF THE ARMS TRADE INDEX

DIRECTORY

AMMUNITION COMPONENTS, SHOTSHELL

Claybuster Wads & Harvester Bullets
Garcia National Gun Traders, Inc.
Precision Reloading, Inc.
Tar-Hunt Custom Rifles, Inc.
Vitt/Boos

AMMUNITION COMPONENTS-- BULLETS, POWDER, PRIMERS, CASES

3-D Ammunition & Bullets
A.W. Peterson Gun Shop, Inc.
Acadian Ballistic Specialties
Accuracy Unlimited
Accurate Arms Co., Inc.
Action Bullets & Alloy Inc
ADCO Sales, Inc.
Alaska Bullet Works, Inc.
Alliant Techsystems Smokeless Powder Group
Allred Bullet Co.
Alpha LaFranck Enterprises
American Products, Inc.
Arizona Ammunition, Inc.
Armfield Custom Bullets
A-Square Co.,Inc.
Atlantic Rose, Inc.
Baer's Hollows
Ballard Rifle & Cartridge Co., LLC
Ballistic Product, Inc.
Barnes
Barnes Bullets, Inc.
Beartooth Bullets
Beeline Custom Bullets Limited
Bell Reloading, Inc.
Berger Bullets Ltd.
Berry's Mfg., Inc.
Big Bore Bullets of Alaska
Big Bore Express
Bitterroot Bullet Co.
Black Belt Bullets (See Big Bore Express)
Black Hills Shooters Supply
Black Powder Products
Blount, Inc., Sporting Equipment Div.
Blue Mountain Bullets
Briese Bullet Co., Inc.
Brown Co, E. Arthur
Brown Dog Ent.
BRP, Inc. High Performance Cast Bullets
Buck Stix--SOS Products Co.
Buckeye Custom Bullets
Buckskin Bullet Co.
Buffalo Arms Co.
Buffalo Rock Shooters Supply
Bullseye Bullets
Bull-X, Inc.
Butler Enterprises
Buzztail Brass (See Grayback Wildcats)
Cambos Outdoorsman
Canyon Cartridge Corp.
Cascade Bullet Co., Inc.
Cast Performance Bullet Company
Casull Arms Corp.
CCI Div. of Blount, Inc.
Champion's Choice, Inc.
Cheddite France S.A.
CheVron Bullets
Chuck's Gun Shop
Clean Shot Technologies
Colorado Sutlers Arsenal (See Cumberland States
Competitor Corp. Inc.
Cook Engineering Service
Cor-Bon Bullet & Ammo Co.
Cumberland States Arsenal
Cummings Bullets
Curtis Cast Bullets
Curtis Gun Shop (See Curtis Cast Bullets)
Custom Bullets by Hoffman
D&J Bullet Co. & Custom Gun Shop, Inc.
Dakota Arms, Inc.
Dick Marple & Associates
Dixie Gun Works, Inc.

DKT, Inc.
Dohring Bullets
Eichelberger Bullets, Wm.
Eldorado Cartridge Corp (See PMC/Eldorado
Elkhorn Bullets
Epps, Ellwood (See "Gramps")
Federal Cartridge Co.
Fiocchi of America Inc.
Fish Mfg. Gunsmith Sptg. Co., Marshall
Forkin, Ben (See Belt MTN Arms)
Forkin Arms
Fowler Bullets
Fowler, Bob (See Black Powder Products)
Foy Custom Bullets
Freedom Arms, Inc.
Garcia National Gun Traders, Inc.
Gehmann, Walter (See Huntington Die Specialties)
GOEX Inc.
Golden Bear Bullets
Gotz Bullets
Grayback Wildcats
Green Mountain Rifle Barrel Co., Inc.
Grier's Hard Cast Bullets
GTB
Gun City
Hammets VLD Bullets
Hardin Specialty Dist.
Harris Enterprises
Harrison Bullets
Hart & Son, Inc.
Hawk Laboratories, Inc. (See Hawk, Inc.)
Hawk, Inc.
Haydon Shooters Supply, Russ
Heidenstrom Bullets
Hercules, Inc. (See Alliant Techsystems, Smokeless
Hi-Performance Ammunition Company
Hirtenberger Aktiengesellschaft
Hobson Precision Mfg. Co.
Hodgdon Powder Co.
Hornady Mfg. Co.
HT Bullets
Hunterjohn
Hunters Supply, Inc.
Huntington Die Specialties
Impact Case Co.
Imperial Magnum Corp.
IMR Powder Co.
Intercontinental Distributors, Ltd.
J&D Components
J&L Superior Bullets (See Huntington Die Special)
J.R. Williams Bullet Co.
J-4 Inc.
James Calhoon Varmint Bullets
Jensen Bullets
Jensen's Firearms Academy
Jericho Tool - Magna Shock Ind
Jester Bullets
JLK Bullets
John Walters Wads
JRP Custom Bullets
Ka Pu Kapili
Kasmarsik Bullets
Kaswer Custom, Inc.
Keith's Bullets
Keng's Firearms Specialty, Inc./US Tactical Systems
Ken's Kustom Kartridges
Kent Cartridge Mfg. Co. Ltd.
KLA Enterprises
Knight Rifles
Knight Rifles (See Modern Muzzle Loading, Inc.)
Lage Uniwad
Lapua Ltd.
Lawrence Brand Shot (See Precision Reloading)
Legend Products Corp.
Liberty Shooting Supplies
Lightfield Ammunition Corp. (See Slug Group, Inc.)
Lightning Performance Innovations, Inc.
Lindsley Arms Cartridge Co.
Littleton, J. F.
Lomont Precision Bullets

Loweth, Richard H.R.
Magnus Bullets
Maine Custom Bullets
Maionchi-L.M.I.
Marchmon Bullets
Markesbery Muzzle Loaders, Inc.
MarMik, Inc.
MAST Technology
McMurdo, Lynn (See Specialty Gunsmithing)
Meister Bullets (See Gander Mountain)
Men-Metallwerk Elisenhuette GmbH
Merkuria Ltd.
Michael's Antiques
Mitchell Bullets, R.F.
MI-TE Bullets
Montana Armory, Inc (See C. Sharps Arms Co. Inc.)
Montana Precision Swaging
Mountain State Muzzleloading Supplies, Inc.
Mt. Baldy Bullet Co.
Mulhern, Rick
Murmur Corp.
Nagel's Custom Bullets
National Bullet Co.
Naval Ordnance Works
Necromancer Industries, Inc.
North American Shooting Systems
North Devon Firearms Services
Northern Precision Custom Swaged Bullets
Nosler, Inc.
OK Weber,Inc.
Oklahoma Ammunition Co.
Old Wagon Bullets
Old Western Scrounger,Inc.
Oregon Trail Bullet Company
Pacific Cartridge, Inc.
Pacific Rifle Co.
Page Custom Bullets
Pease Accuracy
Penn Bullets
Petro-Explo Inc.
Phillippi Custom Bullets, Justin
Pinetree Bullets
PMC/Eldorado Cartridge Corp.
Polywad, Inc.
Power Plus Enterprises, Inc.
Precision Components and Guns
Precision Delta
Precision Munitions, Inc.
Prescott Projectile Co.
Price Bullets, Patrick W.
PRL Bullets, c/o Blackburn Enterprises
Professional Hunter Supplies (See Star Custom Bull)
Proofmark Corp.
R.I.S. Co., Inc.
R.M. Precision
Rainier Ballistics Corp.
Ravell Ltd.
Redwood Bullet Works
Reloading Specialties, Inc.
Remington Arms Co., Inc.
Rhino
Robinson H.V. Bullets
Rubright Bullets
SAECO (See Redding Reloading Equipment)
Scharch Mfg., Inc.
Schneider Bullets
Schroeder Bullets
Schumakers Gun Shop
Scot Powder
Seebeck Assoc., R.E.
Shappy Bullets
Sharps Arms Co., Inc., C.
Shilen, Inc.
Sierra Bullets
SOS Products Co. (See Buck Stix-SOS Products Co.)
Southern Ammunition Co., Inc.
Specialty Gunsmithing
Speer Products Div. of Blount Inc. Sporting Equipm
Spencer's Custom Guns
Stanley Bullets
Star Ammunition, Inc.
Star Custom Bullets
Starke Bullet Company

Starline, Inc.
Stewart's Gunsmithing
Swift Bullet Co.
T.F.C. S.p.A.
Taracorp Industries, Inc.
TCCI
TCSR
The Ordnance Works
Thompson Precision
TMI Products (See Haselbauer Products, Jerry)
Traditions Performance Firearms
Trophy Bonded Bullets, Inc.
True Flight Bullet Co.
Tucson Mold, Inc.
Unmussig Bullets, D. L.
USAC
Vann Custom Bullets
Vihtavuori Oy/Kaltron-Pettibone
Vincent's Shop
Viper Bullet and Brass Works
Vom Hoffe (See Old Western Scrounger, Inc., The)
Warren Muzzleloading Co., Inc.
Watson Trophy Match Bullets
Weatherby, Inc.
Western Nevada West Coast Bullets
Widener's Reloading & Shooting Supply, Inc.
Winchester Div. Olin Corp.
Winkle Bullets
Woodleigh (See Huntington Die Specialties)
Worthy Products, Inc.
Wosenitz VHP, Inc.
Wyant Bullets
Wyoming Custom Bullets
Zero Ammunition Co., Inc.

AMMUNITION, COMMERCIAL

"Su-Press-On",Inc.
3-D Ammunition & Bullets
3-Ten Corp.
A.W. Peterson Gun Shop, Inc.
Ace Custom 45's, Inc.
Air Arms
American Ammunition
Arizona Ammunition, Inc.
Arms Corporation of the Philippines
Arundel Arms & Ammunition, Inc., A.
A-Square Co.,Inc.
Atlantic Rose, Inc.
Badger Shooters Supply, Inc.
Ballistic Product, Inc.
Ben William's Gun Shop
Benjamin/Sheridan Co., Crossman
Big Bear Arms & Sporting Goods, Inc.
Black Hills Ammunition, Inc.
Blammo Ammo
Blount, Inc., Sporting Equipment Div.
Brenneke GmBH
Brown Dog Ent.
Buffalo Bullet Co., Inc..
Bull-X, Inc.
Cambos Outdoorsman
Casull Arms Corp.
CBC
Champion's Choice, Inc.
Cor-Bon Bullet & Ammo Co.
Creekside Gun Shop Inc.
Crosman Airguns
Cubic Shot Shell Co., Inc.
Cumberland States Arsenal
Daisy Mfg. Co.
Dead Eye's Sport Center
Delta Arms Ltd.
Delta Frangible Ammunition LLC
Diana (See U.S. Importer - Dynamit Nobel-RWS, Inc.)
Dynamit Nobel-RWS, Inc.
Effebi SNC-Dr. Franco Beretta
Eley Ltd.
Elite Ammunition
Estate Cartridge, Inc.
Federal Cartridge Co.
Fiocchi of America Inc.
Fish Mfg. Gunsmith Sptg. Co., Marshall
Garcia National Gun Traders, Inc.
Garrett Cartridges Inc.
Garthwaite Pistolsmith, Inc., Jim
Gibbs Rifle Co., Inc.

Gil Hebard Guns
Glaser Safety Slug, Inc.
GOEX Inc.
Groenewold, John
Gun City
Gunsmithing, Inc.
Hansen & Co. (See Hansen Cartridge Co.)
Hart & Son, Inc.
Hi-Performance Ammunition Company
Hirtenberger Aktiengesellschaft
Hornady Mfg. Co.
Hunters Supply, Inc.
IMX LLC
Intercontinental Distributors, Ltd.
Ion Industries, Inc
Jones, J.D./SSK Industries
Keng's Firearms Specialty, Inc./US Tactical Systems
Kent Cartridge America, Inc
Kent Cartridge Mfg. Co. Ltd.
Knight Rifles
Lapua Ltd.
Lethal Force Institute (See Police Bookshelf)
Lightfield Ammunition Corp. (See Slug Group, Inc.)
Lock's Philadelphia Gun Exchange
Magnum Research, Inc.
MagSafe Ammo Co.
Magtech Ammunition Co. Inc.
Maionchi-L.M.I.
Markell,Inc.
McBros Rifle Co.
Men-Metallwerk Elisenhuette GmbH
Mullins Ammunition
New England Ammunition Co.
Oklahoma Ammunition Co.
Omark Industries,Div. of Blount,Inc.
Outdoor Sports Headquarters,Inc.
P.S.M.G. Gun Co.
Pacific Cartridge, Inc.
Paragon Sales & Services, Inc.
Parker & Sons Shooting Supply
PMC/Eldorado Cartridge Corp.
Polywad, Inc.
Pony Express Reloaders
Precision Delta
Pro Load Ammunition, Inc.
R.E.I.
Ravell Ltd.
Remington Arms Co., Inc.
Rucker Dist. Inc.
RWS (See US Importer-Dynamit Nobel-RWS, Inc.)
Sellier & Bellot, USA Inc
Southern Ammunition Co., Inc.
Speer Products Div. of Blount Inc. Sporting Equipm
TCCI
The BulletMakers Workshop
Thompson Bullet Lube Co.
USAC
Valor Corp.
VAM Distribution Co LLC
Victory USA
Vihtavuori Oy/Kaltron-Pettibone
Visible Impact Targets
Voere-KGH m.b.H.
Vom Hoffe (See Old Western Scrounger, Inc., The)
Weatherby, Inc.
Westley Richards & Co.
Widener's Reloading & Shooting Supply, Inc.
Winchester Div. Olin Corp.
Zero Ammunition Co., Inc.

AMMUNITION, CUSTOM

3-D Ammunition & Bullets
3-Ten Corp.
Accuracy Unlimited
AFSCO Ammunition
Allred Bullet Co.
American Derringer Corp.
American Products, Inc.
Arizona Ammunition, Inc.
Arms Corporation of the Philippines
A-Square Co.,Inc.
Atlantic Rose, Inc.
Belding's Custom Gun Shop
Berger Bullets Ltd.
Big Bore Bullets of Alaska

Black Hills Ammunition, Inc.
Blue Mountain Bullets
Brynin, Milton
Buckskin Bullet Co.
CBC
Cubic Shot Shell Co., Inc.
Custom Tackle and Ammo
Dakota Arms, Inc.
Dead Eye's Sport Center
Delta Frangible Ammunition LLC
DKT, Inc.
Elite Ammunition
Estate Cartridge, Inc.
Freedom Arms, Inc.
GDL Enterprises
GOEX Inc.
Grayback Wildcats
Gun Accessories (See Glaser Safety
    Slug, Inc.)
Hirtenberger Aktiengesellschaft
Hobson Precision Mfg. Co.
Hoelscher, Virgil
Horizons Unlimited
Hornady Mfg. Co.
Hunters Supply, Inc.
IMX LLC
James Calhoon Varmint Bullets
Jensen Bullets
Jensen's Custom Ammunition
Jensen's Firearms Academy
John Walters Wads
Kaswer Custom, Inc.
Keeler, R. H.
Kent Cartridge Mfg. Co. Ltd.
L E Jurras & Assoc
L.A.R. Mfg., Inc.
Lethal Force Institute (See Police
    Bookshelf)
Lindsley Arms Cartridge Co.
Linebaugh Custom Sixguns
MagSafe Ammo Co.
MAST Technology
McBros Rifle Co.
McMurdo, Lynn (See Specialty
    Gunsmithing)
Men-Metallwerk Elisenhuette GmbH
Milstor Corp.
Mountain Rifles, Inc.
Mullins Ammunition
Naval Ordnance Works
Nygord Precision Products
Oklahoma Ammunition Co.
Old Western Scrounger,Inc.
P.S.M.G. Gun Co.
Phillippi Custom Bullets, Justin
Power Plus Enterprises, Inc.
Precision Munitions, Inc.
Professional Hunter Supplies (See
    Star Custom Bull)
R.E.I.
Ramon B. Gonzalez Guns
Sanders Custom Gun Service
Sanders Gun and Machine Shop
Sandia Die & Cartridge Co.
SOS Products Co. (See Buck Stix-
    SOS Products Co.)
Specialty Gunsmithing
Spencer's Custom Guns
Star Custom Bullets
State Arms Gun Co.
Stewart's Gunsmithing
The BulletMakers Workshop
The Country Armourer
Unmussig Bullets, D. L.
Vitt/Boos
Vom Hoffe (See Old Western
    Scrounger, Inc., The)
Vulpes Ventures, Inc. Fox Cartridge
    Division
Warren Muzzleloading Co., Inc.
Weaver Arms Corp. Gun Shop
Worthy Products, Inc.

AMMUNITION, FOREIGN

A.W. Peterson Gun Shop, Inc.
AFSCO Ammunition
Armscorp USA, Inc.
A-Square Co.,Inc.
Atlantic Rose, Inc.
B & P America
Beeman Precision Airguns
CBC
Cheddite France S.A.
Cubic Shot Shell Co., Inc.

Dead Eye's Sport Center
Diana (See U.S. Importer - Dynamit
    Nobel-RWS, Inc.)
DKT, Inc.
Dynamit Nobel-RWS, Inc.
E. Arthur Brown Co.
Fiocchi of America Inc.
First Inc, Jack
Fisher Enterprises, Inc.
Fisher, R. Kermit (See Fisher
    Enterprises, Inc)
Gamebore Division, Polywad Inc
Gibbs Rifle Co., Inc.
GOEX Inc.
Gunsmithing, Inc.
Hansen & Co. (See Hansen Cartridge
    Co.)
Heidenstrom Bullets
Hirtenberger Aktiengesellschaft
Hornady Mfg. Co.
IMX LLC
Intrac Arms International
Johnson's Gunsmithing, Inc, Neal
K.B.I. Inc
MagSafe Ammo Co.
Maionchi-L.M.I.
Marksman Products
MAST Technology
Merkuria Ltd.
Mullins Ammunition
Naval Ordnance Works
Navy Arms Co.
Navy Arms Company
Neal Johnson's Gunsmithing, Inc.
Oklahoma Ammunition Co.
Old Western Scrounger,Inc.
P.S.M.G. Gun Co.
Paragon Sales & Services, Inc.
Petro-Explo Inc.
R.E.T. Enterprises
Ravell Ltd.
RWS (See US Importer-Dynamit
    Nobel-RWS, Inc.)
Samco Global Arms, Inc.
Sentinel Arms
Southern Ammunition Co., Inc.
Speer Products Div. of Blount Inc.
    Sporting Equipm
Stratco, Inc.
SwaroSports, Inc. (See JagerSport
    Ltd.)
T.F.C. S.p.A.
The BulletMakers Workshop
The Paul Co.
Victory Ammunition
Vihtavuori Oy/Kaltron-Pettibone
Vom Hoffe (See Old Western
    Scrounger, Inc., The)

ANTIQUE ARMS DEALER

Ackerman & Co.
Ad Hominem
Antique American Firearms
Antique Arms Co.
Aplan Antiques & Art, James O.
Arundel Arms & Ammunition, Inc., A.
Ballard Rifle & Cartridge Co., LLC
Bear Mountain Gun & Tool
Bill Johns Master Engraver
Bob's Tactical Indoor Shooting Range
    & Gun Shop
British Antiques
Buckskin Machine Works, A.
    Hunkeler
Bustani, Leo
Cape Outfitters
Carlson, Douglas R, Antique
    American Firearms
CBC-BRAZIL
Chadick's Ltd.
Chambers Flintlocks Ltd., Jim
Champlin Firearms, Inc.
Chuck's Gun Shop
Clements' Custom Leathercraft, Chas
Cole's Gun Works
Collectors Firearms Etc.
Custom Single Shot Rifles
David R. Chicoine
Dixie Gun Works, Inc.
Dixon Muzzleloading Shop, Inc.
Duffy, Charles E (See Guns Antique &
    Modern DBA)
Enguix Import-Export
Fagan & Co.Inc

Fish Mfg. Gunsmith Sptg. Co.,
    Marshall
Flayderman & Co., Inc.
Frielich Police Equipment
Fulmer's Antique Firearms, Chet
Getz Barrel Co.
Glass, Herb
Goergen's Gun Shop
Golden Age Arms Co.
Goodwin, Fred
Gun Hunter Books (See Gun Hunter
    Trading Co)
Gun Hunter Trading Co.
Guns Antique & Modern DBA/Charles
    E. Duffy
Hallowell & Co.
HandCrafts Unltd (See Clements'
    Custom Leather)
Handgun Press
Hansen & Co. (See Hansen Cartridge
    Co.)
Hunkeler, A (See Buckskin Machine
    Works)
James Wayne Firearms for Collectors
    and Investors
Kelley's
Knight's Mfg. Co.
Ledbetter Airguns, Riley
LeFever Arms Co., Inc.
Lever Arms Service Ltd.
Lock's Philadelphia Gun Exchange
Lodgewood Mfg.
Log Cabin Sport Shop
Mandall Shooting Supplies Inc.
Martin's Gun Shop
Michael's Antiques
Montana Outfitters, Lewis E. Yearout
Muzzleloaders Etcetera, Inc.
Navy Arms Company
New England Arms Co.
Pony Express Sport Shop
Powder Horn Antiques
Ravell Ltd.
Retting, Inc., Martin B
Sarco, Inc.
Scott Fine Guns Inc., Thad
Shootin' Shack, Inc.
Sportsmen's Exchange & Western
    Gun Traders, Inc.
Steves House of Guns
Stott's Creek Armory, Inc.
Strawbridge, Victor W.
The Gun Room
The Gun Room Press
The Gun Works
Turnbull Restoration, Doug
Vic's Gun Refinishing
Vintage Arms, Inc.
Wallace, Terry
Westley Richards & Co.
Wiest, M. C.
William Fagan & Co.
Winchester Sutler, Inc., The
Wood, Frank (See Classic Guns, Inc.)
Yearout, Lewis E. (See Montana
    Outfitters)

APPRAISER - GUNS,
ETC.

A.W. Peterson Gun Shop, Inc.
Ackerman & Co.
Antique Arms Co.
Arundel Arms & Ammunition, Inc., A.
Barta's Gunsmithing
Beitzinger, George
Blue Book Publications, Inc.
Bob's Tactical Indoor Shooting Range
    & Gun Shop
British Antiques
Bullet'n Press
Bustani, Leo
Butterfield & Butterfield
Camilli, Lou
Cannon's
Cape Outfitters
Chadick's Ltd.
Champlin Firearms, Inc.
Christie's East
Clark Firearms Engraving
Clements' Custom Leathercraft, Chas
Cole's Gun Works
Collectors Firearms Etc.
Colonial Arms, Inc.

Colonial Repair
Corry, John
Creekside Gun Shop Inc.
Custom Arms Company
Custom Tackle and Ammo
D&D Gunsmiths, Ltd.
David R. Chicoine
DGR Custom Rifles
Dixon Muzzleloading Shop, Inc.
Duane's Gun Repair (See DGR
    Custom Rifles)
Epps, Ellwood (See "Gramps")
Eversull Co., Inc., K.
Fagan & Co.Inc
Ferris Firearms
Fish Mfg. Gunsmith Sptg. Co.,
    Marshall
Flayderman & Co., Inc.
Forty Five Ranch Enterprises
Francotte & Cie S.A. Auguste
Frontier Arms Co.,Inc.
Gene's Custom Guns
George E. Mathews & Son, Inc.
Gerald Pettinger Books
Getz Barrel Co.
Gillmann, Edwin
Gilmore Sports Concepts
Goergen's Gun Shop
Golden Age Arms Co.
Goodwin, Fred
Griffin & Howe, Inc.
Gun City
Gun Hunter Books (See Gun Hunter
    Trading Co)
Gun Hunter Trading Co.
Guns
Hallowell & Co.
Hammans, Charles E.
HandCrafts Unltd (See Clements'
    Custom Leather)
Handgun Press
Hank's Gun Shop
Hansen & Co. (See Hansen Cartridge
    Co.)
Hughes, Steven Dodd
Irwin, Campbell H.
Island Pond Gun Shop
Jackalope Gun Shop
James Wayne Firearms for Collectors
    and Investors
Jensen's Custom Ammunition
Kelley's
L.L. Bean, Inc.
Lampert, Ron
LaRocca Gun Works
Ledbetter Airguns, Riley
LeFever Arms Co., Inc.
Lock's Philadelphia Gun Exchange
Lodgewood Mfg.
Log Cabin Sport Shop
Lomont Precision Bullets
Long, George F.
Madis, George
Mahony, Philip Bruce
Mandall Shooting Supplies Inc.
Martin's Gun Shop
Mathews & Son, Inc., George E.
McCann Industries
McCann's Machine & Gun Shop
McCann's Muzzle-Gun Works
Mercer Custom Guns
Montana Outfitters, Lewis E. Yearout
Muzzleloaders Etcetera, Inc.
Navy Arms Company
New England Arms Co.
Nitex, Inc.
Pasadena Gun Center
Pentheny de Pentheny
Perazzi USA, Inc.
Pony Express Sport Shop
Powder Horn Antiques
R.A. Wells Custom Gunsmith
R.E.T. Enterprises
Ramon B. Gonzalez Guns
Retting, Inc., Martin B
River Road Sporting Clays
Robert Valade Engraving
Safari Outfitters Ltd.
Scott Fine Guns Inc., Thad
Shootin' Shack, Inc.
Spencer Reblue Service
Sportsmen's Exchange & Western
    Gun Traders, Inc.

Stott's Creek Armory, Inc.
Stratco, Inc.
Strawbridge, Victor W.
Ten-Ring Precision, Inc.
The Gun Room Press
The Gun Shop
The Orvis Co.
The Swampfire Shop (See Peterson
    Gun Shop, Inc.)
Thurston Sports, Inc.
Vic's Gun Refinishing
Walker Arms Co., Inc.
Wasmundt, Jim
Werth, T. W.
Whildin & Sons Ltd, E.H.
Wichita Arms, Inc.
Wiest, M. C.
William Fagan & Co.
Williams Shootin' Iron Service, The
    Lynx-Line
Winchester Sutler, Inc., The
Wood, Frank (See Classic Guns, Inc.)
Yearout, Lewis E. (See Montana
    Outfitters)
Yee, Mike

AUCTIONEER - GUNS,
ETC.

"Little John's" Antique Arms
Buck Stix--SOS Products Co.
Butterfield & Butterfield
Christie's East
Fagan & Co.Inc
Kelley's
Sotheby's

BOOKS & MANUALS
(PUBLISHERS &
DEALERS)

"Su-Press-On",Inc.
A.W. Peterson Gun Shop, Inc.
Accurate Arms Co., Inc.
Alpha 1 Drop Zone
American Handgunner Magazine
Armory Publications
Arms & Armour Press
Ballistic Product, Inc.
Ballistic Product, Inc.
Barnes Bullets, Inc.
Bauska Barrels
Beartooth Bullets
Beeman Precision Airguns
Blacksmith Corp.
Blacktail Mountain Books
Blue Book Publications, Inc.
Blue Ridge Machinery & Tools, Inc.
Boone's Custom Ivory Grips, Inc.
Brown Co, E. Arthur
Brownells, Inc.
Bullet'n Press
Calibre Press, Inc.
Cape Outfitters
Cheyenne Pioneer Products
Colonial Repair
Colorado Sutlers Arsenal (See
    Cumberland States
Corbin Mfg. & Supply, Inc.
Cumberland States Arsenal
DBI Books Division of Krause
    Publications
Dixie Gun Works, Inc.
Dixon Muzzleloading Shop, Inc.
Ed~ Brown Products, Inc.
Executive Protection Institute
Flores Publications Inc, J (See Action
    Direct Inc)
Galati International
Gerald Pettinger Books
Golden Age Arms Co.
Gun City
Gun List (See Krause Publications)
Guncraft Sports Inc
Gunnerman Books
GUNS Magazine
Gunsmithing, Inc.
H&P Publishing
Handgun Press
Harris Publications
Hawk Laboratories, Inc. (See Hawk,
    Inc.)
Hawk, Inc.
Haydon Shooters Supply, Russ
Heritage/VSP Gun Books

PRODUCT & SERVICE DIRECTORY

High North Products, Inc.
Hodgdon Powder Co.
Home Shop Machinist The Village Press Publications
Hornady Mfg. Co.
Hungry Horse Books
Huntington Die Specialties
I.D.S.A. Books
Info-Arm
Ironside International Publishers
J Martin Inc
Jantz Supply
Kelley's
King & Co.
Koval Knives
Krause Publications, Inc.
Lapua Ltd.
Lethal Force Institute (See Police Bookshelf)
Madis Books
Magma Engineering Co.
MarMik, Inc.
Milberry House Publishing
Montana Armory, Inc (See C. Sharps Arms Co. Inc.)
Mountain South
Mountain State Muzzleloading Supplies, Inc.
Navy Arms Company
New Win Publishing, Inc.
Outdoor Sports Headquarters,Inc.
Paintball Games International Magazine Aceville
Pejsa Ballistics
Petersen Publishing Co. (See Emap USA)
Police Bookshelf
Precision Shooting,Inc.
Professional Hunter Supplies (See Star Custom Bull)
Ray Riling Arms Books Co.
Remington Double Shotguns
Riling Arms Books Co., Ray
Rocky Mountain Wildlife Products
Rutgers Book Center
S&S Firearms
Safari Press, Inc.
Saunders Gun & Machine Shop
Scharch Mfg., Inc.
Semmer, Charles (See Remington Double Shotguns)
Sharps Arms Co., Inc., C.
Shootin' Accessories, Ltd.
Sierra Bullets
Speer Products Div. of Blount Inc. Sporting Equipm
SPG LLC
Stackpole Books
Stewart Game Calls, Inc., Johnny
Stoeger Industries
Stoeger Publishing Co. (See Stoeger Industries)
The Gun Parts Corp.
The Gun Room Press
The Gun Works
The NgraveR Co.
The Outdoorsman's Bookstore
Thomas, Charles C.
Track of the Wolf, Inc.
Trafalgar Square
Trotman, Ken
Tru-Balance Knife Co.
Vega Tool Co.
Vintage Industries, Inc.
VSP Publishers (See Heritage/VSP Gun Books)
W. Square Enterprises
W.E. Brownell Checkering Tools
WAMCO--New Mexico
Wells Creek Knife & Gun Works
Wilderness Sound Products Ltd.
Winchester Press (See New Win Publishing, Inc.)
Wolfe Publishing Co.
Wolf's Western Traders

BULLET CASTING, ACCESSORIES

Ballisti-Cast, Inc.
Beartooth Bullets
Bullet Metals
CFVentures
Ferguson, Bill

Lee Precision, Inc.
Lyman Products Corporation
Magma Engineering Co.
Ox-Yoke Originals, Inc.
Rapine Bullet Mould Mfg. Co.
SPG LLC
The Hanned Line
Thompson Bullet Lube Co.
United States Products Co.

BULLET CASTING, FURNACES & POTS

Ballisti-Cast, Inc.
Bullet Metals
Ferguson, Bill
Lee Precision, Inc.
Lyman Products Corporation
Magma Engineering Co.
Rapine Bullet Mould Mfg. Co.

BULLET CASTING, LEAD

Action Bullets & Alloy Inc
Ames Metal Products
Belltown Ltd.
Buckskin Bullet Co.
Buffalo Arms Co.
Bullet Metals
Bullseye Bullets
Hunters Supply, Inc.
Jericho Tool - Magna Shock Ind
John Walters Wads
Lee Precision, Inc.
Magma Engineering Co.
Montana Precision Swaging
Muzzleloading Technologies, Inc
Ox-Yoke Originals, Inc.
Penn Bullets
Proofmark Corp.
SPG LLC
W. Square Enterprises

BULLET PULLERS

Battenfeld Technologies
Royal Arms Gunstocks

BULLET TOOLS

Brynin, Milton
Bullet Swaging Supply Inc.
Camdex, Inc.
Corbin Mfg. & Supply, Inc.
Cumberland Arms
Eagan, Donald V.
Holland's Gunsmithing
Hollywood Engineering
Lee Precision, Inc.
Necromancer Industries, Inc.
Niemi Engineering, W. B.
North Devon Firearms Services
Rorschach Precision Products
Sport Flite Manufacturing Co.
The Hanned Line
WTA Manufacturing

BULLET, CASE & DIE LUBRICANTS

Bonanza (See Forster Products)
Brown Co, E. Arthur
Buckskin Bullet Co.
Camp-Cap Products
CH Tool & Die Co (See 4-D Custom Die Co)
Cooper-Woodward
CVA
Elkhorn Bullets
E-Z-Way Systems
Ferguson, Bill
Forster Products
Guardsman Products
HEBB Resources
Heidenstrom Bullets
Hollywood Engineering
Hornady Mfg. Co.
Imperial (See E-Z-Way Systems)
Knoell, Doug
Le Clear Industries (See E-Z-Way Systems)
Lee Precision, Inc.
Lithi Bee Bullet Lube
MI-TE Bullets
Paco's (See Small Custom Mould & Bullet Co)
RCBS Div. of Blount
Reardon Products

Rooster Laboratories
Shay's Gunsmithing
Small Custom Mould & Bullet Co.
Tamarack Products, Inc.
Uncle Mike's (See Michaels of Oregon Co)
Warren Muzzleloading Co., Inc.
Widener's Reloading & Shooting Supply, Inc.
Young Country Arms

CARTRIDGES FOR COLLECTORS

"Gramps" Antique Cartridges
Ackerman & Co.
Ad Hominem
Armory Publications
British Antiques
Cameron's
Campbell, Dick
Cartridge Transfer Group, Pete de Coux
Cherry Creek State Park Shooting Center
Cole's Gun Works
Colonial Repair
Cubic Shot Shell Co., Inc.
de Coux, Pete (See Cartridge Transfer Group)
Duane's Gun Repair (See DGR Custom Rifles)
Enguix Import-Export
Epps, Ellwood (See "Gramps")
First Inc, Jack
Fitz Pistol Grip Co.
Forty Five Ranch Enterprises
Goergen's Gun Shop
Grayback Wildcats
Gun City
Gun Hunter Books (See Gun Hunter Trading Co)
Gun Hunter Trading Co.
Liberty Shooting Supplies
Mandall Shooting Supplies Inc.
MAST Technology
Michael's Antiques
Montana Outfitters, Lewis E. Yearout
Pasadena Gun Center
Samco Global Arms, Inc.
SOS Products Co. (See Buck Stix-SOS Products Co.)
Stone Enterprises Ltd.
The Country Armourer
The Gun Parts Corp.
Vom Hoffe (See Old Western Scrounger, Inc., The)
Ward & Van Valkenburg
Yearout, Lewis E. (See Montana Outfitters)

CASE & AMMUNITION PROCESSORS, INSPECTORS, BOXERS

Ammo Load, Inc.
Ben's Machines
Hafner World Wide, Inc.
Scharch Mfg., Inc.

CASE CLEANERS & POLISHING MEDIA

3-D Ammunition & Bullets
Battenfeld Technologies
Belltown Ltd.
Chem-Pak Inc.
G96 Products Co., Inc.
Lee Precision, Inc.
Penn Bullets
VibraShine, Inc.

CASE PREPARATION TOOLS

CONKKO
Haydon Shooters Supply, Russ
High Precision
Hoehn Sales, Inc.
J. Dewey Mfg. Co., Inc.
K&M Services
Lee Precision, Inc.
Match Prep--Doyle Gracey
Plum City Ballistic Range
RCBS Div. of Blount
Sinclair International, Inc.
Stoney Point Products, Inc.

CASE TRIMMERS, TRIM DIES & ACCESSORIES

Fremont Tool Works
K&M Services
Match Prep--Doyle Gracey
OK Weber,Inc.
Ozark Gun Works

CASE TUMBLERS, VIBRATORS, MEDIA & ACCESSORIES

4-D Custom Die Co.
Battenfeld Technologies
Berry's Mfg., Inc.
Dillon Precision Products, Inc.
Penn Bullets
VibraShine, Inc.

CASES, CABINETS, RACKS & SAFES - GUN

All Rite Products, Inc.
Allen Co., Bob
Allen Co., Inc.
Allen Sportswear, Bob (See Allen Co., Bob)
Alumna Sport by Dee Zee
American Display Co.
American Security Products Co.
Americase
Art Jewel Enterprises Ltd.
Ashby Turkey Calls
Bagmaster Mfg., Inc.
Barramundi Corp.
Berry's Mfg., Inc.
Big Sky Racks, Inc.
Big Spring Enterprises "Bore Stores"
Bill's Custom Cases
Bison Studios
Black Sheep Brand
Brauer Bros. Mfg. Co.
Brown, H. R. (See Silhouette Leathers)
Browning Arms Co.
Bushmaster Hunting & Fishing
Cannon Safe, Inc.
Chipmunk (See Oregon Arms, Inc.)
Cobalt Mfg., Inc.
CONKKO
Connecticut Shotgun Mfg. Co.
D&L Industries (See D.J. Marketing)
D.J. Marketing
Dara-Nes, Inc. (See Nesci Enterprises, Inc.)
Deepeeka Exports Pvt. Ltd.
Doskocil Mfg. Co., Inc.
DTM International, Inc.
Elk River, Inc.
English, Inc., A.G.
Enhanced Presentations, Inc.
Eversull Co., Inc., K.
Fort Knox Security Products
Frontier Safe Co.
Galati International
GALCO International Ltd.
Gun Locker Div. of Airmold W.R. Grace & Co.-Conn.
Gun-Ho Sports Cases
Hall Plastics, Inc., John
Hastings Barrels
Homak
Hoppe's Div. Penguin Industries, Inc.
Huey Gun Cases
Hugger Hooks Co.
Hunter Co., Inc.
Hydrosorbent Products
Impact Case Co.
Johanssons Vapentillbehor, Bert
Johnston Bros. (See C&T Corp. TA Johnson Brothers)
Jumbo Sports Products
Kalispel Case Line
Kane Products, Inc.
KK Air International (See Impact Case Co.)
Knock on Wood Antiques
Kolpin Mfg., Inc.
Lakewood Products LLC
Liberty Safe
Marsh, Mike
McWelco Products
Morton Booth Co.
MPC

MTM Molded Products Co., Inc.
Nalpak
Necessary Concepts, Inc.
Nesci Enterprises Inc.
Outa-Site Gun Carriers
Palmer Security Products
Perazzi USA, Inc.
Pflumm Mfg. Co.
Poburka, Philip (See Bison Studios)
Powell & Son (Gunmakers) Ltd., William
Prototech Industries, Inc.
Quality Arms, Inc.
Rogue Rifle Co., Inc.
Schulz Industries
Silhouette Leathers
Southern Security
Sportsman's Communicators
Sun Welding Safe Co.
Sweet Home, Inc.
Talmage, William G.
The Eutaw Co., Inc.
The Outdoor Connection,Inc.
The Surecase Co.
Tinks & Ben Lee Hunting Products (See Wellington)
W. Waller & Son, Inc.
Wilson Case, Inc.
Woodstream
Zanotti Armor, Inc.
Ziegel Engineering

CHOKE DEVICES, RECOIL ABSORBERS & RECOIL PADS

3-Ten Corp.
Accuright
Action Products, Inc.
Allen Co., Bob
Allen Sportswear, Bob (See Allen Co., Bob)
Answer Products Co.
Arms Ingenuity Co.
Baer Custom, Inc, Les
Baker, Stan
Bansner's Gunsmithing Specialties
Bartlett Engineering
Battenfeld Technologies
Briley Mfg. Inc.
Brooks Tactical Systems
B-Square Company, Inc.
Buffer Technologies
Bull Mountain Rifle Co.
C&H Research
Cation
Chicasaw Gun Works
Clearview Products
Colonial Arms, Inc.
Connecticut Shotgun Mfg. Co.
CRR, Inc./Marble's Inc.
Danuser Machine Co.
Dina Arms Corporation
Frank Custom Classic Arms, Ron
Graybill's Gun Shop
Guns
Harry Lawson Co.
Hastings Barrels
Hogue Grips
Holland's Gunsmithing
I.N.C. Inc (See Kickeez Inc.)
J.P. Enterprises Inc.
Jackalope Gun Shop
Jenkins Recoil Pads, Inc.
KDF, Inc.
Kickeez Inc
Lawson Co., Harry
London Guns Ltd.
Lyman Products Corporation
Mag-Na-Port International, Inc.
Marble Arms (See CRR, Inc./Marble's Inc.)
Menck, Gunsmith Inc., T.W.
Middlebrooks Custom Shop
Morrow, Bud
Nelson/Weather-Rite, Inc.
Nu-Line Guns,Inc.
Oakland Custom Arms,Inc.
One Of A Kind
Original Box, Inc.
Palsa Outdoor Products
Precision Reloading, Inc.
Pro-Port Ltd.
Protektor Model

Que Industries, Inc.
R.M. Precision
Shotguns Unlimited
Simmons Gun Repair, Inc.
Sound Technology
Stone Enterprises Ltd.
Time Precision, Inc.
Truglo, Inc
Trulock Tool
Uncle Mike's (See Michaels of Oregon Co)
Universal Sports
Virgin Valley Custom Guns
Vortek Products, Inc.
Williams Gun Sight Co.
Wilson Gun Shop
Wise Guns, Dale

CHRONOGRAPHS & PRESSURE TOOLS

Air Rifle Specialists
Brown Co, E. Arthur
Canons Delcour
Clearview Products
Competition Electronics, Inc.
Custom Chronograph, Inc.
D&H Precision Tooling
Hege Jagd-u. Sporthandels GmbH
Hornady Mfg. Co.
Hutton Rifle Ranch
Kent Cartridge Mfg. Co. Ltd.
Oehler Research,Inc.
P.A.C.T., Inc.
Savage Arms, Inc.
Shooting Chrony, Inc.
SKAN A.R.
Stratco, Inc.
Tepeco

CLEANERS & DEGREASERS

Belltown Ltd.
Camp-Cap Products
G96 Products Co., Inc.
Hafner World Wide, Inc.
Kleen-Bore,Inc.
Lestrom Laboratories, Inc.
Mac-1 Airgun Distributors
Modern Muzzleloading, Inc
Northern Precision Custom Swaged Bullets
Prolixrr Lubricants
R&S Industries Corp.
Sheffield Knifemakers Supply, Inc.
United States Products Co.

CLEANING & REFINISHING SUPPLIES

AC Dyna-tite Corp.
Accupro Gun Care
Alpha 1 Drop Zone
American Gas & Chemical Co., Ltd
Answer Products Co.
Armite Laboratories
Armsport, Inc.
Atlantic Mills, Inc.
Atsko/Sno-Seal, Inc.
Barnes Bullets, Inc.
Battenfeld Technologies
Beeman Precision Airguns
Belltown Ltd.
Bill's Gun Repair
Birchwood Casey
Blount, Inc., Sporting Equipment Div.
Blue and Gray Products Inc (See Ox-Yoke Originals)
Break-Free, Inc.
Bridgers Best
Brown Co, E. Arthur
Brownells, Inc.
C.S. Van Gorden & Son, Inc.
Cambo's Outdoorsman
Camp-Cap Products
Chem-Pak Inc.
CONKKO
Connecticut Shotgun Mfg. Co.
Creedmoor Sports, Inc.
CRR, Inc./Marble's Inc.
Custom Products (See Jones Custom Products)
Cylinder & Slide, Inc., William R. Laughridge
D&H Prods. Co., Inc.

Dara-Nes, Inc. (See Nesci Enterprises, Inc.)
Decker Shooting Products
Deepeeka Exports Pvt. Ltd.
Desert Mountain Mfg.
Dewey Mfg. Co., Inc., J.
Du-Lite Corp.
Dykstra, Doug
E&L Mfg., Inc.
Ed King Office
Eezox, Inc.
Ekol Leather Care
Faith Associates
Flitz International Ltd.
Fluoramics, Inc.
Frontier Products Co.
G96 Products Co., Inc.
Golden Age Arms Co.
Guardsman Products
Gunsmithing, Inc.
Hafner World Wide, Inc.
Half Moon Rifle Shop
Haydon Shooters Supply, Russ
Heatbath Corp.
Hoppe's Div. Penguin Industries, Inc.
Hornady Mfg. Co.
Hydrosorbent Products
Iosso Products
J. Dewey Mfg. Co., Inc.
James Calhoon Varmint Bullets
Jantz Supply
Johnston Bros. (See C&T Corp. TA Johnson Brothers)
Jonad Corp.
K&M Industries, Inc.
Kellogg's Professional Products
Kent Cartridge Mfg. Co. Ltd.
Kesselring Gun Shop
Kleen-Bore,Inc.
Knight Rifles
Laurel Mountain Forge
LEM Gun Specialties Inc. The Lewis Lead Remover
List Precision Engineering
LPS Laboratories, Inc.
Lyman Products Corporation
Marble Arms (See CRR, Inc./Marble's Inc.)
Mark Lee Supplies
Micro Sight Co.
Minute Man High Tech Industries
Mountain State Muzzleloading Supplies, Inc.
Mountain View Sports, Inc.
MTM Molded Products Co., Inc.
Muscle Products Corp.
Muzzleloading Technologies, Inc
Neal Johnson's Gunsmithing, Inc.
Nesci Enterprises Inc.
Northern Precision Custom Swaged Bullets
Now Products, Inc.
October Country Muzzleloading
Old World Oil Products
Omark Industries,Div. of Blount,Inc.
Original Mink Oil,Inc
Otis Technology, Inc
Outers Laboratories Div. of Blount, Inc.Sporting
Ox-Yoke Originals, Inc.
P&M Sales and Service
Parker & Sons Shooting Supply
Parker Gun Finishes
Pendleton Royal, c/o Swingler Buckland Ltd.
Pete Rickard, Inc.
Precision Airgun Sales, Inc.
Prolixrr Lubricants
Pro-Shot Products, Inc.
R&S Industries Corp.
Radiator Specialty Co.
Redfield/Blount
Rickard, Inc., Pete
Rooster Laboratories
Rusty Duck Premium Gun Care Products
Saunders Gun & Machine Shop
Schumakers Gun Shop
Sheffield Knifemakers Supply, Inc.
Shiloh Creek
Shooter's Choice
Shootin' Accessories, Ltd.
Silencio/Safety Direct

Sno-Seal, Inc. (See Atsko/Sno-Seal)
Southern Bloomer Mfg. Co.
Starr Trading Co., Jedediah
Svon Corp.
T.F.C. S.p.A.
TDP Industries, Inc.
Tetra Gun Lubricants (See FTI, Inc.)
Texas Platers Supply Co.
The Dutchman's Firearms, Inc.
The Lewis Lead Remover (See LEM Gun Specialties)
The Paul Co.
Thompson Bullet Lube Co.
Thompson/Center Arms
Track of the Wolf, Inc.
United States Products Co.
Venco Industries, Inc. (See Shooter's Choice)
VibraShine, Inc.
Volquartsen Custom Ltd.
Vom Hoffe (See Old Western Scrounger, Inc., The)
Warren Muzzleloading Co., Inc.
Watson Trophy Match Bullets
WD-40 Co.
Wick, David E.
Willow Bend
Wolf's Western Traders
Young Country Arms

COMPUTER SOFTWARE - BALLISTICS

Action Target, Inc.
AmBr Software Group Ltd.
Arms Software
Arms, Programming Solutions (See Arms Software)
Barnes Bullets, Inc.
Canons Delcour
Corbin Mfg. & Supply, Inc.
Data Tech Software Systems
Hodgdon Powder Co.
Huntington Die Specialties
J.I.T. Ltd.
Jensen Bullets
Kent Cartridge Mfg. Co. Ltd.
Maionchi-L.M.I.
Oehler Research,Inc.
Outdoor Sports Headquarters,Inc.
P.A.C.T., Inc.
Pejsa Ballistics
Powley Computer (See Hutton Rifle Ranch)
RCBS Div. of Blount
Sierra Bullets
The Ballistic Program Co., Inc.
The Country Armourer
Tioga Engineering Co., Inc.
Vancini, Carl (See Bestload, Inc.)
W. Square Enterprises

CUSTOM GUNSMITH

A&W Repair
A.A. Arms, Inc.
A.W. Peterson Gun Shop, Inc.
Acadian Ballistic Specialties
Accuracy Unlimited
Ace Custom 45's, Inc.
Acra-Bond Laminates
Actions by "T" Teddy Jacobson
Ad Hominem
Adair Custom Shop, Bill
Ahlman Guns
Aldis Gunsmithing & Shooting Supply
Alpha Gunsmith Division
Alpha Precision, Inc.
Alpine Indoor Shooting Range
American Custom Gunmakers Guild
Amrine's Gun Shop
Answer Products Co.
Antique Arms Co.
Armament Gunsmithing Co., Inc.
Arms Craft Gunsmithing
Arms Ingenuity Co.
Armscorp USA, Inc.
Arnold Arms Co., Inc.
Artistry Inwood
Art's Gun & Sport Shop, Inc.
Arundel Arms & Ammunition, Inc., A.
Autauga Arms, Inc.
Baelder, Harry
Baer Custom, Inc, Les
Bain & Davis, Inc.

Bansner's Gunsmithing Specialties
Barnes Bullets, Inc.
Baron Technology
Barta's Gunsmithing
Bear Arms
Bear Mountain Gun & Tool
Beaver Lodge (See Fellowes, Ted)
Behlert Precision, Inc.
Beitzinger, George
Belding's Custom Gun Shop
Ben William's Gun Shop
Bengtson Arms Co., L.
Biesen, Al
Biesen, Roger
Bill Adair Custom Shop
Billings Gunsmiths Inc.
BlackStar AccuMax Barrels
BlackStar Barrel Accurizing (See BlackStar AccuMax
Bob Rogers Gunsmithing
Boltin, John M.
Bond Custom Firearms
Borden Rifles Inc
Borovnik KG, Ludwig
Bowen Classic Arms Corp.
Brace, Larry D.
Brian Perazone-Gunsmith
Briese Bullet Co., Inc.
Briganti, A.J.
Briley Mfg. Inc.
Broad Creek Rifle Works, Ltd.
Brockman's Custom Gunsmithing
Broken Gun Ranch
Brown Precision,Inc.
Buckhorn Gun Works
Buckskin Machine Works, A. Hunkeler
Budin, Dave
Bull Mountain Rifle Co.
Bullberry Barrel Works, Ltd.
Burkhart Gunsmithing, Don
Cache La Poudre Rifleworks
Cambos Outdoorsman
Cambo's Outdoorsman
Camilli, Lou
Cannon's
Carolina Precision Rifles
Carter's Gun Shop
Caywood, Shane J.
CBC-BRAZIL
Chambers Flintlocks Ltd., Jim
Champlin Firearms, Inc.
Chicasaw Gun Works
Chuck's Gun Shop
Clark Custom Guns, Inc.
Clark Firearms Engraving
Classic Arms Company
Classic Arms Corp.
Clearview Products
Cleland's Outdoor World, Inc
Cloward's Gun Shop
Coffin, Charles H.
Cogar's Gunsmithing
Coleman's Custom Repair
Cole's Gun Works
Colonial Arms, Inc.
Colonial Repair
Colorado Gunsmithing Academy
Colorado School of Trades
Colt's Mfg. Co., Inc.
Conrad, C. A.
Corkys Gun Clinic
Cox, Ed. C.
Craig Custom Ltd., Research & Development
Creekside Gun Shop Inc.
Cullity Restoration
Curtis Custom Shop
Custom Arms Company
Custom Checkering Service, Kathy Forster
Custom Gun Products
Custom Gun Stocks
Custom Single Shot Rifles
Cylinder & Slide, Inc., William R. Laughridge
D&D Gunsmiths, Ltd.
D&J Bullet Co. & Custom Gun Shop, Inc.
Dangler, Homer L.
Darlington Gun Works, Inc.
Dave's Gun Shop
David Miller Co.

David R. Chicoine
David W. Schwartz Custom Guns
Davis, Don
Delorge, Ed
Del-Sports, Inc.
DGR Custom Rifles
DGS, Inc., Dale A. Storey
Dietz Gun Shop & Range, Inc.
Dilliott Gunsmithing, Inc.
Donnelly, C. P.
Duane A. Hobbie Gunsmithing
Duane's Gun Repair (See DGR Custom Rifles)
Duffy, Charles E (See Guns Antique & Modern DBA)
Duncan's Gun Works, Inc.
E. Arthur Brown Co.
Echols & Co., D'Arcy
Eckelman Gunsmithing
Ed Brown Products, Inc.
Ed~ Brown Products, Inc.
Eggleston, Jere D.
EGW Evolution Gun Works
Entre'prise Arms, Inc.
Erhardt, Dennis
Eskridge Rifles
Eversull Co., Inc., K.
Eyster Heritage Gunsmiths, Inc., Ken
Ferris Firearms
Fish Mfg. Gunsmith Sptg. Co., Marshall
Fisher, Jerry A.
Fisher Custom Firearms
Fleming Firearms
Flynn's Custom Guns
Forkin, Ben (See Belt MTN Arms)
Forkin Arms
Forster, Kathy (See Custom Checkering)
Forster, Larry L.
Forthofer's Gunsmithing & Knifemaking
Francesca, Inc.
Francotte & Cie S.A. Auguste
Frank Custom Classic Arms, Ron
Fred F. Wells/Wells Sport Store
Frontier Arms Co.,Inc.
Fullmer, Geo. M.
G.G. & G.
Gary Reeder Custom Guns
Gator Guns & Repair
Genecco Gun Works
Gentry Custom Gunmaker, David
George E. Mathews & Son, Inc.
Gillmann, Edwin
Gilman-Mayfield, Inc.
Gilmore Sports Concepts
Giron, Robert E.
Goens, Dale W.
Gonic Arms/North American Arm
Goodling's Gunsmithing
Goodwin, Fred
Grace, Charles E.
Graybill's Gun Shop
Green, Roger M.
Greg Gunsmithing Repair
GrE-Tan Rifles
Griffin & Howe, Inc.
Griffin & Howe, Inc.
Gruning Precision Inc
Guncraft Sports Inc
Guns
Guns Antique & Modern DBA/Charles E. Duffy
Gunsite Custom Shop
Gunsite Gunsmithy (See Gunsite Custom Shop)
Gunsite Training Center
Gunsmithing Ltd.
Hagn Rifles & Actions, Martin
Hamilton, Alex B (See Ten-Ring Precision, Inc)
Hammans, Charles E.
Hammond Custom Guns Ltd.
Hank's Gun Shop
Hanson's Gun Center, Dick
Hanus Birdguns Bill
Harris Gunworks
Harry Lawson Co.
Hart & Son, Inc.
Hartmann & Weiss GmbH
Harwood, Jack O.

Hawken Shop, The (See Dayton Traister)
Hecht, Hubert J, Waffen-Hecht
Heilmann, Stephen
Heinie Specialty Products
Heppler, Keith M, Keith's Custom Gunstocks
Heydenberk, Warren R.
High Bridge Arms, Inc
High Performance International
High Precision
Highline Machine Co.
Hill, Loring F.
Hiptmayer, Armurier
Hiptmayer, Klaus
Hoag Gun Wks
Hodgson, Richard
Hoehn Sales, Inc.
Hoelscher, Virgil
Hoenig & Rodman
Holland's Gunsmithing
Hollis Gun Shop
Huebner, Corey O.
Hughes, Steven Dodd
Hunkeler, A (See Buckskin Machine Works
Hyper-Single, Inc.
IAI
Imperial Magnum Corp.
Irwin, Campbell H.
Island Pond Gun Shop
Ivanoff, Thomas G (See Tom's Gun Repair)
J J Roberts Firearm Engraver
J&S Heat Treat
J.J. Roberts/Engraver
Jack Dever Co.
Jackalope Gun Shop
Jagdwaffen, P. Hofer
Jamison's Forge Works
Jarrett Rifles, Inc.
Jarvis, Inc.
Jay McCament Custom Gun Maker
Jeffredo Gunsight
Jensen's Custom Ammunition
Jim Norman Custom Gunstocks
Jim's Gun Shop (See Spradlin's)
Jim's Precision, Jim Ketchum
John Norrell Arms
John Rigby & Co.
Jones Custom Products, Neil A.
Jones, J.D./SSK Industries
Juenke, Vern
KDF, Inc.
Keith's Custom Gunstocks
Ken Eyster Heritage Gunsmiths, Inc.
Ken Starnes Gunmaker
Ken's Gun Specialties
Ketchum, Jim (See Jim's Precision)
Kilham & Co.
Kimball, Gary
King's Gun Works
KLA Enterprises
Klein Custom Guns, Don
Kleinendorst, K. W.
Knippel, Richard
KOGOT
Korzinek Riflesmith, J
L E Jurras & Assoc
LaFrance Specialties
Lair, Sam
Lampert, Ron
LaRocca Gun Works
Larry Lyons Gunworks
Lathrop's, Inc.
Laughridge, William R (See Cylinder & Slide Inc)
Lawson Co., Harry
Lazzeroni Arms Co.
Lee's Red Ramps
LeFever Arms Co., Inc.
Lind Custom Guns, Al
Linebaugh Custom Sixguns
List Precision Engineering
Lock's Philadelphia Gun Exchange
Long, George F.
Mag-Na-Port International, Inc.
Mahony, Philip Bruce
Mahovsky's Metalife
Makinson, Nicholas
Mandall Shooting Supplies Inc.
Marent, Rudolf
Martin's Gun Shop

Martz, John V.
Mathews & Son, Inc., George E.
Mazur Restoration, Pete
McCann's Muzzle-Gun Works
McCluskey Precision Rifles
McFarland, Stan
McGowen Rifle Barrels
McKinney, R.P. (See Schuetzen Gun Co.)
McMillan Rifle Barrels
MCS, Inc.
Mercer Custom Guns
Michael's Antiques
Mid-America Recreation, Inc.
Middlebrooks Custom Shop
Miller Arms, Inc.
Miller Custom
Mills Jr., Hugh B.
Moeller, Steve
Monell Custom Guns
Montgomery Community College
Morrison Custom Rifles, J. W.
Morrow, Bud
Mo's Competitor Supplies (See MCS Inc)
Mowrey's Guns & Gunsmithing
Mullis Guncraft
Muzzleloading Technologies, Inc
NCP Products, Inc.
Nelson's Custom Guns
Nettestad Gun Works
New England Arms Co.
New England Custom Gun Service
Newman Gunshop
Nicholson Custom
Nickels, Paul R.
Nicklas, Ted
Nitex, Inc.
North American Shooting Systems
Nu-Line Guns,Inc.
Oakland Custom Arms,Inc.
Old World Gunsmithing
Olson, Vic
Ottmar, Maurice
Ox-Yoke Originals, Inc.
Ozark Gun Works
P.S.M.G. Gun Co.
Pac-Nor Barreling
Pagel Gun Works, Inc.
Parker Gun Finishes
Pasadena Gun Center
Paterson Gunsmithing
Paulsen Gunstocks
PEM's Mfg. Co.
Pence Precision Barrels
Penrod Precision
Pentheny de Pentheny
Perazone-Gunsmith, Brian
Performance Specialists
Pete Mazur Restoration
Powell & Son (Gunmakers) Ltd., William
Power Custom, Inc.
Professional Hunter Supplies (See Star Custom Bull)
Quality Custom Firearms
Quality Firearms of Idaho, Inc.
R&J Gun Shop
Ray's Gunsmith Shop
Renfrew Guns & Supplies
Ridgetop Sporting Goods
Ries, Chuck
River Road Sporting Clays
RMS Custom Gunsmithing
Robert Valade Engraving
Robinson, Don
Rocky Mountain Arms, Inc.
Rocky Mountain Rifle Works Ltd.
Romain's Custom Guns, Inc.
RPM
Rupert's Gun Shop
Ryan, Chad L.
Sanders Custom Gun Service
Sanders Gun and Machine Shop
Savage Arms, Inc.
Schiffman, Mike
Schumakers Gun Shop
Score High Gunsmithing
Scott McDougall & Associates
Sharp Shooter Supply
Shaw, Inc., E. R. (See Small Arms Mfg. Co.)
Shay's Gunsmithing

Shockley, Harold H.
Shooters Supply
Shootin' Shack, Inc.
Shooting Specialties (See Titus, Daniel)
Shotguns Unlimited
Sile Distributors, Inc.
Silver Ridge Gun Shop (See Goodwin, Fred)
Simmons Gun Repair, Inc.
Singletary, Kent
Sipes Gun Shop
Siskiyou Gun Works (See Donnelly, C. P.)
Skeoch, Brian R.
Sklany's Machine Shop
Slezak, Jerome F.
Small Arms Mfg. Co.
Small Arms Specialists
Smith, Art
Smith, Sharmon
Snapp's Gunshop
Sound Technology
Speiser, Fred D.
Spencer Reblue Service
Spencer's Custom Guns
Sportsmen's Exchange & Western Gun Traders, Inc.
Springfield, Inc.
SSK Industries
Star Custom Bullets
Steelman's Gun Shop
Steffens, Ron
Stiles Custom Guns
Storey, Dale A. (See DGS Inc.)
Stott's Creek Armory, Inc.
Strawbridge, Victor W.
Sturgeon Valley Sporters
Sullivan, David S .(See Westwind Rifles Inc.)
Swann, D. J.
Swenson's 45 Shop, A. D.
Swift River Gunworks
Szweda, Robert (See RMS Custom Gunsmithing)
Taconic Firearms Ltd., Perry Lane
Talmage, William G.
Tank's Rifle Shop
Tar-Hunt Custom Rifles, Inc.
Tarnhelm Supply Co., Inc.
Taylor & Robbins
Ten-Ring Precision, Inc.
Terry K. Kopp Professional Gunsmithing
Terry Theis-Engraver
The Competitive Pistol Shop
The Custom Shop
The Gun Shop
The Gun Works
The Orvis Co.
The Robar Co.'s, Inc.
The Swampfire Shop (See Peterson Gun Shop, Inc.)
Thompson, Randall (See Highline Machine Co.)
Thurston Sports, Inc.
Time Precision, Inc.
Toms Gun Repair, Inc.
Tom's Gunshop
Trevallion Gunstocks
Trulock Tool
Tucker, James C.
Turnbull Restoration, Doug
Unmussig Bullets, D. L.
Upper Missouri Trading Co.
Van Horn, Gil
Van Patten, J. W.
Van's Gunsmith Service
Vest, John
Vic's Gun Refinishing
Vintage Arms, Inc.
Virgin Valley Custom Guns
Volquartsen Custom Ltd.
Walker Arms Co., Inc.
Wallace, Terry
Wasmundt, Jim
Wayne E. Schwartz Custom Guns
Weaver Arms Corp. Gun Shop
Weber & Markin Custom Gunsmiths
Weems, Cecil
Weigand Combat Handguns, Inc.
Werth, T. W.
Wessinger Custom Guns & Engraving

Western Design (See Alpha Gunsmith Division)
Westley Richards & Co.
Westwind Rifles, Inc., David S. Sullivan
White Barn Wor
White Shooting Systems, Inc. (See White Muzzleload
Wichita Arms, Inc.
Wiebe, Duane
Wiest, M. C.
Wild West Guns
Williams Gun Sight Co.
Williams Shootin' Iron Service, The Lynx-Line
Williamson Precision Gunsmithing
Wilson Gun Shop
Winter, Robert M.
Wise Guns, Dale
Wiseman and Co., Bill
Wood, Frank (See Classic Guns, Inc.)
Working Guns
Wright's Hardwood Gunstock Blanks
Yankee Gunsmith
Yee, Mike
Zeeryp, Russ

CUSTOM METALSMITH

A&W Repair
Ackerman & Co.
Ahlman Guns
Aldis Gunsmithing & Shooting Supply
Alpha Precision, Inc.
American Custom Gunmakers Guild
Amrine's Gun Shop
Answer Products Co.
Antique Arms Co.
Arnold Arms Co., Inc.
Artistry Inwood
Baer Custom, Inc, Les
Bansner's Gunsmithing Specialties
Baron Technology
Bear Mountain Gun & Tool
Behlert Precision, Inc.
Beitzinger, George
Bengtson Arms Co., L.
Biesen, Al
Bill Adair Custom Shop
Billings Gunsmiths Inc.
Billingsley & Brownell
Bob Rogers Gunsmithing
Bone Engraving, Ralph
Bowen Classic Arms Corp.
Brace, Larry D.
Briganti, A.J.
Broad Creek Rifle Works, Ltd.
Brown Precision,Inc.
Buckhorn Gun Works
Bull Mountain Rifle Co.
Bullberry Barrel Works, Ltd.
Burkhart Gunsmithing, Don
Bustani, Leo
Campbell, Dick
Carter's Gun Shop
Caywood, Shane J.
Checkmate Refinishing
Cleland's Outdoor World, Inc
Colonial Repair
Colorado Gunsmithing Academy
Craftguard
Crandall Tool & Machine Co.
Cullity Restoration
Custom Arms Company
Custom Gun Products
Custom Single Shot Rifles
D&D Gunsmiths, Ltd.
D&H Precision Tooling
Dave's Gun Shop
Delorge, Ed
DGS, Inc., Dale A. Storey
Dilliott Gunsmithing, Inc.
Duane's Gun Repair (See DGR Custom Rifles)
Duncan's Gun Works, Inc.
Echols & Co., D'Arcy
Erhardt, Dennis
Eyster Heritage Gunsmiths, Inc., Ken
Ferris Firearms
Forster, Larry L.
Forthofer's Gunsmithing & Knifemaking
Francesca, Inc.
Frank Custom Classic Arms, Ron
Frank Knives

Fred F. Wells/Wells Sport Store
Fullmer, Geo. M.
Gary Reeder Custom Guns
Genecco Gun Works
Gene's Custom Guns
Gentry Custom Gunmaker, David
Grace, Charles E.
Grayback Wildcats
Graybill's Gun Shop
Green, Roger M.
Griffin & Howe, Inc.
Guns
Gunsmithing Ltd.
Hagn Rifles & Actions, Martin
Hamilton, Alex B (See Ten-Ring Precision, Inc)
Harry Lawson Co.
Hartmann & Weiss GmbH
Harwood, Jack O.
Hecht, Hubert J, Waffen-Hecht
Heilmann, Stephen
Highline Machine Co.
Hiptmayer, Armurier
Hiptmayer, Klaus
Hoag Gun Wks
Hoelscher, Virgil
Holland's Gunsmithing
Hollis Gun Shop
Hyper-Single, Inc.
Island Pond Gun Shop
Ivanoff, Thomas G (See Tom's Gun Repair)
J J Roberts Firearm Engraver
J&S Heat Treat
Jack Dever Co.
Jamison's Forge Works
Jay McCament Custom Gun Maker
Jeffredo Gunsight
Ken Eyster Heritage Gunsmiths, Inc.
Ken Starnes Gunmaker
Ken's Gun Specialties
Kilham & Co.
Klein Custom Guns, Don
Kleinendorst, K. W.
Knippel, Richard
Lampert, Ron
Larry Lyons Gunworks
Lawson Co., Harry
List Precision Engineering
Mahovsky's Metalife
Makinson, Nicholas
Mazur Restoration, Pete
McCann Industries
McCann's Machine & Gun Shop
McFarland, Stan
Miller Arms, Inc.
Montgomery Community College
Morrison Custom Rifles, J. W.
Morrow, Bud
Mullis Guncraft
Nelson's Custom Guns
Nettestad Gun Works
New England Custom Gun Service
Nicholson Custom
Nitex, Inc.
Noreen, Peter H.
Oakland Custom Arms,Inc.
Olson, Vic
Ozark Gun Works
Pagel Gun Works, Inc.
Parker Gun Finishes
Pasadena Gun Center
Penrod Precision
Pete Mazur Restoration
Precise Metalsmithing Enterprises
Precision Specialties
Rice, Keith (See White Rock Tool & Die)
River Road Sporting Clays
Rocky Mountain Arms, Inc.
Romain's Custom Guns, Inc.
Score High Gunsmithing
Simmons Gun Repair, Inc.
Singletary, Kent
Sipes Gun Shop
Skeoch, Brian R.
Sklany's Machine Shop
Small Arms Specialists
Smith, Art
Smith, Sharmon
Snapp's Gunshop
Spencer Reblue Service
Spencer's Custom Guns

Sportsmen's Exchange & Western Gun Traders, Inc.
Steffens, Ron
Stiles Custom Guns
Storey, Dale A. (See DGS Inc.)
Strawbridge, Victor W.
Taylor & Robbins
Ten-Ring Precision, Inc.
Terry K. Kopp Professional Gunsmithing
The Alaskan Silversmith
The Custom Shop
The Gun Shop
The Robar Co.'s, Inc.
Thompson, Randall (See Highline Machine Co.)
Toms Gun Repair, Inc.
Van Horn, Gil
Van Patten, J. W.
Waldron, Herman
Wallace, Terry
Weber & Markin Custom Gunsmiths
Werth, T. W.
Wessinger Custom Guns & Engraving
Westrom, John (See Precision Metal Finishing)
White Rock Tool & Die
Wiebe, Duane
Wild West Guns
Williams Shootin' Iron Service, The Lynx-Line
Williamson Precision Gunsmithing
Winter, Robert M.
Wise Guns, Dale
Wood, Frank (See Classic Guns, Inc.)
Wright's Hardwood Gunstock Blanks
Zufall, Joseph F.

DECOYS

A&M Waterfowl,Inc.
Baekgaard Ltd.
Belding's Custom Gun Shop
Carry-Lite, Inc.
Fair Game International
Farm Form Decoys, Inc.
Feather, Flex Decoys
Flambeau Products Corp.
G&H Decoys,Inc.
Herter's Manufacturing, Inc.
Hiti-Schuch, Atelier Wilma
Klingler Woodcarving
L.L. Bean, Inc.
Molin Industries, Tru-Nord Division
North Wind Decoy Co.
Quack Decoy & Sporting Clays
Russ Trading Post
Sports Innovations Inc.
Tanglefree Industries
Woods Wise Products

DIE ACCESSORIES, METALLIC

MarMik, Inc.
Rapine Bullet Mould Mfg. Co.
Sport Flite Manufacturing Co.
Wolf's Western Traders

DIES, METALLIC

4-D Custom Die Co.
Dakota Arms, Inc.
Dillon Precision Products, Inc.
Fremont Tool Works
Gruning Precision Inc
King & Co.
Lyman Products Corporation
Montana Precision Swaging
Ozark Gun Works
Rapine Bullet Mould Mfg. Co.
RCBS Div. of Blount
Redding Reloading Equipment
Romain's Custom Guns, Inc.
Sport Flite Manufacturing Co.
Vega Tool Co.
Wolf's Western Traders

DIES, SHOTSHELL

MEC, Inc.

DIES, SWAGE

4-D Custom Die Co.
Bullet Swaging Supply Inc.
Sport Flite Manufacturing Co.

ENGRAVER, ENGRAVING TOOLS

Ackerman & Co.
Adair Custom Shop, Bill
Ahlman Guns
Alfano, Sam
Allard, Gary/Creek Side Metal & Woodcrafters
Allen Firearm Engraving
Altamont Co.
American Custom Gunmakers Guild
American Pioneer Video
Anthony and George Ltd.
Baron Technology
Barraclough, John K.
Bill Adair Custom Shop
Bill Johns Master Engraver
Billy Bates Engraving
Blair Engraving, J. R.
Bleile, C. Roger
Boessler, Erich
Bone Engraving, Ralph
Bratcher, Dan
Brooker, Dennis
Churchill, Winston
Clark Firearms Engraving
Collings, Ronald
Creek Side Metal & Woodcrafters
Cullity Restoration
Cupp, Alana, Custom Engraver
Custom Single Shot Rifles
Custom Single Shot Rifles
Dayton Traister
Delorge, Ed
Dolbare, Elizabeth
Drain, Mark
Dremel Mfg. Co.
Dubber, Michael W.
Engraving Artistry
Evans Engraving, Robert
Eyster Heritage Gunsmiths, Inc., Ken
Firearms Engraver's Guild of America
Flannery Engraving Co., Jeff W
Forty Five Ranch Enterprises
Fountain Products
Francotte & Cie S.A. Auguste
Frank E. Hendricks Master Engravers, Inc.
Frank Knives
Fred F. Wells/Wells Sport Store
French, Artistic Engraving, J. R.
Gary Reeder Custom Guns
Gene's Custom Guns
Glimm's Custom Gun Engraving
Golden Age Arms Co.
Gournet Artistic Engraving
Grant, Howard V.
Griffin & Howe, Inc.
Guns
Gurney, F. R.
Gwinnell, Bryson J.
Hale, Engraver, Peter
Half Moon Rifle Shop
Hands Engraving, Barry Lee
Harris Gunworks
Harris Hand Engraving, Paul A.
Harwood, Jack O.
Hawken Shop, The (See Dayton Traister)
Hendricks, Frank E. Inc., Master Engravers
Hiptmayer, Armurier
Hiptmayer, Heidemarie
Ingle, Ralph W.
J J Roberts Firearm Engraver
J.J. Roberts/Engraver
J.R. Blair Engraving
Jagdwaffen, P. Hofer
Jantz Supply
John Adams & Son Engravers
Kamyk Engraving Co., Steve
Kane, Edward
Kehr Engraving
Kelly, Lance
Ken Eyster Heritage Gunsmiths, Inc.
Kenneth W. Warren Engraver
Klingler Woodcarving
Knippel, Richard
Koevenig's Engraving Service
Larry Lyons Gunworks
LeFever Arms Co., Inc.
Leibowitz, Leonard
Lindsay, Steve

Little Trees Ramble (See Scott Pilkington)
Lutz Engraving, Ron E.
Master Engravers, Inc. (See Hendricks, Frank E)
McCombs, Leo
McDonald, Dennis
McKenzie, Lynton
Mele, Frank
Metals Hand Engraver/European Hand Engraving
Mittermeier, Inc., Frank
Montgomery Community College
Nelson, Gary K.
New England Custom Gun Service
New Orleans Jewelers Supply Co.
Oker's Engraving
Pedersen, C. R.
Pedersen, Rex C.
Peter Hale/Engraver
Pilgrim Pewter,Inc. (See Bell Originals Inc. Sid)
Pilkington, Scott (See Little Trees Ramble)
Piquette's Custom Engraving
Potts, Wayne E.
Rabeno, Martin
Ralph Bone Engraving
Reed, Dave
Reno, Wayne
Riggs, Jim
Robert Valade Engraving
Rohner, Hans
Rohner, John
Rosser, Bob
Rundell's Gun Shop
Runge, Robert P.
Sampson, Roger
San Welch Gun Engraving
Schiffman, Mike
Sheffield Knifemakers Supply, Inc.
Sherwood, George
Singletary, Kent
Smith, Mark A.
Smith, Ron
Smokey Valley Rifles (See Lutz Engraving, Ron E)
Terry Theis-Engraver
The Alaskan Silversmith
The Gun Room
The NgraveR Co.
Thiewes, George W.
Thirion Gun Engraving, Denise
Thompson/Center Arms
Vest, John
Viramontez, Ray
Vorhes, David
W.E. Brownell Checkering Tools
Wagoner, Vernon G.
Wallace, Terry
Warenski, Julie
Warren, Kenneth W. (See Mountain States Engraving)
Weber & Markin Custom Gunsmiths
Wells, Rachel
Wessinger Custom Guns & Engraving
Wood, Mel
Yee, Mike

GAME CALLS

Adventure Game Calls
African Import Co.
Arkansas Mallard Duck Calls
Ashby Turkey Calls
Bostick Wildlife Calls, Inc.
Cedar Hill Game Calls LLC
Crit'R Call (See Rocky Mountain Wildlife Products)
Custom Calls
D&H Prods. Co., Inc.
D-Boone Ent., Inc.
Deepeeka Exports Pvt. Ltd.
Dr. O's Products Ltd.
Duck Call Specialists
Faulhaber Wildlocker
Faulk's Game Call Co., Inc.
Fibron Products, Inc.
Glynn Scobey Duck & Goose Calls
Green Head Game Call Co.
Hally Caller
Haydel's Game Calls, Inc.
Herter's Manufacturing, Inc.
Hunter's Specialties Inc.
Keowee Game Calls

Kingyon, Paul L. (See Custom Calls)
Knight & Hale Game Calls
Lohman Mfg. Co., Inc.
Mallardtone Game Calls
Moss Double Tone, Inc.
Mountain Hollow Game Calls
Oakman Turkey Calls
Outdoor Sports Headquarters,Inc.
Pete Rickard, Inc.
Philip S. Olt Co.
Primos, Inc.
Quaker Boy, Inc.
Rickard, Inc., Pete
Rocky Mountain Wildlife Products
Russ Trading Post
Sceery Game Calls
Sports Innovations Inc.
Stanley Scruggs' Game Calls
Stewart Game Calls, Inc., Johnny
Sure-Shot Game Calls, Inc.
Tanglefree Industries
The Original Deer Formula Co
Tinks & Ben Lee Hunting Products (See Wellington)
Tink's Safariland Hunting Corp.
Wellington Outdoors
Wilderness Sound Products Ltd.
Woods Wise Products
Wyant's Outdoor Products, Inc.

GAUGES, CALIPERS & MICROMETERS

Blue Ridge Machinery & Tools, Inc.
Gruning Precision Inc
K&M Services
Starrett Co., L. S.
Stoney Point Products, Inc.

GUN PARTS, U.S. & FOREIGN

"Su-Press-On",Inc.
A.A. Arms, Inc.
Actions by "T" Teddy Jacobson
Ahlman Guns
Amherst Arms
Antique Arms Co.
Armscorp USA, Inc.
Aro-Tek Ltd.
Auto-Ordnance Corp.
Badger Shooters Supply, Inc.
Bar-Sto Precision Machine
Bear Mountain Gun & Tool
Billings Gunsmiths Inc.
Bill's Gun Repair
Bob's Gun Shop
Brian Perazone-Gunsmith
Briese Bullet Co., Inc.
British Antiques
Brownells, Inc.
Bryan & Assoc.
Buffer Technologies
Bushmaster Firearms (See Quality Parts Co.)
Bustani, Leo
Cambo's Outdoorsman
Cape Outfitters
Caspian Arms, Ltd.
CBC-BRAZIL
Chicasaw Gun Works
Cole's Gun Works
Colonial Arms, Inc.
Colonial Repair
Colt's Mfg. Co., Inc.
Cryo-Accurizing
Custom Riflestocks, Inc., Michael M. Kokolus
Cylinder & Slide, Inc., William R. Laughridge
Delta Arms Ltd.
DGR Custom Rifles
Dibble, Derek A.
Duane's Gun Repair (See DGR Custom Rifles)
Duffy, Charles E (See Guns Antique & Modern DBA)
E.A.A. Corp.
EGW Evolution Gun Works
Elliott Inc., G. W.
EMF Co., Inc.
Enguix Import-Export
Entre'prise Arms, Inc.
European American Armory Corp (See E.A.A. Corp)

Falcon Industries, Inc
Federal Arms Corp. of America
Fleming Firearms
Flintlocks, Etc.
Forrest Inc., Tom
Gentry Custom Gunmaker, David
Glimm's Custom Gun Engraving
Goodwin, Fred
Granite Mountain Arms, Inc
Greider Precision
Groenewold, John
Guns Antique & Modern DBA/Charles E. Duffy
Hammans, Charles E.
Hastings Barrels
Hawken Shop, The (See Dayton Traister)
High Performance International
I.S.S.
Irwin, Campbell H.
J. Dewey Mfg. Co., Inc.
Johnson's Gunsmithing, Inc, Neal
Jonathan Arthur Ciener, Inc.
K.K. Arms Co.
Kimber of America, Inc.
Knight's Mfg. Co.
Krico Deutschland
Lampert, Ron
Laughridge, William R (See Cylinder & Slide Inc)
Leapers, Inc.
List Precision Engineering
Lodewick, Walter H.
Lodgewood Mfg.
Long, George F.
Mandall Shooting Supplies Inc.
Markell,Inc.
Martin's Gun Shop
McCormick Corp., Chip
MCS, Inc.
Merkuria Ltd.
Morrow, Bud
Mo's Competitor Supplies (See MCS Inc)
North Star West
Northwest Arms
Nu-Line Guns,Inc.
Nygord Precision Products
Olympic Arms Inc.
P.S.M.G. Gun Co.
Parts & Surplus
Pennsylvania Gun Parts Inc
Perazone-Gunsmith, Brian
Perazzi USA, Inc.
Performance Specialists
Quality Firearms of Idaho, Inc.
Quality Parts Co./Bushmaster Firearms
Ranch Products
Randco UK
Raptor Arms Co., Inc.
Ravell Ltd.
Retting, Inc., Martin B
Ruger (See Sturm, Ruger & Co., Inc.)
S&S Firearms
Sabatti S.r.l.
Samco Global Arms, Inc.
Sarco, Inc.
Savage Arms (Canada), Inc.
Scherer
Shockley, Harold H.
Shootin' Shack, Inc.
Silver Ridge Gun Shop (See Goodwin, Fred)
Simmons Gun Repair, Inc.
Sipes Gun Shop
Smires, C. L.
Smith & Wesson
Southern Ammunition Co., Inc.
Sportsmen's Exchange & Western Gun Traders, Inc.
Springfield Sporters, Inc.
Springfield, Inc.
Steyr Mannlicher AG & CO KG
STI International
Strayer-Voigt, Inc
Sturm Ruger & Co. Inc.
Sunny Hill Enterprises, Inc.
T&S Industries, Inc.
Tank's Rifle Shop
Tarnhelm Supply Co., Inc.
The Gun Parts Corp.
The Gun Room Press

The Gun Shop
The Southern Armory
The Swampfire Shop (See Peterson Gun Shop, Inc.)
Triple-K Mfg. Co., Inc.
VAM Distribution Co LLC
Vektor USA
Vintage Arms, Inc.
W. Waller & Son, Inc.
W.C. Wolff Co. (Wolff Gunsprings)
Walker Arms Co., Inc.
Weaver Arms Corp. Gun Shop
Wescombe, Bill (See North Star West)
Whitestone Lumber Corp.
Wild West Guns
Williams Mfg. of Oregon
Winchester Sutler, Inc., The
Wise Guns, Dale
Wisners Inc/Twin Pine Armory

GUNS & GUN PARTS, REPLICA & ANTIQUE

Ackerman & Co.
Ahlman Guns
Armi San Paolo
Auto-Ordnance Corp.
Ballard Rifle & Cartridge Co., LLC
Bear Mountain Gun & Tool
Billings Gunsmiths Inc.
Bob's Gun Shop
British Antiques
Buckskin Machine Works, A. Hunkeler
Cache La Poudre Rifleworks
Cash Mfg. Co., Inc.
CBC-BRAZIL
CCL Security Products
Chambers Flintlocks Ltd., Jim
Chicasaw Gun Works
Cogar's Gunsmithing
Cole's Gun Works
Collectors Firearms Etc.
Colonial Repair
Colt Blackpowder Arms Co.
Colt's Mfg. Co., Inc.
Custom Riflestocks, Inc., Michael M. Kokolus
Custom Single Shot Rifles
Dangler, Homer L.
David R. Chicoine
Delhi Gun House
Delta Arms Ltd.
Dilliott Gunsmithing, Inc.
Dixon Muzzleloading Shop, Inc.
Euroarms of America, Inc.
Flintlocks, Etc.
George E. Mathews & Son, Inc.
Getz Barrel Co.
Golden Age Arms Co.
Goodwin, Fred
Groenewold, John
Gun Hunter Books (See Gun Hunter Trading Co)
Gun Hunter Trading Co.
Guns
Hastings Barrels
Hunkeler, A (See Buckskin Machine Works
IAR Inc.
Ken Starnes Gunmaker
Kokolus, Michael M. (See Custom Riflestocks)
L&R Lock Co.
LaPrade
Leonard Day
List Precision Engineering
Lock's Philadelphia Gun Exchange
Lodgewood Mfg.
Lone Star Rifle Company
Lucas, Edward E
Mandall Shooting Supplies Inc.
Martin's Gun Shop
Mathews & Son, Inc., George E.
McKinney, R.P. (See Schuetzen Gun Co.)
Mid-America Recreation, Inc.
Mountain State Muzzleloading Supplies, Inc.
Mowrey Gun Works
Navy Arms Co.
Navy Arms Company
Neumann GmbH
North Star West

Nu-Line Guns,Inc.
Pasadena Gun Center
Pecatonica River Longrifle
PEM's Mfg. Co.
Pennsylvania Gun Parts Inc
Pony Express Sport Shop
Precise Metalsmithing Enterprises
Quality Firearms of Idaho, Inc.
R.A. Wells Custom Gunsmith
Randco UK
Ravell Ltd.
Retting, Inc., Martin B
S&S Firearms
Sarco, Inc.
Shootin' Shack, Inc.
Silver Ridge Gun Shop (See Goodwin, Fred)
Simmons Gun Repair, Inc.
Sklany's Machine Shop
Southern Ammunition Co., Inc.
Starr Trading Co., Jedediah
Stott's Creek Armory, Inc.
Tennessee Valley Mfg.
The Gun Parts Corp.
The Gun Room Press
The Gun Works
Tiger-Hunt Gunstocks
Triple-K Mfg. Co., Inc.
Turnbull Restoration, Doug
Uberti USA, Inc.
Upper Missouri Trading Co.
Vintage Industries, Inc.
Vortek Products, Inc.
Wescombe, Bill (See North Star West)
Winchester Sutler, Inc., The

GUNS, AIR

Air Arms
Air Rifle Specialists
Air Venture Airguns
Airrow
Allred Bullet Co.
Arms Corporation of the Philippines
BEC, Inc.
Beeman Precision Airguns
Benjamin/Sheridan Co., Crossman
Brass Eagle, Inc.
Brocock Ltd.
Bryan & Assoc.
BSA Guns Ltd.
Compasseco, Ltd.
Component Concepts, Inc.
Conetrol Scope Mounts
Creedmoor Sports, Inc.
Crosman Airguns
Crosman Products of Canada Ltd.
Daisy Mfg. Co.
Daystate Ltd.
Diana (See U.S. Importer - Dynamit Nobel-RWS, Inc.
Domino
Dynamit Nobel-RWS, Inc.
European American Armory Corp (See E.A.A. Corp)
Frankonia Jagd Hofmann & Co.
FWB
Gamo USA, Inc.
Gaucher Armes, S.A.
Great Lakes Airguns
Groenewold, John
Hebard Guns, Gil
J.G. Anschuetz GmbH & Co. KG
Labanu, Inc.
Leapers, Inc.
Legacy Sports International
List Precision Engineering
Loch Leven Industries
Mac-1 Airgun Distributors
Marksman Products
Maryland Paintball Supply
Merkuria Ltd.
Neal Johnson's Gunsmithing, Inc.
Nygord Precision Products
Pardini Armi Srl
Precision Airgun Sales, Inc.
Precision Sales International, Inc.
Ripley Rifles
Robinson, Don
RWS (See US Importer-Dynamit Nobel-RWS, Inc.)
S.G.S. Sporting Guns Srl.
Savage Arms, Inc.
SKAN A.R.
Smart Parts

Smith & Wesson
Steyr Mannlicher AG & CO KG
Stone Enterprises Ltd.
The Park Rifle Co., Ltd.
Theoben Engineering
Tippman Pneumatics, Inc.
Tristar Sporting Arms, Ltd.
Trooper Walsh
UltraSport Arms, Inc.
Valor Corp.
Visible Impact Targets
Vortek Products, Inc.
Walther GmbH, Carl
Webley and Scott Ltd.
Weihrauch KG, Hermann
Whiscombe (See U.S. Importer-Pelaire Products)
World Class Airguns

GUNS, FOREIGN MANUFACTURER U.S. IMPORTER

Accuracy Internationl Precision Rifles (See U.S.)
Accuracy Int'l. North America, Inc.
Air Arms
Armas Kemen S. A. (See U.S. Importers)
Armi Perazzi S.p.A.
Armi San Marco (See U.S. Importers-Taylor's & Co I
Armi Sport (See U.S. Importers-Cape Outfitters)
Arms Corporation of the Philippines
Arrieta S.L.
Astra Sport, S.A.
Atamec-Bretton
AYA (See U.S. Importer-New England Custom Gun Serv
B.C. Outdoors
BAC
BEC, Inc.
Benelli Armi S.p.A.
Benelli USA Corp
Beretta S.p.A., Pietro
Beretta U.S.A. Corp.
Bernardelli S.p.A., Vincenzo
Bersa S.A.
Bertuzzi (See U.S. Importer-New England Arms Co)
Bill Hanus Birdguns LLC
Blaser Jagdwaffen GmbH
Borovnik KG, Ludwig
Bosis (See U.S. Importer-New England Arms Co.)
BRNO (See U.S. Importers-Bohemia Arms Co.)
Brocock Ltd.
Browning Arms Co.
Bryan & Assoc.
BSA Guns Ltd.
Cabanas (See U.S. Importer-Mandall Shooting Supply)
CBC
Champlin Firearms, Inc.
Chapuis Armes
Churchill (See U.S. Importer-Ellett Bros)
Cosmi Americo & Figlio s.n.c.
Crucelegui, Hermanos (See U.S. Importer-Mandall)
Cryo-Accurizing
Cubic Shot Shell Co., Inc.
Daewoo Precision Industries Ltd.
Dakota (See U.S. Importer-EMF Co., Inc.)
Davide Pedersoli and Co.
Diana (See U.S. Importer - Dynamit Nobel-RWS, Inc.
Domino
Dumoulin, Ernest
Eagle Imports, Inc.
EAW (See U.S. Importer-New England Custom Gun Serv
Effebi SNC-Dr. Franco Beretta
Euroarms of America, Inc.
Euro-Imports
Eversull Co., Inc., K.
F.A.I.R. Tecni-Mec s.n.c. di Isidoro Rizzini & C.
Fabarm S.p.A.
Fausti Cav. Stefano & Figlie snc
FEG

Felk, Inc.
FERLIB
Fiocchi Munizioni S.p.A. (See U.S. Importer-Fiocch
Firearms Co Ltd/Alpine (See U.S. Importer-Mandall
Firearms International
Flintlocks, Etc.
Franchi S.p.A.
FWB
Galaxy Imports Ltd.,Inc.
Gamba S.p.A. Societa Armi Bresciane Srl
Gamo (See U.S. Importers-Arms United Corp, Daisy M
Garbi, Armas Urki
Gaucher Armes, S.A.
Gibbs Rifle Co., Inc.
Glock GmbH
Goergen's Gun Shop
Great Lakes Airguns
Grulla Armes
Hammerli Ltd.
Hammerli USA
Hartford (See U.S. Importer-EMF Co. Inc.)
Hartmann & Weiss GmbH
Heckler & Koch, Inc.
Hege Jagd-u. Sporthandels GmbH
Helwan (See U.S. Importer-Interarms)
Holland & Holland Ltd.
Howa Machinery, Ltd.
I.A.B. (See U.S. Importer-Taylor's & Co. Inc.)
IGA (See U.S. Importer-Stoeger Industries)
Imperial Magnum Corp.
Import Sports Inc.
IMX LLC
Inter Ordnance of America LP
Intrac Arms International
J.G. Anschuetz GmbH & Co. KG
JSL Ltd (See U.S. Importer-Specialty Shooters)
Kimar (See U.S. Importer-IAR,Inc)
Korth
Korth USA
Krico Deutschland
Krieghoff Gun Co., H.
KSN Industries Ltd (See U.S. Importer-Israel Arms)
Lakefield Arms Ltd (See Savage Arms Inc)
Lapua Ltd.
Laurona Armas Eibar, S.A.L.
Lebeau-Courally
Legacy Sports International
Lever Arms Service Ltd.
Llama Gabilondo Y Cia
London Guns Ltd.
M. Thys (See U.S. Importer-Champlin Firearms Inc)
Madis, George
Magtech Ammunition Co. Inc.
Mandall Shooting Supplies Inc.
Marocchi F.lli S.p.A
Mauser Werke Oberndorf Waffensysteme GmbH
McCann Industries
MEC-Gar S.r.l.
Merkel Freres
Miltex, Inc
Miroku, B C/Daly, Charles (See U.S. Importer)
Morini (See U.S. Importers-Mandall Shooting Supply)
Navy Arms Co.
Navy Arms Company
New SKB Arms Co.
Norica, Avnda Otaola
Norinco
Norma Precision AB (See U.S. Importers-Dynamit)
Northwest Arms
OK Weber,Inc.
Para-Ordnance Mfg., Inc.
Pardini Armi Srl
Pease International
Perazzi USA, Inc.
Perugini Visini & Co. S.r.l.
Peters Stahl GmbH

Pietta (See U.S. Importers-Navy Arms Co, Taylor's
Piotti (See U.S. Importer-Moore & Co, Wm. Larkin)
PMC/Eldorado Cartridge Corp.
Powell & Son (Gunmakers) Ltd., William
Prairie Gun Works
Precision Sales International, Inc.
Rizzini F.lli (See U.S. Importers-Moore & C England)
Rizzini SNC
Robinson Armament Co
Rossi Firearms
Rottweil Compe
Rutten (See U.S. Importer-Labanu Inc)
RWS (See US Importer-Dynamit Nobel-RWS, Inc.)
S.A.R.L. G. Granger
S.I.A.C.E. (See U.S. Importer-IAR Inc)
Sabatti S.r.l.
Sako Ltd (See U.S. Importer-Stoeger Industries)
San Marco (See U.S. Importers-Cape Outfitters-EMF
Sauer (See U.S. Importers-Paul Co., The, Sigarms I
SIG
SIG-Sauer (See U.S. Importer-Sigarms Inc.)
Small Arms Specialists
Societa Armi Bresciane Srl (See U.S. Importer-Cape
Sphinx Engineering SA
Springfield, Inc.
Star Bonifacio Echeverria S.A.
Starr Trading Co., Jedediah
Steyr Mannlicher AG & CO KG
T.F.C. S.p.A.
Tanfoglio Fratelli S.r.l.
Tanner (See U.S. Importer-Mandall Shooting Supply)
Taurus International Firearms (See U.S. Importer)
Taurus S.A. Forjas
Taylor's & Co., Inc.
Techno Arms (See U.S. Importer-Auto-Ordnance Corp
Tikka (See U.S. Importer-Stoeger Industries)
TOZ (See U.S. Importer-Nygord Precision Products)
Ugartechea S. A., Ignacio
Ultralux (See U.S. Importer-Keng's Firearms)
Unique/M.A.P.F.
Valtro USA, Inc
Voere-KGH m.b.H.
Walther GmbH, Carl
Weatherby, Inc.
Webley and Scott Ltd.
Weihrauch KG, Hermann
Westley Richards & Co.
Whiscombe (See U.S. Importer-Pelaire Products)
Wolf (See J.R. Distributing)
Zabala Hermanos S.A.

GUNS, FOREIGN-IMPORTER

Accuracy International
AcuSport Corporation
Air Rifle Specialists
American Arms Inc. (See Tristar)
American Frontier Firearms Mfg., Inc
Armsport, Inc.
Auto-Ordnance Corp.
BAC
Bell's Legendary Country Wear
Benelli USA Corp
Big Bear Arms & Sporting Goods, Inc.
Bill Hanus Birdguns LLC
Brian Perazone-Gunsmith
Bridgeman Products
British Sporting Arms
Browning Arms Co.
Cabela's
Cape Outfitters
Century International Arms, Inc.
Champion Shooters' Supply
Champion's Choice, Inc.
Chapuis USA

Cimarron F.A. Co.
CVA
CZ USA
Dynamit Nobel-RWS, Inc.
E&L Mfg., Inc.
E.A.A. Corp.
Ellett Bros.
EMF Co., Inc.
Eversull Co., Inc., K.
Fiocchi of America Inc.
Fisher, Jerry A.
Flintlocks, Etc.
Franzen International,Inc (See U.S.
   Importer for)
G.U. Inc (See U.S. Importer for New
   SKB Arms Co)
Galaxy Imports Ltd.,Inc.
Gamba, USA
Gamo USA, Inc.
Giacomo Sporting USA
Glock, Inc.
Gremmel Enterprises
Griffin & Howe, Inc.
GSI, Inc.
Gunsite Custom Shop
Gunsite Training Center
Hanus Birdguns Bill
Heckler & Koch, Inc.
I.S.S.
IAR Inc.
Imperial Magnum Corp.
IMX LLC
Intrac Arms International
Ithaca Gun Co. LLC
Johnson's Gunsmithing, Inc, Neal
K.B.I. Inc
Keng's Firearms Specialty, Inc./US
   Tactical Systems
Krieghoff International,Inc.
Labanu, Inc.
Legacy Sports International
Lion Country Supply
London Guns Ltd.
Magnum Research, Inc.
Mandall Shooting Supplies Inc.
Marx, Harry (See U.S. Importer for
   FERLIB)
MCS, Inc.
MEC-Gar U.S.A., Inc.
Navy Arms Company
Neal Johnson's Gunsmithing, Inc.
New England Arms Co.
New England Custom Gun Service
Nygord Precision Products
P.S.M.G. Gun Co.
Para-Ordnance, Inc.
Pelaire Products
Perazzi USA, Inc.
Powell Agency, William
Precision Sales International, Inc.
Quality Arms, Inc.
S.D. Meacham
Samco Global Arms, Inc.
Savage Arms, Inc.
Schuetzen Pistol Works
Scott Fine Guns Inc., Thad
Sigarms, Inc.
SKB Shotguns
Small Arms Specialists
Southern Ammunition Co., Inc.
Specialty Shooters Supply, Inc.
Springfield, Inc.
Stoeger Industries
Stone Enterprises Ltd.
Swarovski Optik North America Ltd.
Taurus Firearms, Inc.
Taylor's & Co., Inc.
The Gun Shop
The Midwest Shooting School
The Orvis Co.
The Paul Co.
Track of the Wolf, Inc.
Traditions Performance Firearms
Tristar Sporting Arms, Ltd.
Trooper Walsh
U.S. Importer-Wm. Larkin Moore
Uberti USA, Inc.
VAM Distribution Co LLC
Vektor USA
Vintage Arms, Inc.
Weatherby, Inc.
Westley Richards Agency USA (See
   U.S. Importer for

Whitestone Lumber Corp.
Wingshooting Adventures
World Class Airguns

GUNS, SURPLUS, PARTS & AMMUNITION

Ad Hominem
Ahlman Guns
Alpha 1 Drop Zone
Armscorp USA, Inc.
Arundel Arms & Ammunition, Inc., A.
Bondini Paolo
Cambos Outdoorsman
Century International Arms, Inc.
Cole's Gun Works
Conetrol Scope Mounts
Delta Arms Ltd.
First Inc, Jack
Fleming Firearms
Forrest Inc., Tom
Frankonia Jagd Hofmann & Co.
Garcia National Gun Traders, Inc.
Gun City
Gun Hunter Books (See Gun Hunter
   Trading Co)
Gun Hunter Trading Co.
Hank's Gun Shop
Hege Jagd-u. Sporthandels GmbH
Jackalope Gun Shop
Ken Starnes Gunmaker
LaRocca Gun Works
Legacy Sports International
Lever Arms Service Ltd.
Log Cabin Sport Shop
Lomont Precision Bullets
Mandall Shooting Supplies Inc.
Martin's Gun Shop
Navy Arms Co.
Navy Arms Company
Nevada Pistol Academy, Inc.
Northwest Arms
Oil Rod and Gun Shop
Paragon Sales & Services, Inc.
Parts & Surplus
Pasadena Gun Center
Perazone-Gunsmith, Brian
Power Plus Enterprises, Inc.
Quality Firearms of Idaho, Inc.
Ravell Ltd.
Retting, Inc., Martin B
Samco Global Arms, Inc.
Sarco, Inc.
Shootin' Shack, Inc.
Silver Ridge Gun Shop (See Goodwin,
   Fred)
Simmons Gun Repair, Inc.
Sportsmen's Exchange & Western
   Gun Traders, Inc.
Springfield Sporters, Inc.
T.F.C. S.p.A.
Tarnhelm Supply Co., Inc.
The Gun Parts Corp.
The Gun Room Press
Thurston Sports, Inc.
Vom Hoffe (See Old Western
   Scrounger, Inc., The)
Whitestone Lumber Corp.
Williams Shootin' Iron Service, The
   Lynx-Line

GUNS, U.S. MADE

3-Ten Corp.
A.A., Inc.
Accu-Tek
Ace Custom 45's, Inc.
Acra-Bond Laminates
Airrow
Allred Bullet Co.
American Arms Inc. (See Tristar)
American Derringer Corp.
American Frontier Firearms Mfg., Inc
AR-7 Industries, LLC
ArmaLite, Inc.
Armscorp USA, Inc.
A-Square Co.,Inc.
Austin & Halleck
Autauga Arms, Inc.
Auto-Ordnance Corp.
Baer Custom, Inc, Les
Ballard Rifle & Cartridge Co., LLC
Barrett Firearms Manufacturer, Inc.
Bar-Sto Precision Machine
Benjamin/Sheridan Co., Crossman

Beretta S.p.A., Pietro
Beretta U.S.A. Corp.
Big Bear Arms & Sporting Goods, Inc.
Bond Arms, Inc.
Borden Ridges Rimrock Stocks
Borden Rifles Inc
Brockman's Custom Gunsmithing
Brown Co, E. Arthur
Browning Arms Co.
Bryan & Assoc.
Bushmaster Firearms (See Quality
   Parts Co.)
Calico Light Weapon Systems
Cambos Outdoorsman
Cape Outfitters
Casull Arms Corp.
CCL Security Products
Century Gun Dist. Inc.
Champlin Firearms, Inc.
Charter 2000
Colt's Mfg. Co., Inc.
Competitor Corp. Inc.
Conetrol Scope Mounts
Connecticut Shotgun Mfg. Co.
Connecticut Valley Classics (See
   CVC)
Cooper Arms
Creekside Gun Shop Inc.
Crosman Airguns
Cryo-Accurizing
Cumberland Arms
Cumberland Mountain Arms
CVA
CVC
Daisy Mfg. Co.
Dakota Arms, Inc.
DAN WESSON FIREARMS
Dangler, Homer L.
Davis Industries
Dayton Traister
Downsizer Corp.
E&L Mfg., Inc.
E. Arthur Brown Co.
Eagle Arms, Inc. (See ArmaLite, Inc.)
Ed Brown Products, Inc.
Ed~ Brown Products, Inc. (See
   Laseraim Technolo
Emerging Technologies, Inc. (See
   Laseraim Technolo
Entre'prise Arms, Inc.
Essex Arms
Excel Industries Inc.
FN Manufacturing
Fort Worth Firearms
Frank Custom Classic Arms, Ron
Freedom Arms, Inc.
Fulton Armory
Galena Industries AMT
Garcia National Gun Traders, Inc.
Genecco Gun Works
Gibbs Rifle Co., Inc.
Gil Hebard Guns
Gilbert Equipment Co., Inc.
Granite Mountain Arms, Inc
Griffin & Howe, Inc.
Gunsite Custom Shop
Gunsite Gunsmithy (See Gunsite
   Custom Shop)
H&R 1871, Inc.
Hammerli USA
Harrington & Richardson (See H&R
   1871, Inc.)
Harris Gunworks
Hart & Son, Inc.
Hawken Shop, The (See Dayton
   Traister)
Henry Repeating Arms Co.
Heritage Firearms (See Heritage Mfg.,
   Inc.)
Heritage Manufacturing, Inc.
Hesco-Meprolight
High Precision
Hi-Point Firearms
HJS Arms,Inc.
H-S Precision, Inc.
Hutton Rifle Ranch
IAI
IAR Inc.
Imperial Miniature Armory
IMX LLC
Intratec
Ithaca Classic Doubles
Ithaca Gun Co. LLC
J.P. Enterprises, Inc.
J.P. Gunstocks, Inc.

John Rigby & Co.
John's Custom Leather
K.K. Arms Co.
Kahr Arms
Kehr Engraving
Kelbly, Inc.
Kel-Tec CNC Industries, Inc.
Kimber of America, Inc.
Knight Rifles
Knight's Mfg. Co.
Kolar
L.A.R. Mfg., Inc.
L.W. Seecamp Co., Inc.
LaFrance Specialties
Lakefield Arms Ltd (See Savage Arms
   Inc)
Laseraim Technologies, Inc.
Lever Arms Service Ltd.
Ljutic Industries, Inc.
Lock's Philadelphia Gun Exchange
Lomont Precision Bullets
Lone Star Rifle Company
M.O.A. Corp.
Madis, George
Mag-Na-Port International, Inc.
Magnum Research, Inc.
Mandall Shooting Supplies Inc.
Marlin Firearms Co.
Maverick Arms, Inc.
McBros Rifle Co.
McCann Industries
Mid-America Recreation, Inc.
Miller Arms, Inc.
MKS Supply, Inc. (See Hi-Point
   Firearms)
Montana Armory, Inc (See C. Sharps
   Arms Co. Inc.)
Mountain Rifles, Inc.
MPI Stocks
NCP Products, Inc.
New England Firearms
Noreen, Peter H.
North American Arms, Inc.
North Star West
Northwest Arms
Nowlin Mfg. Co.
October Country Muzzleloading
Olympic Arms Inc.
Pacific Armament Corp.
Parker & Sons Shooting Supply
Phillips & Rogers, Inc.
Phoenix Arms
Professional Ordnance, Inc.
ProWare, Inc.
Quality Parts Co./Bushmaster
   Firearms
Ramon B. Gonzalez Guns
Rapine Bullet Mould Mfg. Co.
Raptor Arms Co., Inc.
Remington Arms Co., Inc.
Republic Arms, Inc.
Rifles, Inc.
Robinson Armament Co
Rock River Arms
Rocky Mountain Arms, Inc.
Rogue Rifle Co., Inc.
Rogue River Rifleworks
Romain's Custom Guns, Inc.
RPM
Ruger (See Sturm, Ruger & Co., Inc.)
Russ Trading Post
Savage Arms (Canada), Inc.
Scattergun Technologies, Inc.
Searcy Enterprises
Sharps Arms Co., Inc., C.
Shiloh Rifle Mfg.
Shooters Arms Manufacturing Inc.
Sklany's Machine Shop
Small Arms Specialists
Smith & Wesson
Sound Technology
Sporting Arms Mfg., Inc.
Springfield, Inc.
STI International
Stoeger Industries
Strayer-Voigt, Inc
Sturm Ruger & Co. Inc.
Sunny Hill Enterprises, Inc.
T&S Industries, Inc.
Taconic Firearms Ltd., Perry Lane
Talon Industries Inc.
Tank's Rifle Shop
Tar-Hunt Custom Rifles, Inc.

Taurus Firearms, Inc.
Texas Armory (See Bond Arms, Inc.)
Thompson/Center Arms
Time Precision, Inc.
Tristar Sporting Arms, Ltd.
U.S. Patent Fire Arms
U.S. Repeating Arms Co., Inc.
Ultra Light Arms, Inc.
Visible Impact Targets
Volquartsen Custom Ltd.
Wallace, Terry
Walther USA
Weatherby, Inc.
Wescombe, Bill (See North Star West)
Wessinger Custom Guns & Engraving
Whildin & Sons Ltd, E.H.
Wichita Arms, Inc.
Wichita Arms, Inc.
Wildey, Inc.
Wilson Gun Shop
Z-M Weapons

GUNSMITH SCHOOL

American Gunsmithing Institute
Bull Mountain Rifle Co.
Colorado Gunsmithing Academy
Colorado School of Trades
Cylinder & Slide, Inc., William R.
   Laughridge
Lassen Community College,
   Gunsmithing Dept.
Laughridge, William R (See Cylinder
   & Slide Inc)
Log Cabin Sport Shop
Modern Gun Repair School
Montgomery Community College
Murray State College
North American Correspondence
   Schools The Gun Pro
Nowlin Mfg. Co.
NRI Gunsmith School
Pennsylvania Gunsmith School
Piedmont Community College
Pine Technical College
Professional Gunsmiths of
   America,Inc.
Smith & Wesson
Southeastern Community College
Spencer's Custom Guns
Trinidad St. Jr Col Gunsmith Dept.
Wright's Hardwood Gunstock Blanks
Yavapai College

GUNSMITH SUPPLIES, TOOLS & SERVICES

Ace Custom 45's, Inc.
Actions by "T" Teddy Jacobson
Aldis Gunsmithing & Shooting Supply
Alley Supply Co.
Allred Bullet Co.
Alpec Team, Inc.
American Frontier Firearms Mfg., Inc
American Gunsmithing Institute
Baer Custom, Inc, Les
Bar-Sto Precision Machine
Bauska Barrels
Bear Mountain Gun & Tool
Bengtson Arms Co., L.
Biesen, Al
Biesen, Roger
Bill Johns Master Engraver
Bill's Gun Repair
Blue Ridge Machinery & Tools, Inc.
Boyds' Gunstock Industries, Inc.
Break-Free, Inc.
Brian Perazone-Gunsmith
Briley Mfg. Inc.
Brockman's Custom Gunsmithing
Brownells, Inc.
Bryan & Assoc.
B-Square Company, Inc.
Buffer Technologies
Bull Mountain Rifle Co.
Burkhart Gunsmithing, Don
C&H Research
C.S. Van Gorden & Son, Inc.
Carbide Checkering Tools (See J&R
   Engineering)
Caywood, Shane J.
CBC-BRAZIL
Chapman Manufacturing Co.
Chem-Pak, Inc.
Chicasaw Gun Works

Choate Machine & Tool Co., Inc.
Colonial Arms, Inc.
Colorado School of Trades
Colt's Mfg. Co., Inc.
Conetrol Scope Mounts
Craig Custom Ltd., Research & Development
Creekside Gun Shop Inc.
CRR, Inc./Marble's Inc.
Cumberland Arms
Cumberland Mountain Arms
Custom Checkering Service, Kathy Forster
Custom Gun Products
D&J Bullet Co. & Custom Gun Shop, Inc.
Decker Shooting Products
Dem-Bart Checkering Tools, Inc.
Dewey Mfg. Co., Inc., J.
Dixie Gun Works, Inc.
Dremel Mfg. Co.
Du-Lite Corp.
Ed Brown Products, Inc.
EGW Evolution Gun Works
Entre'prise Arms, Inc.
Erhardt, Dennis
Faith Associates
Falcon Industries, Inc
FERLIB
Fisher, Jerry A.
Forgreens Tool Mfg., Inc.
Forkin, Ben (See Belt MTN Arms)
Forkin Arms
Forster, Kathy (See Custom Checkering)
Fortune Products, Inc.
Grace Metal Products
Greider Precision
GrE-Tan Rifles
Groenewold, John
GRS Corp., Glendo
Gruning Precision Inc
Gunline Tools
Half Moon Rifle Shop
Hammond Custom Guns Ltd.
Hastings Barrels
Henriksen Tool Co., Inc.
High Performance International
High Precision
Hoelscher, Virgil
Holland's Gunsmithing
Huey Gun Cases
IAI
Ironsighter Co.
Ivanoff, Thomas G (See Tom's Gun Repair)
J&R Engineering
J&S Heat Treat
J. Dewey Mfg. Co., Inc.
Jantz Supply
Jenkins Recoil Pads, Inc.
JGS Precision Tool Mfg.
Jonathan Arthur Ciener, Inc.
Jones Custom Products, Neil A.
Kasenit Co., Inc.
Kimball, Gary
Kleinendorst, K. W.
Kmount
Korzinek Riflesmith, J
Kwik Mount Corp.
LaBounty Precision Reboring, Inc
Lea Mfg. Co.
Lee's Red Ramps
List Precision Engineering
London Guns Ltd.
Mahovsky's Metalife
Marble Arms (See CRR, Inc./Marble's Inc.)
Mark Lee Supplies
Marsh, Mike
Martin's Gun Shop
Menck, Gunsmith Inc., T.W.
Metalife Industries (See Mahovsky's Metalife)
Metaloy, Inc.
Michael's Antiques
MMC
Morrow, Bud
Mo's Competitor Supplies (See MCS Inc)
Mowrey's Guns & Gunsmithing
N&J Sales
New England Custom Gun Service

Nowlin Mfg. Co.
Nu-Line Guns,Inc.
Ole Frontier Gunsmith Shop
P.M. Enterprises, Inc.
Parker Gun Finishes
PEM's Mfg. Co.
Perazone-Gunsmith, Brian
Piquette's Custom Engraving
Power Custom, Inc.
Practical Tools, Inc.
Precision Specialties
Professional Gunsmiths of America,Inc.
R.A. Wells Custom Gunsmith
Ranch Products
Ransom International Corp.
Reardon Products
Rice, Keith (See White Rock Tool & Die)
Robert Valade Engraving
Rocky Mountain Arms, Inc.
Roto Carve
Royal Arms Gunstocks
Scott McDougall & Associates
Sharp Shooter Supply
Shooter's Choice
Simmons Gun Repair, Inc.
Smith Abrasives, Inc.
Southern Bloomer Mfg. Co.
Spencer Reblue Service
Spencer's Custom Guns
Spradlin's
Starr Trading Co., Jedediah
Starrett Co., L. S.
Stiles Custom Guns
Sullivan, David S .(See Westwind Rifles Inc.)
Sunny Hill Enterprises, Inc.
T&S Industries, Inc.
Terry K. Kopp Professional Gunsmithing
Terry Theis-Engraver
Texas Platers Supply Co.
The Dutchman's Firearms, Inc.
The NgraveR Co.
The Robar Co.'s, Inc.
Toms Gun Repair, Inc.
Track of the Wolf, Inc.
Trulock Tool
United States Products Co.
Van Gorden & Son Inc., C. S.
Venco Industries, Inc. (See Shooter's Choice)
W.C. Wolff Co. (Wolff Gunsprings)
Warne Manufacturing Co.
Washita Mountain Whetstone Co.
Weaver Arms Corp. Gun Shop
Weigand Combat Handguns, Inc.
Wessinger Custom Guns & Engraving
Westrom, John (See Precision Metal Finishing)
Westwind Rifles, Inc., David S. Sullivan
White Rock Tool & Die
Wilcox All-Pro Tools & Supply
Wild West Guns
Will-Burt Co.
Williams Gun Sight Co.
Williams Shootin' Iron Service, The Lynx-Line
Williamson Precision Gunsmithing
Willow Bend
Windish, Jim
Winter, Robert M.
Wise Guns, Dale
Wright's Hardwood Gunstock Blanks
Yavapai College

HANDGUN ACCESSORIES

"Su-Press-On",Inc.
A.A. Arms, Inc.
Ace Custom 45's, Inc.
Action Direct, Inc.
ADCO Sales, Inc.
Adventurer's Outpost
Aimpoint c/o Springfield, Inc.
Aimtech Mount Systems
Ajax Custom Grips, Inc.
Alpha 1 Drop Zone
Alpha Gunsmith Division
American Derringer Corp.
American Frontier Firearms Mfg., Inc

Arms Corporation of the Philippines
Aro-Tek Ltd.
Astra Sport, S.A.
Autauga Arms, Inc.
Baer Custom, Inc, Les
Bagmaster Mfg., Inc.
Bar-Sto Precision Machine
Behlert Precision, Inc.
Berry's Mfg., Inc.
Bill's Custom Cases
Blue and Gray Products Inc (See Ox-Yoke Originals)
Bond Custom Firearms
Bowen Classic Arms Corp.
Bridgeman Products
Broken Gun Ranch
Brooks Tactical Systems
Bucheimer, J. M. (See Jumbo Sports Products)
Bushmaster Firearms (See Quality Parts Co.)
Bushmaster Hunting & Fishing
Butler Creek Corp.
Cannon Safe, Inc.
Catco-Ambush, Inc.
Centaur Systems, Inc.
Central Specialties Ltd (See Trigger Lock Division)
Charter 2000
Cheyenne Pioneer Products
Clark Custom Guns, Inc.
Classic Arms Company
Concealment Shop Inc.
Conetrol Scope Mounts
Craig Custom Ltd., Research & Development
Crimson Trace Lasers
CRR, Inc./Marble's Inc.
Cylinder & Slide, Inc., William R. Laughridge
D&L Industries (See D.J. Marketing)
D.J. Marketing
Dade Screw Machine Products
Delhi Gun House
DeSantis Holster & Leather Goods, Inc.
Doskocil Mfg. Co., Inc.
E&L Mfg., Inc.
E. Arthur Brown Co.
E.A.A. Corp.
Ed Brown Products, Inc.
E~ Brown Products, Inc.
Essex Arms
Euroarms of America, Inc.
European American Armory Corp (See E.A.A. Corp)
Falcon Industries, Inc
Federal Arms Corp. of America
Fisher Custom Firearms
Fleming Firearms
Flores Publications Inc, J (See Action Direct Inc)
Frielich Police Equipment
FWB
G.G. & G.
Galati International
GALCO International Ltd.
Garcia National Gun Traders, Inc.
Garthwaite Pistolsmith, Inc., Jim
Gary Reeder Custom Guns
Gil Hebard Guns
Gilmore Sports Concepts
Glock, Inc.
Gould & Goodrich
Greider Precision
Gremmel Enterprises
Gun-Alert
Gun-Ho Sports Cases
H.K.S. Products
Hafner World Wide, Inc.
Hebard Guns, Gil
Heckler & Koch, Inc.
Heinie Specialty Products
Henigson & Associates, Steve
Hill Speed Leather, Ernie
Hi-Point Firearms
Hobson Precision Mfg. Co.
Hoppe's Div. Penguin Industries, Inc.
H-S Precision, Inc.
Hunter Co., Inc.
Impact Case Co.
J.P. Enterprises Inc.
Jarvis, Inc.

JB Custom
Jeffredo Gunsight
Jim Noble Co.
John's Custom Leather
Jonathan Arthur Ciener, Inc.
Jones, J.D./SSK Industries
Jumbo Sports Products
K.K. Arms Co.
Kalispel Case Line
KeeCo Impressions, Inc.
King's Gun Works
KK Air International (See Impact Case Co.)
L&S Technologies Inc (See Aimtech Mount Systems)
Lakewood Products LLC
LaPrade
LaserMax, Inc.
Lee's Red Ramps
Loch Leven Industries
Lohman Mfg. Co., Inc.
Mag-Na-Port International, Inc.
Magnolia Sports,Inc.
Mahony, Philip Bruce
Marble Arms (See CRR, Inc./Marble's Inc.)
Markell,Inc.
Maxi-Mount
McCormick Corp., Chip
MEC-Gar S.r.l.
Menck, Gunsmith Inc., T.W.
Merkuria Ltd.
Middlebrooks Custom Shop
Millett Sights
Mogul Co./Life Jacket
MTM Molded Products Co., Inc.
No-Sho Mfg. Co.
Omega Sales
Outdoor Sports Headquarters,Inc.
Ox-Yoke Originals, Inc.
Pachmayr Div. Lyman Products
Pacific Armament Corp.
Pager Pal
Pearce Grip, Inc.
Phoenix Arms
Piquette's Custom Engraving
Practical Tools, Inc.
Precision Small Arms
Quality Parts Co./Bushmaster Firearms
Ram-Line Blount, Inc.
Ranch Products
Ransom International Corp.
Redfield, Inc
Ringler Custom Leather Co.
Round Edge, Inc.
RPM
Shooters Arms Manufacturing Inc.
Simmons Gun Repair, Inc.
Sound Technology
Southern Bloomer Mfg. Co.
Southwind Sanctions
Springfield, Inc.
SSK Industries
Sturm Ruger & Co. Inc.
T.F.C. S.p.A.
TacStar
TacTell, Inc.
Tactical Defense Institute
Talon Industries Inc.
Tanfoglio Fratelli S.r.l.
The Gun Parts Corp.
The Keller Co.
The Protector Mfg. Co., Inc.
Thompson/Center Arms
Trigger Lock Division/Central Specialties Ltd.
Trijicon, Inc.
Triple-K Mfg. Co., Inc.
Truglo, Inc
Tyler Manufacturing & Distributing
United States Products Co.
Valor Corp.
Volquartsen Custom Ltd.
W. Waller & Son, Inc.
W.C. Wolff Co. (Wolff Gunsprings)
Walther USA
Weigand Combat Handguns, Inc.
Western Design (See Alpha Gunsmith Division)
Williams Gun Sight Co.
Wilson Gun Shop

HANDGUN GRIPS

A.A. Arms, Inc.
African Import Co.
Ahrends, Kim (See Custom Firearms, Inc)
Ajax Custom Grips, Inc.
Altamont Co.
American Derringer Corp.
American Frontier Firearms Mfg., Inc
American Gripcraft
Arms Corporation of the Philippines
Art Jewel Enterprises Ltd.
Baelder, Harry
Baer Custom, Inc, Les
Bear Hug Grip, Inc.
Big Bear Arms & Sporting Goods, Inc.
Bob's Gun Shop
Boone Trading Co., Inc.
Boone's Custom Ivory Grips, Inc.
Brooks Tactical Systems
Clark Custom Guns, Inc.
Cole-Grip
Colonial Repair
Crimson Trace Lasers
Custom Firearms (See Ahrends, Kim)
E.A.A. Corp.
Ed Brown Products, Inc.
EMF Co., Inc.
Essex Arms
European American Armory Corp (See E.A.A. Corp)
Falcon Industries, Inc
Fibron Products, Inc.
Fisher Custom Firearms
Fitz Pistol Grip Co.
Forrest Inc., Tom
FWB
Garthwaite Pistolsmith, Inc., Jim
Herrett's Stocks, Inc.
HIP-GRIP Barami Corp.
Hogue Grips
H-S Precision, Inc.
Huebner, Corey O.
IAI
Jim Norman Custom Gunstocks
John Masen Co. Inc.
KeeCo Impressions, Inc.
Kim Ahrends Custom Firearms, Inc.
Korth
Lee's Red Ramps
Lett Custom Grips
Linebaugh Custom Sixguns
Lyman Products Corporation
Michaels Of Oregon
Millett Sights
N.C. Ordnance Co.
Newell, Robert H.
Northern Precision Custom Swaged Bullets
Pachmayr Div. Lyman Products
Pardini Armi Srl
Pilgrim Pewter,Inc. (See Bell Originals Inc. Sid)
Precision Small Arms
Radical Concepts
Rosenberg & Son, Jack A
Roy's Custom Grips
Sile Distributors, Inc.
Spegel, Craig
Stoeger Industries
Sturm Ruger & Co. Inc.
Sunny Hill Enterprises, Inc.
Tactical Defense Institute
Taurus Firearms, Inc.
Tirelli
Tyler Manufacturing & Distributing
U.S. Patent Fire Arms
Uncle Mike's (See Michaels of Oregon Co)
Vintage Industries, Inc.
Volquartsen Custom Ltd.
Western Mfg. Co.
Wright's Hardwood Gunstock Blanks

HEARING PROTECTORS

Aero Peltor
Ajax Custom Grips, Inc.
Brown Co, E. Arthur
Browning Arms Co.
David Clark Co., Inc.
Dick Marple & Associates
E-A-R, Inc.
Electronic Shooters Protection, Inc.

Gentex Corp.
Gunsmithing, Inc.
Hoppe's Div. Penguin Industries, Inc.
Huntington Die Specialties
Huntington Die Specialties
Kesselring Gun Shop
North Safety Products
Paterson Gunsmithing
Peltor, Inc. (See Aero Peltor)
R.E.T. Enterprises
Ridgeline, Inc
Rucker Dist. Inc.
Silencio/Safety Direct
Sound Technology
Tactical Defense Institute
Watson Trophy Match Bullets
Willson Safety Prods. Div.

HOLSTERS & LEATHER GOODS

A&B Industries,Inc (See Top-Line USA Inc)
A.A. Arms, Inc.
Action Direct, Inc.
Action Products, Inc.
Alessi Holsters, Inc.
American Sales & Kirkpatrick
Arratoonian, Andy (See Horseshoe Leather Products)
Autauga Arms, Inc.
Bagmaster Mfg., Inc.
Baker's Leather Goods, Roy
Bandcor Industries, Div. of Man-Sew Corp.
Bang-Bang Boutique (See Holster Shop, The)
Bear Hug Grip, Inc.
Beretta S.p.A., Pietro
Bianchi International, Inc.
Brauer Bros. Mfg. Co.
Brocock Ltd.
Brooks Tactical Systems
Brown, H. R. (See Silhouette Leathers)
Browning Arms Co.
Bucheimer, J. M. (See Jumbo Sports Products)
Bull-X, Inc.
Bushwacker Counter Assault
Cathey Enterprises, Inc.
Chace Leather Products
Cimarron F.A. Co.
Classic Old West Styles
Clements' Custom Leathercraft, Chas
Cobra Sport S.r.l.
Colonial Repair
Concealment Shop Inc.
Creedmoor Sports, Inc.
Delhi Gun House
DeSantis Holster & Leather Goods, Inc.
Ekol Leather Care
El Dorado Leather (c/o Dill)
El Paso Saddlery Co.
EMF Co., Inc.
Faust Inc., T. G.
Flores Publications Inc, J (See Action Direct Inc)
Frankonia Jagd Hofmann & Co.
Gage Manufacturing
GALCO International Ltd.
Garcia National Gun Traders, Inc.
Gil Hebard Guns
Gilmore Sports Concepts
GML Products, Inc.
Gould & Goodrich
Gun Leather Limited
Gunfitters
Hafner World Wide, Inc.
HandCrafts Unltd (See Clements' Custom Leather)
Hank's Gun Shop
Hebard Guns, Gil
Heinie Specialty Products
Hellweg Ltd.
Henigson & Associates, Steve
Hill Speed Leather, Ernie
HIP-GRIP Barami Corp.
Hobson Precision Mfg. Co.
Hogue Grips
Horseshoe Leather Products
Hoyt Holster Co., Inc.
Hume, Don

Hunter Co., Inc.
James Churchill Glove Co.
Jim Noble Co.
John's Custom Leather
Jumbo Sports Products
K.L. Null Holsters Ltd.
Kane Products, Inc.
Kirkpatrick Leather Co.
Kolpin Mfg., Inc.
Korth
Kramer Handgun Leather
L.A.R. Mfg., Inc.
Lawrence Leather Co.
Lock's Philadelphia Gun Exchange
Lone Star Gunleather
Magnolia Sports,Inc.
Markell,Inc.
Marksman Products
Michaels Of Oregon
Minute Man High Tech Industries
Navy Arms Company
Nikolai leather
No-Sho Mfg. Co.
Null Holsters Ltd. K.L.
October Country Muzzleloading
Ojala Holsters, Arvo
Oklahoma Leather Products,Inc.
Old West Reproductions,Inc. R.M. Bachman
P.S.M.G. Gun Co.
Pager Pal
Pathfinder Sports Leather
PWL Gunleather
Renegade
Ringler Custom Leather Co.
Rogue Rifle Co., Inc.
Rumanya Inc.
Safariland Ltd., Inc.
Safety Speed Holster, Inc.
Scharch Mfg., Inc.
Schulz Industries
Second Chance Body Armor
Shoemaker & Sons Inc., Tex
Sile Distributors, Inc.
Silhouette Leathers
Smith Saddlery, Jesse W.
Southwind Sanctions
Sparks, Milt
Stalker, Inc.
Starr Trading Co., Jedediah
Strong Holster Co.
Stuart, V. Pat
Tabler Marketing
Tactical Defense Institute
Ted Blocker Holsters, Inc.
Thad Rybka Custom Leather Equipment
The Eutaw Co., Inc.
The Gun Works
The Holster Shop
The Keller Co.
Top-Line USA, Inc.
Torel, Inc.
Triple-K Mfg. Co., Inc.
Tristar Sporting Arms, Ltd.
Tyler Manufacturing & Distributing
Uncle Mike's (See Michaels of Oregon Co)
Valor Corp.
Venus Industries
Walt's Custom Leather, Walt Whinnery
Watson Trophy Match Bullets
Westley Richards & Co.
Whinnery, Walt (See Walt's Custom Leather)
Wild Bill's Originals
Wilson Gun Shop

HUNTING & CAMP GEAR, CLOTHING, ETC.

A&M Waterfowl,Inc.
Ace Sportswear, Inc.
Action Direct, Inc.
Action Products, Inc.
Adventure 16, Inc.
Adventure Game Calls
Allen Co., Bob
Allen Sportswear, Bob (See Allen Co., Bob)
Alpha 1 Drop Zone
Armor (See Buck Stop Lure Co., Inc.)
Atlanta Cutlery Corp.

Atsko/Sno-Seal, Inc.
B.B. Walker Co.
Baekgaard Ltd.
Bagmaster Mfg., Inc.
Barbour, Inc.
Bauer, Eddie
Bear Archery
Beaver Park Product, Inc.
Better Concepts Co.
Bill Johns Master Engraver
Boss Manufacturing Co.
Brown, H. R. (See Silhouette Leathers)
Brown Manufacturing
Browning Arms Co.
Buck Stop Lure Co., Inc.
Bushmaster Hunting & Fishing
C.W. Erickson's Mfg. Inc.
Cambo's Outdoorsman
Camp-Cap Products
Carhartt,Inc.
Clarkfield Enterprises, Inc.
Classic Old West Styles
Clements' Custom Leathercraft, Chas
Coghlan's Ltd.
Cold Steel Inc.
Coleman Co., Inc.
Coulston Products, Inc.
Creedmoor Sports, Inc.
D&H Prods. Co., Inc.
Dakota Corp.
Danner Shoe Mfg. Co.
Deepeeka Exports Pvt. Ltd.
Dr. O's Products Ltd.
Dunham Boots
Duofold, Inc.
Dynalite Products, Inc.
E-A-R, Inc.
Ekol Leather Care
Flores Publications Inc, J (See Action Direct Inc)
Forrest Tool Co.
Fortune Products, Inc.
Fox River Mills, Inc.
Frontier
G&H Decoys,Inc.
Gerber Legendary Blades
Glacier Glove
Hinman Outfitters, Bob
Hodgman, Inc.
Houtz & Barwick
Hunter's Specialties Inc.
James Churchill Glove Co.
K&M Industries, Inc.
Kamik Outdoor Footwear
Kolpin Mfg., Inc.
L.L. Bean, Inc.
LaCrosse Footwear, Inc.
Langenberg Hat Co.
Leapers, Inc.
Lectro Science, Inc.
Liberty Trouser Co.
MAG Instrument, Inc.
Mag-Na-Port International, Inc.
Marathon Rubber Prods. Co., Inc.
McCann Industries
McCann's Machine & Gun Shop
Molin Industries, Tru-Nord Division
Mountain Hollow Game Calls
Nelson/Weather-Rite, Inc.
North Safety Products
Northlake Outdoor Footwear
Original Mink Oil,Inc.
Palsa Outdoor Products
Partridge Sales Ltd., John
Pointing Dog Journal, Village Press Publications
Powell & Son (Gunmakers) Ltd., William
Pro-Mark Div. of Wells Lamont
Pyramid, Inc.
Randolph Engineering, Inc.
Ringler Custom Leather Co.
Robert Valade Engraving
Rocky Shoes & Boots
Russ Trading Post
Scansport, Inc.
Sceery Game Calls
Schaefer Shooting Sports
Servus Footwear Co.
Simmons Outdoor Corp.
Sno-Seal, Inc. (See Atsko/Sno-Seal)

Streamlight, Inc.
Swanndri New Zealand
T.H.U. Enterprises, Inc.
TEN-X Products Group
The Eutaw Co., Inc.
The Original Deer Formula Co
The Orvis Co.
The Outdoor Connection,Inc.
The Outdoor Connection,Inc.
Thompson, Norm
Thompson/Center Arms
Tink's Safariland Hunting Corp.
Torel, Inc.
Triple-K Mfg. Co., Inc.
United Cutlery Corp.
Venus Industries
Wakina by Pic
Walls Industries, Inc.
Wideview Scope Mount Corp.
Wilderness Sound Products Ltd.
Willson Safety Prods. Div.
Winchester Sutler, Inc., The
Wolverine Footwear Group
Woolrich, Inc.
Wyoming Knife Corp.
Yellowstone Wilderness Supply

KNIVES & KNIFEMAKER'S SUPPLIES

A.G. Russell Knives,Inc.
Action Direct, Inc.
Adventure 16, Inc.
African Import Co.
Aitor-Cuchilleria Del Norte S.A.
All Rite Products, Inc.
American Target Knives
Art Jewel Enterprises Ltd.
Atlanta Cutlery Corp.
B&D Trading Co., Inc.
Barteaux Machete
Belltown Ltd.
Benchmark Knives (See Gerber Legendary Blades)
Beretta S.p.A., Pietro
Beretta U.S.A. Corp.
Big Bear Arms & Sporting Goods, Inc.
Bill Johns Master Engraver
Bill's Custom Cases
Boker USA, Inc.
Boone Trading Co., Inc.
Boone's Custom Ivory Grips, Inc.
Bowen Knife Co., Inc.
Brooks Tactical Systems
Brown, H. R. (See Silhouette Leathers)
Browning Arms Co.
Buck Knives, Inc.
Buster's Custom Knives
Camillus Cutlery Co.
Campbell, Dick
Case & Sons Cutlery Co., W R
Chicago Cutlery Co.
Clements' Custom Leathercraft, Chas
Cold Steel Inc.
Coleman Co., Inc.
Colonial Knife Co., Inc.
Compass Industries, Inc.
Crosman Blades (See Coleman Co., Inc.)
CRR, Inc./Marble's Inc.
Cutco Cutlery
DAMASCUS-U.S.A.
Dan's Whetstone Co., Inc.
Deepeeka Exports Pvt. Ltd.
Degen Inc. (See Aristocrat Knives)
Delhi Gun House
DeSantis Holster & Leather Goods, Inc.
Diamond Machining Technology, Inc. (See DMT)
EdgeCraft Corp., S. Weiner
Empire Cutlery Corp.
Eze-Lap Diamond Prods.
Flitz International Ltd.
Flores Publications Inc, J (See Action Direct Inc)
Forrest Tool Co.
Forthofer's Gunsmithing & Knifemaking
Fortune Products, Inc.
Frank Knives
Frost Cutlery Co.

Galati International
George Ibberson (Sheffield) Ltd.
Gerber Legendary Blades
Gibbs Rifle Co., Inc.
Glock, Inc.
Golden Age Arms Co.
H&B Forge Co.
Hafner World Wide, Inc.
HandCrafts Unltd (See Clements' Custom Leather)
Harris Publications
High North Products, Inc.
Hoppe's Div. Penguin Industries, Inc.
Hunter Co., Inc.
Hunting Classics Ltd.
Imperial Schrade Corp.
J.A. Blades, Inc. (See Christopher Firearms Co.)
J.A. Henckels Zwillingswerk Inc.
J.R. Blair Engraving
Jackalope Gun Shop
Jantz Supply
Jenco Sales, Inc.
Johnson Wood Products
KA-BAR Knives, Inc
Kasenit Co., Inc.
Kershaw Knives
Koval Knives
Lamson & Goodnow Mfg. Co.
Lansky Sharpeners
Leapers, Inc.
Leatherman Tool Group, Inc.
Lethal Force Institute (See Police Bookshelf)
Lett Custom Grips
Linder Solingen Knives
Marble Arms (See CRR, Inc./Marble's Inc.)
Matthews Cutlery
McCann Industries
McCann's Machine & Gun Shop
Molin Industries, Tru-Nord Division
Mountain State Muzzleloading Supplies, Inc.
Normark Corp.
October Country Muzzleloading
Outdoor Edge Cutlery Corp.
Pilgrim Pewter,Inc. (See Bell Originals Inc. Sid)
Piquette's Custom Engraving
Plaza Cutlery, Inc.
Queen Cutlery Co.
R&C Knives & Such
R. Murphy Co., Inc.
Randall-Made Knives
Robert Valade Engraving
Rodgers & Sons Ltd., Joseph (See George Ibberson
Russ Trading Post
Scansport, Inc.
Schiffman, Mike
Sheffield Knifemakers Supply, Inc.
Smith Saddlery, Jesse W.
Spyderco, Inc.
T.F.C. S.p.A.
Terry Theis-Engraver
The Creative Craftsman, Inc.
The Gun Room
Traditions Performance Firearms
Traditions Performance Firearms
Tru-Balance Knife Co.
United Cutlery Corp.
Utica Cutlery Co.
Venus Industries
Washita Mountain Whetstone Co.
Weber Jr., Rudolf
Wells Creek Knife & Gun Works
Wenger North America/Precise Int'l
Western Cutlery (See Camillus Cutlery Co.)
Whinnery, Walt (See Walt's Custom Leather)
Wideview Scope Mount Corp.
Wostenholm (See Ibberson [Sheffield] Ltd., George)
Wyoming Knife Corp.

LABELS, BOXES & CARTRIDGE HOLDERS

Berry's Mfg., Inc.
Brocock Ltd.
Brown Co, E. Arthur

DIRECTORY

Cabinet Mtn. Outfitters Scents & Lures
Cheyenne Pioneer Products
Del Rey Products
DeSantis Holster & Leather Goods, Inc.
Ed King Office
Fitz Pistol Grip Co.
Flambeau Products Corp.
J&J Products, Inc.
Kolpin Mfg., Inc.
Liberty Shooting Supplies
Midway Arms, Inc.
MTM Molded Products Co., Inc.
Pendleton Royal, c/o Swingler Buckland Ltd.

LEAD WIRES & WIRE CUTTERS

3-D Ammunition & Bullets
Ames Metal Products
Big Bore Express
Bullet Swaging Supply Inc.
Montana Precision Swaging
Northern Precision Custom Swaged Bullets
Sport Flite Manufacturing Co.
Star Ammunition, Inc.
Unmussig Bullets, D. L.

LOAD TESTING & PRODUCT TESTING

Ballistic Research
Bridgeman Products
Briese Bullet Co., Inc.
Buckskin Bullet Co.
Bull Mountain Rifle Co.
CFVentures
Claybuster Wads & Harvester Bullets
Clearview Products
D&H Precision Tooling
Dead Eye's Sport Center
Defense Training International, Inc.
Duane's Gun Repair (See DGR Custom Rifles)
H.P. White Laboratory, Inc.
Henigson & Associates, Steve
Hoelscher, Virgil
Hutton Rifle Ranch
Jackalope Gun Shop
Jensen Bullets
L E Jurras & Assoc
Liberty Shooting Supplies
Linebaugh Custom Sixguns
Lomont Precision Bullets
Maionchi-L.M.I.
MAST Technology
McMurdo, Lynn (See Specialty Gunsmithing)
Middlebrooks Custom Shop
Modern Gun Repair School
Multiplex International
Northwest Arms
Oil Rod and Gun Shop
Ramon B. Gonzalez Guns
Rupert's Gun Shop
Small Custom Mould & Bullet Co.
SOS Products Co. (See Buck Stix-SOS Products Co.)
Spencer's Custom Guns
Tar-Hunt Custom Rifles, Inc.
Tioga Engineering Co., Inc.
Trinidad St. Jr Col Gunsmith Dept.
Vancini, Carl (See Bestload, Inc.)
Vulpes Ventures, Inc. Fox Cartridge Division
W. Square Enterprises
Wessinger Custom Guns & Engraving
X-Spand Target Systems

LOADING BLOCKS, METALLIC & SHOTSHELL

Battenfeld Technologies
Jericho Tool - Magna Shock Ind

LUBRISIZERS, DIES & ACCESSORIES

Ballisti-Cast, Inc.
Ben's Machines
Buffalo Arms Co.
Cast Performance Bullet Company

Chem-Pak Inc.
Hart & Son, Inc.
Javelina Lube Products
Magma Engineering Co.
NEI Handtools, Inc.
SPG LLC
Thompson Bullet Lube Co.
Time Precision, Inc.
United States Products Co.
WTA Manufacturing

MISCELLANEOUS

Home Shop Machinist The Village Press Publications
Nu-Line Guns,Inc.
Sinclair International, Inc.
Yearout, Lewis E. (See Montana Outfitters)

.22 cal. Conversion Units for Handguns
Gremmel Enterprises

.45 ACP 1911 office magazines
Mag-Pack Corp.

1/4 Rib, Floorplates, etc.etc.
DAMASCUS-U.S.A.

10901 Rt. 164, Lisbon, OH 44432
Cubic Shot Shell Co., Inc.

163 acre Sport Clay & Rifle Range
Cubic Shot Shell Co., Inc.

3 Position Safety For Mauser 98
Gentry Custom Gunmaker, David

44-1/2 rifles, sights, barrels, stocks, exact copi
Mid-America Recreation, Inc.

45-70 Speciality Items
Wolf's Western Traders

Accurigers, Supertunes
Time Precision, Inc.

Actions, Rifle
Hall Manufacturing

Adapters, Cartridge
Alex, Inc.

Adapters, Shotshell
PC Co.

Adjustable Muzzle Brake
Que Industries, Inc.

Air Cartridge Weapons, Weihrauch, Uberti,
Brocock Ltd.

Airgun Accessories
BSA Guns Ltd.

Airgun Repair
Airgun Repair Centre

Airgunsmithing, Pellets (ammo)
Mac-1 Airgun Distributors

All Pedersoli Parts for the US
Flintlocks, Etc.

Aluminum Cases for any firearm
Impact Case Co.

Animal Lure Manufacture
Russ Trading Post

Antique Arms Publications
Bullet'n Press

Antique Firearms Catalogs Subscription $20
Antique American Firearms

Antique Style Cartirdge Boxes
Cheyenne Pioneer Products

Arms Restoration, Rust-Blue
Kehr Engraving

Arrieta Shotguns
Quality Arms, Inc.

Assault Rifle Accessories
Ram-Line Blount, Inc.

Association of Custom Gunmakers & Related Crafts
American Custom Gunmakers Guild

Bags, Cases, custom sewed products
Hafner World Wide, Inc.

Bags, packs
Action Direct, Inc.

Barrel Kits: To Convert To 19 Caliber
James Calhoon Varmint Bullets

Barrel Stress Relieving
300 Below Services (See Cryo-Accurizing)

Baskets
Russ Trading Post

Binoculars & Scopes
Tele-Optics

Black Powder
GOEX Inc.

Black Powder Bullets, Cast & Swaged
Montana Precision Swaging

Blanks & Semi-Inlet Stocks
Acra-Bond Laminates

Blueing-Firearms
Walker Arms Co., Inc.

Body Armor
A&B Industries,Inc (See Top-Line USA Inc)
Faust Inc., T. G.
Second Chance Body Armor
Top-Line USA, Inc.

Bolt Conversions for 5mm Rem Mag rifles
Schroeder Bullets

Book Copyediting Services
CFVentures

Bore Lights
Gremmel Enterprises
MDS

Borelights
Willow Bend

Brass Catcher
Bridgeman Products
Gage Manufacturing

Bullet Casting Machines
Ballisti-Cast, Inc.

Bullet Lubricants
Tamarack Products, Inc.

Bullets for Muzzleloading guns
Big Bore Express

Bullets, Moly Coat
Starke Bullet Company

Bullets, Rubber
CIDCO

Candle Lanterns 1 drop oil can
Cash Mfg. Co., Inc.

Cannons, Miniature Replicas
Furr Arms

Cartridge Case Neck Gauge
Plum City Ballistic Range

Cast bullet lube only for pistol & rifle
Javelina Lube Products

Centered Scope Mount for M-1 Garand
York M-1 Conversions

Civil War Clothing & Supplies
Winchester Sutler, Inc., The

Civilian & Law Enforcement
SAFE

Cleaning Pads & jage
K&M Services

Clear Shot Powder
GOEX Inc.

Complete Custom Rifles
Amrine's Gun Shop

Complete Custom Rifles to order only
Classic Arms Corp.

Concealment Vest, Holstered handbags, gear
Concealment Shop Inc.

Cover Scent
Russ Trading Post

Custom Bullets, Custom Ammunition
Blue Mountain Bullets

Custom Checkering & Refinishing
Custom Gun Stocks

custom checking
RMS Custom Gunsmithing

Custom Firearms or Expensive Fragile Eq
Impact Case Co.

Custom Gunstock Design
Keith's Custom Gunstocks

Custom Knife Maker & Engraver
Frank Knives

Custom Leather goods
Silhouette Leathers

Custom Leupold Scope Reticles
Premier Reticles

Custom Made Cleaning Rods for Cal. 14, 17, 20
Unmussig Bullets, D. L.

Custom Made Kentucky Rifles
Lutz Engraving, Ron E.

Custom Pistol & Revolver Maker
Wessinger Custom Guns & Engraving

Custom Reloading
Blue Mountain Bullets

Custom Rifle Design Classic
Heppler, Keith M, Keith's Custom Gunstocks

Custom Rifle Maker
Wessinger Custom Guns & Engraving

Custom Scope Reticles
T.K. Lee Co.

Custom Throwing Knife Mfg
Tru-Balance Knife Co.

Damascus Bar
DAMASCUS-U.S.A.

Davide Pedersul Co Italy Full Line Importer
Flintlocks, Etc.

Dealer in Machine Guns, Cannon Gatlings
Lomont Precision Bullets

Decker Rifle Vise
Decker Shooting Products

Deer Lure
Russ Trading Post

Dehumidifiers
Buenger Enterprises/Goldenrod Dehumidifier
Hydrosorbent Products

Dryers
Peet Shoe Dryer, Inc.

Electroless Nickel Plating
Spencer Reblue Service

Engraving Instructor
Barraclough, John K.

European Accessories
Quality Arms, Inc.

Export Agent for Various Brands including NAA, PAR
Austin Sheridan USA, Inc.

Exporter
Quality Arms, Inc.

E-Z Loader
Del Rey Products

FFL Record Keeping
Basics Information Systems, Inc.
PFRB Co.
R.E.T. Enterprises

Field Carts
Ziegel Engineering

Fine Shotguns, Gun Cases
Quality Arms, Inc.

Fircourm Engraver
Metals Hand Engraver/European Hand Engraving

Firearm & Scope Refinishing Spradlin's TefCote
Spradlin's

Firearm Refinishers
Armoloy Co. of Ft. Worth

Firearm Restoration
Adair Custom Shop, Bill
Mazur Restoration, Pete
Moeller, Steve
Nicholson Custom

Firearm Restoration Specializing in S&S Shotgun &
Pete Mazur Restoration

Firearms Engraver
Oker's Engraving

Firearms Restoration
Turnbull Restoration, Doug

Fire-Lapping Supplies
Beartooth Bullets

Fully Custom Gunsmithing Gun Maker
P.S.M.G. Gun Co.

Gloves
Russ Trading Post

Gun Hangers
Cash Mfg. Co., Inc.

Gun Lubricant
Muscle Products Corp.

Gun Rights Lobby
Western Missouri Shooters Alliance

Gun Safes, Handgun Safes, Gun Vaults, Safes
English, Inc., A.G.

Gunfitting Service
The Midwest Shooting School

Guns/accessories, knives & swords
Leapers, Inc.

Gunsmithing Machinery
Blue Ridge Machinery & Tools, Inc.

Gunstock Blanks Knife Handles & Pistol Grips
Johnson Wood Products

Gunstock Engraver-Custom
Klingler Woodcarving

Hammer Shrouds for Revolvers
W. Waller & Son, Inc.

Hunting & Game Calling Videos
Woods Wise Products

Hunting & Trapping Supply
Russ Trading Post

Hunting Blinds
Trax America, Inc.

Hunting Trips
J/B Adventures & Safaris Inc.
Professional Hunter Supplies (See Star Custom Bull)
Wild West Guns

Hydraulic or Spring Recoil Reducers
Danuser Machine Co.

Hypodermic Rifles/Pistols
Multipropulseurs

Importer & Maker of Museum Quality
Small Arms Specialists

Importer for Various Brands including Norma
Austin Sheridan USA, Inc.

Importer/Wholesaler of Scopes, Mounts, Airsoft
Leapers, Inc.

Industrial Dessicants
WAMCO--New Mexico

Interior Shotgun Barrel Work
Eyster Heritage Gunsmiths, Inc., Ken

Ivory Legal
African Import Co.

Keeps the barrel of a black powder firearm clean
Lestrom Laboratories, Inc.

Knife Sharpeners
EdgeCraft Corp., S. Weiner

Knives
Russ Trading Post

Knives, Custom Carved Antler Handles
Klingler Woodcarving

Knives, Sport, Pocket, Hunting
A.G. Russell Knives,Inc.

Laser Sights
Alpec Team, Inc.

Lassen Community College
Barraclough, John K.

Letter openers, sportsmens jewelry
The Alaskan Silversmith

Lettering Restoration System
Pranger, Ed G.

Load Development
Dead Eye's Sport Center

Locks, Gun
Brown Manufacturing
Central Specialties Ltd (See Trigger Lock Division
L&R Lock Co.
Master Lock Co.
Trigger Lock Division/Central Specialties Ltd.
Voere-KGH m.b.H.

Lut Fitter's Stove's
McCann Industries

Magazines
Mag-Pack Corp.
Mech-Tech Systems, Inc.

Make distribute trap door grip caps
Heilmann, Stephen

Making Pewter Wildlife coat hooks
The Alaskan Silversmith

Manufacture Custom, Handmade Duck & Goose Calls
Custom Calls

Manufacturer Muzzle Brakes
KDF, Inc.

Manufacturer of complete line of replica Stevens
Mid-America Recreation, Inc.

Manufacturer of Custom Gunstocks for Shotguns
Wenig Custom Gunstocks

Mats
Brigade Quartermasters

Mauser Actions
Granite Mountain Arms, Inc

Military & Police (restricted)
Vulpes Ventures, Inc. Fox Cartridge Division

Military Equipment/Accessories
Amherst Arms

Miniature Guns
Small Arms Specialists

Miruko is Browning SKB is SKB also Weatherby Shotg
SKB Shotguns

Mongoose Slings
High North Products, Inc.

Muzzle Brake & Spring Loaded Recoil Pad
Answer Products Co.

Muzzle Brakes Barrel Fluting
Ozark Gun Works

Muzzle Loader Custom Gun Building
McCann's Muzzle-Gun Works

Muzzle loading projectiles
Buffalo Bullet Co., Inc..

Muzzleloading Leather Goods, Possible bags, etc
The Eutaw Co., Inc.

Nitex E Nickle
Nitex, Inc.

NRA affiliated school
Trinidad St. Jr Col Gunsmith Dept.

NRA Summer Schools
Barraclough, John K.

Octagon Barrel Maker
KOGOT

of Stevens Products Mfg. From 1894 to WWI
Mid-America Recreation, Inc.

Online Firearms Newspaper
Bullet'n Press

Optical Equipment Repair
ABO (USA) Inc

Optics Importer Docter Sports Optics
B.C. Outdoors

Ordnance, Nosler, Stoney Point & Weatherby
Austin Sheridan USA, Inc.

outdoor gears & collectibles gifts
Leapers, Inc.

Pancake Holster, Belts & Other Leather Goods
Baker's Leather Goods, Roy

Parts & Service for the Colt Single Action Army Re
Peacemaker Specialists

Photographers, Gun
Bilal, Mustafa
Hanusin, John
Macbean, Stan
Payne Photography, Robert
Radack Photography
Smith, Michael
Weyer International
White Pine Photographic Services

Pietta Importers
Brocock Ltd.

Pistol Barrel Maker
Aro-Tek Ltd.
Bar-Sto Precision Machine

Powder Measurers
Cash Mfg. Co., Inc.

Power Tools, Rotary Flexible Shaft
Foredom Electric Co.

Precision Cap Dispensers
Cash Mfg. Co., Inc.

Professional lowbolt folging (no welding), longer,
Schumakers Gun Shop

Provide Custom Bullet Alloys
Bullet Metals

Quiet Muzzle Broke
Gentry Custom Gunmaker, David

R&D Work
Genecco Gun Works

Range & shooting bags
Concealment Shop Inc.

Rapid Fire Device for .22 Rifles. Hand crank
B.M.F. Activator, Inc.

Rapid Fire Devise
B.M.F. Activator, Inc.

Reblueing, Parkerizing
Spencer Reblue Service

Rebluing & Color Case harding, Barrel Lining
Toms Gun Repair, Inc.

Reduction System
Answer Products Co.

Rem 700 RH & LH
Gentry Custom Gunmaker, David

Renovation of Quality Classic Guns & Gen Gunsmithi
Bob Rogers Gunsmithing

Repair American Made Weaver Scopes
Weaver Scope Repair Service

Repairs All Makes
Tele-Optics

Restoration
Larry Lyons Gunworks

Restoration Antique Long guns
Antique Arms Co.

Restoration Of European Double Guns & Rifles & Ant
Flynn's Custom Guns

Restorations
Bill Adair Custom Shop

RF Barrel Vibration Reducer
Hoehn Sales, Inc.

RF Device
B.M.F. Activator, Inc.

Rifle & Shotgun Repair
DGR Custom Rifles

Rifle and Shotgun Stock blanks.
Heppler, Keith M, Keith's Custom Gunstocks

Rifle Builder
Sanders Custom Gun Service

Rifle Maker
Jagdwaffen, P. Hofer

Rifles
Pete Mazur Restoration

Rust Blowing & Recondition
Briganti, A.J.

rust Blueing
Spencer Reblue Service

Rust Proofing/applicator
Rusteprufe Laboratories

Sabot Bullets
Northern Precision Custom Swaged Bullets

Saddle Rings, Studs
Silver Ridge Gun Shop (See Goodwin, Fred)

Safeties
P.M. Enterprises, Inc.

safety devices
Boonie Packer Products
P&M Sales and Service

Scent Pads
Russ Trading Post

Scents and Lures
Buck Stop Lure Co., Inc.
Cabinet Mtn. Outfitters Scents & Lures
Dr. O's Products Ltd.
Mountain Hollow Game Calls
Tinks & Ben Lee Hunting Products (See Wellington)
Tink's Safariland Hunting Corp.
Wellington Outdoors
Wildlife Research Center, Inc.
Wyant's Outdoor Products, Inc.

Scope Mounts
McCann Industries

Scrimshaw
Dolbare, Elizabeth
Reno, Wayne

Sell Polymer Finishes
Ten-Ring Precision, Inc.

Shooters Shirts
TEN-X Products Group

Shooting Range Equipment
Caswell Detroit Armor Companies

Shooting Vest, Camo Clothing
TEN-X Products Group

Shotgun Barrel Maker
Baker, Stan

Shotgun Conversion Tubes
Dina Arms Corporation

Sifters
Russ Trading Post

Silencers
AWC Systems Technology
DLO Mfg.
Fleming Firearms
S.C.R.C.
Sound Technology
Ward Machine

Slings and Swivels
DTM International, Inc.
Pathfinder Sports Leather
Schulz Industries
Torel, Inc.

slings, swivels, mag loaders, speedloaders
Boonie Packer Products

Sportsmans Mdse
Sturm Ruger & Co. Inc.

Stakes
Russ Trading Post

Stock Checkering & Carving
Stan De Treville & Co.

stock dup;icating service
RMS Custom Gunsmithing

Stock Duplication Curly Maple for Longrifles
Tiger-Hunt Gunstocks

Stock For Firearms
DAMASCUS-U.S.A.

Stretchers
Russ Trading Post

Tactical Ammunition
Vulpes Ventures, Inc. Fox Cartridge Division

Tim Metal, Antmony Metal
Ames Metal Products

Tool and Press Mounting System
TTM

Tooling for the Firearm Industry
Clymer Mfg. Co.

Training, Defensive Use of Force
SAFE

Traps
Russ Trading Post

Treestands and Accessories and
Trax America, Inc.

Treestands and Steps
Dr. O's Products Ltd.
Silent Hunter
Summit Specialties, Inc.
Treemaster
Warren & Sweat Mfg. Co.

Trinidad State SNR College
Barraclough, John K.

Trophies
V.H. Blackinton & Co., Inc.

Turkish and Cal. English Walnut Stock Blanks
Farmer-Dressel, Sharon

Turkish and Cal. English Walnut, Grip Caps
Dressel Jr, Paul G

Ventilated Rib
Simmons Gun Repair, Inc.

Video Tapes
American Pioneer Video
Calibre Press, Inc.
Cedar Hill Game Calls LLC
Clements' Custom Leathercraft, Chas
Foothills Video Productions, Inc.
HandCrafts Unltd (See Clements' Custom Leather)
Lethal Force Institute (See Police Bookshelf)
Police Bookshelf
Primos, Inc.
R.T. Eastman Products
Trail Visions
Wilderness Sound Products Ltd.

Wads for Lead Bullets tin & Alloyed Metals
John Walters Wads

Walnut Stock Blanks
Keith's Custom Gunstocks

Warranty Repair Remington Winchester & Browning
Island Pond Gun Shop

Warranty Service for Weatherby & Remington
Williamson Precision Gunsmithing

We manufacture Micro Bed. Stock Bedding compound
Micro Sight Co.

Weatherby & Remington
Williamson Precision Gunsmithing

Wipe Away Gun Cleaning Cloth
Belltown Ltd.

World's Finest Recoil
Answer Products Co.

Xythos-Miniature Revolver
Andres & Dworsky

MOULDS & MOULD ACCESSORIES

American Products, Inc.
Ballisti-Cast, Inc.
Buffalo Arms Co.
Cast Performance Bullet Company
Lee Precision, Inc.
Lyman Products Corporation
Magma Engineering Co.
NEI Handtools, Inc.
Old West Bullet Moulds
Penn Bullets
Rapine Bullet Mould Mfg. Co.
Redding Reloading Equipment
S&S Firearms
Small Custom Mould & Bullet Co.
Wolf's Western Traders

MUZZLE-LOADING GUNS, BARRELS & EQUIPMENT

Accuracy Unlimited
Ackerman & Co.
Adkins, Luther
Allen Mfg.
Armi San Paolo
Austin & Halleck
Bauska Barrels
Beaver Lodge (See Fellowes, Ted)
Bentley, John
Big Bore Express
Birdsong & Assoc, W. E.
Black Powder Products
Blue and Gray Products Inc (See Ox-Yoke Originals
Bridgers Best
Buckskin Bullet Co.
Buckskin Machine Works, A. Hunekler
Butler Creek Corp.
Cache La Poudre Rifleworks
California Sights (See Fautheree, Andy)
Cash Mfg. Co., Inc.

PRODUCT & SERVICE DIRECTORY

CBC-BRAZIL
Chambers Flintlocks Ltd., Jim
Cimarron F.A. Co.
Claybuster Wads & Harvester Bullets
Cogar's Gunsmithing
Colonial Repair
Conetrol Scope Mounts
Cousin Bob's Mountain Products
Cumberland Arms
Cumberland Mountain Arms
Curly Maple Stock Blanks (See Tiger-Hunt)
CVA
Dangler, Homer L.
Davide Pedersoli and Co.
Dayton Traister
deHaas Barrels
Delhi Gun House
Dixie Gun Works, Inc.
Dixon Muzzleloading Shop, Inc.
Ed King Office
EMF Co., Inc.
Euroarms of America, Inc.
Feken, Dennis
Fellowes, Ted
Flintlocks, Etc.
Fort Hill Gunstocks
Fowler, Bob (See Black Powder Products)
Frankonia Jagd Hofmann & Co.
Frontier
Getz Barrel Co.
Goergen's Gun Shop
Golden Age Arms Co.
Gonic Arms/North American Arm
Green Mountain Rifle Barrel Co., Inc.
Hastings Barrels
Hawken Shop, The (See Dayton Traister)
Hege Jagd-u. Sporthandels GmbH
Hodgdon Powder Co.
Hoppe's Div. Penguin Industries, Inc.
Hornady Mfg. Co.
Hunkeler, A (See Buckskin Machine Works
Ironsighter Co.
J.P. Gunstocks, Inc.
John Walters Wads
Jones Co., Dale
K&M Industries, Inc.
Kalispel Case Line
Kennedy Firearms
Knight Rifles
Knight Rifles (See Modern Muzzle Loading, Inc.)
Kolar
L&R Lock Co.
L&S Technologies Inc (See Aimtech Mount Systems)
Lakewood Products LLC
Legend Products Corp.
Lestrom Laboratories, Inc.
Lothar Walther Precision Tool Inc.
Lutz Engraving, Ron E.
Lyman Products Corporation
Lyman Products Corporation
Markesbery Muzzle Loaders, Inc.
Marlin Firearms Co.
McCann's Muzzle-Gun Works
Michaels Of Oregon
Millennium Designed Muzzleloaders
MMP
Modern Muzzleloading, Inc
Mountain State Muzzleloading Supplies, Inc.
Mowrey Gun Works
MSC Industrial Supply Co.
Mt. Alto Outdoor Products
Muzzleloading Technologies, Inc
Naval Ordnance Works
Navy Arms Co.
Navy Arms Company
Newman Gunshop
North Star West
October Country Muzzleloading
Oklahoma Leather Products,Inc.
Olson, Myron
Orion Rifle Barrel Co.
Ox-Yoke Originals, Inc.
P.S.M.G. Gun Co.
Pacific Rifle Co.
Parker & Sons Shooting Supply
Parker Gun Finishes

Pecatonica River Longrifle
Pioneer Arms Co.
Piquette's Custom Engraving
Prairie River Arms
Redfield/Blount
Rusty Duck Premium Gun Care Products
S&S Firearms
Selsi Co., Inc.
Shiloh Creek
Shooter's Choice
Simmons Gun Repair, Inc.
Sklany's Machine Shop
Smokey Valley Rifles (See Lutz Engraving, Ron E)
South Bend Replicas, Inc.
Southern Bloomer Mfg. Co.
Starr Trading Co., Jedediah
Stone Mountain Arms
Sturm Ruger & Co. Inc.
Taylor's & Co., Inc.
Tennessee Valley Mfg.
The Eutaw Co., Inc.
The Gun Works
The House of Muskets, Inc.
The House of Muskets, Inc.
Thompson Bullet Lube Co.
Thompson/Center Arms
Thunder Mountain Arms
Tiger-Hunt Gunstocks
Track of the Wolf, Inc.
Traditions Performance Firearms
Truglo, Inc
Uncle Mike's (See Michaels of Oregon Co)
Upper Missouri Trading Co.
Venco Industries, Inc. (See Shooter's Choice)
Virgin Valley Custom Guns
Voere-KGH m.b.H.
W.E. Birdsong & Assoc.
Warne Manufacturing Co.
Warren Muzzleloading Co., Inc.
Wescombe, Bill (See North Star West)
White Owl Enterprises
White Shooting Systems, Inc. (See White Muzzleload
Woodworker's Supply
Wright's Hardwood Gunstock Blanks
Young Country Arms
Ziegel Engineering
Ziegel Engineering

PISTOLSMITH

A.W. Peterson Gun Shop, Inc.
Acadian Ballistic Specialties
Accuracy Unlimited
Ace Custom 45's, Inc.
Actions by "T" Teddy Jacobson
Adair Custom Shop, Bill
Ahlman Guns
Ahrends, Kim (See Custom Firearms, Inc)
Aldis Gunsmithing & Shooting Supply
Alpha Precision, Inc.
Alpine Indoor Shooting Range
Armament Gunsmithing Co., Inc.
Aro-Tek Ltd.
Arundel Arms & Ammunition, Inc., A.
Baer Custom, Inc, Les
Bain & Davis, Inc.
Banks, Ed
Bar-Sto Precision Machine
Behlert Precision, Inc.
Ben William's Gun Shop
Bengtson Arms Co., L.
Bill Adair Custom Shop
Billings Gunsmiths Inc.
Bob Rogers Gunsmithing
Bowen Classic Arms Corp.
Broken Gun Ranch
Burkhart Gunsmithing, Don
Cannon's
Caraville Manufacturing
Carter's Gun Shop
Chicasaw Gun Works
Clark Custom Guns, Inc.
Cleland's Outdoor World, Inc
Colonial Repair
Colorado School of Trades
Colt's Mfg. Co., Inc.
Corkys Gun Clinic
Craig Custom Ltd., Research & Development

Curtis Custom Shop
Custom Arms Company
Custom Firearms (See Ahrends, Kim)
Cylinder & Slide, Inc., William R. Laughridge
D&L Sports
David R. Chicoine
Dayton Traister
Dilliott Gunsmithing, Inc.
Ed Brown Products, Inc.
Ed~ Brown Products, Inc.
EGW Evolution Gun Works
Ellicott Arms, Inc./Woods Pistolsmithing
Ferris Firearms
Fisher Custom Firearms
Forkin, Ben (See Belt MTN Arms)
Forkin Arms
Francesca, Inc.
Frielich Police Equipment
G.G. & G.
Garthwaite Pistolsmith, Inc., Jim
Gary Reeder Custom Guns
Genecco Gun Works
Gentry Custom Gunmaker, David
George E. Mathews & Son, Inc.
Greider Precision
Gunsite Custom Shop
Gunsite Gunsmithy (See Gunsite Custom Shop)
Gunsite Training Center
Hamilton, Alex B (See Ten-Ring Precision, Inc)
Hammond Custom Guns Ltd.
Hank's Gun Shop
Hanson's Gun Center, Dick
Harris Gunworks
Harwood, Jack O.
Hawken Shop, The (See Dayton Traister)
Hebard Guns, Gil
Heinie Specialty Products
High Bridge Arms, Inc
Highline Machine Co.
Hoag Gun Wks
Irwin, Campbell H.
Island Pond Gun Shop
Ivanoff, Thomas G (See Tom's Gun Repair)
J&S Heat Treat
Jarvis, Inc.
Jeffredo Gunsight
Jensen's Custom Ammunition
Jones, J.D./SSK Industries
Jungkind, Reeves C.
Kaswer Custom, Inc.
Ken Starnes Gunmaker
Ken's Gun Specialties
Kilham & Co.
Kim Ahrends Custom Firearms, Inc.
Kimball, Gary
King's Gun Works
La Clinique du .45
LaFrance Specialties
LaRocca Gun Works
Lathrop's, Inc.
Lawson, John G (See Sight Shop, The)
Leckie Professional Gunsmithing
Lee's Red Ramps
Linebaugh Custom Sixguns
List Precision Engineering
Long, George F.
Mag-Na-Port International, Inc.
Mahony, Philip Bruce
Mahovsky's Metalife
Mandall Shooting Supplies Inc.
Marent, Rudolf
Marvel, Alan
Mathews & Son, Inc., George E.
Maxi-Mount
McCann's Machine & Gun Shop
MCS, Inc.
Middlebrooks Custom Shop
Miller Custom
Mitchell's Accuracy Shop
MJK Gunsmithing, Inc.
Modern Gun Repair School
Montgomery Community College
Mo's Competitor Supplies (See MCS Inc)
Mowrey's Guns & Gunsmithing
Mullis Guncraft

NCP Products, Inc.
Novak's, Inc.
Nygord Precision Products
Pace Marketing, Inc.
Paris, Frank J.
Pasadena Gun Center
PEM's Mfg. Co.
Performance Specialists
Pierce Pistols
Power Custom, Inc.
Precision Specialties
Randco UK
Ries, Chuck
Rim Pac Sports, Inc.
Rocky Mountain Arms, Inc.
RPM
Score High Gunsmithing
Scott McDougall & Associates
Seecamp Co. Inc., L. W.
Shooters Supply
Shootin' Shack, Inc.
Singletary, Kent
Sipes Gun Shop
Springfield, Inc.
SSK Industries
Swenson's 45 Shop, A. D.
Swift River Gunworks
Ten-Ring Precision, Inc.
Terry K. Kopp Professional Gunsmithing
The Robar Co.'s, Inc.
The Sight Shop
Thompson, Randall (See Highline Machine Co.)
Thurston Sports, Inc.
Time Precision, Inc.
Vic's Gun Refinishing
Volquartsen Custom Ltd.
Walker Arms Co., Inc.
Walters Industries
Wardell Precision Handguns Ltd.
Weigand Combat Handguns, Inc.
Wessinger Custom Guns & Engraving
White Barn Wor
Wichita Arms, Inc.
Williamson Precision Gunsmithing
Wilson Gun Shop
Wright's Hardwood Gunstock Blanks

POWDER MEASURES, SCALES, FUNNELS & ACCESSORIES

4-D Custom Die Co.
Battenfeld Technologies
Dillon Precision Products, Inc.
Fremont Tool Works
Frontier
High Precision
Lyman Products Corporation
Modern Muzzleloading, Inc
RCBS Div. of Blount
Redding Reloading Equipment
VibraShine, Inc.

PRESS ACCESSORIES, METALLIC

Lyman Products Corporation
R.E.I.
TTM
Vega Tool Co.

PRESS ACCESSORIES, SHOTSHELL

MEC, Inc.
Precision Reloading, Inc.
R.E.I.
TTM

PRESSES, ARBOR

Blue Ridge Machinery & Tools, Inc.
Hoehn Sales, Inc.
K&M Services
Sinclair International, Inc.

PRESSES, METALLIC

4-D Custom Die Co.
Battenfeld Technologies
Dillon Precision Products, Inc.
Fremont Tool Works
RCBS Div. of Blount
Redding Reloading Equipment

PRESSES, SHOTSHELL

Ballistic Product, Inc.
Dillon Precision Products, Inc.
MEC, Inc.
Precision Reloading, Inc.

PRESSES, SWAGE

Bullet Swaging Supply Inc.
MAST Technology

PRIMING TOOLS & ACCESSORIES

Hart & Son, Inc.
K&M Services
RCBS Div. of Blount
Simmons, Jerry
Sinclair International, Inc.
TTM

REBORING & RERIFLING

Ahlman Guns
Bauska Barrels
BlackStar AccuMax Barrels
BlackStar Barrel Accurizing (See BlackStar AccuMax)
Fred F. Wells/Wells Sport Store
H&S Liner Service
Hastings Barrels
Ivanoff, Thomas G (See Tom's Gun Repair)
Jackalope Gun Shop
LaBounty Precision Reboring, Inc
NCP Products, Inc.
Pence Precision Barrels
Redman's Rifling & Reboring
Rice, Keith (See White Rock Tool & Die)
Ridgetop Sporting Goods
Savage Arms, Inc.
Shaw, Inc., E. R. (See Small Arms Mfg. Co.)
Siegrist Gun Shop
Simmons Gun Repair, Inc.
Stratco, Inc.
Terry K. Kopp Professional Gunsmithing
The Gun Works
Time Precision, Inc.
Van Patten, J. W.
White Rock Tool & Die
Zufall, Joseph F.

RELOADING TOOLS AND ACCESSORIES

"Gramps" Antique Cartridges
4-D Custom Die Co.
Accurate Arms Co., Inc.
Advance Car Mover Co., Rowell Div.
Alaska Bullet Works, Inc.
American Products, Inc.
Ames Metal Products
Ammo Load, Inc.
Armfield Custom Bullets
Armite Laboratories
Arms Corporation of the Philippines
Atlantic Rose, Inc.
Atsko/Sno-Seal, Inc.
Bald Eagle Precision Machine Co.
Ballistic Product, Inc.
Belltown Ltd.
Ben William's Gun Shop
Ben's Machines
Berger Bullets Ltd.
Berry's Mfg., Inc.
Blount, Inc., Sporting Equipment Div.
Blue Ridge Machinery & Tools, Inc.
Bonanza (See Forster Products)
Break-Free, Inc.
Brown Co, E. Arthur
BRP, Inc. High Performance Cast Bullets
Brynin, Milton
B-Square Company, Inc.
Buck Stix--SOS Products Co.
Bullseye Bullets
C&D Special Products (See Claybuster Wads & Harves
Camdex, Inc.
Camp-Cap Products
Canyon Cartridge Corp.
Case Sorting System
CFVentures

CH Tool & Die Co (See 4-D Custom Die Co)
Chem-Pak Inc.
CheVron Bullets
Claybuster Wads & Harvester Bullets
CONKKO
Cook Engineering Service
Cooper-Woodward
Crouse's Country Cover
Cumberland Arms
Curtis Cast Bullets
Custom Products (See Jones Custom Products)
CVA
D.C.C. Enterprises
Davide Pedersoli and Co.
Davis, Don
Davis Products, Mike
Denver Instrument Co.
Dewey Mfg. Co., Inc., J.
Dillon Precision Products, Inc.
Dropkick
E&L Mfg., Inc.
Eagan, Donald V.
Ed King Office
Eezox, Inc.
Efficient Machinery Co
Eichelberger Bullets, Wm.
Elkhorn Bullets
Enguix Import-Export
Euroarms of America, Inc.
E-Z-Way Systems
Federated-Fry (See Fry Metals)
Feken, Dennis
Ferguson, Bill
First Inc, Jack
Fisher Custom Firearms
Fitz Pistol Grip Co.
Flambeau Products Corp.
Flitz International Ltd.
Forster Products
Fremont Tool Works
Fry Metals
GAR
Gehmann, Walter (See Huntington Die Specialties)
Graf & Sons
Graphics Direct
Graves Co.
Green, Arthur S.
Greenwood Precision
GTB
Gun City
Hanned Precision (See Hanned Line, The)
Harrell's Precision
Harris Enterprises
Harrison Bullets
Haydon Shooters Supply, Russ
Heidenstrom Bullets
High Precision
Hirtenberger Aktiengesellschaft
Hoch Custom Bullet Moulds (See Colorado Shooter's
Hodgdon Powder Co.
Hoehn Sales, Inc.
Hoelscher, Virgil
Holland's Gunsmithing
Hollywood Engineering
Hondo Ind.
Hornady Mfg. Co.
Howell Machine
Hunters Supply, Inc.
Huntington Die Specialties
Hutton Rifle Ranch
Image Ind. Inc.
Imperial Magnum Corp.
INTEC International, Inc.
Iosso Products
J&L Superior Bullets (See Huntington Die Special)
Javelina Lube Products
JGS Precision Tool Mfg.
JLK Bullets
John Walters Wads
Jonad Corp.
Jones Custom Products, Neil A.
Jones Moulds, Paul
K&M Services
Kapro Mfg.Co. Inc. (See R.E.I.)
Knoell, Doug
Korzinek Riflesmith, J
L.A.R. Mfg., Inc.

L.E. Wilson, Inc.
Lapua Ltd.
LBT
Le Clear Industries (See E-Z-Way Systems)
Lee Precision, Inc.
Legend Products Corp.
Liberty Metals
Liberty Shooting Supplies
Lightning Performance Innovations, Inc.
Lithi Bee Bullet Lube
Littleton, J. F.
Lock's Philadelphia Gun Exchange
Lortone Inc.
Loweth, Richard H.R.
Lyman Instant Targets, Inc. (See Lyman Products)
MA Systems
Magma Engineering Co.
MarMik, Inc.
Marquart Precision Co.
MAST Technology
Match Prep--Doyle Gracey
Mayville Engineering Co. (See MEC, Inc.)
MCS, Inc.
Midway Arms, Inc.
MI-TE Bullets
MMP
Montana Armory, Inc (See C. Sharps Arms Co. Inc.)
Mo's Competitor Supplies (See MCS Inc)
Mountain South
Mountain State Muzzleloading Supplies, Inc.
Mt. Baldy Bullet Co.
MTM Molded Products Co., Inc.
Multi-Scale Charge Ltd.
MWG Co.
Navy Arms Company
Necromancer Industries, Inc.
NEI Handtools, Inc.
Newman Gunshop
North Devon Firearms Services
October Country Muzzleloading
Old West Bullet Moulds
Omark Industries,Div. of Blount,Inc.
Original Box, Inc.
Outdoor Sports Headquarters,Inc.
Paco's (See Small Custom Mould & Bullet Co)
Paragon Sales & Services, Inc.
Pease Accuracy
Peerless Alloy, Inc.
Pinetree Bullets
Ponsness/Warren
Prairie River Arms
Precision Castings & Equipment
Precision Reloading, Inc.
Prime Reloading
Professional Hunter Supplies (See Star Custom Bull)
Prolixrr Lubricants
Pro-Shot Products, Inc.
R.E.I.
R.I.S. Co., Inc.
Rapine Bullet Mould Mfg. Co.
Redding Reloading Equipment
Reloading Specialties, Inc.
Rice, Keith (See White Rock Tool & Die)
Roberts Products
Rochester Lead Works
Rooster Laboratories
Rorschach Precision Products
SAECO (See Redding Reloading Equipment)
Sandia Die & Cartridge Co.
Saunders Gun & Machine Shop
Saville Iron Co. (See Greenwood Precision)
Scharch Mfg., Inc.
Scot Powder Co. of Ohio, Inc.
Seebeck Assoc., R.E.
Sharp Shooter Supply
Sharps Arms Co., Inc., C.
Shiloh Creek
Shiloh Rifle Mfg.
Shooter's Choice
Sierra Specialty Prod. Co.
Silver Eagle Machining

Simmons, Jerry
Sinclair International, Inc.
Skip's Machine
Small Custom Mould & Bullet Co.
Sno-Seal, Inc. (See Atsko/Sno-Seal)
SOS Products Co. (See Buck Stix-SOS Products Co.)
Spencer's Custom Guns
Sportsman Supply Co.
SSK Industries
Stalwart Corporation
Star Custom Bullets
Starr Trading Co., Jedediah
Stillwell, Robert
Stoney Point Products, Inc.
Stratco, Inc.
Tamarack Products, Inc.
Taracorp Industries, Inc.
TCCI
TCSR
TDP Industries, Inc.
Tetra Gun Lubricants (See FTI, Inc.)
The Gun Works
The Hanned Line
The Protector Mfg. Co., Inc.
Thompson Bullet Lube Co.
Thompson/Center Arms
Timber Heirloom Products
Time Precision, Inc.
TMI Products (See Haselbauer Products, Jerry)
Tru-Square Metal Prods., Inc.
Vega Tool Co.
Venco Industries, Inc. (See Shooter's Choice)
VibraShine, Inc.
Vibra-Tek Co.
Vihtavuori Oy/Kaltron-Pettibone
Vitt/Boos
W.B. Niemi Engineering
W.J. Riebe Co.
Waechter
WD-40 Co.
Webster Scale Mfg. Co.
White Rock Tool & Die
Widener's Reloading & Shooting Supply, Inc.
Wise Custom Guns
Wolf's Western Traders
Woodleigh (See Huntington Die Specialties)
WTA Manufacturing
Yesteryear Armory & Supply
Young Country Arms

RESTS BENCH, PORTABLE AND ACCESSORIES

Accuright
Adventure 16, Inc.
Armor Metal Products
Bald Eagle Precision Machine Co.
Bartlett Engineering
Battenfeld Technologies
Borden Rifles Inc
Browning Arms Co.
B-Square Company, Inc.
C.W. Erickson's Mfg. Inc.
Canons Delcour
Chem-Pak Inc.
Clift Mfg., L. R.
Clift Welding Supply & Cases
Decker Shooting Products
Desert Mountain Mfg.
Greenwood Precision
Harris Engineering Inc.
Haydon Shooters Supply, Russ
Hidalgo, Tony
Hoehn Sales, Inc.
Hoelscher, Virgil
Hoppe's Div. Penguin Industries, Inc.
Keng's Firearms Specialty, Inc./US Tactical Systems
Kolpin Mfg., Inc.
Kramer Designs
Midway Arms, Inc.
Millett Sights
P.S.M.G. Gun Co.
Protektor Model
Ransom International Corp.
Redfield/Blount
Saville Iron Co. (See Greenwood Precision)

Sinclair International, Inc.
Stoney Point Products, Inc.
T.H.U. Enterprises, Inc.
The Outdoor Connection,Inc.
Thompson Target Technology
Tonoloway Tack Drives
Varmint Masters, LLC
Wichita Arms, Inc.
Zanotti Armor, Inc.
Ziegel Engineering

RIFLE BARREL MAKER

Airrow
American Safe Arms, Inc.
Bauska Barrels
BlackStar AccuMax Barrels
BlackStar Barrel Accurizing (See BlackStar AccuMax
Border Barrels Ltd.
Brian Perazone-Gunsmith
Brown Co, E. Arthur
Bullberry Barrel Works, Ltd.
Canons Delcour
Carter's Gun Shop
Christensen Arms
Cincinnati Swaging
Cryo-Accurizing
D&J Bullet Co. & Custom Gun Shop, Inc.
deHaas Barrels
Dilliott Gunsmithing, Inc.
DKT, Inc.
Donnelly, C. P.
Douglas Barrels Inc.
Fred F. Wells/Wells Sport Store
Gaillard Barrels
Gary Schneider Rifle Barrels Inc.
Getz Barrel Co.
Granite Mountain Arms, Inc
Green Mountain Rifle Barrel Co., Inc.
Gruning Precision Inc
Half Moon Rifle Shop
Harris Gunworks
Hart Rifle Barrels,Inc.
Hastings Barrels
Hoelscher, Virgil
H-S Precision, Inc.
Jackalope Gun Shop
Jagdwaffen, P. Hofer
Knippel, Richard
Krieger Barrels, Inc.
Lilja Precision Rifle Barrels
Lothar Walther Precision Tool Inc.
McGowen Rifle Barrels
McMillan Rifle Barrels
Mid-America Recreation, Inc.
Modern Gun Repair School
Morrison Precision
Obermeyer Rifled Barrels
Olympic Arms Inc.
Orion Rifle Barrel Co.
Pac-Nor Barreling
Pell, John T. (See KOGOT)
Pence Precision Barrels
Perazone-Gunsmith, Brian
Raptor Arms Co., Inc.
Rocky Mountain Rifle Works Ltd.
Rogue Rifle Co., Inc.
Sabatti S.r.l.
Sanders Custom Gun Service
Savage Arms, Inc.
Schneider Rifle Barrels, Inc, Gary
Shaw, Inc., E. R. (See Small Arms Mfg. Co.)
Shilen, Inc.
Siskiyou Gun Works (See Donnelly, C. P.)
Small Arms Mfg. Co.
Specialty Shooters Supply, Inc.
Spencer's Custom Guns
Strutz Rifle Barrels, Inc., W. C.
Swift River Gunworks
Terry K. Kopp Professional Gunsmithing
The Gun Works
The Wilson Arms Co.
Unmussig Bullets, D. L.
Verney-Carron
Virgin Valley Custom Guns
W.C. Strutz Rifle Barrels, Inc.
Wiseman and Co., Bill

SCOPES, MOUNTS, ACCESSORIES, OPTICAL EQUIPMENT

A.R.M.S., Inc.
ABO (USA) Inc
Accu-Tek
Ackerman, Bill (See Optical Services Co)
Action Direct, Inc.
ADCO Sales, Inc.
Adventurer's Outpost
Aimpoint c/o Springfield, Inc.
Aimtech Mount Systems
Air Rifle Specialists
Air Venture Airguns
Alley Supply Co.
Alpec Team, Inc.
Apel GmbH, Ernst
ArmaLite, Inc.
Arundel Arms & Ammunition, Inc., A.
BAC
Baer Custom, Inc, Les
Barrett Firearms Manufacturer, Inc.
Beaver Park Product, Inc.
BEC, Inc.
Beeman Precision Airguns
Ben William's Gun Shop
Benjamin/Sheridan Co., Crossman
BKL Technologies
Blount, Inc., Sporting Equipment Div.
Boonie Packer Products
Borden Ridges Rimrock Stocks
Borden Rifles Inc
Brockman's Custom Gunsmithing
Brocock Ltd.
Brown Co, E. Arthur
Brownells, Inc.
Brunton U.S.A.
BSA Optics
B-Square Company, Inc.
Burris Co., Inc.
Bushnell Performance Optics
Butler Creek Corp.
Carl Zeiss Inc
Catco-Ambush, Inc.
Celestron International
Center Lock Scope Rings
Chicasaw Gun Works
Chuck's Gun Shop
Clark Custom Guns, Inc.
Clearview Mfg. Co., Inc.
Compass Industries, Inc.
Compasseco, Ltd.
Concept Development Corp.
Conetrol Scope Mounts
Creedmoor Sports, Inc.
Crimson Trace Lasers
Crosman Airguns
Custom Quality Products, Inc.
D&H Prods. Co., Inc.
D.C.C. Enterprises
Daisy Mfg. Co.
Del-Sports, Inc.
DHB Products
E. Arthur Brown Co.
Eclectic Technologies, Inc.
Edmund Scientific Co.
Ednar, Inc.
Eggleston, Jere D.
EGW Evolution Gun Works
Emerging Technologies, Inc. (See Laseraim Technolo
Entre'prise Arms, Inc.
Excalibur Electro Optics Inc
Excel Industries Inc.
Falcon Industries, Inc
Farr Studio,Inc.
Federal Arms Corp. of America
Frankonia Jagd Hofmann & Co.
Fujinon, Inc.
G.G. & G.
Galati International
Gentry Custom Gunmaker, David
Gil Hebard Guns
Gilmore Sports Concepts
GSI, Inc.
Gun South, Inc. (See GSI, Inc.)
Guns
Guns Div. of D.C. Engineering, Inc.
Gunsmithing, Inc.
Hakko Co. Ltd.
Hammerli USA

PRODUCT & SERVICE DIRECTORY

Harris Gunworks
Harvey, Frank
Heckler & Koch, Inc.
Hertel & Reuss
Hiptmayer, Armurier
Hiptmayer, Klaus
HiTek International
Holland's Gunsmithing
Ironsighter Co.
Jeffredo Gunsight
Jena Eur
Jerry Phillips Optics
Jewell Triggers, Inc.
John Masen Co. Inc.
John Unertl Optical Co., Inc.
John's Custom Leather
Johnson's Gunsmithing, Inc, Neal
Jones, J.D./SSK Industries
Kahles A Swarovski Company
Kalispel Case Line
Keng's Firearms Specialty, Inc./US
    Tactical Systems
KenPatable Ent., Inc.
Kesselring Gun Shop
Kimber of America, Inc.
Kmount
Kowa Optimed, Inc.
Kris Mounts
KVH Industries, Inc.
Kwik Mount Corp.
Kwik-Site Co.
L&S Technologies Inc (See Aimtech
    Mount Systems)
L.A.R. Mfg., Inc.
Laser Devices, Inc.
Laseraim Technologies, Inc.
LaserMax, Inc.
Leapers, Inc.
Lectro Science, Inc.
Lee Co., T. K.
Leica USA, Inc.
Leupold & Stevens, Inc.
Lightforce U.S.A. Inc.
List Precision Engineering
Lohman Mfg. Co., Inc.
Lomont Precision Bullets
London Guns Ltd.
Mac-1 Airgun Distributors
Mag-Na-Port International, Inc.
Marksman Products
Maxi-Mount
McBros Rifle Co.
McCann's Machine & Gun Shop
McMillan Optical Gunsight Co.
MCS, Inc.
MDS
Merit Corp.
Military Armament Corp.
Millett Sights
Mirador Optical Corp.
Mitchell Optics, Inc.
Mo's Competitor Supplies (See MCS
    Inc)
Mountain Rifles, Inc.
Muzzleloading Technologies, Inc
MWG Co.
Neal Johnson's Gunsmithing, Inc.
New England Custom Gun Service
Nightforce (See Lightforce USA Inc)
Nikon, Inc.
Nowlin Mfg. Co.
Nygord Precision Products
Olympic Optical Co.
Optical Services Co.
Orchard Park Enterprise
Ozark Gun Works
P.M. Enterprises, Inc.
Parsons Optical Mfg. Co.
PECAR Herbert Schwarz GmbH
PEM's Mfg. Co.
Pentax Corp.
Perazone-Gunsmith, Brian
PMC/Eldorado Cartridge Corp.
Precise Metalsmithing Enterprises
Precision Sport Optics
Premier Reticles
Quarton USA, Ltd. Co.
R.A. Wells Custom Gunsmith
Ram-Line Blount, Inc.
Ramon B. Gonzalez Guns
Ranch Products
Randolph Engineering, Inc.
Redfield, Inc

Redfield/Blount
Rice, Keith (See White Rock Tool &
    Die)
Robinson Armament Co
Rocky Mountain High Sports Glasses
Rogue Rifle Co., Inc.
S&K Mfg. Co.
Sanders Custom Gun Service
Sanders Gun and Machine Shop
Schmidt & Bender, Inc.
Schumakers Gun Shop
Scope Control, Inc.
ScopLevel
Score High Gunsmithing
Segway Industries
Selsi Co., Inc.
Sharp Shooter Supply
Shepherd Enterprises, Inc.
Sightron, Inc.
Simmons Outdoor Corp.
Sinclair International, Inc.
Six Enterprises
SKAN A.R.
Southern Bloomer Mfg. Co.
Sportsmatch U.K. Ltd.
Springfield, Inc.
SSK Industries
Stiles Custom Guns
Stoeger Industries
Stoney Point Products, Inc.
Sturm Ruger & Co. Inc.
Sunny Hill Enterprises, Inc.
SwaroSports, Inc. (See JagerSport
    Ltd.)
Swarovski Optik North America Ltd.
Swift Instruments, Inc.
T.K. Lee Co.
TacStar
Talley, Dave
Tasco Sales, Inc.
Tele-Optics
The Outdoor Connection,Inc.
Thompson/Center Arms
Time Precision, Inc.
Traditions Performance Firearms
Trijicon, Inc.
Truglo, Inc
Ultra Dot Distribution
Uncle Mike's (See Michaels of Oregon
    Co)
Unertl Optical Co. Inc., John
United Binocular Co.
United States Optics Technologies,
    Inc.
Valor Corp.
Virgin Valley Custom Guns
Visible Impact Targets
Voere-KGH m.b.H.
Warne Manufacturing Co.
Warren Muzzleloading Co., Inc.
WASP Shooting Systems
Watson Trophy Match Bullets
Weatherby, Inc.
Weaver Products
Weaver Scope Repair Service
Weigand Combat Handguns, Inc.
Westley Richards & Co.
White Rock Tool & Die
White Shooting Systems, Inc. (See
    White Muzzleload
Wideview Scope Mount Corp.
Wilcox Industries Corp
York M-1 Conversions
Zanotti Armor, Inc.

SHELLHOLDERS

Fremont Tool Works
Hart & Son, Inc.
K&M Services
Redding Reloading Equipment
Vega Tool Co.

SHOOTING/TRAINING
SCHOOL

Alpine Indoor Shooting Range
American Small Arms Academy
Auto Arms
Beretta U.S.A. Corp.
Bob's Tactical Indoor Shooting Range
    & Gun Shop
Bridgeman Products
Cannon's

Chapman Academy of Practical
    Shooting
Chelsea Gun Club of New York City
    Inc.
Cherry Creek State Park Shooting
    Center
Concealment Shop Inc.
CQB Training
Custom Arms Company
Defense Training International, Inc.
Executive Protection Institute
Ferris Firearms
Front Sight Firearms Training
    Institute
G.H. Enterprises Ltd.
Gene's Custom Guns
Griffin & Howe, Inc.
Guncraft Sports Inc
Gunsite Training Center
Henigson & Associates, Steve
Jensen's Custom Ammunition
Jensen's Firearms Academy
L.L. Bean, Inc.
Lethal Force Institute (See Police
    Bookshelf)
Ljutic Industries, Inc.
McMurdo, Lynn (See Specialty
    Gunsmithing)
Mendez, John A.
NCP Products, Inc.
Nevada Pistol Academy, Inc.
North American Shooting Systems
North Mountain Pine Training Center
    (See Executive
Paxton Quigley's Personal Protection
    Strategies
Pentheny de Pentheny
Performance Specialists
River Road Sporting Clays
SAFE
Shoot Where You Look
Shooter's World
Sigarms, Inc.
Smith & Wesson
Specialty Gunsmithing
Starlight Training Center, Inc.
Tactical Defense Institute
The Firearm Training Center
The Midwest Shooting School
The Shooting Gallery
Thunden Ranch
Trinidad St. Jr Col Gunsmith Dept.
Western Missouri Shooters Alliance
Yankee Gunsmith
Yavapai Firearms Academy Ltd.

SHOTSHELL
MISCELLANY

American Products, Inc.
Ballistic Product, Inc.
Bridgeman Products
MEC, Inc.
Precision Reloading, Inc.
R.E.I.
T&S Industries, Inc.
Vitt/Boos

SIGHTS, METALLIC

Accura-Site (See All's, The Jim
    Tembelis Co., Inc.)
Alley Supply Co.
All's, The Jim J. Tembelis Co., Inc.
Alpec Team, Inc.
Andela Tool & Machine, Inc.
Armsport, Inc.
Aro-Tek Ltd.
Ashley Outdoors, Inc
Aspen Outfitting Co
BAC
Baer Custom, Inc, Les
Ballard Rifle & Cartridge Co., LLC
BEC, Inc.
Bob's Gun Shop
Bo-Mar Tool & Mfg. Co.
Bond Custom Firearms
Bowen Classic Arms Corp.
Bradley Gunsight Co.
Brockman's Custom Gunsmithing
Brooks Tactical Systems
Brown Co, E. Arthur
California Sights (See Fautheree,
    Andy)
Cape Outfitters

Cash Mfg. Co., Inc.
Center Lock Scope Rings
Champion's Choice, Inc.
C-More Systems
Colonial Repair
CRR, Inc./Marble's Inc.
Davide Pedersoli and Co.
DHB Products
E. Arthur Brown Co.
EGW Evolution Gun Works
Falcon Industries, Inc
Farr Studio,Inc.
Forkin Arms
G.G. & G.
Garthwaite Pistolsmith, Inc., Jim
Guns Div. of D.C. Engineering, Inc.
Gunsmithing, Inc.
Hank's Gun Shop
Heidenstrom Bullets
Heinie Specialty Products
Hesco-Meprolight
Hiptmayer, Armurier
Hiptmayer, Klaus
IMX LLC
Innovative Weaponry Inc.
J.G. Anschuetz GmbH & Co. KG
J.P. Enterprises Inc.
Johnson's Gunsmithing, Inc, Neal
Keng's Firearms Specialty, Inc./US
    Tactical Systems
Knight Rifles
Kris Mounts
L.P.A. Snc
Leapers, Inc.
Lee's Red Ramps
List Precision Engineering
London Guns Ltd.
Lyman Instant Targets, Inc. (See
    Lyman Products)
Madis, George
Marble Arms (See CRR, Inc./Marble's
    Inc.)
MCS, Inc.
MEC-Gar S.r.l.
Meprolight (See Hesco-Meprolight)
Merit Corp.
Mid-America Recreation, Inc.
Middlebrooks Custom Shop
Millett Sights
MMC
Modern Muzzleloading, Inc
Montana Armory, Inc (See C. Sharps
    Arms Co. Inc.)
Montana Vintage Arms
Mo's Competitor Supplies (See MCS
    Inc)
Navy Arms Company
New England Custom Gun Service
Newman Gunshop
North Pass
Novak's, Inc.
OK Weber,Inc.
P.M. Enterprises, Inc.
PEM's Mfg. Co.
Quarton USA, Ltd. Co.
Redfield, Inc
RPM
Sharps Arms Co., Inc., C.
Slug Site
STI International
T.F.C. S.p.A.
Talley, Dave
The Gun Doctor
The Gun Works
Thompson/Center Arms
Time Precision, Inc.
Trijicon, Inc.
Truglo, Inc
United States Optics Technologies,
    Inc.
Warne Manufacturing Co.
WASP Shooting Systems
Wichita Arms, Inc.
Wild West Guns
Williams Gun Sight Co.
Wilson Gun Shop

STOCK MAKER

Acra-Bond Laminates
Amrine's Gun Shop
Antique Arms Co.
Artistry Inwood
Aspen Outfitting Co
Bain & Davis, Inc.

Baron Technology
Belding's Custom Gun Shop
Billings Gunsmiths Inc.
Bob Rogers Gunsmithing
Boltin, John M.
Bone Engraving, Ralph
Borden Ridges Rimrock Stocks
Bowerly, Kent
Brace, Larry D.
Burkhart Gunsmithing, Don
Cambo's Outdoorsman
Carter's Gun Shop
Caywood, Shane J.
Chuck's Gun Shop
Claro Walnut Gunstock Co.
Clear Creek Outdoors
Coffin, Charles H.
Colorado Gunsmithing Academy
Custom Riflestocks, Inc., Michael M.
    Kokolus
D&D Gunsmiths, Ltd.
D.D. Custom Stocks, R.H. "Dick"
    Devereaux
DGR Custom Rifles
DGS, Inc., Dale A. Storey
Dressel Jr, Paul G
Erhardt, Dennis
Farmer-Dressel, Sharon
Fieldsport Ltd.
Fisher, Jerry A.
Genecco Gun Works
George E. Mathews & Son, Inc.
Gillmann, Edwin
Grace, Charles E.
Great American Gunstock Co.
Gruning Precision Inc
Gunsmithing Ltd.
Harper's Custom Stocks
Harry Lawson Co.
Heilmann, Stephen
Heppler, Keith M, Keith's Custom
    Gunstocks
Heydenberk, Warren R.
Huebner, Corey O.
Island Pond Gun Shop
Jack Dever Co.
Jagdwaffen, P. Hofer
Jamison's Forge Works
Jay McCament Custom Gun Maker
Jim Norman Custom Gunstocks
John Rigby & Co.
Keith's Custom Gunstocks
Klein Custom Guns, Don
Knippel, Richard
L E Jurras & Assoc
Larry Lyons Gunworks
Lind Custom Guns, Al
Mathews & Son, Inc., George E.
McGowen Rifle Barrels
Mercer Custom Guns
Mid-America Recreation, Inc.
Mitchell, Jack
Modern Gun Repair School
Montgomery Community College
Morrow, Bud
Nelson's Custom Guns
Nettestad Gun Works
Nickels, Paul R.
Oakland Custom Arms,Inc.
Paul D. Hillmer Custom Gunstocks
Paulsen Gunstocks
Pawling Mountain Club
Pecatonica River Longrifle
Pentheny de Pentheny
R&J Gun Shop
R.A. Wells Custom Gunsmith
RMS Custom Gunsmithing
Royal Arms Gunstocks
Sanders Custom Gun Service
Sanders Gun and Machine Shop
Six Enterprises
Skeoch, Brian R.
Smith, Art
Smith, Sharmon
Speiser, Fred D.
Stott's Creek Armory, Inc.
Sturgeon Valley Sporters
Talmage, William G.
Taylor & Robbins
Tiger-Hunt Gunstocks
Trico Plastics
Tucker, James C.
Turnbull Restoration, Doug

Ultra Light Arms, Inc.
Vest, John
Walker Arms Co., Inc.
Wayne E. Schwartz Custom Guns
Wenig Custom Gunstocks
Wessinger Custom Guns & Engraving
Williamson Precision Gunsmithing
Winter, Robert M.
Working Guns
Yee, Mike

STOCKS (COMMERCIAL)

3-Ten Corp.
Accuracy Unlimited
Acra-Bond Laminates
Ahlman Guns
Arms Ingenuity Co.
Arundel Arms & Ammunition, Inc., A.
Aspen Outfitting Co
BAC
Baelder, Harry
Balickie, Joe
Bansner's Gunsmithing Specialties
Barnes Bullets, Inc.
Battenfeld Technologies
Beitzinger, George
Belding's Custom Gun Shop
Bell & Carlson, Inc.
Biesen, Al
Biesen, Roger
Billings Gunsmiths Inc.
Blount, Inc., Sporting Equipment Div.
Bob's Gun Shop
Boltin, John M.
Borden Ridges Rimrock Stocks
Borden Rifles Inc
Boyds' Gunstock Industries, Inc.
Brace, Larry D.
Briganti, A.J.
Brockman's Custom Gunsmithing
Brown Co, E. Arthur
Brown Precision,Inc.
Buckhorn Gun Works
Bullberry Barrel Works, Ltd.
Butler Creek Corp.
Cali'co Hardwoods, Inc.
Camilli, Lou
Campbell, Dick
Cape Outfitters
Caywood, Shane J.
Chambers Flintlocks Ltd., Jim
Chicasaw Gun Works
Churchill, Winston
Claro Walnut Gunstock Co.
Clear Creek Outdoors
Cloward's Gun Shop
Coffin, Charles H.
Coffin, Jim (See Working Guns)
Colonial Repair
Colorado Gunsmithing Academy
Colorado School of Trades
Conrad, C. A.
Creedmoor Sports, Inc.
Curly Maple Stock Blanks (See Tiger-Hunt)
Custom Checkering Service, Kathy Forster
Custom Gun Products
Custom Riflestocks, Inc., Michael M. Kokolus
Custom Single Shot Rifles
D&D Gunsmiths, Ltd.
D&G Precision Duplicators (See Greene Precision)
D&J Bullet Co. & Custom Gun Shop, Inc.
D.D. Custom Stocks, R.H. "Dick" Devereaux
Dakota Arms, Inc.
Dangler, Homer L.
David W. Schwartz Custom Guns
Devereaux, R.H. "Dick" (See D.D. Custom)
DGR Custom Rifles
Dick Marple & Associates
Dillon, Ed
Duane's Gun Repair (See DGR Custom Rifles)
Duncan's Gun Works, Inc.
Echols & Co., D'Arcy
Eggleston, Jere D.
Erhardt, Dennis
Falcon Industries, Inc
Falcon Industries, Inc

Farmer-Dressel, Sharon
Fibron Products, Inc.
Fieldsport Ltd.
Folks, Donald E.
Forster, Kathy (See Custom Checkering)
Forster, Larry L.
Forthofer's Gunsmithing & Knifemaking
Francotte & Cie S.A. Auguste
Frank Custom Classic Arms, Ron
Game Haven Gunstocks
Gary Goudy Classic Stocks
Gene's Custom Guns
Gervais, Mike
Gillmann, Edwin
Giron, Robert E.
Goens, Dale W.
Golden Age Arms Co.
Grace, Charles E.
Great American Gunstock Co.
Green, Roger M.
Greenwood Precision
Griffin & Howe, Inc.
Guns
Guns Div. of D.C. Engineering, Inc.
Gunsmithing Ltd.
Hammerli USA
Hanson's Gun Center, Dick
Harper's Custom Stocks
Harris Gunworks
Harry Lawson Co.
Hart & Son, Inc.
Harwood, Jack O.
Hastings Barrels
Hecht, Hubert J, Waffen-Hecht
Heilmann, Stephen
Heppler, Keith M, Keith's Custom Gunstocks
Heydenberk, Warren R.
High Tech Specialties, Inc.
Hiptmayer, Armurier
Hiptmayer, Klaus
Hoelscher, Virgil
Hoenig & Rodman
Hogue Grips
H-S Precision, Inc.
Hughes, Steven Dodd
IAI
Island Pond Gun Shop
Ivanoff, Thomas G (See Tom's Gun Repair)
J.P. Gunstocks, Inc.
Jackalope Gun Shop
Jarrett Rifles, Inc.
Jim Norman Custom Gunstocks
John Masen Co. Inc.
Johnson Wood Products
Kelbly, Inc.
Ken's Rifle Blanks
Kilham & Co.
Klingler Woodcarving
Knippel, Richard
Kokolus, Michael M. (See Custom Riflestocks)
Lawson Co., Harry
Lind Custom Guns, Al
Mazur Restoration, Pete
McBros Rifle Co.
McCann's Muzzle-Gun Works
McDonald, Dennis
McFarland, Stan
McGuire, Bill
McKinney, R.P. (See Schuetzen Gun Co.)
McMillan Fiberglass Stocks, Inc.
Michaels Of Oregon
Miller Arms, Inc.
Mitchell, Jack
Morrison Custom Rifles, J. W.
MPI Stocks
MWG Co.
NCP Products, Inc.
Nettestad Gun Works
New England Arms Co.
New England Custom Gun Service
Newman Gunshop
Nickels, Paul R.
Oakland Custom Arms,Inc.
Oil Rod and Gun Shop
Old World Gunsmithing
One Of A Kind
Ottmar, Maurice

Pacific Research Laboratories, Inc. (See Rimrock)
Pagel Gun Works, Inc.
Paragon Sales & Services, Inc.
Paul D. Hillmer Custom Gunstocks
Paulsen Gunstocks
Pawling Mountain Club
Pecatonica River Longrifle
PEM's Mfg. Co.
Perazone-Gunsmith, Brian
Perazzi USA, Inc.
Pohl, Henry A. (See Great American Gun Co.
Powell & Son (Gunmakers) Ltd., William
Precision Gun Works
Quality Custom Firearms
R&J Gun Shop
Ram-Line Blount, Inc.
Rampart International
Reagent Chemical & Research, Inc. (See Calico Hard)
Redfield/Blount
Reiswig, Wallace E. (See Claro Walnut Gunstock)
Richards Micro-Fit Stocks
RMS Custom Gunsmithing
Robinson, Don
Robinson Armament Co
Robinson Firearms Mfg. Ltd.
Romain's Custom Guns, Inc.
Roto Carve
Ryan, Chad L.
Sanders Gun and Machine Shop
Saville Iron Co. (See Greenwood Precision)
Schiffman, Curt
Schiffman, Mike
Schiffman, Norman
Score High Gunsmithing
Sile Distributors, Inc.
Simmons Gun Repair, Inc.
Six Enterprises
Skeoch, Brian R.
Smith, Sharmon
Speiser, Fred D.
Stan De Treville & Co.
Stiles Custom Guns
Storey, Dale A. (See DGS Inc.)
Strawbridge, Victor W.
Sturgeon Valley Sporters
Swann, D. J.
Swift River Gunworks
Szweda, Robert (See RMS Custom Gunsmithing)
T.F.C. S.p.A.
Talmage, William G.
Taylor & Robbins
Tecnolegno S.p.A.
The Gun Shop
The Orvis Co.
Thompson/Center Arms
Tiger-Hunt Gunstocks
Time Precision, Inc.
Tirelli
Track of the Wolf, Inc.
Trevallion Gunstocks
Tuttle, Dale
Vic's Gun Refinishing
Vintage Industries, Inc.
Virgin Valley Custom Guns
Volquartsen Custom Ltd.
Walker Arms Co., Inc.
Weber & Markin Custom Gunsmiths
Weems, Cecil
Wenig Custom Gunstocks
Werth, T. W.
Wessinger Custom Guns & Engraving
Western Mfg. Co.
Windish, Jim
Winter, Robert M.
Working Guns
Wright's Hardwood Gunstock Blanks
Yee, Mike
York M-1 Conversions
Zeeryp, Russ

STUCK CASE REMOVERS

MarMik, Inc.
Toms Gun Repair, Inc.

TARGETS, BULLET & CLAYBIRD TRAPS

Action Target, Inc.
Air Arms
American Target
A-Tech Corp.
Autauga Arms, Inc.
Beeman Precision Airguns
Benjamin/Sheridan Co., Crossman
Beomat of America, Inc.
Birchwood Casey
Blount, Inc., Sporting Equipment Div.
Blue and Gray Products Inc (See Ox-Yoke Originals)
Brown Manufacturing
Bull-X, Inc.
Caswell Detroit Armor Companies
Champion Target Co.
Crosman Airguns
D.C.C. Enterprises
Datumtech Corp.
Detroit-Armor Corp.
Diamond Mfg. Co.
Federal Champion Target Co.
Freeman Animal Targets
G.H. Enterprises Ltd.
Hiti-Schuch, Atelier Wilma
H-S Precision, Inc.
Hunterjohn
J.G. Dapkus Co., Inc.
Kennebec Journal
Kleen-Bore,Inc.
Lakefield Arms Ltd (See Savage Arms Inc)
Leapers, Inc.
Littler Sales Co.
Lyman Instant Targets, Inc. (See Lyman Products)
Marksman Products
Mendez,M John A.
MSR Targets
N.B.B., Inc.
National Target Co.
North American Shooting Systems
Outers Laboratories Div. of Blount, Inc.Sporting
Ox-Yoke Originals, Inc.
Palsa Outdoor Products
Passive Bullet Traps, Inc. (See Savage Range)
PlumFire Press, Inc.
Precision Airgun Sales, Inc.
Quack Decoy & Sporting Clays
Redfield, Inc
Redfield/Blount
Remington Arms Co., Inc.
Rockwood Corp.
Rocky Mountain Target Co.
Savage Arms (Canada), Inc.
Savage Range Systems, Inc.
Schaefer Shooting Sports
Seligman Shooting Products
Shooters Supply
Shoot-N-C Targets (See Birchwood Casey)
Target Shooting, Inc.
Thompson Target Technology
Trius Traps, Inc.
Universal Sports
Visible Impact Targets
White Flyer Targets
Woods Wise Products
World of Targets (See Birchwood Casey)
X-Spand Target Systems
Zriny's Metal Targets (See Z's Metal Targets)
Z's Metal Targets & Frames

TAXIDERMY

African Import Co.
Kulis Freeze Dry Taxidermy
Montgomery Community College
World Trek, Inc.

TRAP & SKEET SHOOTER'S EQUIPMENT

Accurate Arms Co., Inc.
Allen Co., Bob
Allen Sportswear, Bob (See Allen Co., Bob)
American Products, Inc.

Bagmaster Mfg., Inc.
Baker, Stan
Beomat of America, Inc.
Beretta S.p.A., Pietro
Bridgeman Products
C&H Research
Cape Outfitters
Claybuster Wads & Harvester Bullets
Fiocchi of America Inc.
G.H. Enterprises Ltd.
Game Winner, Inc.
Hastings Barrels
Hoppe's Div. Penguin Industries, Inc.
Hunter Co., Inc.
Jamison's Forge Works
Jenkins Recoil Pads, Inc.
Jim Noble Co.
Kalispel Case Line
Kolar
Lakewood Products LLC
Mag-Na-Port International, Inc.
Maionchi-L.M.I.
MEC, Inc.
Moneymaker Guncraft Corp.
MTM Molded Products Co., Inc.
NCP Products, Inc.
Pachmayr Div. Lyman Products
Palsa Outdoor Products
Perazzi USA, Inc.
Pro-Port Ltd.
Protektor Model
Quack Decoy & Sporting Clays
Redfield/Blount
Remington Arms Co., Inc.
Rhodeside, Inc.
Shootin' Accessories, Ltd.
Shooting Specialties (See Titus, Daniel)
T&S Industries, Inc.
TEN-X Products Group
Trius Traps, Inc.
Truglo, Inc
Universal Sports
Warne Manufacturing Co.
X-Spand Target Systems
Ziegel Engineering

TRIGGERS, RELATED EQUIPMENT

Actions by "T" Teddy Jacobson
B&D Trading Co., Inc.
Baer Custom, Inc, Les
Behlert Precision, Inc.
Bond Custom Firearms
Boyds' Gunstock Industries, Inc.
Dayton Traister
EGW Evolution Gun Works
Electronic Trigger Systems, Inc.
Eversull Co., Inc., K.
FWB
Guns
Hart & Son, Inc.
Hawken Shop, The (See Dayton Traister)
Hoelscher, Virgil
Holland's Gunsmithing
J.P. Enterprises Inc.
Jewell Triggers, Inc.
John Masen Co. Inc.
Jones Custom Products, Neil A.
KK Air International (See Impact Case Co.)
L&R Lock Co.
List Precision Engineering
London Guns Ltd.
M.H. Canjar Co.
Master Lock Co.
Miller Single Trigger Mfg. Co.
NCP Products, Inc.
PEM's Mfg. Co.
Penrod Precision
Perazone-Gunsmith, Brian
Perazzi USA, Inc.
Robinson Armament Co
Schumakers Gun Shop
Sharp Shooter Supply
Shilen, Inc.
Simmons Gun Repair, Inc.
Spencer's Custom Guns
Target Shooting, Inc.
Watson Trophy Match Bullets

MANUFACTURER'S DIRECTORY

A

A Zone Bullets, 2039 Walter Rd., Billings, MT 59105 / 800-252-3111; FAX: 406-248-1961
A&B Industries, Inc. (See Top-Line USA Inc.)
A&M Waterfowl, Inc., R.R. Murphy Co., Inc. Murphy, P.O. Box 102, Ripley, TN 38063 / 901-635-4003; FAX: 901-635-2320
A&W Repair, 2930 Schneider Dr., Arnold, MO 63010 / 314-287-3725
A.A. Arms, Inc., 4811 Persimmon Ct., Monroe, NC 28110 / 704-289-5356 or 800-935-1119; FAX: 704-289-5859
A.B.S. III, 9238 St. Morritz Dr., Fern Creek, KY 40291
A.G. Russell Knives, Inc., 1705 N. Thompson St., Springdale, AR 72764 / 501-751-7341 ag@agrussell.com agrussell.com
A.R.M.S., Inc., 230 W. Center St., West Bridgewater, MA 02379-1620 / 508-584-7816; FAX: 508-588-8045
A.W. Peterson Gun Shop, Inc., 4255 W. Old U.S. 441, Mt. Dora, FL 32757-3299 / 352-383-4258; FAX: 352-735-1001
ABO (USA) Inc., 615 SW 2nd Avenue, Miami, FL 33130 / 305-859-2010; FAX: 305-859-2099
AC Dyna-tite Corp., 155 Kelly St., P.O. Box 0984, Elk Grove Village, IL 60007 / 847-593-5566; FAX: 847-593-1304
Acadian Ballistic Specialties, P.O. Box 787, Folsom, LA 70437 / 504-796-0078 gunsmith@neasolft.com
Accupro Gun Care, 15512-109 Ave., Surrey, BC U3R 7E8 CANADA / 604-583-7807
Accuracy International, Foster, P.O. Box 111, Wilsall, MT 49086-0111 / 406-587-7922; FAX: 406-585-9434
Accuracy International Precision Rifles (See U.S.)
Accuracy Int'l. North America, Inc., P.O. Box 5267, Oak Ridge, TN 37831 / 423-482-0330; FAX: 423-482-0336
Accuracy Unlimited, 16036 N. 49 Ave., Glendale, AZ 85306 / 602-978-9089; FAX: 602-978-9089
Accuracy Unlimited, 7479 S. DePew St., Littleton, CO 80123
Accura-Site (See All's, The Jim J. Tembelis Co., Inc.)
Accurate Arms Co., Inc., 5891 Hwy. 230 West, McEwen, TN 37101 / 800-416-3006; FAX: 931-729-4211
Accuright, RR 2 Box 397, Sebeka, MN 56477 / 218-472-3383
Accu-Tek, 4510 Carter Ct., Chino, CA 91710
Ace Custom 45's, Inc., 1880 1/2 Upper Turtle Creek Rd., Kerrville, TX 78028 / 830-257-4290; FAX: 830-257-5724 www.acecustom45.com
Ace Sportswear, Inc., 700 Quality Rd., Fayetteville, NC 28306 / 919-323-1223; FAX: 919-323-5392
Ackerman & Co., Box 133 US Highway Rt. 7, Pownal, VT 05261 / 802-823-9874 muskets@togsther.net
Ackerman, Bill (See Optical Services Co.)
Acra-Bond Laminates, 134 Zimmerman Rd., Kalispell, MT 59901 / 406-257-9003; FAX: 406-257-9003 merlins@digisys.net
Action Bullets & Alloy Inc., RR 1, P.O. Box 189, Quinter, KS 67752 / 913-754-3609; FAX: 913-754-3629
Action Direct, Inc., P.O. Box 830760, Miami, FL 33283 / 305-559-4652; FAX: 305-559-4652 action-direct.com
Action Products, Inc., 22 N. Mulberry St., Hagerstown, MD 21740 / 301-797-1414; FAX: 301-733-2073
Action Target, Inc., P.O. Box 636, Provo, UT 84603 / 801-377-8033; FAX: 801-377-8096
Actions by "T" Teddy Jacobson, 16315 Redwood Forest Ct., Sugar Land, TX 77478 / 281-277-4008; FAX: 281-277-9112 jaj45f@alltel.net www.actionsbyt.com
AcuSport Corporation, 1 Hunter Pl., Bellefontaine, OH 43311-3001 / 513-593-7010; FAX: 513-592-5625
Ad Hominem, 3130 Gun Club Ln., RR, Orillia, ON L3V 6H3 CANADA / 705-689-5303; FAX: 705-689-5303
Adair Custom Shop, Bill, 2886 Westridge, Carrollton, TX 75006
ADCO Sales, Inc., 4 Draper St. #A, Woburn, MA 01801 / 781-935-1799; FAX: 781-935-1011
Adkins, Luther, 1292 E. McKay Rd., Shelbyville, IN 46176-8706 / 317-392-3795
Advance Car Mover Co., Rowell Div., P.O. Box 1, 240 N. Depot St., Juneau, WI 53039 / 414-386-4464; FAX: 414-386-4416
Adventure 16, Inc., 4620 Alvarado Canyon Rd., San Diego, CA 92120 / 619-283-6314
Adventure Game Calls, R.D. 1, Leonard Rd., Spencer, NY 14883 / 607-589-4611
Adventurer's Outpost, P.O. Box 547, Cottonwood, AZ 86326-0547 / 800-762-7471; FAX: 602-634-8781
Aero Peltor, 90 Mechanic St., Southbridge, MA 01550 / 508-764-5500; FAX: 508-764-0188
African Import Co., 22 Goodwin Rd., Plymouth, MA 02360 / 508-746-8552; FAX: 508-746-0404
AFSCO Ammunition, 731 W. Third St., P.O. Box L, Owen, WI 54460 / 715-229-2516
Ahlman Guns, 9525 W. 230th St., Morristown, MN 55052 / 507-685-4243; FAX: 507-685-4280
Ahrends, Kim (See Custom Firearms, Inc.), Box 203, Clarion, IA 50525 / 515-532-3449; FAX: 515-532-3926
Aimpoint c/o Springfield, Inc., 420 W. Main St., Geneseo, IL 61254 / 309-944-1702
Aimtech Mount Systems, P.O. Box 223, Thomasville, GA 31799-0223 / 912-226-4313; FAX: 912-227-0222 aimtech@surfsouth.com www.aimtech-mounts.com
Air Arms, Hailsham Industrial Park, Diplocks Way, Hailsham, E. Sussex, BN27 3JF ENGLAND / 011-0323-845853
Air Rifle Specialists, P.O. Box 138, 130 Holden Rd., Pine City, NY 14871-0138 / 607-734-7340; FAX: 607-733-3261
Air Venture Airguns, 9752 E. Flower St., Bellflower, CA 90706 / 310-867-6355
Airgun Repair Centre, 3227 Garden Meadows, Lawrenceburg, IN 47025 / 812-637-1463; FAX: 812-637-1463
Airrow, 11 Monitor Hill Rd., Newtown, CT 06470 / 203-270-6343
Aitor-Cuchilleria Del Norte S.A., Izelaieta, 17, 48260, Ermua, S SPAIN / 43-17-08-50 info@aitor.com www.aitor.com
Ajax Custom Grips, Inc., 9130 Viscount Row, Dallas, TX 75247 / 214-630-8893; FAX: 214-630-4942
Aker International, Inc., 2248 Main St., Ste. 6, Chula Vista, CA 91911 / 619-423-5182; FAX: 619-423-1363
Al Lind Custom Guns, 7821 76th Ave. SW, Lakewood, WA 98498 / 206-584-6361
Alana Cupp Custom Engraver, P.O. Box 207, Annabella, UT 84711 / 801-896-4834
Alaska Bullet Works, Inc., 9978 Crazy Horse Dr., Juneau, AK 99801 / 907-789-3834; FAX: 907-789-3433
Aldis Gunsmithing & Shooting Supply, 502 S. Montezuma St., Prescott, AZ 86303 / 602-445-6723; FAX: 602-445-6763
Alessi Holsters, Inc., 2465 Niagara Falls Blvd., Amherst, NY 14228-3527 / 716-691-5615
Alex, Inc., Box 3034, Bozeman, MT 59772 / 406-282-7396; FAX: 406-282-7396
Alfano, Sam, 36180 Henry Gaines Rd., Pearl River, LA 70452 / 504-863-3364; FAX: 504-863-7715
All American Lead Shot Corp., P.O. Box 224566, Dallas, TX 75062
All Rite Products, Inc., 5752 N. Silverstone Circle, Mountain Green, UT 84050 / 801-876-3330; FAX: 801-876-2216
Allard, Gary/Creek Side Metal & Woodcrafters, Fishers Hill, VA 22626 / 703-465-3903
Allen Co., Bob, 214 SW Jackson, P.O. Box 477, Des Moines, IA 50315 / 515-283-2191 or 800-685-7020; FAX: 515-283-0779
Allen Co., Inc., 525 Burbank St., Broomfield, CO 80020 / 303-469-1857 or 800-876-8600; FAX: 303-466-7437
Allen Firearm Engraving, 339 Grove Ave., Prescott, AZ 86301 / 520-778-1237
Allen Mfg., 6449 Hodgson Rd., Circle Pines, MN 55014 / 612-429-8231
Allen Sportswear, Bob (See Allen Co., Bob)
Alley Supply Co., P.O. Box 848, Gardnerville, NV 89410 / 702-782-3800
Alliant Techsystems Smokeless Powder Group, 200 Valley Rd., Ste. 305, Mt. Arlington, NJ 07856 / 800-276-9337; FAX: 201-770-2528
Allred Bullet Co., 932 Evergreen Dr., Logan, UT 84321 / 435-752-6983; FAX: 435-752-6983
All's, The Jim J. Tembelis Co., Inc., 216 Loper Ct., Neenah, WI 54956 / 920-725-5251; FAX: 920-725-5251
Alpec Team, Inc., 201 Ricken Backer Cir., Livermore, CA 94550 / 510-606-8245; FAX: 510-606-4279
Alpha 1 Drop Zone, 2121 N. Tyler, Wichita, KS 67212 / 316-729-0800
Alpha Gunsmith Division, 1629 Via Monserate, Fallbrook, CA 92028 / 619-723-9279 or 619-728-2663
Alpha LaFranck Enterprises, P.O. Box 81072, Lincoln, NE 68501 / 402-466-3193
Alpha Precision, Inc., 3238 Della Slaton Rd., Comer, GA 30629 / 706-783-2131 jim@alphaprecisioninc.com www.alphaprecisioninc.com
Alpine Indoor Shooting Range, 2401 Government Way, Coeur d'Alene, ID 83814 / 208-676-8824; FAX: 208-676-8824
Altamont Co., 901 N. Church St., P.O. Box 309, Thomasboro, IL 61878 / 217-643-3125 or 800-626-5774; FAX: 217-643-7973
Alumna Sport by Dee Zee, 1572 NE 58th Ave., P.O. Box 3090, Des Moines, IA 50316 / 800-798-9899
Amadeo Rossi S.A., Rua: Amadeo Rossi, 143, Sao Leopoldo, RS 93030-220 BRAZIL / 051-592-5566
AmBr Software Group Ltd., P.O. Box 301, Reistertown, MD 21136-0301 / 800-888-1917; FAX: 410-526-7212
American Ammunition, 3545 NW 71st St., Miami, FL 33147 / 305-835-7400; FAX: 305-694-0037
American Arms Inc. (See Tristar Sporting Arms, Inc.)
American Custom Gunmakers Guild, P.O. Box 812, Burlington, IA 52601 / 318-752-6114; FAX: 319-752-6114 acgg@acgg.org acgg.org
American Derringer Corp., 127 N. Lacy Dr., Waco, TX 76705 / 800-642-7817 or 817-799-9111; FAX: 817-799-7935
American Display Co., 55 Cromwell St., Providence, RI 02907 / 401-331-2464; FAX: 401-421-1264
American Frontier Firearms Mfg., Inc., P.O. Box 744, Aguanga, CA 92536 / 909-763-0014; FAX: 909-763-0014
American Gas & Chemical Co., Ltd., 220 Pegasus Ave., Northvale, NJ 07647 / 201-767-7300
American Gunsmithing Institute, 1325 Imola Ave. #504, Napa, CA 94559 / 707-253-0462; FAX: 707-253-7149
American Handgunner Magazine, 591 Camino de la Reina, Ste 200, San Diego, CA 92108 / 619-297-5350; FAX: 619-297-5353
American Pioneer Video, P.O. Box 50049, Bowling Green, KY 42102-2649 / 800-743-4675
American Products, Inc., 14729 Spring Valley Road, Morrison, IL 61270 / 815-772-3336; FAX: 815-772-8046
American Safe Arms, Inc., 1240 Riverview Dr., Garland, UT 84312 / 801-257-7472; FAX: 801-785-8156
American Sales & Kirkpatrick, P.O. Box 677, Laredo, TX 78042 / 956-723-6893; FAX: 956-725-0672 holsters@kirkpatrickleather.com http://kirkpatrickleather.com
American Sales & Kirkpatrick Mfg. Co., P.O. Box 677, Laredo, TX 78042 / 210-723-6893; FAX: 210-725-0672
American Security Products Co., 11925 Pacific Ave., Fontana, CA 92337 / 909-685-9680 or 800-421-6142; FAX: 909-685-9685
American Small Arms Academy, P.O. Box 12111, Prescott, AZ 86304 / 602-778-5623
American Target, 1328 S. Jason St., Denver, CO 80223 / 303-733-0433; FAX: 303-777-0311
American Target Knives, 1030 Brownwood NW, Grand Rapids, MI 49504 / 616-453-1998
Americase, P.O. Box 271, 1610 E. Main, Waxahachie, TX 75165 / 800-880-3629; FAX: 214-937-8373
Ames Metal Products, 4323 S. Western Blvd., Chicago, IL 60609 / 773-523-3230; or 800-255-6937; FAX: 773-523-3854
Amherst Arms, P.O. Box 1457, Englewood, FL 34295 / 941-475-2020; FAX: 941-473-1212
Ammo Load, Inc., 1560 E. Edinger, Ste. G, Santa Ana, CA 92705 / 714-558-8858; FAX: 714-569-0319
Amrine's Gun Shop, 937 La Luna, Ojai, CA 93023 / 805-646-2376
Amsec, 11925 Pacific Ave., Fontana, CA 92337
Analog Devices, Box 9106, Norwood, MA 02062
Andela Tool & Machine, Inc., RD3, Box 246, Richfield Springs, NY 13439
Anderson Manufacturing Co., Inc., 22602 53rd Ave. SE, Bothell, WA 98021 / 206-481-1858; FAX: 206-481-7839
Andres & Dworsky, Bergstrasse 18, 3822 Karlstein, Thaya, AUSTRIA / 0 28 44-285; FAX: 02844 28619 andrews.dworsky@wvnet.as
Angelo & Little Custom Gun Stock Blanks, P.O. Box 240046, Dell, MT 59724-0046
Anics Corp, 28525 Belcourt Rd., Pepper Pike, OH 44124 / 216-464-9562:; FAX: 216-464-9563 anics@aol.com
Answer Products Co., 1519 Westbury Dr., Davison, MI 48423 / 810-653-2911
Anthony and George Ltd., Rt. 1, P.O. Box 45, Evington, VA 24550 / 804-821-8117
Antique American Firearms, P.O. Box 71035, Dept. GD, Des Moines, IA 50325 / 515-224-6552
Antique Arms Co., 1110 Cleveland Ave., Monett, MO 65708 / 417-235-6501
Apel GmbH, Ernst, Am Kirschberg 3, D-97218, Gerbrunn, GERMANY / 0 (931) 707192 info@eaw.de www.eaw.de
Aplan Antiques & Art, James O., HC 80, Box 793-25, Piedmont, SD 57769 / 605-347-5016
AR-7 Industries, LLC, 998 N. Colony Rd., Meriden, CT 06450 / 203-630-3536; FAX: 203-630-3637
Arizona Ammunition, Inc., 21421 No. 14th Ave., Ste. E, Phoenix, AZ 85027 / 623-516-9004; FAX: 623-516-9012 azammo.com
Arkansas Mallard Duck Calls, Rt. Box 182, England, AR 72046 / 501-842-3597
ArmaLite, Inc., P.O. Box 299, Geneseo, IL 61254 / 309-944-6939; FAX: 309-944-6949
Armament Gunsmithing Co., Inc., 525 Rt. 22, Hillside, NJ 07205 / 908-686-0960; FAX: 718-738-5019 armamentgunsmithing@worldnet.att.net
Armas Kemen S. A. (See U.S. Importers)
Armas Urki Garbi, 12-14 20.600, Eibar (Guipuzcoa), / 43-11 38 73
Armfield Custom Bullets, 4775 Caroline Dr., San Diego, CA 92115 / 619-582-7188; FAX: 619-287-3238
Armi Perazzi S.p.A., Via Fontanelle 1/3, 1-25080, Botticino Mattina, / 030-2692591; FAX: 030 2692594+
Armi San Marco (See Taylor's & Co)

DIRECTORY

Armi San Paolo, 172-A, I-25062, via Europa, ITALY / 030-2751725

Armi Sport (See U.S. Importers-Cape Outfitters)

Armite Laboratories, 1560 Superior Ave., Costa Mesa, CA 92627 / 213-587-7768; FAX: 213-587-5075

Armoloy Co. of Ft. Worth, 204 E. Daggett St., Fort Worth, TX 76104 / 817-332-5604; FAX: 817-335-6517

Armor (See Buck Stop Lure Co., Inc.)

Armor Metal Products, P.O. Box 4609, Helena, MT 59604 / 406-442-5560; FAX: 406-442-5650

Armory Publications, 17171 Bothall Way NE, #276, Seattle, WA 98155 / 208-664-5061; FAX: 208-664-9906 armorypub@aol.com www.grocities.com/armorypub

Arms & Armour Press, Wellington House, 125 Strand, London, WC2R 0BB ENGLAND / 0171-420-5555; FAX: 0171-240-7265

Arms Corporation of the Philippines, Bo. Parang Marikina, Metro Manila, PHILIPPINES / 632-941-6243 or 632-941-6244; FAX: 632-942-0682

Arms Craft Gunsmithing, 1106 Linda Dr., Arroyo Grande, CA 93420 / 805-481-2830

Arms Ingenuity Co., P.O. Box 1, 51 Canal St., Weatogue, CT 06089 / 203-658-5624

Arms Software, 4851 SW Madrona St., Lake Oswego, OR 97035 / 800-366-5559 or 503-697-0533; FAX: 503-697-3337

Arms, Programming Solutions (See Arms Software)

Armscorp USA, Inc., 4424 John Ave., Baltimore, MD 21227 / 410-247-6200; FAX: 410-247-6205 info@armscorpusa.com armscorpusa.com

Armsport, Inc., 3950 NW 49th St., Miami, FL 33142 / 305-635-7850; FAX: 305-633-2877

Arnold Arms Co., Inc., P.O. Box 1011, Arlington, WA 98223 / 800-371-1011 or 360-435-1011; FAX: 360-435-7304

Aro-Tek Ltd., 206 Frontage Rd. North, Ste. C, Pacific, WA 98047 / 206-351-2984; FAX: 206-833-4483

Arratoonian, Andy (See Horseshoe Leather Products)

Arrieta S.L., Morkaiko 5, 20870, Elgoibar, SPAIN / 34-43-743150; FAX: 34-43-743154+

Art Jewel Enterprises Ltd., Eagle Business Ctr., 460 Randy Rd., Carol Stream, IL 60188 / 708-260-0400

Artistry Inwood, 134 Zimmerman Rd., Kalispell, MT 59901 / 406-257-9003; FAX: 406-257-9167 merlins@digisys.net

Art's Gun & Sport Shop, Inc., 6008 Hwy. Y, Hillsboro, MO 63050

Arundel Arms & Ammunition, Inc., A., 24A Defense St., Annapolis, MD 21401 / 410-224-8683

Arvo Ojala Holsters, P.O. Box 98, N. Hollywood, CA 91603 / 818-222-9700; FAX: 818-222-0401

Ashby Turkey Calls, P.O. Box 1466, Ava, MO 65608-1466 / 417-967-3787

Ashley Outdoors, Inc., 2401 Ludelle St., Fort Worth, TX 76105 / 888-744-4880; FAX: 800-734-7939

Aspen Outfitting Co, Jon Hollinger, 9 Dean St., Aspen, CO 81611 / 970-925-3406

A-Square Co., Inc., One Industrial Park, Bedford, KY 40006-9667 / 502-255-7456; FAX: 502-255-7657

Astra Sport, S.A., Apartado 3, 48300 Guernica, Espagne, SPAIN / 34-4-6250100; FAX: 34-4-6255186+

Atamec-Bretton, 19 rue Victor Grignard, F-42026, St.-Etienne Cedex 1, FRANCE / 77-93-54-69; FAX: 33-77-93-57-98+

A-Tech Corp., P.O. Box 1281, Cottage Grove, OR 97424

Atlanta Cutlery Corp., 2143 Gees Mill Rd., Box 839 CIS, Conyers, GA 30207 / 800-883-0300; FAX: 404-388-0246

Atlantic Mills, Inc., 1295 Towbin Ave., Lakewood, NJ 08701-5934 / 800-242-7374

Atlantic Rose, Inc., P.O. Box 10717, Bradenton, FL 34282-0717

Atsko/Sno-Seal, Inc., 2664 Russell St., Orangeburg, SC 29115 / 803-531-1820; FAX: 803-531-2139

Auguste Francotte & Cie S.A., rue du Trois Juin 109, 4400 Herstal-Liege, BELGIUM / 32-4-248-13-18; FAX: 32-4-948-11-79

Austin & Halleck, 1099 Welt, Weston, MO 64098 / 816-386-2176; FAX: 816-386-2177

Austin Sheridan USA, Inc., P.O. Box 577, 36 Haddam Quarter Rd., Durham, CT 06422 / 860-349-1772; FAX: 860-349-1771 swalzer@palm.net

Autauga Arms, Inc., Pratt Plaza Mall No. 13, Prattville, AL 36067 / 800-262-9563; FAX: 334-361-2961

Auto Arms, 738 Clearview, San Antonio, TX 78228 / 512-434-5450

Automatic Equipment Sales, 627 E. Railroad Ave., Salesburg, MD 21801

Auto-Ordnance Corp., P.O. Box 220, Blauvelt, NY 10913 / 914-353-7770

Autumn Sales, Inc. (Blaser), 1320 Lake St., Fort Worth, TX 76102 / 817-335-1634; FAX: 817-338-0119

Avnda Otaola Norica, 16 Apartado 68, 20600, Eibar

AWC Systems Technology, P.O. Box 41938, Phoenix, AZ 85080-1938 / 602-780-1050; FAX: 602-780-2967

AYA (See U.S. Importer-New England Custom Gun Service)

B

B & P America, 12321 Brittany Cir., Dallas, TX 75230 / 972-726-9069

B&D Trading Co., Inc., 3935 Fair Hill Rd., Fair Oaks, CA 95628 / 800-334-3790 or 916-967-9366; FAX: 916-967-4873

B.B. Walker Co., P.O. Box 1167, 414 E. Dixie Dr., Asheboro, NC 27203 / 910-625-1380; FAX: 910-625-8125

B.C. Outdoors, Larry McGhee, P.O. Box 61497, Boulder City, NV 89006 / 702-294-3056; FAX: 702-294-0413 jdalton@pmcammo.com www.pmcammo.com

B.M.F. Activator, Inc., 12145 Mill Creek Run, Plantersville, TX 77363 / 936-894-2397 or 800-527-2881; FAX: 936-894-2397

BAC, 17101 Los Modelos St., Fountain Valley, CA 92708 / 719-746-8063

Badger Shooters Supply, Inc., P.O. Box 397, Owen, WI 54460 / 800-424-9069; FAX: 715-229-2332

Baekgaard Ltd., 1855 Janke Dr., Northbrook, IL 60062 / 708-498-3040; FAX: 708-493-3106

Baelder, Harry, Alte Goennebeker Strasse 5, 24635, Rickling, GERMANY / 04328-722732; FAX: 04328-722733

Baer Custom, Inc., Les, 29601 34th Ave., Hillsdale, IL 61257 / 309-658-2716; FAX: 309-658-2610

Baer's Hollows, P.O. Box 284, Eads, CO 81036 / 719-438-5718

Bagmaster Mfg., Inc., 2731 Sutton Ave., St. Louis, MO 63143 / 314-781-8002; FAX: 314-781-3363

Bain & Davis, Inc., 307 E. Valley Blvd., San Gabriel, CA 91776-3522 / 818-573-4241 or 213-283-7449 baindavis@aol.com

Baker, Stan, 10000 Lake City Way, Seattle, WA 98125 / 206-522-4575

Baker's Leather Goods, Roy, P.O. Box 893, Magnolia, AR 71753 / 870-234-0344 pholsters@ipa.net

Balance Co., 340-39 Ave., S.E., Box 505, Calgary, AB T2G 1X6 CANADA

Bald Eagle Precision Machine Co., 101-A Allison St., Lock Haven, PA 17745 / 570-748-6772; FAX: 570-748-4443

Balickie, Joe, 408 Trelawney Ln., Apex, NC 27502 / 919-362-5185

Ballard Industries, P.O. Box 2035, Arnold, CA 95223-2035 / 408-996-0957; FAX: 408-257-6828

Ballard Rifle & Cartridge Co., LLC, 113 W Yellowstone Ave., Cody, WY 82414 / 307-587-4914; FAX: 307-527-6097 ballard@wyoming.com

Ballistic Product, Inc., 20015 75th Ave. North, Corcoran, MN 55340-9456 / 612-494-9237; FAX: 612-494-9236 info@ballisticproducts.com www.ballisticproducts.com

Ballistic Research, 1108 W. May Ave., McHenry, IL 60050 / 815-385-0037

Ballisti-Cast, Inc., 6347 49th St. NW, Plaza, ND 58771 / 701-497-3333; FAX: 701-497-3335

Bandcor Industries, Div. of Man-Sew Corp., 6108 Sherwin Dr., Port Richey, FL 34668 / 813-848-0432

Bang-Bang Boutique (See The Holster Shop)

Banks, Ed, 2762 Hwy. 41 N., Ft. Valley, GA 31030 / 912-987-4665

Bansner's Gunsmithing Specialties, 261 East Main St. Box VH, Adamstown, PA 19501 / 800-368-2379; FAX: 717-484-0523

Barbour, Inc., 55 Meadowbrook Dr., Milford, NH 03055 / 603-673-1313; FAX: 603-673-6510

Barnes, 110 Borner St. S, Prescott, WI 54021-1149 / 608-897-8416

Barnes Bullets, Inc., P.O. Box 215, American Fork, UT 84003 / 801-756-4222 or 800-574-9200; FAX: 801-756-2465 email@barnesbullets.com barnesbullets.com

Baron Technology, 62 Spring Hill Rd., Trumbull, CT 06611 / 203-452-0515; FAX: 203-452-0663 dbaron@baronengraving.com www.baronengraving.com

Barraclough, John K., 55 Merit Park Dr., Gardena, CA 90247 / 310-324-2574

Barramundi Corp., P.O. Drawer 4259, Homosassa Springs, FL 32687 / 904-628-0200

Barrett Firearms Manufacturer, Inc., P.O. Box 1077, Murfreesboro, TN 37133 / 615-896-2938; FAX: 615-896-7313

Barry Lee Hands Engraving, 26192 E. Shore Route, Bigfork, MT 59911 / 406-837-0035

Bar-Sto Precision Machine, P.O. Box 1838, Twentynine Palms, CA 92277 / 760-367-2747; FAX: 760-367-2407 barsto@eee.org www.barsto.com

Barta's Gunsmithing, 10231 US Hwy. 10, Cato, WI 54230-8565 / 920-732-4472

Barteaux Machete, 1916 SE 50th Ave., Portland, OR 97215-3238 / 503-233-5880

Bartlett Engineering, 40 South 200 East, Smithfield, UT 84335-1645 / 801-563-5910

Basics Information Systems, Inc., 1141 Georgia Ave., Ste. 515, Wheaton, MD 20902 / 301-949-1070; FAX: 301-949-5326

Battenfeld Technologies, 5885 W. Van Horn Tavern Rd., Columbia, MO 65203 / 573-445-9200; FAX: 573-447-4158 battenfeldtechnologies.com

Bauer, Eddie, 15010 NE 36th St., Redmond, WA 98052

Baumgartner Bullets, 3011 S. Alane St., W. Valley City, UT 84120

Bauska Barrels, 105 9th Ave. W., Kalispell, MT 59901 / 406-752-7706

Bear Archery, RR 4, 4600 Southwest 41st Blvd., Gainesville, FL 32601 / 904-376-2327

Bear Arms, 121 Rhodes St., Jackson, SC 29831 / 803-471-9859

Bear Hug Grip, Inc., P.O. Box 16649, Colorado Springs, CO 80935-6649 / 800-232-7710

Bear Mountain Gun & Tool, 120 N. Plymouth, New Plymouth, ID 83655 / 208-278-5221; FAX: 208-278-5221

Beartooth Bullets, P.O. Box 491, Dept. HLD, Dover, ID 83825-0491 / 208-448-1865 bullets@beartoothbullets.com beartoothbullets.com

Beaver Lodge (See Fellowes, Ted)

Beaver Park Product, Inc., 840 J St., Penrose, CO 81240 / 719-372-6744

BEC, Inc., 1227 W. Valley Blvd., Ste. 204, Alhambra, CA 91803 / 626-281-5751; FAX: 626-293-7073

Beeline Custom Bullets Limited, P.O. Box 85, Yarmouth, NS B5A 4B1 CANADA / 902-648-3494; FAX: 902-648-0253

Beeman Precision Airguns, 5454 Argosy Dr., Huntington Beach, CA 92649 / 714-890-4800; FAX: 714-890-4808

Behlert Precision, Inc., P.O. Box 288, 7067 Easton Rd., Pipersville, PA 18947 / 215-766-8681 or 215-766-7301; FAX: 215-766-8681

Beitzinger, George, 116-20 Atlantic Ave., Richmond Hill, NY 11419 / 718-847-7661

Belding's Custom Gun Shop, 10691 Sayers Rd., Munith, MI 49259 / 517-596-2388

Bell & Carlson, Inc., Dodge City Industrial Park, 101 Allen Rd., Dodge City, KS 67801 / 800-634-8586 or 620-225-6688; FAX: 620-225-9095 email@bellandcarlson.com www.bellandcarlson.com

Bell Reloading, Inc., 1725 Harlin Lane Rd., Villa Rica, GA 30180

Bell's Gun & Sport Shop, 3309-19 Mannheim Rd., Franklin Park, IL 60131

Bell's Legendary Country Wear, 22 Circle Dr., Bellmore, NY 11710 / 516-679-1158

Belltown Ltd., 11 Camps Rd., Kent, CT 06757 / 860-354-5750; FAX: 860-354-6764

Ben William's Gun Shop, 1151 S. Cedar Ridge, Duncanville, TX 75137 / 214-780-1807

Benchmark Knives (See Gerber Legendary Blades)

Benelli Armi S.p.A., Via della Stazione, 61029, Urbino, ITALY / 39-722-307-1; FAX: 39-722-327427+

Benelli USA Corp, 17603 Indian Head Hwy, Accokeek, MD 20607 / 301-283-6981; FAX: 301-283-6988 benelliusa.com

Bengtson Arms Co., L., 6345-B E. Akron St., Mesa, AZ 85205 / 602-981-6375

Benjamin/Sheridan Co., Crossman, Rts. 5 and 20, E. Bloomfield, NY 14443 / 716-657-6161; FAX: 716-657-5405 www.crosman.com

Ben's Machines, 1151 S. Cedar Ridge, Duncanville, TX 75137 / 214-780-1807; FAX: 214-780-0316

Bentley, John, 128-D Watson Dr., Turtle Creek, PA 15145

Beomat of America, Inc., 300 Railway Ave., Campbell, CA 95008 / 408-379-4829

Beretta S.p.A., Pietro, Via Beretta, 18-25063, Gardone V.T., ITALY / 39-30-8341-1; FAX: 39-30-8341-421

Beretta U.S.A. Corp., 17601 Beretta Dr., Accokeek, MD 20607 / 301-283-2191; FAX: 301-283-0435

Berger Bullets Ltd., 5443 W. Westwind Dr., Glendale, AZ 85310 / 602-842-4001; FAX: 602-934-9083

Bernardelli S.p.A., Vincenzo, 125 Via Matteotti, P.O. Box 74, Brescia, ITALY / 39-30-8912851-2-3; FAX: 39-30-8910249

Berry's Mfg., Inc., 401 North 3050 East St., St. George, UT 84770 / 435-634-1682; FAX: 435-634-1683 sales@berrysmfg.com www.berrysmfg.com

Bersa S.A., Gonzales Castillo 312, 1704, Ramos Mejia, ARGENTINA / 541-656-2377; FAX: 541-656-2093+

Bert Johanssons Vapentillbehor, S-430 20 Veddige, SWEDEN

Bertuzzi (See U.S. Importer-New England Arms Co.)

Better Concepts Co., 663 New Castle Rd., Butler, PA 16001 / 412-285-9000

Beverly, Mary, 3201 Horseshoe Trail, Tallahassee, FL 32312

MANUFACTURER'S DIRECTORY

Bianchi International, Inc., 100 Calle Cortez, Temecula, CA 92590 / 909-676-5621; FAX: 909-676-6777

Biesen, Al, 5021 Rosewood, Spokane, WA 99208 / 509-328-9340

Biesen, Roger, 5021 W. Rosewood, Spokane, WA 99208 / 509-328-9340

Big Bear Arms & Sporting Goods, Inc., 1112 Milam Way, Carrollton, TX 75006 / 972-416-8051 or 800-400-BEAR; FAX: 972-416-0771

Big Bore Bullets of Alaska, P.O. Box 521455, Big Lake, AK 99652-1455 / 907-373-2673; FAX: 907-373-2673 doug@mtaonline.net www.awloo.com/bbb/index

Big Bore Express, 16345 Midway Rd., Nampa, ID 83651 / 208-466-9975; FAX: 208-466-6927 before .com

Big Sky Racks, Inc., P.O. Box 729, Bozeman, MT 59771-0729 / 406-586-9393; FAX: 406-585-7378

Big Spring Enterprises "Bore Stores", P.O. Box 1115, Big Spring Rd., Yellville, AR 72687 / 870-449-5297; FAX: 870-449-4446

Bilal, Mustafa, 908 NW 50th St., Seattle, WA 98107-3634 / 206-782-4164

Bilinski, Bryan (See Fieldsport Ltd.)

Bill Austin's Calls, Box 284, Kaycee, WY 82639 / 307-738-2552

Bill Adair Custom Shop, 2886 Westridge, Carrollton, TX 75006 / 972-418-0950

Bill Hanus Birdguns LLC, P.O. Box 533, Newport, OR 97365 / 541-265-7433; FAX: 541-265-7400 www.billhanusbirdguns.com

Bill Johns Master Engraver, 7927 Ranch Roach 965, Fredericksburg, TX 78624-9545 / 830-997-6795

Bill Wiseman and Co., P.O. Box 3427, Bryan, TX 77805 / 409-690-3456; FAX: 409-690-0156

Billeb, Stephen (See Quality Custom Firearms)

Billings Gunsmiths Inc., 1841 Grand Ave., Billings, MT 59102 / 406-256-8390

Billingsley & Brownell, P.O. Box 25, Dayton, WY 82836 / 307-655-9344

Bill's Custom Cases, P.O. Box 2, Dunsmuir, CA 96025 / 530-235-0177; FAX: 530-235-4959

Bill's Gun Repair, 1007 Burlington St., Mendota, IL 61342 / 815-539-5786

Billy Bates Engraving, 2302 Winthrop Dr., Decatur, AL 35603 / 256-355-3690 bbrn@aol.com www.angelfire.com/al/billybatets

Birchwood Casey, 7900 Fuller Rd., Eden Prairie, MN 55344 / 800-328-6156 or 612-937-7933; FAX: 612-937-7979

Birdsong & Assoc, W. E., 1435 Monterey Rd., Florence, MS 39073-9748 / 601-366-8270

Bismuth Cartridge Co., 3500 Maple Ave., Ste. 1650, Dallas, TX 75219 / 214-521-5880; FAX: 214-521-9035

Bison Studios, 1409 South Commerce St., Las Vegas, NV 89102 / 702-388-2891; FAX: 702-383-9967

Bitterroot Bullet Co., P.O. Box 412, Lewiston, ID 83501-0412 / 208-743-5635; FAX: 208-743-5635 brootbil@lewiston.com

BKL Technologies, P.O. Box 5237, Brownsville, TX 78523

Black Bullets (See Big Bore Express)

Black Hills Ammunition, Inc., P.O. Box 3090, Rapid City, SD 57709-3090 / 605-348-5150; FAX: 605-348-9827

Black Hills Shooters Supply, P.O. Box 4220, Rapid City, SD 57709 / 800-289-2506

Black Powder Products, 67 Township Rd. 1411, Chesapeake, OH 45619 / 614-867-8047

Black Sheep Brand, 3220 W. Gentry Parkway, Tyler, TX 75702 / 903-592-3853; FAX: 903-592-0527

Blacksmith Corp., P.O. Box 280, North Hampton, OH 45349 / 800-531-2665; FAX: 937-969-8399 bcbooks@glasscity.net

BlackStar AccuMax Barrels, 11501 Brittmoore Park Dr., Houston, TX 77041 / 281-721-6040; FAX: 281-721-6041

BlackStar Barrel Accurizing (See BlackStar AccuMax Barrels)

Blacktail Mountain Books, 42 First Ave. W., Kalispell, MT 59901 / 406-257-5573

Blair Engraving, J. R., P.O. Box 64, Glenrock, WY 82637 / 307-436-8115

Blammo Ammo, P.O. Box 1677, Seneca, SC 29679 / 803-882-1768

Blaser Jagdwaffen GmbH, D-88316, Isny Im Allgau, GERMANY

Bleile, C. Roger, 5040 Ralph Ave., Cincinnati, OH 45238 / 513-251-0249

Blount, Inc., Sporting Equipment Div., 2299 Snake River Ave., P.O. Box 856, Lewiston, ID 83501 / 800-627-3640 or 208-746-2351; FAX: 208-799-3904

Blue and Gray Products Inc. (See Ox-Yoke Originals, Inc.)

Blue Book Publications, Inc., 8009 34th Ave. S. Ste. 175, Minneapolis, MN 55425 / 800-877-4867 or 612-854-5229; FAX: 612-853-1486 bluebook@bluebookinc.com www.bluebookinc.com

Blue Mountain Bullets, HCR 77, P.O. Box 231, John Day, OR 97845 / 541-820-4594

Blue Ridge Machinery & Tools, Inc., P.O. Box 536-GD, Hurricane, WV 25526 / 800-872-6500; FAX: 304-562-5311 blueridgemachine@worldnet.att.net blueridgemachinery.com

BMC Supply, Inc., 26051 - 179th Ave. S.E., Kent, WA 98042

Bob Allen Co. 214 SW Jackson, P.O. Box 477, Des Moines, IA 50315 / 800-685-7020; FAX: 515-283-0779

Bob Rogers Gunsmithing, P.O. Box 305, 344 S. Walnut St., Franklin Grove, IL 61031 / 815-456-2685; FAX: 815-288-7142

Bob's Gun Shop, P.O. Box 200, Royal, AR 71968 / 501-767-1970; FAX: 501-767-1970

Bob's Tactical Indoor Shooting Range & Gun Shop, 90 Lafayette Rd., Salisbury, MA 01952 / 508-465-5561

Boessler, Erich, Am Vogeltal 3, 97702, Munnerstadt, GERMANY

Boker USA, Inc., 1550 Balsam Street, Lakewood, CO 80215 / 303-462-0662; FAX: 303-462-0668 bokerusa@worldnet.att.net www.bokerusa.com

Boltin, John M., P.O. Box 644, Estill, SC 29918 / 803-625-2185

Bo-Mar Tool & Mfg. Co., 6136 State Hwy 300, Longview, TX 75604 / 903-759-4784; FAX: 903-759-9141 marxkor@earthlink.net bo-mar.com

Bonanza (See Forster Products)

Bond Arms, Inc., P.O. Box 1296, Granbury, TX 76048 / 817-573-4445; FAX: 817-573-5636

Bond Custom Firearms, 8954 N. Lewis Ln., Bloomington, IN 47408 / 812-332-4519

Bondini Paolo, Via Sorrento 345, San Carlo di Cesena, ITALY / 0547-663-240; FAX: 0547-663-780

Bone Engraving, Ralph, 718 N. Atlanta, Owasso, OK 74055 / 918-272-9745

Boone Trading Co., Inc., P.O. Box 669, Brinnon, WA 98320 / 360-796-4330; or 800-423-1945; FAX: 360-796-4511 sales@boonetrading.com www.boonetrading.com

Boonie Packer Products, P.O. Box 12517, Salem, OR 97309 / 800-477-3244 or 503-581-3244; FAX: 503-581-3191

Borden Ridges Rimrock Stocks, RR 1 Box 250 BC, Springville, PA 18844 / 570-965-2505; FAX: 570-965-2328

Borden Rifles Inc., RD 1, Box 250BC, Springville, PA 18844 / 717-965-2505; FAX: 717-965-2328

Border Barrels Ltd., Riccarton Farm, Newcastleton, SCOTLAND UK

Borovnik KG, Ludwig, 9170 Ferlach, Bahnhofstrasse 7, AUSTRIA / 042 27 24 42; FAX: 042 26 43 49

Bosis (See U.S. Importer-New England Arms Co.)

Boss Manufacturing Co., 221 W. First St., Kewanee, IL 61443 / 309-852-2131 or 800-447-4581; FAX: 309-852-0848

Bostick Wildlife Calls, Inc., P.O. Box 728, Estill, SC 29918 / 803-625-2210 or 803-625-4512

Bowen Classic Arms Corp., P.O. Box 67, Louisville, TN 37777 / 865-984-3583 www.bowenclassicarms.com

Bowen Knife Co., Inc., P.O. Box 590, Blackshear, GA 31516 / 912-449-4794

Bowerly, Kent, 710 Golden Pheasant Dr, Redmond, OR 97756 / 541-595-6028

Boyds' Gunstock Industries, Inc., 25376 403rd Ave., Mitchell, SD 57301 / 605-996-5011; FAX: 605-996-9878

Brace, Larry D., 771 Blackfoot Ave., Eugene, OR 97404 / 541-688-1278; FAX: 541-607-5833

Bradley Gunsight Co., P.O. Box 340, Plymouth, VT 05056 / 860-589-0531; FAX: 860-582-6294

Brass Eagle, Inc., 7050A Bramalea Rd., Unit 19, Mississauga, , ON L4Z 1C7 CANADA / 416-848-4844

Bratcher, Dan, 311 Belle Air Pl., Carthage, MO 64836 / 417-358-1518

Brauer Bros. Mfg. Co., 2020 Delman Blvd., St. Louis, MO 63103 / 314-231-2864; FAX: 314-249-4952

Break-Free, Inc., P.O. Box 25020, Santa Ana, CA 92799 / 714-953-1900; FAX: 714-953-0402

Brenneke GmbH, P.O. Box 1646, 30837, Langenhagen, GERMANY / 0511/97262-0; FAX: 0511/97262-62 info@brenneke.de www.brenneke.com

Brian Perazone-Gunsmith, Cold Spring Rd., Roxbury, NY 12474 / 607-326-4088; FAX: 607-326-3140

Bridgeman Products, Harry Jaffin, 153 B Cross Slope Court, Englishtown, NJ 07726 / 732-536-3604; FAX: 732-972-1004

Bridgers Best, P.O. Box 1410, Berthoud, CO 80513

Briese Bullet Co., Inc., RR1, Box 108, Tappen, ND 58487 / 701-327-4578; FAX: 701-327-4579

Brigade Quartermasters, 1025 Cobb International Blvd., Dept. VH, Kennesaw, GA 30144-4300 / 404-428-1248 or 800-241-3125; FAX: 404-426-7726

Briganti, A.J., 512 Rt. 32, Highland Mills, NY 10930 / 914-928-9573

Briley Mfg. Inc., 1230 Lumpkin, Houston, TX 77043 / 800-331-5718 or 713-932-6995; FAX: 713-932-1043

British Antiques, P.O. Box 35369, Tucson, AZ 85740 / 520-575-9063 britishantiques@hotmail.com

British Sporting Arms, RR1, Box 130, Millbrook, NY 12545 / 914-677-8303

Broad Creek Rifle Works, Ltd., 120 Horsey Ave., Laurel, DE 19956 / 302-875-5446; FAX: 302-875-1449 bcqw4guns@aol.com

Brockman's Custom Gunsmithing, P.O. Box 357, Gooding, ID 83302 / 208-934-5050

Brocock Ltd., 43 River Street, Digbeth, Birmingham, B5 5SA ENGLAND / 011-021-773-1200; FAX: 01217731211 sales@brocock.co.uk www.brocock.co.uk

Broken Gun Ranch, 10739 126 Rd., Spearville, KS 67876 / 316-385-2587; FAX: 316-385-2597

Brooker, Dennis, Rt. 1, Box 12A, Derby, IA 50068 / 515-533-2103

Brooks Tactical Systems, 279-C Shorewood Ct., Fox Island, WA 98333 / 253-549-2866; FAX: 253-549-2703 brooks@brookstactical.com www.brookstactical.com

Brown, H. R. (See Silhouette Leathers)

Brown Co., E. Arthur, 3404 Pawnee Dr., Alexandria, MN 56308 / 320-762-8847

Brown Dog Ent., 2200 Calle Camelia, 1000 Oaks, CA 91360 / 805-497-2318; FAX: 805-497-1618

Brown Manufacturing, P.O. Box 9219, Akron, OH 44305 / 800-837-GUNS

Brown Precision, Inc., 7786 Molinos Ave., Los Molinos, CA 96055; FAX: 916-384-1638

Brownells, Inc., 200 S. Front St., Montezuma, IA 50171 / 641-623-5401; FAX: 641-623-3896 orderdesk@brownells.com www.brownells.com

Browning Arms Co., One Browning Pl., Morgan, UT 84050 / 801-876-2711; FAX: 801-876-3331

Browning Arms Co. (Parts & Service), 3005 Arnold Tenbrook Rd., Arnold, MO 63010 / 314-287-6800; FAX: 314-287-9751

BRP, Inc., High Performance Cast Bullets, 1210 Alexander Rd., Colorado Springs, CO 80909 / 719-633-0658

Brunton U.S.A., 620 E. Monroe Ave., Riverton, WY 82501 / 307-856-6559; FAX: 307-856-1840

Bryan & Assoc., R D Sauls, P.O. Box 5772, Anderson, SC 29623-5772 / 864-261-6810 bryanandac@aol.com www.huntersweb.com/bryanandac

Brynin, Milton, P.O. Box 383, Yonkers, NY 10710 / 914-779-4333

BSA Guns Ltd., Armoury Rd. Small Heath, Birmingham, ENGLAND / 011-021-772-8543; FAX: 011-021-773-084

BSA Optics, 3911 SW 47th Ave #914, Ft Lauderdale, FL 33314 / 954-581-2144; FAX: 954-581-3165 bsaoptic@bellsouth bsaoptics.com

B-Square Company, Inc., ;, P.O. Box 11281, 2708 St. Louis Ave., Ft. Worth, TX 76110 / 817-923-0964 or 800-433-2909; FAX: 817-926-7012

Bucheimer, J. M. (See Jumbo Sports Products)

Buck Knives, Inc., 1900 Weld Blvd., P.O. Box 1267, El Cajon, CA 92020 / 619-449-1100 or 800-326-2825; FAX: 619-562-5774 8

Buck Stix--SOS Products Co., Box 3, Neenah, WI 54956

Buck Stop Lure Co., Inc., 3600 Grow Rd. NW, P.O. Box 636, Stanton, MI 48888 / 517-762-5091; FAX: 517-762-5124

Buckeye Custom Bullets, 6490 Stewart Rd., Elida, OH 45807 / 419-641-4463

Buckhorn Gun Works, 8109 Woodland Dr., Black Hawk, SD 57718 / 605-787-6472

Buckskin Bullet Co., P.O. Box 1893, Cedar City, UT 84721 / 435-586-3286

Buckskin Machine Works, A. Hunkeler, 3235 S. 358th St., Auburn, WA 98001 / 206-927-5412

Budin, Dave, Main St., Margaretville, NY 12455 / 914-586-4103; FAX: 914-586-4105

Buenger Enterprises/Goldenrod Dehumidifier, 3600 S. Harbor Blvd., Oxnard, CA 93035 / 800-451-6797 or 805-985-5828; FAX: 805-985-1534

Buffalo Arms Co., 99 Raven Ridge, Samuels, ID 83864 / 208-263-6953; FAX: 208-265-2096

Buffalo Bullet Co., Inc., 12637 Los Nietos Rd., Unit A., Santa Fe Springs, CA 90670 / 800-426-7082; FAX: 626-944-5054

Buffalo Rock Shooters Supply, R.R. 1, Ottawa, IL 61350 / 815-433-2471

Buffer Technologies, P.O. Box 104930, Jefferson City, MO 65110 / 573-634-8529; FAX: 573-634-8522

Bull Mountain Rifle Co., 6327 Golden West Terrace, Billings, MT 59016 / 406-656-0778

Bullberry Barrel Works, Ltd., 2430 W. Bullberry Ln. 67-5, Hurricane, UT 84737 / 435-635-9866; FAX: 435-635-0348

Bullet Metals, P.O. Box 1238, Sierra Vista, AZ 85636 / 520-458-5321; FAX: 520-458-1421 info@theantiononman.com theantimonyman.com

---

DIRECTORY

MANUFACTURER'S DIRECTORY

Bullet Swaging Supply Inc., P.O. Box 1056, 303 McMillan Rd., West Monroe, LA 71291 / 318-387-3266; FAX: 318-387-7779 leblackmon@colla.com

Bullet'n Press, 1210 Jones St., Gastonia, NC 28052-7520 / 704-853-0265 gnpress@nemaine.com www.nemaine.com/bnpress

Bullseye Bullets, 1808 Turkey Creek Rd #9, Plant City, FL 33567 / 800-741-6343 bbullets8100@aol.com

Bull-X, Inc., 520 N. Main, Farmer City, IL 61842 / 309-928-2574 or 800-248-3845; FAX: 309-928-2130

Burkhart Gunsmithing, Don, P.O. Box 852, Rawlins, WY 82301 / 307-324-6007

Burnham Bros., P.O. Box 1148, Menard, TX 78659 / 915-396-4572; FAX: 915-396-4574

Burris Co., Inc., P.O. Box 1747, 331 E. 8th St., Greeley, CO 80631 / 970-356-1670; FAX: 970-356-8702

Bushmaster Firearms (See Quality Parts Co.)

Bushmaster Hunting & Fishing, 451 Alliance Ave., Toronto, ON M6N 2J1 CANADA / 416-763-4040; FAX: 416-763-0623

Bushnell Performance Optics, 9200 Cody, Overland Park, KS 66214 / 913-752-3400 or 800-423-3537; FAX: 913-752-3550

Bushwacker Counter Assault, 120 Industry Ct, Kalispell, MT 59901-7991 / 406-728-6241; FAX: 406-728-8800

Bustani, Leo, P.O. Box 8125, W. Palm Beach, FL 33410 / 305-622-2710

Buster's Custom Knives, P.O. Box 214, Richfield, UT 84701 / 801-896-5319

Butler Creek Corp., 290 Arden Dr., Belgrade, MT 59714 / 800-423-8327 or 406-388-1356; FAX: 406-388-7204

Butler Enterprises, 834 Oberting Rd., Lawrenceburg, IN 47025 / 812-537-3584

Butterfield & Butterfield, 220 San Bruno Ave., San Francisco, CA 94103 / 415-861-7500

Buzztail Brass (See Grayback Wildcats)

C

C&D Special Products (See Claybuster Wads & Harvester Bullets)

C&H Research, 115 Sunnyside Dr., Box 351, Lewis, KS 67552 / 316-324-5445 www.09.net(chr)

C. Palmer Manufacturing Co., Inc., P.O. Box 220, West Newton, PA 15089 / 412-872-8200; FAX: 412-872-8302

C. Sharps Arms Co. Inc., 100 Centennial, Box 885, Big Timber, MT 59011 / 406-932-4353; FAX: 406-932-4443

C.S. Van Gorden & Son, Inc., 1815 Main St., Bloomer, WI 54724 / 715-568-2612

C.W. Erickson's Mfg. Inc., 530 Garrison Ave. NE, P.O. Box 522, Buffalo, MN 55313 / 612-682-3665; FAX: 612-682-4328

Cabanas (See U.S. Importer-Mandall Shooting Supplies Inc.)

Cabela's, 812-13th Ave., Sidney, NE 69160 / 308-254-6644 or 800-237-4444; FAX: 308-254-6745

Cabinet Mtn. Outfitters Scents & Lures, P.O. Box 766, Plains, MT 59859 / 406-826-3970

Cache La Poudre Rifleworks, 140 N. College, Ft. Collins, CO 80524 / 303-482-6913

Calibre Press, Inc., 666 Dundee Rd., Ste. 1607, Northbrook, IL 60062 / 800-323-0037; FAX: 708-498-6869

Cali'co Hardwoods, Inc., 3580 Westwind Blvd., Santa Rosa, CA 95403 / 707-546-4045; FAX: 707-546-4027 calicohardwoods@msn.com

Calico Light Weapon Systems, 1489 Greg St., Sparks, NV 89431

California Sights (See Fautheree, Andy)

Cambos Outdoorsman, 532 E. Idaho Ave., Ontario, OR 97914 / 541-889-3138; FAX: 541-889-2633

Camdex, Inc., 2330 Alger, Troy, MI 48083 / 810-528-2300; FAX: 810-528-0989

Cameron's, 16690 W. 11th Ave., Golden, CO 80401 / 303-279-7365; FAX: 303-628-5413

Camilli, Lou, 8895 N. Military Trl. Ste. 201E, Palm Beach Gardens, FL 33410-6244

Camillus Cutlery Co., 54 Main St., Camillus, NY 13031 / 315-672-8111; FAX: 315-672-8832

Campbell, Dick, 20000 Silver Ranch Rd., Conifer, CO 80433 / 303-697-0150; FAX: 303-697-0150

Camp-Cap Products, P.O. Box 3805, Chesterfield, MO 63006 / 314-532-4340; FAX: 314-532-4340

Cannon, Andy (See Cannon's)

Cannon Safe, Inc., 216 S. 2nd Ave. #BLD-932, San Bernardino, CA 92400-0181 / 310-692-0636 or 800-242-1055; FAX: 310-692-7252

Cannon's, Andy Cannon, Box 1026, 320 Main St., Polson, MT 59860 / 406-887-2048

Canons Delcour, Rue J.B. Cools, B-4040, Herstal, BELGIUM / +32.(0)42.40.61.40; FAX: +32(0)42.40.22.88

Canyon Cartridge Corp., P.O. Box 152, Albertson, NY 11507; FAX: 516-294-8946

Cape Outfitters, 599 County Rd. 206, Cape Girardeau, MO 63701 / 573-335-4103; FAX: 573-335-1555

Caraville Manufacturing, P.O. Box 4545, Thousand Oaks, CA 91359 / 805-499-1234

Carbide Checkering Tools (See J&R Engineering)

Carhartt, Inc., P.O. Box 600, 3 Parklane Blvd., Dearborn, MI 48121 / 800-358-3825 or 313-271-8460; FAX: 313-271-3455

Carl Walther GmbH, B.P. 4325, D-89033, Ulm, GERMANY

Carl Walther USA, P.O. Box 208, Ten Prince St., Alexandria, VA 22313 / 703-548-1400; FAX: 703-548-7826

Carl Zeiss Inc., 13017 N. Kingston Ave., Chester, VA 23836-2743 / 804-861-0033 or 800-388-2984; FAX: 804-733-4024

Carlson, Douglas R., Antique American Firearms, P.O. Box 71035, Dept. GD, Des Moines, IA 50325 / 515-224-6552

Carolina Precision Rifles, 1200 Old Jackson Hwy., Jackson, SC 29831 / 803-827-2069

Carrell's Precision Firearms, 643 Clark Ave., Billings, MT 59101-1614 / 406-962-3593

Carry-Lite, Inc., 5203 W. Clinton Ave., Milwaukee, WI 53223 / 414-355-3520; FAX: 414-355-4775

Carter's Gun Shop, 225 G St., Penrose, CO 81240 / 719-372-6240

Cartridge Transfer Group, Pete de Coux, 235 Oak St., Butler, PA 16001 / 412-282-3426

Cascade Bullet Co., Inc., 2355 South 6th St., Klamath Falls, OR 97601 / 503-884-9316

Cascade Shooters, 2155 N.W. 12th St., Redwood, OR 97756

Case & Sons Cutlery Co., W. R., Owens Way, Bradford, PA 16701 / 814-368-4123 or 800-523-6350; FAX: 814-768-5369

Case Sorting System, 12695 Cobblestone Creek Rd., Poway, CA 92064 / 619-486-9340

Cash Mfg. Co., Inc., P.O. Box 130, 201 S. Klein Dr., Waunakee, WI 53597-0130 / 608-849-5664; FAX: 608-849-5664

Caspian Arms, Ltd., 14 North Main St., Hardwick, VT 05843 / 802-472-6454; FAX: 802-472-6709

Cast Performance Bullet Company, P.O. Box 153, Riverton, WY 82501 / 307-857-2940; FAX: 307-857-3132 castperform@wyoming.com castperformance.com

Casull Arms Corp., P.O. Box 1629, Afton, WY 83110 / 307-886-0200

Caswell Detroit Armor Companies, 1221 Marshall St. NE, Minneapolis, MN 55413-1055 / 612-379-2000; FAX: 612-379-2367

Catco-Ambush, Inc., P.O. Box 300, Corte Madera, CA 94926

Cathey Enterprises, Inc., P.O. Box 2202, Brownwood, TX 76804 / 915-643-2553; FAX: 915-643-3653

Cation, 2341 Alger St., Troy, MI 48083 / 810-689-0658; FAX: 810-689-7558

Caywood, Shane J., P.O. Box 321, Minocqua, WI 54548 / 715-277-3866

CBC, Avenida Humberto de Campos 3220, 09400-000, Ribeirao Pires, SP, BRAZIL / 55-11-742-7500; FAX: 55-11-459-7385

CBC-BRAZIL, 3 Cuckoo Ln., Honley, Yorkshire HD7 2BR, ENGLAND / 44-1484-661062; FAX: 44-1484-663709

CCG Enterprises, 5217 E. Belknap St., Halton City, TX 76117 / 800-819-7464

CCI Div. of Blount, Inc., Sporting Equipment Div. 2299 Sn, P.O. Box 856, Lewiston, ID 83501 / 800-627-3640 or 208-746-2351; FAX: 208-746-2915

CCL Security Products, 199 Whiting St., New Britain, CT 06051 / 800-733-8588

Cedar Hill Game Calls LLC, 238 Vic Allen Rd., Downsville, LA 71234 / 318-982-5632; FAX: 318-368-2245

Celestron International, P.O. Box 3578, 2835 Columbia St., Torrance, CA 90503 / 310-328-9560; FAX: 310-212-5835

Centaur Systems, Inc., 1602 Foothill Rd., Kalispell, MT 59901 / 406-755-8609; FAX: 406-755-8609

Center Lock Scope Rings, 9901 France Ct., Lakeville, MN 55044 / 612-461-2114

Central Specialties Ltd. (See Trigger Lock Division/Central Specialists Ltc.)

Century Gun Dist. Inc., 1467 Jason Rd., Greenfield, IN 46140 / 317-462-4524

Century International Arms, Inc., 1161 Holland Dr., Boca Raton, FL 33487

CFVentures, 509 Harvey Dr., Bloomington, IN 47403-1715

CH Tool & Die Co. (See 4-D Custom Die Co.)

Chace Leather Products, 507 Alden St., Fall River, MA 02722 / 508-678-7556; FAX: 508-675-9666

Chadick's Ltd., P.O. Box 100, Terrell, TX 75160 / 214-563-7577

Chambers Flintlocks Ltd., Jim, 116 Sams Branch Rd., Candler, NC 28715 / 828-667-8361; FAX: 828-665-0852

Champion Shooters' Supply, P.O. Box 303, New Albany, OH 43054 / 614-855-1603; FAX: 614-855-1209

Champion Target Co., 232 Industrial Parkway, Richmond, IN 47374 / 800-441-4971

Champion's Choice, Inc., 201 International Blvd., LaVergne, TN 37086 / 615-793-4066; FAX: 615-793-4070

Champlin Firearms, Inc., P.O. Box 3191, Woodring Airport, Enid, OK 73701 / 580-237-7388; FAX: 580-242-6922 info@champlinarms.com champlinarms.com

Chapman Academy of Practical Shooting, 4350 Academy Rd., Hallsville, MO 65255 / 573-696-5544 or 573-696-2266

Chapman, J. Ken (See Old West Bullet Moulds)

Chapman Manufacturing Co., 471 New Haven Rd., P.O. Box 250, Durham, CT 06422 / 860-349-9228; FAX: 860-349-0084 sales@chapmanmfg.com www.chapmanmfg.com

Chapuis Armes, 21 La Gravoux, BP15, 42380, St. Bonnet-le-Chatea, FRANCE / (33)77.50.06.96+

Chapuis USA, 416 Business Park, Bedford, KY 40006

Charter 2000, 273 Canal St., Shelton, CT 06484 / 203-922-1652

Checkmate Refinishing, 370 Champion Dr., Brooksville, FL 34601 / 352-799-5774; FAX: 352-799-2986

Cheddite France S.A., 99 Route de Lyon, F-26501, Bourg-les-Valence, FRANCE / 33-75-56-4545; FAX: 33-75-56-3587 export@cheddite.com

Chelsea Gun Club of New York City Inc., 237 Ovington Ave., Apt. D53, Brooklyn, NY 11209 / 718-836-9422 or 718-833-2704

Chem-Pak Inc., P.O. Box 2058, Winchester, VA 22604-1258 / 800-336-9828 or 703-667-1341; FAX: 703-722-3993

Cherry Creek State Park Shooting Center, 12500 E. Belleview Ave., Englewood, CO 80111 / 303-693-1765

Chet Fulmer's Antique Firearms, P.O. Box 792, Rt. 2 Buffalo Lake, Detroit Lakes, MN 56501 / 218-847-7712

CheVron Bullets, RR1, Ottawa, IL 61350 / 815-433-2471

Cheyenne Pioneer Products, P.O. Box 28425, Kansas City, MO 64188 / 816-413-9196; FAX: 816-455-2859 cheyennepp@aol.com www.cartridgeboxes.com

Chicago Cutlery Co., 1536 Beech St., Terre Haute, IN 47804 / 800-457-2665

Chicasaw Gun Works, 4 Mi. Mkr., Pluto Rd. Box 868, Shady Spring, WV 25918-0868 / 304-763-2848; FAX: 304-763-3725

Chipmunk (See Oregon Arms, Inc.)

Choate Machine & Tool Co., Inc., P.O. Box 218, 116 Lovers Ln., Bald Knob, AR 72010 / 501-724-6193 or 800-972-6390; FAX: 501-724-5873

Christensen Arms, 385 N. 3050 E., St. George, UT 84790 / 435-624-9535; FAX: 435-674-9293

Christie's East, 219 E. 67th St., New York, NY 10021 / 212-606-0406

Chu Tani Ind., Inc., P.O. Box 2064, Cody, WY 82414-2064

Chuck's Gun Shop, P.O. Box 597, Waldo, FL 32694 / 904-468-2264

Churchill (See U.S. Importer-Ellett Bros.)

Churchill, Winston, 2838 20 Mile Stream Rd., Proctorsville, VT 05153 / 802-226-7772

CIDCO, 21480 Pacific Blvd., Sterling, VA 22170 / 703-444-5353

Cimarron F.A. Co., P.O. Box 906, Fredericksburg, TX 78624-0906 / 210-997-9090; FAX: 210-997-0802

Cincinnati Swaging, 2605 Marlington Ave., Cincinnati, OH 45208

Clark Custom Guns, Inc., 336 Shootout Ln., Princeton, LA 71067 / 318-949-9884; FAX: 318-949-9829

Clark Firearms Engraving, P.O. Box 80746, San Marino, CA 91118 / 818-287-1652

Clarkfield Enterprises, Inc., 1032 10th Ave., Clarkfield, MN 56223 / 612-669-7140

Claro Walnut Gunstock Co., 1235 Stanley Ave., Chico, CA 95928 / 530-342-5188; FAX: 530-342-5199

Classic Arms Company, Rt 1 Box 120F, Burnet, TX 78611 / 512-756-4001

Classic Arms Corp., P.O. Box 106, Dunsmuir, CA 96025-0106 / 530-235-2000

Classic Old West Styles, 1060 Doniphan Park Circle C, El Paso, TX 79936 / 915-587-0684

Claybuster Wads & Harvester Bullets, 309 Sequoya Dr., Hopkinsville, KY 42240 / 800-922-6287 or 800-284-1746; FAX: 502-885-8088 50

Clean Shot Technologies, 21218 St. Andrews Blvd. Ste 504, Boca Raton, FL 33433 / 888-866-2532

Clear Creek Outdoors, Pat LaBoone, 2550 Hwy 23, Wrenshall, MN 55797 / 218-384-3670

Clearview Mfg. Co., Inc., 413 S. Oakley St., Fordyce, AR 71742 / 501-352-8557; FAX: 501-352-7120

Clearview Products, 3021 N. Portland, Oklahoma City, OK 73107

Cleland's Outdoor World, Inc., 10306 Airport Hwy., Swanton, OH 43558 / 419-865-4713; FAX: 419-865-5865

Clements' Custom Leathercraft, Chas, 1741 Dallas St., Aurora, CO 80010-2018 / 303-364-0403; FAX: 303-739-9824 gryphons@home.com kuntaoslcat.com

Clenzoil Corp., P.O. Box 80226, Sta. C, Canton, OH 44708-0226 / 330-833-9758; FAX: 330-833-4724

Clift Mfg., L. R., 3821 Hammonton Rd., Marysville, CA 95901 / 916-755-3390; FAX: 916-755-3393

Clift Welding Supply & Cases, 1332-A Colusa Hwy., Yuba City, CA 95993 / 916-755-3390; FAX: 916-755-3393

Cloward's Gun Shop, 4023 Aurora Ave. N, Seattle, WA 98103 / 206-632-2072

Clymer Mfg. Co., 1645 W. Hamlin Rd., Rochester Hills, MI 48309-3312 / 248-853-5555; FAX: 248-853-1530

C-More Systems, P.O. Box 1750, 7553 Gary Rd., Manassas, VA 20108 / 703-361-2663; FAX: 703-361-5881

Cobalt Mfg., Inc., 4020 Mcewen Rd. Ste. 180, Dallas, TX 75244-5090 / 817-382-8986; FAX: 817-383-4281

Cobra Sport S.r.l., Via Caduti Nei Lager No. 1, 56020 San Romano, Montopoli v/Arno (Pi, ITALY / 0039-571-450490; FAX: 0039-571-450492

Coffin, Charles H., 3719 Scarlet Ave., Odessa, TX 79762 / 915-366-4729; FAX: 915-366-4729

Coffin, Jim (See Working Guns)

Cogar's Gunsmithing, 206 Redwine Dr., Houghton Lake, MI 48629 / 517-422-4591

Coghlan's Ltd., 121 Irene St., Winnipeg, MB R3T 4C7 CANADA / 204-284-9550; FAX: 204-475-4127

Cold Steel Inc., 3036 Seaborg Ave. Ste. A, Ventura, CA 93003 / 800-255-4716 or 800-624-2363; FAX: 805-642-9727

Coleman Co., Inc., 250 N. St. Francis, Wichita, KS 67201

Coleman's Custom Repair, 4035 N. 20th Rd., Arlington, VA 22207 / 703-528-4486

Cole's Gun Works, Old Bank Building, Rt. 4 Box 250, Moyock, NC 27958 / 919-435-2345

Collectors Firearms Etc., Ed Kukowski, P.O. Box 62, Minnesota City, MN 55959 / 507-689-2925

Collings, Ronald, 1006 Cielta Linda, Vista, CA 92083

Colonial Arms, Inc., P.O. Box 636, Selma, AL 36702-0636 / 334-872-9455; FAX: 334-872-9540 colonialarms@mindspring.com www.colonialarms.com

Colonial Knife Co., Inc., P.O. Box 3327, Providence, RI 02909 / 401-421-1600; FAX: 401-421-2047

Colonial Repair, 47 Navarre St., Roslindale, MA 02131-4725 / 617-469-4951

Colorado Gunsmithing Academy, RR 3 Box 79B, El Campo, TX 77437-9603 / 719-336-4099 or 800-754-2046; FAX: 719-336-9642

Colorado School of Trades, 1575 Hoyt St., Lakewood, CO 80215 / 800-234-4594; FAX: 303-233-4723

Colorado Sutlers Arsenal (See Cumberland States Arsenal)

Colt Blackpowder Arms Co., 110 8th Street, Brooklyn, NY 11215 / 212-925-2159; FAX: 212-966-4986

Colt's Mfg. Co., Inc., P.O. Box 1868, Hartford, CT 06144-1868 / 800-962-COLT or 860-236-6311; FAX: 860-244-1449

Compass Industries, Inc., 104 East 25th St., New York, NY 10010 / 212-473-2614 or 800-221-9904; FAX: 212-353-0826

Compasseco, Ltd., 151 Atkinson Hill Ave., Bardtown, KY 40004 / 502-349-0910

Competition Electronics, Inc., 3469 Precision Dr., Rockford, IL 61109 / 815-874-8001; FAX: 815-874-8181

Competitor Corp. Inc., Appleton Business Center, 30 Tricnit Road Unit 16, New Ipswich, NH 03071 / 603-878-3891; FAX: 603-878-3950

Component Concepts, Inc., 530 S. Springbrook Dr., Newberg, OR 97132-7056 / 503-554-8095; FAX: 503-554-9370

Concealment Shop Inc., 617 W Kearney St., Ste. 205, Mesquite, TX 75149 / 972-289-8997; FAX: 972-289-4410 concealmentshop@email.msn.com www.theconcealmentshop.com

Concept Development Corp., 14715 N. 78th Way, Ste. 300, Scottsdale, AZ 85260 / 800-472-4405; FAX: 602-948-7560

Conetrol Scope Mounts, 10225 Hwy. 123 S., Seguin, TX 78155 / 830-379-3030 or 800-CONETROL; FAX: 830-379-3030

CONKKO, P.O. Box 40, Broomall, PA 19008 / 215-356-0711

Connecticut Shotgun Mfg. Co., P.O. Box 1692, 35 Woodland St., New Britain, CT 06051 / 860-225-6581; FAX: 860-832-8707

Connecticut Valley Classics (See CVC)

Conrad, C. A., 3964 Ebert St., Winston-Salem, NC 27127 / 919-788-5469

Cook Engineering Service, 891 Highbury Rd., Vict, 3133 AUSTRALIA

Cooper Arms, P.O. Box 114, Stevensville, MT 59870 / 406-777-5534; FAX: 406-777-5228

Cooper-Woodward, 3800 Pelican Rd., Helena, MT 59602 / 406-458-3800 dolymama@msn.com

Corbin Mfg. & Supply, Inc., 600 Industrial Circle, P.O. Box 2659, White City, OR 97503 / 541-826-5211; FAX: 541-826-8669

Cor-Bon Bullet & Ammo Co., 1311 Industry Rd., Sturgis, SD 57785 / 800-626-7266; FAX: 800-923-2666

Corkys Gun Clinic, 4401 Hot Springs Dr., Greeley, CO 80634-9226 / 970-330-0516

Corry, John, 861 Princeton Ct., Neshanic Station, NJ 08853 / 908-369-8019

Cosmi Americo & Figlio s.n.c., Via Flaminia 307, Ancona, ITALY / 071-888208; FAX: 39-071-887008+

Coulston Products, Inc., P.O. Box 30, 201 Ferry St. Ste. 212, Easton, PA 18044-0030 / 215-253-0167 or 800-445-9927; FAX: 215-252-1511

Cousin Bob's Mountain Products, 7119 Ohio River Blvd., Ben Avon, PA 15202 / 412-766-5114; FAX: 412-766-5114

Cox, Ed. C., RD 2, Box 192, Prosperity, PA 15329 / 412-228-4984

CP Bullets, 1310 Industrial Hwy. #5-6, South Hampton, PA 18966 / 215-953-7264; FAX: 215-953-7275

CQB Training, P.O. Box 1739, Manchester, MO 63011

Craftguard, 3624 Logan Ave., Waterloo, IA 50703 / 319-232-2959; FAX: 319-234-0804

Craig Custom Ltd., Research & Development, 629 E. 10th, Hutchinson, KS 67501 / 316-669-0601

Crandall Tool & Machine Co., 19163 21 Mile Rd., Tustin, MI 49688 / 616-829-4430

Creedmoor Sports, Inc., P.O. Box 1040, Oceanside, CA 92051 / 619-757-5529

Creek Side Metal & Woodcrafters, Fishers Hill, VA 22626 / 703-465-3903

Creekside Gun Shop Inc., Main St., Holcomb, NY 14469 / 716-657-6338; FAX: 716-657-7900

Creighton Audette, 19 Highland Circle, Springfield, VT 05156 / 802-885-2331

Crimson Trace Lasers, 1433 N.W. Quimby, Portland, OR 97209 / 800-442-2406; FAX: 503-627-0166 www.crimsontrace.com

Crit'R Call (See Rocky Mountain Wildlife Products)

Crosman Airguns, Rts. 5 and 20, E. Bloomfield, NY 14443 / 716-657-6161; FAX: 716-657-5405

Crosman Blades (See Coleman Co., Inc.)

Crosman Products of Canada Ltd., 1173 N. Service Rd. West, Oakville, ON L6M 2V9 CANADA / 905-827-1822

Crouse's Country Cover, P.O. Box 160, Storrs, CT 06268 / 860-423-8736

CRR, Inc./Marble's Inc., 420 Industrial Park, P.O. Box 111, Gladstone, MI 49837 / 906-428-3710; FAX: 906-428-3711

Crucelegui, Hermanos (See U.S. Importer-Mandall)

Cryo-Accurizing, Ms Melissa Sorenson, 2250 N. 1500 W., Ogden, UT 84404

Cubic Shot Shell Co., Inc., 98 Fatima Dr., Campbell, OH 44405 / 330-755-0349

Cullity Restoration, 209 Old Country Rd., East Sandwich, MA 02537 / 508-888-1147

Cumberland Arms, 514 Shafer Road, Manchester, TN 37355 / 800-797-8414

Cumberland Mountain Arms, P.O. Box 710, Winchester, TN 37398 / 615-967-8414; FAX: 615-967-9199

Cumberland States Arsenal, 1124 Palmyra Road, Clarksville, TN 37040

Cummings Bullets, 1417 Esperanza Way, Escondido, CA 92027

Cupp, Alana, Custom Engraver, P.O. Box 207, Annabella, UT 84711 / 801-896-4834

Curly Maple Stock Blanks (See Tiger-Hunt Gunstocks)

Curtis Cast Bullets, 527 W. Babcock St., Bozeman, MT 59715 / 406-587-8117; FAX: 406-587-8117

Curtis Custom Shop, RR1, Box 193A, Wallingford, KY 41093 / 703-659-4265

Curtis Gun Shop (See Curtis Cast Bullets)

Custom Arms Company, James R. Steger, 125 Lincoln Ave., P.O. Box 7212, Penndel, PA 19047 / 215-757-8710; FAX: 215-757-8710

Custom Bullets by Hoffman, 2604 Peconic Ave., Seaford, NY 11783

Custom Calls, 607 N. 5th St., Burlington, IA 52601 / 319-752-4465

Custom Checkering Service, Kathy Forster, 2124 SE Yamhill St., Portland, OR 97214 / 503-236-5874

Custom Chronograph, Inc., 5305 Reese Hill Rd., Sumas, WA 98295 / 360-988-7801

Custom Firearms Inc. (See Ahrends, Kim)

Custom Gun Products, 5021 W. Rosewood, Spokane, WA 99208 / 509-328-9340

Custom Gun Stocks, 3062 Turners Bend Rd., McMinnville, TN 37110 / 615-668-3912

Custom Products (See Jones Custom Products)

Custom Quality Products, Inc., 345 W. Girard Ave., P.O. Box 71129, Madison Heights, MI 48071 / 810-585-1616; FAX: 810-585-0644

Custom Riflestocks, Inc., Michael M. Kokolus, 7005 Herber Rd., New Tripoli, PA 18066 / 610-298-3013; FAX: 610-298-2431 mkokolus@prodigy.net

Custom Single Shot Rifles, Jim Hamilton, 9651 Meadows Ln., Guthrie, OK 73044 / 405-282-3634

Custom Tackle and Ammo, P.O. Box 1886, Farmington, NM 87499 / 505-632-3539

Cutco Cutlery, P.O. Box 810, Olean, NY 14760 / 716-372-3111

CVA, 5988 Peachtree Corners East, Norcross, GA 30071 / 800-251-9412; FAX: 404-242-8546

CVC, 5988 Peachtree Crns East, Norcross, GA 30071

Cylinder & Slide, Inc., William R. Laughridge, 245 E. 4th St., Fremont, NE 68025 / 402-721-4277; FAX: 402-721-0263

CZ USA, P.O. Box 171073, Kansas City, KS 66117 / 913-321-1811; FAX: 913-321-4901

D

D&D Gunsmiths, Ltd., 363 E. Elmwood, Troy, MI 48083 / 810-583-1512; FAX: 810-583-1524

D&H Precision Tooling, 7522 Barnard Mill Rd., Ringwood, IL 60072 / 815-653-4011

D&H Prods. Co., Inc., 465 Denny Rd., Valencia, PA 16059 / 412-898-2840 or 800-776-0281; FAX: 412-898-2013

D&J Bullet Co. & Custom Gun Shop, Inc., 426 Ferry St., Russell, KY 41169 / 606-836-2663; FAX: 606-836-2663

D&L Industries (See D.J. Marketing)

D&L Sports, P.O. Box 651, Gillette, WY 82717 / 307-686-4008

D&R Distributing, 308 S.E. Valley St., Myrtle Creek, OR 97457 / 503-863-6850

D.C.C. Enterprises, 259 Wynburn Ave., Athens, GA 30601

D.D. Custom Stocks, R.H. "Dick" Devereaux, 5240 Mule Deer Dr., Colorado Springs, CO 80919 / 719-548-8468

D.J. Marketing, 10602 Horton Ave., Downey, CA 90241 / 310-806-0891; FAX: 310-806-6231

Dade Screw Machine Products, 2319 NW 7th Ave., Miami, FL 33127 / 305-573-5050

Daewoo Precision Industries Ltd., 34-3 Yeoeuido-Dong, Yeongdeungoo-GU 15th Fl., Seoul, KOREA

Daisy Mfg. Co., P.O. Box 220, Rogers, AR 72757 / 501-621-4210; FAX: 501-636-0573

Dakota (See U.S. Importer-EMF Co., Inc.)

Dakota Arms, Inc., HC 55, Box 326, Sturgis, SD 57785 / 605-347-4686; FAX: 605-347-4459

Dakota Corp., 77 Wales St., P.O. Box 543, Rutland, VT 05701 / 802-775-6062 or 800-451-4167; FAX: 802-773-3919

Da-Mar Gunsmith's Inc., 102 1st St., Solvay, NY 13209

Damascus-U.S.A., 149 Deans Farm Rd., Tyner, NC 27980 / 252-221-2010; FAX: 252-221-2009

Dan Wesson Firearms, 119 Kemper Ln., Norwich, NY 13815 / 607-336-1174; FAX: 607-336-2730

Danforth, Mikael (See Vektor USA)

Dangler, Homer L., 2870 Lee Marie Dr., Adrian, MI 49221 / 517-547-6745

Danner Shoe Mfg. Co., 12722 NE Airport Way, Portland, OR 97230 / 503-251-1100 or 800-345-0430; FAX: 503-251-1119

Dan's Whetstone Co., Inc., 130 Timbs Pl., Hot Springs, AR 71913 / 501-767-1616; FAX: 501-767-9598 questions@danswhetstone.com danswhetstone.com

Danuser Machine Co., 550 E. Third St., P.O. Box 368, Fulton, MO 65251 / 573-642-2246; FAX: 573-642-2240

Dara-Nes, Inc. (See Nesci Enterprises, Inc.)

Darlington Gun Works, Inc., P.O. Box 698, 516 S. 52 Bypass, Darlington, SC 29532 / 803-393-3931

Darwin Hensley Gunmaker, P.O. Box 329, Brightwood, OR 97011 / 503-622-5411

Data Tech Software Systems, 19312 East Eldorado Dr., Aurora, CO 80013

Datumtech Corp., 2275 Wehrle Dr., Buffalo, NY 14221

Dave Norin Schrank's Smoke & Gun, 2010 Washington St., Waukegan, IL 60085 / 708-662-4034

Dave's Gun Shop, 555 Wood Street, Powell, WY 82435 / 307-754-9724

David Clark Co., Inc., P.O. Box 15054, Worcester, MA 01615-0054 / 508-756-6216; FAX: 508-753-5827 sales@davidclark.com davidclark.com

David Condon, Inc., 109 E. Washington St., Middleburg, VA 22117 / 703-687-5642

David Miller Co., 3131 E. Greenlee Rd., Tucson, AZ 85716 / 520-326-3117

David R. Chicoine, 19 Key St., Eastport, ME 04631 / 207-853-4116 gnpress@nemaine.com

David W. Schwartz Custom Guns, 2505 Waller St., Eau Claire, WI 54703 / 715-832-1735

Davide Pedersoli and Co., Via Artigiani 57, Gardone VT, Brescia 25063, ITALY / 030-8912402; FAX: 030-8911019

Davis, Don, 1619 Heights, Katy, TX 77493 / 713-391-3090

MANUFACTURER'S DIRECTORY

Davis Industries, 15150 Sierra Bonita Ln., Chino, CA 91710 / 909-597-4726; FAX: 909-393-9771
Davis Products, Mike, 643 Loop Dr., Moses Lake, WA 98837 / 509-765-6178 or 509-766-7281
Daystate Ltd., Birch House Lanee, Cotes Heath Staffs, ST15.022, ENGLAND / 01782-791755; FAX: 01782-791617
Dayton Traister, 4778 N. Monkey Hill Rd., P.O. Box 593, Oak Harbor, WA 98277 / 360-679-4657; FAX: 360-675-1114
DBI Books Division of Krause Publications, 700 E State St., Iola, WI 54990-0001 / 715-445-2214
D-Boone Ent., Inc., 5900 Colwyn Dr., Harrisburg, PA 17109
de Coux, Pete (See Cartridge Transfer Group)
Dead Eye's Sport Center, 76 Baer Rd., Shickshinny, PA 18655 / 570-256-7432 deadeyeprizz@aol.com
Decker Shooting Products, 1729 Laguna Ave., Schofield, WI 54476 / 715-359-5873; FAX: 715-355-7319
Deepeeka Exports Pvt. Ltd., D-78, Saket, Meerut-250-006, INDIA / 011-91-121-640363; FAX: 011-91-121-640988 deepeeka@poboxes.com www.deepeeka.com
Defense Training International, Inc., 749 S. Lemay, Ste. A3-337, Ft. Collins, CO 80524 / 303-482-2520; FAX: 303-482-0548
deHaas Barrels, RR 3, Box 77, Ridgeway, MO 64481 / 816-872-6308
Del Rey Products, P.O. Box 5134, Playa Del Rey, CA 90296-5134 / 213-823-0494
Delhi Gun House, 1374 Kashmere Gate, Delhi, 0110 006 INDIA; FAX: 91-11-2917344
Delorge, Ed, 6734 W. Main, Houma, LA 70360 / 504-223-0206
Del-Sports, Inc., Box 685, Main St., Margaretville, NY 12455 / 845-586-4103; FAX: 845-586-4105
Delta Arms Ltd., P.O. Box 1000, Delta, VT 84624-1000
Delta Enterprises, 284 Hagemann Dr., Livermore, CA 94550
Delta Frangible Ammunition LLC, P.O. Box 2350, Stafford, VA 22555-2350 / 540-720-5778 or 800-339-1933; FAX: 540-720-5667 dfa@dfanet.com www.dfanet.com
Dem-Bart Checkering Tools, Inc., 6807 Bickford Ave., Old Hwy. 2, Snohomish, WA 98290 / 360-568-7356; FAX: 360-568-1798 dembartco.com
Denver Instrument Co., 6542 Fig St., Arvada, CO 80004 / 800-321-1135 or 303-431-7255; FAX: 303-423-4831
DeSantis Holster & Leather Goods, Inc., P.O. Box 2039, 149 Denton Ave., New Hyde Park, NY 11040-0701 / 516-354-8000; FAX: 516-354-7501
Desert Mountain Mfg., P.O. Box 130184, Coram, MT 59913 / 800-477-0762 or 406-387-5361; FAX: 406-387-5361
Detroit-Armor Corp., 720 Industrial Dr. No. 112, Cary, IL 60013 / 708-639-7666; FAX: 708-639-7694
Devereaux, R.H. "Dick" (See D.D. Custom Stocks)
Dewey Mfg. Co., Inc., J., P.O. Box 2014, Southbury, CT 06488 / 203-264-3064; FAX: 203-262-6907 deweyrods@worldnet.att.net www.deweyrods.com
DGR Custom Rifles, 4191 37th Ave SE, Tappen, ND 58487 / 701-327-8135
DGS, Inc., Dale A. Storey, 1117 E. 12th, Casper, WY 82601 / 307-237-2414; FAX: 307-237-2414 dalest@trib.com www.dgsrifle.com
DHB Products, P.O. Box 3092, Alexandria, VA 22302 / 703-836-2648
Diamond Machining Technology, Inc. (See DMT)
Diamond Mfg. Co., P.O. Box 174, Wyoming, PA 18644 / 800-233-9601
Diana (See U.S. Importer - Dynamit Nobel-RWS, Inc.)
Dibble, Derek A., 555 John Downey Dr., New Britain, CT 06051 / 203-224-2630
Dick Marple & Associates, 21 Dartmouth St., Hooksett, NH 03106 / 603-627-1837; FAX: 603-627-1837
Dietz Gun Shop & Range, Inc., 421 Range Rd., New Braunfels, TX 78132 / 210-885-4662
Dilliott Gunsmithing, Inc., 657 Scarlett Rd., Dandridge, TN 37725 / 865-397-9204 gunsmithd@aol.com dilliottgunsmithing.com
Dillon, Ed, 1035 War Eagle Dr. N., Colorado Springs, CO 80919 / 719-598-4929; FAX: 719-598-4929
Dillon Precision Products, Inc., 8009 East Dillon's Way, Scottsdale, AZ 85260 / 480-948-8009 or 800-762-3845; FAX: 480-998-2786 sales@dillonprecision.com www.dillonprecision.com
Dina Arms Corporation, P.O. Box 46, Royersford, PA 19468 / 610-287-0266; FAX: 610-287-0266
Division Lead Co., 7742 W. 61st Pl., Summit, IL 60502
Dixie Gun Works, Inc., Hwy. 51 South, Union City, TN 38261 / order 800-238-6785; FAX: 901-885-0440
Dixon Muzzleloading Shop, Inc., 9952 Kunkels Mill Rd., Kempton, PA 19529 / 610-756-6271 dixonmuzzleloading.com
DKT, Inc., 14623 Vera Dr., Union, MI 49130-9744 / 800-741-7083 orders; FAX: 616-641-2015
DLO Mfg., 10807 SE Foster Ave., Arcadia, FL 33821-7304

DMT--Diamond Machining Technology Inc., 85 Hayes Memorial Dr., Marlborough, MA 01752; FAX: 508-485-3924
Dohring Bullets, 100 W. 8 Mile Rd., Ferndale, MI 48220
Dolbare, Elizabeth, P.O. Box 222, Sunburst, MT 59482-0222
Domino, P.O. Box 108, 20019 Settimo Milanese, Milano, ITALY / 1-39-2-33512040; FAX: 1-39-2-33511587
Donnelly, C. P., 405 Kubli Rd., Grants Pass, OR 97527 / 541-846-6604
Doskocil Mfg. Co., Inc., P.O. Box 1246, 4209 Barnett, Arlington, TX 76017 / 817-467-5116; FAX: 817-472-9810
Douglas Barrels Inc., 5504 Big Tyler Rd., Charleston, WV 25313-1398 / 304-776-1341; FAX: 304-776-8560
Downsizer Corp., P.O. Box 710316, Santee, CA 92072-0316 / 619-448-5510; FAX: 619-448-5780 www.downsizer.com
Dr. O's Products Ltd., P.O. Box 111, Niverville, NY 12130 / 518-784-3333; FAX: 518-784-2800
Drain, Mark, SE 3211 Kamilche Point Rd., Shelton, WA 98584 / 206-426-5452
Dremel Mfg. Co., 4915-21st St., Racine, WI 53406
Dressel Jr, Paul G, 209 N. 92nd Ave., Yakima, WA 98908 / 509-966-9233; FAX: 509-966-3365 dressels@nwinfo.net dressels.com
Dri-Slide, Inc., 411 N. Darling, Fremont, MI 49412 / 616-924-3950
Dropkick, 1460 Washington Blvd., Williamsport, PA 17701 / 717-326-6561; FAX: 717-326-4950
DTM International, Inc., 40 Joslyn Rd., P.O. Box 5, Lake Orion, MI 48362 / 313-693-6670
Duane A. Hobbie Gunsmithing, 2412 Pattie Ave., Wichita, KS 67216 / 316-264-8266
Duane's Gun Repair (See DGR Custom Rifles)
Dubber, Michael W., P.O. Box 312, Evansville, IN 47702 / 812-424-9000; FAX: 812-424-6551
Duck Call Specialists, P.O. Box 124, Jerseyville, IL 62052 / 618-498-9855
Duffy, Charles E. (See Guns Antique & Modern DBA), Williams Ln., P.O. Box 2, West Hurley, NY 12491 / 914-679-2997
Du-Lite Corp., 171 River Rd., Middletown, CT 06457 / 203-347-2505; FAX: 203-347-9404
Dumoulin, Ernest, Rue Florent Boclinville 8-10, 13-4041, Votten, BELGIUM / 41 27 78 92
Duncan's Gun Works, Inc., 1619 Grand Ave., San Marcos, CA 92069 / 619-727-0515
Dunham Boots, 1 Keuka Business Park #300, Penn Yan, NY 14527-8995 / 802-254-2316
Duofold, Inc., RD 3 Rt. 309, Valley Square Mall, Tamaqua, PA 18252 / 717-386-2666; FAX: 717-386-3652
Dybala Gun Shop, P.O. Box 1024, FM 3156, Bay City, TX 77414 / 409-245-0866
Dykstra, Doug, 411 N. Darling, Fremont, MI 49412 / 616-924-3950
Dynalite Products, Inc., 215 S. Washington St., Greenfield, OH 45123 / 513-981-2124
Dynamit Nobel-RWS, Inc., 81 Ruckman Rd., Closter, NJ 07624 / 201-767-7971; FAX: 201-767-1589

E

E&L Mfg., Inc., 4177 Riddle By Pass Rd., Riddle, OR 97469 / 541-874-2137; FAX: 541-874-3107
E. Arthur Brown Co., 3404 Pawnee Dr., Alexandria, MN 56308 / 320-762-8847
E.A.A. Corp., P.O. Box 1299, Sharpes, FL 32959 / 407-639-4842 or 800-536-4442; FAX: 407-639-7006
Eagan, Donald V., P.O. Box 196, Benton, PA 17814 / 717-925-6134
Eagle Arms, Inc. (See ArmaLite, Inc.)
Eagle Grips, Eagle Business Center, 460 Randy Rd., Carol Stream, IL 60188 / 800-323-6144 or 708-260-0400; FAX: 708-260-0486
Eagle Imports, Inc., 1750 Brielle Ave., Unit B1, Wanamassa, NJ 07712 / 908-493-0333
E-A-R, Inc., Div. of Cabot Safety Corp., 5457 W. 79th St., Indianapolis, IN 46268 / 800-327-3431; FAX: 800-488-8007
EAW (See U.S. Importer-New England Custom Gun Service)
Echols & Co., D'Arcy, P.O. Box 421, Millville, UT 84326 / 435-755-6812
Eckelman Gunsmithing, 3125 133rd St. SW, Fort Ripley, MN 56449 / 218-829-3176
Eclectic Technologies, Inc., 45 Grandview Dr., Ste. A, Farmington, CT 06034
Ed Brown Products, Inc., 43825 Muldrow Trail, Perry, MO 63462 / 573-565-3261; FAX: 573-565-2791
Ed King Office, P.O. Box 1242, Bloomington, IL 61701
Ed Brown Products, Inc., 43825 Muldrow Trail, Perry, MO 63462 / 573-565-3261; FAX: 573-565-2791

Edenpine, Inc. c/o Six Enterprises, Inc., 320 D Turtle Creek Ct., San Jose, CA 95125 / 408-999-0201; FAX: 408-999-0216
EdgeCraft Corp., S. Weiner, 825 Southwood Road, Avondale, PA 19311 / 610-268-0500 or 800-342-3255; FAX: 610-268-3545 www.edgecraft.com
Edmisten Co., P.O. Box 1293, Boone, NC 28607
Edmund Scientific Co., 101 E. Gloucester Pike, Barrington, NJ 08033 / 609-543-6250
Ednar, Inc., 2-4-8 Kayabacho, Nihonbashi Chuo-ku, Tokyo, JAPAN / 81(Japan)-3-3667-1651; FAX: 81-3-3661-8113
Eezox, Inc., P.O. Box 772, Waterford, CT 06385-0772 / 800-462-3331; FAX: 860-447-3484
Effebi SNC-Dr. Franco Beretta, via Rossa, 4, 25062, ITALY / 030-2751955; FAX: 030-2180414
Efficient Machinery Co., 12878 NE 15th Pl., Bellevue, WA 98005
Eggleston, Jere D., 400 Saluda Ave., Columbia, SC 29205 / 803-799-3402
EGW Evolution Gun Works, 4050 B-8 Skyron Dr., Doylestown, PA 18901 / 215-348-9892; FAX: 215-348-1056
Eichelberger Bullets, Wm., 158 Crossfield Rd., King Of Prussia, PA 19406
Ekol Leather Care, P.O. Box 2652, West Lafayette, IN 47906 / 317-463-2250; FAX: 317-463-7004
El Dorado Leather (c/o Dill), P.O. Box 566, Benson, AZ 85602 / 520-586-4791; FAX: 520-586-4791
El Paso Saddlery Co., P.O. Box 27194, El Paso, TX 79926 / 915-544-2233; FAX: 915-544-2535
Eldorado Cartridge Corp. (See PMC/Eldorado Cartridge Corp.)
Electro Prismatic Collimators, Inc., 1441 Manatt St., Lincoln, NE 68521
Electronic Shooters Protection, Inc., 11997 W. 85th Pl., Arvada, CO 80005 / 800-797-7791; FAX: 303-456-7179
Electronic Trigger Systems, Inc., P.O. Box 13, 230 Main St. S., Hector, MN 55342 / 320-848-2760; FAX: 320-848-2760
Eley Ltd., P.O. Box 705, Witton, Birmingham, B6 7UT ENGLAND / 021-356-8899; FAX: 021-331-4173
Elite Ammunition, P.O. Box 3251, Oakbrook, IL 60522 / 708-366-9006
Elk River, Inc., 1225 Paonia St., Colorado Springs, CO 80915 / 719-574-4407
Elkhorn Bullets, P.O. Box 5293, Central Point, OR 97502 / 541-826-7440
Ellett Bros., 267 Columbia Ave., P.O. Box 128, Chapin, SC 29036 / 803-345-3751 or 800-845-3711; FAX: 803-345-1820
Ellicott Arms, Inc./Woods Pistolsmithing, 8390 Sunset Dr., Ellicott City, MD 21043 / 410-465-7979
Elliott Inc., G. W., 514 Burnside Ave., East Hartford, CT 06108 / 203-289-5741; FAX: 203-289-3137
EMAP USA, 6420 Wilshire Blvd., Los Angeles, CA 90048 / 213-782-2000; FAX: 213-782-2867
Emerging Technologies, Inc. (See Laseraim Technologies, Inc.)
EMF Co., Inc., 1900 E. Warner Ave., Ste. 1-D, Santa Ana, CA 92705 / 949-261-6611; FAX: 949-756-0133
Empire Cutlery Corp., 12 Kruger Ct., Clifton, NJ 07013 / 201-472-5155; FAX: 201-779-0759
English, Inc., A.G., 708 S. 12th St., Broken Arrow, OK 74012 / 918-251-3399 agenglish@webzone.net www.agenglish.com
Engraving Artistry, 36 Alto Rd., Burlington, CT 06013 / 203-673-6837 bobburt44@hotmail.com
Enguix Import-Export, Alpujarras 58, Alzira, Valencia, SPAIN / (96) 241 43 95; FAX: (96) (241 43 95
Enhanced Presentations, Inc., 5929 Market St., Wilmington, NC 28405 / 910-799-1622; FAX: 910-799-5004
Enlow, Charles, 895 Box, Beaver, OK 73932 / 405-625-4487
Entre'prise Arms, Inc., 15861 Business Center Dr., Irwindale, CA 91706
EPC, 1441 Manatt St., Lincoln, NE 68521 / 402-476-3946
Epps, Ellwood (See "Gramps" Antique Cartridges)
Erhardt, Dennis, 4508 N Montana Ave., Helena, MT 59602-7237 / 406-442-4533
Erma Werke GmbH, Johan Ziegler St., 13/15/FeldiglSt., D-8060 Dachau, GERMANY
Eskridge Rifles, Steven Eskridge, 218 N. Emerson, Mart, TX 76664 / 817-876-3544
Eskridge, Steven (See Eskridge Rifles)
Essex Arms, P.O. Box 363, Island Pond, VT 05846 / 802-723-6203; FAX: 802-723-6203
Essex Metals, 1000 Brighton St., Union, NJ 07083 / 800-282-8369
Estate Cartridge, Inc., 12161 FM 830, Willis, TX 77378 / 409-856-7277; FAX: 409-856-5486
Euber Bullets, No. Orwell Rd., Orwell, VT 05760 / 802-948-2621
Euroarms of America, Inc., P.O. Box 3277, Winchester, VA 22604 / 540-662-1863; FAX: 540-662-4464

Euro-Imports, 905 West Main St. Ste. E, El Cajon, CA 92020 / 619-442-7005; FAX: 619-442-7005
European American Armory Corp. (See E.A.A. Corp.)
Evans Engraving, Robert, 332 Vine St., Oregon City, OR 97045 / 503-656-5693
Eversull Co., Inc., K., 1 Tracemont, Boyce, LA 71409 / 318-793-8728; FAX: 318-793-5483 bestguns@aol.com
Excalibur Electro Optics Inc., P.O. Box 400, Fogelsville, PA 18051-0400 / 610-391-9105; FAX: 610-391-9220
Excel Industries Inc., 4510 Carter Ct., Chino, CA 91710 / 909-627-2404; FAX: 909-627-7817
Executive Protection Institute, P.O. Box 802, Berryville, VA 22611 / 540-955-1128 rwk@crosslink.com
Eyster Heritage Gunsmiths, Inc., Ken, 6441 Bishop Rd., Centerburg, OH 43011 / 614-625-6131
Eze-Lap Diamond Prods., P.O. Box 2229, 15164 West State St., Westminster, CA 92683 / 714-847-1555; FAX: 714-897-0280
E-Z-Way Systems, P.O. Box 4310, Newark, OH 43058-4310 / 740-345-6645 or 800-848-2072; FAX: 740-345-6600

F

F.A.I.R. Tecni-Mec s.n.c. di Isidoro Rizzini & C., Via Gitti, 41 Zona Industrial 25060, Marcheno (Brescia), ITALY / 030/861162; FAX: 030/8610179 info@fair.it www.fair.it
Fabarm S.p.A., Via Averolda 31, 25039 Travagliato, Brescia, ITALY / 030-6863629; FAX: 030-6863684
Fagan & Co. Inc., 22952 15 Mile Rd., Clinton Township, MI 48035 / 810-465-4637; FAX: 810-792-6996
Fair Game International, P.O. Box 77234-34053, Houston, TX 77234 / 713-941-6269
Faith Associates, P.O. Box 549, Flat Rock, NC 28731-0549 / 828-692-1916; FAX: 828-697-6827
Falcon Industries, Inc., P.O. Box 1060, Tijeras, NM 87059 / 505-281-3783
Far North Outfitters, Box 1252, Bethel, AK 99559
Farm Form Decoys, Inc., 1602 Biovu, P.O. Box 748, Galveston, TX 77553 / 409-744-0762 or 409-765-6361; FAX: 409-765-8513
Farmer-Dressel, Sharon, 209 N. 92nd Ave., Yakima, WA 98908 / 509-966-9233; FAX: 509-966-3365 dressels@nwinfo.net dressels.com
Farr Studio, Inc., 1231 Robinhood Rd., Greeneville, TN 37743 / 615-638-8825
Farrar Tool Co., Inc., 12150 Bloomfield Ave., Ste. E, Santa Fe Springs, CA 90670 / 310-863-4367; FAX: 310-863-5123
Faulhaber Wildlocker, Dipl.-Ing. Norbert Wittasek, Seilergasse 2 A-1010 Wien, Wien, AUSTRIA / OM-43-1-5137001; FAX: OM-43-1-5137001
Faulk's Game Call Co., Inc., 616 18th St., Lake Charles, LA 70601 / 318-436-9726; FAX: 318-494-7205
Faust Inc., T. G., 544 Minor St., Reading, PA 19602 / 610-375-8549; FAX: 610-375-4488
Fausti Cav. Stefano & Figlie snc, Via Martiri Dell Indipendenza, 70, Marcheno, 25060 ITALY
Fautheree, Andy, P.O. Box 4607, Pagosa Springs, CO 81157 / 970-731-5003; FAX: 970-731-5009
Feather, Flex Decoys, 4500 Doniphan Dr., Neosho, MO 64850 / 318-746-8596; FAX: 318-742-4815
Federal Arms Corp. of America, 7928 University Ave., Fridley, MN 55432 / 612-780-8780; FAX: 612-780-8780
Federal Cartridge Co., 900 Ehlen Dr., Anoka, MN 55303 / 612-323-2300; FAX: 612-323-2506
Federal Champion Target Co., 232 Industrial Parkway, Richmond, IN 47374 / 800-441-4971; FAX: 317-966-7747
Federated-Fry (See Fry Metals)
FEG, Budapest, Soroksariut 158, H-1095, HUNGARY
Feken, Dennis, Rt. 2, Box 124, Perry, OK 73077 / 405-336-5611
Felk, Inc., 2121 Castlebridge Rd., Midlothian, VA 23113 / 804-794-3744
Fellowes, Ted, Beaver Lodge, 9245 16th Ave. SW, Seattle, WA 98106 / 206-763-1698
Ferguson, Bill, P.O. Box 1238, Sierra Vista, AZ 85636 / 520-458-5321; FAX: 520-458-9125
FERLIB, Via Costa 46, 25063, Gardone V.T., ITALY / 30-89-12-586; FAX: 30-89-12-586
Ferris Firearms, 7110 F.M. 1863, Bulverde, TX 78163 / 210-980-4424
Fibron Products, Inc., P.O. Box 430, Buffalo, NY 14209-0430 / 716-886-2378; FAX: 716-886-2394
Fieldsport Ltd., Bryan Bilinski, 3313 W South Airport Rd., Traverse City, MI 49684 / 616-933-0767
Fiocchi Munizioni S.p.A. (See U.S. Importer-Fiocchi)
Fiocchi of America Inc., 5030 Fremont Rd., Ozark, MO 65721 / 417-725-4118 or 800-721-2666; FAX: 417-725-1039
Firearms Co Ltd/Alpine (See U.S. Importer-Mandall Shooting Supplies Inc.)

Firearms Engraver's Guild of America, 332 Vine St., Oregon City, OR 97045 / 503-656-5693
Firearms International, 5709 Hartsdale, Houston, TX 77036 / 713-460-2447
First Inc., Jack, 1201 Turbine Dr., Rapid City, SD 57701 / 605-343-9544; FAX: 605-343-9420
Fish Mfg. Gunsmith Sptg. Co., Marshall, Rd. Box 2439, Rt. 22 N, Westport, NY 12993 / 518-962-4897; FAX: 518-962-4897
Fisher, Jerry A., 631 Crane Mt. Rd., Big Fork, MT 59911 / 406-837-2722
Fisher Custom Firearms, 2199 S. Kittredge Way, Aurora, CO 80013 / 303-755-3710
Fisher Enterprises, Inc., 1071 4th Ave. S., Ste. 303, Edmonds, WA 98020-4143 / 206-771-5382
Fisher, R. Kermit (See Fisher Enterprises, Inc.)
Fitz Pistol Grip Co., P.O. Box 744, Lewiston, CA 96052-0744 / 916-778-0240
Flambeau Products Corp., 15981 Valplast Rd., Middlefield, OH 44062 / 216-632-1631; FAX: 216-632-1581
Flannery Engraving Co., Jeff W, 11034 Riddles Run Rd., Union, KY 41091 / 606-384-3127
Flayderman & Co., Inc., P.O. Box 2446, Ft. Lauderdale, FL 33303 / 954-761-8855
Fleming Firearms, 7720 E. 126th St. N, Collinsville, OK 74021-7016 / 918-665-3624
Flintlocks, Etc., 160 Rossiter Rd., P.O. Box 181, Richmond, MA 01254 / 413-698-3822; FAX: 413-698-3866 flintetc@vgernet.net pedersoli
Flitz International Inc., 821 Mohr Ave., Waterford, WI 53185 / 414-534-5898; FAX: 414-534-2991
Flores Publications Inc., J. (See Action Direct Inc.)
Fluoramics, Inc., 18 Industrial Ave., Mahwah, NJ 07430 / 800-922-0075; FAX: 201-825-7035
Flynn's Custom Guns, P.O. Box 7461, Alexandria, LA 71306 / 318-455-7130
FN Manufacturing, P.O. Box 24257, Columbia, SC 29224 / 803-736-0522
Folks, Donald E., 205 W. Lincoln St., Pontiac, IL 61764 / 815-844-7901
Foothills Video Productions, Inc., P.O. Box 651, Spartanburg, SC 29304 / 803-573-7023 or 800-782-5358
Foredom Electric Co., Rt. 6, 16 Stony Hill Rd., Bethel, CT 06801 / 203-792-8622
Forgett, Valmore (See Navy Arms Company)
Forgreens Tool Mfg., Inc., P.O. Box 955, Robert Lee, TX 76945-0955 / 915-453-2800; FAX: 915-453-2460
Forkin Arms, 205 10th Ave SW, White Sulphur Spring, MT 59645 / 406-547-2344; FAX: 406-547-2456
Forrest Inc., Tom, P.O. Box 326, Lakeside, CA 92040 / 619-561-5800; FAX: 619-561-0227
Forrest Tool Co., P.O. Box 768, 44380 Gordon Ln., Mendocino, CA 95460 / 707-937-2141; FAX: 717-937-1817
Forster, Kathy (See Custom Checkering Service)
Forster, Larry L., P.O. Box 212, 220 First St. NE, Gwinner, ND 58040-0212 / 701-678-2475
Forster Products, 310 E Lanark Ave., Lanark, IL 61046 / 815-493-6360; FAX: 815-493-2371
Fort Hill Gunstocks, 12807 Fort Hill Rd., Hillsboro, OH 45133 / 513-466-2763
Fort Knox Security Products, 1051 N. Industrial Park Rd., Orem, UT 84057 / 801-224-7233 or 800-821-5216; FAX: 801-226-5493
Fort Worth Firearms, 2006-B, Martin Luther King Fwy., Ft. Worth, TX 76104-6303 / 817-536-0718; FAX: 817-535-0290
Forthofer's Gunsmithing & Knifemaking, 5535 U.S. Hwy 93S, Whitefish, MT 59937-8411 / 406-862-2674
Fortune Products, Inc., 205 Hickory Creek Rd., Marble Falls, TX 78654 / 210-693-6111; FAX: 210-693-6394
Forty Five Ranch Enterprises, Box 1080, Miami, OK 74355-1080 / 918-542-5875
Foster (See Accuracy International)
Fountain Products, 492 Prospect Ave., West Springfield, MA 01089 / 413-781-4651; FAX: 413-733-8217
4-D Custom Die Co., 711 N. Sandusky St., P.O. Box 889, Mt. Vernon, OH 43050-0889 / 740-397-7214; FAX: 740-397-6600 info@ch4d.com ch4d.com
Fowler Bullets, 806 Dogwood Dr., Gastonia, NC 28054 / 704-867-3259
Fowler, Bob (See Black Powder Products)
Fox River Mills, Inc., P.O. Box 298, 227 Poplar St., Osage, IA 50461 / 515-732-3798; FAX: 515-732-5128
Foy Custom Bullets, 104 Wells Ave., Daleville, AL 36322
Francesca, Inc., 3115 Old Ranch Rd., San Antonio, TX 78217 / 512-826-2584; FAX: 512-826-8211
Franchi S.p.A., Via del Serpente 12, 25131, Brescia, ITALY / 030-3581833; FAX: 030-3581554

Francotte & Cie S.A. Auguste, rue de Trois Juin 109, 4400 Herstal-Liege, BELGIUM / 32-4-248-13-18; FAX: 32-4-948-11-79
Frank Custom Classic Arms, Ron, 7131 Richland Rd., Ft Worth, TX 76118 / 817-284-9300; FAX: 817-284-9300
Frank E. Hendricks Master Engravers, Inc., HC03, Box 434, Dripping Springs, TX 78620 / 512-858-7828
Frank Knives, 13868 NW Keleka Pl., Seal Rock, OR 97376 / 541-563-3041; FAX: 541-563-3041
Frank Mittermeier, Inc., P.O. Box 2G, 3577 E. Tremont Ave., Bronx, NY 10465 / 718-828-3843
Frankonia Jagd Hofmann & Co., D-97064 Wurzburg, Wurzburg, GERMANY / 09302-200; FAX: 09302-20200
Fred F. Wells/Wells Sport Store, 110 N Summit St., Prescott, AZ 86301 / 520-445-3655
Freedom Arms, Inc., P.O. Box 150, Freedom, WY 83120 / 307-883-2468 or 800-833-4432; FAX: 307-883-2005
Freeman Animal Targets, 5519 East County Road, 100 South, Plainsfield, IN 46168 / 317-272-2663; FAX: 317-272-2674 signs@indy.net www.freemansigns.com
Fremont Tool Works, 1214 Prairie, Ford, KS 67842 / 316-369-2327
French, Artistic Engraving, J. R., 1712 Creek Ridge Ct., Irving, TX 75060 / 214-254-2654
Frielich Police Equipment, 211 East 21st St., New York, NY 10010 / 212-254-3045
Front Sight Firearms Training Institute, P.O. Box 2619, Aptos, CA 95001 / 800-987-7719; FAX: 408-684-2137
Frontier, 2910 San Bernardo, Laredo, TX 78040 / 956-723-5409; FAX: 956-723-1774
Frontier Arms Co., Inc., 401 W. Rio Santa Cruz, Green Valley, AZ 85614-3932
Frontier Products Co., 2401 Walker Rd., Roswell, NM 88201-8950 / 614-262-9357
Frontier Safe Co., 3201 S. Clinton St., Fort Wayne, IN 46806 / 219-744-7233; FAX: 219-744-6678
Frost Cutlery Co., P.O. Box 22636, Chattanooga, TN 37422 / 615-894-6079; FAX: 615-894-9576
Fry Metals, 4100 6th Ave., Altoona, PA 16602 / 814-946-1611
Fujinon, Inc., 10 High Point Dr., Wayne, NJ 07470 / 201-633-5600; FAX: 201-633-5216
Fullmer, Geo. M., 2499 Mavis St., Oakland, CA 94601 / 510-533-4193
Fulmer's Antique Firearms, Chet, P.O. Box 792, Rt 2 Buffalo Lake, Detroit Lakes, MN 56501 / 218-847-7712
Fulton Armory, 8725 Bollman Place No. 1, Savage, MD 20763 / 301-490-9485; FAX: 301-490-9547
Furr Arms, 91 N. 970 W., Orem, UT 84057 / 801-226-3877; FAX: 801-226-3877
FWB, Neckarstrasse 43, 78727, Oberndorf a. N., GERMANY / 07423-814-0; FAX: 07423-814-89

G

G&H Decoys, Inc., P.O. Box 1208, Hwy. 75 North, Henryetta, OK 74437 / 918-652-3314; FAX: 918-652-3400
G.C.C.T., 4455 Torrance Blvd., Ste. 453, Torrance, CA 90503-4398
G.G. & G., 3602 E. 42nd Stravenue, Tucson, AZ 85713 / 520-748-7167; FAX: 520-748-7583
G.H. Enterprises Ltd., Bag 10, Okotoks, AB T0L 1T0 CANADA / 403-938-6070
G.U. Inc. (See U.S. Importer for New SKB Arms Co.)
G.W. Elliott, Inc., 514 Burnside Ave., East Hartford, CT 06108 / 203-289-5741; FAX: 203-289-3137
G96 Products Co., Inc., 85 5th Ave., Bldg #6, Paterson, NJ 07544 / 973-684-4050; FAX: 973-684-4050
Gage Manufacturing, 663 W. 7th St., A, San Pedro, CA 90731 / 310-832-3546
Gaillard Barrels, P.O. Box 21, Pathlow, SK S0K 3B0 CANADA / 306-752-3769; FAX: 306-752-5969
Gain Twist Barrel Co. Rifle Works and Armory, 707 12th Street, Cody, WY 82414 / 307-587-4919; FAX: 307-527-6097
Galati International, P.O. Box 10, 616 Burley Ridge Rd., Wesco, MO 65586 / 573-775-2308; FAX: 573-775-4308 support@galatiinternational.com www.galatiinternational.com
Galaxy Imports Ltd., Inc., P.O. Box 3361, Victoria, TX 77903 / 361-573-4867; FAX: 361-576-9622 galaxy@tisd.net
GALCO International Ltd., 2019 W. Quail Ave., Phoenix, AZ 85027 / 602-258-8295 or 800-874-2526; FAX: 602-582-6854
Galena Industries AMT, 5463 Diaz St., Irwindale, CA 91706 / 626-856-8883; FAX: 626-856-8878
Gamba S.p.A. Societa Armi Bresciane Srl, Renato, Via Artigiani 93, ITALY / 30-8911640; FAX: 30-8911648
Gamba, USA, P.O. Box 60452, Colorado Springs, CO 80960 / 719-578-1145; FAX: 719-444-0731

Game Haven Gunstocks, 13750 Shire Rd., Wolverine, MI 49799 / 616-525-8257
Game Winner, Inc., R 1 Box Industrial Park, Opp, AL 36467 / 770-434-9210; FAX: 770-434-9215
Gamebore Division, Polywad Inc., P.O. Box 7916, Macon, GA 31209 / 912-477-0669
Gamo USA, Inc., 3911 SW 47th Ave., Ste. 914, Ft. Lauderdale, FL 33314 / 954-581-5822; FAX: 954-581-3165; gamousa@gate.net www.gamo.com
Gander Mountain, Inc., 12400 Fox River Rd., Wilmont, WI 53192 / 414-862-6848
GAR, 590 McBride Avenue, West Paterson, NJ 07424 / 973-754-1114; FAX: 973-754-1114
Garbi, Armas Urki, 12-14 20.600 Eibar, Guipuzcoa, SPAIN
Garcia National Gun Traders, Inc., 225 SW 22nd Ave., Miami, FL 33135 / 305-642-2355
Garrett Cartridges Inc., P.O. Box 178, Chehalis, WA 98532 / 360-736-0702 garrettcartridges.com
Garthwaite Pistolsmith, Inc., Jim, Rt 2 Box 310, Watsontown, PA 17777 / 570-538-1566; FAX: 570-538-2965
Gary Goudy Classic Stocks, 1512 S. 5th St., Dayton, WA 99328-1716 / 415-322-1338
Gary Reeder Custom Guns, 2710 N. Steves Blvd. #22, Flagstaff, AZ 86004 / 520-526-3313; FAX: 520-527-0840 gary@reedercustomguns.com www.reedercustomguns.com
Gary Schneider Rifle Barrels Inc., 12202 N. 62nd Pl., Scottsdale, AZ 85254 / 602-948-2525
Gator Guns & Repair, 6255 Spur Hwy., Kenai, AK 99611 / 907-283-7947
Gaucher Armes, S.A., 46 rue Desjoyaux, 42000, Saint-Etienne, FRANCE / 04-77-33-38-92; FAX: 04-77-61-95-72
GDL Enterprises, 409 Le Gardeur, Slidell, LA 70460 / 504-649-0693
Gehmann, Walter (See Huntington Die Specialties)
Genco, P.O. Box 5704, Asheville, NC 28803
Genecco Gun Works, 10512 Lower Sacramento Rd., Stockton, CA 95210 / 209-951-0706; FAX: 209-931-3872
Gene's Custom Guns, P.O. Box 10534, White Bear Lake, MN 55110 / 612-429-5105
Gentex Corp., 5 Tinkham Ave., Derry, NH 03038 / 603-434-0311; FAX: 603-434-3002 sales@derry.gentexcorp.com www.derry.gentexcorp.com
Gentner Bullets, 109 Woodlawn Ave., Upper Darby, PA 19082 / 610-352-9396
Gentry Custom Gunmaker, David, 314 N Hoffman, Belgrade, MT 59714 / 406-388-GUNS davidgent@mon.net gentrycustom.com
George & Roy's, P.O. Box 2125, Sisters, OR 97759-2125 / 503-228-5424 or 800-553-3022; FAX: 503-225-9409
George E. Mathews & Son, Inc., 10224 S. Paramount Blvd., Downey, CA 90241 / 562-862-6719; FAX: 562-862-6719
George Ibberson (Sheffield) Ltd., 25-31 Allen St., Sheffield, S3 7AW ENGLAND / 0114-2766123; FAX: 0114-2738465
Gerald Pettinger Books, Rte. 2 Box 125, Russell, IA 50238 / 641-535-2239 gretinger@lisco.com
Gerber Legendary Blades, 14200 SW 72nd Ave., Portland, OR 97223 / 503-639-6161 or 800-950-6161; FAX: 503-684-7008
Gervais, Mike, 3804 S. Cruise Dr., Salt Lake City, UT 84109 / 801-277-7729
Getz Barrel Co., P.O. Box 88, Beavertown, PA 17813 / 717-658-7263
Giacomo Sporting USA, 6234 Stokes Lee Center Rd., Lee Center, NY 13363
Gibbs Rifle Co., Inc., 211 Lawn St., Martinsburg, WV 25401 / 304-262-1651; FAX: 304-262-1658
Gil Hebard Guns, 125-129 Public Square, Knoxville, IL 61448 / 309-289-2700; FAX: 309-289-2233
Gilbert Equipment Co., Inc., 960 Downtowner Rd., Mobile, AL 36609 / 205-344-3322
Gillmann, Edwin, 33 Valley View Dr., Hanover, PA 17331 / 717-632-1662
Gilman-Mayfield, Inc., 3279 E. Shields, Fresno, CA 93703 / 209-221-9415; FAX: 209-221-9419
Gilmore Sports Concepts, 5949 S. Garnett, Tulsa, OK 74146 / 918-250-3810; FAX: 918-250-3845 gilmore@webzone.net www.gilmoresports.com
Giron, Robert E., 12671 Cousins Rd., Peosta, IA 52068-9752 / 412-731-6041
Glacier Glove, 4890 Aircenter Circle, Ste. 210, Reno, NV 89502 / 702-825-8225; FAX: 702-825-6544
Glaser Safety Slug, Inc., P.O. Box 8223, Foster City, CA 94404 / 800-221-3489; FAX: 510-785-6685 safetyslug.com
Glass, Herb, P.O. Box 25, Bullville, NY 10915 / 914-361-3021
Glimm, Jerome (See Glimm's Custom Gun Engraving)
Glimm's Custom Gun Engraving, Jerome C. Glimm, 19 S. Maryland, Conrad, MT 59425 / 406-278-3574 jandiglimm@mcn.net

Glock GmbH, P.O. Box 50, A-2232, Deutsch Wagram, AUSTRIA
Glock, Inc., P.O. Box 369, Smyrna, GA 30081 / 770-432-1202; FAX: 770-433-8719
Glynn Scobey Duck & Goose Calls, Rt. 3, Box 37, Newbern, TN 38059 / 901-643-6241
GML Products, Inc., 394 Laredo Dr., Birmingham, AL 35226 / 205-979-4867
Gner's Hard Cast Bullets, 1107 11th St., LaGrande, OR 97850 / 503-963-8796
Goens, Dale W., P.O. Box 224, Cedar Crest, NM 87008 / 505-281-5419
Goergen's Gun Shop, 17985 538th Ave., Austin, MN 55912 / 507-433-9280; FAX: 507-433-9280
GOEX Inc., P.O. Box 659, Doyline, LA 71023-0659 / 318-382-9300; FAX: 318-382-9303
Golden Age Arms Co., 115 E. High St., Ashley, OH 43003 / 614-747-2488
Golden Bear Bullets, 3065 Fairfax Ave., San Jose, CA 95148 / 408-238-9515
Gonic Arms/North American Arm, 134 Flagg Rd., Gonic, NH 03839 / 603-332-8456 or 603-332-8457
Goodling's Gunsmithing, R.D. 1, Box 1097, Spring Grove, PA 17362 / 717-225-3350
Goodwin, Fred, Silver Ridge Gun Shop, Sherman Mills, ME 04776 / 207-365-4451
Gotz Bullets, 7313 Rogers St., Rockford, IL 61111
Gould & Goodrich, 709 E. McNeil, Lillington, NC 27546 / 910-893-2071; FAX: 910-893-4742
Gournet Artistic Engraving, Geoffroy Gournet, 820 Paxinosa Ave., Easton, PA 18042 / 610-559-0710
Gournet, Geoffroy (See Gournet Artistic Engraving)
Grace, Charles E., 1305 Arizona Ave., Trinidad, CO 81082 / 719-846-9435
Grace Metal Products, P.O. Box 67, Elk Rapids, MI 49629 / 616-264-8133
Graf & Sons, 4050 S. Clark St., Mexico, MO 65265 / 573-581-2266; FAX: 573-581-2875
"Gramps" Antique Cartridges, Box 341, Washago, ON L0K 2B0 CANADA / 705-689-5348
Granite Mountain Arms, Inc., 3145 W Hidden Acres Trail, Prescott, AZ 86305 / 520-541-9758; FAX: 520-445-6826
Grant, Howard V., Hiawatha 15, Woodruff, WI 54568 / 715-356-7146
Graphics Direct, P.O. Box 372421, Reseda, CA 91337-2421 / 818-344-9002
Graves Co., 1800 Andrews Ave., Pompano Beach, FL 33069 / 800-327-9103; FAX: 305-960-0301
Grayback Wildcats, 5306 Bryant Ave., Klamath Falls, OR 97603 / 541-884-1072
Graybill's Gun Shop, 1035 Ironville Pike, Columbia, PA 17512 / 717-684-2739
Great American Gunstock Co., 3420 Industrial Dr., Yuba City, CA 95993 / 530-671-4570; FAX: 530-671-3906
Great Lakes Airguns, 6175 S. Park Ave., New York, NY 14075 / 716-648-6666; FAX: 716-648-5279
Green, Arthur S., 485 S. Robertson Blvd., Beverly Hills, CA 90211 / 310-274-1283
Green, Roger M., P.O. Box 984, 435 E. Birch, Glenrock, WY 82637 / 307-436-9804
Green Genie, Box 114, Cusseta, GA 31805
Green Head Game Call Co., RR 1, Box 33, Lacon, IL 61540 / 309-246-2155
Green Mountain Rifle Barrel Co., Inc., P.O. Box 2670, 153 West Main St., Conway, NH 03818 / 603-447-1095; FAX: 603-447-1099
Greenwood Precision, P.O. Box 407, Rogersville, MO 65742 / 417-725-2330
Greg Gunsmithing Repair, 3732 26th Ave. North, Robbinsdale, MN 55422 / 612-529-8103
Greg's Superior Products, P.O. Box 46219, Seattle, WA 98146
Greider Precision, 431 Santa Marina Ct., Escondido, CA 92029 / 619-480-8892; FAX: 619-480-9800
Gremmel Enterprises, 2111 Carriage Dr., Eugene, OR 97408-7537 / 541-302-3000
GrE-Tan Rifles, 29742 W.C.R. 50, Kersey, CO 80644 / 970-353-6176; FAX: 970-356-9133
Grier's Hard Cast Bullets, 1107 11th St., LaGrande, OR 97850 / 503-963-8796
Griffin & Howe, Inc., 36 W. 44th St., Ste. 1011, New York, NY 10036 / 212-921-0980
Griffin & Howe, Inc., 33 Claremont Rd., Bernardsville, NJ 07924 / 908-766-2287
Grifon, Inc., 58 Guinam St., Waltham, MS 02154
Groenewold, John, P.O. Box 830, Mundelein, IL 60060 / 847-566-2365
GRS Corp., Glendo, P.O. Box 1153, 900 Overlander St., Emporia, KS 66801 / 316-343-1084 or 800-835-3519
Grulla Armes, Apartado 453, Avda Otaloa 12, Eibar, SPAIN

Gruning Precision Inc., 7101 Jurupa Ave., No. 12, Riverside, CA 92504 / 909-689-6692; FAX: 909-689-7791 gruningprecision@earthlink.net www.gruningprecision.com
GSI, Inc., 7661 Commerce Ln., Trussville, AL 35173 / 205-655-8299
GTB, 482 Comerwood Court, San Francisco, CA 94080 / 650-583-1550
Guarasi, Robert (See Wilcox Industries Corp.)
Guardsman Products, 411 N. Darling, Fremont, MI 49412 / 616-924-3950
Gun Accessories (See Glaser Safety Slug, Inc.)
Gun City, 212 W. Main Ave., Bismarck, ND 58501 / 701-223-2304
Gun Hunter Books (See Gun Hunter Trading Co.)
Gun Hunter Trading Co., 5075 Heisig St., Beaumont, TX 77705 / 409-835-3006; FAX: 409-838-2266 gunhuntertrading@hotmail.com
Gun Leather Limited, 116 Lipscomb, Ft. Worth, TX 76104 / 817-334-0225; FAX: 800-247-0609
Gun List (See Krause Publications)
Gun Locker Div. of Airmold W.R. Grace & Co.-Conn., Becker Farms Ind. Park, P.O. Box 610, Roanoke Rapids, NC 27870 / 800-344-5716; FAX: 919-536-2201
Gun South, Inc. (See GSI, Inc.)
Gun Vault, 7339 E. Acoma Dr., Ste. 7, Scottsdale, AZ 85260 / 602-951-6855
Gun-Alert, 1010 N. Maclay Ave., San Fernando, CA 91340 / 818-365-0864; FAX: 818-365-1308
Guncraft Sports Inc., 10737 Dutchtown Rd., Knoxville, TN 37932 / 865-966-4545; FAX: 865-966-4500 findit@guncraft.com www.usit.net/guncraft
Gunfitters, P.O. 426, Cambridge, WI 53523-0426 / 608-764-8128 gunfitters@aol.com www.gunfitters.com
Gun-Ho Sports Cases, 110 E. 10th St., St. Paul, MN 55101 / 612-224-9491
Gunline Tools, 2950 Saturn St., "O", Brea, CA 92821 / 714-993-5100; FAX: 714-572-4128
Gunnerman Books, P.O. Box 217, Owosso, MI 48867 / 517-729-7018; FAX: 517-725-9391
Guns Antique & Modern DBA/Charles E. Duffy, Williams Ln., West Hurley, NY 12491 / 914-679-2997
Guns Div. of D.C. Engineering, Inc., 8633 Southfield Fwy., Detroit, MI 48228 / 313-271-7111 or 800-886-7623; FAX: 313-271-7112 guns@rifletech.com rifletech.com
GUNS Magazine, 591 Camino de la Reina, Ste. 200, San Diego, CA 92108 / 619-297-5350; FAX: 619-297-5353
Guns, John C Pevear, 81 E. Streetsboro St., Hudson, OH 44236 / 330-650-4563 jcpevear@aol.com
Gunsite Custom Shop, P.O. Box 451, Paulden, AZ 86334 / 520-636-4104; FAX: 520-636-1236
Gunsite Gunsmithy (See Gunsite Custom Shop)
Gunsite Training Center, P.O. Box 700, Paulden, AZ 86334 / 520-636-4565; FAX: 520-636-1236
Gunsmithing Ltd., 57 Unquowa Rd., Fairfield, CT 06430 / 203-254-0436; FAX: 203-254-1535
Gunsmithing, Inc., 30 W Buchanan St., Colorado Springs, CO 80907 / 719-632-3795; FAX: 719-632-3493
Gurney, F. R., Box 13, Sooke, BC V0S 1N0 CANADA / 604-642-5282; FAX: 604-642-7859
Gwinnell, Bryson J., P.O. Box 1307, Kilauea, HI 96754-1307 / 802-767-3664

H

H&B Forge Co., Rt. 2, Geisinger Rd., Shiloh, OH 44878 / 419-895-1856
H&P Publishing, 7174 Hoffman Rd., San Angelo, TX 76905 / 915-655-5953
H&R 1871, Inc., 60 Industrial Rowe, Gardner, MA 01440 / 978-632-9393; FAX: 978-632-2300
H&S Liner Service, 515 E. 8th, Odessa, TX 79761 / 915-332-1021
H. Krieghoff Gun Co., Boschstrasse 22, D-89079, Ulm, GERMANY / 731-401820; FAX: 731-4018270
H.K.S. Products, 7841 Founion Dr., Florence, KY 41042 / 606-342-7841 or 800-354-9814; FAX: 606-342-5865
H.P. White Laboratory, Inc., 3114 Scarboro Rd., Street, MD 21154 / 410-838-6550; FAX: 410-838-2802
Hafner World Wide, Inc., P.O. Box 1987, Lake City, FL 32055 / 904-755-6481; FAX: 904-755-6595 hafner@isgroupe.net
Hagn Rifles & Actions, Martin, P.O. Box 444, Cranbrook, BC V1C 4H9 CANADA / 604-489-4861
Hakko Co. Ltd., 1-13-12, Narimasu, Itabashiku Tokyo, JAPAN / 03-5997-7870/2; FAX: 81-3-5997-7840
Hale, Engraver, Peter, 800 E Canyon Rd., Spanish Fork, UT 84660 / 801-798-8215
Half Moon Rifle Shop, 490 Halfmoon Rd., Columbia Falls, MT 59912 / 406-892-4409

MANUFACTURER'S DIRECTORY

Hall Manufacturing, 142 CR 406, Clanton, AL 35045 / 205-755-4094

Hall Plastics, Inc., John, P.O. Box 1526, Alvin, TX 77512 / 713-489-8709

Hallowell & Co., P.O. Box 1445, Livingston, MT 59047 / 406-222-4770; FAX: 406-222-4792 morris@hallowellco.com hallowellco.com

Hally Caller, 443 Wells Rd., Doylestown, PA 18901 / 215-345-6354

Hamilton, Jim (See Custom Single Shot Rifles)

Hamilton, Alex B. (See Ten-Ring Precision, Inc.)

Hammans, Charles E., P.O. Box 788, 2022 McCracken, Stuttgart, AR 72106 / 870-673-1388

Hammerli Ltd., Seonerstrasse 37, CH-5600, SWITZERLAND / 064-50 11 44; FAX: 064-51 38 27

Hammerli USA, 19296 Oak Grove Circle, Groveland, CA 95321; FAX: 209-962-5311

Hammets VLD Bullets, P.O. Box 479, Rayville, LA 71269 / 318-728-2019

Hammond Custom Guns Ltd., 619 S. Pandora, Gilbert, AZ 85234 / 602-892-3437

Hammonds Rifles, RD 4, Box 504, Red Lion, PA 17356 / 717-244-7879

HandCrafts Unltd. (See Clements' Custom Leathercraft)

Handgun Press, P.O. Box 406, Glenview, IL 60025 / 847-657-6500; FAX: 847-724-8831 jschroed@inter-access.com

Hands Engraving, Barry Lee, 26192 E. Shore Route, Bigfork, MT 59911 / 406-837-0035

Hank's Gun Shop, Box 370, 50 West 100 South, Monroe, UT 84754 / 801-527-4456

Hanned Precision (See The Hanned Line)

Hansen & Co. (See Hansen Cartridge Co.)

Hanson's Gun Center, Dick, 233 Everett Dr, Colorado Springs, CO 80911

Hanus Birdguns Bill, P.O. Box 533, Newport, OR 97365 / 541-265-7433; FAX: 541-265-7400

Hanusin, John, 3306 Commercial, Northbrook, IL 60062 / 708-564-2706

Hardin Specialty Dist., P.O. Box 338, Radcliff, KY 40159-0338 / 502-351-6649

Harford (See U.S. Importer-EMF Co. Inc.)

Harper's Custom Stocks, 928 Lombrano St., San Antonio, TX 78207 / 210-732-5780

Harrell's Precision, 5756 Hickory Dr., Salem, VA 24133 / 703-380-2683

Harrington & Richardson (See H&R 1871, Inc.)

Harris Engineering Inc., Dept GD54, Barlow, KY 42024 / 502-334-3633; FAX: 502-334-3000

Harris Enterprises, P.O. Box 105, Bly, OR 97622 / 503-353-2625

Harris Gunworks, 11240 N. Cave Creek Rd., Ste 104, Phoenix, AZ 85020 / 602-582-9627; FAX: 602-582-5178

Harris Hand Engraving, Paul A., 113 Rusty Ln., Boerne, TX 78006-5746 / 512-391-5121

Harris Publications, 1115 Broadway, New York, NY 10010 / 212-807-7100; FAX: 212-627-4678

Harrison Bullets, 6437 E. Hobart St., Mesa, AZ 85205

Harry Lawson Co., 3328 N. Richey Blvd., Tucson, AZ 85716 / 520-326-1117

Hart & Son, Inc., Robert W., 401 Montgomery St., Nescopeck, PA 18635 / 717-752-3655; FAX: 717-752-1088

Hart Rifle Barrels, Inc., P.O. Box 182, 1690 Apulia Rd., Lafayette, NY 13084 / 315-677-9841; FAX: 315-677-9610 hartrb@aol.com hartbarrels.com

Hartford (See U.S. Importer-EMF Co. Inc.)

Hartmann & Weiss GmbH, Rahlstedter Bahnhofstr. 47, 22143, Hamburg, GERMANY / (40) 677 55 85; FAX: (40) 677 55 92

Harvey, Frank, 218 Nightfall, Terrace, NV 89015 / 702-558-6998

Harwood, Jack O., 1191 S. Pendlebury Ln., Blackfoot, ID 83221 / 208-785-5368

Hastings Barrels, 320 Court St., Clay Center, KS 67432 / 913-632-3169; FAX: 913-632-6554

Hawk Laboratories, Inc. (See Hawk, Inc.)

Hawk, Inc., 849 Hawks Bridge Rd., Salem, NJ 08079 / 609-299-2700; FAX: 609-299-2800

Hawken Shop, The (See Dayton Traister)

Haydel's Game Calls, Inc., 5018 Hazel Jones Rd., Bossier City, LA 71111 / 800-HAYDELS; FAX: 318-746-3711

Haydon Shooters Supply, Russ, 15018 Goodrich Dr. NW, Gig Harbor, WA 98329-9738 / 253-857-7557; FAX: 253-857-7884

Heatbath Corp., P.O. Box 2978, Springfield, MA 01101 / 413-543-3381

Hebard Guns, Gil, 125-129 Public Square, Knoxville, IL 61448

HEBB Resources, P.O. Box 999, Mead, WA 99021-0999 / 509-466-1292

Hecht, Hubert J., Waffen-Hecht, P.O. Box 2635, Fair Oaks, CA 95628 / 916-966-1020

Heckler & Koch GmbH, P.O. Box 1329, 78722 Oberndorf, Neckar, GERMANY / 49-7423179-0; FAX: 49-7423179-2406

Heckler & Koch, Inc., 21480 Pacific Blvd., Sterling, VA 20166-8900 / 703-450-1900; FAX: 703-450-8160 www.hecklerkoch.usa.com

Hege Jagd-u. Sporthandels GmbH, P.O. Box 101461, W-7770, Ueberlingen a. Boden, GERMANY

Heidenstrom Bullets, Urdngt 1, 3937 Heroya, NORWAY

Heilmann, Stephen, P.O. Box 657, Grass Valley, CA 95945 / 530-272-8758

Heinie Specialty Products, 301 Oak St., Quincy, IL 62301-2500 / 217-228-9500; FAX: 217-228-9502 rheinie@heinie.com www.heinie.com

Hellweg Ltd., 40356 Oak Park Way, Ste. W, Oakhurst, CA 93644 / 209-683-3030; FAX: 209-683-3422

Hendricks, Frank E. Inc., Master Engravers, HC 03, Box 434, Dripping Springs, TX 78620 / 512-858-7828

Henigson & Associates, Steve, P.O. Box 2726, Culver City, CA 90231 / 310-305-8288; FAX: 310-305-1905

Henriksen Tool Co., Inc., 8515 Wagner Creek Rd., Talent, OR 97540 / 541-535-2309; FAX: 541-535-2309

Henry Repeating Arms Co., 110 8th St., Brooklyn, NY 11215 / 718-499-5600

Heppler, Keith (See Keith's Custom Gunstocks)

Heppler, Keith M., Keith's Custom Gunstocks, 540 Banyan Cir., Walnut Creek, CA 94598 / 510-934-3509; FAX: 510-934-3143 kmheppler@hotmail.com

Hercules, Inc. (See Alliant Techsystems, Smokeless Powder Group)

Heritage Firearms (See Heritage Mfg., Inc.)

Heritage Manufacturing, Inc., 4600 NW 135th St., Opa Locka, FL 33054 or 305-685-5966; FAX: 305-687-6721

Heritage/VSP Gun Books, P.O. Box 887, McCall, ID 83638 / 208-634-4104; FAX: 208-634-3101

Herrett's Stocks, Inc., P.O. Box 741, Twin Falls, ID 83303 / 208-733-1498

Hertel & Reuss, Werk fr Optik und Feinmechanik GmbH, Quellhofstrasse 67, 34 127, GERMANY / 0561-83006; FAX: 0561-893308

Hesco-Meprolight (See Kimber)

Heydenberk, Warren R., 1059 W. Sawmill Rd., Quakertown, PA 18951 / 215-538-2682

Hickman, Jaclyn, Box 1900, Glenrock, WY 82637

Hidalgo, Tony, 12701 SW 9th Pl., Davie, FL 33325 / 954-476-7645

High Bridge Arms, Inc., 3185 Mission St., San Francisco, CA 94110 / 415-282-8358

High North Products, Inc., P.O. Box 2, Antigo, WI 54409 / 715-627-2331; FAX: 715-623-5451

High Performance International, 5734 W. Florist Ave., Milwaukee, WI 53218 / 414-466-9040

High Precision, Bud Welsh, 80 New Road, E. Amherst, NY 14051 / 716-688-6344; FAX: 716-688-0425

High Standard Mfg. Co., Inc., 10606 Hempstead Hwy., Ste. 116, Houston, TX 77092 / 713-462-4200; FAX: 713-462-6437

High Tech Specialties, Inc., P.O. Box 387R, Adamstown, PA 19501 / 215-484-0405 or 800-231-9385

Highline Machine Co., Randall Thompson, 654 Lela Pl., Grand Junction, CO 81504 / 970-434-4971

Hi-Grade Imports, 8655 Monterey Rd., Gilroy, CA 95021 / 408-842-9301; FAX: 408-842-2374

Hill, Loring F., 304 Cedar Rd., Elkins Park, PA 19027

Hill Speed Leather, Ernie, 4507 N. 195th Ave., Litchfield Park, AZ 85340 / 602-853-9222; FAX: 602-853-9235

Hinman Outfitters, Bob, 107 N. Sanderson Ave., Bartonville, IL 61607-1839 / 309-691-8132

Hi-Performance Ammunition Company, 484 State Route 366, Apollo, PA 15613 / 412-327-8100

HIP-GRIP Barami Corp., 6689 Orchard Lake Rd. No. 148, West Bloomfield, MI 48322 / 248-738-0462; FAX: 248-738-2542

Hi-Point Firearms, 5990 Philadelphia Dr., Dayton, OH 45415 / 513-275-4991; FAX: 513-522-8330

Hiptmayer, Armurier, RR 112 750, P.O. Box 136, Eastman, PQ J0E 1P0 CANADA / 514-297-2492

Hiptmayer, Heidemarie, RR 112 750, P.O. Box 136, Eastman, PQ J0E 1P0 CANADA / 514-297-2492

Hiptmayer, Klaus, RR 112 750, P.O. Box 136, Eastman, PQ J0E 1P0 CANADA / 514-297-2492

Hirtenberger Aktiengesellschaft, Leobersdorferstrasse 31, A-2552, Hirtenberg, Austria / 43(0)2256 81184; FAX: 43(0)2256 81807

HiTek International, 484 El Camino Real, Redwood City, CA 94063 / 415-363-1404 or 800-54-NIGHT; FAX: 415-363-1408

Hiti-Schuch, Atelier Wilma, A-8863 Predlitz, Pirming, Y1 AUSTRIA / 0353418278

HJS Arms, Inc., P.O. Box 3711, Brownsville, TX 78523-3711 / 800-453-2767; FAX: 210-542-2767

Hoag Gun Wks, James W. Hoag, 8523 Canoga Ave., Ste. C, Canoga Park, CA 91304 / 818-998-1510

Hoag, James (See Hoag Gun Wks)

Hobson Precision Mfg. Co., 210 Big Oak Ln, Brent, AL 35034 / 205-926-4662; FAX: 205-926-3193 cahobbob@dbtech.net

Hodgdon Powder Co., 6231 Robinson, Shawnee Mission, KS 66202 / 913-362-9455; FAX: 913-362-1307

Hodgman, Inc., 1750 Orchard Rd., Montgomery, IL 60538 / 708-897-7555; FAX: 708-897-7558

Hodgson, Richard, 9081 Tahoe Ln., Boulder, CO 80301

Hoehn Sales, Inc., 2045 Kohn Road, Wright City, MO 63390 / 636-745-8144; FAX: 636-745-7868 hoehnsal@usmo.com benchrestcentral

Hoelscher, Virgil; 1804 S. Valley View Blvd., Las Vegas, NV 89102-3972 / 310-631-8545

Hoenig & Rodman, 6521 Morton Dr., Boise, ID 83704 / 208-375-1116

Hoffman New Ideas, 821 Northmoor Rd., Lake Forest, IL 60045 / 312-234-4075

Hogue Grips, P.O. Box 1138, Paso Robles, CA 93447 / 800-438-4747 or 805-239-1440; FAX: 805-239-2553

Holland & Holland Ltd., 33 Bruton St., London, ENGLAND / 44-171-499-4411; FAX: 44-171-408-7962

Holland's Gunsmithing, P.O. Box 69, Powers, OR 97466 / 541-439-5155; FAX: 541-439-5155

Hollinger, Jon (See Aspen Outfitting Co.)

Hollis Gun Shop, 917 Rex St., Carlsbad, NM 88220 / 505-885-3782

Hollywood Engineering, 10642 Arminta St., Sun Valley, CA 91352 / 818-842-8376

Homak, 5151 W. 73rd St., Chicago, IL 60638-6613 / 312-523-3100; FAX: 312-523-9455

Home Shop Machinist The Village Press Publications, P.O. Box 1810, Traverse City, MI 49685 / 800-447-7367; FAX: 616-946-3289

Hondo Ind., 510 S. 52nd St., I04, Tempe, AZ 85281

Hoppe's Div. Penguin Industries, Inc., Airport Industrial Mall, Coatesville, PA 19320 / 610-384-6000

Horizons Unlimited, P.O. Box 426, Warm Springs, GA 31830 / 706-655-3603; FAX: 706-655-3603

Hornady Mfg. Co., P.O. Box 1848, Grand Island, NE 68802 / 800-338-3220 or 308-382-1390; FAX: 308-382-5761

Horseshoe Leather Products, Andy Arratoonian, The Cottage Sharow, Ripon, ENGLAND / 44-1765-605858 andy@horseshoe.co.uk www.horseshoe.co.uk

Houtz & Barwick, P.O. Box 435, W. Church St., Elizabeth City, NC 27909 / 800-775-0337 or 919-335-4191; FAX: 919-335-1152

Howa Machinery, Ltd., Sukaguchi, Shinkawa-cho Nishikasugai-gun, Aichi 452, JAPAN

Howell Machine, 815 1/2 D St., Lewiston, ID 83501 / 208-743-7418

Hoyt Holster Co., Inc., P.O. Box 69, Coupeville, WA 98239-0069 / 360-678-6640; FAX: 360-678-6549

H-S Precision, Inc., 1301 Turbine Dr., Rapid City, SD 57701 / 605-341-3006; FAX: 605-342-8964

HT Bullets, 244 Belleville Rd., New Bedford, MA 02745 / 508-999-3338

Hubert J. Hecht Waffen-Hecht, P.O. Box 2635, Fair Oaks, CA 95628 / 916-966-1020

Huebner, Corey O., P.O. Box 564, Frenchtown, MT 59834 / 406-721-7168

Huey Gun Cases, P.O. Box 22456, Kansas City, MO 64113 / 816-444-1637; FAX: 816-444-1637 hueycases@aol.com www.hueycases.com

Hugger Hooks Co., 3900 Easley Way, Golden, CO 80403 / 303-279-0600

Hughes, Steven Dodd, P.O. Box 545, Livingston, MT 59047 / 406-222-9377; FAX: 406-222-9377

Hume, Don, P.O. Box 351, Miami, OK 74355 / 800-331-2686; FAX: 918-542-4340

Hungry Horse Books, 4605 Hwy. 93 South, Whitefish, MT 59937 / 406-862-7997

Hunkeler, A. (See Buckskin Machine Works)

Hunter Co., Inc., 3300 W. 71st Ave., Westminster, CO 80030 / 303-427-4626; FAX: 303-428-3980

Hunterjohn, P.O. Box 771457, St. Louis, MO 63177 / 314-531-7250

Hunter's Specialties Inc., 6000 Huntington Ct. NE, Cedar Rapids, IA 52402-1268 / 319-395-0321; FAX: 319-395-0326

Hunters Supply, Inc., P.O. Box 313, Tioga, TX 76271 / 940-437-2458; FAX: 940-437-2228 hunterssupply@hotmail.com hunterssupply.net
Hunting Classics Ltd., P.O. Box 2089, Gastonia, NC 28053 / 704-867-1307; FAX: 704-867-0491
Huntington Die Specialties, 601 Oro Dam Blvd., Oroville, CA 95965 / 530-534-1210; FAX: 530-534-1212
Hutton Rifle Ranch, P.O. Box 45236, Boise, ID 83711 / 208-345-8781
Hydrosorbent Products, P.O. Box 437, Ashley Falls, MA 01222 / 413-229-2967; or 800-448-7903; FAX: 413-229-8743 orders@dehumidify.com www.dehumidify.com
Hyper-Single, Inc., 520 E. Beaver, Jenks, OK 74037 / 918-299-2391

I

I.A.B. (See U.S. Importer-Taylor's & Co. Inc.)
I.D.S.A. Books, 1324 Stratford Dr., Piqua, OH 45356 / 937-773-4203; FAX: 937-778-1922
I.N.C. Inc. (See Kickeez Inc.)
I.S.S., P.O. Box 185234, Ft. Worth, TX 76181 / 817-595-2090
I.S.W., 106 E. Cairo Dr., Tempe, AZ 85282
IAI, 5709 Hartsdale, Houston, TX 77036 / 713-789-0745; FAX: 713-789-7513 iaipro@wt.net www.israelarms.com
IAR Inc., 33171 Camino Capistrano, San Juan Capistrano, CA 92675 / 949-443-3642; FAX: 949-443-3647
Ide, K. (See Sturgeon Valley Sporters)
IGA (See U.S. Importer-Stoeger Industries)
Ignacio Ugartechea S.A., Chonta 26, Eibar, 20600 SPAIN / 43-121257; FAX: 43-121669
Illinois Lead Shop, 7742 W. 61st Pl., Summit, IL 60501
Image Ind. Inc., 382 Balm Court, Wood Dale, IL 60191 / 630-766-2402; FAX: 630-766-7373
Impact Case Co., P.O. Box 9912, Spokane, WA 99209-0912 / 800-262-3322 or 509-467-3303; FAX: 509-326-5436 info@kkair.com www.kkair.com
Imperial (See E-Z-Way Systems)
Imperial Magnum Corp., P.O. Box 249, Oroville, WA 98844 / 604-495-3131; FAX: 604-495-2816
Imperial Miniature Armory, 10547 S. Post Oak Rd., Houston, TX 77035 / 713-729-8428; FAX: 713-729-2274 wayne@1800miniature.com www.1800miniature.com
Imperial Schrade Corp., 7 Schrade Ct., Box 7000, Ellenville, NY 12428 / 914-647-7601; FAX: 914-647-8701 csc@schradeknives.com www.schradeknives.com
Import Sports Inc., 1750 Brielle Ave., Unit B1, Wanamassa, NJ 07712 / 908-493-0302; FAX: 908-493-0301
IMR Powder Co., 1080 Military Turnpike, Ste. 2, Plattsburgh, NY 12901 / 518-563-2253; FAX: 518-563-6916
IMX LLC, 2169 Greenville Rd., La Grange, GA 30241 / 706-882-8070; FAX: 706-882-9050
Info-Arm, P.O. Box 1262, Champlain, NY 12919 / 514-955-0355; FAX: 514-955-0357
Ingle, Ralph W., Engraver, 112 Manchester Ct., Centerville, GA 31028 / 478-953-5824 riengraver@aol.com
Innovative Weaponry Inc., 2513 E. Loop 820 N., Fort Worth, TX 76118 / 817-284-0099; or 800-334-3573
INTEC International, Inc., P.O. Box 5708, Scottsdale, AZ 85261 / 602-483-1708
Inter Ordnance of America LP, 3305 Westwood Industrial Dr., Monroe, NC 28110-5204 / 704-821-8337; FAX: 704-821-8523
Intercontinental Distributors, Ltd., P.O. Box 815, Beulah, ND 58523
Intrac Arms International, 5005 Chapman Hwy., Knoxville, TN 37920
Intratec, 12405 SW 130th St., Miami, FL 33186-6224 / 305-232-1821; FAX: 305-253-7207
Ion Industries, Inc., 3508 E. Allerton Ave., Cudahy, WI 53110 / 414-486-2007; FAX: 414-486-2017
Iosso Products, 1485 Lively Blvd., Elk Grove Village, IL 60007 / 847-437-8400; FAX: 847-437-8478
Iron Bench, 12619 Bailey Rd., Redding, CA 96003 / 916-241-4623
Ironside International Publishers, 3000 S. Eads St., Arlington, VA 22202 / 703-684-6111; FAX: 703-683-5486
Ironsighter Co., P.O. Box 85070, Westland, MI 48185 / 734-326-8731; FAX: 734-326-3378 www.ironsighter.com
Irwin, Campbell H., 140 Hartland Blvd., East Hartland, CT 06027 / 203-653-3901
Island Pond Gun Shop, Cross St., Island Pond, VT 05846 / 802-723-4546
Israel Arms International, Inc. (See IAI)
Ithaca Classic Doubles, Stephen Lamboy, The Old Station, No. 5 Railroad St., Victor, NY 14564 / 716-924-2710
Ithaca Gun Co. LLC, 891 Route 34-B, King Ferry, NY 13081 / 888-9ITHACA; FAX: 315-364-5134
Ivanoff, Thomas G. (See Tom's Gun Repair)

J

J J Roberts Firearm Engraver, 7808 Lake Dr., Manassas, VA 20111 / 703-330-0448; FAX: 703-264-8600 james.roberts@angelfire.com www.angelfire.com/va2/engraver
J Martin Inc., P.O. Drawer AP, Beckley, WV 25802 / 304-255-4073; FAX: 304-255-4077
J&D Components, 75 East 350 North, Orem, UT 84057-4719 / 801-225-7007
J&J Products, Inc., 9240 Whitmore, El Monte, CA 91731 / 818-571-5228; FAX: 800-927-8361
J&J Sales, 1501 21st Ave. S., Great Falls, MT 59405 / 406-453-7549
J&L Superior Bullets (See Huntington Die Specialties)
J&R Engineering, P.O. Box 77, 200 Lyons Hill Rd., Athol, MA 01331 / 508-249-9241
J&R Enterprises, 4550 Scotts Valley Rd., Lakeport, CA 95453
J&S Heat Treat, 803 S. 16th St., Blue Springs, MO 64015 / 816-229-2149; FAX: 816-228-1135
J. Dewey Mfg. Co., Inc., P.O. Box 2014, Southbury, CT 06488 / 203-264-3064; FAX: 203-262-6907
J. Korzinek Riflesmith, RD 2, Box 73D, Canton, PA 17724 / 717-673-8512
J.A. Henckels Zwillingswerk Inc., 9 Skyline Dr., Hawthorne, NY 10532 / 914-592-7370
J.G. Dapkus Co., Inc., Commerce Circle, P.O. Box 293, Durham, CT 06422
J.G. Anschuetz GmbH & Co. KG, Daimlerstr.12, 89079 Ulm, Elm, GERMANY / 731-40120; FAX: 731 4012700 JGA-info@anschuetz-sport.com anschuetz-sport.com
J.I.T. Ltd., P.O. Box 230, Freedom, WY 83120 / 708-494-0937
J.J. Roberts/Engraver, 7808 Lake Dr., Manassas, VA 22111 / 703-330-0448
J.M. Bucheimer Jumbo Sports Products, 721 N. 20th St., St. Louis, MO 63103 / 314-241-1020
J.P. Enterprises Inc., 7605 N. 128th St., White Bear Lake, MN 55110 / 651-426-9196; FAX: 651-426-2472
J.P. Gunstocks, Inc., 4508 San Miguel Ave., North Las Vegas, NV 89030 / 702-645-0718
J.R. Blair Engraving, P.O. Box 64, Glenrock, WY 82637 / 307-436-8115
J.R. Williams Bullet Co., 2008 Tucker Rd., Perry, GA 31069 / 912-987-0274
J.W. Morrison Custom Rifles, 4015 W. Sharon, Phoenix, AZ 85029 / 602-978-3754
J/B Adventures & Safaris Inc., 2275 E. Arapahoe Rd., Ste. 109, Littleton, CO 80122-1521 / 303-771-0977
J-4 Inc., 1700 Via Burton, Anaheim, CA 92806 / 714-254-8315; FAX: 714-956-4421
Jack A. Rosenberg & Sons, 12229 Cox Ln., Dallas, TX 75234 / 214-241-6302
Jack Dever Co., 8590 NW 90, Oklahoma City, OK 73132 / 405-721-6393
Jack First, Inc., 1201 Turbine Dr., Rapid City, SD 57701 / 605-343-9544; FAX: 605-343-9420
Jackalope Gun Shop, 1048 S. 5th St., Douglas, WY 82633 / 307-358-3441
Jaffin, Harry (See Bridgeman Products)
Jagdwaffen, P. Hofer, Buchsenmachermeister, Kirchgasse 24 A-9170, Austria, AUSTRIA / 43 4227 3683; FAX: 43 4227 368330 peterhofer@hoferwaffen.com www.hoferwaffen.com
James Calhoon Varmint Bullets, Shambo Rt., 304, Havre, MT 59501 / 406-395-4079 www.jamescalhoon.com
James Churchill Glove Co., P.O. Box 298, Centralia, WA 98531 / 360-736-2816; FAX: 360-330-0151 churchillglove@localaccess.com
James Wayne Firearms for Collectors and Investors, 2608 N. Laurent, Victoria, TX 77901 / 361-578-1258; FAX: 361-578-3559
Jamison's Forge Works, 4527 Rd. 6.5 NE, Moses Lake, WA 98837 / 509-762-2659
Jantz Supply, 309 West Main Dept. HD, Davis, OK 73030-0584 / 580-369-2316; FAX: 580-369-3082 jantz@brightok.net www.knifemaking.com
Jarrett Rifles, Inc., 383 Brown Rd., Jackson, SC 29831 / 803-471-3616
Jarvis, Inc., 1123 Cherry Orchard Ln., Hamilton, MT 59840 / 406-961-4392
JAS, Inc., P.O. Box 0, Rosemount, MN 55068 / 952-890-7631
Javelina Lube Products, P.O. Box 337, San Bernardino, CA 92402 / 714-882-5847; FAX: 714-434-6937
Jay McCament Custom Gun Maker, Jay McCament, 1730-134th St. Ct. S., Tacoma, WA 98444 / 253-531-8832
JB Custom, P.O. Box 6912, Leawood, KS 66206 / 913-381-2329
Jeff W. Flannery Engraving Co., 11034 Riddles Run Rd., Union, KY 41091 / 606-384-3127

Jeffredo Gunsight, P.O. Box 669, San Marcos, CA 92079 / 619-728-2695
Jena Eur, P.O. Box 319, Dunmore, PA 18512
Jenco Sales, Inc., P.O. Box 1000, Manchaca, TX 78652 / 800-531-5301; FAX: 800-266-2373
Jenkins Recoil Pads, Inc., 5438 E. Frontage Ln., Olney, IL 62450 / 618-395-3416
Jensen Bullets, RR 1 Box 187, Arco, ID 83213-9720 / 208-785-5590
Jensen's Custom Ammunition, 5146 E. Pima, Tucson, AZ 85712 / 602-325-3346; FAX: 602-322-5704
Jensen's Firearms Academy, 1280 W. Prince, Tucson, AZ 85705 / 602-293-8516
Jericho Tool - Magna Shock Ind, 2917 St Hwy 7, Bainbridge, NY 13733-9496 / 607-563-8222; FAX: 607-563-8560 www.jerichotool.com
Jerry Phillips Optics, P.O. Box L632, Langhorne, PA 19047 / 215-757-5037; FAX: 215-757-7097
Jesse W. Smith Saddlery, 0499 County Road J, Pritchett, CO 81064-9604 / 509-325-0622
Jester Bullets, Rt. 1 Box 27, Orienta, OK 73737
Jewell Triggers, Inc., 3620 Hwy. 123, San Marcos, TX 78666 / 512-353-2999
J-Gar Co., 183 Turnpike Rd., Dept. 3, Petersham, MA 01366-9604
JGS Precision Tool Mfg., 100 Main Sumner, Coos Bay, OR 97420 / 541-267-4331; FAX: 541-267-5996
Jim Chambers Flintlocks Ltd., Rt. 1, Box 513-A, Candler, NC 28715 / 704-667-8361
Jim Garthwaite Pistolsmith, Inc., Rt. 2 Box 310, Watsontown, PA 17777 / 717-538-1566
Jim Noble Co., 1305 Columbia St., Vancouver, WA 98660 / 360-695-1309; FAX: 360-695-6835 jnobleco@aol.com
Jim Norman Custom Gunstocks, 14281 Cane Rd., Valley Center, CA 92082 / 619-749-6252
Jim's Gun Shop (See Spradlin's)
Jim's Precision, Jim Ketchum, 1725 Moclips Dr., Petaluma, CA 94952 / 707-762-3014
JLK Bullets, 414 Turner Rd., Dover, AR 72837 / 501-331-4194
Johanssons Vapentillbehor, Bert, S-430 20, Veddige, SWEDEN
John Hall Plastics, Inc., Inc., P.O. Box 1526, Alvin, TX 77512 / 713-489-8709
John Adams & Son Engravers, 7040 Vt. Rt. 113, Vershire, VT 05079 / 802-685-0019; FAX: 802-685-0019
John Masen Co. Inc., 1305 Jelmak, Grand Prairie, TX 75050 / 817-430-8732; FAX: 817-430-1715
John Norrell Arms, 2608 Grist Mill Rd., Little Rock, AR 72207 / 501-225-7864
John Partridge Sales Ltd., Trent Meadows Rugeley, Staffordshire, WS15 2HS ENGLAND
John Rigby & Co., 500 Linne Rd. Ste. D, Paso Robles, CA 93446 / 805-227-4236; FAX: 805-227-4723 jrigby@calinet www.johnrigbyandco.com
John Unertl Optical Co., Inc., 308-310 Clay Ave., Mars, PA 16046-0818 / 724-625-3810
John Walters Wads, 500 N. Avery Dr., Moore, OK 73160 / 405-799-0376; FAX: 405-799-7727 www.tinwadman@cs.com
Johnny Stewart Game Calls, Inc., P.O. Box 7954, 5100 Fort Ave., Waco, TX 76714 / 817-772-3261; FAX: 817-772-3670
John's Custom Leather, 523 S. Liberty St., Blairsville, PA 15717 / 724-459-6802; FAX: 724-459-5996
Johnson Wood Products, 34968 Crystal Road, Strawberry Point, IA 52076 / 319-933-4930
Johnson's Gunsmithing, Inc., Neal, 208 W Buchanan St., Ste B, Colorado Springs, CO 80907 / 800-284-8671; FAX: 719-632-3493
Jonad Corp., 2091 Lakeland Ave., Lakewood, OH 44107 / 216-226-3161
Jonathan Arthur Ciener, Inc., 8700 Commerce St., Cape Canaveral, FL 32920 / 321-868-2200; FAX: 321-868-2201
Jones Co., Dale, 680 Hoffman Draw, Kila, MT 59920 / 406-755-4684
Jones Custom Products, Neil A., 17217 Brookhouser Rd., Saegertown, PA 16433 / 814-763-2769; FAX: 814-763-4228
Jones Moulds, Paul, 4901 Telegraph Rd., Los Angeles, CA 90022 / 213-262-1510
Jones, J.D./SSK Industries, 590 Woodvue Ln., Wintersville, OH 43953 / 740-264-0176; FAX: 740-264-2257
JP Sales, Box 307, Anderson, TX 77830
JRP Custom Bullets, RR2 2233 Carlton Rd., Whitehall, NY 12887 / 518-282-0084 or 802-438-5548
JSL Ltd. (See U.S. Importer-Specialty Shooters Supply Inc.)
Juenke, Vern, 25 Bitterbush Rd., Reno, NV 89523 / 702-345-0225
Jumbo Sports Products, J. M. Bucheimer, 721 N. 20th St., St. Louis, MO 63103 / 314-241-1020

Jungkind, Reeves C., 5001 Buckskin Pass, Austin, TX 78745-2841 / 512-442-1094

Justin Phillippi Custom Bullets, P.O. Box 773, Ligonier, PA 15658 / 412-238-9671

K

K&M Industries, Inc., Box 66, 510 S. Main, Troy, ID 83871 / 208-835-2281; FAX: 208-835-5211

K&M Services, 5430 Salmon Run Rd., Dover, PA 17315 / 717-292-3175; FAX: 717-292-3175

K. Eversull Co., Inc., 1 Tracemont, Boyce, LA 71409 / 318-793-8728

K.B.I. Inc., P.O. Box 6625, Harrisburg, PA 17112 / 717-540-8518; FAX: 717-540-8567

K.K. Arms Co., Star Route Box 671, Kerrville, TX 78028 / 210-257-4718; FAX: 210-257-4891

K.L. Null Holsters Ltd., 161 School St. NW, Hill City Station, Resaca, GA 30735 / 706-625-5643; FAX: 706-625-9392

Ka Pu Kapili, P.O. Box 745, Honokaa, HI 96727 / 808-776-1644; FAX: 808-776-1731

KA-BAR Knives, Inc., 1125 E. State St., Olean, NY 14760 / 800-282-0130; FAX: 716-373-6245 info@ka-bar.com www.ka-bar.com

Kahles A Swarovski Company, 2 Slater Rd., Cranston, RI 02920 / 401-946-2220; FAX: 401-946-2587

Kahr Arms, P.O. Box 220, 630 Route 303, Blauvelt, NY 10913 / 845-353-5996; FAX: 845-353-7833 www.kahr.com

Kalispel Case Line, P.O. Box 267, Cusick, WA 99119 / 509-445-1121

Kamik Outdoor Footwear, 554 Montee de Liesse, Montreal, PQ H4T 1P1 CANADA / 514-341-3950; FAX: 514-341-1861

Kamyk Engraving Co., Steve, 9 Grandview Dr., Westfield, MA 01085-1810 / 413-568-0457

Kane, Edward, P.O. Box 385, Ukiah, CA 95482 / 707-462-2937

Kane Products, Inc., 5572 Brecksville Rd., Cleveland, OH 44131 / 216-524-9962

Kapro Mfg.Co. Inc. (See R.E.I.)

Kasenit Co., Inc., 13 Park Ave., Highland Mills, NY 10930 / 914-928-9595; FAX: 914-928-7292

Kasmarsik Bullets, 4016 7th Ave. SW, Puyallup, WA 98373

Kaswer Custom, Inc., 13 Surrey Dr., Brookfield, CT 06804 / 203-775-0564; FAX: 203-775-6872

KDF, Inc., 2485 Hwy. 46 N., Seguin, TX 78155 / 830-379-8141; FAX: 830-379-5420

KeeCo Impressions, Inc., 346 Wood Ave., North Brunswick, NJ 08902 / 800-468-0546

Keeler, R. H., 817 "N" St., Port Angeles, WA 98362 / 206-457-4702

Kehr Engraving, Roger Kehr, 2131 Agate Ct. SE, Lacy, WA 98503 / 360-491-0691

Kehr, Roger (See Kehr Engraving)

Keith's Bullets, 942 Twisted Oak, Algonquin, IL 60102 / 708-658-3520

Keith's Custom Gunstocks, Keith M Heppler, 540 Banyan Circle, Walnut Creek, CA 94598 / 925-934-3509; FAX: 925-934-3143

Kelbly, Inc., 7222 Dalton Fox Lake Rd., North Lawrence, OH 44666 / 216-683-4674; FAX: 216-683-7349

Kelley's, P.O. Box 125, Woburn, MA 01801 / 617-935-3389

Kellogg's Professional Products, 325 Pearl St., Sandusky, OH 44870 / 419-625-6551; FAX: 419-625-6167

Kelly, Lance, 1723 Willow Oak Dr., Edgewater, FL 32132 / 904-423-4933

Kel-Tec CNC Industries, Inc., P.O. Box 236009, Cocoa, FL 32923-6009 / 407-631-0068; FAX: 407-631-1169

Ken Eyster Heritage Gunsmiths, Inc., 6441 Bishop Rd., Centerburg, OH 43011 / 614-625-6131

Ken Starnes Gunmaker, 15940 SW Holly Hill Rd., Hillsboro, OR 97123-9033 / 503-628-0705; FAX: 503-628-6005

Keng's Firearms Specialty, Inc./US Tactical Systems, 875 Wharton Dr., P.O. Box 44405, Atlanta, GA 30336-1405 / 404-691-7611; FAX: 404-505-8445

Kennebec Journal, 274 Western Ave., Augusta, ME 04330 / 207-622-6288

Kennedy Firearms, 10 N. Market St., Muncy, PA 17756 / 717-546-6695

Kenneth W. Warren Engraver, P.O. Box 2842, Wenatchee, WA 98807 / 509-663-6123; FAX: 509-665-6123

KenPatable Ent., Inc., P.O. Box 19422, Louisville, KY 40259

Ken's Gun Specialties, Rt. 1, Box 147, Lakeview, AR 72642 / 501-431-5606

Ken's Kustom Kartridges, 331 Jacobs Rd., Hubbard, OH 44425 / 216-534-4595

Ken's Rifle Blanks, Ken McCullough, Rt. 2, P.O. Box 85B, Weston, OR 97886 / 503-566-3879

Kent Cartridge America, Inc., P.O. Box 849, 1000 Zigor Rd., Kearneysville, WV 25430

Kent Cartridge Mfg. Co. Ltd., Unit 16 Branbridges Industrial Esta, Tonbridge, Kent, ENGLAND / 622-872255; FAX: 622-872645

Keowee Game Calls, 608 Hwy. 25 North, Travelers Rest, SC 29690 / 864-834-7204; FAX: 864-834-7831

Kershaw Knives, 25300 SW Parkway Ave., Wilsonville, OR 97070 / 503-682-1966 or 800-325-2891; FAX: 503-682-7168

Kesselring Gun Shop, 400 Hwy. 99 North, Burlington, WA 98233 / 206-724-3113; FAX: 206-724-7003

Ketchum, Jim (See Jim's Precision)

Kickeez Inc., 301 Industrial Dr., Carl Junction, MO 64834-8806 / 419-649-2100; FAX: 417-649-2200 kickey@ipa.net

Kilham & Co., Main St., P.O. Box 37, Lyme, NH 03768 / 603-795-4112

Kim Ahrends Custom Firearms, Inc., Box 203, Clarion, IA 50525 / 515-532-3449; FAX: 515-532-3926

Kimar (See U.S. Importer-IAR, Inc.)

Kimball, Gary, 1526 N. Circle Dr., Colorado Springs, CO 80909 / 719-634-1274

Kimber of America, Inc., 1 Lawton St., Yonkers, NY 10705 / 800-880-2418; FAX: 914-964-9340

King & Co., P.O. Box 1242, Bloomington, IL 61702 / 309-473-2161

King's Gun Works, 1837 W. Glenoaks Blvd., Glendale, CA 91201 / 818-956-6010; FAX: 818-548-8606

Kingyon, Paul L. (See Custom Calls)

Kirkpatrick Leather Co., P.O. Box 677, Laredo, TX 78040 / 956-723-6631; FAX: 956-725-0672

KK Air International (See Impact Case Co.)

KLA Enterprises, P.O. Box 2028, Eaton Park, FL 33840 / 941-682-2829; FAX: 941-682-2829

Kleen-Bore, Inc., 16 Industrial Pkwy., Easthampton, MA 01027 / 413-527-0300; FAX: 413-527-2522 info@kleen-bore.com www.kleen-bore.com

Klein Custom Guns, Don, 433 Murray Park Dr., Ripon, WI 54971 / 920-748-2931

Kleinendorst, K. W., RR 1, Box 1500, Hop Bottom, PA 18824 / 717-289-4687

Klingler Woodcarving, P.O. Box 141, Thistle Hill, Cabot, VT 05647 / 802-426-3811

Kmount, P.O. Box 19422, Louisville, KY 40259 / 502-239-5447

Knight & Hale Game Calls, Box 468, Industrial Park, Cadiz, KY 42211 / 502-924-1755; FAX: 502-924-1763

Knight Rifles, 21852 Hwy. J46, P.O. Box 130, Centerville, IA 52544 / 515-856-2626; FAX: 515-856-2628

Knight Rifles (See Modern Muzzleloading, Inc.)

Knight's Mfg. Co., 7750 9th St. SW, Vero Beach, FL 32968 / 561-562-5697; FAX: 561-569-2955

Knippel, Richard, 500 Gayle Ave. Apt. 213, Modesto, CA 95350-4241 / 209-869-1469

Knock on Wood Antiques, 355 Post Rd., Darien, CT 06820 / 203-655-9031

Knoell, Doug, 9737 McCardle Way, Santee, CA 92071

Knopp, Gary (See Super 6 LLC)

Koevenig's Engraving Service, Box 55 Rabbit Gulch, Hill City, SD 57745 / 605-574-2239

KOGOT, 410 College, Trinidad, CO 81082 / 719-846-9406; FAX: 719-846-9406

Kokolus, Michael M. (See Custom Riflestocks Inc.)

Kolar, 1925 Roosevelt Ave., Racine, WI 53406 / 414-554-0800; FAX: 414-554-9093

Kolpin Mfg., Inc., P.O. Box 107, 205 Depot St., Fox Lake, WI 53933 / 414-928-3118; FAX: 414-928-3687

Korth, Robert-Bosch-Str. 4, P.O. Box 1320, 23909 Ratzeburg, GERMANY / 451-4991497; FAX: 451-4993230

Korth USA, 437R Chandler St., Tewksbury, MA 01876 / 978-851-8656; www.korthusa.com

Korzinek Riflesmith, J., RD 2, Box 73D, Canton, PA 17724 / 717-673-8512

Koval Knives, 5819 Zarley St., Ste. A, New Albany, OH 43054 / 614-855-0777; FAX: 614-855-0945

Kowa Optimed, Inc., 20001 S. Vermont Ave., Torrance, CA 90502 / 310-327-1913; FAX: 310-327-4177

Kramer Designs, P.O. Box 129, Clancy, MT 59634 / 406-933-8658; FAX: 406-933-8658

Kramer Handgun Leather, P.O. Box 112154, Tacoma, WA 98411 / 206-564-6652; FAX: 206-564-1214

Krause Publications, Inc., 700 E. State St., Iola, WI 54990-0001 / 715-445-2214; FAX: 715-445-4087

Krico Deutschland, Nuernbergerstrasse 6, D-90602, Pyrbaum, GERMANY / 09180-2780; FAX: 09180-2661

Krieger Barrels, Inc., N114 W18697 Clinton Dr., Germantown, WI 53022 / 414-255-9593; FAX: 414-255-9586

Krieghoff Gun Co., H., Boschstrasse 22, D-89079 Elm, GERMANY or 731-4018270

Krieghoff International, Inc., 7528 Easton Rd., Ottsville, PA 18942 / 610-847-5173; FAX: 610-847-8691

Kris Mounts, 108 Lehigh St., Johnstown, PA 15905 / 814-539-9751

KSN Industries Ltd. (See U.S. Importer-Israel Arms International Inc.)

Kukowski, Ed (See Collectors Firearms Etc.)

Kulis Freeze Dry Taxidermy, 725 Broadway Ave., Bedford, OH 44146 / 216-232-8352; FAX: 216-232-7305 jkulis@kastaway.com

KVH Industries, Inc., 110 Enterprise Center, Middletown, RI 02842 / 401-847-3327; FAX: 401-849-0045

Kwik Mount Corp., P.O. Box 19422, Louisville, KY 40259 / 502-239-5447

Kwik-Site Co., 5555 Treadwell, Wayne, MI 48184 / 734-326-1500; FAX: 734-326-4120

L

L E Jurras & Assoc., P.O. Box 680, Washington, IN 47501 / 812-254-6170; FAX: 812-254-6170 jurasgun@rtcc.net

L&R Lock Co., 1137 Pocalla Rd., Sumter, SC 29150 / 803-775-6127; FAX: 803-775-5171

L&S Technologies (See Aimtech Mount Systems)

L. Bengtson Arms Co., 6345-B E. Akron St., Mesa, AZ 85205 / 602-981-6375

L.A.R. Mfg., Inc., 4133 W. Farm Rd., West Jordan, UT 84088 / 801-280-3505; FAX: 801-280-1972

L.E. Wilson, Inc., Box 324, 404 Pioneer Ave., Cashmere, WA 98815 / 509-782-1328; FAX: 509-782-7200

L.L. Bean, Inc., Freeport, ME 04032 / 207-865-4761; FAX: 207-552-2802

L.P.A. Snc, Via Alfieri 26, Gardone V.T., Brescia, ITALY / 30-891-14-81; FAX: 30-891-09-51

L.R. Clift Mfg., 3821 Hammonton Rd., Marysville, CA 95901 / 916-755-3390; FAX: 916-755-3393

L.S. Starrett Co., 121 Crescent St., Athol, MA 01331 / 617-249-3551

L.W. Seecamp Co., Inc., P.O. Box 255, New Haven, CT 06502 / 203-877-3429

La Clinique du .45, 1432 Rougemont, Chambly, , PQ J3L 2L8 CANADA / 514-658-1144

Labanu, Inc., 2201-F Fifth Ave., Ronkonkoma, NY 11779 / 516-467-6197; FAX: 516-981-4112

LaBoone, Pat (See Clear Creek Outdoors)

LaBounty Precision Reboring, Inc., 7968 Silver Lake Rd., P.O. Box 186, Maple Falls, WA 98266 / 360-599-2047; FAX: 360-599-3018

LaCrosse Footwear, Inc., P.O. Box 1328, La Crosse, WI 54602 / 608-782-3020 or 800-323-2668; FAX: 800-658-9444

LaFrance Specialties, P.O. Box 87933, San Diego, CA 92138-7933 / 619-293-3373; FAX: 619-293-7087

Lage Uniwad, P.O. Box 2302, Davenport, IA 52809 / 319-388-LAGE; FAX: 319-388-LAGE

Lair, Sam, 520 E. Beaver, Jenks, OK 74037 / 918-299-2391

Lake Center, P.O. Box 670, St. Charles, MO 63302 / 314-946-7500

Lakefield Arms Ltd. (See Savage Arms Inc.)

Lakewood Products LLC, 275 June St., Berlin, WI 54923 / 800-872-8458; FAX: 920-361-7719

Lamboy, Stephen (See Ithaca Classic Doubles)

Lampert, Ron, Rt. 1, 44857 Schoolcraft Trl, Guthrie, MN 56461 / 218-854-7345

Lamson & Goodnow Mfg. Co., 45 Conway St., Shelburne Falls, MA 03170 / 413-625-6564; or 800-872-6564; FAX: 413-625-9816 www.lamsonsharp.com

Langenberg Hat Co., P.O. Box 1860, Washington, MO 63090 / 800-428-1860; FAX: 314-239-3151

Lanphert, Paul, P.O. Box 1985, Wenatchee, WA 98807

Lansky Levine, Arthur (See Lansky Sharpeners)

Lansky Sharpeners, Arthur Lansky Levine, P.O. Box 50830, Las Vegas, NV 89016 / 702-361-7511; FAX: 702-896-9511

LaPrade, P.O. Box 250, Ewing, VA 24248 / 423-733-2615

Lapua Ltd., P.O. Box 5, Lapua, FINLAND / 6-310111; FAX: 6-4388991

LaRocca Gun Works, 51 Union Pl., Worcester, MA 01608 / 508-754-2887; FAX: 508-754-2887

Larry Lyons Gunworks, 110 Hamilton St., Dowagiac, MI 49047 / 616-782-9478

Laser Devices, Inc., 2 Harris Ct. A-4, Monterey, CA 93940 / 408-373-0701; FAX: 408-373-0903

Laseraim Technologies, Inc., P.O. Box 3548, Little Rock, AR 72203 / 501-375-2227

LaserMax, Inc., 3495 Winton Pl., Bldg. B, Rochester, NY 14623-2807 / 800-527-3703; FAX: 716-272-5427

Lassen Community College, Gunsmithing Dept., P.O. Box 3000, Hwy. 139, Susanville, CA 96130 / 916-251-8800; FAX: 916-251-8838

Lathrop's, Inc., 5146 E. Pima, Tucson, AZ 85712 / 520-881-0266 or 800-875-4867; FAX: 520-322-5704

Laughridge, William R. (See Cylinder & Slide, Inc.)

Laurel Mountain Forge, P.O. Box 52, Crown Point, IN 48065 / 219-548-2950; FAX: 219-548-2950

Laurona Armas Eibar, S.A.L., Avenida de Otaola 25, P.O. Box 260, Eibar 20600, SPAIN / 34-43-700600; FAX: 34-43-700616

Lawrence Brand Shot (See Precision Reloading, Inc.)

Lawrence Leather Co., P.O. Box 1479, Lillington, NC 27546 / 910-893-2071; FAX: 910-893-4742

Lawson Co., Harry, 3328 N Richey Blvd., Tucson, AZ 85716 / 520-326-1117; FAX: 520-326-1117

Lawson, John G. (See The Sight Shop)

Lazzeroni Arms Co., P.O. Box 26696, Tucson, AZ 85726 / 888-492-7247; FAX: 520-624-4250

LBT, HCR 62, Box 145, Moyie Springs, ID 83845 / 208-267-3588

Le Clear Industries (See E-Z-Way Systems)

Lea Mfg. Co., 237 E. Aurora St., Waterbury, CT 06720 / 203-753-5116

Leapers, Inc., 7675 Five Mile Rd., Northville, MI 48167 / 248-486-1231; FAX: 248-486-1430

Leatherman Tool Group, Inc., 12106 NE Ainsworth Cir., P.O. Box 20595, Portland, OR 97294 / 503-253-7826; FAX: 503-253-7830

Lebeau-Courally, Rue St. Gilles, 386 4000, Liege, BELGIUM / 042-52-48-43; FAX: 32-042-52-20-08

Leckie Professional Gunsmithing, 546 Quarry Rd., Ottsville, PA 18942 / 215-847-8594

Lectro Science, Inc., 6410 W. Ridge Rd., Erie, PA 16506 / 814-833-6487; FAX: 814-833-0447

Ledbetter Airguns, Riley, 1804 E. Sprague St., Winston Salem, NC 27107-3521 / 919-784-0676

Lee Co., T. K., 1282 Branchwater Ln., Birmingham, AL 35216 / 205-913-5222

Lee Precision, Inc., 4275 Hwy. U, Hartford, WI 53027 / 262-673-3075; FAX: 262-673-9273 info@leeprecision.com leeprecision.com

Lee's Red Ramps, P.O. Box 294210, 13223 Sheepcreek Rd., Phelan, CA 92329 / 505-538-8529

LeFever Arms Co., Inc., 6234 Stokes, Lee Center Rd., Lee Center, NY 13363 / 315-337-6722; FAX: 315-337-1543

Legacy Sports International, P.O. Box 208, Ten Prince St., Alexandria, VA 22313 / 703-548-4837; FAX: 703-549-7826

Legend Products Corp., 21218 Saint Andrews Blvd., Boca Raton, FL 33433-2435

Leibowitz, Leonard, 1205 Murrayhill Ave., Pittsburgh, PA 15217 / 412-361-5455

Leica USA, Inc., 156 Ludlow Ave., Northvale, NJ 07647 / 201-767-7500; FAX: 201-767-8666

LEM Gun Specialties Inc. The Lewis Lead Remover, P.O. Box 2855, Peachtree City, GA 30269-2024

Leonard Day, 6 Linseed Rd. Box 1, West Hatfield, MA 01088-7505 / 413-337-8369

Les Baer Custom, Inc., 29601 34th Ave., Hillsdale, IL 61257 / 309-658-2716; FAX: 309-658-2610

Lestrom Laboratories, Inc., P.O. Box 628, Mexico, NY 13114-0628 / 315-343-3076; FAX: 315-592-3370

Lethal Force Institute (See Police Bookshelf)

Lett Custom Grips, 672 Currier Rd., Hopkinton, NH 03229-2652 / 800-421-5388; FAX: 603-226-4580 info@lettgrips.com www.lettgrips.com

Leupold & Stevens, Inc., 14400 NW Greenbrier Pky., Beaverton, OR 97006 / 503-646-9171; FAX: 503-526-1455

Lever Arms Service Ltd., 2131 Burrard St., Vancouver, BC V6J 3H7 CANADA / 604-736-2711; FAX: 604-738-3503

Lew Horton Dist. Co., Inc., 15 Walkup Dr., Westboro, MA 01581 / 508-366-7400; FAX: 508-366-5332

Liberty Metals, 2233 East 16th St., Los Angeles, CA 90021 / 213-581-9171; FAX: 213-581-9351

Liberty Safe, 1060 N. Spring Creek Pl., Springville, UT 84663 / 800-247-5625; FAX: 801-489-6409

Liberty Shooting Supplies, P.O. Box 357, Hillsboro, OR 97123 / 503-640-5518; FAX: 503-640-5518

Liberty Trouser Co., 3500 6 Ave S., Birmingham, AL 35222-2406 / 205-251-9143

Lightforce U.S.A. Inc., 19226 66th Ave. So., L-103, Kent, WA 98032 / 206-656-1577; FAX: 206-656-1578

Lightning Performance Innovations, Inc., RD1 Box 555, Mohawk, NY 13407 / 800-242-5873; FAX: 315-866-1578

Lilja Precision Rifle Barrels, P.O. Box 372, Plains, MT 59859 / 406-826-3084; FAX: 406-826-3083 lilja@riflebarrels.com www.riflebarrel.com

Lincoln, Dean, Box 1886, Farmington, NM 87401

Lind Custom Guns, Al, 7821 76th Ave. SW, Lakewood, WA 98498 / 253-584-6361 lindcustguns@worldnot.att.net

Linder Solingen Knives, 4401 Sentry Dr., Tucker, GA 30084 / 770-939-6915; FAX: 770-939-6738

Lindsay, Steve, RR 2 Cedar Hills, Kearney, NE 68847 / 308-236-7885

Lindsley Arms Cartridge Co., P.O. Box 757, 20 College Hill Rd., Henniker, NH 03242 / 603-428-3127

Linebaugh Custom Sixguns, Route 2, Box 100, Maryville, MO 64468 / 660-562-3031 sitgunner.com

Lion Country Supply, P.O. Box 480, Port Matilda, PA 16870

List Precision Engineering, Unit 1 Ingley Works, 13 River Road, Barking, ENGLAND / 011-081-594-1686

Lithi Bee Bullet Lube, 1728 Carr Rd., Muskegon, MI 49442 / 616-788-4479

"Little John's" Antique Arms, 1740 W. Laveta, Orange, CA 92668

Littler Sales Co., 20815 W. Chicago, Detroit, MI 48228 / 313-273-6889; FAX: 313-273-1099 littlerptg@aol.com

Littleton, J. F., 275 Pinedale Ave., Oroville, CA 95966 / 916-533-6084

Ljutic Industries, Inc., 732 N. 16th Ave., Ste. 22, Yakima, WA 98907 / 509-248-0476; FAX: 509-576-8233 www.ljuticgun.com

Llama Gabilondo Y Cia, Apartado 290, E-01080, Victoria, SPAIN

Loch Leven Industries, P.O. Box 2751, Santa Rosa, CA 95405 / 707-573-8735; FAX: 707-573-0369

Lock's Philadelphia Gun Exchange, 6700 Rowland Ave., Philadelphia, PA 19149 / 215-332-6225; FAX: 215-332-4800

Lodewick, Walter H., 2816 NE Halsey St., Portland, OR 97232 / 503-284-2554

Lodgewood Mfg., P.O. Box 611, Whitewater, WI 53190

Log Cabin Sport Shop, 8010 Lafayette Rd., Lodi, OH 44254 / 330-948-1082; FAX: 330-948-4307

Logan, Harry M., Box 745, Honokaa, HI 96727 / 808-776-1644

Lohman Mfg. Co., Inc., 4500 Doniphan Dr., P.O. Box 220, Neosho, MO 64850 / 417-451-4438; FAX: 417-451-2576

Lomont Precision Bullets, 278 Sandy Creek Rd., Salmon, ID 83467 / 208-756-6819; FAX: 208-756-6824 klomont.com

London Guns Ltd., Box 3750, Santa Barbara, CA 93130 / 805-683-4141; FAX: 805-683-1712

Lone Star Gunleather, 1301 Brushy Bend Dr., Round Rock, TX 78681 / 512-255-1805

Lone Star Rifle Company, 11231 Rose Road, Conroe, TX 77303 / 409-856-3363

Long, George F., 1500 Rogue River Hwy., Ste. F, Grants Pass, OR 97527 / 541-476-7552

Lortone Inc., 2856 NW Market St., Seattle, WA 98107

Lothar Walther Precision Tool Inc., 3425 Hutchinson Rd., Cumming, GA 30040 / 770-889-9998; FAX: 770-889-4918 lotharwalther@mindspring.com www.lothar-walther.com

Loweth, Richard H.R., 29 Hedgerow Ln., Kirby Muxloe, Leics, LE9 2BN ENGLAND / (0) 116 238 6295

LPS Laboratories, Inc., 4647 Hugh Howell Rd., P.O. Box 3050, Tucker, GA 30084 / 404-934-7800

Lucas, Edward E, 32 Garfield Ave., East Brunswick, NJ 08816 / 201-251-5526

Lupton, Keith (See Pawling Mountain Club)

Lutz Engraving, Ron E., E1998 Smokey Valley Rd., Scandinavia, WI 54977 / 715-467-2674

Lyman Instant Targets, Inc. (See Lyman Products Corporation)

Lyman Products Corporation, 475 Smith Street, Middletown, CT 06457-1529 / 800-22-LYMAN or 860-632-2020; FAX: 860-632-1699

M

M. Thys (See U.S. Importer-Champlin Firearms, Inc.)

M.H. Canjar Co., 6510 Raleigh St., Arvada, CO 80003 / 303-295-2638; FAX: 303-295-2638

M.O.A. Corp., 2451 Old Camden Pike, Eaton, OH 45320 / 937-456-3669

MA Systems, P.O. Box 1143, Chouteau, OK 74337 / 918-479-6378

Mac-1 Airgun Distributors, 13974 Van Ness Ave., Gardena, CA 90249 / 310-327-3581; FAX: 310-327-0238 mac1@mac1airgun.com mac1airgun.com

Macbean, Stan, 754 North 1200 West, Orem, UT 84057 / 801-224-6446

Madis, George, P.O. Box 545, Brownsboro, TX 75756 / 903-852-6480

Madis Books, 2453 West Five Mile Pkwy., Dallas, TX 75233 / 214-330-7168

MAG Instrument, Inc., 1635 S. Sacramento Ave., Ontario, CA 91761 / 909-947-1006; FAX: 909-947-3116

Magma Engineering Co., P.O. Box 161, 20955 E. Ocotillo Rd., Queen Creek, AZ 85242 / 602-987-9008; FAX: 602-987-0148

Mag-Na-Port International, Inc., 41302 Executive Dr., Harrison Twp., MI 48045-1306 / 810-469-6727; FAX: 810-469-0425 email@magnaport.com www.magnaport.com

Magnolia Sports, Inc., 211 W. Main, Magnolia, AR 71753 / 501-234-8410 or 800-530-7816; FAX: 501-234-8117

Magnum Power Products, Inc., P.O. Box 17768, Fountain Hills, AZ 85268

Magnum Research, Inc., 7110 University Ave. NE, Minneapolis, MN 55432 / 800-772-6168 or 763-574-1868; FAX: 763-574-0109 magnumresearch.com

Magnus Bullets, P.O. Box 239, Toney, AL 35773 / 256-420-8359; FAX: 256-420-8360

Mag-Pack Corp., P.O. Box 846, Chesterland, OH 44026

MagSafe Ammo Co., 4700 S. US Highway 17/92, Casselberry, FL 32707-3814 / 407-834-9966; FAX: 407-834-8185

Magtech Ammunition Co. Inc., 837 Boston Rd. #12, Madison, CT 06443 / 203-245-8983; FAX: 203-245-2883 rfine@magtechammunition www.magtech.com.br

Mahony, Philip Bruce, 67 White Hollow Rd., Lime Rock, CT 06039-2418 / 203-435-9341

Mahovsky's Metalife, R.D. 1, Box 149a Eureka Road, Grand Valley, PA 16420 / 814-436-7747

Maine Custom Bullets, RFD 1, Box 1755, Brooks, ME 04921

Maionchi-L.M.I., Via Di Coselli-Zona, Industriale Di Guamo 55060, Lucca, ITALY / 011 39-583 94291

Makinson, Nicholas, RR 3, Komoka, ON N0L 1R0 CANADA / 519-471-5462

Malcolm Enterprises, 1023 E. Prien Lake Rd., Lake Charles, LA 70601

Mallardtone Game Calls, 2901 16th St., Moline, IL 61265 / 309-762-8089

Mandall Shooting Supplies Inc., 3616 N. Scottsdale Rd., Scottsdale, AZ 85252 / 480-945-2553; FAX: 480-949-0734

Marathon Rubber Prods. Co., Inc., 1009 3rd St., Wausau, WI 54403-4765 / 715-845-6255

Marble Arms (See CRR, Inc./Marble's Inc.)

Marchmon Bullets, 8191 Woodland Shore Dr., Brighton, MI 48116

Marent, Rudolf, 9711 Tiltree St., Houston, TX 77075 / 713-946-7028

Mark Lee Supplies, 9901 France Ct., Lakeville, MN 55044 / 612-461-2114

Markell, Inc., 422 Larkfield Center 235, Santa Rosa, CA 95403 / 707-573-0792; FAX: 707-573-9867

Markesbury Muzzle Loaders, Inc., 7785 Foundation Dr., Ste. 6, Florence, KY 41042 / 606-342-5553; or 606-342-2380

Marksman Products, 5482 Argosy Dr., Huntington Beach, CA 92649 / 714-898-7535 or 800-822-8005; FAX: 714-891-0782

Marlin Firearms Co., 100 Kenna Dr., North Haven, CT 06473 / 203-239-5621; FAX: 203-234-7991

MarMik, Inc., 2116 S. Woodland Ave., Michigan City, IN 46360 / 219-872-7231; FAX: 219-872-7231

Marocchi F.lli S.p.A, Via Galileo Galilei 8, I-25068 Zanano, ITALY

Marquart Precision Co., P.O. Box 1740, Prescott, AZ 86302 / 520-445-5646

Marsh, Mike, Croft Cottage, Main St., Derbyshire, DE4 2BY ENGLAND / 01629 650 669

Marshall Enterprises, 792 Canyon Rd., Redwood City, CA 94062

Marshall F. Fish Mfg. Gunsmith Sptg. Co., Rd. Box 2439, Rt. 22 North, Westport, NY 12993 / 518-962-4897; FAX: 518-962-4897

Martin B. Retting Inc., 11029 Washington, Culver City, CA 90232 / 213-837-2412

Martin Hagn Rifles & Actions, P.O. Box 444, Cranbrook, BC V1C 4H9 CANADA / 604-489-4861

Martin's Gun Shop, 937 S. Sheridan Blvd., Lakewood, CO 80226 / 303-922-2184

Martz, John V., 8060 Lakeview Ln., Lincoln, CA 95648; FAX: 916-645-3815

Marvel, Alan, 3922 Madonna Rd., Jarretsville, MD 21084 / 301-557-6545

Marx, Harry (See U.S. Importer for FERLIB)

Maryland Paintball Supply, 8507 Harford Rd., Parkville, MD 21234 / 410-882-5607

MAST Technology, 4350 S. Arville, Ste. 3, Las Vegas, NV 89103 / 702-362-5043; FAX: 702-362-9554

Master Engravers, Inc. (See Hendricks, Frank E. Inc.)

Master Lock Co., 2600 N. 32nd St., Milwaukee, WI 53245 / 414-444-2800

Match Prep--Doyle Gracey, P.O. Box 155, Tehachapi, CA 93581 / 661-822-5383; FAX: 661-823-8680

Mathews & Son, Inc., George E., 10224 S. Paramount Blvd., Downey, CA 90241 / 562-862-6719; FAX: 562-862-6719

Matthews Cutlery, 4401 Sentry Dr., Tucker, GA 30084 / 770-939-6915

Mauser Werke Oberndorf Waffensysteme GmbH, Postfach 1349, 78722, Oberndorf/N., GERMANY

Maverick Arms, Inc., 7 Grasso Ave., P.O. Box 497, North Haven, CT 06473 / 203-230-5300; FAX: 203-230-5420

Maxi-Mount, P.O. Box 291, Willoughby Hills, OH 44094-0291 / 216-944-9456; FAX: 216-944-9456

Mayville Engineering Co. (See MEC, Inc.)

Mazur Restoration, Pete, 13083 Drummer Way, Grass Valley, CA 95949 / 530-268-2412

McBros Rifle Co., P.O. Box 86549, Phoenix, AZ 85080 / 602-582-3713; FAX: 602-581-3825

McCament, Jay (See Jay McCament Custom Gun Maker)

McCann Industries, P.O. Box 641, Spanaway, WA 98387 / 253-537-6919; FAX: 253-537-6919 mccann.machine@worldnet.att.net www.mccannindustries.com

McCann's Machine & Gun Shop, P.O. Box 641, Spanaway, WA 98387 / 253-537-6919; FAX: 253-537-6993 mccann.machine@worldnet.att.net www.mccannindustries.com

McCann's Muzzle-Gun Works, 14 Walton Dr., New Hope, PA 18938 / 215-862-2728

McCluskey Precision Rifles, 10502 14th Ave. NW, Seattle, WA 98177 / 206-781-2776

McCombs, Leo, 1862 White Cemetery Rd., Patriot, OH 45658 / 614-256-1714

McCormick Corp., Chip, P.O. Box 1560, 1715 W FM 1626 Ste 105, Manchaca, TX 78652 / 800-328-CHIP; FAX: 512-462-0009

McCullough, Ken (See Ken's Rifle Blanks)

McDonald, Dennis, 8359 Brady St., Peosta, IA 52068 / 319-556-7940

McFarland, Stan, 2221 Idella Ct., Grand Junction, CO 81505 / 970-243-4704

McGhee, Larry (See B.C. Outdoors)

McGowen Rifle Barrels, 5961 Spruce Ln., St. Anne, IL 60964 / 815-937-9816; FAX: 815-937-4024

McGuire, Bill, 1600 N. Eastmont Ave., East Wenatchee, WA 98802 / 509-884-6021

Mchalik, Gary (See Rossi Firearms)

McKenzie, Lynton, 6940 N. Alvernon Way, Tucson, AZ 85718 / 520-299-5090

McMillan Fiberglass Stocks, Inc., 1638 W. Knudsen Dr., #102, Phoenix, AZ 85027 / 602-582-9635; FAX: 602-581-3825

McMillan Optical Gunsight Co., 28638 N. 42nd St., Cave Creek, AZ 85331 / 602-585-7868; FAX: 602-585-7872

McMillan Rifle Barrels, P.O. Box 3427, Bryan, TX 77805 / 409-690-3456; FAX: 409-690-0156

McMurdo, Lynn (See Specialty Gunsmithing)

MCS, Inc., 34 Delmar Dr., Brookfield, CT 06804 / 203-775-1013; FAX: 203-775-9462

McWelco Products, 6730 Santa Fe Ave., Hesperia, CA 92345 / 619-244-8876; FAX: 619-244-9398

MDS, P.O. Box 1441, Brandon, FL 33509-1441 / 813-653-1180; FAX: 813-684-5953

Measurement Group Inc., Box 27777, Raleigh, NC 27611

Measures, Leon (See Shoot Where You Look)

MEC, Inc., 715 South St., Mayville, WI 53050 / 414-387-4500; FAX: 414-387-5802 reloaders@mayul.com www.mayvl.com

MEC-Gar S.r.l., Via Madonnina 64, Gardone V.T. Brescia, ITALY / 39-30-8912687; FAX: 39-30-8910065

MEC-Gar U.S.A., Inc., Box 112, 500B Monroe Turnpike, Monroe, CT 06468 / 203-635-8662; FAX: 203-635-8662

Mech-Tech Systems, Inc., 1602 Foothill Rd., Kalispell, MT 59901 / 406-755-8055

Meister Bullets (See Gander Mountain Inc.)

Mele, Frank, 201 S. Wellow Ave., Cookeville, TN 38501 / 615-526-4860

Menck, Gunsmith Inc., T.W., 5703 S. 77th St., Ralston, NE 68127

Mendez, John A., P.O. Box 620984, Orlando, FL 32862 / 407-344-2791

Men-Metallwerk Elisenhuette GmbH, P.O. Box 1263, Nassau/Lahn, D-56372 GERMANY / 2604-7819

Meprolight (See Kimber)

Mercer Custom Guns, 216 S. Whitewater Ave., Jefferson, WI 53549 / 920-674-3839

Merit Corp., Box 9044, Schenectady, NY 12309 / 518-346-1420 www.meritcorportation.com

Merkel Freres, Strasse 7 October, 10, Suhl, GERMANY

Merkuria Ltd., Argentinska 38, 17005, Praha 7 CZECH, REPUBLIC / 422-875117; FAX: 422-809152

Metal Merchants, P.O. Box 186, Walled Lake, MI 48390-0186

Metalife Industries (See Mahovsky's Metalife)

Metaloy, Inc., Rt. 5, Box 595, Berryville, AR 72616 / 501-545-3611

Metals Hand Engraver/European Hand Engraving, Ste. 216, 12 South First St., San Jose, CA 95113 / 408-293-6559

Michael's Antiques, Box 591, Waldoboro, ME 04572

Michaels Of Oregon, 1710 Red Soils Ct., Oregon City, OR 97045

Micro Sight Co., 242 Harbor Blvd., Belmont, CA 94002 / 415-591-0769; FAX: 415-591-7531

Microfusion Alfa S.A., Paseo San Andres N8, P.O. Box 271, Eibar, 20600 SPAIN / 34-43-11-89-16; FAX: 34-43-11-40-38

Mid-America Recreation, Inc., 1328 5th Ave., Moline, IL 61265 / 309-764-5089; FAX: 309-764-2722

Middlebrooks Custom Shop, 7366 Colonial Trail East, Surry, VA 23883 / 757-357-0881; FAX: 757-365-0442

Midway Arms, Inc., 5875 W. Van Horn Tavern Rd., Columbia, MO 65203 / 800-243-3220 or 573-445-6363; FAX: 573-446-1018

Midwest Gun Sport, 1108 Herbert Dr., Zebulon, NC 27597 / 919-269-5570

Midwest Sport Distributors, Box 129, Fayette, MO 65248

Mike Davis Products, 643 Loop Dr., Moses Lake, WA 98837 / 509-765-6178 or 509-766-7281

Milberry House Publishing, P.O. Box 575, Corydon, IN 47112 / 888-738-1567; FAX: 888-738-1567

Military Armament Corp., P.O. Box 120, Mt. Zion Rd., Lingleville, TX 76461 / 817-965-3253

Millennium Designed Muzzleloaders, P.O. Box 536, Routes 11 & 25, Limington, ME 04049 / 207-637-2316

Miller Arms, Inc., P.O. Box 260 Purl St., St. Onge, SD 57779 / 605-642-5160; FAX: 605-642-5160

Miller Custom, 210 E. Julia, Clinton, IL 61727 / 217-935-9362

Miller Single Trigger Mfg. Co., Rt. 209, Box 1275, Millersburg, PA 17061 / 717-692-3704

Millett Sights, 7275 Murdy Circle, Adm. Office, Huntington Beach, CA 92647 / 714-842-5575 or 800-645-5388; FAX: 714-843-5707

Mills Jr., Hugh B., 3615 Canterbury Rd., New Bern, NC 28560 / 919-637-4631

Milstor Corp., 80-975 Indio Blvd., Indio, CA 92201 / 760-775-9998; FAX: 760-775-5229 milstor@webtv.net

Miltex, Inc., 700 S. Lee St., Alexandria, VA 22314-4332 / 888-642-9123; FAX: 301-645-1430

Minute Man High Tech Industries, 10611 Canyon Rd. E., Ste. 151, Puyallup, WA 98373 / 800-233-2734

Mirador Optical Corp., P.O. Box 11614, Marina Del Rey, CA 90295-7614 / 310-821-5587; FAX: 310-305-0386

Mitchell, Jack, c/o Geoff Gaebe, Addieville East Farm, 200 Pheasant Dr., Mapleville, RI 02839 / 401-568-3185

Mitchell Bullets, R.F., 430 Walnut St., Westernport, MD 21562

Mitchell Optics, Inc., 2072 CR 1100 N., Sidney, IL 61877 / 217-688-2219 or 217-621-3018; FAX: 217-688-2505

Mitchell's Accuracy Shop, 68 Greenridge Dr., Stafford, VA 22554 / 703-659-0165

MI-TE Bullets, 1396 Ave. K, Ellsworth, KS 67439 / 785-472-4575; FAX: 785-472-5579

Mittermeier, Inc., Frank, P.O. Box 2G, 3577 E. Tremont Ave., Bronx, NY 10465 / 718-828-3843

Mixson Corp., 7635 W. 28th Ave., Hialeah, FL 33016 / 305-821-5190 or 800-327-0078; FAX: 305-558-9318

MJK Gunsmithing, Inc., 417 N. Huber Ct., E. Wenatchee, WA 98802 / 509-884-7683

MKS Supply, Inc. (See Hi-Point Firearms)

MMC, 2513 East Loop 820 North, Ft. Worth, TX 76118 / 817-595-0404; FAX: 817-595-3074

MMP, Rt. 6, Box 384, Harrison, AR 72601 / 501-741-5019; FAX: 501-741-3104

Modern Gun Repair School, P.O. Box 846, Saint Albans, VT 05478-0846 / 802-524-2223; FAX: 802-524-2053 jfwp@dlilearn.com www.mgsinfowdfilearn.com

Modern Muzzleloading, Inc., P.O. Box 130, Centerville, IA 52544 / 641-856-2626

Moeller, Steve, 1213 4th St., Fulton, IL 61252 / 815-589-2300

Mogul Co./Life Jacket, 500 N. Kimball Rd. Ste. 109, South Lake, TX 76092

Molin Industries, Tru-Nord Division, P.O. Box 365, 204 North 9th St., Brainerd, MN 56401 / 218-829-2870

Monell Custom Guns, 228 Red Mills Rd., Pine Bush, NY 12566 / 914-744-3021

Moneymaker Guncraft Corp., 1420 Military Ave., Omaha, NE 68131 / 402-556-0226

Montana Armory, Inc. (See C. Sharps Arms Co. Inc.)

Montana Outfitters, Lewis E. Yearout, 308 Riverview Dr. E., Great Falls, MT 59404 / 406-761-0859

Montana Precision Swaging, P.O. Box 4746, Butte, MT 59702 / 406-484-0600; FAX: 406-494-0600

Montana Vintage Arms, 2354 Bear Canyon Rd., Bozeman, MT 59715

Montgomery Community College, P.O. Box 787-GD, Troy, NC 27371 / 910-576-6222 or 800-839-6222; FAX: 910-576-2176 hammondp@mcc.montgomery.cc.nc.us www.montgomery.cc.nc.us

Morini (See U.S. Importers-Mandall Shooting Supplies Inc.)

Morrison Custom Rifles, J. W., 4015 W Sharon, Phoenix, AZ 85029 / 602-978-3754

Morrison Precision, 6719 Calle Mango, Hereford, AZ 85615 / 520-378-6207 morprec@c2i2.com

Morrow, Bud, 11 Hillside Ln., Sheridan, WY 82801-9729 / 307-674-8360

Morton Booth Co., P.O. Box 123, Joplin, MO 64802 / 417-673-1962; FAX: 417-673-3642

Mo's Competitor Supplies (See MCS, Inc.)

Moss Double Tone, Inc., P.O. Box 1112, 2101 S. Kentucky, Sedalia, MO 65301 / 816-827-0827

Mountain Hollow Game Calls, Box 121, Cascade, MD 21719 / 301-241-3282

Mountain Plains, Inc., 244 Glass Hollow Rd., Alton, VA 22920 / 800-687-3000

Mountain Rifles, Inc., HC 5 Box 9900, Palmer, AK 99645-9511 / 907-373-4194; FAX: 907-373-4195

Mountain South, P.O. Box 381, Barnwell, SC 29812 /; FAX: 803-259-3227

Mountain State Muzzleloading Supplies, Inc., Box 154-1, Rt. 2, Williamstown, WV 26187 / 304-375-7842; FAX: 304-375-3737

Mountain View Sports, Inc., Box 188, Troy, NH 03465 / 603-357-9690; FAX: 603-357-9691

Mowrey Gun Works, P.O. Box 246, Waldron, IN 46182 / 317-525-6181; FAX: 317-525-9595

Mowrey's Guns & Gunsmithing, 119 Fredericks St., Canajoharie, NY 13317 / 518-673-3483

MPC, P.O. Box 450, McMinnville, TN 37110-0450 / 615-473-5513; FAX: 615-473-5516

MPI Stocks, P.O. Box 83266, Portland, OR 97283 / 503-226-1215; FAX: 503-226-2661

MSC Industrial Supply Co., 151 Sunnyside Blvd., Plainview, NY 11803-9915 / 516-349-0330

MSR Targets, P.O. Box 1042, West Covina, CA 91793 / 818-331-7840

Mt. Alto Outdoor Products, Rt. 735, Howardsville, VA 24562

Mt. Baldy Bullet Co., 12981 Old Hill City Rd., Keystone, SD 57751-6623 / 605-666-4725

MTM Molded Products Co., Inc., 3370 Obco Ct., Dayton, OH 45414 / 937-890-7461; FAX: 937-890-1747

Mulhern, Rick, Rt. 5, Box 152, Rayville, LA 71269 / 318-728-2688

Mullins Ammunition, Rt. 2, Box 304K, Clintwood, VA 24228 / 540-926-6772; FAX: 540-926-6092

Mullis Guncraft, 3523 Lawyers Road E., Monroe, NC 28110 / 704-283-6683

Multiplex International, 26 S. Main St., Concord, NH 03301 /; FAX: 603-796-2223

Multipropulseurs, La Bertrandiere, 42580, FRANCE / 77 74 01 30; FAX: 77 93 19 34

Multi-Scale Charge Ltd., 3269 Niagara Falls Blvd., N. Tonawanda, NY 14120 / 905-566-1255; FAX: 905-276-6295

Mundy, Thomas A., 69 Robbins Road, Somerville, NJ 08876 / 201-722-2199

Murmur Corp., 2823 N. Westmoreland Ave., Dallas, TX 75222 / 214-630-5400

Murphy, R.R. Murphy Co., Inc. (See A&M Waterfowl, Inc.)

Murray State College, 1 Murray Campus St., Tishomingo, OK 73460 / 508-371-2371

Muscle Products Corp., 112 Fennell Dr., Butler, PA 16002 / 800-227-7049 or 724-283-0567; FAX: 724-283-8310 mpcsales@mpc-home.com mpc-home.com

Muzzleloaders Etcetera, Inc., 9901 Lyndale Ave. S., Bloomington, MN 55420 / 612-884-1161 muzzleloaders-etcetera.com

Muzzleloading Technologies, Inc., 25 E. Hwy. 40, Ste. 330-12, Roosevelt, UT 84066 / 801-722-5996; FAX: 801-722-5909

MWG Co., P.O. Box 971202, Miami, FL 33197 / 800-428-9394 or 305-253-8393; FAX: 305-232-1247

N

N&J Sales, Lime Kiln Rd., Northford, CT 06472 / 203-484-0247

N.B.B., Inc., 24 Elliot Rd., Sterling, MA 01564 / 508-422-7538 or 800-942-9444

N.C. Ordnance Co., P.O. Box 3254, Wilson, NC 27895 / 919-237-2440; FAX: 919-243-9845

Nagel's Custom Bullets, 100 Scott St., Baytown, TX 77520-2849

Nalpak, 1937-C Friendship Dr., El Cajon, CA 92020 / 619-258-1200

National Bullet Co., 1585 E. 361 St., Eastlake, OH 44095 / 216-951-1854; FAX: 216-951-7761

National Target Co., 4690 Wyaconda Rd., Rockville, MD 20852 / 800-827-7060 or 301-770-7060; FAX: 301-770-7892

Naval Ordnance Works, Rt. 2, Box 919, Sheperdstown, WV 25443 / 304-876-0998

Navy Arms Co., 689 Bergen Blvd., Ridgefield, NJ 07657 / 201-945-2500; FAX: 201-945-6859

Navy Arms Company, Valmore J. Forgett Jr., 689 Bergen Blvd., Ridgefield, NJ 07657 / 201-945-2500; FAX: 201-945-6859 info@navyarms.com www.navyarms.com

NCP Products, Inc., 3500 12th St. N.W., Canton, OH 44708 / 330-456-5130; FAX: 330-456-5234

Neal Johnson's Gunsmithing, Inc., 208 W. Buchanan St., Ste. B, Colorado Springs, CO 80907 / 800-284-8671; FAX: 719-632-3493

Necessary Concepts, Inc., P.O. Box 571, Deer Park, NY 11729 / 516-667-8509; FAX: 516-667-8588

Necromancer Industries, Inc., 14 Communications Way, West Newton, PA 15089 / 412-872-8722

NEI Handtools, Inc., 51583 Columbia River Hwy., Scappoose, OR 97056 / 503-543-6776; FAX: 503-543-6799

Neil A. Jones Custom Products, 17217 Brookhouser Road, Saegertown, PA 16433 / 814-763-2769; FAX: 814-763-4228

Nelson, Gary K., 975 Terrace Dr., Oakdale, CA 95361 / 209-847-4590

Nelson, Stephen (See Nelson's Custom Guns)

Nelson/Weather-Rite, Inc., 14760 Santa Fe Trail Dr., Lenexa, KS 66215 / 913-492-3200; FAX: 913-492-8749

Nelson's Custom Guns, Stephen Nelson, 7430 NW Valley View Dr., Corvallis, OR 97330 / 541-745-5232 nelsons-custom@home.com

Nesci Enterprises Inc., P.O. Box 119, Summit St., East Hampton, CT 06424 / 203-267-2588

Nesika Bay Precision, 22239 Big Valley Rd., Poulsbo, WA 98370 / 206-697-3830

Nettestad Gun Works, RR 1, Box 160, Pelican Rapids, MN 56572 / 218-863-4301

Neumann GmbH, Am Galgenberg 6, 90575, GERMANY / 09101/8258; FAX: 09101/6356

Nevada Pistol Academy, Inc., 4610 Blue Diamond Rd., Las Vegas, NV 89139 / 702-897-1100

New England Ammunition Co., 1771 Post Rd. East, Ste. 223, Westport, CT 06880 / 203-254-8048

New England Arms Co., Box 278, Lawrence Ln., Kittery Point, ME 03905 / 207-439-0593; FAX: 207-439-0525 info@newenglandarms.com www.newenglandarms.com

New England Custom Gun Service, 438 Willow Brook Rd., Plainfield, NH 03781 / 603-469-3450; FAX: 603-469-3471 bestguns@cyberportal.net www.newenglandcustom.com

New England Firearms, 60 Industrial Rowe, Gardner, MA 01440 / 508-632-9393; FAX: 508-632-2300

New Orleans Jewelers Supply Co., 206 Charters St., New Orleans, LA 70130 / 504-523-3839; FAX: 504-523-3836

New SKB Arms Co., C.P.O. Box 1401, Tokyo, JAPAN / 81-3-3943-9550; FAX: 81-3-3943-0695

New Win Publishing, Inc., 186 Center St., Clinton, NJ 08809 / 908-735-9701; FAX: 908-735-9703

Newark Electronics, 4801 N. Ravenswood Ave., Chicago, IL 60640

Newell, Robert H., 55 Coyote, Los Alamos, NM 87544 / 505-662-7135

Newman Gunshop, 119 Miller Rd., Agency, IA 52530 / 515-937-5775

Nicholson Custom, 17285 Thornlay Road, Hughesville, MO 65334 / 816-826-8746

Nickels, Paul R., 4328 Seville St., Las Vegas, NV 89121 / 702-435-5318

Nicklas, Ted, 5504 Hegel Rd., Goodrich, MI 48438 / 810-797-4493

Niemi Engineering, W. B., Box 126 Center Rd., Greensboro, VT 05841 / 802-533-7180; FAX: 802-533-7141

Nightforce (See Lightforce USA Inc.)

Nikolai Leather, 15451 Electronic ln, Huntington Beach, CA 92649 / 714-373-2721; FAX: 714-373-2723

Nikon, Inc., 1300 Walt Whitman Rd., Melville, NY 11747 / 516-547-8623; FAX: 516-547-0309

Nitex, Inc., P.O. Box 1706, Uvalde, TX 78801 / 888-543-8843

Noreen, Peter H., 5075 Buena Vista Dr., Belgrade, MT 59714 / 406-586-7383

Norica, Avnda Otaola, 16 Apartado 68, Eibar, SPAIN

Norinco, 7A Yun Tan N, Beijing, CHINA

Norma Precision AB (See U.S. Importers-Dynamit Nobel-RWS, Inc.)

Normark Corp., 10395 Yellow Circle Dr., Minnetonka, MN 55343-9101 / 612-933-7060; FAX: 612-933-0046

North American Arms, Inc., 2150 South 950 East, Provo, UT 84606-6285 / 800-821-5783 or 801-374-9990; FAX: 801-374-9998

North American Correspondence Schools The Gun Pro, Oak & Pawney St., Scranton, PA 18515 / 717-342-7701

North American Shooting Systems, P.O. Box 306, Osoyoos, BC V0H 1V0 CANADA / 604-495-3131; FAX: 604-495-2816

North Devon Firearms Services, 3 North St., Braunton, EX33 1AJ ENGLAND / 01271 813624; FAX: 01271 813624

North Mountain Pine Training Center (See Executive Protection Institute)

North Pass, 425 South Bowen St., Ste. 6, Longmount, CO 80501 / 303-682-4315; FAX: 303-678-7109

North Safety Products, 10091 Stageline St., Corona, CA 92883-5100 / 714-524-1665

North Star West, P.O. Box 488, Glencoe, CA 95232 / 209-293-7010

North Wind Decoy Co., 1005 N. Tower Rd., Fergus Falls, MN 56537 / 218-736-4378; FAX: 218-736-7060

Northern Precision Custom Swaged Bullets, 329 S. James St., Carthage, NY 13619 / 315-493-1711

Northlake Outdoor Footwear, P.O. Box 10, Franklin, TN 37065-0010 / 615-794-1556; FAX: 615-790-8005

Northside Gun Shop, 2725 NW 109th, Oklahoma City, OK 73120 / 405-840-2353

Northwest Arms, 26884 Pearl Rd., Parma, ID 83660 / 208-722-6771; FAX: 208-722-1062

No-Sho Mfg. Co., 10727 Glenfield Ct., Houston, TX 77096 / 713-723-5332

Nosler, Inc., P.O. Box 671, Bend, OR 97709 / 800-285-3701 or 541-382-3921; FAX: 541-388-4667

Novak's, Inc., 1206 1/2 30th St., P.O. Box 4045, Parkersburg, WV 26101 / 304-485-9295; FAX: 304-428-6722

Now Products, Inc., P.O. Box 27608, Tempe, AZ 85285 / 800-662-6063:; FAX: 480-966-0890

Nowlin Mfg. Co., 20622 S. 4092 Rd., Claremore, OK 74017 / 918-342-0689; FAX: 918-342-0624 nowl.nguns@msn.com nowlinguns.com

NRI Gunsmith School, 4401 Connecticut Ave. NW, Washington, DC 20008

Nu-Line Guns, Inc., 1053 Caulks Hill Rd., Harvester, MO 63304 / 314-441-4500 or 314-447-4501; FAX: 314-447-5018

Null Holsters Ltd. K.L., 161 School St NW, Resaca, GA 30735 / 706-625-5643; FAX: 706-625-9392

Numrich Arms Corp., 203 Broadway, W. Hurley, NY 12491

NW Sinker and Tackle, 380 Valley Dr., Myrtle Creek, OR 97457-9717

Nygord Precision Products, P.O. Box 12578, Prescott, AZ 86304 / 520-717-2315; FAX: 520-717-2198

O

O.F. Mossberg & Sons, Inc., 7 Grasso Ave., North Haven, CT 06473 / 203-230-5300; FAX: 203-230-5420

Oakland Custom Arms, Inc., 4690 W. Walton Blvd., Waterford, MI 48329 / 810-674-8261

Oakman Turkey Calls, RD 1, Box 825, Harrisonville, PA 17228 / 717-485-4620

Obermeyer Rifled Barrels, 23122 60th St., Bristol, WI 53104 / 262-843-3537; FAX: 262-843-2129

October Country Muzzleloading, P.O. Box 969, Dept. GD, Hayden, ID 83835 / 208-772-2068; FAX: 208-772-9230 octobercountry.com

Oehler Research, Inc., P.O. Box 9135, Austin, TX 78766 / 512-327-6900 or 800-531-5125; FAX: 512-327-6903

Oil Rod and Gun Shop, 69 Oak St., East Douglas, MA 01516 / 508-476-3687

Ojala Holsters, Arvo, P.O. Box 98, N Hollywood, CA 91603 / 503-669-1404

OK Weber, Inc., P.O. Box 7485, Eugene, OR 97401 / 541-747-0458; FAX: 541-747-5927 okweber@pacinfo okweber.com

Oker's Engraving, P.O. Box 126, Shawnee, CO 80475 / 303-838-6042

Oklahoma Ammunition Co., 3701A S. Harvard Ave., No. 367, Tulsa, OK 74135-2265 / 918-396-3187; FAX: 918-396-4270

Oklahoma Leather Products, Inc., 500 26th NW, Miami, OK 74354 / 918-542-6651; FAX: 918-542-6653

Old Wagon Bullets, 32 Old Wagon Rd., Wilton, CT 06897

Old West Bullet Moulds, J Ken Chapman, P.O. Box 519, Flora Vista, NM 87415 / 505-334-6970

Old West Reproductions, Inc. R.M. Bachman, 446 Florence S. Loop, Florence, MT 59833 / 406-273-2615; FAX: 406-273-2615

Old Western Scrounger, Inc., 12924 Hwy. A-I2, Montague, CA 96064 / 916-459-5445; FAX: 916-459-3944

Old World Gunsmithing, 2901 SE 122nd St., Portland, OR 97236 / 503-760-7681

Old World Oil Products, 3827 Queen Ave. N., Minneapolis, MN 55412 / 612-522-5037

Ole Frontier Gunsmith Shop, 2617 Hwy. 29 S., Cantonment, FL 32533 / 904-477-8074

Olson, Myron, 989 W. Kemp, Watertown, SD 57201 / 605-886-9787

Olson, Vic, 5002 Countryside Dr., Imperial, MO 63052 / 314-296-8086

Olympic Arms Inc., 620-626 Old Pacific Hwy. SE, Olympia, WA 98513 / 360-491-3447; FAX: 360-491-3447

Olympic Optical Co., P.O. Box 752377, Memphis, TN 38175-2377 / 901-794-3890 or 800-238-7120; FAX: 901-794-0676 80

Omark Industries, Div. of Blount, Inc., 2299 Snake River Ave., P.O. Box 856, Lewiston, ID 83501 / 800-627-3640 or 208-746-2351

Omega Sales, P.O. Box 1066, Mt. Clemens, MI 48043 / 810-469-7323; FAX: 810-469-0425

One Of A Kind, 15610 Purple Sage, San Antonio, TX 78255 / 512-695-3364

Op-Tec, P.O. Box L632, Langhorn, PA 19047 / 215-757-5037

Optical Services Co., P.O. Box 1174, Santa Teresa, NM 88008-1174 / 505-589-3833

Orchard Park Enterprise, P.O. Box 563, Orchard Park, NY 14227 / 616-656-0356

Oregon Trail Bullet Company, P.O. Box 529, Dept. P, Baker City, OR 97814 / 800-811-0548; FAX: 514-523-1803

Original Box, Inc., 700 Linden Ave., York, PA 17404 / 717-854-2897; FAX: 717-845-4276

Original Mink Oil, Inc., 10652 NE Holman, Portland, OR 97220 / 503-255-2814 or 800-547-5895; FAX: 503-255-2487

Orion Rifle Barrel Co., RR2, 137 Cobler Village, Kalispell, MT 59901 / 406-257-5649

Otis Technology, Inc., RR 1, Box 84, Boonville, NY 13309 / 315-942-3320

Ottmar, Maurice, Box 657, 113 E. Fir, Coulee City, WA 99115 / 509-632-5717

Outa-Site Gun Carriers, 219 Market St., Laredo, TX 78040 / 210-722-4678 or 800-880-9715; FAX: 210-726-4858

Outdoor Edge Cutlery Corp., 6395 Gunpark Dr., Unit Q, Boulder, CO 80301 / 303-652-8212; FAX: 303-652-8238

Outdoor Enthusiast, 3784 W. Woodland, Springfield, MO 65807 / 417-883-9841

Outdoor Sports Headquarters, Inc., 967 Watertower Ln., West Carrollton, OH 45449 / 513-865-5855; FAX: 513-865-5962

Outers Laboratories Div. of Blount, Inc.Sporting, Route 2, P.O. Box 39, Onalaska, WI 54650 / 608-781-5800; FAX: 608-781-0368

Ox-Yoke Originals, Inc., 34 Main St., Milo, ME 04463 / 800-231-8313 or 207-943-7351; FAX: 207-943-2416

Ozark Gun Works, 11830 Cemetery Rd., Rogers, AR 72756 / 501-631-6944; FAX: 501-631-6944 ogw@hotmail.com www.geocities.com/ozarkgunworks

P

P&M Sales and Service, 5724 Gainsborough Pl., Oak Forest, IL 60452 / 708-687-7149

P.A.C.T., Inc., P.O. Box 531525, Grand Prairie, TX 75053 / 214-641-0049

P.M. Enterprises, Inc., 146 Curtis Hill Rd., Chehalis, WA 98532 / 360-748-3743; FAX: 360-748-1802 precise1@quik.com

P.S.M.G. Gun Co., 10 Park Ave., Arlington, MA 02174 / 617-646-8845; FAX: 617-646-2133

Pace Marketing, Inc., P.O. Box 2039, Stuart, FL 34995 / 561-871-9682; FAX: 561-871-6552

Pachmayr Div. Lyman Products, 475 S. Mountain Ave., Monrovia, CA 91016 / 626-357-7771

Pacific Armament Corp., 4813 Enterprise Way Unit K, Modesto, CA 95356 / 209-545-2800 gunparts@att.net

Pacific Cartridge, Inc., 2425 Salashan Loop Road, Ferndale, WA 98248 / 360-366-4444; FAX: 360-366-4445

Pacific Rifle Co., P.O. Box 1473, Lake Oswego, OR 97035 / 503-538-7437

Pac-Nor Barreling, 99299 Overlook Rd., P.O. Box 6188, Brookings, OR 97415 / 503-469-7330; FAX: 503-469-7331

Paco's (See Small Custom Mould & Bullet Co.)

Page Custom Bullets, P.O. Box 25, Port Moresby, NEW GUINEA

Pagel Gun Works, Inc., 1407 4th St. NW, Grand Rapids, MN 55744 / 218-326-3003

Pager Pal, 200 W Pleasantview, Hurst, TX 76054 / 800-561-1603; FAX: 817-285-8769 www.pagerpal.com

Paintball Games International Magazine Aceville, Castle House 97 High St., Essex, ENGLAND / 011-44-206-564840

Palmer Security Products, 2930 N. Campbell Ave., Chicago, IL 60618 / 800-788-7725; FAX: 773-267-8080 info@palmersecurity.com www.palmersecurity.com

Palsa Outdoor Products, P.O. Box 81336, Lincoln, NE 68501 / 402-488-5288; FAX: 402-488-2321

Paragon Sales & Services, Inc., 2501 Theodore St., Crest Hill, IL 60435-1613 / 815-725-9212; FAX: 815-725-8974

Para-Ordnance Mfg., Inc., 980 Tapscott Rd., Scarborough, ON M1X 1E7 CANADA / 416-297-7855; FAX: 416-297-1289

Para-Ordnance, Inc., 1919 NE 45th St., Ste. 215, Ft. Lauderdale, FL 33308

Pardini Armi Srl, Via Italica 154, 55043, Lido Di Camaiore Lu, ITALY / 584-90121; FAX: 584-90122

Paris, Frank J., 17417 Pershing St., Livonia, MI 48152-3822

Parker & Sons Shooting Supply, 9337 Smoky Row Rd., Straw Plains, TN 37871-1257

Parker Gun Finishes, 9337 Smokey Row Rd., Strawberry Plains, TN 37871 / 423-933-3286

Parker Reproductions, 114 Broad St., Flemington, NJ 08822 / 908-284-2800; FAX: 908-284-2113

Parsons Optical Mfg. Co., P.O. Box 192, Ross, OH 45061 / 513-867-0820; FAX: 513-867-8380

Partridge Sales Ltd., John, Trent Meadows, Rugeley, ENGLAND

Parts & Surplus, P.O. Box 22074, Memphis, TN 38122 / 901-683-4007

Pasadena Gun Center, 206 E. Shaw, Pasadena, TX 77506 / 713-472-0417; FAX: 713-472-1322

Passive Bullet Traps, Inc. (See Savage Range Systems, Inc.)

Paterson Gunsmithing, 438 Main St., Paterson, NJ 07502 / 201-345-4100

Pathfinder Sports Leather, 2920 E. Chambers St., Phoenix, AZ 85040 / 602-276-0016

Patrick W. Price Bullets, 16520 Worthley Dr., San Lorenzo, CA 94580 / 510-278-1547

Pattern Control, 114 N. Third St., P.O. Box 462105, Garland, TX 75046 / 214-494-3551; FAX: 214-272-8447

Paul A. Harris Hand Engraving, 113 Rusty Ln., Boerne, TX 78006-5746 / 512-391-5121

Paul D. Hillmer Custom Gunstocks, 7251 Hudson Heights, Hudson, IA 50643 / 319-988-3941

Paul Jones Moulds, 4901 Telegraph Rd., Los Angeles, CA 90022 / 213-262-1510

Paulsen Gunstocks, Rt. 71, Box 11, Chinook, MT 59523 / 406-357-3403

Pawling Mountain Club, Keith Lupton, P.O. Box 573, Pawling, NY 12564 / 914-855-3825

Paxton Quigley's Personal Protection Strategies, 9903 Santa Monica Blvd., 300, Beverly Hills, CA 90212 / 310-281-1762 www.defend-net.com/paxton

Payne Photography, Robert, P.O. Box 141471, Austin, TX 78714 / 512-272-4554

PC Co., 5942 Secor Rd., Toledo, OH 43623 / 419-472-6222

Peacemaker Specialists, P.O. Box 157, Whitmore, CA 96096 / 916-472-3438

Pearce Grip, Inc., P.O. Box 40367, Fort Worth, TX 76140-0367 / 206-485-5488; FAX: 206-488-9497

Pease Accuracy, Bob, P.O. Box 310787, New Braunfels, TX 78131 / 210-625-1342

Pease International, 53 Durham St., Portsmouth, NH 03801 / 603-431-1331; FAX: 603-431-1221

PECAR Herbert Schwarz GmbH, Kreuzbergstrasse 6, 10965, Berlin, GERMANY / 004930-785-7383; FAX: 004930-785-1934 michael.schwart@pecar-berlin.de www.pecar-berlin.de

Pecatonica River Longrifle, 5205 Nottingham Dr., Rockford, IL 61111 / 815-968-1995; FAX: 815-968-1996

Pedersen, C. R., 2717 S. Pere Marquette Hwy., Ludington, MI 49431 / 231-843-2061; FAX: 231-845-7695 fegafega.com

Pedersen, Rex C., 2717 S. Pere Marquette Hwy., Ludington, MI 49431 / 616-843-2061

Peerless Alloy, Inc., 1445 Osage St., Denver, CO 80204-2439 / 303-825-6394 or 800-253-1278

Peet Shoe Dryer, Inc., 130 S. 5th St., P.O. Box 618, St. Maries, ID 83861 / 208-245-2095 or 800-222-PEET; FAX: 208-245-5441

Peifer Rifle Co., P.O. Box 192, Nokomis, IL 62075-0192 / 217-563-7050; FAX: 217-563-7060

Pejsa Ballistics, 1314 Marquette Ave Apt 807, Minneapolis, MN 55403-4121 / 612-374-3337; FAX: 612-374-5383

Pelaire Products, 5346 Bonky Ct., W. Palm Beach, FL 33415 / 561-439-0691; FAX: 561-967-0052

Pell, John T. (See KOGOT)

Peltor, Inc. (See Aero Peltor)

PEM's Mfg. Co., 5063 Waterloo Rd., Atwater, OH 44201 / 216-947-3721

Pence Precision Barrels, 7567 E. 900 S., S. Whitley, IN 46787 / 219-839-4745

Pendleton Royal, c/o Swingler Buckland Ltd., 4/7 Highgate St., Birmingham, ENGLAND / 44 121 440 3060 or 44 121 446 5898; FAX: 44 121 446 4165

Pendleton Woolen Mills, P.O. Box 3030, 220 N.W. Broadway, Portland, OR 97208 / 503-226-4801

Penn Bullets, P.O. Box 756, Indianola, PA 15051

Pennsylvania Gun Parts Inc., P.O. Box 665, 300 Third St., East Berlin, PA 17316-0665 / 717-259-8010; FAX: 717-259-0057

Pennsylvania Gunsmith School, 812 Ohio River Blvd., Avalon, Pittsburgh, PA 15202 / 412-766-1812; FAX: 412-766-0855 pgs@pagunsmith.com www.pagunsmith.com

Penrod Precision, 312 College Ave., P.O. Box 307, N. Manchester, IN 46962 / 219-982-8385

Pentax Corp., 35 Inverness Dr. E., Englewood, CO 80112 / 303-799-8000; FAX: 303-790-1131

Pentheny de Pentheny, 2352 Baggett Ct, Santa Rosa, CA 95401 / 707-573-1390; FAX: 707-573-1390

Perazone-Gunsmith, Brian, Cold Spring Rd., Roxbury, NY 12474 / 607-326-4088; FAX: 607-326-3140

Perazzi USA, Inc., 855 N Todd Ave., Azusa, CA 91702-2224 / 626-303-0068; FAX: 626-303-2081

Performance Specialists, 308 Eanes School Rd., Austin, TX 78746 / 512-327-0119

Perugini Visini & Co. S.r.l., Via Camprelle, 126, 25080 Nuvolera, ITALY / 30-6897535; FAX: 30-6897821

Pete Elsen, Inc., 1523 S. 113th St., West Allis, WI 53214 / 414-476-4660; FAX: 414-476-5160

Pete Mazur Restoration, 13083 Drummer Way, Grass Valley, CA 95949 / 916-268-2412

Pete Rickard, Inc., 115 Roy Walsh Rd., Cobleskill, NY 12043 / 518-234-2731:; FAX: 518-234-2454 rickard@telenet.net peterickard.com

Peter Dyson & Son Ltd., 3 Cuckoo Ln., Honley Huddersfield, Yorkshire, HD7 2BR ENGLAND / 44-1484-661062; FAX: 44-1484-663709

Peter Hale/Engraver, 800 E. Canyon Rd., Spanish Fork, UT 84660 / 801-798-8215

Peters Stahl GmbH, Stettiner Strasse 42, D-33106, Paderborn, GERMANY / 05251-750025; FAX: 05251-75611

Petersen Publishing Co. (See Emap USA)

Petro-Explo Inc., 7650 U.S. Hwy. 287, Ste. 100, Arlington, TX 76017 / 817-478-8888

Pevear, John (See Guns, John C. Pevear)

Pflumm Mfg. Co., 10662 Widmer Rd., Lenexa, KS 66215 / 800-888-4867; FAX: 913-451-7857

PFRB Co., P.O. Box 1242, Bloomington, IL 61702 / 309-473-3964; FAX: 309-473-2161

Philip S. Olt Co., P.O. Box 550, 12662 Fifth St., Pekin, IL 61554 / 309-348-3633; FAX: 309-348-3300

Phillippi Custom Bullets, Justin, P.O. Box 773, Ligonier, PA 15658 / 724-238-2962; FAX: 724-238-9671 jrp@wpa.net http://www.wpa.net-jrphil

Phillips & Rogers, Inc., 100 Hilbig #C, Conroe, TX 77301 / 409-435-0011

Phoenix Arms, 1420 S. Archibald Ave., Ontario, CA 91761 / 909-937-6900; FAX: 909-937-0060

Photronic Systems Engineering Company, 6731 Via De La Reina, Bonsall, CA 92003 / 619-758-8000

Piedmont Community College, P.O. Box 1197, Roxboro, NC 27573 / 336-599-1181; FAX: 336-597-3817 www.piedmont.cc.nc.us

Pierce Pistols, 55 Sorrellwood Ln., Sharpsburg, GA 30277-9523 / 404-253-8192

Pietta (See U.S. Importers-Navy Arms Co, Taylor's)

Pine Technical College, 1100 4th St., Pine City, MN 55063 / 800-521-7463; FAX: 612-629-6766

Pinetree Bullets, 133 Skeena St., Kitimat, BC V8C 1Z1 CANADA / 604-632-3768; FAX: 604-632-3768

Pioneer Arms Co., 355 Lawrence Rd., Broomall, PA 19008 / 215-356-5203

Piotti (See U.S. Importer-Moore & Co., Wm. Larkin)

Piquette, Paul (See Piquette's Custom Engraving)

Piquette's Custom Engraving, Paul R. Piquette, 80 Bradford Dr., Feeding Hills, MA 01030 / 413-786-8118; FAX: 413-786-8118

Plaza Cutlery, Inc., 3333 Bristol, 161 South Coast Plaza, Costa Mesa, CA 92626 / 714-549-3932

Plum City Ballistic Range, N2162 80th St., Plum City, WI 54761 / 715-647-2539

PlumFire Press, Inc., 30-A Grove Ave., Patchogue, NY 11772-4112 / 800-695-7246; FAX: 516-758-4071

PMC/Eldorado Cartridge Corp., P.O. Box 62508, 12801 U.S. Hwy. 95 S., Boulder City, NV 89005 / 702-294-0025; FAX: 702-294-0121 kbauer@pmcammo.com pmcammo.com

Poburka, Philip (See Bison Studios)

Pohl, Henry A. (See Great American Gunstock Co.)

Pointing Dog Journal, Village Press Publications, P.O. Box 968, Dept. PGD, Traverse City, MI 49685 / 800-272-3246; FAX: 616-946-3289

Police Bookshelf, P.O. Box 122, Concord, NH 03301 / 603-224-6814; FAX: 603-226-3554

Polywad, Inc., P.O. Box 7916, Macon, GA 31209 / 912-477-0669 polywadmpb@aol.com www.polywad.com

Ponsness/Warren, P.O. Box 8, Rathdrum, ID 83858 / 208-687-2231; FAX: 208-687-2233

Pony Express Reloaders, 608 E. Co. Rd. D, Ste. 3, St. Paul, MN 55117 / 612-483-9406; FAX: 612-483-9884

Pony Express Sport Shop, 16606 Schoenborn St., North Hills, CA 91343 / 818-895-1231

Potts, Wayne E., 912 Poplar St., Denver, CO 80220 / 303-355-5462

Powder Horn Antiques, P.O. Box 4196, Ft. Lauderdale, FL 33338 / 305-565-6060

Powder Horn Ltd., P.O. Box 565, Glenview, IL 60025 / 404-989-3257

Powell & Son (Gunmakers) Ltd., William, 35-37 Carrs Ln., Birmingham, B4 7SX ENGLAND / 121-643-0689; FAX: 121-631-3504

Powell Agency, William, 22 Circle Dr., Bellmore, NY 11710 / 516-679-1158

Power Custom, Inc., 29739 Hwy. J, Gravois Mills, MO 65037 / 513-372-5684; FAX: 573-372-5799 pwpowers@laurie.net www.powercustom.com

Power Plus Enterprises, Inc., P.O. Box 38, Warm Springs, GA 31830 / 706-655-2132

Powley Computer (See Hutton Rifle Ranch)

Practical Tools, Inc., 7067 Easton Rd., P.O. Box 133, Pipersville, PA 18947 / 215-766-7301; FAX: 215-766-8681

Prairie Gun Works, 1-761 Marion St., Winnipeg, MB R2J 0K6 CANADA / 204-231-2976; FAX: 204-231-8566

Prairie River Arms, 1220 N. Sixth St., Princeton, IL 61356 / 815-875-1616 or 800-445-1541; FAX: 815-875-1402

Pranger, Ed G., 1414 7th St., Anacortes, WA 98221 / 206-293-3488

Precise Metalsmithing Enterprises, 146 Curtis Hill Rd., Chehalis, WA 98532 / 206-748-3743; FAX: 206-748-8102

Precision Airgun Sales, Inc., 5247 Warrensville Ctr. Rd., Maple Hts., OH 44137 / 216-587-5005; FAX: 216-587-5005

Precision Cast Bullets, 101 Mud Creek Ln., Ronan, MT 59864 / 406-676-5135

Precision Castings & Equipment, P.O. Box 326, Jasper, IN 47547-0135 / 812-634-9167

Precision Components and Guns, Rt. 55, P.O. Box 337, Pawling, NY 12564 / 914-855-3040

Precision Delta, P.O. Box 128, Ruleville, MS 38771 / 662-756-2810; FAX: 662-756-2590

Precision Gun Works, 104 Sierra Rd. Dept. GD, Kerrville, TX 78028 / 830-367-4587

Precision Munitions, Inc., P.O. Box 326, Jasper, IN 47547

Precision Reloading, Inc., P.O. Box 122, Stafford Springs, CT 06076 / 860-684-5680; FAX: 860-684-6788 www.precisionreloading.com

Precision Sales International, Inc., P.O. Box 1776, Westfield, MA 01086 / 413-562-5055; FAX: 413-562-5056 precision-sales.com

Precision Shooting, Inc., 222 McKee St., Manchester, CT 06040 / 860-645-8776; FAX: 860-643-8215 www.precisionshooting.com

Precision Small Arms, 9777 Wilshire Blvd., Ste. 1005, Beverly Hills, CA 90212 / 310-859-4867; FAX: 310-859-2868

Precision Specialties, 131 Hendom Dr., Feeding Hills, MA 01030 / 413-786-3365; FAX: 413-786-3365

Precision Sport Optics, 15571 Producer Ln., Unit G, Huntington Beach, CA 92649 / 714-891-1309; FAX: 714-892-6920

Premier Reticles, 920 Breckinridge Ln., Winchester, VA 22601-6707 / 540-722-0601; FAX: 540-722-3522

Prescott Projectile Co., 1808 Meadowbrook Road, Prescott, AZ 86303

Preslik's Gunstocks, 4245 Keith Ln., Chico, CA 95926 / 916-891-8236

Price Bullets, Patrick W., 16520 Worthley Dr., San Lorenzo, CA 94580 / 510-278-1547

Prime Reloading, 30 Chiswick End, Meldreth, ROYSTON UK / 0763-260636

Primos, Inc., P.O. Box 12785, Jackson, MS 39236-2785 / 601-366-1288; FAX: 601-362-3274

PRL Bullets, c/o Blackburn Enterprises, 114 Stuart Rd., Ste. 110, Cleveland, TN 37312 / 423-559-0340

Pro Load Ammunition, Inc., 5180 E. Seltice Way, Post Falls, ID 83854 / 208-773-9444; FAX: 208-773-9441

Professional Gunsmiths of America, Inc., Route 1, Box 224F, Lexington, MO 64067 / 816-259-2636

Professional Hunter Supplies (See Star Custom Bullets)

Professional Ordnance, Inc., 1070 Metric Dr., Lake Havasu City, AZ 86403 / 520-505-2420; FAX: 520-505-2141 www.professional-ordnance.com

Prolixr Lubricants, P.O. Box 1348, Victorville, CA 92393 / 800-248-5823 or 760-243-3129; FAX: 760-241-0148 prolix@accex.net www.prolixlubricant.com

Pro-Mark Div. of Wells Lamont, 6640 W. Touhy, Chicago, IL 60648 / 312-647-8200

Proofmark Corp., P.O. Box 610, Burgess, VA 22432 / 804-453-4337; FAX: 804-453-4337 proofmark@rivnet.net

Pro-Port Ltd., 41302 Executive Dr., Harrison Twp., MI 48045-1306 / 810-469-7323; FAX: 810-469-0425 e-mail@magnaport.com www.magnaport.com

Pro-Shot Products, Inc., P.O. Box 763, Taylorville, IL 62568 / 217-824-9133; FAX: 217-824-8861

Protektor Model, 1-11 Bridge St., Galeton, PA 16922 / 814-435-2442 hrk@penn.com www.protektormodel.com

Prototech Industries, Inc., Rt. 1, Box 81, Delia, KS 66418 / 913-771-3571; FAX: 913-771-2531

ProWare, Inc., 15847 NE Hancock St., Portland, OR 97230 / 503-239-0159

PWL Gunleather, P.O. Box 450432, Atlanta, GA 31145 / 770-822-1640; FAX: 770-822-1704 covert@pwlusa.com www.pwlusa.com

Pyromid, Inc., P.O. Box 6466, Bend, OR 97708 / 503-548-1041; FAX: 503-923-1004

Q

Quack Decoy & Sporting Clays, 4 Ann & Hope Way, P.O. Box 98, Cumberland, RI 02864 / 401-723-8202; FAX: 401-722-5910

Quaker Boy, Inc., 5455 Webster Rd., Orchard Parks, NY 14127 / 716-662-3979; FAX: 716-662-9426

Quality Arms, Inc., Box 19477, Dept. GD, Houston, TX 77224 / 281-870-8377; FAX: 281-870-8524 arrieta2@excite.com www.gunshop.com

Quality Custom Firearms, Stephen L. Billeb, 22 Vista View Ln., Cody, WY 82414 / 307-587-4278; FAX: 307-587-4297 sbilleb@hotmail.com

Quality Firearms of Idaho, Inc., 659 Harmon Way, Middleton, ID 83644-3065 / 208-466-1631

Quality Parts Co./Bushmaster Firearms, 999 Roosevelt Trail Bldg. 3, Windham, ME 04062 / 207-892-2005; FAX: 207-892-8068

Quarton USA, Ltd. Co., 7042 Alamo Downs Pkwy., Ste. 370, San Antonio, TX 78238-4518 / 800-520-8435 or 210-520-8430; FAX: 210-520-8433

Que Industries, Inc., P.O. Box 2471, Everett, WA 98203 / 800-769-6930 or 206-347-9843; FAX: 206-514-3266 queinfo@queindustries.com

Queen Cutlery Co., P.O. Box 500, Franklinville, NY 14737 / 800-222-5233; FAX: 800-299-2618

R

R&C Knives & Such, 2136 Candy Cane Walk, Manteca, CA 95336-9501 / 209-239-3722; FAX: 209-825-6947

R&D Gun Repair, Kenny Howell, RR1 Box 283, Beloit, WI 53511

R&J Gun Shop, 337 S. Humbolt St., Canyon City, OR 97820 / 541-575-2130 rjgunshop@highdestertnet.com

R&S Industries Corp., 8255 Brentwood Industrial Dr., St. Louis, MO 63144 / 314-781-5400 polishingcloth.com

R. Murphy Co., Inc., 13 Groton-Harvard Rd., P.O. Box 376, Ayer, MA 01432 / 617-772-3481

R.A. Wells Custom Gunsmith, 3452 1st Ave., Racine, WI 53402 / 414-639-5223

R.E. Seebeck Assoc., P.O. Box 59752, Dallas, TX 75229

R.E.I., P.O. Box 88, Tallevast, FL 34270 / 813-755-0085

R.E.T. Enterprises, 2608 S. Chestnut, Broken Arrow, OK 74012 / 918-251-GUNS; FAX: 918-251-0587

R.F. Mitchell Bullets, 430 Walnut St., Westernport, MD 21562

R.I.S. Co., Inc., 718 Timberlake Circle, Richardson, TX 75080 / 214-235-0933

R.M. Precision, P.O. Box 210, LaVerkin, UT 84745 / 801-635-4656; FAX: 801-635-4430

R.T. Eastman Products, P.O. Box 1531, Jackson, WY 83001 / 307-733-3217 or 800-624-4311

Rabeno, Martin, 92 Spook Hole Rd., Ellenville, NY 12428 / 845-647-2129; FAX: 845-647-2129 fancygun@aol.com

Radack Photography, Lauren, 21140 Jib Court L-12, Aventura, FL 33180 / 305-931-3110

Radiator Specialty Co., 1900 Wilkinson Blvd., P.O. Box 34689, Charlotte, NC 28234 / 800-438-6947; FAX: 800-421-9525

Radical Concepts, P.O. Box 1473, Lake Grove, OR 97035 / 503-538-7437

Rainier Ballistics Corp., 4500 15th St. East, Tacoma, WA 98424 / 800-638-8722 or 206-922-7589; FAX: 206-922-7854

Ralph Bone Engraving, 718 N. Atlanta, Owasso, OK 74055 / 918-272-9745

Ram-Line Blount, Inc., P.O. Box 39, Onalaska, WI 54650

Ramon B. Gonzalez Guns, P.O. Box 370, 93 St. Joseph's Hill Road, Monticello, NY 12701 / 914-794-4515

Rampart International, 2781 W. MacArthur Blvd., B-283, Santa Ana, CA 92704 / 800-976-7240 or 714-557-6405

Ranch Products, P.O. Box 145, Malinta, OH 43535 / 313-277-3118; FAX: 313-565-8536

Randall-Made Knives, P.O. Box 1988, Orlando, FL 32802 / 407-855-8075

Randco UK, 286 Gipsy Rd., Welling, DA16 1JJ ENGLAND / 44 81 303 4118

Randolph Engineering, Inc., 26 Thomas Patten Dr., Randolph, MA 02368 / 800-541-1405; FAX: 800-875-4200

Randy Duane Custom Stocks, 110 W. North Ave., Winchester, VA 22601 / 703-667-9461; FAX: 703-722-3993

Range Brass Products Company, P.O. Box 218, Rockport, TX 78381

Ranger Shooting Glasses, 26 Thomas Patten Dr., Randolph, MA 02368 / 800-541-1405; FAX: 617-986-0337

Ransom International Corp., 1027 Spire Dr., Prescott, AZ 86302 / 520-778-7899; FAX: 520-778-7993 ransom@primenet.com www.ransom-intl.com

Rapine Bullet Mould Mfg. Co., 9503 Landis Ln., East Greenville, PA 18041 / 215-679-5413; FAX: 215-679-9795

Raptor Arms Co., Inc., 273 Canal St., #179, Shelton, CT 06484 / 203-924-7618; FAX: 203-924-7624

Ravell Ltd., 289 Diputacion St., 08009, Barcelona, SPAIN / 34(3) 4874486; FAX: 34(3) 4881394

Ray Riling Arms Books Co., 6844 Gorsten St., P.O. Box 18925, Philadelphia, PA 19119 / 215-438-2456; FAX: 215-438-5395

Ray's Gunsmith Shop, 3199 Elm Ave., Grand Junction, CO 81504 / 970-434-6162; FAX: 970-434-6162

Raytech Div. of Lyman Products Corp., 475 Smith Street, Middletown, CT 06457-1541 / 860-632-2020; FAX: 860-632-1699

RCBS Div. of Blount, 605 Oro Dam Blvd., Oroville, CA 95965 / 800-533-5000 or 916-533-5191; FAX: 916-533-1647 www.rcbs.com

Reagent Chemical & Research, Inc. (See Cali'co Hardwoods, Inc.)

Reardon Products, P.O. Box 126, Morrison, IL 61270 / 815-772-3155

Red Diamond Dist. Co., 1304 Snowdon Dr., Knoxville, TN 37912

Redding Reloading Equipment, 1089 Starr Rd., Cortland, NY 13045 / 607-753-3331; FAX: 607-756-8445 techline@redding-reloading.com www.redding-reloading.com

Redfield Media Resource Center, 4607 N.E. Cedar Creek Rd., Woodland, WA 98674 / 360-225-5000; FAX: 360-225-7616

Redfield, Inc., 5800 E. Jewell Ave., Denver, CO 80224 / 303-757-6411; FAX: 303-756-2338

Redfield/Blount, P.O. Box 39, Onalaska, WI 54650 / 608-781-5800; FAX: 608-781-0368

Redman's Rifling & Reboring, 189 Nichols Rd., Omak, WA 98841 / 509-826-5512

Redwood Bullet Works, 3559 Bay Rd., Redwood City, CA 94063 / 415-367-6741

Reed, Dave, Rt. 1, Box 374, Minnesota City, MN 55959 / 507-689-2944

Reiswig, Wallace E. (See Claro Walnut Gunstock Co.)

Reloaders Equipment Co., 4680 High St., Ecorse, MI 48229

Reloading Specialties, Inc., Box 1130, Pine Island, MN 55463 / 507-356-8500; FAX: 507-356-8800

Remington Arms Co., Inc., 870 Remington Dr., P.O. Box 700, Madison, NC 27025-0700 / 800-243-9700; FAX: 910-548-8700

Remington Double Shotguns, 7885 Cyd Dr., Denver, CO 80221 / 303-429-6947

Renato Gamba S.p.A.-Societa Armi Bresciane Srl., Via Artigiani 93, 25063 Gardone, Val Trompia (BS), ITALY / 30-8911640; FAX: 30-8911648

Renegade, P.O. Box 31546, Phoenix, AZ 85046 / 602-482-6777; FAX: 602-482-1952

Renfrew Guns & Supplies, R.R. 4, Renfrew, ON K7V 3Z7 CANADA / 613-432-7080

Reno, Wayne, 2808 Stagestop Rd., Jefferson, CO 80456 / 719-836-3452

Republic Arms, Inc., 15167 Sierra Bonita Ln., Chino, CA 91710 / 909-597-3873; FAX: 909-597-2612

Retting, Inc., Martin B, 11029 Washington, Culver City, CA 90232 / 213-837-2412

RG-G, Inc., P.O. Box 935, Trinidad, CO 81082 / 719-845-1436

RH Machine & Consulting Inc., P.O. Box 394, Pacific, MO 63069 / 314-271-8465

Rhino, P.O. Box 787, Locust, NC 28097 / 704-753-2198

Rhodeside, Inc., 1704 Commerce Dr., Piqua, OH 45356 / 513-773-5781

Rice, Keith (See White Rock Tool & Die)

Richard H.R. Loweth (Firearms), 29 Hedgegrow Ln., Kirby Muxloe, Leics. LE9 2BN, ENGLAND

Richards Micro-Fit Stocks, 8331 N. San Fernando Ave., Sun Valley, CA 91352 / 818-767-6097; FAX: 818-767-7121

Rickard, Inc., Pete, RD 1, Box 292, Cobleskill, NY 12043 / 800-282-5663; FAX: 518-234-2454

Ridgeline, Inc., Bruce Sheldon, P.O. Box 930, Dewey, AZ 86327-0930 / 800-632-5900; FAX: 520-632-5900

Ridgetop Sporting Goods, P.O. Box 306, 42907 Hilligoss Ln. East, Eatonville, WA 98328 / 360-832-6422; FAX: 360-832-6422

Ries, Chuck, 415 Ridgecrest Dr., Grants Pass, OR 97527 / 503-476-5623

Rifles, Inc., 873 W. 5400 N., Cedar City, UT 84720 / 801-586-5996; FAX: 801-586-5996

Riggs, Jim, 206 Azalea, Boerne, TX 78006 / 210-249-8567

Riley Ledbetter Airguns, 1804 E. Sprague St., Winston Salem, NC 27107-3521 / 919-784-0676

Riling Arms Books Co., Ray, 6844 Gorsten St., P.O. Box 18925, Philadelphia, PA 19119 / 215-438-2456; FAX: 215-438-5395

Rim Pac Sports, Inc., 1034 N. Soldano Ave., Azusa, CA 91702-2135

Ringler Custom Leather Co., 31 Shining Mtn. Rd., Powell, WY 82435 / 307-645-3255

Ripley Rifles, 42 Fletcher Street, Ripley, Derbyshire, DE5 3LP ENGLAND / 011-0773-748353

River Road Sporting Clays, Bruce Barsotti, P.O. Box 3016, Gonzales, CA 93926 / 408-675-2473

Rizzini SNC, Via 2 Giugno, 7/7Bis-25060, Marcheno (Brescia), ITALY

RLCM Enterprises, 110 Hill Crest Dr., Burleson, TX 76028

RMS Custom Gunsmithing, 4120 N. Bitterwell, Prescott Valley, AZ 86314 / 520-772-7626

Robert Evans Engraving, 332 Vine St., Oregon City, OR 97045 / 503-656-5693

Robert Valade Engraving, 931 3rd Ave., Seaside, OR 97138 / 503-738-7672

Roberts Products, 25328 SE Iss. Beaver Lk. Rd., Issaquah, WA 98029 / 206-392-8172

Robinett, R. G., P.O. Box 72, Madrid, IA 50156 / 515-795-2906

Robinson, Don, Pennsylvania Hse., 36 Fairfax Crescent, W Yorkshire, ENGLAND / 0422-364458

Robinson Armament Co., P.O. Box 16776, Salt Lake City, UT 84116-0776 / 801-355-0401; FAX: 801-355-0402 zdf@robarm.com www.robarm.com

Robinson Firearms Mfg. Ltd., 1699 Blondeaux Crescent, Kelowna, BC V1Y 4J8 CANADA / 604-868-9596

Robinson H.V. Bullets, 3145 Church St., Zachary, LA 70791 / 504-654-4029

Rochester Lead Works, 76 Anderson Ave., Rochester, NY 14607 / 716-442-8500; FAX: 716-442-4712

Rock River Arms, 101 Noble St., Cleveland, IL 61241

Rockwood Corp., Speedwell Division, 136 Lincoln Blvd., Middlesex, NJ 08846 / 800-243-8274; FAX: 980-560-7475

Rocky Mountain Arms, Inc., 1813 Sunset Pl, Unit D, Longmont, CO 80501 / 800-375-0846; FAX: 303-678-8766

Rocky Mountain High Sports Glasses, 8121 N. Central Park Ave., Skokie, IL 60076 / 847-679-1012 or 800-323-1418; FAX: 847-679-0184

Rocky Mountain Rifle Works Ltd., 1707 14th St., Boulder, CO 80302 / 303-443-9189

Rocky Mountain Target Co., 3 Aloe Way, Leesburg, FL 34788 / 352-365-9598

Rocky Mountain Wildlife Products, P.O. Box 999, La Porte, CO 80535 / 970-484-2768; FAX: 970-484-0807

Rocky Shoes & Boots, 294 Harper St., Nelsonville, OH 45764 / 800-848-9452 or 614-753-1951; FAX: 614-753-4024

Rodgers & Sons Ltd., Joseph (See George Ibberson (Sheffield) Ltd.)

Rogue Rifle Co., Inc., P.O. Box 20, Prospect, OR 97536 / 541-560-4040; FAX: 541-560-4041

Rogue River Rifleworks, 1317 Spring St., Paso Robles, CA 93446 / 805-227-4706; FAX: 805-227-4723

Rohner, Hans, 1148 Twin Sisters Ranch Rd., Nederland, CO 80466-9600

Rohner, John, 186 Virginia Ave., Asheville, NC 28806 / 303-444-3841

Romain's Custom Guns, Inc., RD 1, Whetstone Rd., Brockport, PA 15823 / 814-265-1948 romwhetstone@penn.com

Ron Frank Custom Classic Arms, 7131 Richland Rd., Ft. Worth, TX 76118 / 817-284-9300; FAX: 817-284-9300

Ron Lutz Engraving, E. 1998 Smokey Valley Rd., Scandinavia, WI 54977 / 715-467-2674

Rooster Laboratories, P.O. Box 412514, Kansas City, MO 64141 / 816-474-1622; FAX: 816-474-1307

Rorschach Precision Products, 417 Keats Cir., Irving, TX 75061-6754 / 214-790-3487

Rosenberg & Son, Jack A, 12229 Cox Ln., Dallas, TX 75234 / 214-241-6302

Ross, Don, 12813 West 83 Terrace, Lenexa, KS 66215 / 913-492-6982

Rosser, Bob, 1824 29th Ave., Ste. 214, Birmingham, AL 35209 / 205-870-4422; FAX: 205-870-4421

Rossi Firearms, Gary Mchalik, 16175 NW 49th Ave., Miami, FL 33014-6314 / 305-474-0401; FAX: 305-623-7506 rossiusa.com

Roto Carve, 2754 Garden Ave., Janesville, IA 50647

Rottweil Compe, 1330 Glassell, Orange, CA 92667

Round Edge, Inc., P.O. Box 723, Lansdale, PA 19446 / 215-361-0859

Royal Arms Gunstocks, 919 8th Ave. NW, Great Falls, MT 59404 / 406-453-1149; FAX: 406-453-1194 royalarms@lmt.net lmt.net/~royalarms

Roy's Custom Grips, Rt. 3, Box 174-E, Lynchburg, VA 24504 / 804-993-3470

RPM, 15481 N. Twin Lakes Dr., Tucson, AZ 85739 / 520-825-1233; FAX: 520-825-3333

Rubright Bullets, 1008 S. Quince Rd., Walnutport, PA 18088 / 215-767-1339

Rucker Dist. Inc., P.O. Box 479, Terrell, TX 75160 / 214-563-2094

Ruger (See Sturm, Ruger & Co., Inc.)

Rumanya Inc., 11513 Piney Lodge Rd., Gaithersburg, MD 20878-2443 / 281-345-2077; FAX: 281-345-2005

Rundell's Gun Shop, 6198 Frances Rd., Clio, MI 48420 / 313-687-0559

Runge, Robert P., 94 Grove St., Ilion, NY 13357 / 315-894-3036

Rupert's Gun Shop, 2202 Dick Rd., Ste. B, Fenwick, MI 48834 / 517-248-3252

Russ Haydon Shooters' Supply, 15018 Goodrich Dr. NW, Gig Harbor, WA 98329 / 253-857-7557; FAX: 253-857-7884

Russ Trading Post, William A. Russ, 23 William St., Addison, NY 14801-1326 / 607-359-3896

Russ, William (See Russ Trading Post)

Rusteprufe Laboratories, 1319 Jefferson Ave., Sparta, WI 54656 / 608-269-4144; FAX: 608-366-1972 rusteprufe@centurytel.net

Rusty Duck Premium Gun Care Products, 7785 Foundation Dr., Ste. 6, Florence, KY 41042 / 606-342-5553; FAX: 606-342-5556

Rutgers Book Center, 127 Raritan Ave., Highland Park, NJ 08904 / 732-545-4344; FAX: 732-545-6686

Rutten (See U.S. Importer-Labanu, Inc.)

RWS (See US Importer-Dynamit Nobel-RWS, Inc.)

Ryan, Chad L., RR 3, Box 72, Cresco, IA 52136 / 319-547-4384

S

S&K Mfg. Co., RR 2 Box 72E, Sugar Grove, PA 16350-9201 / 814-563-7808; FAX: 814-563-4067

S&S Firearms, 74-11 Myrtle Ave., Glendale, NY 11385 / 718-497-1100; FAX: 718-497-1105

S.A.R.L. G. Granger, 66 cours Fauriel, 42100, Saint Etienne, FRANCE / 04 77 25 14 73; FAX: 04 77 38 66 99

S.C.R.C., P.O. Box 660, Katy, TX 77492-0660; FAX: 713-578-2124

S.D. Meacham, 1070 Angel Ridge, Peck, ID 83545

S.G.S. Sporting Guns Srl., Via Della Resistenza, 37 20090, Buccinasco, ITALY / 2-45702446; FAX: 2-45702464

S.I.A.C.E. (See U.S. Importer-IAR Inc.)

Sabatti S.r.l., via Alessandro Volta 90, 25063 Gardone V.T., Brescia, ITALY / 030-8912207-831312; FAX: 030-8912059

SAECO (See Redding Reloading Equipment)

Safari Outfitters Ltd., 71 Ethan Allan Hwy., Ridgefield, CT 06877 / 203-544-9505

Safari Press, Inc., 15621 Chemical Ln. B, Huntington Beach, CA 92649 / 714-894-9080; FAX: 714-894-4949

Safariland Ltd., Inc., 3120 E. Mission Blvd., P.O. Box 51478, Ontario, CA 91761 / 909-923-7300; FAX: 909-923-7400

SAFE, P.O. Box 864, Post Falls, ID 83877 / 208-773-3624; FAX: 208-773-6819 staysafe@safe-llc.com www.safe-llc.com

Safety Speed Holster, Inc., 910 S. Vail Ave., Montebello, CA 90640 / 323-723-4140; FAX: 323-726-6973

Saf-T-Lok, 5713 Corporate Way, Ste. 100, W. Palm Beach, FL 33407

Sako Ltd. (See U.S. Importer-Stoeger Industries)

Samco Global Arms, Inc., 6995 NW 43rd St., Miami, FL 33166 / 305-593-9782; FAX: 305-593-1014 samco@samcoglobal.com samcoglobal.com

Sampson, Roger, 2316 Mahogany St., Mora, MN 55051 / 612-679-4868

San Marco (See U.S. Importers-Cape Outfitters-EMF Co., Inc.)

San Welch Gun Engraving, Sam Welch, HC 64 Box 2110, Moab, UT 84532 / 435-259-8131

Sanders Custom Gun Service, 2358 Tyler Ln., Louisville, KY 40205 / 502-454-3338; FAX: 502-451-8857

Sanders Gun and Machine Shop, 145 Delhi Road, Manchester, IA 52057 / 502-454-3338; FAX: 502-451-8857

Sandia Die & Cartridge Co., 37 Atancacio Rd. NE, Albuquerque, NM 87123 / 505-298-5729

Sarco, Inc., 323 Union St., Stirling, NJ 07980 / 908-647-3800; FAX: 908-647-9413

Sauer (See U.S. Importers-Paul Co., The, Sigarms)

Sauls, R. (See Bryan & Assoc.)

Saunders Gun & Machine Shop, R.R. 2, Delhi Rd., Manchester, IA 52057

Savage Arms (Canada), Inc., 248 Water St., P.O. Box 1240, Lakefield, ON K0L 2H0 CANADA / 705-652-8000; FAX: 705-652-8431

Savage Arms, Inc., 100 Springdale Rd., Westfield, MA 01085 / 413-568-7001; FAX: 413-562-7764

Savage Range Systems, Inc., 100 Springdale Rd., Westfield, MA 01085 / 413-568-7001; FAX: 413-562-1152

Saville Iron Co. (See Greenwood Precision)

Savino, Barbara J., P.O. Box 51, West Burke, VT 05871-0051

Scansport, Inc., P.O. Box 700, Enfield, NH 03748 / 603-632-7654

Scattergun Technologies, Inc., 620 8th Ave. S., Nashville, TN 37203 / 615-254-1441; FAX: 615-254-1449

Sceery Game Calls, P.O. Box 6520, Sante Fe, NM 87502 / 505-471-9110; FAX: 505-471-3476

Schaefer Shooting Sports, P.O. Box 1515, Melville, NY 11747-0515 / 516-643-5466; FAX: 516-643-2426 rschaefe@optonline.net, www.schaefershooting.com

Scharch Mfg., Inc., 10325 CR 120, Salida, CO 81201 / 719-539-7242 or 800-836-4683; FAX: 719-539-3021

Scherer, Box 250, Ewing, VA 24248 / 615-733-2615; FAX: 615-733-2073

Schiffman, Curt, 3017 Kevin Cr., Idaho Falls, ID 83402 / 208-524-4684

Schiffman, Mike, 8233 S. Crystal Springs, McCammon, ID 83250 / 208-254-9114

Schiffman, Norman, 3017 Kevin Cr., Idaho Falls, ID 83402 / 208-524-4684

Schmidt & Bender, Inc., 438 Willow Brook Rd., P.O. Box 134, Meriden, NH 03770 / 800-468-3450 or 800-468-3450; FAX: 603-469-3471; scopes@cyberportal.net, schmidtbender.com

Schmidtke Group, 17050 W. Salentine Dr., New Berlin, WI 53151-7349

Schneider Bullets, 3655 W. 214th St., Fairview Park, OH 44126

Schneider Rifle Barrels, Inc., Gary, 12202 N. 62nd Pl., Scottsdale, AZ 85254 / 602-948-2525

Schroeder Bullets, 1421 Thermal Ave., San Diego, CA 92154 / 619-423-3523; FAX: 619-423-8124

Schuetzen Pistol Works, 620-626 Old Pacific Hwy. SE, Olympia, WA 98513 / 360-459-3471; FAX: 360-491-3447

Schulz Industries, 16247 Minnesota Ave., Paramount, CA 90723 / 213-439-5903

Schumakers Gun Shop, 512 Prouty Corner Lp. A, Colville, WA 99114 / 509-684-4848

Scope Control, Inc., 5775 Co. Rd. 23 SE, Alexandria, MN 56308 / 612-762-7295

ScopLevel, 151 Lindbergh Ave., Ste. C, Livermore, CA 94550 / 925-449-5052; FAX: 925-373-0861

Score High Gunsmithing, 9812-A, Cochiti SE, Albuquerque, NM 087123 / 800-326-5632 or 505-292-5532; FAX: 505-292-2592

Scot Powder, Rt.1 Box 167, McEwen, TN 37101 / 800-416-3006; FAX: 615-729-4211

Scot Powder Co. of Ohio, Inc., Box GD96, Only, TN 37140 / 615-729-4207 or 800-416-3006; FAX: 615-729-4217

Scott Fine Guns Inc., Thad, P.O. Box 412, Indianola, MS 38751 / 601-887-5929

Scott McDougall & Associates, 7950 Redwood Dr., Ste. 13, Cotati, CA 94931 / 707-546-2264; FAX: 707-795-1911 www.colt380.com

Searcy Enterprises, P.O. Box 584, Boron, CA 93596 / 760-762-6771; FAX: 760-762-0191

Second Chance Body Armor, P.O. Box 578, Central Lake, MI 49622 / 616-544-5721; FAX: 616-544-9824

Seebeck Assoc., R.E., P. O. Box 59752, Dallas, TX 75229

Seecamp Co. Inc., L. W., P.O. Box 255, New Haven, CT 06502 / 203-877-3429

Segway Industries, P.O. Box 783, Suffern, NY 10901-0783 / 914-357-5510

Seligman Shooting Products, Box 133, Seligman, AZ 86337 / 602-422-3607

Sellier & Bellot, USA Inc., P.O. Box 27006, Shawnee Mission, KS 66225 / 913-685-0916; FAX: 913-685-0917

Selsi Co., Inc., P.O. Box 10, Midland Park, NJ 07432-0010 / 201-935-0388; FAX: 201-935-5851

Semmer, Charles (See Remington Double Shotguns), 7885 Cyd Dr., Denver, CO 80221 / 303-429-6947

Sentinel Arms, P.O. Box 57, Detroit, MI 48231 / 313-331-1951; FAX: 313-331-1456

Service Armament, 689 Bergen Blvd., Ridgefield, NJ 07657

Servus Footwear Co., 1136 2nd St., Rock Island, IL 61204 / 309-786-7741; FAX: 309-786-9808

Shappy Bullets, 76 Milldale Ave., Plantsville, CT 06479 / 203-621-3704

Sharp Shooter Supply, 4970 Lehman Road, Delphos, OH 45833 / 419-695-3179

Sharps Arms Co., Inc., C., 100 Centennial, Box 885, Big Timber, MT 59011 / 406-932-4353

Shaw, Inc., E. R. (See Small Arms Mfg. Co.)

Shay's Gunsmithing, 931 Marvin Ave., Lebanon, PA 17042

Sheffield Knifemakers Supply, Inc., P.O. Box 741107, Orange City, FL 32774-1107 / 904-775-6453; FAX: 904-774-5754

Sheldon, Bruce (See Ridgeline, Inc.)

Shepherd Enterprises, Inc., Box 189, Waterloo, NE 68069 / 402-779-2424; FAX: 402-779-4010 sshepherd@shepherdscopes.com www.shepherdscopes.com

Sherwood, George, 46 N. River Dr., Roseburg, OR 97470 / 541-672-3159

Shilen, Inc., 205 Metro Park Blvd., Ennis, TX 75119 / 972-875-5318; FAX: 972-875-5402

Shiloh Creek, Box 357, Cottleville, MO 63338 / 314-925-1842; FAX: 314-925-1842

Shiloh Rifle Mfg., 201 Centennial Dr., Big Timber, MT 59011 / 406-932-4454; FAX: 406-932-5627

Shockley, Harold H., 204 E. Farmington Rd., Hanna City, IL 61536 / 309-565-4524

Shoemaker & Sons Inc., Tex, 714 W. Cienega Ave., San Dimas, CA 91773 / 909-592-2071; FAX: 909-592-2378

Shoot Where You Look, Leon Measures, Dept GD, 408 Fair, Livingston, TX 77351

Shooters Arms Manufacturing, Inc., Rivergate Mall, Gen. Maxilom Ave., Cebu City 6000, PHILIPPINES / 6332-254-8478 www.shootersarms.com.ph

Shooter's Choice, 16770 Hilltop Park Pl., Chagrin Falls, OH 44023 / 216-543-8808; FAX: 216-543-8811

Shooter's Edge Inc., 3313 Creekstone Dr., Fort Collins, CO 80525-6169

Shooters Supply, 1120 Tieton Dr., Yakima, WA 98902 / 509-452-1181

Shooter's World, 3828 N. 28th Ave., Phoenix, AZ 85017 / 602-266-0170

Shootin' Accessories, Ltd., P.O. Box 6810, Auburn, CA 95604 / 916-889-2220

Shootin' Shack, Inc., 1065 Silver Beach Rd., Riviera Beach, FL 33403 / 561-842-0990

Shooting Chrony, Inc., 3269 Niagara Falls Blvd., N. Tonawanda, NY 14120 / 905-276-6292; FAX: 416-276-6295

Shooting Specialties (See Titus, Daniel)

Shooting Star, 1715 FM 1626 Ste. 105, Manchaca, TX 78652 / 512-462-0009

Shoot-N-C Targets (See Birchwood Casey)

Shotgun Sports, P.O. Box 6810, Auburn, CA 95604 / 530-889-2220; FAX: 530-889-9106

Shotguns Unlimited, 2307 Fon Du Lac Rd., Richmond, VA 23229 / 804-752-7115

Siegrist Gun Shop, 8752 Turtle Rd., Whittemore, MI 48770

Sierra Bullets, 1400 W. Henry St., Sedalia, MO 65301 / 816-827-6300; FAX: 816-827-6300

Sierra Specialty Prod. Co., 1344 Oakhurst Ave., Los Altos, CA 94024; FAX: 415-965-1536

SIG, CH-8212 Neuhausen, SWITZERLAND

Sigarms, Inc., Corporate Park, Exeter, NH 03833 / 603-772-2302; FAX: 603-772-9082 www.sigarms.com

Sightron, Inc., 1672B Hwy. 96, Franklinton, NC 27525 / 919-528-8783; FAX: 919-528-0995 info@sightron.com www.sightron.com

Signet Metal Corp., 551 Stewart Ave., Brooklyn, NY 11222 / 718-384-5400; FAX: 718-388-7488

SIG-Sauer (See U.S. Importer-Sigarms Inc.)

Sile Distributors, Inc., 7 Centre Market Pl., New York, NY 10013 / 212-925-4111; FAX: 212-925-3149

Silencio/Safety Direct, 56 Coney Island Dr., Sparks, NV 89431 / 800-648-1812 or 702-354-4451; FAX: 702-359-1074

Silent Hunter, 1100 Newton Ave., W. Collingswood, NJ 08107 / 609-854-3276

Silhouette Leathers, P.O. Box 1161, Gunnison, CO 81230 / 303-641-6639, oldshooter@yahoo.com

Silver Eagle Machining, 18007 N. 69th Ave., Glendale, AZ 85308

Silver Ridge Gun Shop (See Goodwin, Fred)

Simmons, Jerry, 715 Middlebury St., Goshen, IN 46526 / 219-533-8546

Simmons Gun Repair, Inc., 700 S. Rogers Rd., Olathe, KS 66062 / 913-782-3131; FAX: 913-782-4189

Simmons Outdoor Corp., P.O. Box 217, Heflin, AL 36264

Sinclair International, Inc., 2330 Wayne Haven St., Fort Wayne, IN 46803 / 219-493-1858; FAX: 219-493-2530 sinclair@ctlnet.com www.sinclairintl.com

Singletary, Kent, 2915 W. Ross, Phoenix, AZ 85027 / 602-582-4900

Sipes Gun Shop, 7415 Asher Ave., Little Rock, AR 72204 / 501-565-8480

Siskiyou Gun Works (See Donnelly, C. P.)

Six Enterprises, 320-D Turtle Creek Ct., San Jose, CA 95125 / 408-999-0201; FAX: 408-999-0216

SKAN A.R., 4 St. Catherines Road, Long Melford, Suffolk, O10 9JU ENGLAND / 011-0787-312942

SKB Shotguns, 4325 S. 120th St., Omaha, NE 68137 / 800-752-2767; FAX: 402-330-8040 skb@radiks.net skbshotguns.com

Skeoch, Brian R., P.O. Box 279, Glenrock, WY 82637 / 307-436-9655; FAX: 307-436-9034

Skip's Machine, 364 29th Rd., Grand Junction, CO 81501 / 303-245-5417

Sklany's Machine Shop, 566 Birch Grove Dr., Kalispell, MT 59901 / 406-755-4257

Slezak, Jerome F., 1290 Marlowe, Lakewood (Cleveland), OH 44107 / 216-221-1668

Slug Site, Ozark Wilds, 21300 Hwy. 5, Versailles, MO 65084 / 573-378-6430 john.ebeling.com

Small Arms Mfg. Co., 5312 Thoms Run Rd., Bridgeville, PA 15017 / 412-221-4343; FAX: 412-221-4303

Small Arms Specialists, 443 Firchburg Rd., Mason, NH 03048 / 603-878-0427; FAX: 603-878-3905 miniguns@empire.net miniguns.com

Small Custom Mould & Bullet Co., Box 17211, Tucson, AZ 85731

Smart Parts, 1203 Spring St., Latrobe, PA 15650 / 412-539-2660; FAX: 412-539-2298

Smires, C. L., 5222 Windmill Ln., Columbia, MD 21044-1328

Smith & Wesson, 2100 Roosevelt Ave., Springfield, MA 01104 / 413-781-8300; FAX: 413-731-8980

Smith, Art, 230 Main St. S., Hector, MN 55342 / 320-848-2760; FAX: 320-848-2760

Smith, Mark A., P.O. Box 182, Sinclair, WY 82334 / 307-324-7929

Smith, Michael, 2612 Ashmore Ave., Red Bank, TN 37415-6353 / 615-267-8341

Smith, Ron, 5869 Straley, Ft. Worth, TX 76114 / 817-732-6768

Smith, Sharmon, 4545 Speas Rd., Fruitland, ID 83619 / 208-452-6329

Smith Abrasives, Inc., 1700 Sleepy Valley Rd., P.O. Box 5095, Hot Springs, AR 71902-5095 / 501-321-2244; FAX: 501-321-9232

Smith Saddlery, Jesse W., 0499 Cty. Rd. J, Pritchett, CO 81064-9604 / 509-325-0622

Smokey Valley Rifles (See Lutz Engraving, Ron E)

Snapp's Gunshop, 6911 E. Washington Rd., Clare, MI 48617 / 517-386-9226

Sno-Seal, Inc. (See Atsko/Sno-Seal)

Societa Armi Bresciane Srl (See U.S. Importer-Cape Outfitters)

Sorenson, Ms Melissa (See Cryo-Accurizing)

SOS Products Co. (See Buck Stix-SOS Products Co.), Box 3, Neenah, WI 54956

Sotheby's, 1334 York Ave. at 72nd St., New York, NY 10021 / 212-606-7260

Sound Technology, Box 391, Pelham, AL 35124 / 205-664-5860 or 907-486-2825; soundtechsilencers.com

South Bend Replicas, Inc., 61650 Oak Rd., South Bend, IN 46614 / 219-289-4500

Southeastern Community College, 1015 S. Gear Ave., West Burlington, IA 52655 / 319-752-2731

Southern Ammunition Co., Inc., 4232 Meadow St., Loris, SC 29569-3124 / 803-756-3262; FAX: 803-756-3583

Southern Bloomer Mfg. Co., P.O. Box 1621, Bristol, TN 37620 / 615-878-6660; FAX: 615-878-8761

Southern Security, 1700 Oak Hills Dr., Kingston, TN 37763 / 423-376-6297; FAX: 800-251-9992

Southwind Sanctions, P.O. Box 445, Aledo, TX 76008 / 817-441-8917

Sparks, Milt, 605 E. 44th St. No. 2, Boise, ID 83714-4800

Spartan-Realtree Products, Inc., 1390 Box Circle, Columbus, GA 31907 / 706-569-9101; FAX: 706-569-0042

Specialty Gunsmithing, Lynn McMurdo, P.O. Box 404, Afton, WY 83110 / 307-886-5535

Specialty Shooters Supply, Inc., 3325 Griffin Rd., Ste. 9mm, Fort Lauderdale, FL 33317

Speedfeed Inc., P.O. Box 1146, Rocklin, CA 95677 / 916-630-7720; FAX: 916-630-7719

Speer Products, Div. of Blount, Inc. Sporting Equipment, P.O. Box 856, Lewiston, ID 83501 / 208-746-2351; FAX: 208-746-2915

Spegel, Craig, P.O. Box 387, Nehalem, OR 97131 / 503-368-5653

Speiser, Fred D., 2229 Dearborn, Missoula, MT 59801 / 406-549-8133

Spencer Reblue Service, 1820 Tupelo Trail, Holt, MI 48842 / 517-694-7474

Spencer's Custom Guns, 4107 Jacobs Creek Dr., Scottsville, VA 24590 / 804-293-6836; FAX: 804-293-6836

SPG LLC, P.O. Box 1625, Cody, WY 82414 / 307-587-7621; FAX: 307-587-7695

Sphinx Engineering SA, Ch. des Grandex-Vies 2, CH-2900, Porrentruy, SWITZERLAND / FAX: 41 66 66 30 90

Sport Flite Manufacturing Co., P.O. Box 1082, Bloomfield Hills, MI 48303 / 248-647-3747

Sporting Arms Mfg., Inc., 801 Hall Ave., Littlefield, TX 79339 / 806-385-5665; FAX: 806-385-3394

Sporting Clays Of America, 9257 Buckeye Rd., Sugar Grove, OH 43155-9632 / 740-746-8334; FAX: 740-746-8605

Sports Innovations Inc., P.O. Box 5181, 8505 Jacksboro Hwy., Wichita Falls, TX 76307 / 817-723-6015

Sportsman Safe Mfg. Co., 6309-6311 Paramount Blvd., Long Beach, CA 90805 / 800-266-7150 or 310-984-5445

Sportsman Supply Co., 714 E. Eastwood, P.O. Box 650, Marshall, MO 65340 / 816-886-9393

Sportsman's Communicators, 588 Radcliffe Ave., Pacific Palisades, CA 90272 / 800-538-3752

Sportsmatch U.K. Ltd., 16 Summer St., Leighton Buzzard, Bedfordshire, LU7 1HT ENGLAND / 01525-381638; FAX: 01525-851236 info@sportsmatch-uk.com, www.sportsmatch-uk.com

Sportsmen's Exchange & Western Gun Traders, Inc., 560 S. C St., Oxnard, CA 93030 / 805-483-1917

Spradlin's, 457 Shannon Rd., Texas Creek, CO 81223 / 719-275-7105; FAX: 719-275-3852; spradlins@prodigy.net, jimspradlin.com

Springfield Sporters, Inc., RD 1, Penn Run, PA 15765 / 412-254-2626; FAX: 412-254-9173

Springfield, Inc., 420 W. Main St., Geneseo, IL 61254 / 309-944-5631; FAX: 309-944-3676

Spyderco, Inc., 4565 N. Hwy. 93, P.O. Box 800, Golden, CO 80403 / 303-279-8383 or 800-525-7770; FAX: 303-278-2229

SSK Industries, 590 Woodvue Ln., Wintersville, OH 43953 / 740-264-0176; FAX: 740-264-2257

Stackpole Books, 5067 Ritter Rd., Mechanicsburg, PA 17055-6921 / 717-796-0411; FAX: 717-796-0412

Stalker, Inc., P.O. Box 21, Fishermans Wharf Rd., Malakoff, TX 75148 / 903-489-1010

Stalwart Corporation, P.O. Box 46, Evanston, WY 82931-0046 / 307-789-7687; FAX: 307-789-7688

Stan De Treville & Co., 4129 Normal St., San Diego, CA 92103 / 619-298-3393

Stanley Bullets, 2085 Heatheridge Ln., Reno, NV 89509

Stanley Scruggs' Game Calls, Rt. 1, Hwy. 661, Cullen, VA 23934 / 804-542-4241 or 800-323-4828

Star Ammunition, Inc., 5520 Rock Hampton Ct., Indianapolis, IN 46268 / 800-221-5927; FAX: 317-872-5847

Star Bonifacio Echeverria S.A., Torrekva 3, Eibar, 20600 SPAIN / 43-107340; FAX: 43-101524

Star Custom Bullets, P.O. Box 608, 468 Main St., Ferndale, CA 95536 / 707-786-9140; FAX: 707-786-9117

Star Machine Works, P.O. Box 1872, Pioneer, CA 95666 / 209-295-5000

Starke Bullet Company, P.O. Box 400, 605 6th St. NW, Cooperstown, ND 58425 / 888-797-3431

Starkey Labs, 6700 Washington Ave. S., Eden Prairie, MN 55344

Starkey's Gun Shop, 9430 McCombs, El Paso, TX 79924 / 915-751-3030

Starlight Training Center, Inc., Rt. 1, P.O. Box 88, Bronaugh, MO 64728 / 417-843-3555

Starline, Inc., 1300 W. Henry St., Sedalia, MO 65301 / 660-827-6640; FAX: 660-827-6650; info@starlinebrass.com http://www.starlinebrass.com

Starr Trading Co., Jedediah, P.O. Box 2007, Farmington Hills, MI 48333 / 810-683-4343; FAX: 810-683-3282

Starrett Co., L. S., 121 Crescent St., Athol, MA 01331 / 978-249-3551; FAX: 978-249-8495

State Arms Gun Co., 815 S. Division St., Waunakee, WI 53597 / 608-849-5800

Steelman's Gun Shop, 10465 Beers Rd., Swartz Creek, MI 48473 / 810-735-4884

Steffens, Ron, 18396 Mariposa Creek Rd., Willits, CA 95490 / 707-485-0873

Stegall, James B., 26 Forest Rd., Wallkill, NY 12589

Steger, James (See Custom Arms Company)

Steve Henigson & Associates, P.O. Box 2726, Culver City, CA 90231 / 310-305-8288; FAX: 310-305-1905

Steve Kamyk Engraver, 9 Grandview Dr., Westfield, MA 01085-1810 / 413-568-0457

Steve Nastoff's 45 Shop, Inc., 1057 Laverne Dr., Youngstown, OH 44511-3405 / 330-538-2977

Steve's House of Guns, Rt. 1, Minnesota City, MN 55959 / 507-689-2573

Stewart Game Calls, Inc., Johnny, P.O. Box 7954, 5100 Fort Ave., Waco, TX 76714 / 817-772-3261; FAX: 817-772-3670

Stewart's Gunsmithing, P.O. Box 5854, Pietersburg North 0750, Transvaal, SOUTH AFRICA / 01521-89401

Steyr Mannlicher AG & CO KG, Mannlicherstrasse 1, A-4400, Steyr, AUSTRIA / 0043-7252-78621; FAX: 0043-7252-68621

STI International, 114 Halmar Cove, Georgetown, TX 78628 / 800-959-8201; FAX: 512-819-0465

Stiles Custom Guns, 76 Cherry Run Rd., Box 1605, Homer City, PA 15748 / 712-479-9945

Stillwell, Robert, 421 Judith Ann Dr., Schertz, TX 78154

Stoeger Industries, 5 Mansard Ct., Wayne, NJ 07470 / 201-872-9500 or 800-631-0722; FAX: 201-872-2230

Stoeger Publishing Co. (See Stoeger Industries)

Stone Enterprises Ltd., 426 Harveys Neck Rd., P.O. Box 335, Wicomico Church, VA 22579 / 804-580-5114; FAX: 804-580-8421

Stone Mountain Arms, 5988 Peachtree Corners E., Norcross, GA 30071 / 800-251-9412

Stoney Point Products, Inc., 1822 N. Minnesota St., New Ulm, MN 56073-0234 / 507-354-3360; FAX: 507-354-7236; stoney@newulmtel.net www.stoneypoint.com

Storage Tech, 1254 Morris Ave., N. Huntingdon, PA 15642 / 800-437-9393

Storey, Dale A. (See DGS, Inc.)

Storm, Gary, P.O. Box 5211, Richardson, TX 75083 / 214-385-0862

Stott's Creek Armory, Inc., 2526 S. 475W, Morgantown, IN 46160 / 317-878-5489; FAX: 317-878-9489 www.sccalendar.com

Stratco, Inc., P.O. Box 2270, Kalispell, MT 59901 / 406-755-1221; FAX: 406-755-1226

Strawbridge, Victor W., 6 Pineview Dr., Dover, NH 03820 / 603-742-0013

Strayer, Sandy (See Strayer-Voigt, Inc.)

Strayer-Voigt, Inc., Sandy Strayer, 3435 Ray Orr Blvd., Grand Prairie, TX 75050 / 972-513-0575

Streamlight, Inc., 1030 W. Germantown Pike, Norristown, PA 19403 / 215-631-0600; FAX: 610-631-0712

Strong Holster Co., 39 Grove St., Gloucester, MA 01930 / 508-281-3300; FAX: 508-281-6321

Strutz Rifle Barrels, Inc., W. C., P.O. Box 611, Eagle River, WI 54521 / 715-479-4766

Stuart, V. Pat, Rt.1, Box 447-S, Greenville, VA 24440 / 804-556-3845

Sturgeon Valley Sporters, K. Ide, P.O. Box 283, Vanderbilt, MI 49795 / 517-983-4338

Sturm, Ruger & Co. Inc., 200 Ruger Rd., Prescott, AZ 86301 / 520-541-8820; FAX: 520-541-8850

"Su-Press-On", Inc., P.O. Box 09161, Detroit, MI 48209 / 313-842-4222

Sullivan, David S. (See Westwind Rifles Inc.)

Summit Specialties, Inc., P.O. Box 786, Decatur, AL 35602 / 205-353-0634; FAX: 205-353-9818

Sun Welding Safe Co., 290 Easy St. No. 3, Simi Valley, CA 93065 / 805-584-6678 or 800-729-SAFE; FAX: 805-584-6169; sunwelding.com

Sunny Hill Enterprises, Inc., W1790 Cty. HHH, Malone, WI 53049 / 920-795-4722; FAX: 920-795-4822

Super 6 LLC, Gary Knopp, 3806 W. Lisbon Ave., Milwaukee, WI 53208 / 414-344-3343

Sure-Shot Game Calls, Inc., P.O. Box 816, 6835 Capitol, Groves, TX 77619 / 409-962-1636; FAX: 409-962-5465

Survival Arms, Inc., 273 Canal St., Shelton, CT 06484-3173 / 203-924-6533; FAX: 203-924-2581

Svon Corp., 2107 W. Blue Heron Blvd., Riviera Beach, FL 33404-5005 / 508-881-8852

Swann, D. J., 5 Orsova Close, Eltham North Vic., 3095 AUSTRALIA / 03-431-0323

Swanndri New Zealand, 152 Elm Ave., Burlingame, CA 94010 / 415-347-6158

Swarovski Optik North America Ltd., 2 Slater Rd., Cranston, RI 02920 / 401-946-2220 or 800-426-3089; FAX: 401-946-2587

Sweet Home, Inc., P.O. Box 900, Orrville, OH 44667-0900

Swenson's 45 Shop, A. D., 3839 Ladera Vista Rd., Fallbrook, CA 92028-9431

Swift Bullet Co., P.O. Box 27, 201 Main St., Quinter, KS 67752 / 913-754-3959; FAX: 913-754-2359

Swift Instruments, Inc., 952 Dorchester Ave., Boston, MA 02125 / 617-436-2960; FAX: 617-436-3232

Swift River Gunworks, 450 State St., Belchertown, MA 01007 / 413-323-4052

Szweda, Robert (See RMS Custom Gunsmithing)

T

T&S Industries, Inc., 1027 Skyview Dr., West Carrollton, OH 45449 / 513-859-8414

T.F.C. S.p.A., Via G. Marconi 118, B, Villa Carcina 25069, ITALY / 030-881271; FAX: 030-881826

T.G. Faust, Inc., 544 Minor St., Reading, PA 19602 / 610-375-8549; FAX: 610-375-4488

T.H.U. Enterprises, Inc., P.O. Box 418, Lederach, PA 19450 / 215-256-1665; FAX: 215-256-9718

T.K. Lee Co., 1282 Branchwater Ln., Birmingham, AL 35216 / 205-913-5222; odonmich@aol.com, scopedot.com

T.W. Menck Gunsmith Inc., 5703 S. 77th St., Ralston, NE 68127

Tabler Marketing, 2554 Lincoln Blvd., Ste. 555, Marina Del Rey, CA 90291 / 818-755-4565; FAX: 818-755-0972

Taconic Firearms Ltd., Perry Ln., P.O. Box 553, Cambridge, NY 12816 / 518-677-2704; FAX: 518-677-5974

MANUFACTURER'S DIRECTORY

TacStar, P.O. Box 547, Cottonwood, AZ 86326-0547 / 602-639-0072; FAX: 602-634-8781

TacTell, Inc., P.O. Box 5654, Maryville, TN 37802 / 615-982-7855; FAX: 615-558-8294

Tactical Defense Institute, 574 Miami Bluff Ct., Loveland, OH 45140 / 513-677-8229; FAX: 513-677-0447

Talley, Dave, P.O. Box 821, Glenrock, WY 82637 / 307-436-8724 or 307-436-9315

Talmage, William G., 10208 N. Cty. Rd. 425 W., Brazil, IN 47834 / 812-442-0804

Talon Industries Inc., P.O. Box 626, Ennis, MT 59729 / 406-682-7515; talonind@3rivers.net

Tamarack Products, Inc., P.O. Box 625, Wauconda, IL 60084 / 708-526-9333; FAX: 708-526-9353

Tanfoglio Fratelli S.r.l., via Valtrompia 39, 41, Brescia, ITALY / 30-8910361; FAX: 30-8910183

Tanglefree Industries, 1261 Heavenly Dr., Martinez, CA 94553 / 800-982-4868; FAX: 510-825-3874

Tank's Rifle Shop, P.O. Box 474, Fremont, NE 68026-0474 / 402-727-1317; FAX: 402-721-2573 www.tanksrifleshop.com

Tanner (See U.S. Importer-Mandall Shooting Supply)

Taracorp Industries, Inc., 1200 Sixteenth St., Granite City, IL 62040 / 618-451-4400

Target Shooting, Inc., P.O. Box 773, Watertown, SD 57201 / 605-882-6955; FAX: 605-882-8840

Tar-Hunt Custom Rifles, Inc., 101 Dogtown Rd., Bloomsburg, PA 17815 / 570-784-6368; FAX: 570-784-6368 www.tar-hunt.com

Tarnhelm Supply Co., Inc., 431 High St., Boscawen, NH 03303 / 603-796-2551; FAX: 603-796-2918

Tasco Sales, Inc., 2889 Commerce Pky., Miramar, FL 33025

Taurus Firearms, Inc., 16175 NW 49th Ave., Miami, FL 33014 / 305-624-1115; FAX: 305-623-7506

Taurus International Firearms (See U.S. Importer)

Taurus S.A. Forjas, Avenida Do Forte 511, Porto Alegre, RS BRAZIL 91360 / 55-51-347-4050; FAX: 55-51-347-3065

Taylor & Robbins, P.O. Box 164, Rixford, PA 16745 / 814-966-3233

Taylor's & Co., Inc., 304 Lenoir Dr., Winchester, VA 22603 / 540-722-2017; FAX: 540-722-2018

TCCI, P.O. Box 302, Phoenix, AZ 85001 / 602-237-3823; FAX: 602-237-3858

TCSR, 3998 Hoffman Rd., White Bear Lake, MN 55110-4626 / 800-328-5323; FAX: 612-429-0526

TDP Industries, Inc., 606 Airport Blvd., Doylestown, PA 18901 / 215-345-8687; FAX: 215-345-6057

Techno Arms (See U.S. Importer-Auto-Ordnance Corp.)

Tecnolegno S.p.A., Via A. Locatelli, 6 10, 24019 Zogno, I ITALY / 0345-55111; FAX: 0345-55155

Ted Blocker Holsters, Inc., 9396 SW Tigard St., Tigard, OR 97223 / 503-557-7757; FAX: 503-557-3771

Tele-Optics, 630 E. Rockland Rd., P.O. Box 6313, Libertyville, IL 60048 / 847-362-7757

Tennessee Valley Mfg., 14 Cty. Rd. 521, Corinth, MS 38834 / 601-286-5014

Ten-Ring Precision, Inc., Alex B. Hamilton, 1449 Blue Crest Ln., San Antonio, TX 78232 / 210-494-3063; FAX: 210-494-3066

TEN-X Products Group, 1905 N. Main St., Ste. 133, Cleburne, TX 76031-1305 / 972-243-4016 or 800-433-2225; FAX: 972-243-4112

Tepeco, P.O. Box 342, Friendswood, TX 77546 / 713-482-2702

Terry K. Kopp Professional Gunsmithing, Rt 1 Box 224F, Lexington, MO 64067 / 816-259-2636

Terry Theis-Engraver, Terry Theis, 21452 FM 2093, Harper, TX 78631 / 830-864-4438

Testing Systems, Inc., 220 Pegasus Ave., Northvale, NJ 07647

Teton Arms, Inc., P.O. Box 411, Wilson, WY 83014 / 307-733-3395

Tetra Gun Lubricants (See FTI, Inc.)

Tex Shoemaker & Sons, Inc., 714 W. Cienega Ave., San Dimas, CA 91773 / 909-592-2071; FAX: 909-592-2378

Texas Armory (See Bond Arms, Inc.)

Texas Platers Supply Co., 2453 W. Five Mile Parkway, Dallas, TX 75233 / 214-330-7168

Thad Rybka Custom Leather Equipment, 134 Havilah Hill, Odenville, AL 35120

Thad Scott Fine Guns, Inc., P.O. Box 412, Indianola, MS 38751 / 601-887-5929

The Accuracy Den, 25 Bitterbrush Rd., Reno, NV 89523 / 702-345-0225

The Alaskan Silversmith, 2145 Wagner Hollow Rd., Fort Plain, NY 13339 / 518-993-3983 sidbell@capital.net

The Ballistic Program Co., Inc., 2417 N. Patterson St., Thomasville, GA 31792 / 912-228-5739 or 800-368-0835

The BulletMakers Workshop, RFD 1 Box 1755, Brooks, ME 04921

The Competitive Pistol Shop, 5233 Palmer Dr., Ft. Worth, TX 76117-2433 / 817-834-8479

The Country Armourer, P.O. Box 308, Ashby, MA 01431-0308 / 508-827-6797; FAX: 508-827-4845

The Creative Craftsman, Inc., 95 Hwy. 29 N., P.O. Box 331, Lawrenceville, GA 30246 / 404-963-2112; FAX: 404-513-9488

The Custom Shop, 890 Cochrane Crescent, Peterborough, ON K9H 5N3 CANADA / 705-742-6693

The Dutchman's Firearms, Inc., 4143 Taylor Blvd., Louisville, KY 40215 / 502-366-0555

The Ensign-Bickford Co., 660 Hopmeadow St., Simsbury, CT 06070

The Eutaw Co., Inc., 7522 Old State Rd., Holly Hill, SC 29059 / 803-496-3341

The Firearm Training Center, 9555 Blandville Rd., West Paducah, KY 42086 / 502-554-5886

The Fouling Shot, 6465 Parfet St., Arvada, CO 80004

The Gun Doctor, P.O. Box 39242, Downey, CA 90242 / 310-862-3158

The Gun Doctor, 435 E. Maple, Roselle, IL 60172 / 708-894-0668

The Gun Parts Corp., 226 Williams Ln., West Hurley, NY 12491 / 914-679-2417; FAX: 914-679-5849

The Gun Room, 1121 Burlington, Muncie, IN 47302 / 765-282-9073; FAX: 765-282-5270 bshstleguns@aol.com

The Gun Room Press, 127 Raritan Ave., Highland Park, NJ 08904 / 732-545-4344; FAX: 732-545-6656 gunbooks@rutgersgunbooks.com www.rutgersgunbooks.com

The Gun Shop, 716-A S. Rogers Rd., Olathe, KS 66062

The Gun Shop, 62778 Spring Creek Rd., Montrose, CO 81401

The Gun Shop, 5550 S. 900 East, Salt Lake City, UT 84117 / 801-263-3633

The Gun Works, 247 S. 2nd, Springfield, OR 97477 / 541-741-4118; FAX: 541-988-1097 gunworks@worldnet.att.net www.thegunworks.com

The Gunsight, 1712 N. Placentia Ave., Fullerton, CA 92631

The Gunsmith in Elk River, 14021 Victoria Ln., Elk River, MN 55330 / 612-441-7761

The Hanned Line, P.O. Box 2387, Cupertino, CA 95015-2387 smith@hanned.com, www.hanned.com

The Holster Shop, 720 N. Flagler Dr., Ft. Lauderdale, FL 33304 / 305-463-7910; FAX: 305-761-1483

The House of Muskets, Inc., P.O. Box 4640, Pagosa Springs, CO 81157 / 970-731-2295

The House of Muskets, Inc., P.O. Box 4640, Pagosa Springs, CO 81157 / 303-731-2295

The Keller Co., 4215 McEwen Rd., Dallas, TX 75244 / 214-770-8585

The Lewis Lead Remover (See LEM Gun Specialties)

The Midwest Shooting School, 2550 Hwy. 23, Wrenshall, MN 55797 / 218-384-3670 patrick@midwestshootingschool.com midwestshootingschool.com

The NgraveR Co., 67 Wawecus Hill Rd., Bozrah, CT 06334 / 860-823-1533

The Ordnance Works, 2969 Pidgeon Point Rd., Eureka, CA 95501 / 707-443-3252

The Original Deer Formula Co, P.O. Box 1705, Dickson, TN 37056 / 615-446-8346 or 800-874-6965; FAX: 615-446-0646; deerformula@aol.com, fishformula.com

The Orvis Co., Rt. 7, Manchester, VT 05254 / 802-362-3622; FAX: 802-362-3525

The Outdoor Connection, Inc., 7901 Panther Way, P.O. Box 7751, Waco, TX 76714-7751 / 800-533-6076 or 254-772-5575; FAX: 254-776-3553 floyd@outdoorconnection.com www.outdoorconnection.com

The Outdoorsman's Bookstore, Llangorse, Brecon, LD3 7UE United Kingdom / 44-1874-658-660; FAX: 44-1874-658-650

The Park Rifle Co., Ltd., Unit 6a Dartford Trade Park, Power Mill Ln., Dartford DA7 7NX, ENGLAND / 011-0322-222512

The Paul Co., 27385 Pressonville Rd., Wellsville, KS 66092 / 785-883-4444; FAX: 785-883-2525

The Protector Mfg. Co., Inc., 443 Ashwood Pl., Boca Raton, FL 33431 / 407-394-6011

The Robar Co.'s, Inc., 21438 N. 7th Ave., Ste. B, Phoenix, AZ 85027 / 602-581-2648; FAX: 602-582-0059

The School of Gunsmithing, 6065 Roswell Rd., Atlanta, GA 30328 / 800-223-4542

The Shooting Gallery, 8070 Southern Blvd., Boardman, OH 44512 / 216-726-7788

The Sight Shop, John G. Lawson, 1802 E. Columbia Ave., Tacoma, WA 98404 / 206-474-5465

The Southern Armory, 25 Millstone Road, Woodlawn, VA 24381 / 703-238-1343; FAX: 703-238-1453

The Surecase Co., 233 Wilshire Blvd., Ste. 900, Santa Monica, CA 90401 / 800-92ARMLOC

The Swampfire Shop (See Peterson Gun Shop, Inc.)

The Wilson Arms Co., 63 Leetes Island Rd., Branford, CT 06405 / 203-488-7297; FAX: 203-488-0135

Theis, Terry (See Terry Theis-Engraver)

Theoben Engineering, Stephenson Rd., St. Ives Huntingdon, Cambs., PE17 4WJ ENGLAND / 011-0480-461718

Thiewes, George W., 14329 W. Parada Dr., Sun City West, AZ 85375

Things Unlimited, 235 N. Kimbau, Casper, WY 82601 / 307-234-5277

Thirion Gun Engraving, Denise, P.O. Box 408, Graton, CA 95444 / 707-829-1876

Thomas, Charles C., 2600 S. First St., Springfield, IL 62794 / 217-789-8980; FAX: 217-789-9130

Thompson, Norm, 18905 NW Thurman St., Portland, OR 97209

Thompson Bullet Lube Co., P.O. Box 409, Wills Point, TX 75169 / 972-271-8063; FAX: 972-840-6743; thomlube@flash.net, www.thompsonbulletlube.com

Thompson Precision, 110 Mary St., P.O. Box 251, Warren, IL 61087 / 815-745-3625

Thompson, Randall (See Highline Machine Co.)

Thompson Target Technology, 618 Roslyn Ave., SW, Canton, OH 44710 / 216-453-7707; FAX: 216-478-4723

Thompson/Center Arms, P.O. Box 5002, Rochester, NH 03867 / 603-332-2394; FAX: 603-332-5133; tech@tcarms.com, www.tcarms.com

300 Below Services (See Cryo-Accurizing)

3-D Ammunition & Bullets, P.O. Box 433, Doniphan, NE 68832 / 402-845-2285 or 800-255-6712; FAX: 402-845-6546

3-Ten Corp., P.O. Box 269, Feeding Hills, MA 01030 / 413-789-2086; FAX: 413-789-1549

Thunder Ranch, HCR 1, Box 53, Mt. Home, TX 78058 / 830-640-3138

Thunder Mountain Arms, P.O. Box 593, Oak Harbor, WA 98277 / 206-679-4657; FAX: 206-675-1114

Thurston Sports, Inc., RD 3 Donovan Rd., Auburn, NY 13021 / 315-253-0966

Tiger-Hunt Gunstocks, Box 379, Beaverdale, PA 15921 / 814-472-5161; tigerhunt4@aol.com, www.gunstockwood.com

Tikka (See U.S. Importer-Stoeger Industries)

Timber Heirloom Products, 618 Roslyn Ave. SW, Canton, OH 44710 / 216-453-7707; FAX: 216-478-4723

Time Precision, Inc., 640 Federal Rd., Brookfield, CT 06804 / 203-775-8343

Tinks & Ben Lee Hunting Products (See Wellington)

Tink's Safariland Hunting Corp., P.O. Box 244, 1140 Monticello Rd., Madison, GA 30650 / 706-342-4915; FAX: 706-342-7568

Tioga Engineering Co., Inc., P.O. Box 913, 13 Cone St., Wellsboro, PA 16901 / 570-724-3533; FAX: 570-724-3895 tiogaeng@epix.net

Tippman Pneumatics, Inc., 3518 Adams Center Rd., Ft. Wayne, IN 46806 / 219-749-6022; FAX: 219-749-6619

Tirelli, Snc Di Tirelli Primo E.C., Via Matteotti No. 359, Gardone V.T. Brescia, I ITALY / 030-8912819; FAX: 030-832240

TM Stockworks, 6355 Maplecrest Rd., Fort Wayne, IN 46835 / 219-485-5389

TMI Products (See Haselbauer Products, Jerry)

Tom Forrest, Inc., P.O. Box 326, Lakeside, CA 92040 / 619-561-5800; FAX: 619-561-0227

Tombstone Smoke 'n' Deals, P.O. Box 31298, Phoenix, AZ 85046 / 602-905-7013; FAX: 602-443-1998

Tom's Gun Repair, Inc., Thomas G. Ivanoff, 76-6 Route, Cody, WY 82414 / 307-587-6949

Tom's Gunshop, 3601 Central Ave., Hot Springs, AR 71913 / 501-624-3856

Tonoloway Tack Drives, HCR 81, Box 100, Needmore, PA 17238

Top-Line USA, Inc., 7920-28 Hamilton Ave., Cincinnati, OH 45231 / 513-522-2992 or 800-346-6699; FAX: 513-522-0916

Torel, Inc., 1708 N. South St., P.O. Box 592, Yoakum, TX 77995 / 512-293-2341; FAX: 512-293-3413

TOZ (See U.S. Importer-Nygord Precision Products)

Track of the Wolf, Inc., P.O. Box 6, Osseo, MN 55369-0006 / 612-424-2500; FAX: 612-424-9860

Traditions Performance Firearms, P.O. Box 776, 1375 Boston Post Rd., Old Saybrook, CT 06475 / 860-388-4656; FAX: 860-388-4657; trad@ctz.nai.net, www.traditionsmuzzle.com

Trafalgar Square, P.O. Box 257, N. Pomfret, VT 05053 / 802-457-1911

Traft Gunshop, P.O. Box 1078, Buena Vista, CO 81211

Trail Visions, 5800 N. Ames Ter., Glendale, WI 53209 / 414-228-1328

Trax America, Inc., P.O. Box 898, 1150 Eldridge, Forrest City, AR 72335 / 870-633-0410 or 800-232-2327; FAX: 870-633-4788; trax@ipa.net, www.traxamerica.com

Treadlok Gun Safe, Inc., 1764 Granby St. NE, Roanoke, VA 24012 / 800-729-8732 or 703-982-6881; FAX: 703-982-1059

Treemaster, P.O. Box 247, Guntersville, AL 35976 / 205-878-3597

Trevallion Gunstocks, 9 Old Mountain Rd., Cape Neddick, ME 03902 / 207-361-1130

Trico Plastics, 28061 Diaz Rd., Temecula, CA 92590 / 909-676-7714; FAX: 909-676-0267; ustinfo@ustplastics.com, www.tricoplastics.com

Trigger Lock Division/Central Specialties Ltd., 220-D Exchange Dr, Crystal Lake, IL 60014 / 847-639-3900; FAX: 847-639-3972

Trijicon, Inc., 49385 Shafer Ave., P.O. Box 930059, Wixom, MI 48393-0059 / 810-960-7700; FAX: 810-960-7725

Trilux, Inc., P.O. Box 24608, Winston-Salem, NC 27114 / 910-659-9438; FAX: 910-768-7720

Trinidad St. Jr. Col. Gunsmith Dept., 600 Prospect St., Trinidad, CO 81082 / 719-846-5631; FAX: 719-846-5667

Triple-K Mfg. Co., Inc., 2222 Commercial St., San Diego, CA 92113 / 619-232-2066; FAX: 619-232-7675

Tristar Sporting Arms, Ltd., 1814-16 Linn St., P.O. Box 7496, N. Kansas City, MO 64116 / 816-421-1400; FAX: 816-421-4182

Trius Traps, Inc., P.O. Box 25, 221 S. Miami Ave., Cleves, OH 45002 / 513-941-5682; FAX: 513-941-7970 triustraps@fuse.net triustraps.com

Trooper Walsh, 2393 N. Edgewood St., Arlington, VA 22207

Trophy Bonded Bullets, Inc., 900 S. Loop W., Ste. 190, Houston, TX 77054 / 713-645-4499 or 888-308-3006; FAX: 713-741-6393

Trotman, Ken, 135 Ditton Walk, Unit 11, Cambridge, CB5 8PY ENGLAND / 01223-211030; FAX: 01223-212317

Tru-Balance Knife Co., P.O. Box 140555, Grand Rapids, MI 49514 / 616-453-3679

True Flight Bullet Co., 5581 Roosevelt St., Whitehall, PA 18052 / 610-262-7630; FAX: 610-262-7806

Truglo, Inc., P.O. Box 1612, McKinna, TX 75070 / 972-774-0300; FAX: 972-774-0323; www.truglosights.com

Trulock Tool, P.O. Box 530, Whigham, GA 31797 / 229-762-4678; FAX: 229-762-4050; trulockchokes@hotmail.com, trulockchokes.com

Tru-Square Metal Prods., Inc., 640 First St. SW, P.O. Box 585, Auburn, WA 98071 / 206-833-2310; FAX: 206-833-2349

TTM, 1550 Solomon Rd., Santa Maria, CA 93455 / 805-934-1281 ttm@pronet.net, thompsontoolmount.com

Tucker, James C., P.O. Box 1212, Paso Robles, CA 93447-1212

Tucson Mold, Inc., 930 S. Plumer Ave., Tucson, AZ 85719 / 520-792-1075; FAX: 520-792-1075

Turnbull Restoration, Doug, 6680 Rt. 58 & 20 Dept. SM 2000, P.O. Box 471, Bloomfield, NY 14469 / 716-657-6338; turnbullrest@mindspring.com, www.turnbullrestoration.com

Tuttle, Dale, 4046 Russell Rd., Muskegon, MI 49445 / 616-766-2250

Tyler Manufacturing & Distributing, 3804 S. Eastern, Oklahoma City, OK 73129 / 405-677-1487 or 800-654-8415

U

U.S. Importer-Wm. Larkin Moore, 8430 E. Raintree Ste. B-7, Scottsdale, AZ 85260

U.S. Patent Fire Arms, 55 Van Dyke Ave., Hartford, CT 06106 / 877-227-6901; FAX: 800-644-7265; usfirearms.com

U.S. Repeating Arms Co., Inc., 275 Winchester Ave., Morgan, UT 84050-9333 / 801-876-3440; FAX: 801-876-3737

U.S. Tactical Systems (See Keng's Firearms Specialty)

U.S.A. Magazines, Inc., P.O. Box 39115, Downey, CA 90241 / 800-872-2577

Uberti USA, Inc., P.O. Box 469, Lakeville, CT 06039 / 860-435-8068; FAX: 860-435-8146

Ugartechea S. A., Ignacio, Chonta 26, Eibar, SPAIN / 43-121257; FAX: 43-121669

Ultra Dot Distribution, 2316 N.E. 8th Rd., Ocala, FL 34470

Ultra Light Arms, Inc., 1024 Grafton Rd., Morgantown, WV 26508 / 304-292-0600; FAX: 304-292-9662 newultralightarm@cs.com www.newultralightarm

Ultralux (See U.S. Importer-Keng's Firearms)

UltraSport Arms, Inc., 1955 Norwood Ct., Racine, WI 53403 / 414-554-3237; FAX: 414-554-9731

Uncle Bud's, HCR 81, Box 100, Needmore, PA 17238 / 717-294-6000; FAX: 717-294-6005

Uncle Mike's (See Michaels of Oregon Co.)

Unertl Optical Co. Inc., John, 308 Clay Ave., P.O. Box 818, Mars, PA 16046-0818 / 412-625-3810

Unique/M.A.P.F., 10 Les Allees, 64700, Hendaye, FRANCE / 33-59-20-71-93

UniTec, 1250 Bedford SW, Canton, OH 44710 / 216-452-4017

United Binocular Co., 9043 S. Western Ave., Chicago, IL 60620

United Cutlery Corp., 1425 United Blvd., Sevierville, TN 37876 / 865-428-2532 or 800-548-0835; FAX: 865-428-2267

United States Optics Technologies, Inc., 5900 Dale St., Buena Park, CA 90621 / 714-994-4901; FAX: 714-994-4904

United States Products Co., 518 Melwood Ave., Pittsburgh, PA 15213 / 412-621-2130; FAX: 412-621-8740

Universal Sports, P.O. Box 532, Vincennes, IN 47591 / 812-882-8680; FAX: 812-882-8680

Unmussig Bullets, D. L., 7862 Brentford Dr., Richmond, VA 23225 / 804-320-1165

Upper Missouri Trading Co., Box 100, Crofton, NE 68730 / 402-388-4844

USAC, 4500-15th St. E., Tacoma, WA 98424 / 206-922-7589

Utica Cutlery Co., 820 Noyes St., Utica, NY 13503 / 315-733-4663; FAX: 315-733-6602

V

V.H. Blackinton & Co., Inc., 221 John L. Dietsch, Attleboro Falls, MA 02763-0300 / 508-699-4436; FAX: 508-695-5349

Valor Corp., 5555 NW 36th Ave., Miami, FL 33142 / 305-633-0127; FAX: 305-634-4536

Valtro USA, Inc., 1281 Andersen Dr., San Rafael, CA 94901 / 415-256-2575; FAX: 415-256-2576

VAM Distribution Co. LLC, 1141-B Mechanicsburg Rd., Wooster, OH 44691 www.rex10.com

Van Gorden & Son Inc., C. S., 1815 Main St., Bloomer, WI 54724 / 715-568-2612

Van Horn, Gil, P.O. Box 207, Llano, CA 93544

Van Patten, J. W., P.O. Box 145, Foster Hill, Milford, PA 18337 / 717-296-7069

Vancini, Carl (See Bestload, Inc.)

Vann Custom Bullets, 330 Grandview Ave., Novato, CA 94947

Van's Gunsmith Service, 224 Rt. 69-A, Parish, NY 13131 / 315-625-7251

Varmint Masters, LLC, Rick Vecqueray, P.O. Box 6724, Bend, OR 97708 / 541-318-7306; FAX: 541-318-7306 varmintmasters@bendnet.com www.varmintmasters.net

Vecqueray, Rick (See Varmint Masters, LLC)

Vega Tool Co., c/o T.R. Ross, 4865 Tanglewood Ct., Boulder, CO 80301 / 303-530-0174

Vektor USA, Mikael Danforth, 5139 Stanart St., Norfolk, VA 23502 / 888-740-0837 or 757-455-8895; FAX: 757-461-9155

Venco Industries, Inc. (See Shooter's Choice)

Venus Industries, P.O. Box 246, Sialkot-1, PAKISTAN; FAX: 92-432-85579

Verney-Carron, B.P. 72, 54 Boulevard Thiers, 42002, FRANCE / 33-477791500; FAX: 33-477790702

Vest, John, 1923 NE 7th St., Redmond, OR 97756-8342 / 541-923-8898; FAX: 541-923-8898

VibraShine, Inc., P.O. Box 577, Taylorsville, MS 39168 / 601-785-9854; FAX: 601-785-9874

Vibra-Tek Co., 1844 Arroya Rd., Colorado Springs, CO 80906 / 719-634-8611; FAX: 719-634-6886

Vic's Gun Refinishing, 6 Pineview Dr., Dover, NH 03820-6422 / 603-742-0013

Victory Ammunition, P.O. Box 1022, Milford, PA 18337 / 717-296-5768; FAX: 717-296-9298

Victory USA, P.O. Box 1021, Pine Bush, NY 12566 / 914-744-2060; FAX: 914-744-5181

Vihtavuori Oy, FIN-41330 Vihtavuori, FINLAND, / 358-41-3779211; FAX: 358-41-3771643

Vihtavuori Oy/Kaltron-Pettibone, 1241 Ellis St., Bensenville, IL 60106 / 708-350-1116; FAX: 708-350-1606

Viking Video Productions, P.O. Box 251, Roseburg, OR 97470

Vincent's Shop, 210 Antoinette, Fairbanks, AK 99701

Vincenzo Bernardelli S.p.A., 125 Via Matteotti, P.O. Box 74, Gardone V.T., Bresci, 25063 ITALY / 39-30-8912851-2-3; FAX: 39-30-8910249

Vintage Arms, Inc., 6003 Saddle Horse, Fairfax, VA 22030 / 703-968-0779; FAX: 703-968-0780

Vintage Industries, Inc., 781 Big Tree Dr., Longwood, FL 32750 / 407-831-8949; FAX: 407-831-5346

Viper Bullet and Brass Works, 11 Brock St., Box 582, Norwich, ON N0J 1P0 CANADA

Viramontez, Ray, 601 Springfield Dr., Albany, GA 31707 / 912-432-9683

Virgin Valley Custom Guns, 450 E 800 N #20, Hurricane, UT 84737 / 435-635-8941; FAX: 435-635-8943; vvcguns@infowest.com, www.virginvalleyguns.com

Visible Impact Targets, Rts. 5 & 20, E. Bloomfield, NY 14443 / 716-657-6161; FAX: 716-657-5405

Vitt/Boos, 1195 Buck Hill Rd., Townshend, VT 05353 / 802-365-9232

Voere-KGH m.b.H., P.O. Box 416, A-6333 Kufstein, Tirol, AUSTRIA / 0043-5372-62547; FAX: 0043-5372-65752

Volquartsen Custom Ltd., 24276 240th St., P.O. Box 397, Carroll, IA 51401 / 712-792-4238; FAX: 712-792-2542; vcl@netins.net, www.volquartsen.com

Vom Hoffe (See Old Western Scrounger, Inc.)

Vorhes, David, 3042 Beecham St., Napa, CA 94558 / 707-226-9116; FAX: 707-253-7334

Vortek Products, Inc., P.O. Box 871181, Canton, MI 48187-6181 / 313-397-5656; FAX: 313-397-5656

VSP Publishers (See Heritage/VSP Gun Books), P.O. Box 887, McCall, ID 83638 / 208-634-4104; FAX: 208-634-3101

Vulpes Ventures, Inc., Fox Cartridge Division, P.O. Box 1363, Bolingbrook, IL 60440-7363 / 630-759-1229; FAX: 815-439-3945

W

W. Square Enterprises, 9826 Sagedale, Houston, TX 77089 / 713-484-0935; FAX: 281-484-0935

W. Waller & Son, Inc., 2221 Stoney Brook Rd., Grantham, NH 03753-7706 / 603-863-4177; waller@wallerandson.com, wallerandson

W.B. Niemi Engineering, Box 126 Center Rd., Greensboro, VT 05841 / 802-533-7180 or 802-533-7141

W.C. Strutz Rifle Barrels, Inc., P.O. Box 611, Eagle River, WI 54521 / 715-479-4766

W.C. Wolff Co. (Wolff Gunsprings), P.O. Box 458, Newtown Square, PA 19073 / 610-359-9600 or 800-545-0077; FAX: 610-359-9496; mail@gunsprings.com, www.gunsprings.com

W.E. Birdsong & Assoc., 1435 Monterey Rd., Florence, MS 39073-9748 / 601-366-8270

W.E. Brownell Checkering Tools, 9390 Twin Mountain Cir, San Diego, CA 92126 / 858-695-2479; FAX: 858-695-2479

W.J. Riebe Co., 3434 Tucker Rd., Boise, ID 83703

W.R. Case & Sons Cutlery Co., Owens Way, Bradford, PA 16701 / 814-368-4123 or 800-523-6350; FAX: 814-768-5369

Waechter, 43 W. South St. #1FL, Nanticoke, PA 18634 / 717-864-3967; FAX: 717-864-2669

Wagoner, Vernon G., 2325 E. Encanto, Mesa, AZ 85213 / 480-835-1307

Wakina by Pic, 24813 Alderbrook Dr., Santa Clarita, CA 91321 / 800-295-8194

Waldron, Herman, Box 475, 80 N. 17th St., Pomeroy, WA 99347 / 509-843-1404

Walker Arms Co., Inc., 499 Cty. Rd. 820, Selma, AL 36701 / 334-872-6231; FAX: 334-872-6262

Walker Mfg., Inc., 8296 S. Channel, Harsen's Island, MI 48028

Wallace, Terry, 385 San Marino, Vallejo, CA 94589 / 707-642-7041

Walls Industries, Inc., P.O. Box 98, 1905 N. Main, Cleburne, TX 76031 / 817-645-4366; FAX: 817-645-7946

Walters Industries, 6226 Park Ln., Dallas, TX 75225 / 214-691-6973

Walther GmbH, Carl, B.P. 4325, D-89033 Ulm, GERMANY

Walther USA, P.O. Box 2208, Springfield, MA 01102-2208 / 413-747-3443; www.walther-usa.com

Walt's Custom Leather, Walt Whinnery, 1947 Meadow Creek Dr., Louisville, KY 40218 / 502-458-4361

WAMCO--New Mexico, P.O. Box 205, Peralta, NM 87042-0205 / 505-869-0826

Ward & Van Valkenburg, 114 32nd Ave. N., Fargo, ND 58102 / 701-232-2351

Ward Machine, 5620 Lexington Rd., Corpus Christi, TX 78412 / 512-992-1221

Wardell Precision Handguns Ltd., 48851 N. Fig Springs Rd., New River, AZ 85027-8513 / 602-465-7995

Warenski, Julie, 590 E. 500 N., Richfield, UT 84701 / 801-896-5319; FAX: 801-896-5319

Warne Manufacturing Co., 9039 SE Jannsen Rd., Clackamas, OR 97015 / 503-657-5590 or 800-683-5590; FAX: 503-657-5695

Warren & Sweat Mfg. Co., P.O. Box 350440, Grand Island, FL 32784 / 904-669-3166; FAX: 904-669-7272

Warren Muzzleloading Co., Inc., Hwy. 21 N., P.O. Box 100, Ozone, AR 72854 / 501-292-3268

Warren, Kenneth W. (See Mountain States Engraving)

Washita Mountain Whetstone Co., P.O. Box 378, Lake Hamilton, AR 71951 / 501-525-3914

Wasmundt, Jim, P.O. Box 511, Fossil, OR 97830

WASP Shooting Systems, Rt. 1, Box 147, Lakeview, AR 72642 / 501-431-5606

Watson Bros., 39 Redcross Way, London Bridge, LONDON United Kingdom; FAX: 44-171-403-336

Manufacturer's Directory

Watson Trophy Match Bullets, 500 US 27 S. 19, Frostproof, FL 33843 / 864-244-7948 or 941-635-7948

Wayne E. Schwartz Custom Guns, 970 E. Britton Rd., Morrice, MI 48857 / 517-625-4079

Wayne Reno, 2808 Stagestop Rd., Jefferson, CO 80456 / 719-836-3452

Wayne Specialty Services, 260 Waterford Dr., Florissant, MO 63033 / 413-831-7083

WD-40 Co., 1061 Cudahy Pl., San Diego, CA 92110 / 619-275-1400; FAX: 619-275-5823

Weatherby, Inc., 3100 El Camino Real, Atascadero, CA 93422 / 805-466-1767 or 800-227-2016; FAX: 805-466-2527

Weaver Arms Corp. Gun Shop, RR 3, P.O. Box 266, Bloomfield, MO 63825-9528

Weaver Products, P.O. Box 39, Onalaska, WI 54650 / 800-648-9624 or 608-781-5800; FAX: 608-781-0368

Weaver Scope Repair Service, 1121 Larry Mahan Dr., Ste. B, El Paso, TX 79925 / 915-593-1005

Webb, Bill, 6504 N. Bellefontaine, Kansas City, MO 64119 / 816-453-7431

Weber & Markin Custom Gunsmiths, 4-1691 Powick Rd., Kelowna, BC V1X 4L1 CANADA / 250-762-7575; FAX: 250-861-3655

Weber Jr., Rudolf, P.O. Box 160106, D-5650 GERMANY / 0212-592136

Webley and Scott Ltd., Frankley Industrial Park, Tay Rd., Birmingham, B45 0PA ENGLAND / 011-021-453-1864; FAX: 021-457-7846

Webster Scale Mfg. Co., P.O. Box 188, Sebring, FL 33870 / 813-385-6362

Weems, Cecil, 510 W. Hubbard St., Mineral Wells, TX 76067-4847 / 817-325-1462

Weigand Combat Handguns, Inc., 685 S. Main Rd., Mountain Top, PA 18707 / 570-868-8358; FAX: 570-868-5218; sales@jackweigand.com, www.scopemount.com

Weihrauch KG, Hermann, Industriestrasse 11, 8744 Mellrichstadt, Mellrichstadt, GERMANY

Welch, Sam (See San Welch Gun Engraving)

Wellington Outdoors, P.O. Box 244, 1140 Monticello Rd., Madison, GA 30650 / 706-342-4915; FAX: 706-342-7568

Wells, Rachel, 110 N. Summit St., Prescott, AZ 86301 / 520-445-3655

Wells Creek Knife & Gun Works, 32956 State Hwy. 38, Scottsburg, OR 97473 / 541-587-4202; FAX: 541-587-4223

Welsh, Bud (See High Precision)

Wenger North America/Precise Int'l, 15 Corporate Dr., Orangeburg, NY 10962 / 800-431-2996; FAX: 914-425-4700

Wenig Custom Gunstocks, 103 N. Market St., P.O. Box 249, Lincoln, MO 65338 / 660-547-3679; FAX: 660-547-2881; gunstock@wenig.com, www.wenig.com

Werth, T. W., 1203 Woodlawn Rd., Lincoln, IL 62656 / 217-732-1300

Wescombe, Bill (See North Star West)

Wessinger Custom Guns & Engraving, 268 Limestone Rd., Chapin, SC 29036 / 803-345-5677

West, Jack L., 1220 W. Fifth, P.O. Box 427, Arlington, OR 97812

Western Cutlery (See Camillus Cutlery Co.)

Western Design (See Alpha Gunsmith Division)

Western Mfg. Co., 550 Valencia School Rd., Aptos, CA 95003 / 831-688-5884; lotsabears@earthlink.net

Western Missouri Shooters Alliance, P.O. Box 11144, Kansas City, MO 64119 / 816-597-3950; FAX: 816-229-7350

Western Nevada West Coast Bullets, P.O. Box 2270, Dayton, NV 89403-2270 / 702-246-3941; FAX: 702-246-0836

Westley Richards & Co., 40 Grange Rd., Birmingham, ENGLAND / 010-214722953

Westrom, John (See Precision Metal Finishing)

Westwind Rifles, Inc., David S. Sullivan, P.O. Box 261, 640 Briggs St., Erie, CO 80516 / 303-828-3823

Weyer International, 2740 Nebraska Ave., Toledo, OH 43607 / 419-534-2020; FAX: 419-534-2697

Whildin & Sons Ltd., E.H., RR 2 Box 119, Tamaqua, PA 18252 / 717-668-6743; FAX: 717-668-6745

Whinnery, Walt (See Walt's Custom Leather)

Whiscombe (See U.S. Importer-Pelaire Products)

White Barn Wor, 431 Cty. Rd., Broadlands, IL 61816

White Flyer Targets, 1300 Post Oak Blvd., Ste 680, Houston, TX 77056 / 800-322-7855; FAX: 713-963-0951; whflyer@aol.com

White Owl Enterprises, 2583 Flag Rd., Abilene, KS 67410 / 913-263-2613; FAX: 913-263-2613

White Pine Photographic Services, Hwy. 60, General Delivery, Wilno, ON K0J 2N0 CANADA / 613-756-3452

White Rock Tool & Die, 6400 N. Brighton Ave., Kansas City, MO 64119 / 816-454-0478

Whitestone Lumber Corp., 148-02 14th Ave., Whitestone, NY 11357 / 718-746-4400; FAX: 718-767-1748

Wichita Arms, Inc., 923 E. Gilbert, P.O. Box 11371, Wichita, KS 67211 / 316-265-0661; FAX: 316-265-0760

Wick, David E., 1504 Michigan Ave., Columbus, IN 47201 / 812-376-6960

Widener's Reloading & Shooting Supply, Inc., P.O. Box 3009 CRS, Johnson City, TN 37602 / 615-282-6786; FAX: 615-282-6651

Wideview Scope Mount Corp., 13535 S. Hwy. 16, Rapid City, SD 57701 / 605-341-3220; FAX: 605-341-9142; wvdon@rapidnet.com

Wiebe, Duane, 846 Holly WYA, Placerville, CA 95667-3415

Wiest, M. C., 10737 Dutchtown Rd., Knoxville, TN 37932 / 423-966-4545

Wilcox All-Pro Tools & Supply, 4880 147th St., Montezuma, IA 50171 / 515-623-3138; FAX: 515-623-3104

Wilcox Industries Corp., Robert F. Guarasi, 53 Durham St., Portsmouth, NH 03801 / 603-431-1331; FAX: 603-431-1221

Wild Bill's Originals, P.O. Box 13037, Burton, WA 98013 / 206-463-5738; FAX: 206-465-5925

Wild West Guns, 7521 Old Seward Hwy., Unit A, Anchorage, AK 99518 / 800-992-4570 or 907-344-4500; FAX: 907-344-4005

Wilderness Sound Products Ltd., 4015 Main St. A, Springfield, OR 97478 / 503-741-0263 or 800-437-0006; FAX: 503-741-7648

Wildey, Inc., 45 Angevine Rd., Warren, CT 06754-1818 / 860-355-9000; FAX: 860-354-7759; www.wildeyguns.com

Wildlife Research Center, Inc., 1050 McKinley St., Anoka, MN 55303 / 612-427-3350 or 800-USE-LURE; FAX: 612-427-8354

Will-Burt Co., 169 S. Main, Orrville, OH 44667

William Fagan & Co., 22952 15 Mile Rd., Clinton Township, MI 48035 / 810-465-4637; FAX: 810-792-6996

William Powell & Son (Gunmakers) Ltd., 35-37 Carrs Ln., Birmingham, B4 7SX ENGLAND / 121-643-0689; FAX: 121-631-3504

William Powell Agency, 22 Circle Dr., Bellmore, NY 11710 / 516-679-1158

Williams Gun Sight Co., 7389 Lapeer Rd., Box 329, Davison, MI 48423 / 810-653-2131 or 800-530-9028; FAX: 810-658-2140; williamsgunsight.com

Williams Mfg. of Oregon, 110 East B St., Drain, OR 97435 / 503-836-7461; FAX: 503-836-7245

Williams Shootin' Iron Service, The Lynx-Line, Rt. 2, Box 223A, Mountain Grove, MO 65711 / 417-948-0902; FAX: 417-948-0902

Williamson Precision Gunsmithing, 117 W. Pipeline, Hurst, TX 76053 / 817-285-0064; FAX: 817-280-0044

Willow Bend, P.O. Box 203, Chelmsford, MA 01824 / 978-256-8508; FAX: 978-256-8508

Willson Safety Prods. Div., P.O. Box 622, Reading, PA 19603-0622 / 610-376-6161; FAX: 610-371-7725

Wilson Case, Inc., P.O. Box 1106, Hastings, NE 68902-1106 / 800-322-5493; FAX: 402-463-5276 sales@wilsoncase.com www.wilsoncase.com

Wilson Gun Shop, 2234 Cty. Rd. 719, Berryville, AR 72616 / 870-545-3618; FAX: 870-545-3310

Winchester Div. Olin Corp., 427 N. Shamrock, East Alton, IL 62024 / 618-258-3566; FAX: 618-258-3599

Winchester Press (See New Win Publishing, Inc.)

Winchester Sutler, Inc., The, 270 Shadow Brook Ln., Winchester, VA 22603 / 540-888-3595; FAX: 540-888-4632

Windish, Jim, 2510 Dawn Dr., Alexandria, VA 22306 / 703-765-1994

Wingshooting Adventures, 0-1845 W. Leonard, Grand Rapids, MI 49544 / 616-677-1980; FAX: 616-677-1986

Winkle Bullets, R.R. 1, Box 316, Heyworth, IL 61745

Winter, Robert M., P.O. Box 484, 42975-287th St., Menno, SD 57045 / 605-387-5322

Wise Custom Guns, 1402 Blanco Rd., San Antonio, TX 78212-2716 / 210-828-3388

Wise Guns, Dale, 333 W. Olmos Dr, San Antonio, TX 78212 / 210-828-3388

Wiseman and Co., Bill, P.O. Box 3427, Bryan, TX 77805 / 409-690-3456; FAX: 409-690-0156

Wisners Inc./Twin Pine Armory, P.O. Box 58, Hwy. 6, Adna, WA 98522 / 360-748-4590; FAX: 360-748-1802

Wolf (See J.R. Distributing)

Wolfe Publishing Co., 6471 Airpark Dr., Prescott, AZ 86301 / 520-445-7810 or 800-899-7810; FAX: 520-778-5124

Wolf's Western Traders, 1250 Santa Cord Ave., #613, Chula Vista, CA 91913 / 619-482-1701; patwolf4570book@aol.com

Wolverine Footwear Group, 9341 Courtland Dr. NE, Rockford, MI 49351 / 616-866-5500; FAX: 616-866-5658

Wood, Mel, P.O. Box 1255, Sierra Vista, AZ 85636 / 602-455-5541

Wood, Frank (See Classic Guns, Inc.), 3230 Medlock Bridge Rd., Ste. 110, Norcross, GA 30092 / 404-242-7944

Woodleigh (See Huntington Die Specialties)

Woods Wise Products, P.O. Box 681552, Franklin, TN 37068 / 800-735-8182; FAX: 615-726-2637

Woodstream, P.O. Box 327, Lititz, PA 17543 / 717-626-2125; FAX: 717-626-1912

Woodworker's Supply, 1108 N. Glenn Rd., Casper, WY 82601 / 307-237-5354

Woolrich, Inc., Mill St., Woolrich, PA 17701 / 800-995-1299; FAX: 717-769-6234/6259

Working Guns, Jim Coffin, 1224 NW Fernwood Cir., Corvallis, OR 97330-2909 / 541-928-4391

World Class Airguns, 2736 Morningstar Dr., Indianapolis, IN 46229 / 317-897-5548

World of Targets (See Birchwood Casey)

World Trek, Inc., 7170 Turkey Creek Rd., Pueblo, CO 81007-1046 / 719-546-2121; FAX: 719-543-6886

Worthy Products, Inc., RR 1, P.O. Box 213, Martville, NY 13111 / 315-324-5298

Wosenitz VHP, Inc., Box 741, Dania, FL 33004 / 305-923-3748; FAX: 305-925-2217

Wostenholm (See Ibberson [Sheffield] Ltd., George)

Wright's Hardwood Gunstock Blanks, 8540 SE Kane Rd., Gresham, OR 97080 / 503-666-1705

WTA Manufacturing, P.O. Box 164, Kit Carson, CO 80825 / 800-700-3054; FAX: 719-962-3570

Wyant Bullets, Gen. Del., Swan Lake, MT 59911

Wyant's Outdoor Products, Inc., P.O. Box 9, Broadway, VA 22815

Wyoming Custom Bullets, 1626 21st St., Cody, WY 82414

Wyoming Knife Corp., 101 Commerce Dr., Ft. Collins, CO 80524 / 303-224-3454

X

X-Spand Target Systems, 26-10th St. SE, Medicine Hat, AB T1A 1P7 CANADA / 403-526-7997; FAX: 403-528-2362

Y

Yankee Gunsmith, 2901 Deer Flat Dr., Copperas Cove, TX 76522 / 817-547-8433

Yavapai College, 1100 E. Sheldon St., Prescott, AZ 86301 / 520-776-2353; FAX: 520-776-2355

Yavapai Firearms Academy Ltd., P.O. Box 27290, Prescott Valley, AZ 86312 / 520-772-8262; info@yfainc.com, www.yfainc.com

Yearout, Lewis E. (See Montana Outfitters), 308 Riverview Dr. E., Great Falls, MT 59404 / 406-761-0859

Yee, Mike, 29927 56 Pl. S., Auburn, WA 98001 / 206-839-3991

Yellowstone Wilderness Supply, P.O. Box 129, West Yellowstone, MT 59758 / 406-646-7613

Yesteryear Armory & Supply, P.O. Box 408, Carthage, TN 37030

York M-1 Conversions, 803 Mill Creek Run, Plantersville, TX 77363 / 800-527-2881 or 713-477-8442

Young Country Arms, William, 1409 Kuehner Dr. #13, Simi Valley, CA 93063-4478

Z

Zabala Hermanos S.A., P.O. Box 97, Eibar, 20600 SPAIN / 43-768085 or 43-768076; FAX: 34-43-768201

Zander's Sporting Goods, 7525 Hwy. 154 West, Baldwin, IL 62217-9706 / 800-851-4373; FAX: 618-785-2320

Zanotti Armor, Inc., 123 W. Lone Tree Rd., Cedar Falls, IA 50613 / 319-232-9650

Zeeryp, Russ, 1601 Foard Dr., Lynn Ross Manor, Morristown, TN 37814 / 615-586-2357

Zero Ammunition Co., Inc., 1601 22nd St. SE, P.O. Box 1188, Cullman, AL 35056-1188 / 800-545-9376; FAX: 205-739-4683

Ziegel Engineering, 2108 Lomina Ave., Long Beach, CA 90815 / 562-596-9481; FAX: 562-598-4734; ziegel@aol.com, www.ziegelerg.com

Zim's, Inc., 4370 S. 3rd W., Salt Lake City, UT 84107 / 801-268-2505

Z-M Weapons, 203 South St., Bernardston, MA 01337 / 413-648-9501; FAX: 413-648-0219

Zriny's Metal Targets (See Z's Metal Targets)

Z's Metal Targets & Frames, P.O. Box 78, South Newbury, NH 03255 / 603-938-2826

Zufall, Joseph F., P.O. Box 304, Golden, CO 80402-0304

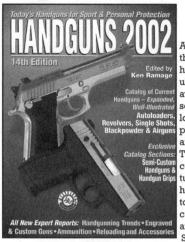
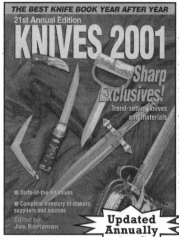
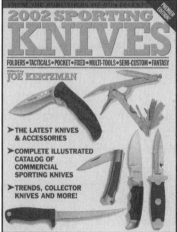

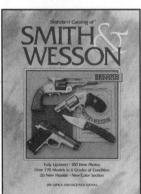
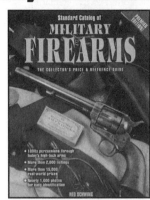
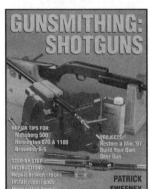